INTERNATIONAL FINANCIAL MANAGEMENT

Jeff Madura *Florida Atlantic University*

Roland Fox *Salford University*

SOUTH-WESTERN
CENGAGE Learning

Australia · Brazil · Japan · Korea · Mexico · Singapore · Spain · United Kingdom · United States

SOUTH-WESTERN
CENGAGE Learning™

International Financial Management
Jeff Madura and Roland Fox

Publishing Director: Linden Harris

Publisher: Brendan George

Development Editor: Laura Priest

Production Editor: Lucy Mills

Production Controller: Eyvett Davis

Marketing Manager: Anne-Marie Scoones

Typesetter: Saxon Graphics Ltd

Cover design: Landy-Sky

Text design: Design Deluxe Ltd, Bath, UK

© 2007, Cengage Learning EMEA

For product information and technology assistance,
contact **emea.info@cengage.com**.

For permission to use material from this text or product,
and for permission queries,
email **clsuk.permissions@cengage.com**.

British Library Cataloguing-in-Publication Data
A catalogue record for this book is available from the British Library.

ISBN: 978-1-84480-360-6

Cengage Learning EMEA
Cheriton House, North Way, Andover, Hampshire, SP10 5BE
United Kingdom

Cengage Learning products are represented in Canada by Nelson Education Ltd.

For your lifelong learning solutions, visit
www.cengage.co.uk

Purchase e-books or e-chapters at:
www.cengagebrain.com

Printed by Seng Lee Press, Singapore
3 4 5 6 7 8 9 10 – 12 11 10

Jeff Madura:

To My Parents

Roland Fox:

To Marlene, Anna and Joe

About the authors

Jeff Madura is presently the SunTrust Bank Professor of Finance at Florida Atlantic University. He has written several textbooks, including *Financial Markets and Institutions*. His research on international finance has been published in numerous journals, including *Journal of Financial and Quantitative Analysis*, *Journal of Money, Credit and Banking*, *Journal of Banking and Finance*, *Journal of International Money and Finance*, *Journal of Financial Research*, *Financial Review*, *Journal of Multinational Financial Management*, and *Global Finance Journal*. He has received awards for excellence in teaching and research, and has served as a consultant for international banks, securities firms, and other multi-national corporations. He has served as a director for the Southern Finance Association and Eastern Finance Association, and also served as president of the Southern Finance Association.

Roland Fox graduated from Manchester University and joined PriceWaterhouseCoopers. He subsequently worked in insurance and for a multinational company, Invensys, before taking up a lecturing post. He is currently a senior lecturer in finance at Salford University. He has published a number of papers on management accounting, finance and education.

Brief Contents

Contents

PART 4
LONG-TERM ASSET AND LIABILITY MANAGEMENT 461

13 FOREIGN DIRECT INVESTMENT 463

14 MULTINATIONAL CAPITAL BUDGETING 482

15 MULTINATIONAL RESTRUCTURING 523

Preface

Multinational Corporations (MNCs) continue to expand their operations globally. They must not only be properly managed to apply their comparative advantages in foreign countries, but must also manage their exposure to many forms and sources of risk. These firms' exposure is especially pronounced in developing countries where currency values and economies are volatile. As international conditions change, so do opportunities and risk. Those MNCs that are most capable of responding to changes in the international financial environment will be rewarded. The same can be said for today's students who become the MNC managers of the future.

LECTURER NOTES

Intended market and teaching strategy

This text presumes an understanding of basic corporate finance. It is suitable for both final year undergraduate and master's level courses in international financial management. The text is not directed at the wider business community but may nevertheless be of interest.

The text offers an intuitive and real world grasp of the concepts and issues in international finance. A wealth of examples are provided to enable the student to see the implications of the subject to business, mostly from an MNC perspective. This fuller explanation serves as a support for the lecturer who has increasingly to deliver to students from diverse backgrounds.

Links to the academic literature are provided by a selection of peer reviewed articles from academic journals with related questions provided at the end of each part of the book. These articles have been specially selected for their quality and accessibility to the typical final year and master's student. Giving academic articles a stronger pedagogic role in this way recognizes the now widely available e-journal access which allows such material to be an integral part of the learning programme.

The selection of academic articles is part of an extensive array of support material designed to ensure that the student is able to reflect on and evaluate issues and problems in the subject to a high academic level. Addressing the more technical aspects of the subject first, at the end of each chapter graded questions are provided. The last questions have been given the subtitle of "Project Workshop"; they enable the student to apply ideas in the chapter directly to real world sources. These questions can be used as the basis of project work that can constitute part of the final assessment of the course. At master's level the workshop exercises may be used to form the element of research around which a dissertation can be written. A general framework for projects is provided in the "Project Workshop Notes" section on the companion website. Spreadsheet and statistical packages combined with economic and exchange rate databases made available to your students by your institution can be used with good effect to support such work.

The more discursive aspects of the subject constitute a second route to achieving a high quality of academic study. The "Critical Debate" topics at the end of each chapter give the student the opportunity to discuss contentious issues in the chapter. The continuing case study, also at the end of each chapter, may be used to help bring the subject within the students' grasp.

At the end of each of the five parts of the book there is an integrative problem that is mainly but not wholly technically based. As noted above, the more discursive elements are reviewed in a section entitled "Essays/Discussion and Articles" also at the end of each part. These articles, some 36 in total, can be read and understood without further support material by final year and master's level students. More particularly, they are not the listing of principal articles in the field which generally require specialist knowledge of a number of papers; such articles are widely quoted elsewhere. Most institutions have e-journal access and it will therefore be possible for all students in the class to have easy access to these papers. Essay questions, for the most part based exclusively on the article, follow many of the article references. Aligning student work directly with the sources in this way is an effective way of ensuring academic standards.

The difference between undergraduate level and master's is seen here as one of degree. Both levels require clear, extended explanations. However, final year undergraduate courses may omit some of the appendices and make occasional use of articles and workshop exercises and discussions; master's level courses can be expected to make greater use of the higher level material.

On the companion website "Supplemental Cases", "Project Workshop Notes" and "Discussion in the Boardroom" offer further teaching material. Appendix B entitled "Maths and Statistics Support" is a useful way of ensuring that all students have an adequate technical background for this subject.

Further support material is available on the internet from: http://www.cengage.co.uk/madura_fox. These include:

- Instructor's Manual
- Online quizzes.
- PowerPoint lecture slides.
- Spreadsheets illustrating examples in the text including option diagrams and portfolio modelling.

Other supplements include an Exam View test bank (CD). The Instructor's Manual contains the chapter theme topics to stimulate class discussion and answers to end of chapter questions.

The European edition

Existing users of the text will be acquainted with the Madura US edition which this text replaces. Almost all of the changes are additions or alterations to the US text and hence this edition is slightly longer.

Examples have been changed to UK and Continental Europe contexts. In defence of the greater use of the pound rather than the euro, all that can be said is that the text is in English and the second author is half French! A choice had to be made. Other changes add some topics of a slightly more advanced nature, generally for their real world relevance. Other sections have been rewritten mainly to give a rather more frank and at times sceptical approach that is more in line with the European tradition. Topics such as the euro and European financial integration and a history of exchange rates have been given fuller treatment for obvious reasons. Assessment material generally, and the academic paper programme in particular, has been added to develop the reflective and evaluative aspects of study as interpreted in academia on this side of the Atlantic.

A number of other changes have also been made. Diagrams are more self-contained. There have been some technical extensions. A fuller portfolio model is presented here simply so that students know how to handle more than two investments! Real exchange rates are given greater prominence; the role of the random walk in forecasting risk has been included; as has the calculation of optimal cross-currency hedges. Cylinder or range forward options have been added to the existing list. Volume effects in scenario analysis are worked out in greater detail. The international capital asset pricing model has been added. All of the content related developments have been taught to specialist and non-specialist students by the second author for many years. The project workshop exercises have been extended and reflect the second author's experience in supervising countless projects. The maths and statistics support section has been enlarged from the original as has the project-based appendix (which can be found on the companion website). And finally, the glossary has been extended particularly to include those statistical and technical terms that appear in articles and confuse the student. As most terms are defined throughout the text (highlighted in bold), the comprehensive glossary can be found on the companion website.

The overall intention has been to preserve the clarity of the original text whilst offering a closer fit to the demands of Higher Education in Europe.

ACKNOWLEDGEMENTS

For the European edition I would like to thank the reviewers for their sterling work and the publishing team at Cengage, in particular, Pat Bond, Laura Priest and Lucy Mills. My colleagues at Salford University have been very encouraging; my particular thanks go to Dr Neil Thompson for comments on economic aspects and to Professor Rose Baker who checked over some of the more advanced statistics. I, of course, take responsibility for any inaccuracies.

Finally, I would like to thank my wife, Marlene, and two children, Anna and Joe, for their forbearance in what is a very time consuming and absorbing process.

Roland Fox
Salford University

The publisher would like to thank the following reviewers for their comments:

Peter Roosenboom, Erasmus University, Rotterdam
Anders Karlsson, Stockholm University School of Business
Kevin Campbell, University of Stirling

Walk through tour

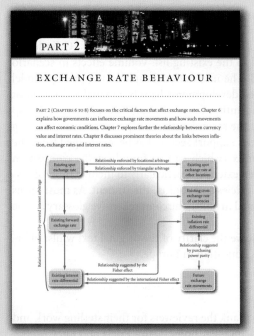

Part opening diagram A diagram at the beginning of each part illustrates how the key concepts relate to one another.

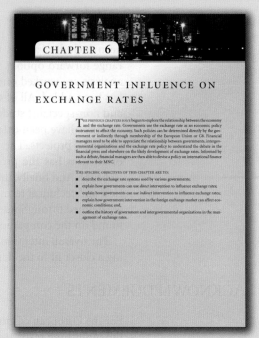

Objectives These define what you can expect to achieve as you read the chapter and what will be assessed by the exercises and other assessments as the chapter proceeds.

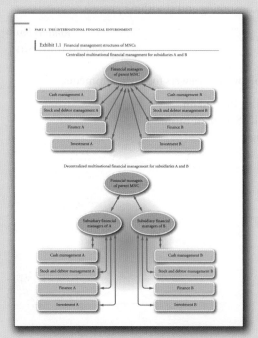

Exhibits These give a visual representation of key concepts or data.

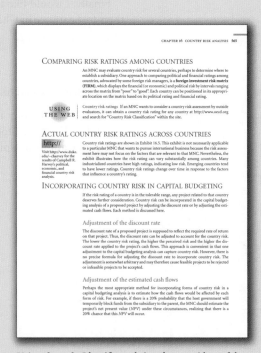

Using the web Identifies websites that provide useful information related to key concepts.

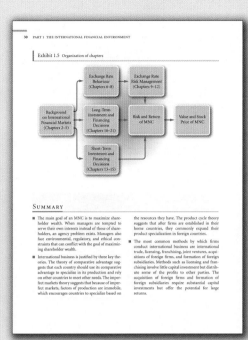

Summary Found at the end of each chapter, the summary offers a useful method of reviewing knowledge for exams by reminding students of what they have learned so far.

Critical debate A controversial topic is introduced, two opposing views are provided and students must decide which view they support and why.

Self tests A self test at the end of each chapter challenges the students on the key concepts. The answers are provided in Appendix A.

Questions and applications A variety of questions and other applications designed to give students a thorough familiarity with the chapter material and to open up areas of further discovery.

Case studies Allow students to apply chapter concepts to a specific situation of an MNC.

Small business dilemma Students use the knowledge they have learned so far to make decisions about a small MNC.

Integrative problem Found at the end of each part, this feature integrates the key concepts across chapters in that part.

Essays/discussion and academic articles At the end of each Part, a list of articles allows students access to the literature and get essay practice.

PART 1

THE INTERNATIONAL FINANCIAL ENVIRONMENT

PART 1 (CHAPTERS 1 TO 5) provides an overview of the multinational corporation (MNC) and the environment in which it operates. Chapter 1 explains the goals of the MNC, along with the motives and risks of international business. Chapter 2 describes the international flow of funds between countries. Chapter 3 describes the international financial markets and how these markets facilitate ongoing operations. Chapter 4 explains how exchange rates are determined, while Chapter 5 provides a background on the currency futures and options markets. Managers of MNCs must understand the international environment described in these chapters in order to make proper decisions.

CHAPTER 1

MULTINATIONAL FINANCIAL MANAGEMENT: AN OVERVIEW

THE COMMONLY STATED GOAL of a firm is to maximize its value and thereby maximize shareholder wealth. This goal is applicable not only to firms that focus on domestic business, but also to firms that focus on international business. Developing business at an international level is an important means of enhancing value for many firms. Since foreign markets can be distinctly different from local markets, they create opportunities for improving the firm's cash flows. Many barriers to entry into foreign markets have been reduced or removed recently, thereby encouraging firms to pursue international business (producing and/or selling goods in foreign countries). Consequently, many firms have evolved into multinational corporations (MNCs), which are defined as firms that engage in some form of international business. Their managers conduct international financial management, which involves international investing and financing decisions that are intended to enhance the value of the MNC.

Initially, firms may merely attempt to export products to a particular country or import supplies from a foreign manufacturer. Over time, however, many recognize additional foreign opportunities and eventually establish subsidiaries in foreign countries. Large European MNCs such as BP plc (United Kingdom) Renault (France) and Koninklijke Philips Electronics N.V. (Netherlands) and many other firms have more than half of their assets in foreign (non-euro) countries. Businesses, such as Nokia (Finland), Diageo (United Kingdom), ThyssenKrupp Group (Germany), Alcatel (France) and Cadbury Schweppes (United Kingdom), Adidas (Germany), commonly generate more than a third of their sales outside Europe. The Cadbury Schweppes Group, for instance, has 57% of its sales in the Americas and Asia Pacific regions. It has 103 manufacturing plants less than 50 of which are in Europe. Risk is worldwide rather than purely domestic for these firms, for instance, the weakness of the dollar in 2004 reduced Cadbury's overall pre-tax profit by 7%.

An understanding of international financial management is crucial not only for the largest MNCs with numerous foreign subsidiaries but also for small- and medium-sized enterprises (SMEs). They tend to penetrate specialty markets where they will not have to compete with large firms that could capitalize on economies of scale. While some SMEs have established subsidiaries, many of them penetrate foreign markets through exports. International financial management is important even to companies that have no international business because these companies must recognize how their foreign competitors will be affected by movements in exchange rates, foreign interest rates, labour costs, and inflation. Such economic characteristics can affect the foreign competitors' costs of production and pricing policies.

Companies must also recognize how domestic competitors that obtain foreign supplies or foreign financing will be affected by economic conditions in foreign countries. If these domestic competitors are able to reduce their costs by capitalizing on opportunities in international markets, they may be able to reduce their prices without reducing their profit margins. This could allow them to increase market share at the expense of the purely domestic companies.

This chapter provides a background on the goals of an MNC and the potential risk and returns from engaging in international business.

THE SPECIFIC OBJECTIVES OF THIS CHAPTER ARE TO:

■ identify the main goal of the MNC and potential conflicts with that goal,

■ describe the key theories that seek to explain international business, and

■ outline the common methods used to conduct international business.

GOAL OF THE MNC

The focus of this text is on MNCs that are quoted on the world's stock exchanges. They will almost always have numerous wholly owned foreign subsidiaries. The commonly accepted goal of such an MNC is to maximize shareholder wealth. Some MNCs are former state owned companies where governments remain an important shareholder (e.g. Renault and Petro China). Such companies seek stock market quotes to raise finance and therefore have to demonstrate by means of the annual accounts and report that they are maximizing shareholder wealth in the same way as a wholly private owned company. Such companies may benefit more from government support, but in all other respects there is little to suggest that they are in any way different from other MNCs.

Shareholder influence is another major difference between MNCs. Continental Europe has what has been termed the blockholder system: fewer, larger stakeholders in companies with corporate governance laws that seek to protect creditors and employees. The UK-US market-based approach has far more dispersed ownership and much greater emphasis on shareholders' rights. In the long run profit maximization is in the interests of all groups, but as ever it is the short term that provides key differences in areas such as employee rights and representation at Board level. In offering greater non-shareholder participation, the Continental system gives greater emphasis on long-term profitability, and this is borne out by the generally longer payback periods of Continental European companies compared to the UK.

Conflicts with the MNC goal

It has often been argued that managers of a firm may make decisions that conflict with the firm's goal to maximize shareholder wealth. For example, a decision to establish a subsidiary in one location versus another may be based on the location's appeal to a particular manager rather than on its potential benefits to shareholders. A decision to expand may be determined by a manager's desire to make the division grow in order to receive more responsibility and compensation. When a firm has only one owner who is also the sole manager, such a conflict of goals does not occur. However, when a corporation's shareholders differ from its managers, a conflict of goals can exist. This conflict is often referred to as the **agency problem**.

The costs of ensuring that managers maximize shareholder wealth (referred to as *agency costs*) are normally larger for MNCs than for purely domestic firms for several reasons. First, MNCs with subsidiaries scattered around the world may experience larger agency problems because monitoring managers of distant subsidiaries in foreign countries is more difficult. Second, foreign subsidiary managers raised in different cultures may not follow uniform goals. Third, the sheer size of the larger MNCs can also create large agency problems. The sales of the larger MNCs compare with the value of production of a small country. Fourth, some non-UK managers tend to downplay the short-term effects of decisions, which may result in decisions for foreign subsidiaries of the UK-based MNCs that are inconsistent with maximizing shareholder wealth. Financial managers of an MNC with several subsidiaries may be tempted to make decisions that maximize the values of their respective subsidiaries. This objective will not necessarily coincide with maximizing the value of the overall MNC.

EXAMPLE

A subsidiary manager obtained financing from the parent firm (headquarters) to develop and sell a new product. The manager estimated the costs and benefits of the project from the subsidiary's perspective and determined that the project was feasible. However, the manager neglected to realize that any earnings from this project remitted to the parent would be heavily taxed by the host government. The estimated after-tax benefits received by the parent were more than offset by the cost of financing the project. While the subsidiary's individual value was enhanced, the MNC's overall value was reduced.

If financial managers are to maximize the wealth of their MNC's shareholders, they must implement policies that maximize the value of the overall MNC rather than the value of their respective subsidiaries. Many MNCs require major decisions by subsidiary managers to be approved by the parent. However, it is difficult for the parent to monitor all decisions made by subsidiary managers.

At times it can appear that the headquarters of an MNC (the parent company) is pursuing other goals, for example, environmental concerns, funding community projects or maximizing market share or directors' bonuses. The counter argument is that these are really proxy or operational goals necessary for long-term profit maximization. The sheer size of MNCs makes what are small payments in relation to overall profits, seem very large. Motives can always be questioned and there will always be the view that shareholders' interests could be more vigorously pursued. In some respects it is assuring to note that the US company Enron's demise (the most recent major case of corporate misbehaviour where shareholders' wealth was being sacrificed for managerial rewards) involved misleading shareholders by false accounting and deception. If there had been a more honest disclosure of information, as is required, the abuses would most likely not have taken place. The same can be said of the Italian food giant Parmalat which collapsed in December 2003 with a 14.3 billion euro hole in its accounts. As with Enron the accounts had been materially misstated. The lesson to be learnt from such scandals is that relevant information must be disclosed to the market. Legislation (in the US, the Sarbanes-Oxley Act of 2002) an active financial press and improved accounting regulations help shareholders make informed decisions.

Impact of management control

The magnitude of agency costs can vary with the management style of the MNC. A centralized management style, as illustrated in the top section of Exhibit 1.1, can reduce agency costs because it allows managers of the parent direct control of foreign subsidiaries and therefore reduces the power of subsidiary managers. However, the parent's managers may make poor decisions for the subsidiary if they are not as informed as subsidiary managers about local financial conditions.

Alternatively, an MNC can use a decentralized management style, as illustrated in the bottom section of Exhibit 1.1. This style is more likely to result in higher agency costs because subsidiary managers may make decisions that do not focus on maximizing the value of the entire MNC. Yet, this style gives more control to those managers who are closer to the subsidiary's operations and environment. To the extent that subsidiary managers recognize the goal of maximizing the value of the overall MNC and are compensated in accordance with that goal, the decentralized management style can be more effective.

Given the obvious tradeoff between centralized and decentralized management styles, some MNCs attempt to achieve the advantages of both styles. That is, they allow subsidiary managers to make the key decisions about their respective operations, but the parent's management monitors the decisions to ensure that they are in the best interests of the entire MNC.

How the Internet facilitates management control. The Internet is making it easier for the parent to monitor the actions and performance of its foreign subsidiaries.

EXAMPLE

The parent of Jersey plc., has subsidiaries in India and Australia. The subsidiaries are in different time zones, so communicating frequently by phone is inconvenient and expensive. In addition, financial reports and designs of new products or plant sites cannot be easily communicated over the phone. The Internet allows the foreign subsidiaries to e-mail updated information in a standardized format to avoid language problems and to send images of financial reports and product designs. The parent can easily track inventory, sales, expenses, and earnings of each subsidiary on a weekly or monthly basis. Thus, the use of the Internet can reduce agency costs due to international business.

Impact of corporate control

Various forms of corporate control can be used to reduce agency problems in MNCs. The agency problem that exists for management control also exists for control of the organization as a whole. Well motivated directors need to work in an environment that is not over regulated and rewards them for good performance. At the same time shareholders need reassurance that there are safeguards to prevent their interests being ignored.

Share options. A form of corporate control, based on motivation, is to partially compensate the board members and executives with share options. Such incentive packages, which may include shares as well, can encourage directors to make decisions that maximize the MNC's share price. However, this strategy may effectively control only decisions by directors and board members who receive such incentives. This higher level of management is then in turn faced with a similar problem of motivating the lower levels. Share options can again be used. In many organizations employees also hold shares in the company.

Exhibit 1.1 Financial management structures of MNCs

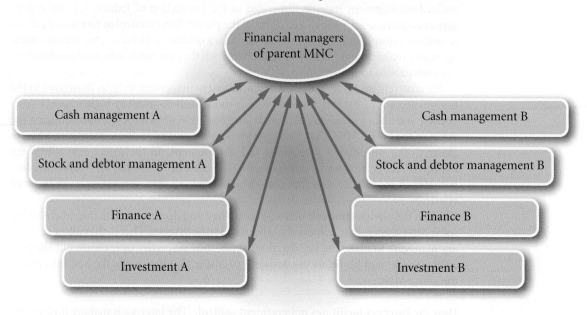

Centralized multinational financial management for subsidiaries A and B

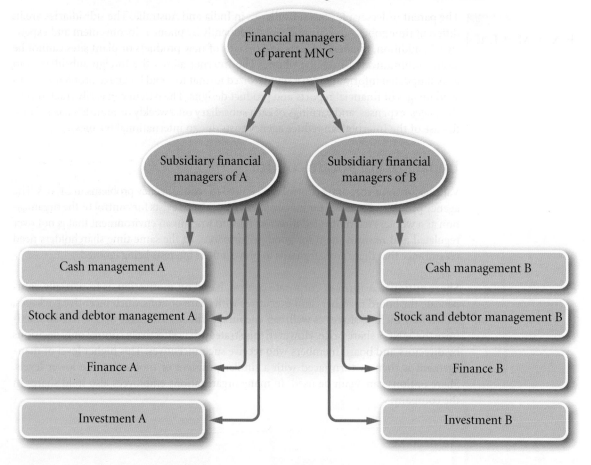

Decentralized multinational financial management for subsidiaries A and B

Hostile takeover threat. A second form of corporate control is the threat of a hostile takeover if the MNC is inefficiently managed. Stock market analysts and shareholders will sell the shares of companies they believe to be badly run. If this view is widespread in the market, the share price will fall. Another firm might then acquire the MNC at a low price and are likely to terminate the contracts of the existing directors who have not already resigned. In theory, this threat is supposed to encourage directors to make decisions that enhance the value of MNCs. It is also in the interests of the directors to ensure good motivation and control of lower levels of management. In the past, this threat was not so great for managers of subsidiaries in many countries because their governments commonly protected employees, thereby effectively eliminating the potential benefits from a takeover – France and Germany being notable examples. Recently, however, governments have recognized that such protectionism may promote inefficiencies, and they are now more willing to accept takeovers and the subsequent layoffs that occur. In Europe there is currently much debate about the extent to which employees rights can be maintained in a world economy where production has to compete with goods made in countries with poor employee rights. Hostile takeovers are governed by the Thirteenth Directive of the European Union. Generally it imposes more restictions on both the raider and the target compared to the US legislation.

Investor monitoring. A third form of corporate control is monitoring by individuals, pressure groups and institutions, including investment trusts, pension funds and insurance companies, all of whom are major shareholders in the stock market. Their monitoring by means of the financial press, annual and interim reports and, rather more controversially, by investor briefings given by companies, tends to focus on broad issues such as: motivation packages; use of excess cash for repurchasing shares; investing in questionable projects; ethical behaviour; and attempts by MNCs to insulate themselves from the threat of a takeover (by implementing anti-takeover amendments, for example). An MNC whose decisions appear inconsistent with maximizing shareholder wealth will be subjected to shareholder activism as pension funds and other large institutional shareholders lobby for management changes and threaten votes of no confidence at the MNC's annual general meeting (AGM). MNCs that have been subjected to various forms of shareholder activism include Eastman Kodak, Adidas, Shell and IBM.

Non-US banks also maintain large share portfolios (unlike US commercial banks, which do not use deposited funds to purchase shares). Such banks are large and hold a sufficient proportion of shares of numerous firms (including some US-based MNCs) to have some influence on key corporate policies. In Germany, banks are often represented on the Supervisory Board of companies and will play a part in their management. The concern is that either as lender or as a member of the management, banks will have access to private or insider information. The relationship is uneasy in that stock markets around the world forbid the use of such information when taking investment decisions. If some investors used private information, other investors would be disadvantaged and may sell shares to the informed investor at a price that the informed investor knows for sure is undervalued. It would be like playing poker against someone who knew which cards were going to be dealt next. The banks are supposed to have "Chinese walls" inside the organization so that insider information cannot be used to make investment decisions. To date, the rather difficult distinction between investor monitoring and insider information via briefings or lending, has not caused difficulties.

Constraints interfering with the MNC's goal

When financial managers of MNCs attempt to maximize their firm's value, they are confronted with various constraints that can be classified as environmental, regulatory, or ethical in nature.

Environmental constraints. Each country enforces its own environmental constraints. Building codes, disposal of production waste materials, and pollution controls are examples of restrictions that force subsidiaries to incur additional costs. The threat by MNCs to locate elsewhere in the face of overly harsh local environmental laws acts as a significant restraint to countries wishing to pursue a strong environmental policy. The failure of the US and Australia to sign the Kyoto protocol on global warming further weakens the environmental movement.

Regulatory constraints. Each country also enforces its own regulatory constraints pertaining to taxes, currency convertibility, earnings remittance, employee rights, and other policies that can affect cash flows of a subsidiary established there. Because these regulations can influence cash flows, financial managers must consider them when assessing policies. Also, any change in these regulations may require revision of existing financial policies, so financial managers should monitor the regulations for any potential changes over time.

To recognize the potential impact of regulations, consider the regulation of employee rights. Although it is understandable that every country attempts to ensure employee rights, countries are limited by the threat of multinationals investing elsewhere.

EXAMPLE | Eurenza, a subsidiary of an MNC is manufacturing in Eastern Europe. Recently, the government in Eastern Europe has imposed a tax on employers that is designed to finance an improved state pension. Production by Eurenza is now less profitable than production in the Far East. The MNC wishes to improve productivity at Eurenza with a plan that will involve laying off some employees. Under the current law in that country, redundancy is an expensive and long process. As a result, the MNC has ceased all new investment in Eurenza and is planning to halt production altogether.

Ethical constraints. There is no consensus standard of business conduct that applies to all countries. A business practice that is perceived to be unethical in one country may be totally ethical in another. For example, MNCs are well aware that certain business practices that are accepted in some less developed countries would be illegal in their home country. Bribes to governments in order to receive special tax breaks or other favours are common in some countries. Dieter Frisch, a former director-general of development at the European Commission, estimates that on average at least 10–20% of total government contract costs are bribes. The MNCs face a dilemma. If they do not participate in such practices, they may be at a competitive disadvantage. Yet, if they do participate, their reputations will suffer in countries that do not approve of such practices.

Managing within the constraints. Some MNCs have made the costly choice to refrain from business practices that are legal in certain foreign countries but not legal in their home country. Thus, they follow a worldwide code of ethics. This may enhance their worldwide credibility, which can increase global demand for their products. Recently, McKinsey & Co. found that investors assigned a higher value to firms that exhibit high corporate governance standards and are likely to obey ethical constraints. The premiums that investors would pay for these firms averaged 12% in North America, 20 to 25% in Asia and Latin America, and more than 30% in Europe.

THEORIES OF INTERNATIONAL BUSINESS

Theories in this area seek to explain the level and nature of international business. There are two broad categories, economic and business related theories. Economic theories address the problem at national level, looking at how countries can increase their overall level of wealth through international trade. In this respect the theories are normative, they examine the logic of international trade but do not necessarily explain actual trade levels. These theories are of particular importance in practice as a response to those who argue that international trade is creating poverty. Business theories are based on observation, they seek to find common patterns of development of international business and model these patterns into a coherent explanation. These theories are valuable in that they provide a compact explanation of observed practice.

Economic theories

Theory of absolute and comparative advantage. The theory of **absolute advantage** was first formally stated by Adam Smith and conforms to what most non-specialists would advance as an explanation and justification for international trade. Suppose that Country A is more efficient at producing food, and Country B is more efficient at producing machinery, in a two country world. The world production of food and machinery (the overall size of the "cake") can be increased by specialization. Country A should produce more food than it needs at the expense of some machinery production; and country B should produce more machinery than it needs at the expense of some food production. Country A can then trade some of its surplus food for some of Country B's surplus machinery. The important point here is that through better use of resources by means of specialization, the world totals of food and machinery are now higher than before specialization. It is easy to show (see the example below) that from such trade, it is possible for both countries to increase their levels of consumption of food and machinery. This is termed a Pareto optimal solution; both parties are better off through specialization and international trade.

The economist, David Ricardo, extended this analysis to the law of **comparative advantage**. He asked the equivalent question to: "what if A were less efficient at producing food as well as being less efficient at producing machinery?". He showed that if Country A produced more of the product at which it was comparatively *less inefficient*, it was still possible for world production levels of food and machinery to increase and both parties could still benefit through international trade. Suppose in this example that Country B developed its food production and became slightly more efficient than Country A and remained much more efficient at producing machinery. There would still be benefits to both parties if A specialized more in food and B more in machinery. As well as productivity it may be the case that resources for production are more abundant in some countries than others. International trade allows use of resources that otherwise may have been unused. Thus it is argued, in almost all cases countries can benefit through international trade.

In practice, countries in the developed world have a technology advantage, while other countries, such as India and China, have an advantage in the cost of labour. Since these advantages cannot be easily transported, countries tend to use their advantages to specialize in the production of goods that can be produced with their relative advantages. This explains why Europe and the United States are large producers of aircraft, computer components and other highly technical equipment, while countries such as India and China are large producers of clothes, basic computers and other lower technology equipment. Many of the island economies (Martinique, the Seychelles and Virgin Islands), for example, specialize in tourism and rely completely on international trade for most products. Although these islands could produce some goods, it is more efficient for them to specialize in tourism. That is, the islands are better off using some revenues earned from tourism to import products rather than attempting to produce all the products that they need.

There are also more difficult to explain examples. Although there are exceptions with regard to individual products, on average, imports into the United States are more capital intensive than their exports. One would expect this of a developing country rather than the world's most developed country (this observation is known as the Leontief paradox). There are further developments to trade theory related to the pricing mechanism and availability of resources. The underlying rationale nevertheless remains the same. International trade increases world production and all can benefit through international trade. Thus trade theory provides a basic economic rationale and justification for multinational activity. Note that it does not say that all countries will necessarily benefit, only that countries can benefit. There is further support from history. Countries that have been excluded from international trade (e.g. North Korea, Libya, Cuba and arguably Eastern Europe) have all suffered from backward economies and there have been clear benefits when restrictions have been eased. Also, when there have been increased restrictions on international trade as in the 1930s, overall output and wealth has declined.

EXAMPLE

From the above discussion, suppose that Countries A and B produce all their own food and machinery, producing about as much food and as much machinery as each other – these equal size assumptions are to simplify calculations and are otherwise not important. Country A is more efficient at food production and Country B more efficient at machinery production. Then international trade is introduced. Country A reduces its machinery production by 4% to 96% and with those resources increases its food production by 20% to 120% of before trade levels. Country B reduces its food production to 95% and increases its machinery production to 114% of before trade levels. They then trade as in the following diagram.

	Country A		Country B	
Gains from international trade	**machinery**	**food**	**machinery**	**food**
Before international trade A and B self-sufficient producing about the same amounts of food and machinery as each other	100%	100%	100%	100%
Specialization due to international trade (A in food, B in machinery)	96%	120%	114%	95%
Exchange: B trades surplus machinery for A's surplus food	+7%	−10%	−7%	+10%
After international trade	103%	110%	107%	105%

Notes:

■ Country A can reduce its production of machinery by 4% and increase its production of food by 20% because the resources released through reducing machinery production can be more productively used in producing food.

■ Country B releases resources by reducing its food production by 5% and uses those resources more productively to produce machinery.

■ Country A exchanges 10% of its food surplus in exchange for 7% of B's machinery surplus. Both countries are now better off as they now have more food and machinery than before trade.

■ Country A can be less productive than B at both machinery and food and there still be gains from international trade, similarly B can be less productive than A. Alternatively, A may have more abundant food resources and B more abundant machinery resources.

Imperfect markets theory. Countries differ with respect to resources available for the production of goods. Yet, even with such comparative advantages, the volume of international business would be limited if all resources could be easily transferred among countries. If markets were perfect, factors of production (except land) would be mobile and freely transferable. The unrestricted mobility of factors would create equality in costs and returns and remove the comparative cost advantage – rather than the rationale for international trade and investment. However, the real world suffers from **imperfect market** conditions where factors of production are somewhat immobile. There are costs and often restrictions related to the transfer of labour and other resources used for production. There may also be restrictions on transferring funds and other resources among countries. For example, tariffs and restrictions on imports that can only be overcome by producing in the relevant country. The European Union is often cited as an example of such a restricted market. Because markets for the various resources used in production are "imperfect", firms often capitalize on a foreign country's resources. Overall, wealth can be increased as imperfect markets provide an incentive for firms to seek out foreign opportunities and produce wealth that otherwise would not have been created.

Business theories

Product cycle theory. One of the more popular explanations as to why firms evolve into MNCs is the **product cycle theory.** According to this theory, firms first become established in the home market to meet local demand. A lack of information and a lack of resources creates a preference for single market development. Where the product is successful, the firm will experience foreign demand for its products from exporters, foreign companies or even via the Internet from foreign customers. As time passes, the firm may feel the only way to retain its advantage over competition in foreign countries is to produce the product in foreign markets, thereby reducing its transportation costs. The competition in the foreign markets may increase as other producers become more familiar with the firm's product. The firm may develop strategies to prolong the foreign demand for its product. A common approach is to attempt to differentiate the product so that other competitors cannot offer exactly the same product. These phases of the cycle are illustrated in Exhibit 1.2. Most of the established MNCs today have followed this route. Greater availability of finance, knowledge and better communications as well as the Internet suggests that in future more developments may start at an international level, but currently the product life cycle theory remains a good description.

Global strategies. International business is seen as a product of global strategies being pursued by MNCs. The large investments required for medical research can only be recouped by patenting and marketing the products worldwide. Similarly for the aircraft industry and big budget films. Prestigious brand names (France's Louis Vuitton, Ralph Lauren in the US, Swiss Rolex watches) require a worldwide market as part of their attraction. Where there is already a strong international market, firms need to produce and sell internationally to protect their sales. For example, computer chip production and car production cannot be profitably viewed as single country products unless catering for a niche market only.

INTERNATIONAL BUSINESS METHODS

Firms use several methods to conduct international business. The most common methods are:

- International trade
- Licensing
- Franchising
- Joint ventures
- Acquisitions of existing operations
- Establishing new foreign subsidiaries

Each method is discussed in turn, with emphasis on its risk and return characteristics.

Exhibit 1.2 International product life cycle

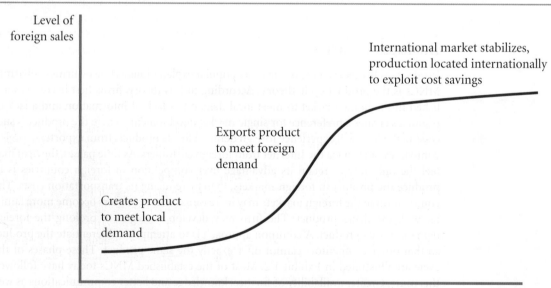

International trade

Trading rather than investing abroad is a relatively conservative approach to international business that can be used by firms to penetrate markets (by exporting) or to obtain supplies at a low cost (by importing). The risk is minimal because the firm does not invest any of its capital abroad. If the firm experiences a decline in its exporting or importing, it can normally reduce or discontinue this part of its business at a low cost.

USING THE WEB

Trade conditions for industries An outlook of international trade conditions for each of several industries is provided at http://www.ita.doc.gov/td/industry/otea.

Many large MNCs, including Boeing (US), BP (UK), DaimlerChrysler (Germany), France Telecom, Nestlé (Switzerland), generate more than £3 billion in annual sales from exporting. None the less, small businesses generally account for a significant proportion of exports (20% in the US).

How the Internet facilitates international trade. Many firms use their websites to list the products that they sell, along with the price for each product. This allows them to easily advertise their products to potential importers anywhere in the world without mailing brochures to various countries. In addition, a firm can add to its product line or change prices by simply revising its website. Thus, importers need only monitor an exporter's website periodically to keep abreast of its product information.

Firms can also use their websites to accept orders online. Some products such as software can be delivered directly to the importer over the Internet in the form of a file that lands in the importer's computer. Other products must be shipped, but the Internet makes it easier to track the shipping process. An importer can transmit its order for products via e-mail to the exporter. The exporter's warehouse fills orders. When the warehouse ships the products, it can send an e-mail message to the importer and to the exporter's headquarters. The warehouse may even use technology to monitor its inventory of products so that suppliers are automatically notified to send more supplies once the inventory is reduced to a specific level. If the exporter uses multiple warehouses, the Internet allows them to work as a network so that if one warehouse cannot fill an order, another warehouse will.

Licensing

Licensing involves selling copyrights, patents, trademarks, or trade names or legal rights in exchange for fees known as royalties. Thus a company is selling the right to produce their goods. For example, Pepsi-Cola licenses Heineken to make and sell Pepsi-Cola in the Netherlands. Oil companies need a licence from the host government to drill for oil. Eli Lilly & Co. (US) has a licensing agreement to produce drugs for Hungary and other countries. Licensing allows firms to use their technology in foreign markets without a major investment in foreign countries and without the transportation costs that result from exporting. A major disadvantage of licensing is that it is difficult for the firm providing the technology to ensure quality control in the foreign production process.

How the Internet facilitates licensing. Some firms with an international reputation use their brand name to advertise products over the Internet. They may use manufacturers in foreign countries to produce some of their products subject to their specifications.

Springs SA has set up a licensing agreement with a manufacturer in the Czech Republic. When Springs receives orders for its products from customers in Eastern Europe, it relies on this manufacturer to produce and deliver the products ordered. This expedites the delivery process and may even allow Springs to have the products manufactured at a lower cost than if it produced them itself. Springs has nevertheless to carefully monitor the quality of production in the Czech Republic.

Franchising

Under a **franchising** agreement the franchisor provides a specialized sales or service strategy, support assistance, and possibly an initial investment in the franchise in exchange for periodic fees. For example, McDonald's, Pizza Hut, Subway sandwiches, Blockbuster video, and Dairy Queen are franchisors who sell franchises that are owned and managed by local residents in many foreign countries. Like licensing, franchising allows firms to penetrate foreign markets without a major investment in foreign countries. The recent relaxation of barriers in foreign countries throughout Eastern Europe and South America has resulted in numerous franchising arrangements.

Joint ventures

A **joint venture** is a venture that is owned and operated by two or more firms. Many firms penetrate foreign markets by engaging in a joint venture with firms that reside in those markets. In China it is currently a requirement that one of the partners of a joint venture is a government owned company. Most joint ventures allow two firms to apply their respective comparative advantages in a given project. For example, General Mills, Inc., joined in a venture with Nestlé SA, so that the cereals produced by General Mills could be sold through the overseas sales distribution network established by Nestlé. Xerox Corp. and Fuji Co. (of Japan) engaged in a joint venture that allowed Xerox Corp. to penetrate the Japanese market and allowed Fuji to enter the photocopying business. Joint ventures between automobile manufacturers are numerous, as each manufacturer can offer its technological advantages. General Motors has ongoing joint ventures with automobile manufacturers in several different countries, including Hungary and the former Soviet states.

Acquisitions of existing operations

Firms frequently acquire other firms in foreign countries as a means of penetrating foreign markets. Acquisitions allow firms to have full control over their foreign businesses and to quickly obtain a large portion of foreign market share.

Cadbury Schweppes has grown mainly through acquisitions in recent years including Wedel chocolate (Poland, 1999), Hollywood chewing gum (France, 2000), a buyout of minority shareholders of Cadbury India (2002), Dandy chewing gum from Denmark (2002) and the Adams chewing gum business ($4.2bn, 2003). Clearly they are seeking synergies by being dominant in the chewing gum business.

An acquisition of an existing corporation is a quick way to grow. An MNC that grows in this way also partly protects itself from adverse actions from the host government of the acquired company. The MNC has control of a usually well-established firm with good connections to its government. The risk is that too much has been paid for the acquisition, also that there are unforeseen problems with the acquired company. It has to be remembered that the sellers of the company have a thorough knowledge of the business and the price at which they are selling is presumably higher than their estimate. The acquiring company is therefore to a certain extent outguessing the local owners – a risky proposition.

Some firms engage in partial international acquisitions in order to obtain a stake in foreign operations. This requires a smaller investment than full international acquisitions and therefore exposes the firm to less risk. On the other hand, the firm will not have complete control over foreign operations that are only partially acquired.

Establishing new foreign subsidiaries

Firms can also penetrate foreign markets by establishing new operations in foreign countries to produce and sell their products. Like a foreign acquisition, this method requires a large investment. Establishing new subsidiaries may be preferred to foreign acquisitions because the operations can be tailored exactly to the firm's needs. Development will be slower, however, in that the firm will not reap any rewards from the investment until the subsidiary is built and a customer base established.

Summary of methods

The methods of increasing international business extend from the relatively simple approach of international trade to the more complex approach of acquiring foreign firms or establishing new subsidiaries. Any method of increasing international business that requires a direct investment in foreign operations normally is referred to as a **foreign direct investment (FDI)**. International trade and licensing usually are not considered to be FDI because they do not involve direct investment in foreign operations. Franchising and joint ventures tend to require some investment in foreign operations, but to a limited degree. Foreign acquisitions and the establishment of new foreign subsidiaries require substantial investment in foreign operations and represent the largest portion of FDI.

Many MNCs use a combination of methods to increase international business. Motorola and IBM, for example, have substantial direct foreign investment, but also derive some of their foreign revenue from various licensing agreements, which require less FDI to generate revenue.

EXAMPLE

The evolution of Nike began in 1962, when Phil Knight, a business student at Stanford's business school, wrote a paper on how a US firm could use Japanese technology to break the German dominance of the athletic shoe industry in the United States. After graduation, Knight visited the Unitsuka Tiger shoe company in Japan. He made a licensing agreement with that company to produce a shoe that he sold in the United States under the name Blue Ribbon Sports (BRS). In 1972, Knight exported his shoes to Canada. In 1974, he expanded his operations into Australia. In 1977, the firm licensed factories in Taiwan and Korea to produce athletic shoes and then sold the shoes in Asian countries. In 1978, BRS became Nike, Inc., and began to export shoes to Europe and South America. As a result of its exporting and its direct foreign investment, Nike's international sales reached $1 billion by 1992 and were about $5 billion by 2004.

INTERNATIONAL OPPORTUNITIES

Because of possible cost advantages from producing in foreign countries or possible revenue opportunities from demand by foreign markets, the growth potential becomes much greater for firms that consider international business.

Investment opportunities

http://

Foreign Direct investment analysis and trends can be obtained at: **http://www.unctad.org/Templates/webflyer.asp?docid=5209&intItemID=3235&lang=1&mode=downloads.** Or search under the keywords "UNCTAD World Investment report". For a broader view see "IMF World Economic Outlook" to be found at: **http://www.imf.org/external/pubs/ft/weo/2005/01/** or by using the title as the keywords.

Investment opportunities in real assets (i.e. factories, labour, machinery and offices) are greater for MNCs than for purely domestic companies in that MNCs supply world markets and take advantage of benefits on a worldwide basis. MNCs can take advantage of cheaper labour in one market and easily available natural resources in another. By supplying different markets, MNCs also benefit from greater diversification and hence lower risk. In the Cadbury Schweppes example, by selling chocolate in many different countries, a decline in one market can be offset by an increase in demand in another market.

Portfolio investment, that is investment in stocks and shares by banks and insurance companies, also offer better returns in the international markets. Investors can benefit from a booming economy in one part of the world and again spread their risk by investing in differing economies. The IMF estimate that between 1990 and 2003 portfolio investments of European countries increased by nearly 4 ½ times. This rate of increase is larger than the increase in equivalent domestic investments. Institutions are therefore becoming more international in their investment outlook.

Financing opportunities

An MNC has greater access to funding than its smaller domestic counterpart. In particular the large foreign currency lending market in London (the Eurodollar market) is open to large companies only, at reduced interest rates. The security rating of large MNCs is also likely to be higher and therefore a lower risk premium is paid. A drawback is that individual international projects are riskier than their domestic equivalent. There are greater business risks in dealing with a less familiar market, greater financial risks when using a different currency and greater credit risk. As with investment, MNCs are more able to diversify exchange rate risk by borrowing in different currencies.

Opportunities in Europe

Over time, economic and political conditions can change, creating new opportunities in international business. Four events have had a major impact on opportunities in Europe: (1) the Single European Act, (2) the removal of the Berlin Wall, (3) the inception of the euro, and (4) the expansion of the European Union.

Single European Act. In the late 1980s, industrialized countries in Europe agreed to make regulations more uniform and to remove many taxes on goods traded between these countries. This agreement, supported by the Single European Act of 1987, was followed by a series of negotiations among the countries to achieve uniform policies by 1992. The act allows MNCs with subsidiaries in a given European country greater access to European markets than MNCs with no presence in Europe.

Many firms, including European subsidiaries of major MNCs, have capitalized on the agreement by streamlining their production within Europe and are now better able to achieve economies of scale.

Removal of the Berlin Wall. In 1989, another historic event occurred in Europe when the Berlin Wall separating East Germany from West Germany was torn down. This was symbolic of new relations between East Germany and West Germany and was followed by the reunification of the two countries. In addition, it encouraged free enterprise in all Eastern European countries and the privatization of businesses that were owned by the government. A key motive for pursuing opportunities in Eastern Europe was the lack of products available there. Coca-Cola Co., Reynolds Metals Co., General Motors, and numerous other MNCs aggressively pursued expansion in Eastern Europe as a result of the momentum toward free enterprise.

While the Single European Act of 1987 and the move toward free enterprise in Eastern Europe offered new opportunities to MNCs, they also posed new risks. Firms doing business in Europe were subjected to more competition. As in other historical examples of deregulation, the more efficient firms have benefited at the expense of less efficient firms.

<table>
<tr><td>

http://

Updated euro information An update of information on the euro is provided at **http://www.ecb.int** and also at **http:// www.just-in-case. tmfweb.nl/eurosite. htm#EMU-Members.**

</td></tr>
</table>

Inception of the euro. In 1999, the 11 EMU (European and Monetary Union) countries: The Netherlands, Germany, France, Austria, Luxembourg, Ireland, Portugal, Italy, Belgium, Finland, Spain adopted the euro as their currency for business transactions between these countries (Greece joined later in 2001). The euro was phased in as a currency for other transactions during 2001 and completely replaced the currencies of the participating countries on 1 January 2002. Consequently, only the euro is used for transactions in these countries. MNCs now have reduced costs in having to deal with fewer currencies. There is also a benefit in not having to use the less stable currencies of smaller European countries. The single currency system in most of Europe should encourage more trade among European countries. In addition, the use of a single currency allows for a single monetary policy in those countries (i.e. a single interest rate and increasing harmony in tax and financial regulations). Therefore, in assessing the economic growth in Europe, MNCs can focus on only one monetary policy rather than the country-specific monetary policies that were prevalent before 1999.

Expansion of the European Union. In the late 1990s, the European Union (EU) made plans to allow more countries to become members (see Exhibit 1.3). In 2004, the plans became a reality, as Cyprus, the Czech Republic, Estonia, Hungary, Latvia, Lithuania, Malta, Poland, Slovakia, and Slovenia were admitted to the EU. These countries continued to use their own currencies, but may be able to adopt the euro as their currency in the future if they meet specified guidelines regarding budget deficits and other financial conditions. Nevertheless, their admission into the EU is relevant because restrictions on their trade with the EU will be reduced. Since wages in these countries are substantially lower than in Western European countries, many MNCs have established manufacturing plants there to produce products and export them to the rest of the EU. The governments in some of the new EU countries have reduced corporate tax rates and offered other incentives to encourage MNCs to establish facilities there.

The conditions for joining the euro amount to a stable economy with relatively low levels of government intervention. The terms as set out in the 1992 Maastricht Treaty are as follows:

- Inflation no more than 1.5% greater than the average of the three member countries with the lowest inflation rates.

- Long-term interest rates not in excess of 2% above the average of the three member countries with the lowest inflation.

- Membership of the European mechanism of exchange rates for two years implying no change in the exchange rate with the euro by more than 15% in two years.

- Net government spending (fiscal deficit) of no more than 3% of GDP.

- A ratio of general government debt to GDP of no more than 60% or approaching this value.

Also as the national banks become an integral part of the European Central Bank, they must have authority over the countries' monetary policy, in particular have the ability to set interest rates.

The UK, whilst not wanting to apply for euro membership, has nevertheless kept to within the spirit of the rules. The Bank of England's Monetary Policy Committee sets

Exhibit 1.3 The European Union

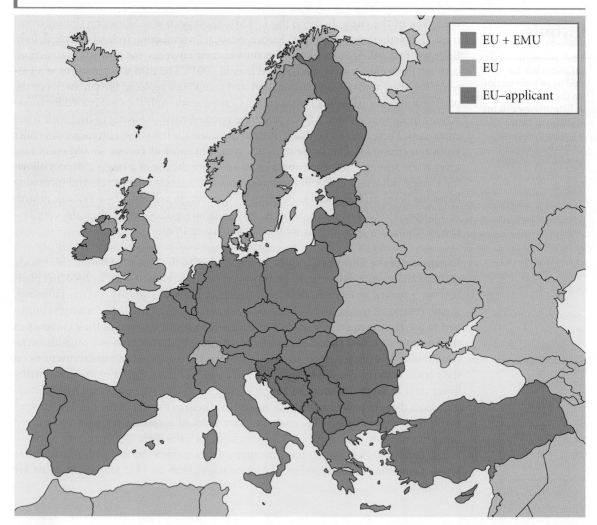

interest rates, a power previously held by the government. The Chancellor's "Golden Rule" aims to keep government spending on current as opposed to capital items at the same level as tax revenue over an economic cycle.

The central problem of economic integration between differing economies is that member countries are affected by each other's debt in having to pay a common interest rate. High government expenditure is also likely to be seen as a source of unfair competition in that the spending might be indirectly subsidizing industry. The solution is therefore to advocate conservative economic policies by member states. The Stability and Growth pact agreed in 1997 extends the prudent economic policies of joining to members once they have joined. This agreement has been the source of open controversy between member states as greater government expenditure is seen by some members as necessary for the promotion of economic growth.

Opportunities in North and South America

Like Europe, America offers more business opportunities now because of a reduction in restrictions.

NAFTA. As a result of the North American Free Trade Agreement (NAFTA) of 1993, trade barriers between the United States and Mexico were eliminated. Some US firms attempted to capitalize on this by exporting goods that had previously been restricted by barriers to Mexico. Other firms established subsidiaries in Mexico to produce their goods at a lower cost than was possible in the United States and then sell the goods in the United States. The removal of trade barriers essentially allowed US firms to penetrate product and labour markets that previously had not been accessible.

The removal of trade barriers between the United States and Mexico allows Mexican firms to export some products to the United States that were previously restricted. Thus, US firms that produce these goods are now subject to competition from Mexican exporters. Given the low cost of labour in Mexico, some US firms have lost some of their market share. The effects are most pronounced in the labour-intensive industries.

Within a month after the NAFTA accord, the momentum for free trade continued with a GATT (General Agreement on Tariffs and Trade) accord. This accord was the conclusion of trade negotiations from the so-called Uruguay Round that had begun seven years earlier. It called for the reduction or elimination of trade restrictions on specified imported goods over a ten-year period across 117 countries. The accord has generated more international business for firms that had previously been unable to penetrate foreign markets because of trade restrictions.

Removal of investment restrictions. Many Latin American countries have made it easier for MNCs to engage in direct foreign investment thereby allowing MNCs more ownership rights if they acquire a local company. MNCs with technological advantages are now able to capitalize on their comparative advantages in Latin America. The flow of direct foreign investment into Latin America has not only been beneficial to MNCs, but has also improved the level of technology there.

Opportunities in Asia

MNCs have commonly identified Asia as having tremendous business potential because of its large population base. Yet, MNCs had difficulty pursuing growth opportunities in Asia because of excessive restrictions on investment there. Some of the restrictions were explicit, while others were implicit (major bureaucratic delays).

Removal of investment restrictions. During the 1990s, many Asian countries reduced the restrictions imposed on investment by MNCs based in other countries. Consequently, MNCs can now acquire companies in Asia more easily or create licensing agreements with Asian companies without government interference.

Since the reduction in restrictions, MNCs have increased their international business in Asia. In 2004, 51% of Adidas (Germany) footwear was made in China and 21% in Vietnam, Shell (UK, Netherlands) is building a petrochemical complex in Nanhai, China. Heineken, Europe's largest brewer, has breweries in Shanghai and has acquired the major brewery in Guandong province. All major MNCs view China as the country with the most potential for growth and have invested billions of euros in projects.

Impact of the Asian crisis. In 1997, several Asian countries including Indonesia, Malaysia, and Thailand experienced severe economic problems. Many local companies went bankrupt, and concerns about the countries caused financial outflows of funds. These outflows left limited funds to support the economy. Interest rates increased because of the outflow of funds; this placed even more strain on firms that needed to borrow money. This so-called Asian crisis lingered into 1998 and adversely affected numerous MNCs conducting business in South East Asia.

Yet, the crisis also created international business opportunities. The values of local firms were depressed, and Asian governments reduced restrictions on acquisitions, which allowed MNCs from Europe and the United States to pursue acquisitions in the Asian countries. Some MNCs were able to purchase local companies at a relatively low cost, improve the efficiency of the firms, and benefit from future economic growth. For example, during the Asian crisis in 1997–98, South Korea's large conglomerate firms (called *chaebols*) experienced financial problems and began to sell many of their business units to obtain cash.

<table>
<tr><td>

http://

Background material on the Asian crisis may be found at **http://www.asienhaus.org/links /crisis.htm.**

</td></tr>
</table>

EXPOSURE TO INTERNATIONAL RISK

Although international business can reduce an MNC's exposure to its home country's economic conditions, it usually increases an MNC's exposure to (1) exchange rate movements, (2) foreign economic conditions, and (3) political risk. Each of these forms of exposure is briefly described here and is discussed in more detail in later sections of the text. MNCs that plan to pursue international business should consider these potential risks.

Exposure to exchange rate movements

Most international business results in the exchange of one currency for another to make the payment. Since exchange rates fluctuate on a daily basis, the cash outflows required to make payments change accordingly. Consequently, the number of units of a firm's home currency needed to purchase foreign supplies can change even if the suppliers have not adjusted their prices.

E X A M P L E

Burt plc, a UK importer, buys rice from the United States at $10 a sack. For each sack, Burt has to purchase $10 dollars with British pounds and then with the $10 buy the rice from the US company. The transaction is a double purchase, first the dollars then the rice. If the value of the dollar increases by 10%, the effective cost of the sack of imported rice for Burt plc will also increase by 10%. So both the cost of the foreign currency and the cost of the product are important to the overall cost of the rice for Burt.

Exporters selling goods in their own currency will be exposed to exchange rate fluctuations. A German company selling goods in euros to a British company, for example, will require the British company to purchase euros and then purchase the goods. In this case, if the value of the euro goes up (strengthens), the British company will have to pay more for the goods. The German exporter may well find that there is a decline in the order book as customers who do not use euros find the goods too expensive. To avoid the risk of currency changes for its customers, the German company may seek to invoice goods in the currency of its customers, in this case the British pound. In effect it would now be the German company that would bear the cost of exchange rate risk. If the value of the euro strengthens, the German company would now suffer in that the foreign currency would convert into fewer euros. In this case, the British pounds would convert into fewer euros. Either the exporter or the importer or the international financial markets must bear the exchange rate risk.

For MNCs with subsidiaries in foreign countries, exchange rate fluctuations affect the value of cash flows remitted by subsidiaries to the parent. When the parent's home currency goes up in value, the remitted foreign funds will convert to a smaller amount of the home currency.

E X A M P L E

The French subsidiary of Burt plc wishes to pay a dividend of 150,000 euros to Burt at an exchange rate of 1.5 euros for each British pound (£1) – a potential payment of £100,000 (being 150,000 euros / 1.5 = £100,000). If the value of the £ increases to 2 euros for each £1, the value of the payment will be only £75,000 (i.e. 150,000 euros / 2 = £75,000)

Exposure to foreign economies

When MNCs enter foreign markets to sell products, the demand for these products is dependent on the economic conditions in those markets. Thus, the cash flows of the MNC are subject to foreign economic conditions. For example, Michelin (France) the world's largest tyre manufacturer, experienced a 40% drop in lorry tyre sales in South East Asia due to the Asian crisis in 1998 but in the United States that year their lorry tyre sales were up by 14%.

Exposure to political risk

When MNCs establish subsidiaries in foreign countries, they become exposed to **political risk**, which arises because the host government or the public may take actions that affect the MNC's cash flows (political risk is often viewed as a subset of **country risk**, which is discussed in detail in a later chapter). For example, South Africa passed a law (the Medicines and Related Substances Control Amendment Act) in 1997 to allow generic substitutes (copies) of patented drugs to be used. The following year 41 pharmaceutical companies including large multinationals brought an action against the South African government. The law in South Africa had allowed their patented products to be copied legally – this is just one of the many forms of political risk. The United States government also became involved by putting the South African government on its special "watch list" – but it was later removed. A compromise solution was eventually achieved. Generally, governments cannot act on the world stage in an unrestrained manner for fear of being isolated. Even where host governments have sought to nationalize subsidiaries of MNCs, compensation will be paid.

Terrorism and war. One form of an exposure to political risk is terrorism. A terrorist attack can affect a firm's operations or its employees. The September 11, 2001 terrorist attack on the World Trade Center reminded MNCs around the world of the exposure to terrorism. MNCs from more than 50 countries were directly affected because they occupied space in the World Trade Center. In addition, other MNCs were also affected because they engage in trade or have direct foreign investment in foreign countries that may also experience an increase in terrorism.

Wars can also adversely affect an MNC's cash flows. During the war in Iraq in 2003, anti-American protests against the war in countries in the Middle East and elsewhere forced some US-based MNCs to temporarily shut down their operations in some countries. In addition, the protests led to a decline in the demand for products produced by some US-based MNCs.

OVERVIEW OF AN MNC'S CASH FLOWS

Most MNCs have some local business similar to other purely domestic firms. Because of the MNCs' international operations, however, their cash flow streams differ from those of purely domestic firms. Exhibit 1.4 shows cash flow diagrams for three common profiles of MNCs. Profile A in this exhibit reflects an MNC whose only international business is international trade. Thus, its international cash flows result from either paying for imported supplies or receiving payment in exchange for products that it exports.

Profile B reflects an MNC that engages in both international trade and some international arrangements (which can include international licensing, franchising, or joint ventures). Any of these international arrangements can require cash outflows by the MNC in foreign countries to comply with the arrangement, such as the expenses incurred from transferring technology or funding partial investment in a franchise or joint venture. These arrangements generate cash flows to the MNC in the form of fees for services (such as technology or support assistance) it provides.

Profile C reflects an MNC that engages in international trade, international arrangements, and direct foreign investment. This type of MNC has one or more foreign subsidiaries. There can be cash outflows from the parent to its foreign subsidiaries in the form of invested funds to help finance the operations of the foreign subsidiaries. There

Exhibit 1.4 Cash flow diagrams for UK MNCs

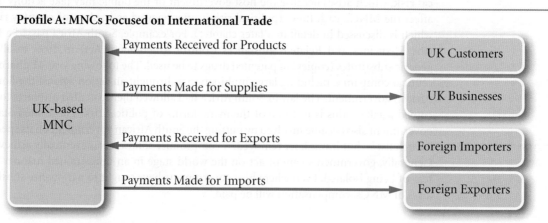

Profile A: MNCs Focused on International Trade

Profile B: MNCs Focused on International Trade and International Arrangements

**Profile C: MNCs Focused on International Trade International Arrangements,
and Direct Foreign Investment**

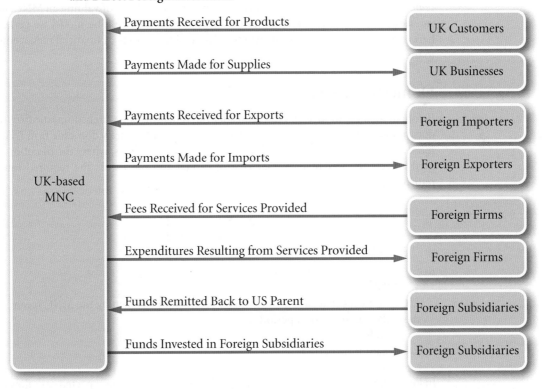

are also cash flows from the foreign subsidiaries to the parent in the form of remitted earnings and fees for services provided by the parent, which can all be classified as remitted funds from the foreign subsidiaries. In general, the cash outflows associated with international business by the parent are to pay for imports, to comply with its international arrangements, or to support the creation or expansion of foreign subsidiaries. Conversely, it will receive cash flows in the form of payment for its exports, fees for the services it provides within its international arrangements, and remitted funds from the foreign subsidiaries.

Many MNCs initially conduct international business in the manner illustrated by Profile A. Some of these MNCs develop international arrangements and foreign subsidiaries over time; others are content to focus on exporting or importing as their only method of international business. Although the three profiles vary, they all show how international business generates cash flows. These cash flows represent the cash inflows received by the MNC minus the cash outflows.

VALUATION MODEL FOR AN MNC

The value of an MNC is relevant to its shareholders and debtholders. As shareholders are the owners of the company, when managers make decisions that maximize the value of the firm, they maximize shareholder wealth. Since international financial management should be conducted with the goal of increasing the value of the MNC, it is useful to review some basics of valuation. There are numerous methods of valuing an MNC, here we use the most widely accepted valuation model in finance. The model we generate here will be used throughout the text to relate various aspects of financial management to the overall goal of wealth maximization.

Domestic model

Before modelling an MNC's value, consider the valuation of a purely domestic firm that does not engage in any foreign transactions. The value of a purely domestic firm is commonly specified as the present value of its expected cash flows, where the discount rate used reflects the weighted average cost of capital and represents the required rate of return by investors:

$$V = \sum_{t=1}^{n} \left[\frac{E(CF_{£,t})}{(1+k)^t} \right]$$

Key:
V = MNC value;
$E(CF_{£,t})$ = expected cash flows from all projects undertaken by the MNC received at the end of period t for n periods;
k = overall cost of capital
n = distant time period

In longer form: the value of a company (V) is the total ($\sum$) of the expected cash flows for each period ($E(CF_{£,t})$), discounted by the cost of capital for that period $(1+k)^t$.

Cash flows in period t represent funds received by the firm minus funds needed to pay expenses or taxes, or to reinvest in the firm (such as an investment to replace old computers or machinery). Valuation is based on cash flows rather than allocated costs such

MANAGING FOR VALUE
Yahoo!'s decision to expand internationally

Many MNCs have penetrated foreign markets in recent years. Like domestic projects, foreign projects involve an investment decision and a financing decision. The investment decision to engage in a foreign project results in revenue and expenses that are denominated in a foreign currency. The decision of how to finance a foreign project affects the MNC's cost of capital. Most foreign projects are assessed on the basis of their potential to attract new demand and therefore generate additional cash flows. Consider Yahoo! (US-based), which has expanded its portal services in numerous foreign countries. For example, it has established main pages in Canada, Latin America, Europe, and Asia. It generates cash inflows from these foreign projects in the form of advertising fees paid by local merchants who purchase space on Yahoo!'s website. It incurs cash outflows from these foreign projects in the form of expenses incurred from providing information. It needs funding to finance these foreign projects and hopes that its cash flows will generate a return that exceeds the cost of financing.

Every foreign project considered by Yahoo! is subject to conditions specific to that country, resulting in a unique estimate of net cash flows. Every foreign project is also subject to a cost of financing that is specific to the country. Thus, Yahoo!'s decision regarding a possible project in Argentina may not necessarily be the same as its decision regarding a similar project in Australia.

Once an MNC such as Yahoo! has decided to pursue a foreign project, it must continually consider a set of multinational finance decisions, such as these:

- How to forecast exchange rates of the currencies it uses.
- How to assess its exposure to exchange rate movements.
- Whether and how to hedge its exposure to exchange rate movements.
- How to pursue additional foreign expansion.
- How to finance its foreign expansion.
- How to manage its international cash and liquidity.

These are the key multinational finance decisions that are made by Yahoo! and other MNCs, and they are therefore given much attention in this text. To the extent that Yahoo!'s managers can make multinational finance decisions that increase the overall present value of its future cash flows, they can maximize the firm's value.

Before financial managers of Yahoo! and other MNCs make these multinational finance decisions, they need to understand how international financial markets can facilitate their business and must recognize the forces that affect exchange rates. These macroeconomic concepts, which are discussed in the first two parts of the text, set the stage for understanding how the performance of any business is influenced by local country conditions. Then, in the last three parts of the text, multinational finance decisions are examined.

as depreciation. The expected cash flows are estimated from knowledge about various existing projects as well as other projects that will be implemented in the future. A firm's decisions about how it should invest funds to expand its business can affect its expected future cash flows and therefore can affect the firm's value.

The required rate of return (k) in the denominator of the valuation equation represents the cost of capital to the firm and is essentially a weighted average of the cost of capital based on all of the firm's projects. It can be calculated without reference to individual projects by calculating the cost of share capital and fixed interest debt and taking a weighted average based on their respective market values. Thus the overall cost of financing the projects can be worked out directly without reference to the cost of individual projects.

If the firm's credit rating is suddenly lowered because the market judges that its projects are now riskier, its cost of capital will increase and so will the required rate of return for the now riskier projects. Holding other factors constant, an increase in the firm's required rate of return will reduce the value of the firm, because expected cash flows must be discounted at a higher interest rate. Conversely, a decrease in the firm's required rate of return will increase the value of the firm because expected cash flows are discounted at a lower required rate of return.

The two major factors in valuing an MNC are therefore returns as measured by the expected cash flows, and risk, as included in the discount rate. Expected cash flows are normally taken to be a matter of business estimation that is beyond the scope of finance and is therefore a given input into financial management. By far the greater emphasis in finance is on risk – the required discount rate.

Valuing international cash flows

Unlike their domestic equivalents, MNCs engage in projects with a wider range of risk. Even where the product is relatively homogeneous, markets in different economies will differ more than in the same economy and, where relevant, the value of foreign currencies will affect revenues and costs. It is important therefore to distinguish between project discount rates and overall company discount rates, they will not be the same. Projects must be discounted using the risk premium relevant to that project and must not be discounted using the average rate or overall cost of capital irrespective of the project. Furthermore, the discount rate for a project is not affected by the financing of the project or the company – a point made by Modigliani and Miller. Fortunately these assertions make good sense. A risky project does not become acceptable merely because it is being valued by a company that normally undertakes safe projects (i.e. has a low cost of capital). Nor is a safe project unacceptable because it is being considered by a company with a high cost of capital, i.e. that normally undertakes risky projects. Both such companies should discount the project at the same discount rate, which is derived from the risk of the project itself. The level of borrowing (gearing) of a company should not affect the acceptance or rejection of a project. As Modigliani and Miller[1] showed, shareholders can adjust their investments to effectively choose their own level of gearing, so it can hardly play a part in valuation. A minor exception to this picture are tax savings from borrowing, these affect the level of cash flows to shareholders and may differ between companies.

EXAMPLE

The Managing Director (MD) of Builders plc specializes in constructing apartments in the UK. The discount rate applied is normally the risk free rate with a premium of 6%. Recently, they have been approached with a project to build apartment blocks in a South American country. The MD applies the normal premium and finds the project very profitable. The Finance Director thinks that the project is far riskier and applies a 15% premium. She calculates that the project has a negative value. The MD agrees that he should have applied a higher rate.

Part of the greater risk of foreign investment derives from variability in currency values. MNCs will be earning and paying amounts in various foreign currencies. The foreign currency cash flows will then be valued in the home currency. Thus, the expected home currency cash flows to be received at the end of period t are equal to the sum of the products of cash flows denominated in each currency j times the expected exchange rate at which currency j could be converted into pounds by the MNC at the end of period t.

---

[1]   For example, see P. Vernimmen (2005) *Corporate Finance: Theory and Practice*, New York: Wiley, pp. 660 *et seq.*

$$E(CF_{\pounds,t}) = \sum_{j=1}^{m}[E(CF_{j,t}) \times E(ER_{j,t})]$$

Key:

$E(CF_{\pounds,t})$ = expected value in home currency of the cash flows across all projects for period t;

$CF_{j,t}$ = cash flow projects in currency j time t;

$E(ER_{j,t})$ = relevant expected exchange rate conversions into £'s for cash flow for project j.

For the sake of convenience, it is assumed that each project is in a single currency. The word relevant has been added to expected exchange rate to indicate that the exchange rate may be contractually fixed or limited by means of a financial guarantee as outlined in the following chapters.

For example, an MNC that does business in two currencies could measure the expected cash flow in pounds in any period by multiplying the expected cash flow in each currency times the expected exchange rate at which that currency could be converted to pounds and then summing those two products. If the firm does not use various techniques (discussed later in the text) to hedge its transactions in foreign currencies, the expected exchange rate in a given period would be used in the valuation equation to estimate the corresponding expected exchange rate at which the foreign currency can be converted into pounds in that period. Conversely, if the MNC hedges these transactions, the exchange rate at which it can hedge would be used in the valuation equation.

It may help to think of an MNC as a portfolio of currency cash flows, one for each currency in which it conducts business. The expected pound cash flows derived from each of those currencies can be combined to determine the total expected pound cash flows in each future period. The present value of those cash flows serves as the estimate of the MNC's value. It is easier to derive an expected pound cash flow value for each currency before combining the cash flows among currencies within a given period, because each currency's cash flow amount must be converted to a common unit (the pound) before combining the amounts.

To illustrate how the pound cash flows of an MNC can be measured, consider a UK firm that expects to earn £1,000,000 in the UK and 1,500,000 euros from the euro currency area. Assuming that a euro is worth 60 pence (£0.60), the expected cash flows are:

$$E(CF_{\pounds,t}) = \sum_{j=1}^{m}[E(CF_{j,t}) \times E(ER_{j,t})]$$
$$= [\pounds1,000,000] + [1,500,000 \times 0.60]$$
$$= [\pounds1,000,000] + [900,000]$$
$$= \pounds1,900,000.$$

The earnings already in the home currency do not need to be converted. Alternatively, one could say that there is a one unit for one unit exchange rate.

The MNC's pound cash flows at the end of every period in the future can be estimated in the same manner. Then, the MNC's value can be measured by determining the present value of the expected pound cash flows, which is the sum of the discounted pound cash flows that are expected in all future periods. This example uses only two currencies, but if the MNC had transactions involving 4 currencies, the same process could be used. The expected pound cash flows for each of the 4 currencies would be estimated separately for each future period. The expected pound cash flows for each of the 4 currencies within each period could then be combined to derive the total pound cash flows per period. Finally, the cash flows in each period would be discounted to derive the value of the MNC.

The general formula for the cash flows received by an MNC in any particular period can be written as:

$$E(CF_{£,t}) = \sum_{j=1}^{n} [E(CF_{j,t}) \times E(ER_{j,t})]$$

The value of an MNC can be more clearly differentiated from the value of a purely domestic firm by substituting the expression $[E(CF_{j,t}) \times E(ER_{j,t})]$ for $E(CF_{£,t})$ in the valuation model, as shown here:

$$V = \sum_{t=1}^{} \frac{\sum_{j=1}^{n} [E(CF_{j,t}) \times E(ER_{j,t})]}{(1+k)^t}$$

where $CF_{j,t}$ represents the cash flow denominated in a particular currency (including pounds), and $ER_{j,t}$ represents the exchange rate at which the MNC can convert the foreign currency at the end of period t. Thus, the value of an MNC can be affected by a change in expectations about $CF_{j,t}$ or $ER_{j,t}$. Only those cash flows that are to be received by the MNC's parent in the period of concern should be counted. To avoid double-counting, cash flows of the MNC's subsidiaries are considered in the valuation model only when they reflect transactions with the parent company. Thus, any expected cash flows received by foreign subsidiaries should not be counted in the valuation equation until they are expected to be remitted to the parent.

The denominator of the valuation model for the MNC remains unchanged from the original valuation model for the purely domestic firm. However, recognize that the weighted average cost of capital for the MNC is based on funding some projects that reflect business in different countries. Thus, any decision by the MNC's parent that affects the cost of its capital supporting projects in a specific country can affect its weighted average cost of capital (and its required rate of return) and therefore can affect its value.

In general, the valuation model shows that an MNC's value can be affected by forces that influence the amount of its cash flows in a particular currency (CF_j), the exchange rate at which that currency is converted into pounds (ER_j), or the MNC's weighted average cost of capital (k).

Impact of financial management and international conditions on value

MNCs recognize that they may increase their value by increasing their cash flows (return) or by reducing their cost of capital (risk). Hence, their challenge is to make decisions that will accomplish one or both of these objectives. An MNC's financial decisions include how much business to conduct in each country and how much financing to obtain in each currency. Its financial decisions determine its exposure to the international environment. If it conducts very little international business, its potential for enhancing its value is limited, but so is its vulnerability to changes in exchange rate movements or other international conditions. Conversely, if an MNC pursues substantial international business in markets where there are opportunities, it may be able to substantially increase its pound cash flows and therefore increase its value, but it will be highly exposed to exchange rate effects, economic conditions, and political conditions in these markets. As in all finance, there is a trade off between risk and return. International investment entails higher risks; but higher returns. Effective international financial management minimizes the risk for the expected return net of interest charges.

The uncertainty surrounding an MNC's cash flows is influenced by the composition of its international business, as well as by the amount of that business. Exchange rates, economic conditions, and political conditions are much more volatile in some countries than in others. Therefore, two MNCs of the same size and in the same industry may have the same volume of foreign business, but one of them might be less risky because it conducts business in more stable countries.

Though an MNC does not have control over a country's exchange rate, economic conditions, or political conditions, it can control its degree of exposure to those conditions with its financial management. Two MNCs of the same size and in the same industry could have the exact same composition of international business, but one of them might be less risky because it makes financial decisions that reduce its exposure to exchange rates, economic conditions, or political conditions.

ORGANIZATION OF THE TEXT

The organization of the chapters in this text is shown in Exhibit 1.5. Chapters 2 to 8 discuss international markets and conditions from a macroeconomic perspective, focusing on external forces that can affect the value of an MNC. Though financial managers may not have control over these forces, they do have some control over their degree of exposure to these forces. These macroeconomic chapters provide the background necessary to make financial decisions.

Chapters 9 to 21 take a microeconomic perspective and focus on how the financial management of an MNC can affect its value. Financial decisions by MNCs are commonly classified as either investing decisions or financing decisions. In general, investing decisions by an MNC tend to affect the numerator of the valuation model because such decisions affect expected cash flows. In addition, if investing decisions by the MNC's parent alter the firm's weighted average cost of capital, they may also affect the denominator of the valuation model. Long-term financing decisions by an MNC's parent tend to affect the denominator of the valuation model because they affect the MNC's cost of capital.

Exhibit 1.5 Organization of chapters

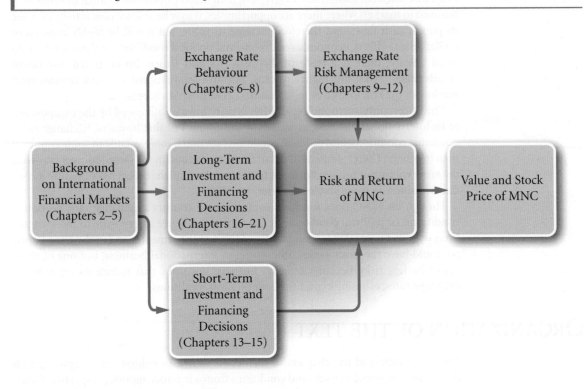

SUMMARY

- The main goal of an MNC is to maximize shareholder wealth. When managers are tempted to serve their own interests instead of those of shareholders, an agency problem exists. Managers also face environmental, regulatory, and ethical constraints that can conflict with the goal of maximizing shareholder wealth.

- International business is justified by three key theories. The theory of comparative advantage suggests that each country should use its comparative advantage to specialize in its production and rely on other countries to meet other needs. The imperfect markets theory suggests that because of imperfect markets, factors of production are immobile, which encourages countries to specialize based on

the resources they have. The product cycle theory suggests that after firms are established in their home countries, they commonly expand their product specialization in foreign countries.

- The most common methods by which firms conduct international business are international trade, licensing, franchising, joint ventures, acquisitions of foreign firms, and formation of foreign subsidiaries. Methods such as licensing and franchising involve little capital investment but distribute some of the profits to other parties. The acquisition of foreign firms and formation of foreign subsidiaries require substantial capital investments but offer the potential for large returns.

CRITICAL DEBATE

Proposition. When a European-based MNC competes in foreign countries it pays wages comparable with local rates and obeys environmental and other laws that can be less restrictive than in their home country. Bribes, in some countries regarded as a tradition, may also be paid to local government officials. In Europe, the picture is not so different, an MNC may contribute to local facilities and put pressure on local government not to oppose planning applications. MNCs do not exist to teach the world morality, they merely conform to local tradition – they have to do this in order to compete.

Opposing view. European-based MNCs should maintain a standard code of ethics that applies to any country, even if it is at a disadvantage in a foreign country that allows activities that might be viewed as unethical. In this way, the MNC establishes more credibility worldwide.

Critically evaluate these arguments. Which argument do you support? Offer your own opinion on this issue based on the information you have obtained.

To add content to your evaluation, review the annual reports of large European multinationals; where these are pdf files, conduct searches using the Acrobat "binoculars" logo with the words "responsibility" and "environment" within the report. Some counter ideas may be gleaned from http://corporatewatch.com and from http://web.amnesty.org where you should search for "UN Global Contract" as well as the previous key words. All these sources are pursuing a particular goal and must be viewed critically.

SELF TEST

Answers are provided in Appendix A at the back of the text.

1. What are typical reasons why MNCs expand internationally?

2. Describe the changes in Europe that have created new opportunities for MNCs.

3. Identify the more obvious risks faced by MNCs that expand internationally.

QUESTIONS AND APPLICATIONS

1. **Agency problems of MNCs.**
   a. Explain the agency problem of MNCs.
   b. Why might agency costs be larger for an MNC than for a purely domestic firm?

2. **Comparative advantage.**
   a. Explain how the theory of comparative advantage relates to the need for international business.
   b. Explain how the product cycle theory relates to the growth of an MNC.

3. **Imperfect markets.**
   a. Explain how the existence of imperfect markets has led to the establishment of subsidiaries in foreign markets.
   b. If perfect markets existed, would wages, prices, and interest rates among countries be more similar or less similar than under conditions of imperfect markets? Why?

4. **International opportunities.**
   a. How does access to international opportunities affect the size of corporations?
   b. Describe a scenario in which the size of a corporation is not affected by access to international opportunities.
   c. Outline the opportunities available to MNCs.

5. **International opportunities due to the Internet.**
   a. What factors cause some firms to become more internationalized than others?
   b. Offer your opinion on why the Internet may result in more international business.

6. **Impact of the euro.** Explain how the adoption of the euro as the single currency by European countries could be beneficial to MNCs based in Europe and elsewhere.

7. **Benefits and Risks of International Business.** As an overall review of this chapter, identify possible reasons for growth in international business. Then, list the various disadvantages that may discourage international business.

8. **Motives of an MNC.** Describe constraints that interfere with an MNC's objective.

9. **Centralization and agency costs.** Would the agency problem be more pronounced for an MNC which has its parent company make most major decisions for its foreign subsidiaries, or for an MNC which uses a decentralized approach?

10. **Global competition.** Explain why more standardized product specifications across countries can increase global competition.

11. **Impact of the euro on US subsidiaries.** Drinkalot Ltd has a French subsidiary that produces wine and exports to various European countries. Explain how the subsidiary's business may have been affected since the conversion of many European currencies into a single European currency (the euro) in 1999.

12. **Macro versus micro topics.** Review the table of contents and indicate whether each of the chapters from Chapter 2 through Chapter 21 has a macro or micro perspective.

13. **Methods used to conduct international business.** Durve Ltd desires to penetrate a foreign market with either a licensing agreement with a foreign firm or by acquiring a foreign firm. Explain the differences in potential risk and return between a licensing agreement with a foreign firm and the acquisition of a foreign firm.

14. **International business methods.** Snyder GmbH a German firm that sells high-quality golf clubs in Europe, wants to expand further by selling the same golf clubs in Brazil.
    a. Describe the tradeoffs that are involved for each method (such as exporting, direct foreign investment, etc.) that Snyder could use to achieve its goal.
    b. Which method would you recommend for this firm? Justify your recommendation.

15. **Impact of political risk.** Explain why political risk may discourage international business.

16. **International joint venture.** Scottish and Newcastle breweries (a real UK company) have joint ventures with United Breweries in India, Chongquin (the fifth largest brewer in China) and Baltic Beverages and Holdings in Eastern Europe.
    a. Explain how the joint venture can enable Scottish and Newcastle breweries to achieve its objective of maximizing shareholder wealth.
    b. Explain how the joint venture can limit the risk of the international business.
    c. Many international joint ventures are intended to circumvent barriers (business and cultural) that normally prevent foreign competition. What barriers might Scottish and Newcastle breweries be circumventing as a result of the joint venture?

17. **Impact of Eastern European growth.** The managers of VGood Corp. (a US fictitious company) recently had a meeting to discuss new opportunities in Europe as a result of the recent integration among Eastern European countries. They decided not to penetrate new markets because of their present focus on expanding market share in the United States. VGood's financial managers have developed forecasts for earnings based on the 12% market share (defined here as its percentage of total European sales) that VGood currently has in Eastern Europe. Is 12% an appropriate estimate for next year's Eastern European market share? If not, does it likely overestimate or underestimate the actual Eastern European market share next year?

18. **Valuation of an MNC.** Turnip plc (a UK fictitious company), based in Birmingham, considers several international opportunities in Europe that could affect the value of its firm. The valuation of its firm is dependent on four factors: (1) expected cash flows in pounds, (2) expected cash flows in euros that are ultimately converted into pounds, (3) the rate at which it can convert euros to pounds, and (4) Turnip's weighted average cost of capital. For each opportunity, identify the factors that would be affected.

a. Turnip plans a licensing deal in which it will sell technology to a firm in Germany for £3,000,000; the payment is invoiced in pounds, and this project has the same risk level as its existing businesses.

b. Turnip plans to acquire a large firm in Portugal that is riskier than its existing businesses.

c. Turnip plans to discontinue its relationship with a US supplier so that it can import a small amount of supplies (denominated in euros) at a lower cost from a Belgian supplier.

d. Turnip plans to export a small amount of materials to Ireland that are denominated in euros.

19. **Assessing motives for international business.** Pliny Inc. (a US fictitious company), specializes in manufacturing some basic parts for sports utility vehicles that are produced and sold in the United States. Its main advantage in the United States is that its production is efficient and less costly than that of some other unionized manufacturers. It has a substantial market share in the United States. Its manufacturing process is labour-intensive. It pays relatively low wages compared to US competitors, but has guaranteed the local workers that their job positions will not be eliminated for the next 30 years. It hired a consultant to determine whether it should set up a subsidiary in Mexico, where the parts would be produced. The consultant suggested that Pliny should expand for the following reasons. Offer your opinion on whether the consultant's reasons are logical.

a. Theory of competitive advantage: There are not many SUVs sold in Mexico, so Pliny, Inc., would not have to face much competition there.

b. Imperfect markets theory: Pliny cannot easily transfer workers to Mexico, but it can establish a subsidiary there in order to penetrate a new market.

c. Product cycle theory: Pliny has been successful in the United States. It has limited growth opportunities because it already controls much of the US market for the parts it produces. Thus, the natural next step is to conduct the same business in a foreign country.

d. Exchange rate risk: the exchange rate of the peso has weakened recently, so this would allow Pliny to build a plant at a very low cost (by exchanging dollars for the cheap pesos to build the plant).

e. Political risk: the political conditions in Mexico have stabilized in the last few months, so Pliny should attempt to penetrate the Mexican market now.

20. **Valuation of Carrefour's international business.** In addition to all of its stores in France, Carrefour has 24 hypermarkets in Argentina, 85 in Brazil, 27 in Mexico, 41 in China, 27 in Korea, a total of 823 stores in 29 countries. Consider the value of Carrefour as being composed of two parts, a euro area part and a non-euro area part. Explain how to determine the present value (in euros) of the non-euro part assuming that you had access to all the details of Carrefour businesses outside the euro area.

21. **Impact of international business on cash flows and risk.** Slowman Travel Agency specializes in tours for American tourists. Until recently all of its business was in Switzerland. It has just established a subsidiary in Athens, Greece, which provides tour services in the Greek islands for American tourists. It rented a shop near the port of Athens. It also hired residents of Athens, who could speak English and provide tours of the Greek islands. The subsidiary's main costs are rent and salaries for its employees and the lease of a few large boats in Athens that it uses for tours. American tourists pay for the entire tour in dollars at Slowman's US office before they depart for Greece.

a. Explain why Slowman may be able to effectively capitalize on international opportunities such as the Greek island tours.

b. Slowman is privately owned by owners who reside in Switzerland and work in the main office. Explain possible agency problems associated with the creation of a subsidiary in Athens, Greece. How can Slowman attempt to reduce these agency costs?

c. Greece's cost of labour and rent are relatively low. Explain why this information is relevant to Slowman's decision to establish a tour business in Greece.

d. Explain how the cash flow situation of the Greek tour business exposes Slowman to exchange rate risk. Is Slowman favourably or unfavourably affected when the euro (Greece's currency) appreciates against the dollar? Explain.

e. Slowman plans to finance its Greek tour business. Its subsidiary could obtain loans in euros from a bank in Greece to cover its rent, and its main office could pay off the loans over time. Alternatively, its main office could borrow dollars and would periodically convert dollars to euros to pay the expenses in Greece. Does either type of loan reduce the exposure of Slowman to exchange rate risk? Explain.

f. Explain how the Greek island tour business could expose Slowman to country risk.

PROJECT WORKSHOP

22. **Assessing direct foreign investment trends.** The website address of the Bureau of Economic Analysis is http://www.bea.doc.gov.

    For UK data see http://www.statistics.gov.uk/StatBase/Product.asp?vlnk=1140 or search for "Pink Book 2004"

    a. Use this website to assess recent trends in direct foreign investment (FDI) abroad by US or UK firms. Compare the FDI in the United Kingdom with the FDI in France. Offer a possible reason for the large difference.

    b. Based on the recent trends in FDI, are UK-based MNCs pursuing opportunities in Asia? In Eastern Europe? In Latin America?

23. Select a firm from the top ten firms from a European country (exclude financial institutions,

a list may be found at http://www.forbes.com/lists/ choose the country option for selection). Go to the company website and download the most recent annual report. Before selecting the company, ensure that it is engaged in international business. From a reading of this document and with particular reference to this chapter:

a. Review the Goals of the MNC. Is there a mission statement? Are there notes as to the company's policy towards the environment, its workforce etc.? Generally review statements of intent in the document.

b. How far do you think that the company development can be explained by theories of international business as outlined in this chapter?

c. What international business methods does this company principally employ? What do you think is the reason for their international business strategy (i.e. why do they not pursue other strategies)?

d. Outline the international opportunities and international risks faced by this company. Where these are not specifically stated, outline what you think are the likely opportunities and risks. In your view, how great are these international risks and international opportunities?

DISCUSSION IN THE BOARDROOM

This exercise can be found on the companion website at www.cengage.co.uk/madura_fox.

RUNNING YOUR OWN MNC

This exercise can be found on the companion website at www.cengage.co.uk/madura_fox.

Essays/discussion and articles can be found at the end of Part 1

BLADES PLC CASE STUDY
Decision to expand internationally

Blades plc is a UK-based company that has been incorporated in the United Kingdom for three years. Blades is a relatively small company, with total assets of only £15 million. The company produces a single type of product, roller blades. Due to the booming skateboard market in the United Kingdom at the time of the company's establishment, Blades has been quite successful. For example, in its first year of operation, it reported a net income of £3.5 million. Recently, however, the demand for Blades' "Speedos", the company's primary product in the United Kingdom, has been slowly tapering off, and Blades has not been performing well. Last year, it reported a return on assets of only 7%. In response to the company's annual report for its most recent year of operations, Blades' shareholders have been pressuring the company to improve its performance; its share price has fallen from a high of £20 per share three years ago to £12 last year. Blades produces high-quality skateboards and employs a unique production process, but the prices it charges are among the top 5% in the industry.

In light of these circumstances, Ben Holt, the company's director of finance, is contemplating his alternatives for Blades' future. There are no other cost-cutting measures that Blades can implement in the United Kingdom without affecting the quality of its product. Also, production of alternative products would require major modifications to the existing plant setup. Furthermore, and because of these limitations, expansion within the United Kingdom at this time seems pointless.

Ben Holt is considering the following: if Blades cannot penetrate the UK market further or reduce costs here, why not import some parts from overseas and/or expand the company's sales to foreign countries? Similar strategies have proved successful for numerous companies that expanded into Asia in recent years to increase their profit margins. The Managing Director's initial focus is on Thailand. Thailand has recently experienced weak economic conditions, and Blades could purchase components there at a low cost. Ben Holt is aware that many of Blades' competitors have begun importing production components from Thailand.

Not only would Blades be able to reduce costs by importing rubber and/or plastic from Thailand due to the low costs of these inputs, but it might also be able to augment weak UK sales by exporting to Thailand, an economy still in its infancy and just beginning to appreciate leisure products such as roller blades. While several of Blades' competitors import components from Thailand, few are exporting to the country. Long-term decisions would also eventually have to be made; maybe Blades, plc, could establish a subsidiary in Thailand and gradually shift its focus away from the United Kingdom if its UK sales do not rebound. Establishing a subsidiary in Thailand would also make sense for Blades due to its superior production process. Ben Holt is reasonably sure that Thai firms could not duplicate the high-quality production process employed by Blades. Furthermore, if the company's initial approach of exporting works well, establishing a subsidiary in Thailand would preserve Blades' sales before Thai competitors are able to penetrate the Thai market.

As a financial analyst for Blades, plc, you are assigned to analyze international opportunities and risk resulting from international business. Your initial assessment should focus on the barriers and opportunities that international trade may offer. Ben Holt has never been involved in international business in any form and is unfamiliar with any constraints that may inhibit his plan to export to and import from a foreign country. Mr Holt has presented you with a list of initial questions you should answer.

1. What are the advantages Blades could gain from importing from and/or exporting to a foreign country such as Thailand?
2. What are some of the disadvantages Blades could face as a result of foreign trade in the short run? In the long run?
3. Which theories of international business described in this chapter apply to Blades plc in the short run? In the long run?
4. What long-range plans other than establishment of a subsidiary in Thailand are an option for Blades and may be more suitable for the company?

SMALL BUSINESS DILEMMA
Developing a multinational sporting goods industry

In every chapter of this text, some of the key concepts are illustrated with an application to a small sporting goods firm that conducts international business. These "Small Business Dilemma" features allow students to recognize the dilemmas and possible decisions that firms (such as this sporting goods firm) may face in a global environment. For this chapter, the application is on the development of the sporting goods firm that would conduct international business.

Last month, Jim Logan from Ireland completed his undergraduate degree in finance and decided to pursue his dream of managing his own sporting goods business. Jim had worked in a sporting goods shop while going to university in Ireland, and he had noticed that many customers wanted to purchase a low-priced basketball. However, the sporting goods store where he worked, like many others, sold only top-of-the-line basketballs. From his experience, Jim was aware that top-of-the-line basketballs had a high markup and that a low-cost basketball could possibly penetrate the UK market. He also knew how to produce cricket balls. His goal was to create a firm that would produce low-priced basketballs and sell them on a wholesale basis to various sporting goods stores in the United Kingdom. Unfortunately, many sporting goods stores began to sell low-priced basketballs just before Jim was about to start his business. The firm that began to produce the low-cost basketballs already provided many other products to sporting goods stores in the United Kingdom and therefore had already established a business relationship with these stores. Jim did not believe that he could compete with this firm in the UK market.

Rather than pursue a different business, Jim decided to implement his idea on a global basis. While basketball has not been a traditional sport in many countries, it has become more popular in some countries in recent years. Furthermore, the expansion of cable networks in many countries would allow for much more exposure to basketball games in those countries in the future. Jim asked many of his foreign friends from college days if they recalled seeing basketballs sold in their home countries. Most of them said they rarely noticed basketballs being sold in sporting goods stores but that they expected the demand for basketballs to increase in their home countries. Consequently, Jim decided to start a business of producing low-priced basketballs and exporting them to sporting goods distributors in foreign countries. Those distributors would then sell the basketballs at the retail level. Jim planned to expand his product line over time once he identified other sports products that he might sell to foreign sporting goods stores. He decided to call his business "Sports Exports Company". To avoid any rent and labour expenses, Jim planned to produce the basketballs in his garage and to perform the work himself. Thus, his main business expenses were the cost of the material used to produce basketballs and expenses associated with finding distributors in foreign countries who would attempt to sell the basketballs to sporting goods stores.

1. Is Sports Exports Company a multinational corporation?
2. Why are the agency costs lower for Sports Exports Company than for most MNCs?
3. Does Sports Exports Company have any comparative advantage over potential competitors in foreign countries that could produce and sell basketballs there?
4. How would Jim Logan decide which foreign markets he would attempt to enter? Should he initially focus on one or many foreign markets?
5. The Sports Exports Company has no immediate plans to conduct direct foreign investment. However, it might consider other less costly methods of establishing its business in foreign markets. What methods might the Sports Exports Company use to increase its presence in foreign markets by working with one or more foreign companies?

CHAPTER 2

INTERNATIONAL FLOW OF FUNDS

INTERNATIONAL BUSINESS IS FACILITATED by markets that allow for the flow of funds between countries. The principal international transactions are: borrowing from abroad, lending abroad, investing in foreign shares, setting up foreign subsidiaries, paying dividends to foreign parent companies, payments for imports and receipts for exports. The balance of payments is a record of these international money flows and is discussed in this chapter.

Financial managers of MNCs monitor the balance of payments so that they can determine the nature of international transactions for a particular country and how they are changing over time. The balance of payments is an indicator of the health of the economy and may even signal potential shifts in exchange rates.

THE SPECIFIC OBJECTIVES OF THIS CHAPTER ARE TO:

- explain the key components of the balance of payments,
- explain how the international trade flows are influenced by economic and political factors, and
- explain how the international capital flows are influenced by country characteristics.

BALANCE OF PAYMENTS

The **balance of payments** is a summary of transactions between domestic and foreign *residents* over a specified period of time. It represents an accounting of a country's international transactions for a period, usually a quarter or a year.

A resident is an individual or business or any organization operating in the particular country. For an organization, this will normally entail setting up a company in the country under the commercial company laws of that country. Individuals who earn their income and live in the country are residents though they might be foreign nationals. A business that is resident is registered in the country and is a legal, tax paying entity. Such businesses include all the national companies, so for the UK, British Petroleum plc, Tesco plc, Barclays Bank plc and so on are resident companies. Subsidiaries of foreign multinationals are also residents of the country like any other registered company in the country. For example, Matsushita Electric Industrial in Japan supplies consumer and business related electronics products in the UK. The operation is more than direct exporting from

Japan, so they have set up Panasonic (UK) ltd (a wholly owned subsidiary) to manage the operation. Panasonic (UK) ltd is registered and located in the UK, pays taxes to the UK government on its profits and pays dividends to its parent company in Japan. Exports from Panasonic (UK) ltd will count as UK exports in the balance of payments statement. In this way, multinationals play a full part in the economies in which they operate.

Data for the balance of payments is collected via questionnaires and returns to governments. Although it is described in terms of a double entry system, it is not the same as a set of accounts in this respect. The figures are therefore really estimates and there is a balancing account "net errors and omissions", in the UK 2004 accounts for 2003 the net error was £1,732m. The figures will also be adjusted over the years, so the exports for 2002 in the 2004 accounts will be slightly different from 2002 exports in the 2003 accounts.

A balance-of-payments statement can be broken down into various components. Those that receive the most attention are the current account and the financial account (sometimes referred to as the capital account). Taking the UK as an example, the **current account** represents mainly export and import payments for goods and services between the UK and the rest of the world. The **financial account** represents principally a summary of investments in stocks and shares between the UK and the rest of the world – investments into the UK and investments from the UK to the rest of the world. Balance of payments are normally prepared for individual countries, but may also be prepared for currency areas such as the euro, or for multinational entities such as the European Union.

Exhibit 2.1 A foreign currency transaction

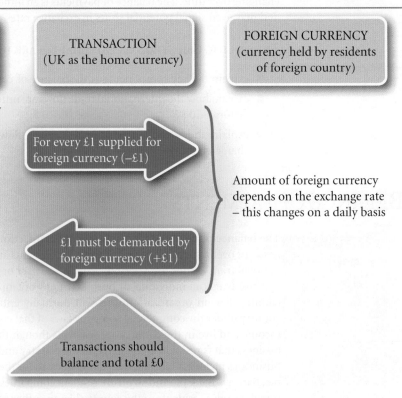

Notes:
- The Balance of Payments is a record of the demand and supply of currency held by home residents in transactions with non-residents.
- Particularly for EU countries, both the home currency and the foreign currency could be euros.

The transactions between home and foreign residents often involve different currencies, national residents offering their home currency in exchange for foreign currency and foreign residents offering their foreign currency for home currency. For countries trading in the euro area, many of the transactions will be in the same currency; but there is no fundamental difference to the recording process. The domestic or home currency side involved in the transaction (or more formally, currency held by the resident) is recorded twice in the balance of payments in a similar manner to double entry bookkeeping (see Exhibit 2.1). It therefore does not matter how much or what currency is involved on the other side of the transaction, only what is happening to the currency held by residents is of interest.

One aspect of the domestic held currency side of the transaction is recorded as a credit or plus (+), and the other aspect is recorded as a debit or negative (−). As each transaction balances, i.e. the plus figure equals the negative figure, so the balance of payments as a total of such transactions should also balance.

Generally, transactions that create a supply of domestic currency seeking foreign currency are recorded as a negative or debit; transactions that create a demand for domestic currency are recorded as a positive or credit. So, taking the UK as the home country, exports from the UK (creates demand for British pounds to pay for the exports) are positive; imports into the UK (creates supply of British pounds to pay foreign suppliers) are negative; investment into the UK (creates demand for British pounds to pay for shares etc.) is positive; investment out of the UK (creates supply of British pounds to pay for foreign shares etc.) is negative. Further examples are given in Exhibit 2.2.

EXAMPLE

Suppose, for the sake of clarity, that there are no financial intermediaries such as banks and therefore trading has to be direct. Wavy plc has to pay 150 euros for imports. It offers over the Internet £100 in exchange for 150 euros. That offer is accepted by Francophile SA of France who want £100 to pay for a British export. The supply of UK currency by Wavy is recorded as a debit or negative in the imports account, and the demand for the UK currency by Francophile is recorded as an export – a plus or credit. Both transactions are at £100 – note that it does not matter as far as the balance is concerned how many euros were exchanged for the £100.

Exhibit 2.2 Examples of balance of payment transactions

International trade transaction with UK as the home country	Demand or supply of British pounds	Entry on UK balance of payments
UK importer purchases radios from Singapore	Supply of British pounds	Debit or −
Spanish importer pays UK company for goods supplied	Demand for British pounds	Credit or +
French company pays insurance premium to Lloyds insurance in London	Demand for British pounds	Credit or +
Foreign workers resident in the UK send money home	Supply of British pounds	Debit or −
French company buys shares on the London Stock Exchange	Demand for British pounds	Credit or +
UK company loans money to its American subsidiary	Supply of British pounds	Debit or −
Australian subsidiary pays dividends to its UK parent company	Demand for British pounds	Credit or +
Italian company lends money to its UK subsidiary	Demand for British pounds	Credit or +

Current account

Current accounts are described in various ways in differing balance of payments accounts. The distinguishing feature of current account transactions is that they are international payments for goods and services between nationals and non-nationals. The UK balance of payments report a balance of trade (exports of goods less imports of goods), a balance of services (the export less import of insurance, banking, tourism and other services); a balance of income (the balance of dividend, interest payments and salary payments); and current transfers (sundry transactions including payments and receipts from the EU and charity payments). In total these balances add up to the overall current account balance.

A deficit in the balance of trade means that the value of goods and services exported by the home country is less than the imports. On the financial markets there would have been a net supply of home currency seeking foreign currency to pay for the larger value of

Exhibit 2.3 UK balance of payments

UK balance of payments for 2003	£million	Balance	Notes
Current Account			
Exports of goods	187,846		
Imports of goods	−235,136		
Balance		−47,290	Net importer of goods
Exports of services	89,693		
Imports of services	−75,076		
Balance		14,617	Net exporter of services
Interest and dividends received	126,340		
Interest and dividends paid	−104,243		
Balance		22,097	Net earner on investments
Current transfers balance		−9,854	Net transfers out
Overall balance on current account		**−20,430**	
Capital and Financial account			
Direct investment abroad	−32,052		
Direct investment in the UK	9,765		
Balance		−22,287	Net direct investor abroad
Portfolio investment abroad	−34,748		
Portfolio investment in the UK	91,257		
Balance		56,509	Net buying of UK shares, bonds and other instruments from abroad
Trade credit		−12,925	Net lender of trade credit abroad
Sundry		−2,599	
Errors and omissions		1,732	Error from estimates
Overall balance on capital and financial account		**20,430**	

■ A negative figure represents an increase in the demand for foreign currency by British pounds. A positive figure is a demand for British pounds by foreign currency.

■ To put these figures in perspective, gross domestic product (total value of output) was about £1,100,000m

Source: *The Pink Book*, ONS

imported goods and services. A negative balance on the current account has to be met by a positive balance on the financial account. A positive balance on the financial account represents a net demand for the home currency to pay for investments into the home country. Taken together excess imports are being financed by borrowing from abroad (i.e. investments into the home country). The UK balance of payments (Exhibit 2.3) shows just such a picture.

Financial account

The key components of the financial account (sometimes called the capital account) are direct foreign investment, portfolio investment, and other capital investment. Direct foreign investment represents the investment in fixed assets in foreign countries that can be used to conduct business operations. Examples of direct foreign investment include a firm's acquisition of part or all of a foreign company, the construction of a new manufacturing plant, or the expansion of an existing plant in a foreign country. The investment will typically either be lending to an existing subsidiary or the acquisition of sufficient shares in a foreign company to be involved in the management (usually regarded as above 10%) or setting up a new company and buying the shares and lending to that company to operate.

Portfolio investment represents transactions involving long-term financial assets (such as stocks and bonds) between countries. The key difference with direct foreign investment is that there is no participation in the management. The level of investment in any one company is therefore much lower than in the case of direct investment (below 10%). Thus, a purchase of 1% of Heineken (Netherlands) shares by a UK investor is classified as portfolio investment because it represents a purchase of foreign financial assets without changing control of the company. If a UK firm purchased all of Heineken's shares in an acquisition, this transaction would result in a transfer of control and therefore would be classified as direct foreign investment instead of portfolio investment.

A third component of the capital account consists of other capital investment, which represents transactions involving short-term financial assets (such as money market securities) between countries. In general, direct foreign investment measures the expansion of firms' foreign operations, whereas portfolio investment and other capital investment measure the net flow of funds due to financial asset transactions between individual or institutional investors.

Overall balance of payments

The balance of payments account can be described in three broad categories:

- Current account in surplus, financial account in deficit.
- Current account in deficit, financial account in surplus.
- Current account and financial account in balance.

Current account in surplus, financial account in deficit (Type 1, Exhibit 2.4). Ideally one would want to see these balances in a developed country. A mature economy should be able to generate surplus goods and surplus savings. A surplus on the current account would be expected from such a productive economy, more exports of high tech, high value added goods and imports of low tech goods and raw materials. The consequent deficit on the financial account means that there is a net demand for foreign currency. Such demand would be required if a developed country were to invest its surplus savings in a developing country.

However, an alternative less appealing scenario is of a developing country that has a surplus on the current account (a positive figure), driven by the need to earn foreign currency in order to repay loans on the financial account (equivalent to investment out, a balancing negative figure).

Current account in deficit, financial account in surplus (Type 2, Exhibit 2.4). Reflecting the previous discussion, this result could be a good scenario for a developing nation. The current account deficit would ideally be due to imports of machinery. The finance for such imports would be through international borrowing resulting in a surplus on the financial account. A deficit on the current account can, however, all too easily be due to high interest payments on loans, or import of relatively unproductive goods.

Developed countries often overconsume resulting in excess imports leading to a current account deficit (a net supply of home currency for foreign currency). This deficit is financed by a demand by foreign currency for home currency to invest in deposit accounts, shares and bonds of the developed country. Such investments are in a secure currency that may hold its value far better than the home currency of the MNC and be more useful to finance international trade. The developed country may even offer better interest rates to attract foreign deposits in order to finance the excess of imports.

The US has for many years run a large currency account deficit, over 5% of its gross national product. This net supply of US dollars for foreign currency is met by foreign investment in US Treasury bonds and other securities. One third of US public debt is held abroad, net financial liabilities are $2.6 trillion from zero in 1980. There is also significant foreign investment in US real estate (ranches, shopping malls etc.). The value of the US dollar is not affected; the supply of dollars for imports is met by a demand for dollars to invest in deposit accounts, bonds etc. It may be argued that by running a deficit, the US is providing a market for developing countries. The resulting foreign holdings of dollar deposits also help international liquidity; effectively the dollar is acting as a world currency. But some may argue that there is a cost to the US in that it could be seen as selling its assets to fund short-term purchases from abroad.

Current account and financial account in balance (see Type 3, Exhibit 2.4). The balance of payments must be seen within the context of the economy as a whole. Being in balance is not an especially desirable goal. Large deficits and surpluses may be quite

Exhibit 2.4 Types of balance of payments

Defining characteristic:	Type 1 Positive current account balance, negative financial account balance	Type 2 Negative current account balance, positive financial account balance	Type 3 Both accounts more or less in balance
Exports	+100	+65	+80
Imports	−60	−100	−78
Current account balance	+40	−35	+2
Investment in	+50	+80	−52
Investment out	−90	−45	+50
Financial account balance	−40	+35	−2

■ The figures are illustrative only.

small in the context of the economy as a whole. It is quite possible for a country to maintain a current account deficit in much the same way as a company can sustain an increasing overdraft as it grows in size.

INTERNATIONAL TRADE FLOWS

France, UK, Germany, and other European countries rely more heavily on international trade than the United States. The trade volume of European countries is typically between 30 and 40% of their respective GDPs. The trade volume of the United States and Japan is typically between 10 and 20% of their respective GDPs. Nevertheless, for all countries, the volume of trade has grown over time (see Exhibits 2.5, 2.6 and 2.7).

Distribution of exports and imports for major countries

The themes to note from the bar charts (Exhibit 2.5) are:

1. The relatively low level of trade with Japan for the European countries.
2. The high levels of trade with Asia.
3. The relatively low involvement of France with the US and Asia compared to Germany and the UK.
4. The generally low level of trade with Africa compared to other countries.
5. The much greater significance of the Pacific Rim (Japan and Asia) than Europe for the US.
6. The persistence of traditional trading partners. The relatively high levels of French trade with Africa reflects its colonial ties with North Africa (Algeria) in particular. The UK's trade with Ireland and the US trade with Mexico are further examples.

Exhibit 2.5 Direction of trade statistics 2003

UK exports and imports by country 2003

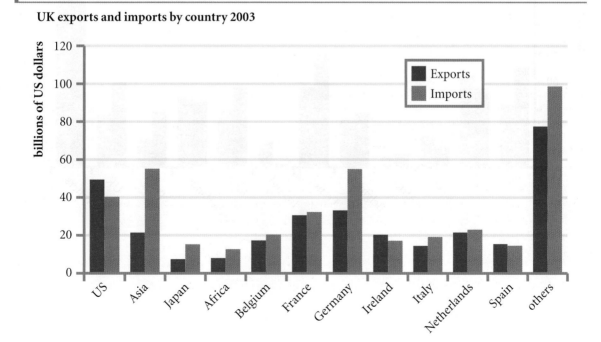

French exports and imports by country 2003

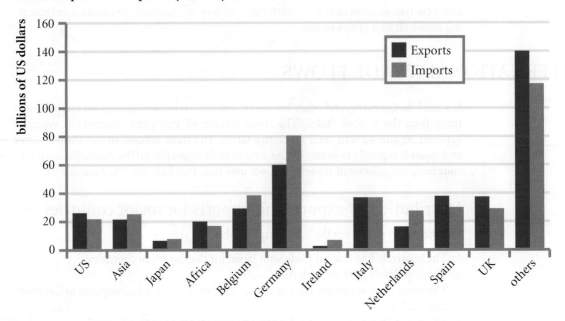

German exports and imports by country 2003

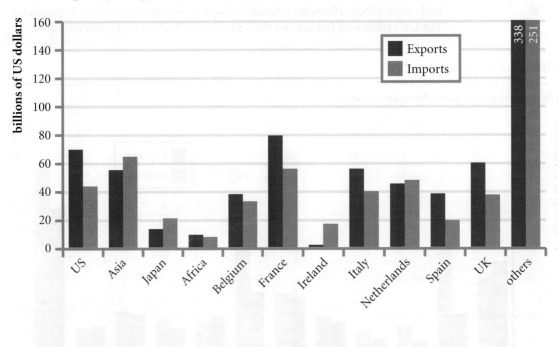

US exports and imports 2003

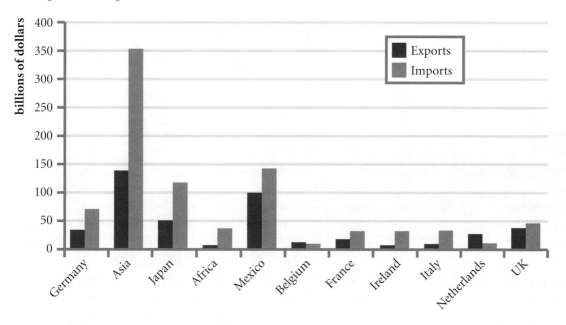

Balance of trade trends

The themes on the balance of trade trends from Exhibit 2.6 are:

1. Germany has for many years operated with a surplus on the balance of payments account.
2. France's balance of payments has deteriorated in recent years.
3. The UK has operated for a number of years with a balance of payments deficit.
4. The US runs an increasingly large balance of payments deficit.

Source: *IMF Balance of Payments Yearbook.*

Exhibit 2.6 Trends in trade

		Exports and imports of goods – billions of US dollars							
		1996	**1997**	**1998**	**1999**	**2000**	**2001**	**2002**	**2003**
UK	exports	261	282	272	269	284	274	280	307
	imports	282	301	308	316	334	332	350	384
France	exports	282	286	303	300	298	294	307	361
	imports	267	259	278	282	301	291	300	360
Germany	exports	523	510	543	543	550	571	617	753
	imports	453	440	466	473	492	481	489	601
US	exports	614	680	672	686	775	722	685	716
	imports	803	876	917	1030	1224	1146	1165	1261

Source: *IMF Balance of Payments Yearbook.*

Exhibit 2.7 Comparison of balance of payments for selected countries 2003

	billions of dollars					
Exports	UK	France	Germany	US	Japan	Uganda
goods	307	362	753	716	449	0.6
services	147	100	123	304	78	0.3
income	206	89	111	294	95	0.3
Imports						
goods	−384	−361	−601	−1261	−343	−1.3
services	−123	−85	−173	−256	−112	−0.5
income	−170	−81	−124	−261	−24	−0.2
other transactions	−16	−20	−34	−67	−7	0.4
Current a/c balance	−33	4	55	−531	136	−0.4
direct investment out	−51	−57	−2	−174	−29	0
direct investment in	16	48	11	40	6	0.2
Portfolio investment out	−56	−148	−38	−72	−176	0
Portfolio investment in	149	136	104	544	81	0
net errors and omissions	2	6	24	−12	−17	0
other transactions	−27	11	−154	205	−1	0.2
Financial and other a/cs balance	33	−4	−55	531	−136	0.4
GDP	1794	1760	2403	11004	4294	39
Population	59	60	82	294	128	26
conversion rates per $1	0.61247	0.886	0.886	1	115.93	1964

Note

1. Other transaction accounts includes transfers between accounts

The main points to note from the table of international trade data (Exhibit 2.7) are:

1. The UK has relatively high exports of services (insurance, banking, finance etc.) and high levels of investment abroad.
2. French data is similar to that of the UK but with a greater emphasis on goods rather than services and finance. The portfolio figures for France were exceptionally high (the average for the previous five years was $100bn).
3. Germany has a very high surplus on goods offset in part by deficits on services and income – these are typical figures of recent times.
4. US balance of payments account is characterized by very large deficit on the currency account, though as a percent of GDP the US figures are much smaller than the UK.
5. Japan's economy is characterized by a very large surplus on the current account.
6. The Ugandan data shows a deficit on the current account and a surplus on the financial account as would be expected of a developing country. What is remarkable is the difference in the level of economic activity for a country whose population is 40% of that of the UK, its GDP is just over 2% of the UK's and imports (its highest figure), just over 0.3% of the UK level.

Source: *IMF Balance of Payments Yearbook.*

UPDATED TRADE AND INVESTMENT CONDITIONS

USING THE WEB

An update of exports and imports of goods and services is provided at: http://www.wto.org/english/res_e/statis_e/its2003_e/its03_toc_e.htm, The World Trade Organization site (http://www.wto.org) is a good source for trade information generally.

An update of foreign direct investment (FDI) is available at: http://www.unctad.org/en/docs/wir2004overview_en.pdf, the UNCTAD site (United Nations Conference on Trade and Development http://www.unctad.org) is a good source of information generally about FDI.

Portfolio investment data can be found at: http://www.imf.org/external/pubs/ft/weo/2005/01/pdf/chapter3.pdf (the International Monetary Fund site, http://www.imf.org generally is a good source of financial data).

The UK government provides a detailed and well explained view of their investment and trade published as "The Pink Book" at: http://www.statistics.gov.uk/downloads/theme_economy/PinkBook04.pdf.

Trade agreements

http://

For further information on EU trade agreements consult: **http://europa.eu.int/comm/trade/index_en.htm** and the homepage of the World Trade Organization at **http://www.wto.org/**.

Many trade agreements have occurred over the years in an effort to reduce trade restrictions. Throughout the 1990s, trade restrictions between European countries were removed. One implicit trade barrier was the different regulations among countries. MNCs were unable to sell products across all European countries because each country required different specifications (related to the size or composition of the products). The standardization of product specifications throughout Europe during the 1990s removed a very large trade barrier. The adoption of the euro as a single currency in much of Europe also encouraged trade between European countries. It removed the transaction costs associated with the conversion of one currency to another. It also removed concerns about exchange rate risk for producers or customers based in Europe that were selling to other countries in Europe. The EU conducts a number of summits and meetings with countries and trading areas such as Latin America, Mercosur (Brazil, Argentina, Paraguay, Uruguay) designed to further trade relations by means of lowering tariffs (a tariff is a tax on imported goods), or in the recent case of a textile agreement with China in Shanghai, 10 June 2005, to limit the growth of textile imports from China until 2008.

In June 2003, the United States and Chile signed a free trade agreement to remove tariffs on more than 90% of the products traded between the two countries. In January 1988, the United States and Canada agreed to a free trade pact, which was completely phased in by 1998. This agreement reduced trade barriers on many products and increased global competition within some industries.

General negotiations are now under the auspices of the World Trade Organization (WTO), which was set up after the Uruguay Round of trade talks (1986 – 94) held by the now disbanded General Agreement on Tariffs and Trade (GATT). Currrently the WTO is overseeing the Doha Development Agenda set up in November 2001 to focus in particular on the problems of developing nations.

Trade disagreements

Countries seek to promote free trade so that their companies seeking to export goods are able to compete in foreign markets without discrimination. Economic theories (see above) also advocate free trade as the basis of greater wealth for all. For this reason countries are members of organizations such as the World Trade Organization and the Organisation for Economic Cooperation and Development (OECD), which seek to encourage free trade for just these reasons. Yet countries also seek to restrict free trade in order to protect domestic industry from foreign competition and at the same time seek to promote exports and in doing so cause trade disagreements.

It is the specific task of the WTO to resolve multilateral trade disputes through an adjudication process. The main problems with this process are firstly that it takes time, and secondly the disputed unfair trade practice remains in place during the consultation procedure. The WTO itself gives as a case study of a dispute over discrimination against the import of Venezuelan petrol in January 1995 that took two and a half years to settle. Bringing cases may also be used as a way of justifying actions. The WTO allows a certain degree of retaliation including actions taken against dumping (selling at an unfairly low price), actions to counteract subsidies by foreign countries to promote their exports and emergency measures to limit imports in order to give temporary protection to domestic industries. Thus a kind of low level "trade war" is permitted within the negotiating framework. It is important to remember that the WTO is a member driven organization, there are no powers of enforcement. All settlements are by agreement. Thus most countries, including the US and EU, have at various times been accused of unfair trade practices. The job of the WTO is to prevent such actions escalating to the point where countries impose tariffs and quotas indiscriminately. The reason why countries do not want to be seen to be overtly in breach of WTO decisions is partly because of the risk of retaliation, but also history. The Smoot Hawley Act of 1930 raised tariffs to their highest level and provoked retaliation by other major industrialized countries, followed by a catastrophic collapse in world trade; thus in trying to protect against imports, the US suffered a decline in exports as well and an overall adverse effect on economic activity. Real exports (after adjusting for general price changes) fell by over 30% and GDP fell by over 25% between 1930 and 1933, events that have always been seen as closely linked. This example above all others serves as a warning from history.

The argument about imports, however, remains. Foreign imports compete with local production causing unemployment, sometimes in areas of high unemployment. In theory, such workers should retrain for more productive employment and the unemployment should be temporary. The loss of salary should therefore only be short term and in the long run such workers should be better off. Unfortunately the theory does not specify the length of time for the short term. Governments are often in power only for the short term and have to address these problems. Thus the problem is finely balanced as countries try to argue that their exports should not be restricted but the exports of certain other countries (imports to them) should be restricted.

Consider the following situations that commonly occur:

1. The firms based in one country are not subject to environmental restrictions and, therefore, can produce at a lower cost than firms in other countries.
2. The firms based in one country are not subject to child labour laws and are able to produce products at a lower cost than firms in other countries by relying mostly on children to produce the products.
3. The firms based in one country are allowed by their government to offer bribes to large customers when pursuing business deals in a particular industry. They have a

competitive advantage over firms in other countries that are not allowed to offer bribes.

4. The firms in one country receive subsidies from the government, as long as they export the products. The exporting of products that were produced with the help of government subsidies is commonly referred to as **dumping**. These firms may be able to sell their products at a lower price than any of their competitors in other countries.

5. The firms in one country receive tax breaks if they are in specific industries. This practice is not necessarily a subsidy, but it still is a form of government financial support.

In all of these situations, firms in one country may have an advantage over firms in other countries. Every government uses some strategies that may give its local firms an advantage in the fight for global market share. Thus, the playing field in the battle for global market share is probably not even across all countries. Yet, there is no formula that will ensure a fair battle for market share. Regardless of the progression of international trade treaties, governments will always be able to find strategies that can give their local firms an edge in exporting. Suppose, as an extreme example, that a new international treaty outlawed all of the strategies described above. One country's government could still try to give its local firms a trade advantage by attempting to maintain a relatively weak currency. This strategy can increase foreign demand for products produced locally because products denominated in a weak currency can be purchased at a low price.

Using the exchange rate as a policy. At any given point in time, a group of exporters may claim that they are being mistreated and lobby their government to adjust the currency so that their exports will not be so expensive for foreign purchasers. Note that when exports are purchased, the foreign purchaser has in effect to buy the currency and then with that currency buy the product or service. So a cheaper currency will be the same as lowering the price of the product. In 2004, European exporters claimed that they were at a disadvantage because the euro was too strong. Meanwhile, US exporters claimed that they could not compete with China because the Chinese currency (yuan) was maintained at an artificially weak level. In July 2005 the Chinese yuan abandoned its peg to the dollar and is now pegged to a basket of currencies. The mechanism includes setting a central parity rate to the dollar, currently at 8.004 yuan to the dollar. There are however in 2006 still accusations that the yuan is undervalued and is a cause of excessive imports of Chinese goods by the US. One effect of these accusations is to encourage hot money (speculative investment funds) into the country. Some commentators believe this to be the source of recent rises in the Chinese A-share market. Chinese foreign exchange controls and limits on foreign stock market investment are designed to limit the effect of such speculative investment.

Outsourcing. One of the most recent issues related to trade is outsourcing. Multinational companies relocate their production to countries such as Bulgaria, China, India, Vietnam to take advantage of lower labour costs. Even services can be outsourced, for example, telephone booking systems for airlines may be outsourced to India. This form of international trade allows MNCs to conduct operations at a lower cost. The consumer also benefits through lower prices. However, it shifts jobs to other countries and is criticized by the people who lose their jobs due to the outsourcing.

EXAMPLE

As a French citizen, Dominic says he is embarrassed by French firms that outsource their labour services to other countries as a means of increasing their value, because this practice eliminates jobs in France. Dominic is president of Atlantic Company and says the company will never outsource its services. Atlantic Company imports most of its materials from a foreign company. It also owns a factory in Morocco, and the clothing produced in Morocco is exported to France.

Dominic recognizes that outsourcing may replace jobs in France. Yet, he does not realize that importing materials or operating a factory in Morocco is outsourcing and may also have replaced jobs in France. If questioned about his use of foreign labour markets for materials or production, he would likely explain that the high manufacturing wages in France force him to rely on lower cost labour in foreign countries. Yet, the same argument could be used by other French firms that outsource services.

Dominic owns a Toyota, a Nokia cell phone, a Toshiba computer, and Adidas clothing. He argues that these non-French products are better value for money than French products. Nicole, a friend of Dominic, suggests that his consumption choices are inconsistent with his "create French jobs" philosophy. She explains that she only purchases French products. Yet she owns a Ford (produced in Morocco), a Motorola telephone (components produced in Asia), a Compaq computer (produced in China), and Nike clothing (produced in Indonesia)!

Trade policies and political issues. The actions of MNCs designed to maximize profits are seen by many as having strong political consequences for which governments and MNCs should be held to account. People expect imports to be restricted from countries that fail to enforce environmental laws or child labour laws or from countries whose governments commit large scale abuse of human rights. Every international trade convention now attracts a large number of protesters, all of whom have their own agendas.

The problem for MNCs is whether they should follow relative or universal values. Should they respect or comply with the values and practices of the countries in which they operate, which may include low environmental standards, child labour and corrupt payments to government officials (relative values); or should they adopt universal values of good practice and behave in the same way wherever they operate. Relative values are in one sense non-political in that they respect the traditions and culture of the countries in which they operate. The counter argument is that MNCs become a strong moral force in these countries. Should a country wish to improve its environmental laws, for instance, there is the implied threat that a profit-making MNC will move to another location where the laws are more lax (sometimes referred to as the "race to the bottom"). Thus countries feel pressured to maintain low standards. So it is argued that there is a political consequence even to relative values.

The other approach is to adopt universal values and standards, or at least minimum levels which MNCs apply wherever they operate. A small step was taken in this direction by the UN Sub-Commission on the Promotion and Protection of Human Rights, which in 2003 approved the UN Norms on the Responsibilities of Transnational Corporations and Other Business Enterprises with regard to human rights (see: http://web.amnesty.org/aidoc/aidoc_pdf.nsf/Index/IOR420022004ENGLISH/$File/IOR4200204.pdf or search on the paper title). These appear to be no more than a set of aspirations, and as with much UN work, of uncertain practical implications. There would nevertheless be real difficulties if these values were to be actively enforced. Universal values are more obviously political and may be seen as interfering in the governance of countries. Also, the status of UN rules in a sense undermines that of governments in that many would argue that it is for governments to regulate MNCs not the UN. Such initiatives are therefore likely to remain purely voluntary.

Disagreements within the European Union. In 2004, ten countries from Eastern Europe joined the European Union (EU). Firms based in these newer participating countries in the EU are now subject to reduced trade barriers on EU-related trade. However, these countries are now also subject to the EU tariffs on products that enter the EU. For example, the EU places a 75% tax (tariff) on bananas that are imported by all EU countries. Consequently, the retail price of bananas will likely increase, as the tax is passed on to the consumers. This type of tariff has caused some friction between EU countries that commonly import products and other EU countries.

The philosophy behind the EU trade agreements is that firms within the EU can compete on a level playing field with zero or standardized restrictions across countries. However, governments still claim that some countries have advantages over others. For example, the German government suggested that firms in Poland have an unfair advantage because the Polish government imposes a relatively lower corporate tax rate on its corporations than other EU countries.

FACTORS AFFECTING INTERNATIONAL TRADE FLOWS

Because international trade can significantly affect a country's economy, it is important to identify and monitor the important factors. The most influential factors are:

- Inflation
- National income
- Government restrictions
- Exchange rates

Impact of inflation

If a country's inflation rate increases relative to the countries with which it trades, its current account will be expected to decrease, other things being equal. Consumers and corporations in that country will most likely purchase more goods overseas (due to high local inflation), while the country's exports to other countries will decline.

Impact of national income

If a country's income level (national income) increases by a higher percentage than those of other countries, its current account is expected to decrease, other things being equal. As the real income level (adjusted for inflation) rises, so does consumption of goods. A percentage of that increase in consumption (sometimes referred to as the marginal propensity to import) will most likely reflect an increased demand for foreign goods.

Impact of government restrictions

A country's government can prevent or discourage imports from other countries. By imposing such restrictions, the government disrupts trade flows. Among the most commonly used trade restrictions are tariffs and quotas.

Tariffs and quotas. If a country's government imposes a tax on imported goods (i.e. a **tariff**), the prices of foreign goods to consumers are effectively increased. Tariffs imposed by the US government are on average lower than those imposed by other governments. Some industries, however, are more highly protected by tariffs than others. American apparel products and farm products have historically received more protection against foreign competition through high tariffs on related imports.

In addition to tariffs, a government can reduce its country's imports by enforcing a **quota**, or a maximum limit that can be imported. Quotas have been commonly applied to a variety of goods imported by the United States and other countries.

Other types of restrictions. Some **trade sanctions** may be imposed on products for health and safety reasons.

In 2001, an outbreak of foot-and-mouth disease occurred in the United Kingdom and eventually spread to several other European countries. This disease can spread by direct or indirect contact with infected animals. The US government imposed trade restrictions on some products produced in the United Kingdom for health reasons. Consequently, UK exports to the United States declined abruptly. In 2004 the EU banned the import of tuna and swordfish products from countries who did not manage fish stocks in a sustainable manner.

These examples illustrate how uncontrollable factors besides inflation, national income, tariffs and quotas, and exchange rates can affect the balance of trade between two countries.

Impact of exchange rates

Each currency is valued in terms of other currencies through the use of exchange rates so that currencies can be exchanged to facilitate international transactions. The values of most currencies fluctuate over time because of market and government forces (as discussed in detail in Chapter 4). If a *currency*, for example Currency A as used by Country A, begins to rise in value against other currencies, goods exported in Currency A will become more expensive for the foreign purchasers using a different currency. As a consequence, the demand for such goods may well decrease and value of exports for Country A will decline. At the same time, the higher value of currency A will mean that imports in foreign currency will cost less – the value of imports is likely to rise. A fall in exports and a rise in imports will result in a worsening balance of payments on the current account.

A tennis racket that sells in the UK for £100 will require a payment of 150 euros by a French importer if the euro is valued at 1.5 euros = £1. If the British pound then becomes more expensive, costing say 1.8 euros, then the French importer will have to pay 180 euros to buy the tennis racket. The French importer may be willing to pay the extra 180 – 150 = 30 euros, in which case UK's exports will not be affected. But the cost of the racket for the French importer has increased by (180 – 150) / 150 = 0.20 or 20%, so it seems likely that the French importer will look elsewhere and the UK will experience a fall in export quantities and value.

By the same token, a devaluation or fall in the value of Currency A will make the currency cheaper and make imports denominated in foreign currency more expensive and

http://

Information about tariffs on imported products and anti-dumping orders by the US is provided at: **http://www.dataweb.usitc.gov**. The European equivalent is at: **http://www.eurunion.org/legislat/customs.htm#** TARIFFSCHEDULE (this is part of the US view of the EU which is rather clearer than the EU's own version). There is an excellent introduction to trade in Europe at: **http://europa.eu.int/comm/publications/booklets/move/19/txt_en.htm**. As always, reduced versions of these links will normally lead to more general pages, e.g. **http://europa.eu.int/comm/publications**. Tariff Rates: detailed information about tariffs imposed by each country is provided at: **http://www.worldbank.org/data/wdi2000/pdfs/tab6_6.pdf**.

E X A M P L E

exports less expensive. Imports are likely to *fall*; whereas the cheaper currency will make exports denominated in Currency A less expensive for foreign purchasers resulting in an *increase* in exports. So a fall in imports and an increase in exports will improve the balance of payments, but this has to be set against the increase in the cost of imports as a result of the devaluation (see Exhibit 2.8 for a summary).

The relationship crucially depends on the price sensitivity (or price elasticity) of exports and imports. If they are both very price sensitive, then an increase in the value of Currency A will lead to exports falling dramatically and imports rising steeply; a devaluation will imply a steep rise in exports and a dramatic fall in imports. But if demand did not change much as a result of the change in price (price inelasticity), a devaluation, for instance, could mean simply more expensive imports and no change in exports resulting in a worsening rather than an improvement in the balance of payments.

The elasticity argument is important because an increasing value of a currency (revaluation) does not always mean a worsening current account balance and a devaluation does not always improve the balance. In the 1970s and 1980s the West German Deutschmark increased significantly in value on a number of occasions and yet the current account remained strong. So although a devaluing currency is normally associated with an improvement in the current account balance (and the opposite for an appreciation), the relationship is not automatic. A developing country exporting a basic commodity such as copper may experience an adverse rather than a positive effect from devaluation. Cheaper copper exports from a devaluation does not necessarily increase the demand as developed countries will not want to store up copper simply because it is cheap. On the other hand a devaluation will have made essential imports more expensive with little chance of switching supplies to home sources. So a devaluation could result in

---

Exhibit 2.8 Current account balance for UK, effects of exchange rate revaluation and devaluation

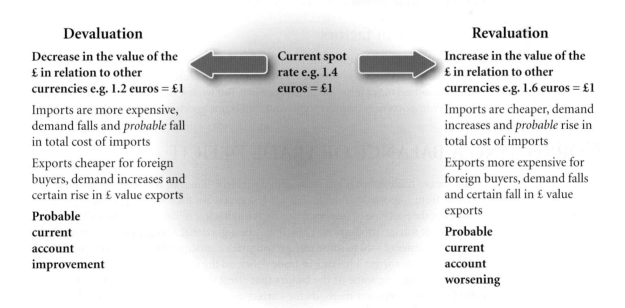

Devaluation

Decrease in the value of the £ in relation to other currencies e.g. 1.2 euros = £1

Current spot rate e.g. 1.4 euros = £1

Revaluation

Increase in the value of the £ in relation to other currencies e.g. 1.6 euros = £1

Imports are more expensive, demand falls and *probable* fall in total cost of imports

Imports are cheaper, demand increases and *probable* rise in total cost of imports

Exports cheaper for foreign buyers, demand increases and certain rise in £ value exports

Exports more expensive for foreign buyers, demand falls and certain fall in £ value exports

Probable current account improvement

Probable current account worsening

Notes:
- The total value of imports depends on the quantity reaction to changes in their price (elasticity) due to the change in the value of the pound.
- Although the increase and decrease in exports is certain, the size of the change is not certain.

higher import costs and not much of an increase in exports, overall a fall in the current account balance. The elasticity of exports and imports must be such that when a currency devalues the favourable volume reactions, a decline in imports and a rise in exports, must be able to offset the increase in the cost of imports.

EXAMPLE

During the 1997–98 Asian crisis, the exchange rates of Asian currencies declined substantially against the dollar, which caused the prices of Asian products to decline from the perspective of the United States and many other countries. Consequently, the demand for Asian products increased and sometimes replaced the demand for products of other countries. For example, the weakness of the Thai baht during this period caused an increase in the global demand for fish from Thailand and a decline in the demand for similar products from the United States (Seattle).

EXAMPLE

The President looked across the table at his Chief Economist and mused: "So, if we devalue our currency from 1 lira to the US dollar to 1.15 liras to the dollar you are saying that all our exports will be cheaper to buy." The Chief Economist looked pleased: "Yes, holders of dollars will have to pay about 15% less to buy a lira. Our tobacco, cars and clothing will all be much cheaper for them – we should be able to export more." The President looked out of the window and eyed a passing plane: "Imports are going to be more expensive – the dollar costs more, so fewer mobile phones and foreign cars." "Yes, if they want to buy a foreign car it is now going to cost them 15% more." The President sensed that his Economist was simply trying to get him to agree: "But what if they don't want to give up their phones and foreign cars, our import bill could go up." The Chief Economist suddenly felt that the President was about to dismiss his advice: "Sir, a cheaper currency should increase our exports, yet our existing levels of imports will be more expensive, but we confidently expect that the demand for imports on average will fall and that the increase in exports and fall in import quantities will offset the increase in import prices. Our balance of payments should improve." The President noted the caution: "Should, should … what are the other factors?"

Interaction of factors

Because the factors that affect the balance of trade interact, their simultaneous influence on the balance of trade is complex. For example, devaluing the home currency on its own will indeed make imports more expensive. But what if there is inflation in the home country? Imports may be more expensive; but home goods even more expensive.

CORRECTING A BALANCE OF TRADE DEFICIT

A balance of trade deficit is not necessarily a problem; it may be that a country's consumers benefit from imported products that are less expensive than locally produced products. However, the purchase of imported products implies less reliance on domestic production in favour of foreign production. Thus, it may be argued that a large balance of trade deficit causes a transfer of jobs to some foreign countries. Consequently, a country's government may attempt to correct a balance of trade deficit on the current account.

By reconsidering some of the factors that affect the balance of trade, it is possible to develop some common methods for correcting a deficit. Any policy that will increase foreign demand for the country's goods and services will improve its balance of trade position. Foreign demand may increase if export prices become more attractive. This can occur when the country's inflation is low or when its currency's value is reduced, thereby making the prices cheaper from a foreign perspective.

A floating exchange rate could possibly correct any international trade imbalances in the following way. A deficit in a country's balance of trade suggests that the country is spending more funds on foreign products than it is receiving from exports to foreign countries. Because it is selling its currency (to buy foreign goods) in greater volume than the foreign demand for its currency, the value of its currency should decrease. This decrease in value should encourage more foreign demand for its goods in the future. While this theory seems rational, it does not always work as just described. It is possible that, instead, a country's currency will remain stable or appreciate even when the country has a balance of trade deficit. The negative balance on the current account can be sustained by positive balance on the financial account representing a net inflow of investment into the country.

The United States normally experiences a large balance of trade deficit, which should place downward pressure on the value of the dollar. Yet, in some years, there is substantial investment in dollar-denominated securities by foreign investors. This foreign demand for the dollar places upward pressure on its value, thereby offsetting the downward pressure caused by the trade imbalance. So, on the international exchanges the excess of dollars being offered for foreign currency to pay for imports is met by a demand by holders of foreign currency to buy dollars in order to buy bonds, shares and deposit accounts in the US. The deficit on the current account due to the surplus imports is being met by a positive balance on the financial account due to surplus investment into the US. Thus, a balance of trade deficit will not always be corrected by a currency adjustment.

This particular scenario is unique to the US and possibly may be the case with the euro in the future. In effect, the US dollar is acting as a world currency. The US can print dollars (expand its money supply), import goods with that money, and the money is not exchanged but simply deposited back in the US by a foreign institution and used for international trade. This relationship relies on the confidence of foreign investors in the dollar. If that confidence is lost, then the value of the dollar could fall rapidly as happened in the early 1970s. It is currently thought that these large imbalances may be a feature of the world economy, especially as investment becomes increasingly international.

Why a weak home currency is not a perfect solution

Even if a country's home currency weakens, its balance of trade deficit will not necessarily be corrected for the following reasons.

Counterpricing by competitors. When a country's currency weakens, its prices become more attractive to foreign customers, and many foreign companies lower their prices to remain competitive with the country's firms.

Impact of other weak currencies. The currency does not necessarily weaken against all currencies at the same time.

EXAMPLE

When the British pound weakens in Europe, the British pound's exchange rates with the currencies of Hong Kong, Singapore, South Korea, and Taiwan may remain more stable. As some UK firms reduce their demand for supplies produced in European countries, they may increase their demand for goods produced in Asian countries. Consequently, the British pound's weakness in European countries causes a change in international trade behaviour but does not eliminate the UK trade deficit.

Exhibit 2.9 J-curve effect

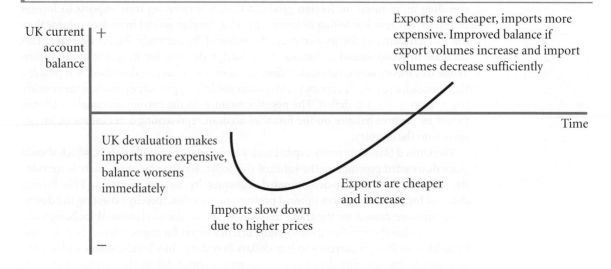

Prearranged international transactions. Many international trade transactions are prearranged and cannot be immediately adjusted. Thus, a weaker British pound may attract foreign purchasers who cannot immediately sever their relationships with suppliers from other countries. Over time, they may begin to take advantage of the weaker British pound by purchasing UK imports, if they believe that the weakness will continue. The lag time between the British pound's weakness and the foreign purchasers' increased demand for UK products could be as long as 18 months or even longer.

The UK balance of trade may actually deteriorate in the short run as a result of British pound depreciation. The price effects (increased cost of imports) are likely to occur more quickly than the more favourable quantity effects (reduction in quantity of imports and increase in the quantity of exports). This pattern is called the **J-curve effect**, and it is illustrated in Exhibit 2.9. The further decline in the trade balance before a reversal creates a trend that can look like the letter J.

Intercompany trade. A fourth reason why a weak currency will not always improve a country's balance of trade is that importers and exporters that are under the same ownership have unique relationships. Many firms purchase products that are produced by their subsidiaries in what is referred to as **intracompany trade** (intra means within and inter means between). This type of trade makes up more than 50% of all international trade. The trade between the two parties will normally continue regardless of exchange rate movements. Thus, the impact of exchange rate movements on intracompany trade patterns is limited.

INTERNATIONAL CAPITAL FLOWS

| | Direct inflows and outflows | | | | |
| | billions of dollars | | | | |
	1999	2000	2001	2002	2003
US Direct Foreign Investment in	289	321	167	72	40
US Direct Foreign Investment out	225	159	142	135	174
UK Direct Foreign Investment in	90	122	54	29	15
UK Direct Foreign Investment out	202	245	60	34	51
French Direct Foreign Investment in	47	42	50	49	48
French Direct Foreign Investment out	119	174	87	50	57
German Direct Foreign Investment in	56	210	21	35	11
German Direct Foreign Investment out	110	60	37	9	2

Source: *IMF Balance of Payments Yearbook*

Direct foreign investment is typically the acquisition of shares with direct management interest (defined by the OECD as 10% or more of the share ownership) and subsequent transactions with such entities – that may be subsidiaries for example. UK direct inward investment appears to have fallen in recent years and the claim may be made that this is the result of Britain not joining the euro. A recent report by the accountants Ernst and Young, however, suggests that lower outward investment from the US is more likely the cause, German inward investment appears to have suffered a similar fate. The UK's share of non-European investment inwards according to the same report remains healthy.

| | Portfolio inflows and outflows | | | | |
| | billions of dollars | | | | |
	1999	2000	2001	2002	2003
US Portfolio Foreign Investment in	286	437	428	428	544
US Portfolio Foreign Investment out	116	122	85	−16	72
UK Portfolio Foreign Investment in	184	256	70	77	149
UK Portfolio Foreign Investment out	34	97	125	−1	56
French Portfolio Foreign Investment in	118	132	107	68	136
French Portfolio Foreign Investment out	127	97	85	85	148
German Portfolio Foreign Investment in	178	41	133	102	104
German Portfolio Foreign Investment out	190	192	112	60	38

Source: *IMF Balance of Payments Yearbook*

The UK and France have high relative foreign portfolio investments (defined as the acquisition of equity and debt securities without ownership interest). Foreign investments out are referred to as the acquisition of assets and investment in as liabilities. Between 1990 and 2003 average external assets and liabilities of major countries have tripled (these figures include direct investment). This increase has been accompanied by

http://

FDI by multinationals including lists of major multinational companies listed by foreign investment can be found in the UN Commission on Trade and Development (UNCTAD) World Investment Report 2004. The download is currently available at: **http://www.unctad. org/Templates/ webflyer.asp?docid= 5209&intItemID= 3235&lang=1&mode,** downloads more easily retrieved through using a search engine.

http://

FDI information
Further information on foreign direct investment can be obtained from the World Bank website at **http://rru.worldbank. org/Themes/ ForeignDirect Investment/**
The "Investment Policy Review" and "The World Investment Directory" are useful further links from this page. The OECD offers a developed country viewpoint at **http:// www.oecd.org/home/,** choose the "By Topic" option. Finally, the search engine at **http:// www.corporatewatch. org.uk/** offers a decidedly alternative (dissident) view of investment.

a decline in home bias of investments as the increase overseas investments is much more than the increase in the total value of domestic investment markets. Portfolio investment overseas was estimated by the IMF to be about 48% of UK domestic capital market, Germany 31%, Japan 17%, US 7%, whereas in 1980 all percentages were below 3% except for the UK at 11%. Location of international portfolio investment is still, however, dominated by proximity.

The top ten multinationals' rates by their investments abroad are: General Electric (US), Vodafone (UK), Ford Motor Co. (US), BP (UK), General Motors (US), Royal Dutch /Shell Group (UK, Netherlands), Toyota (Japan), Total (France), France Telecom (France) and ExxonMobil (US). The annual report of these companies and all major companies discloses the geographical location of foreign investments and reports on the investment policies of the company.

Factors affecting FDI

Capital flows resulting from FDI change whenever conditions in a country change the desire of firms to conduct business operations there. Some of the more common factors that could affect a country's appeal for FDI are identified here.

Changes in restrictions. During the 1990s, many countries lowered their restrictions on FDI, thereby opening the way to more FDI in those countries. Many MNCs, have been penetrating less developed countries such as Argentina, Chile, Mexico, India and China. New opportunities in these countries have arisen from the removal of government barriers.

Privatization. Several national governments have recently engaged in **privatization**, or the selling of some of their operations to corporations and other investors. Privatization is popular in Brazil and Mexico, in Eastern European countries such as Poland and Hungary, and in such Caribbean territories as the Virgin Islands. It allows for greater international business as foreign firms can acquire operations sold by national governments.

Privatization was used in Chile to prevent a few investors from controlling all the shares and in France to prevent a possible reversion to a more nationalized economy. In the United Kingdom, privatization was promoted to spread stock ownership across investors, which allowed more people to have a direct stake in the success of British industry.

The primary reason that the market value of a firm may increase in response to privatization is the anticipated improvement in managerial efficiency. Managers in a privately owned firm can focus on the goal of maximizing shareholder wealth, whereas in a state-owned business, the state must consider the economic and social ramifications of any business decision. Also, managers of a privately owned enterprise are more motivated to ensure profitability because their careers may depend on it. For these reasons, privatized firms will search for local and global opportunities that could enhance their value. The trend toward privatization will undoubtedly create a more competitive global marketplace.

Potential economic growth. Countries that have greater potential for economic growth are more likely to attract FDI because firms recognize that they may be able to capitalize on that growth by establishing more business there.

Tax rates. Countries that impose relatively low tax rates on corporate earnings are more likely to attract FDI. When assessing the feasibility of FDI, firms estimate the after-tax cash flows that they expect to earn.

Exchange rates. Firms typically prefer to direct FDI to countries where the local currency is expected to strengthen against their own. Under these conditions, they can invest funds to establish their operations in a country while that country's currency is relatively cheap (weak). Then, earnings from the new operations can periodically be converted back to the firm's currency at a more favourable exchange rate.

Factors affecting international portfolio investment

The desire by individual or institutional investors to direct international portfolio investment to a specific country is influenced by the following factors.

Tax rates on interest or dividends. Investors normally prefer to invest in a country where the taxes on interest or dividend income from investments are relatively low. Investors assess their potential after-tax earnings from investments in foreign securities.

Interest rates. Portfolio investment can also be affected by interest rates. Money tends to flow to countries with high interest rates, as long as the local currencies are not expected to weaken.

http://

Information on capital flows and international portfolio transactions is provided at **http://www.worldbank.org** and at the website for the Bank for International Settlements **http://www.bis.org/**, follow the "statistics" link.

Exchange rates. When investors invest in a security in a foreign country, their return is affected by: (1) the change in the value of the security; and (2) the change in the value of the currency in which the security is denominated. If a country's home currency is expected to strengthen, foreign investors may be willing to invest in the country's securities to benefit from the currency movement. Conversely, if a country's home currency is expected to weaken, foreign investors may decide to purchase securities in other countries.

AGENCIES THAT FACILITATE INTERNATIONAL FLOWS

A variety of agencies have been established to facilitate international trade and financial transactions. These agencies often represent a group of nations. A description of some of the more important agencies follows.

International Monetary Fund

The United Nations Monetary and Financial Conference held in Bretton Woods, New Hampshire, in July 1944, was called to develop a structured international monetary system. As a result of this conference, the **International Monetary Fund (IMF)** was formed. The major objectives of the IMF, as set by its charter, are to: (1) promote cooperation among countries on international monetary issues, (2) promote stability in exchange rates, (3) provide temporary funds to member countries attempting to correct imbalances of international payments, (4) promote free mobility of capital funds across countries, and (5) promote free trade. It is clear from these objectives that the IMF's goals encourage increased internationalization of business.

The IMF is overseen by a Board of Governors, composed of finance officers (such as the head of the central bank) from each of the 184 member countries. It also has an executive board composed of 24 executive directors representing the member countries. This board is based in Washington, DC, and meets at least three times a week to discuss ongoing issues.

One of the key duties of the IMF is its **compensatory financing facility (CFF)**, which attempts to reduce the impact of export instability on country economies. Although it is available to all IMF members, this facility is used mainly by developing countries. A country experiencing financial problems due to reduced export earnings must demonstrate that the reduction is temporary and beyond its control. In addition, it must be willing to work with the IMF in resolving the problem.

Each member country of the IMF is assigned a quota based on a variety of factors reflecting that country's economic size as an economy and involvement in international trade and investment. Members are required to pay this assigned quota. The amount of funds that each member can borrow from the IMF depends on its particular quota.

The financing by the IMF is measured in **special drawing rights (SDRs)**. The SDR is an international reserve asset created by the IMF and allocated to member countries to supplement currency reserves. The SDR is not an issued currency but simply a unit of account, a weighted basket of currencies. It is like a currency for measuring only, to turn it into currency one has to convert it to an issued currency such as the euro at the calculated exchange rate. The SDR's value fluctuates in accordance with the value of the currencies in the basket.

The IMF played an active role in attempting to reduce the adverse effects of the Asian crisis. In 1997 and 1998, it provided funding to various Asian countries in exchange for promises from the respective governments to take specific actions intended to improve economic conditions.

Funding dilemma of the IMF. The IMF typically specifies economic reforms that a country must satisfy to receive IMF funding (the term "conditionality" refers to IMF requests attached to lending). In this way, the IMF attempts to ensure that the country uses the funds responsibly. Although its lending powers have not kept pace with the growth of the international economy, the IMF retains great authority. Banks are generally unwilling to lend unless the IMF has agreed terms with the country.

During the Asian crisis, the IMF agreed to provide $43 billion to Indonesia. The negotiations were tense, as the IMF demanded that President Suharto break up some of the monopolies run by his friends and family members and close a number of weak banks. Citizens of Indonesia interpreted the bank closures as a banking crisis and began to withdraw their deposits from all banks. In January 1998, the IMF demanded many types of economic reform, and Suharto agreed to them. The reforms may have been overly ambitious, however, and Suharto failed to institute them. The IMF agreed to renegotiate the terms in March 1998 in a continuing effort to rescue Indonesia, but this effort signalled that a country did not have to meet the terms of its agreement to obtain funding. A new agreement was completed in April, and the IMF resumed its payments to support a bailout of Indonesia. In May 1998, Suharto abruptly discontinued subsidies for gasoline and food, which led to riots. Suharto blamed the riots on the IMF and on foreign investors who wanted to acquire assets in Indonesia at depressed prices.

The dilemma for the IMF is that its terms for lending (conditionality) have inevitable political consequences. Developing countries feel aggrieved that a body with no democratic status (votes are proportional to SDR quotas, i.e. to the financial contribution of the country) should have a greater influence on their lives than the UN. The UN website has expressed the view that IMF and World Bank economic conditionality packages increase levels of poverty and inequality in developing countries.

World Bank

The **International Bank for Reconstruction and Development (IBRD)**, also referred to as the **World Bank**, was established in 1944. Its primary objective is to make loans to countries to enhance economic development. For example, the World Bank recently extended a loan to Mexico for about $4 billion over a ten-year period for environmental projects to facilitate industrial development near the US border. Its main source of funds is the sale of bonds and other debt instruments to private investors and governments. The World Bank has a profit-oriented philosophy. Therefore, its loans are not subsidized but are extended at market rates to governments (and their agencies) that are likely to repay them.

A key aspect of the World Bank's mission is the **Structural Adjustment Loan (SAL)**, established in 1980. The SALs are intended to enhance a country's long-term economic growth. For example, SALs have been provided to Turkey and to some less developed countries that are attempting to improve their balance of trade.

Because the World Bank provides only a small portion of the financing needed by developing countries, it attempts to spread its funds by entering into **cofinancing agreements**. Cofinancing is performed in the following ways:

- *Official aid agencies.* Development agencies may join the World Bank in financing development projects in low-income countries.

- *Export credit agencies.* The World Bank cofinances some capital-intensive projects that are also financed through export credit agencies.

- *Commercial banks.* The World Bank has joined with commercial banks to provide financing for private-sector development. In recent years, more than 350 banks from all over the world have participated in cofinancing.

The World Bank recently established the **Multilateral Investment Guarantee Agency (MIGA)**, which offers various forms of political risk insurance. This is an additional means (along with its SALs) by which the World Bank can encourage the development of international trade and investment.

The World Bank is one of the largest borrowers in the world; its borrowings have amounted to the equivalent of $70 billion. Its loans are well diversified among numerous currencies and countries. It has received the highest credit rating (AAA) possible.

World Trade Organization

The **World Trade Organization (WTO)** was created as a result of the Uruguay Round of trade negotiations that led to the GATT accord in 1993. This organization was established to provide a forum for multilateral trade negotiations and to settle trade disputes (see Trade disputes section above) related to the GATT accord. It began its operations in 1995 with 81 member countries, and more countries have joined since then. Member countries are given voting rights that are used to make judgements about trade disputes and other issues.

International Financial Corporation

In 1956 the **International Financial Corporation (IFC)** was established to promote private enterprise within countries. Composed of a number of member nations, the IFC works to promote economic development through the private rather than the government sector. It not only provides loans to corporations but also purchases stock, thereby becoming part owner in some cases rather than just a creditor. The IFC typically provides 10 to 15% of the necessary funds in the private enterprise projects in which it invests, and the remainder of the project must be financed through other sources. Thus, the IFC acts as a catalyst, as opposed to a sole supporter, for private enterprise development projects. It traditionally has obtained financing from the World Bank but can borrow in the international financial markets.

International Development Association

The **International Development Association (IDA)** was created in 1960 with country development objectives somewhat similar to those of the World Bank. Its loan policy is more appropriate for less prosperous nations, however. The IDA extends loans at low interest rates to poor nations that cannot qualify for loans from the World Bank.

Bank for International Settlements

The **Bank for International Settlements (BIS)** attempts to facilitate cooperation among countries with regard to international transactions. It also provides assistance to countries experiencing a financial crisis. The BIS is sometimes referred to as the "central banks' central bank" or the "lender of last resort". It played an important role in supporting some of the less developed countries during the international debt crisis in the early and mid-1980s. It commonly provides financing for central banks in Latin American and Eastern European countries.

Regional development agencies

Several other agencies have more regional (as opposed to global) objectives relating to economic development. These include, for example, the Inter-American Development Bank (focusing on the needs of Latin America), the Asian Development Bank (established to enhance social and economic development in Asia), and the African Development Bank (focusing on development in African countries).

In 1990, the European Bank for Reconstruction and Development was created to help the Eastern European countries adjust from communism to capitalism. Twelve Western European countries hold a 51% interest, while Eastern European countries hold a 13.5% interest. The United States is the biggest shareholder, with a 10% interest. There are 40 member countries in aggregate.

HOW INTERNATIONAL TRADE AFFECTS AN MNC'S VALUE

An MNC's value can be affected by international trade in several ways. The increased revenues from international trade are a clear source of increased value. International investments, exploiting resources and new investment opportunities should increase profits. The risk reduction effects of diversifying on the international stage serve to increase the value of the company by making its profits more stable.

SUMMARY

- The key components of the balance of payments are the current account and the financial account. The financial account is a broad measure of the country's international trade balance. The financial account is a measure of the country's long-term and short-term capital investments, including direct foreign investment and investment in securities (portfolio investment).

- A country's international trade flows are affected by inflation, national income, government restrictions, and exchange rates. High inflation, a high national income, low or no restrictions on imports, and a strong local currency tend to result in a strong demand for imports and a current account deficit. Although some countries attempt to correct current account deficits by reducing the value of their currencies, this strategy is not always successful.

- A country's international capital flows are affected by any factors that influence direct foreign investment or portfolio investment. Direct foreign investment tends to occur in those countries that have no restrictions and much potential for economic growth. Portfolio investment tends to occur in those countries where taxes are not excessive, where interest rates are high, and where the local currencies are not expected to weaken.

CRITICAL DEBATE

Trade and human rights.

Proposition. Some countries do not protect human rights in the same manner as European countries. At times, European countries should threaten to restrict EU imports from or investment to a particular country if it does not correct human rights violations. The EU should use its large international trade and investment as leverage to ensure that human rights violations do not occur. Other countries with a history of human rights violations are more likely to honour human rights if their economic conditions are threatened.

Opposing view. No. International trade and human rights are two separate issues. International trade should not be used as the weapon to enforce human rights. Firms engaged in international trade should not be penalized for the human rights violations of a government. If the EU imposes trade restrictions to enforce human rights, the country will retaliate. Thus, the EU firms that export to that foreign country will be adversely affected. By imposing trade sanctions, the EU is indirectly penalizing the MNCs that are attempting to conduct business in specific foreign countries. Trade sanctions cannot solve every difference in beliefs or morals between the more developed countries and the developing countries. By restricting trade, the EU will slow down the economic progress of developing countries.

Who has the better argument and why? Search under "UN Norms on the Responsibilities of Transnational Corporations and Other Business Enterprises with regard to Human Rights" and "UN Norms on the Responsibilities of Transnational Corporations problems".

International finance and accountability.

Proposition. The sheer size of the foreign currency markets make MNCs and their free market philosophy intimidating even for developed countries. Countries can in effect no longer regulate their financial institutions or their currencies. Only the IMF and the G8 have any influence and neither of those are democratic bodies. The UN has tried, but frankly, its charter for Transnational Corporations is not very strong. Although MNCs do not want to give the impression that they are above the law, it is difficult to see what law they are obeying.

Opposing view. Nonsense. Companies are registered in their home country and their subsidiaries are registered in their country of operation, they obey all the laws of those countries and more – the transgressions of MNCs, if you look on the Web, are remarkably few. MNCs in their Annual Reports demonstrate that not only do they comply with all local laws but also they have overriding concerns about the environment and working conditions. If countries wanted to stop trading in foreign assets, they could pass laws and ban the practice. But all countries know that MNCs are a source of wealth and prosperity and that their standards are higher than the local equivalent.

With whom do you agree? You may Google "MNCs", "accountability", "+OECD" and "+pdf" as one search and "UN global Compact", "OECD Guidelines for Multinational Enterprises" and finally FTSE4Good, but be aware that there is a bias towards the proposer's viewpoint.

SELF TEST

Answers are provided in Appendix A at the back of the text.

1. Briefly explain how changes in various economic factors affect the UK current account balance.

2. Explain why UK tariffs may change the composition of UK exports but will not necessarily reduce a UK balance of trade deficit.

3. Explain how a financial crisis can affect international trade.

QUESTIONS AND APPLICATIONS

1. **Balance of payments.**
   a. What is the current account generally composed of?
   b. What is the financial account generally composed of?

2. **Inflation effect on trade.**
   a. How would a relatively high home inflation rate affect the home country's current account, other things being equal?
   b. Is a negative current account harmful to a country? Discuss.

3. **Government restrictions.** How can government restrictions affect international payments among countries?

4. **IMF.**
   a. What are some of the major objectives of the IMF?
   b. How is the IMF involved in international trade?

5. **Exchange rate effect on trade balance.** Would the UK balance of trade deficit be larger or smaller if the pound depreciates against all currencies, versus depreciating against some currencies but appreciating against others? Explain.

6. **Demand for exports.** A relatively small UK balance of trade deficit is commonly attributed to a strong demand for UK exports. What do you think is the underlying reason for the strong demand for UK exports?

7. **Demand for imports.** Explain why a devaluation may result in a higher total import value. Why do we expect it to be lower?

8. **Effects of the euro.** Explain how the euro may affect UK international trade.

9. **Currency effects.** When South Korea's export growth stalled, some South Korean firms suggested that South Korea's primary export problem was the weakness in the Japanese yen. How would you interpret this statement?

10. **Effects of tariffs.** Assume a simple world in which the United Kingdom exports soft drinks and beer to France and imports wine from France. If the United Kingdom imposes large tariffs on the French wine, explain the likely impact on the values of the UK beverage firms, UK wine producers, the French beverage firms, and the French wine producers.

ADVANCED QUESTIONS

11. **Free trade.** There has been considerable momentum to reduce or remove trade barriers in an effort to achieve "free trade". Yet, one disgruntled executive of an exporting firm stated, "Free trade is not conceivable; we are always at the mercy of the exchange rate. Any country can use this mechanism to impose trade barriers." What does this statement mean?

12. **International investments.** In recent years many UK-based MNCs have increased their investments in foreign securities, which are not as susceptible to the negative shocks of the UK market. Also, when MNCs believe that UK securities are overvalued, they can pursue non-UK securities that are driven by a different market. Moreover, in periods of low UK interest rates, UK corporations tend to seek investments in foreign securities. In general, the flow of funds into foreign countries tends to decline when UK investors anticipate a strong pound.

a. Explain how expectations of a strong pound can affect the tendency of UK investors to invest abroad.

b. Explain how low UK interest rates can affect the tendency of UK-based MNCs to invest abroad.

c. In general terms, what is the attraction of foreign investments to UK investors?

13. **Exchange rate effects on trade.**

a. Explain why a stronger dollar could enlarge the UK balance of trade deficit. Explain why a weaker dollar could affect the UK balance of trade deficit.

b. It is sometimes suggested that a floating exchange rate will adjust to reduce or eliminate any current account deficit. Explain why this adjustment would occur.

c. Why does the exchange rate not always adjust to a current account deficit?

PROJECT WORKSHOP

14. **UK balance of trade.** Consult the Pink Book 2004 at:http://www.statistics.gov.uk/StatBase/Product. asp?vlnk=1140

a. Use this website to assess recent trends in exporting and importing by UK firms. How has the balance of trade changed over the last ten years?

b. Offer possible reasons for this change in the balance of trade.

15. Using the financial data packages at your institution or by consulting the *International Monetary Fund Balance of Payments Statistics Yearbook* and web references in the chapter, explore further the international trade and investment themes suggested in the notes to the bar charts.

16. Using the *UNCTAD World Investment Report 2004* or the Forbes lists at http://www.forbes. com/lists/, consult the annual reports of ten large multinational companies and examine their foreign investment policies. Forbes provides direct links, otherwise a search using the companies' names and the word "homepage" then look for the download of the annual report.

DISCUSSION IN THE BOARDROOM

This exercise can be found on the companion website at www.cengage.co.uk/madura_fox.

RUNNING YOUR OWN MNC

This exercise can be found on the companion website at www.cengage.co.uk/madura_fox.

Essays / discussion and articles can be found at the end of Part 1

BLADES PLC CASE STUDY
Exposure to international flow of funds

Ben Holt, the finance director of Blades plc, has decided to counteract the decreasing demand for "Speedos" roller blades by exporting this product to Thailand. Furthermore, due to the low cost of rubber and plastic in Southeast Asia, Holt has decided to import some of the components needed to manufacture "Speedos" from Thailand. Holt feels that importing rubber and plastic components from Thailand will provide Blades with a cost advantage (the components imported from Thailand are about 20% cheaper than similar components in the United Kingdom). Currently, approximately $15 million, or 10%, of Blades' sales are contributed by its sales in Thailand. Only about 4% of Blades' cost of goods sold is attributable to rubber and plastic imported from Thailand.

Blades faces little competition in Thailand from other UK roller blades manufacturers. Those competitors that export roller blades to Thailand invoice their exports in British pounds. Currently, Blades follows a policy of invoicing in Thai baht (Thailand's currency). Ben Holt felt that this strategy would give Blades a competitive advantage, since Thai importers can plan more easily when they do not have to worry about paying differing amounts due to currency fluctuations. Furthermore, Blades' primary customer in Thailand (a retail store) has committed itself to purchasing a certain amount of "Speedos" annually if Blades will invoice in baht for a period of three years. Blades' purchases of components from Thai exporters are currently invoiced in Thai baht.

Ben Holt is rather content with current arrangements and believes the lack of competitors in Thailand, the quality of Blades' products, and its approach to pricing will ensure Blades' position in the Thai roller blade market in the future. Holt also feels that Thai importers will prefer Blades over its competitors because Blades invoices in Thai baht.

As Blades' financial analyst, you have doubts as to Blades' "guaranteed" future success. Although you believe Blades' strategy for its Thai sales and imports is sound, you are concerned about current expectations for the Thai economy. Current forecasts indicate a high level of anticipated inflation, a decreasing level of national income, and a continued depreciation of the Thai baht. In your opinion, all of these future developments could affect Blades financially given the company's current arrangements with its suppliers and with the Thai importers. Both Thai consumers and firms might adjust their spending habits should certain developments occur.

In the past, you have had difficulty convincing Ben Holt that problems could arise in Thailand. Consequently, you have developed a list of questions for yourself, which you plan to present to the company's CFO after you have answered them. Your questions are listed here:

1. How could a higher level of inflation in Thailand affect Blades (assume UK inflation remains constant)?
2. How could competition from firms in Thailand and from UK and European firms conducting business in Thailand affect Blades?
3. How could a decreasing level of national income in Thailand affect Blades?
4. How could a continued depreciation of the Thai baht affect Blades? How would it affect Blades relative to UK exporters invoicing their roller blades in British pounds?
5. If Blades increases its business in Thailand and experiences serious financial problems, are there any international agencies that the company could approach for loans or other financial assistance?

SMALL BUSINESS DILEMMA
Developing a multinational sporting goods industry

Recall from Chapter 1 that Jim Logan planned to pursue his dream of establishing his own business in Ireland (called the Sports Exports Company) of exporting basketballs to one or more foreign markets. Jim has decided to initially pursue the market in the United Kingdom because British citizens appear to have some interest in basketball as a possible hobby, and no other firm has capitalized on this idea in the United Kingdom. (The sporting goods shops in the United Kingdom do not sell basketballs but might be willing to sell them.) Jim has contacted one sporting goods distributor that has agreed to purchase basketballs on a monthly basis and distribute (sell) them to sporting goods stores throughout the United Kingdom.

The distributor's demand for basketballs is ultimately influenced by the demand for basketballs by British citizens who shop in British sporting goods stores. The Sports Exports Company will receive British pounds when it sells the basketballs to the distributor and will then convert the pounds into euros. Jim recognizes that products (such as the basketballs his firm will produce) exported from Ireland to foreign countries can be affected by various factors.

Identify the factors that affect the current account balance between Ireland and the United Kingdom. Explain how each factor may possibly affect the British demand for the basketballs that are produced by the Sports Exports Company.

CHAPTER 3

INTERNATIONAL FINANCIAL MARKETS

DUE TO THE GROWTH in international business and investment over the last 30 years, there has been a large increase in the size and variety of international financial markets. The main functions of these markets are borrowing, lending and risk reduction. A complicating factor compared to their domestic equivalent is the exchange rate. Financial managers of MNCs need to understand these markets in order to operate effectively.

THE SPECIFIC OBJECTIVES OF THIS CHAPTER ARE TO DESCRIBE THE BACKGROUND AND CORPORATE USE OF THE FOLLOWING INTERNATIONAL FINANCIAL MARKETS:

- foreign exchange market,
- international money market,
- international credit market,
- international bond market, and
- international stock markets.

MOTIVES FOR USING INTERNATIONAL FINANCIAL MARKETS

There are a number of barriers that prevent markets in different countries for real or financial assets from becoming completely integrated; these barriers include tax differentials, tariffs, quotas, labour immobility, cultural differences, financial reporting differences, and significant costs of communicating information across countries. Nevertheless, the barriers can also create unique opportunities for specific geographic markets that will attract foreign creditors and investors. For example, barriers such as tariffs, quotas, and labour immobility can cause a given country's economic conditions to be distinctly different from others. Investors and creditors may want to do business in that country to capitalize on favourable conditions unique to that country. At the same time these imperfections have also been a motive for developing larger international markets.

Motives for investing in foreign markets

Investors invest in foreign markets for one or more of the following motives:

- *Economic conditions.* Investors may expect firms in a particular foreign country to achieve a more favourable performance than those in the investor's home country. For example, the relaxing of restrictions in Eastern European countries created favourable economic conditions there. Such conditions attracted foreign investors and creditors.

- *Exchange rate expectations.* Some investors purchase financial securities denominated in a currency that is expected to appreciate against their own. The performance of such an investment is highly dependent on the currency movement over the investment horizon.

- *International diversification.* Investors may achieve benefits from internationally diversifying their asset portfolio. When an investor's entire portfolio does not depend solely on a single country's economy, cross-border differences in economic conditions can allow for risk-reduction benefits. A share portfolio representing firms across European countries is less risky than a share portfolio representing firms in any single European country. Furthermore, access to foreign markets allows investors to spread their funds across a more diverse group of industries than may be available domestically. This is especially true for investors residing in countries where firms are concentrated in a relatively small number of industries.

Motives for providing credit in foreign markets

Creditors (including individual investors who purchase debt securities) have one or more of the following motives for providing credit in foreign markets:

- *High foreign interest rates.* Some countries experience a shortage of loanable funds, which can cause market interest rates to be relatively high, even after considering default risk. Foreign creditors may attempt to capitalize on the higher rates, thereby providing capital to overseas markets. Often, however, relatively high interest rates are perceived to reflect relatively high inflationary expectations in that country. To the extent that inflation can cause depreciation of the local currency against others, high interest rates in the country may be somewhat offset by a weakening of the local currency over the time period of concern. The relation between a country's expected inflation and its local currency movements is not precise, however, because several other factors can influence currency movements as well. Thus, some creditors may believe that the interest rate advantage in a particular country will not be offset by a local currency depreciation over the period of concern.

■ *Exchange rate expectations.* Creditors may consider supplying capital to countries whose currencies are expected to appreciate against their own. Whether the form of the transaction is a bond or a loan, the creditor benefits when the currency of denomination appreciates against the creditor's home currency.

■ *International diversification.* Creditors can benefit from international diversification, which may have the effect of reducing the probability of simultaneous bankruptcy across its borrowers. The effectiveness of such a strategy depends on the correlation between the economic conditions of countries. If the countries of concern tend to experience somewhat similar business cycles, diversification across countries will be less effective.

Motives for borrowing in foreign markets

Borrowers may have one or more of the following motives for borrowing in foreign markets:

■ *Exchange rate expectations.* When a company borrows from abroad, there are two "costs" that must be taken into account. The first is the interest rate, as with any borrowing. The second is unique to international borrowing and is the effect of changes in the exchange rate. When money is borrowed in a foreign currency, it must be converted into the home currency to be usable. At the end of the borrowing period, the repayment must be in the foreign currency for the exact amount of the foreign currency loan. So the loan must be converted back into the foreign currency plus or minus amounts due to exchange rate changes. If the value of the foreign currency has, say, increased in the intervening period, the cost of borrowing will have effectively increased. If, for example, a UK company borrows from abroad and converts the loan into £100,000 at the start of the period, but at the end of the borrowing period it costs £120,000 to repay the amount lent in the foreign currency because the foreign currency has gone up in value, then the cost of borrowing from abroad is the £20,000 increase in repayment due to exchange rate movement, plus any interest payments made. On the other hand, if a foreign currency declines in value over the borrowing period, the cost of repayment could be less than the original converted cost of the loan. In the example above, if the foreign currency has fallen in value by say 5%, then the cost of repayment will be £95,000 (i.e. $(1-0.05) \times 100,000$), a saving of £100,000–£95,000 = £5,000. Such savings will reduce and even offset interest payments, making foreign borrowing potentially very cheap. So, because exchange rate movements can make borrowing cheaper or more expensive all that can be said overall is that it is more risky.

When a foreign subsidiary of an MNC remits funds to its parent, the funds must be converted to the home currency and are subject to exchange rate risk. The MNC will be adversely affected if the foreign currency depreciates at that time. If the MNC expects that the foreign currency may depreciate against the dollar, it can reduce the exchange rate risk by having the subsidiary borrow funds locally to support its business. The subsidiary will remit less funds to the parent if it must pay interest on local debt before remitting the funds. Thus, the amount of funds converted to home currency will be smaller, resulting in less exposure to exchange rate risk.

■ *Low interest rates.* Some countries have a large supply of funds available to lend compared to the demand by borrowers for these funds. Interest rates, the price of borrowing, would in such circumstances, be low. Borrowers may attempt to borrow funds from creditors in these countries because the interest rate charged is lower. A country with relatively low interest rates is often expected to have a relatively low rate of inflation, which can place upward pressure on the foreign currency's value and offset any advantage of lower interest rates. The relation between expected inflation differentials and currency movements is not precise, however, so some borrowers will choose to borrow from a market where nominal interest rates are low, since they do not expect an adverse currency movement to fully offset this advantage.

FOREIGN EXCHANGE MARKET

When MNCs or other participants invest or borrow in foreign markets, they commonly rely on the foreign exchange market to obtain the currencies that they need. Thus, the act of borrowing or investing internationally typically requires the use of the foreign exchange market. By allowing currencies to be exchanged, the **foreign exchange market** facilitates international trade and financial transactions. MNCs rely on the foreign exchange market to exchange their home currency for a foreign currency that is needed to purchase imports or to use for direct foreign investment. Alternatively, they may need the foreign exchange market to convert foreign revenues to their home currency. The difference between the market for foreign currency and any other market is that the price of currency has been subject to far more government intervention. The reason is simple. The price of a currency affects the price of all goods denominated in that currency. Thus if the value of the euro goes up in relation to the British pound, all goods in Europe will cost more for the British purchaser as the more expensive euro has to be purchased in order to purchase the goods. The pervasive effect of a change in the value of a currency naturally makes its price of great interest to a government.

A brief history of foreign exchange for developed countries

The history of foreign exchange is essentially a history of the degree of government involvement. It varies from an exchange rate that governments keep fixed, such as the gold standard and more recently the euro area, to a wholly variable system where the forces of supply and demand are allowed to operate freely in the foreign markets without government intervention. Governments can have a potentially large effect on the exchange rate, they are the printers of the currency, the holders of large amounts of gold and the main borrowers in the currency. Generally, governments have used their influence to reduce currency fluctuations and have been advocates of fixed rate systems. Their motive is stability. That exchange rates are not fixed has been due to two main factors. Firstly, the sheer size of the foreign exchange markets – one day's trading is now larger than the annual gross domestic product for the UK. Governments cannot influence markets as easily as 20 or more years ago. Secondly, governments have not always wanted to face the consequences of protecting the value of a currency – increasing interest rates and increasing unemployment are possibilities.

History offers snapshots of various exchange rate regimes and their problems. For the MNC, such history is useful as it shows possible futures.

Gold standard. From 1876 to 1913, exchange rates were dictated by the **gold standard**. Each currency was convertible into gold at a specified rate. This reflects the origins of paper money, notes were essentially receipts for holdings of precious metal by gold-smiths and silversmiths. On UK currency, the words "I promise to pay the bearer" reflects its origins as a receipt. Convertibility into gold was seen as essential for maintaining confidence in a currency. If the holder did not like the currency, a commodity of universal value, gold, was offered as an alternative. The US dollar, was convertible into gold by governments as late as 1971. Exchange rates between currencies in such a system are fixed by the exchange rate into gold. If currency A is convertible into twice as much gold as currency B, currency A in the foreign exchange markets must be worth twice as much as currency B. At any other rate, riskless profits are possible (sometimes termed arbitrage). The market does not allow a profit to be made without the possibility of a loss.

When World War I began in 1914, the gold standard was suspended. Some countries reverted to the gold standard in the 1920s but abandoned it as a result of a banking panic in the United States and Europe during the Great Depression. The problem was that governments did not have sufficient gold to fulfil all the promises, it was not "fully backed". In the 1930s, some countries attempted to peg their currency to the dollar or the British pound instead of gold, but there were frequent revisions as governments found difficulties in converting to dollars or British pounds at the promised exchange rate. As a result of the instability in the foreign exchange market and the severe restrictions on international transactions during this period, the volume of international trade declined.

Agreements on fixed exchange rates. In 1944, an international agreement (known as the **Bretton Woods Agreement**) called for fixed exchange rates between currencies. This agreement lasted until 1971. During this period, governments would intervene to prevent exchange rates from moving more than 1% above or below their initially established levels. The dollar was convertible into gold hence the term gold exchange system for this regime.

Because of the confidence in the dollar, the US was able to maintain large current account deficits on its balance of payments. Exporting countries were by and large happy to hold dollars as an international medium of exchange. Thus a deficit on the current account (a net supply of dollars to pay for imports) was financed by a positive balance on the financial account (a net demand for dollars to invest in the US). However, the size of the deficits eventually led some governments to exchange their reserves of dollars for gold. By 1971, the US dollar appeared to be overvalued; the supply of US dollars for foreign currency was greater than the foreign demand for dollars. To maintain the exchange rate, the difference had to be met from reserves of foreign exchange held by the US government or "Fed" (the money supply in the US is controlled by a government agency called the "Fed" or Board of Governors of the Federal Reserve System, a network of major US banks). Representatives from the major nations met to discuss this dilemma. As a result of this conference, which led to the **Smithsonian Agreement**, the US dollar was devalued relative to the other major currencies and was no longer convertible into gold. The degree to which the dollar was devalued varied with each foreign currency. Not only was the dollar's value reset, but exchange rates were also allowed to fluctuate by 2.25% in either direction from the newly set rates. This was the first post World War II step in letting market forces (supply and demand) determine the appropriate price of a currency and marked the end of gold conversion. Although boundaries still existed for exchange rates, they were widened, allowing the currency values to move more freely toward their appropriate levels.

At this time, countries who were members of the equivalent of the European Union (the European Economic Community) decided to create a fixed exchange rate system between themselves (the European Common Margins Agreement). They modelled it on the gold exchange system and sought to maintain a more or less fixed rate with the dollar. Such financial conditions were seen as an important part of the policy of free trade within the Union. Unfortunately the system failed due to the large devaluations of the dollar.

The system (the European Monetary System or Exchange Rate Mechanism) was resurrected by the then President of the EU, Roy Jenkins, in 1979. This time the currencies of the EEC were linked only to each other by an exchange rate grid, along with the creation of a numeraire currency the European Currency Unit or ECU – similar to the Special Drawing Right only made up of European currencies. The Delors report in 1989 set out the procedure for full integration (European and Monetary Union – EMU) that eventually led to the formation of the euro on 1 January 1999. The euro is the equivalent of a wholly fixed exchange rate regime between its members who are currently: Germany, France, Italy, Spain, Portugal, Belgium, Luxembourg, the Netherlands, Austria, Finland, Greece and Ireland. EMU outlines the process for joining what is seen as an expanding currency area. Little is new in finance, from 1865 to 1927 there was a Latin Monetary Union made up of France, Switzerland, Greece, Italy, Romania and a number of smaller countries. As ever, the British response to joining was lukewarm.

Floating Exchange Rate System. Returning to the Smithsonian Agreement in 1971, governments still had difficulty maintaining exchange rates within the stated boundaries. By March 1973, the more widely traded currencies were allowed to fluctuate in accordance with market forces, and the official boundaries were eliminated.

The modern era is usually dated from the Plaza Accord (1985) attended by the then G5 nations (France, West Germany, Japan, the United States and the United Kingdom). Amongst a number of market liberalization measures the countries expressed the view that the dollar was overvalued (US current account deficits were once again large). Over the following two years the dollar devalued in an orderly manner by over 50%. The novel features of this approach were that it was a joint international declaration, that the rationale was well explained, and that there were no targets – the so called "soft barriers approach". The financial markets, by then increasing in size, had less opportunity for speculation given that there was no commitment either to a time schedule or a rate. The Exchange Rate Mechanism was to learn a similar lesson in 1992 when membership of the ERM was challenged by the international financial markets. Britain left, never to return. Italy also left but returned later and France resisted the speculative attacks. But after that event (sometimes termed Black Wednesday, a reference to the most dramatic episode when the UK left the ERM) the parity grid was given much wider bands and speculative attacks were allowed to exhaust themselves before adjustments were made.

As a postscript, exchange rate movements are caused in the main by "fundamental factors", events in the economy. A major factor in the turbulence of modern times was the price of oil, then largely under the control of a cartel of Middle Eastern countries who were members of OPEC (Organisation of Petroleum Exporting Countries). Over the 1970s and 1980s, Saudi Light oil went from $1.80 per barrel, peaked in February 1981 at $39 per barrel and ended the 1980s at $20 per barrel. It is currently back to near $40 per barrel, but in real terms it was much higher in 1981 (i.e. $39 in 1981 could purchase much more than $39 today due to inflation).

Currently, exchange rates have enjoyed a period of relative stability. But the usual warning signs are there, namely, large US current account deficits and surging oil prices. The now G8 (United States, Japan, Germany, France, Britain, Italy, Canada and Russia) remains the likely deciding body for further exchange rate management of the world's developed nations.

Foreign exchange transactions

The "foreign exchange market" should not be thought of as a specific building or location where traders exchange currencies. Companies normally exchange one currency for another through a commercial bank over a telecommunications network.

Spot market. The most common type of foreign exchange transaction is for immediate exchange at the so-called **spot rate** (immediate is interpreted as being within two days). The market where these transactions occur is known as the **spot market**. The average daily foreign exchange trading by banks around the world now exceeds $1.5 trillion (that is 1.5 million million). About 28% of transactions are US dollar–euro transactions, 17% US dollar–Yen and 14% US dollar–British pound.

**USING
THE WEB**

Historical exchange rates Historical exchange rate movements are provided at http://
www.oanda.com. Data are available on a daily basis for most currencies.

Some commodities such as oil are traditionally traded in US dollars. The US dollar may also be an intermediary currency, for example British pounds could be converted to Malaysian ringitt by first converting to US dollars and then to Malaysian ringitt – simply because it is cheaper. Although banks in London, New York, and Tokyo, the three largest foreign exchange trading centres, conduct much of the foreign exchange trading, many foreign exchange transactions occur outside these trading centres. Banks in virtually every major city facilitate foreign exchange transactions between MNCs. Trading also takes place outside the market, known as the Over The Counter or OTC market. The process of trading can also take place without a middle man, the process is known as disintermediation. Buyers and sellers of currencies can trade directly with each other, a process made much easier with the development of the Internet.

EXAMPLE

Max N.V. a Dutch firm purchases supplies priced at $100,000 from Amerigo, a US supplier, on the first day of every month. Max instructs its bank to transfer funds from its account to the supplier's account also on the first day of each month. It only has euros in its account, whereas Amerigo's invoices are in dollars. When payment was made one month ago, the dollar was worth 1.08 euros, so Max N.V. needed 108,000 euros to pay for the supplies ($100,000 × 1.08 = 108,000 euros). The bank reduced Max's account balance by 108,000 euros, which was exchanged at the bank for $100,000. The bank then sent the $100,000 electronically to Amerigo by increasing Amerigo's account balance by $100,000. Today, a new payment needs to be made. The dollar is currently valued at 1.12 euros, so the bank will reduce Max's account balance by 112,000 euros ($100,000 × 1.12 euros = 112,000 euros) and exchange it for $100,000, which will be sent electronically to Amerigo.

The bank not only executes the transactions but also serves as the foreign exchange dealer. Each month the bank receives euros from Max N.V. in exchange for the dollars it provides. In addition, the bank facilitates other transactions for MNCs in which it receives euros in exchange for dollars. The bank maintains a stock of euros, dollars, and other currencies to facilitate these foreign exchange transactions. If the transactions cause it to buy as many euros as it sells to MNCs, its stock of euros will not change. If the bank sells more euros than it buys, however, its stock of euros will be reduced.

Other intermediaries also serve the foreign exchange market. Some other financial institutions such as securities firms can provide the same services described in the previous example. In addition, most major airports around the world have foreign exchange centres, where individuals can exchange currencies. In many cities, there are retail foreign exchange offices where tourists and other individuals can exchange currencies.

Use of the dollar in the spot market. Many foreign transactions do not require an exchange of currencies but will accept foreign currency. For example, the US dollar is commonly accepted as a medium of exchange by merchants in many countries, especially in countries such as Bolivia, Brazil, China, Cuba, Indonesia, Russia, and Vietnam where the home currency is either weak or subject to foreign exchange restrictions. Many merchants accept US dollars because they can use them to purchase goods from other countries. The US dollar is the official currency of Ecuador, Liberia, and Panama.

Spot market structure. Hundreds of banks facilitate foreign exchange transactions, but the top 20 handle about 50% of the transactions. Deutsche Bank (Germany), Citibank (a subsidiary of Citigroup, US), and J.P. Morgan Chase are the largest traders of foreign exchange. Some banks and other financial institutions have formed alliances (one example is FX Alliance LLC) to offer currency transactions over the Internet.

At any given point in time, the exchange rate between two currencies should be similar across the various banks that provide foreign exchange services. If there is a large discrepancy, customers or other banks will purchase large amounts of a currency from whatever bank quotes a relatively low price and immediately sell it to whatever bank quotes a relatively high price. Such actions cause adjustments in the exchange rate quotations that eliminate any discrepancy.

If a bank begins to experience a shortage in a particular foreign currency, it can purchase that currency from other banks. This trading between banks occurs in what is often referred to as the **interbank market**. Within this market, banks can obtain quotes, or they can contact brokers who sometimes act as intermediaries, matching one bank desiring to sell a given currency with another bank desiring to buy that currency. About ten foreign exchange brokerage firms handle much of the interbank transaction volume.

Although foreign exchange trading is conducted only during normal business hours in a given location, these hours vary among locations due to different time zones. Thus, at any given time on a weekday, somewhere around the world a bank is open and ready to accommodate foreign exchange requests.

When the foreign exchange market opens in the United States each morning, the opening exchange rate quotations are based on the prevailing rates quoted by banks in London and other locations where the foreign exchange markets have opened earlier. Suppose the quoted spot rate of the British pound was $1.80 at the previous close of the US foreign exchange market, but by the time the market opens the following day, the opening spot rate is $1.76. News occurring in the morning before the US market opened could have changed the supply and demand conditions for British pounds in the London foreign exchange market, reducing the quoted price for the pound.

With the newest electronic devices, foreign currency trades are negotiated on computer terminals, and a push of a button confirms the trade. Traders now use electronic trading boards that allow them to instantly register transactions and check their bank's positions in various currencies. Also, several US banks have established night trading desks. The largest banks initiated night trading to capitalize on foreign exchange movements at night and to accommodate corporate requests for currency trades. Even some medium-sized banks now offer night trading to accommodate corporate clients.

Spot market liquidity. The spot market for each currency can be described by its liquidity, which reflects the level of trading activity. The more willing buyers and sellers there are, the more liquid a market is. The spot markets for heavily traded currencies such as the euro, the British pound, and the Japanese yen are very liquid. Conversely, the spot markets for currencies of less developed countries are less liquid. A currency's liquidity affects the ease with which an MNC can obtain or sell that currency. If a currency is illiquid, the number of willing buyers and sellers is limited, and an MNC may be unable to quickly purchase or sell that currency at a reasonable exchange rate. About a third of transactions are at spot.

Forward transactions. In addition to the spot market, a forward market for currencies enables an MNC to lock in the exchange rate (called a **forward rate**) at which it will buy or sell a currency. A **forward contract** specifies the amount of a particular currency that will be purchased or sold by the MNC at a specified future point in time and at a specified exchange rate. Commercial banks accommodate the MNCs that desire forward contracts. MNCs commonly use the forward market to hedge future payments that they expect to make or receive in a foreign currency. In this way, they do not have to worry about fluctuations in the spot rate until the time of their future payments. The liquidity of the forward market varies among currencies. The forward market for euros is very liquid because many MNCs take forward positions to hedge their future payments in euros. In contrast, the forward markets for Latin American and Eastern European currencies are less liquid because there is less international trade with those countries and therefore MNCs take fewer forward positions. For some currencies, there is no forward market.

Attributes of banks that provide foreign exchange. The following characteristics of banks are important to customers in need of foreign exchange:

1. *Competitiveness of quote.* For example, a saving of 1 pence per unit on an order of one million units of currency is worth £10,000.
2. *Special relationship with the bank.* The bank may offer cash management services or be willing to make a special effort to obtain even hard-to-find foreign currencies for the corporation.
3. *Speed of execution.* Banks may vary in the efficiency with which they handle an order. A corporation needing the currency will prefer a bank that conducts the transaction promptly and handles any paperwork properly.
4. *Advice about current market conditions.* Some banks may provide assessments of foreign economies and relevant activities in the international financial environment that relate to corporate customers.
5. *Forecasting advice.* Some banks may provide forecasts of the future state of foreign economies, the future value of exchange rates, and the like.

    This list suggests that a corporation needing a foreign currency should not automatically choose a bank that will sell that currency at the lowest price. Most corporations that often need foreign currencies develop a close relationship with at least one major bank in case they ever need favours from a bank.

MANAGING FOR VALUE
Intel's currency trading

When Intel needs to exchange foreign currency, it no longer calls a bank to request an exchange of currencies. Instead, it logs on to an online currency trader that serves as an intermediary between Intel and member banks. One popular online currency trader is Currenex, which conducts more than $300 million in foreign exchange transactions per day. If Intel needs to purchase a foreign currency, it logs on and specifies its order. Currenex relays the order to various banks that are members of its system and are allowed to bid for the orders. When Currenex relays the order, member banks have 25 seconds to specify a quote online for the currency that the customer (Intel) desires. Then, Currenex displays the quotes on a screen, ranked from highest to lowest. Intel has 5 seconds to select one of the quotes provided, and the deal is completed. This process is much more transparent than traditional foreign exchange market transactions because Intel can review quotes of many competitors at one time.

Interpreting foreign exchange quotations

Exchange rate quotations for widely traded currencies are published in the *Financial Times* and in business sections of many newspapers on a daily basis. With some exceptions, each country has its own currency. In 1999, several European countries (comprising Germany, France, Italy, Spain, Portugal, Belgium, Luxembourg, the Netherlands, Austria, Finland, Ireland and later Greece) adopted the euro as their new currency replacing their own currencies. Their own currencies were phased out by the year 2002.

A quote is written as so many units of one currency (the term currency) for one unit of another (the base currency), so 60 pence or £0.60 to the dollar is written as £0.60:$1. To convert, say, $100 into British pounds at this rate is simply $100 × 0.60 = £60. To convert, say, £150 into dollars at this rate is £150 / 0.60 = $250. Note that conversion is achieved either by multiplying or dividing; it is important not to apply the wrong operation!

Choosing the right operation, multiplying or dividing, always poses a small problem for most students. There are various ways of avoiding error, a simple mnemonic is offered here. If a currency conversion is seen as a source currency ("from") to a destination currency ("to"), then in the exchange rate quote, if the source currency is on the left (term) one divides; if the source currency is on the right (base) one multiplies. A number of examples are given in Exhibit 3.1.

Exhibit 3.1 Currency conversion

Conversion		Exchange rate	Operation	Converted Value
From (*source*)	To (*destination*)			
£100	dollars	$1.85:£1	Multiply	£100 × 1.85 = $185
£60	euros	1.25 euro:£1	Multiply	£60 × 1.25 = 75 euros
250 euros	British pounds	1.25 euro:£1	Divide	250 euros / 1.25 = £200
$1,000	euros	$1.11:1 euro	Divide	$1,000 / 1.11 = 901 euros

Direct and indirect quotations.

- **direct quote**: the number of units of home currency for one of the foreign currency,

- **indirect quote**: the number of units of foreign currency for one unit of the home currency.

There is a reciprocal relationship between the two:

Indirect quotation = 1/direct quotation

So   8 Rand:£1   is the same as   £0.125:1 Rand   as 1/8 = 0.125
      5 peso:£1   is the same as   £0.20:1 peso   as 1/5 = 0.20
    135 Yen:1 euro is the same as   0.0074 euro:1 Yen as 1/135 = 0.0074

A direct quote can be described as "the value of foreign currency", and an indirect quote can be described as "how much home currency will buy abroad". The indirect quote tends to be used in the UK and parts of the former British Empire. It is a relic of the days when the British pound was non-decimal and it was easier to apply fractions to decimal currency than the then complex UK currency. Elsewhere it is normal to find the direct quote being used.

Much analysis in international finance seeks to explain the value of foreign currency and account for the variation in its value. The direct quote is the natural rate to use. If the value of foreign currency goes up, the direct rate goes up. So, taking the British pound as the home currency and an exchange rate of £0.56:$1, if the value of the dollar increases by 10% then the new rate will be £0.56 × (1 + 0.10) = £0.616, that is £0.616:$1. Similarly, if the value of the dollar falls, the direct rate will fall. If the rates used were indirect, the relationship would be the opposite, an increase in the rate would mean a fall in the value of foreign currency – not surprisingly this is very confusing and should be avoided. In equations therefore, the more straightforward direct rate is used. Also as a consequence of this problem, when discussing exchange rates it is better to talk about changes in the value of currencies and not the rate – an increase in value is unequivocal.

EXAMPLE

Mr Y a Finance Director has been given the following rates from his bank: 4 zloty:1 euro; £0.68:1 euro and 6 zloty:£1. He wonders if he changed £1,000 into Polish zloty, converted his Polish zloty into euros and then converted the euros back into British pounds, would he have the £1,000 he started with? He works out that £1,000 would buy him 6,000 zloty, then 6,000 zloty would buy 1,500 euro (i.e. 6,000 zloty/4 = 1,500) and finally 1,500 euro would buy £1,020 (i.e. 1,500 euros × 0.68) a profit of £20 or 2% ([1,020 − 1,000]/1,000). "Great" he thinks, I can earn certain money just by picking up the phone. When he tells the Bank Manager, she laughs: "You've forgotten the transaction costs, we would charge nearly 2% for those transactions and then your zloty euro rate is for converting euros into zloty not zloty into euros. All told, you would make a loss. Don't worry we would not allow you to make a profit for nothing – you've got to take a risk to do that."

Quotations of spot and forward rates. The spot rate normally means delivery within two days and are quoted for all the major currencies in the financial press. Some quotations of exchange rates include forward rates for the most widely traded currencies. Other forward rates are not quoted in business newspapers but are quoted by the banks

POUND SPOT FORWARD AGAINST THE POUND

Mar 29		Closing mid-point	Change on day	Bid/offer spread	Day's Mid high	low	One month Rate	%PA	Three months Rate	%PA	One year Rate	%PA	Bank of Eng. Index
Europe													
Czech Rep.	(Koruna)	41.4617	-0.0889	286 - 948	41.8130	41.3610	41.3833	2.3	41.2111	2.4	40.5568	2.2	-
Denmark	(DKr)	10.7812	-0.0218	783 - 841	10.8399	10.7680	10.7669	1.6	10.7381	1.6	10.6434	1.3	106.7
Hungary	(Forint)	385.902	+1.3430	585 - 218	388.370	384.710	386.342	-1.4	387.568	-1.7	394.197	-2.1	-
Norway	(NKr)	11.5303	+0.0362	242 - 364	11.5372	11.4763	11.5143	1.7	11.4775	1.8	11.3497	1.6	101.8
Poland	(Zloty)	5.7115	+0.0137	068 - 163	5.7659	5.6945	5.7096	0.4	5.7046	0.5	5.6806	0.5	-
Russia	(Rouble)	48.2314	-0.2413	189 - 439	48.5057	48.1527	48.2653	-0.8	48.3276	-0.8	48.6415	-0.9	-
Slovakia	(Koruna)	54.5921	-0.0191	429 - 414	54.9760	54.4950	54.5483	1.0	54.4825	0.8	54.3036	0.5	-
Slovenia	(Tolar)	346.159	-0.6900	024 - 295	348.052	345.827	345.798	1.3	345.056	1.3	340.939	1.5	-
Sweden	(SKr)	13.6252	+0.0517	197 - 307	13.6625	13.5888	13.6	2.2	13.5455	2.3	13.3472	2.0	78.7
Switzerland	(SFr)	2.2740	-0.0010	732 - 748	2.2838	2.2718	2.2681	3.1	2.2553	3.3	2.2079	2.9	110.6
Turkey	(Lira)	2.3596	-0.0080	576 - 616	2.3804	2.3515	2.3777	-9.2	2.4084	-8.3	2.5423	-7.7	-
UK	(£)	-	-	-	-	-	-	-	-	-	-	-	98.2
Euro	(Euro)	1.4448	-0.0031	445 - 452	1.4529	1.4431	1.4427	1.7	1.4385	1.7	1.4243	1.4	91.81
SDR	(€)	1.207000	-	-	-	-	-	-	-	-	-	-	-
Argentina	(Peso)	5.3376	-0.0534	348 - 404	5.3721	5.3339	5.3499	-2.8	5.3849	-3.5	5.6087	-5.1	-
Americas													
Brazil	(R$)	3.8678	-0.0253	657 - 699	3.8969	3.8494	3.9013	-10.4	3.9681	-10.4	4.2447	-9.7	-
Canada	(C$)	2.0351	-0.0118	344 - 359	2.0437	2.0294	2.0339	0.7	2.0322	0.6	2.0264	0.4	99.1
Mexico	(New Peso)	19.0228	-0.1965	163 - 294	19.2991	18.9996	19.071	-3.0	19.1753	-3.2	19.639	-3.2	-
Peru	(New Sol)	5.7568	-0.1124	535 - 600	5.7928	5.7535	5.7687	-2.5	5.7855	-2.0	5.8484	-1.6	-
USA	($)	1.7337	-0.0159	335 - 339	1.7443	1.7318	1.7342	-0.3	1.7356	-0.4	1.7431	-0.5	97.1
Australia	(A$)	2.4642	-0.0028	631 - 654	2.4844	2.4579	2.4661	-0.9	2.4705	-1.0	2.488	-1.0	86.4
Pacific/Middle East/Africa													
Hong Kong	(HK$)	13.4540	-0.1217	521 - 559	13.5352	13.4400	13.4512	0.3	13.4521	0.1	13.4565	0.0	-
India	(Rs)	77.4270	-0.6926	834 - 707	77.9780	77.2730	77.5991	-2.7	77.9002	-2.4	79.2138	-2.3	-
Indonesia	(Rupiah)	15863.4	+24.30	529 - 739	15921.8	15788.0	15867.57	-0.3	15881.22	-0.4	15950.01	-0.5	-
Iran	(Rial)	15834.8	-151.3000	182 - 513									-
Israel	(Shk)	8.1545	-0.0262	466 - 623	8.1967	8.1466	8.1578	-0.5	8.1708	-0.8	8.2334	-1.0	-
Japan	(Y)	204.793	+0.4130	744 - 843	205.600	204.440	204.093	4.1	202.528	4.4	196.273	4.2	125.5
Kuwait	(Kuwaiti D)	0.5064	-0.0046	062 - 065	0.5098	0.5058	0.5068	-0.9	0.5078	-1.1	0.5114	-1.0	-
Malaysia	(M$)	6.4078	-0.0570	053 - 102	6.4466	6.4025	6.4009	1.3	6.3875	1.3	6.3355	1.1	-
New Zealand	(NZ$)	2.8830	+0.0002	815 - 845	2.9081	2.8704	2.8895	-2.7	2.9037	-2.9	2.9535	-2.4	99.1
Philippines	(Peso)	88.9041	-0.5792	245 - 837	89.3841	88.8245	89.0905	-2.5	89.5004	-2.7	91.327	-2.7	-
Saudi Arabia	(SR)	6.5019	-0.0596	008 - 030	6.5413	6.4949	6.5035	-0.3	6.5103	-0.5	6.5496	-0.7	-
Singapore	(S$)	2.8125	-0.0168	116 - 133	2.8298	2.8088	2.8102	1.0	2.8055	1.0	2.7827	1.1	-
South Africa	(R)	10.9925	+0.0269	826 - 025	11.0332	10.9334	11.0157	-2.5	11.066	-2.7	11.2826	-2.6	-
South Korea	(Won)	1690.62	-18.3000	016 - 107	1707.67	1689.02	1689.85	0.5	1688.61	0.5	1684.42	0.4	-
Taiwan	(T$)	56.5056	-0.4990	306 - 806	56.8730	56.4306	56.3904	2.4	56.1005	2.9	54.9402	2.8	-
Thailand	(Bt)	67.5363	-0.4873	852 - 874	68.2520	67.4852	67.5714	-0.6	67.6773	-0.8	68.1491	-0.9	-
U A E	(Dirham)	6.3674	-0.0583	663 - 684	6.4059	6.3607	6.3694	-0.4	6.3756	-0.5	6.4074	-0.6	-

Bid/offer spreads in the Pound Spot table show only the last three decimal places. New Sterling ERI calculated by the Bank of England. Base 2005 = 100. Other Indices Base average 1990 = 100. Indices rebased 1/2/95.

Source: *Financial Times*, reprinted with kind permission.

that offer forward contracts in various currencies. Quoted rates are normally for one month, three months and one year, but may be tailored by a bank to a MNC's individual needs. The above is the online quote given by the *Financial Times* at http://news.ft.com/markets/spotpound.

The "%PA" column is the calculation of the premium or discount in the rate compared to the spot expressed as an annual percentage rate. So for the Czech koruna, the one month rate is 41.3833 and the spot is 41.4617. If you invest £1 now in koruna you will receive 41.4617 koruna and when you convert back one month later, you will receive 41.4617/41.3833 = £1.001894484. The annual interest rate equivalent is £1.001894484^{12}−1 = 0.023 or 2.3%. Note that from the perspective of the pound, these are indirect quotes.

Bid/ask spread of banks. Commercial banks charge fees for conducting foreign exchange transactions. At any given point in time, a bank's **bid** (buy) direct quote for a foreign currency will be less than its **ask** (sell) direct quote. As with the retail of any other product the retailer (bank) will buy the product (currency) at the lower price and sell at the higher price. The service offered by the bank is availability, convenience and a competitive price. The **bid/ask spread** represents the differential between the bid and ask quotes, and is intended to cover the costs involved in accommodating requests to exchange currencies. The bid/ask spread is normally expressed as a percentage of the ask quote.

EXAMPLE

To understand how a bid/ask spread could affect you, assume you live in France and have 1,000 euros and plan to travel from France to the United States. Assume further that the bank's bid (buy) rate for the US dollar is 1.28 euros:$1 and its ask (sell) rate is 1.31 euros:$1. Before leaving on your trip, you go to this bank to exchange euros for dollars. Your 1,000 euros will be converted to $763.36 as follows:

$$\text{euros} \rightarrow \text{US dollars: } 1,000 \text{ euros} / 1.31 \text{ euros:}\$1 = \$763.36$$

The bank's ask rate is relevant here because that is the rate at which it is selling dollars. Note that the conversion is rounded to the smallest unit of currency $0.01 or 1 cent. Now suppose that because of an emergency you cannot take the trip, and you reconvert the $763.36 back to euros, just after purchasing the US dollars. If the exchange rate has not changed, you will be quoted the bank's bid rate for buying dollars and receive:

$$\text{US dollars} \rightarrow \text{euros: } \$763.36 \times 1.28 \text{ euros:}\$1 = \$977.10$$

Due to the bid/ask spread, you have 22.90 euros less (1,000 euros − 977.10 euros = 22.90 euros) or 2.29% less. Obviously, the euro amount of the loss would be larger if you originally converted more than 1,000 euros into dollars. The loss can be worked out directly as a percentage by measuring the percentage difference between the two rates thus:

$$(1.31 - 1.28) / 1.31 = 2.29\%$$

Comparison of bid/ask spread among currencies. The differential between a bid quote and an ask quote will look much smaller for currencies that have a smaller value. As stated above, this differential can be standardized by measuring it as a percentage difference between the two rates divided by the ask rate (the first part of the transaction).

EXAMPLE

Somerset Bank quotes a bid price for yen of £0.005 and an ask price of £0.0052. In this case, the nominal bid/ask spread is £0.005 − £0.0052, or just two-hundredths of a penny. Yet, the bid/ask spread in percentage terms is actually slightly higher for the yen in this example than for the dollar in the previous example. To prove this, consider a traveller who sells £1,000 for yen at the bank's ask price of £0.0052. The traveller receives about ¥192,308 (computed as £1,000/£0.0052). If the traveller cancels the trip and converts the yen back to pounds, then, assuming no changes in the bid/ask quotations, the bank will buy these yen back at the bank's bid price of £0.005 for a total of about £961.54 (computed by ¥192,308 × £0.005), this is £38.46 (or 3.846%) less than what the traveller started with – measured directly as (0.0052 − 0.005) / 0.0052 = 0.03846 or 3.846%. This spread exceeds that of the British pound (2.29% in the previous example) although the figures are much smaller. The size of a currency unit is no more significant than whether your height is measured in metres or millimeters, it is the percentage movement in a currency that matters.

Both the previous examples calculated the bid/ask spread as a percentage. The following is the general formula for calculating the spread:

$$\text{Bid/Ask spread} = \frac{\text{Ask rate} - \text{Bid rate}}{\text{Ask rate}}$$

Using this formula, the bid/ask spreads are computed in Exhibit 3.2 for a selection of currency quotes.

Notice that the spread represents the bank's profit margin. Sometimes travel firms who similarly buy and sell currencies will also add a commission or ostentatiously advertise zero commission. In all cases, however, money is made through buying more cheaply than selling. For larger so-called wholesale transactions between banks or for large corporations, the spread will be much smaller. The bid/ask spread for small retail transactions is commonly in the range of 3 to 7%; for wholesale transactions requested by MNCs, the spread is between 0.01 and 0.03%. The spread is normally larger for illiquid currencies that are less frequently traded. Commercial banks are normally exposed to more exchange rate risk when maintaining these currencies.

In the following discussion and in examples throughout much of the text, the bid/ask spread will be ignored. That is, only one price will be shown for a given currency to allow you to concentrate on understanding other relevant concepts. These examples depart slightly from reality because the bid and ask prices are, in a sense, assumed to be equal. Although the ask price will always exceed the bid price by a small amount in reality, the implications from examples should nevertheless hold, even though the bid/ask spreads are not accounted for. In particular examples where the bid/ask spread can contribute significantly to the concept, it will be accounted for.

Various websites, including bloomberg.com, provide bid/ask quotations. To conserve space, some quotations show the entire bid price followed by a slash and then only the last two or three digits of the ask price (known as the "pips").

E X A M P L E

Assume that the prevailing quote for wholesale transactions by a commercial bank for the euro is $1.0876/78. This means that a US commercial bank is willing to buy euros for

Exhibit 3.2 Computation of the bid/ask spread

Currency	Bid rate	Ask rate	$\dfrac{\text{Ask rate} - \text{bid rate}}{\text{Ask rate}} = spread$
Dollar	£0.54:$1	£0.56:$1	$\dfrac{£0.56 - £0.54}{£0.56} = 0.03571 \text{ or } 3.571\%$
Nigerian Naira	£0.004:1 Naira	£0.0042:1 Naira	$\dfrac{£0.0042 - £0.004}{£0.0042} = 0.04762 \text{ or } 4.762\%$
British pound	1.46 euro:£1	1.48:£1	$\dfrac{£1.48 - £1.46}{£1.48} = 0.01351 \text{ or } 1.351\%$

$1.0876 per euro. Alternatively, it is willing to sell euros for $1.0878. The bid/ask spread in this example is:

$$\text{Bid/Ask spread} = \frac{\$1.0878 - \$1.0876}{\$1.0878} = 0.00018438 \text{ or } 0.0184\% \text{ to 4 decimal places}$$

Factors that affect the spread. The spread on currency quotations is influenced by the following factors:

$$\text{Spread} = f(\underset{+}{\text{Order costs}}, \underset{+}{\text{Inventory costs}}, \underset{-}{\text{Competition}}, \underset{-}{\text{Volume}}, \underset{+}{\text{Currency risk}})$$

- *Order costs.* Order costs are the costs of processing orders, including clearing costs and the costs of recording transactions.
- *Inventory costs.* Inventory costs are the costs of maintaining an inventory of a particular currency. Holding an inventory involves an opportunity cost because the funds could have been used for some other purpose. If interest rates are relatively high, the opportunity cost of holding an inventory should be relatively high. The higher the inventory costs, the larger the spread that will be established to cover these costs.
- *Competition.* The more intense the competition, the smaller the spread quoted by intermediaries. Competition is more intense for the more widely traded currencies because there is more business in those currencies.
- *Volume.* More liquid currencies are less likely to experience a sudden change in price. Currencies that have a large trading volume are more liquid because there are numerous buyers and sellers at any given time. This means that the market has sufficient depth that a few large transactions are unlikely to cause the currency's price to change abruptly.
- *Currency risk.* Some currencies exhibit more volatility than others because of economic or political conditions that cause the demand for and supply of the currency to change abruptly. For example, currencies in countries that have frequent political crises are subject to abrupt price movements. Intermediaries that are willing to buy or sell these currencies could incur large losses due to an abrupt change in the values of these currencies.

Cross exchange rates. Most tables of exchange rate quotations express currencies relative to the British pound, US dollar or euro or all three. But in some instances, a firm will want or be concerned about the exchange rate between two other currencies. For example, if a UK firm wants to convert earnings in Mexican pesos to Australian dollars (A$) to pay for imports from Australia, an estimate of the likely rate can be calculated as a **cross exchange rate**. The diagram in Exhibit 3.3 illustrates the relationship:

USING THE WEB   Cross exchange rates Cross exchange rates for several currencies are provided at http://www.bloomberg.com.

Exhibit 3.3 Cross exchange rates

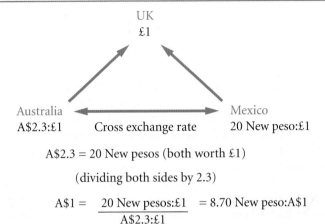

A$2.3 = 20 New pesos (both worth £1)

(dividing both sides by 2.3)

$$A\$1 = \frac{20 \text{ New pesos:£1}}{A\$2.3:£1} = 8.70 \text{ New peso:A\$1}$$

Note:
- For an implied or cross rate, the right hand side of the quote (the base) must be the same currency for both rates and the denominator (lower half) of the ratio becomes the base of the new quote.

Currency futures and options markets

A **currency futures contract** specifies a standard volume of a particular currency to be exchanged on a specific settlement date. Some MNCs involved in international trade use the currency futures markets to hedge their positions.

EXAMPLE

Paris SA has ordered supplies from the US that are denominated in dollars. It expects the dollar to increase in value over time and therefore desires to hedge its payables in dollars. Paris buys futures contracts on dollars to lock in the price that it will pay for dollars at a future point in time. Meanwhile, it will receive Mexican pesos in the future and wants to hedge these receivables. Paris sells futures contracts on pesos to lock in the euros that it will receive when it sells the pesos for euros at a specified point in the future.

Futures contracts are somewhat similar to forward contracts except that they are sold on an exchange whereas forward contracts are offered by commercial banks. Additional details on futures contracts, including other differences from forward contracts, are provided in Chapter 5.

Currency options contracts can be classified as calls or puts. A **currency call option** provides the right to buy a specific currency at a specific price (called the **strike price** or **exercise price**) within a specific period of time. It is used to hedge future payables. A **currency put option** provides the right to sell a specific currency at a specific price within a specific period of time. It is used to hedge future receivables.

Currency call and put options can be purchased on an exchange. They offer more flexibility than forward or futures contracts because they do not require any obligation. That is, the firm can elect not to exercise the option.

Currency options have become a popular means of hedging, particularly in the US. The Coca-Cola Co. has replaced about 30 to 40% of its forward contracting with currency options. FMC, a US manufacturer of chemicals and machinery, now hedges its foreign sales with currency options instead of forward contracts. A recent study by the Whitney Group found that 85% of US-based MNCs use currency options. Additional details about currency options, including other differences from futures and forward contracts, are provided in Chapter 5.

INTERNATIONAL MONEY MARKET

Financial markets exist in every country to ensure that funds are transferred efficiently from surplus units (savers) to deficit units (borrowers). These markets are overseen by various regulators that attempt to enhance the markets' creditworthiness (ensuring that purchasers are able to pay) and efficiency. The financial institutions that serve these financial markets exist primarily to provide information and expertise. The increase in international business has resulted in the development of an international money market. Financial institutions in this market serve MNCs by accepting deposits and offering loans in a variety of currencies. In general, the international money market is distinguished from domestic money markets by the types of transactions between the participating financial institutions and the MNCs. The financial transactions are in a wide variety of currencies, and large, often the equivalent of $1 million or more.

Market efficiency

One of the major concepts in finance is that of market efficiency. The term is not used to refer to the operational efficiency, though that is important. Rather efficiency refers to how well information is used in the marketplace. Originally the concept was applied to stock markets but the ideas refer to any market, but most particularly to markets of "financial promises". A share is a promise of future dividends, a currency is also a financial promise, simply of value. Currency markets are the most sophisticated in the world, the promise of value can be for value now (the spot market) or value in the future (the futures market). The valuation of currencies requires that the traders look into the future, and using the information to hand, estimate the value of the currency. Information plays a key role in the valuation process. The value of a currency may fall if a current account deficit is larger than expected. The value may rise if there is an economic report that is better than expected. Or, the value may fall if a good economic forecast was not as good as expected. Thus, as information flows into the market on a daily basis, traders in the marketplace buy and sell currencies on the strength of that information and as a result, the price changes. Note that the definition of good and bad information is always in relation to expectations. In finance, information is not inherently good or bad. As noted above, a piece of good news may bring about a fall in the value of a currency if it is not as good as expected; bad news a rise in the value of the currency if it is not as bad as expected.

The role of the market, is to ensure that information is available to all traders. In the market for shares this requirement implies strict rules on the disclosure of information to ensure that some traders do not have access to private company information and therefore have an unfair advantage. There is no real equivalent for currencies, private information of relevance to currencies is held by governments and major economic institutions. Governments are keen to avoid speculation in their currency and are therefore likely to ensure that private information is kept confidential until announced to the market as a whole. Major institutions would lose status if their reports were leaked to the market.

All information relevant to valuing a currency is about the future. It is tempting to think that a spot price only reflects current information and, say, a one month futures price will reflect future information. This would be wrong. All prices reflect the same information set. The only difference is that the information's effect on value will be discounted to the present for the spot price and will be discounted to the one month value for the one month futures price. Because these prices draw on the same information set, it is not unreasonable to suggest that a spot rate may be a good predictor of future rates. This and other consequences of market efficiency will be commented on in later chapters.

Tests for market efficiency have been developed in relation to the stock market, here we apply the concepts to currencies. There are three types: weak form efficiency, semi strong form efficiency and strong form efficiency.

Weak form efficiency requires that currency prices move randomly, at least in the short term. It may seem strange that analysts would expect that such a sophisticated market should produce currency values that change randomly. Information, however, is by definition random because it is in relation to expectations. Tomorrow's information may be better than expected (implying a rise in currency value) or may be worse than expected (implying a fall in currency value), one cannot tell at the end of any particular trading day whether information will be better or worse than expected. If a rise or fall are equally likely at any point in time, one has a price that is moving randomly. Tests for randomness as such do not exist, one can only test for an absence of patterns (the opposite of randomness). In general, patterns are not found, so the market is weak form efficient.

The qualification made above was that this was at least in the short term. Indeed, until the 1990s, researchers could not distinguish exchange rate movements from a random information process as described. Nowadays, there is some belief that relative inflation rates offer some longer-term guidance as to the future exchange rate. The current debate is over the length of time of the adjustment process. Given that many studies indicate that half the adjustment would take three to four years, this is clearly a medium- to long-term process. Relevant research articles are given at the end of Part 2.

The other two types of efficiency are called semi strong efficiency and strong form efficiency. Both refer to the disclosure of information. Semi strong efficiency requires that prices reflect all published information; strong form efficiency requires that prices reflect all published and private information. Markets desire semi strong form of efficiency, namely that the value of currencies reflect all known published information. If prices were influenced by private, unpublished information, market traders would feel that the market was unfair as they would lose profits to other traders who had such information. Such insider knowledge would lead to certain or near certain profits, a situation that would not be deemed fair.

EXAMPLE

The trading department of Anybank plc is actively buying and selling Currency A. It expects good balance of payments figures to be announced tomorrow. The manager explains to a new recruit: "Everyone expects that the figures will be good, we have already bought Currency A on this expectation. The point is, will it be better than the market expects or worse? I don't really know. The Prime Minister has been a bit pessimistic on the economy of late, maybe the results are very good and he is trying to lower our expectations so that the results are a nice surprise." The recruit replies: "Maybe the results aren't really that good and he is trying to avoid a big disappointment", the manager responds: "Mmm … who knows …OK, we haven't really got any fresh information on this currency, we will not make any further purchases or sales."

Published information in the international arena is a matter for governments and international institutions. Generally, one can expect that the officials of both types of institutions will not trade on information before it is published.

Origins and development

The international money market includes large banks in countries around the world. Large financial institutions such as Deutsche Bank and J.P. Morgan Chase are major participants. Two other important elements of the international money market are the European money market and the Asian money market.

European money market. The origins of the European money market can be traced to the Eurocurrency market that developed during the 1960s and 1970s. As MNCs expanded their operations during that period, international financial intermediation emerged to accommodate their needs. Because the US dollar was widely used even between non US countries as a medium for international trade, there was a consistent need for dollars in Europe and elsewhere. Some foreign depositors in US banks were worried that their assets might be frozen for political reasons due to the Cold War. Other depositors were unhappy with the US government restrictions on banks. For example, when the United States limited foreign lending by US banks in 1968, foreign subsidiaries of US-based MNCs could obtain US dollars from banks in Europe via the Eurocurrency market. Similarly, when ceilings were placed on the interest rates paid on dollar deposits in the United States, MNCs transferred their funds to European banks, which were not subject to the ceilings. A significant number of foreign depositors in US banks also transferred their dollar deposits to London. In effect they sold their accounts to a London bank who held the deposit in the US bank and in return gave the sellers an account in London denominated in US dollars. Soon, London banks were using their dollar deposits to lend to corporate customers based in Europe. These dollar deposits in banks in Europe (and on other continents as well) came to be known as **Eurodollars**, and the market for Eurodollars came to be known as the **Eurocurrency market**. ("Eurodollars" and "Eurocurrency" should not be confused with the "euro", which is the currency.)

The growing importance of the Organization of Petroleum Exporting Countries (OPEC) also contributed to the growth of the Eurocurrency market. Because OPEC generally requires payment for oil in dollars, the OPEC countries began to use the Eurocurrency market to deposit a portion of their oil reserves. These dollar-denominated deposits are sometimes known as **petrodollars**. Oil revenues deposited in banks have sometimes been lent to oil-importing countries that are short of cash. As these countries purchase more oil, funds are again transferred to the oil-exporting countries, which in turn create new deposits. This recycling process has been an important source of funds for some countries.

Today, the Eurocurrency market is not used as often as in the past because domestic markets are now more competitive. Governments are aware that they cannot restrict bank operations without distorting the market and disadvantaging their own banks. The European money market nevertheless remains an important part of the network of international money markets. Participation is limited to large MNCs and financial institutions who can benefit from rates that are better than elsewhere because the amounts traded are large and there is a very low risk of bankruptcy.

Asian money market. Like the European money market, the Asian money market originated as a market involving mostly dollar-denominated deposits. Hence, it was originally known as the **Asian dollar market**. The market emerged to accommodate the needs of businesses that were using the US dollar (and some other foreign currencies) as a medium of exchange for international trade. These businesses could not rely on banks in Europe because of the distance and different time zones. Today, the Asian money market, as it is now called, is centred in Hong Kong and Singapore, where large banks accept deposits and make loans in various foreign currencies.

Functions of the international money market. Today, both the Asian money market and the European money market are key components of the international money market. The primary function of banks in this market is to channel funds from depositors to borrowers. For example, the major sources of deposits in the Asian money market are MNCs with excess cash and government agencies. Manufacturers are major borrowers in this market. Another function is interbank lending and borrowing. Banks that have more qualified loan applicants than they can accommodate use the interbank market to obtain additional funds. Banks in the Asian money market commonly borrow from or lend to banks in the European market.

Standardizing global bank regulations

The growing standardization of regulations around the world has contributed to the trend toward globalization in the banking industry. Three of the more significant regulatory events allowing for a more competitive global playing field are: (1) the Single European Act, (2) the Basel Accord, and (3) the Basel II Accord.

Banks are central to international finance, exchanging currencies, speculating, investing internationally, trading in derivatives and so on. The balance sheet of banks is very unusual due to the nature of their trade. On the financing side, shareholder capital is relatively small compared to the very large current liabilities created by the deposit accounts. In effect the bank owes you the money you have deposited and that is much more than the shareholder value. On the assets side, most of the money is in lending to clients. In fact very little of the money deposited with banks is kept as cash. This is potentially a very risky position. If depositors all asked to withdraw their money (known as a run on the bank) the bank would not have the money. Also, if a few large clients went bankrupt, those loans would have to be written off against reserves, i.e. shareholder capital. Because shareholder capital is relatively small, it is possible that a bank could become bankrupt by having negative shareholder capital. This would occur if the amount of the write off were larger than the shareholder value. Arguably, during the Third World Debt Crisis which began in 1982, many banks found that sovereign loans (loans to countries) of doubtful quality were greater in value than their shareholding. The share capital inadequacy of banks became apparent. Interest rates also became more volatile making it more possible that banks might be in a position of having to offer rates to customers that would threaten their profits. Off balance sheet activities resulting in financial guarantees also increase the risk of banking.

Basel Accord. Before 1988, share capital standards imposed on banks varied across countries, which allowed some banks to have a comparative global advantage over others. As an example, suppose that banks in the United States were required to maintain more capital than foreign banks. Foreign banks would grow more easily, as they would need a relatively small amount of capital to support an increase in assets. Despite their low share capital, such banks were not necessarily perceived as too risky because the governments in those countries were likely to back banks that experienced financial problems.

Therefore, some non-US banks had globally competitive advantages over US banks, without being subject to excessive risk. In December 1987, 12 major industrialized countries attempted to resolve the disparity by proposing uniform bank standards. In July 1988, in the **Basel Accord**, central bank governors of the 12 countries agreed on standardized guidelines. Under these guidelines, banks must maintain share capital equal to at least 8% of their assets. For this purpose, banks' assets are weighted by risk – the higher the risk the higher the weighting. This essentially results in a higher required capital ratio for riskier assets. Off-balance sheet items are also accounted for so that banks cannot circumvent capital requirements by focusing on services that are not explicitly shown as assets on a balance sheet.

Basel II Accord. Banking regulators that form the so-called Basel Committee have agreed a new accord (known as Basel II) to correct some inconsistencies that still existed. For example, banks in some countries have required better collateral (security) to back their loans – if the borrower from the bank cannot pay, the banks have a lien (ownership right) on the collateral and can sell the assets pledged to the bank in the event of non-payment.

The agreement, effective from December 2006 is based on three "pillars":

- Minimum capital requirements. Share capital must be at least 8% of a special valuation of lending. The formula for valuing lending is made up of credit risk (the risk that the borrower, e.g. a business, will not pay), market risk (exposure to uncertain market value of investments by the bank in shares, bonds etc.) and operational risk (the risk from fraud and failing operational processes internal to the bank).
- Supervisory review. Banking supervisors have powers to ask a bank to increase its share capital requirements if there are found to be weaknesses in its capital assessment processes.
- Market discipline. Let investors decide on the risk of buying shares in the bank by requiring greater disclosure of their risk management policies in the annual report. The Barclays Bank plc Annual Report for 2005, for instance, devotes 49 pages to risk management. For a non-bank operation the report would normally have about one to five pages.

Single European Act. One of the most significant events affecting international banking was the **Single European Act**, which was phased in by 1992 throughout the European Union (EU) countries. The following are some of the more relevant provisions of the Single European Act for the banking industry:

- Capital can flow freely throughout Europe.
- Banks can offer a wide variety of lending, leasing, and securities activities in the EU.
- Regulations regarding competition, mergers, and taxes are similar throughout the EU.
- A bank established in any one of the EU countries has the right to expand into any or all of the other EU countries.

As a result of this act, banks have expanded across European countries. Efficiency in the European banking markets has increased because banks can more easily cross countries without concern for country-specific regulations that prevailed in the past.

Another key provision of the act is that banks entering Europe receive the same banking powers as other banks there. Similar provisions apply to non-US banks that enter the United States.

INTERNATIONAL CREDIT MARKET

Multinational corporations and domestic firms sometimes obtain medium-term funds through loans from local financial institutions or through the issuance of notes (medium-term debt obligations) in their local markets. However, MNCs also have access to medium-term funds through banks located in foreign markets. Loans of one year or longer extended by banks to MNCs or government agencies in Europe are commonly called Eurocredits or **Eurocredit loans**. These loans are provided in the so-called **Eurocredit market**. The loans can be denominated in dollars or many other currencies and commonly have a maturity of five years.

Because banks accept short-term deposits and sometimes provide longer-term loans, their asset and liability maturities do not match. This can adversely affect a bank's performance during periods of rising interest rates, since the bank may have locked in a rate on its longer-term loans while the rate it pays on short-term deposits is rising over time. To avoid this risk, banks commonly use floating rate loans. The loan rate floats in accordance with the movement of some market interest rate, such as the **London Interbank Offer Rate (LIBOR)**, which is the rate commonly charged for loans between banks. For example, a Eurocredit loan may have a loan rate that adjusts every six months and is set at "LIBOR plus 3%". The premium paid above LIBOR will depend on the credit risk of the borrower. The LIBOR varies among currencies because the market supply of and demand for funds vary among currencies.

The international credit market is well developed in Asia and is developing in South America. Periodically, some regions are affected by an economic crisis, which increases the credit risk. Financial institutions tend to reduce their participation in those markets when credit risk increases. Thus, even though funding is widely available in many markets, the funds tend to move toward the markets where economic conditions are strong and credit risk is tolerable.

Syndicated loans

Sometimes a single bank is unwilling or unable to lend the amount needed by a particular corporation or government agency. In this case, a **syndicate** of banks may be organized. Each bank within the syndicate participates in the lending. A lead bank is responsible for negotiating terms with the borrower. Then the lead bank organizes a group of banks to underwrite the loans. The syndicate of banks is usually formed in about six weeks, or less if the borrower is well known because the credit evaluation can then be conducted more quickly.

Borrowers that receive a syndicated loan incur various fees besides the interest on the loan. Front-end management fees are paid to cover the costs of organizing the syndicate and underwriting the loan. In addition, a commitment fee of about 0.25% or 0.50% is charged annually on the unused portion of the available credit extended by the syndicate.

Syndicated loans can be denominated in a variety of currencies. The interest rate depends on the currency denominating the loan, the maturity of the loan, and the creditworthiness of the borrower. Interest rates on syndicated loans are commonly adjustable according to movements in an interbank lending rate, and the adjustment may occur every six months or every year.

Syndicated loans not only reduce the default risk of a large loan to the degree of participation for each individual bank, but they can also add an extra incentive for the borrower to repay the loan. If a government defaults on a loan to a syndicate, word will quickly spread among banks, and the government will likely have difficulty obtaining future loans. Borrowers are therefore strongly encouraged to repay syndicated loans promptly. From the perspective of the banks, syndicated loans increase the probability of prompt repayment.

INTERNATIONAL BOND MARKET

Bonds or debentures or bills are issues by companies and governments. A bond typically offers a fixed interest payment for a number of years or term, combined with a repayment (redemption) of the nominal amount borrowed at the end of the term. They may be secured on the assets of the company in case of non-payment. Unlike shares, there is no ownership interest, and so no voting rights. Although MNCs, like domestic firms, can obtain long-term debt by issuing bonds in their local markets, MNCs can also access long-term funds in foreign markets. MNCs may choose to issue bonds in the international bond markets for three reasons. First, issuers recognize that they may be able to attract a stronger demand by issuing their bonds in a particular foreign country rather than in their home country. Some countries have a limited investor base, so MNCs in those countries seek financing elsewhere. Second, MNCs may prefer to finance a specific foreign project in a particular currency and therefore may attempt to obtain funds where that currency is widely used. Third, financing in a foreign currency with a lower interest rate may enable an MNC to reduce its cost of financing, although it may be exposed to exchange rate risk (as explained in later chapters). Some institutional investors prefer to invest in international bond markets rather than their respective local markets when they can earn a higher return on bonds denominated in foreign currencies.

International bonds are typically classified as either foreign bonds or Eurobonds. A **foreign bond** is issued by a borrower foreign to the country where the bond is placed. For example, a US corporation may issue a bond denominated in Japanese yen, which is sold to investors in Japan. In some cases, a firm may issue a variety of bonds in various countries. The currency denominating each type of bond is determined by the country where it is sold. These foreign bonds are sometimes specifically referred to as **parallel bonds**.

Eurobond market

Eurobonds are bonds that are sold in countries other than the country of the currency denominating the bonds. The emergence of the Eurobond market was partially the result of the **Interest Equalization Tax (IET)** imposed by the US government in 1963 to discourage US investors from investing in foreign securities. Thus, non-US borrowers that historically had sold foreign securities to US investors began to look elsewhere for funds. Further impetus to the market's growth came in 1984 when the US government abolished a withholding tax that it had formerly imposed on some non-US investors and allowed US corporations to issue bearer bonds directly to non-US investors.

Eurobonds have become very popular as a means of attracting funds, perhaps in part because they circumvent registration requirements. US-based MNCs such as McDonald's and Walt Disney commonly issue Eurobonds. Non-US firms such as Guinness, Nestlé, and Volkswagen also use the Eurobond market as a source of funds.

In recent years, governments and corporations from emerging markets such as Croatia, Ukraine, Romania, and Hungary have frequently utilized the Eurobond market. New corporations that have been established in emerging markets rely on the Eurobond market to finance their growth. They have to pay a risk premium of at least three percentage points annually above the US Treasury bond rate on dollar-denominated Eurobonds.

Features of Eurobonds. Eurobonds have several distinctive features. They are usually issued in bearer form, and coupon payments are made yearly. Some Eurobonds carry a convertibility clause allowing them to be converted into a specified number of shares of common share. An advantage to the issuer is that Eurobonds typically have few, if any, protective covenants. Furthermore, even short-maturity Eurobonds include call provisions. Some Eurobonds, called **floating rate notes** (**FRNs**), have a variable rate provision that adjusts the coupon rate over time according to prevailing market rates.

Denominations. Eurobonds are commonly denominated in a number of currencies. Although the US dollar is used most often, denominating 70 to 75% of Eurobonds, the euro will likely also be used to a significant extent in the future. Recently, some firms have issued debt denominated in Japanese yen to take advantage of Japan's extremely low interest rates. Because interest rates for each currency and credit conditions change constantly, the popularity of particular currencies in the Eurobond market changes over time.

Underwriting process. Eurobonds are underwritten by a multinational syndicate of investment banks and simultaneously placed in many countries, providing a wide spectrum of fund sources to tap. The underwriting process takes place in a sequence of steps. The multinational managing syndicate sells the bonds to a large underwriting crew. In many cases, a special distribution to regional underwriters is allocated before the bonds finally reach the bond purchasers. One problem with the distribution method is that the second- and third-stage underwriters do not always follow up on their promise to sell the bonds. The managing syndicate is therefore forced to redistribute the unsold bonds or to sell them directly, which creates "digestion" problems in the market and adds to the distribution cost. To avoid such problems, bonds are often distributed in higher volume to underwriters that have fulfilled their commitments in the past at the expense of those that have not. This has helped the Eurobond market maintain its desirability as a bond placement centre.

Secondary market. Eurobonds also have a secondary market. The market makers are in many cases the same underwriters who sell the primary issues. A technological advance called **Euro-clear** helps to inform all traders about outstanding issues for sale, thus allowing a more active secondary market. The intermediaries in the secondary market are based in ten different countries, with those in the United Kingdom dominating the action. They can act not only as brokers but also as dealers that hold inventories of Eurobonds. Many of these intermediaries, such as Bank of America International, Salomon Smith Barney, and Citicorp International, are subsidiaries of US corporations.

Before the adoption of the euro in much of Europe, MNCs in European countries commonly preferred to issue bonds in their own local currency. The market for bonds in each currency was limited. Now, with the adoption of the euro, MNCs from many different countries can issue bonds denominated in euros, which allows for a much larger and more liquid market. MNCs have benefited because they can more easily obtain debt by issuing bonds, as investors know that there will be adequate liquidity in the secondary market.

Development of other bond markets

Bond markets have developed in Asia and South America. Government agencies and MNCs in these regions use international bond markets to issue bonds when they believe they can reduce their financing costs. Investors in some countries use international bond markets because they expect their local currency to weaken in the future and prefer to invest in bonds denominated in a strong foreign currency. The South American bond market has experienced limited growth because the interest rates in some countries there are usually high. MNCs and government agencies in those countries are unwilling to issue bonds when interest rates are so high, so they rely heavily on short-term financing.

COMPARING INTEREST RATES AMONG CURRENCIES

Recently quoted annualized interest rates are shown in Exhibit 3.4. Notice the wide disparity among interest rates of different countries. At one extreme, Japan's annualized interest rate was about 1%, whereas Brazil's annualized interest rate was 19%.

The interest rates in debt markets are crucial because they affect the MNC's cost of financing. Since interest rates can vary substantially among currencies, the cost of local financing for foreign projects varies among countries. The interest rate on a debt instrument denominated in a specific currency is determined by the demand for funds denominated in that currency and the supply of funds available in that currency.

The supply and demand schedules for the British pound and for Mexico's currency (the peso) are compared for a given point in time in Exhibit 3.5. The demand schedule for loanable funds is downward sloping for any currency, which simply means that the quantity of funds demanded at any point in time is inversely related to the interest rate level. That is, the total amount of loanable funds demanded (borrowed) at a given point in time is higher if the cost of borrowing is lower.

The supply schedule for loanable funds denominated in a given currency is upward sloping, which means that the total amount of loanable funds supplied (such as savings by individuals) at a given point in time is positively related to the interest rate level. That is, the total amount of loanable funds supplied to the market is higher if the interest rate offered on savings accounts is higher.

Though the demand schedule for loanable funds should be downward sloping for every currency and the supply schedule of loanable funds should be upward sloping for every currency, the actual positions of these schedules vary among currencies. First, notice that the demand and supply curves are further to the right for the British pound than for the Mexican peso. The amount of British pound-denominated loanable funds supplied and demanded is much greater than the amount of peso-denominated loanable funds because the UK economy is much larger than Mexico's economy.

Also notice that the positions of the demand and supply schedules for loanable funds are much higher for the Mexican peso than for the British pound. The supply schedule for loanable funds denominated in Mexican pesos shows that hardly any amount of savings would be supplied at low interest rate levels because the high inflation in Mexico encourages households to spend all of their disposable income before prices increase more. It discourages households from saving unless the interest rate is sufficiently high.

Exhibit 3.4 Comparison of annualized short-term interest rates among countries in 2004. (Rates are rounded to the nearest %)

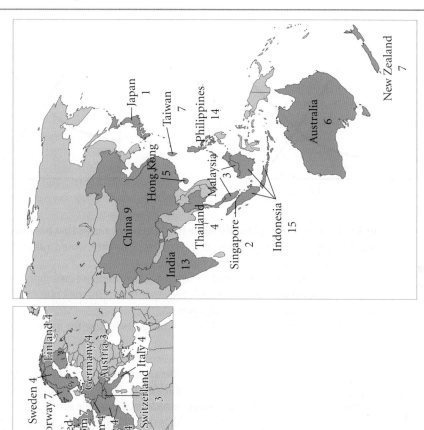

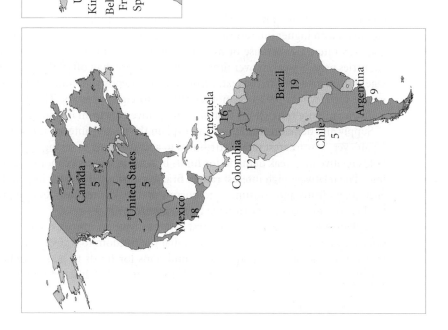

Exhibit 3.5 Why UK interest rates differ from Mexican peso interest rates

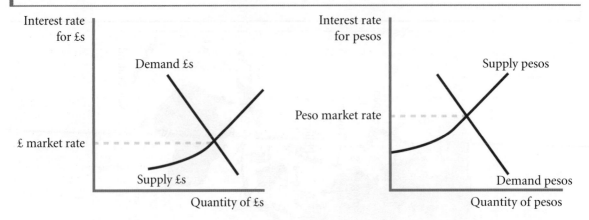

In addition, the demand for loanable funds in pesos shows that borrowers are willing to borrow even at very high rates of interest because they would rather borrow funds to make purchases now before prices increase.

Because of the differences in the positions of the demand and supply schedules for the two currencies shown in Exhibit 3.5, the equilibrium interest rate for the Mexican peso is much higher than for the British pound.

As the demand and supply schedules change over time for a specific currency, so will the equilibrium interest rate.

EXAMPLE

Suppose that Mexico's government is able to substantially reduce the local inflation. In that case, the supply schedule of loanable funds denominated in pesos would shift out (to the right). Conversely, the demand schedule of loanable funds denominated in pesos would shift in (to the left). The two shifts would result in a lower equilibrium interest rate.

One might think that investors from other countries should invest in savings accounts in countries with higher interest rates. However, higher interest rates are given for a reason, and very often it is because of higher inflation. The currencies of these high-inflation countries usually weaken over time, which may more than offset the interest rate advantage as explained later in the text. Second, savings deposits in some of these countries are not insured, which presents another risk to foreign investors. Third, some emerging countries impose restrictions that discourage investors from investing funds there.

Supply and demand conditions can explain the relative interest rate for any currency. Japan's very low interest rate is attributed to a large supply of savings by Japanese households relative to a weak demand for funds because of a weak economy (limited borrowing). The relatively high interest rate in Brazil is attributed to both high inflation, which encourages firms and consumers to borrow and make purchases before prices increase further, and to excessive borrowing by the government.

A change in one currency's interest rate can have an impact on another within the same day, week, or month. The point is that the freedom to transfer funds across countries causes the demand and supply conditions for funds to be somewhat integrated, which can cause interest rate movements to be integrated. Interest rates in the European countries participating in the euro are similar because they are subject to the same money supply and demand conditions.

INTERNATIONAL STOCK MARKETS

MNCs and domestic firms commonly obtain long-term funding by issuing shares locally. Yet, MNCs can also attract funds from foreign investors by issuing shares in international markets. The shares offering may be more easily digested when it is issued in several markets. In addition, the issuance of shares in a foreign country can enhance the firm's image and name recognition there.

The recent conversion of many European countries to a single currency (the euro) has resulted in more share offerings in Europe by US- and European-based MNCs. In the past, an MNC needed a different currency in every country where it conducted business and therefore borrowed currencies from local banks in those countries. Now, it can use the euro to finance its operations across several European countries and may be able to obtain all the financing it needs with one share or bond offering denominated in euros. The MNCs can then use a portion of the revenue (in euros) to pay dividends to shareholders and interest to bondholders.

Issuance of foreign shares in the United States

Non-US corporations or governments that need large amounts of funds sometimes issue shares in the United States (these are called **Yankee stock offerings**, note that "**stock**" is the US term for share in this context) due to the liquidity of the new-issues market there. In other words, a foreign corporation or government may be more likely to sell an entire issue of shares in the US market, whereas in other, smaller markets, the entire issue may not necessarily sell.

When a non-US firm issues shares in its own country, its shareholder base is quite limited, as a few large institutional investors may own most of the shares. By issuing shares in the United States, such a firm diversifies its shareholder base, which can reduce share price volatility caused when large investors sell shares.

The US investment banks commonly serve as underwriters of the shares targeted for the US market and receive underwriting fees representing about 7% of the value of shares issued. Since many financial institutions in the United States purchase non-US shares as investments, non-US firms may be able to place an entire share offering within the United States.

Firms that issue shares in the United States typically are required to satisfy stringent disclosure rules on their financial condition. However, they are exempt from some of these rules when they qualify for a Securities and Exchange Commission guideline (called Rule 144a) through a direct placement of shares to institutional investors.

Many of the recent share offerings in the United States by non-US firms have resulted from privatization programmes in Latin America and Europe. Thus, businesses that were previously government owned are being sold to US shareholders. Given the large size of some of these businesses, the local stock markets are not large enough to digest the share offerings. Consequently, US investors are financing many privatized businesses based in foreign countries.

American depository receipts. Non-US firms also obtain equity financing by using **American depository receipts (ADRs)**, which are certificates representing bundles of shares. The use of ADRs circumvents some disclosure requirements imposed on share offerings in the United States, yet enables non-US firms to tap the US market for funds. The ADR market grew after businesses were privatized in the early 1990s, as some of these businesses issued ADRs to obtain financing.

Since ADR shares can be traded just like shares, the price of an ADR changes each day in response to demand and supply conditions. Over time, however, the value of an ADR should move in tandem with the value of the corresponding share that is listed on the foreign stock exchange, after adjusting for exchange rate effects. The formula for calculating the price of an ADR is:

$$P_{ADR} = Conv \times P_{fs} \times S$$

Where: P_{ADR} = the price of the ADR in dollars,
$Conv$ = number of foreign shares that can be obtained for one ADR
P_{fs} = the price of the foreign shares measured in foreign currency, and
S = the spot rate of the foreign currency i.e. foreign currency units:$1.

EXAMPLE

A share of the ADR of the French firm Pari represents one share of this firm that is traded on a French stock exchange. The share price of Pari was 20 euros when the French market closed. As the US stock market opens, the euro is worth $1.05, so the ADR price should be:

$$
\begin{aligned}
P_{ADR} &= Conv \times P_{fs} \times S \\
&= 1 \times 20 \times \$1.05 \\
&= \$21
\end{aligned}
$$

If there is a discrepancy between the ADR price and the price of the foreign share (after adjusting for the exchange rate), investors can use arbitrage to capitalize on the discrepancy between the prices of the two assets. The act of arbitrage should realign the prices.

EXAMPLE

Assume no transaction costs. If $P_{ADR} < (P_{fs} \times S)$, then ADR shares will flow back to France. They will be converted to shares of the French company and will be traded in the French market. Investors can engage in arbitrage by buying the ADR shares in the United States, converting them to shares of the French company, and then selling those shares on the French stock exchange where the share is listed.

The arbitrage will: (1) reduce the supply of ADRs traded in the US market, thereby putting upward pressure on the ADR price, and (2) increase the supply of the French shares traded in the French market, thereby putting downward pressure on the share price in France. The arbitrage will continue until the discrepancy in prices disappears.

ADRs are a good example of the subtlety and international nature of financial markets. Their regulation has equally to be on an international scale to be effective.

Issuance of shares in foreign markets

The locations of an MNC's operations can influence the decision about where to place its shares, as the MNC may desire a country where it is likely to generate enough future cash flows to cover dividend payments. The shares of the largest MNCs are widely traded on numerous stock exchanges around the world. For example, Alcatel (France), Nokia (Finland), Coca-Cola Co., IBM, and many other MNCs have their shares listed on several different stock exchanges. When an MNC's shares are listed on foreign stock exchanges, it can easily be traded by foreign investors who have access to those exchanges.

Exhibit 3.6 Stock exchanges around the world

Country	Stock market capitalization (in millions of $)
Argentina	$ 192,499
Australia	372,974
Austria	29,935
Belgium	182,481
Brazil	186,238
Chile	56,310
Finland	293,635
France	1,146,634
Germany	1,270,243
Greece	86,538
Hungary	10,637
India	110,396
Indonesia	23,006
Ireland	81,882
Israel	55,964
Italy	768,364
Japan	3,157,222
Luxembourg	34,016
Malaysia	120,007
Mexico	121,403
Netherlands	640,456
New Zealand	18,613
Nigeria	5,404
Norway	65,034
Pakistan	4,944
Peru	11,134
Philippines	41,523
Poland	26,017
Portugal	60,681
South Africa	139,750
Spain	504,219
Sweden	328,339
Switzerland	792,316
Thailand	36,340
Turkey	47,150
United Kingdom	2,576,992
United States	15,104,037
Yugoslavia	10,817
Zimbabwe	7,972

Source: International Bank for Reconstruction and Development, 2002.

Impact of the euro. The adoption of the euro by many European countries has encouraged MNCs based in Europe to issue shares. Investors throughout Europe are more willing to invest in shares when they do not have to worry about exchange rate effects. For example, a German insurance company may be more willing to buy shares issued by a firm in Portugal now that the same currency is used in both countries. The secondary market for shares denominated in euros is more liquid as a result of the participation by investors from several different countries that have adopted the euro.

Comparison of stock markets. Exhibit 3.6 provides a summary of the major stock markets, but there are numerous other exchanges. Some stock markets are much smaller reflecting the greater reliance on debt financing than equity financing in the past. Recently, however, firms have been issuing shares more frequently, which has resulted in the growth of the smaller stock markets. The percentage of individual versus institutional ownership of shares varies across stock markets. Generally financial institutions and other firms own a much larger proportion of the shares than individuals.

Large MNCs have begun to float new share issues simultaneously in various countries. Investment banks underwrite shares through one or more syndicates across countries. The global distribution of shares can reach a much larger market, so greater quantities of shares can be issued at a given price.

USING THE WEB

Stock market trading information. Information about the market capitalization, share trading volume, and turnover for each stock market is provided at http://www.worldbank.org/data.

In 2000, the Amsterdam, Brussels, and Paris stock exchanges merged to create the Euronext market. Since then, the Lisbon stock exchange has joined as well. As of 2004, the Euronext market had about 1,500 firms listed, about 300 of them from other countries. Most of the largest firms based in Continental Europe have listed their shares on the Euronext market. This market is likely to grow over time as other stock exchanges may join it. A single European stock market with similar guidelines for all shares regardless of their home country would make it easier for those investors who prefer to do all of their trading in one market.

In recent years, many new stock markets have been developed. These so-called emerging markets enable foreign firms to raise large amounts of capital by issuing shares. These markets may enable MNCs doing business in emerging markets to raise funds by issuing shares there and listing their shares on the local stock exchanges. Market characteristics such as the amount of trading relative to market capitalization and the applicable tax rates can vary substantially among emerging markets.

INTERNATIONAL FINANCIAL MARKETS AND THE MNC

Exhibit 3.7 illustrates the foreign cash flow movements of a typical MNC. These cash flows can be classified into four corporate functions, all of which generally require use of the foreign exchange markets. The spot market, forward market, currency futures market, and currency options market are all classified as foreign exchange markets.

The first function is foreign trade with business clients. Exports generate foreign cash inflows, while imports require cash outflows. A second function is direct foreign investment, or the acquisition of foreign real assets. This function requires cash outflows but generates future inflows through remitted dividends back to the MNC parent or the sale of these foreign assets. A third function is short-term investment or financing in foreign

Exhibit 3.7   Foreign cash flow chart of an MNC

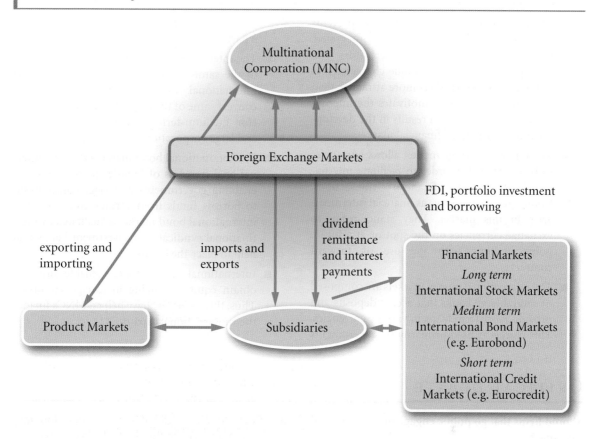

securities. A fourth function is longer-term financing in the international bond or stock markets.

HOW FINANCIAL MARKETS AFFECT AN MNC'S VALUE

Since interest rates commonly vary among countries, an MNC's parent may use international money or bond markets to obtain funds at a lower cost than they can be obtained locally. By doing so, it reduces its cost of debt and therefore reduces its weighted average cost of capital, which results in a higher valuation. An MNC's parent may be able to achieve a lower weighted average cost of capital by issuing equity in some foreign markets rather than issuing equity in its local market. If the MNC achieves a lower cost of capital, it can achieve a higher valuation.

SUMMARY

■ The existence of market imperfections prevents markets from being completely integrated. Consequently, investors and creditors can attempt to capitalize on unique characteristics that make foreign markets more attractive than domestic markets. This motivates the international flow of funds and results in the development of international financial markets.

■ The foreign exchange market allows currencies to be exchanged in order to facilitate international trade or financial transactions. Commercial banks serve as financial intermediaries in this market. They stand ready to exchange currencies on the spot or at a future point in time with the use of forward contracts.

■ The international money markets are composed of several large banks that accept deposits and provide short-term loans in various currencies. This market is used primarily by governments and large corporations. The European market is a part of the international money market.

■ The international credit markets are composed of the same commercial banks that serve the international money market. These banks convert some of the deposits received into loans (for medium-term periods) to governments and large corporations.

■ The international bond markets facilitate international transfers of long-term credit, thereby enabling governments and large corporations to borrow funds from various countries. The international bond market is facilitated by multinational syndicates of investment banks that help to place the bonds.

■ International stock markets enable firms to obtain equity financing in foreign countries. Thus, these markets have helped MNCs finance their international expansion.

CRITICAL DEBATE

Should firms that go public engage in international offerings?

Proposition. Yes. When a firm issues shares to the public for the first time in an initial public offering (IPO), it is naturally concerned about whether it can place all of its shares at a reasonable price. It will be able to issue its shares at a higher price by attracting more investors. It will increase its demand by spreading the shares across countries. The higher the price at which it can issue shares, the lower is its cost of using equity capital. It can also establish a global name by spreading shares across countries.

Opposing view. No. If a firm spreads its shares across different countries at the time of the IPO, there will be less publicly traded shares in the home country. Thus, it will not have as much liquidity in the secondary market. Investors desire shares that they can easily sell in the secondary market, which means that they require that the shares have liquidity. To the extent that a firm reduces its liquidity in the home country by spreading its share across countries, it may not attract sufficient home demand for the shares. Thus, its efforts to create global name recognition may reduce its name recognition in the United States.

With whom do you agree? State your reasons. Use InfoTrac or some other search engine to learn more about this issue. Which argument do you support? Offer your own opinion on this issue.

Stock Markets are inefficient.

Proposition. I cannot believe that if the value of the euro in terms of, say, the British pound increases three days in a row, on the fourth day there is still a 50:50 chance that it will go up or down in value. I think that most investors will see a trend and will buy, therefore the price is more likely to go up. Also, if the forward market predicts a rise in value, on average, surely it is going to rise in value. In other words, currency prices are predictable. And finally, if it were so unpredictable and therefore unprofitable to the speculator, how is it that there is such a vast sum of money being traded every day for speculative purposes – there is no smoke without fire.

Opposing view. The simple answer is that if that is what you believe, buy currencies that have increased three days in a row and on average you should make a profit, buy currencies where the forward market shows an increase in value. The fact is that there are a lot of investors with just your sort of views. The market traders know all about such beliefs and will price the currency so that such easy profit (their loss) cannot be made. Look at past currency rates for yourself, check all fourth day changes after three days of rises, any difference is going to be not enough to cover transaction costs or trading expenses and the slight inaccuracy in your figures which are likely to be closing day mid point of the bid/ask spread. No, all currency movements are related to information and no one knows if tomorrows news will be better or worse than expected.

With whom do you agree? Could there be undiscovered patterns? Could some movements not be related to information? Could some private news be leaking out?

SELF TEST

Answers are provided in Appendix A at the back of the text.

1. Sunny Bank quotes a bid rate of £0.58 for the US dollar and an ask rate of £0.60. What is the bid/ask percentage spread?

2. Cloudy Bank quotes an ask rate of £0.12 for the Peruvian currency (new sol) and a bid rate of £0.09. Determine the bid/ask percentage spread. Briefly give reasons for the difference with Q1.

3. Briefly explain how MNCs can make use of each international financial market described in this chapter.

QUESTIONS AND APPLICATIONS

1. **Motives for investing in foreign money markets.** Explain why an MNC may invest funds in a financial market outside its own country.

2. **Motives for providing credit in foreign markets.** Explain why some financial institutions prefer to provide credit in financial markets outside their own country.

3. **Exchange rate effects on investing.** Explain how the appreciation of the Australian dollar against the euro would affect the return to a French firm that invested in an Australian money market security.

4. **Exchange rate effects on borrowing.** Explain how the appreciation of the Japanese yen against the UK pound would affect the return to a UK firm that borrowed Japanese yen and used the proceeds for a UK project.

5. **Bank services.** List some of the important characteristics of bank foreign exchange services that MNCs should consider.

6. **Bid/ask spread.** Delay Bank's bid price for US dollars is £0.53 and its ask price is £0.55. What is the bid/ask percentage spread?

7. **Bid/ask spread.** Compute the bid/ask percentage spread for Mexican peso in which the ask rate is 20.6 New peso to the dollar and the bid rate is 21.5 New peso.

8. **Forward contract.** The Wolfpack ltd is a UK exporter that invoices its exports to the United States in dollars. If it expects that the dollar will appreciate against the pound in the future, should it hedge its exports with a forward contract? Explain.

9. **Euro.** Explain the foreign exchange situation for countries that use the euro when they engage in international trade among themselves.

10. **Indirect exchange rate.** If the direct exchange rate of the euro is worth £0.685, what is the indirect rate of the euro? Note that the pound is the home currency.

11. **Cross exchange rate.** Assume Poland's currency (the zloty) is worth £0.17 and the Japanese yen is worth £0.005. What is the cross (implied) rate of the zloty with respect to yen?

12. **Syndicated loans.** Explain how syndicated loans are used in international markets.

13. **Loan rates.** Explain the process used by banks in the Eurocredit market to determine the rate to charge on loans.

14. **International markets.** What is the function of the international money markets? Briefly describe the reasons for the development and growth of the European money market. Explain how the international money, credit, and bond markets differ from one another.

15. **Evolution of floating rates.** Briefly describe the historical developments that led to floating exchange rates as of 1973.

16. **International diversification.** Explain how the Asian crisis would have affected the returns to a UK firm investing in the Asian stock markets as a means of international diversification. (See the chapter appendix.)

17. **Eurocredit loans.**
    a. With regard to Eurocredit loans, who are the borrowers?
    b. Why would a bank desire to participate in syndicated Eurocredit loans?
    c. What is LIBOR, and how is it used in the Eurocredit market?

18. **Foreign exchange.** You just came back from Canada, where the Canadian dollar was worth £0.43. You still have C$200 from your trip and could exchange them for pounds at the airport, but the airport foreign exchange desk will only buy them for £0.40. Next week, you will be going to Mexico and will need pesos. The airport foreign exchange desk will sell you pesos for £0.055 per peso. You met a tourist at the airport who is from Mexico and is on his way to Canada. He is willing to buy your C$200 for 1500 New Pesos. Should you accept the offer or cash the Canadian dollars in at the airport? Explain.

19. **Foreign stock markets.** Explain why firms may issue shares in foreign markets. Why might MNCs issue more shares in Europe since the conversion to a single currency in 1999?

20. **Stock market integration.** Bullet plc a UK firm, is planning to issue new shares on the London Stock Exchange this month. The only decision still to be made is the specific day on which the shares will be issued. Why do you think Bullet monitors results of the Tokyo stock market every morning?

ADVANCED QUESTIONS

21. **Effects of September 11.** Why do you think the terrorist attack on the United States was expected to cause a decline in US interest rates? Given the expectations for a decline in US interest rates and share prices, how were capital flows between the United States and other countries likely to be affected?

22. **International financial markets.** Carrefour the French Supermarket chain has established retail outlets worldwide. These outlets are massive and contain products purchased locally as well as imports. As Carrefour generates earnings beyond what it needs abroad, it may remit those earnings back to France. Carrefour is likely to build additional outlets especially in China.
    a. Explain how the Carrefour outlets in China would use the spot market in foreign exchange.
    b. Explain how Carrefour might utilize the international money markets when it is establishing other Carrefour stores in Asia.
    c. Explain how Carrefour could use the international bond market to finance the establishment of new outlets in foreign markets.

23. **Interest rates.** Why do interest rates vary among countries? Why are interest rates normally similar for those European countries that use the euro as their currency? Offer a reason why the government interest rate of one country could be slightly higher than that of the government interest rate of another country, even though the euro is the currency used in both countries.

24. **Market information on the Internet.** Use your own institution's currency database or visit http://www.oanda.com/convert/fxhistory, to obtain exchange rate data covering at least one year, copy and paste the results into Excel and answer the following questions:

   a. Determine the cross exchange rate between the Japanese yen and the Australian dollar. Compare the cross exchange rate with the direct rate. Are there any differences? Evaluate the significance of your results.

   b. Select a pattern, for example two days of consecutive falls, then select and check the movements on the following day (the third day in this case). Are the following day movements unusual in any way? Evaluate the significance of your results.

It is helpful to use nested "if" instructions in Excel. In this example two days of consecutive falls is the criteria for selecting the third day's price movement. An instruction placed in C4 and copied and pasted to C365 with exchange rates from B1 to B365 would be: =IF(B3>B2,IF(B2>B1,B4,""),"")

a run of three days would be:

=IF(B4>B3,IF(B3>B2,IF(B2>B1,B5,""),""),"")

note that "" is simply a double inverted comma, Excel ignores gaps so " " will also work. Once applied, choose "Data" and "sort" from the toolbar to get rid of the blanks.

Note that the Excel formula can be varied so that for instance < may be used and other operands =, +, – and so on. Formulas may also be incorporated so that if only large movements were of interest one could write:

=IF(B4>B3*1.1,IF(B3>B2*1.1,IF(B2>B1*1.1,B5,""),""),"")

Experiment with the formula to obtain the desired pattern.

25. From Appendix 3, imagine that you are a UK investor, construct an international portfolio of shares. Is the standard deviation of your international portfolio greater or less than an equivalent domestic portfolio? Evaluate the significance of your results.

You will need a database of a history of the share prices of large companies (Perfect Analysis and Datastream are examples). The history of exchange rates with the British pound for the currencies quoted, e.g. \$:£, euro:£, C\$:£ and so on.

The return on a share for a month will be $(1+R) \times (1+e)$ – see appendix for more on the formula. You may then calculate the variance and covariance matrix of a portfolio of these returns month on month (the portfolio calculator may help).

26. From Appendix 3, compare the return and the risk of investing in the NYSE with investing in the London Stock Exchange for a UK investor. Evaluate the significance of your results.

   You will need a FTSE stock exchange index, the Dow Jones index or NASDAQ index and the £:\$ exchange rate.

   Analysis can be made using Excel. The process is to invest in the US index at the start of the period and convert back at the end of the period. Then work out the percentage change in the value. To "buy the index" you can in effect treat the index as the dollar price of a share, so buy the currency, then buy the share at the beginning of the period, then at the end of the period reverse the process.

   Alternatively, you can work out the percentage change in the index over the period and the percentage change in the value of the currency over the year, then use the formula as in the text:

$$R_£ = (1+R)(1+e)$$

Note that you can work out the risk in approximate fashion by working out the percentage changes in the value of the currency and index then applying the model for combining variances, as:

VAR (index) + Var (£:\$ rate) + 2 × SD (£:\$ rate) × SD (index) × Corr (£:\$ rate, index)

This is not exact but relies on the approximation that at low levels of change i.e. below 10% :

$(1+R) \times (1+e) - 1$ roughly equals $R + e$

so the formula is the same as adding two investments as the returns are roughly additive.

27. From Appendix 3. Calculate the percentage changes (returns on a period by period basis)

between any two major currencies for a ten year period on a rolling basis. You may choose the length of the return period. Thus, if your data is monthly, say, the last day of each month then your first return would be the percentage change from 31 December to 31 January, the second return would be from the 31 January to 28 February and so on – there is a note on returns in Appendix B at the end of the book. Then calculate the variances and correlations between the returns.

a. Using graphs, examine the predictability of the standard deviation of each currency and the predictability of the correlation between the two currencies.

b. Examine a period where there has been a significant change in the value of the standard deviations and correlations. Look at the financial news about this time and see whether or not there is any suggestion in the press that might indicate a change in the behaiour of the currencies.

DISCUSSION IN THE BOARDROOM

This exercise can be found on the companion website at www.cengage.co.uk/madura_fox.

RUNNING YOUR OWN MNC

This exercise can be found on the companion website at www.cengage.co.uk/madura_fox.

Essays/discussion and articles can be found at the end of Part 1

BLADES PLC CASE STUDY
Decisions to use international financial markets

As a financial analyst for Blades plc you are reasonably satisfied with Blades' current setup of exporting "Speedos" (roller blades) to Thailand. Due to the unique arrangement with Blades' primary customer in Thailand, forecasting the revenue to be generated there is a relatively easy task. Specifically, your customer has agreed to purchase 180,000 pairs of Speedos annually, for a period of three years, at a price of THB4,594 (THB = Thai baht) per pair. The current direct quotation of the pound–baht exchange rate is £0.016.

The cost of goods sold incurred in Thailand (due to imports of the rubber and plastic components from Thailand) runs at approximately THB2,871 per pair of Speedos, but Blades currently only imports materials sufficient to manufacture about 72,000 pairs of Speedos. Blades' primary reasons for using a Thai supplier are the high quality of the components and the low cost, which has been facilitated by a continuing depreciation of the Thai baht against the pound. If the pound cost of buying components becomes more expensive in Thailand than in the United Kingdom, Blades is contemplating providing its UK supplier with the additional business.

Your plan is quite simple; Blades is currently using its Thai-denominated revenues to cover the cost of goods sold incurred there. During the last year, excess revenue was converted to pounds at the prevailing exchange rate. Although your cost of goods sold is not fixed contractually as the Thai revenues are, you expect them to remain relatively constant in the near future. Consequently, the baht-denominated cash inflows are fairly predictable each year because the Thai customer has committed to the purchase of 180,000 pairs of Speedos at a fixed price. The excess pound revenue resulting from the conversion of baht is used either to support the UK production of Speedos if needed or to invest in the United Kingdom. Specifically, the revenues are used to cover cost of goods sold in the UK manufacturing plant.

Ben Holt, Blades' finance director, notices that Thailand's interest rates are approximately 15% (versus 8% in the United Kingdom). You interpret the high interest rates in Thailand as an indication of the uncertainty resulting from Thailand's unstable economy. Holt asks you to assess the feasibility of investing Blades' excess funds from Thailand operations in Thailand at an interest rate of 15%. After you express your opposition to his plan, Holt asks you to detail the reasons in a detailed report.

1. One point of concern for you is that there is a tradeoff between the higher interest rates in Thailand and the delayed conversion of baht into pounds. Explain what this means.
2. If the net baht received from the Thailand operation are invested in Thailand, how will UK operations be affected? (Assume that Blades is currently paying 10% on pounds borrowed and needs more financing for its firm.)
3. Construct a spreadsheet to compare the cash flows resulting from two plans. Under the first plan, net baht-denominated cash flows (received today) will be invested in Thailand at 15% for a one-year period, after which the baht will be converted to pounds. The expected spot rate for the baht in one year is about £0.0147 (Ben Holt's plan). Under the second plan, net baht-denominated cash flows are converted to pounds immediately and invested in the United Kingdom for one year at 8%. For this question, assume that all baht-denominated cash flows are due today. Does Holt's plan seem superior in terms of pound cash flows available after one year? Compare the choice of investing the funds versus using the funds to provide needed financing to the firm.

SMALL BUSINESS DILEMMA
Developing a multinational sporting goods industry

Each month, the Sports Exports Company (an Irish firm) receives an order for basketballs from a British sporting goods distributor. The monthly payment for the basketballs is denominated in British pounds, as requested by the British distributor. Jim Logan, owner of the Sports Exports Company, must convert the pounds received into euros.

1. Explain how the Sports Exports Company could utilize the spot market to facilitate the exchange of currencies. Be specific.
2. Explain how the Sports Exports Company is exposed to exchange rate risk and how it could use the forward market to hedge this risk.

INVESTING IN INTERNATIONAL FINANCIAL MARKETS

The trading of financial assets (such as shares or bonds) by investors in international financial markets has a major impact on MNCs. First, this type of trading can influence the level of interest rates in a specific country (and therefore the cost of debt to an MNC) because it affects the amount of funds available there. Second, it can affect the price of an MNC's shares (and therefore the cost of equity to an MNC) because it influences the demand for the MNC's shares. Third, it enables MNCs to sell securities in foreign markets. So, even though international investing in financial assets is not the most crucial activity of MNCs, international investing by individual and institutional investors can indirectly affect the actions and performance of an MNC. Consequently, an understanding of the motives and methods of international investing is necessary to anticipate how the international flow of funds may change in the future and how that change may affect MNCs.

BACKGROUND ON INTERNATIONAL STOCK EXCHANGES

The international trading of shares has grown over time but has been limited by three barriers: transaction costs, information costs, and exchange rate risk. In recent years, however, these barriers have been reduced as explained here.

USING THE WEB

Stock exchange information It is best to use Google for the homepage of the Stock Exchange. For example the London Stock Exchange can be found at http://www.london-stockexchange.com/en-gb, go to the bottom of the page and jump to statistics. Or choose the NYSE at http://www.nyse.com and search the index on the left. In both cases pdf or Excel files offer the best quality data.

Reduction in transaction costs

Most countries tend to have their own stock exchanges, where the shares of local publicly held companies are traded. In recent years, exchanges have been consolidated within a country, which has increased efficiency and reduced transaction costs. Some European stock exchanges now have extensive cross-listings so that investors in a given European country can easily purchase shares of companies based in other European countries.

In particular, because of its efficiency, the stock exchange of Switzerland may serve as a model that will be applied to many other stock exchanges around the world. The Swiss stock exchange is now fully computerized, so a trading floor is not needed. Orders by investors to buy or sell flow to financial institutions that are certified members of the

Swiss stock exchange. These institutions are not necessarily based in Switzerland. The details of the orders, such as the name of the shares, the number of shares to be bought or sold, and the price at which the investor is willing to buy or sell, are fed into a computer system. The system matches buyers and sellers and then sends information confirming the transaction to the financial institution, which informs the investor that the transaction is completed.

When there are many more buy orders than sell orders for a given share, the computer is unable to accommodate all orders. Some buyers will then increase the price they are willing to pay for the shares. Thus, the price adjusts in response to the demand (buy orders) for the shares and the supply (sell orders) of the shares for sale recorded by the computer system. Similar dynamics occur when a trading floor is used, but the computerized system has documented criteria by which it prioritizes the execution of orders; traders on a trading floor may execute some trades in ways that favour themselves at the expense of investors.

In recent years, electronic communications networks (ECNs) have been created in many countries to match orders between buyers and sellers. Like the Swiss stock exchange, ECNs do not have a visible trading floor: the trades are executed by a computer network. Examples of popular ECNs include Archipelago, Instinet, and Tradebook. With an ECN, investors can place orders on their computers that are then executed by the computer system and confirmed through the Internet to the investor. Thus, all parts of the trading process from the placement of the order to the confirmation that the transaction has been executed are conducted by computer. The ease with which such orders can occur, regardless of the locations of the investor and the stock exchange, is sure to increase the volume of international share transactions in the future.

Impact of alliances. Several stock exchanges have created international alliances with the stock exchanges of other countries, thereby enabling firms to more easily cross-list their shares among various stock markets. This gives investors easier and cheaper access to foreign shares. The alliances also allow greater integration between markets. At some point in the future, there may be one global stock market in which any shares of any country can be easily purchased or sold by investors around the world. A single global stock market would allow US investors to easily purchase any shares, regardless of where the corporation is based or the currency in which the share is denominated. The international alliances are a first step toward a single global stock market. The costs of international share transactions have already been substantially reduced as a result of some of the alliances.

Reduction in information costs

The Internet provides investors with access to much information about foreign shares, enabling them to make more informed decisions without having to purchase information about these shares. Consequently, investors should be more comfortable assessing foreign shares. Although differences in accounting rules still limit the degree to which financial data about foreign companies can be interpreted or compared to data about firms in other countries, there is some momentum toward making accounting standards uniform across some countries.

Exchange rate risk

When investing in a foreign share that is denominated in a foreign currency, investors are subject to the possibility that the currency denominating the share may depreciate against the investor's currency over time.

The potential for a major decline in the share's value simply because of a large degree of depreciation is more likely for emerging markets, such as Indonesia or Russia, where the local currency can change by 10% or more on a single day.

Measuring the impact of exchange rates. The return to a UK investor from investing in a foreign share is influenced by the return on the share itself which includes the dividend, and the percentage change in the exchange rate, as shown here:

$$R_{UK} = (1+R)(1+e) - 1$$

Where:

R_{UK} = Overall return to the UK investor over the time period $t-1$ to t, the time periods subscript has not been included, it is assumed that the return must be defined over a period!

R = return on the foreign investment itself measured as

$$\frac{P_t - P_{t-1} + D_t}{P_t}$$

Where:

P_t =   price at time t
P_{t-1} = price at time $t-1$
D_t = dividend

e = percentage change in the value of the foreign currency over period $t-1$ to t.

E X A M P L E

A year ago, Rob Grady invested in the share of Vopka, a Russian company. Over the last year, the share increased in value by 35%. Over this same period, however, the Russian rouble's value declined by 30%. Rob sold the Vopka shares today. His return is:

$$R_{UK} = (1+R)(1+e) - 1$$
$$R_{UK} = (1+0.35)(1-0.30) - 1$$
$$= -0.055 \text{ or } -5.5\%$$

Even though the return on the share was more pronounced than the exchange rate movement, Rob lost money on his investment. The reason is that the exchange rate movement of −30% wiped out not only 30% of his initial investment but also 30% of the share's return.

As the preceding example illustrates, investors should consider the potential influence of exchange rate movements on foreign shares before investing in those shares. Foreign investments are especially risky in developing countries, where exchange rates tend to be very volatile.

Reducing exchange rate risk of foreign shares. One method of reducing exchange rate risk is to take what are termed short positions in the foreign currencies denominating the foreign shares. A short position in this context means a selling contract dated in the future. For example, a US investor holding Mexican shares who expects the shares to be worth 10 million Mexican pesos one year from now could sell forward contracts (or futures contracts) to sell 10 million pesos. The shares could be sold at that time for pesos, and the pesos could be exchanged for dollars at a locked-in price.

Although hedging the exchange rate risk of an international share portfolio can be effective, it has three limitations. First, the number of foreign currency units to be converted to dollars at the end of the investment horizon is unknown as the exact price will not be known. Nevertheless, though the hedge may not be perfect for this reason, investors normally should be able to hedge most of their exchange rate risk.

A second limitation of hedging exchange rate risk is that the investors may decide to retain the foreign shares beyond the initially planned investment horizon. Of course, they can reverse (or close out) the existing position and create another forward sale, albeit at a different rate.

A third limitation of hedging is that forward rates for currencies that are less widely traded may not exist or may exhibit a large discount.

INTERNATIONAL SHARE DIVERSIFICATION

A substantial amount of research has demonstrated that investors in shares can benefit by diversifying internationally. The philosophy of diversification is very simple. An investor will normally invest in a portfolio, which is no more than saying that investment will be in the shares of more than one company. A well diversified portfolio will be made up of investments in shares whose performance is not well correlated. If the value of one share in the portfolio falls there will be other shares in the portfolio that will be increasing in value. Looking from the other point of view, there will be falls in the value of some shares in the portfolio which will limit the effect of rises. So a well diversified portfolio experiences lower overall falls in value but less steep rises in value than a poorly diversified portfolio. The general wisdom is that a portfolio should be well diversified to lessen the effect of individual problems of any one investment. Note that a well diversified portfolio may be risky if made up of volatile shares (i.e. prone to large gains or losses) or may be relatively safe depending on the nature of the shares in the portfolio. Diversification merely gets rid of individual share effects but keeps the common trait in the portfolio.

Investing in a portfolio is a choice between risk (as measured by expected volatility measures such as variance – see below) and return (as defined in the previous equation). Exhibit 3.8 outlines the choice for an investor. In an efficient market (where goods are priced according to all available information) the choice is between greater return and greater risk or lesser return but lesser risk. Portfolios C and E in Exhibit 3.8 are mispriced in relation to portfolio A – we will assume that A is correctly priced.

Portfolio E should be offering a higher return. As the future value is a given estimate, the only way to increase the return is to pay less for that future value – so portfolio E is overvalued with respect to A. Lowering the amount paid for E and hence raising the return would move it into the B quadrant. By the same reasoning portfolio C is undervalued, more should be paid for the given expected value – the higher price of C would lower the return and move it down into the D quadrant. Portfolios B and D may or may not be attractive to the holder of portfolio A depending on the holder's level of risk aversion. A risk averse investor will prefer portfolio D to A and an investor wanting to take on more risk will prefer B to A. When selecting portfolios, choice and value depends on risk and return.

Exhibit 3.8 Risks return choice for an investor – a comparison of portfolios A, B, C, D and E

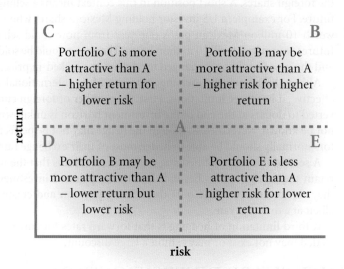

Measuring portfolio risk and return. As shown in the previous equation, the return on an individual share is measured by its movement in value plus any dividends all measured as a percentage return. Because the value of the currency may have changed, the return must be multiplied by currency movement. If the investment were in bonds, interest payments would replace dividends. Also, returns can be expressed in monetary terms as well.

EXAMPLE

Sunny investments plc a UK company has purchased 150,000 euros worth of shares in Sensible SA a French company when the exchange rate was 1.5 euros:£1. At the end of the year, Sunny receives 7,000 euros from Sensible in dividend payments and sells its shares for 160,000 euros. Its returns are then converted at 1.4 euros:£1.

The returns calculated in monetary terms are:

Original investment 150,000 euros / 1.5 = £100,000

Converted sale price of shares 160,000 euros / 1.4 = £114,285.71

Converted value of dividends 7,000 euros / 1.4 = £5000

Monetary return = £114,285.71 + £5000 – £100,000 = £19,285.71 which is a return in percentage terms of £19,295.71 / £100,000 = 0.1928571 or 19.29%

Or

Percentage return on investment in Sensible: (160,000 euros – 150,000 euros + 7,000 euros) / 150,000 euros = 11.3333%

Percentage movement in currency value: opening value of the euro 1/1.5 = £0.666666; closing value of the euro: 1/1.4 = £0.714285; percentage change in value of the euro: (£0.714285 – £0.666666) / £0.666666 = 0.071428571 or 7.14286%

Overall return is R_{UK} $= (1+R)\ (1+e) -1$

$= (1+0.113333)\ (1+0.0714286) - 1$

$= 0.1928568$ or $\underline{19.29\%}$

(note that the difference between 0.1928571 and 0.1928568 of 0.0000003 is a rounding error).

The percentage approach as in the above example of Sunny plc will be used here.

The formula for the return on a portfolio is: the weighted average return on investments.

Weights are defined as the percentage original investment in a share. This is a small approximation in that weights change with changes in the value of the shares in the portfolio, the original value is sufficient. For international investments the return includes percentage changes in the value of the currency as outlined in the preceding example (Sunny Investments). The following example (Investor Morse) illustrates the calculation of the expected return on a portfolio.

EXAMPLE

If Investor Morse invests a quarter of the initial sum in share A offering a 20% return and three quarters in share B offering a 10% return, the weights are 25% and 75% for shares A and B respectively and the overall return will be:

$$0.25 \times 20\% + 0.75 \times 10\% = 12.5\% \text{ for the portfolio}$$

The overall risk of a portfolio is, however, more problematic. Risk for an individual investment is normally thought of as an expected standard deviation – a measure of potential variability (sometimes termed volatility in the literature). For portfolios there is a need to combine the risk measure of differing investments to obtain the overall risk of the portfolio. If there were a perfect correlation between investments in a portfolio – see Appendix B for notes on correlation – the overall risk of a portfolio would be simply the weighted average of the expected standard deviations of the investments in the portfolio. But in virtually all portfolios the returns on individual investments are not perfectly correlated. The more diversified the portfolio, the lower the overall variability of the portfolio. Diversification as well as standard deviation is therefore an important factor in taking into account the overall level of risk in a portfolio. It is not enough just to look at the individual variability of investments in a portfolio. Calculations must include correlation or covariability as a measure of diversification. Conceptually the formula is not difficult.

The formula for the overall standard deviation of a portfolio is: the square root of the weighted average of all possible variances and covariances in the portfolio.

A correlation is simply a covariance mapped onto a scale going from –1 to +1. A covariance can therefore be thought of as a correlation. Thus a high correlation or covariance exists between two shares A and B in a portfolio when the returns on share A are above its expected return, the return on share B is also almost always above its expected return; and similarly if share A is below its expected return, share B too will be below its expected return almost always. A low correlation would exist if share A were above its expected return, share B is only sometimes above its expected return. Thus correlation is the same idea as diversification, the advantage of a correlation or covariance is that it is a statistical measure. High correlation indicates low diversification, there is not much offsetting effect; low correlation indicates high diversification – when share A is performing badly share B may be performing well.

The calculation of the standard deviation of a portfolio of share A and share B can be written in the form of a matrix to ensure that all possible variances and covariances are included as shown in Exhibit 3.9.

Thus the standard deviation of a portfolio made up of two shares can also be written (with references to the matrix in Exhibit 3.9) as:

$$SD_p = \sqrt{\underbrace{w_A^2 \times Var(A)}_{\text{Top left}} + \underbrace{w_B^2 \times Var(B)}_{\text{Bottom right}} + \underbrace{2 \times w_A \times w_B SD_A \times SD_B \times Corr(A,B)}_{\text{top right and bottom left}}}$$

This rather long formula is no more than the square root of the total of the cells in the matrix in Exhibit 3.9. The advantage of using a matrix is that it is easy now to see how to calculate the standard deviation of portfolios made up of three or more shares or, more generally, international investments.

An example of an extended matrix is shown in Exhibit 3.10. Note that this powerful formula, in many ways the basis of finance, applies to all types of investment: ADRs, Eurobonds, US treasury bonds etc. Although the value in their own currency terms will not change greatly, the returns here are translated into the home currency of the investor and will therefore be subject to changes in the value of the foreign currency. Thus the formula applies to international investments in general.

Exhibit 3.9   Calculating the variance of a two share portfolio – the variance covariance matrix

	Share A	Share B
Share A	$w_A^2 \times Var(A)$	$w_A \times w_B \times Cov(A,B)$
Share B	$w_B \times w_A \times Cov(B,A)$	$w_B^2 \times Var(B)$

Notes:

- This is a variance (*Var*) and Covariance (*Cov*) matrix of returns, where returns are defined as:
  $R_{UK} = (1+R)(1+e) - 1$ (where R_{UK} are the translated foreign returns (R) affected by currency changes (e) – see above);

- w_A and w_B are weights, the percentage of original investment in share A and share B;

- The top right and bottom left values are the same i.e. $w_A \times w_B \times Cov(A,B) = w_B \times w_A \times Cov(B,A)$;

- Covariances can be written using more familiar terms:
  $Cov(A,B) = SD_A \times SD_B \times Corr(A,B)$
  where:
  SD_A, SD_B = standard deviations of A and B
  $Corr(A,B)$ = correlation of A and B

- The standard deviation of the portfolio is simply the square root of the total of all the values in the cells of the above matrix.

Exhibit 3.10 Calculating the variance of a portfolio of three or more international investments

	International investment A	International investment B	International investment C	International investment D	International investment E
International investment A	$w_A^2 \times Var(A)$	$w_A \times w_B \times Cov(A,B)$	$w_A \times w_C \times Cov(A,C)$	$w_A \times w_D \times Cov(A,D)$	$w_A \times w_E \times Cov(A,E)$
International investment B	$w_A \times w_B \times Cov(A,B)$	$W_B^2 \times Var(B)$	$w_B \times w_C \times Cov(B,C)$	$w_B \times w_D \times Cov(B,D)$	$w_B \times w_E \times Cov(B,E)$
International investment C	$w_A \times w_C \times Cov(A,C)$	$w_B \times w_C \times Cov(B,C)$	$W_C^2 \times Var(C)$	$w_C \times w_D \times Cov(C,D)$	$w_C \times w_D \times Cov(C,E)$
International investment D	$w_A \times w_D \times Cov(A,D)$	$w_B \times w_D \times Cov(B,D)$	$w_C \times w_D \times Cov(C,D)$	$W_D^2 \times Var(D)$	$w_D \times w_E \times Cov(D,E)$
International investment E	$w_A \times w_E \times Cov(A,E)$	$w_B \times w_E \times Cov(B,E)$	$w_C \times w_D \times Cov(C,E)$	$w_D \times w_E \times Cov(D,E)$	$W_E^2 \times Var(E)$

Notes:

■ The overall variance is simply the total value of all the cells in the matrix, for an explanation of the symbols see previous exhibit. Note that this matrix simply extends the pattern of Exhibit 3.9.

■ The pattern can be extended to any number of investments, the lead diagonal is top left to bottom right (in bold) the values above the lead diagonal are a mirror image (the same), as the values below the lead diagonal – hence the 2 in the equation above.

■ Note that the lead diagonal represents individual risk of the investments and will become progressively less important compared to their joint risk as the portfolio grows – at present five cells compared to 20 covariance cells – hence the diversifying effect.

■ The order of the investments in the covariance term is the same, but note that the operation is commutative i.e. $Cov(A,B) = Cov(B,A)$ and so on.

The formula is the same as for domestic investment, the difference is that the sources of variability are increased as the returns are denominated in foreign currency and have to be translated.

Since stock markets partially reflect the current and/or forecasted state of their countries' economies, they do not move in tandem. Thus, the returns of shares in different markets are not expected to be highly correlated. In Exhibit 3.10 the off diagonal values are therefore likely to be lower than for a purely domestic portfolio – the diversification effect larger.

Crucial to the measurement of risk is an understanding as to how to predict variances and covariances of shares. Also, as these investments are foreign, the variance and covariance of exchange rates as well as shares is important. Sophisticated techniques such as Generalized Autoregressive Conditional Heteroskedasticity (GARCH) can be employed to predict volatility (i.e. standard deviation). Predicting covariances or correlations, however, is currently on the frontier of statistical modelling.

As an alternative to statistical modelling, businesses have to resort to subjective judgements on the future value of these variables. Aids to such judgements can be gleaned from simply modelling volatilities and correlations over time in Excel. Even in these circumstances, the model is useful in that it provides the "language" for estimating portfolio risk.

The concept of an efficient market says that prices move randomly and unpredictably and it may seem therefore that any prediction is not possible. But the randomness refers to the direction of movement, variance is a non-directional statement and says nothing about whether the currency values will go up or down. So predicting variances and indeed covariances and the derived measures of correlations, standard deviations or volatilities does not mean that the markets are inefficient.

EXAMPLE

Guess Investments plc wants to invest £100,000 in a portfolio of two foreign shares. The following are estimates of their returns translated into British pounds:

Investment in: share X £60,000; share Y £40,000

Expected return: share X 15%; share Y 45%

Standard deviation: share X 10%; share Y 50%

Correlation share X with share Y: 0.25

The weights are: $w_X = 60,000 / 100,000 = 0.60$; $w_Y = 40,000 / 100,000 = 0.40$

The expected returns on the portfolio are: $0.60 \times 15\% + 0.40 \times 45\% = 27\%$

The standard deviation of the portfolio is:

$$\sqrt{0.60^2 \times 0.10^2 + 0.40^2 \times 0.50^2 + 2 \times 0.40 \times 0.60 \times 0.10 \times 0.50 \times 0.25} = 0.22$$

or 22%.

So, assuming that the returns are jointly normally distributed (that is when their returns are considered jointly the overall returns are normally distributed), the 95% confidence interval (see Appendix B) for the expected portfolio returns is:

$$1.96 \times 0.22 = 43\%$$

$$-16\% \xleftarrow{-43\%} 27\% \xrightarrow{+43\%} 70\%$$

The Guess director observes: "There isn't much of a diversification effect as the weighted average of the standard deviations (i.e. assuming perfect correlation and hence no diversification) is $0.6 \times 10\% + 0.4 \times 50\% = 26\%$ as opposed to the 22% above". His bright young assistant replies: "True, but two investments hardly make a portfolio. Now if you didn't invest in X as your 'safe' share, but just looked for security in diversification and invested only in four shares similar to Y, in four different stock markets, with say a correlation of 0.1 between any two, your overall standard deviation would be about ... 0.285 or 28.5%. An expected return of 45% with a standard deviation of 28.5% not bad, certainly better than this expected return of 27% for a standard deviation of 22%" (you may check this calculation on the Portfolio Calculator). The Guess Director replies: "And what if all the markets collapse together? It has happened."

Limitations of international diversification

Correlations between share indexes in differing stock markets are a proxy measure for the kind of correlation of returns one can expect from investing in shares in the differing stock markets – the correlation is therefore important. In general, correlations between share indexes have been higher in recent years than they were several years ago. The general increase in correlations among stock market returns reduces the opportunity to lower risk through international diversification unless exchange rate movements offer further reductions in co-movement.

Exhibit 3.11 Integration among foreign stock markets during the 1987 crash

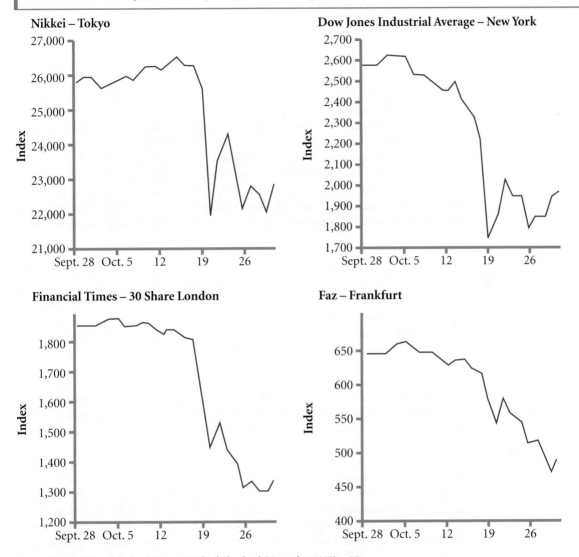

Source: *Economic Trends* Federal Reserve Bank of Cleveland (November 1987), p.17.

USING THE WEB

Stock market performance Charts showing recent stock market performance for each market can be found at http://finance.yahoo.com/intlindices?u. The prevailing share index level is shown for each country, as well as the performance of each market during the previous day. For some markets, you can assess the performance over the last year by clicking on Chart next to the country's name.

One reason for the increased correlations among stock market returns is increased integration of business between countries. Foreign portfolio investments between 1985 and 2003 have increased globally at an estimated annual average rate of 13½%. Institutional investors are increasingly holding international portfolios. Increased integration also results in more intercountry trade flows. In particular, many European countries have become more integrated as regulations have been standardized throughout Europe to facilitate trade between countries. In addition, the adoption of the euro has removed exchange rate risk due to trade between participating countries.

The conversion to the euro also allows portfolio managers in European countries to invest in shares of other participating European countries without concern for exchange rate risk, because these shares are also denominated in euros. This facilitates a more regional approach for European investors, who are not restricted to shares within their respective countries.

Since some stock market correlations may become more pronounced during a crisis, international diversification will not necessarily be as effective during a downturn as it is during more favourable conditions. This is an important point. The statistics used to capture the idea of diversification (covariance and correlation) are averages of co-movement. They assume that overall conditions are relatively constant and that the differing movements happen for temporary reasons. But clearly, if there is a major regime shift, as in a financial crisis, all markets are going to be affected and the kind of assumptions behind correlation type measures may well not hold. Two such events that had just such an adverse effect on many markets, the 1987 crash and the Asian crisis, are discussed next.

Market movements during the 1987 crash. Further evidence on the relationships between stock markets is obtained by assessing market movements during the stock market crash in October 1987. Exhibit 3.11 shows the stock market movements for four major countries during the crash. While the magnitude of the decline was not exactly the same, all four markets were adversely affected. When institutional investors anticipated a general decline in shares, they sold some shares from all markets, instead of just their home market.

Many stock markets experienced larger declines in prices than US stock markets. For example, during the month of October 1987, the US market index declined by about 21%, while the German market index declined by about 23% and the United Kingdom index by 26%. The stock market indexes of Australia and Hong Kong decreased by more than 50% over this same month.

Market movements during the Asian crisis. In the summer of 1997, Thailand experienced severe economic problems, which were followed by economic downturns in several other Asian countries. Investors revalued shares downward because of weakened economic conditions, more political uncertainty, and a lack of confidence that the problems would be resolved. The effects during the first year of the Asian crisis are summarized in Exhibit 3.12. This crisis demonstrated how quickly share prices could adjust to changing conditions and how adverse market conditions could spread across countries. Thus, diversification across Asia did not effectively insulate investors during the Asian crisis. Diversification across all continents would have been a more effective method of diversification during the crisis.

Although there has not been another world stock market crash since 1987, there have been several mini-crashes. For example, on 27 August 1998 (referred to as "Bloody Thursday"), Russian shares and currency values declined abruptly in response to severe financial problems in Russia, and most stock markets around the world experienced losses on that day. US shares declined by more than 4% on this day. The adverse effects extended beyond shares that would be directly affected by financial problems in Russia as paranoia caused investors to sell shares across all markets due to fears that all shares might be overvalued.

Exhibit 3.12 How stock markets changed during the Asian crisis

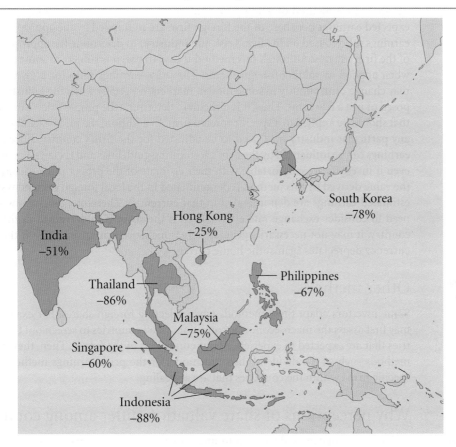

In response to the September 11, 2001, terrorist attacks on the United States, many stock markets experienced declines of more than 10% over the following week. Diversification among markets was not very effective in reducing risk in this case.

VALUATION OF FOREIGN SHARES

When investors consider investing in foreign shares, they need methods for valuing those shares. The methods are no different to the valuation of domestic shares except that there are added complications from exchange rate movements.

Dividend discount model

One possibility is to use the dividend discount model with an adjustment to account for expected exchange rate movements. Foreign shares pay dividends in the currency in which they are denominated. Thus, the cash flow per period to European investors is the dividend (denominated in the foreign currency) converted to euros. Because of exchange rate uncertainty, the value of the foreign shares from a home investor's perspective is subject to exchange rate uncertainty as well as uncertainty over dividends.

Price-earnings method

An alternative method of valuing foreign shares is to apply price-earnings ratios. The expected earnings per share of the foreign firm are multiplied by the appropriate price-earnings ratio (based on the firm's risk and industry) to determine the appropriate price of the firm's shares. Although this method is easy to use, it is subject to some limitations when applied to valuing foreign shares. The price-earnings ratio for a given industry may change continuously in some foreign markets, especially when the industry is composed of just a few firms. Thus, it is difficult to determine the proper price-earnings ratio that should be applied to a specific foreign firm. In addition, the price-earnings ratio for any particular industry may need to be adjusted for the firm's country, since reported earnings can be influenced by the firm's accounting guidelines and tax laws. Furthermore, even if investors are comfortable with their estimate of the proper price-earnings ratio, the value derived by this method is denominated in the local foreign currency (since the estimated earnings are denominated in that currency). Therefore, investors would still need to consider exchange rate effects. Even if the share is undervalued in the foreign country, it may not necessarily generate a reasonable return for investors if the foreign currency depreciates against the home currency.

Other methods

Some investors adapt these methods when selecting foreign shares. For example, they may first assess the macroeconomic conditions of all countries to screen out those countries that are expected to experience poor conditions in the future. Then, they use other methods such as the dividend discount model or the price-earnings method to value specific firms within the countries that are appealing.

Why perceptions of share valuation differ among countries

A share that appears undervalued to investors in one country may seem overvalued to investors in another country. Some of the more common reasons why perceptions of a share's valuation may vary among investors in different countries are identified here.

Required rate of return. Some investors attempt to value a share according to the present value of the future cash flows that it will generate. The dividend discount model is one of many models that use this approach. The required rate of return that is used to discount the cash flows can vary substantially among countries. The rate is based on the prevailing risk-free interest rate available to investors, plus a risk premium.

Do countries apply the same risk premium to identical projects? Are some investment communities more risk averse than others? These are not settled questions. What can be said is that the more risky the project the lower the value of its share as a higher discount rate is applied. A foreign investor may think that the risk has been overpriced and that the share is a bargain and hence worth purchasing. Or the investor may see higher returns than are currently estimated for that share. Such judgements are the stuff of investment. For international investment it is this risk plus exchange rate risk.

The other element of the discount rate used to discount future dividends is the risk free rate. This interest rate is the newspaper rate quoted as the market rate between large banks. The rate includes an allowance for inflation and for the inconvenience of lending (sometimes called time preference). The rate is risk free in the sense that the investor is more or less guaranteed to receive the money as promised in the investment, as banks rarely go bankrupt. This rate differs between currencies (not countries). Thus, there is a single rate for the euro and a single rate for the British pound and one rate for the dollar, yen and so on. The rates differ, the rate for the euro LIBOR (London Interbank Offered Rate) is about 2%, but is 4.8% for the British pound and 3% for the US dollar. Given that these are equilibrium rates in that they are determined by supply and demand in the marketplace, one might ask why everyone does not invest in the UK rather than in the euro, dollar and so on? From the point of view of the international investor seeking to obtain the highest return on investment, UK rates are higher for a given level of risk. Shares and bonds should be offering a higher rate of return as a result and therefore be good value.

One way of explaining the difference in the risk free rate is to look at differences in the constituent parts. Time preference probably does not vary between countries but inflation clearly does vary and may explain differences. But the fact that inflation may be higher in the UK is of little consequence to an investor who simply wants to buy shares, receive dividends and then convert the dividends to their home currency and then, at some later date, sell the shares and convert back. For the foreign investor the rationale for a difference lies in changes in the value of the currency between conversion dates – once again we return to the concept of exchange rate risk.

Exchange rate risk. Returns are determined by the rate earned in the local currency *and* any changes in the value of the currency between the investment date and the conversion back to home currency date (see the Sunny Investments example above). The conversion process is termed exchange rate risk. The relationship between currency values, interest rates and inflation is explained further in the following chapter. But for the moment one can see that where a currency is suffering high inflation its value may well fall in relation to other currencies over time – as one unit of the currency buys less. A higher interest rate may well be needed to compensate for the expected loss in value of the currency. Hence interest rates between currencies may differ.

Taxes. The tax effects of dividends and capital gains also vary among countries. The lower a country's tax rates, the greater the proportion of the pre-tax cash flows received that the investor can retain. Other things being equal, investors based in low-tax countries should value shares higher. Differences in particular countries between the taxes levied on dividends and taxes on capital gains will create preferences within that country for shares that pay high dividends or shares that pay low dividends but have higher capital gains. A change in the tax laws of, say, the UK may make investments in that country more or less attractive to the UK.

METHODS USED TO INVEST INTERNATIONALLY

For investors attempting international share diversification, five common approaches are available:

- Direct purchases of foreign shares
- Investment in MNC shares
- American depository receipts (ADRs)
- Exchange-traded funds (ETFs)
- International mutual funds (IMFs)

Each approach is discussed in turn.

Direct purchases of foreign shares

Foreign shares can be purchased on foreign stock exchanges. This requires the services of brokerage firms that can contact floor brokers who work on the foreign stock exchange of concern. However, this approach is inefficient because of market imperfections such as insufficient information, transaction costs, and tax differentials among countries.

An alternative method of investing directly in foreign shares is to purchase shares of foreign companies that are sold on the local stock exchange. In the United States, for example, Royal Dutch Shell (of the Netherlands), Sony (of Japan), and many other foreign shares are sold on US stock exchanges. Because the number of foreign shares listed on any local stock exchange is typically quite limited, this method by itself may not be adequate to achieve the full benefits of international diversification.

Investment in MNC shares

The operations of an MNC represent international diversification. Like an investor with a well-managed share portfolio, an MNC can reduce risk (variability in net cash flows) by diversifying sales not only among industries but also among countries. In this sense, the MNC as a single firm can achieve stability similar to that of an internationally diversified share portfolio. By investing in an MNC, the investor should gain from the diversification by having a share that behaves rather differently from local investments in non-MNCs. Perhaps surprisingly, the evidence is that MNC shares tend to behave in much the same way as less international shares on the same stock exchange and are not affected as might be expected by movements on other stock markets. This suggests that the diversification benefits from investing in an MNC are limited.

American depository receipts

Another approach is to purchase American depository receipts (ADRs), which are certificates representing ownership of foreign shares. More than 1,000 ADRs are available in the United States, primarily traded on the over-the-counter (OTC) stock market. An investment in ADRs may be an adequate substitute for direct investment in foreign shares. Only a limited number of ADRs are available, however.

USING THE WEB

ADR performance The performance of ADRs is provided at http://www.adr.com. Click on Industry to review the share performance of ADRs within each industry. The website provides a table that shows information about the industry, including the number of ADRs in that industry, and the 6-month and 12-month returns. Click on any particular industry of interest to review the performance of individual ADRs in that industry.

Exchange-traded funds (ETFs)

Although investors have closely monitored international share indexes for years, they were typically unable to invest directly in these indexes. The index was simply a measure of performance for a set of shares but was not traded. Exchange-traded funds (ETFs) represent indexes that reflect composites of shares for particular countries; they were created to allow investors to invest directly in a share index representing any one of several countries. ETFs are sometimes referred to as world equity benchmark shares (WEBS) or as iShares.

International mutual funds

A final approach to consider is purchasing shares of **international mutual funds (IMFs)**, which are portfolios of shares from various countries. Like domestic mutual funds, IMFs are popular due to: (1) the low minimum investment necessary to participate in the funds, (2) the presumed expertise of the portfolio managers, and (3) the high degree of diversification achieved by the portfolios' inclusion of several shares. Many investors believe an IMF can better reduce risk than a purely domestic mutual fund because the IMF includes foreign securities. An IMF represents a prepackaged portfolio, so investors who use it do not need to construct their own portfolios. Although some investors prefer to construct their own portfolios, the existence of numerous IMFs on the market today allows investors to select the one that most closely resembles the type of portfolio they would have constructed on their own. Moreover, some investors feel more comfortable with a professional manager managing the international portfolio.

CHAPTER 4

EXCHANGE RATE DETERMINATION

FINANCIAL MANAGERS OF MNCS must continuously monitor exchange rates because their cash flows are highly dependent on changes in the rates. In a matter of days the value of a currency can fall by 5%, 10% or more. As a result, a potentially profitable contract or transaction can become unprofitable unless the risk has been managed in some way so that the effect is lessened without making the underlying business unprofitable. Financial managers therefore need to understand what factors influence exchange rates so that they can anticipate how exchange rates may change in response to specific conditions. This chapter provides a foundation for understanding how exchange rates are determined.

THE SPECIFIC OBJECTIVES OF THIS CHAPTER ARE TO:

- explain how exchange rate movements are measured,
- explain how the equilibrium exchange rate is determined, and
- examine factors that affect the equilibrium exchange rate.

MEASURING EXCHANGE RATE MOVEMENTS

Exchange rate movements affect an MNC's value because they can affect the amount of cash inflows received from exporting or from a subsidiary, and the amount of cash outflows needed to pay for imports. An exchange rate measures the value of one currency in units of another currency. As economic conditions change, exchange rates can change substantially. A decline in a currency's value is often referred to as **depreciation**. When the British pound depreciates against the US dollar, this means that the US dollar is strengthening relative to the pound. The increase in a currency value is often referred to as **appreciation**.

When a foreign currency's spot rates are compared at two specific points in time, the spot rate at the more recent date is denoted as S_t and the spot rate at the earlier date is denoted as S_{t-1}. The percentage change in the value of the foreign currency is computed as follows:

$$\text{Percent change in a foreign currency value} = \frac{S_t - S_{t-1}}{S_{t-1}}$$

Using direct exchange rates positive percentage change indicates that the foreign currency has appreciated, while a negative percentage change indicates that it has depreciated. As has been indicated, the values of currencies can vary greatly over a short time. For popular currencies there will be changes every day indeed every hour on the foreign currency exchanges. Taking the British pound as an example, on some days, most foreign currencies appreciate against the pound, although by different degrees. On other days, most currencies depreciate against the pound, but by different degrees. There are also days when some currencies appreciate while others depreciate against the pound; the media describe this scenario by stating that "the pound was *mixed* in trading".

Exhibit 4.1 illustrates how the euro changed on an annual basis from 2000 to 2004. Some currencies that are less frequently traded are even more volatile. The changes in a currency's value can have a major impact on costs and revenue.

EXAMPLE

Consider the impact of the euro's change in value from the beginning of 2004 to the end of that year. Assume that a hotel in France charged 100 euros for a room on these two dates. If a UK resident had visited France and stayed in that hotel, the cost would have been £70 (see Exhibit 4.1) at the beginning of 2004 and £71 at the end of the year. The hotel receives the same amount of euros, but the cost in British pounds was over 1.4% more ((71–70)/70 = 0.0413) because the euro had appreciated against the pound. Prices generally in France would have increased by 1.4% for a UK purchaser as a result of the euro appreciation.

Now consider the effect of the euro's fluctuation on an MNC. If a UK-based MNC purchased products priced at 1 million euros at the beginning of 2003, the British pound cost would have been £650,000. If it purchased the same products at the beginning of 2005, the UK cost would have been £710,000. The increase in cost over this period (assuming no change in the actual price of the product) was over 9% due to the increase in the value of the euro; meanwhile a French based MNC would have to pay less for goods being sold in British pounds.

The potential impact of exchange rate movements on an MNC's costs and revenue is obvious and is reinforced throughout the text. Consequently, it is important to understand the forces that can cause an exchange rate to change over time. MNCs that

Exhibit 4.1   Annual changes in the value of the euro from the perspective of the British pound and US dollar

Date	Exchange rate £s: euro	Annual percentage change in terms of British pounds	Exchange rate $s: euro	Annual percentage change in terms of dollars
01/01/2000	£0.63:1 euro	–	$1.001:1 euro	–
01/01/2001	£0.63:1 euro	0.0%	$0.94:1 euro	–6.1%
01/01/2002	£0.61:1 euro	–3.2%	$0.89:1 euro	–5.3%
01/01/2003	£0.65:1 euro	+6.6%	$1.05:1 euro	+18%
01/01/2004	£0.70:1 euro	+7.7%	$1.26:1 euro	+20%
01/01/2005	£0.71:1 euro	+1.4%	$1.36:1 euro	+8%

Notes:
■ All figures have been rounded, e.g. the first of the percentage changes in the dollar value of the euro: (0.94 − 1.001) / 1.001 = −0.0609 ≈ −6.1%

■ The value of the euro has moved in the same direction in terms of the dollar and British pound, but clearly the relationship with the British pound has been more stable.

understand how currencies might be affected by existing forces can prepare for possible adverse effects on their expenses or revenue and may be able to reduce their exposure.

EXCHANGE RATE EQUILIBRIUM

Although it is easy to measure the percentage change in the value of a currency, it is more difficult to explain why the value changed or to forecast how it may change in the future. To achieve either of these objectives, the concept of an **equilibrium exchange rate** must be understood, as well as the factors that affect the equilibrium rate.

Before considering why an exchange rate changes, realize that an exchange rate at a given point in time represents the *price* of a currency. Like any other products sold in markets, the price of a currency is determined by the demand for that currency relative to supply. Thus, for each possible price of a British pound, there is a corresponding demand for pounds and a corresponding supply of pounds for sale. At any point in time, a currency should exhibit the price at which the demand for that currency is equal to supply, and this represents the equilibrium exchange rate. Of course, conditions can change over time, causing the supply or demand for a given currency to adjust, and thereby causing movement in the currency's price. This topic is more thoroughly discussed in this section.

Demand for a currency

The US dollar is used here to explain exchange rate equilibrium. Exhibit 4.2 shows a hypothetical number of dollars that would be demanded under various possibilities for the exchange rate. At any one point in time, there is only one exchange rate. The exhibit shows the quantity of dollars that would be demanded at various exchange rates. The demand schedule is downward sloping because UK corporations will be encouraged to purchase more US goods when the dollar is worth less, as it will take fewer British pounds to obtain the desired amount of dollars.

Exhibit 4.2 UK demand schedule for US dollars

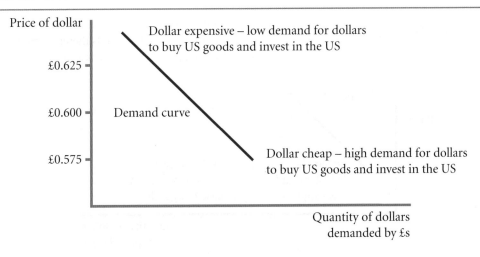

Note:

■ Moving from an exchange rate of £0.625:$1 to £0.575:$1, US goods are (0.575 − 0.625) / 0.625 = −0.08 or are 8% cheaper.

Supply of a currency for sale

Up to this point, only the UK demand for dollars has been considered, but the US demand for British pounds must also be considered. From the UK perspective, the US demand for the British pound results in a *supply of dollars for sale*, since dollars are supplied in the foreign exchange market in exchange for British pounds.

A supply schedule of dollars for sale in the foreign exchange market can be developed in a manner similar to the demand schedule for dollars. Exhibit 4.3 shows the quantity of dollars for sale (supplied to the foreign exchange market in exchange for pounds) corresponding to each possible exchange rate. Notice from the supply schedule in Exhibit 4.3 that there is a positive relationship between the value of the US dollar and the quantity of US dollars for sale (supplied), which can be explained as follows. When the dollar is valued high, US consumers and firms are more likely to purchase UK goods. Thus, they supply a greater number of dollars to the market, to be exchanged for pounds. Conversely, when the dollar is valued low, the supply of dollars for sale is smaller, reflecting less US desire to obtain the relatively more expensive UK goods.

Equilibrium

The demand and supply schedules for pounds by US dollars are combined in Exhibit 4.4. At an exchange rate of £0.575:$1, the quantity of dollars demanded would exceed the supply of dollars for sale. Consequently, banks providing foreign exchange services would experience a shortage of dollars at that exchange rate. At an exchange rate of £0.625:$1, the quantity of dollars demanded would be less than the supply of dollars for sale. Therefore, banks providing foreign exchange services would experience a surplus of dollars at that exchange rate. According to Exhibit 4.4, the equilibrium exchange rate is £0.600:$1 because this rate equates the quantity of dollars demanded with the supply of dollars for sale.

Exhibit 4.3 US supply schedule for British pounds

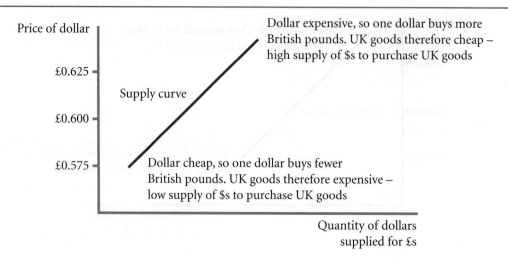

Notes

■ Adding some figures to the relationship, moving from an exchange rate of £0.625:$1 to £0.575:$1 means that for holders of US dollars the British pound will have increased in cost from $1.60:£1 to $1.74:£1 an increase of $(1.74 - 1.60) / 1.60 \approx 0.0875$ or 8.75% hence a low supply of dollars (note that these rates are the inverse of the $ rates, i.e. £0.625:$1 implies $1.60:£1 as $1/0.625 = 1.60$ and $1/0.575 \approx 1.74$ see direct and indirect rates in the previous chapter).

■ Compare these notes with the notes of Exhibit 4.2. For exactly the same change in exchange rates from £0.625:$1 to £0.575:$1, US goods have become 8% cheaper for holders of British pounds; whereas UK goods have become 8.75% more expensive for holders of US dollars. Surely the percentage changes should be the same! In fact they are not, the difference is known as Siegal's paradox and is currently thought to be of little consequence other than in explaining differences between calculations of the same events but viewed from differing home currencies.

Exhibit 4.4 Equilibrium exchange rate determination

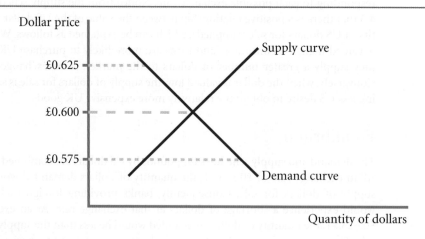

Note:

■ The quantity of dollars now represents dollars demanded by British pounds and dollars offered or supplied for British pounds.

Impact of liquidity. For all currencies, the equilibrium exchange rate is reached through transactions in the foreign exchange market, but for some currencies, the adjustment process is more volatile than for others. If the currency's spot market is liquid, its exchange rate will not be highly sensitive to a single large purchase or sale of the currency, such markets are termed "deep". Therefore, the change in the equilibrium exchange rate will be relatively small and the currency movement will not be volatile. With many willing buyers and sellers of the currency, transactions can be easily accommodated at the given rate. Conversely, if the currency's spot market is illiquid, its exchange rate may be highly sensitive to a single large purchase or sale transaction. There are not sufficient buyers or sellers to accommodate a large transaction, which means that the price of the currency must change to attract sufficient buyers and sellers to rebalance the supply and demand for the currency. Consequently, illiquid currencies tend to exhibit more volatile exchange rate movements, as the equilibrium prices of their currencies adjust to even minor changes in supply and demand conditions. Ideally, markets should be deep and broad. A deep market is liquid and can cope with large transactions. There is also the need for markets to be broad. A broad market has many different views as to the correct market price, and is not going to overreact to information. Therefore breadth is also important to stability.

FACTORS THAT INFLUENCE EXCHANGE RATES

The equilibrium exchange rate will change over time as supply and demand schedules change. The factors that cause currency supply and demand schedules to change are discussed here by relating each factor's influence to the demand and supply schedules graphically displayed in Exhibit 4.4. The following equation summarizes the factors that can influence a currency's spot rate:

$$e = f(\Delta INF, \Delta INT, \Delta INC, \Delta GC, \Delta EXP)$$

where:

e	=	percentage change in the spot rate;
Δ	=	Greek letter for delta where "d" stands for difference or change;
ΔINF	=	change in the differential between UK inflation and the foreign country's inflation;
ΔINT	=	change in the differential between the UK interest rate and the foreign country's interest rate;
ΔINC	=	change in the differential between the UK income level and the foreign country's income level;
ΔGC	=	change in government controls;
ΔEXP	=	change in expectations of future exchange rates.

Relative inflation rates

Changes in relative inflation rates can affect international trade activity, which influences the demand for and supply of currencies and therefore influences exchange rates.

EXAMPLE

Consider how the demand and supply schedules displayed in Exhibit 4.4 would be affected if UK inflation suddenly increased substantially while US inflation remained the same. (Assume that both British and US firms sell goods that can serve as substitutes for each other.) The sudden jump in UK inflation should cause an increase in the UK demand for US goods and therefore also cause an increase in the UK demand for US dollars.

In addition, the jump in UK inflation should reduce the US desire for British goods and therefore reduce the supply of dollars wanting British pounds. These market reactions are illustrated in Exhibit 4.5. The increased UK demand for dollars and the reduced supply of dollars for sale place upward pressure on the value of the dollar. According to Exhibit 4.5, the new equilibrium value is £0.610:$1.

Exhibit 4.5 Impact of rising UK inflation on the equilibrium value of the US dollar

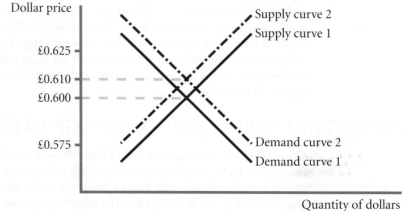

Note:

■ The equilibrium rate changes from £0.600:$1 to £06610:$1.

If US inflation increased (rather than UK inflation), the opposite forces would occur. Assume there is a sudden and substantial increase in US inflation while UK inflation is low. Based on this information, answer the following questions: (1) How is the demand schedule for dollars affected? (2) How is the supply schedule of dollars for sale affected? (3) Will the new equilibrium value of the pound increase, decrease, or remain unchanged? Based on the information given, the answers are (1) the demand schedule for dollars should shift inward, (2) the supply schedule of dollars for sale should shift outward, and (3) the new equilibrium value of the dollar will decrease. Of course, the actual amount by which the dollar's value will decrease depends on the magnitude of the shifts. There is not enough information to determine their exact magnitude.

In reality, the actual demand and supply schedules, and therefore the true equilibrium exchange rate, will reflect several factors simultaneously. The point of the preceding example is to demonstrate how to logically work through the mechanics of the effect that higher inflation in a country can have on an exchange rate. Each factor is assessed one at a time to determine its separate influence on exchange rates, holding all other factors constant. Then, all factors can be tied together to fully explain why an exchange rate moves the way it does.

Relative interest rates

Changes in relative interest rates affect investment in foreign securities, which influences the demand for and supply of currencies and therefore influences exchange rates.

EXAMPLE

Assume that UK interest rates rise while US interest rates remain constant. In this case, UK investors are likely to reduce their demand for dollars, since UK rates are now more attractive relative to US rates, and there is therefore less desire for US bank deposits. Because UK rates will now look more attractive to US investors with excess cash, the supply of dollars for sale by US investors should increase as they establish more bank deposits in the United Kingdom. Due to an inward shift in the demand for dollars and an outward shift in the supply of dollars for sale, the equilibrium exchange rate or the value of the dollar should decrease. This is graphically represented in Exhibit 4.6. If UK interest rates decreased relative to US interest rates, the opposite shifts would be expected.

In some cases, an exchange rate between two countries' currencies can be affected by changes in a third country's interest rate.

EXAMPLE

When the euro interest rate increases, it can become more attractive to UK investors than the US rate. This encourages UK investors to purchase fewer dollar-denominated securities. Thus, the demand for dollars would be smaller than it would have been without the increase in euro interest rates for all given exchange rates, which places downward pressure on the value of the dollar in terms of the British pound.

In the 1999–2000 period, European interest rates were relatively low compared to US interest rates. This interest rate differential encouraged European investors to invest money in dollar-denominated debt securities. This activity resulted in a large supply of euros in the foreign exchange market and put downward pressure on the euro. In the 2002–03 period, US interest rates were lower than European interest rates. Consequently, there was a large US demand for euros to capitalize on the higher interest rates, which placed upward pressure on the euro. It must be remembered that portfolio investment flows are very large in the international money markets, interest rates will therefore be an important part in determining the value of a currency.

Exhibit 4.6 Impact of rising UK interest rates on the equilibrium value of the US dollar in terms of British pounds

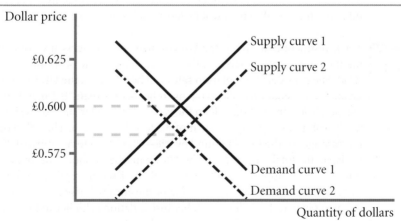

Notes:
- Demand and supply curves move from curve 1 to curve 2.
- Demand for dollars falls as home investments now seem relatively more attractive.
- Dollars supplied for British pounds increases in order to purchase UK securities offering the higher interest rate.

Real interest rates. High interest rates on their own cannot be the only factor in determining the value of a currency, otherwise the currency offering the highest interest rate would attract all investment. So there must be factors that make a manager of a portfolio refrain from investing all funds in the currency offering the highest interest rate. That factor is a concern that although the interest rate is higher, there could well be an offsetting fall in the value of the currency with the higher interest rate. So if the UK is offering a LIBOR rate of 5% and the US is offering a rate of 3%, a US portfolio manager who decides *not* to invest in the UK must be expecting the British pound to lose value against the dollar by at least 2% (calculated as 5% − 3% = 2%), so that the net returns from investing in the UK would be the 5% from the investment less at least the 2% loss in the value of the British pound. The net return would therefore be no more than 5% − 2% = 3% the same as investing in the US. So a higher interest rate would not attract all international investments as many investors would think that there is likely to be an even greater offsetting fall in the value of the currency.

Such reasoning leads to the question as to why the value of the British pound should be expected to fall causing interest rates to be higher? An American economist Irving Fisher suggested that interest rates were compensation for three elements: time, risk and inflation – the details are discussed in Chapter 7. For the LIBOR rates, time and risk elements of the interest rate (known as the real interest rate) should be the same between the US and the UK, the only rationale for a difference is therefore inflation according the Fisher. If, for example, interest rates are expected to be higher in the UK after adjustment for inflation (i.e. higher expected real interest rates), there will be an increased supply of dollars for British pounds and a reduced demand for dollars by British pounds as investment prefers the UK to the US. As shown in Exhibit 4.6 there would be a consequent leftward shift in the demand for dollars and rightward shift in the supply of dollars for British pounds resulting in a fall in the value of the dollar.

The US portfolio manager should, by this reasoning, only invest in the UK if he or she feels that the interest rate less inflation (or real interest rate) is going to be higher in the UK than in the US. For the US portfolio manager, countries with higher expected real interest rates are offering a higher return after allowing for loss in currency value due to higher expected inflation. The currencies of such countries should be attractive and increase in value; though not all managers will agree, so the rise will be limited. But where a higher interest rate does not offset an expected fall in the currency value due to inflation, the overall return will be less than home investment.

EXAMPLE

The investment manager at the UK company of BadGuess Investments plc is considering the interest rates offered in the US (3.5%), the UK (4%), the euro (2%) and Japan (0%). She considers the inflation rates will be US (2%), the UK (3%) the euro (0%) and Japan (−1%, deflation). She explains to her senior that: "If I invest in the US, inflation will be 1% less than in the UK so the value of the dollar should rise by about 1% against the British pound giving a return of 3.5% + 1% = 4.5%. The value of the euro should increase against the British pound by 3% − 0% = 3% a total return of 2% + 3% = 5% and for Japan the total return should be 4%. So maybe we should be investing in the euro, it's offering 5% as opposed to 4% in the UK." Her senior replies: "Well OK, but your estimate is really a gamble that the value of the euro will rise against the British pound by 3%, you say that this will happen because inflation is higher in the UK by 3%, but there are many other factors that cause the value of currencies to change in relation to each other, such as the current problems of the constitution in the euro area."

Relative income levels

A third factor affecting exchange rates is relative income levels. Because income can affect the amount of imports demanded, it can affect exchange rates.

EXAMPLE

Assume that the UK income level rises substantially while the US income level remains unchanged. Consider the impact of this scenario on: (1) the demand schedule for dollars, (2) the supply schedule of dollars for sale, and (3) the equilibrium exchange rate. First, the demand schedule for dollars will shift rightwards, reflecting the increase in UK income and therefore increased demand for US goods. Second, the supply schedule of dollars for sale is not expected to change as income levels do not affect prices. Therefore, the equilibrium exchange rate and value of the dollar are expected to rise, as shown in Exhibit 4.7.

Changing income levels can also affect exchange rates indirectly through effects on interest rates. When this effect is considered, the impact may differ from the theory presented here, as will be explained shortly.

Government controls

A fourth factor affecting exchange rates is government controls. The governments of foreign countries can influence the equilibrium exchange rate in many ways, including: (1) imposing foreign exchange barriers, (2) imposing foreign trade barriers, (3) intervening (buying and selling currencies) in the foreign exchange markets, and (4) affecting macro variables such as inflation, interest rates, and income levels. Chapter 6 covers these activities in detail.

EXAMPLE

Suppose the US real interest rates rose relative to British real interest rates. The expected reaction would be an increase in the British supply of pounds for sale to obtain more US dollars (in order to capitalize on high US money market yields). Yet, if the British government placed a heavy tax on interest income earned from foreign investments, this could discourage the exchange of pounds for dollars.

Exhibit 4.7 Impact of rising UK income levels relative to the US on the equilibrium value of the US dollar

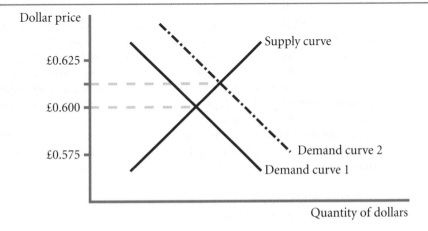

Note:

■ Increase in UK income increases demand for goods generally including US imports, hence the higher demand for dollars.

Expectations

A fifth factor affecting exchange rates is market expectations. Like other efficient financial markets, foreign exchange markets react immediately to any news that may have a future effect. By definition in finance, news is information that differs from expectations. This further complicates relationships in that an announcement of high inflation in the US, if unexpected, may cause currency traders to sell dollars, anticipating a future decline in the dollar's value. But if the high inflation was less than expected then traders may buy dollars because the situation is better than at first thought. If in line with expectations, there may be no movement. So, an announcement of high inflation could have a positive, negative or no effect on the value of the dollar! The solution is that when analyzing the effect of factors on the value of a currency, the "measure" must always be in relation to expectations. Unfortunately expectations are hard to measure and for the most part models use actual values such as interest rates and inflation rather than expected interest rates and inflation.

Many institutional investors (such as commercial banks and insurance companies) take currency positions based on anticipated interest rate movements in various countries.

EXAMPLE   Investors may temporarily invest funds in France if they expect euro interest rates to increase. Such a rise may cause further capital flows into the euro area, which could place upward pressure on the euro's value. By taking a position based on expectations, investors can fully benefit from the rise in the euro's value because they will have purchased euros before the change occurred. Although the investors face the obvious risk that their expectations may be wrong, the point is that expectations can influence exchange rates because they commonly motivate institutional investors to take foreign currency positions.

Impact of signals on currency speculation. Day-to-day speculation on future exchange rate movements is commonly driven by signals of future interest rate movements, but it can also be driven by other factors. Signals of the future economic conditions that affect exchange rates can change quickly, so the speculative positions in currencies may adjust quickly, causing unclear patterns in exchange rates. It is not unusual for the dollar to strengthen substantially on a given day, only to weaken substantially on the next day. This can occur when speculators overreact to news on one day (causing the dollar to be overvalued), which results in a correction on the next day. Overreactions occur because speculators are commonly taking positions based on signals of future actions (rather than the confirmation of actions), and these signals may be misleading.

When speculators speculate on currencies in emerging markets, they can have a substantial impact on exchange rates. Those markets have a smaller amount of foreign exchange trading for other purposes (such as international trade) and therefore are less liquid than the larger markets.

The abrupt decline in the Russian rouble on some days during 1998 was partially attributed to speculative trading (although the decline might have occurred anyway over time). The decline in the rouble created a lack of confidence in other emerging markets as well and caused speculators to sell off other emerging market currencies, such as those of Poland and Venezuela. The market for the rouble is not very active, so a sudden shift in positions by speculators can have a substantial impact.

Interaction of factors

Transactions within the foreign exchange markets facilitate either trade or financial flows. Trade-related foreign exchange transactions are generally less responsive to news. Financial flow transactions are very responsive to news, however, because decisions to hold securities denominated in a particular currency are often dependent on anticipated changes in currency values. Sometimes trade-related factors and financial factors interact and simultaneously affect exchange rate movements.

An increase in income levels sometimes causes expectations of higher interest rates. So, even though a higher income level can result in more imports, it may also indirectly attract more financial inflows (assuming interest rates increase). Because the favourable financial flows may overwhelm the unfavourable trade flows, an increase in income levels is frequently expected to strengthen the local currency.

Exhibit 4.8 separates payment flows between countries into trade-related and finance-related flows and summarizes the factors that affect these flows. Over a particular period, some factors may place upward pressure on the value of a foreign currency while other factors place downward pressure on the currency's value.

EXAMPLE

Assume the simultaneous existence of: (1) a sudden increase in UK inflation, and (2) a sudden increase in UK interest rates. If the US economy is relatively unchanged, the increase in UK inflation will place upward pressure on the dollar's value while the increase in UK interest rates places downward pressure on the dollar's value.

Exhibit 4.8 Summary of factors affecting exchange rates

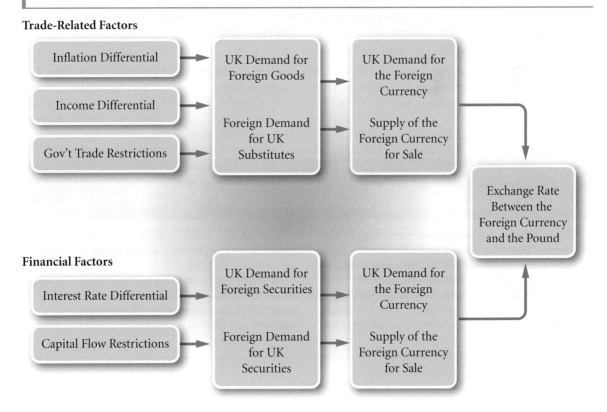

The sensitivity of an exchange rate to these factors is dependent on the volume of international transactions between the two countries. If the two countries engage in a large volume of international trade but a very small volume of international capital flows, the relative inflation rates will likely be more influential. If the two countries engage in a large volume of capital flows, however, interest rate fluctuations may be more influential.

EXAMPLE

Assume that Morgan AG, a German-based MNC, commonly purchases supplies from Venezuela and Bahrain and therefore desires to forecast the value of the Venezuelan bolivar and the Bahrain dinar in terms of euros.

Assume that Germany and Venezuela conduct a large volume of international trade but engage in minimal capital flow transactions. Venezuelan inflation is expected to be 5% higher than in Germany.

Also, assume that Germany and Bahrain conduct very little international trade but frequently engage in capital flow transactions. Interest rates are expected to be 2% higher in Germany than in Bahrain.

What should Morgan expect regarding the future value of the Venezuelan bolivar and the Bahranian dinar?

The bolivar should be influenced most by trade-related factors because of Venezuela's assumed heavy trade with Germany. The expected inflationary changes should place downward pressure on the value of the bolivar. Interest rates are expected to have little direct impact on the bolivar because of the assumed infrequent capital flow.

The Bahrainian dinar should be most influenced by interest rates because of Bahrain's assumed heavy capital flow transactions with Germany. The expected interest rate changes should place upward pressure on the value of the euro in terms of the dinar. The inflationary changes are expected to have little direct impact on the dinar because of the assumed infrequent trade between the two countries.

Capital flows have become larger over time and can easily overwhelm trade flows. For this reason, the influence of factors such as inflation on interest rates has become increasingly important.

MANAGING FOR VALUE
Impact of exchange rate changes on cash flows for Renault, Nestlé and Philips

Renault SA the French car maker chooses not to hedge its operations and accepts that there will be variation in profits due to exchange rate changes that over the long term will even out. The company estimated in 2004 that a 1% appreciation of the euro against all other currencies had a negative impact of 41 million euros on its operating margin due mainly to the British pound (accounting for about half the change) and the Turkish lira and Central European currencies.

Nestlé adopts a similar policy but noted in 2004 that exchange rate variability had a negative impact on sales of 3.5%.

The Philips group on the other hand notes that it has a significant mismatch in its costs and revenues. Its costs are mostly in euros and significant revenues are in dollars. It has a policy of hedging its cash flows using currency derivatives of up to 18 months (see Chapter 5).

An understanding of exchange rate equilibrium does not guarantee accurate forecasts of future exchange rates because that will depend in part on how the factors that affect exchange rates will change in the future. Even if analysts fully realize how factors influence exchange rates, they may not be able to predict how those factors will change. Even if they can predict factors such as future economic growth and inflation, the effect on the exchange rate is not clear in that it is the difference with market expectations that affects the exchange rate. A high growth prediction may have a negative effect on the value of the currency if that expectation is lower than expectations. Estimating whether or not economic growth is higher or lower than market expectations is even harder than trying to predict those variables on their own.

Speculating on anticipated exchange rates

Many commercial banks attempt to capitalize on their forecasts of anticipated exchange rate movements in the foreign exchange market, as illustrated in this example.

- The European Bank expects the exchange rate of the New Zealand dollar (NZ$) to appreciate from its present level of 0.50 euros to 0.52 euros in 30 days.

- The European Bank is able to borrow $20 million on a short-term basis from other banks.

- Present short-term interest rates (annualized) in the interbank market are as follows:

Currency	Lending rate	Borrowing rate
Euro	6.72%	7.20%
New Zealand dollars (NZ$)	6.48%	6.96%

Because brokers sometimes serve as intermediaries between banks, the lending rate differs from the borrowing rate. Given this information, the European Bank could:

1. Borrow 20 million euros.
2. Convert the 20 million euros to NZ$40 million (computed as 20,000,000 euros/ 0.50).
3. Lend the New Zealand dollars at 6.48% annualized, which represents a 0.54% return over the 30-day period [computed as 6.48% × (30/360)]. After 30 days, the bank will receive NZ$40,216,000 [computed as NZ$40,000,000 × (1 + 0.0054)].
4. Use the proceeds from the New Zealand dollar loan repayment (on day 30) to repay the euros borrowed. The annual interest on the euros borrowed is 7.2%, or 0.6% over the 30-day period [computed as 7.2% × (30/360)]. The total NZ$ amount necessary to repay the loan is therefore NZ$38,692,308 [computed as 20,000,000 euros × (1 + 0.006) / 0.52].
5. Given that the bank accumulated NZ$40,216,000 from its New Zealand dollar loan, it would earn a speculative profit of NZ$1,523,692 (being NZ$40,216,000 − NZ$38,692,308) which is the equivalent of 792,320 euros (given a spot rate of 0.52 euros per New Zealand dollar on day 30). The bank would earn this speculative profit without using any funds from deposit accounts because the funds would have been borrowed through the interbank market.

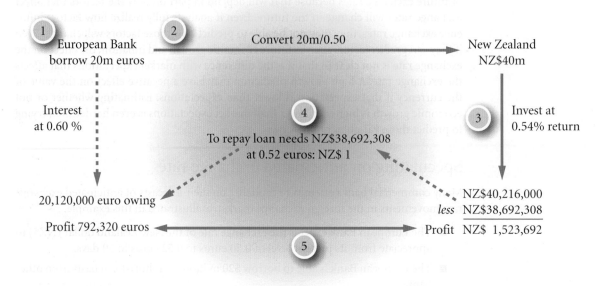

A simple schema of the above events is shown above.

If instead the European Bank expects that the New Zealand dollar will depreciate, it can attempt to make a speculative profit by taking positions opposite to those just described. To illustrate, assume that the bank expects an exchange rate of 0.48 euros for the New Zealand dollar on day 30. It can borrow New Zealand dollars, convert them to euros, and lend the euros out. On day 30, it will close out these positions. Using the rates quoted in the previous example, and assuming the bank can borrow NZ$40 million, the bank takes the following steps:

1. Borrow NZ$40 million.
2. Convert the NZ$40 million to 20 million euros (computed as NZ$40,000,000 × 0.50 euro).
3. Lend the euros at 6.72%, which represents a 0.56% return over the 30-day period. After 30 days, the bank will receive 20,112,000 euros [computed as 20,000,000 euros × (1 + 0.0056)].
4. Use the proceeds of the euro loan repayment (on day 30) to repay the New Zealand dollars borrowed. The annual interest on the New Zealand dollars borrowed is 6.96%, or 0.58% over the 30-day period [computed as 6.96 × (30/360)]. The total New Zealand dollar amount necessary to repay the loan is therefore NZ$40,232,000 [computed as NZ$40,000,000 × (1 + 0.0058)].
5. Assuming that the exchange rate on day 30 is 0.48 euros per New Zealand dollar as anticipated, the number of euros necessary to repay the NZ$ loan is 19,311,360 euros (computed as NZ$40,232,000 × 0.48 euros per New Zealand dollar). Given that the bank accumulated 20,112,000 euros from its euro loan, it would earn a speculative profit of 800,640 euros without using any of its own money (computed as 20,112,000 euros − 19,311,360 euros).

Most banks continue to take some speculative positions in foreign currencies. In fact, some banks' currency trading profits have exceeded $100 million per quarter lately.

The potential returns from foreign currency speculation are high for banks that have large borrowing capacity. Nevertheless, foreign exchange rates are very volatile and a poor forecast could result in a large loss. One of the best-known bank failures, Franklin National Bank in 1974, was primarily attributed to massive speculative losses from foreign currency positions.

SUMMARY

■ Exchange rate movements are commonly measured by the percentage change in their values over a specified period, such as a month or a year. MNCs closely monitor exchange rate movements over the period in which they have cash flows denominated in the foreign currencies of concern.

■ The equilibrium exchange rate between two currencies at any point in time is based on the demand and supply conditions. Changes in the demand for a currency or the supply of a currency for sale will affect the equilibrium exchange rate.

■ The key economic factors that can influence exchange rate movements through their effects on demand and supply conditions are relative inflation rates, interest rates, and income levels, as well as government controls. As these factors cause a change in international trade or financial flows, they affect the demand for a currency or the supply of currency for sale and therefore affect the equilibrium exchange rate.

■ The two factors that are most closely monitored by foreign exchange market participants are relative inflation and interest rates.

If a country experiences higher inflation than other countries, its exports should decrease (demand for its currency decreases), its imports should increase (supply of its currency increases), and there is downward pressure on its currency's equilibrium value.

If a country experiences higher real interest rates (i.e. interest rate returns less expected loss in currency value due to inflation), the inflow of funds to purchase its securities should increase (demand for its currency increases), the outflow of its funds to purchase foreign securities should decrease (supply of its currency to be exchanged for foreign currency decreases), and there is upward pressure on its currency's equilibrium value.

■ All relevant factors must be considered simultaneously to assess the likely movement in a currency's value.

CRITICAL DEBATE

The currencies of some Latin American countries depreciate against other currencies on a consistent basis. How can persistently weak currencies be stabilized?

Proposition. The governments of these countries need to increase the demand for their currency by attracting more capital flows. Raising interest rates will make their currencies more attractive to foreign investors. They also need to insure bank deposits so that foreign investors who invest in large bank deposits do not need to worry about default risk. In addition, they could impose capital restrictions on local investors to prevent capital outflows.

Opposing view. The governments of these countries print too much money because they make too many promises to the electorate that would otherwise have to be funded by higher taxes or borrowing at high interest rates. Printing money is the easy way out; but prices rise, exports decrease and imports increase. Thus, these countries could relieve the downward pressure on their local currencies by printing less money and thereby reducing the money supply and hence inflation. The outcome is likely to be a temporary reduction in economic growth and business failures. Higher interest rates would merely increase inflation.

Reply. Solutions that cause riots are not very clever.

With whom do you agree? Which argument do you support? Offer your own opinion on this issue.

SELF TEST

Answers are provided in Appendix A at the back of the text.

1. Briefly describe how various economic factors can affect the equilibrium exchange rate of the Japanese yen's value with respect to that of the pound.

2. A recent shift in the interest rate differential between the United Kingdom and Country A had a large effect on the value of Currency A. However, the same shift in the interest rate differential between the United Kingdom and Country B had no effect on the value of Currency B. Explain why the effects may vary.

3. Smart Banking plc can borrow £5 million at 6% annualized. It can use the proceeds to invest in US dollars at 9% per year over a six-day period. The US dollar is worth £0.60 and is expected to be worth £0.59 in six days. Based on this information, should Smart Banking plc borrow pounds and invest in US dollars? What would be the gain or loss in pounds?

QUESTIONS AND APPLICATIONS

1. **Percentage depreciation.** Assume the spot rate of the US dollar is £0.54. The expected spot rate one year from now is assumed to be £0.51. What percentage depreciation does this reflect?

2. **Inflation effects on exchange rates.** Assume that the UK inflation rate becomes high relative to euro inflation. Other things being equal, how should this affect the: (a) UK demand for euros, (b) supply of euros for foreign currency, and (c) equilibrium value of the euro?

3. **Interest rate effects on exchange rates.** Assume euro interest rates fall relative to British interest rates. Other things being equal, how should this affect the: (a) euro demand for British pounds, (b) supply of pounds for sale, and (c) equilibrium value of the pound?

4. **Income effects on exchange rates.** Assume that the income level in the euro area rises at a much higher rate than does the UK income level. Other things being equal, how should this affect the: (a) euro area demand for British pounds, (b) supply of British pounds for sale, and (c) equilibrium value of the British pound in terms of the euro?

5. **Trade restriction effects on exchange rates.** Assume that the Japanese government relaxes its controls on imports by Japanese companies. Other things being equal, how should this affect the: (a) UK demand for Japanese yen, (b) supply of yen for sale, and (c) equilibrium value of the yen?

6. **Effects of real interest rates.** What is the expected relationship between the relative real interest rates of two countries and the exchange rate of their currencies?

7. **Speculative effects on exchange rates.** Explain why a public forecast about the future value of the euro by a respected economist about future interest rates could affect the value of the euro today. Why do some forecasts by well-respected economists have no impact on today's value of the euro?

8. **Factors affecting exchange rates.** What factors affect the future movements in the value of the euro against the dollar?

9. **Interaction of exchange rates.** Assume that there are substantial capital flows among the United Kingdom, the United States, and the euro area. If interest rates in the United Kingdom decline to a level below the US interest rate, and inflationary expectations remain unchanged, how could this affect the value of the euro against the US dollar? How might this decline in the United Kingdom's interest rate possibly affect the value of the British pound against the euro?

10. **Trade deficit effects on exchange rates.** Every month, the UK trade deficit figures are announced. Foreign exchange traders often react to this announcement and even attempt to forecast the figures before they are announced.

a. Why do you think the trade deficit announcement sometimes has such an impact on foreign exchange trading?

b. In some periods, foreign exchange traders do not respond to a trade deficit announcement, even when the announced deficit is very large. Offer an explanation for such a lack of response.

11. **Comovements of exchange rates.** Explain why the value of the British pound against the dollar will not always move in tandem with the value of the euro against the dollar.

12. **Factors affecting exchange rates.** In the 1990s, Russia was attempting to import more goods but had little to offer other countries in terms of potential exports. In addition, Russia's inflation rate was high. Explain the type of pressure that these factors placed on the Russian currency.

13. **National income effects.** Analysts commonly attribute the appreciation of a currency to expectations that economic conditions will strengthen. Yet, this chapter suggests that when other factors are held constant, increased national income could increase imports and cause the local currency to weaken. In reality, other factors are not constant. What other factor is likely to be affected by increased economic growth and could place upward pressure on the value of the local currency?

14. **Factors affecting exchange rates.** If the Asian countries experience a decline in economic growth (and experience a decline in inflation and interest rates as a result), how will their currency values (relative to the British pound) be affected?

15. **Impact of crises.** Why do you think most crises in countries (such as the Asian crisis) cause the local currency to weaken abruptly? Is it because of trade or capital flows?

16. How do you think the weaker economic conditions would affect trade flows in a **developing country**? How would weaker conditions affect the value of its currency (holding other factors constant)? How do you think interest rates would be?

17. **Measuring effects on exchange rates.** Tarheel Co. plans to determine how changes in UK and euro real interest rates will affect the value of the British pound.

a. Describe a regression model that could be used to achieve this purpose. Also explain the expected sign of the regression coefficient. (See Appendix B.)

b. If Tarheel Co. thinks that the existence of a quota in particular historical periods may have affected exchange rates, how might this be accounted for in the regression model?

18. **Factors affecting exchange rates.** Mexico tends to have much higher inflation than the United States and also much higher interest rates than the United States. Inflation and interest rates are much more volatile in Mexico than in industrialized countries. The value of the Mexican peso is typically more volatile than the currencies of industrialized countries from a US perspective; it has typically depreciated from one year to the next, but the degree of depreciation has varied substantially. The bid/ask spread tends to be wider for the peso than for currencies of industrialized countries.

a. Identify the most obvious economic reason for the persistent depreciation of the peso.

b. High interest rates are commonly expected to strengthen a country's currency because they can encourage foreign investment in securities in that country, which results in the exchange of other currencies for that currency. Yet, the peso's value has declined against the dollar over most years even though Mexican interest rates are typically much higher than US interest rates. Thus, it appears that the high Mexican interest rates do not attract substantial US investment in Mexico's securities. Why do you think US investors do not try to capitalize on the high interest rates in Mexico?

c. Why do you think the bid/ask spread is higher for pesos than for currencies of industrialized countries? How does this affect a US firm that does substantial business in Mexico?

19. **Aggregate effects on exchange rates.** Assume that the United Kingdom invests heavily in government and corporate securities of Country K. In addition, residents of Country K invest heavily in the United Kingdom. Approximately £10 billion worth of investment transactions occur between these two countries each year. The total value of trade transactions per year is about £8 million. This information is expected to also hold in the future.

Because your firm exports goods to Country K, your job as international cash manager requires you to forecast the value of Country K's currency (the "krank") with respect to the dollar. Explain how each of the following conditions will affect the value of the krank, holding other things equal. Then, aggregate all of these impacts to develop an overall forecast of the krank's movement against the dollar.

a. UK inflation has suddenly increased substantially, while Country K's inflation remains low.

b. UK interest rates have increased substantially, while Country K's interest rates remain low. Investors of both countries are attracted to high interest rates.

c. The UK income level increased substantially, while Country K's income level has remained unchanged.

d. The United Kingdom is expected to impose a small tariff on goods imported from Country K.

e. Combine all expected impacts to develop an overall forecast.

20. **Speculation.** Blue Demon Bank expects that the Mexican peso will depreciate against the dollar from its spot rate of $0.15 to $0.14 in ten days. The following interbank lending and borrowing rates exist:

Currency	Lending rate	Borrowing rate
US dollar	8%	8.3%
Mexican peso	8.5%	8.7%

Assume that Blue Demon Bank has a borrowing capacity of either $10 million or 70 million pesos in the interbank market, depending on which currency it wants to borrow.

a. How could Blue Demon Bank attempt to capitalize on its expectations without using deposited funds? Estimate the profits that could be generated from this strategy.

b. Assume all the preceding information with this exception: Blue Demon Bank expects the peso to appreciate from its present spot rate of $0.15 to $0.17 in 30 days. How could it attempt to capitalize on its expectations without using deposited funds? Estimate the profits that could be generated from this strategy.

21. **Speculation.** Diamond Bank expects that the Singapore dollar will depreciate against the euro from its spot rate of 0.48 euros to 0.45 euros in 60 days. The following interbank lending and borrowing rates exist:

Currency	Lending rate	Borrowing rate
euro	7.0%	7.2%
Singapore dollar	22.0%	24.0%

Diamond Bank considers borrowing 10 million Singapore dollars in the interbank market and investing the funds in euros for 60 days. Estimate the profits (or losses) that could be earned from this strategy. Should Diamond Bank pursue this strategy?

PROJECT WORKSHOP

22. **Exchange rates online.** Download the exchange rate between any two major currencies on a daily basis for the last five years. You may download exchange rates either from your institution or from http://www.oanda.com. You will then need to load the figures into Excel.

a. Select the days with the ten largest percentage changes in the exchange rate. Consult via online newspapers (provided by your institution) the financial news related to the change in the exchange rate. Then examine and critically comment on the reasons for the change in the exchange rate as given in the financial press.

b. How is the exercise in part a of this question related to the concept of market efficiency?

BLADES PLC CASE STUDY
Assessment of future exchange rate movements

As the chief financial officer of Blades plc Ben Holt is pleased that his current system of exporting "Speedos" to Thailand seems to be working well. Blades' primary customer in Thailand, a retailer called Entertainment Products, has committed itself to purchasing a fixed number of Speedos annually for the next three years at a fixed price denominated in baht, Thailand's currency. Furthermore, Blades is using a Thai supplier for some of the components needed to manufacture Speedos. Nevertheless, Holt is concerned about recent developments in Asia. Foreign investors from various countries had invested heavily in Thailand to take advantage of the high interest rates there. As a result of the weak economy in Thailand, however, many foreign investors have lost confidence in Thailand and have withdrawn their funds.

Ben Holt has two major concerns regarding these developments. First, he is wondering how these changes in Thailand's economy could affect the value of the Thai baht and, consequently, Blades. More specifically, he is wondering whether the effects on the Thai baht may affect Blades even though its primary Thai customer is committed to Blades over the next three years.

Second, Holt believes that Blades may be able to speculate on the anticipated movement of the baht, but he is uncertain about the procedure needed to accomplish this. To facilitate Holt's understanding of exchange rate speculation, he has asked you, Blades' financial analyst, to provide him with detailed illustrations of two scenarios. In the first, the baht would move from a current level of £0.0147 to £0.0133 within the next 30 days. Under the second scenario,

the baht would move from its current level to £0.0167 within the next 30 days.

Based on Holt's needs, he has provided you with the following list of questions to be answered:

1. How are percentage changes in a currency's value measured? Illustrate your answer numerically by assuming a change in the Thai baht's value from a value of £0.0147 to £0.0173.

2. What are the basic factors that determine the value of a currency? In equilibrium, what is the relationship between these factors?

3. How might the relatively high levels of inflation and interest rates in Thailand have affected the baht's value? (Assume a constant level of UK inflation and interest rates.)

4. How do you think the loss of confidence in the Thai baht, evidenced by the withdrawal of funds from Thailand, affected the baht's value? Would Blades be affected by the change in value, given the primary Thai customer's commitment?

5. Assume that Thailand's central bank wishes to prevent a withdrawal of funds from its country in order to prevent further changes in the currency's value. How could it accomplish this objective using interest rates?

6. Construct a spreadsheet illustrating the steps Blades' treasurer would need to follow in order to speculate on expected movements in the baht's value over the next 30 days. Also show the speculative profit (in pounds) resulting from each scenario. Use both of Ben Holt's examples to illustrate possible speculation. Assume that Blades can borrow either £7 million or the baht equivalent

of this amount. Furthermore, assume that the following short-term interest rates (annualized) are available to Blades:

Currency	Lending rate	Borrowing rate
British pounds	8.10%	8.20%
Thai baht	14.80%	15.40%

SMALL BUSINESS DILEMMA
Assessment by the Sports Exports Company of Factors that affect the British pound's value

Because the Sports Exports Company (an Irish firm) receives payments in British pounds every month and converts those pounds into euros, it needs to closely monitor the value of the British pound in the future. Jim Logan, owner of the Sports Exports Company, expects that inflation will rise substantially in the United Kingdom, while inflation in Ireland will remain low. He also expects that the interest rates in both countries will rise by about the same amount.

1. Given Jim's expectations, forecast whether the pound will appreciate or depreciate against the euro over time.
2. Given Jim's expectations, will the Sports Exports Company be favourably or unfavourably affected by the future changes in the value of the pound?

CHAPTER 5

CURRENCY DERIVATIVES

T HIS CHAPTER IS DEVOTED entirely to currency derivatives, often used by speculators interested in trading currencies simply to achieve profits but also used by firms to cover the risk of their foreign currency positions. A currency derivative is a contract whose price is derived from the value and price behaviour of the underlying currency that it represents. MNCs commonly take positions in currency derivatives to reduce the risk of (or hedge) their exposure to exchange rate risk. Their managers must understand how these derivatives can be used to achieve corporate goals.

THE SPECIFIC OBJECTIVES OF THIS CHAPTER ARE TO:

■ explain how forward contracts are used to hedge based on anticipated exchange rate movements,

■ describe how currency futures contracts are used to speculate or hedge based on anticipated exchange rate movements, and

■ explain how currency options contracts are used to speculate or hedge based on anticipated exchange rate movements.

FORWARD MARKET

The forward market facilitates the trading of forward contracts on currencies. A forward contract is an agreement between a corporation and a commercial bank to exchange a specified amount of a currency at a specified exchange rate (called the forward rate) on a specified date in the future. When multinational corporations (MNCs) anticipate a future need for or future receipt of a foreign currency, they can set up forward contracts to lock in the rate at which they can purchase or sell a particular foreign currency. Virtually all large MNCs use forward contracts. Some MNCs have forward contracts outstanding worth more than £100 million to hedge various positions.

Because forward contracts accommodate large corporations, the forward transaction will often be valued for very large sums. Forward contracts normally are not used by consumers or small firms. In cases when a bank does not know a corporation well or fully trust it, the bank may request that the corporation make an initial deposit to assure that it will fulfil its obligation. Such a deposit is called a compensating balance and typically does not pay interest.

The most common forward contracts are for 30, 60, 90, 180, and 360 days, although other periods (including longer periods) are available. The forward rate of a given currency will typically vary with the length (number of days) of the forward period.

How MNCs use forward contracts

MNCs use forward contracts to hedge their imports. They can lock in the rate at which they obtain a currency needed to purchase imports.

EXAMPLE

Freeze plc is an MNC based in Birmingham that will need 1,000,000 Singapore dollars in 90 days to purchase Singapore imports. It can buy Singapore dollars for immediate delivery at the spot rate of £0.35 per Singapore dollar (S$). At this spot rate, the firm would need £350,000 (computed as S$1,000,000 × £0.35 per Singapore dollar). However, it does not have the funds right now to exchange for Singapore dollars. It could wait 90 days and then exchange pounds for Singapore dollars at the spot rate existing at that time. But Freeze does not know what the spot rate will be at that time. If the rate rises to £0.40 by then, Freeze will need £400,000 (computed as S$1,000,000 × £0.40 per Singapore dollar), an additional outlay of £50,000 due to the appreciation of the Singapore dollar.

To avoid exposure to exchange rate risk, Freeze can lock in the rate it will pay for Singapore dollars 90 days from now without having to exchange British pounds for Singapore dollars immediately. Specifically, Freeze can negotiate a forward contract with a bank to purchase S$1,000,000 90 days forward.

The ability of a forward contract to lock in an exchange rate can create an opportunity cost in some cases.

EXAMPLE

Assume that in the previous example, Freeze negotiated a 90-day forward rate of £0.38 to purchase S$1,000,000. If the spot rate in 90 days is £0.37, Freeze will have paid £0.01 per unit or £10,000 (1,000,000 units × £0.01) more for the Singapore dollars as a result of taking out a forward contract. But this cost can also be seen as something of an insurance payment in that Freeze avoided the possibility of having to pay much more on the spot market.

Corporations also use the forward market to lock in the rate at which they can sell foreign currencies. This strategy is used to hedge against the possibility of those currencies depreciating over time.

EXAMPLE

Scanlon, plc, based in the UK, exports products to a French firm and will receive payment of 400,000 euros in four months. It can lock in the British pounds to be received from this transaction by selling euros forward. That is, Scanlon can negotiate a forward contract with a bank to sell the 400,000 euros for British pounds at a specified forward rate today. Assume the prevailing four-month forward rate on euros is £0.60:1 euro. In four months, Scanlon will exchange its 400,000 euros for £240,000 (computed as 400,000 euros × £0.60 = £240,000).

Bid/Ask spread. Like spot rates, forward rates have a bid/ask spread. For example, a bank may set up a contract with one firm agreeing to sell the firm Singapore dollars 90 days from now at £0.36 per Singapore dollar. This represents the ask rate. At the same time, the bank may agree to purchase (bid) Singapore dollars 90 days from now from some other firm at £0.35 per Singapore dollar.

The spread between the bid and ask prices is wider for forward rates of currencies of developing countries, such as Chile, Mexico, South Korea, Taiwan, and Thailand. Because these markets have relatively few orders for forward contracts, banks are less able to match up willing buyers and sellers. This lack of liquidity causes banks to widen the bid/ask spread when quoting forward contracts. The wider spread gives banks more profit to cope with the greater risk of having to buy the currency from another bank to complete the deal – an unprofitable course of action. The contracts in these countries are generally available only for short-term horizons.

Premium or discount on the forward rate. A forward rate for buying or selling currency is said to be at a premium or discount compared to the current spot rate.

Where the forward rate is at a premium, the foreign currency is more expensive than the current cost as given by the spot rate.

Where the forward rate is at a discount, the foreign currency is less expensive than the current cost as given by the spot rate.

The premium and discount are usually expressed as a percentage movement from the current spot price. Measuring the difference as a percentage helps in estimating the effect on proposed transactions. So if the US dollar is at a premium of 2% in 60 days time against the euro, buying dollars in 60 days time will be 2% more expensive than buying today.

More formally, the forward rate is equal to the spot rate multiplied by a premium or discount:

$$F = S(1 + p)$$

Where:

F = forward rate (in direct form, i.e. so many units of domestic currency for one unit of foreign currency);

S = spot rate (in direct form, i.e. so many units of domestic currency for one unit of foreign currency);

p = the forward premium (+) or discount (−) expressed as 0.05 for 5% etc.

EXAMPLE

If the euro's spot rate is £0.70, and its one-year forward rate has a forward premium of 2%, the one-year forward rate is:

$$F = s(1+p)$$
$$= 0.70(1+0.002)$$
$$= £0.714$$

Given quotations for the spot rate and the forward rate at a given point in time, the premium can be determined by rearranging the above equation:

$$F = S(1+p)$$
$$F/S = 1+p$$
$$F/S - 1 = p$$

EXAMPLE

If the euro's one-year forward rate is quoted at £0.714 and the euro's spot rate is quoted at £0.70, the euro's forward premium is:

$$F/S - 1 = p$$
$$0.714/0.70 = 1.02 \text{ or } 2\%$$

When the forward rate is less than the prevailing spot rate, the forward premium is negative. Another term used for a negative premium is a discount.

EXAMPLE

If the euro's one-year forward rate is quoted at £0.6596 and the euro's spot rate is quoted at £0.68, the euro's forward premium is:

$$F/S - 1 = p$$
$$0.6596/0.68 - 1 = -0.03 \text{ or } -3\%$$

Since p is negative, the forward rate contains a discount.

Assume the forward exchange rates of the British pound for various maturities as shown in the second column of Exhibit 5.1. Based on each forward exchange rate, the forward discount can be computed on an annualized basis, as shown in Exhibit 5.1.

Exhibit 5.1 Computation of forward rate premiums or discounts

Type of exchange rate for the euro	Market quote: value of 1 euro	Maturity	Annualized premium (+) or discount (−)
Spot	£0.6813	now	0
30-day forward rate	£0.6829	30 days	$\dfrac{(0.6829-0.6813)}{0.6813} \times \dfrac{360}{30} = 2.8\%$
90-day forward rate	£0.6859	90 days	$\dfrac{(0.6859-0.6813)}{0.6813} \times \dfrac{360}{90} = 2.7\%$
180-day forward rate	£0.6977	180 days	$\dfrac{(0.6977-0.6813)}{0.677} \times \dfrac{360}{180} = 4.8\%$

In some situations, a firm may prefer to assess the premium or discount on an unannual-ized basis. In this case, it would not include the fraction that represents the number of periods per year in the formula. Note that the formula uses an approximate basis as often found in practice, the actuarial approach is also to be found (see Appendix B).

Arbitrage. Forward rates typically differ from the spot rate for any given currency. The difference is dictated by arbitrage possibilities. It should *not* be possible to make a risk-less profit through buying and selling currencies. In the case of forward rates, the arbitrageur could borrow in the country with the lower interest rate, invest in the country with the higher interest rate and arrange a conversion back into the original currency using the forward rate. So, borrow, convert to foreign currency, invest, then convert back at the forward rate. The "round trip" would be without risk as interest rates and exchange rates would all be guaranteed at the outset. Although the arbitrageur would earn more interest than he or she is paying, that benefit would almost certainly be lost by the forward discount (or exchange rate loss) of the currency offering the higher interest rate. Transaction costs can also be significant in preventing profit possibilities. Consequently, the forward rate usually contains a premium (or discount) that reflects the difference between the home interest rate and the foreign interest rate.

Movements in the forward rate over time. Because of the arbitrage possibilities (above), the forward exchange rate between any two currencies will depend on the interest rates in those countries and the current spot rate. Any movement over time in the spot rate and the interest rates of the two countries will affect the forward rate. For example, if the spot rate of the euro (the value of the euro in terms of British pounds) increased by 4% from a month ago, the forward rate would have also increased by 4% providing that the difference between the interest rates remained the same. The effect of interest rates will be investigated further in Chapter 7. The forward rate is only a good predictor of the spot in so far as the difference in interest rates and the spot rate is a good predictor of the future spot rate. Arbitrage ties the forward rate to the spot and interest rates. As a result, although it sounds like a prediction, the forward rate is not an independent forecast.

<table>
<tr><td>

USING THE WEB

</td><td>

Forward rates Forward rates of the Canadian dollar, British pound, euro, and Japanese yen are provided for various periods at:

http://www.bmo.com/economic/regular/fxrates.html. The website shows the forward rate of the Canadian dollar for many time horizons. It also shows the forward rate of the British pound, the euro, and the Japanese yen against the Canadian dollar and against the US dollar.

</td></tr>
</table>

Offsetting a forward contract. In some cases, an MNC may desire to offset a forward contract that it previously created. This is a common way in the financial markets of ending a contract. The simple idea is that if Company M owes 1 million Argentine pesos at some future point in time (t) as with a future contract to buy from Bank A (see Exhibit 5.2), the obligation can be effectively ended by taking out a future contract to sell 1 million pesos to, say, Bank B. Both contracts can be satisfied if Bank A sells to Bank B without any involvement of Company M. In the terminology, Company M's position will be "closed out". Importantly, if a bank negotiates a separate fee for ending a contract (and that may well be the case), that fee should be no more than the cost of closing out.

Closing out is the underlying process that determines the cost. The following example (Green Bay) illustrates that cost. Closing out is a general financial technique used in particular for futures contracts. Its use is not frequent for forward contracts but is most easily demonstrated using forwards.

E X A M P L E

On 10 March, Green Bay plc hired a French construction company to expand its office and agreed to pay 200,000 euros for the work on 10 September. It negotiated a six-month forward contract with Bank A to buy 200,000 euros at £0.70 per euro, which would be used to pay the French firm in six months. On 10 April, the French construction company informed Green Bay that it would not be able to perform the work as promised. Therefore, Green Bay offset its existing contract by negotiating a forward contract with Bank B to sell 200,000 euros for the date of 10 September. However, the spot rate of the euro had decreased over the last month, and the prevailing forward contract price for 10 September was £0.66. Green Bay now has a forward contract to sell 200,000 euros on 10 September, which offsets the other contract it has to buy 200,000 euros on 10 September. However, Green Bay is buying at £0.70 per euro and selling at £0.66 per euro a loss of £0.04 per euro. The total loss on the contract would be £0.04 × 200,000 = 8,000 euros. This loss would be paid to the holder of the first contract at £0.70 (Bank A) who would then be happy to sell to Bank B at the rate of the second contract of £0.66.

If Green Bay in the preceding example negotiates the forward sale with the same bank where it negotiated the forward purchase, it may simply be able to request that its initial forward contract be offset. The bank will charge a fee of at least 8,000 euros for this service, reflecting the underlying closing out process. Thus, the MNC cannot just ignore its obligation, but must pay a fee to offset its original obligation.

Exhibit 5.2 Closing out

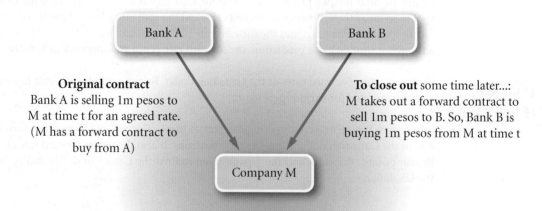

Original contract
Bank A is selling 1m pesos to
M at time t for an agreed rate.
(M has a forward contract to
buy from A)

To close out some time later...:
M takes out a forward contract to
sell 1m pesos to B. So, Bank B is
buying 1m pesos from M at time t

Closed out position:
Bank A can sell 1m pesos directly to Bank B at time t for the rate agreed between M and B.
M will have already settled with A any difference between the price with A and the price with B
(see Green Bay example).

Using forward contracts for swap transactions. A swap transaction involves a spot transaction along with a corresponding forward contract that will ultimately reverse the spot transaction. Many forward contracts are negotiated for this purpose.

EXAMPLE

Soho plc needs to invest 1 million Chilean pesos in its Chilean subsidiary for the production of additional products. It wants the subsidiary to repay the pesos in one year. Soho wants to lock in the rate at which the pesos can be converted back into British pounds in one year, and it uses a one-year forward contract for this purpose. Soho contacts its bank and requests the following swap transaction:

1. *Today.* The bank should withdraw British pounds from Soho's UK account, convert the British pounds to pesos in the spot market, and transmit the pesos to the subsidiary's account.
2. *In one year.* The bank should withdraw 1 million pesos from the subsidiary's account, convert them to British pounds at today's forward rate, and transmit them to Soho's UK account.

Soho plc is not exposed to exchange rate movements due to the transaction because it has locked in the rate at which the pesos will be converted back to British pounds. If the one-year forward rate exhibits a discount, however, Soho will receive fewer British pounds in one year than it invested in the subsidiary today. It may still be willing to engage in the swap transaction under these circumstances in order to remove the possibility of receiving even fewer British pounds in one year's time.

Non-deliverable forward contracts

A new type of forward contract called a **non-deliverable forward contract (NDF)** is frequently used for currencies in emerging markets. Like a regular forward contract, an NDF represents an agreement regarding a position in a specified amount of a specified currency, a specified exchange rate, and a specified future settlement date. However, an NDF does not result in an actual exchange of the currencies at the future date. That is, there is no delivery. Instead, one party to the agreement makes a payment to the other party based on the exchange rate at the future date.

At first an NDF might sound rather odd as a contract, but it is really no more than a contract that is closed out at maturity date (see the Green Bay example above). The purpose of a forward contract is to protect against *changes* in the value of the currency. An NDF provides payment based on the change to the value of the currency, effectively locking in the purchaser (a multinational company) to a fixed rate. Thus if an MNC is buying a currency and takes out an NDF and the rate rises above the agreed future rate, the MNC will receive compensation for the difference. The cost of the currency less the compensation will be the same as purchasing at the agreed future rate. If there were a fall in the value of the currency, the MNC would have to pay the difference, again the total cost would be the equivalent of buying at the agreed future rate.

EXAMPLE

Jackson AG, a German company, determines as of 1 April that it will need 50 million Kenyan shillings to purchase coffee on 1 July. It can negotiate an NDF with a local bank as follows. The NDF will specify the currency (Kenyan shilling), the settlement date (90 days from now), and a so-called reference rate, which identifies the type of exchange rate that will be marked to market at the settlement. Specifically, the NDF will contain the following information:

- Buy 50 million Kenyan shilling.
- Settlement date: 1 July.
- Reference index: Kenyan shilling's closing exchange rate (in euros) quoted by Kenya's central bank in 90 days.

Assume that the Kenyan shilling (which is the reference index) is currently valued at 0.01 euros, so the euro amount of the position is 50 million × 0.01 = 500,000 euros at the time of the agreement. At the time of the settlement date (1 July), the value of the reference index is determined, and a payment is made between the two parties to settle the NDF. For example, if the shilling value increases to 0.012 euros by 1 July, the value of the position specified in the NDF will be 600,000 euros (0.012 euros × 50 million shillings). Since the cost of the 50 million shillings is 100,000 euros higher than when the agreement was created, Jackson will receive a payment of 100,000 euros from the bank.

Recall that Jackson needs 50 million shillings to buy imports. Since the shilling's spot rate rose from 1 April to 1 July, Jackson will need to pay 100,000 euros more for the imports than if it had paid for them on 1 April. At the same time, however, Jackson will have received a payment of 100,000 euros due to its NDF. Thus, the NDF hedged (offset) the exchange rate risk.

If the Kenyan shilling had depreciated to 0.009 euros instead of rising, Jackson's position in its NDF would have been valued at 450,000 euros (50 million shillings × 0.009 euros) at the settlement date, which is 50,000 euros less than the value when the agreement was created. Therefore, Jackson would have owed the bank 50,000 euros at that time to settle the NDF. However, the decline in the spot rate of the shilling means that Jackson would pay 50,000 euros less for the imports than if it had paid for them on 1 April. Thus, an offsetting effect would also occur in this example.

In both cases the net payment made by Jackson is 500,000 euros made up of purchasing the shilling at the market rate and then paying or receiving from the bank the difference between the market rate in euros and the NDF rate of 500,000 euros.

As these examples show, although an NDF does not involve delivery, it can effectively hedge future foreign currency payments that are anticipated by an MNC. The non-deliverable aspect of the contract may be attractive if the other party wants to be paid the equivalent value of their local currency in dollars, pounds or euros at the time of the transaction. There may therefore be no actual delivery of local currency in the underlying transaction.

CURRENCY FUTURES MARKET

Currency futures contracts are contracts specifying a standard volume of a particular currency to be exchanged on a specific settlement date. Thus, currency futures contracts are similar to forward contracts in terms of their obligation, but differ from forward contracts in the way they are traded. They are commonly used by MNCs to hedge their foreign currency positions. In addition, they are traded by speculators who hope to capitalize on their expectations of exchange rate movements. Unlike forward contracts, active trading determines the price of a futures contract. Trading is made possible because of the standard nature of the contracts.

The contracts are person to person, a buyer's gain is a seller's loss and vice versa. A buyer of a currency futures contract locks in the exchange rate to be paid for a foreign currency at a future point in time. Alternatively, a seller of a currency futures contract locks in the exchange rate at which a foreign currency can be exchanged for the home currency. In the United Kingdom, currency futures contracts are purchased to lock in the amount of British pounds needed to obtain a specified amount of a particular foreign currency; they are sold to lock in the amount of British pounds to be received from selling a specified amount of a particular foreign currency.

Contract specifications

Currency futures contracts are available for several widely traded currencies at the Chicago Mercantile Exchange (CME – the original futures exchange and the market that serves as a model for all others); the contract for each currency specifies a standardized number of units (see Exhibit 5.3). The standard size of a contract enables traders to deal in contracts without having to ask for the size of the contract, this speeds up the trading process.

On the Chicago Exchange, the typical currency futures contract is based on a currency value in terms of US dollars. However, futures contracts are also available on some cross-rates, such as the exchange rate between the Australian dollar and the Canadian dollar. Thus, speculators who expect that the Australian dollar will move substantially against the Canadian dollar can take a futures position to capitalize on their expectations. In addition, Australian firms that have exposure in Canadian dollars or Canadian firms that have exposure in Australian dollars may use this type of futures contract to hedge their exposure.

http://

The *Futures* magazine website is at http://www.futuresmag.com/library/contents.html.

Visit the Chicago Mercantile Exchange site at http://www.cme.com for a time series on financial futures and option prices (see below). The site allows for the generation of historic price charts.

See http://www.cme.com/prd/fx/crossrate2625.html for more information about futures on cross exchange rates.

Exhibit 5.3 Currency futures contracts traded on the Chicago Mercantile Exchange

Currency	Units per Contract
Australian dollar	100,000
Brazilian real	100,000
British pound	62,500
Canadian dollar	100,000
Euro	125,000
Japanese yen	12,500,000
Mexican peso	500,000
New Zealand dollar	100,000
Norwegian krone	2,000,000
Russian ruble	2,500,000
South African rand	500,000
Swedish krona	2,000,000
Swiss franc	125,000
Czech koruna	4,000,000
Polish zloty	500,000
Hungarian forint	30,000,000

Notes:

■ The Czech Republic, Poland and Hungary joined the European Union in 2004 but will still use their currencies until at least 2006.

■ Underlying currencies are referred to as units, this practice avoids having to refer to too many currencies when specifying contracts.

Currency futures contracts typically specify the third Wednesday in March, June, September, or December as the settlement date. There is also an over-the-counter currency futures market, where various financial intermediaries facilitate trading of currency futures contracts with specific settlement dates. As noted above, contracts have to be standardized to ensure that floor trading (known as "open outcry in the pit") can be carried out quickly and efficiently.

Trading futures

Firms or individuals can execute orders for currency futures contracts by calling brokerage firms that serve as intermediaries. The order to buy or sell a currency futures contract for a specific currency and a specific settlement date is communicated to the brokerage firm, which in turn communicates the order to the CME. A floor broker at the CME who specializes in that type of currency futures contract stands at a specific spot at the trading pit where that type of contract is traded and attempts to find a counterparty to fulfil the order. For example, if an MNC wants to purchase a Mexican peso futures contract with a December settlement date, the floor broker assigned to execute this order will look for another floor broker who has an order to sell a Mexican peso futures contract with a December settlement date.

Trading on the floor (in the trading pits) of the CME takes place from 7:20am to 2:00pm (Chicago time) Monday through Friday. Currency futures contracts can also be traded on the CME's automated order-entry and matching system called GLOBEX, which typically is open 23 hours per day (closed from 4pm to 5pm). The GLOBEX system matches buy and sell orders for each type of currency futures contract. E-mini futures for some currencies are also traded on the GLOBEX system; they specify half the number of units of the standard futures contract.

When participants in the currency futures market take a position, they need to establish an initial margin (deposit an amount of money with the clearing house), which may represent as little as 10% of the contract value. The margin required is in the form of cash for small investors or Treasury securities for institutional investors. In addition to the initial margin, participants are subject to a variation margin, which is intended to accumulate a sufficient amount of funds to back the futures position. Depositing such funds with the clearing house ensures that losses are debited to the customer account as and when they occur – thus bad debts are avoided. Full-service brokers typically charge a commission of about $50 for a round-trip trade in currency futures, while discount brokers charge a commission of about $20. Some Internet brokers also trade currency futures.

EXAMPLE

Assume that as of 10 February, a futures contract on $20,000 on the Euronext Liffe European market with a March settlement date is priced at 0.80 euros per dollar. Consider the positions of two different firms on the opposite sides of this contract. The buyer of this currency futures contract will receive $20,000 on the March settlement date and will pay 16,000 euros (computed as $20,000 × 0.80 euros per dollar). The seller of this contract is obliged to sell $20,000 at a price of 0.80 euros per dollar and therefore will receive 16,000 euros on the settlement date. See http://www.euronext.com for further details.

Comparison of currency futures and forward contracts

Currency futures contracts are similar to forward contracts in that they allow a customer to lock in the exchange rate at which a specific currency is purchased or sold for a specific date in the future. Nevertheless, there are some differences between currency futures contracts and forward contracts, which are summarized in Exhibit 5.4. Currency futures contracts are sold on an exchange, while each forward contract is negotiated between a firm and a commercial bank over a telecommunications network. Thus, forward contracts can be tailored to the needs of the firm, while currency futures contracts are standardized.

Corporations that have established relationships with large banks tend to use forward contracts rather than futures contracts because forward contracts are tailored to the precise amount of currency to be purchased or sold in the future and the precise forward date that they prefer. Conversely, small firms and individuals who do not have established relationships with large banks or prefer to trade in smaller amounts tend to use currency futures contracts.

Pricing currency futures

The price of currency futures normally will be similar to the forward rate for a given currency and settlement date. This relationship is enforced by the potential arbitrage activity that would occur if there were significant discrepancies. Once again we see arbitrage processes determining market prices.

Exhibit 5.4 Comparison of the forward and futures markets

	Forward	Futures
Size of contract	Tailored to individual needs.	Standardized.
Delivery date	Tailored to individual needs.	Standardized.
Participants	Banks, brokers, and multinational companies. Public speculation not encouraged.	Banks, brokers, and multinational companies. Qualified public speculation encouraged.
Security deposit	None as such, but compensating bank balances or lines of credit required.	Small security deposit required.
Clearing operation	Handling contingent on individual banks and brokers. No separate clearing house function.	Handled by exchange clearing house. Daily settlements to the market price.
Marketplace	Over the telephone worldwide.	Central exchange floor with worldwide communications.
Regulation	Self-regulating.	Commodity Futures Trading Commission; National Futures Association.
Liquidation	Most settled by actual delivery. Some by offset, at a cost.	Most by offset, very few by delivery.
Transaction costs	Set by 'spread' between bank's buy and sell prices.	Negotiated brokerage fees.

Source: Chicago Mercantile Exchange.

EXAMPLE

Assume that the currency futures price on the pound is $1.50 and that forward contracts for a similar period are available for $1.48. Firms may attempt to purchase forward contracts and simultaneously sell currency futures contracts. If they can exactly match the settlement dates of the two contracts, they can generate guaranteed profits of $0.02 per unit. These actions will place downward pressure on the currency futures price. The futures contract and forward contracts of a given currency and settlement date should have the same price, or else guaranteed profits are possible (assuming no transaction costs).

The currency futures price differs from the spot rate for the same reasons that a forward rate differs from the spot rate. If a currency's spot and futures prices were the same and the currency's interest rate were higher than the UK rate, UK speculators could lock in a higher return than they would receive on UK investments. They could:

1. purchase the foreign currency at the spot rate,
2. invest the funds in that foreign country at the attractive interest rate,
3. simultaneously sell currency futures for a maturity date that coincides with the end of the investment period to lock in the exchange rate at which they could reconvert the currency back to British pounds.

If the spot and futures rates were the same, there would be neither a gain nor a loss on the currency conversion. Thus, the higher foreign interest rate would provide a higher yield on this type of investment. The actions of investors to capitalize on this opportunity would place upward pressure on the spot rate increasing the value now of the foreign currency and downward pressure on the future value of the currency, causing the futures price to fall below the spot rate. There would then be a currency loss on conversion that should match the difference in interest rates, otherwise arbitrage profits would be possible.

Credit risk of currency futures contracts

Each currency futures contract represents an agreement between a client and the exchange clearing house, even though the exchange has not taken a position (see Exhibit 5.5). To illustrate, assume you call a broker to request the purchase of a euro futures contract with a March settlement date. Meanwhile, another person unrelated to you calls a broker to request the sale of a similar futures contract. Neither party needs to worry about the credit risk of the counterparty. The exchange clearing house assures that you will receive whatever is owed to you as a result of your currency futures position.

To minimize its risk in such a guarantee, the CME imposes **margin requirements** to cover fluctuations in the value of a contract, meaning that the participants must make a deposit with their respective brokerage firms when they take a position. The initial margin requirement is typically between $1,000 and $2,000 per currency futures contract. Charges and credits are made on a daily basis to the accounts of the buyer and seller depending on the movement of the value of the futures contract.

Thus if a US speculator purchases a futures contract on British pounds and the futures price of the pound goes up the following day by ½ a cent ($0.005), the purchaser has a potential gain as the contract enables him to buy British pounds for ½ a cent less than the market. The purchaser could "close out" (see below) by taking out a futures contract to sell at the higher rate. As this is a zero sum game between the buyer and seller (one's loss is the other's gain) – the seller is selling at ½ a cent below the current futures price.

Exhibit 5.5 Contractual positions for futures contract

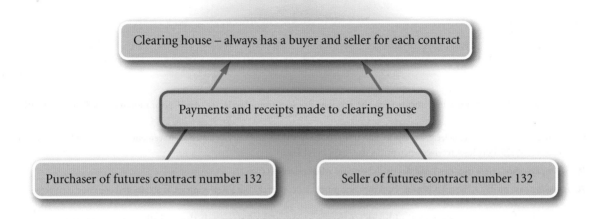

So the seller (if nothing else happened) owes the purchaser ½ a cent per pound. The clearing house would charge the seller £62,500 × $0.005 = $312.5 and credit the amount to the purchaser *the next day*. The clearing house debits and credits each account in this way on a daily basis. This is a process used by most market trading organizations including those trading over the Internet (see Exhibit 5.6).

The obvious question is why settle on a daily basis? Why not wait to the end of the contract, after all the positions may reverse the following day and the payment be made in the other direction. The reason for daily settlement is to ensure the creditworthiness of both parties. If the sellers margin went below a safety level with the $312.5 payment and the seller refused to top up the account, the clearing house could terminate the contract and the purchaser buy a futures at the current price. Having already received the difference between the current price and the original purchase price from the daily settlement process, the purchaser will not lose out by having the contract at the higher price. In technical terms, the contract is effectively closed out on a daily basis. Exhibit 5.6 illustrates the daily closing out procedure.

Unlike futures contracts, margin requirements are not always required for forward contracts due to the more personal nature of the agreement; the bank knows the firm it is dealing with and may trust it to fulfil its obligation.

Speculation with currency futures

Currency futures contracts are often purchased by speculators who are simply attempting to capitalize on their expectation of a currency's future movement.

Assume that a UK speculator expects the US dollar to appreciate in the future. They can purchase a futures contract that will lock in the price at which they buy dollars at a specified settlement date. On the settlement date, they can purchase their dollars at the

Exhibit 5.6 Currency futures contract on British pounds (£62,500), example of daily settlement on the Chicago Mercantile Exchange

Day	Price per £1 (or unit) of futures contract	Purchaser pays (–) or receives (+)	Seller pays (–) or receives (+)
0	$0.503		
1	$0.504	($0.504 – $0.503) × 62500 = +$62.5 ⟵——— –$62.5	
2	$0.502	($0.502 – $0.504) × 62500 = –$125 ———⟶ +$125	
3	$0.505	($0.505 – $0.502) × 62500 =+$187.5 ⟵——— –$187.5	

Notes:

- Payments are based on price movements from the previous day (*not* from day 1), e.g. day 3 price movement is $0.505 – $0.502 = $0.003.

- Purchaser pays when prices fall, e.g. day 2 price falls from $0.504 to $0.502, amount calculated as movement × units i.e. ($0.502 – $0.504) × 62500 = –$125. Purchaser receives when prices rise (days 1 and 3).

- Seller pays when prices rise (day 1 and day 3) and receives when prices fall (day 2).

- If, having paid on day 3, the seller became bankrupt, the purchaser could take out a new contract at $0.505 and continue unaffected.

rate specified by the futures contract and then sell these dollars at the spot rate. If the spot rate has appreciated by this time in accordance with their expectations, they will profit from this strategy. Alternatively, rather than actually dealing in the currencies, speculators can simply close out by selling an offsetting futures contract (similar to the offsetting forward contract, see below). Daily settlement will have ensured that they will have already received the gain.

Currency futures are often sold by speculators who expect that the spot rate of a currency will be less than the rate at which they would be obliged to sell it.

EXAMPLE

Assume that as of 4 April, a futures contract specifying 125,000 euros and a June settlement date is priced at £0.6813. On 4 April, speculators who expect the euro will decline sell futures contracts on euros. Assume that on 17 June (the settlement date), the spot rate of the euro is £0.6810. The gain on the futures position is £37.5, which represents the difference between the amount received (£85,162.5) when selling the euros in accordance with the futures contract versus the amount paid (£85,125) for those euros in the spot market. In practice, the speculator will have received the £37.5 from daily settlement.

Of course, expectations are often incorrect. It is because of different expectations that some speculators decide to purchase futures contracts while other speculators decide to sell the same contracts at a given point in time.

Currency futures market efficiency. If the currency futures market is efficient, the futures price for a currency at any given point in time should reflect all available information. Both the spot rate and the futures rate will be derived from the same information set. The only difference is that expected events of significance will be discounted to the future date for the futures and the present for the spot. An exception is the cost of time itself, the interest rate. As has been shown, arbitrage ensures that the futures price differs from the spot by the interest rate differential. If interest rates are higher in Brazil, the futures price will be at a discount so that the higher interest rate earned through investing in Brazil is lost by the discount on the futures price. Otherwise, riskless profits would be possible. By and large, when adjusted for this known difference, the futures should be an unbiased estimate of the future spot. But it is unlikely to be a better estimate than the present spot (i.e. the prediction of no change in the exchange rate). This is because there is nothing that the futures price "knows" that is not "known" by the spot rate.

How firms use currency futures

Corporations that have open positions in foreign currencies can consider purchasing or selling futures contracts to offset their positions.

Purchasing futures to hedge payables. The purchase of futures contracts locks in the price at which a firm can purchase a currency.

EXAMPLE

Tetoni s.a. (Italy) orders Canadian goods and upon delivery will need to send C$500,000 to the Canadian exporter. Thus, Tetoni purchases Canadian dollar futures contracts today, thereby locking in the price to be paid for Canadian dollars at a future settlement date. By holding futures contracts, Tetoni does not have to worry about changes in the spot rate of the Canadian dollar over time.

Selling futures to hedge receivables. The sale of futures contracts locks in the price at which a firm can sell a currency.

EXAMPLE

Karla ltd sells futures contracts when it plans to receive a currency from exporting that it will not need (it accepts a foreign currency when the importer prefers that type of payment). By selling a futures contract, Karla ltd locks in the price at which it will be able to sell this currency as of the settlement date. Such an action can be appropriate if Karla expects the foreign currency to depreciate against Karla's home currency.

The use of futures contracts to cover, or **hedge**, a firm's currency positions is described more thoroughly in Chapter 11.

Closing out a futures position

If a firm holding a currency futures contract to purchase decides before the settlement date that it no longer wants to maintain its position, it can close out the position by selling an identical futures contract. The process is the same as the offsetting of forward contracts. With forward contracts closing out was unusual, with futures, closing out is normal. One reason is that a futures contract is much used for speculation where the interest is in the currency movements rather than actual buying or selling of the currency. A second reason, of interest to MNCs, is that a futures contract has fixed settlement dates (the third Wednesday of every quarter month). Companies will normally want protection to a different date, closing out enables a company to obtain protection up to a precise date and thereafter have no further obligations. Companies need to choose settlement dates beyond the date when a purchase or sale of currency is required. Closing out then enables protection to the precise date. The clearing house will offset the equal and opposite contracts and no further daily settlement receipts or payments will be made. The gain or loss to the firm will have been already paid or received from daily settlement before closing out.

The price of a futures contract changes over time in accordance with movements in the spot rate and interest rates and also with changing expectations about the spot rate and interest rates.

If the spot rate of a currency increases substantially over a one-month period, the futures price is likely to increase by about the same amount. In this case, the purchase and subsequent sale of a futures contract would be profitable. Conversely, a decline in the spot rate over time will correspond with a decline in the currency futures price, meaning that the purchase and subsequent sale of a futures contract would result in a loss. While the purchasers of the futures contract could decide not to close out their position under such conditions, the losses from that position could increase over time.

EXAMPLE

On January 10, Tacoma ltd anticipates that it will need Australian dollars (A$) in March when it orders supplies from an Australian supplier. Consequently, Tacoma purchases a futures contract specifying A$100,000 and a March settlement date (which is 19 March for this contract). On 10 January, the futures contract is priced at £0.41 per A$. On 15 February, Tacoma realizes that it will not need to order supplies because it has reduced its production levels. Therefore, it has no need for A$ in March. It sells a futures contract on A$ with the March settlement date to offset the contract it purchased in January. At this time, the futures contract is priced at £0.39 per A$. On 19 March (the settlement date), Tacoma has offsetting positions in futures contracts. However, the price when the futures contract was purchased was higher than the price when an identical contract was sold, so Tacoma incurs a loss from its futures positions. Tacoma's transactions are summarized in Exhibit 5.7. Move from left to right along the time line to review the transactions. The example does not include margin requirements.

Sellers of futures contracts can close out their positions by purchasing currency futures contracts with similar settlement dates. Although most contracts are closed out before the settlement date, delivery is possible but the terms of delivery are usually not particularly attractive. The market prefers contracts to be closed out.

Exhibit 5.7 Closing out a futures contract

10 January	10 February	19 March
Futures contract price:		
£0.41	£0.39	£0.36
1. Takes out a contract to buy on 19 March A$100,000 at £0.41 per A$.	2. Will have paid out net £0.39 – £0.41 = –£0.02 × A$100,000 = £2,000 in daily settlement charges. 3. Takes out a contract to sell on 19 March on A$100,000 at £0.39 per A$. 4. Contracts offset by clearing house, the holder will not have any further commitments.	5. The contracts are offset so no further payments required. As a note, the contract to buy would have paid out a further (£0.36 – £0.39) × A$100,000 = £3,000 but the contract to sell will have earned (£0.39 – £0.36) × A$100,000 = £3,000. In fact, whatever the spot price on settlement the contracts will have earned equal and opposite amounts. Closing out merely recognizes that the holder of equal and opposite contracts will not have to make further payments.

Transaction costs of currency futures

Brokers who fulfil orders to buy or sell futures contracts charge a transaction or brokerage fee in the form of a bid/ask spread. That is, they buy a futures contract for one price (their "bid" price) and simultaneously sell the contract to someone else for a slightly higher price (their "ask" price). The difference between a bid and an ask price on a futures contract may be as little as £5.00 in total. Yet, even this amount can be larger in percentage terms than the transaction fees for forward contracts.

CURRENCY OPTIONS MARKET

Currency options provide the right but not the obligation to purchase or sell currencies at specified prices. The main difference with futures and forward contracts is that, in the case of an option, a range of prices are offered and also that the purchaser does not have to fulfil the contract, it can be allowed to lapse. For MNCs it can be used as a kind of insurance policy. When buying foreign currency an option contract can be used to ensure that the company will not have to pay more than a certain amount. When selling foreign currency, a minimum value can be established. Thus an MNC can limit its exposure to exchange rate fluctuations but not *eliminate* exposure as with a fully covered futures position. Where the market goes above or below the guaranteed price (known as the strike or exercise price) the options policy pays out the difference, as with any insurance policy where a claim is made. There are two types of options, an American option that allows the purchaser of the contract to buy or sell at any time before the settlement or exercise date, and a European option that allows purchase or sale of the currency only at the exercise date. Options are available for many currencies, including the US dollar, Australian dollar, British pound, Brazilian real, Canadian dollar, euro, Japanese yen, Mexican peso, New Zealand dollar, Russian rouble, South African rand, and Swiss franc.

Option exchanges

In late 1982, exchanges in Amsterdam, Montreal, and Philadelphia first allowed trading in standardized foreign currency options. Since that time, options have been offered on the Chicago Mercantile Exchange and the Chicago Board Options Exchange. Currency options are traded through the GLOBEX system at the Chicago Mercantile Exchange, even after the trading floor is closed. Thus, currency options are traded virtually around the clock.

The options exchanges in the United States are regulated by the Securities and Exchange Commission. Options can be purchased or sold through brokers for a commission. The commission per transaction is commonly $30 to $60 for a single currency option, but it can be much lower per contract when the transaction involves multiple contracts. Brokers require that a margin be maintained during the life of the contract and daily settlement is made as with futures contracts. The margin is increased for clients whose option positions have deteriorated. This protects against possible losses if the clients do not fulfil their obligations.

In September 2000 the exchanges of Amsterdam, Brussels and Paris merged to form Euronext N.V., a Dutch holding company. In 2002 the LIFFE (London International Financial Futures and Options Exchange) was acquired. Subsequent years have seen the merger of clearing house services as well.

Over-the-counter market

In addition to the exchanges where currency options are available, there is an over-the-counter market where currency options are offered by commercial banks and brokerage firms. Unlike the currency options traded on an exchange, currency options are tailored to the specific needs of the firm. Since these options are not standardized, all the terms must be specified in the contracts. The number of units, desired strike price, and expiration date can be tailored to the specific needs of the client. When currency options are not standardized, there is less liquidity and a wider bid/ask spread.

The minimum size of currency options offered by financial institutions is normally more than £1 million. Since these transactions are conducted with a specific financial institution rather than an exchange, there are no credit guarantees. Thus, the agreement made is only as safe as the parties involved. For this reason, financial institutions may require some collateral from individuals or firms desiring to purchase or sell currency options. Currency options are classified as either **calls** or **puts**, as discussed in the next section.

CURRENCY CALL OPTIONS

A currency call option grants the right to buy a specific currency at a designated price within a specific period of time if it is an American option or at a certain time if it is a European option. The price at which the owner is allowed to buy that currency is known as the exercise price or strike price, and there are monthly expiration dates for each option.

Call options are desirable when one wishes to lock in a maximum price to be paid for a currency in the future. If the spot rate of the currency rises above the strike price, owners of call options can "exercise" their options by purchasing the currency at the strike price, which will be cheaper than the prevailing spot rate. This strategy is somewhat similar to that used by purchasers of futures contracts, except that:

- The futures contracts do not offer a range of prices, forward and futures only offer the expected price.
- Forward and future contracts require an obligation to buy or sell, while the currency option does not. The owner can choose to let the option expire on the expiration date without ever exercising it.
- Owners of expired call options will have lost the premium they initially paid, but that is the most they can lose. Losses are potentially unlimited for purchasers of futures contracts – though losses can be halted by closing out.

Although currency options typically expire near the middle of the specified month, some of them expire at the end of the specific month and are designated as EOM (end of month). Some options are listed as "European style", which means that they can be exercised only upon expiration.

A currency call option is said to be *in the money* when the present exchange rate exceeds the strike price. The term "in the money" is being used in the normal sense in that if the present exchange or spot rate exceeds the strike price, the holder of the call option is due to be paid the difference. In Exhibit 5.8 a quote on a range of call options on the dollar is given. Imagine that the situation is of a UK speculator wanting to buy dollars. Call options at strike prices of £0.60:$1 and £0.65:$1 are both in the money as the spot is £0.67:$1. At these lower strike prices, the holder is in effect able to buy dollars at below the spot or market price (note that the premium prevents an immediate profit

Exhibit 5.8 Call option quote

Stock Exchange £/$ quote for call options for $50,000 – European style options		
Spot: £0.67:$1		
current date: November		
Strike price value of $1 in pounds	Premiums £s per $1	
	December	January
£0.60	£0.076	£0.085
£0.65	£0.040	£0.052
£0.70	£0.017	£0.029

Notes:

- A January call option at a strike price of £0.65 would incur a cost £0.052 × 50,000 = £2,600 known as the contract premium.
- The buyer of the January call option at a strike price of £0.65 will collect £0.01 × 50,000 = £500 for every penny (£0.01) the spot rate of the dollar is above £0.65 at the designated date in January.
- If the spot rate is below £0.65 in January, the option will not be exercised and will be allowed to lapse, the premium will have been forfeited by the purchaser of the call option.
- A European option can only be exercised at the exercise date – an American option any time up to the exercise date.

being made). Options are *at the money* when the present exchange rate equals the strike price, and *out of the money* when the present exchange rate is less than the strike price (Exhibit 5.8 strike price of £0.70 is out of the money). For a given currency and expiration date, an in-the-money call option will require a higher premium than options that are at the money or out of the money. The premium will also be higher for longer expiration dates as evidenced in Exhibit 5.8.

Factors affecting currency call option premiums

The premium on a call option represents the cost of having the right to buy the underlying currency at a specified price. For MNCs that use currency call options to hedge, the premium reflects a cost of insurance or protection for MNCs.

The call option premium in general terms is influenced by the probability of a payout. Thus in Exhibit 5.8 the premium for the right to buy British pounds at £0.70:$1 is very small for December because it is very unlikely that the spot rate will increase by about 4½% from £0.67 to £0.70 in such a short space of time. Longer term options are more expensive because there is a greater probability of a payout, i.e. being in the money.

As with all insurance type contracts, the greater the likelihood of a payout, the higher the premium.

Three factors influence the option premium (referred to as C):

$$C = f(S - X, T, \sigma)$$

Where:

$S - X$ = the difference between the spot exchange rate (S) and the strike or exercise price (X),

T = the time to maturity,

σ = the volatility of the currency, as measured by the standard deviation of the movements in the currency.

The relationships between the call option premium and these factors are summarized next.

- *Level of existing spot price relative to strike price.* The higher the spot rate relative to the strike price, the more likely a payout. Where the spot is above the strike, the option contract is going to enable the holder to buy the currency at below the current price. The premium should at least cover this difference plus a small extra to cover for the possibility of being even deeper in the money (i.e. the payout being even higher).

- *Length of time before the expiration date.* It is generally expected that the spot rate has a greater chance of rising high above the strike price if it has a longer period of time to do so. The premiums for the January settlement dates are all higher than for the December dates.

- *Potential variability of currency.* The greater the variability of the changes in currency, the higher the probability that the spot rate will be above the strike price. Thus, more volatile currencies have higher call option prices. For example, changes in the euro Swiss franc exchange rate is more stable than most other currencies. If all other factors are similar, euro call options on Swiss francs should be less expensive than call options on other non-euro currencies.

The potential variability of returns or changes in the currency can also vary over time for a particular currency. For example, at the beginning of the Asian crisis in 1997, the Asian countries experienced financial problems, and their currency values were subject to much more uncertainty. Consequently, the premium on over-the-counter options of Asian currencies such as the Thai baht, Indonesian rupiah, and Korean won increased. The higher premium was necessary to compensate those who were willing to sell options in these currencies, as the risk to sellers had increased because the currencies had become more volatile.

Note here that we are talking about volatility of the *changes* in the value of the currency, whether the daily *changes* in the value of the currency are high or low. This is closely linked to the standard deviation of the actual values of the currency, but there is an important difference. If there is a trend in the figures, the standard deviation of the actual values will be distorted upwards by out of date figures, whereas looking at just the movements will get rid of this distortion. The *changes* approach is sometimes referred to as detrended.

How firms use currency call options

Corporations with open positions in foreign currencies can sometimes use currency call options to cover these positions.

Using call options to hedge payables. MNCs can purchase call options on a currency to hedge future payables.

EXAMPLE

When Pike ltd (UK) orders Australian goods, it makes a payment in Australian dollars to the Australian exporter upon delivery. An Australian dollar call option locks in a maximum rate at which Pike can exchange British pounds for Australian dollars. The call option contract specifies the maximum price that Pike must pay to obtain these Australian dollars. If the Australian dollar's value remains below the strike price, Pike can purchase Australian dollars at the prevailing spot rate when it needs to pay for its imports and simply let its call option expire.

Options may be more appropriate than futures or forward contracts for some situations. Adidas in their 2004 annual report state that they use options up to 18 months in advance to protect against their significant dollar denominated purchases whilst at the same time being able to benefit from the continuing depreciation of the dollar.

Using call options to hedge project bidding. MNCs bidding for foreign projects may purchase call options to lock in the cost of the potential expenses.

EXAMPLE

Kelly plc is an MNC based in Scotland that has bid on a project sponsored by the Canadian government. If the bid is accepted, Kelly will need approximately C$500,000 to purchase Canadian materials and services. However, Kelly will not know whether the bid is accepted until three months from now. Kelly expects the value of the Canadian dollar to fall; but it may rise. If it rises above a certain level the project will no longer be profitable. In this case, it can purchase call options with a three-month expiration date at a strike price that will guarantee a minimum level of profit. Ten call option contracts will cover the entire amount of potential exposure. If the bid is accepted, Kelly can use the options to purchase the Canadian dollars needed if the value of the Canadian dollar has risen above the strike price. If the Canadian dollar has depreciated over time or has not risen above the strike price, Kelly will let the options expire.

Assume that the strike or exercise price on Canadian dollars is £0.43 and the call option premium is £0.005 per unit. Kelly will pay £250 per option (since there are 50,000 units per Canadian dollar option and 50,000 × 0.005 = £250), or £2,500 for the ten option contracts. With options, the maximum amount necessary to purchase the C$500,000 is £215,000 (computed as £0.43 per Canadian dollar × C$500,000) plus the cost of the options £2,500. So a maximum total of £217,500 would be needed. The cost of the options (£2,500) would be less the higher the exercise price, simply because the protection would be less and therefore the probability of a payout less.

Even if Kelly's bid is rejected, it will exercise the currency call option if the Canadian dollar's spot rate exceeds the exercise price before the option expires and sell the Canadian dollars in the spot market. Any gain from exercising may partially or even fully offset the premium paid for the options. Alternatively, there is an active secondary market for options and they may simply be sold on that market.

This type of example is quite common. When Air Products and Chemicals was hired to undertake some projects, it needed capital equipment from Germany. The purchase of equipment was contingent on whether the firm was hired for the projects. The company used options to hedge this possible future purchase.

Using call options to hedge target bidding. Firms can also use call options to hedge a possible acquisition.

EXAMPLE

Mumble plc is attempting to acquire a French firm and has submitted its bid in euros. Mumble has purchased call options on the euro because it will need euros to purchase the French company's stock. The call options hedge the UK firm against the potential appreciation of the euro by the time the acquisition occurs. Whether or not the acquisition goes ahead, if the euro remains below the strike price, Mumble can let the call options expire. If the euro exceeds the strike price at maturity, Mumble can exercise the options and sell the euros in the spot market. Alternatively, Mumble can sell the call options it is holding. Either of these actions may offset part or all of the premium paid for the options. In these circumstances Mumble may also take out options on the price of the target company if they are traded or options on the Paris DAX index to provide partial protection against price rises in the shares of the target company.

Speculating with currency call options

Because this text focuses on multinational financial management, the corporate use of currency options is more important than the speculative use. The use of options for hedging is discussed in detail in Chapter 11. Speculative trading is discussed here in order to provide a greater insight into the workings of the market. Speculators play an important role in setting prices and ensuring that the market is responsive to new information. Also, particularly with options, the dividing line between commercial and speculative use is somewhat blurred, only guaranteeing a price if it goes above a certain rate is to accept a degree of speculation on the future price.

Individuals may speculate in the currency options market based on their expectation of the future movements in a particular currency. Speculators who expect that a foreign currency will appreciate can purchase call options on that currency. Once the spot rate of that currency appreciates, the speculators can exercise their options by purchasing that currency at the strike price and then sell the currency at the prevailing spot rate. This assumes that the speculator holds an American option which can be exercised up to the expiration date. Holders of European options, which can only be exercised at the maturity date, can nevertheless sell their options on the second hand market before that date and achieve similar gains.

Just as with currency futures, for every buyer of a currency call option there must be a seller. A seller (called a **writer**) of a call option is obliged to sell a specified currency at a specified price (the strike price) up to a specified expiration date (in the case of an American option or at a specified date in the case of a European option) *if the option is exercised*. It is the buyer of the option who decides whether or not the option is exercised not the writer.

Speculators may sometimes want to sell a currency call option on a currency that they expect will depreciate in the future. The only way a currency call option will be exercised is if the spot rate is higher than the strike price. Thus, a seller of a currency call option will receive the premium when the option is purchased and will profit by the entire amount if the option is not exercised. When it appears that an option will be exercised, there will still be sellers of options. However, such options will sell for premiums that will include the profit that can be made on the option now (the intrinsic element) plus an extra amount to pay for the risk of even higher profits (the time element).

The net profit to a speculator who purchases call options on a currency is based on a comparison of the selling price of the currency in the foreign exchange market versus the exercise price paid for the currency and the premium paid for the call option.

EXAMPLE

Jim is a speculator who buys a call option on euros with a strike price of £0.700 and a December settlement date. The current spot price as of that date is about £0.682. Jim pays a premium of £0.005 per unit (euro) for the call option. Assume there are no brokerage fees. At the expiration date, the spot rate of the euro reaches £0.724. *Where the spot rate is above the strike price, the call option will be exercised.* Jim exercises the call option and then immediately sells the pounds at the spot rate to a bank. To determine Jim's profit or loss, first compute his revenues from selling the currency. Then, subtract from this amount the purchase price of the euros when exercising the option, and also subtract the purchase price of the option (the premium). The computations follow. Assume one option contract specifies 150,000 units.

Position at settlement for Jim as PURCHASER of a European call option on 150,000 euros	Per Unit	Per Contract Decision: EXERCISE OPTION
Selling price of euro (on the currency markets)	£0.724	£108,600 (£0.724 × 150,000 units)
−Purchase price of euro (by exercising the option)	−0.700	−£105,000 (£0.700 × 150,000 units)
−Premium paid for option	−0.005	−£750 (£0.005 × 150,000 units)
=Net profit	£0.019	£2,850 (£0.019 × 150,000 units)

Assume that Linda was the seller of the call option purchased by Jim. Also assume that Linda would purchase euros only if and when the option was exercised, at which time she must provide the euros at the exercise price of £0.700. Using the information in this example, Linda's net loss from selling the call option is derived here:

Position at settlement for Linda as SELLER (or writer) of a European call option	Per Unit	Per Contract
Selling price of euro (as per option contract)	£0.700	£105,000 (£0.700 × 150,000 units)
−Purchase price of euro (on the currency markets)	−0.724	−£108,600 (£0.724 × 150,000 units)
+Premium received for option	0.005	£750 (£0.005 × 150,000 units)
=Net profit (+) or loss (−)	−£0.019	£2,850 (£0.019 × 150,000 units)

As a second example, assume Jim tries his luck again:

- Call option premium on euros = £0.005 per unit.
- Strike price = $0.730.
- One option contract represents 150,000 euros.

In his previous contract Jim took out a strike price above the current spot and the value of the euro rose above the strike price and a profit was made. Here he is trying to do the same thing and hoping that the spot will rise above the level it was at the end of his previous contract. Only this time, at the settlement date the spot rate is £0.720, well below the strike price. *Where the spot rate is below the strike price, the call option will not be exercised and allowed to lapse.* The net position to speculator Jim is computed as follows:

Position at settlement for Jim as PURCHASER of a European call option	Per Unit	Per Contract Decision: DO NOT EXERCISE OPTION
Selling price of euro (on the currency markets)	£0.720	Option allowed to lapse
−Purchase price of euro (by exercising the option)	£0.730	Option allowed to lapse

−Premium paid for option	−0.005	−£750 (£0.005 × 150,000 units)
=Net profit (+) or loss (−)	−£0.005	£2,850 (£0.019 × 150,000 units)

For the seller or writer of the call option, Jim's losses are the writers gains:

Position at settlement for Linda as SELLER or writer of a European call option	Per Unit	Per Contract
Selling price of euro (as per option contract)	£0.730	Option allowed to lapse by purchaser
Purchase price of euro (as per the markets)	£0.720	Option allowed to lapse by purchaser
+Premium received for option	+0.005	£750 (£0.005 × 150,000 units)
=Net profit (+) or loss (−)	+£0.005	£750 (£0.005 × 150,000 units)

Further points:

■ When brokerage fees are ignored, the currency call purchaser's gain will be the seller's loss. The currency call purchaser's expenses represent the seller's revenues, and the purchaser's revenues represent the seller's expenses. Yet, because it is possible for purchasers and sellers of options to close out their positions, the relationship described here will not hold unless both parties begin and close out their positions at the same time.

  An owner of a currency option may simply sell the option to someone else before the expiration date rather than exercising it. The owner can still earn profits, since the option premium changes over time, reflecting the probability that the option can be exercised and the potential profit from exercising it.

■ Where the spot rate is above the strike price, the call option will be exercised. Where the spot rate is below the strike price, the call option will not be exercised and allowed to lapse. This relationship holds even where there is an overall loss as exercising makes a contribution – the loss would be greater if the option were not exercised.

■ The purchaser of the call option is the party that decides whether or not the option is to be exercised. The purchaser cannot lose more than his or her premium – it is a common error when making calculations of gains or losses to forget this point and forget that where an option is not exercised there will be no purchase or sale of currency.

Profit and break-even point from speculation. Regardless of the number of units in a contract, a purchaser of a call option will break even if the spot rate less the strike price equals the premium.

E X A M P L E

Based on the information in the previous example (a strike price of £0.73 and a premium of £0.005), the actions and profit or loss for the purchaser of a call option at varying strike prices including the break even level would be as in the following table. Note that transaction costs have not been taken into account – the administration costs brokerage fees etc. Also, where the spot price equals the strike price, there is no point in exercising. As a check on the calculations, note that losses cannot exceed the premium.

Position at settlement for purchaser of a European call option for a range of potential selling prices	Per Unit Do not exercise	Per Unit Do not exercise	Per Unit Do not exercise	Per Unit Exercise	Per Unit Exercise	Per Unit Exercise
Selling price of euro (on the currency markets) if option exercised	£0.720	£0.728	£0.730	£0.732	£0.735	£0.740
−Purchase price of euro (by exercising the option)	£0.730	£0.730	£0.730	£0.730	£0.730	£0.730
−Premium paid for option	−0.005	−0.005	−0.005	−0.005	−0.005	−0.005
=Net profit (+) or loss (−) per unit	−£0.005	−£0.005	−£0.005	−£0.003	£0.000	+£0.005

CURRENCY PUT OPTIONS

The purchaser of a currency put option receives the right to *sell* a currency at a specified price (the strike price) within a specified period of time for an American option or at the settlement date in the case of a European option. The reason for using the terms calls and puts should now be a little clearer. Options offer the right to buy and sell the right to buy, and buy and sell the right to sell! It is less confusing to say that options offer the right to buy and sell calls and puts. As with currency call options, the purchaser of a put option is not obliged to exercise the option. Therefore, the maximum potential loss to the owner of the put option is the price (or premium) paid for the option contract.

A currency put option is said to be *in the money* (i.e. profitable) when the present exchange rate is less than the strike price. Again the term "in the money" simply refers to the fact that, at these prices, the purchaser of the option is due to be paid. This means that the purchaser of the put option has the right to sell at the strike price which is above the current market price. Where a put option is *at the money*, the present exchange rate equals the strike price, and *out of the money* when the present exchange rate exceeds the strike price. For a given currency and settlement or expiration date, an in-the-money put option will require a higher premium than options that are at the money or out of the money.

Factors affecting currency put option premiums

The put option premium (referred to as P) is primarily influenced by three factors:

$$P = f(S - X, T, \sigma)$$

Where:

$S - X$ = the difference between the spot exchange rate (S) and the strike or exercise price (X),
T = the time to maturity,
σ = the volatility of the currency changes, as measured by the standard deviation of the movements in the currency.

The relationships between the put option premium and these factors, which also influence call option premiums as described earlier, are summarized next.

First, the spot rate of a currency relative to the strike price is important. The lower the spot rate relative to the strike price, the more valuable the put option will be, because

> ### Exhibit 5.9 Put option quote
>
> | Stock Exchange £/$ quote for put options for $50,000 – European style options | | |
> |---|---|---|
> | Spot: £0.67:$1 | | |
> | current date: November | | |
> | Strike price value of $1 in pounds | Strike Price value of $1 in pounds | |
> | | December | January |
> | £0.60 | £0.003 | £0.010 |
> | £0.65 | £0.018 | £0.027 |
> | £0.70 | £0.044 | £0.053 |

Notes:

- A January put option at a strike price of £0.65 would incur a cost £0.027 × 50,000 = £1,350 known as the contract premium.

- The buyer of the January put option at a strike price of £0.65 will collect £0.01 × 50,000 = £2,500 for every penny (£0.01) the spot rate is below £0.65 at the designated date in January.

- If the spot rate is above £0.65 in January, the option will not be exercised and will be allowed to lapse, the premium will have been forfeited by the purchaser of the call option.

- A European option can only be exercised at the exercise date – an American option any time up to the exercise date.

there is a higher probability that the option will be exercised. Recall that just the opposite relationship held for call options. A second factor influencing put option premium is the length of time until the expiration date. As with currency call options, the longer the time to expiration, the greater the put option premium as a payout is more likely due to the greater uncertainty of prices over time. In other words we can be relatively sure that a spot rate that is say 5% out of the money is not going to be in the money tomorrow. So if settlement were tomorrow the premium would be very small. But if settlement were to be a year hence, the possibility of being in the money is much greater. A longer period creates a higher probability that the currency will move into a range where it will be feasible to exercise the option (whether it is a put or a call). These relationships can be verified by assessing quotations of put option premiums for a specified currency (see Exhibit 5.9). A third factor that influences the put option premium is the variability of a currency. As with currency call options, the greater the variability, the greater the put option premium will be, again reflecting a higher probability that the option may be exercised.

Hedging with currency put options

Corporations with open positions in foreign currencies can use currency put options in some cases to cover these positions.

EXAMPLE

Assume that Hookway ltd (UK) has exported products to Canada and invoiced the products in Canadian dollars (at the request of the Canadian importers). Hookway is concerned that the Canadian dollars it is receiving may depreciate to a level that would severely affect its profits. To insulate itself against possible depreciation, Hookway purchases Canadian dollar put options, which entitle it to sell Canadian dollars at a strike price that would avoid such losses. In essence, Hookway locks in the minimum rate at which it can exchange Canadian dollars for British pounds over a specified period of time. If the Canadian dollar appreciates over this time period, Hookway can let the put options expire and sell the Canadian dollars it receives at the prevailing spot rate.

Speculating with currency put options

Individuals may speculate with currency put options based on their expectations of the future movements in a particular currency. For example, speculators who expect that the British pound will depreciate can purchase British pound put options, which will entitle them to sell British pounds at a specified strike price. If the pound's spot rate depreciates as expected, the speculators can in theory purchase pounds at the spot rate and exercise their put options by selling these pounds at the strike price. In practice, the current market premium of the option they are holding will include this profit, so they could simply sell their put option.

Speculators can also attempt to profit from selling currency put options. The seller of such options is obliged to purchase the specified currency at the strike price from the owner who exercises the put option. Speculators who believe the currency will appreciate (or at least will not depreciate) may sell a currency put option. If the currency appreciates over the entire period, the option will not be exercised. This is an ideal situation for put option sellers, since they keep the premiums received when selling the options and bear no cost.

EXAMPLE

A put option contract on US dollars specifies the following information:

- Put option premium on the US dollar ($) = £0.02 per unit.
- Strike price = £0.60.
- One option contract represents $50,000.

A speculator who had purchased this put option decided to exercise the option at the expiration date, when the spot rate of the dollar was £0.55. The speculator purchased the pounds in the spot market at that time. Given this information, the net profit to the purchaser of the put option is calculated as follows:

MANAGING FOR VALUE
Cisco's dilemma when hedging with put options

When Cisco Systems' European subsidiaries remit funds to their US parent, Cisco may consider purchasing put options to lock in the rate at which the euros will convert to dollars. The put options also offer the flexibility of letting the options expire if the prevailing exchange rate of the euro is higher than the options' exercise price. Several put options are available to Cisco and other MNCs that wish to hedge their currency positions. At a given point in time, some put options are deep out of the money, meaning that the prevailing exchange rate is high above the exercise price. These options are cheaper (have a lower premium), as they are unlikely to be exercised because their exercise price is too low. At the same time, other put options have an exercise price that is currently above the prevailing exchange rate and are therefore more likely to be exercised. Consequently, these options are more expensive.

Cisco must weigh the tradeoff when using put options to hedge. It can create a hedge that is cheap, but the options can be exercised only if the currency's spot rate declines substantially. Alternatively, Cisco can create a hedge that can be exercised at a more favourable exchange rate, but it must pay a higher premium for the options. If Cisco's goal in using put options is simply to prevent a major loss if the currency weakens substantially, it may be willing to use an inexpensive put option (low exercise price, low premium). However, if its goal is to ensure that the currency can be exchanged at a more favourable exchange rate, Cisco will use a more expensive put option (high exercise price, high premium). By selecting currency options with an exercise price and premium that fits their objectives, Cisco and other MNCs can increase their value.

The net profit to a speculator from purchasing put options on a currency is based on a comparison of the exercise price at which the currency can be sold versus the purchase price of the currency and the premium paid for the put option.

Position at settlement for PURCHASER of a European put option	Per Unit	Per Contract
Selling price of $ from exercising the put option	£0.60	£30,000 (£0.60 × 50,000 units)
−Purchase price of $	£0.55	−£27,500 (−£0.55 × 50,000 units)
−Premium paid	−£0.02	−£1,000 (−£0.02 × 50,000 units)
=Net profit	£0.03	£1,500 (£0.03 × 50,000 units)

Assuming that the seller of the put option sold the pounds received immediately after the option was exercised, the net loss to the seller of the put option is calculated as follows:

Position at settlement for SELLER of a European put option	Per Unit	Per Contract
Selling price of $	£0.55	£27,500 (−£0.55 × 50,000 units)
−Purchase price of $ from the put option having been exercised	−£0.60	−£30,000 (£0.60 × 50,000 units)
+Premium received	+£0.02	+£1,000 (−£0.02 × 50,000 units)
=Net profit	−£0.03	−£1,500 (£0.03 × 50,000 units)

The seller of the put options could simply refrain from selling the dollars (after being forced to buy them at £0.60 per dollar) until the spot rate of the dollar rises. However, there is no guarantee that the dollar will reverse its direction and begin to appreciate. The seller's net loss could potentially be greater if the dollar's spot rate continued to fall, unless the dollars were sold immediately.

With the simplifying assumptions of the previous example, whatever an owner of a put option gains, the seller loses, and vice versa. This relationship would hold if brokerage costs did not exist and if the buyer and seller of options entered and closed their positions at the same time. Brokerage fees for currency options exist, however, and are very similar in magnitude to those of currency futures contracts.

Speculating with combined put and call options. For volatile currencies, one possible speculative strategy is to create a **straddle**, which uses both a put option and a call option at the same exercise price. This may seem unusual because owning a put option is appropriate for expectations that the currency will depreciate, while owning a call option is appropriate for expectations that the currency will appreciate. However, a company may simply wish to protect against volatility in the markets which of itself may affect profits. For example a sharply appreciating dollar will be good for the translated dollar revenues of a MNC; but may adversely affect its US sales due to cheap imports into the US. A similar argument can be made for a depreciating dollar. The overall effect of large changes may therefore be indeterminate and worthwhile hedging.

USING
THE WEB

Options prices Information on currency options can be obtained on the website of the Philadelphia Stock Exchange. In particular, the link http://www.phlx.com/products/currency/currency.html provides contract specifications and volume information for the currency options contracts that are traded on that exchange.

Alternatively, a speculator might anticipate that a currency will be substantially affected by current economic events yet be uncertain of the exact way it will be affected. By purchasing a put option and a call option, the speculator will gain if the currency moves substantially in either direction. Although two options are purchased and only one is exercised, the gains could more than offset the costs.

Currency options market efficiency. If the currency options market is efficient, the premiums on currency options properly reflect all available information. Under these conditions, it may be difficult for speculators to consistently generate abnormal profits when speculating in this market. Research has found that the currency options market is efficient after controlling for transaction costs. Although some trading strategies could have generated abnormal gains in specific periods, they would have generated large losses if implemented in other periods. It is difficult to know which strategy would generate abnormal profits in future periods.

CONTINGENCY GRAPHS FOR CURRENCY OPTIONS

A contingency graph for currency options illustrates the potential gain or loss for various exchange rate scenarios.

Contingency graph for a purchaser of a call option

A contingency graph for a purchaser of a call option compares the price paid for the call option to potential payoffs to be received for a range of future exchange rate rates.

Suppose a European style call option on dollars is available with a strike price of £0.65 and a call premium of £0.03. The speculator plans to exercise the option on the expiration date (if appropriate at that time) and then immediately sell the dollars received in the spot market. Under these conditions, a **contingency graph** can be created to measure the profit or loss per unit (see Exhibit 5.10a). Notice that if the future spot rate is £0.65 or less, the net loss per unit is £0.03 (ignoring transaction costs). This represents the loss of the premium per unit paid for the option, as the option would not be exercised. At all rates above £0.65 per unit the option will be exercised. Between the future spot prices of £0.65 and £0.68 exercising the option reduces the losses and is therefore worthwhile. Note that it is a common mistake to think that because an overall loss per unit is being made the option should still not be exercised. The important point here is that the loss is reduced through exercising, i.e. it will be less than the premium of £0.03. Breakeven is at £0.68. Here the gains from exercising the option are £0.68 − £0.65 = £0.03 and exactly match the premium paid. Breakeven for a call option is therefore the strike price plus the premium.

Contingency graph for a seller of a call option

A contingency graph for the seller of a call option compares the premium received from selling a call option to the potential payoffs made to the buyer of the call option for various exchange rate scenarios. Remember that the seller or writer of an option hopes that the option will not be exercised and that the option will be out of the money for the purchaser.

E X A M P L E

Exhibit 5.10b provides a contingency graph for a speculator who sold the call option described in the previous example. It assumes that this seller, if the option were to be

Exhibit 5.10a Contingency graph for the purchaser of the call option

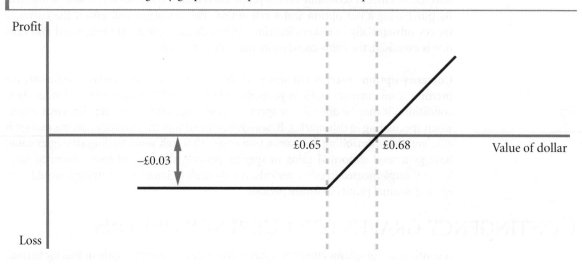

Exhibit 5.10b Contingency graph for the seller (or writer) of the call option

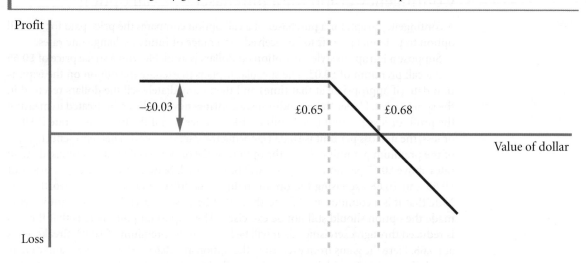

exercised, would purchase the pounds in the spot market at the exercise date (transaction costs have not been included). At future spot rates of less than £0.65, the net gain to the seller would be the premium of £0.03 per unit, as the option would not have been exercised. If the future spot rate is £0.67, the seller would gain £0.01 per unit on the option transaction paying £0.67 for the dollars in the spot market and selling dollars for £0.65 to fulfil the exercise request. This loss would be offset by the premium of £0.03 per unit received, resulting in a net gain of £0.01 per unit.

The breakeven point is at £0.68 as outlined in the previous example, and the net gain to the seller of a call option becomes negative at all future spot rates higher than that point. Notice that the contingency graphs for the buyer and seller of call options are mirror images of one another. This reflects the fact that in this simplified scenario the

Exhibit 5.10c Contingency graph for the purchaser of the put option

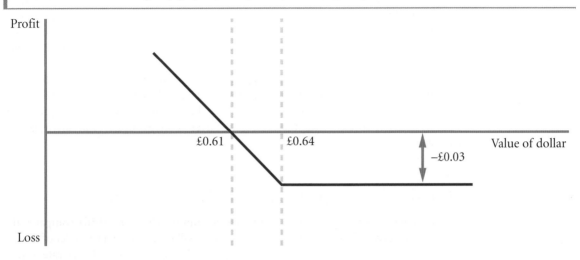

Exhibit 5.10d Contingency graph for the seller (or writer) of the put option

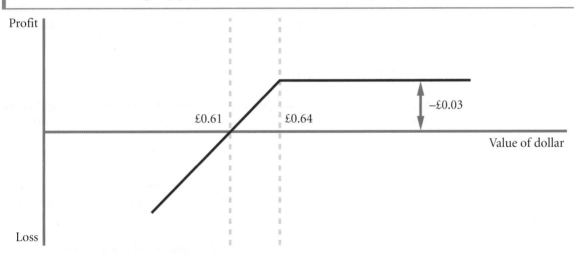

seller's gain is the purchaser's loss and vice versa – this phenomenon is sometimes termed a zero sum game. The same applies to put options.

The seller of the call option faces potentially unlimited losses. This exposure can be limited by buying a call option at a higher strike price (say, £0.72 for $1) at rates above the higher strike price the losses from selling the call will be offset by the gains on the purchased call.

Contingency graph for a buyer of a put option

A contingency graph for a buyer of a put option compares the premium paid for the put option to potential payoffs received for a range of future exchange rates.

Exhibit 5.10c shows the net gains to a buyer of a US dollar put option with an exercise price of £0.64 and a premium of £0.03 per unit. If the future spot rate is above £0.64, the option will not be exercised – the purchaser of the option will make more money by selling on the spot market than by selling to the writer or seller of the put option. At any rate below £0.64 the option will be exercised. So, at a future spot rate of £0.63, the put option will be exercised even though there is an overall loss of £0.02 per unit (£0.64 – £0.63 – £0.03). The point here is that exercise is still worthwhile as the loss has been reduced. The breakeven point in this example is £0.61, since this is the future spot rate that will generate £0.03 per unit from exercising the option to offset the £0.03 premium. At any future spot rates of less than £0.61, the buyer of the put option will earn a positive net gain.

Contingency graph for a seller of a put option

A contingency graph for the seller of this put option (Exhibit 10.5d) compares the premium received from selling the option to the possible payoffs that the seller of the put option will have to make to the buyer of the put option for various exchange rate scenarios. As with call option writers, the hope is that the option will be out of the money and the seller will retain the premium.

Note that the graph for the seller of a put option is the mirror image of the contingency graph for the buyer of the same put option. Again as with call options, the seller's position is essentially speculative. Such speculation offers a service to MNCs who may be purchasing the option to protect against a loss of profits on international transactions.

CONDITIONAL CURRENCY OPTIONS

A currency option can be structured with a conditional premium, meaning that the premium paid for the option is conditioned on the actual movement in the currency's value over the period of concern. This kind of option enables the instrument to compete more with futures where there is no premium (but remember that futures does not offer a range of strike prices nor the possibility of not exercising). The basic idea is to charge a higher premium than a traditional option when conditions are favourable and no premium when conditions are less favourable. It is rather like giving an option on an option!

Jensen ltd a UK-based MNC, needs to sell dollars that it will receive in 60 days. It can negotiate a traditional currency put option on dollars in which the exercise price is £0.60 and the premium is £0.03 per unit.

Alternatively, it can negotiate a conditional currency option with a commercial bank. The exercise price of £0.60 is supplemented by a so-called trigger of £0.62. If the dollar's value falls below the exercise price by the expiration date, Jensen will exercise the option, thereby receiving £0.60 per pound, and it will not have to pay a premium for the option. These will be unexpectedly bad circumstances for Jensen, so not paying the premium will be a welcome relief.

If the dollar's value is between the exercise price (£0.60) and the trigger (£0.62), the option will not be exercised, and Jensen will not need to pay a premium. For Jensen these will be circumstances that the company will judge to be very likely – so the judgement will be that the company will probably not have to pay the premium. If the dollar's value exceeds the trigger of £0.62, Jensen will pay a premium of £0.04 per unit. Notice that this premium will be higher than the premium that would be paid for a basic put option. Jensen may not mind this outcome, however, because it will be receiving a high price for the dollar from converting its dollar receivables on the spot market.

Jensen must determine whether the potential advantage of the conditional option (avoiding the payment of a premium under some conditions) outweighs the potential disadvantage (paying a higher premium than the premium for a traditional put option on US dollars).

The potential advantage and disadvantage are illustrated in Exhibit 5.11. At exchange rates less than or equal to the trigger level (£0.62), the conditional option results in a larger payment to Jensen by the amount of the premium that would have been paid for the basic option. Conversely, at exchange rates above the trigger level, the conditional option results in a lower payment to Jensen, as its premium of £0.04 exceeds the premium of £0.03 per unit paid on a basic option. With the ordinary put option the minimum net conversion price of the dollar will be £0.57 (i.e. £0.60 – £0.03), the conditional option has a minimum price of £0.58 (i.e. £0.62 – £0.04).

The choice of a basic option versus a conditional option is dependent on expectations of the currency's exchange rate over the period of concern and the firm's level of risk aversion. A firm that was very confident that the pound's value would not exceed £0.64 and did not want to convert the dollars at anything less than £0.58 in the previous example would prefer the conditional currency option.

Conditional currency options are also available for firms needing to purchase a foreign currency in the near future. There are variations, some conditional options require a premium if the trigger is reached anytime up until the expiration date; others require a premium only if the exchange rate is beyond the trigger as of the expiration date.

Another variation is a cylinder option (typically between a bank and an MNC) or zero cost option that guarantees an exchange rate between two agreed limits (see Appendix 5B for further details).

Taken together the zero cost option and the contingency option show that sophisticated insurance contracts can be built from using basic calls and puts. The term "financial engineering" has been used to describe the complexity of such options.

Exhibit 5.11 Comparison of conditional and basic currency options

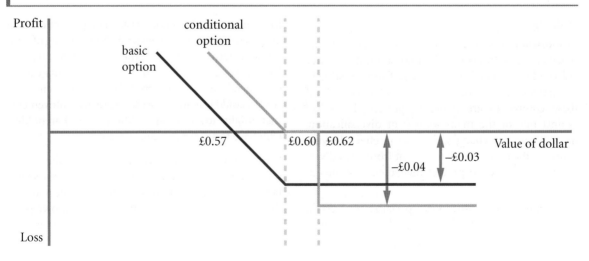

European and American currency options

The discussion of currency options has used a mixture of American and European style options. European style options can be exercised only at the settlement or expiration date, whereas American options can be exercised up to and including the settlement date. If a company wishes to terminate a European style option before the settlement date, the option can be sold in the secondary market. If the option is "in the money" at the time of sale, the price of the option will take the "in the money" position into account, so some but not all of the potential benefit will be recovered.

SUMMARY

- A forward contract specifies a standard volume of a particular currency to be exchanged on a particular date. Such a contract can be purchased by a firm to hedge payables or sold by a firm to hedge receivables.

- A currency futures contract can be purchased by speculators who expect the currency to appreciate. Conversely, it can be sold by speculators who expect that currency to depreciate. If the currency depreciates, the value of the futures contract declines, allowing those speculators to benefit when they close out their positions.

- Futures contracts on a particular currency can be purchased by corporations that have payables in that currency and wish to hedge against the possible appreciation of that currency. Conversely, these contracts can be sold by corporations that have receivables in that currency and wish to hedge against the possible depreciation of that currency.

- Currency options are classified as call options or put options. Call options allow the right to purchase a specified currency at a specified exchange rate by a specified expiration date. Put options allow the right to sell a specified currency at a specified exchange rate by a specified expiration date.

- Call options on a specific currency can be purchased by speculators who expect that currency to appreciate. Put options on a specific currency can be purchased by speculators who expect that currency to depreciate.

- Currency call options are commonly purchased by corporations that have payables in a currency that is expected to appreciate. Currency put options are commonly purchased by corporations that have receivables in a currency that is expected to depreciate.

CRITICAL DEBATE

Hedging.

Proposition. MNCs should not protect against currency changes. Investors take into account currency risks and the diversification benefits from investing in companies that conduct international business. But if these companies are going to protect themselves against one of the main sources of diversification, namely currency changes, they are in effect denying investors the opportunity to benefit from such diversification in order to protect their own positions as directors.

Opposing view. Companies specialize in certain activities that generally do not include currency speculation. Derivatives enable such companies to special-

ize in more clearly defined risks. The protection is in any case only short term, no protection is being offered for long-term changes in the value of a currency. Derivatives simply avoid distortion to profits caused by unusual changes to currency values. Such currency shocks could lead to abnormal share price movements that might adversely affect individual shareholders who have to sell for personal reasons.

With whom do you agree? How should the investment community view business risk? Should shareholders be more aware of the currency risk policy of the company? Are directors protecting their own positions at the expense of the shareholder? Offer your own opinion on this issue.

SELF TEST

Answers are provided in Appendix A at the back of the text.

1. A call option on US dollars with a strike price of £0.60 is purchased by a speculator for a premium of £0.06 per unit. Assume there are 50,000 units in this option contract. If the US dollar's spot rate is £0.65 at the time the option is exercised, what is the net profit or loss per unit to the speculator if the option were to be exercised now? What is the net profit or loss for one contract? What would the spot rate need to be at the time the option is exercised for the speculator to break even? What is the net profit per unit to the seller of this option if exercised now?

2. A put option on Australian dollars with a strike price of £0.53 is purchased by a speculator for a premium of £0.02. If the Australian dollar's spot rate is £0.50 on the expiration date, should the speculator exercise the option on this date or let the option expire? What is the net profit or loss per unit to the speculator? What is the net profit or loss per unit to the seller of this put option?

3. Longer-term currency options are becoming more popular for hedging exchange rate risk. Why do you think some firms decide to hedge by using other techniques instead of purchasing long-term currency options?

QUESTIONS AND APPLICATIONS

1. **Forward versus futures contracts.** Compare and contrast forward and futures contracts.

2. **Using currency futures.**
   a. How can currency futures be used by corporations?
   b. How can currency futures be used by speculators?

3. **Currency options.** Differentiate between a currency call option and a currency put option.

4. **Forward premium.** Compute the forward discount or premium for the Mexican peso whose 90-day forward rate is £0.05 and spot rate is £0.051. State whether your answer is a discount or premium.

5. **Effects of a forward contract.** How can a forward contract backfire?

6. **Hedging with currency options.** When would a US firm consider purchasing a call option on euros for hedging? When would a US firm consider purchasing a put option on euros for hedging?

7. **Speculating with currency options.** When should a speculator purchase a call option on Australian dollars? When should a speculator purchase a put option on Australian dollars?

8. **Currency call option premiums.** List the factors that affect currency call option premiums and briefly explain the relationship that exists for each. Do you think an at-the-money call option in euros has a higher or lower premium than an at-the-money call option on dollars (assuming the expiration date and the total dollar value represented by each option are the same for both options)?

9. **Currency put option premiums.** List the factors that affect currency put options and briefly explain the relationship that exists for each.

10. **Speculating with currency call options.** Randy Rudecki purchased a call option on British pounds for 0.02 euros per unit. The strike price was 1.45 euros, and the spot rate at the time the option was exercised was 1.46 euros. Assume there are 31,250 units in a British pound option. What was Randy's net profit on this option?

11. **Speculating with currency put options.** Alice Duever purchased a put option on dollars for £0.04 per unit. The strike price was £0.55, and the spot rate at the time the dollar option was exercised was £0.63. Assume there are 50,000 units in a US dollar option. What was Alice's net profit on the option?

12. **Selling currency call options.** Mike Suerth sold a call option on Canadian dollars for £0.01 per unit. The strike price was £0.42, and the spot rate at the time the option was exercised was £0.46. Assume Mike did not obtain Canadian dollars until the option was exercised. Also assume that there are 50,000 units in a Canadian dollar option. What was Mike's net profit on the call option?

13. **Selling currency put options.** Brian Tull sold a put option on Canadian dollars for £0.02 per unit. The strike price was £0.42, and the spot rate at the time the option was exercised was £0.40. Assume Brian immediately sold off the Canadian dollars received when the option was exercised. Also assume that there are 50,000 units in a Canadian dollar option. What was Brian's net profit on the put option?

14. **Forward versus currency option contracts.** What are the advantages and disadvantages to an MNC that uses currency options on dollars rather than a forward contract on dollars to hedge its exposure in dollars? Explain why an MNC may use forward contracts to hedge committed transactions and use currency options to hedge contracts that are anticipated but not committed. Why might forward contracts be advantageous for committed transactions, and currency options be advantageous for anticipated transactions?

15. **Speculating with currency futures.** Assume that the euro's spot rate has moved in cycles over time. How might you try to use futures contracts on euros to capitalize on this tendency? How could you determine whether such a strategy would have been profitable in previous periods?

16. **Hedging with Currency Derivatives.** Assume that the transactions listed in the first column of the following table are anticipated by US firms that have no other foreign transactions. Place an "X" in the table wherever you see possible ways to hedge each of the transactions.

17. **Price movements of currency futures.** Assume that on 1 November, the spot rate of the British pound was £0.63 and the price on a December futures contract was £0.64. Assume that the pound depreciated during November so that by 30 November it was worth £0.60.
    a. What do you think happened to the futures price over the month of November? Why?
    b. If you had known that this would occur, would you have purchased or sold a December futures contract in pounds on 1 November? Explain.

18. **Speculating with currency futures.** Assume that a March futures contract on Mexican pesos was available in January for $0.09 per unit. Also assume that forward contracts were available for the same settlement date at a price of $0.092 per peso. How could speculators capitalize on this situation, assuming zero transaction costs? How would such speculative activity affect the difference between the forward contract price and the futures price?

	Forward Contract		Futures Contract		Options Contract	
	Forward purchase	Forward sale	Buy futures	Sell futures	Purchase call	Purchase put
a. George ltd plans to purchase Japanese goods denominated in yen.						
b. Harvard ltd will sell goods to Japan, denominated in yen.						
c. Yale plc has a subsidiary in Australia that will be remitting funds to the UK parent.						
d. Brown ltd needs to pay off existing loans that are denominated in Canadian dollars.						
e. Princeton ltd may purchase a company in Japan in the near future (but the deal may not go through).						

19. **Speculating with currency call options.** LSU Corp purchased Canadian dollar call options for speculative purposes. If these options are exercised, LSU will immediately sell the Canadian dollars in the spot market. Each option was purchased for a premium of $0.03 per unit, with an exercise price of $0.75. LSU plans to wait until the expiration date before deciding whether to exercise the options. Of course, LSU will exercise the options at that time only if it is feasible to do so. In the following table, fill in the net profit (or loss) per unit to LSU Corp based on the listed possible spot rates of the Canadian dollar on the expiration date.

Possible spot rate on Canadian dollar on expiration date	Net profit (loss) per unit to LSU corporation
$0.76	
$0.78	
$0.80	
$0.82	
$0.85	
$0.87	

20. **Speculating with currency put options.** Auburn ltd has purchased Canadian dollar put options for speculative purposes. Each option was purchased for a premium of £0.02 per unit, with an exercise price of £0.48 per unit. Auburn ltd will purchase the Canadian dollars just before it exercises the options (if it is feasible to exercise the options). It plans to wait until the expiration date before deciding whether to exercise the options. In the following table, fill in the net profit (or loss) per unit to Auburn ltd based on the listed possible spot rates of the Canadian dollar on the expiration date.

Possible spot rate on Canadian dollar on expiration date	Net profit (loss) per unit to Auburn ltd
£0.42	
£0.44	
£0.46	
£0.48	
£0.50	
£0.52	

21. **Speculating with currency call options.** Bama plc has sold dollar call options for speculative purposes. The option premium was £0.04 per unit, and the exercise price was £0.54. Bama will purchase the dollars on the day the options are exercised (if the options are exercised) in order to fulfil its obligation. In the following table, fill in the net profit (or loss) to Bama plc if the listed spot rate exists at the time the purchaser of the call options considers exercising them.

Possible spot rate at the time the purchaser of the call option (American style) considers exercising them	Net profit (loss) per unit to Bama plc
£0.48	
£0.50	
£0.52	
£0.54	
£0.56	
£0.58	
£0.60	

22. **Speculating with currency put options.** Bulldog ltd has sold Australian dollar put options at a premium of £0.01 per unit, and an exercise price of £0.42 per unit. It has forecasted the Australian dollar's lowest level over the period of concern as shown in the following table. Determine the net profit (or loss) per unit to Bulldog ltd if each level occurs and the put options are exercised at that time.

Possible value of Australian dollar	Net profit (loss) per unit to Bulldog ltd if value occurs
£0.38	
£0.39	
£0.40	
£0.41	
£0.42	

23. **Hedging with currency derivatives.** A US professional football team plans to play an exhibition game in the United Kingdom next year. Assume that all expenses will be paid by the British government, and that the team will receive a cheque for 1 million pounds. The team anticipates that the pound will depreciate substantially by the scheduled date of the game. In addition, the

National Football League must approve the deal, and approval (or disapproval) will not occur for three months. How can the team hedge its position? What is there to lose by waiting three months to see if the exhibition game is approved before hedging?

ADVANCED QUESTIONS

24. **Risk of currency futures.** Currency futures markets are commonly used as a means of capitalizing on shifts in currency values, because the value of a futures contract tends to move in line with the change in the corresponding currency value. Recently, many currencies appreciated against the dollar. Most speculators anticipated that the dollar's value would continue to decline. However, the Fed intervened in the foreign exchange market by immediately buying dollars with foreign currency, causing an abrupt halt in the decline in the value of the dollar. Participants that had sold dollar futures contracts for a range of other currencies incurred large losses.

    a. Explain why the central bank's intervention caused such panic among currency futures traders with buy positions.

    b. Some traders with sell positions on dollars may have responded immediately to the central bank's intervention by buying futures contracts. Why would some speculators with buy positions leave their positions unchanged or even increase their positions by purchasing more futures contracts in response to the central bank's intervention?

25. **Currency straddles.** Reska ltd has constructed a long euro straddle. A call option on euros with an exercise price of £0.61 has a premium of £0.015 per unit. A euro put option has a premium of $0.008 per unit. Some possible euro values at option expiration are shown in the following table. (See Appendix B in this chapter.)

    a. Complete the worksheet and determine the net profit per unit to Reska ltd for each possible future spot rate.

Value of euro at option expiration			
	£0.50	£0.55	£0.60	£0.65
Call				
Put				
Net				

b. Determine the breakeven point(s) of the long straddle. What are the breakeven points of a short straddle using these options?

26. **Currency straddles.** Refer to the previous question, but assume that the call and put option premiums are $0.01 per unit and $0.006 per unit, respectively. (See Appendix B in this chapter.)

    a. Construct a contingency graph for a long euro straddle (call options).

    b. Construct a contingency graph for a short euro straddle (put options).

27. **Currency option contingency graphs.** (See Appendix B in this chapter.) The current spot rate of the Singapore dollar (S$) is £0.34. The following option information is available:

■ Call option premium on Singapore dollar (S$) = £0.015.

■ Put option premium on Singapore dollar (S$) = £0.009.

■ Call and put option strike price = £0.36.

■ One option contract represents S$70,000.

Construct a contingency graph for a short straddle using these options.

28. **Speculating with currency straddles.** Maggie Hawthorne is a currency speculator. She has noticed that recently the dollar has depreciated substantially against the euro. The current exchange rate of the dollar is 0.78 euro. After reading a variety of articles on the subject, she believes that the euro will continue to fluctuate substantially in the months to come. Although most forecasters believe that the euro will depreciate against the dollar in the near future, Maggie thinks that there is also a good possibility of further appreciation. Currently, a call option on euros is available with an exercise price of 0.80 euro and a premium of 0.04 euro. A euro put option with an exercise price of 0.80 euro and a premium of 0.03 euro is also available. (See Appendix B in this chapter.)

    a. Describe how Maggie could use straddles to speculate on the dollar's value.

    b. At option expiration, the value of the dollar is 0.90 euro. What is Maggie's total profit or loss from a long straddle position?

c. What is Maggie's total profit or loss from a long straddle position if the value of the dollar is 0.60 euro at option expiration?

d. What is Maggie's total profit or loss from a long straddle position if the value of the dollar at option expiration is still 0.78 euro?

e. Given your answers to the questions above, when is it advantageous for a speculator to engage in a long straddle? When is it advantageous to engage in a short straddle?

29. **Currency strangles.** (See Appendix B in this chapter.) Assume the following options are currently available for British pounds (£):

■ Call option premium on dollars = £0.04 per unit.

■ Put option premium on dollars = £0.03 per unit.

■ Call option strike price = £0.64.

■ Put option strike price = £0.62.

■ One option contract represents $50,000.

a. Construct a worksheet for a long strangle using these options.

b. Determine the breakeven point(s) for a strangle.

c. If the spot price of the dollar at option expiration is £0.63, what is the total profit or loss to the strangle buyer?

d. If the spot price of the dollar at option expiration is £0.60, what is the total profit or loss to the strangle writer?

30. **Currency straddles.** Refer to the previous question, but assume that the call and put option premiums are £0.035 per unit and £0.025 per unit, respectively. (See Appendix B in this chapter.)
a. Construct a contingency graph for a long pound straddle.
b. Construct a contingency graph for a short pound straddle.

31. **Currency strangles.** The following information is currently available for Canadian dollar (C$) options (see Appendix B in this chapter):
■ Put option exercise price = £0.45.
■ Put option premium = £0.014 per unit.
■ Call option exercise price = £0.46.
■ Call option premium = £0.01 per unit.
■ One option contract represents C$50,000.

a. What is the maximum possible gain the purchaser of a strangle can achieve using these options?

b. What is the maximum possible loss the writer of a strangle can incur?

c. Locate the breakeven point(s) of the strangle.

32. **Currency strangles.** For the following options available on Australian dollars (A$), construct a worksheet and contingency graph for a long strangle. Locate the breakeven points for this strangle. (See Appendix B in this chapter.)
■ Put option strike price = £0.42.
■ Call option strike price = £0.40.
■ Put option premium = £0.01 per unit.
■ Call option premium = £0.02 per unit.

33. **Speculating with currency options.** Barry Egan is a currency speculator. Barry believes that the Japanese yen will fluctuate widely against the euro in the coming month. Currently, one-month call options on Japanese yen (¥) are available with a strike price of 0.0085 euro and a premium of 0.0007 euro per unit. One-month put options on Japanese yen are available with a strike price of 0.0084 euro and a premium of 0.0005 euro per unit. One option contract on Japanese yen contains ¥6.25 million. (See Appendix B in this chapter.)

a. Describe how Barry Egan could utilize these options to speculate on the movement of the Japanese yen.

b. Assume Barry decides to construct a long strangle in yen. What are the breakeven points of this strangle?

c. What is Barry's total profit or loss if the value of the yen in one month is 0.0070 euro?

d. What is Barry's total profit or loss if the value of the yen in one month is $0.0090 euro?

34. **Currency bull spreads and bear spreads.** A call option on dollars exists with a strike price of £0.64 and a premium of £0.04 per unit. Another call option on dollars has a strike price of £0.66 and a premium of £0.03 per unit. (See Appendix B in this chapter.)
a. Complete the worksheet for a bull spread below.

Value of British pound at option expiration				
	£0.58	£0.64	£0.66	£0.72
Call@0.64				
Call@0.66				
Net				

b. What is the breakeven point for this bull spread?

c. What is the maximum profit of this bull spread? What is the maximum loss?

d. If the dollar spot rate is £0.65 at option expiration, what is the total profit or loss for the bull spread?

e. If the dollar spot rate is £0.63 at option expiration, what is the total profit or loss for a bear spread?

35. **Bull spreads and bear spreads.** Two dollar put options are available with exercise prices of £0.70 and £0.72. The premiums associated with these options are £0.02 and £0.03 per unit, respectively. (See Appendix B in this chapter.)

Value of British pound at option expiration				
	£0.65	£0.70	£0.75	£0.80
Put@0.70				
Put@0.72				
Net				

a. Describe how a bull spread can be constructed using these put options. What is the difference between using put options versus call options to construct a bull spread?

b. Complete the worksheet.

c. At option expiration, the spot rate of the pound is £0.70. What is the bull spreader's total gain or loss?

d. At option expiration, the spot rate of the pound is £0.66. What is the bear spreader's total gain or loss?

36. **Profits from using currency options and futures.** On 2 July, the two-month futures rate of the Argentine peso contained a 2% discount (unannualized). There was a call option on pesos with an exercise price that was equal to the spot rate. There was also a put option on pesos with an exercise price equal to the spot rate. The premium

on each of these options was 3% of the spot rate at that time. On 2 September, the option expired. Go to http://www.oanda.com (or any website that has foreign exchange rate quotations) and determine the direct quote of the Argentine peso. You exercised the option on this date if it was feasible to do so.

a. What was your net profit per unit if you had purchased the call option?

b. What was your net profit per unit if you had purchased the put option?

c. What was your net profit per unit if you had purchased a futures contract on 2 July that had a settlement date of 2 September?

d. What was your net profit per unit if you sold a futures contract on 2 July that had a settlement date of 2 September?

37. A UK MNC takes out a cylinder option to buy dollars between the rates of £0.75 and £0.85 per US dollar. (See Appendix B in this chapter.)

a. Describe the implied options in the contract.

b. Explain potential payoffs from the options and their total effect on the MNC's cost of purchasing the dollar.

PROJECT WORKSHOP

38. **Currency futures online.** The website of the Chicago Mercantile Exchange provides information about currency futures and options. Its address is http://www.cme.com.

a. Use this website to review the prevailing prices of currency futures contracts. Do today's futures prices (for contracts with the closest settlement date) generally reflect an increase or decrease from the day before? Is there any news today that might explain the change in the futures prices?

b. Does it appear that futures prices among currencies (for the closest settlement date) are changing in the same direction? Explain.

c. If you purchase a British pound futures contract with the closest settlement date, what is the futures price? Given that a contract is based on 62,500 pounds, what is the dollar amount you will need at the settlement date to fulfil the contract?

DISCUSSION IN THE BOARDROOM

This exercise can be found on the companion website at www.cengage.co.uk/madura_fox.

RUNNING YOUR OWN MNC

This exercise can be found on the companion website at www.cengage.co.uk/madura_fox.

Essays/discussion and articles can be found at the end of Part 1

BLADES PLC CASE STUDY
Use of currency derivative instruments

Blades plc needs to order supplies two months ahead of the delivery date. It is considering an order from a Japanese supplier that requires a payment of 12.5 million yen payable as of the delivery date. Blades has two choices:

- Purchase two call options contracts (since each option contract represents 6,250,000 yen).
- Purchase one futures contract (which represents 12.5 million yen).

The futures price on yen has historically exhibited a slight discount from the existing spot rate. However, the firm would like to use currency options to hedge payables in Japanese yen for transactions two months in advance. Blades would prefer hedging its yen payable position because it is uncomfortable leaving the position open given the historical volatility of the yen. Nevertheless, the firm would be willing to remain unhedged if the yen becomes more stable someday.

Ben Holt, Blades' finance director, prefers the flexibility that options offer over forward contracts or futures contracts because he can let the options expire if the yen depreciates. He would like to use an exercise price that is about 5% above the existing spot rate to ensure that Blades will have to pay no more than 5% above the existing spot rate for a transaction two months beyond its order date, as long as the option premium is no more than 1.6% of the price it would have to pay per unit when exercising the option.

In general, options on the yen have required a premium of about 1.5% of the total transaction amount that would be paid if the option is exercised. For example, recently the yen spot rate was £0.0048 and the firm purchased a call option with an exercise price of £0.00504, which is 5% above the existing spot rate. The premium for this option was £0.000089, which is 1.5% of the price to be paid per yen if the option is exercised.

A recent event caused more uncertainty about the yen's future value, although it did not affect the spot rate or the forward or futures rate of the yen. Specifically, the yen's spot rate was still £0.0048, but the option premium for a call option with an exercise price of $0.00756 was now £0.00010. An alternative call option is available with an expiration date of two months from now; it has a premium of £0.0000756 (which is the size of the premium that would have existed for the option desired before the event), but it is for a call option with an exercise price of £0.00528.

The table below summarizes the option and futures information available to Blades.

	Before Event	After Event	
Spot rate	£0.0048	£0.0048	£0.0048
Option Information:			
Exercise price (£)	£0.00504	£0.00504	£0.00504
Exercise price (% above spot)	5%	5%	10%
Option premium per yen (£)	£0.000076	£0.00010	£0.0000756
Option premium (% of exercise price)	1.5%	2.0%	1.5%
Futures Contract Information:			
Futures price	£0.004608	£0.004608	

As an analyst for Blades, you have been asked to offer insight on how to hedge. Use a spreadsheet to support your analysis of questions 4 and 6.

1. If Blades uses call options to hedge its yen payables, should it use the call option with the exercise price of £0.00504 or the call option with the exercise price of £0.0048? Describe the tradeoff.
2. Should Blades allow its yen position to be unhedged? Describe the tradeoff.
3. Assume there are speculators who attempt to capitalize on their expectation of the yen's movement over the two months between the order and delivery dates by either buying or selling yen futures now and buying or selling yen at the future spot rate. Given this information, what is the *expectation* on the order date of the yen spot rate by the delivery date? (Your answer should consist of one number.)

4. Assume that the firm shares the market consensus of the future yen spot rate. Given this expectation and given that the firm makes a decision (i.e., option, futures contract, remain unhedged) purely on a cost basis, what would be its optimal choice?
5. Will the choice you made as to the optimal hedging strategy in question 4 definitely turn out to be the lowest-cost alternative in terms of actual costs incurred? Why or why not?
6. Now assume that you have determined that the historical standard deviation of the yen is about £0.0003. Based on your assessment, you believe it is highly unlikely that the future spot rate will be more than two standard deviations above the expected spot rate by the delivery date. Also assume that the futures price remains at its current level of £0.004608. Based on this expectation of the future spot rate, what is the optimal hedge for the firm?

SMALL BUSINESS DILEMMA
Use of currency futures and options by the Sports Exports Company

The Sports Exports Company receives pounds each month as payment for the footballs that it exports. It anticipates that the pound will depreciate over time against the dollar.

1. How can the Sports Exports Company use currency futures contracts to hedge against exchange rate risk? Are there any limitations of using currency futures contracts that would prevent the Sports Exports Company from locking in a specific exchange rate at which it can sell all the pounds it expects to receive in each of the upcoming months?
2. How can the Sports Exports Company use currency options to hedge against exchange rate risk? Are

there any limitations of using currency options contracts that would prevent the Sports Exports Company from locking in a specific exchange rate at which it can sell all the pounds it expects to receive in each of the upcoming months?
3. Jim Logan, owner of the Sports Exports Company, is concerned that the pound may depreciate substantially over the next month, but he also believes that the pound could appreciate substantially if specific situations occur. Should Jim use currency futures or currency options to hedge the exchange rate risk? Is there any disadvantage of selecting this method for hedging?

CURRENCY OPTION PRICING

The premiums paid for currency options depend on various factors that must be monitored when anticipating future movements in currency option premiums. Since participants in the currency options market typically take positions based on their expectations as to how the premiums will change over time, they can benefit from understanding how options are priced.

BOUNDARY CONDITIONS

The first step in pricing currency options is to recognize boundary conditions that force the option premium to be within lower and upper bounds.

Lower bounds

The call option premium (C) has a lower bound of at least zero or the spread between the underlying spot exchange rate (S) and the exercise price (X), whichever is greater, as shown below:

$$C = \text{MAX}(0, S - X)$$

This floor is enforced by arbitrage restrictions. For example, assume that the premium on a British pound call option is $0.01, while the spot rate of the pound is $1.62 and the exercise price is $1.60. In this example, the spread ($S - X$) exceeds the call premium, which would allow for arbitrage. One could purchase the call option for $0.01 per unit, immediately exercise the option at $1.60 per pound, and then sell the pounds in the spot market for $1.62 per unit. This would generate an immediate profit of $0.01 per unit. Arbitrage would continue until the market forces realigned the spread ($S - X$) to be less than or equal to the call premium.

The put option premium (P) has a lower bound of zero or the spread between the exercise price (X) and the underlying spot exchange rate (S), whichever is greater, as shown below:

$$P = \text{MAX}(0, X - S)$$

This floor is also enforced by arbitrage restrictions. For example, assume that the premium on a British pound put option is $0.02, while the spot rate of the pound is $1.60 and the exercise price is $1.63. One could purchase the pound put option for $0.02 per unit, purchase pounds in the spot market at $1.60, and immediately exercise the option by selling the pounds at $1.63 per unit. This would generate an immediate profit of $0.01 per unit. Arbitrage would continue until the market forces realigned the spread $(X - S)$ to be less than or equal to the put premium.

Upper bounds

The upper bound for a call option premium is equal to the spot exchange rate (S):

$$C = S$$

If the call option premium ever exceeds the spot exchange rate, one could engage in arbitrage by selling call options for a higher price per unit than the cost of purchasing the underlying currency. Even if those call options are exercised, one could provide the currency that was purchased earlier (the call option was covered). The arbitrage profit in this example is the difference between the amount received when selling the premium and the cost of purchasing the currency in the spot market. Arbitrage would occur until the call option's premium was less than or equal to the spot rate.

The upper bound for a put option is equal to the option's exercise price (X):

$$P = X$$

If the put option premium ever exceeds the exercise price, one could engage in arbitrage by selling put options. Even if the put options are exercised, the proceeds received from selling the put options exceed the price paid (which is the exercise price) at the time of exercise.

Given these boundaries that are enforced by arbitrage, option premiums lie within these boundaries.

APPLICATION OF PRICING MODELS

Although boundary conditions can be used to determine the possible range for a currency option's premium, they do not precisely indicate the appropriate premium for the option. However, pricing models have been developed to price currency options. Based on information about an option (such as the exercise price and time to maturity) and about the currency (such as its spot rate, standard deviation, and interest rate), pricing models can derive the premium on a currency option. The currency option pricing model of Biger and Hull[1] is shown below:

$$C = e^{-r^*T}S . N(d_1) - e^{-rT}X . N(d_1 - \sigma \sqrt{T})$$

d_1	=	$\{[\ln(S/X) + (r - r^* + (\sigma^2/2))\sqrt{T}]/\sigma\}$
C	=	price of the currency call option
S	=	underlying spot exchange rate
X	=	exercise price
r	=	US riskless rate of interest
r^*	=	foreign riskless rate of interest
σ	=	instantaneous standard deviation of the return on a holding of foreign currency

---

1 Nahum Biger and John Hull, "The Valuation of Currency Options", *Financial Management* (Spring 1983), 24–8.

T = option's time maturity expressed as a fraction of a year

$N(\cdot)$ = standard normal cumulative distribution function

This equation is based on the stock option pricing model (OPM) when allowing for continuous dividends. Since the interest gained on holding a foreign security (r^*) is equivalent to a continuously paid dividend on a stock share, this version of the OPM holds completely. The key transformation in adapting the stock OPM to value currency options is the substitution of exchange rates for stock prices. Thus, the percentage change of exchange rates is assumed to follow a diffusion process with constant mean and variance.

Bodurtha and Courtadon[2] have tested the predictive ability of the currency option of the pricing model. They computed pricing errors from the model using 3,326 call options. The model's average percentage pricing error for call options was −6.90%, which is smaller than the corresponding error reported for the dividend-adjusted Black-Scholes stock OPM. Hence, the currency option pricing model has been more accurate than the counterpart stock OPM.

The model developed by Biger and Hull is sometimes referred to as the European model because it does not account for early exercise. European currency options do not allow for early exercise (before the expiration date), while American currency options do allow for early exercise. The extra flexibility of American currency options may justify a higher premium on American currency options than on European currency options with similar characteristics. However, there is not a closed-form model for pricing American currency options. Although various techniques are used to price American currency options, the European model is commonly applied to price American currency options because the European model can be just as accurate.

Bodurtha and Courtadon found that the application of an American currency options pricing model does not improve predictive accuracy. Their average percentage pricing error was −7.07% for all sample call options when using the American model.

Given all other parameters, the currency option pricing model can be used to impute the standard deviation σ. This implied parameter represents the option's market assessment of currency volatility over the life of the option.

Pricing currency put options according to put-call parity

Given the premium of a European call option (called C), the premium for a European put option (called P) on the same currency and same exercise price (X) can be derived from put-call parity, as shown below:

$$P = c + Xe^{-rT} - Se^{-r^*T}$$

Where:

r = US riskless rate of interest

r^* = foreign riskless rate of interest

T = option's time to maturity expressed as a fraction of the year

---

2 James Bodurtha and Georges Courtadon, "Tests of an American Option Pricing Model on the Foreign Currency Options Market", *Journal of Financial Quantitative Analysis* (June 1987): 153–68.

If the actual put option premium is less than what is suggested by the put-call parity equation above, arbitrage can be conducted. Specifically, one could: (1) buy the put option, (2) sell the call option, and (3) buy the underlying currency. The purchases are financed with the proceeds from selling the call option and from borrowing at the rate r. Meanwhile, the foreign currency that was purchased can be deposited to earn the foreign rate r^*. Regardless of the scenario for the path of the currency's exchange rate movement over the life of the option, the arbitrage will result in a profit. First, if the exchange rate is equal to the exercise price such that each option expires worthless, the foreign currency can be converted in the spot market to dollars, and this amount will exceed the amount required to repay the loan. Second, if the foreign currency appreciates and therefore exceeds the exercise price, there will be a loss from the call option being exercised.

Although the put option will expire, the foreign currency will be converted in the spot market to dollars, and this amount will exceed the amount required to repay the loan and the amount of the loss on the call option. Third, if the foreign currency depreciates and therefore is below the exercise price, the amount received from exercising the put option plus the amount received from converting the foreign currency to dollars will exceed the amount required to repay the loan. Since the arbitrage generates a profit under any exchange rate scenario, it will force an adjustment in the option premiums so that put-call parity is no longer violated.

If the actual put option premium is more than what is suggested by put-call parity, arbitrage would again be possible. The arbitrage strategy would be the reverse of that used when the actual put option premium was less than what is suggested by put-call parity (as just described). The arbitrage would force an adjustment in option premiums so that put-call parity is no longer violated. The arbitrage that can be applied when there is a violation of put-call parity on American currency options differs slightly from the arbitrage applicable to European currency options. Nevertheless, the concept still holds that the premium of a currency put option can be determined according to the premium of a call option on the same currency and the same exercise price.

CURRENCY OPTION COMBINATIONS

In addition to the basic call and put options just discussed, a variety of currency option combinations are available to the currency speculator and hedger. A currency option combination uses simultaneous call and put option positions to construct a unique position to suit the hedger's or speculator's needs. A currency option combination may include both long (buying) and short (selling) positions and will itself either cost money in the hope of earning revenue or earn revenue in the hope of not costing money, i.e. be either long or short. As a note, the term long can be equated with buying or owning assets and the term short with selling or incurring liabilities. Typically, a currency option combination will result in a unique contingency graph.

Currency option combinations can be used both to hedge cash inflows and outflows denominated in a foreign currency and to speculate on the future movement of a foreign currency. More specifically, both MNCs and individual speculators can construct a currency option combination to accommodate expectations of either appreciating or depreciating foreign currencies.

In this appendix, four of the most popular currency option combinations are discussed. These are straddles, strangles, spreads and zero premium options. For each of these combinations, the following topics will be discussed:

- The composition of the combination.
- The worksheet and contingency graph for the long combination.
- The worksheet and contingency graph for the short combination.
- Uses of the combination to speculate on the movement of a foreign currency.

CURRENCY STRADDLES

Long currency straddle

A straddle is essentially a bet on the standard deviation or variability of a currency. To construct a long straddle in a foreign currency, an MNC or individual would buy (take a long position in) both a call option and a put option for that currency; the call and the put option have the same expiration date and strike price.

When constructing a long straddle, the buyer purchases both the right to buy the foreign currency and the right to sell the foreign currency. Since the call option will become profitable if the foreign currency appreciates, and the put option will become profitable if the foreign currency depreciates, a long straddle becomes profitable when the foreign currency *either* appreciates or depreciates. Obviously, this is a huge advantage for the individual or entity that constructs a long straddle, since it appears that it would benefit from the position as long as the foreign currency exchange rate does not remain constant. The disadvantage of a long straddle position is that it is expensive to construct, because it involves the purchase of two separate options, each of which requires payment of the option premium. Therefore, a long straddle becomes profitable only if the foreign currency appreciates or depreciates substantially. The holder of a straddle is therefore betting that the currency will become volatile.

Long currency straddle worksheet. To determine the profit or loss associated with a long straddle (or any combination), it is easiest to first construct a profit or loss worksheet for several possible currency values at option expiration. The worksheet can be set up to show each individual option position and the net position. The worksheet will also help in constructing a contingency graph for the combination.

Put and call options are available for dollars with the following information:

- Call option premium on dollar = £0.03 per unit.
- Put option premium on dollar = £0.02 per unit.
- Strike price = £0.60.
- One option contract represents $50,000.

To construct a long straddle, the buyer would purchase both a dollar call and a dollar put option, paying £0.03 + £0.02 = £0.05 per unit. If the value of the dollar at option expiration is above the strike price of £0.60, the call option is in the money, but the put option is out of the money. Conversely, if the value of the dollar at option expiration is below £0.60, the put option is in the money, but the call option is out of the money.

A possible worksheet for the long straddle that illustrates the profitability of the individual components is shown below:

Value of dollar at option expiration	£0.50	£0.55	£0.60	£0.65	£0.70
Profit (loss) from purchasing a call	−£0.03	−£0.03	−£0.03	+£0.02	+£0.07
Profit (loss) from purchasing a put	+£0.08	+£0.03	−£0.02	−£0.02	−£0.02
Net	+£0.05	£0.00	−£0.05	£0.00	+£0.05

Long currency straddle contingency graph. A contingency graph for the long currency straddle is shown in Exhibit 5B.1. This graph includes more extreme possible outcomes than are shown in the table. Either the call or put option on the foreign currency will be in the money at option expiration as long as the foreign currency value at option expiration differs from the strike price.

There are two breakeven points for a long straddle position – one below the strike price and one above the strike price. The lower breakeven point is equal to the strike price less both premiums; the higher breakeven point is equal to the strike price plus both premiums. Thus, for the above example, the two breakeven points are located at £0.55 = £0.60 − £0.05 and at £0.65 = £0.60 + £0.05.

The maximum loss for the long straddle in the example occurs at a dollar value at option expiration equal to the strike price, when both options are at the money. At that point, the straddle buyer would lose both option premiums. The maximum loss for the straddle buyer is thus equal to $0.05 = $0.03 + $0.02.

Exhibit 5B.1 Contingency graph for a long currency straddle (note that the breakeven rates are for individual options not the combined options)

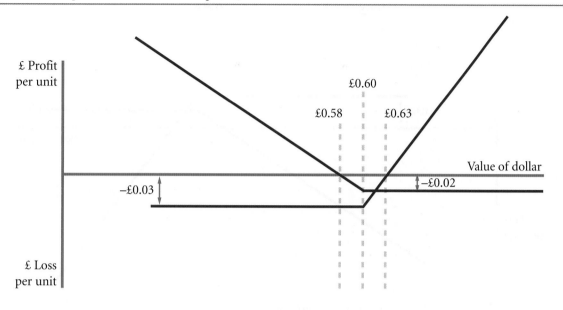

Short currency straddle

Constructing a short straddle in a foreign currency involves selling (taking a short position in) both a call option and a put option for that currency. As in a long straddle, the call and put option have the same expiration date and strike price.

The advantage of a short straddle is that it provides the option writer with income from two separate options. The disadvantage is the possibility of substantial losses if the underlying currency moves substantially away from the strike price.

Short currency straddle worksheet and contingency graph. A short straddle results in a worksheet and contingency graph that are exactly opposite to those of a long straddle.

Assuming the same information as in the previous example, a short straddle would involve writing both a call option on dollars and a put option on dollars. A possible worksheet for the resulting short straddle is shown below:

Value of dollar at option expiration	£0.50	£0.55	£0.60	£0.65	£0.70
Profit (loss) from selling a call	+£0.03	+£0.03	+£0.03	+£0.02	−£0.07
Profit (loss) from selling a put	−£0.08	−£0.03	+£0.02	+£0.02	+£0.02
Net	−£0.05	£0.00	+£0.05	£0.00	−£0.05

The worksheet also illustrates that there are two breakeven points for a short straddle position – one below the strike price and one above the strike price. The lower breakeven point is equal to the strike price less both premiums; the higher breakeven point is equal to the strike price plus both premiums. Thus, the two breakeven points are located at $1.00 = $1.05 − $0.05 and at $1.10 = $1.05 + $0.05. This is the same relationship as for the long straddle position.

Exhibit 5B.2 Contingency graph for a short currency straddle (note that the breakeven rates are for the individual options not the combined options)

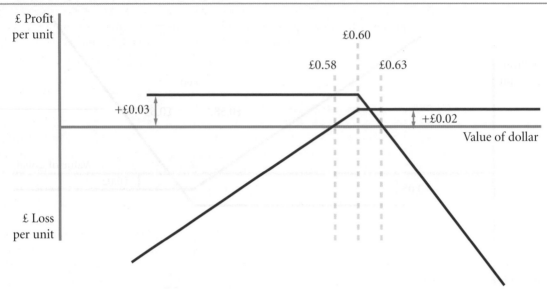

The maximum gain occurs at a dollar value at option expiration equal to the strike price of £0.60 and is equal to the sum of the two option premiums (£0.03 + £0.02 = £0.05).

The resulting contingency graph is shown in Exhibit 5B.2.

Speculating with currency straddles

Individuals can speculate using currency straddles based on their expectations of the future movement in a particular foreign currency. For example, speculators who expect that the British pound will appreciate or depreciate substantially can buy a straddle. If the pound appreciates substantially, the speculator will let the put option expire and exercise the call option. If the pound depreciates substantially, the speculator will let the call option expire and exercise the put option.

Speculators may also profit from short straddles. The writer of a short straddle believes that the value of the underlying currency will remain close to the exercise price until option expiration. If the value of the underlying currency is equal to the strike price at option expiration, the straddle writer would collect premiums from both options. However, this is a rather risky position; if the currency appreciates or depreciates substantially, the straddle writer will lose money. If the currency appreciates substantially, the straddle writer will have to sell the currency for the strike price, since the call option will be exercised. If the currency depreciates substantially, the straddle writer has to buy the currency for the strike price, since the put option will be exercised.

CURRENCY STRANGLES

Currency strangles are very similar to currency straddles, with one important difference: the call and put options of the underlying foreign currency have different exercise prices. Nevertheless, the underlying security and the expiration date for the call and put options are identical.

Long currency strangle

Since the call and put options used in a strangle can have different exercise prices, a long strangle can be constructed in a variety of ways. For example, a strangle could be constructed in which the call option has a higher exercise price than the put option and vice versa. The most common type of strangle, and the focus of this section, is a strangle that involves buying a put option with a lower strike price than the call option that is purchased. To construct a long strangle in a foreign currency, an MNC or individual would thus take a long position in a call option and a long position in a put option for that currency. The call option has the higher exercise price.

An advantage of a long strangle relative to a comparable long straddle is that it is cheaper to construct. From previous sections, recall that there is an inverse relationship between the spot price of the currency relative to the strike price and the call option premium: the lower the spot price relative to the strike price, the lower the option premium will be. Therefore, if a long strangle involves purchasing a call option with a relatively high exercise price, it should be cheaper to construct than a comparable straddle, everything else being equal.

The disadvantage of a strangle relative to a straddle is that the underlying currency has to fluctuate more prior to expiration. As with a long straddle, the reason for constructing a long strangle is the expectation of a substantial currency fluctuation in either direction prior to the expiration date. However, since the two options involved in a strangle have different exercise prices, the underlying currency has to fluctuate to a larger extent before the strangle is in the money at future spot prices. The smaller likelihood of making a profit is matched by the lower cost of a strangle relative to the straddle.

Long currency strangle worksheet. The worksheet for a long currency strangle is similar to the worksheet for a long currency straddle, as the following example shows.

Put and call options are available for dollars with the following information:

- Call option premium on dollar = £0.015 per unit.
- Put option premium on dollar = £0.025 per unit.
- Call option strike price = £0.625.
- Put option strike price = £0.575.
- One option contract represents $50,000.

Note that this example is almost identical to the earlier straddle example, except that the call option has a higher exercise price than the put option and the call option premium is slightly lower.

A possible worksheet for the long strangle is shown here:

Value of dollar at option expiration	£0.525	£0.575	£0.625	£0.675
Profit (loss) from buying a call	−£0.015	−£0.015	−£0.015	+£0.035
Profit (loss) from buying a put	+£0.025	−£0.025	−£0.025	−£0.025
Net	+£0.010	−£0.040	−£0.040	+£0.010

Long currency strangle contingency graph. Exhibit 5B.3 shows a contingency graph for the long currency strangle. Again, the graph includes more extreme values than are shown in the worksheet. The call option will be in the money when the foreign currency

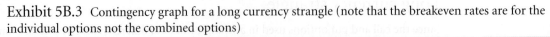

Exhibit 5B.3   Contingency graph for a long currency strangle (note that the breakeven rates are for the individual options not the combined options)

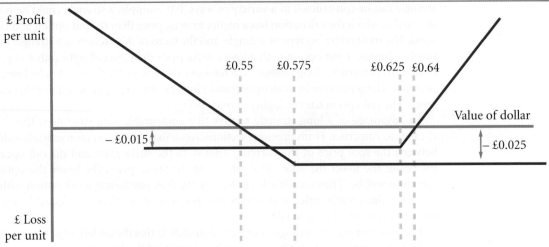

value is higher than its strike price at option expiration, and the put option will be in the money when the foreign currency value is below the put option strike price at option expiration. Thus, the long call position is in the money at dollar values above the £0.625 call option exercise price at option expiration. Conversely, the put option is in the money at dollar values below the put option exercise price of £0.575.

The two breakeven points for a long strangle position are located below the put option premium and above the call option premium. The lower breakeven point for both the contracts together is equal to the put option strike price less both premiums (£0.535 = £0.575 − £0.04); the higher breakeven point is equal to the call option strike price plus both premiums (£0.665 = £0.625 + £0.040).

The maximum loss for a long strangle occurs at dollar values at option expiration between the two strike prices. At any future spot price between the two exercise prices, the straddle buyer would lose both option premiums (−£0.040 = −(£0.025 − £0.015)).

The contingency graph for the long strangle illustrates that the dollar must fluctuate more widely than with a straddle before the position becomes profitable. However, the maximum loss is only £0.04 per unit, whereas it was £0.05 per unit for the long straddle.

Short currency strangle

Analogous to a short currency straddle, a short strangle involves taking a short position in both a call option and a put option for that currency. As with a short straddle, the call and put options have the same expiration date. However, the call option has the higher exercise price in a short strangle.

Relative to a short straddle, the disadvantage of a short strangle is that it provides less income, since the call option premium will be lower, everything else being equal. However, the advantage of a short strangle relative to a short straddle is that the underlying currency has to fluctuate more before the strangle writer is in danger of losing money.

Short currency strangle worksheet and contingency graph.   The euro example is next used to show that the worksheet and contingency graph for the short strangle are exactly opposite to those of a long strangle.

Continuing with the information in the preceding example, a short strangle can be constructed by writing a call option on euros and a put option on euros. The resulting worksheet is shown below:

Value of euro at option expiration	£0.525	£0.575	£0.625	£0.675
Profit (loss) from buying a call	+£0.015	+£0.015	+£0.015	−£0.035
Profit (loss) from buying a put	−£0.025	+£0.025	+£0.025	+£0.025
Net	−£0.010	+£0.040	+£0.040	−£0.010

The table shows that there are two breakeven points for the short strangle. The lower breakeven point is equal to the put option strike price less both premiums; the higher breakeven point is equal to the call option strike price plus both premiums. The two breakeven points are thus identical to the breakeven points for the long strangle position (see above).

The maximum gain for a short strangle (£0.040 = £0.015 + £0.025) occurs at a value of the euro at option expiration between the two exercise prices.

The short strangle contingency graph is shown in Exhibit 5B.4.

Speculating with currency strangles

As with straddles, individuals can speculate using currency strangles based on their expectations of the future movement in a particular foreign currency. For instance, speculators who expect the dollar to appreciate or depreciate substantially can construct a long strangle. Speculators can benefit from short strangles if the future spot price of the underlying currency is between the two exercise prices.

Compared to a straddle, the speculator who buys a strangle believes that the underlying currency will fluctuate even more widely prior to expiration. In return, the speculator pays less to construct the long strangle. A speculator who writes a strangle will receive both option premiums as long as the future spot price is between the two exercise prices. Compared to a straddle, the total amount received from writing the two options is less. However, the range of future spot prices between which no option is exercised is much wider for a short strangle.

Exhibit 5B.4 Contingency graph for a short currency strangle (note that the breakeven rates are for the individual options not the combined options)

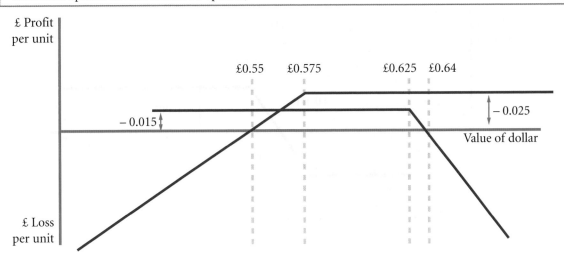

CURRENCY SPREADS

A variety of currency spreads exist that can be used by both MNCs and individuals to hedge cash inflows or outflows or to profit from an anticipated movement in a foreign currency. This section covers two of the most popular types of spreads: bull spreads and bear spreads. Bull spreads are profitable when a foreign currency appreciates, whereas bear spreads are profitable when a foreign currency depreciates.

Currency bull spreads with call options

A currency bull spread is constructed by buying a call option for a particular underlying currency and simultaneously writing a call option for the same currency with a higher exercise price. A bull spread can also be constructed using currency put options, as will be discussed shortly.

With a bull spread, the spreader believes that the underlying currency will appreciate modestly, but not substantially.

Assume two call options on Australian dollars (A$) are currently available. The first option has a strike price of £0.41 and a premium of £0.010. The second option has a strike price of £0.42 and a premium of $0.005. The bull spreader buys the £0.41 option and sells the £0.42 option. An option contract on Australian dollars consists of 50,000 units (see Exhibit 5B.5).

Currency bull spread worksheet and contingency graph. For the Australian dollar example, a worksheet and contingency graph can be constructed. One possible worksheet is shown below:

Value of Australian dollar at option expiration	£0.40	£0.41	£0.415	£0.42	£0.43	£0.44
Profit (loss) from buying a call	−£0.010	−£0.010	−£0.005	£0.00	+£0.010	+£0.020
Profit (loss) from selling a call	+£0.005	+£0.005	+£0.005	+£0.005	−£0.005	−£0.015
Net	−£0.005	−£0.005	£0.000	+£0.005	+£0.005	+£0.005

Exhibit 5B.5 Contingency graph for a currency bull spread

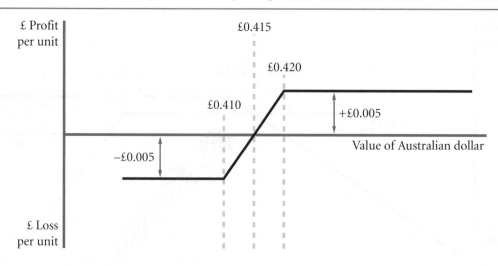

The worksheet and contingency graph show that the maximum loss for the bull spreader is limited to the difference between the two option premiums of −£0.005 = −$0.010 + $0.005. This maximum loss occurs at future spot prices equal to the lower strike price or below.

Also note that for a bull spread the gain is limited to the difference between the strike prices less the difference in the option premiums and is equal to £0.005 = £0.42 − £0.41 − £0.005. This maximum gain occurs at future spot prices equal to the higher exercise price or above.

The breakeven point for the bull spread is located at the lower exercise price plus the difference in the two option premiums and is equal to £0.415 = £0.41 + £0.05.

Currency bull spreads with put options

As mentioned previously, currency bull spreads can be constructed just as easily with put options as with call options. To construct a put bull spread, the spreader would buy a put option with a lower exercise price and write a put option with a higher exercise price. The basic arithmetic involved in constructing a put bull spread is thus essentially the same as for a call bull spread, with one important difference, as discussed next.

Recall that there is a positive relationship between the level of the existing spot price relative to the strike price and the call option premium. Consequently, the option with the higher exercise price that is written in a call bull spread will have the lower option premium, everything else being equal. Thus, buying the call option with the lower exercise price and writing the call option with the higher exercise price involves a cash outflow for the bull spreader. For this reason, call bull spreads fall into a broader category of spreads called debit spreads. Also recall that the lower the spot rate relative to the strike price, the higher the put option premium will be. Consequently, the option with the higher strike price that is written in a put bull spread will have the higher option premium, everything else being equal. Thus, buying the put option with the lower exercise price and writing the put option with the higher exercise price in a put bull spread results in a cash inflow for the bull spreader. For this reason, put bull spreads fall into a broader category of spreads called credit spreads.

Speculating with currency bull spreads

The speculator who constructs a currency bull spread trades profit potential for a reduced cost of establishing the position. Ideally, the underlying currency will appreciate to the higher exercise price but not far above it. Although the speculator would still realize the maximum gain of the bull spread in this case, he or she would incur significant opportunity costs if the underlying currency appreciates much above the higher exercise price. Speculating with currency bull spreads is appropriate for currencies that are expected to appreciate slightly until the expiration date. Since the bull spread involves both buying and writing options for the underlying currency, bull spreads can be relatively cheap to construct and will not result in large losses if the currency depreciates. Conversely, bull spreads are useful tools to generate additional income for speculators.

Currency bear spreads

The easiest way to think about a currency bear spread is as a short bull spread. That is, a currency bear spread involves taking exactly the opposite positions involved in a bull spread. The bear spreader writes a call option for a particular underlying currency and simultaneously buys a call option for the same currency with a higher exercise price. Consequently, the bear spreader anticipates a modest depreciation in the foreign currency; but limits the losses should the currency move in the other direction.

Currency bear spread worksheet and contingency graph. For the Australian dollar example above, the bear spreader writes the £0.41 option and buys the £0.42 option. A worksheet and contingency graph can be constructed (see Exhibit 5B.6). One possible worksheet is shown below:

Value of Australian dollar at option expiration	£0.40	£0.41	£0.415	£0.42	£0.43
Profit (loss) from selling a call	+£0.010	+£0.010	+£0.005	£0.00	−£0.010
Profit (loss) from buying a call	−£0.005	−£0.005	−£0.005	−£0.005	+£0.005
Net	+£0.005	+£0.005	£0.000	−£0.005	−£0.005

The corresponding contingency graph is shown in Exhibit 5B.6.

Notice that the worksheet and contingency graph for the bear spread are the mirror image of the worksheet and contingency graph for the bull spread. Consequently, the maximum gain for the bear spreader is limited to the difference between the two exercise prices of £0.005 = £0.015 − £0.005, and the maximum loss for a bear spread (−£0.005 = £0.41 − £0.42 − £0.005.) occurs when the Australian dollar's value is equal to or above the higher exercise price at option expiration.

Also, the breakeven point is located at the lower exercise price plus the difference in the two option premiums and is equal to £0.415 = £0.41 + £0.05, which is the same breakeven point as for the bull spread.

It is evident from the above illustration that the bear spreader hopes for a currency depreciation. An alternative way to profit from a depreciation would be to buy a put option for the currency. A bear spread, however, is typically cheaper to construct, since it involves buying one call option and writing another call option. The disadvantage of the bear spread compared to a long put position is that opportunity costs can be significant if the currency depreciates dramatically. Consequently, the bear spreader hopes for a modest currency depreciation.

Exhibit 5B.6 Contingency graph for a currency bear spread

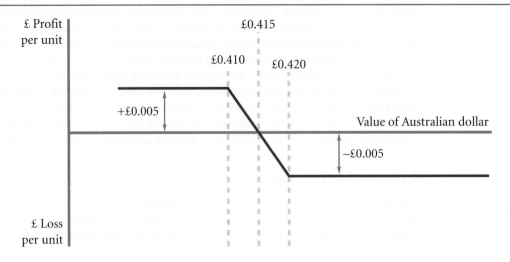

Cylinder or zero cost option

This option is included because it is of interest to treasurers. If an MNC is purchasing goods, a useful form of protection would be if a bank guaranteed or compensated the MNC if the value of the currency went above a certain level. In effect a call option. The zero cost element (i.e. there is no charge for the options) exploits the fact that an MNC would probably not mind losing some of the benefits if a currency fell in value. If a treasurer of an MNC is purchasing, the concern is that the cost of the currency does not go above an upper limit. The MNC would be happy to see the rate fall, but if the currency fell below a lower limit the MNC would probably not be too worried if they did not benefit by the drop below the lower limit, so long as it is protected against rises above the upper limit. In effect the bank is saying: "if the price of the currency goes above the upper limit, we will compensate you; but in return, if the price goes below the lower limit, you will have to buy at the lower limit price and we the bank will gain by the difference between the lower limit price at which we sell the currency to you and the even lower market price". Thus although the option itself does not cost money, the bank does stand to gain if the currency price moves in the case of buying currency to make a payment below the lower limit. A similar argument can be made out for revenues in foreign currency. Increases above the upper limit would be collected by the bank (the MNC writes a call to the bank); but if the value of the foreign currency fell below a lower limit, the bank would compensate the MNC for the difference (the MNC would hold a put funded by the bank). The limits are again set so that there is no net payment to be made.

EXAMPLE

Suppose a UK MNC is expecting to make a payment in dollars and takes out a cylinder option for zero cost against a bank with the purchase of a call option on dollars at a strike price of, say, £0.80 that could be financed by selling a put option on dollars at, say, £0.70. The upper limit is therefore £0.80, and the lower limit is £0.70 per dollar.

The arrangement would result in three possible scenarios: 1) the spot rate at settlement is above £0.80:$1 in which case the call option is exercised and the bank pays the MNC the difference between the spot and the strike of £0.80. The MNC is therefore guaranteed a maximum price of £0.80 to pay for a US dollar; 2) the spot price is at or between £0.80 and £0.70. Both contracts would be out of the money and as the premiums offset, no payment would be required; 3) the spot rate is below £0.70 in which case the MNC honours the put option it sold to the bank and the bank sells the dollars to the MNC for £0.70. Thus possible payment by the MNC under (3) offsets possible payment to the MNC under (1). Put simply the treasurer of the MNC would be saying to the bank: "you pay the difference in cost if the price of the dollar is above £0.80 and in return I will pay you the difference if the price falls below £0.70". The value of expressing this arrangement in terms of options, is that the appropriate strike prices can be approximated reasonably well using the option pricing formula. The contingency position is shown in Exhibit 5B.7 and Exhibit 5B.8.

Exhibit 5B.7 Using a cylinder option contract – a UK MNC seeking to convert pound revenue into dollars

Column number	1	2	3	4	5
Value of US dollar at settlement to pay	−£0.65	−£0.70	−£0.75	−£0.80	−£0.85
MNC profit (loss) from purchasing a call on dollars	not exercised	not exercised	not exercised	not exercised	+£0.05
MNC profit (loss) from selling a put on dollars	−£0.05	not exercised	not exercised	not exercised	not exercised
Net rate for the US dollar for MNC	−£0.70	−£0.70	−£0.75	−£0.80	−£0.80

Exhibit 5B.8 Contingency graph for a cylinder option guaranteeing purchase cost of dollars of between £0.70 and £0.80

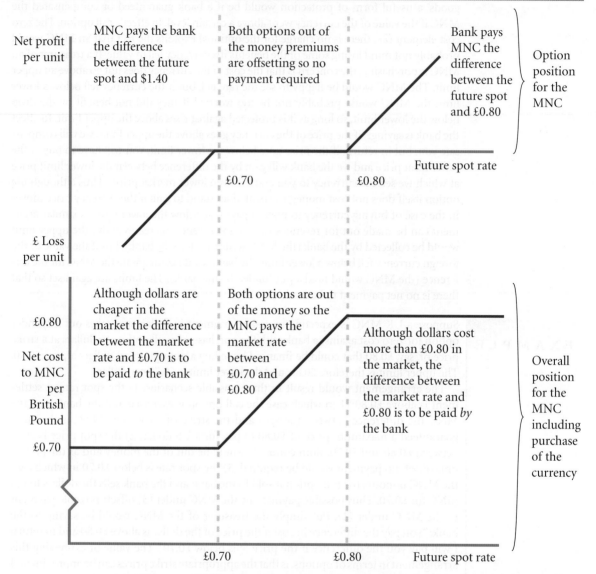

The guaranteed limits can also apply to MNCs intending to sell currency. Suppose a UK MNC wanted to sell dollars earned in the US for British pounds and was offered an upper limit to the value of the dollars converted of £0.80, in return the bank would guarantee a lower limit to the value of the dollars of £0.70. The MNC would in effect purchase a put at the lower limit to benefit from falls below £0.70, and sell or write a call at the higher limit where the bank would now benefit by being able to buy dollars from the MNC at a top limited rate of £0.80 if the market rate is even higher. Between those limits the transaction would be at the market rate.

The following spreadsheet in Exhibit 5B.9 is available on the companion website www.cengage.co.uk/madura_fox.

Exhibit 5B.9 Option calculator spreadsheet

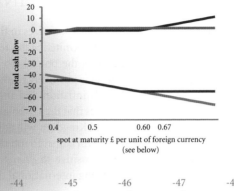

Option Calculator *				
	strike price	call buy (1) call write (−1) put buy (2) put write (−2)	premium	Units of foreign currency
option1	£0.55	1	£0.01	100
option2	£0.45	−2	£0.01	100
revenue (+) or cost (-) due in foreign currency				−100

* You may alter all the numbers in this table
** Total represents net payment or receipt
  when holding both options with revenue or cost due.

	revenue(+) cost(−) £'s								
		−40	−41	−42	−43	−44	−45	−46	−47	−48
	option 1	−1	−1	−1	−1	−1	−1	−1	−1	−1
	option 2	−4	−3	−2	−1	0	1	1	1	1
	total**	−45	−45	−45	−45	−45	−45	−46	−47	−48
	Maturity	0.4	0.41	0.42	0.43	0.44	0.45	0.46	0.47	0.48

Data (leave)

THE INTERNATIONAL FINANCIAL ENVIRONMENT

Mesa Co. specializes in the production of small fancy picture frames, which are exported from the United States to the United Kingdom. Mesa invoices the exports in pounds and converts the pounds to dollars when they are received. The British demand for these frames is positively related to economic conditions in the United Kingdom. Assume that British inflation and interest rates are similar to the rates in the United States. Mesa believes that the US balance of trade deficit from trade between the United States and the United Kingdom will adjust to changing prices between the two countries, while capital flows will adjust to interest rate differentials. Mesa believes that the value of the pound is very sensitive to changing international capital flows and is moderately sensitive to changing international trade flows. Mesa is considering the following information:

- The UK inflation rate is expected to decline, while the US inflation rate is expected to rise.

- British interest rates are expected to decline, while US interest rates are expected to increase.

Questions

1. Explain how the international trade flows should initially adjust in response to the changes in inflation (holding exchange rates constant). Explain how the international capital flows should adjust in response to the changes in interest rates (holding exchange rates constant).

2. Using the information provided, will Mesa expect the pound to appreciate or depreciate in the future? Explain.

3. Mesa believes international capital flows shift in response to changing interest rate differentials. Is there any reason why the changing interest rate differentials in this example will not necessarily cause international capital flows to change significantly? Explain.

4. Based on your answer to question 2, how would Mesa's cash flows be affected by the expected exchange rate movements? Explain.

5. Based on your answer to question 4, should Mesa consider hedging its exchange rate risk? If so, explain how it could hedge using forward contracts, futures contracts, and currency options.

1. Goergan, M., M. Martynove and L. Renneboog (2005) "Corporate Governance: Convergence evidence from takeover regulation reforms in Europe", *Oxford Economic Review*, 20 (2), 243–68.
   Q *Evaluate the advantages and disadvantages of the two corporate governance models outlined by Goergan et al.*

2. Woods, N. (2000) "The Challenge of Good Governance for the IMF and the World Bank Themselves", *World Development*, 28 (5), 823–41. A discussion of the problems facing these institutions.
   Q *From a reading of the Woods article, outline the pressures for reform of the IMF and World Bank. Discuss the advantages and disadvantages of democratizing decisions.*

3. Critin, D. and S. Fischer (2000) "Strengthening the International Financial System: Key Issues", *World Development*, 28 (6), 1133–42. The role of the IMF, capital flows and exchange rate regimes.
   Q *Private sector involvement is essential to economic development; but exchange rate volatility, moral hazard and capital flow restrictions limit its contribution. Explain and discuss possible solutions.*

4. Conway, P. (2006) "The International Monetary Fund in a Time of Crisis: a review of Stanley Fisher's essays from a time of crisis: The International Financial System and Development", *Journal of Economic Literature*, XLIV, 115–44.
   Q *Reviewing the crises of the 1990s, is the IMF part of the problem? Discuss.*

5. Morgan, R.E. and C.S. Katsikeas (1997) "Theories of International Trade, Foreign Investment and Firm Internationalization: a critique", *Management Decision*, 35 (1), 68–78. A clear and relatively brief tour around the area.
   Q *What can we reasonably expect from trade and investment theories? Outline and discuss*

6. Cyr, A.I. (2003) "The euro: faith, hope and parity", *International Affairs*, 75 (5), 979–92. An excellent historical context and analysis.
   Q *Consider and evaluate possible future scenarios for the euro.*

EXCHANGE RATE BEHAVIOUR

PART 2 (CHAPTERS 6 TO 8) focuses on the critical factors that affect exchange rates. Chapter 6 explains how governments can influence exchange rate movements and how such movements can affect economic conditions. Chapter 7 explores further the relationship between currency value and interest rates. Chapter 8 discusses prominent theories about the links between inflation, exchange rates and interest rates.

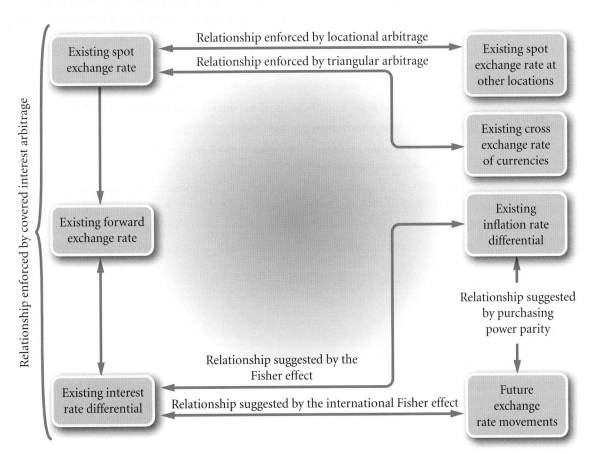

CHAPTER 6

GOVERNMENT INFLUENCE ON EXCHANGE RATES

THE PREVIOUS CHAPTERS HAVE begun to explore the relationship between the economy and the exchange rate. Governments use the exchange rate as an economic policy instrument to affect the economy. Such policies can be determined directly by the government or indirectly through membership of the European Union or G8. Financial managers need to be able to appreciate the relationship between governments, intergovernmental organizations and the exchange rate policy to understand the debate in the financial press and elsewhere on the likely development of exchange rates. Informed by such a debate, financial managers are then able to devise a policy on international finance relevant to their MNC.

THE SPECIFIC OBJECTIVES OF THIS CHAPTER ARE TO:

- describe the exchange rate systems used by various governments;
- explain how governments can use *direct* intervention to influence exchange rates;
- explain how governments can use *indirect* intervention to influence exchange rates;
- explain how government intervention in the foreign exchange market can affect economic conditions; and,
- outline the history of government and intergovernmental organizations in the management of exchange rates.

EXCHANGE RATE SYSTEMS

Exchange rate systems can be classified according to the degree by which exchange rates are controlled by the government. Exchange rate systems normally fall into one of the following categories:

- Fixed
- Managed float
- Pegged
- Freely floating

Each of these exchange rate systems is discussed in turn.

Fixed exchange rate system

http://

Visit the European Union site at **http://europa.eu.int/index_en.htm** for access to the server of the European Union's Parliament, Council, Commission, Court of Justice, and other bodies. It includes basic information on all related political and economic issues.

In a **fixed exchange rate system**, exchange rates are either held constant or allowed to fluctuate only within very narrow boundaries. If an exchange rate begins to move too much, governments, via their central banks, intervene to maintain it within the boundaries. In some situations, a government will devalue or reduce the value of its currency against other currencies. In other situations, it will revalue or increase the value of its currency against other currencies. A central bank's actions to devalue a currency is referred to as devaluation. The term *depreciation* is also used, but in a different context. Devaluation refers to a downward adjustment of the exchange rate by the central bank. Depreciation refers to a change caused by exchange rate markets. Revaluation refers to an upward adjustment of the exchange rate by the central bank. An upward adjustment by the market is referred to as an *appreciation* in the value of the currency.

Advantages of a fixed exchange rate system. In a fixed exchange rate environment, MNCs can engage in international trade without worrying about the future exchange rate. Consequently, the managerial duties of an MNC are less difficult.

EXAMPLE

When UK companies imported materials from abroad during the fixed exchange rate era after World War II (see history below), it could anticipate the amount of British pounds it would need to pay for the imports. When the British pound devalued in the late 1960s, however, UK companies needed more British pounds to purchase imports.

A second advantage is that where the currency of a small economy with high inflation fixes its exchange rate to a large currency with low inflation, the inflation in the small currency is restrained. Prices in the small currency are now in direct competition with imports that are not increasing in price because of the fixed exchange rate. As the economy is smaller, the possible extra demand for imports from the large economy will not affect the price of imports.

Disadvantages of a fixed exchange rate system. Although an MNC is not exposed to continual movements in an exchange rate, it does continuously face the possibility that the government will devalue or revalue its currency. In this respect the difference with a variable exchange rate system is not so great.

A second disadvantage is that from a macro viewpoint, a fixed exchange rate system may make each country more vulnerable to economic conditions in other countries.

EXAMPLE

Assume that there are only two countries in the world: the United States and the United Kingdom. Also assume a fixed exchange rate system, and that these two countries trade frequently with each other. If the United States experiences a much higher inflation rate than the United Kingdom, US consumers should buy more goods from the United Kingdom and British consumers should reduce their imports of US goods (due to the high US prices). This reaction would force US production down and unemployment up. It could also cause higher inflation in the United Kingdom due to the excessive demand for British goods relative to the supply of British goods produced. Thus, the high inflation in the United States could cause high inflation in the United Kingdom. In the mid and late 1960s, the United States experienced relatively high inflation and was accused of "exporting" that inflation to some European countries due to the fixed exchange rate.

Alternatively, a high unemployment rate in the United States will cause a reduction in US income and a decline in US purchases of British goods. Consequently, productivity in the United Kingdom may decrease and unemployment may rise. In this case, the United States may "export" unemployment to the United Kingdom.

However if a fixed exchange rate is accompanied by appropriate policies, good rather than bad economic conditions may spread.

EXAMPLE

Rerun the previous example and assume that there is only the United States and the United Kingdom. The much higher inflation in the United States causes the demand for British pounds to rise and the exchange rate to move outside its set limits. Initially, the United States will use its reserves of British pounds to meet the demand in the market place; but reserves of British pounds are bound to run low. Subsequently, the United States raises interest rates to make the dollar more attractive. The higher interest rates reduces spending in the US as consumers lower their credit card debt and companies borrow less and defer investment spending plans. Demand decreases in the United States, inflation slows down and as a result unemployment increase temporarily. Financial stability is restored, some may say at the expense of economic activity.

Where different countries share the same currency as in the European Union it is very clearly the case that members are subject to the economic conditions in each other's countries. If a member government such as Italy decided to borrow excessively to promote its own economy, interest rates may well increase. As a common currency area can only support one interest rate, it would mean that people in France could be paying more on their borrowing for credit cards and houses etc. due to the excessive borrowing in Italy. The solution in the European Union is to harmonize economic policies. To this end, member states signed up to the Stability and Growth Pact in 1997. The main terms are that government budgets must balance in the medium term and that there are penalties for excessive annual borrowing (more than 3% of GDP). As yet such penalties have yet to be levied despite rules being broken repeatedly by France and Germany.

Thus a fixed currency implies interdependency of the economic systems. It is possible for good economic conditions such as low inflation to spread, or bad conditions such as high inflation and unemployment to spread. The relative size of the countries, or rather, currency areas is an important factor as well as the economic policies of the countries concerned and the nature of the co-operation between the policies.

Managed float exchange rate system

The exchange rate system that exists today for the major currencies lies somewhere between fixed and freely floating. It resembles the freely floating system in that exchange rates are allowed to fluctuate on a daily basis and there are no official boundaries. It is similar to the fixed rate system in that governments can and sometimes do intervene to prevent their currencies from moving too far in a certain direction. This type of system is known as a **managed float** or "dirty" float (as opposed to a "clean" float where rates float freely without government intervention).

Criticism of a managed float system. The main problem of a managed float is whether or not it works. Interventions at the time of the Louvre Accord were not found to be statistically significant. Economic fundamentals, that is the view that the dollar economy was being undervalued, was probably more responsible for stabilizing the value of the dollar. At best it seems a very weak form of control of variable rate systems that achieves little. However, it is probably all that is available given that market volumes greatly exceed reserves of foreign exchange held by governments.

Pegged exchange rate system

Some countries use a **pegged exchange rate** arrangement, in which their home currency's value is pegged to a foreign currency or a basket of foreign currencies. While the home currency's value is fixed in terms of the foreign currency to which it is pegged, it moves in line with that currency against other currencies.

Some Asian countries such as Malaysia and Thailand had pegged their currency's value to the dollar. During the Asian crisis, though, they were unable to maintain the peg and allowed their currencies to float against the dollar.

Currency boards

A currency board is a system for pegging the value of the local currency to some other specified currency. The board must maintain currency reserves of the specified currency for all the local currency that it has issued. In one sense it may appear that the currency value is safe in that the currency board can replace the currency it has issued with the foreign currency. Cash is, however, only a small part of the total "money" or credit in an economy. Banks hold only about 10% of deposits in the form of cash. The currency board could therefore only convert 10% of bank balances into the chosen foreign currency.

EXAMPLE

Hong Kong has tied the value of its currency (the Hong Kong dollar) to the US dollar (HK$7.80 = $1.00) since 1983. Every Hong Kong dollar in circulation is backed by a US dollar in reserve.

A currency board can stabilize a currency's value. This is important because investors generally avoid investing in a country if they expect the local currency will weaken substantially. If a currency board is expected to remain in place for a long period, it may reduce fears that the local currency will weaken and thus may encourage investors to maintain their investments within the country. However, a currency board is worth considering only if the government can convince investors that the exchange rate will be maintained.

When Indonesia was experiencing financial problems during the 1997–98 Asian crisis, businesses and investors sold the local currency (rupiah) because of expectations that it would weaken further. Such actions perpetuated the weakness, as the exchange of rupiah for other currencies placed more downward pressure on the value of the rupiah. Indonesia considered implementing a currency board to stabilize its currency and discourage the flow of funds out of the country. Businesses and investors had no confidence in the Indonesian government's ability to maintain a fixed exchange rate and feared that economic pressures would ultimately lead to a decline in the rupiah's value. Thus, Indonesia's government did not implement a currency board.

A currency board is effective only if investors believe that it will last. If investors expect that market forces will prevent a government from maintaining the local currency's exchange rate, they will attempt to move their funds to other countries where they expect the local currency to be stronger. When foreign investors withdraw their funds from a country and convert the funds into a different currency, they place downward pressure on the local currency's exchange rate. If the supply of the currency for sale continues to exceed the demand, the government will be forced to devalue its currency.

EXAMPLE

In 1991, Argentina established a currency board that pegged the Argentine peso to the dollar. In 2002, Argentina was suffering from major economic problems, and its government was unable to repay its debt. Foreign investors and local investors began to transfer their funds to other countries because they feared that their investments would earn poor returns. These actions required the exchange of pesos into other currencies such as the dollar and caused an excessive supply of pesos for sale in the foreign exchange market. The government could not maintain the exchange rate of 1 peso = 1 dollar, because the supply of pesos for sale exceeded the demand at that exchange rate. In March 2002, the government devalued the peso to 1 peso = \$0.71 (1.4 pesos per dollar). Even at this new exchange rate, the supply of pesos for sale exceeded the demand, so the Argentine government decided to let the peso's value float in response to market conditions rather than set the peso's value.

Once again, the dominance of the markets over government management is evident. Where the market takes the view that the currency is overvalued, the volume of selling of that currency is such that governments are unable to resist the pressure for a devaluation.

Exposure of a pegged currency to interest rate movements. A country that uses a currency board does not have complete control over its local interest rates, because its rates must be aligned with the interest rates of the currency to which it is tied.

Recall that the Hong Kong dollar is pegged to the US dollar. If Hong Kong lowers its interest rates to stimulate its economy, its interest rate would then be lower than US interest rates. Investors based in Hong Kong would be enticed to exchange Hong Kong dollars for US dollars and invest in the United States where interest rates are higher. Since the Hong Kong dollar is tied to the US dollar, the investors could exchange the proceeds of their investment back to Hong Kong dollars at the end of the investment period without concern about exchange rate risk because the exchange rate is fixed.

If the United States raises its interest rates, Hong Kong would be forced to raise its interest rates (on securities with similar risk as those in the United States). Otherwise, investors in Hong Kong could invest their money in the United States and earn a higher rate.

Even though a country may not have control over its interest rate when it establishes a currency board, its interest rate may be more stable than if it did not have a currency board. Its interest rate will move in tandem with the interest rate of the currency to which it is tied. The interest rate may include a risk premium that could reflect either default risk or the risk that the currency board will be discontinued.

EXAMPLE

While the Hong Kong interest rate moves in tandem with the US interest rate, specific investment instruments may have a slightly higher interest rate in Hong Kong than in the United States. For example, a Treasury bill may offer a slightly higher rate in Hong Kong than in the United States. While this allows for possible arbitrage by US investors who wish to invest in Hong Kong, they will face two forms of risk. First, some investors may believe that there is a slight risk that the Hong Kong government could default on its debt. Second, if there is sudden downward pressure on the Hong Kong dollar, the currency board could be discontinued. In this case, the Hong Kong dollar's value would be reduced, and US investors would earn a lower return than they could have earned in the United States.

Exposure of a pegged currency to exchange rate movements. A currency that is pegged to another currency cannot be pegged against all other currencies. If it is pegged to the US dollar, it is forced to move in tandem with the dollar against other currencies. Since a country cannot peg its currency to all currencies, it is exposed to movements of currencies against the currency to which it is pegged. In 2005 the Chinese announced that the yuan would no longer be pegged to the dollar but to a basket of currencies. As well as the dollar, the euro, the yen and the South Korean won, the basket includes the Australian, Canadian and Singapore dollars, the British pound, the Malaysian ringgit, the Russian rouble and the Thai baht. The weights in the basket have not been disclosed other than to say that the weights in general reflect the level of trade with those currencies. In effect, the yuan will only be presenting a soft target to the foreign exchange market. Traders will not know exactly what value the Bank of China seeks against any one currency. Such a strategy is designed to deter speculators in the manner of the soft targets in the Exchange Rate Mechanism (see below).

EXAMPLE

As mentioned earlier, from 1991 to 2002, the Argentine peso's value was set to equal one US dollar. Thus, if the dollar strengthened against the Brazilian real by 10% in a particular month, the Argentine peso strengthened against the Brazilian real by the exact same amount. During the 1991–2002 period, the dollar commonly strengthened against the Brazilian real and some other currencies in South America; therefore, the Argentine peso also strengthened against those currencies. Many exporting firms in Argentina were adversely affected by the strong Argentine peso because it made their products too expensive for importers. Now that Argentina's currency board has been eliminated, the Argentine peso is no longer forced to move in tandem with the dollar against other currencies.

Pressures can also exist for appreciation. The Chinese central bank revalued the yuan against the dollar (to which it was then pegged) in July 2005. The Chinese government faces speculative purchase of Chinese securities to profit from an expected further appreciation in the value of the yuan. Exporters will also find that their products cost more and must decide whether to compensate by lowering their prices of pass the higher cost on to the foreign importer.

Dollarization

Dollarization is the replacement of a foreign currency with US dollars. This process is a step beyond a currency board, because it forces the local currency to be replaced by the US dollar. Although dollarization and a currency board both attempt to peg the local currency's value, the currency board does not replace the local currency with dollars. The decision to use US dollars as the local currency cannot be easily reversed because the country no longer has a local currency.

From 1990 to 2000, Ecuador's currency (the sucre) depreciated by about 97% against the dollar. The weakness of the currency caused unstable trade conditions, high inflation, and volatile interest rates. In 2000, in an effort to stabilize trade and economic conditions, Ecuador replaced the sucre with the US dollar as its currency. By November 2000, inflation had declined and economic growth had increased. Thus, it appeared that dollarization had favourable effects.

Freely floating exchange rate system

In a **freely floating exchange rate system**, exchange rate values are determined by market forces without intervention by governments. Whereas a fixed exchange rate system allows no flexibility for exchange rate movements, a freely floating exchange rate system allows complete flexibility. A freely floating exchange rate adjusts on a continual basis in response to demand and supply conditions for that currency.

Advantages of a freely floating exchange rate system. One advantage of a freely floating exchange rate system is that a country is more insulated from the inflation of other countries.

EXAMPLE

Return to the previous example in which there are only two countries, but now assume a freely floating exchange rate system. If the United States experiences a high rate of inflation, the increased US demand for British goods will place upward pressure on the value of the British pound. As a second consequence of the high US inflation, the reduced British demand for US goods will result in a reduced supply of pounds for sale (exchanged for dollars), which will also place upward pressure on the British pound's value. The pound will appreciate due to these market forces (it was not allowed to appreciate under the fixed rate system). This appreciation will make British goods more expensive for US consumers, even though British producers did not raise their prices. The higher prices will simply be due to the pound's appreciation; that is, a greater number of US dollars are required to buy the same number of pounds as before.

In the United Kingdom, the actual price of the goods as measured in British pounds may be unchanged. Even though US prices have increased, British consumers will continue to purchase US goods because they can exchange their pounds for more US dollars (due to the British pound's appreciation against the US dollar).

Another advantage of freely floating exchange rates is that a country is more insulated from unemployment problems in other countries.

EXAMPLE

Under a floating rate system, the decline in US purchases of British goods, caused by US unemployment, will reflect a reduced US demand for British pounds. Such a shift in demand can cause the pound to depreciate against the dollar (under the fixed rate system, the pound would not be allowed to depreciate). The depreciation of the pound will make British goods look cheap to US consumers, offsetting the possible reduction in demand for these goods resulting from a lower level of US income. As was true with inflation, a sudden change in unemployment will have less influence on a foreign country under a floating rate system than under a fixed rate system.

As these examples illustrate, in a freely floating exchange rate system, problems experienced in one country will not necessarily be contagious. The exchange rate adjustments serve as a form of protection against "exporting" economic problems to other countries.

An additional advantage of a freely floating exchange rate system is that a central bank is not required to constantly maintain exchange rates within specified boundaries. It can therefore hold lower levels of foreign exchange that would be needed under a fixed rate regime to meet surplus demand for foreign currency at the fixed rate. It also need not adjust interest rates and the money supply just to control exchange rates. Furthermore, governments can implement policies without concern as to whether the policies will maintain the exchange rates within specified boundaries. Restrictions on investments can be reduced and markets as a result are freer and more efficient.

Disadvantages of a freely floating exchange rate system. In the previous example, the United Kingdom was somewhat insulated from the problems experienced in the United States due to the freely floating exchange rate system. Although this is an advantage for the country that is protected (the United Kingdom), it can be a disadvantage for the country that initially experienced the economic problems.

EXAMPLE

If the United Kingdom experiences high inflation, the British pound may weaken. A weaker UK British pound causes import prices to be higher. This can increase the price of UK materials and supplies causing "cost push" inflation. In addition, higher foreign prices (from the UK perspective) can force UK consumers to purchase domestic products. As UK producers recognize that foreign competition has been reduced due to the weak British pound, they can more easily raise the prices of their finished goods without losing their customers to foreign competition.

In a similar manner, a freely floating exchange rate system can adversely affect a country that has high unemployment.

EXAMPLE

If the UK unemployment rate is rising, UK demand for imports will decrease. As a result, the reduced supply of British pounds on the foreign exchange will place upward pressure on the value of the British pound. A stronger British pound will then cause UK consumers to purchase foreign products rather than UK products because the foreign products can be purchased cheaply. Yet, such a reaction can actually be detrimental to the United Kingdom during periods of high unemployment.

As these examples illustrate, a country's economic problems can sometimes be compounded by freely floating exchange rates. Under such a system, MNCs will need to devote substantial resources to measuring and managing exposure to exchange rate fluctuations. Thus although cheaper for governments, variable rates are more expensive for industry.

Comparing fixed and floating rates in outline, governments want the certainty of fixed rates with the low cost and greater independence of variable rates. Managed floats offer the prospect of benefiting from both systems.

Classification of exchange rate arrangements

Exhibit 6.1 identifies the currencies and exchange rate arrangements used by various countries. Many countries allow the value of their currency to float against others but intervene periodically to influence its value. Several small countries peg their currencies to the US dollar.

The Mexican peso has a controlled exchange rate that applies to international trade and a floating market rate that applies to tourism. The floating market rate is influenced by central bank intervention. Chile intervenes to maintain its currency within 10% of a specified exchange rate with respect to major currencies. Venezuela intervenes to limit exchange rate fluctuations within wide bands.

Some Eastern European countries that recently opened their markets have tied their currencies to a single widely traded currency. The arrangement was sometimes temporary, as these countries were searching for the proper exchange rate that would stabilize or enhance their economic conditions. For example, in 1998 when the currency account deficit of the Slovakian balance of payments exceeded 10% of GDP, the

Exhibit 6.1 Exchange rate arrangements

Floating Rate System			
Country	**Currency**	**Country**	**Currency**
Afghanistan	new afghani	Norway	krone
Argentina	peso	Paraguay	guarani
Australia	dollar	Peru	new sol
Bolivia	boliviano	Poland	zloty
Brazil	real	Romania	leu
Canada	dollar	Russia	rouble
Chile	peso	Singapore	dollar
Euro participants (12 European countries)	euro	South Africa	rand
Hungary	forint	South Korea	won
India	rupee	Sweden	krona
Indonesia	rupiah	Switzerland	franc
Israel	new shekel	Taiwan	new dollar
Jamaica	dollar	Thailand	baht
Japan	yen	United Kingdom	pound
Mexico	peso	Venezuela	bolivar

Pegged Rate System		
The following currencies are pegged to a currency or a composite of currencies.		
Country	**Currency**	**Currency is Pegged to**
Bahamas	dollar	US dollar
Barbados	dollar	US dollar
Bermuda	dollar	US dollar
China	yuan	Basket of currencies
Hong Kong	dollar	US dollar
Saudi Arabia	riyal	US dollar

government unpegged to currency and allowed it to devalue in an attempt to reduce demand for foreign goods and increase foreign demand for its own goods.

Many governments attempt to impose exchange controls to prevent their exchange rates from fluctuating. When these governments remove the controls, however, the exchange rates abruptly adjust to a new market-determined level. For example, in October 1994, the Russian authorities allowed the Russian rouble to fluctuate, and the rouble depreciated by 27% against the dollar on that day. In April 1996, Venezuela's government removed controls on the bolivar (its currency), and the bolivar depreciated by 42% on that day.

After the 2001 war in Afghanistan, an exchange rate system was needed. In October 2002, a new currency, called the new afghani, was created to replace the old afghani. The old currency was exchanged for the new money at a ratio of 1,000 to 1. Thus, 30,000 old afghanis were exchanged for 30 new afghanis. The new money was printed with water-marks to deter counterfeits.

At the end of the 2003 war in Iraq, an exchange rate system was also needed. At that time, three different currencies were being used in Iraq. The Swiss dinar (so called because it was designed in Switzerland) was created before the Gulf War, but had not been printed since then. It traded at about 8 dinars per dollar and was used by the Kurds in northern Iraq. The Saddam dinar, which was used extensively before 2003, was printed in excess to finance Iraq's military budget and was easy to counterfeit. Its value relative to the dollar was very volatile over time. The US dollar was frequently used in the black market in Iraq even before the 2003 war. Just after the war, the dollar was used more frequently, as merchants were unwilling to accept Saddam dinars out of fear that their value was declining.

Although Iraq is not the best example, mention should be made of the possibility of multicurrency arrangements. In 1989 the UK government proposed a "hard ecu", a European currency to be used as an alternative alongside the domestic currencies that made up the Ecu. Indeed, in the UK and in most other countries there is nothing to stop MNCs and individuals settling their debts in any currency, providing both parties are agreed. A number of retail chains in the UK will accept euros as payment and it may be that the UK converts to the euro in this way. The danger of such arrangements is that individuals become exposed to currency fluctuations in their own personal finances, for example, earning in one currency and borrowing in another. This was the case in the Argentinian crisis of 2001/2 where some 70% of loans were denominated in dollars.

GOVERNMENT INTERVENTION – THE PROCESS

Each country has a central bank that may intervene in the foreign exchange markets to control its currency's value. In the United States, for example, the central bank is made up of a network of major banks referred to as the Federal Reserve System (the Fed). In Europe the European Central Bank is a separate bank situated in Frankfurt, Germany. The main decision-making body, the Governing Council, includes the governors of all the national central banks from the 12 euro area countries. Central banks have other duties besides intervening in the foreign exchange market. In particular, they control interest rates and attempt to control the growth of the money supply. The central bank is in charge of printing the money and controlling the amount of lending in the currency. The immediate objectives are to maintain stable prices, economic growth and low unemployment. The precise nature of government spending is, of course, the responsibility of governments. The Central Bank's role is to control the overall levels.

USING
THE WEB

Central bank website links The Bank for International Settlements website http://
www.bis.org/cbanks.htm provides links to websites of central banks around the
world.

Reasons for government intervention

The degree to which the home currency is controlled, or "managed", varies among central
banks. Central banks commonly manage exchange rates for three reasons:

- To smooth exchange rate movements.
- To establish implicit exchange rate boundaries.
- To respond to temporary disturbances.

Smooth exchange rate movements. If a central bank is concerned that its economy will
be affected by abrupt movements in its home currency's value, it may attempt to smooth
the currency movements over time. Its actions may keep business cycles less volatile. The
central bank may also encourage international trade by reducing exchange rate uncertainty. Furthermore, smoothing currency movements may reduce fears in the financial
markets and speculative activity that could cause a major decline in a currency's value.

Establish implicit exchange rate boundaries. Some central banks attempt to maintain
their home currency rates within some unofficial, or implicit, boundaries. Analysts are
commonly quoted as forecasting that a currency will not fall below or rise above a particular benchmark value because the central bank would intervene to attempt to prevent
that. It should be remembered that the volumes of transactions on the international
financial markets are very much greater than the reserves of the central banks. Any
attempt by central banks to influence the value of its currency may well fail.

Respond to temporary disturbances. In some cases, a central bank may intervene to
insulate a currency's value from a temporary disturbance. Because of the size of the
international currency markets, central banks will often act in unison. The European
Central Bank may therefore use its reserves of euros to buy British pounds to support the
value of the pound at the request of the Bank of England.

EXAMPLE

News that oil prices might rise could cause expectations of a future decline in the value
of the Japanese yen because Japan exchanges yen for dollars to purchase oil from oil-
exporting countries (oil is always paid for in dollars). Foreign exchange market speculators may exchange yen for dollars in anticipation of this decline. Central banks may
therefore intervene to offset the immediate downward pressure on the yen caused by
such market transactions.

Several studies have found that government intervention does not have a permanent
impact on exchange rate movements. In many cases, intervention is overwhelmed by
market forces. In the absence of intervention, however, currency movements would be
even more volatile.

Direct intervention

To force the British pound to depreciate, the Bank of England can intervene directly by
exchanging pounds that it holds as reserves for other foreign currencies in the foreign

Exhibit 6.2 Effects of direct central bank intervention in the foreign exchange market

Bank of England exchanges reserves of foreign currency for £s thereby increasing the demand for £s by foreign currency

Bank of England exchanges £s for foreign currency thereby increasing the supply of £s for foreign currency

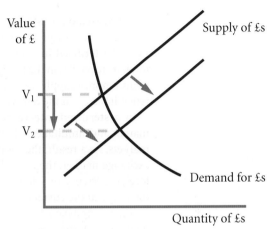

exchange market. By "flooding the market with pounds" in this manner, the Bank of England puts downward pressure on the pound. If the Bank of England desires to strengthen the pound, it can use its reserves of foreign exchange to buy pounds in the foreign exchange market, thereby putting upward pressure on the pound.

The effects of direct intervention on the value of the British pound are illustrated in Exhibit 6.2. To strengthen the pound's value, the Bank of England draws on its reserves of foreign currency (an item in the balance of payments account) to buy British pounds. As a result, there is an outward shift in the demand for pounds in the foreign exchange market (as shown in the graph on the left). Conversely, to weaken the pound's value, the Bank of England sells pounds for foreign currency, which causes an outward shift in the supply of pounds for sale in the foreign exchange market (as shown in the graph on the right).

E X A M P L E

During early 2004, Japan's central bank, the Bank of Japan, intervened on several occasions to lower the value of the yen. In the first two months of 2004, the Bank of Japan sold yen in the foreign exchange market in exchange for $100 billion. Then, on 5 March, 2004, the Bank of Japan sold yen in the foreign exchange market in exchange for $20 billion, which put immediate downward pressure on the value of the yen.

Direct intervention is usually most effective when there is a coordinated effort among central banks. If all central banks simultaneously attempt to strengthen or weaken the currency in the manner just described, they can exert greater pressure on the currency's value.

Reliance on reserves. The effectiveness of a central bank's direct intervention depends on the amount of reserves it can use. If the central bank has a low level of reserves, it may not be able to exert much pressure on the currency's value. Market forces are likely to overwhelm its actions.

As foreign exchange activity has grown, central bank intervention has become less effective. The volume of foreign exchange transactions on a single day now exceeds the combined values of reserves at all central banks. Consequently, the number of direct interventions has declined. In 1989, for example, the Fed (the US central banking system) intervened on 97 different days. Since then, the Fed has not intervened on more than 20 days in any year.

Nonsterilized versus sterilized intervention. When central banks intervene in the foreign exchange market without adjusting for the change in the money supply, they are engaging in a **nonsterilized intervention**. For example, if the Bank of England sells pounds for foreign currencies in the foreign exchange markets in an attempt to weaken the pound, the pound money supply increases. Effectively, the Bank of England as the printer of the currency, has created the reserve of pounds to use on the exchange markets.

In a **sterilized intervention**, the central bank intervenes in the foreign exchange market and simultaneously engages in offsetting transactions in the treasury securities markets. As a result, the money supply is unchanged. When intervening in the foreign exchange market, the central bank can either buy its own currency with its reserves of foreign currency or sell its currency from the reserves that it creates by virtue of being the issuer of the currency.

If the central bank buys its own currency, it creates an artificial demand that will help to maintain its value. There will also be a reduction in the money supply as the central bank in effect "buys back" its own currency. This effect can be negated by using the money it has bought back to purchase its own treasury securities from commercial banks. Redeeming treasury securities in this way increases the money supply in the economy as money is paid by the central bank to the commercial banks for the securities.

If the central bank, in simple terms, prints money and sells it for foreign currency, the effect is to increase the money supply. This effect can be negated by issuing treasury securities. Payment for securities by banks will reduce the money supply as banks pay the central bank for the securities. The central bank can then retire the payments it receives from circulation.

EXAMPLE

If the Bank of England desires to strengthen the British pound without affecting the pound money supply, it: (1) buys pounds with foreign currency, thus maintaining the foreign currency demand for pounds and hence the pound's value; and (2), with the pounds it receives for foreign currency buy or redeem its own treasury bills (securities). Thus there will be no net change in the holding of pounds in the economy (see Exhibit 6.3, top right hand section).

The balance of payments would show a reduction in the Bank of England's reserves of foreign currency. This would be noted with a plus sign indicating the resulting demand for pounds (similar to the effect of exports).

The difference between nonsterilized and sterilized intervention is illustrated in Exhibit 6.3. In the top half of the exhibit, the Bank of England attempts to strengthen the British pound, and in the bottom half, the Bank of England attempts to weaken or lower the value of the pound. For each scenario, the right hand side shows a sterilized intervention involving an exchange of Treasury bills for British pounds that offsets the pound flows resulting from the exchange of currencies. Thus, the sterilized intervention achieves the same exchange of currencies in the foreign exchange market as the nonsterilized intervention, but it involves an additional transaction to prevent changes to the pound money supply.

Exhibit 6.3 Forms of central bank intervention in the foreign exchange market

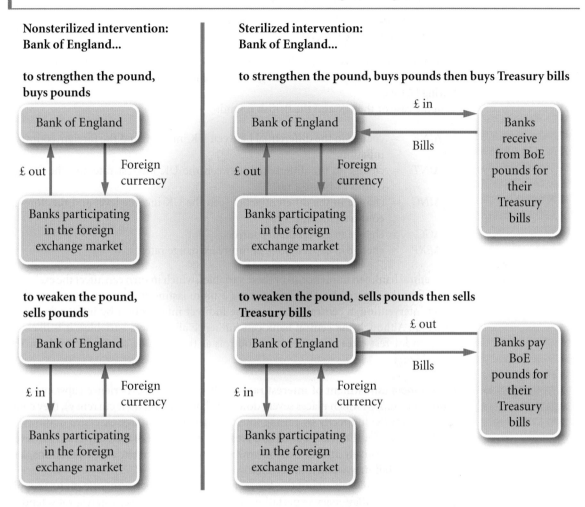

Notes:
£ out = £s taken out of circulation and held by the Bank of England.
£ in = £s put in to circulation by the Bank of England.

Speculating on direct intervention. Some traders in the foreign exchange market attempt to determine when central bank intervention is occurring, and the extent of the intervention, in order to capitalize on the anticipated results of the intervention effort. Normally, the central banks attempt to intervene without being noticed. However, dealers at the major banks often pass the information to other market participants. Also, when central banks deal directly with the numerous commercial banks, markets are well aware that the central bank is intervening. To hide its strategy, a central bank may pretend to be interested in selling when it is actually buying or vice versa. It calls commercial banks and obtains both bid and ask quotes on currencies, so the banks will not know whether the central bank is considering purchases or sales of these currencies.

Intervention strategies vary among central banks. Some arrange for one large order when they intervene; others use several smaller orders equivalent to 5 million euros to

10 million euros. Even if traders determine the extent of central bank intervention, they still cannot know with certainty what impact it will have on exchange rates.

Indirect intervention

A central bank can also affect its currency's value indirectly by influencing the factors that determine it. Recall that the change in a currency's spot rate is influenced by the following factors:

in the case of the UK and the British pound:

ΔINF = change in the differential between UK inflation and the foreign country's inflation;

ΔINT = change in the differential between the UK interest rate and the foreign country's interest rate;

ΔINC = change in the differential between the UK income level and the foreign country's income level;

ΔGC = change in government controls;

ΔEXP = change in expectations of future exchange rates.

The central bank can influence all of these variables, which in turn can affect the exchange rate. Since these variables are likely to have a more lasting impact on a spot rate than direct intervention, a central bank may use indirect intervention by influencing these variables. Although the central bank can influence all of these variables, it is likely to focus on interest rates or government controls as these can be changed directly by the central bank.

Government adjustment of interest rates. When countries experience substantial net outflows of funds (which places severe downward pressure on their currency), they commonly intervene indirectly by raising interest rates to discourage excessive outflows of funds and therefore limit any downward pressure on the value of their currency. However, this strategy adversely affects local borrowers (government agencies, corporations, and consumers) and may weaken the economy.

The central bank can attempt to lower interest rates by increasing the money supply (assuming that inflationary expectations are not affected). Lower interest rates tend to discourage foreign investors from investing in home securities, thereby placing downward pressure on the value of the home currency. Or, to boost a currency's value, the central bank can attempt to increase interest rates by reducing the money supply.

In the UK, interest rates are set by the Bank of England's Monetary Policy Committee. The minutes of the meeting including the vote of whether the interest rates should rise, fall or stay the same are published. Markets can include expectations in their interest rate sensitive prices (the price of the currency and shares) thus discouraging speculation.

EXAMPLE

In October 1997, there was concern that the Asian crisis might adversely affect Brazil and other Latin American countries. Speculators pulled funds out of Brazil and reinvested them in other countries, causing major capital outflows and therefore placing extreme downward pressure on the Brazilian currency (the real). The central bank of Brazil responded at the end of October by doubling its interest rates from about 20% to about 40%. This action discouraged investors from pulling funds out of Brazil because they could now earn twice the interest from investing in some securities there. Although the bank's action was successful in defending the real, it reduced economic growth because the cost of borrowing funds was too high for many firms.

In another example, during the Asian crisis in 1997 and 1998, central banks of some Asian countries increased their interest rates to prevent their currencies from weakening. The higher interest rates were expected to make the local securities more attractive and therefore encourage investors to maintain their holdings of securities, which would reduce the exchange of the local currency for other currencies. This effort was not successful for most Asian countries, although it worked for China and Hong Kong.

As a third example, in May 1998, the Russian currency (the rouble) had consistently declined, and Russian stock prices had fallen by more than 50% from their level four months earlier. Fearing that the lack of confidence in Russia's currency and stocks would cause massive outflows of funds, the Russian central bank attempted to prevent further outflows by tripling interest rates (from about 50% to 150%). The rouble was temporarily stabilized, but stock prices continued to decline because investors were concerned that the high interest rates would reduce economic growth.

Government use of foreign exchange controls. Some governments attempt to use foreign exchange controls (such as restrictions on the exchange of the currency) as a form of indirect intervention to maintain the exchange rate of their currency. A control exists where a resident has to obtain permission to buy foreign currency and where a foreign national needs permission to buy a currency. Exchange controls tend to affect the capital account rather than the current account. China, for example, allowed its currency to be bought and sold for current account transactions involving goods and services in 1996. But only in 2001 were Chinese residents allowed to purchase foreign exchange to pay for their own studies abroad. In 2002 the Qualified Foreign Investor Initiative was introduced in China to allow non-residents, under certain conditions, to invest in the Chinese Stock Market. Exchange rate controls require government permission to exchange the domestic currency for foreign currency. Sometimes the rates may differ depending on the purpose of the transaction. Under severe pressure, however, governments tend to let the currency float temporarily toward its market-determined level and set new bands around that level.

EXAMPLE

During the mid-1990s, Venezuela imposed foreign exchange controls on its currency (the bolivar). In April 1996, Venezuela removed its controls on foreign exchange, and the bolivar declined by 42% the next day. This result suggests that the market-determined exchange rate of the bolivar was substantially lower than the exchange rate at which the government artificially set the bolivar.

EXCHANGE RATE TARGET ZONES

In recent years, many economists have criticized the present exchange rate system because of the wide swings in exchange rates of major currencies. Some have suggested that **target zones** be used for these currencies. An initial exchange rate would be established, with specific boundaries surrounding that rate. Such a target zone is similar to the bands used in a fixed exchange rate system, but would likely be wider. Proponents of the target zone system suggest that it would stabilize international trade patterns by reducing exchange rate volatility.

Implementing a target zone system could be complicated, however. First, what initial exchange rate should be established for each country? Second, how wide should the target zone be? The ideal target zone would allow exchange rates to adjust to economic factors without causing wide swings in international trade and arousing fear in financial markets.

If target zones were implemented, governments would be responsible for intervening to maintain their currencies within the zones. If the zones were sufficiently wide, government intervention would rarely be necessary; however, such wide zones would basically resemble the exchange rate system as it exists today. Governments tend to intervene when a currency's value moves outside some implicitly acceptable zone. Unless governments could maintain their currency's value within the target zone, this system could not ensure stability in international markets. A country experiencing a large balance of trade deficit might intentionally allow its currency to float below the lower boundary in order to stimulate foreign demand for its exports. Wide swings in international trade patterns could result. Furthermore, financial market prices would be more volatile because financial market participants would expect some currencies to move outside their zones. The result would be a system no different from what exists today.

In February 1987, representatives of the United States, Japan, West Germany, France, Canada, Italy, and the United Kingdom (also known as the Group of Seven or G7 countries) signed the **Louvre Accord** to establish acceptable ranges (not disclosed to the public) for the dollar's value relative to other currencies. The Federal Reserve intervened heavily in the foreign exchange market for two years after the Louvre Accord, but it has generally intervened only in small doses in recent years. Thus, recent central bank intervention policy has been similar to the policy that existed before the Louvre Accord.

INTERVENTION AS A POLICY TOOL

The government of any country can implement its own fiscal and monetary policies to control its economy. In addition, it may attempt to influence the value of its home currency in order to improve its economy, weakening its currency under some conditions and strengthening it under others. In essence, the exchange rate becomes a tool, like tax laws and the money supply, that the government can use to achieve its desired economic objectives.

Influence of a weak home currency on the economy

A weak home currency can stimulate foreign demand for products. A weak euro, for example, can substantially boost euro-zone exports and euro-zone jobs. In addition, it may also reduce imports.

Though a weak currency can reduce unemployment at home, it can lead to higher inflation. In the early 1990s, the US dollar was weak, causing US imports from foreign countries to be highly priced. This situation priced firms such as Bayer, Volkswagen, and Volvo out of the US market. Under these conditions, US companies were able to raise their domestic prices because it was difficult for foreign producers to compete. In addition, US firms that are heavy exporters, such as Goodyear Tire & Rubber Co., Litton Industries, Merck, and Maytag Corp, also benefit from a weaker dollar.

Influence of a strong home currency on the economy

A strong home currency can encourage consumers and corporations of that country to buy goods from other countries. This situation intensifies foreign competition and forces domestic producers to refrain from increasing prices. Therefore, the country's overall inflation rate should be lower if its currency is stronger, other things being equal.

Though a strong currency is a possible cure for high inflation, it may cause higher unemployment due to the attractive foreign prices that result from a strong home cur-

Exhibit 6.4 Impact of government actions on exchange rates

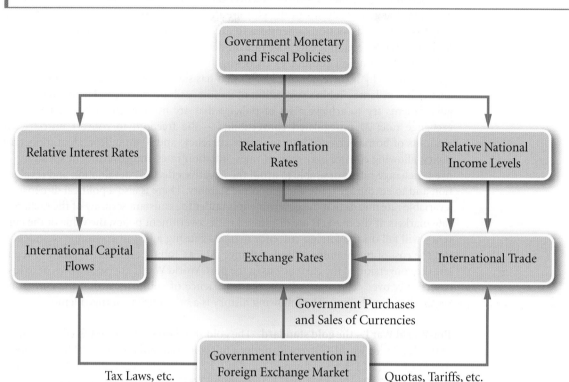

rency. The ideal value of the currency depends on the perspective of the country and the officials who must make these decisions. The strength or weakness of a currency is just one of many factors that influence a country's economic conditions.

By combining this discussion of how exchange rates affect inflation with the discussion in Chapter 4 of how inflation can affect exchange rates, a more complete picture of the dynamics of the exchange rate–inflation relationship can be achieved. A weak pound places upward pressure on UK inflation, which in turn places further downward pressure on the value of the pound. A strong pound places downward pressure on inflation and on UK economic growth. The interaction among exchange rates, government policies, and economic factors is illustrated in Exhibit 6.4. As already mentioned, factors other than the home currency's strength affect unemployment and/or inflation. Likewise, factors other than unemployment and the inflation level influence a currency's strength. The cycles that have been described here will often be interrupted by these other factors and therefore will not continue indefinitely.

A BRIEF HISTORY OF EXCHANGE RATES

The history of exchange rates is mainly an account of the attempt by governments to manage exchange rates in increasingly free market economies. Exchange rates are primarily affected by economic developments. The exchange rate accompanies these developments, but on occasion can be the cause when there is a financial crisis. For financial managers knowledge of the history of exchange rates is important in that it shows in a way that theory does not, what can happen to exchange rates. Although transactions have become increasingly sophisticated over the years, the role of money in the economy has little changed. Solutions in the past are therefore still relevant today. Also, history suggests social and political dimensions to exchange rate behaviour that is not reflected in the primarily economic exchange rate models.

Perhaps the simplest question to ask is why there are so many changes to the exchange rate system? Why is there not one system that has slowly evolved over time? Part of the answer lies in James Tobin's suggestion of an impossibility theorem. He maintains that governments try to achieve a set of policies that are not consistent being: 1) a fixed exchange rate; 2) unregulated convertibility – the freedom to convert unrestricted amounts of home currency into any other currency; and 3) an independent monetary policy, allowing control over interest rates, inflation rates and government spending. A fixed exchange rate is desirable to avoid the negative effects of devaluation and revaluation and to encourage trade and economic stability. There is also a political dimension, a variable rate means that the government is under the constant scrutiny of the exchange rate markets. If the markets are displeased with government policy, the value of the currency will fall on the foreign currency markets causing a loss of economic confidence. But the cost of maintaining a fixed exchange rate, as Tobin points out, is either to regulate the conversion of the currency, as in the post-World War II era (see below), or to lose sovereignty over economic policy – the experience of countries within the euro zone (again discussed below). The following history is a brief outline of this dilemma.

Pre-World War I – the gold standard. The gold standard is the earliest fixed rate system of the developed world. Currencies under a full gold standard are convertible into a fixed weight of gold of a defined fineness (quality). Before World War I, the Bank of England sold gold at £3 17s 10½d (£3.89375) per ounce (28.35 grammes). Gold could serve as an alternative currency, if businesses feared that their paper money would buy less gold in future (a devaluation), it could always convert its money into gold now. The gold standard was an insurance against the temptation by central banks to print too much money – the main cause of a devaluation. As all currencies adopting the gold standard were convertible into an ounce of gold at a set price, the exchange rate between these currencies was also fixed. As stated in an earlier chapter, a currency unit that could buy twice as much gold as a unit of another currency had to be worth twice as much as the other currency unit.

The UK adopted the gold standard in 1816 and the United States and Europe converted in the 1870s. This was a period of great financial stability, although there were large fluctuations in economic activity – trade cycles. As exchange rates were fixed and free trade was actively encouraged, an excess of imports could only be corrected by reducing the level of economic activity in order to reduce imports. This was achieved automatically in that excess imports meant money and gold flowing out of the economy to pay for the imports. The consequent reduction in the money supply led directly to a reduction in economic activity. On the plus side, exchange rate stability encourages international investment, and it is one of the surprising facts that nearly 50% of the savings of the developed world before World War I was invested in the developing world. The ratio nowadays is about a tenth of that figure, i.e. 5%.

The interwar period. Economic disruption after World War I caused intermittent periods of free floating exchange rates and fixed gold standard rates for the major currencies. Germany experienced hyperinflation caused in part by unrealistic reparation payments after the War. In 1919 there were 8.9 German marks to the dollar, by October

1922, that figure had risen to 4,500 and in 1923 reached 4.2 trillion (million million) marks to the dollar! Inflation rose by the hour, a meal was more expensive by the end than at the beginning. A loaf of bread cost 200 billion marks. In 1923 a new currency the rentenmark was introduced, supposedly backed by property (it could be exchanged for land). In 1924 the reichsmark replaced the rentenmark and was backed 30% by gold (i.e. gold reserves amounted to 30% in value of notes in circulation). Inflation came to an abrupt end, and then gold had brought currency stability. The legacy of German hyper-inflation in Europe is great caution on the part of the German government with regard to monetary policy (government borrowing and lending). The conservatism of the Growth and Stability pact (1997 – see below) is in part due to this experience.

In the mid 1920s there was an attempt by European countries to return to the gold standard. In the UK the return to the gold standard in 1925 limited the money supply and hence government spending. This and the overvalued rate of the pound was in part responsible for the general strike of 1926 and the Great Depression resulting in high unemployment. Deflationary pressures and rising unemployment forced governments to spend more, hence increasing the money supply. The consequence was devaluation on the international exchange markets and/or shortage of gold as confidence was lost in the currency. The 1930s saw competitive devaluations and suspension of convertibility into gold. The fixed exchange rate regime was incompatible with the need for governments to control their money supply and thereby manage their economies. The US dollar floated in 1933 and generally there was a reduced commitment to gold.

Bretton Woods Agreement. Towards the end of World War II, there was a desire to establish a stable exchange rate system. In particular, countries wanted to avoid the financial chaos after World War I. The Bretton Woods Conference resulted in the setting up of the International Monetary Fund (IMF) and the International Bank for Reconstruction and Development (now the World Bank). The IMF was charged with overseeing a fixed exchange rate with the dollar. From 1944 to 1971, exchange rates were typically fixed to within 1% of the dollar which alone was redeemable into gold at 35 dollars an ounce. Governments intervened in the foreign exchange markets to ensure that the exchange rates remained within the 1% band. As with the gold standard, a fixed exchange rate with the dollar implies a fixed exchange rate with all other currencies in the system. In addition to the fixed exchange rate there were also restrictions on the amount of currency that could be used in international transactions. These restrictions on convertibility helped to support the currency in the marketplace. For example, until 1967 foreign investors in the UK were allowed to sell their stocks and shares to other foreign investors but not to UK residents. Such a sale would have created a demand for foreign currency to pay the foreign investors. There were also restrictions on investments abroad that were only lifted in 1979.

Smithsonian Agreement. The problem with the Bretton Woods Agreement was that all currencies except the dollar were pegged or fixed in a way that was tested by market trading each day. The dollar's peg was with gold, and that link was not tested as few in the immediate post-war era wanted to change dollars for the far less easily handled commodity, gold. The Fed or Federal Reserve Board in the United States, charged with managing monetary policy, were constrained by the need to ensure that there were sufficient gold reserves to meet any demands to convert dollars into gold. In 1958 their reserves of gold were more than the rest of the world's banks put together and were ample, though the reserves were not sufficient to change all dollars into gold. But as there were very few demands to convert dollars into gold, the Fed found that in practice the dollars could be issued without increasing the reserves of gold, and that the gold to dollar ratio could be allowed to fall. The resulting increase in the money supply was needed to finance large current account deficits and the Vietnam War.

In effect the United States was benefiting from international seigniorage. The dollar was becoming a world currency and the US was able to profit from issuing the currency. In very simple terms, the US could print dollars and spend the money and associated credit created on imports. For other currencies this would have resulted in an oversupply of domestic currency and devaluation. But the US position was different. Because international trade needed accounts denominated in a stable, acceptable currency, the dollars offered for imports were deposited back in the US in the form of short-term deposits. The current account deficits therefore did not appear to lead to devaluation pressures. Increased supply was met by increased demand. The deficit on the current account was met by a surplus on the financial or capital account due to the demand for deposits in the US. When the IMF was set up at Bretton Woods, a plan by the British economist J.M. Keynes wanted to create a world currency, the bancor. It was intended that the benefits from issuing the bancor would go to developing countries. In the event this plan was rejected and the numeraire currency of the SDR (Special Drawing Right) was created which did not have a separate seigniorage effect. It was the dollar that became the prime beneficiary of the increase in world trade.

Eventually the current account deficits and evident over issuing of dollars led to a loss of confidence in its value and two European countries, Germany and France, began to prefer gold as a reserve to dollars. The resulting loss of confidence ending the long period of relative calm in exchange rates, came to an abrupt end on 14 March 1968 when President Johnson suspended the gold pool operation as it was known. $2.8 billion had been converted into gold in the previous six months. The price of gold was allowed to float freely, though central banks continued to trade gold at $35 an ounce.

Eventually, the United States on 15 August 1971, suspended convertibility into gold, imposed a 10% surcharge on imports, and limited tax relief on imported machinery. Unfortunately these measures prompted restrictions on the international flow of investments, as investment institutions sought to move their funds out of dollars in anticipation of a devaluation of the dollar. A meeting was called of the ten largest economies at the Smithsonian Institute in Washington. As a result, the dollar was devalued against the yen by 17%, the German mark by 14%, the French franc and the UK pound by 8%. The margin of variation around the dollar was increased to 2¼% from 1%. The official price of gold was raised to $38 an ounce. This move was of little significance as the market price was well above this rate – newly mined gold went on to the non-bank market, and banks were unwilling to use gold at this rate to settle accounts. Finally, in August 1971, with much depleted gold reserves, convertibility of the dollar into gold between Central Banks was suspended.

The fixed exchange rates between currencies continued in this now weakened form. However, there was still an excessive demand by dollar holders for foreign currency. As of February 1973, the dollar was again devalued. By March 1973, most governments of the major countries were no longer attempting to maintain their home currency values within the boundaries established by the Smithsonian Agreement. The world financial system had changed from a fixed rate regime to a freely floating exchange rate system between the major currencies.

The members of what is now termed the European Union, at this point, set up a system of managing exchange rates between their currencies in what proved to be the start of the long road that led to the creation of the euro (see below). Their reasons were simply that a fixed exchange rate between members was seen as necessary for promoting free trade.

Creation of Europe's snake arrangement. In the late 1960s it became evident that the gold exchange standard was not going to last in its present form. The European Economic Community (now the European Union) commissioned the Werner report which came out in 1970. The report recommended a process of monetary union within Europe by means of a parity grid system. By narrowing the band of variation, a single currency was planned to be achieved by 1980 – some 19 years before the actual achievement of fixed rates on 1 January 1999. In the spirit of the Werner plan, and in response to the Smithsonian arrangements, the European Economic Community (EEC) set up what came to be known as the "snake in the tunnel" or simply, the "snake" system. Currencies, as under the Smithsonian Agreement, were allowed to vary 2¼% either side of the dollar, allowing currencies to rise or fall a total of 4½%. If a currency moved from its ceiling to its floor whilst another currency went from the floor to the ceiling the total movement between the two currencies would be 2 × 4½% = 9%. Such potential variation was considered to be too much between members of the EEC. They therefore agreed in addition that they would maintain a 2¼% (half the Smithsonian band) with each other. When one currency rose to the top of its band with the dollar, it would buy the weakest of the currencies. The snake came into operation in March 1972, the UK, Denmark and Ireland joined in May 1972. The UK left the following month when the £ was floated, Italy left in 1973 and France in 1976. When the European monetary system was established in 1979, members of the snake were Germany, Benelux, Denmark and Norway.

The failure to develop a stable system in the 1970s was in no small part due to the large increases in oil prices. In response to the Arab-Israeli war in October 1973 oil prices were increased by the Arab dominated Organization of Petroleum Exporting Countries (OPEC). Prices increased in real terms (after adjusting for inflation) by 126% in 1974. Over the 1970s oil prices increased by 300% again in real terms. Oil is paid for in dollars, therefore the devaluation of the dollar helped to offset the oil price changes. Being linked to the dollar, however, meant that the beneficial effect of dollar devaluation was less than if currencies floated freely against the dollar.

Creation of the European Monetary System (EMS). Despite the gradual disintegration of the snake, the UK president of the European Commission, Roy Jenkins, relaunched the monetary union project by initiating the European Monetary System in March 1979. This was a parity grid system that did not include the dollar. Thus each country faced a central rate, upper and lower rates with each other member of the system. Originally, the currencies were allowed to diverge by 2¼% above and below the central rate and a wider band of 6% for the Italian lira. The system became known as the Exchange Rate Mechanism or ERM. In addition a numeraire currency (a weighted basket of currencies) was created known as the European Currency Unit (the ECU). The new currency, later to become the euro, was used in the parity system as a measure for determining intervention and also served to measure expenditure of the European Economic Community.

A weighted basket of currencies can be thought of literally as a basket containing currencies. In this case there were 1.15 French francs, 109 Italian lira, 0.82 of a German mark and so on. The value of the ECU could be translated into any one currency simply by converting the currencies in the basket at the market exchange rates to the desired currency. The amount of each currency in the basket was determined by the level of trade undertaken by each country within the community. The lira had a low value, so 109 lira amounted to less than 10% of the value of the ECU in 1979. The German mark had a high value and was about 33% of the value of the ECU. The currency values in the basket were periodically readjusted. The Special Drawing Right (SDR) is also a numeraire currency and serves a similar purpose for the International Monetary Fund. The value of the euro was originally set at 1SDR, and the value of the euro was set at the then value of an ECU in 1999.

Managed float. This system is usually dated from the Plaza Accord (September 1985) between the US, France, Germany and the UK. The view was expressed at the meeting that the dollar was overvalued, but no specific targets or timetable was offered. By early 1987 the dollar had lost more than 40% against its highs in 1985 with the German mark and the Japanese yen. In February 1987 there was another meeting in Paris (the Louvre Accord, this time including Canada) where it was jointly agreed that the value of the dollar should be stabilized, but gave no indication as to how this was to be achieved. The dollar continued to fall and only began to stabilize following a further meeting amongst the major nations that Christmas (the "Telephone Accord"). Unlike previous attempts to influence the exchange rate no specific targets were given to the market. The concept of soft targets was born. The advantage was that the very large funds on the foreign exchange markets had no targets against which to speculate. Intervention by the central banks initially tried to oppose market movements but later was refined to move rates in relatively quiet periods with market trends that they approved of rather than contest bouts of speculation. The technique was later adopted by the Exchange Rate Mechanism of the EU to good effect.

Demise of the European Monetary System. At first the system worked well. Between 1979 and 1983 there were 27 realignments averaging 5.3% and between 1984 and 1987, 12 realignments averaging 3.8%. The UK joined the ERM on 8 October 1990 after a period of high interest rates in order to maintain the value of the British pound. The consensus was that the British pound was overvalued in the parity grid. This was, in fact, a deliberate policy designed to keep inflation low. The reason was that by making the British pound relatively expensive, prices in the UK would have to compete with imports that were at an artificially low price. France had taken much the same action when it joined in 1979 and had successfully reduced its inflation. The stratagem was nevertheless vulnerable. Measures needed to protect the value of the British pound would now have to be that much stronger given that the starting point was already one of overvaluation. Needless to say, the market tested this vulnerability in 1992. A major difference between 1979 and 1992 was that the international financial markets were much larger and hence powerful, boosted in part by the relaxation of restrictions on portfolio investment. The breaking point came as a result of German unification following the fall of the Berlin Wall in 1989. East Germany was allowed to convert its currency to West German marks at a very favourable rate causing a 20% jump in the money supply, growth was insufficient to absorb this increase. Government borrowing in Germany was also higher to help finance the rebuilding of East Germany following years of neglect under communist rule. As a result, the German government increased its interest rates. In order to prevent the value of the British pound falling against the other currencies in the ERM, it was necessary to increase UK interest rates as well. The currencies in the ERM were having to pay higher interest rates for reasons that were purely concerned with the German economy.

The effect of an interest rate rise in the UK is very different from other members due to the tradition of borrowing to purchase houses in the UK. On the continent renting is the norm. Householders in the UK typically borrow up to five years' income to purchase their house on variable interest loans (mortgages). A 1% increase in a 6% 25 year loan of £100,000 to buy a house (i.e. a mortgage) is approximately £64 per month, a 2% increase £129. An increase in interest rates directly affects householders far more in the UK than in the rest of Europe. Against this background, the market came to believe that UK politicians would prefer to devalue the British pound rather than raise interest rates. The trial of strength with the markets came on 16 September, 1992 ("Black Wednesday"). Speculators, treasurers of MNCs, and investors all converted British pounds into foreign currency in the belief that the pound was about to devalue. At 2.15pm interest rates were raised to 15% from 10% that morning. By 5.15pm after using over £8billion in the foreign currency reserves of the Bank of England and other European central banks to support the value of the pound, it was suspended from the ERM and allowed to devalue. The British pound devalued by over 5% in one day and by a further 5% over the next month. The Italian lira suffered a similar fate (Italy had also followed the UK out of the snake system). An attempt was then made to speculate on a fall in the value of the French franc. The attempt failed, though at 30 January 1993 central bank interest rates were: France 10%, Germany 8.25% and the UK 6.0625%. The fluctuation margins were increased to 15% in August 1993 effectively ending the rigid form of the ERM. Italy later rejoined the ERM. However, for the British pound, Black Wednesday marked the end of formal participation in the European currency project – a position that is little changed today.

After 1992, greater variation of currencies in the looser form of the ERM did not ensue. A policy of soft exchange rate targets was pursued. Occasional variations were not contested by the central banks, when the market was quieter, intervention was made to encourage the markets to move in the approved direction.

The relative calm amongst European currencies after 1992 was in part due to the clear commitment to create a single European currency by the end of the decade. The Maastricht Treaty was signed in February 1992 and amongst other provisions "Resolved to achieve the strengthening and the convergence of their economies and to establish an economic and monetary union including, in accordance with the provisions of this Treaty, a single and stable currency." By stressing economic convergence, the lesson had been learnt that exchange rate policy had to reflect economic realities.

Unlike many previous exchange rate agreements, the ERM came to an orderly end with the creation of the euro in 1999.

European Monetary Union. The creation of the euro on 1 January 1999 meant the fixing of exchange rates of the then 11 participating nations: Austria, Belgium, Finland, France, Germany, Ireland, Italy, Luxembourg, Netherlands, Portugal, Spain, and later, Greece. Subsequently, in January and early February 2002 these nations withdrew their national currencies and issued a common currency.

Together, the participating countries in the euro comprise almost 20% of the world's gross domestic product – a proportion similar to that of the United States. Three countries that were members of the EU in 1999 (the United Kingdom, Denmark, and Sweden) decided not to adopt the euro at that time. The ten countries in Eastern Europe (including the Czech Republic and Hungary) that joined the EU in 2004 will be eligible to participate in the euro in the future if they meet specific economic goals. Countries that participate in the EU are supposed to abide by the Stability and Growth pact before they adopt the euro. This pact requires that the country's budget deficit be less than 3% of its gross domestic product. However, there is already some question about the budget deficit exceeding the limit of the EU countries that presently participate in the euro.

Four of the ten countries that became part of the EU in May 2004 (Cyprus, Estonia, Lithuania, and Slovenia) are planning to take the first step in adopting the euro. To do so, they must restrict the movements of the euro relative to their home currency within a range of plus or minus 15% from an initially set exchange rate. This will allow them to

http://

The website **http://www.ecb.int/home/html/index.en.html** provides information on the euro and monetary policy conducted by the European Central Bank.

monitor the exchange movements within this range before they permanently convert their currency into euros at a particular exchange rate. Assuming that they also comply with other specified macroeconomic conditions, such as limiting inflation and their budget deficit, these countries could adopt the euro in 2007.

As an historical note suggesting that little is new in finance, a similar form of standardization was attempted in 1865 with the formation of the Latin Monetary Union. The principal members were France, Belgium, Switzerland, Italy and Greece. Each member issued standard coins that were allowed to circulate freely throughout the Union. Later, other countries, in particular, Austria, Bulgaria, Romania, Spain, and Venezuela issued coins of similar denomination and value without formally joining.

The relatively harmonious progress to the development of the euro is in contrast to crises elsewhere.

How Mexico's pegged system led to the Mexican peso crisis. In 1994, Mexico's central bank used a special pegged exchange rate system that linked the peso to the US dollar but allowed the peso's value to fluctuate against the dollar within a band. The Mexican central bank enforced the link through frequent intervention. In fact, it partially supported its intervention by issuing short-term debt securities denominated in dollars and using the dollars to purchase pesos in the foreign exchange market. Limiting the depreciation of the peso was intended to reduce inflationary pressure that can be caused by a very weak home currency. The argument is that a weak home currency leads to more expensive imports creating a cost push effect thereby increasing inflation. Keeping the price of imports down, however, led in part to a large balance of trade deficit in 1994. Because the peso was stronger than it should have been, Mexican firms and consumers were encouraged to buy an excessive amount of imports.

Many speculators based in Mexico recognized that the peso was being maintained at an artificially high level, and they speculated on its potential decline by investing their funds in the United States. They planned to sell their US investments if and when the peso's value weakened so that they could convert the dollars from their US investments into pesos at a favourable exchange rate. As with the speculation against the British pound on Black Wednesday, the selling of the peso for the dollar put even more downward pressure on the peso.

On 20 December 1994, Mexico's central bank devalued the peso by about 13%. Mexico's stock prices plummeted, as many foreign investors sold their shares and withdrew their funds from Mexico in anticipation of further devaluations. On 22 December the central bank allowed the peso to float freely, and it declined by 15%. This was the beginning of the so-called Mexican peso crisis. In an attempt to discourage foreign investors from withdrawing their investments in Mexico's debt securities, the central bank increased interest rates, but the higher rates increased the cost of borrowing for Mexican firms and consumers, thereby slowing economic growth.

As Mexico's short-term debt obligations denominated in dollars matured, the Mexican central bank used its weak pesos to obtain dollars and repay the debt. Since the peso had weakened, the effective cost of financing with dollars was very expensive for the central bank. Mexico's financial problems caused investors to lose confidence in peso-denominated securities, so they liquidated their peso-denominated securities and transferred their funds to other countries. These actions put additional downward pressure on the peso. In the four months after 20 December 1994, the value of the peso declined by more than 50%. Over time, Mexico's economy improved, and the paranoia that had led to the withdrawal of funds by foreign investors subsided. The Mexican crisis might not have occurred if the peso had been allowed to float throughout 1994, because the peso would have gravitated toward its natural level. The crisis illustrates that central bank intervention will not necessarily be able to overwhelm market forces; thus, the crisis may serve as an argument for letting a currency float freely.

The end of Argentina's pegged system. In 1991 Argentina set up a currency board which linked the peso to the dollar on a one to one basis. The money supply was limited to purchasing dollars. Strong economic growth was checked in 1994 by the Mexican crisis and a decline in Argentina's GDP. Growth subsequently resumed but at the cost of increasing indebtedness. In 1998, Argentina was in recession made worse by the devaluation of the Brazilian real, about a third of Argentina's exports were to Brazil. In 2001 Argentina defaulted on its international loan repayments. As many loans were denominated in dollars and earnings were in pesos, loss of confidence in the peso led to a run on the banks. Withdrawals were limited to $1,000 per month. In early 2002 the currency board was terminated and the peso was allowed to devalue, by March the peso had lost nearly 70% of its value. The government implemented legislation on the conversion rate to be used in converting dollar debts to pesos. The burden of devaluation was mainly placed on the lender, especially for the smaller debts.

In many ways the Argentina crisis is an illustration of Tobin's proposition that a fixed exchange rate is incompatible with free convertibility *and* an independent money supply and hence borrowing policy. It also illustrates the risk involved of a supposedly riskless fixed exchange rate.

The Asian crisis. From 1990 to 1997, Asian countries achieved higher economic growth than any other countries. They were viewed as models for advances in technology and economic improvement. In the summer and fall of 1997, however, they experienced financial problems, leading to what is commonly referred to as the "Asian crisis", and resulting in bailouts of several countries by the International Monetary Fund (IMF).

Much of the crisis is attributed to the substantial depreciation of Asian currencies, which caused severe financial problems for firms and governments throughout Asia, as well as some other regions. This crisis demonstrated how exchange rate movements can affect country conditions and therefore affect the firms that operate in those countries.

Crisis in Thailand. Until July 1997, Thailand was one of the world's fastest growing economies. In fact, Thailand grew faster than any other country over the 1985–94 period. Thai consumers spent freely, which resulted in lower savings compared to other South East Asian countries. The high level of spending and low level of saving put upward pressure on prices of real estate and products and on the local interest rate. Normally, countries with high inflation tend to have weak currencies because of forces from purchasing power parity. Prior to July 1997, however, Thailand's currency was linked to the dollar, which made Thailand an attractive site for foreign investors; they could earn a high interest rate on invested funds while being protected (until the crisis) from a large depreciation in the baht.

Normally, countries desire a large inflow of funds because it can help support the country's growth. In Thailand's case, however, the inflow of funds provided Thai banks with more funds than the banks could use for making loans. Consequently, in an attempt to use all the funds, the banks made many very risky loans. Commercial developers borrowed heavily without having to prove that the expansion was feasible. Lenders were willing to lend large sums of money based on the previous success of the developers. The loans may have seemed feasible based on the assumption that the economy would continue its high growth, but such high growth could not last forever. The corporate structure of Thailand also led to excessive lending. Many corporations are tied in with banks, such that some bank lending is not an "arm's-length" business transaction, but a loan to a friend that needs funds.

In addition to the lending situation, the large inflow of funds made Thailand more susceptible to a massive outflow of funds if foreign investors ever lost confidence in the Thai economy. Given the large amount of risky loans and the potential for a massive outflow of funds, Thailand was sometimes described as a "house of cards", waiting to collapse.

While the large inflow of funds put downward pressure on interest rates, the supply was offset by a strong demand for funds as developers and corporations sought to capitalize on the growth economy by expanding. Thailand's government was also borrowing heavily to improve the country's infrastructure. Thus, the massive borrowing was occurring at relatively high interest rates, making the debt expensive to the borrowers.

During the first half of 1997, the dollar strengthened against the Japanese yen and European currencies, which reduced the prices of Japanese and European imports. Although the dollar was linked to the baht over this period, Thailand's products were not priced as competitively to US importers.

Pressure on the Thai baht. The baht experienced downward pressure in July 1997 as some foreign investors recognized its potential weakness. The outflow of funds expedited the weakening of the baht, as foreign investors exchanged their baht for their home currencies. The baht's value relative to the dollar was pressured by the large sale of baht in exchange for dollars. On July 2, 1997, the baht was detached from the dollar. Thailand's central bank then attempted to maintain the baht's value by intervention. Specifically, it swapped its baht reserves for dollar reserves at other central banks and then used its dollar reserves to purchase the baht in the foreign exchange market (this swap agreement required Thailand to reverse this exchange by exchanging dollars for baht at a future date). The intervention was intended to offset the sales of baht by foreign investors in the foreign exchange market, but market forces overwhelmed the intervention efforts. As the supply of baht for sale exceeded the demand for baht in the foreign exchange market, the government eventually had to surrender in its effort to defend the baht's value. In July 1997, the value of the baht plummeted. Over a five-week period, it declined by more than 20% against the dollar.

Thailand's central bank used more than $20 billion to purchase baht in the foreign exchange market as part of its direct intervention efforts. Due to the decline in the value of the baht, Thailand needed more baht to be exchanged for the dollars to repay the other central banks.

Thailand's banks estimated the amount of their defaulted loans at over $30 billion. Meanwhile, some corporations in Thailand had borrowed funds in other currencies (including the dollar) because the interest rates in Thailand were relatively high. This strategy backfired because the weakening of the baht forced these corporations to exchange larger amounts of baht for the currencies needed to pay off the loans. Consequently, the corporations incurred a much higher effective financing rate (which accounts for the exchange rate effect to determine the true cost of borrowing) than they would have paid if they had borrowed funds locally in Thailand. The higher borrowing cost was an additional strain on the corporations.

On 5 August 1997, the IMF and several countries agreed to provide Thailand with a $16 billion rescue package. Japan provided $4 billion, while the IMF provided $4 billion. At the time, this was the second largest bailout plan ever put together for a single country (Mexico had received a $50 billion bailout in 1994). In return for this monetary support,

Thailand agreed to reduce its budget deficit, prevent inflation from rising above 9%, raise its value-added tax from 7% to 10%, and clean up the financial statements of the local banks, which had many undisclosed bad loans.

The rescue package took time to finalize because Thailand's government was unwilling to shut down all the banks that were experiencing financial problems as a result of their overly generous lending policies. Many critics have questioned the efficacy of the rescue package because some of the funding was misallocated due to corruption in Thailand.

Spread of the crisis throughout South East Asia. The crisis in Thailand was contagious to other countries in South East Asia. The South East Asian economies are somewhat integrated because of the trade between countries. The crisis was expected to weaken Thailand's economy, which would result in a reduction in the demand for products produced in the other countries of South East Asia. As the demand for those countries' products declined, so would their national income and their demand for products from other South East Asian countries. Thus, the effects could perpetuate. Like Thailand, the other South East Asian countries had very high growth in recent years, which had led to overly optimistic assessments of future economic conditions and thus to excessive loans being extended for projects that had a high risk of default.

These countries were also similar to Thailand in that they had relatively high interest rates, and their governments tended to stabilize their currencies. Consequently, these countries had attracted a large amount of foreign investment as well. Thailand's crisis made foreign investors realize that such a crisis could also hit the other countries in South East Asia. Consequently, they began to withdraw funds from these countries.

In July and August of 1997, the values of the Malaysian ringgit, Singapore dollar, Philippine peso, Taiwan dollar, and Indonesian rupiah also declined. The Philippine peso was devalued in July. Malaysia initially attempted to maintain the ringgit's value within a narrow band but then surrendered and let the ringgit float to its market-determined level. In August 1997, Bank Indonesia (the central bank) used more than $500 million in direct intervention to purchase rupiah in the foreign exchange market in an attempt to boost the value of the rupiah. By mid August, however, it gave up its effort to maintain the rupiah's value within a band and let the rupiah float to its natural level. This decision by Bank Indonesia to let the rupiah float may have been influenced by the failure of Thailand's costly efforts to maintain the baht. The market forces were too strong and could not be offset by direct intervention. On 30 October 1997, a rescue package for Indonesia was announced, but the IMF and Indonesia's government did not agree on the terms of the $43 billion package until the spring of 1998. One of the main points of contention was that President Suharto wanted to peg the rupiah's exchange rate, but the IMF believed that Bank Indonesia would not be able to maintain the rupiah's exchange rate at a fixed level and that it would come under renewed speculative attack.

As the South East Asian countries gave up their fight to maintain their currencies within bands, they imposed restrictions on their forward and futures markets to prevent excessive speculation. For example, Indonesia and Malaysia imposed a limit on the size of forward contracts created by banks for foreign residents. These actions limited the degree to which speculators could sell these currencies forward based on expectations that the currencies would weaken over time. In general, efforts to protect the currencies failed because investors and firms had no confidence that the fundamental factors causing weakness in the currencies were being corrected. Therefore, the flow of funds out of the Asian countries continued; this outflow led to even more sales of Asian currencies in exchange for other currencies, which put additional downward pressure on the values of the currencies.

As the values of the South East Asian currencies declined, speculators responded by withdrawing more of their funds from these countries, which led to further weakness in the currencies. As in Thailand, many corporations had borrowed in other countries (such as the United States) where interest rates were relatively low. The decline in the values of their local currencies caused the corporations' effective rate of financing to be excessive, which strained their cash flow situation.

Due to the integration of South East Asian economies, the excessive lending by the local banks across the countries, and the susceptibility of all these countries to massive fund outflows, the crisis was not really focused on one country. What was initially referred to as the Thailand crisis became the Asian crisis.

Impact of the Asian crisis on Hong Kong. On 23 October 1997, prices in the Hong Kong stock market declined by 10.2% on average; considering the three trading days before that, the cumulative four-day effect was a decline of 23.3%. The decline was primarily attributed to speculation that Hong Kong's currency might be devalued and that Hong Kong could experience financial problems similar to the South East Asian countries. The fact that the market value of Hong Kong companies could decline by almost one-fourth over a four-day period demonstrated the perceived exposure of Hong Kong to the crisis.

During this period, Hong Kong maintained its pegged exchange rate system with the Hong Kong dollar tied to the US dollar. However, it had to increase interest rates to discourage investors from transferring their funds out of the country.

Impact of the Asian crisis on Russia. The Asian crisis caused investors to reconsider other countries where similar effects might occur. In particular, they focused on Russia. As investors lost confidence in the Russian currency (the rouble), they began to transfer funds out of Russia. In response to the downward pressure this outflow of funds placed on the rouble, the central bank of Russia engaged in direct intervention by using dollars to purchase roubles in the foreign exchange market. It also used indirect intervention by raising interest rates to make Russia more attractive to investors, thereby discouraging additional outflows.

In July 1998, the IMF (with some help from Japan and the World Bank) organized a loan package worth $22.6 billion for Russia. The package required that Russia boost its tax revenue, reduce its budget deficit, and create a more capitalist environment for its businesses.

During August 1998, Russia's central bank commonly intervened to prevent the rouble from declining substantially. On 26 August, however, it gave up its fight to defend the rouble's value, and market forces caused the rouble to decline by more than 50% against most currencies on that day. This led to fears of a new crisis, and the next day (called "Bloody Thursday"), paranoia swept stock markets around the world. Some stock markets (including the US stock market) experienced declines of more than 4%.

Impact of the Asian crisis on South Korea. By November 1997, seven of South Korea's conglomerates (called *chaebols*) had collapsed. The banks that financed the operations of the *chaebols* were stuck with the equivalent of $52 billion in bad debt as a result. Like banks in the South East Asian countries, South Korea's banks had been too willing to provide loans to corporations (especially the chaebols) without conducting a thorough credit analysis. The banks had apparently engaged in such risky lending because they assumed that economic growth would continue at a rapid pace and therefore exaggerated the future cash flows that borrowers would have available to pay off their loans. In addition, South Korean banks had traditionally extended loans to the conglomerates without assessing whether the loans could be repaid. In November, South Korea's currency (the won) declined substantially, and the central bank attempted to use its reserves to prevent a free fall in the won but with little success. Meanwhile, the credit ratings of several banks were downgraded because of their bad loans.

On 3 December 1997, the IMF agreed to enact a $55 billion dollar rescue package for South Korea. The World Bank and the Asian Development Bank joined with the IMF to provide a standby credit line of $35 billion. If that amount was not sufficient, other countries (including Japan and the United States) had agreed to provide a credit line of $20 billion. The total available credit (assuming it was all used) exceeded the credit provided in the Mexican bailout of 1994 and made this the largest bailout ever. In exchange for the funding, South Korea agreed to reduce its economic growth and to restrict the conglomerates from excessive borrowing. This restriction resulted in some bankruptcies and unemployment, as the banks could not automatically provide loans to all conglomerates needing funds unless the funding was economically justified.

Impact of the Asian crisis on China. Ironically, China did not experience the adverse economic effects of the Asian crisis because it had grown less rapidly than the South East Asian countries in the years prior to the crisis. The Chinese government had more control over economic conditions because it still owned most real estate and still controlled most of the banks that provided credit to support growth. Thus, there were fewer bankruptcies resulting from the crisis in China. In addition, China's government was able to maintain the value of the yuan against the dollar, which limited speculative flows of funds out of China. Though interest rates increased during the crisis, they remained relatively low. Consequently Chinese firms could obtain funding at a reasonable cost and could continue to meet their interest payments.

Nevertheless, concerns about China mounted because it relies heavily on exports to stimulate its economy; China was now at a competitive disadvantage relative to the South East Asian countries whose currencies had depreciated. Thus, importers from the United States and Europe shifted some of their purchases to those countries. In addition, the decline in the other Asian currencies against the Chinese yuan encouraged Chinese consumers to purchase imports instead of locally manufactured products.

Lessons about exchange rates and intervention from the Asian crisis. The Asian crisis demonstrated the degree to which currencies could depreciate in response to a lack of confidence by investors and firms in a central bank's ability to stabilize its local currency. If investors and firms had believed the central banks could prevent the free fall in currency values, they would not have transferred their funds to other countries, and South East Asian currency values would not have experienced such downward pressure.

Exhibit 6.5 shows how exchange rates of some Asian currencies changed against the US dollar during one year of the crisis (from June 1997 to June 1998). In particular, the currencies of Indonesia, Malaysia, South Korea, and Thailand declined substantially.

The Asian crisis also demonstrated how interest rates could be affected by flows of funds out of countries. Exhibit 6.6 illustrates how interest rates changed from June 1997 (just before the crisis) to June 1998 for various Asian countries. The increase in interest rates can be attributed to the indirect interventions intended to prevent the local currencies from depreciating further, or to the massive outflows of funds, or to both of these conditions. In particular, interest rates of Indonesia, Malaysia, and Thailand increased

Exhibit 6.5 How exchange rates changed during the Asian Crisis (June 1997–June 1998)

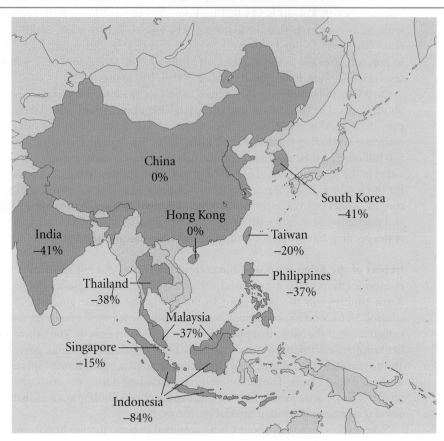

substantially from their pre-crisis levels. Those countries whose local currencies experienced more depreciation had higher upward adjustments. Since the substantial increase in interest rates (which tends to reduce economic growth) may have been caused by the outflow of funds, it may have been indirectly due to the lack of confidence by investors and firms in the ability of the Asian central banks to stabilize the local currencies.

Finally, the Asian crisis demonstrated how integrated country economies are, especially during a crisis. Just as the US and European economies can affect emerging markets, they are susceptible to conditions in emerging markets. Even if a central bank can withstand the pressure on its currency caused by conditions in other countries, it cannot necessarily insulate its economy from other countries that are experiencing financial problems.

The recent decline of the dollar. Between January 2001 and January 2005 the dollar had lost 30% against the euro and over 22% against the British pound. The US government has, as part of its management strategy, chosen not to reverse this change. One explanation for the fall is that the balance of payments in goods and services had risen from $363 billion (i.e. $363,000,000,000) to $618 billion in 2004. The oversupply of dollars for foreign currency can be expected to lower the price of a free floating currency such as the dollar. The problem for the US is that imports over the same period increased by 30% and exports by only 18%. A depreciating dollar should make imports more expensive,

Exhibit 6.6 How interest rates changed during the Asian crisis (number before "/" represents annualized interest rate as of June 1997; number after the "/" represents annualized interest rate as of June 1998)

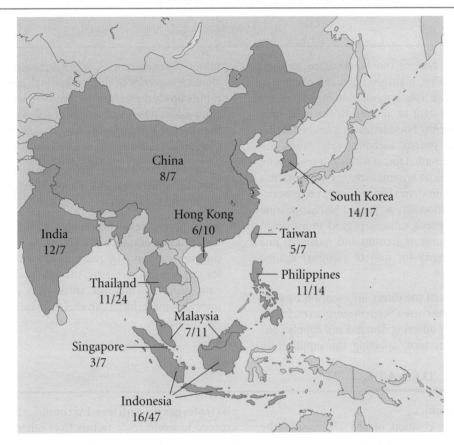

exports cheaper and therefore correct the balance of payments deficit. There are a number of possible explanations as to why this did not happen:

- GDP increased by 16% in monetary terms, a fixed propensity to import means that imports will increase along with other expenditure.

- Multinationals increasingly source their production from all over the world. Exchange rates are only one of the considerations in locating production. A large but possibly temporary adverse movement of the dollar is an insufficient motive to reorganize production.

- Oil is priced in dollars. As one quarter of imports is on oil which is priced in dollars, a devaluing dollar, it has been suggested, has been the cause of recent large increases in the price of oil which clearly does not help US imports.

- Relatively low domestic savings in America has forced the US government to borrow from overseas. The ready supply of foreign currency to buy US Treasury Bills has prevented the dollar from declining further, as a result imports have also not declined by as much as would have been expected.

One scenario is that ever increasing indebtedness of the US to the rest of the world, caused by the positive balance on the financial account, will become unsustainable. As at the end of the 1960s, a rapid sale of the dollar could bring about a collapse in its value. However, a more optimistic scenario is that the US is providing a secure place for the world's surplus savings and is therefore helping growth in the world economy.

SUMMARY

- Exchange rate systems can be classified as fixed rate, freely floating, managed float, and pegged. In a fixed exchange rate system, exchange rates are either held constant or allowed to fluctuate only within very narrow boundaries. In a freely floating exchange rate system, exchange rate values are determined by market forces without intervention. In a managed float system, exchange rates are not restricted by boundaries but are subject to government intervention. In a pegged exchange rate system, a currency's value is pegged to a foreign currency or a unit of account and moves in line with that currency (or unit of account) against other currencies.

- Governments can use direct intervention by purchasing or selling currencies in the foreign exchange market, thereby affecting demand and supply conditions and, in turn, affecting the equilibrium values of the currencies. When a government purchases a currency in the foreign exchange market, it puts upward pressure on the currency's equilibrium value. When a government sells a currency in the foreign exchange market, it puts downward pressure on the currency's equilibrium value.

- Governments can use indirect intervention by influencing the economic factors that affect equilibrium exchange rates.

- When government intervention is used to weaken the euro, for example, a weak euro can stimulate the euro economy by reducing the euro demand for imports and increasing the foreign demand for euro exports. Thus, the weak euro can reduce unemployment, but it can also increase inflation in the euro-zone.

CRITICAL DEBATE

To join or not to join...

Proposition. The position of the UK within the European Union (EU) is untenable. Whereas the UK enjoys the economic trade and investment benefits of being in the EU, by having a separate currency, it reserves for itself the right to make all its goods cheaper than other countries within the EU by devaluing against the euro. Since 2001 it has been as high as 1.6 euros:£1 and as low as 1.4 euros:£1. Harmonizing taxation, trade and competition within the EU makes little sense when one of the players has this enormous advantage. Furthermore, the ability of the UK to lower its prices is slowly forcing the EU to adopt the "Anglo-Saxon" model of the economy (low wages, little worker protection and wider gaps between rich and poor) in order to compete. The whole EU project is being undermined.

Opposing view. The status of the British pound does not confer benefits, rather it avoids injustice. UK residents borrow far more than in the EU, the euro interest rate policy could easily severely disadvantage the UK as was illustrated by "Black Wednesday". The UK

also trades heavily with non-EU countries and is more exposed to world trade factors than other EU countries. Given that the UK is a net contributor to the EU and that it runs a trade deficit with the EU, the benefits seem rather limited.

With whom do you agree? (Remember to include Appendix 6 in your reading.)

1. Is a single currency necessary for further EU integration?

2. Does the UK economy necessarily need a separate currency?

3. Is a separate currency really the cause of the spread of the Anglo-Saxon model; what other factors underlie the Anglo-Saxon model?

The gold standard

Proposition. Developing countries should adopt the gold standard! History shows that a lack of confidence in the currencies of developing countries is the major cause of the financial crises. Under the gold standard currencies would be convertible into gold. Currency value would be more stable, countries would be less likely to borrow excessively. More investment would be attracted to developing countries as in the pre-World War I era.

Opposing view. Credit would be restricted to the reserves of gold and would arrest development. Alternatively, convertibility would be limited. The large level of imports needed for a developing country would lead to balance of payments difficulties which in turn would lead to a reduction in the money supply as sterilization would not be possible. The consequent deflation would be disastrous for a developing country.

SELF TEST

Answers are provided in Appendix A at the back of the text.

1. Explain why it would be difficult to maintain a fixed exchange rate between the euro and the dollar.

2. Assume the European Central Bank (ECB) believes that the dollar should be weakened against the euro. Explain how the ECB could use direct and indirect intervention to weaken the dollar's value with respect to the euro. Assume that future inflation in the EU is expected to be low, regardless of the ECB's actions.

3. Briefly explain why a central bank may wish to weaken the value of its currency.

QUESTIONS AND APPLICATIONS

1. **Exchange rate systems.** Compare and contrast the fixed, freely floating, and managed float exchange rate systems. What are some advantages and disadvantages of a freely floating exchange rate system versus a fixed exchange rate system?

2. **Intervention with euros.** Assume that Belgium, one of the European countries that uses the euro as its currency, would prefer that its currency depreciate against the dollar. Can it apply central bank intervention to achieve this objective? Explain.

3. **Direct intervention.** How can a central bank use direct intervention to change the value of a currency? Explain why a central bank may desire to smooth exchange rate movements of its currency.

4. **Indirect intervention.** How can a central bank use indirect intervention to change the value of a currency?

5. **Intervention effects.** Assume there is concern that the United States may experience a recession. How should the Federal Reserve influence the dollar to prevent a recession? How might US exporters react to this policy (favourably or unfavourably)? What about US importing firms?

6. **Currency effects on economy.** What is the impact of a weak home currency on the home economy, other things being equal? What is the impact of a strong home currency on the home economy, other things being equal?

7. **Feedback effects.** Explain the potential feedback effects of a currency's changing value on inflation.

8. **Indirect intervention.** Why would indirect intervention by a central bank have a stronger impact on some currencies than others? Why would a central bank's indirect intervention have a stronger impact than its direct intervention?

9. **Effects on currencies tied to the dollar.** The Hong Kong dollar's value is tied to the US dollar. Explain how the following trade patterns would be affected by the appreciation of the Japanese yen against the dollar:
   a. Hong Kong exports to Japan.
   b. Hong Kong exports to the United States.

10. **Intervention effects on bond prices.** UK Treasury bill prices are normally inversely related to UK Treasury bill. If the Bank of England planned to use intervention to weaken the British pound, how might bond prices be affected?

11. **Direct intervention in Europe.** If most countries in Europe experience a recession, how might the European Central Bank use direct intervention to stimulate economic growth?

12. **Sterilized intervention.** Explain the difference between sterilized and nonsterilized intervention.

13. **Effects of indirect intervention.** Suppose that the government of Chile reduces one of its key interest rates. The values of several other Latin American currencies are expected to change substantially against the Chilean peso in response to the news.
    a. Explain why other Latin American currencies could be affected by a cut in Chile's interest rates.
    b. How would the central banks of other Latin American countries likely adjust their interest rates? How would the currencies of these countries respond to the central bank interventions?
    c. How would a US firm that exports products to Latin American countries be affected by the central bank interventions? (Assume the exports are denominated in the corresponding Latin American currency for each country.)

14. **Freely floating exchange rates.** Should the governments of Asian countries allow their currencies to float freely? What would be the advantages of letting their currencies float freely? What would be the disadvantages?

15. **Indirect intervention.** During the Asian crisis, some Asian central banks raised their interest rates to prevent their currencies from weakening. Yet, the currencies weakened anyway. Offer your opinion as to why the central banks' efforts at indirect intervention did not work.

ADVANCED QUESTIONS

16. **Monitoring of the central bank intervention.** Why do foreign market participants attempt to monitor the European Central Bank's direct intervention efforts? How does the ECB attempt to hide its intervention actions? The media frequently report that "the euro's value strengthened ahead of moves by the ECB to..." Explain why the euro's value may change even before the ECB takes action (for example a change in interest rates).

17. **Effects of September 11.** Within a few days after the September 11, 2001 terrorist attack on the United States, the Federal Reserve reduced short-term interest rates to stimulate the US economy. How might this action have affected the foreign flow of funds into the United States and affected the value of the dollar? How could such an effect on the dollar have increased the probability that the US economy would strengthen?

18. **Intervention effects on corporate performance.** Assume you have a subsidiary in Australia. The subsidiary sells mobile homes to local consumers in Australia, who buy the homes using mostly borrowed funds from local banks. Your subsidiary purchases all of its materials from Hong Kong. The Hong Kong dollar is tied to the US dollar. Your subsidiary borrowed funds from the US parent, and must pay the parent $100,000 in interest each month. Australia has just raised its interest rate in order to boost the value of its currency (Australian dollar, A$). The Australian dollar appreciates against the dollar as a result. Explain whether these actions would increase, reduce, or have no effect on:
    a. The volume of your subsidiary's sales in Australia (measured in A$).
    b. The cost to your subsidiary of purchasing materials (measured in A$).
    c. The cost to your subsidiary of making the interest payments to the US parent (measured in A$).
    Briefly explain each answer.

19. **Pegged currencies.** Why do you think a country suddenly decides to peg its currency to the dollar or some other currency? When a currency is unable to maintain the peg, what do you think are the typical forces that break the peg?

20. **Impact of intervention on currency option premiums.** Assume that the central bank of the country Zakow periodically intervenes in the foreign exchange market to prevent large upward or downward fluctuations in its currency (called the zak) against the US dollar. Today, the central bank announced that it will no longer intervene in the foreign exchange market. The spot rate of

the zak against the dollar was not affected by this news. Will the news affect the premium on currency call options that are traded on the zak? Will the news affect the premium on currency put options that are traded on the zak? Explain.

PROJECT WORKSHOP

21. **Bank of Japan.** The website for Japan's central bank, the Bank of Japan, provides information about its mission and its policy actions. Its address is http://www.boj.or.jp/en/index.htm.
    a. Use this website to summarize the mission of the Bank of Japan. How does this mission relate to intervening in the foreign exchange market?
    b. Review the minutes of recent meetings by Bank of Japan officials. Summarize at least one recent meeting that was associated with possible or actual intervention to affect the yen's value.
    c. Why might the foreign exchange intervention strategies of the Bank of Japan be relevant to the European governments and to European-based MNCs?

22. Use newspaper resources at your institution to summarize the arguments around one of the following groups of keywords:
    a. "Polish plumber" and "euro". In particular, focus on the need for cohesion in Europe to support the euro.
    b. "yuan" and "revaluation" and "trade restrictions". In particular, focus on the issues surrounding a revaluation (increase in value) of the Chinese currency.
    c. "imf" and "conditionality" and "Africa" and "exchange rate". In particular, focus on the problems of managing a weak currency.

One year, 2005, should be sufficient. You will need to choose the articles carefully. Avoid articles that are too detailed or not relevant. Try to sort out the main themes surrounding the issue. Include detailed references to source articles – it is a good idea to cut and paste all articles referred to into one Word file. Try to include at least one very recent article as evidence against plagiarism. Finally, you may vary the keywords to refine your theme; but do not spend hours looking for the elusive perfect article.

DISCUSSION IN THE BOARDROOM

This exercise can be found on the companion website at www.cengage.co.uk/madura_fox.

RUNNING YOUR OWN MNC

This exercise can be found on the companion website at www.cengage.co.uk/madura_fox.

Essays/discussion and articles can be found at the end of Part 2

BLADES PLC CASE STUDY
Assessment of government influence on exchange rates

Recall that Blades, the UK manufacturer of roller blades, generates most of its revenue and incurs most of its expenses in the United Kingdom. However, the company has recently begun exporting roller blades to Thailand. The company has an agreement with Entertainment Products, Inc., a Thai importer, for a three-year period. According to the terms of the agreement, Entertainment Products will purchase 180,000 pairs of "Speedos", Blades' primary product, annually at a fixed price of 4,594 Thai baht per pair. Due to quality and cost considerations, Blades is also importing certain rubber and plastic components from a Thai exporter. The cost of these components is approximately 2,871 Thai baht per pair of Speedos. No contractual agreement exists between Blades plc and the Thai exporter. Consequently, the cost of the rubber and plastic components imported from Thailand is subject not only to exchange rate considerations but to economic conditions (such as inflation) in Thailand as well.

Shortly after Blades began exporting to and importing from Thailand, Asia experienced weak economic conditions. Consequently, foreign investors in Thailand feared the baht's potential weakness and withdrew their investments, resulting in an excess supply of Thai baht for sale. Because of the resulting downward pressure on the baht's value, the Thai government attempted to stabilize the baht's exchange rate. To maintain the baht's value, the Thai government intervened in the foreign exchange market. Specifically, it swapped its baht reserves for dollar reserves at other central banks and then used its dollar reserves to purchase the baht in the foreign exchange market. However, this agreement required Thailand to reverse this transaction by exchanging dollars for baht at a future date. Unfortunately, the Thai government's intervention was unsuccessful, as it was overwhelmed by market forces. Consequently, the Thai government ceased its intervention efforts, and the value of the Thai baht declined substantially against the dollar over a three-month period.

When the Thai government stopped intervening in the foreign exchange market, Ben Holt, Blades' finance director, was concerned that the value of the Thai baht would continue to decline indefinitely. Since Blades generates net inflow in Thai baht, this would seriously affect the company's profit margin. Furthermore, one of the reasons Blades had expanded into Thailand was to appease the company's shareholders. At last year's annual shareholder meeting, they had demanded that senior management take action to improve the firm's low profit margins. Expanding into Thailand had been Holt's suggestion, and he is now afraid that his career might be at stake. For these reasons, Holt feels that the Asian crisis and its impact on Blades demand his serious attention. One of the factors Holt thinks he should consider is the issue of government intervention and how it could affect Blades in particular. Specifically, he wonders whether the decision to enter into a fixed agreement with Entertainment Products was a good idea under the circumstances. Another issue is how the future completion of the swap agreement initiated by the Thai government will affect Blades. To address these issues and to gain a little more understanding of the process of government intervention, Holt has prepared the following list of questions for you, Blades' financial analyst, since he knows that you understand international financial management.

1. Did the intervention effort by the Thai government constitute direct or indirect intervention? Explain.
2. Did the intervention by the Thai government constitute sterilized or nonsterilized intervention? What is the difference between the two types of intervention? Which type do you think would be more effective in increasing the value of the baht? Why? (Hint: think about the effect of nonsterilized intervention on UK interest rates.)
3. If the Thai baht is virtually fixed with respect to the dollar, how could this affect UK levels of inflation? Do you think these effects on the UK economy will be more pronounced for companies such as Blades that operate under trade arrangements involving commitments or for firms that do not? How are companies such as Blades affected by a fixed exchange rate?
4. What are some of the potential disadvantages for Thai levels of inflation associated with the floating exchange rate system that is now used in Thailand?

Do you think Blades contributes to these disadvantages to a great extent? How are companies such as Blades affected by a freely floating exchange rate?

5. What do you think will happen to the Thai baht's value when the swap arrangement is completed? How will this affect Blades?

SMALL BUSINESS DILEMMA
Assessment of central bank intervention by the Sports Exports Company

Jim Logan, owner of the Sports Exports Company, is concerned about the value of the British pound over time because his firm receives pounds as payment for basketballs exported to the United Kingdom. He recently read that the Bank of England (the central bank of the United Kingdom) is likely to intervene directly in the foreign exchange market by flooding the market with British pounds.

1. Forecast whether the British pound will weaken or strengthen based on the information provided.
2. How would the performance of the Sports Exports Company be affected by the Bank of England's policy of flooding the foreign exchange market with British pounds (assuming that it does not hedge its exchange rate risk)?

ECONOMIC CONSIDERATIONS OF THE EURO

Optimum currency areas. In 1961 Robert Mundell advanced the notion of an optimal currency area. He argued that if either labour and machinery were mobile and/or prices were flexible, the cost of joining a monetary union would be very low. The benefits of a union are those of a fixed exchange rate regime, in particular, less uncertainty and more competition.

Labour mobility has been questioned during the referendums that led to the recent rejection of a new constitution for Europe. The possibility of labour mobility expressed in the form of a "Polish plumber" in the French referendum. The notion that the local plumber might come from Poland caught the public imagination and was seen by many in France as unacceptable. Price flexibility is another difficulty. The high cost of labour in France and Germany compared to Spain and East European countries is in part responsible for the increase in unemployment in those countries. A lower cost of employment along with the resultant lower protection of workers rights is seen by many countries as leading to US-style or "Anglo-Saxon" economy.

The picture is rather brighter with regard to capital mobility. One way to assess such mobility is to measure the correlation of savings with investment within a country. If it is high, then investment is self funded within a country and there is deemed to be low capital mobility. Studies in the 1990s suggest that countries within the then European Monetary System had a low correlation compared to European countries outside the system (Sarno and Taylor 1998 and Bayoumi *et al.* 1999). Such results suggest that capital moves relatively freely within the currency area and therefore would not be correlated with any one country's savings. The sharing out of capital within the EU is helped by regional development grants giving aid to poorer areas. This is a relatively static part of EU expenditure being between 32% to 38% of EU operating expenditure compared to agriculture which is between 55% and 60%.

Reasons for joining a currency area in the case of the EU include wanting to create ever closer economic and social cohesion. Capital and labour mobility within a currency area has social as well as economic consequences that are entirely in line with the original aims of the EU as laid out in the Maastricht Treaty. There are also more immediate financial gains and some costs. On the plus side, there are the gains of having a fixed exchange rate with other countries in the exchange rate area – low price uncertainty and lower reserves of foreign exchange are needed. On the negative side is the centralization and potential loss of seigniorage (the profit from printing money). Regional grants from the EU offer limited recompense. Another benefit of being able to print money is that governments can fund operations. Where this is to excess, the result is inflation. But such inflation can be seen as a tax on the real value of savings. The decline in value of a balance of, say, 1,000 units of local currency due to inflation is the cost or "tax" that funds the excessive government money creation to fund projects. A higher inflation, lower direct tax country may have to alter its taxes to compensate the loss of the "inflation tax" as it is sometimes called. More generally, the loss of seigniorage is part of the development of a single monetary policy which is a direct consequence of a currency area such as the EU.

Impact on European monetary policy

The euro allows for a single money supply throughout the euro zone, rather than a separate money supply for each participating currency. This means that levels of government borrowing must be similar across participating countries. To this end the Stability and Growth pact was signed in 1997. The conditions of the pact, a balanced budget in the medium term and limited government borrowing to 3% of GDP, are very restrictive and have presented difficulties especially to members of the euro zone facing an economic slowdown. Even the UK in 2005 had to redefine the medium term in order to claim a balanced budget in the medium term under its parallel "Golden Rule". There is a certain irony in the fact that Germany, the country seen as sponsoring the pact, was in fact the country that in the early 1990s through monetary indiscipline during the unification of Germany was the cause of the break up of the narrow form of the ERM and to a certain extent the cause of Black Wednesday as explained above.

European Central Bank. The European Central Bank (ECB) is based in Frankfurt and is responsible for setting monetary policy for all participating European countries. Its objective is to control inflation in the participating countries and to stabilize (within reasonable boundaries) the value of the euro with respect to other major currencies. Thus, the ECB's monetary goals of price stability and currency stability are similar to those of individual countries around the world, but differ in that they are focused on a group of countries instead of a single country.

Implications of a European monetary policy. Although a single European monetary policy may allow for more consistent economic conditions across countries, it prevents any individual European country from solving local economic problems with its own unique monetary policy. European governments may disagree on the ideal monetary policy to enhance their local economies, but they must agree on a single European monetary policy.

The degree to which countries can pursue different *economic* policies whilst maintaining a common currency and monetary policy is something of an unanswered question. Crucial to any government policy is the level of government spending. Given that the amount of borrowing is controlled by being in the euro, further spending has to be financed by taxation (fiscal policy). For high tax countries (often cited as the Scandinavian countries and more generally all EU countries apart from the UK) the concern is that as barriers come down, businesses and higher earners will opt for lower tax countries within the EU (such an economy is often referred to as the "Anglo-Saxon model"). For governments wishing to increase spending to help a sluggish economy (France and Germany being examples in 2005), raising taxes is not a good policy as it takes money out of the economy that the government is trying to energize. Thus it is perhaps understandable that the Stability and Growth pact rules are being broken by a number of countries and also that the next step in integration that was represented by the European Constitution has met considerable resistance. The danger for the EU is that exchange rate policy (in this case the euro and the implied common monetary policy) and economic policy are beginning to diverge. At the heart of many a crisis is just such a divergence.

Impact on business within Europe

The euro enables residents of participating countries to engage in cross-border trade flows and capital flows throughout the euro zone (participating countries) without converting to a different currency. The elimination of currency movements among European countries also encourages more long-term business arrangements between firms of different countries, as they no longer have to worry about adverse effects due to currency movements. Thus, firms in different European countries are increasingly engaging in all types of business arrangements including licensing, joint ventures, and acquisitions.

Prices of products are now more comparable among European countries, as the exchange rate between the countries is fixed. Thus, buyers can more easily determine where they can obtain products at the lowest cost.

Trade flows between the participating European countries have increased because exporters and importers can conduct trade without concern about exchange rate movements. To the extent that there are more trade flows between these countries, economic conditions in each of these countries should have a larger impact on the other European countries, and economies of these countries may become more integrated. Yet, as noted above, the degree of integration and its speed are now in question.

Impact on the valuation of businesses in Europe

When non-EU firms consider acquiring targets in Europe, they can more easily compare the prices (market values) of targets among countries because their values are denominated in the same currency (the euro). In addition, the future currency movements of the target's currency against any non-European currency will be the same. Therefore, MNCs can more easily conduct valuations of firms across the participating European countries.

European firms face more pressure to perform well because they can be measured against all other firms in the same industry throughout the participating countries, not just within their own country. The influence of firms on individual governments is less in that specific help is likely to breach European competition rules. On the other hand the collective bargaining strength of the EU is much greater than the individual power of the constituent governments. As such EU firms offer stronger competition in the international marketplace than prior to the introduction of the euro and can be expected to increase in value.

Impact on financial flows

A single European currency forces the risk free interest rate offered on government securities to be similar across the participating European countries. Any discrepancy in rates would encourage investors within these European countries to invest in the currency with the highest rate, which would realign the interest rates among these countries. Any small differences are most likely due to technical reasons such as slightly differing conditions on the bond.

Stock prices are now more comparable among the European countries because they are denominated in the same currency. Investors in the participating European countries are now able to invest in stocks throughout these countries without concern about exchange rate risk. Thus, there is more cross-border investing than there was in the past.

Since stock market prices are influenced by expectations of economic conditions, the stock prices among the European countries may become more highly correlated if economies among these countries become more highly correlated. Investors from other countries who invest in European countries may not achieve as much diversification as in the past because of the integration and because the exchange rate effects will be the same for all markets whose stocks are denominated in euros. Stock markets in these European countries are also likely to consolidate over time now that they use the same currency. Bond investors based in these European countries can now invest in bonds issued by governments and corporations in these countries without concern about exchange rate risk, as long as the bonds are denominated in euros. Some European governments have already issued bonds that are redenominated in euros, because the secondary market for some bonds issued in Europe with other currency denominations is now less active. The bond yields in participating European countries are not necessarily similar even though they are now denominated in the same currency; the credit risk may still be higher for issuers in a particular country.

Impact on exchange rate risk

One major advantage of a single European currency is the complete elimination of exchange rate risk between the participating European countries, which could encourage more trade and capital flows across European borders. In addition, foreign exchange transaction costs associated with transactions between European countries have been eliminated. The single European currency is consistent with the goal of the Single European Act to remove trade barriers between European borders, since exchange rate risk is an implicit trade barrier.

The euro's value with respect to other currencies changes continuously. The euro's value is influenced by the trade flows and capital flows between the set of participating European countries and the other countries, since these flows affect supply and demand conditions. Its value with respect to the Japanese yen, for instance, is influenced by the trade flows and capital flows between the set of participating European countries and Japan.

Status report on the euro

The euro has experienced a volatile ride since it was introduced in 1999. Its value initially declined substantially against the British pound, the dollar, and many other currencies. In October 2001, for example, 33 months after it was introduced, its value was $0.88, or about 27% less than its initial value. The weakness was partially attributed to capital outflows from Europe. By June 2004, however, the euro was valued at $1.22, or 42% above its value in October 2001. The strength in the euro was partially due to the relatively high European interest rates compared to US interest rates in this period, which attracted capital inflows into Europe.

The main problem for the euro is the status of the Stability and Growth pact, in particular its borrowing restrictions. In 2005, Germany faces the fourth year of failing to comply with restrictions on government borrowing and is predicting similar problems for the foreseeable future. There is now open criticism of the euro and its attendant borrowing restrictions, first voiced at ministerial level in Italy (Roberto Maroni, the

Italian Welfare Minister in 2005). The governor of the Bank of France, Christian Noyer, has also in 2005 openly discussed the possibility of countries leaving the euro. The restrictions of the Stability and Growth pact, designed to maintain order between countries were set at a very conservative level – too conservative even for the German government. Many members of the euro-zone regard a measure of increased borrowing and government intervention as being needed to help sluggish economies. The European Commission in response has eased the restrictions of the Stability and Growth pact and some now regard it as effectively inoperative. At a time when a euro-zone macroeconomic policy needs to be negotiated to replace the pact, there is no effective forum and level of agreement among member states to decide on a policy. The issue is in some ways a playing out of the debate in the early 1990s at to whether there should be economic union (sometimes termed political union as the union is essentially about agreeing common economic policies – a political process) before monetary union or, as happened, monetary union before economic union. The European Constitution was designed to allow greater central decision-making powers that would have eased political and economic union. Its rejection, along with an easing of the Stability and Growth pact now leaves a currency with an uncertain management structure made up of the European Central Bank, the Commission and individual governments all having a significant independent influence. To be optimistic, the need for a coordinated fiscal policy (borrowing and taxation) is now self-evident and is being called for by academics and the IMF. A process of informal cooperation between central banks, the European Central Bank, the Commission and individual governments may well emerge to provide, de facto, the level of coordination not achieved by more formal agreement.

References

Sarno, L. and M.P. Taylor (1998) "Savings – Investment Correlations: Transitory versus Permanent", *Manchester Business School*, 66, 17–38.

Bayoumi, T.A., L. Sarno and M.P. Taylor (1999) "Macro Economic Shocks, the ERM, and Tripolarity", *Review of Economics and Statistics*, 77, 321–31.

Mundell, R.A. (1961) "A Theory of Optimal Currency Areas", *American Economic Review*, 51, 657–65.

CHAPTER 7

INTERNATIONAL ARBITRAGE AND INTEREST RATE PARITY

THE FOREIGN EXCHANGE MARKET is one of the most sophisticated of all world markets. If inconsistencies occur within the foreign exchange market, rates will be realigned by market traders. The process is termed international arbitrage. Financial managers of MNCs must understand how international arbitrage realigns exchange rates in order to begin to predict exchange rate behaviour. Arbitrage processes are therefore fundamental to assessing the foreign exchange risk faced by MNCs.

THE SPECIFIC OBJECTIVES OF THIS CHAPTER ARE TO:

■ explain the conditions that will result in various forms of international arbitrage, along with the realignments that will occur in response to various forms of international arbitrage, and

■ explain the concept of interest rate parity and how it prevents arbitrage opportunities.

INTERNATIONAL ARBITRAGE

Arbitrage can be loosely defined as making a profit from a discrepancy in quoted prices. The strategy does not involve risk (or at least the risk is trivially small) and, in many cases, does not require an investment of funds to be tied up for a length of time.

EXAMPLE

Two coin shops buy and sell coins. If Shop A is willing to sell a particular coin for £120, while Shop B is willing to buy that same coin for £130, a person can execute arbitrage by purchasing the coin at Shop A for £120 and selling it to Shop B for £130. The profit is certain (£10 less any travel costs) and the risk trivial – the trader might be mugged going from one shop to the other! The prices at coin shops can nevertheless vary because demand conditions may vary among shop locations. But if two coin shops are not aware of each other's prices and are sufficiently close to each other, the opportunity for arbitrage may occur. The act of arbitrage will cause prices to realign. In our example, arbitrage would cause Shop A to raise its price (due to high demand for the coin). At the same time, Shop B would reduce its buying price after receiving a surplus of coins as arbitrage occurs.

Arbitrage is therefore a very simple mechanism for determining prices and price behaviour and is a fundamental process in many financial proofs. The reasoning is that if the price in shop A can be calculated, then by arbitrage processes, it should be possible to predict the price in Shop B. In finance, the two "shops" may be two financial packages that offer the same benefits. Modigliani and Miller's[1] propositions and the Black Scholes option pricing model both use this argument.

The type of arbitrage discussed in this chapter is primarily international in scope; it is applied to foreign exchange and international money markets and takes three common forms:

- Locational arbitrage
- Triangular arbitrage
- Covered interest arbitrage

Each form will be discussed in turn.

Locational arbitrage

Commercial banks providing foreign exchange services normally quote about the same rates as each other on currencies, so shopping around may not necessarily lead to a more favourable rate. If the demand and supply conditions for a particular currency vary among banks, the banks may price that currency at different rates, and market forces will force realignment. That is to say, traders will change the market conditions when exploiting the price differences, ultimately forcing the same price for the same "product".

When quoted exchange rates vary among locations, participants in the foreign exchange market can capitalize on the discrepancy. Specifically, they can use **locational arbitrage**, which is the process of buying a currency at the location where it is priced cheaply and immediately selling it at another location where the price is higher.

---

1 For example see P. Vernimmen (2005) *Corporate Finance: Theory and Practice*, New York: Wiley, pp. 660 *et seq.*

EXAMPLE

Akron Bank and Zyn Bank serve the foreign exchange market by buying and selling currencies. Assume that there is no bid/ask spread. The exchange rate quoted at Akron Bank is £0.62 for $1, while the exchange rate quoted at Zyn Bank is £0.63. You could conduct locational arbitrage by purchasing dollars at Akron Bank for £0.62 per dollar and then selling them to Zyn Bank for £0.63 per dollar. Under the condition that there is no bid/ask spread and there are no other costs to conducting this arbitrage strategy, your gain would be £0.01 per dollar. The gain is risk-free in that you knew when you purchased the dollars how much you could sell them for. Also, you did not have to tie your funds up for any length of time.

Locational arbitrage is normally conducted by banks or other foreign exchange dealers whose computers can continuously monitor the quotes provided by other banks. If other banks noticed a discrepancy between Akron Bank and Zyn Bank, they would quickly engage in locational arbitrage to earn an immediate risk-free profit. Since banks have a bid/ask spread on currencies, this next example accounts for the spread.

Exhibit 7.1 Currency quotes for locational arbitrage example

	Akron Bank			Zyn Bank	
	Bid (bank *buys* dollars)	Ask (bank *sells* dollars)		Bid (bank *buys* dollars)	Ask (bank *sells* dollars)
Dollar quote	£0.61	£0.62	Dollar quote	£0.62	£0.63

EXAMPLE

The information on British pounds at both banks is revised to include the bid/ask spread in Exhibit 7.1. Based on these quotes, you can no longer profit from locational arbitrage. If you buy pounds from Akron Bank at £0.62 (the bank's ask price) and then sell the pounds at Zyn Bank at its bid price of £0.62, you just break even. If you tried it the other way around and buy from Zyn bank at £0.63 and sell to Akron bank at £0.61 you would make a loss. As this example demonstrates, even when the bid or ask prices of two banks are different, locational arbitrage will not always be possible. To achieve profits from locational arbitrage, the bid price of one bank must be higher than the ask price of another bank.

Gains from locational arbitrage. Gains from locational arbitrage are based on the amount of money used to capitalize on the exchange rate discrepancy, along with the size of the discrepancy.

EXAMPLE

Quotations for the New Zealand dollar (NZ$) at two banks are shown in Exhibit 7.2. You can obtain New Zealand dollars from North Bank at the ask price of £0.38 and then sell New Zealand dollars to South Bank at the bid price of £0.39. This represents one "round-trip" transaction in locational arbitrage. If you start with £10,000 and conduct one round-trip transaction, how many British pounds will you end up with? The £10,000 is initially exchanged for NZ$26,316 (£10,000/£0.38 per New Zealand dollar) at North Bank. Then the NZ$26,316 are sold for £0.39 each, for a total of £10,263. Thus, your gain from locational arbitrage is £263.

A briefer calculation is to observe that for every £0.38 a profit of £0.39 − £0.38 = £0.01 is made. As a percentage, this profit is £0.01 / £0.38 = 2.63%, which for £10,000 is £10,000 × 0.0263 = £263. As a note of caution, it is advisable to avoid short cuts unless very familiar with the calculation, the safer, longer route of calculating a "round-trip" is preferable!

Exhibit 7.2 Locational arbitrage

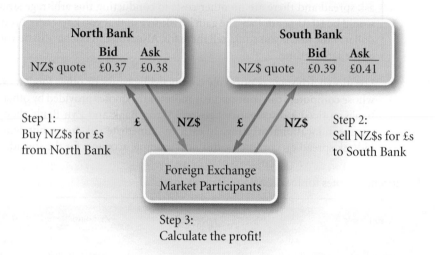

North Bank

	Bid	Ask
NZ$ quote	£0.37	£0.38

South Bank

	Bid	Ask
NZ$ quote	£0.39	£0.41

Step 1:
Buy NZ$s for £s
from North Bank

£   NZ$ £   NZ$

Step 2:
Sell NZ$s for £s
to South Bank

Foreign Exchange
Market Participants

Step 3:
Calculate the profit!

The gain of £263 may appear to be small relative to the investment of $10,000. However, consider that funds were not tied up for any length of time and that there was no risk. The round-trip transaction could take place over a telecommunications network within a matter of seconds for hundreds of times a day. Also, if a larger sum of money were used the gain would be larger each "round-trip". In financial terms, this transaction amounts to earning limitless amounts of money for no risk – the financial equivalent of a "free lunch" and there are no "free lunches" in finance! It is important to emphasize, therefore, that such a misalignment of prices is only likely to last for a very short period of time.

If you notice an apparent misalignment of prices in the financial press, the likely explanations are that:

1. the prices are not accurate (for example they may have been taken at different times of the day);
2. there are regulations and restrictions concerning the purchase and selling of the currencies that make the proposed round-trip impossible;
3. the difference does not cover transaction costs which include commissions;
4. you have not identified the element of risk.

Unfortunately, the press often uses the word "arbitrage" for transactions that are risky and therefore give the impression that such profits are common. In any event do not attempt to pay for your education through part-time locational arbitrage!

Realignment due to locational arbitrage. Quoted prices will react to the locational arbitrage strategy used by foreign exchange market participants.

EXAMPLE

In the previous example, the high demand for New Zealand dollars at North Bank (resulting from arbitrage activity) will cause a shortage of New Zealand dollars there. As a result of this shortage, North Bank will raise its ask price for New Zealand dollars. The excess supply of New Zealand dollars at South Bank (resulting from sales of New Zealand dollars to South Bank in exchange for US dollars) will force South Bank to lower its bid price. As the currency prices are adjusted, gains from locational arbitrage will be reduced. Once the ask price of North Bank is not any lower than the bid price of South Bank, locational arbitrage will no longer occur. Prices may adjust in a matter of seconds or minutes from the time when locational arbitrage occurs.

The concept of locational arbitrage is relevant in that it explains why exchange rate quotations among banks at different locations normally will not differ by a significant amount. This applies not only to banks on the same street or within the same city but to all banks across the world. Technology allows banks to be electronically connected to foreign exchange quotations at any time. Thus, banks can ensure that their quotes are in line with those of other banks. They can also immediately detect any discrepancies among quotations as soon as they occur, and capitalize on those discrepancies. Thus, technology enables more consistent prices among banks and reduces the likelihood of significant discrepancies in foreign exchange quotations among locations.

Triangular arbitrage

Cross exchange rates represent the relationship between two currencies that are different from the chosen base currency. Taking the UK as the base currency, the term *cross exchange rate* refers to the implied exchange rate between two foreign currencies that exists when there are two quotes for foreign currencies in terms of British pounds. The calculation is illustrated by the following example.

EXAMPLE

If the US dollar is worth £0.50 and the euro is worth £0.80 there is an implied or cross exchange rate between the euro and the dollar. This is because the holder of euros wanting to convert to dollars could do so directly or indirectly by converting into British pounds and then converting the pounds into dollars. This second method uses the cross exchange rate. To calculate the rate we can use a simple equation approach.

The above exchange rates can be written as:

£0.50 = $1 or taking the inverse £1 = $2.0 (see Chapter 3)

£0.80 = 1 euro or taking the inverse £1 = 1.25 euro

Therefore $2.0 = 1.25 euro as they are both worth £1.

Putting this exchange rate in more traditional form:

$2.0 = 1.25 euro → divide both sides by 1.25 → $1.6 equals 1 euro

or

$2.0 = 1.25 euro → divide both sides by 2.00 → $1 equals 0.625 euros

Therefore, to calculate the cross exchange rate, find out the value of the currencies to one unit of the common currency. Then equate those values and convert the equation to traditional form.

If a quoted direct exchange rate differs from the appropriate cross exchange rate (as determined by the preceding formula), you can attempt to capitalize on the discrepancy. Specifically, you can use **triangular arbitrage**, in which currency transactions are conducted in the spot market to capitalize on a discrepancy in the cross exchange rate between two currencies.

EXAMPLE

Assume that a UK bank has quoted the US dollar at $1.60 to the British pound, the Malaysian ringgit (MYR) at MYR8.1 to the pound, and the third exchange rate at $0.20 for one Malaysian ringgit. If, as a UK businessman or businesswoman, you wanted to convert 100,000 ringgit to pounds, would it be preferable to convert at the direct rate of £1 = MYR8.1 or use the cross exchange rate by converting the ringgit into dollars and then the dollars into pounds (see Exhibit 7.3)?

Looking at the rates involved in the cross rate calculation, $0.20 = 1MYR and $1.60 = £1 or taking the inverses $1 = £0.625 and $1 = 5MYR the implied pound to ringgit rate is £0.625 = 5 MYR or (dividing both sides by 0.625) 8 MYR = £1. So the pound is cheaper when the cross exchange route (8 MYR) is taken compared to the direct route (8.1 MYR). Taking the calculation step by step:

1. Convert ringgit to dollars: 100,000 MYR × $0.20 = $20,000.
2. Convert the $20,000 to pounds: $20,000 / $1.60 = £12,500.
3. Compare with direct conversion: 100,000MYR / 8.1 MYR = £12,346. So using the cross exchange rate is better by £12,500 − £12,346 = £154

Speculators using the arbitrage process could borrow in pounds for a very short period. Convert to ringgit at the rate of 8.1MYR, convert the ringgit to dollars and then from dollars back into pounds (anticlockwise around the triangle). This is equivalent to con-

Exhibit 7.3 Converting ringgit to pounds

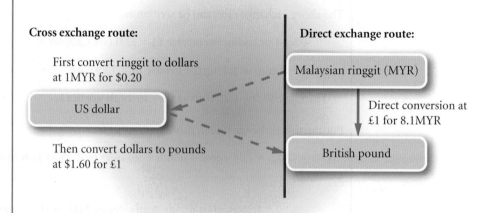

Cross exchange route:

First convert ringgit to dollars at 1MYR for $0.20

US dollar

Then convert dollars to pounds at $1.60 for £1

Direct exchange route:

Malaysian ringgit (MYR)

Direct conversion at £1 for 8.1MYR

British pound

verting into ringgit at 8.1MYR to the pound and converting back at 8.0MYR to the pound (the cross exchange rate calculated above). For every £100 converted in this way the gain would be £1.25 or 1.25% of the initial investment. Assuming no transaction costs, the rates would eventually change so that there was no profit to be gained in this way. With transaction costs, the cross exchange route might not be cheaper and these rates may remain.

Like locational arbitrage, triangular arbitrage does not tie up funds. Also, the strategy is risk-free, since there is no uncertainty about the prices at which you will buy and sell the currencies. As the market does not like profit to be earned for no risk, any gains are likely to be for a very short period of time.

Accounting for the bid/ask spread. As noted, the previous example was simplified in that it did not account for transaction costs. In reality, there is a bid and ask quote for each currency, which means that the arbitrageur incurs transaction costs that can reduce or even eliminate the gains from triangular arbitrage. The following example illustrates how bid and ask prices can affect arbitrage profits.

E X A M P L E Using Exhibit 7.4, you can determine whether or not triangular arbitrage is possible by starting with some fictitious amount (say £10,000) of British pounds and estimating the number of pounds you would generate by going "around the triangle" in Exhibit 7.4. Note that the task has changed from the previous example only in that the speculator is simply interested in the consistency of the exchange rates and can test the rates by converting pounds to ringgit, then ringgit to dollars and finally dollars to pounds. If the rates are not aligned, a profit or loss will be made. If there is a loss, then going the other way around the triangle will yield a profit.

Exhibit 7.4 Currency quotes for a triangular arbitrage example

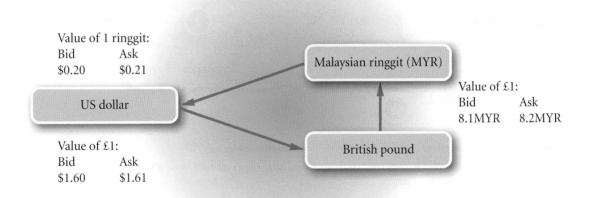

The initial £10,000 will be converted into ringgit at the bid rate (bank buys) of 8.1MYR so 81,000MYR. Then convert the ringgit to dollars at the bid rate of $0.20 yielding 81,000MYR × $0.20 = $16,200. Finally, convert the $16,200 into pounds at the ask rate (bank sells) of $1.61, so $16,200 / 1.61 = £10,062.11, a profit of £62.11. This profit is less than the previous example due to the bid ask spread (which is a profit margin or transaction cost) charged by the banks.

Realignment due to triangular arbitrage. The realignment that results from the triangular arbitrage activity is summarized in Exhibit 7.5. The realignment is likely to occur quickly to prevent continued benefits from triangular arbitrage. The discrepancies assumed here are unlikely to occur within a single bank. More likely, triangular arbitrage would require three transactions at three separate banks.

The exchange rate between the three currencies is displayed in Exhibit 7.5. If any two of these three exchange rates are known, the exchange rate of the third pair can be determined. When the actual exchange rate differs from the implied cross exchange rate, the exchange rates of the currencies are not in equilibrium. Triangular arbitrage would force the exchange rates back into equilibrium.

Like locational arbitrage, triangular arbitrage is a strategy that few of us can ever take advantage of because the computer technology available to foreign exchange dealers can easily detect misalignments in cross exchange rates. It is because of triangular arbitrage that cross exchange rates are usually aligned correctly. If they are not, triangular arbitrage will take place until the rates are aligned correctly.

Exhibit 7.5 Currency quotes for a triangular arbitrage example

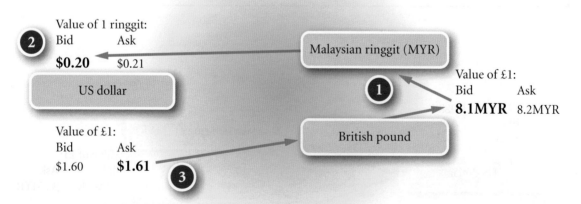

One or more of theses effect should occur such that profits are no longer possible:

1. High demand for ringgit from pounds, results in pressure for a fall in ringgit offered to make it less attractive. Arbitrageur gets fewer ringgit.

2. High demand for dollars from ringgit, results in pressure for a fall in dollars offered to make it less attractive. Arbitrageur gets fewer dollars.

3. High demand for pounds at this rate, bank makes pound more expensive by raising the rate. Arbitrageur gets fewer pounds.

Covered interest arbitrage

Covered interest arbitrage is the process of capitalizing on interest rate differences between two countries while covering exchange rate risk. The logic of the term *covered interest arbitrage* becomes clear when it is broken into two parts: "interest arbitrage" refers to the process of capitalizing on the difference between the interest rates of two countries; "covered" refers to hedging your position against exchange rate risk by converting at today's quote for a forward exchange transaction rather than taking a risk and converting at whatever the spot rate is at the future point in time.

Covered interest arbitrage differs from conventional arbitrage in that investment and a period of time is required in the process. However, the profit is made at the moment of concluding the arbitrage package in much the same way as any other arbitrage operation. An arbitrageur can always sell the package and obtain the discounted value of the profit immediately as with other arbitrage arrangements. The following is an example of such an arbitrage operation:

E X A M P L E

As a UK currency trader, you desire to capitalize on relatively high rates of interest in the United States compared with the United Kingdom and have funds available for 90 days. The interest rate is certain; only the future exchange rate from dollars into pounds is uncertain. You can use a forward sale of dollars to guarantee the rate at which you can exchange dollars for pounds at a future point in time (see Exhibit 7.6). The strategy is as follows:

1. On day 1, convert your British pounds into dollars and set up a 90-day deposit account in a US bank. Work out value of the account after 90 days.
2. On day 1, engage in a 90-day forward contract to sell the dollars accumulated in step 1 for pounds. The arbitrage deal is now complete and the profit guaranteed.
3. In 90 days, when the deposit matures, fulfil the 90-day forward contract and convert the dollars back into pounds at the agreed forward rate.

Exhibit 7.6 Covered interest arbitrage

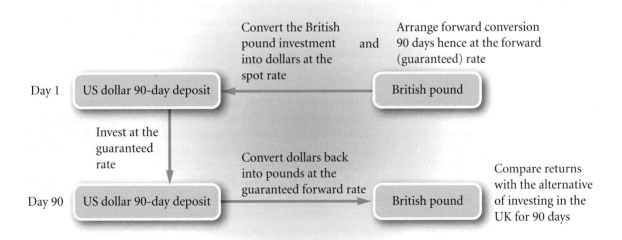

If the proceeds from engaging in covered interest arbitrage exceed the proceeds from investing in a domestic bank deposit, and assuming neither deposit is subject to default risk, covered interest arbitrage is feasible. The feasibility of covered interest arbitrage is based on the interest rate differential and the forward rate premium. To illustrate, consider the following numerical example.

Assume the following information:

EXAMPLE

- You have £800,000 to invest.
- The current spot rate of the dollar is £0.625.
- The 90-day forward rate of the pound is £0.625.
- The 90-day interest rate in the United Kingdom is 2%.
- The 90-day interest rate in the United States is 4%.

These interest rates are rather high and are for illustrative purposes only. 90 days is 90/360 or ¼ of a year so the annual rate in the US is approximately 16% (i.e. 4 × 4%)!
Based on this information, you should proceed as follows:

1. On day 1, convert the £800,000 to $1,280,000 and deposit the $1,280,000 in a US bank.
2. On day 1, sell $1,331,200 at the 90-days forward rate at the contract rate of £0.625 to the dollar. Note that by the time the deposit matures, you will have $1,280,000 × 1.04 = $1,331,200 (including interest).
3. In 90 days when the deposit matures, you can fulfil your forward contract obligation by converting your $1,331,200 into £832,000 (based on the forward contract rate of £0.625 per dollar).

This reflects a 4% return over the three-month period (calculated as (£832,000 − £800,000)/£800,000 = 4%), which is twice as much as the 2% return on the UK investment over a similar period. The return on the foreign deposit is known on day 1, since you know when you make the deposit exactly how many dollars you will get back from your 90-day investment.

Recall that locational and triangular arbitrage do not tie up funds; thus, any profits are achieved instantaneously. In the case of covered interest arbitrage, the funds are tied up for a period of time (90 days in our example). This strategy would not be advantageous if it earned 2% per annum or less, since you could earn 2% on a domestic deposit for the same level of (no) risk.

Realignment due to covered interest arbitrage. The comments made about previous arbitrage operations apply here as well. The market does not allow profit to be made without taking a risk. So if this were a real example, one would only see the misalignment very briefly and probably not at all. Only if there were transaction costs would the forward rate not be in alignment with the interest rate differential.

Covered interest arbitrage affects four variables (if between the UK and US): pound spot rate, British interest rate, US interest rate, and the pound forward rate. The normal assumption is that the forward rate adjusts to the other variables. In practice, future expectations drives all four variables at the same time and a more accurate description would be to say that the variables are codetermined. One would therefore expect the variables to change together such that there is a reduction in excess arbitrage profits.

EXAMPLE

Using the information from the previous example, Exhibit 7.7 summarizes the potential impact of covered interest arbitrage on exchange rates and interest rates and the forward rate. For the sake of explanation, the assumption is made here that all variables except the forward rate are fixed and that it is the forward rate alone that adjusts. But it should be remembered that in practice the process of adjustment is more complex.

In the previous example, if we assume no adjustment to interest rates, covered interest arbitrage will be feasible until the loss in value of the dollar on the forward exchange exactly offsets the gain in interest rates. Here we work out the forward rate that yields no profit. Given that the US interest rate is 2% above the British rate, UK investors can benefit from covered interest arbitrage until the forward rate of the dollar is 2% less in value than the spot rate.

The spot rate is £0.625 to the dollar. The offsetting 2% fall in the value of the dollar on the forward market is calculated as follows:

$$£0.625 \times (1.02/1.04) = £0.61298 \text{ to the dollar.}$$

(Note that the approximate approach is to say that the value of the dollar will be 2% − 4% = −2% or 2% less, so 98% of £0.625 is £0.6125. The exact relationship is to divide rather than subtract so 1.02/1.04 = 0.980769, so 98.0769% of £0.625 which is £0.61298. The very small rounding error of £1 is due to rounding to five decimal places! See the interest rate parity derivation below for a more formal derivation of this relationship.)

The arbitrage operation now appears as follows:

1. On day 1, convert the £800,000 to $1,280,000 and deposit the $1,280,000 in a US bank.
2. On day 1, sell the amount deposited plus the interest that will be credited to the account, i.e. $1,331,200 (note that $1,280,000 × 1.04 = $1,331,200) at the new 90-day forward rate of £0.61298 to the dollar.

Exhibit 7.7 Covered interest arbitrage market pressures from profitable arbitrage (in italics)

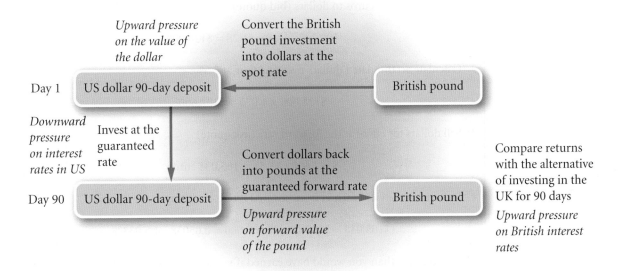

3. In 90 days when the deposit matures, you can fulfil your forward contract obligation by converting your $1,331,200 at the forward rate of £0.61298 into £816,000 (there is a £1.024 rounding error).

The £816,000 is a return of (£816,000 − £800,000) / £800,000 = 0.02 or 2% the same return as investing in the UK. So there are now no gains through interest rate arbitrage.

As this example shows, those individuals who initially conduct covered interest arbitrage cause exchange rates and possibly interest rates to move in such a way that future attempts at covered interest arbitrage provide a return that is no better than what is possible domestically. Due to the market forces from covered interest arbitrage, a relationship between the forward rate premium and interest rate differentials should exist. This relationship is discussed shortly.

Consideration of spreads. One more example is provided to illustrate the effects of the spread between the bid and ask quotes and the spread between deposit and loan rates.

EXAMPLE

Suppose that a holder of euros is considering investing in the US to exploit the higher interest rate. A US bank has quoted the following details:

	Bid Quote	Ask Quote
Euro spot	$1.28	$1.30
Euro one-year forward	$1.30	$1.31
	Deposit Rate	
Interest rate on dollars	7.5%	
Interest rate on euros	6.5%	

You have 100,000 euros to invest for one year. Would you benefit from engaging in covered interest arbitrage?

1. Convert 100,000 euros to dollars (bid quote):

$$100,000 \text{ euros} \times \$1.28 = \$128,000$$

2. Calculate accumulated dollars over one year at 7.5%:

$$\$128,000 \times 1.075 = \$137,600$$

3. Sell dollars for euros at the forward rate (ask quote):

$$\$137,600 / \$1.31 = 105,038 \text{ euros}$$

4. Determine the yield earned from covered interest arbitrage:

$$(\$105,038 − \$100,000)/ \$100,000 = 0.05038, \text{ or } 5.038\%$$

The yield is less than you would have earned if you had invested the funds in the eurozone. Thus, covered interest arbitrage is not profitable.

There are two sources of gain or loss in covered interest arbitrage, the first is the interest rate differential and the second is the gain or loss from currency conversion. The two can be separated in approximate terms:

Interest rate differential   7.5% – 6.5%   =   1% gain

Currency conversion: the investment was

multiplied by 1.28 and converted back by

dividing by 1.31. The net change is:

$$\$1.28 / 1.31 - 1 \quad = \quad \underline{2.3\% \text{ loss}}$$

Approximate net gain or loss   1.3% loss

The actual loss would have been 6.5% – 5.038% = 1.462%. The analysis, though approximate, is useful in that it shows that the gain in interest rates is more than offset by the loss in value of the dollar on the forward market. Where there are no gains or losses overall in the arbitrage operation, the two sources will offset each other.

Finally, note that the arbitrage operation shows that there are powerful market forces to ensure that the forward rate is linked to the spot rate by the interest rate differential. Interest rates are rather slow to move, being adjusted once a month in the UK by the Bank of England. Reasons for moving the rates will often have little to do directly with the future value of the currency. Therefore, any news about the future value of a currency that affects the forward rate will almost certainly affect the spot rate. They both look to the future value of the currency. Using the current spot rate to predict changes to the future spot rate (i.e. a prediction of no change in the rate) may therefore be a good predictor in practice and possibly no worse than using the forward rate.

COMPARISON OF ARBITRAGE EFFECTS

Exhibit 7.8 provides a comparison of the three types of arbitrage. The threat of locational arbitrage ensures that quoted exchange rates are similar across banks in different locations. The threat of triangular arbitrage ensures that exchanging money via another currency is in line with direct conversion. The threat of covered interest arbitrage ensures that forward exchange rates offset interest rate differentials.

INTEREST RATE PARITY (IRP)

Once market forces cause interest rates and exchange rates to adjust such that covered interest arbitrage is no longer feasible, there is an equilibrium state referred to as **interest rate parity (IRP)**. In equilibrium, the forward rate differs from the spot rate by a sufficient amount to offset the interest rate differential between two currencies. In the previous example, the European investor receives a higher interest rate from the investment in the US, but there is an offsetting effect because the investor finds that the euro has increased in value against the dollar over the period (or equivalently, the dollar has fallen in value or devalued against the euro).

Exhibit 7.8 Comparing arbitrage operations

Locational arbitrage: Capitalizes on discrepancies in exchange rates between two locations.

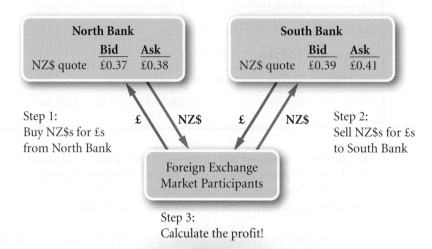

Step 1:
Buy NZ$s for £s
from North Bank

Step 2:
Sell NZ$s for £s
to South Bank

Step 3:
Calculate the profit!

Triangular arbitrage: Capitalizes on discrepancies in cross exchange rates.

If the exchange rates are properly aligned, apart
from transaction costs, £100 converted to MYR
then to $s, should then convert back to £100.

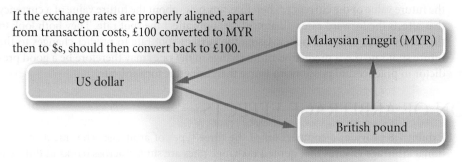

Covered interest arbitrage: Capitalizes on discrepancies between the forward rate and
interest rate differentials.

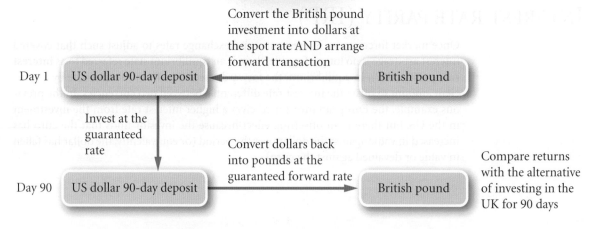

Derivation of interest rate parity

Recall that the forward rate is at a premium when the foreign currency is more expensive in the future and at a discount when the foreign currency is less expensive in the future. So, from the previous example taking the euro as the home currency, one can say that the dollar discount more than offset the interest rate differential. Interest rate parity (IRP) maintains that the return from investing abroad and converting back to the home currency at the forward rate (covered interest arbitrage) is the same as investing domestically. A currency forward premium or discount should exactly offset any difference in interest rates otherwise arbitrage profits will be possible.

The following analysis takes a more formal look at the elements of return from covered interest rate arbitrage and its relation with returns from home investment. A practical example then follows.

Consider a UK investor who attempts covered interest arbitrage. The investor's return from using covered interest arbitrage can be determined given the following:

- The amount of the home currency (UK pounds in our example) that is initially invested (A_h).
- The spot rate (S) in direct form, i.e. pounds to a single unit of foreign currency.
- The interest rate on the foreign deposit (i_f).
- The forward rate (F) in pounds to a single unit of foreign currency.

The amount of the home currency received after investing A_h in a foreign deposit and converting back at the forward rate is denoted as A_n:

$$A_n = (A_h / S)(1 + i_f) F$$

Since F, the forward rate, can be written as the spot rate (S) times one plus the forward premium (called p), i.e. $F = S(1 + p)$, we can rewrite this equation as:

$$A_n = (A_h / S)(1 + i_f)[(S(1 + p)]$$

S cancels out so:

$$A_n = A_h(1 + i_f)(1 + p)$$

The rate of return from investing abroad (called R) is as follows:

$$R = \frac{A_n - A_h}{A_h}$$

Expanding, using the above formula for A_n

$$R = \frac{A_h(1 + i_f)(1 + p) - A_h}{A_h}$$

A_h cancels out, not surprising in that one would not expect return to depend on the amount invested, so:

$$R = (1 + i_f)(1 + p) - 1$$

Returns from covered interest rate arbitrage is made up of the foreign interest rate (i_f) and the movement in the value of the foreign currency (p). Home investment (i_h) should yield a return that is the same as that on foreign investment (R) according to IRP:

$$R = i_h$$

Expanding the return on foreign investment (R) using the above formula we have:

$$(1 + i_f)\,(1 + p) - 1 = i_h$$

By rearranging terms, we can determine what the forward premium (p) of the foreign currency should be under conditions of IRP:

$$(1+i_f)(1+p)-1=i_h$$

$$(1+i_f)(1+p)=1+i_h$$

$$(1+p)=\frac{(1+i_h)}{(1+i_f)}$$

$$p=\frac{(1+i_h)}{(1+i_f)}-1$$

In words, where interest rate parity exists, the premium (p) is determined by the ratio of the interest rates. This relationship was used informally in the above example of covered interest rate arbitrage and is illustrated further below.

Determining the forward premium

From the above, the premium or discount can be simply determined.

EXAMPLE

Assume that the South African rand offers a six-month interest rate of 6%, while the British pound offers a six-month interest rate of 5%. From a UK investor's perspective, the British pound is the home currency. According to IRP, the forward rate premium of the rand with respect to the pound should be:

$$p=\frac{(1+i_h)}{(1+i_f)}-1$$

$$p=\frac{1+0.05}{1+0.06}-1=-0.0094339\,(\text{not annualized})$$

Thus, the rand should exhibit a forward discount of about 0.943% (rounded) over the six months. This implies that UK investors would receive 0.943% less when selling rands six months from now (based on a forward sale) than the price they pay for rands today at the spot rate. Such a discount would offset the interest rate advantage of the rand. If the rand's spot rate is £0.10, a forward discount of 0.943% means that the six-month forward rate is as follows:

$$F = S(1+p)$$
$$F = £0.10(1-0.00943) = £0.099057$$

At this forward rate, covered interest arbitrage would not be any more profitable than domestic investment. As a brief check: £100 would convert to £100/£0.10 = 1000 rand which would earn 1000 (1.06) = 1060 rand and convert back to pounds at the forward rate calculated above at £0.099057 so 1060 × £0.099057 = £105.00042 a rounding error of £0.00042 means that the absolute returns of £105.00042 – 0.00042 = £105 are the same as investing domestically at 5%.

Note that the relationship also means that South African investors would get the same return as domestic investment in South Africa, i.e. 6%. Again, a brief check will confirm this relationship. A South African investor with 1000 rand will convert at the spot rate of £0.10 to the rand, so 1000 × £0.10 = £100, which will earn 5% in the UK so the investor will end up with £100 × 1.05 = £105 and convert back at the forward rate of £0.099057 producing absolute returns of £105 / £0.099057 = 1059.99576 rand, a rounding error of 0.00424 rand means that the return will be 1059.99576 + 0.00424 = 1060 rand, the same amount as would be achieved domestically by investing at 6%.

This is a slightly counter intuitive result in that the forward rate allows UK investors (or rather holders of British pounds) to earn 5% and South African investors to earn 6%. The point is that the 5% is earned in pounds and the 6% is earned in rand. The arbitrage argument would suggest that although the rates may differ, relative inflation rates would result in the purchasing power of pounds and rand increasing at the same rate using covered interest arbitrage, otherwise there would be arbitrage possibilities from trading goods – this is confirmed more formally below. So the positions of the two investors are not quite as different as first might seem.

The approximate relationship between forward premium and interest rate differential. The forward premium (p), as a reminder, is derived from

$$F = S(1+p)$$

where F is the forward rate and S the spot rate. The premium is simply the amount by which the forward rate is more or less than the spot.

The exact relationship between the forward premium (or discount) and the interest rate differential according to IRP is as given above:

$$p = \frac{(1+i_h)}{(1+i_f)} - 1$$

Note that the right hand side is approximately equal to $i_h - i_f$ when the interest rates are low. So, where home interest rates are 6% and foreign interest rates are 4%, the premium on the value of foreign currency should be:

$$p = \frac{(1+0.06)}{(1+0.04)} - 1 = 0.01923 \text{ or } 1.923\%$$

In approximate form, the premium should be home less foreign interest rates:

$$p = i_h - i_f$$
$$= 6\% - 4\%$$
$$= 2\%$$

Note that the two results are about the same:

$$1.923\% \approx 2\%$$

In many calculations this approximate relationship will suffice, particularly where the interest rate differential is small.

EXAMPLE

Reworking the previous example where:

the South African rand has a six-month interest rate of 6%, the British pound has a six-month interest rate of 5% and the rand's spot rate is £0.10. Suppose a UK investor has £100:

Step 1: On day 1 the £100 are converted into rand at £0.10 per rand.

$$£100 / £0.10 \text{ per rand} = 1,000 \text{ rand}$$

Step 2. On the first day, the UK investor also sells rand six months forward. The number of rand to be sold forward is the anticipated accumulation of rand over the six-month period, which is estimated as:

$$1000 \text{ rand} \times (1 + 0.06) = 1,060 \text{ rand}$$

Step 3. After six months, the UK investor withdraws the initial deposit of rand along with the accumulated interest, amounting to a total of 1,060 rand. The investor converts the rand into pounds in accordance with the forward contract agreed upon six months earlier. The premium for the forward rate using the approximate process is:

$$p \approx i_h - i_f = 0.05 = 0.06 = -1\%$$

therefore, the actual forward rate is:

$$F = S\,(1 + p) = £0.10\,(1 - 0.01) = 0.099$$

the forward is £0.099 per rand. So the UK investor can expect to receive 1060 rand × £0.099 = £104.94 which is approximately equal to £105, the same return as investing in the UK. The rounding error is only £0.04 and is sufficiently small for most purposes.

Graphic analysis of interest rate parity

The interest rate differential can be compared to the forward premium (or discount) with the use of a graph. All the possible points that represent interest rate parity are plotted on Exhibit 7.9 by using the approximation expressed earlier and plugging in numbers.

Points representing a discount. For all situations in which the foreign interest rate exceeds the home interest rate, the forward rate should exhibit a discount approximately equal to that differential. When the foreign interest rate (i_f) exceeds the home interest rate (i_h) by 1% ($i_h - i_f = -1\%$), then the forward value of the foreign currency should exhibit a discount of 1%. This is represented by point A on the graph. If the foreign

Exhibit 7.9   Illustration of interest rate parity

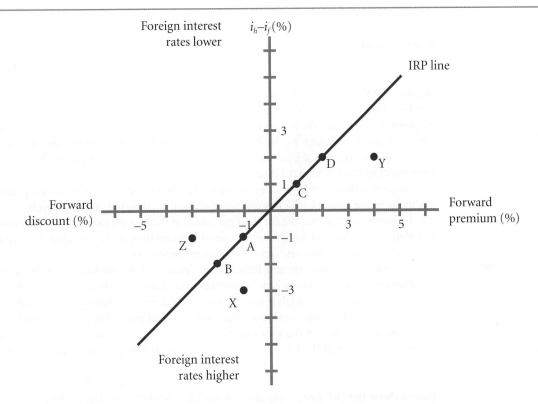

interest rate exceeds the home rate by 2%, then the forward value of the foreign currency should exhibit a discount of 2%, as represented by point B on the graph, and so on.

Points representing a premium. For all situations in which the foreign interest rate is less than the home interest rate, the forward value of the home currency should exhibit a premium approximately equal to that differential. For example, if the home interest rate exceeds the foreign rate by 1% ($i_h - i_f = 1\%$), then the forward premium should be 1%, as represented by point C. If the home interest rate exceeds the foreign rate by 2% ($i_h - i_f = 2\%$), then the forward premium should be 2%, as represented by point D, and so on.

Points representing IRP. Any points lying on the diagonal line cutting the intersection of the axes represent IRP. For this reason, that diagonal line is referred to as the **interest rate parity (IRP) line**. Covered interest arbitrage is not possible for points on the IRP line.

An individual or corporation can at any time examine all currencies to compare forward rate premiums (or discounts) to interest rate differentials. From a UK perspective, interest rates in Japan are usually lower than the home interest rates. Consequently, the forward rate of the Japanese yen usually exhibits a premium and may be represented by points such as C or D or even points above D along the diagonal line in Exhibit 7.9. Conversely, South American and African currencies often have higher interest rates than the United Kingdom, so the pound's forward rate often exhibits a discount, represented by point A or B.

Exhibit 7.9 can be used whether or not you annualize the rates, as long as you are consistent. That is, if you annualize the interest rates to determine the interest rate differential, you should also annualize the forward premium or discount.

Points below the IRP line. What if a three-month deposit represented by a foreign currency offers an annualized interest rate of 10% versus an annualized interest rate of 7% in the home country? Such a scenario is represented on the graph by $i_h - i_f = -3\%$. Also assume that the foreign currency exhibits an annualized forward discount of 1%. The combined interest rate differential and forward discount information can be represented by point X on the graph. Since point X is not on the IRP line, we should expect that covered interest arbitrage will be beneficial for some investors. The investor attains an additional 3 percentage points for the foreign deposit, and this advantage is only partially offset by the 1% forward discount.

Assume that the annualized interest rate in the foreign currency is 5%, as compared to 7% in the home country. The interest rate differential expressed on the graph is $i_h - i_f = 2\%$. However, assume that the forward premium of the foreign currency is 4% (point Y in Exhibit 7.9). Thus, the high forward premium more than makes up what the investor loses on the lower interest rate from the foreign investment.

If the current interest rate and forward rate situation is represented by point X or Y, home country investors can engage in covered interest arbitrage. By investing in a foreign currency, they will earn a higher return (after considering the foreign interest rate and forward premium or discount) than the home interest rate. This type of activity will place upward pressure on the spot rate of the foreign currency, and downward pressure on the forward rate of the foreign currency, until covered interest arbitrage is no longer feasible.

Points above the IRP line. Now shift to the left side of the IRP line. Take point Z, for example. This represents a foreign interest rate that exceeds the home interest rate by 1%, while the forward rate exhibits a 3% discount. This point, like all points to the left of the IRP line, represents a situation in which investors would achieve a lower return on a foreign investment than on a domestic one.

For points such as these, however, covered interest arbitrage is feasible from the perspective of foreign investors. Consider South African investors whose interest rate is 1% higher than the UK interest rate, and the forward rate (with respect to the pound) contains a 3% discount (as represented by point Z). South African investors will sell their home currency in exchange for pounds, invest in pound-denominated securities, and engage in a forward contract to purchase rand forward. Though they earn 1% less on the UK investment, they are able to purchase their home currency for 3% less than what they initially sold it for. This type of activity will place downward pressure on the spot rate of the rand (as it is sold now to invest in the pound) and upward pressure on the pound's forward rate (as investors seek to convert back to rand and consolidate their gain), until covered interest arbitrage is no longer feasible.

How to test whether interest rate parity exists

An investor or firm can plot all realistic points for various currencies on a graph such as that in Exhibit 7.9 to determine whether gains from covered interest arbitrage can be achieved. The location of the points provides an indication of whether covered interest arbitrage is worthwhile. For points to the right of the IRP line, investors in the home country should consider using covered interest arbitrage, since a return higher than the home interest rate (i_h) is achievable. Of course, as investors and firms take advantage of such opportunities, the point will tend to move toward the IRP line. Covered interest arbitrage should continue until the interest rate parity relationship holds.

Interpretation of interest rate parity

As pointed out in the previous example, interest rate parity means that holders of, say, British pounds who invest abroad at a higher interest rate will not get a higher overall return compared to home investment. This is because the forward rate will be at a discount such that any interest rate gain is exactly offset by a fall in the value of the foreign currency in the forward market.

Also, as pointed out in the South African example (above), interest rate parity does *not* mean that all currencies must have the *same* interest rate. One of the major benefits of having an independent currency is that a separate interest rate can be set for that currency and hence the economy where the currency is used. A currency experiencing high inflation and high interest rates, as a result, can neutralize the effect with other currencies by devaluing. Hot money will not flow into the country to exploit the high interest rates because the currency will be quoted at a devalued, lower rate on the forward market.

Does interest rate parity hold?

To determine conclusively whether interest rate parity holds, it is necessary to compare the forward rate (or discount) with interest rate quotations occurring at the same time. If the forward rate and interest rate quotations do not reflect the same time of day, then results could be somewhat distorted. Due to limitations in access to data, it is difficult to obtain quotations that reflect the same point in time.

A comparison of annualized forward rate premiums and annualized interest rate differentials for seven widely traded currencies as of 10 February 2004, is provided in Exhibit 7.10 from a US perspective. At this time, the US interest rate was higher than the Japanese interest rate and lower than the interest rates in other countries. The exhibit shows that the yen exhibited a forward premium, while all other currencies exhibited a discount. The Brazilian real exhibited the most pronounced forward discount, which is attributed to its relatively high interest rate. The forward premium or discount of each currency is in line with the interest rate differential and therefore reflects IRP.

At different points in time, the position of a country may change. For example, if Mexico's interest rate increased while other countries' interest rates stayed the same, Mexico's position would move down along the *y*-axis. Yet, its forward discount would likely be more pronounced (farther to the left along the *x*-axis) as well, since covered interest arbitrage would occur otherwise. Therefore, its new point would be farther to the left but would still be along the 45° line.

Numerous academic studies have conducted empirical examination of IRP in several periods. The actual relationship between the forward rate premium and interest rate differentials generally supports IRP. Although there are deviations from IRP, they are often not large enough to make covered interest arbitrage worthwhile, as we will now discuss in more detail.

Exhibit 7.10   Forward rate premiums and interest rate differentials for seven currencies

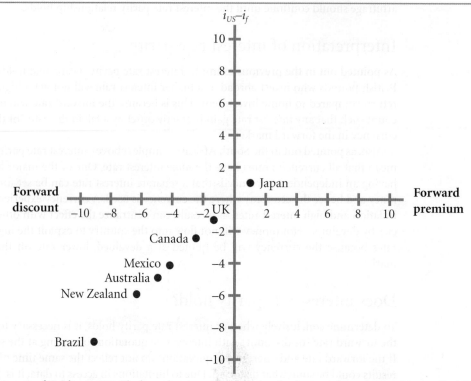

Note: The data are as of 10 February 2004. The forward rate premium is based on the six-month forward rate and is annualized. The interest rate differential represents the difference between the six-month annualized US interest rate and the six-month foreign interest rate.

Considerations when assessing interest rate parity

If interest rate parity does not hold, covered interest arbitrage still may not be worthwhile due to various characteristics of foreign investments, including transaction costs, political risk, and differential tax laws.

Transaction costs. If an investor wishes to account for transaction costs, the actual point reflecting the interest rate differential and forward rate premium must be farther from the IRP line to make covered interest arbitrage worthwhile. Exhibit 7.11 identifies the areas that reflect potential for covered interest arbitrage *after* accounting for transaction costs. Notice the band surrounding the IRP line. For points not on the IRP line but within this band, covered interest arbitrage is not worthwhile (because the excess return is offset by costs). For points to the right of (or below) the band, investors residing in the home country could gain through covered interest arbitrage. For points to the left of (or above) the band, foreign investors could gain through covered interest arbitrage.

Political risk. Even if covered interest arbitrage appears feasible after accounting for transaction costs, investing funds overseas is subject to political risk. Though the forward contract locks in the rate at which the foreign funds should be reconverted, there is no guarantee that the foreign government will allow the funds to be reconverted. A crisis in the foreign country could cause its government to restrict any exchange of the local currency for other currencies. In this case, the investor would be unable to use these funds until the foreign government eliminated the restriction.

Exhibit 7.11 Potential for covered interest arbitrage when considering transaction costs

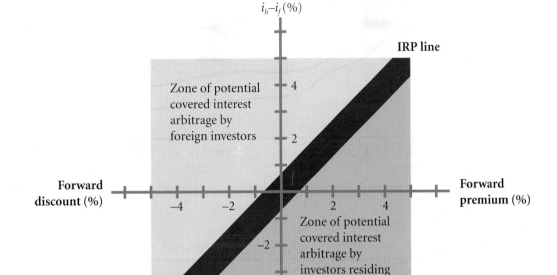

Investors may also perceive a slight default risk on foreign investments such as foreign Treasury bills, since they may not be assured that the foreign government will guarantee full repayment of interest and principal upon default. Therefore, because of concern that the foreign Treasury bills may default, they may accept a lower interest rate on their domestic Treasury bills rather than engage in covered interest arbitrage in an effort to obtain a slightly higher expected return.

Differential tax laws. Because tax laws vary among countries, investors and firms that set up deposits in other countries must be aware of the existing tax laws. Covered interest arbitrage might be feasible when considering before-tax returns but not necessarily when considering after-tax returns. Such a scenario would be due to differential tax rates.

Changes in forward premiums

Exhibit 7.12 illustrates the relationship between interest rate differentials and the forward premium over time. In the fourth quarter of 2000, the US interest rate was higher than the interest rate on euros, and the forward rate of the euro exhibited a premium. During the next two years, the US interest rate declined to a greater degree than the euro's interest rate. As the US interest rate declined below the euro's interest rate in 2001, the euro's forward rate exhibited a discount, as the forward rate was lower than the prevailing spot rate. The larger the degree to which the euro's interest rate exceeded the US interest rate, the more pronounced was the euro's forward discount.

Exhibit 7.12   Relationship between interest rate differentials and forward rate premiums over time

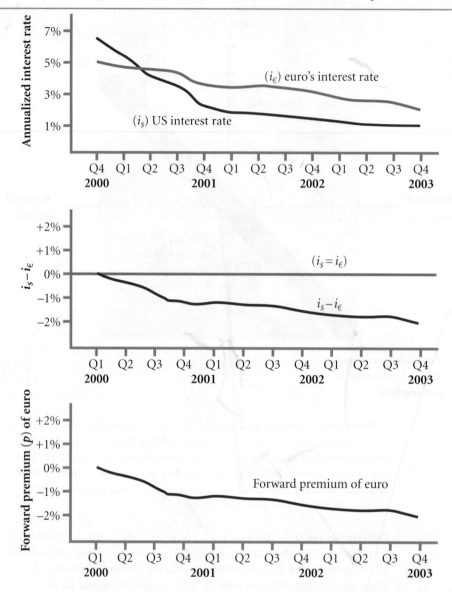

During the 2000–03 period, the interest rate on the Japanese yen was near 0.5%. The US interest rate exceeded the Japanese interest rate throughout this entire period, which caused the Japanese yen's forward rate to exhibit a premium throughout the period. Yet, as the US interest rate declined during the period, the differential between the Japanese and US interest rates narrowed, and the yen's forward rate premium declined as a result.

USING THE WEB

Forward rates Forward rates of the Canadian dollar, British pound, euro, and Japanese yen are provided for various periods at http://www.marketprices.ft.com/markets/currencies/ab.

Managing for value
How interest rate parity affects IBM's hedge

Many MNCs (and one may think of a multinational company such as Renault or IBM) have subsidiaries based in Brazil. Since the Brazilian real has historically depreciated against the dollar, MNCs naturally consider hedging any funds that its Brazilian subsidiaries plan to remit to the parent. Forward and futures contracts can be used to hedge the future transactions in which the Brazilian real will be converted into dollars. Due to interest rate parity, however, the forward or futures rate of the Brazilian real is unfavourable relative to its spot rate. Since the Brazilian interest rate is higher than the European interest rate, IRP forces the forward rate of the Brazilian real to exhibit a discount. The discount is especially pronounced when the Brazilian interest rate is very high. Thus, if an MNC hedges its future conversions

of Brazilian real to dollars, it must accept a heavily discounted exchange rate for conversion in the future. This exchange rate may not be as favourable as the prevailing spot rate at that future time, even if today's spot rate declines over time. This is an important cost of doing business in countries with high interest rates. Since high interest rates are usually caused by a high level of expected inflation, this example illustrates the indirect effect that a foreign country's expected inflation can have on an MNC. IBM, Renault and other MNCs can increase their value by identifying countries that will have a high degree of expected inflation and limiting their exchange rate exposure in those countries.

Summary

- Locational arbitrage may occur if foreign exchange quotations differ among banks. The act of locational arbitrage should force the foreign exchange quotations of banks to become realigned, and locational arbitrage will no longer be possible.

- Triangular arbitrage is related to cross exchange rates. A cross exchange rate between two currencies is determined by the values of these two currencies with respect to a third currency. If the actual cross exchange rate of these two currencies differs from the rate that should exist, triangular arbitrage is possible. The act of triangular arbitrage should force cross exchange rates to become realigned, at which time triangular arbitrage will no longer be possible.

- Covered interest arbitrage is based on the relationship between the forward rate premium and the interest rate differential. The size of the premium or discount exhibited by the forward rate of a currency should be about the same as the differential between the interest rates of the two countries of concern. In general terms, the forward rate of the

foreign currency will contain a discount (premium) if its interest rate is higher (lower) than the US interest rate. If the forward premium deviates substantially from the interest rate differential, covered interest arbitrage is possible. In this type of arbitrage, a foreign short-term investment in a foreign currency is covered by a forward sale of that foreign currency in the future. In this manner, the investor is not exposed to fluctuation in the foreign currency's value.

- Interest rate parity (IRP) is a theory that states that the size of the forward premium (or discount) should be equal to the interest rate differential between the two countries of concern. When IRP exists, covered interest arbitrage is not feasible because any interest rate advantage in the foreign country will be offset by the discount on the forward rate. Thus, the act of covered interest arbitrage would generate a return that is no higher than what would be generated by a domestic investment.

CRITICAL DEBATE

Should arbitrage be more regulated?

Proposition. Yes. Large financial institutions have the technology to recognize when one participant in the foreign exchange market is trying to sell a currency for a higher price than another participant. They also recognize when the forward rate does not properly reflect the interest rate differential. They use arbitrage to capitalize on these situations, which results in large foreign exchange transactions. In some cases, their arbitrage involves taking large positions in a currency and then reversing their positions a few minutes later. This jumping in and out of currencies can cause abrupt price adjustments of currencies and may create more volatility in the foreign exchange market. Regulations should be created that would force financial institutions to maintain their currency positions for at least one month. This would result in a more stable foreign exchange market.

Opposing view. No. When financial institutions engage in arbitrage, they create pressure on the price of a currency that will remove any pricing discrepancy. If arbitrage did not occur, pricing discrepancies would become more pronounced. Consequently, firms and individuals who use the foreign exchange market would have to spend more time searching for the best exchange rate when trading a currency. The market would become fragmented, and prices could differ substantially among banks in a region, or among regions. If the discrepancies became large enough, firms and individuals might even attempt to conduct arbitrage themselves. The arbitrage conducted by banks allows for a more integrated foreign exchange market, which ensures that foreign exchange prices quoted by any institution are in line with the market.

With whom do you agree? State your reasons. Use InfoTrac or search engines recommended by your institution to access academic journals subscribed to by your institution. The keyword "arbitrage" is probably the best means of selecting relevant articles. Such articles often conduct statistical tests of some sophistication. It is the conclusions from these tests and the discussion surrounding their design and the literature review that is the real contribution to the debate. Do not be put off by the rather more obscure aspects of the statistical tests. For this subject, newspapers are *not* a good source as they often confuse speculation with arbitrage. Speculation is considered in the next chapter.

SELF TEST

Answers are provided in Appendix A at the back of the text.

1. Assume that the following spot exchange rates exist today:

   £1   = $1.50
   C$1 = $0.75
   £1   = C$2

   Assume no transaction costs. Based on these exchange rates, can triangular arbitrage be used to earn a profit? Explain.

2. Assume the following information:

   Spot rate of $1 = £0.625
   180 day forward rate of $1 = £0.641
   180 day British interest rate = 4%
   180 day US interest rate = 3%

   Explain in words what is happening to the value of the dollar over the 180-day period.

   Calculate the change in the value of the dollar as a percentage and compare with the difference in interest rates

   Based on this information, is covered interest arbitrage by UK investors feasible (assume a UK investor has £100 to possibly invest in the US)? Explain.

3. Using the information in the previous question, outline how the market might react to the given rates.

4. Explain in general terms how various forms of arbitrage can remove any discrepancies in the pricing of currencies.

5. Assume that the US dollar's one-year forward rate exhibits a premium. Assume that interest rate parity continually exists. Explain how the premium on the US dollars one-year forward rate would change if British one-year interest rates rose by 3 percentage points while US one-year interest rates rose by 2 percentage points.

QUESTIONS AND APPLICATIONS

1. **Locational arbitrage.** Explain the concept of locational arbitrage and the scenario necessary for it to be plausible.

2. **Locational arbitrage.** Assume the following information:

	Beal Bank	Yardley Bank
Bid price of New Zealand dollar	£0.020	£0.018
Ask price of New Zealand dollar	£0.022	£0.019

Given this information, is locational arbitrage possible? If so, explain the steps involved in locational arbitrage, and compute the profit from this arbitrage if you had £1,000,000 to invest. What market forces would occur to eliminate any further possibilities of locational arbitrage?

3. **Triangular arbitrage.** Explain the concept of triangular arbitrage and the scenario necessary for it to be plausible.

4. **Triangular arbitrage.** Assume the following information:

	Quoted Price
Value of Canadian dollar in British pounds	£0.60
Value of New Zealand dollar in British pounds	$0.20
Value of Canadian dollar in New Zealand dollars	NZ$3.02

Given this information, is triangular arbitrage possible? If so, explain the steps that would reflect triangular arbitrage, and compute the profit from this strategy if you had £1,000,000 to invest.

What market forces would occur to eliminate any further possibilities of triangular arbitrage?

5. **Covered interest arbitrage.** Explain the concept of covered interest arbitrage and the scenario necessary for it to be plausible.

6. **Covered interest arbitrage.** Assume the following information:

Spot rate of Canadian dollar	= £0.4400
90-day forward rate of Canadian dollar	= £0.4345
90-day Canadian interest rate	= 4%
90-day UK interest rate	= 2.5%

Given this information, what would be the yield (percentage return) to a UK investor who used covered interest arbitrage? (Assume the investor invests £1,000,000.)

What market forces would occur to eliminate any further possibilities of covered interest arbitrage?

7. **Covered interest arbitrage.** Assume the following information:

Spot rate of Mexican peso	= 14.00 euros
180-day forward rate of Mexican peso	= 13.72 euros
180-day Mexican interest rate	= 6%
180-day euro interest rate	= 5%

Given this information, is covered interest arbitrage worthwhile for Mexican investors who have pesos to invest? Explain your answer.

8. **Effects of September 11.** The terrorist attack on the United States on September 11, 2001, caused expectations of a weaker US economy. Explain how such expectations could have affected US interest rates and therefore have affected the forward rate premium (or discount) on various foreign currencies.

9. **Interest rate parity.** Explain the concept of interest rate parity. Provide the rationale for its possible existence.

10. **Inflation effects on the forward rate.** Why do you think currencies of countries with high inflation rates tend to have forward discounts?

11. **Covered interest arbitrage in both directions.** Assume that the existing UK one-year interest rate is 10% and the EU one-year interest rate is 11%. Also assume that interest rate parity exists. Should the forward rate of the euro exhibit a discount or a premium?

If UK investors attempt covered interest arbitrage, what will be their return?

If euro-zone investors attempt covered interest arbitrage, what will be their return?

12. **Interest rate parity.** Why would UK investors consider covered interest arbitrage in France when the interest rate on euros in France is lower than the UK interest rate?

13. **Interest rate parity.** Consider investors who invest in either US or British one-year Treasury bills. Assume zero transaction costs and no taxes.
    a. "If interest rate parity exists, then the return for UK investors who use covered interest arbitrage will be the same as the return for US investors who invest in UK Treasury bills."

    Is this statement true or false? If false, correct the statement.

    b. "If interest rate parity exists, then the return for British investors who use covered interest arbitrage will be the same as the return for British investors who invest in British Treasury bills."

    Is this statement true or false? If false, correct the statement.

14. **Changes in forward premiums.** Assume that the Japanese yen's forward rate currently exhibits a premium of 6% and that interest rate parity exists. If euro-zone interest rates decrease, how must this premium change to maintain interest rate parity? Why might we expect the premium to change?

15. **Changes in forward premiums.** Assume that the forward rate premium of the euro was higher last month than it is today. What does this imply about interest rate differentials between the United States and Europe today compared to those last month?

16. **Interest rate parity.** If the relationship that is specified by interest rate parity does not exist at any period but does exist on average, then covered interest arbitrage should not be considered by MNCs. Do you agree or disagree with this statement? Explain.

17. **Covered interest arbitrage in both directions.** The one-year interest rate in New Zealand is 6%.

The one-year UK interest rate is 10%. The spot rate of the New Zealand dollar (NZ$) is $0.25. The forward rate of the New Zealand dollar is £0.27. Is covered interest arbitrage feasible for UK investors? Is it feasible for New Zealand investors? In each case, explain why covered interest arbitrage is or is not feasible.

18. **Limitations of covered interest arbitrage.** Assume that the one-year UK interest rate is 11%, while the one-year interest rate in Malaysia is 40%. Assume that a UK bank is willing to purchase the currency of that country from you one year from now at a discount of 13%. Would covered interest arbitrage be worth considering? Is there any reason why you should not attempt covered interest arbitrage in this situation? (Ignore tax effects.)

19. **Covered interest arbitrage in both directions.** Assume that the annual US interest rate is currently 8% and Germany's annual interest rate is currently 9%. The euro's one-year forward rate currently exhibits a discount of 2%.
    a. Does interest rate parity exist?
    b. Can a US firm benefit from investing funds in Germany using covered interest arbitrage?
    c. Can a German subsidiary of a US firm benefit by investing funds in the United States through covered interest arbitrage?

20. **Covered interest arbitrage.** The South African rand has a one-year forward premium of 2%. One-year interest rates in France are 3 percentage points higher than in South Africa. Based on this information, is covered interest arbitrage possible for a French investor if interest rate parity holds?

21. **Deriving the forward rate.** Assume that annual interest rates in the United Kingdom are 4%, while interest rates in France are 6%.
    a. According to IRP, what should the forward rate premium or discount of the euro be?
    b. If the euro's spot rate is £0.66, what should the one-year forward rate of the euro be?

22. **Covered interest arbitrage in both directions.** The following information is available:

■ You have £500,000 to invest.

■ The current spot rate of the Moroccan dirham is £0.06.

- The 60-day forward rate of the Moroccan dirham is £0.05.
- The 60-day interest rate in the United States is 1%.
- The 60-day interest rate in Morocco is 2%.

a. What is the yield to a US investor who conducts covered interest arbitrage?
   Did covered interest arbitrage work for the investor in this case?

b. Would covered interest arbitrage be possible for a Moroccan investor in this case?

ADVANCED QUESTIONS

23. **Economic effects on the forward rate.** Assume that Mexico's economy has expanded significantly, causing a high demand for loanable funds there by local firms. How might these conditions affect the forward discount of the Mexican peso?

24. **Differences among forward rates.** Assume that the 30-day forward premium of the euro with the British pound is −1%, while the 90-day forward premium of the euro is 2%. Explain the likely interest rate conditions that would cause these premiums. Does this ensure that covered interest arbitrage is worthwhile?

25. **Testing interest rate parity.** Describe a method for testing whether interest rate parity exists. Why are transaction costs, currency restrictions, and differential tax laws important when evaluating whether covered interest arbitrage can be beneficial?

26. **Deriving the forward rate.** Before the Asian crisis began, Asian central banks were maintaining a somewhat stable value for their respective currencies. Nevertheless, the forward rate of South East Asian currencies exhibited a discount. Explain.

27. **Interpreting changes in the forward premium.** Assume that interest rate parity holds. At the beginning of the month, the spot rate of the Canadian dollar is £0.35, while the one-year forward rate is £0.34. Assume that UK interest rates increase steadily over the month. At the end of the month, the one-year forward rate is higher (foreign currency costs more) than it was at the beginning of the month. Yet, the one-year forward discount is larger (the one-year premium is more negative) at the end of the month than it was at the beginning of the month. Explain how the relationship between the UK interest rate and the Canadian interest rate changed from the beginning of the month until the end of the month.

28. **Interpreting a large forward discount.** The interest rate in Indonesia is commonly higher than the interest rate in the UK and the eurozone, which reflects a high expected rate of inflation there. Why should European MNCs consider hedging its future remittances from Indonesia to their parent even when the forward discount on the currency (rupiah) is so large?

29. **Change in the forward premium.** At the end of this month, you (the owner of a German firm) are meeting with a Japanese firm to which you will try to sell supplies. If you receive an order from that firm, you will obtain a forward contract to hedge the future receivables in yen. As of this morning, the forward rate of the yen and spot rate are the same. You believe that interest rate parity holds.

    This afternoon, news occurs that makes you believe that the euro-zone interest rates will increase substantially by the end of this month, and that the Japanese interest rate will not change. However, your expectations of the spot rate of the Japanese yen are not affected at all in the future. How will your expected dollar amount of receivables from the Japanese transaction be affected (if at all) by the news that occurred this afternoon? Explain.

30. **Testing IRP.** The one-year interest rate in Singapore is 11%. The one-year interest rate in the United States is 6%. The spot rate of the Singapore dollar (S$) is $0.50 and the forward rate of the S$ is $0.46. Assume zero transactions costs.

    a. Does interest rate parity exist?
    b. Can a US firm benefit from investing funds in Singapore using covered interest arbitrage?

PROJECT WORKSHOP

31. **Forward rates.** Using interest rates (preferably LIBOR) from the newspaper or other source, and

forward rates from the website: http://www.bmo.com/economic/regular/fxrates.html or http://www.ft.com or using your own institutions data sources, calculate whether the one year forward premium between the British pound and the US dollar is in the right direction (note that all required data can be found in a financial newspaper such as the *Financial Times*):

a. Estimate the accuracy of your calculations and suggest reasons for the inaccuracy.

b. Perform the same calculation for other currencies.

Essays/discussion and articles can be found at the end of Part 2

BLADES PLC CASE STUDY
Assessment of potential arbitrage opportunities

Recall that Blades, a UK manufacturer of roller blades, has chosen Thailand as its primary export target for "Speedos", Blades' primary product. Moreover, Blades' primary customer in Thailand, Entertainment Products, has committed itself to purchase 180,000 Speedos annually for the next three years at a fixed price denominated in baht, Thailand's currency. Because of quality and cost considerations, Blades also imports some of the rubber and plastic components needed to manufacture Speedos.

Lately, Thailand has experienced weak economic growth and political uncertainty. As investors lost confidence in the Thai baht as a result of the political uncertainty, they withdrew their funds from the country. This resulted in an excess supply of baht for sale over the demand for baht in the foreign exchange market, which put downward pressure on the baht's value. As foreign investors continued to withdraw their funds from Thailand, the baht's value continued to deteriorate. Since Blades has net cash flows in baht resulting from its exports to Thailand, a deterioration in the baht's value will affect the company negatively.

Ben Holt, Blades' finance director, would like to ensure that the spot and forward rates Blades' bank has quoted are reasonable. If the exchange rate quotes are reasonable, then arbitrage will not be possible. If the quotations are not appropriate, however, arbitrage may be possible. Under these conditions, Holt would

like Blades to use some form of arbitrage to take advantage of possible mispricing in the foreign exchange market. Although Blades is not an arbitrageur, Holt believes that arbitrage opportunities could offset the negative impact resulting from the baht's depreciation, which would otherwise seriously affect Blades' profit margins.

Ben Holt has identified three arbitrage opportunities as profitable and would like to know which one of them is the most profitable. Thus, he has asked you, Blades' financial analyst, to prepare an analysis of the arbitrage opportunities he has identified. This would allow Holt to assess the profitability of arbitrage opportunities very quickly.

1. The first arbitrage opportunity relates to locational arbitrage. Holt has obtained spot rate quotations from two banks in Thailand: Minzu Bank and Sobat Bank, both located in Bangkok. The bid and ask prices of Thai baht for each bank are displayed in the table below:

	Minzu Bank	Sobat Bank
Bid	£0.0149	£0.0152
Ask	£0.0151	£0.0153

Determine whether the foreign exchange quotations are appropriate. If they are not appropriate, determine the profit you could generate by withdrawing £100,000 from Blades' cheque account and engaging in arbitrage before the rates are adjusted.

2. Besides the bid and ask quotes for the Thai baht provided in the previous question, Minzu Bank has provided the following quotations for the pound and the Japanese yen:

	Quoted Bid Price	Quoted Ask Price
Value of a Japanese yen in British pounds	£0.0057	£0.0058
Value of a Thai baht in Japanese yen	¥2.69	¥2.70

Determine whether the cross exchange rate between the Thai baht and Japanese yen is appropriate. If it is not appropriate, determine the profit you could generate for Blades by withdrawing £100,000 from Blades' current account and engaging in triangular arbitrage before the rates are adjusted.

3. Ben Holt has obtained several forward contract quotations for the Thai baht to determine whether covered interest arbitrage may be possible. He was quoted a forward rate of £0.015 per Thai baht for a 90-day forward contract. The current spot rate is £0.0151. Ninety-day interest rates available to Blades in the United Kingdom are 2%, while 90-day interest rates in Thailand are 3.75% (these rates are not annualized). Holt is aware that covered interest arbitrage, unlike locational and triangular arbitrage, requires an investment of funds. Thus, he would like to be able to estimate the dollar profit resulting from arbitrage over and above the dollar amount available on a 90-day UK deposit.

Determine whether the forward rate is priced appropriately. If it is not priced appropriately, determine the profit you could generate for Blades by withdrawing £100,000 from Blades' current account and engaging in covered interest arbitrage. Measure the profit as the excess amount above what you could generate by investing in the US money market.

4. Why are arbitrage opportunities likely to disappear soon after they have been discovered? To illustrate your answer, assume that covered interest arbitrage involving the immediate purchase and forward sale of baht is possible. Discuss how the baht's spot and forward rates would adjust until covered interest arbitrage is no longer possible. What is the resulting equilibrium state called?

SMALL BUSINESS DILEMMA
Assessment of prevailing spot and forward rates by the Sports Exports Company

As the Sports Exports Company from Ireland exports footballs to the United Kingdom, it receives British pounds. The cheque (denominated in pounds) for last month's exports just arrived. Jim Logan (owner of the Sports Exports Company) normally deposits the cheque with his local bank and requests that the bank convert the cheque to euros at the prevailing spot rate (assuming that he did not use a forward contract to hedge this payment). Jim's local bank provides foreign exchange services for many of its business customers who need to buy or sell widely traded currencies. Today, however, Jim decided to check the quotations of the spot rate at other banks before converting the payment into euros.

1. Do you think Jim will be able to find a bank that provides him with a more favourable spot rate than his local bank? Explain.

2. Do you think that Jim's bank is likely to provide more reasonable quotations for the spot rate of the British pound if it is the only bank in town that provides foreign exchange services? Explain.

3. Jim is considering using a forward contract to hedge the anticipated receivables in pounds next month. His local bank quoted him a spot rate of 1.45 euros and a one-month forward rate of 1.4435 euros. Before Jim decides to sell pounds one month forward, he wants to be sure that the forward rate is reasonable, given the prevailing spot rate. A one-month Treasury security in Ireland currently offers a yield (not annualized) of 1%, while a one-month Treasury security in the United Kingdom offers a yield of 1.4%. Do you believe that the one-month forward rate is reasonable given the spot rate of 1.45 euros?

CHAPTER 8

RELATIONSHIPS AMONG INFLATION, INTEREST RATES, AND EXCHANGE RATES

INFLATION RATES AND INTEREST rates can have a significant impact on exchange rates (as explained in Chapter 4) and therefore can influence the value of MNCs. Here, the concern is exclusively with how the spot or present rate behaves over time. MNC treasurers who do not take out forward rate protection (see previous chapter) will need to understand the relationship between exchange rates, interest rates and inflation in order to understand how the extensive debates in the financial press over inflation and interest rates are likely to affect exchange rates. Also, where a government seeks to control exchange rates, it is important to understand the effect on inflation and interest rates in that country. We assume in this chapter, unless stated otherwise, that exchange rates are free floating and wholly determined by non-government market forces.

THE SPECIFIC OBJECTIVES OF THIS CHAPTER ARE TO:

- explain the purchasing power parity (PPP) theory and its implications for exchange rate changes,

- explain the international Fisher effect (IFE) theory and its implications for exchange rate changes, and

- compare the PPP theory, the IFE theory, and the theory of interest rate parity (IRP), which was introduced in the previous chapter.

PURCHASING POWER PARITY (PPP)

In Chapter 4, the expected impact of relative inflation rates on exchange rates was discussed. Recall from this discussion that when the inflation rate in country A (for example) rises, the demand for its currency declines as its exports decline (due to its higher prices). In addition, consumers and firms in country A tend to increase their importing (increasing the supply of home currency for foreign currency). The reduced demand for country A's currency and the increased supply of country A's home currency for foreign currency, both place downward pressure on A's currency.

Inflation rates often vary among countries, causing international trade patterns and exchange rates to adjust accordingly. One of the most popular and controversial theories in international finance is the **purchasing power parity (PPP) theory**. The theory bases its predictions of exchange rate movement on changing patterns of trade due to different inflation rates between countries.

Interpretations of purchasing power parity

There are two forms of PPP theory the absolute form and the broader relative form.

Absolute form of PPP. The **absolute form of PPP** is based on the notion that without international trade barriers and transport costs, consumers shift their demand to wherever prices are lower. It suggests that prices of the same basket of products in two different countries should be equal when measured in a common currency. If there is a discrepancy in prices as measured by a common currency, demand should shift so that these prices converge.

EXAMPLE

If the same basket of products is produced by the United States and the United Kingdom, and the price in the United Kingdom is lower when measured in a common currency, US consumers should seek to import the cheaper UK products. Consequently, the actual price charged in each country may be affected, and/or the exchange rate may adjust. Remember that for a US resident seeking to import the cheaper goods from the UK, an increase in the value of the British pound represents a price rise just as much as an increase in the price of the goods themselves. There are two purchases by the US importer; the currency has to be purchased in order to buy the goods. Overall, market demand would cause the prices of the baskets to be similar when measured in a common currency. Exchange rates are a part of the price adjustment process.

Realistically, the existence of transportation costs, tariffs and quotas may prevent the absolute form of PPP. If transportation costs were high in the preceding example, the demand for the baskets of products might not shift as suggested. Thus, the discrepancy in prices would continue.

Relative form of PPP. The **relative form of PPP** accounts for the possibility of market imperfections such as transportation costs, tariffs, and quotas. This version acknowledges that because of these market imperfections, prices of the same basket of products in different countries will not necessarily be the same when measured in a common currency. It does state, however, that the *rate of change* in the prices of the baskets should be similar when measured in a common currency, as long as the transportation costs and trade barriers are unchanged.

Assume that the United States and the United Kingdom trade extensively with each other and initially have zero inflation. Now assume that the United States experiences a 9% inflation rate, while the United Kingdom experiences a 5% inflation rate. All goods in the US are going to appear to be 9%–5% = 4% more expensive to the UK resident. Under these conditions, PPP theory suggests that the US dollar should depreciate by approximately 4% – the difference in inflation rates. The reduced demand for dollars by British pounds and the increased supply of dollars for pounds will, in a free floating exchange rate regime, lower the value of the dollar against the pound. Thus, the exchange rate should adjust to offset the differential in the inflation rates of the two countries. If this occurs, then the difference in prices that existed before the inflation changes will remain after the inflation changes. If a particular washing machine costs 6% more in the US before the inflation change, it will still cost 6% more after the inflation change.

Therefore the exchange rate adjusts so that *relative* prices are undisturbed by inflation differences. Relative PPP does not require that prices translated into one currency are the same, merely that the differences remain constant.

Rationale behind purchasing power parity theory

PPP is based on international trade in goods and services rather than investment in stocks and shares. In our previous example, the relatively high US inflation should cause US consumers to increase imports from the United Kingdom and British consumers to lower their demand for US goods (since prices of British goods have increased by a lower rate). Such forces place downward pressure on the value of the dollar when measured in pounds. As a result, US importers will find that the pound is becoming more expensive.

The shifting in consumption spending from the United States to the United Kingdom will continue until the British pound's value has appreciated to the extent that the price of British goods relative to US goods is not altered by the different inflation rates. Absolute PPP states that the relative prices should be such that the same goods cost the same whether purchased in the US or the UK (after allowing for transport costs) – a relative difference of zero. Relative PPP states merely that whatever differences exist should remain constant – goods costing x% more should remain costing x% more.

The relationship between exchange rates and inflation, as will be shown more formally, is approximately additive (see Appendix B). To get an intuitive feel for the problem, refer back to the previous example. The conclusion was that the value of the British pound would increase relative to the dollar by about 4%. Assume an exchange rate of $1.8 to the pound. For a US consumer, goods costing £100 in the UK would, before inflation, cost £100 × 1.8 = $180. After UK inflation of 5%, the UK cost would be £105 or in dollars £105 × 1.8 = $189. But as the value of the pound had increased by 4% the exchange rate would have changed. A 4% increase in the value of the pound would mean that the pound would cost 1.8 × 1.04 = $1.872 to the pound. So the full cost to the US importer of the British goods would be £105 × 1.872 = $196.56. The total increase in cost to the US importer would be ($196.56 – $180)/$180 = 9.2%. In approximate terms this is the increase in the value of the British pound of 4% plus the increase in British prices of 5%, a total of 9%.

From the British point of view, the pound will now buy $1.872 or 4% more dollars than before the inflation. Goods costing $1,000 will now cost $1,090 after the 9% inflation in the US. But as the dollar is now cheaper for the UK importer, the total cost to the UK importer will be $1,090/$1.872 = £582.26. Before inflation, the cost in terms of pounds would have been $1,000/1.8 = £555.56. So the net increase taking into account US inflation and the change in the value of the dollar would be (£582.26 – £555.56)/£555.56

= 4.8%. The 9% US inflation less the 4% fall in the value of the dollar results in a net increase in the value of US goods to UK importers of approximately 5% or more exactly 4.8% as calculated above (see Appendix B for an explanation of the difference).

So, reviewing the figures, the exchange rate has performed a neat trick. Both the US and the UK can have their own inflation rates – an important element in having independent economic policies. Yet the relative price of imports compared to domestic goods remains unchanged. Goods imported into the UK from the US go up by 5% the same rate as UK goods. UK exports to the US go up by 9%, the same rate as US goods. The exchange rate adjusts for the difference in inflation rates. The important conditions to this result are that the exchange rate is allowed to float freely and that investment flows guided by interest rates do not disturb the relationship. Conversely one can begin to see that controlling the exchange rate will affect inflation. A fixed exchange rate in the previous example would put downward pressure on the price of US goods to compete with UK goods rising at a lower rate. The interest rate effect is discussed later. For now, a more general derivation of PPP is required.

Derivation of purchasing power parity

Inflation is usually measured as a change in the price index of a country, where a price index can be thought of as a scale which measures the average price. Assume that before inflation, the price indexes of the home country (h) and a foreign country (f) are both set at 100. Now assume that over time, the home country experiences an inflation rate of I_h, while the foreign country experiences an inflation rate of I_f. Due to inflation, the price index of goods in the consumer's home country (P_h) becomes:

$$P_h (1 + I_h)$$

The price index of the foreign country (P_f) will also change due to inflation in that country:

$$P_f (1 + I_f)$$

If home inflation is greater than foreign inflation, $I_h > I_f$, and the exchange rate between the currencies of the two countries does not change, then the consumer's purchasing power is greater when buying foreign goods than buying home goods. In this case, PPP does not exist. If $I_h < I_f$, and the exchange rate between the currencies of the two countries does not change, then the consumer's purchasing power is greater when buying home goods than buying foreign goods. In this case also, PPP does not exist.

The PPP theory suggests that the exchange rate will not remain constant but will adjust to maintain the parity in purchasing power. If inflation occurs and the exchange rate of the foreign currency changes, the foreign price index from the home consumer's perspective becomes:

$$P_f (1 + I_f) (1 + e_f)$$

where e_f represents the percentage change in the value of the foreign currency.

According to PPP theory, the percentage change in the foreign currency (e_f) should change to maintain parity between the new price indexes of the two countries. We can solve for e_f under conditions of PPP by setting the formula for the new price index of the foreign country equal to the formula for the new price index of the home country, as follows:

$$P_f (1 + I_f)(1 + e_f) = P_h (1 + I_h)$$

Solving for e_f, we obtain:

$$(1 + e_f) = \frac{P_h (1 + I_h)}{P_f (1 + I_f)}$$

$$e_f = \frac{P_h (1 + I_h)}{P_f (1 + I_f)} - 1$$

Since P_h equals P_f (because price indexes were initially assumed equal in both countries), they cancel, leaving:

$$e_f = \frac{(1 + I_h)}{(1 + I_f)} - 1$$

This formula reflects the relationship between relative inflation rates and the exchange rate according to PPP. Notice that if $I_h > I_f$, e_f should be positive. This implies that the foreign currency will appreciate when the home country's inflation exceeds the foreign country's inflation. Conversely, if $I_h < I_f$, then e_f should be negative. This implies that the foreign currency will depreciate when the foreign country's inflation exceeds the home country's inflation.

In approximate terms for relatively low levels of inflation:

$$e_f = \frac{(1 + I_h)}{(1 + I_f)} - 1 \approx I_h - I_f$$

Thus if $I_h = 4\%$ and $I_f = 3\%$ the exact approach gives 0.0097 whereas the approximate approach is 0.01 (i.e. $4\% - 3\% = 1\%$), a difference of 0.0003. Whereas if the inflation rates were 54% and 53% the error would be 0.0034, over ten times greater but still possibly not too large (see rounding in Appendix B). From now on we follow the convention that "=" will replace "≈" for the approximate approach.

A useful way of thinking about the relationship is to separate the foreign and home effects:

$$I_h = I_f + e_f$$

The offsetting effect of percentage changes in the value of foreign currency (e_f) and foreign inflation (I_f) become clear.

Using PPP to estimate exchange rate effects

The relative form of PPP can be used to estimate how an exchange rate will change in response to differential inflation rates between countries.

EXAMPLE

Assume that the exchange rate is in equilibrium initially. Then the home currency experiences a 5% inflation rate, while the foreign country experiences a 3% inflation rate. According to PPP, the foreign currency will adjust as follows:

$$e_f = \frac{(1 + I_h)}{(1 + I_f)} - 1$$

$$e_f = \frac{(1 + 0.05)}{(1 + 0.03)} - 1$$

$$= 0.0194 \text{ or } 1.94\%$$

Thus, according to this example, the foreign currency should appreciate by 1.94% in response to the higher inflation of the home country relative to the foreign country. If this exchange rate change does occur, the effective price index of the foreign country will be as high as the index in the home country from the perspective of home country consumers. Even though inflation is lower in the foreign country, appreciation of the foreign currency pushes the foreign country's price index up from the perspective of consumers in the home country. When considering the exchange rate effect, price indexes of both countries rise by 5% from the home country perspective. Thus, consumers' purchasing power is the same for foreign goods and home goods.

EXAMPLE

This example examines the situation when foreign inflation exceeds home inflation. Assume that the exchange rate is in equilibrium initially. Then the home country experiences a 4% inflation rate, while the foreign country experiences a 7% inflation rate. According to PPP, the foreign currency will adjust as follows:

$$ef = \frac{(1+I_h)}{(1+I_f)} - 1$$

$$ef = \frac{(1+0.04)}{(1+0.07)} - 1$$

$$= -0.028 \text{ or } - 2.8\%$$

Thus, according to this example, the foreign currency should depreciate by 2.8% in response to the higher inflation of the foreign country relative to the home country. Even though the inflation is lower in the home country, the depreciation of the foreign currency places downward pressure on the foreign country's prices from the perspective of consumers in the home country. When considering the exchange rate impact, prices of both countries rise by 4%. Thus, PPP still exists due to the adjustment in the exchange rate.

Using a simplified PPP relationship. The simplified relationship derived above is:

$$e_f = I_h - I_f$$

or

$$I_h = I_f + e_f$$

Applied to the first of the two previous examples where home inflation is 5% and foreign inflation is 3%, in approximate terms, the change in the value of one unit of foreign currency (e_f) is $I_h - I_f = 5\% - 3\% = 2\%$ so that $I_h = 5\%$ and $I_f + e_f = 3\% + 2\% = 5\%$. Foreign goods increase in price at the same rate as home goods.

In the second example, home inflation is 4% and foreign inflation is 7%, in approximate terms, the change in the value of one unit of foreign currency (e_f) is $I_h - I_f = 4\% - 7\% = -3\%$ so that $I_h = 4\%$ and $I_f + e_f = 7\% - 3\% = 4\%$. Again foreign goods increase in price at the same rate as home goods.

Graphic analysis of purchasing power parity

Using PPP theory, we should be able to assess the potential impact of inflation on exchange rates. Exhibit 8.1 is a graphic representation of PPP theory. The points on the exhibit suggest that given an inflation differential between the home and the foreign country of X%, the foreign currency should adjust by X% due to that inflation differential.

PPP line. The diagonal line connecting all these points together is known as the **PPP line**. Point A represents our earlier example in which the US and British inflation rates were assumed to be 9% and 5%, respectively, so that $I_h - I_f = -4\%$ (taking the home country to be the UK). Recall that this led to the anticipated depreciation in the US dollar of 4%, as illustrated by point A. Point B reflects a situation in which the UK and foreign inflation rates are 5% and 2%, respectively, so that $I_h - I_f = 3\%$. This leads to anticipated appreciation of the foreign currency by 3%, as illustrated by point B. If the exchange rate does respond to inflation differentials as PPP theory suggests, the actual points should lie on or close to the PPP line.

Purchasing power disparity. Exhibit 8.2 identifies areas of purchasing power disparity. Assume an initial equilibrium situation, then a change in the inflation rates of the two countries. If the exchange rate does not move as PPP theory suggests, there is a disparity in the purchasing power of the two countries.

Point C in Exhibit 8.2 represents a situation where home inflation (I_h) exceeds foreign inflation (I_f) by 3%. Yet, the foreign currency appreciated by only 1% in response to this inflation differential. Consequently, purchasing power disparity exists. Home country consumers' purchasing power for foreign goods has become more favourable relative to their purchasing power for the home country's goods. The PPP theory suggests that such a disparity in purchasing power should exist only in the short run. Over time, as the

Exhibit 8.1 Illustration of purchasing power parity

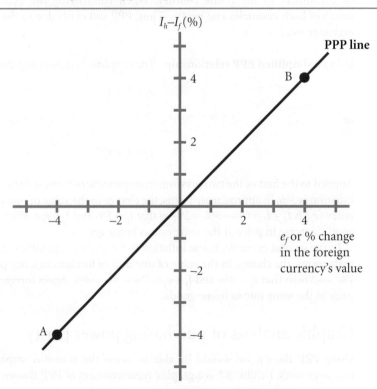

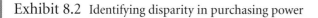

Exhibit 8.2 Identifying disparity in purchasing power

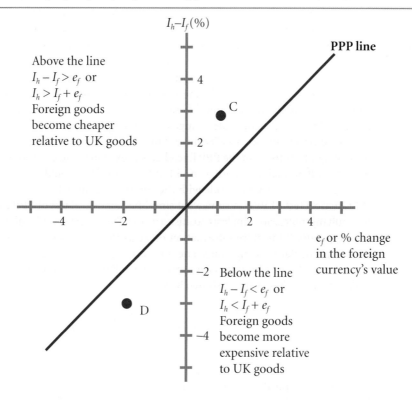

home country consumers take advantage of the disparity by purchasing more foreign goods, upward pressure on the foreign currency's value will cause point C to move toward the PPP line. All points to the left of (or above) the PPP line represent more favourable purchasing power for foreign goods than for home goods.

Point D in Exhibit 8.2 represents a situation where home inflation is 3% below foreign inflation. Yet, the foreign currency has depreciated by only 2%. Again, purchasing power disparity exists. The purchasing power for foreign goods has become less favourable relative to the purchasing power for the home country's goods. The PPP theory suggests that the foreign currency in this example should have depreciated by 3% to fully offset the 3% inflation differential. Since the foreign currency did not weaken to this extent, the home country consumers may cease purchasing foreign goods, causing the foreign currency to weaken to the extent anticipated by PPP theory. If so, point D would move toward the PPP line. All points to the right of (or below) the PPP line represent more favourable purchasing power for home country goods than for foreign goods.

Testing the purchasing power parity theory

The PPP theory not only provides an explanation as to how relative inflation rates between two countries can influence an exchange rate, but it also provides information that can be used to forecast exchange rates.

Conceptual tests of PPP. One way to test the PPP theory is to choose two countries (say, the United Kingdom and another country) and compare the differential in their inflation rates to the percentage change in the foreign currency's value during several time periods. Using a graph similar to Exhibit 8.2, each point representing the inflation differential and exchange rate percentage change for each specific time period could be plotted. The result could then be compared to the PPP line as drawn in Exhibit 8.2. If the points deviate significantly from the PPP line, then the percentage change in the foreign currency is not being influenced by the inflation differential in the manner PPP theory suggests.

As an alternative test (known as cross sectional analysis), several foreign countries could be compared with the home country over a given time period. Each foreign country will exhibit an inflation differential relative to the home country, which can be compared to the exchange rate change during the period of concern. Thus, a point can be plotted on a graph such as Exhibit 8.2 for each foreign country analyzed. If the points deviate significantly from the PPP line, then the exchange rates are not responding to the inflation differentials in accordance with PPP theory. One would suspect from the theory that the greater the level of trade with the country the more likely PPP will hold.

Statistical test of PPP. A somewhat simplified statistical test of PPP can be developed by applying regression analysis to historical exchange rates and inflation differentials (see Appendix B for more information on regression analysis). To illustrate, let's focus on one particular exchange rate. The quarterly percentage changes in the foreign currency value (e_f) can be regressed against the inflation differential that existed at the beginning of each quarter, as shown here:

$$e_f = a_0 + a_1 \left[\frac{(1 + I_{UK})}{(1 + I_f)} - 1 \right] + \mu$$

where a_0 is a constant, a_1 is the slope coefficient, and μ is an error term. Regression analysis could be applied to quarterly data to determine the regression coefficients. The hypothesized values of a_0 and a_1 are 0 and 1.0, respectively. These coefficients imply that for a given inflation differential, there is an equal offsetting percentage change in the exchange rate, on average. The appropriate t-test for each regression coefficient requires a comparison to the hypothesized value and division by the standard error (s.e.) of the coefficient as follows:

$$\text{Test for } a_0 = 0 \quad \text{Test for } a_1 = 1$$

$$t = \frac{a_0 - 0}{\text{s.e of } a_0} \qquad t = \frac{a_1 - 0}{\text{s.e. of } a_1}$$

Then the t-table is used to find the critical t-value. If either t-test finds that the coefficients differ significantly from what is expected, the relationship between the inflation differential and the exchange rate differs from that stated by PPP theory. Further problems with testing for PPP are discussed below.

Results of tests of PPP. Much research has been conducted to test whether PPP exists. Studies by Mishkin, Adler and Dumas, and Abuaf and Jorion[1] found evidence of

---

1. Frederic S. Mishkin (1984) "Are Real Interest Rates Equal Across Countries? An Empirical Investigation of International Parity Conditions", *Journal of Finance*, December, 1345–57; M. Adler and B. Dumas (1983) "International Portfolio Choice and Corporate Finance: A Synthesis", *Journal of Finance*, June, 925–84; N. Abuaf and P. Jorion (1990) "Purchasing Power in the Long Run", *Journal of Finance*, March, 157–74.

Exhibit 8.3 Comparison of annual inflation differentials and exchange rate movements for four major countries from 1982 to 2004

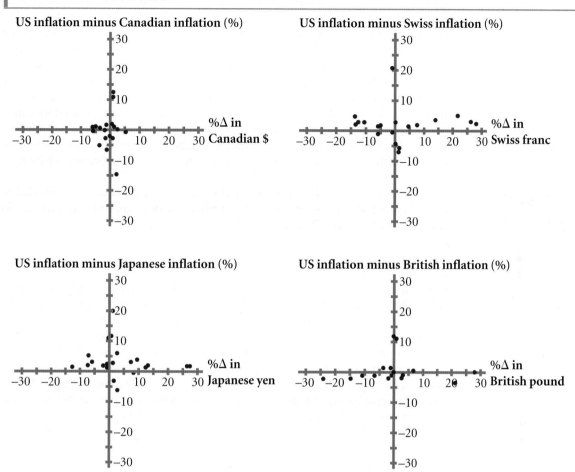

significant deviations from PPP that persisted for lengthy periods. A related study by Adler and Lehman[2] provided evidence against PPP even over the long term.

Hakkio,[3] however, found that when an exchange rate deviated far from the value that would be expected according to PPP, it moved toward that value. Although the relationship between inflation differentials and exchange rates is not perfect even in the long run, it supports the use of inflation differentials to forecast long-run movements in exchange rates. A review paper is included at the end of Part 2.

Tests of PPP for each currency. To further examine whether PPP is valid, Exhibit 8.3 illustrates the relationship between relative inflation rates and exchange rate movements over time taking the US as the home currency. The inflation differential shown in each of the four graphs (each graph represents one foreign currency) is measured as the US

2. M. Adler and B. Lehman (1983) "Deviations from Purchasing Power Parity in the Long Run", *Journal of Finance*, December, 1471–87.
3. Craig S. Hakkio (1986) "Interest Rates and Exchange Rates – What Is the Relationship?", *Economic Review*, Federal Reserve Bank of Kansas City, November, 33–43.

inflation rate minus the foreign inflation rate. The annual differential in inflation between the United States and each foreign country is represented on the vertical axis. The annual percentage change in the exchange rate of each foreign currency (relative to the US dollar) is represented on the horizontal axis. The annual inflation differentials and percentage changes in exchange rates from 1982 to 2004 are plotted. If PPP existed during the period examined, the points plotted on the graph should be near an imaginary 45° line, which would split the axes (like the PPP line shown in Exhibit 8.2).

Although each graph shows different results, some general comments apply to all four graphs. The percentage changes in exchange rates are typically much more volatile than the inflation differentials. Thus, the exchange rates are changing to a greater degree than PPP theory would predict. In some years, even the direction of a currency could not have been anticipated by PPP theory. The results in Exhibit 8.3 suggest that the relationship between inflation differentials and exchange rate movements often becomes distorted.

USING THE WEB

Country inflation rates Information about inflation for each country is provided at http://www.imf.org/external/pubind.htm in the statistical appendix of the World Economic Outlook Report.

Why purchasing power parity does not occur

Statistical tests are a joint test of the theory and the model. If results prove to be poor, it may be the model that is at fault rather than the theory. One obvious problem with the model is that there is an unspecified period of change. Although an arbitrage (riskless) trade process according to the theory drives the relationship, it is not clear how long it takes for an exchange rate to adjust to an imbalance of prices. Should an exchange rate in the third quarter of the year change according to inflation differences in the third, second or first quarter of the year, or some other time period? The measurement of inflation is also problematic. Should the index include goods and services not exported? Preferably not, but then the index will not be weighted according to trade levels appropriate to any single exchange rate. So there will always be an element of approximation. The theory also has important *ceteris paribus* assumptions – other factors such as interest rates are assumed to not affect the relationship. In the real world, of course, other factors are changing all the time and will affect the exchange rate. It would not be unreasonable to argue, in view of these problems, that the relationship may well be untestable in many circumstances. However, where the foreign country experiences much higher inflation than the home country it is observably the case that the foreign currency depreciates. In extreme conditions, therefore, where inflation is clearly the most important economic phenomenon, PPP will hold. In less extreme conditions, the importance of inflation differences is less clear. A more detailed consideration follows.

Confounding effects. The PPP theory presumes that exchange rate movements are driven completely by the inflation differential between two countries. Yet, recall from Chapter 4 that a change in a currency's spot rate is influenced by the following factors:

$$e = f(\Delta INF, \Delta INT, \Delta INC, \Delta GC, \Delta EXP)$$

where

$$e = \text{percentage change in the spot rate}$$

ΔINF = change in the differential between US inflation and the foreign country's inflation

ΔINT = change in the differential between the US interest rate and the foreign country's interest rate

ΔINC = change in the differential between the US income level and the foreign country's income level

ΔGC = change in government controls

ΔEXP = change in expectations of future exchange rates

Since the exchange rate movement is not driven solely by ΔINF, the relationship between the inflation differential and the exchange rate movement is not as simple as suggested by PPP.

EXAMPLE

Assume that Venezuela's inflation rate is 5% above the euro zone inflation rate. From this information, PPP theory would suggest that the Venezuelan bolivar should depreciate by about 5% against the euro. Yet, if the government of Venezuela imposes trade barriers against Europe, Venezuela's consumers and firms will not be able to adjust their spending in reaction to the inflation differential. Therefore, the exchange rate will not adjust as suggested by PPP.

No substitutes for traded goods. The idea behind PPP theory is that as soon as the prices become relatively higher in one country, consumers in the other country will stop buying imported goods and shift to purchasing domestic goods instead. This shift influences the exchange rate. But, if substitute goods are not available domestically, consumers may not stop buying imported goods.

EXAMPLE

Reconsider the previous example in which Venezuela's inflation is 5% higher than the euro zone rate. If European consumers do not find suitable substitute goods at home, they may continue to buy the highly priced goods from Venezuela, and the bolivar may not depreciate as expected according to PPP theory.

The real exchange rate

Discussion of purchasing power parity in newspapers and the press is usually in terms of the real exchange rate. The real exchange rate is the exchange rate adjusted for inflationary effects in the two countries of concern. As it is not an actual exchange rate but rather an adjusted rate, it is normally expressed as an index. Rather than consider just one currency the rate is usually measured against a basket of currencies weighted according to the level of trade. Thus for the British pound, the exchange rate with the euro would be given the highest weighting in the basket, followed by the US dollar and so on. The strict term for such a rate is the "real effective exchange rate". But this is often abbreviated to the "real exchange rate" or "the real value of the currency". It is this value that is important in foreign trade and investment.

As is normally the case, the significance of the index number is not the actual number itself but how it has changed. Thus, if the real (effective) exchange rate of the British pound increases from 120 to 132, there has been an increase in the purchasing power of the pound compared to foreign currencies by 10% ((132 − 120)/120 = 0.10). That is, holders of pounds will find that they can now buy 10% more foreign goods (on average). But also, foreign earners will find that they can on average buy 10% fewer British goods. So an increase in the real value of a currency is associated with decreased competitiveness of the home currency. Similarly, a decrease in the real exchange rate index of a currency would be associated with an increase in competitiveness, as goods would become relatively cheaper for foreign currency holders.

There are two causes of a change in the real value of a currency, a change in the exchange rate (e) and relative inflation. The similarity with purchasing power parity (PPP) should now be apparent. If a home currency weakens (lowers in value) by 10% but its inflation is 10% more than foreign inflation, the real exchange rate has not changed. From the foreign perspective, the weakness of the currency is offset by the higher inflation. In other words, an unchanged real value of a currency means that PPP has been maintained.

The link between the real exchange rate and PPP can be worked out more formally in the following.

The first cause of a change in the real value of a home currency (the pound) is e_h – the percentage change in the exchange rate value of the pound or home currency. This is an indirect quote rather than the more normal direct quote. The second factor outlined above is the effect of inflation. Remember that inflation is inflation of prices *and* incomes. So higher domestic inflation means *on its own* that the real value of the home currency will increase – residents will be able to buy more goods abroad as their earnings will have increased (as well as domestic prices) but the pound will still be buying the same number of euros, dollars, pesos etc. Relative inflation is therefore $I_h - I_f$, if home inflation is higher, the real value of the home currency will be greater. We can therefore add the two sources of a change in the real value together as follows:

$$\Delta R_h = e_h + (I_h - I_f)$$

where

ΔR_h	=	percentage change in the real value of the home currency,
e_h	=	percentage change in the exchange rate value of one unit of *home* currency,
I_h, I_f	=	the home inflation rate and foreign inflation rate respectively.

What is the relation between this equation and PPP? We have asserted that PPP implies that there is no change in the real value of the home currency, so we can set

$$\Delta R_h = 0$$

which implies that

$$e_h = I_f - I_h,$$

using approximate processes, e_h is roughly equal to $-e_f$. As an example, a 5% depreciation in the pound (as home currency) against all foreign currencies is approximately the same as a 5% appreciation in foreign currencies against the pound. Therefore

$$-e_f = I_f - I_h$$

and therefore

$$e_f = I_h - I_f$$

which is the PPP formulation. Therefore testing for changes in the real exchange rate and testing for PPP are one and the same thing. No change in the real exchange rate implies that PPP holds. Also, as is evident in many academic papers, volatility in the real exchange rate is rather more relevant for an economy than just changes in the exchange rate. The real exchange rate addresses purchasing power and therefore has direct trade implications. The two are often not so very different as inflation rates change far less often than exchange rates.

EXAMPLE

Armington ltd is seeking to export slimming products to the United States. Over the last year the value of the pound increased from \$1.5 to \$1.65 or 10%. Inflation in the UK for this particular year was 1% and in the US was 4%. Using the formula: $\Delta R_h = e_h + (I_h - I_f)$ the real value of the pound increased by $10\% + (1\% - 4\%) = 7\%$ making the exports less competitive. The Finance Director explained to the Managing Director: "The pound cost them 10% more, on top of that, our prices went up by 1%. However, their domestic prices went up by 4%, but that still left a 7% increase in our prices relative to theirs. Of course, if we priced the goods in dollars, then we would lose 7% compared to selling here. The real value of the pound goes up which is fine for holiday makers and importers, but we are less competitive.'

Purchasing power parity in the long run

Purchasing power parity can be tested over the long run by assessing a "real" exchange rate between two currencies over time. If the real exchange rate reverts to some mean level over time, this suggests that it is constant (or stationary) in the long run, and any deviations from the mean are temporary. Conversely, if the real exchange rate follows a random walk, this implies that it moves randomly without any predictable pattern. That is, it does not tend to revert to some mean level and therefore cannot be viewed as constant in the long run. Under these conditions, the notion of PPP is rejected because the movements in the real exchange rate appear to be more than temporary deviations from some equilibrium value.

The study by Abuaf and Jorion,[4] mentioned earlier, tested PPP by assessing the long-run pattern of the real exchange rate. Abuaf and Jorion state that the typical findings rejecting PPP in previous studies are questionable because of limitations in the methods used to test PPP. They suggest that deviations from PPP are substantial in the short run but are reduced by about half in three years. Thus, even though exchange rates deviate from the levels predicted by PPP in the short run, their deviations are reduced over the long run.

It should be stressed that the deviations are at times large and persistent over many years. For the purposes of planning, the random walk model can serve as a model of exchange rate behaviour that may err on the side of overstating the potential variation of a currency, but will provide a simply calculated prediction – this is dealt with in Part 3.

USING
THE WEB

Inflation and exchange rate forecasts Information about anticipated inflation and exchange rates is available at http://www.worldbank.org click on "data and research", "prospects" and "prospects for the Global Economy" for a US and euro prediction of inflation and other economic factors.

---

4. N. Abuaf and P. Jorion (1990) "Purchasing Power in the Long Run", *Journal of Finance*, March, 157–74.

The purchasing power parity relationship, though not exact, can explain how some events can have major effects on MNCs through their impact on exchange rates. One common example is the impact of oil prices on inflation and therefore on exchange rates. During the year 2000, the market price of oil increased substantially, placing upward pressure on inflation rates in countries that import oil. The European countries that participate in the euro import oil and were subjected to the higher prices of oil. Since the United Kingdom produces its own oil, it was not directly affected by the higher market price of oil. Its MNCs, however, were adversely affected as a result of their business with the other European countries. Inflation increased in Europe during 2000, which placed downward pressure on the euro relative to the British pound. MNCs in the United Kingdom that export to these euro-zone countries were adversely affected because the pound became more expensive relative to the euro, reducing the demand for British products.

MNCs based in euro-zone countries were also affected. Those that export to the United Kingdom benefited because their products became cheaper to British consumers. However, the inflation in the euro-zone countries caused the European Central Bank to raise interest rates in an attempt to reduce the inflationary pressure. Consequently, the economies of these countries weakened, and the local demand for the products produced by the MNCs was reduced.

MNCs that recognize their susceptibility to foreign inflation rates are motivated to monitor foreign inflation and limit their exposure to countries that may experience an abrupt increase in inflation.

INTERNATIONAL FISHER EFFECT (IFE)

Along with PPP theory, another major theory in international finance is the **international Fisher effect (IFE)** theory. It uses interest rate rather than inflation rate differentials to explain why exchange rates change over time. The theory is closely related to the PPP theory because interest rates are often highly correlated with inflation rates. High inflation is typically accompanied by high interest rates. According to Fisher the monetary or nominal rate is approximately the sum of the real and inflation rates. If it is assumed that investors in different countries require the same real (non-inflation) return for the same level of risk, then the only reason for interest rates to differ for a given risk is differences in expected inflation.

Relationship with purchasing power parity

Recall that PPP theory suggests that exchange rate movements are caused by inflation rate differentials. If differences in expected inflation are the only reason for any difference in nominal *interest* rates then interest rates and inflation differences should be the same. The IFE theory suggests that foreign currencies with relatively high interest rates will depreciate in much the same way as currencies with high inflation rates. The following analysis will concentrate on investments that are risk free, in the sense of guaranteeing the monetary or nominal return – the actual cash. The rates offered by a central bank would be one such example.

EXAMPLE

The nominal interest rate is 8% in the United Kingdom. Investors in the United Kingdom expect a 6% rate of inflation, which means that they expect to earn a real return of 2% over one year. The nominal interest rate in Canada is 13%. Given that investors in Canada also require a real return of 2%, the expected inflation rate in Canada must be 11%. According to PPP theory, the Canadian dollar is expected to depreciate by approximately 5% against the British pound (i.e. 6% − 11% = −5%, Canadian inflation rate is 5% higher). Therefore, UK investors would not benefit from investing in Canada because they would earn 13% from their investment in Canada but find that when the Canadian dollar is converted back into pounds it is worth 5% less, giving a net return of 13% − 5% = 8%, the same rate as investing in the UK.

The link with PPP is therefore that inflation differences provide a rationale for interest rate differences. In this sense PPP enriches the IFE theory. But it should be stated that the Fisher interpretation of interest rates is not necessary in the use of interest rates to explain exchange rate movements. If interest rates are higher in country H than in country L, and funds are *not* moving from L to H, there must be the market expectation that the value of country H's currency will fall relative to L for whatever reason. Expressed in this manner the relationship is termed uncovered interest rate parity. Investing abroad with no exchange rate protection (uncovered) yields a net return (interest rate plus exchange rate movement) that has parity with the domestic return.

Implications of the IFE for the foreign investment market

The IFE theory disagrees with the notion introduced in Chapter 4 that a high interest rate may entice investors from various countries to invest there and could place upward pressure on the currency. This would only happen where the high interest rate was *unexpected*. The term unexpected in this context means that the exchange rate has not adjusted to the change. Where the higher interest rate is expected there is no reason to believe that there will be upward pressure placed on the currency as the high interest rate compensates for an expected devaluation of the currency as suggested by PPP. The following example illustrates this effect.

EXAMPLE

Brazil's prevailing nominal interest rate is frequently very high because of the high inflation there. With inflation levels sometimes exceeding 100% annually, people tend to spend now before prices rise. Rather than saving, they are very willing to borrow even at high interest rates to buy products now because the alternative is to defer the purchase and have to pay a much higher price later. Thus, the high nominal interest rate is attributed to the high expected inflation. Given these expectations of high inflation, even interest rates exceeding 50% will not entice foreign investors because they recognize that high inflation could cause Brazil's currency (the Brazilian real) to decline by more than 50% in a year, fully offsetting the high interest rate. Thus, the high interest rate in Brazil does not attract investment from foreign investors and therefore will not cause the Brazilian real to strengthen. Instead, the high interest rate in Brazil may indicate potential depreciation of the Brazilian real, which places downward pressure on the currency's value. Thus, as with IFE theory, a higher interest rate compensates for an expected fall in the value of the currency.

Now consider a second currency, the Chilean peso and assume that there is a sudden increase in interest rates to a higher level than in the developed world. Chile normally has relatively low inflation, so foreign investors are not as concerned that the Chilean peso's value will decline due to inflationary pressure. In this context, any increase in

Chilean interest rates would be unexpected, investors would have no reason to expect a compensating fall in the value of the Chilean peso. Therefore, they may attempt to capitalize on the higher interest rate in Chile. The increase in investment in Chile would not amount to a deluge as there is always the risk that expectations may be wrong and that the peso does indeed devalue. More cautious money would stay at home!

Exchange rates reflect market expectations; the IFE is a theory of market expectations. It maintains that *on average* changes in the exchange rate offset interest rate differences. The example of Chile above does not therefore contradict the example of Brazil due to the fact that, in Chile, the changes were not anticipated by the market.

In addition, one should caution against over simple analysis. Here it has been suggested that an unexpected increase in interest rates in Chile would attract foreign investment. But one could also argue that the market would take this unexpected piece of news as a signal that the Chilean government, in possession of more information than the market, has reason to believe that the value of the peso will fall. Existing investors, particularly the least content, may decide that this is a hint to the market and pull out. The reaction of the market is rarely simple and rarely unified. Some may increase their investment in Chile, others may withdraw their funds. The spot exchange rate will reflect the net effect of these varying reactions. Perhaps the only safe conclusion is that any test of the theory cannot be expected to yield particularly strong evidence in normal times.

The implications are similar for foreign investors who attempt to capitalize on relatively high home interest rates. Foreign investors may wish to invest in the home market to take advantage of the high interest rates, but where there is no flood of inward investment, the market must be expecting that the value of the home currency will fall. On average across different time periods, the currency value will fall if the foreign exchange market is efficient.

These possible investment opportunities are summarized in Exhibit 8.4. Note that whether investors of a given country invest their funds at home or abroad, the expected nominal or market return to the investor is the same.

Exhibit 8.4 Illustration of the international Fisher effect (IFE) from various investor perspectives

Investors residing in …	Home interest rate (1)	= expected inflation	+ real return	Invest in…	Interest rate earned abroad	+ Expected change in value of foreign currency $(e_f)^{(2)}$	= Net return from foreign investment (3)
UK	5%	3%	2%	Euro	8%	−3%	5%
				US	13%	−8%	5%
Euro zone	8%	6%	2%	UK	5%	3%	8%
				US	13%	−5%	8%
US	13%	11%	2%	UK	5%	8%	13%
				Euro	8%	5%	13%

Notes:
1. Using the approximate method.
2. Calculated as $e_f = I_h - I_f$ so 3% −6% = −3%; 3% − 11% = −8% and so on.
3. Note that the expected return from foreign investment according to IFE is the same as the home interest rate.

Derivation of the international Fisher effect

The precise relationship between the interest rate differential of two countries and the expected exchange rate change according to the IFE can be derived more formally as follows. First, the actual return to investors who invest in money market securities (such as short-term bank deposits) in their home country is simply the interest rate offered on those securities. The actual return to investors who invest in a foreign money market security, however, depends on not only the foreign interest rate (i_f) but also the percentage change in the value of the foreign currency (e_f) denominating the security. The formula for the actual or "effective" (exchange-rate-adjusted) return on a foreign bank deposit (or any money market security) is:

$$r = (1 + i_f)(1 + e_f) - 1$$

According to the IFE, the effective return on a foreign investment should, on average, be equal to the effective return on a domestic investment. Therefore, the IFE suggests that the expected return on a foreign money market investment is equal to the interest rate on a local money market investment:

$$E(r) = i_h$$

where r is the effective return on the foreign deposit and i_h is the interest rate on the home deposit. We can determine the degree by which the foreign currency must change in order to make investments in both countries generate similar returns. Take the expansion of r from the previous formula, and set it equal to i_h as follows:

$$r = i_h$$
$$(1 + i_f)(1 + e_f) - 1 = i_h$$

Now solve for e_f:

$$(1 + i_f)(1 + e_f) = (1 + i_h)$$

$$(1 + e_f) = \frac{(1 + i_h)}{(1 + i_f)}$$

$$e_f = \frac{(1 + i_h)}{(1 + i_f)} - 1$$

As verified here, the IFE theory contends that when $i_h > i_f$, e_f will be positive because the lower foreign interest rate reflects lower inflationary expectations in the foreign country. That is, the foreign currency will appreciate when the foreign interest rate is lower than the home interest rate. This appreciation will improve the foreign return to investors from the home country, making returns on foreign securities similar to returns on home securities. Conversely, when $i_f > i_h$, e_f will be negative. That is, the foreign currency will depreciate when the foreign interest rate exceeds the home interest rate. This depreciation will reduce the return on foreign securities from the perspective of investors in the home country, making returns on foreign securities no higher than returns on home securities.

Numerical example based on the derivation of IFE. Given two interest rates, the value of e_f can be determined from the formula that was just derived, and used to forecast the exchange rate.

Assume that the interest rate on a one-year insured home country bank deposit is 11%, and the interest rate on a one-year insured foreign bank deposit is 12%. For the actual returns of these two investments to be similar from the perspective of investors in the home country, the foreign currency would have to change over the investment horizon by the following percentage:

$$e_f = \frac{(1+i_h)}{(1+i_f)} - 1$$

$$= \frac{(1+0.11)}{(1+0.12)} - 1$$

$$= -0.0089, \text{ or } -89\%$$

The implications are that the foreign currency denominating the foreign deposit would need to depreciate by 0.89% to make the actual return on the foreign deposit equal to 11% from the perspective of investors in the home country. This would make the return on the foreign investment equal to the return on a domestic investment.

Simplified relationship. A more simplified but less precise relationship specified by the IFE is:

$$e_f \approx i_h - i_f$$

That is, the percentage change in the exchange rate over the investment horizon will equal the interest rate differential between two countries. This approximation provides reasonable estimates only when the interest rate differential is small. The similarity with the PPP approximate formula is apparent, interest rates are substituted for inflation rates.

Graphic analysis of the international Fisher effect

Exhibit 8.5 displays the set of points that conform to the argument behind IFE theory. For example, point E reflects a situation where the foreign interest rate exceeds the home interest rate by three percentage points. Yet, the foreign currency has depreciated by 3% to offset its interest rate advantage. Thus, an investor setting up a deposit in the foreign country achieves a return similar to what is possible domestically. Point F represents a home interest rate 2% above the foreign interest rate. If investors from the home country establish a foreign deposit, they are at a disadvantage regarding the foreign interest rate. However, IFE theory suggests that the currency should appreciate by 2% to offset the interest rate disadvantage.

Point F in Exhibit 8.5 also illustrates the IFE from a foreign investor's perspective. The home interest rate will appear attractive to the foreign investor. However, IFE theory suggests that the foreign currency will appreciate by 2%, which, from the foreign investor's perspective, implies that the home country's currency denominating the investment instruments will depreciate to offset the interest rate advantage.

Points on the IFE line. All the points along the so-called **IFE line** in Exhibit 8.5 reflect exchange rate adjustments to offset the differential in interest rates. This means investors

Exhibit 8.5 Illustration of IFE line (when exchange rate changes perfectly offset interest rate differentials)

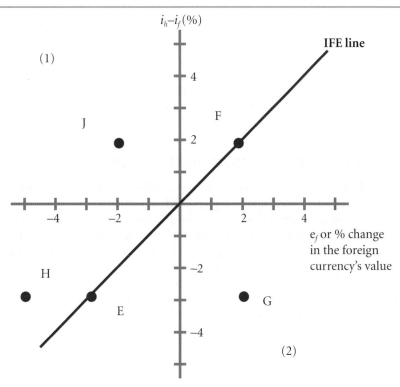

Notes:
■ Above the line $(i_h - i_f) > e_f$ or $i_h > (e_f + i_f)$, in words, the returns from investing at home are greater than investing abroad.
■ Below the line $(i_h - i_f) < e_f$ or $i_h < (e_f + i_f)$, in words, the returns from at home are less than investing abroad.

will end up achieving the same yield (adjusted for exchange rate fluctuations) whether they invest at home or in a foreign country.

To be precise, IFE theory does not suggest that this relationship will exist continuously over each time period. The point of IFE theory is that if an MNC periodically makes foreign investments to take advantage of higher foreign interest rates, it will achieve a yield that is sometimes above and sometimes below the domestic yield. Periodic investments by an MNC corporation in an attempt to capitalize on the higher interest rates will, on average, achieve a yield similar to that by a corporation simply making domestic deposits periodically.

Points below the IFE line. Points below the IFE line generally reflect the higher returns from investing in foreign deposits. For example, point G in Exhibit 8.5 indicates that the foreign interest rate exceeds the home interest rate by 3%. In addition, the foreign currency has appreciated by 2%. The combination of the higher foreign interest rate plus the appreciation of the foreign currency will cause the foreign yield to be higher than what is possible domestically. If actual data were compiled and plotted, and the vast majority of points were below the IFE line, this would suggest that investors of the home country could consistently increase their investment returns by establishing foreign bank deposits. Such results would refute the IFE theory.

Points above the IFE line. Points above the IFE line generally reflect returns from foreign deposits that are lower than the returns possible domestically. For example, point

H reflects a foreign interest rate that is 3% above the home interest rate. Yet, point H also indicates that the exchange rate of the foreign currency has depreciated by 5%, more than offsetting its interest rate advantage.

As another example, point J represents a situation in which an investor of the home country is hampered in two ways by investing in a foreign deposit. First, the foreign interest rate is lower than the home interest rate. Second, the foreign currency depreciates during the time the foreign deposit is held. If actual data were compiled and plotted, and the vast majority of points were above the IFE line, this would suggest that investors of the home country would receive consistently lower returns from foreign investments as opposed to investments in the home country. Such results would refute the IFE theory.

Tests of the international Fisher effect

If the actual points (one for each period) of interest rates and exchange rate changes were plotted over time on a graph such as Exhibit 8.5, we could determine whether the points are systematically below the IFE line (suggesting higher returns from foreign investing), above the line (suggesting lower returns from foreign investing), or evenly scattered on both sides (suggesting a balance of higher returns from foreign investing in some periods and lower foreign returns in other periods).

Exhibit 8.6 is an example of a set of points that tend to support the IFE theory. It implies that returns from short-term foreign investments are, on average, about equal to the returns that are possible domestically. Notice that each individual point reflects a change in the exchange rate that does not exactly offset the interest rate differential. In

Exhibit 8.6 Illustration of IFE concept (when exchange rate changes perfectly offset interest rate differentials on average

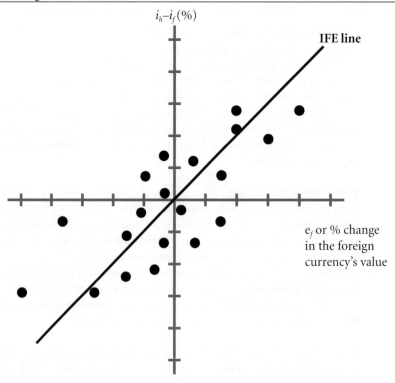

some cases, the exchange rate change does not fully offset the interest rate differential. In other cases, the exchange rate change more than offsets the interest rate differential. Overall, the results balance out such that the interest rate differentials are, *on average*, offset by changes in the exchange rates. Thus, foreign investments have generated yields that are, on average, equal to those of domestic investments.

Risk premiums. If foreign yields are expected to be about equal to domestic yields, an MNC would probably prefer the domestic investments. The firm would know the yield on domestic short-term securities (such as bank deposits) in advance, whereas the yield to be attained from foreign short-term securities would be uncertain because the firm would not know what spot exchange rate would exist at the securities' maturity. Investors generally prefer an investment whose return is known over an investment whose return is uncertain, assuming that all other features of the investments are similar. The approximate equation can be developed to include a risk premium (by tradition, the term premium is used to include a negative premium or discount):

$$e_f + \rho = i_h - i_f$$

where ρ is the risk premium for the period of investment being considered. Risk premiums in international finance, and one might add in finance generally, are not well understood. Theoretical models including premiums are not well supported in practice.

Results from testing the IFE. Whether the IFE holds in reality depends on the particular time period examined. Although the IFE theory may hold during some time frames, there is evidence that it does not consistently hold. A study by Thomas[5] tested the IFE theory by examining the results of: (1) purchasing currency futures contracts of currencies with high interest rates that contained discounts (relative to the spot rates); and (2) selling futures on currencies with low interest rates that contained premiums. If the high-interest-rate currencies depreciated and the low-interest-rate currencies appreciated to the extent suggested by the IFE theory, this strategy would not generate significant profits. However, 123 (57%) of the 216 transactions created by this strategy were profitable. In addition, the average gain was much higher than the average loss. This study indicates that the IFE relationship in practice is more complex than the simple form would suggest. For example, a risk premium may indicate why high interest rate currencies are apparently a better investment on average. On average, insurance is not worthwhile, but it is still purchased to guard against a sudden fall. The same argument may apply to futures contracts, though the exact relationship has yet to be clearly established.

Statistical test of the IFE. A somewhat simplified statistical test of the IFE can be developed by applying regression analysis to historical exchange rates and the nominal interest rate differential:

$$e_f = a_0 + a_1\left(\frac{(1+i_h)}{(1+i_f)} - 1\right) + \mu$$

5. Lee R. Thomas (1985) "A Winning Strategy for Currency – Futures Speculation", *Journal of Portfolio Management*, Fall, 65–9.

where a_0 is a constant, a_1 is the slope coefficient, and μ is an error term. Regression analysis would determine the regression coefficients. The hypothesized values of a_0 and a_1 are 0 and 1.0, respectively.

The appropriate t-test for each regression coefficient requires a comparison to the hypothesized value and then division by the standard error (s.e.) of the coefficients, as follows:

$$\text{Test for } a_0 = 0 \quad \text{Test for } a_1 = 1$$

$$t = \frac{a_0 - 0}{\text{s.e of } a_0} \quad t = \frac{a_1 - 0}{\text{s.e. of } a_1}$$

The t-table is then used to find the critical t-value. If either t-test finds that the coefficients differ significantly from what was hypothesized, the IFE is not supported by the data.

Why the international Fisher effect does not occur

The IFE model cannot be rejected, only not supported by tests. Poor performance may be due to an over simplistic model or measurement problems. Indeed, much of the academic literature in this area is taken up with tests of increasing sophistication.

Exchange rates can be affected by factors other than interest rates. The relation between interest rates and inflation rates suggested by Fisher may not always hold. Assume a nominal interest rate in a foreign country that is 3% above the US rate because expected inflation in that country is 3% above expected US inflation. Even if these nominal rates properly reflect inflationary expectations, the exchange rate of the foreign currency will react to other factors in addition to the inflation differential. If these other factors put upward pressure on the foreign currency's value, they will offset the downward pressure from the inflation differential. Consequently, foreign investments will achieve higher returns for the US investors than domestic investments.

COMPARISON OF THE IRP, PPP, AND IFE THEORIES

At this point, it may be helpful to compare three related theories of international finance: (1) interest rate parity (IRP) or covered interest rate arbitrage, discussed in Chapter 7, (2) purchasing power parity (PPP), and (3) the international Fisher effect (IFE), sometimes referred to as uncovered interest rate arbitrage, uncovered because the investor takes the risk that the future spot rate (value) of the currency of an investment may fall. Exhibit 8.7 summarizes the main themes of each theory. Note that although all three theories relate to the determination of exchange rates, they have different implications. The IRP theory focuses on why the forward rate differs from the spot rate and on the degree of difference that should exist. It relates to a specific point in time. In contrast, the PPP theory and IFE theory focus on how a currency's spot rate will change over time. Whereas PPP theory suggests that the spot rate will change in accordance with inflation differentials, IFE theory suggests that it will change in accordance with interest rate differentials.

Nevertheless, PPP is related to IFE because expected inflation differentials influence the nominal interest rate differentials between two countries.

Some generalizations about national economies can be made from these theories. High-inflation countries tend to have high nominal interest rates (due to the Fisher

Exhibit 8.7 Comparison of the IRP, PPP, and IFE theories

Theory	Key Variables of Theory		Summary of Theory
Interest rate parity (IRP) or covered interest rate arbitrage	Forward rate premium (or discount)	Interest rate differential	The forward rate of one currency with respect to another will contain a premium (or discount) that is determined by the differential in interest rates between the two countries. As a result, covered interest arbitrage will provide a return that is no higher than a domestic return.
Purchasing power parity (PPP)	Percentage change in spot exchange rate	Inflation rate differential	The spot rate of one currency with respect to another will change in reaction to the differential in inflation rates between the two countries. Consequently, the purchasing power for consumers when purchasing goods in their own country will be similar to their purchasing power when importing goods from the foreign country.
International Fisher effect	Percentage change in spot exchange rate	Interest rate differential	The spot rate of one currency with respect to another will change in accordance with the differential in interest rates between the two countries. Consequently, the return on uncovered foreign money market securities will, on average, be no higher than the return on domestic money market securities from the perspective of investors in the home country.

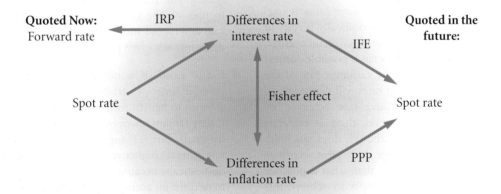

effect). In other words, investors want to be compensated for the high level of inflation. The currencies of high inflation countries tend to weaken over time (because of the PPP and IFE), and the forward rates of their currencies normally exhibit large discounts (due to IRP). There is no doubt that inflation and interest rates play a part in affecting the value of a currency when these values are large.

Where the interest rate and inflation rate differential are smaller the relationships are far less clear. It seems unlikely that the fundamentals of interest rates and inflation rates are no longer relevant, but other factors become relatively more significant. Models that predict future spot rates effectively at lower levels of interest and inflation rates have yet to be developed. The general problems of prediction are examined in the following section. The contribution of the basic theory, as outlined in this chapter, is to provide a strong logical argument for exchange rate behaviour that can serve as the starting point for prediction. In the appendix to this chapter we move on a little more and consider some of the more recent attempts to understand exchange rate behaviour.

Summary

- Purchasing power parity (PPP) theory specifies a precise relationship between relative inflation rates of two countries and their exchange rate. In inexact terms, PPP theory suggests that the equilibrium exchange rate will adjust by the same magnitude as the differential in inflation rates between two countries. Though PPP continues to be a valuable concept, there is evidence of sizable deviations from the theory in the real world.

- The international Fisher effect (IFE) specifies a precise relationship between relative interest rates of two countries and their exchange rates. It suggests that an investor who periodically invests in foreign interest-bearing securities will, on average, achieve a return similar to what is possible domestically. This implies that the exchange rate of the country with high interest rates will depreciate to offset the interest rate advantage achieved by foreign investments. However, there is evidence that during some periods the IFE does not hold. Thus, investment in foreign short-term securities may achieve a higher return than what is possible domestically. If a firm attempts to achieve this higher return, however, it does incur the risk that

the currency of the foreign security might depreciate against the investor's home currency during the investment period. In this case, the foreign security could generate a lower return than a domestic security, even though it exhibits a higher interest rate.

- The PPP theory focuses on the relationship between the inflation rate differential and future exchange rate movements. The IFE focuses on the interest rate differential and future exchange rate movements. The theory of interest rate parity (IRP) focuses on the relationship between the interest rate differential and the forward rate premium (or discount) at a given point in time.

- If IRP exists, it is not possible to benefit from covered interest arbitrage. Investors can still attempt to benefit from high foreign interest rates if they remain uncovered (do not sell the currency forward). But IFE suggests that this strategy will not generate higher returns than what are possible domestically because the exchange rate is expected to decline, on average, by the amount of the interest rate differential.

CRITICAL DEBATE

Does PPP eliminate concerns about long-term exchange rate risk?

Proposition. Yes. Studies have shown that exchange rate movements are related to inflation differentials in the long run. Based on PPP, the currency of a high-inflation country will depreciate against the home currency. A subsidiary in that country should generate inflated revenue from the inflation, which will help offset the adverse exchange effects when its earnings are remitted to the parent. If a firm is focused on long-term performance, the deviations from PPP will offset over time. In some years, the exchange rate effects may exceed the inflation effects, and in other years the inflation effects will exceed the exchange rate effects.

Opposing view. No. Even if the relationship between inflation and exchange rate effects is consistent, this does not guarantee that the effects on the firm will be offsetting. A subsidiary in a high-inflation country will not necessarily be able to adjust its price level to keep up with the increased costs of doing business there. The effects vary with each MNC's situation. Even if the subsidiary can raise its prices to match the rising costs, there are short-term deviations from PPP. The investors who invest in an MNC's stock may be concerned about short-term deviations from PPP, because they will not necessarily hold the stock for the long term. Thus, investors may prefer that firms manage in a manner that reduces the volatility in their performance in short-run and long-run periods.

With whom do you agree? State your reasons. Examine the exchange rate policies of the major multinationals by referring to their annual reports. The Forbes listing of major multinationals on the web is a good starting point. In particular, consult the reports of Renault (France) and Philips (Holland).

SELF TEST

Answers are provided in Appendix A at the back of the text.

1. A UK importer of Japanese computer components pays for the components in yen. The importer is not concerned about a possible increase in Japanese prices (charged in yen) because of the likely offsetting effect caused by purchasing power parity (PPP). Explain what this means.

2. Use what you know about tests of PPP to answer this question. Using the information in the first question, explain why the UK importer of Japanese computer components should be concerned about its future payments.

3. Use PPP to explain how the values of the currencies of Eastern European countries might change if those countries experience high inflation, whilst the UK and the euro zone experience low inflation.

4. Assume that the Canadian dollar's spot rate is £0.57 and that the Canadian and US inflation rates are similar. Then assume that Canada experiences 4% inflation, while the United Kingdom experiences 3% inflation. According to PPP, what will be the new value of the Canadian dollar after it adjusts to the inflationary changes? (You may use the approximate formula to answer this question.)

5. Assume that the Australian dollar's spot rate is £0.30 and that the Australian and UK one-year interest rates are initially 6%. Then assume that the Australian one-year interest rate increases by 5 percentage points, while the UK one-year interest rate remains unchanged. Using this information and the international Fisher effect (IFE) theory, forecast the spot rate for one-year ahead.

6. In the previous question, the Australian interest rates increased from 6% to 11%. According to the IFE, what is the underlying factor that would cause such a change? Give an explanation based on the IFE of the forces that would cause a change in the Australian dollar. If UK investors believe in the IFE, will they attempt to capitalize on the higher Australian interest rates? Explain.

QUESTIONS AND APPLICATIONS

1. **PPP.** Explain the theory of purchasing power parity (PPP). Based on this theory, what is a general forecast of the values of currencies in countries with high inflation?

2. **Rationale of PPP.** Explain the rationale of the PPP theory.

3. **Testing PPP.** Explain how you could determine whether PPP exists. Describe a limitation in testing whether PPP holds.

4. **Testing PPP.** Inflation differentials between the United States and other industrialized countries have typically been a few percentage points in any given year. Yet, in many years annual exchange rates between the corresponding currencies have changed by 10% or more. What does this information suggest about PPP?

5. **Limitations of PPP.** Explain why PPP does not hold.

6. **Implications of IFE.** Explain the international Fisher effect (IFE). What is the rationale for the existence of the IFE? What are the implications of the IFE for firms with excess cash that consistently invest in foreign Treasury bills? Explain why the IFE may not hold.

7. **Implications of IFE.** Assume UK interest rates are generally above foreign interest rates. What does this suggest about the future strength or weakness of the British pound based on the IFE? Should UK investors invest in foreign securities if they believe in the IFE? Should foreign investors invest in UK securities if they believe in the IFE?

8. **Comparing parity theories.** Compare and contrast interest rate parity (discussed in the previous chapter), purchasing power parity (PPP), and the international Fisher effect (IFE).

9. **Real interest rate.** One assumption made in developing the IFE is that all investors in all countries have the same real interest rate. What does this mean?

10. **Interpreting inflationary expectations.** If investors in the United Kingdom and Canada require the same real interest rate, and the nominal rate of interest is 2% higher in Canada, what does this imply about expectations of UK inflation and Canadian inflation? What do these inflationary expectations suggest about future exchange rates?

11. **PPP applied to the euro.** Assume that several European countries that use the euro as their currency experience higher inflation than the United States, while two other European countries that use the euro as their currency experience lower inflation than the United States. According to PPP, how will the euro's value against the dollar be affected?

12. **Source of weak currencies.** Currencies of some Latin American countries, such as Brazil and Venezuela, frequently weaken against most other currencies. What concept in this chapter explains this occurrence? Why don't all US-based MNCs use forward contracts to hedge their future remittances of funds from Latin American countries to the United States if they expect depreciation of the currencies against the dollar?

13. **PPP.** Japan has typically had lower inflation than the United States. How would one expect this to affect the Japanese yen's value? Why does this expected relationship not always occur?

14. **IFE.** Assume that the nominal interest rate in Mexico is 48% and the interest rate in the United States is 8% for one-year securities that are free from default risk. What does the IFE suggest about the differential in expected inflation in these two countries? Using this information and the PPP theory, describe the expected nominal return to US investors who invest in Mexico.

15. **IFE.** Shouldn't the IFE discourage investors from attempting to capitalize on higher foreign interest rates? Why do some investors continue to invest overseas, even when they have no other transactions overseas?

16. **Changes in inflation.** Assume that the inflation rate in Brazil is expected to increase substantially. How will this affect Brazil's nominal interest rates and the value of its currency (called the real)? If the IFE holds, how will the nominal return to UK investors who invest in Brazil be affected by the higher inflation in Brazil? Explain.

17. **Comparing PPP and IFE.** How is it possible for PPP to hold if the IFE does not?

18. **Estimating depreciation due to PPP.** Assume that the spot exchange rate of the British pound is $1.73. How will this spot rate adjust according to PPP if the United Kingdom experiences an inflation rate of 7% while the United States experiences an inflation rate of 2%?

19. **Forecasting the future spot rate based on IFE.** Assume that the spot exchange rate of the Singapore dollar is £0.35. The one-year interest rate is 11% in the United Kingdom and 7% in Singapore. What will the spot rate be in one year according to the IFE? (You may use the approximate formula to answer this question.)

20. **Deriving forecasts of the future spot rate.** As of today, assume the following information is available:

	UK	Mexico
Real rate of interest required by investors	2%	2%
Nominal interest rate	11%	15%
Spot rate	—	£0.05
One-year forward rate	—	£0.049

  a. Use the forward rate to forecast the percentage change in the Mexican peso over the next year.
  b. Use the differential in expected inflation to forecast the percentage change in the Mexican peso over the next year.
  c. Use the spot rate to forecast the percentage change in the Mexican peso over the next year.

21. **Inflation and interest rate effects.** The opening of Russia's market has resulted in a highly volatile Russian currency (the rouble). Russia's inflation has commonly exceeded 20% per month. Russian interest rates commonly exceed 150%, but this is sometimes less than the annual inflation rate in Russia.
  a. Explain why the high Russian inflation has put severe pressure on the value of the Russian rouble.
  b. Does the effect of Russian inflation on the decline in the rouble's value support the PPP theory? How might the relationship be distorted by political conditions in Russia?
  c. Does it appear that the prices of Russian goods will be equal to the prices of UK goods from the perspective of Russian consumers (after considering exchange rates)? Explain.
  d. Will the effects of the high Russian inflation and the decline in the rouble offset each other for UK importers? That is, how will UK importers of Russian goods be affected by the conditions?

22. **IFE application to Asian crisis.** Before the Asian crisis, many investors attempted to capitalize on the high interest rates prevailing in the South East Asian countries although the level of interest rates primarily reflected expectations of inflation. Explain why investors behaved in this manner. Why does the IFE suggest that the South East Asian countries would not have attracted foreign investment before the Asian crisis despite the high interest rates prevailing in those countries?

23. **IFE applied to the euro.** Given the recent conversion of several European currencies to the euro, explain what would cause the euro's value to change against the dollar according to the IFE.

ADVANCED QUESTIONS

24. **IFE.** Beth Miller does not believe that the international Fisher effect (IFE) holds. Current one-year interest rates in Europe are 5%, while one-year interest rates in the United States are 3%. Beth converts $100,000 to euros and invests them in Germany. One year later, she converts the euros back to dollars. The current spot rate of the euro is $1.10.
  a. According to the IFE, what should the spot rate of the euro in one year be?
  b. If the spot rate of the euro in one year is $1.00, what is Beth's percentage return from her strategy?
  c. If the spot rate of the euro in one year is $1.08, what is Beth's percentage return from her strategy?
  d. What must the spot rate of the euro be in one year for Beth's strategy to be successful?

25. **Integrating IRP and IFE.** Assume the following information is available for the United States and Europe:

	US	Europe
Nominal interest rate	4%	6%
Expected inflation	2%	5%
Spot rate	—	$1.13
One-year forward rate	—	$1.10

a. Does IRP hold?

b. According to PPP, what is the expected spot rate of the euro in one year?

c. According to the IFE, what is the expected spot rate of the euro in one year?

d. Reconcile your answers to parts (a) and (c).

26. **IRP.** The one-year risk-free interest rate in Mexico is 10%. The one-year risk-free rate in the United Kingdom is 2%. Assume that interest rate parity exists. The spot rate of the Mexican peso is £0.14.

a. What is the forward rate premium?

b. What is the one-year forward rate of the peso?

c. Based on the international Fisher effect, what is the expected change in the spot rate over the next year?

d. If the spot rate changes as expected according to the IFE, what will be the spot rate in one year?

e. Compare your answers to (b) and (d) and explain the relationship.

27. **Testing the PPP.** How could you use regression analysis to determine whether the relationship specified by PPP exists on average? Specify the model, and describe how you would assess the regression results to determine if there is a *significant* difference from the relationship suggested by PPP.

28. **Testing the IFE.** Describe a statistical test for the IFE.

29. **Impact of barriers on PPP and IFE.** Would PPP be more likely to hold between the United Kingdom and Hungary if trade barriers were completely removed and if Hungary's currency were allowed to float without any government intervention? Would the IFE be more likely to hold between the United States and Hungary if trade barriers were completely removed and if Hungary's currency were allowed to float without any government intervention? Explain.

30. **Interactive effects of PPP.** Assume that the inflation rates of the countries that use the euro are very low, while other European countries that have their own currencies experience high inflation. Explain how and why the euro's value could be expected to change against these currencies according to the PPP theory.

31. **Applying IRP and IFE.** Assume that Mexico has a one-year interest rate that is higher than the UK one-year interest rate. Assume that you believe in the international Fisher effect (IFE) and interest rate parity. Assume zero transactions costs.

Ed is based in the United Kingdom and attempts to speculate by purchasing Mexican pesos today, investing the pesos in a risk-free asset for a year, and then converting the pesos to pounds at the end of one year. Ed did not cover his position in the forward market.

Maria is based in Mexico and attempts covered interest arbitrage by purchasing pounds today and simultaneously selling pounds one-year forward, investing the pounds in a risk-free asset for a year, and then converting the pounds back to pesos at the end of one year.

Do you think the rate of return on Ed's investment will be higher than, lower than, or the same as the rate of return on Maria's investment? Explain.

32. **Arbitrage and PPP.** Assume that locational arbitrage ensures that spot exchange rates are properly aligned. Also assume that you believe in purchasing power parity. The spot rate of the British pound is $1.80. The spot rate of the Swiss franc is £0.3. You expect that the one-year inflation rate will be 7% in the United Kingdom, 5% in Switzerland, and 1% in the United States. The one-year interest rate is 6% in the United Kingdom, 2% in Switzerland, and 4% in the United States. What is your expected spot rate of the Swiss franc in one year with respect to the US dollar? Show your work.

33. **IRP versus IFE.** You believe that interest rate parity and the international Fisher effect hold. Assume that the UK interest rate is presently much higher than the New Zealand interest rate. You have receivables of 1 million New Zealand dollars that you will receive in one year. You could hedge the receivables with the one-year forward contract. Or, you could decide to not hedge. Is

your expected British pound amount of the receivables in one year from hedging higher, lower, or the same as your expected British pound amount of the receivables without hedging? Explain.

34. **IRP, PPP, and speculating in currency derivatives.** The UK three-month interest rate (unannualized) is 1%. The Canadian three-month interest rate (unannualized) is 4%. Interest rate parity exists. The expected inflation over this period is 5% in the United Kingdom and 2% in Canada. A call option with a three-month expiration date on Canadian dollars is available for a premium of £0.02 and a strike price of £0.44. The spot rate of the Canadian dollar is £0.45. Assume that you believe in purchasing power parity.
    a. Determine the pound amount of your profit or loss from buying a call option contract specifying C$100,000.
    b. Determine the dollar amount of your profit or loss from buying a futures contract specifying C$100,000.

> **PROJECT WORKSHOP**

35. Using a graph similar to Exhibit 8.2, represent the inflation differential and exchange rate percentage change for at least ten time periods between two chosen currencies. Plot the results and compare with the PPP line. Where there are deviations, consult e-newspaper sources (available at your institution) to try to determine causes of misalignment. If your institution does not provide these resources, search the Internet for causes.

36. **Currency interest rates.** The "Market" section of the Bloomberg website provides interest rate quotations for numerous currencies. Its address is http://www.bloomberg.com.
    a. Go to the "Markets" section and then to "International Yield Curves". Determine the prevailing one-year interest rate of the Australian dollar, the Japanese yen, and the British pound. Assuming a 2% real rate of interest for savers in any country, determine the expected rate of inflation over the next year in each of these countries that is implied by the nominal interest rate (according to the Fisher effect).

    b. What is the approximate expected percentage change in the value of each of these currencies against the dollar over the next year, when applying PPP to the inflation level of each of these currencies versus the dollar?

37. Using your institutions databases, test one of the following equations:

$$e_f = a_0 + a_1 (i_h - i_f) + \varepsilon$$

or

$$e_f = a_0 + a_1 (I_h - I_f) + \varepsilon$$

where

e	=	percentage change in the value of foreign currency
i	=	interest rate
I	=	inflation rate
f	=	foreign country
h	=	home country
a_0, a_1	=	parameters
μ	=	residual term

choose:

- Two countries (one exchange rate)
- A time period, e.g. 1990 to 2005
- A frequency (annually, quarterly, monthly, daily).

Review your results, then perform a secondary test in response to your findings. The secondary test may, for example:

- Alter the lag structure of the explanatory variables, e.g. quarter 4 exchange rate change regressed against quarter 1 inflation differential.
- Alter the time periods
- Alter the frequency.

Compare your secondary test with the first test to see if there has been an improvement.

38. From a reading of Appendix 8, carry out a variance ratio test measuring Z(k) for a particular

currency chosen from your institution's database or from Oanda.com. Choose at least 30 observations for the longer time period (e.g. 30 months or 30 quarters).

a. Carry out the test for real exchange rates and nominal exchange rates.

b. Explain the meaning of your results.

As a practical note you will need to convert daily data into monthly quarterly data or even simply take every fifth or tenth etc. quote. This can be done using a basic EXCEL package. The following is a guide suitable only for those familiar with EXCEL. Typically the information is in two columns "mm/dd/yy" and the "exchange rate" in columns A and B respectively. To select the first exchange rate in every month use the "text to columns" feature under the "data" heading and isolate the month, day and year into separate columns. Then in blank columns copy the date and exchange rate if the exchange rate is the first of the month as follows. The formula: "=IF(A2 = A1,''',B2 or whatever you want to copy) will copy the data into the blank cell *if* it is the first quote of the month *otherwise*

the cell will be left blank. Create the first line and Block Copy down the column. Then Block Copy all these cells and paste them as a block into their existing location using the paste special formula checking the "values" radio button, this gets rid of the IF formulas. Block the whole area and sort on the year in ascending order. Exchange rates are now in monthly intervals!

To get every fifth or tenth quote etc. replace the months column as follows: put a 1 in the top cell, say A1, below that in A2 enter "=IF(A1 =5, 1,A1+1)" and block copy down the column. Then proceed as above from the amended formula "=IF(A2 = 5,''', B2 or whatever you want to copy)!

DISCUSSION IN THE BOARDROOM

This exercise can be found on the companion website at www.cengage.co.uk/madura_fox.

RUNNING YOUR OWN MNC

This exercise can be found on the companion website at www.cengage.co.uk/madura_fox.

Essays/discussion and articles can be found at the end of Part 2

BLADES PLC CASE STUDY
Assessment of purchasing power parity

Blades, the UK-based roller blades manufacturer, is currently both exporting to and importing from Thailand. The company has chosen Thailand as an export target for its primary product, "Speedos", because of Thailand's growth prospects and the lack of competition from both Thai and UK roller blade manufacturers in Thailand. Under an existing arrangement, Blades sells 180,000 pairs of Speedos annually to Entertainment Products, Inc., a Thai retailer. The arrangement involves a fixed, baht-denominated price and will last for three years. Blades generates approximately 10% of its revenue in Thailand.

Blades has also decided to import certain rubber and plastic components needed to manufacture

Speedos because of cost and quality considerations. Specifically, the weak economic conditions in Thailand resulting from recent events have allowed Blades to import components from the country at a relatively low cost. However, Blades did not enter into a long-term arrangement to import these components and pays market prices (in baht) prevailing in Thailand at the time of purchase. Currently, Blades incurs about 4% of its cost of goods sold in Thailand.

Although Blades has no immediate plans for expansion in Thailand, it may establish a subsidiary there in the future. Moreover, even if Blades does not establish a subsidiary in Thailand, it will continue exporting to and importing from the country for several years. Due to these considerations, Blades' management is very concerned about recent events in Thailand and neighbouring countries, as they may affect both Blades' current performance and its future plans.

Ben Holt, Blades' finance director, is particularly concerned about the level of inflation in Thailand. Blades' export arrangement with Entertainment Products, while allowing for a minimum level of revenue to be generated in Thailand in a given year, prevents Blades from adjusting prices according to the level of inflation in Thailand. In retrospect, Holt is wondering whether Blades should have entered into the export arrangement at all. Because Thailand's economy was growing very fast when Blades agreed to the arrangement, strong consumer spending there resulted in a high level of inflation and high interest rates. Naturally, Blades would have preferred an agreement whereby the price per pair of Speedos would be adjusted for the Thai level of inflation. However, to take advantage of the growth opportunities in Thailand, Blades accepted the arrangement when Entertainment Products insisted on a fixed price level. Currently, however, the baht is freely floating, and Holt is wondering how a relatively high level of Thai inflation may affect the baht–pound exchange rate and, consequently, Blades' revenue generated in Thailand.

Ben Holt is also concerned about Blades' cost of goods sold incurred in Thailand. Since no fixed-price arrangement exists and the components are invoiced in Thai baht, Blades has been subject to increases in the prices of rubber and plastic. Holt is wondering how a potentially high level of inflation will impact the baht–pound exchange rate and the cost of goods sold incurred in Thailand now that the baht is freely floating.

When Holt started thinking about future economic conditions in Thailand and the resulting impact on Blades, he found that he needed your help. In particular, Holt is vaguely familiar with the concept of purchasing power parity (PPP) and is wondering about this theory's implications, if any, for Blades. Furthermore, Holt also remembers that relatively high interest rates in Thailand will attract capital flows and put upward pressure on the baht.

Because of these concerns, and to gain some insight into the impact of inflation on Blades, Ben Holt has asked you to provide him with answers to the following questions:

1. What is the relationship between the exchange rates and relative inflation levels of the two countries? How will this relationship affect Blades' Thai revenue and costs given that the baht is freely floating? What is the net effect of this relationship on Blades?

2. What are some of the factors that prevent PPP from occurring in the short run? Would you expect PPP to hold better if countries negotiate trade arrangements under which they commit themselves to the purchase or sale of a fixed number of goods over a specified time period? Why or why not?

3. How do you reconcile the high level of interest rates in Thailand with the expected change of the baht–pound exchange rate according to PPP?

4. Given Blades' future plans in Thailand, should the company be concerned with PPP? Why or why not?

5. PPP may hold better for some countries than for others. Given that the Thai baht has been freely floating for only a short period of time, how do you think Blades can gain insight into whether PPP will hold for Thailand?

SMALL BUSINESS DILEMMA

Assessment of the IFE by the Sports Exports Company

Every month, the Sports Exports Company receives a payment denominated in British pounds for the footballs it exports to the United Kingdom. Jim Logan, owner of the Sports Exports Company, decides each month whether to hedge the payment with a forward contract for the following month. Now, however, he is questioning whether this process is worth the trouble. He suggests that if the international Fisher effect (IFE) holds, the pound's value should change (on average) by an amount that reflects the differential between the interest rates of the two countries of concern. Since the forward premium reflects that same interest rate differential, the results from hedging should equal the results from not hedging on average.

1. Is Jim's interpretation of the IFE theory correct?
2. If you were in Jim's position, would you spend time trying to decide whether to hedge the receivables each month, or do you believe that the results would be the same (on average) whether you hedged or not?

APPENDIX 8

FURTHER NOTES ON
EXCHANGE RATE MODELS

One would have thought that after over 50 years of research during which time space travel and convincing explanations of the origins of the universe have been accomplished, the relatively small matter of explaining the movement of exchange rates would by now be a settled matter. Unfortunately human financial behaviour appears to be even more complex than the aforementioned problems. There are as yet no models that convincingly explain the movements of the exchange rate. Results are found that are statistically significant, but the term must not be misinterpreted. Such results are better described as discernable rather than significant, certainly they are not sufficient to predict results in a useful manner. In this section we restate the problem and add in a few more attempts to explain matters.

The problem of using PPP to predict exchange rates is that the exchange rate changes far too often to be explained by a model whose explanatory variables (inflation rates) change infrequently, or at least are measured at relatively infrequent intervals. One argument has been that other influences have only been temporary and that PPP represents a long-term equilibrium. To test this proposition, statisticians measure the unexplained element or residual or error term of the PPP model. The argument is that if there are only temporary disturbances, the residual element at time t may well be correlated with t+1, t+2 but then any correlation should fade away (the term mean reverting is used to describe the process). So if the model predicted a 0.5% change in the pound value of the dollar in June of a particular year, and the actual change was 0.58%, the error term was 0.08%. If in the next two months the error terms were 0.04% and then 0.01% and then varied pretty randomly about the model prediction, one has a pattern of correlated errors over time that fade. In a sense one must expect short-term correlation of errors where they represent disturbances as there is nothing special about any one time period, e.g. one year as opposed to 18 months. So, with respect to the June variation, after a couple of months its influence had gone and subsequent monthly error terms were not correlated with the June error. If the pattern of June's error term with the following months is generally true for all months, the model exhibits stationarity and it can be argued that the PPP effect is true for the medium to long term because other disturbances are either random or temporary. Note that this is not saying that the model is accurate over the medium to long term. In our example, there may be different disturbances in the months after June that have their own influence and rate of decay. As far as explaining or predicting changes in the exchange rate, one would want to know the cause of such deviations from the model and obtain a better prediction.

We have expressed these results in terms of the error term of the PPP model. Academic papers sometimes express the same relationship as the variation in the real exchange rate. As established in the main text, if PPP holds, the real exchange rate should be constant. Any movement in the actual real exchange rate can therefore be interpreted as an error in the PPP prediction.

During the 1980s and 1990s a large number of econometric studies were reported attempting to establish stationarity. The results (see Rogoff article in the Essays/discussion and articles section at the end of this chapter) were mixed. Many studies were unable to distinguish their results from a random walk. The term "unit root" is used in such studies to describe the random walk – the variation in one month can be measured as a random step from the previous month's exchange rate. Such a process has no correcting or mean reversion tendency as described above.

What can only be described as a marginal rejection of the random walk hypothesis has been achieved by using extended data sets going back to 1900 and before in some studies. Another approach has been to use panel data, that is data from several exchange rates, and devise a joint test over the data. The decay rate suggested is about 15% per year or 50% of the correction achieved in about 3 years – a rate described as "glacial" by Rogoff. There is some evidence that it might be less if the adjustment process is non-linear – greater at first for larger deviations (Sarno and Taylor 2002).

A simple test of the behaviour of exchange rates was proposed by Cochrane (1988). If the exchange rate behaves as a random walk and there is no mean reverting process, then the variance (var) of, say, daily exchange rate changes should be 1/30th of the variance of monthly exchange rate changes (there being about 30 days in the average month). This is a basic property of a random walk – variance of monthly data should be 30 times the variance of daily data, the variance of half yearly data should be six times the variance of monthly data and so on. Put more succinctly:

$$Z(k) = 1/k \frac{\text{var}[(q_t - q_{t-k})/q_{t-k}]}{\text{var}[(q_t - q_{t-1})/q_{t-1}]} = 1/k \frac{\text{var}(q_t/q_{t-k})}{\text{var}(q_t/q_{t-1})}$$

where q is the exchange rate adjusted for relative inflation (i.e. the real exchange rate) and k is the number of smaller time periods in the larger time period and is therefore greater than 1. So if the top is looking at months and the lower half is looking at days as suggested above, k will be 30. By applying the scaling factor $1/k$, a random walk should approximate $Z(k)$ as 1. If it is less than 1, then over time there is a dampening or mean reversion effect because the variance does not increase by as much as a random walk process predicts. If $Z(k)$ is greater than 1 the system is growing by more than even a random walk would suggest and is clearly unstable.

There is also a simple practical point to be made here. MNCs using the random walk to approximate the uncertainty of exchange rate changes into the future are likely to be slightly overestimating the risk. As an error it is likely to lead to rejection of a profitable opportunity which is somewhat less expensive than an MNC accepting an unprofitable opportunity – a likely consequence of underestimating uncertainty. The random walk approach therefore is a good practical model of future uncertainty.

Of course, it is possible to interpret deviations from PPP as a change in the fundamental PPP relationship. Productivity increases could be one such cause. But the daily nature of movements in the exchange rate suggests that this is unlikely. A better source of explanation is based on models concerned with the money supply and portfolio investment. Because investment flows are large and take place on a daily basis, there is a chance that they may be able to explain exchange rate variability. To get a flavour of such approaches it is instructive to consult the UK Government's Debt and Reserve Management Report 2004–5 currently at http://www.hm-treasury.gov.uk/media/92B/27/debt_res.pdf. The report records issues of government debt thus:

Exhibit 8A.1 Government Treasury bill offers and acceptance (by auction)

Date	Interest on nominal and maturity	Amount £ million	Times oversubscribed	Implied interest rate of average accepted price
29 July 2003	5% 2014	£2,500	2.67	4.57
14 August 2003	4% 2009	£3,250	2.03	4.38
10 September 2003	4¼% 2036	£2,500	2.05	4.77

Source: UK Government Debt and Reserves Management Report 2004–5, p.24

We also learn that:

> The level of the UKs net reserves increased over the year from US$15.6 billion at end-December 2002 to US$17.9 billion at end-December 2003. The value of the gross reserves also rose over the year from US$42.4 billion at end-December 2002 to US$45.9 billion at end-December 2003. This increase reflected, in part, the temporary effect of the issue of the US$3 billion 5-year eurobond in June 2003 (which substituted dollar financing for sterling financing that was due to mature in the course of the financial year).
>
> (Debt and Reserves Management Report, 2004–5, 34)

So the government repaid pound denominated debt and then took out dollar debt and presumably converted the dollar borrowing into pounds thereby creating a demand for the pound.

This is just one small snapshot of the workings of the money markets, their size and influence. The oversubscription in Exhibit 8A.1 suggests that many institutions (mainly insurance and pension companies) have funds that will have to be invested elsewhere. The portfolio balance model suggests that investments abroad are very much part of the portfolio of investments made by such companies. A change in the risk return features in the UK or foreign markets will alter the relative attractiveness of investing abroad. Insurance companies may move funds abroad if investment there becomes relatively more attractive or repatriate funds if UK investment returns improve. Clearly there are exchange rate implications. The Dornbusch "sticky price model" argues that a shock to the money supply (e.g. a sudden greater availability of cash and credit due to government open market operations) will initially lead to portfolio investments such as Treasury bills and shares and will affect interest rates and therefore exchange rates. There are also inflationary effects that take longer to develop (hence the "sticky price"). Such price effects again have exchange rate implications. Exchange rates may therefore have to adjust quite frequently to balance monetary and inflationary effects. Although these are persuasive arguments, attempts to model their predicted effects on the exchange rate have not been particularly successful – but this is not to say that such influences are unimportant.

The predictive ability of a model is a test both of the underlying theory that gives rise to the model and the model's ability to measure the variables. In the last couple of decades theory has remained relatively static whilst most of the effort has gone into modelling. It is not surprising that two of the last four Nobel prizes for economics have gone to econometricians and the third (Edward Prescott) raised a famous problem from measurement rather than theory (the share premium puzzle).

The question remains as to why measurement is so difficult. To understand something of the possible answer, suppose we were given the "right" model for predicting exchange rates. Looking at the variables, all correctly measured, suppose we noted that over the months of April to June for a particular year there was no change in the variables. Would the exchange rate have changed? The answer is probably "yes". The market price reflects not just the actual values but also speculation as to what those values might be in the future. Such speculation may be affected by the quality of the information, a new newspaper, or an article that changes the views of influential investors. The result is that even in periods where economic factors (fundamentals) do not change, the exchange rate can be expected to vary due to changes in beliefs about a future that may or may not occur.

The term "news models" has been applied to an approach that looks at the broad information set that might inform the market opinion forming process. On the left hand side of a regression equation is the difference between the spot and the forward prediction of that spot as a percentage of the previous spot rate, or similar measure. On the right hand side is news. Potentially, this could be an article expressing a different opinion – clearly there are measurement problems. Often economic data is used; to be news, such data must be unexpected and there are ways of measuring differences between actual figures and expectations. Empirical results are mixed; sometimes news is relevant, sometimes not. But even if results were strong, from a more applied MNC point of view, such tests appear to be no more than semi-strong market efficiency tests. What is being tested is whether or not the exchange rate changes as a result of market information – the semi-strong hypothesis. One form of uncertainty, the movement of the exchange rate, is being substituted for another form of uncertainty, unexpected information about employment, inflation rates, growth and so on. Predictive ability is not greatly advanced.

In general it is difficult to see how the opinion forming process itself can be modelled, certainly there is no consistent measurable model of such processes. As a result, predicting exchange rates accurately on a consistent basis may well have to remain a largely unaccomplished goal. Instead, models offer explanations of linkages in the economic system which in extreme circumstances may on occasion be measurable (e.g. a devaluing currency when there is hyperinflation) but ordinarily a model's predictions will be part of a noisy process. At least we can attempt to model uncertainty itself using ideas such as random walks and stationarity and learn to manage the result – hence the emphasis on scenarios in this and succeeding chapters.

References

Sarno, L. and M.P. Taylor (2002) "Purchasing Power Parity and the Real Exchange Rate", *IMF Staff Papers*, 49 (1), 65–105.

Cochrane, J.H. (1988) "How Big Is the Random Walk in GNP?", *Journal of Political Economy*, 96, 893–920.

Exchange rate behaviour

Questions

1. As an employee of the foreign exchange department for a large company, you have been given the following information:

   Beginning of Year

   Spot rate of £ = **$1.596**

   Spot rate of Australian dollar (A$) = **$0.70**

   Cross exchange rate: £1 = **A$2.28**

   One-year forward rate of A$ = **$0.71**

   One-year forward rate of £ = **$1.58004**

   One-year US interest rate = **8.00%**

   One-year British interest rate = **9.09%**

   One-year Australian interest rate = **7.00%**

   Suppose you are a foreign currency trader and that you are managing £100,000:

   a. Determine whether triangular arbitrage is feasible and, if so, how it should be conducted to make a profit.

   b. Determine whether covered interest arbitrage is feasible and, if so, how it should be conducted to make a profit.

   c. For the beginning of the year, use the international Fisher effect (IFE) theory to forecast the annual percentage change in the British pound's value over the year.

   d. Assume that at the beginning of the year, the pound's value is in equilibrium. Assume that over the year the British inflation rate is 6%, while the US inflation rate is 4%. Assume that any change in the pound's value due to the inflation differential has occurred by the end of the year. Using this information and the information provided in question 1, determine how the pound's value changed over the year.

   e. Assume that the pound's depreciation over the year was attributed directly to central bank intervention. Explain the type of direct intervention that would place downward pressure on the value of the pound.

1. Eichengren, B. (1999) "Kicking The Habit Moving From Pegged Exchange Rates To Greater Exchange Rate Flexibility", *The Economic Journal*, 109, C1–C9. A non-technical discussion reflecting on (relatively) recent economic history.

2. Willet, T.D. (1998) "Credibility and Discipline Effects of Exchange Rates as Nominal Anchors: The Need to Distinguish Temporary from Permanent Pegs. A Discussion on the Problems and Reasons for Government Management of Exchange Rates", *World Economy*, 21 (6), 803–26.
   Q   *"Developing countries need fixed exchange rates." Discuss (article 1 or 2).*

3. Amann, E. and W. Baer (2000) "The Illusion of Stability: The Brazilian Economy under Cardoso", *World Development*, 28 (10), 1805–18. A look at the relationship between government and the exchange rate.
   Q   *Explain how the exchange rate can act as an economic instrument – does the failure of the Plano Real suggest that exchange rates should not be managed? Discuss.*

4. Eichengren, B. (2000) "Taming Capital Flows", *World Development*, 28 (6), 1105–16. A look at the disruptive effect of massive flows of portfolio investment.
   Q   *Explain why capital flows are seen by some authors as disruptive – evaluate Eichengren's proposed solution.*

5. Lenain, P. and A. de Serres (2002) "Is The Euro Area Converging or Diverging? Implication for Policy Coordination", *The World Economy*, 25 (10), 1501–19. The start of a proper analysis of the actual as opposed to the intended effects of monetary union.

6. Wyplosz, C. (2006) "European Monetary Union: The Dark Sides of a Major Success", *Economic Policy*, 21 (46), 207–61.

7. Mussa, Michael (1997) "Political and Institutional Commitment to a Common Currency", *The American Economic Review*, 87 (2), 217–20. A commentary on the political implications of the euro.
   Q   *Far from creating unity, is the euro becoming another vehicle for creating further divisions in Europe? Discuss (articles 5, 6, 7 or 11).*

8. Tobin, J. (2000) "Financial Globalisation", *World Development*, 28 (6), 1101–04. Nobel prize winning economist considers the relative merits of exchange rate regimes and the problem of capital flows using an impossibility theorem.
   Q   *Outline Tobin's impossibility theorem. Consider the possible solutions.*

9. Rogoff, K. (1996) "The Purchasing Power Parity Puzzle", *Journal of Economic Literature*, 34 (2), 647–68. An excellent review of PPP.
   Q   *Evaluate the attempts to explain why exchange rates can be so volatile and PPP adjustment so slow.*

10. LeBaron, B. and R. McCulloch (2000) "Floating, Fixed, or Super-Fixed? Dollarization Joins the Menu of Exchange-Rate Options", *The American Economic Review*, 90 (2), 32–7. The effects of dollarization.

11. Mundell, R.A. (1961) "A Theory of Optimum Currency Areas", *The American Economic Review*, 51 (4), 657–65. The original article.

Q *Describe and evaluate the effects of adopting the currency of another country (article 11 or 12).*

12. Reinhart, C.M. and K.S. Rogoff (2004), "The Modern History of Exchange Rate Arrangements: A Reinterpretation", *The Quarterly Journal of Economics*, 119 (1), 1–48. Examines the reality behind general exchange rate classifications.
    Q *Evaluate the evidence provided to justify the claim the IMF classifications are misleading.*

13. Gulcin Ozkan, F. (2005) "Currency and Financial Crises in Turkey 2000–2001: Bad Fundamentals or Bad Luck?", *World Economy*, 28 (4), 541–72. An examination of one particular crisis with reflections on other crises.
    Q *In what sense can the Turkish currency crisis be described as a typical currency crisis? Discuss.*

PART 3

EXCHANGE RATE RISK MANAGEMENT

• •

PART 3 (CHAPTERS 9 TO 12) explains the various functions involved in managing exposure to exchange rate risk. Chapter 9 describes various methods used to forecast exchange rates and explains how to assess forecasting performance. Chapter 10 demonstrates how to measure exposure to exchange rate movements. Given a firm's exposure and forecasts of future exchange rates, Chapters 11 and 12 explain how to hedge that exposure.

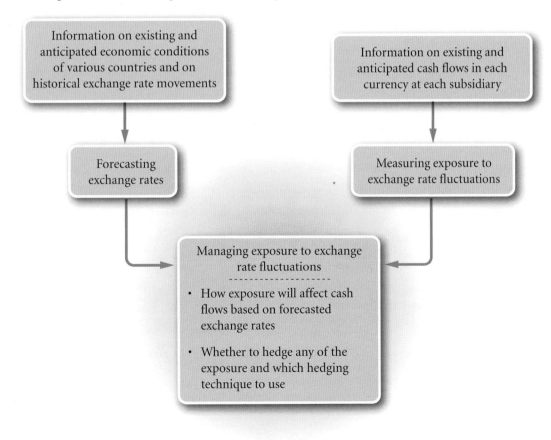

CHAPTER 9

FORECASTING EXCHANGE RATES

MANY DECISIONS OF MNCs are influenced by exchange rate projections. Financial managers must understand how to forecast exchange rates so that they can make decisions that maximize the value of their MNCs.

THE SPECIFIC OBJECTIVES OF THIS CHAPTER ARE TO:

- explain how firms can benefit from forecasting exchange rates,
- describe the common techniques used for forecasting, and
- explain how forecasting performance can be evaluated.

WHY FIRMS FORECAST EXCHANGE RATES

Virtually every operation of an MNC can be influenced by changes in exchange rates. The following are some of the corporate functions for which exchange rate forecasts are necessary:

- *Hedging decision.* MNCs constantly face the decision as to whether to hedge future payments and receipts in foreign currencies. Whether a firm hedges may be determined by its forecasts of foreign currency values.

EXAMPLE

Pierre S.A. based in France, plans to pay for clothing imported from Mexico in 90 days. If the forecasted value of the peso in 90 days is sufficiently below the 90-day forward rate, the MNC may decide not to hedge. In other words it will not have to pay insurance (hedge) to protect against the possibility of a price rise. Forecasting may therefore enable the firm to make a successful forecast that will reduce expenditure for the firm and increase its cash flows.

- *Short-term financing decision.* When large corporations borrow, they have access to several different currencies. The currency they borrow will ideally: (1) exhibit a low interest rate, and (2) weaken in value over the financing period and therefore be cheaper to repay.

EXAMPLE

Luigi SpA, an Italian based company, considers borrowing Japanese yen to finance its European operations because the yen has a low interest rate. If the yen depreciates against the euro over the financing period, the firm can pay back the loan with fewer euros (when converting those euro in exchange for the amount owed in yen). The decision as to whether to finance with yen or euro is dependent on a forecast of the future value of the yen.

- *Short-term investment decision.* Corporations sometimes have a substantial amount of excess cash available for a short time period. Large deposits can be established in several currencies. The ideal currency for deposits will: (1) exhibit a high interest rate, and (2) strengthen in value over the investment period.

EXAMPLE

Roar ASA, a Norwegian-based company, has excess cash and considers depositing the cash into a British bank account. If the British pound appreciates against the Norwegian krone by the end of the deposit period when pounds will be withdrawn and exchanged for krone, more krone will be received than was invested. Thus, the firm can use forecasts of the pound's exchange rate when determining whether to invest the short-term cash in a British account or a Norwegian account.

- *Capital budgeting decision.* When an MNC's parent assesses whether to invest funds in a foreign project, the firm takes into account that the project may periodically require the exchange of currencies. The capital budgeting analysis can be completed only when all estimated cash flows are measured in the parent's local currency.

EXAMPLE

Decker B.V. from Belgium wants to determine whether to establish a subsidiary in Thailand. Forecasts of the future cash flows used in the capital budgeting process will be dependent on the future exchange rate of Thailand's currency (the baht) against the euro. This dependency can be due to: (1) future inflows denominated in baht that will require conversion to euros, and/or (2) the influence of future exchange rates on demand for the subsidiary's products. Accurate forecasts of currency values will improve the estimates of the cash flows and therefore enhance the MNC's decision making.

■ *Earnings assessment.* The parent's decision about whether a foreign subsidiary should reinvest earnings in a foreign country or remit earnings back to the parent may be influenced by exchange rate forecasts. If a strong foreign currency is expected to weaken substantially against the parent's currency, the parent may prefer to convert the foreign earnings before the foreign currency weakens.

Exchange rate forecasts are also useful for forecasting an MNC's earnings. When earnings of an MNC are reported, subsidiary earnings are consolidated and translated into the currency representing the parent firm's home country.

EXAMPLE

Monroe ltd has its home office in the United Kingdom and subsidiaries in Canada and the United States. It must decide whether its Canadian and US subsidiaries should remit their earnings. This involves comparing the amount of dollar cash flows that would be received today (if the subsidiaries remit the earnings) to the potential dollar cash flows that would be received in the future (if the subsidiaries reinvest the earnings). The decision is influenced by Monroe's forecast of the value of the Canadian dollar and the US dollar at the time when the future earnings of the subsidiaries would be remitted.

For accounting purposes, the Canadian subsidiary's earnings in Canadian dollars must be measured by translating them to British pounds. The US subsidiary's earnings in dollars must also be measured by translation to pounds. "Translation" does not mean that the earnings are physically converted to British pounds. It is simply a periodic recording process so that consolidated earnings can be reported in a single currency. In this case, appreciation of the Canadian dollar will boost the Canadian subsidiary's earnings when they are reported in (translated to) pounds. Forecasts of exchange rates thus play an important role in the overall forecast of an MNC's consolidated earnings.

■ *Long-term financing decision.* Corporations that issue bonds to secure long-term funds may consider denominating the bonds in foreign currencies. They prefer the currency borrowed to depreciate over time against the currency they are receiving from sales. To estimate the cost of issuing bonds denominated in a foreign currency, forecasts of exchange rates are required.

EXAMPLE

Harold plc, a UK-based company needs long-term funds to support its UK business. It can issue ten-year bonds denominated in Japanese yen at a 1% coupon rate, which is 5 percentage points less than the prevailing coupon rate on British pound-denominated bonds. However, Harold will need to convert pounds to yen to make the coupon or principal payments on the yen-denominated bond. So if the yen's value rises, the yen-denominated bond could be more costly to Harold than a pound-denominated bond. Harold's decision to issue yen-denominated bonds versus pound-denominated bonds will be dependent on its forecast of the yen's exchange rate over the ten-year period.

Exhibit 9.1 Corporate motives for forecasting exchange rates

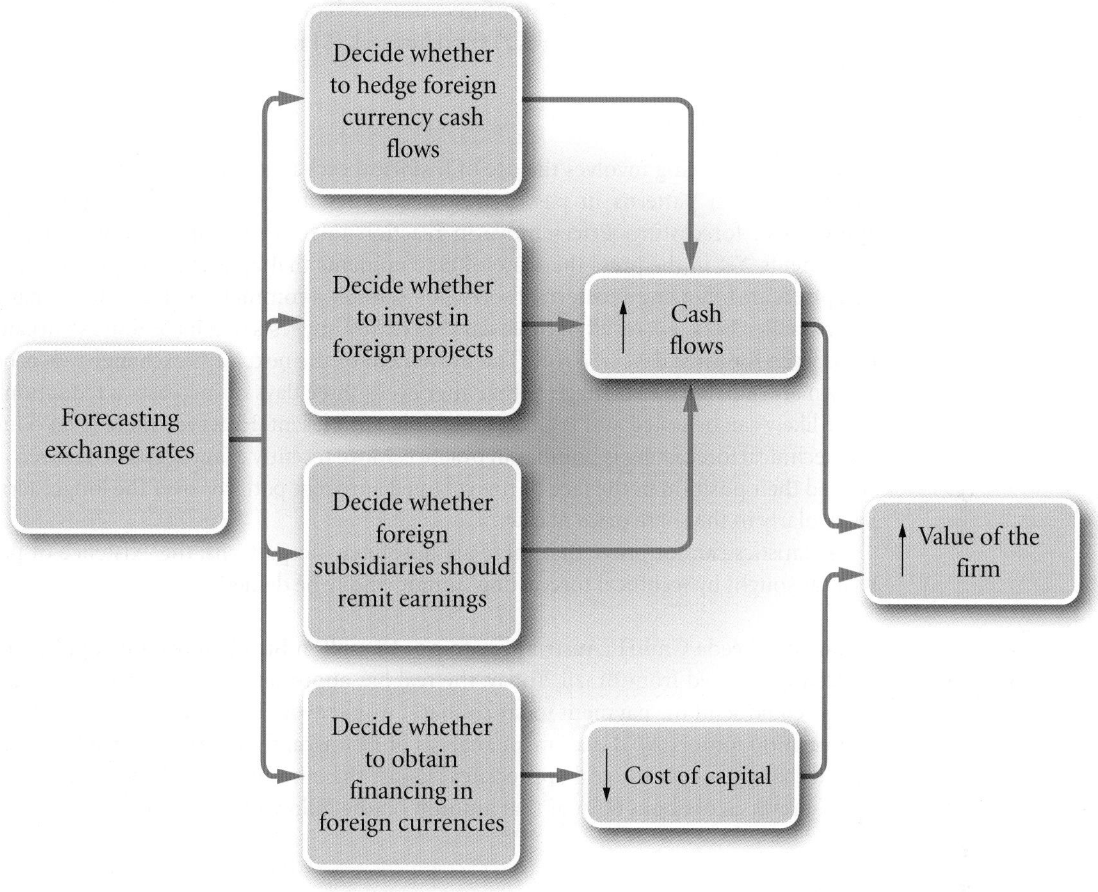

Although most forecasting is applied to currencies whose exchange rates fluctuate continuously, forecasts are also derived for currencies whose exchange rates are fixed at the time of investigation.

EXAMPLE

Even though the Argentine peso's value was still pegged to the US dollar in 2001, some MNCs anticipated that it would be devalued. They therefore made forecasts of its unpegged value. The peso was devalued in 2002, and its exchange rate is no longer tied to the US dollar (see Chapter 6). The Hong Kong dollar has been tied to the US dollar since 1983, but some MNCs still prepare long-term forecasts of the Hong Kong dollar in anticipation that it may be revalued.

An MNC's motives for forecasting exchange rates are summarized in Exhibit 9.1. The motives are distinguished according to whether they can enhance the MNC's value by influencing its cash flows or its cost of capital. The need for accurate exchange rate projections should now be clear. The following section describes the forecasting methods available.

FORECASTING TECHNIQUES

The numerous methods available for forecasting exchange rates can be categorized into four general groups: (1) technical, (2) fundamental, (3) market-based, and (4) mixed.

Technical forecasting

Technical forecasting involves the use of historical exchange rate data to predict future values based on patterns in past prices. Academics in general do not support this approach to forecasting. Prices move in reaction to information and not past price movements. Yet in the press there are often comments that appear to support the view that prices are following a pattern of sorts. For example a comment such as: "the exchange rate has fallen back as a result of three days' increases" suggests that it has done so because it has risen for three days in a row. The movement of the next day's exchange rate is not known and a pattern that suggests that after every three days of increases a reduction is more likely can be tested and is almost certainly not present. However, there is no doubt that technical forecasting is popular in practice. More recently many sceptics have reconsidered their position in the face of unexplained apparent patterns over the longer term, particularly in the share price market.

As statistics cannot prove that there are absolutely no patterns; the existence of patterns as sought by technical forecasting cannot wholly be denied.

EXAMPLE

Tomorrow Freeda GmbH (Austria) has to pay 10 million Brazilian real for supplies that it recently received from Brazil. Today, the real has appreciated by 3% against the euro. Freeda could send the payment today so that it would avoid the effects of any additional appreciation tomorrow. Based on an analysis of historical time series, Freeda has determined that whenever the real appreciates against the euro by more than 1%, it experiences a reversal of about 60% of that amount on the following day. That is:

$$e_{t+1} = e_t \times (-60\%) \text{ when } e_t > 1\%$$

Applying this tendency to the current situation in which the peso appreciated by 3% today, Freeda. forecasts that tomorrow's exchange rate will change by:

$$
\begin{aligned}
e_{t+1} &= e_t \times (-60\%) \\
&= (3\%) \times (-60\%) \\
&= -1.8\%
\end{aligned}
$$

Given this forecast that the real will depreciate tomorrow, Freeda decides that it will make its payment tomorrow instead of today.

http://

http://www.ny.frb.
org/markets/
foreignex.html and
http://www.oanda.
com provide historical
exchange rate data that
may be used to create
technical forecasts of
exchange rates.

Corporations tend to make only limited use of technical forecasting because it typically focuses on the near future, which is not very helpful for developing corporate policies. Most technical forecasts apply to very short-term periods such as one day or one week. A short-term forecast obviously yields quicker returns and more limited losses and is therefore attractive to potential clients.

Both sceptics and proponents would agree that even if technical forecasting cannot provide accurate predictions of the exchange rate itself, it can give some idea of the *range* of possible future rates. Random price movements can move within a predictable range of prices. For example, spinning a coin yields an outcome that one cannot predict with certainty; but one can predict that the outcome will be either heads or tails (barring some freak accident of physics). These matters are discussed further when considering market efficiency later in this chapter. Because technical analysis typically cannot estimate future exchange rates in precise terms, it is not, by itself, an adequate forecasting tool for financial managers of MNCs.

As noted above, technical factors are often cited in the financial press as the main reason for changing speculative positions that cause an adjustment in a currency's value. For example, headlines often attribute a change in the dollar's value to technical factors, typical examples are:

- Technical factors overwhelmed economic news.
- Technical factors triggered sales of pounds.
- Technical factors indicated that euros had been recently oversold, triggering purchases of euros.

As these examples suggest, technical forecasting appears to be widely used by speculators who attempt to capitalize on day-to-day exchange rate movements.

Technical forecasting models have helped some speculators in the foreign exchange market at various times. However, a model that has worked well in one particular period will not necessarily work well in another. With the abundance of technical models existing today, some are bound to generate speculative profits in any given period. If the pattern of currency values over time appears to be random, then technical forecasting is not appropriate. Unless historical trends in exchange rate movements can be identified, examination of past movements will not be useful for indicating future movements.

Finally, mention should be made of the trading effects of technical forecasting models. Many foreign exchange participants argue that even if a particular technical forecasting model is shown to lead consistently to speculative profits, it will no longer be useful once other participants begin to use it. Trading based on the model's recommendation will push the currency value to a position that negates the profit. For example, if a method identifies that the prices always rise on a Tuesday, the extra demand on a Monday that is seeking to exploit the pattern will, of itself, push up the price and destroy the very pattern it is seeking to exploit. The notion that something as public and valuable as a pattern in prices can remain undetected by all but the few is rather fanciful. Technical forecasting nevertheless remains popular in practice. Perhaps like gambling, its justification is behavioural rather than logical.

MANAGING FOR VALUE
How MNC's earnings depend on currency values

Like many publicly traded companies, Renault S.A., the French vehicle manufacturer, analyze their exposure to currency changes in their accounts. The calculation is not easy. In some countries, or more relevantly, in some currency areas Renault will produce as well as sell cars and lorries. Devaluation in such a currency would reduce the value of the revenues in terms of Renault's home currency, the euro; but also, there would be an offsetting reduction in the value of the costs. So the exposure is the net of the revenue figure less the costs in the foreign currency. In other currency areas there may be an excess of purchases and in yet others, an excess of sales. To help investors

appreciate how currency changes affect earnings, Renault calculate in their 2004 Annual Report that a 1% increase in the value of the euro against all other currencies would result in a 41 million euro decrease in profits. They also reveal that a 1% increase in the value of the euro against the British pound alone would lead to a 22 million euro decrease in profits. This implies that Renault is a net earner outside the euro area and is a particularly strong earner in British pounds with relatively few costs denominated in pounds. A decrease in pounds will therefore adversely affect the value of sales with a low offsetting effect from costs.

Fundamental forecasting

Fundamental forecasting is based on fundamental relationships between economic variables and exchange rates. Recall from Chapter 4 that a change in a currency's spot rate is influenced by the following factors:

$$e = f(\Delta INF, \Delta INT, \Delta INC, \Delta GC, \Delta EXT)$$

where:

e	=	percentage change in the spot rate
ΔINF	=	the difference between home inflation and the foreign country's inflation
ΔINT	=	the difference between the home interest rate and the foreign country's interest rate
ΔINC	=	the difference between the home income level and the foreign country's income level
ΔGC	=	change in government controls
ΔEXT	=	change in expectations of future exchange rates

Given current values of these variables along with their historical impact on a currency's value, corporations can develop exchange rate projections.

A forecast may arise simply from a subjective assessment of the degree to which general movements in economic variables in one country are expected to affect exchange rates. MNCs typically use in-house economists to make such projections. From a statistical perspective, a forecast would be based on quantitatively measured impacts of factors on exchange rates. Although some of the full-blown fundamental models are beyond the scope of this text, a simplified discussion follows.

EXAMPLE

The focus here is on only two of the many factors that affect currency values. Before identifying them, consider that the corporate objective is to forecast the percentage change (rate of appreciation or depreciation) in the US dollar with respect to the British pound during the next quarter. For simplicity, assume the firm's forecast for the dollar is dependent on only two factors that affect the dollar's value:

1. Inflation in the United States relative to inflation in the United Kingdom.
2. Income growth in the United States relative to income growth in the United Kingdom (measured as a percentage change).

The first step is to determine how these variables have affected the percentage change in the dollar's value based on historical data. This is commonly achieved with regression analysis. First, quarterly data are compiled for the inflation and income growth levels of both the United Kingdom and the United States. The dependent variable (the left-hand side of a regression) is the quarterly percentage change in the dollar value. The independent variables (the right-hand side of a regression) may be set up as follows:

1. Previous quarterly percentage inflation differential (British inflation rate minus US inflation rate), referred to as INF_{t-1}.
2. Previous quarterly percentage income growth differential (British income growth minus US income growth), referred to as INC_{t-1}.

The regression equation can be defined as:

$$e_{\$,t} = b_0 + b_1 INF_{t-1} + b_2 INC_{t-1} + \mu_t$$

Where:

INF_{t-1} = British inflation less US inflation for time t–1, the previous period to time t,

INC_{t-1} = British income growth less US income growth for time t–1, the previous period to time t,

$e_{\$,t}$ = percentage change in the value of the dollar over time t,

b_0 = a constant,

b_1 = the sensitivity of $e_{\$,t}$ to changes in INF_{t-1},

b_2 = the sensitivity of $e_{\$,t}$ to changes in INC_{t-1},

μ_t = the error term.

A set of historical data is used to obtain previous values of dollar, INF, and INC. Using this data set, regression analysis will generate the values of the regression coefficients (b_0, b_1, and b_2). That is, regression analysis determines the direction and degree to which *changes* in the dollar are affected by each independent variable over the sample. The coefficient b_1 will exhibit a positive sign if, when INF_{t-1} and $e_{\$t}$ change in the same direction over time (other things held constant). A negative sign indicates that $e_{\$t}$ and INF_{t-1} move in opposite directions. In the equation given, b_1 is expected to exhibit a positive sign because when UK inflation increases relative to inflation in the United States, upward pressure is exerted on the dollar's value (dollar goods appear cheaper leading to a greater demand for dollars).

The regression coefficient b_2 (which measures the impact of INC_{t-1} on $e_{\$t}$) is expected to be positive because when British income growth exceeds US income growth, there is upward pressure on the dollar's value. These relationships have already been thoroughly discussed in Chapter 4.

Once regression analysis is employed to generate values of the coefficients, these coefficients can be used to forecast. To illustrate, assume the following values: $b_0 = 0.002$, $b_1 = 0.8$, and $b_2 = 1.0$. The coefficients can be interpreted as follows. For a one-unit percentage change in the inflation differential, the dollar is expected to change by 0.8% in the same direction, other things held constant. For a one-unit percentage change in the income differential, the dollar is expected to change by 1.0% in the same direction, other things held constant. To develop forecasts, assume that the most recent quarterly percentage change in INF_{t-1} (the inflation differential) is 4%, and that INC_{t-1} (the income growth differential) is 2%. Using this information along with our estimated regression coefficients, the forecast for $e_{\$t}$ is:

$$
\begin{aligned}
e_{\$,t} &= b_0 + b_1 INF_{t-1} + b_2 INC_{t-1} + \mu_t \\
&= 0.002 + 0.8(4\%) + 1(2\%) \\
&= 0.2\% + 3.2\% + 2\% \\
&= 5.4\%
\end{aligned}
$$

Thus, given the current figures for inflation rates and income growth, the dollar should appreciate by 5.4% during the next quarter.

This example is simplified to illustrate how fundamental analysis can be implemented for forecasting. A full-blown model might include many more than two factors, but the application would still be similar. Unfortunately, a relationship that held in the past is not necessarily going to hold in the future. Models that have in a sense "thrown in" all relevant variables into the right-hand side of the equation are likely to produce a reasonably good prediction, given that the model chooses the parameters b_1, b_2 etc. that offer the best fit as measured by the adjusted R^2. But the more variables included in the right-hand side the weaker the rationale and the greater the statistical problem of multicollinearity (correlation amongst the explanatory variables). One can have little confidence in the longevity of a model that has no clear justification other than that it worked well over a particular time period.

Use of sensitivity analysis for fundamental forecasting. When a regression model is used for forecasting, and the values of the influential factors have a lagged impact on exchange rates, the actual value of those factors can be used as input for the forecast. For example, if the inflation differential has a lagged impact on exchange rates, the inflation differential in the previous period may be used to forecast the percentage change in the exchange rate over the future period. Some factors, however, have an instantaneous influence on exchange rates. Since these factors obviously cannot be known, forecasts must be used. Firms recognize that poor forecasts of these factors can cause poor forecasts of the exchange rate movements, so they may attempt to account for the uncertainty by using **sensitivity analysis**, which considers more than one possible outcome for the factors exhibiting uncertainty.

Phoenix GmbH (Germany) develops a regression model to forecast the percentage change in the Mexican peso's value. It believes that the real interest rate differential and the inflation differential are the only factors that affect exchange rate movements, as shown in this regression model:

$$e_{p,t} = a_0 + a_1 INT_t + a_2 INF_{t-1} + \mu_t$$

where:

INT_t	=	euro interest rate less Mexican interest rate for time t,
INF_{t-1}	=	euro inflation rate less Mexican inflation rate for the previous period time $t-1$,
$e_{p,t}$	=	percentage change in the value of the peso over time t,
a_0	=	a constant,
a_1	=	the sensitivity of $e_{p,t}$ to changes in INF_{t-1},
a_2	=	the sensitivity of $e_{p,t}$ to changes in INC_{t-1},
μ_t	=	the error term.

Historical data are used to determine values for $e_{p,t}$ along with values for INT_t and INF_{t-1} for several periods (preferably, 30 or more periods are used to build the database). The length of each historical period (quarter, month, etc.) should match the length of the period for which the forecast is needed. The historical data needed per period for the Mexican peso model are: (1) the percentage change in the peso's value, (2) the euro real interest rate minus the Mexican real interest rate, and (3) the euro inflation rate in the previous period minus the Mexican inflation rate in the previous period. Assume that regression analysis has provided the following estimates for the regression coefficients:

Regression Coefficient	Estimate
a_0	0.001
a_1	−0.7
a_2	0.6

The negative sign of a_1 indicates a negative relationship between INT_t and the peso's movements, while the positive sign of a_2 indicates a positive relationship between INF_{t-1} and the peso's movements.

To forecast the peso's percentage change over the upcoming period, INT_t and INF_{t-1} must be estimated. Assume that INF_{t-1} was 1%. However, INT_t is not known at the beginning of the period and must therefore be forecasted. Assume that Phoenix GmbH has developed the following probability distribution for INT_t:

Probability	Possible Outcome
20%	−3%
50%	−4%
30%	−5%
100%	

A separate forecast of e_t can be developed from each possible outcome of INT_t as follows:

Forecast of INT	Forecast of e_t	Probability
−3%	0.1% + (−0.7)(−3%) + 0.6(1%) = 2.8%	20%
−4%	0.1% + (−0.7)(−4%) + 0.6(1%) = 3.5%	50%
−5%	0.1% + (−0.7)(−5%) + 0.6(1%) = 4.2%	30%

If the firm needs forecasts for other currencies, it can develop the probability distributions of their movements over the upcoming period in a similar manner.

EXAMPLE

Phoenix GmbH can forecast the percentage change in the Japanese yen by regressing historical percentage changes in the yen's value against: (1) the differential between euro real interest rates and Japanese real interest rates, and (2) the differential between euro inflation in the previous period and Japanese inflation in the previous period. The regression coefficients estimated by regression analysis for the yen model will differ from those for the peso model. The firm can then use the estimated coefficients along with estimates for the interest rate differential and inflation rate differential to develop a forecast of the percentage change in the yen. Sensitivity analysis can be used to reforecast the yen's percentage change based on alternative estimates of the interest rate differential.

Use of PPP for fundamental forecasting. Recall that the theory of purchasing power parity (PPP) specifies the fundamental relationship between the inflation differential and the exchange rate. In simple terms, PPP states that the currency of the relatively inflated country will depreciate by an amount that reflects that country's inflation differential. Recall that according to PPP, the percentage change in the foreign currency's value (e_f) over a period should reflect the differential between the home inflation rate (I_h) and the foreign inflation rate (I_f) over that period.

EXAMPLE

The UK inflation rate is expected to be 1% over the next year, while the Australian inflation rate is expected to be 6%. According to PPP, the Australian dollar's exchange rate
should change as follows:

$$e_f = \frac{(1+I_{UK})}{(1+I_A)} - 1$$

$$= \frac{(1.01)}{(1.06)} - 1$$

$$\approx -4.7\%$$

This forecast of the percentage change in the Australian dollar can be applied to its existing spot rate to forecast the future spot rate at the end of one year. If the existing spot rate
(S_t) of the Australian dollar is £0.40, the expected spot rate at the end of one year, $E(S_{t+1})$,
will be about 0.3812:

$$e(S_{t+1}) = S_t (1+e_f)$$
$$= £0.40[1+-0.047)]$$
$$= £0.3812$$

In reality, the inflation rates of two countries over an upcoming period are uncertain and
therefore would have to be forecasted when using PPP to forecast the future exchange
rate at the end of the period. This complicates the use of PPP to forecast future exchange
rates. Even if the inflation rates in the upcoming period were known with certainty, PPP
might not be able to forecast exchange rates accurately.

If the PPP theory were accurate in reality, there would be no need to even consider
alternative forecasting techniques. However, using the inflation differential of two countries to forecast their exchange rate is not always accurate. Problems arise for several
reasons: (1) the timing of the impact of inflation fluctuations on changing trade patterns, and therefore on exchange rates, is not known with certainty; (2) data used to
measure relative prices of two countries may be somewhat inaccurate; (3) barriers to
trade can disrupt the trade patterns that should emerge in accordance with PPP theory;
and (4) other factors, such as the interest rate differential between countries, can also
affect exchange rates. For these reasons, the inflation differential by itself is not sufficient
to accurately forecast exchange rate movements. Nevertheless, it should be included in
any fundamental forecasting model.

Limitations of fundamental forecasting. Although fundamental forecasting accounts
for the expected fundamental relationships between factors and currency values, the following limitations exist:

1. The precise timing of the impact of some factors on a currency's value is not known.
   It is possible that the full impact of inflation on exchange rates will not occur until
   two, three, or four quarters later. The regression model would need to be adjusted
   accordingly.
2. As mentioned earlier, some factors exhibit an immediate impact on exchange rates.
   They can be usefully included in a fundamental forecasting model only if forecasts
   can be obtained for them. Forecasts of these factors should be developed for a period
   that corresponds to the period for which a forecast of exchange rates is necessary. In
   this case, the accuracy of the exchange rate forecasts will be somewhat dependent on
   the accuracy of these factors. Even if a firm knows exactly how movements in these

factors affect exchange rates, its exchange rate projections may be inaccurate if it cannot predict the values of the factors.

3. Some factors that deserve consideration in the fundamental forecasting process cannot be easily quantified. For example, what if large Australian exporting firms experience an unanticipated labour strike, causing shortages? This will reduce the availability of Australian goods for British consumers and therefore reduce British demand for Australian dollars. Such an event, which would put downward pressure on the Australian dollar value, normally is not incorporated into the forecasting model.

4. Coefficients derived from the regression analysis will not necessarily remain constant over time. In the previous example, the coefficient for INF_{t-1} was 0.6, suggesting that for a one-unit change in INF_{t-1}, the Mexican peso would appreciate by 0.6%. Yet, if the Mexican government or the EU imposed new trade barriers, or eliminated existing barriers, the impact of the inflation differential on trade (and therefore on the Mexican peso's exchange rate) could be affected.

These limitations of fundamental forecasting have been discussed to emphasize that even the most sophisticated forecasting techniques (fundamental or otherwise) cannot provide consistently accurate forecasts. MNCs that develop forecasts must allow for some margin of error and recognize the possibility of error when implementing corporate policies.

Market-based forecasting

The process of developing forecasts from market indicators, known as **market-based forecasting**, is usually based on either: (1) the spot rate or (2) the forward rate. In this section we examine in greater detail matters first raised in Chapter 7.

Use of the spot rate. Today's spot rate may be used as a forecast of the spot rate that will exist on a future date. Using the spot rate is the same as forecasting that there will be no change in the exchange rate. To see why the spot rate can serve as a market-based forecast, assume the dollar was expected to appreciate against the pound in the very near future. This expectation will have encouraged speculators to buy the dollar with pounds today in anticipation of its appreciation, and these purchases will have forced the dollar's value up immediately. So the current price of the dollar will include the expectation that the value of the dollar will rise.

Conversely, if the dollar was expected to depreciate against the pound, speculators will have sold off dollars hoping to purchase them back at a lower price after their decline in value. Such actions will have forced the dollar to depreciate immediately. Thus, the current value of the dollar should reflect the expectation of the dollar's decline in value. Corporations can use the spot rate to forecast, since it represents the market's expectation of the spot rate in the near future.

Use of the forward rate. A forward rate quoted for a specific date in the future is commonly used as the forecasted spot rate on that future date. That is, a 30-day forward rate provides a forecast for the spot rate in 30 days, a 90-day forward rate provides a forecast of the spot rate in 90 days, and so on. Recall that the forward rate is measured as

$$F = S \, (1 + p)$$

where p represents the forward premium (which may be positive or negative). Since p represents the percentage by which the forward rate differs from the spot rate, it serves as the expected percentage change in the exchange rate:

$$
\begin{aligned}
E(e_f) &= p \\
&= (F/S - 1) \text{ [by rearranging the terms]}
\end{aligned}
$$

EXAMPLE

If the one-year forward rate of the Australian dollar is £0.42, while the spot rate is £0.40, the expected percentage change in the Australian dollar is:

$$
\begin{aligned}
E(e_f) &= p \\
&= (F/S - 1) \\
&= (0.42/0.40) - 1 \\
&= 0.05 \text{ or 5\% appreciation}
\end{aligned}
$$

Rationale for using the forward rate. To understand why the forward rate can serve as a forecast of the future spot rate, consider the following example.

EXAMPLE

If speculators expect the spot rate of the US dollar in 30 days to be 1.28 euros, and the prevailing forward rate is lower at 1.25 euros, they might buy dollars 30 days forward at 1.25 euros and then sell them when received (in 30 days) at the spot rate existing then. If a large number of speculators implement this strategy, the substantial forward purchases of dollars will cause the forward rate to increase until this speculative demand stops. Assuming interest rates do not change, the spot rate will also increase by the same percentage change to avoid the possibility of covered interest rate arbitrage (see Chapter 7). The premium would therefore be unaltered. Thus, as discussed above, the spot rate would also contain the expectation of an appreciation of the dollar.

Perhaps this speculative demand will terminate when the forward rate reaches 1.28 euros to the dollar, since at this rate, no profits will be expected by implementing the strategy. Thus, the forward rate should move toward the market's general expectation of the future spot rate. In this sense, the forward rate serves as a market-based forecast, since it reflects the market's expectation of the spot rate at the end of the forward horizon (30 days from now in this example).

Although the focus of this chapter is on corporate forecasting rather than speculation, it is speculation that helps to push the forward rate to the level that reflects the general expectation of the future spot rate. If corporations are convinced that the forward rate is a reliable indicator of the future spot rate, they can simply monitor this publicly quoted rate to develop exchange rate projections.

Long-term forecasting with forward rates. Long-term exchange rate forecasts can be derived from long-term forward rates.

EXAMPLE

Assume that the spot rate of the dollar is currently 1.20 euros, while the five-year forward rate of the dollar is 1.02 euros. This forward rate can serve as a forecast of 1.02 euros for the dollar in five years, which reflects a 15% depreciation in the dollar over the next five years.

Forward rates are normally available for periods of two to five years or even longer, but the bid/ask spread is wide because of the limited trading volume. Although such rates are rarely quoted in financial newspapers, the quoted interest rates on risk-free instruments of various countries can be used to determine what the forward rates would be under conditions of interest rate parity. The wider bid ask spread ensures that covered interest arbitrage is not possible and that only risk averse investors wanting to insure against a large fall in the value of the currency would be interested in buying forward in this way.

EXAMPLE

Raymond plc a UK company is expecting to have to make a large contract payment in dollars in five years' time. The company has been quoted a five-year forward *ask* rate on dollars of £0.70 and a *bid* rate of £0.52 by a UK bank. Interest rates in the US are quoted at 30% over the five years and in the UK a rate of 40% has been quoted (note that this is not a per year interest rate but the total interest rate charge over the five years). The current spot rate is £0.59 to the dollar.

Raymond notes that £100 would convert now to $169 (£100/0.59) and be worth $220 at the end of the five-year investment period in the US ($169 × 1.30); the investment would then convert back to £114 ($220 × 0.52), a return of only 14% and considerably less than investing in the UK.

Also, $100 would convert to £59 ($100 × 0.59) and be worth £83 (£59 × 1.4) at the end of the five year investment period in the UK. The investment would then convert back to $119 at the end of the period (£83/0.70), a return of only 19% and considerably less than investing in the US. So covered interest rate arbitrage is not possible.

Raymond, however, is thinking of taking out a forward contract to sell dollars at the bank bid rate of £0.52 for a dollar as the discount on the current spot rate of 12% ([£0.52 − £0.59]/£0.59) is considered worthwhile to protect against an even further possible fall in value of the dollar. Raymond's financial manager predicts that such a fall might well be possible and that the company should insure its returns in this way.

As a note, the governments of some emerging markets (such as those in Latin America) do not issue long-term fixed-rate bonds very often. Consequently, long-term interest rates are not available and covered interest rate arbitrage would not be possible.

USING THE WEB

Forward rates as forecasts Forward rates are available for the euro, British pound, Canadian dollar, and Japanese yen for 1-month, 3-month, 6-month, and 12-month maturities at http://www.bmo.com/economic/regular/fxrates.html. These forward rates may serve as forecasts of future spot rates.

The forward rate is easily accessible and therefore serves as a convenient and free forecast. Like any method of forecasting exchange rates, the forward rate is typically more accurate when forecasting exchange rates for short-term horizons than for long-term horizons. Exchange rates tend to wander farther from expectations over longer periods of time.

Implications of the IFE and IRP for forecasts using the forward rate. Recall that if interest rate parity (IRP) holds, the forward rate premium reflects the interest rate differential between two countries. Also recall that if the international Fisher effect (IFE) holds, a currency that has a higher interest rate than the UK interest rate should depreciate against the pound because the higher interest rate implies a higher level of expected inflation in that country than in the United Kingdom. Since the forward rate captures the nominal interest rate (and therefore the expected inflation rate) between two countries, it should provide more accurate forecasts for currencies in high-inflation countries than the spot rate.

Alvi SpA is an Italian firm that does business in Brazil, and it needs to forecast the exchange rate of the Brazilian real for one year ahead. It considers using either the spot rate or the forward rate to forecast the real. The spot rate of the Brazilian real is 0.30 euros. The one-year interest rate in Brazil is 20%, versus 5% in Italy. The one-year forward rate is 0.2625 euros, which reflects a discount to offset the interest rate differential according to IRP (check this yourself using the exact method). Alvi believes that the future exchange rate of the real will be driven by the inflation differential between Brazil and Italy. It also believes that the real rate of interest (i.e. the without inflation rate) in both Brazil and Italy is 3%. This implies that the expected inflation rate for next year is 17% in Brazil and 2% in Italy. The forward rate discount is based on the interest rate differential, which in turn is related to the inflation differential. In this example, the forward rate of the Brazilian real reflects a large discount, which means that it implies a forecast of substantial depreciation of the real against the euro. Conversely, using the spot rate of the real as a forecast would imply that the exchange rate at the end of the year will be what it is today. Since the forward rate forecast indirectly captures the differential in expected inflation rates, it is a more appropriate forecast method than the spot rate.

Firms may not always believe that the forward rate provides more accurate forecasts than the spot rate. If a firm is forecasting over a very short-term horizon such as a day or a week, the interest rate (and therefore expected inflation) differential may not be as influential. Second, some firms may believe that the interest rate differential may not even be influential in the long run. Third, if the foreign country's interest rate is usually similar to the US rate, the forward rate premium or discount will be close to zero, meaning that the forward rate and spot rate will provide similar forecasts.

Mixed forecasting

Because no single forecasting technique has been found to be consistently superior to the others, some MNCs prefer to use a combination of forecasting techniques. This method is referred to as **mixed forecasting**. Various forecasts for a particular currency value are developed using several forecasting techniques. The techniques used are assigned weights in such a way that the weights total 100%, with the techniques considered more reliable being assigned higher weights. The actual forecast of the currency is a weighted average of the various forecasts developed.

Pergreen plc needs to assess the value of the Mexican peso because it is considering expanding its business in Mexico. The conclusions drawn from each forecasting technique are shown in Exhibit 9.2. Notice that, in this example, the forecasted direction of the peso's value is dependent on the technique used. The fundamental forecast predicts the peso will appreciate, but the technical forecast and the market-based forecast predict it will depreciate. Also, notice that even though the fundamental and market-based forecasts are both driven by the same factor (interest rates), the results are distinctly different.

Sometimes MNCs assign one technique a lower weight when forecasting in one period, but a higher weight when forecasting in a later period. Some firms even weight a given technique more for some currencies than for others at a given point in time. For example, a firm may decide that a market-based forecast provides the best prediction for the pound, but that fundamental forecasting works best for the New Zealand dollar, and technical forecasting for the Mexican peso.

While each forecasting method has its merits, some changes in exchange rates are not anticipated by any method.

Exhibit 9.2 Forecasts of the Mexican peso drawn from each forecasting technique

	Factors Considered	Situation	Forecast
Technical Forecast	Recent movement in peso	The peso's value declined below a specific threshold level in the last few weeks.	The peso's value will continue to fall now that it is beyond the threshold level.
Fundamental Forecast	Economic growth, inflation, interest rates	Mexico's interest rates are high and inflation should remain low.	The peso's value will rise as euro investors capitalize on the high interest rates by investing in Mexican securities.
Market-based Forecast	Spot rate, forward rate	The peso's forward rate exhibits a significant discount which is attributed to Mexico's relatively high interest rates.	Based on the forward rate, which provides a forecast of the future spot rate, the peso's value will decline.

EXAMPLE

During the Asian crisis, the Indonesian rupiah depreciated by more than 80% against the dollar within a nine-month period. Before the rupiah's decline, neither technical factors, nor fundamental factors, nor the forward rate indicated any potential weakness. The depreciation of the rupiah was primarily attributed to concerns by institutional investors about the safety of their investments in Indonesia, which encouraged them to liquidate the investments and convert the rupiah into other currencies, putting downward pressure on the rupiah.

Weakness in some currencies may best be anticipated by a subjective assessment of conditions in a particular country and not by the quantitative methods described here. Thus, MNCs may benefit from using the methods described in this chapter along with their own sense of the conditions in a particular country. Nevertheless, it is still difficult to anticipate that a currency will weaken before a speculative outflow occurs. By that time, the currency will have weakened as a result of the outflow.

FORECASTING SERVICES

The corporate need to forecast currency values has prompted the emergence of several forecasting service firms, including Business International, Conti Currency, Predex, and Wharton Econometric Forecasting Associates. In addition, large investment banks offer forecasting services. Many consulting services use at least two different types of analysis to generate separate forecasts and then determine the weighted average of the forecasts. Some forecasting services focus on technical forecasting, while others focus on fundamental forecasting.

USING THE WEB

Exchange rate forecasts A portal for foreign exchange predictions by a range of world banks can be found at: http://www.fxstreet.com/nou/continguts/forecasts.asp?publicitat1=cmesky the home site being http://www.fxstreet.com.

Forecasts are even provided for currencies that are not widely traded. Forecasting service firms provide forecasts on any currency for time horizons of interest to their clients, ranging from one day to ten years from now. In addition, some firms offer advice on international cash management, assessment of exposure to exchange rate risk, and hedging. Many of the firms provide their clients with forecasts and recommendations monthly, or even weekly, for an annual fee.

Performance of forecasting services

Given the recent volatility in foreign exchange markets, it is quite difficult to forecast currency values. One way for a corporation to determine whether a forecasting service is valuable is to compare the accuracy of its forecasts to that of publicly available and free forecasts. The forward rate serves as a benchmark for comparison here, since it is quoted in many newspapers and magazines.

Some studies have compared several forecasting services' forecasts for different currencies to the forward rate, and found that the forecasts provided by services are no better than using the forward rate. Such results are frustrating for the corporations that have paid substantial amounts for expert opinions.

Perhaps some corporate clients of these forecasting services believe the fee is justified even when the forecasting performance is poor, if other services (such as cash management) are included in the package. Alternatively, one may argue that the value of the services is not in necessarily being able to predict exchange rates on a day-to-day basis, but rather being able to anticipate high-risk situations and predict large changes in the exchange rate as with Black Wednesday 1992 in the UK, or the unpegging of the Argentine peso with the dollar in 2002 (see Chapter 6). It is also possible that a corporate treasurer, in recognition of the potential for error in forecasting exchange rates, may prefer to pay a forecasting service firm for its forecasts. Then the treasurer is not directly responsible for corporate problems that result from inaccurate currency forecasts. Not all MNCs hire forecasting service firms to do their forecasting, some may have in-house economists, others may hedge as a matter of policy.

EVALUATION OF FORECAST PERFORMANCE

An MNC that forecasts exchange rates must monitor its performance over time to determine whether the forecasting procedure is satisfactory. For this purpose, a measurement of the forecast error is required. There are various ways to compute forecast errors. One popular measurement will be discussed here and is defined as follows:

$$\text{Absolute forecast error as a percentage of the realized value} = \frac{|\text{Forecasted value} - \text{Realized value}|}{\text{Realized value}}$$

The error is computed using an absolute value because this avoids a possible offsetting effect when determining the mean forecast error. If the forecast error is 0.05 in the first period and −0.05 in the second period (if the absolute value is not taken), the mean error is zero. Yet, that is misleading because the forecast was not perfectly accurate in either period. The absolute value avoids such a distortion.

When comparing a forecasting technique's performance among different currencies, it is often useful to adjust for their relative sizes.

EXAMPLE

Consider the following forecasted and realized values by Old Hampshire plc during one period:

	Forecasted Value	Realized Value
US dollar	£0.60	£0.58
Japanese yen	£0.005	£0.006

In this case, the difference between the forecasted value and the realized value is £0.02 for the dollar and £0.001 for the yen. This does not necessarily mean that the forecast for the yen is more accurate. When the *relative* size of what is forecasted is considered (by dividing the difference by the realized value), one can see that the dollar has been predicted with more accuracy on a percentage basis. With the data given, the forecasting error (as defined earlier) of the British pound is:

$$\text{Absolute forecast error as a percentage of the realized value} = \frac{|£0.60 - £0.58|}{£0.58}$$

$$= £3.4\%$$

In contrast, the forecast error of the Japanese yen is:

$$\text{Absolute forecast error as a percentage of the realized value} = \frac{|£0.005 - £0.006|}{£0.006}$$

$$= 16.7\%$$

It is the percentage difference between actual and forecast that matters when translating large sums of money not the absolute amount. Thus, the yen has been predicted with less accuracy as a percentage even though the absolute error in the exchange rate is a smaller number. Translating yen into pounds would differ from expectations by 16.7% as opposed to only 3.4% if translating the US dollar into pounds.

Forecast accuracy over time

MNCs are likely to have more confidence in their measurement of the forecast error when they measure it over each of several periods. The absolute forecast error as a percentage of the realized value can be estimated for each period to derive the mean error over all of these periods. If an MNC is most interested in forecasting the value of a currency 90 days (one quarter) from now, it will assess errors from the application of various forecast procedures over the last several quarters.

Have forecasts improved in recent years? The answer depends on the method used to develop forecasts. Exhibit 9.3 shows the magnitude of the absolute errors when the forward rate is used as a predictor for the British pound over time. The size of the errors changes over time. The errors are larger in periods when the pound's value was more volatile.

Forecast accuracy among currencies

The ability to forecast currency values may vary with the currency of concern. The US dollar exchange rate with the Canadian dollar is a particularly stable rate over the years and is relatively easy to predict with a reasonable degree of accuracy. A less stable currency as in a developing country is likely to vary more over time or have stable periods followed by brief turbulent readjustments. The absolute forecast errors of currencies can therefore change over time as a result of unpegging a currency, a currency crisis, a change of government policy or other economic developments.

Search for forecast bias

The difference between the forecasted and realized exchange rates for a given point in time is a nominal forecast error. A time series of nominal forecast errors for the British pound

Exhibit 9.3   Absolute forecast errors over time for the British pound (using the forward rate to forecast)

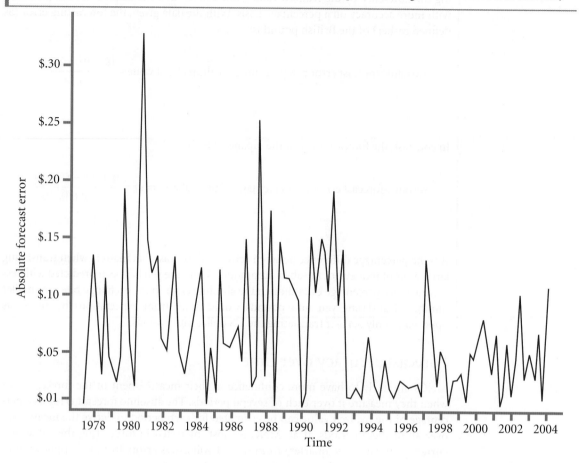

is illustrated in Exhibit 9.4. Negative errors over time indicate underestimating, while positive errors indicate overestimating. If the errors are consistently positive or negative over time, then a bias in the forecasting procedure exists. It appears that a bias did exist in distinct periods. During the strong-pound periods, the forecasts underestimated, while in weak-pound periods, the forecasts overestimated. Such serial correlation over time is known as autocorrelation and violates a basic assumption of the regression equation, causing amongst other effects an underestimate of the variance of the error term.

Statistical test of forecast bias

If the forward rate is a biased predictor of the future spot rate, this implies that there is a systematic forecast error, which could be corrected to improve forecast accuracy. If the forward rate is unbiased, it fully reflects all available information about the future spot rate. In any case, any forecast errors would be the result of events that could not have been anticipated from existing information at the time of the forecast. A conventional method of testing for a forecast bias is to apply the following regression model to historical data:

$$S_t = a_0 + a_1 F_{t-1} + \mu_t$$

Exhibit 9.4 Comparison of forecasted and realized spot rates over time for the British pound (using the forward rate to forecast)

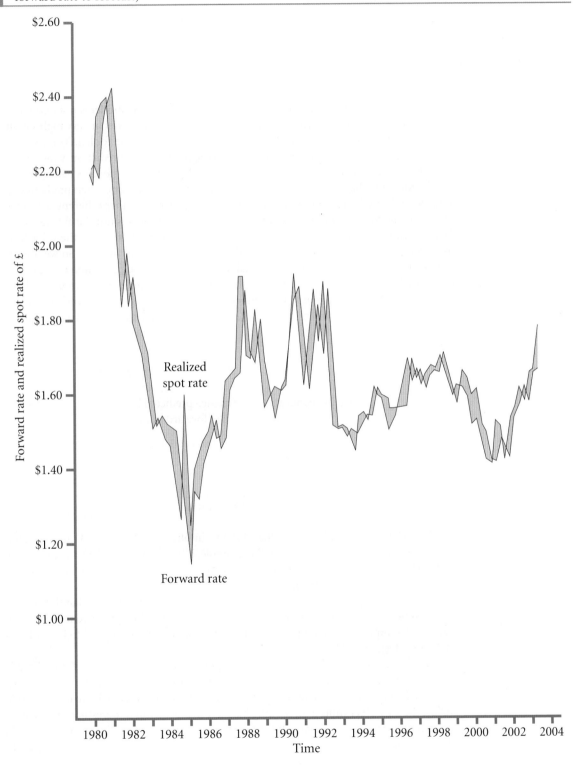

Where:

S_t = the spot rate in direct form (i.e. per unit of foreign currency) at time t,

F_{t-1} = the forward rate prediction, again in direct form, for time t made at time $t-1$,

μ_t = error term for period t,

a_0 = the intercept,

a_1 = the regression coefficient.

The problem with this model as a prediction model is that the model is not detrended. The results appear to produce in most instances a regression model of very high significance and therefore good prediction with a high R^2. Do not be fooled. The model is measuring absolute error compared to the error made by no prediction which is the overall average exchange rate of the whole sample. Of course the model is better than no prediction; but what we want to know is whether the model is better than predicting no change in the exchange rate from the *previous period*. That is rather different. The alternative prediction we would make if we did not have the model is not the average of the whole sample, but the exchange rate from the previous period. If we use the value from the previous period we are making a prediction of *no change* in the rate. So we want to know whether or not the forward rate enables us to make a good prediction of the *change* in the exchange rate. Such a model uses the same variables and e_f the percentage change in the value of foreign currency. Remember that this has always been the variable that we have sought to predict when looking at exchange rate behaviour. A de-trended model appears thus:

$$\underbrace{\frac{S_t - S_{t-1}}{S_t}}_{\text{(actual change)}} = e_f = a_0 + a_1 \underbrace{\frac{F_{t-1} - S_t}{S_t}}_{\substack{\text{(change predicted by} \\ \text{the forward rate)}}} + \mu_t$$

If the forward rate is unbiased, the intercept should equal zero, and the regression coefficient a_1 should equal 1.0. The t-test for a_1 is:

$$t = \frac{a_1 - 1}{\text{Standard error of } a_1}$$

If $a_0 = 0$ and a_1 is significantly less than 1.0, this implies that the forward rate is systematically overestimating the spot rate. For example, if $a_0 = 0$ and $a_1 = 0.90$, the prediction of the change in the spot rate (as in the de-trended model) is estimated to be 90% of the change forecast generated by the forward rate.

Conversely, if $a_0 = 0$ and a_1 is significantly greater than 1.0, this implies that the forward rate is systematically underestimating the value of 1 unit of foreign currency – the spot rate. For example, if $a = 0$ and $a_1 = 1.1$, the future spot rate is estimated to be 1.1 times the forecast generated by the forward rate.

When a bias is detected and anticipated to persist in the future, an MNC may be able to adjust for the bias so that it can improve its forecasting accuracy. For example, if the errors are consistently positive, an MNC could adjust today's forward rate downward to reflect the bias. Over time, a forecasting bias can change (from underestimating to overestimating, or vice versa). Any adjustment to the forward rate used as a forecast would need to reflect the anticipated bias for the period of concern. Thus prediction may result in part statistics and part subjective estimate.

Graphic evaluation of forecast performance

Forecast performance can be examined with the use of a graph that compares forecasted values with the realized values for various time periods.

E X A M P L E

For eight quarters, Tunek ltd used the three-month forward rate of Currency Q to forecast Q's value three months ahead. The results from this strategy are shown in Exhibit 9.5, and the predicted and realized exchange rate values in Exhibit 9.5 are compared graphically in Exhibit 9.6.

Exhibit 9.5 Evaluation of forecast performance

	Predicted Value of Currency Q for End of Period	Realized Value of Currency Q as of End of Period
1	£0.20	£0.16
2	0.18	0.14
3	0.24	0.16
4	0.26	0.22
5	0.30	0.28
6	0.22	0.26
7	0.16	0.14
8	0.14	0.10

The 45° line in Exhibit 9.6 represents perfect forecasts. If the realized value turned out to be exactly what was predicted over several periods, all points would be located on that 45° line in Exhibit 9.6. For this reason, the 45° line is referred to as the **perfect forecast line.** The closer the points reflecting the eight periods are vertically to the 45° line, the better the forecast. The vertical distance between each point and the 45° line is the forecast error. If the point is £0.04 above the 45° line, this means that the realized spot rate was £0.04 higher than the exchange rate forecasted. All points above the 45° line reflect underestimation, while all points below the 45° line reflect overestimation.

If points appear to be scattered evenly on both sides of the 45° line, then the forecasts are said to be *unbiased*, since they are not consistently above or below the realized values. Whether evaluating the size of forecast errors or attempting to search for a bias, more reliable results are obtained when examining a large number of forecasts.

A more thorough assessment of a forecast bias can be conducted by separating the entire period into sub-periods as shown in Exhibit 9.7 for the British pound. Each graph reflects a particular sub-period. Some graphs show a general underestimation while others show overestimation, which means that the forecast bias changed from one sub-period to another.

Comparison of forecasting methods

An MNC can compare forecasting methods by plotting the points relating to two methods on a graph similar to Exhibit 9.6. The points pertaining to each method can be distinguished by a particular mark or colour. The performance of the two methods can be evaluated by comparing distances of points from the 45° line. In some cases, neither

Exhibit 9.6 Graphic evaluation of forecast performance

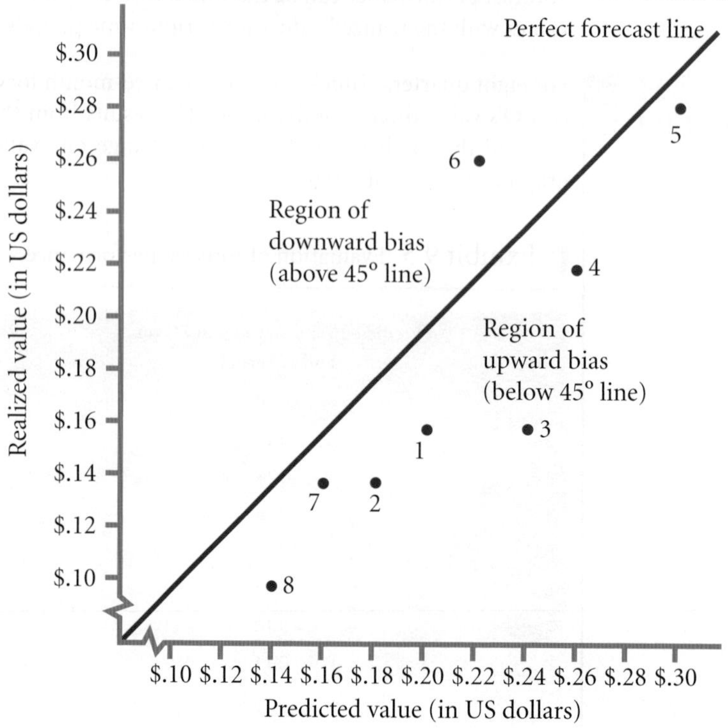

forecasting method may stand out as superior when compared graphically. If so, a more precise comparison can be conducted by computing the forecast errors for all periods for each method and then comparing these errors.

EXAMPLE

Xavier ltd uses a fundamental forecasting method to forecast the Polish currency (zloty), which it will need to purchase to buy imports from Poland. Xavier also derives a second forecast for each period based on an alternative forecasting model. Its previous forecasts of the zloty, using Model 1 (the fundamental method) and Model 2 (the alternative method), are shown in Columns 2 and 3, respectively, of Exhibit 9.8, along with the realized value of the zloty in Column 4.

The absolute forecast errors of forecasting with Model 1 and Model 2 are shown in Columns 5 and 6, respectively. Notice that Model 1 outperformed Model 2 in six of the eight periods. The mean absolute forecast error when using Model 1 is £0.04, meaning that forecasts with Model 1 are off by £0.04 on average. Although Model 1 is not perfectly accurate, it does a better job than Model 2, whose mean absolute forecast error is £0.07. Overall, predictions with Model 1 are on average £0.03 closer to the realized value.

For a complete comparison of performance among forecasting methods, an MNC should evaluate as many periods as possible. Only eight periods are used in our example because that is enough to illustrate how to compare forecasting performance. If the MNC has a large number of periods to evaluate, it could statistically test for significant differences in forecasting errors.

Exhibit 9.7 Graphic comparison of forecasted and realized spot rates in different sub-periods for the British pound (using the forward rate as the forecast)

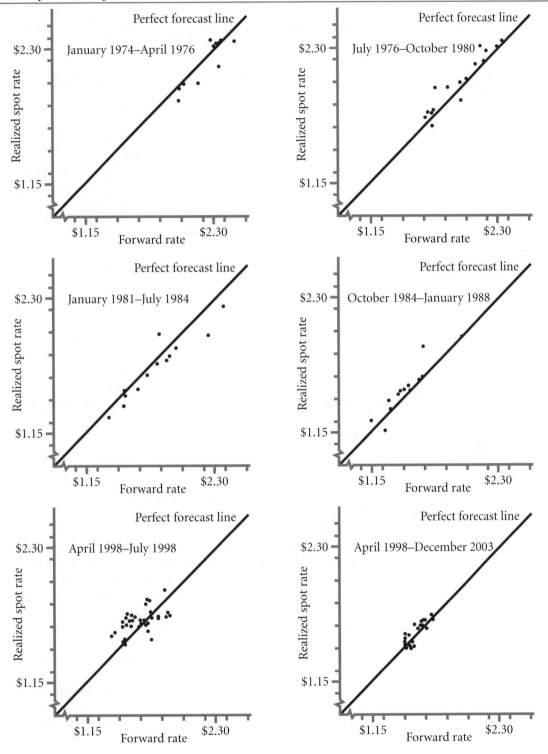

Exhibit 9.8 Comparison of forecast techniques

(1) Period	(2) Predicted value of zloty by Model 1	(3) Predicted value of zloty by Model 2	(4) Realized value of zloty	(5) Absolute forecast error using Model 1	(6) Absolute forecast error using Model 2	(7) = (5) − (6) Difference in absolute forecast errors (Model 1 − Model 2)
1	£0.2	£0.24	£0.16	£0.04	£0.08	£−.04
2	.18	.20	.14	.04	.06	−.02
3	.24	.20	.16	.08	.04	.04
4	.26	.20	.22	.04	.02	.02
5	.30	.18	.28	.02	.10	−.08
6	.22	.32	.26	.04	.06	−.02
7	.16	.20	.14	.02	.06	−.04
8	.14	.24	.10	.04	.14	−.10
				Sum = .32	Sum = .56	Sum = −.24
				Mean =.04	Mean = .07	Mean = −.03

Forecasting under market efficiency

The efficiency of the foreign exchange market also has implications for forecasting. If the foreign exchange market is **weak-form efficient**, then historical and current exchange rate information is not useful for forecasting exchange rate movements because today's exchange rates reflect all of this information. That is, technical analysis would not be capable of improving forecasts. If the foreign exchange market is **semistrong-form efficient**, then all relevant public information is already reflected in today's exchange rates. If today's exchange rates fully reflect any historical trends in exchange rate movements, but not other public information on expected interest rate movements, the foreign exchange market is weak-form efficient, but not semistrong-form efficient. Much research has tested the efficient market hypothesis for foreign exchange markets. Research suggests that foreign exchange markets appear to be weak-form efficient *and* semistrong-form efficient. However, there is some evidence of inefficiencies for some currencies in specific periods.

If foreign exchange markets are **strong-form efficient**, then all relevant public and private information is already reflected in today's exchange rates. This form of efficiency is difficult to test with regard to exchange rates as it is difficult to clearly define private information, unlike say shares where private information becomes public on specified announcement dates.

Even though foreign exchange markets are generally found to be at least semistrong-form efficient, forecasts of exchange rates by MNCs may still be worthwhile. Their goal is not necessarily to earn speculative profits but to use reasonable exchange rate forecasts to implement policies. When MNCs assess proposed policies, they usually prefer to develop their own forecasts of exchange rates over time rather than simply use market-based rates as a forecast of future rates. MNCs are often interested in more than a point estimate of an exchange rate one year, three years, or five years from now. They prefer to develop a variety of scenarios and assess how exchange rates may change for each scenario. Even if today's forward exchange rate properly reflects all available information, it does not indicate to the MNC the possible deviation of the realized future exchange rate from what is expected. MNCs need to determine the range of various possible exchange rate movements in order to assess the degree to which their operating performance could be affected.

EXCHANGE RATE VOLATILITY

Stock market efficiency suggests that an MNC, like an investor, cannot outpredict the market in attempting to forecast the actual future exchange rate. The efficiency concept in a sense does not allow anyone to consistently outpredict the market. But predicting volatility is still "allowable" in that knowledge of future volatility does not suggest any particular buying or selling strategy that will affect prices. Speculators may take out straddles (see Chapter 8) but this is not, of itself, a hedge on a price rise or fall. For an MNC, the knowledge that an exchange rate is going to become more volatile is nevertheless useful for managing uncertainty; it can take the market forecast and the range around the forecast. Where volatility is predicted to increase, an MNC can take a more cautious strategy to protect itself from the effects of exchange rate movements and, where known, the cause of such movements. So a change in expected volatility is useful knowledge.

E X A M P L E

Harp plc is based in Shropshire and imports products from Canada. It uses the spot rate of the Canadian dollar (valued at £0.70) to forecast the value of the Canadian dollar one month from now. It also specifies a range around its forecasts, based on the historical volatility of the Canadian dollar. The more volatile the currency, the more likely it is to wander far from the forecasted value in the future (the larger is the expected forecast error). Harp determines that the standard deviation of the Canadian dollar's movements over the last 12 months is 2%. Thus, assuming the movements are normally distributed, it expects that there is a 68% chance that the actual value will be within 1 standard deviation (2%) of its forecast, which results in a range from £0.686 to £0.714. In addition, it expects that there is a 95% chance that the Canadian dollar will be within 2 standard deviations (4%) of the predicted value, which results in a range from £0.672 to £0.728. By specifying a range, Harp can more properly anticipate how far the actual value of the currency might deviate from its predicted value. If the currency was more volatile, its standard deviation would be larger, and the range surrounding the forecast would also be larger.

As this example shows, the measurement of a currency's volatility is useful for specifying a range around a forecast. However, a currency's volatility can change over time, which means that past volatility levels will not necessarily be the optimal method of establishing a range around a forecast. Therefore, MNCs may prefer to forecast exchange rate volatility using estimates of future exchange rate conditions to determine the potential range surrounding their forecast.

The first step in forecasting exchange rate volatility is to determine the relevant period of concern. If an MNC is forecasting the value of the Canadian dollar each day over the next quarter, it may also attempt to forecast the standard deviation of daily exchange rate movements over this quarter. This information could be used along with the point estimate forecast of the Canadian dollar for each day to derive confidence intervals around each forecast.

Methods of forecasting exchange rate volatility

The volatility of exchange rate movements for a future period can be forecast using: (1) recent exchange rate volatility, (2) historical time series of volatilities, and (3) the implied standard deviation derived from currency option prices.

Use of short-term volatility to predict long-term volatility. The volatility of historical exchange rate movements over a recent period can be used to forecast the short-, medium- and long-term future. In our example, the standard deviation of monthly exchange rate movements in the Canadian dollar during the previous 12 months could be used to estimate the future volatility of the Canadian dollar over the next month. If the volatility conditions of the monthly figures in the sample 12 months is thought to be typical for the next year, the predicted monthly standard deviation can be converted to an annual predicted standard deviation by the simple formula:

$$\text{s.d.}_t = \text{s.d.}_m \times \sqrt{(t/m)}$$

where:

  s.d. = standard deviation

  t, m = time periods in the same unit of time where t is the longer time period and m the shorter time period (so a monthly prediction converted to a prediction of the standard deviation for a year can be calculated by setting $t = 12$ months and $m = 1$ month).

The assumptions are that the exchange rate movements are not correlated over time and follow a random walk. In practice, levels of stationarity will mean that this is a slight overestimate of future volatility (see Appendix 8).

EXAMPLE

The standard deviation of monthly changes in the value of currency Y for the last 12 months has been 1%. Winston ltd estimate that these conditions will last for at least one year and wants to know the estimated standard deviation for the exchange rate one year hence rather than one month hence. Using the above equation, $t = 12$ months and $m = 1$ month. So the implied annual standard deviation of the one year estimate is:

$$\text{s.d.}_t = \text{s.d.}_m \times \sqrt{(t/m)}$$
$$3.46\% = 1\% \times \sqrt{(12/1)}$$

Assuming a random walk and a current spot of £0.50:1 Y, the 95% confidence interval for Y will be:

1.96 standard deviations × 3.46% = 6.78% of the expected value, so:

£0.50 × (1 − 6.78%) < £0.50 < £0.50 × (1 + 6.78%)

£0.4661 < £0.50 < £0.5339

Use of a historical pattern of volatilities. Since historical volatility can change over time, the standard deviation of monthly exchange rate movements in the last 12 months is not necessarily an accurate predictor of the volatility of exchange rate movements in the next month. To the extent that there is a pattern to the changes in exchange rate volatility over time, a series of time periods may be used to forecast volatility in the next period. Being able to predict stock market volatility does not violate weak-form efficiency. The actual value of a currency may not follow a pattern or be predictable but the variance can be predictable. Just as with a lottery, knowing the range of outcomes and their equal probability does not (alas) help to predict the actual number.

EXAMPLE

The standard deviation of monthly exchange rate movements in the dollar can be determined for each of the last several years. Then, a time series trend of these standard deviation levels can be used to form an estimate for the volatility of the dollar over the next month. The forecast may be based on a weighting scheme such as 60% times the standard deviation in the last year, plus 30% times the standard deviation in the year before that, plus 10% times the standard deviation in the year before that. This scheme places more weight on the most recent data to derive the forecast but allows data from the last three years to influence the forecast. Normally, the weights that achieved the most accuracy (lowest forecast error) over previous periods and the number of previous periods (lags) would be used when applying this method.

Various economic and political factors can cause exchange rate volatility to change abruptly, however, so even sophisticated time series models do not necessarily generate accurate forecasts of exchange rate volatility. This method differs from the first method in that it uses information from periods beyond the previous 12 months.

Implied standard deviation. A third method for forecasting exchange rate volatility is to derive the exchange rate's implied standard deviation (ISD) from the currency option pricing model. Recall that the premium on a call option for a currency is dependent on factors such as the relationship between the spot exchange rate and the exercise (strike) price of the option, the number of days until the expiration date of the option, and the anticipated volatility of the currency's exchange rate movements. The actual values of each of these factors are known, except for the anticipated volatility. By plugging in the prevailing option premium paid by investors for that specific currency option, however, it is possible to derive the market's anticipated volatility for that currency. The volatility is measured by the standard deviation, which can be used to develop a probability distribution surrounding the forecast of the currency's exchange rate.

USING THE WEB

Implied volatilities Implied volatilities of major currencies are provided at http://www.fednewyork.org/markets/impliedvolatility.html. The implied volatility can be used to measure the market's expectations of a specific currency's volatility in the future. Implied volatilities are shown for different expiration dates, which allows for forecasts of volatility over periods up to those expiration dates.

SUMMARY

- Multinational corporations need exchange rate forecasts to make decisions on hedging payables and receivables, short-term financing and investment, capital budgeting, and long-term financing.

- The most common forecasting techniques can be classified as: (1) technical, (2) fundamental, (3) market-based, and (4) mixed. Each technique has limitations, and the quality of the forecasts produced varies. Yet, due to the high variability in exchange rates, it should not be surprising that forecasts are not always accurate.

- Forecasting methods can be evaluated by comparing the actual values of currencies to the values predicted by the forecasting method. To be meaningful, this comparison should be conducted over several periods. Two criteria used to evaluate performance of a forecast method are bias and accuracy. When comparing the accuracy of forecasts for two currencies, the absolute forecast error should be divided by the realized value of the currency to control for differences in the relative values of currencies.

CRITICAL DEBATE

What should an MNC use to forecast when budgeting?

Proposition: use the spot rate to forecast. When an MNC firm conducts financial budgeting, it must estimate the values of its foreign currency cash flows that will be received by the parent. Since it is well documented that firms cannot accurately forecast future values, MNCs should use the spot rate for budgeting. Changes in economic conditions are difficult to predict, and the spot rate reflects the best guess of the future spot rate if there are no changes in economic conditions.

Opposing view: use the forward rate to forecast. The spot rates of some currencies do not represent accurate or even unbiased estimates of the future spot rates. Many currencies of developing countries have generally declined over time. These currencies tend to be in countries that have high inflation rates. If the spot rate had been used for budgeting, the dollar cash flows resulting from cash inflows in these currencies would have been highly overestimated. The expected inflation in a country can be accounted for by using the nominal interest rate. A high nominal interest rate implies a high level of expected inflation. Based on interest rate parity, these currencies will have pronounced discounts. Thus, the forward rate captures the expected inflation differential between countries because it is influenced by the nominal interest rate differential. Since it captures the inflation differential, it should provide a more accurate forecast of currencies, especially those currencies in high-inflation countries.

With whom do you agree? Use InfoTrac or some other search engine to learn more about this issue. Which argument do you support? Offer your own opinion on this issue.

SELF TEST

Answers are provided in Appendix A at the back of the text.

1. Assume that the annual UK interest rate is expected to be 7% for each of the next four years, while the annual interest rate in India is expected to be 20%. Determine the appropriate four-year forward rate premium or discount on the Indian rupee, which could be used to forecast the percentage change in the rupee over the next four years.

2. Consider the following information:

Currency	90-day Forward Rate	Spot Rate That Occurred 90-Days Later
Canadian dollar	0.80 euros	0.82 euros
Japanese yen	0.012 euros	0.011 euros

Assuming the forward rate was used to forecast the future spot rate, determine whether the Canadian dollar or the Japanese yen was forecasted with more accuracy, based on the absolute forecast error as a percentage of the realized value.

3. An analyst has stated that the British pound seems to increase in value over the two weeks following announcements by the Bank of England (the British central bank) that it will raise interest rates. If this statement is true, what are the inferences regarding weak-form or semistrong-form efficiency?

4. Assume that Russian interest rates are much higher than UK interest rates. Also assume that interest rate parity (discussed in Chapter 7) exists. Would you expect the rouble to appreciate or depreciate? Explain.

5. Warden plc is considering a project in Venezuela, which will be very profitable if the local currency (bolivar) appreciates against the British pound. If the bolivar depreciates, the project will result in losses. Warden plc forecasts that the bolivar will appreciate. The bolivar's value historically has been very volatile. As a manager of Warden plc, would you be comfortable with this project? Explain.

QUESTIONS AND APPLICATIONS

1. **Motives for forecasting.** Explain corporate motives for forecasting exchange rates.

2. **Technical forecasting.** Explain the technical technique for forecasting exchange rates. What are some limitations of using technical forecasting to predict exchange rates?

3. **Fundamental forecasting.** Explain the fundamental technique for forecasting exchange rates. What are some limitations of using a fundamental technique to forecast exchange rates?

4. **Market-based forecasting.** Explain the market-based technique for forecasting exchange rates. What is the rationale for using market-based forecasts? If the euro appreciates substantially against the dollar during a specific period, would market-based forecasts have overestimated or underestimated the realized values over this period? Explain.

5. **Mixed forecasting.** Explain the mixed technique for forecasting exchange rates.

6. **Detecting a forecast bias.** Explain how to assess performance in forecasting exchange rates. Explain how to detect a bias in forecasting exchange rates.

7. **Measuring forecast accuracy.** You are hired as a consultant to assess a firm's ability to forecast. The firm has developed a point forecast for two different currencies presented in the following table. The firm asks you to determine which currency was forecasted with greater accuracy.

Period	Yen forecast	Actual yen value	Dollar forecast	Actual dollar value
1	£0.0050	£0.0051	£0.60	£0.61
2	0.0048	0.0052	0.62	0.61
3	0.0053	0.0052	0.63	0.65
4	0.0055	0.0056	0.58	0.62

8. **Limitations of a fundamental forecast.** Wellington ltd believes that future real interest rate movements will affect exchange rates, and it has applied regression analysis to historical data to assess the relationship. It will use regression coefficients derived from this analysis, along with forecasted real interest rate movements, to predict exchange rates in the future. Explain at least three limitations of this method.

9. **Consistent forecasts.** Brinnington plc is a UK-based MNC with subsidiaries in most major countries. Each subsidiary is responsible for forecasting the future exchange rate of its local currency relative to the British pound. Comment on this policy. How might Brinnington ensure consistent forecasts among the different subsidiaries?

10. **Forecasting with a forward rate.** Assume that the four-year annualized interest rate in the United Kingdom is 9% and the four-year annualized interest rate in Singapore is 6%. Assume interest rate parity holds for a four-year horizon. Assume that the spot rate of the Singapore dollar is £0.40. If the forward rate is used to forecast exchange rates, what will be the forecast for the Singapore dollar's spot rate in four years? What percentage appreciation or depreciation does this forecast imply over the four-year period?

11. **Foreign exchange market efficiency.** Assume that foreign exchange markets were found to be weak-form efficient. What does this suggest about utilizing technical analysis to speculate in euros? If MNCs believe that foreign exchange markets are strong-form efficient, why would they develop their own forecasts of future exchange rates? That is, why wouldn't they simply use today's quoted rates as indicators about future rates? After all, today's quoted rates should reflect all relevant information.

12. **Forecast error.** The director of currency forecasting at Champaign-Urbana ltd says, "The most critical task of forecasting exchange rates is not to derive a point estimate of a future exchange rate but to assess how wrong our estimate might be". What does this statement mean?

13. **Forecasting exchange rates of currencies that previously were fixed.** When some countries in Eastern Europe initially allowed their currencies to fluctuate against the dollar, would the fundamental technique based on historical relationships have been useful for forecasting future exchange rates of these currencies? Explain.

14. **Forecast error.** Royce ltd is a UK firm with future receivables one year from now in Canadian dollars and Brazilian real. Its Brazilian real receivables are known with certainty, and its estimated Canadian dollar receivables are subject to a 2% error in either direction. The pound values of both types of receivables are similar. There is no chance of default by the customers involved. Royce's treasurer says that the estimate of pound cash flows to be generated from the Brazilian real receivables is subject to greater uncertainty than that of the Canadian dollar receivables. Explain the rationale for the treasurer's statement.

15. **Forecasting the euro.** Cooper, plc, periodically obtains euros to purchase German products. It assesses UK and German trade patterns and inflation rates to develop a fundamental forecast for the euro. How could Cooper possibly improve its method of fundamental forecasting as applied to the euro?

16. **Forward rate forecast.** Assume that you obtain a quote for a one-year forward rate on the Mexican peso. Assume that Mexico's one-year interest rate is 40%, while the UK one-year interest rate is 7%. Over the next year, the peso depreciates by 12%. Do you think the forward rate overestimated the spot rate one year ahead in this case? Explain.

17. **Forecasting based on PPP versus the forward rate.** You believe that the Singapore dollar's exchange rate movements are mostly attributed to purchasing power parity. Today, the nominal annual interest rate in Singapore is 18%. The nominal annual interest rate in the United Kingdom is 3%. You expect that annual inflation will be about 4% in Singapore and 1% in the United Kingdom. Assume that interest rate parity holds. Today the spot rate of the Singapore dollar is £0.41. Do you think the one-year forward rate would underestimate, overestimate, or be an unbiased estimate of the future spot rate in one year? Explain.

18. **Interpreting an unbiased forward rate.** Assume that the forward rate is an unbiased but not necessarily accurate forecast of the future exchange rate of the yen over the next several years. Based on this information, do you think Raven ltd should hedge its remittance of expected Japanese yen profits to the UK parent by selling yen forward

contracts? Why would this strategy be advantageous? Under what conditions would this strategy backfire?

ADVANCED QUESTIONS

19. **Probability distribution of forecasts.** Assume that the following regression model was applied to historical quarterly data:

$$e_t = a_0 + a_1 INT_t + a2INF_{t-1} + \mu_t$$

where

e_t	=	percentage change in the exchange rate of the Japanese yen in period t
INT_t	=	average real interest rate differential (UK interest rate minus Japanese interest rate) over period t
INF_{t-1}	=	inflation differential (UK inflation rate minus Japanese inflation rate) in the previous period
a_0, a_1, a_2	=	regression coefficients
μ_t	=	error term

Assume that the regression coefficients were estimated as follows:

$a_0 = 0.0$

$a_1 = 0.9$

$a_2 = 0.8$

Also assume that the inflation differential in the most recent period was 3%. The real interest rate differential in the upcoming period is forecasted as follows:

Interest Rate Differential	Probability
0%	30%
1	60
2	10

If Stillwater ltd uses this information to forecast the Japanese yen's exchange rate, what will be the probability distribution of the yen's percentage change over the upcoming period?

20. **Testing for a forecast bias.** You must determine whether there is a forecast bias in the forward

rate. You apply regression analysis to test the relationship between the actual spot rate and the forward rate forecast (F):

$$S = a_0 + a_1 (F)$$

The regression results are as follows:

Coefficient	Standard Error
$a_0 = 0.006$	0.011
$a_1 = 0.800$	0.05

Based on these results, is there a bias in the forecast? Verify your conclusion. If there is a bias, explain whether it is an overestimate or an underestimate.

21. **Effect of September 11 on forward rate forecasts.** The September 11, 2001 terrorist attack on the United States was quickly followed by lower interest rates in the United States. How would this affect a fundamental forecast of foreign currencies? How would this affect the forward rate forecast of foreign currencies?

22. **Interpreting forecast bias information.** The treasurer of Glencoe ltd detected a forecast bias when using the 30-day forward rate of the euro to forecast future spot rates of the euro over various periods. He believes he can use this information to determine whether imports ordered every week should be hedged (payment is made 30 days after each order). Glencoe's managing director says that in the long run the forward rate is unbiased and that the treasurer should not waste time trying to "beat the forward rate" but should just hedge all orders. Who is correct?

23. **Forecasting Latin American currencies.** The value of each Latin American currency relative to the euro is dictated by supply and demand conditions between that currency and the dollar. The values of Latin American currencies have generally declined substantially against the euro over time. Most of these countries have high inflation rates and high interest rates. The data on inflation rates, economic growth, and other economic indicators are subject to error, as limited resources are used to compile the data.
   a. If the forward rate is used as a market-based forecast, will this rate result in a forecast of appreciation, depreciation, or no change in any particular Latin American currency? Explain.
   b. If technical forecasting is used, will this result in a forecast of appreciation, depreciation, or no change in the value of a specific Latin American currency? Explain.
   c. Do you think that UK firms can accurately forecast the future values of Latin American currencies? Explain.

24. **Selecting between forecast methods.** Bolivia currently has a nominal one-year risk-free interest rate of 40%, which is primarily due to the high level of expected inflation. The euro nominal one-year risk-free interest rate is 8%. The spot rate of Bolivia's currency (called the boliviana) is 0.14 euro. The one-year forward rate of the boliviana is 0.108 euro. What is the forecasted percentage change in the boliviana if the spot rate is used as a one-year forecast? What is the forecasted percentage change in the boliviana if the one-year forward rate is used as a one-year forecast? Which forecast do you think will be more accurate? Why?

25. **Comparing market-based forecasts.** For all parts of this question, assume that interest rate parity exists, the prevailing one-year UK nominal interest rate is low, and that you expect UK inflation to be low this year.
   a. Assume that the country Dinland engages in much trade with the United Kingdom and the trade involves many different products. Dinland has had a zero trade balance with the United Kingdom (the value of exports and imports is about the same) in the past. Assume that you expect a high level of inflation (about 40%) in Dinland over the next year because of a large increase in the prices of many products that Dinland produces. Dinland presently has a one-year risk-free interest rate of more than 40%. Do you think that the prevailing spot rate or the one-year forward rate would result in a more accurate forecast of Dinland's currency (the din) one year from now? Explain.
   b. Assume that the country Freeland engages in much trade with the United Kingdom and the trade involves many different products. Freeland has had a zero trade balance with

the United Kingdom (the value of exports and imports is about the same) in the past. You expect high inflation (about 40%) in Freeland over the next year because of a large increase in the cost of land (and therefore housing) in Freeland. You believe that the prices of products that Freeland produces will not be affected. Freeland presently has a one-year risk-free interest rate of more than 40%. Do you think that the prevailing one-year forward rate of Freeland's currency (the fre) would overestimate, underestimate, or be a reasonably accurate forecast of the spot rate one year from now? (Presume a direct quotation of the exchange rate, so that if the forward rate underestimates, it means that its value is less than the realized spot rate in one year. If the forward rate overestimates, it means that its value is more than the realized spot rate in one year.)

PROJECT WORKSHOP

26. CME exchange rates. The website of the Chicago Mercantile Exchange (CME) provides information about the exchange and the futures contracts offered on the exchange. Its address is http://www.cme.com.
   a. Go to the section on "Prices" and then to the "Daily and Weekly Charts". Describe the trend of a peso futures contract over the last few months. What does this trend suggest about changes in forecasts of the peso over the period assessed (assuming that the futures rate was used as a forecasting method)? What do you think caused the futures prices to change over the last few months?
   b. Select a peso futures contract that has at least one month until its settlement date. Determine whether that futures contract would have underestimated or overestimated the spot rate as of the settlement date if it

had been used to forecast the future spot rate. Was the forecast accurate?

27. Select an exchange rate and a forward rate for a given period.
   a. Calculate:

$$S_t = a_0 + a_1 F_{t-1} + \mu_t$$

   Where:

S_t	=	the spot rate at time t,
F_{t-1}	=	the forward rate prediction for time t made at time $t-1$,
μ_t	=	error term for period t,
a_0	=	the intercept,
a_1	=	the regression coefficient, and note the R^2. Does this prove that the future is a good predictor?

   b. Now calculate the equation:

$$S_t = a_0 + a_1 S_{t-1} + \mu_t$$

   compare your result with the equation in section (a). How do you explain the good performance of the model in this section, given that it is only using an old rate ($t-1$) to predict the rate at time t?
   c. Finally calculate the equation:

$$\frac{S_t - S_{t-1}}{S_t} = a_0 + a_1 \frac{F_{t-1} - S_t}{S_t} + \mu_t$$

   is this a bettter model? Explain

DISCUSSION IN THE BOARDROOM

This exercise can be found on the companion website at www.thomsonlearning.co.uk/madura_fox.

RUNNING YOUR OWN MNC

This exercise can be found on the companion website at www.thomsonlearning.co.uk/madura_fox.

Essays/discussion and articles can be found at the end of Part 3

BLADES PLC CASE STUDY
Forecasting exchange rates

Recall that Blades plc the UK-based manufacturer of roller blades, is currently both exporting to and importing from Thailand. Ben Holt, Blades' chief financial officer (CFO), and you, a financial analyst at Blades plc are reasonably happy with Blades' current performance in Thailand. Entertainment Products, Inc., a Thai retailer for sporting goods, has committed itself to purchase a minimum number of Blades' "Speedos" annually. The agreement will terminate after three years. Blades also imports certain components needed to manufacture its products from Thailand. Both Blades" imports and exports are denominated in Thai baht. Because of these arrangements, Blades generates approximately 10% of its revenue and 4% of its cost of goods sold in Thailand.

Currently, Blades' only business in Thailand consists of this export and import trade. Ben Holt, however, is thinking about using Thailand to augment Blades' UK business in other ways as well in the future. For example, Holt is contemplating establishing a subsidiary in Thailand to increase the percentage of Blades' sales to that country. Furthermore, by establishing a subsidiary in Thailand, Blades will have access to Thailand's money and capital markets. For instance, Blades could instruct its Thai subsidiary to invest excess funds or to satisfy its short-term needs for funds in the Thai money market. Furthermore, part of the subsidiary's financing could be obtained by utilizing investment banks in Thailand.

Due to Blades' current arrangements and future plans, Ben Holt is concerned about recent developments in Thailand and their potential impact on the company's future in that country. Economic conditions in Thailand have been unfavourable recently. Movements in the value of the baht have been highly volatile, and foreign investors in Thailand have lost confidence in the baht, causing massive capital outflows from Thailand. Consequently, the baht has been depreciating.

When Thailand was experiencing a high economic growth rate, few analysts anticipated an economic downturn. Consequently, Holt never found it necessary to forecast economic conditions in Thailand even though Blades was doing business there. Now, however, his attitude has changed. A continuation of the unfavourable economic conditions prevailing in Thailand could affect the demand for Blades" products in that country. Consequently, Entertainment Products may not renew its commitment for another three years.

Since Blades generates net cash inflows denominated in baht, a continued depreciation of the baht could adversely affect Blades, as these net inflows would be converted into fewer pounds. Thus, Blades is also considering hedging its baht-denominated inflows.

Because of these concerns, Holt has decided to reassess the importance of forecasting the baht-pound exchange rate. His primary objective is to forecast the baht-pound exchange rate for the next quarter. A secondary objective is to determine which forecasting technique is the most accurate and should be used in future periods. To accomplish this, he has asked you, a financial analyst at Blades, for help in forecasting the baht-pound exchange rate for the next quarter.

Holt is aware of the forecasting techniques available. He has collected some economic data and conducted a preliminary analysis for you to use in your analysis. For example, he has conducted a time series analysis for the exchange rates over numerous quarters. He then used this analysis to forecast the baht's value next quarter. The technical forecast indicates a depreciation of the baht by 6% over the next quarter from the baht's current level of £0.015 to £0.014. He has also conducted a fundamental forecast of the baht-pound exchange rate using historical inflation and interest rate data. The fundamental forecast, however, depends on what happens to Thai interest rates during the next quarter and therefore reflects a probability distribution. There is a 30% chance that Thai interest rates will be such that the baht will depreciate by 2%, a 15% chance that the baht will depreciate by 5%, and a 55% chance that the baht will depreciate by 10%.

Ben Holt has asked you to answer the following questions:

1. Considering both Blades' current practices and future plans, how can it benefit from forecasting the baht-pound exchange rate?

2. Which forecasting technique (i.e., technical, fundamental, or market-based) would be easiest to use in forecasting the future value of the baht? Why?

3. Blades is considering using either current spot rates or available forward rates to forecast the future value of the baht. Available forward rates currently exhibit a large discount. Do you think the spot or the forward rate will yield a better market-based forecast? Why?

4. The current 90-day forward rate for the baht is £0.014. By what percentage is the baht expected to change over the next quarter according to a market-based forecast using the forward rate? What will be the value of the baht in 90 days according to this forecast?

5. Assume that the technical forecast has been more accurate than the market-based forecast in recent weeks. What does this indicate about market efficiency for the baht–pound exchange rate? Do you think this means that technical analysis will always be superior to other forecasting techniques in the future? Why or why not?

6. What is the expected percentage change in the value of the baht during the next quarter based on the fundamental forecast? What is the forecasted value of the baht using this forecast? If the value of the baht 90 days from now turns out to be £0.0147, which forecasting technique is the most accurate? (Use the absolute forecast error as a percentage of the realized value to answer the last part of this question.)

7. Do you think the technique you have identified in question 6 will always be the most accurate? Why or why not?

Small business dilemma
Exchange rate forecasting by the Sports Exports Company

The Sports Exports Company converts euros into British pounds every month. The prevailing spot rate is about 1.45 euros, but there is much uncertainty about the future value of the euro. Jim Logan, owner of the Sports Exports Company, expects that British inflation will rise substantially in the future. In previous years when British inflation was high, the pound depreciated. The prevailing British interest rate is slightly higher than the prevailing euro interest rate. The pound has risen slightly over each of the last several months. Jim wants to forecast the value of the pound for each of the next 20 months.

1. Explain how Jim can use technical forecasting to forecast the future value of the euro. Based on the information provided, do you think that a technical forecast will predict future appreciation or depreciation in the pound?

2. Explain how Jim can use fundamental forecasting to forecast the future value of the euro. Based on the information provided, do you think that a fundamental forecast will predict appreciation or depreciation in the pound?

3. Explain how Jim can use a market-based forecast to forecast the future value of the euro. Do you think the market-based forecast will predict appreciation, depreciation, or no change in the value of the pound?

4. Does it appear that all of the forecasting techniques will lead to the same forecast of the euro's future value? Which technique would you prefer to use in this situation?

CHAPTER 10

MEASURING EXPOSURE TO EXCHANGE RATE FLUCTUATIONS

EXCHANGE RATE RISK CAN be broadly defined as the risk that a company's perform-ance will be affected by exchange rate movements. Multinational corporations (MNCs) closely monitor their operations to determine how they are exposed to various forms of exchange rate risk. Financial managers must understand how to measure the exposure of their MNCs to exchange rate fluctuations so that they can determine whether and how to protect their companies from such exposure.

THE SPECIFIC OBJECTIVES OF THIS CHAPTER ARE TO:

- discuss the relevance of an MNC's exposure to exchange rate risk,
- explain how transaction exposure can be measured,
- explain how economic exposure can be measured, and
- explain how translation exposure can be measured.

IS EXCHANGE RATE RISK RELEVANT?

Some have argued that exchange rate risk is irrelevant. These contentions, in turn, have resulted in counterarguments, as summarized here.

Purchasing power parity argument

One argument for exchange rate irrelevance is that, according to purchasing power parity (PPP) theory, exchange rate movements are just a response to differentials in price changes between countries. Therefore, the exchange rate effect is offset by the change in prices.

EXAMPLE

Hokkaido ltd of Japan denominates its exports to Europe in euros. If the euro weakens by 3% due to purchasing power parity, that implies that European inflation is about 3% higher than Japanese inflation. If European competitors raise their prices in line with European inflation, Hokkaido can increase its euro prices by 3% without losing any customers. Thus, the increase in its price of 3% offsets the 3% reduction in the value of the euro.

PPP does not necessarily hold, however, so the exchange rate will not necessarily change in accordance with the inflation differential between the two countries. Since a perfect offsetting effect is unlikely, the firm's competitive capabilities may indeed be influenced by exchange rate movements. Even if PPP did hold over a very long period of time, this would not comfort managers of MNCs that are focusing on the next quarter or year.

The investor hedge argument

A second argument for exchange rate irrelevance is that investors in MNCs can hedge exchange rate risk on their own. Therefore companies need not concern themselves with currency risk. The investor hedge argument assumes that investors have sufficient information on corporate exposure to exchange rate fluctuations as well as the capabilities to correctly insulate their individual exposure. To the extent that investors prefer that corporations perform the hedging for them, exchange rate exposure is relevant to corporations. An MNC may be able to hedge at a lower cost than individual investors. In addition, it has more information about its exposure and can more effectively hedge its exposure.

Currency diversification argument

Another argument is that if an MNC is well diversified across numerous countries, its value will not be affected by exchange rate movements because of offsetting effects. Correlations between currencies can be high and complete offsetting impossible.

Stakeholder diversification argument

Some critics also argue that if stakeholders (such as creditors or shareholders) are well diversified, they will be somewhat insulated against losses experienced by an MNC due to exchange rate risk. The exact nature of the currency risk of MNC's is not disclosed so protection can only be approximate.

Response from MNCs

Creditors who provide loans to MNCs can experience large losses if the MNCs experience financial problems. Thus, creditors may prefer that the MNCs maintain low exposure to exchange rate risk.

To the extent that MNCs can stabilize their earnings over time by hedging their exchange rate risk, they may also reduce their general operating expenses over time (by avoiding costs of downsizing and restructuring caused by more variable earnings over time). Many MNCs show concern over the need to avoid excessive swings in earnings caused by exchange rate risk and engage in relatively short-term hedging (12 months or less). The following extracts from the annual accounts of selected MNCs gives a flavour of their attitude to currency risk:

> *material transaction foreign exchange exposures are hedged... Exposures are mainly hedged with derivative financial instruments such as forward foreign exchange contracts and foreign exchange options. The majority of financial instruments hedging exchange have a duration of less than a year. The group does not hedge forecasted foreign currency cash flows beyond two years.*

(Nokia Annual Financial Reports 2004, 31)

> *With respect to currency exposure linked to long term assets in foreign currencies, the Company makes an effort to reduce the associated currency exposure by financing in the same currency ... Short term currency exposure is periodically monitored with limits set by the Company's management. The Group's treasury department manages this currency exposure.*

(Total Annual Financial Report, 2004, 173)

> *Foreign exchange risk management. Our principal objective is to reduce the risk to short term profits of exchange rate volatility. Transactional currency exposures that could impact the profit and loss account are hedged, typically using forward purchases or sales of foreign currencies and currency options ...We hedge the majority of our investment in our international subsidiaries via foreign exchange transactions in matching currencies. Our objective is to maintain a low cost of borrowing and hedge against material movements to our balance sheet value ... We translate overseas profits at average exchange rates which we do not currently seek to hedge.*

(Tesco Annual Financial Report, 2005, 7)

These major MNCs have attempted to stabilize their earnings with hedging strategies because they believe exchange rate risk is relevant. All annual reports of major companies contain sections on exchange risk management.

TYPES OF EXPOSURE

As mentioned in the previous chapter, exchange rates cannot be forecasted with perfect accuracy, but the firm can at least measure its exposure to exchange rate fluctuations. If the firm is highly exposed to exchange rate fluctuations, it can consider techniques to reduce its exposure. Such techniques are identified in the following chapter. Before choosing among them, the firm should first measure its degree of exposure.

Exposure to exchange rate fluctuations comes in three forms:

- Transaction exposure
- Economic exposure
- Translation exposure

Each type of exposure will be discussed in turn.

TRANSACTION EXPOSURE

The value of a firm's cash *inflows* received in various currencies will be affected by the respective exchange rates of these currencies when they are converted typically into the home currency. Similarly, the value of a firm's cash *outflows* in various currencies will be dependent on the respective exchange rates of these currencies. The degree to which the value of future cash transactions can be affected by exchange rate fluctuations is referred to as **transaction exposure**.

Transaction exposure can have a substantial impact on a firm's earnings. It is not unusual for a currency to change by as much as 10% in a given year. If an exporter denominates its exports in a foreign currency, a 10% decline in that currency will reduce the dollar value of its receivables by 10%. This effect could possibly eliminate any profits from exporting.

To assess transaction exposure, an MNC needs to: (1) estimate its net cash flows in each currency, and (2) measure the potential impact of the currency exposure.

Estimating "net" cash flows in each currency

MNCs tend to focus on transaction exposure over an upcoming short-term period (such as the next month or the next quarter) for which they can anticipate foreign currency cash flows with reasonable accuracy. Since MNCs commonly have foreign subsidiaries spread around the world, they need an information system that can track their currency positions.

To measure its transaction exposure, an MNC needs to project the consolidated net amount in currency inflows or outflows for all its subsidiaries, categorized by currency. One foreign subsidiary may have inflows of a foreign currency while another has outflows of that same currency. In that case, the MNC's net cash flows of that currency overall may be negligible. If most of the MNC's subsidiaries have future inflows in another currency, however, the net cash flows in that currency could be substantial. Estimating the consolidated net cash flows per currency is a useful first step when assessing an MNC's exposure because it helps to determine the MNC's overall position in each currency.

EXAMPLE

Youth plc, a UK company, conducts its international business in four currencies. Its objective is first to measure its exposure in each currency in the next quarter and then estimate its consolidated cash flows for one quarter ahead, as shown in Exhibit 10.1. For example, Youth expects Swiss franc inflows of 12,000,000 SFr and outflows of 2,000,000 SFr over the next quarter. Thus, Youth expects net inflows of 10,000,000 SFr. Given an expected exchange rate of £0.44 to the Swiss franc at the end of the quarter, it can convert the expected net inflow of Swiss francs into an expected net inflow of £4,400,000 (estimated as 10,000,000 SFr × £0.44).

The same process is used to determine the net cash flows of each of the other three currencies. Notice from the last column of Exhibit 10.1 that the expected net cash flows in three of the currencies are positive, while the net cash flows in Japanese yen are negative (reflecting cash outflows). Thus, Youth will be favourably affected by the

Exhibit 10.1	Consolidated net cash flow assessment of Youth plc

Currency	Total inflow	Total outflow	Net inflow or outflow	Expected exchange rate at end of quarter	Net inflow or outflow as measured in £s
euros	17,000,000 euros	7,000,000 euros	+10,000,000 euros	£0.68	+£6,800,000
Swiss francs	12,000,000 SFr	2,000,000 SFr	+ 10,000,000 SFr	£0.44	+£4,400,000
Japanese yen	200,000,000 yen	900,000,000 yen	−700,000,000 yen	£0.005	−£3,500,000
US dollars	$10,000,000	$7,000,000	+$3,000,000	£0.55	+£ 1,650,000

Exhibit 10.2	Estimating the range of net inflows or outflows for Youth plc

Currency	Expected net inflow or outflow	Range of possible exchange rates at end of quarter (company is 95% confident that the exchange rate will lie between these values)	Range of possible net inflows or outflows in British pounds (based on the range of possible exchange rates)
euros	+10,000,000 euros	£0.65 to £0.71	+£6,500,000 to +£7,100,000
Swiss francs	+ 10,000,000 SFr	£0.40 to £0.48	+£4,000,000 to +£4,800,000
Japanese yen	−700,000,000 yen	£0.004 to £0.006	−£2,800,000 to −£4,200,000
US dollars	+$3,000,000	£0.52 to £0.58	+£1,560,000 to +£1,740,000

appreciation of the euro, US dollar, and Swiss franc. Conversely, it will be adversely affected by the appreciation of the yen.

E X A M P L E

The information in Exhibit 10.1 has been converted into British pounds so that Youth plc can assess the exposure of each currency by using a common measure. Notice that Youth has a smaller pound amount of exposure in yen and US dollars than in the other currencies. However, this does not necessarily mean that Youth will be less affected by these exposures, as will be explained shortly.

Recognize that the net inflows or outflows in each foreign currency and the exchange rates at the end of the period are uncertain. Thus, Youth might develop a range of possible exchange rates for each currency, as shown in Exhibit 10.2, instead of a point estimate. In this case, there is a range of net cash flows in pounds rather than a point estimate. Notice that the range of pound cash flows resulting from Youth's transactions is variable. Where uncertainty is high, there is a wide range of exchange rate estimates and as a consequence a wide range of possible pound values over the next quarter.

Youth plc assessed its net cash flow situation for only one quarter. It could also derive its expected net cash flows for other periods, such as a week or a month. Some MNCs assess their transaction exposure during several periods by applying the methods just described to each period. The further into the future an MNC attempts to measure its transaction exposure, the less accurate will be the measurement due to the greater uncertainty about inflows or outflows in each foreign currency, as well as future exchange rates, over periods further into the future. An MNC's overall exposure can be assessed only after considering each currency's variability and the correlations among currencies. The overall exposure of Youth plc will be assessed after the following discussion of currency variability and correlations.

Measuring the potential impact of the currency exposure

The net cash flows of an MNC can be viewed as streams of cash flows in differing currencies. Their value converted into the home currency will vary due to both business risk and exchange rate risk. The currency values over time are bound to be correlated to some degree. If there is inflation in the UK, for instance, the pound will depreciate against all currencies, not just one currency. Business risk may also be correlated between different countries, recession can affect economic areas made up of many countries. A successful new drug, for instance, will be effective in a range of markets in different countries. Here we look just at currency exposure and assume that the cash flow in the foreign currency is known and it is only the exchange rate that is uncertain. A company needs to be able to assess its overall exposure to exchange rate variation. To do this it needs to be able to combine the individual estimates of variation due to exchange rate changes as outlined in Exhibit 10.2.

One way of combining the risk from different sources to achieve an overall estimate is to see the returns as a portfolio of cash flows and use the model developed in Chapter 3 to assess the overall portfolio risk of the cash flows. Here the absolute form of the model (see Appendix B) is used. Thus the standard deviation in terms of the converted value of the foreign cash flows is used rather than a percentage. So, absolute cash flows are used rather than percentages and weights. Combining the variability of cash flows originating from two different currencies can be achieved as follows:

$$\sigma_p = \sqrt{\sigma_X^2 + \sigma_Y^2 + 2\sigma_X^2 \sigma_Y^2 CORR_{XY}}$$

where:

σ_p	=	the standard deviation of the converted value of foreign cash flows,
$\sigma_{X,Y}^2$	=	the variance in terms of converted net cash flows from currencies X and Y,
$CORR_{XY}$	=	correlation coefficient of monthly percentage changes between currencies X and Y.

In practice companies will want to assess the overall variability from more than just two different currency sources. Here again, approaches from earlier chapters are adapted as outlined in the next sections.

Measurement of currency variability. The standard deviation statistic measures the degree of movement for each currency. In any given period, some currencies clearly fluctuate much more than others. The exact causes of fluctuation and hence standard deviation in a currency are not well understood. Where countries trade extensively with each other, the standard deviation tends to be lower, though other factors may intervene. Also where there are stable economies, variation in the value of the currency tends to be lower, thus: the US dollar–Canadian dollar exchange rate has always been stable; the British pound–US dollar rate has been less stable given recent problems with the dollar (see Chapter 3); the British pound–euro exchange rate has been relatively stable. Currencies in emerging markets can be very unstable. It is also easy to underestimate the variability due to the "peso effect" or "the dog that never barked". Such currencies can have long quiet periods followed by episodes of complete collapse. If measurement is taken during the long quiet period, the fear of collapse will not be recorded in the sample and the expected variability underestimated.

As well as crises being able to change currency variability, a change of government policy or a change of economic policy or external changes such as an oil price rise, or war, can have an effect on measures of variability. It should be remembered that the object of measuring variability is to try to predict *future* variation. In looking at historic periods, it is important to select a time span that represents conditions likely to prevail in the future.

Measurement of currency correlations. The correlation coefficient measures the degree to which two currencies move in relation to each other. As noted in an earlier chapter a correlation is the same as a covariance except that a correlation is mapped on to a scale of −1.0 through to +1.0. The extreme case is perfect positive correlation, which is represented by a correlation coefficient equal to 1.00. In such cases when the change in one currency is a little above its mean, the change in the other currency is also a little above its mean. When one currency change is very much below its mean, the change in the other currency is also very much below its mean. Correlations can also be negative, reflecting an inverse relationship between individual movements, the extreme case being −1.00. When the change in one currency is a little *above* its mean, the change in the other currency is a little *below* its mean. Here they move in opposite directions and offset each other. Negative correlations are obviously useful in reducing risk; but so are poor correlations instead of high correlations. Exhibit 10.5 shows the correlation coefficients (based on daily data) for several currency pairs. It is clear that some currency pairs exhibit a much higher correlation than others. The £:euro and £:SFr are highly correlated whereas the £:dollar and the $:SFr had almost zero correlation over the time in question. As there is no clear understanding as to what causes a correlation, prediction and stability of correlations must be treated with great caution.

Applying currency correlations to net cash flows. The implications of currency correlations for a particular MNC depend on the cash flow characteristics of that MNC.

Positive cash flows in highly correlated currencies result in higher exchange rate risk for the MNC. However, many MNCs have negative net cash flow positions in some currencies; in these situations, the correlations can have different effects on the MNC's exchange rate risk. To measure currency correlations in a relatively practical way we now turn to an extended multicurrency example.

Exhibit 10.3 Variance covariance matrix for MNC cash flows

	Currency A	Currency B	Currency C
Currency A	**Var(A)**	Cov(A,B)	Cov(A,C)
Currency B	Cov(A,B)	**Var(B)**	Cov(B,C)
Currency C	Cov(A,C)	Cov(B,C)	**Var(C)**

Notes:
- The overall variance is the total of all the values in the matrix. The overall standard deviation is the square root of the overall variance.
- Values of (A) (B) (C) (A,B) (A,C) etc. are measured as cash flows converted into the home currency.
- Var(A) etc. is the variance of the converted value of currency A etc.
- Cov(A,B) etc. stands for the covariance between converted cash flows of currency A and B, it can be calculated as $Cov(A,B) = \sigma_A \times \sigma_B \times$ Correlation (A,B). Also, cov(A,B) = cov(B,A) where σ_A is the standard deviation of A, σ_B the standard deviation of B.
- Extending the analysis to more than three currencies simply requires an extension of the pattern of variances and covariances.

Multicurrency exposure. In practice, MNCs will want to value the cash flows from more than just two currencies as in the above model. The extension to a multicurrency position as in Exhibit 10.3 requires the use of a variance covariance model as first developed in Chapter 3 (see also Appendix B) as follows:

As an example, the variance covariance matrix can be applied to Youth plc.

E X A M P L E

The expected cash flows anticipated by Youth plc are given in Exhibit 10.4. The spread of outcomes represent a subjective estimate with 95% confidence that the true value will lie between the limits. If this notion is translated into the statistical 95% confidence interval then the standard deviation can be estimated as there are 3.92 standard deviations in a 95% confidence interval i.e. $1.96 \times 2 = 3.92$. With this assumption, Exhibit 10.4 gives the expected value and calculates the standard deviation of each of the foreign cash flows. The *expected* cash flows are additive, so Youth can expect to receive £9,350,000 at the end of the next month. The standard deviation of the combined receipts are *not* additive and must be calculated using a variance covariance matrix. As a covariance $(A,B) = $ correlation $(A,B) \times \sigma_A \times \sigma_B$, and we have estimates of the standard deviations σ_A and σ_B, the correlation is all that is required to complete the calculation.

The Exhibit in 10.6 simply applies the variance covariance matrix as in 10.3 to Youth plc, using the correlations and standard deviations calculated in 10.4 and 10.5. Note that

Exhibit 10.4 Expected cash flows and standard deviations for Youth plc

Source of foreign cash flow	Expected converted value of cash flow	Subjective estimate of standard deviation of cash flows (see notes below)
euros	+£6,800,000	£153,061
Swiss francs	+£4,400,000	£204,082
Japanese yen	−£3,500,000	£357,143
US dollars	+£1,650,000	£45,918
Total Expected Return	£9,350,000	

Note:
■ Standard deviation estimate assumes a normal distribution about the expected value, hence the 95% confidence interval spread is 1.96 standard deviations above *and* below the mean, therefore:

$$\text{spread} = 1.96 \times 2 \times \text{standard deviation}$$
$$\text{standard deviation} = \text{spread}/(1.96 \times 2)$$
$$\text{e.g. } (£7,100,000 - £6,500,000)/(1.96 \times 2) = £153,061.$$

Exhibit 10.5 Correlations of exchange rate movements of rates with the British pound (daily percentage changes October 2004 to October 2005)

euros	Swiss francs	Japanese yen	US dollars
euros	1	0.76	0.29	0.22
Swiss francs		1	0.27	0.04
Japanese yen			1	0.32
US dollars				1

Exhibit 10.6 Overall cash flow risk faced by Youth plc

	euros	Swiss francs	Japanese yen	US dollars
euros	23,427,669,721	23,740,116,202	−15,852,752,770	1,546,216,100
Swiss francs	23,740,116,202	41,649,462,724	−19,679,343,586	374,841,491
Japanese yen	−15,852,752,770	−19,679,343,586	127,551,122,449	−5,247,773,528
US dollars	1,546,216,100	374,841,491	−5,247,773,528	2,108,462,724

Expected value (from Exhibit 10.5)	£9,350,000
variance of combined cash flows (total of matrix)	£164,499,325,436
Standard deviation of combined cash flows (square root of variance)	£405,585
Standard deviation / expected return =	0.04 or 4%

Notes:

■ The variance of the portfolio is the sum of all the values of the matrix.

■ The matrix is normally calculated using a spreadsheet (see Appendix C).

■ Japanese covariances are negative as they relate to a cash outflow.

■ Calculation: as an example, top left, variance of euros: $153,061^2 = 23,427,669,721$.
 Second column top row, correlation (SFr, euro) $\times \sigma_{SFr} \times \sigma_{euro} = 0.76 \times 153,061 \times 204,082 = 23,740,116,202$

as the Japanese yen is an *outflow* so the correlations are *negative for this example*, this is simply the positive correlation of Exhibit 10.5 multiplied by −1.0.

These calculations involve large numbers and would normally be done using a spreadsheet (see support material for an example). Looking at the calculation overall, Youth plc is expecting a cash inflow of £9,350,000 (Exhibit 10.4) and a standard deviation of £405,585 or 4% of that expected value (Exhibit 10.6). The confidence interval of 1.96 standard deviations implies a spread of outcomes of:

$$£8,555,053 \xleftarrow[-1.96 \times £405,585]{} £9,350,000 \xleftarrow[+1.96 \times £405,585]{} £10,144,947$$

for Youth plc. The decision is whether to hedge or not hedge. That decision depends on whether a potential return of only £8,555,053 is acceptable. The value at risk approach discussed below, elaborates on this decision.

More generally, one can see from the example of Youth plc that:

1. Setting cash outflows against inflows of foreign currency helps to offset the overall currency risk. In simple terms, the negative values in the matrix in 10.6 represent the outflows and lower the overall variance and hence the risk. If the cash flows were predominantly negative, then inflows would offset the outflows and lower the risk.
2. In the case of cash flows that are either all negative or all positive, higher positive correlations implies higher risk and lower correlations lower risk. Again looking at the variance covariance matrix, correlation is part of the covariance calculation and affects all the off diagonal entries. The closer the correlation coefficient is to zero the lower the overall risk.

Exhibit 10.7 summarizes the combined effect.

Exhibit 10.7　Impact of cash flow and correlation conditions on an MNC's exposure

If the MNC's expected cash flow situation is:	And the currencies are:	The MNC's exposure is relatively:
Equal amounts of net inflows in two currencies	Highly correlated	High
Equal amounts of net inflows in two currencies	Slightly positively correlated	Moderate
Equal amounts of net inflows in two currencies	Negatively correlated	Low
A net inflow in one currency and a net outflow of about the same amount in another currency	Highly correlated	Low
A net inflow in one currency and a net outflow of about the same amount in another currency	Slightly positively correlated	Moderate
A net inflow in one currency and a net outflow of about the same amount in another currency	Negatively correlated	High

Exhibit 10.8　Movements of major currencies against the British pound

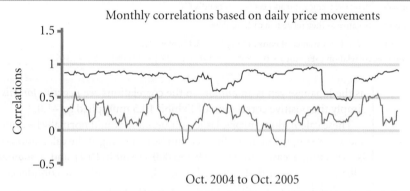

Monthly correlations based on daily price movements

Oct. 2004 to Oct. 2005

Note: The top line represents the correlation of the value of euro and Swiss franc in terms of the British pound. The bottom line the correlation of the value of dollar and euro value in terms of the pound.

Currency correlations over time. Exhibit 10.8 shows the trends of exchange rate movements of various currencies against the pound.

Assessing transaction exposure based on value-at-risk

A related method for assessing exposure is the value-at-risk (VAR) method, which incorporates volatility and currency correlations to determine the potential maximum one-day loss on the value of positions of an MNC that is exposed to exchange rate movements.

EXAMPLE

Celia ltd will receive 10 million Norwegian Krone (NKr) tomorrow as a result of providing consulting services to a Norwegian oil firm. It wants to determine the maximum one-day loss due to a potential decline in the value of the krone, based on a 95% confidence level, i.e. a 5% chance only of the krone being a lower value. It estimates the standard deviation of daily percentage changes of the Noregian krone to be 1.2% over the last 100 days. If these daily percentage changes are normally distributed, the maximum one-day loss is determined by the lower boundary (the left tail) of the probability distribution, which is about 1.65 standard deviations away from the expected percentage change in the krone (this is a one tail distribution as we are only interested in a fall in value, so it is not the more familiar 1.96 standard deviations). Assuming an expected percentage change of 0% (implying no expected change in the krone) during the next day, the maximum one-day loss is:

Maximum one-day loss

$$= E(e_t) - (1.65 \times \sigma_{krone})$$
$$= 0\% - (1.65 \times 1.2\%)$$
$$= -0.0198, \text{ or } -1.98\%$$

Assume the spot rate of the krone is £0.09. The maximum one-day loss of −1.98% implies a krone value of:

Krone based on maximum one-day loss

$$= S \times [1 + E(e_t)]$$
$$= £0.09 \times [1 + (-0.0198)]$$
$$= £0.088218$$

Thus, if the maximum one-day loss occurs, the krone's value will have declined to £0.088218. If Celia has 10 million NKr, this represents an expected value of £900,000 (at £0.09 per krone), so a decline in the krone's value to £0.088218 would result in a loss of 10 million krone × (£0.088218 − £0.09) = −£17,820.

Factors that affect the maximum one-day loss. The maximum one-day loss of a currency is dependent on three factors. First, it is dependent on the expected percentage change in the currency for the next day. If the expected outcome in the previous example is −0.2% instead of 0%, the maximum loss over the one-day period is

Maximum one-day loss

$$= E(e_t) - (1.65 \times \sigma_{krone})$$
$$= -0.2\% - (1.65 \times 1.2\%)$$
$$= -0.0218, \text{ or } -2.18\%$$

Second, the maximum one-day loss is dependent on the confidence level used. A higher confidence level will cause a more pronounced maximum one-day loss, holding other factors constant. If the confidence level in the example is 97.5% instead of 95%, the lower boundary is 1.96 standard deviations from the expected percentage change in the krone. Thus, the maximum one-day loss is

Maximum one-day loss

$$= E(e_t) - (1.96 \times \sigma_{krone})$$
$$= -0\% - (1.96 \times 1.2\%)$$
$$= -0.02352, \text{ or } -2.352\%$$

Third, the maximum one-day loss is dependent on the standard deviation of the daily percentage changes in the currency over a previous period. If the krone's standard deviation in the example is 1% instead of 1.2%, the maximum one-day loss is:

Maximum one-day loss

$$= E(e_t) - (1.65 \times \sigma_{krone})$$
$$= -0\% - (1.65 \times 1.0\%)$$
$$= -0.0165, \text{ or } -1.65\%$$

Applying VAR to longer time horizons. The VAR method can also be used to assess exposure over longer time horizons. To predict monthly standard deviation it seems sensible to take monthly observations, but to predict the standard deviation five years' hence, taking five yearly observations would be impractical, 30 observations would go back 150 years! The following example resolves this problem.

EXAMPLE

Laffe SA (France) expects to receive US dollars in one month for products that it exported. It wants to determine the maximum one-month loss due to a potential decline in the value of the dollar, based on a 95% confidence level. It estimates the standard deviation of the percentage changes of the US dollar to be 2% per month over the last 40 months. If these monthly percentage changes are normally distributed, the maximum one-month loss is determined by the lower boundary (the left tail) of the probability distribution, which is about 1.65 standard deviations away from the expected percentage change in the dollar. Assuming an expected percentage change of −1% during the next month, the maximum one-month loss is:

Maximum one-month loss
$$
\begin{aligned}
&= E(e_t) - (1.65 \times \sigma_\$) \\
&= -1\% - (1.65 \times 2.0\%) \\
&= -0.043, \text{ or } -4.3\%
\end{aligned}
$$

If Laffe is uncomfortable with the magnitude of the potential loss, it can hedge its position as explained in the next chapter.

Laffe is also wondering about the change in the value of the dollar in five years' time as it is thinking of undertaking a long-term contract in the United States. It considers that the last 40 months are representative of the future conditions over the next five years. We could not take 40 observations or even ten observations of five year changes as the exchange rates would reach back to different times. However, given that the last 40 months are seen as representing future conditions, we can easily solve this very practical problem by assuming that the future possible returns are normally distributed and that the currency is weak form efficient and follows a random walk. Note that these assumptions are approximate and err on the side of caution. As a reminder, the formula for calculating long time horizons from shorter periods under these conditions is:

$$
\sigma_t = \sigma_m \times \sqrt{(t/m)}
$$

where:

  t = the longer time period,
  m = shorter time period, both expressed in common time units,
  σ = standard deviation of the foreign currency.

In this case m is one month and t is 60 months (i.e. five years × 12 months) so $t/m = 60$. The five year standard deviation is therefore:

Five year standard deviation $= 2\% \times \sqrt{(60)} = 15.5\%$

If our expected value is no change in the exchange rate over the five years, the maximum five year loss under such conditions is:

Maximum five year loss
$$
\begin{aligned}
&= E(e_t) - (1.65 \times \sigma_\$) \\
&= 0\% - (1.65 \times 15.5\%) \\
&= -0.256, \text{ or } -25.6\%
\end{aligned}
$$

Laffe might want to take measures to protect itself from this potential risk. Longer-term hedging is possible, also it may wish to protect structure its operations to minimize the risk as explained in the next chapter. Note from Chapter 9 that the exchange rate variance increases at slightly less than that predicted by the random walk model.

Applying VAR to transaction exposure of a portfolio. Since MNCs are commonly exposed to more than one currency, they may apply the VAR method to a currency portfolio. Once the standard deviation of the portfolio is calculated (see above) the VAR approach can proceed as for one currency. An example of applying VAR to a two-currency portfolio is provided here.

EXAMPLE

Benny AB, a Swedish exporting firm, expects to receive substantial payments denominated in Indonesian rupiah and Thai baht in one month. Based on today's spot rates, the Swedish krone value of the funds to be received is estimated at 600,000SKr for the rupiah and 400,000SKr for the baht. Thus, Benny is exposed to a currency portfolio weighted 60% in rupiah and 40% in baht. Benny wants to determine the maximum one-month loss due to a potential decline in the value of these currencies, based on a 95% confidence level. Based on data for the last 20 months, it estimates the standard deviation of monthly percentage changes to be 7% for the rupiah and 8% for the baht, and a correlation coefficient of 0.50 between the rupiah and baht. The portfolio's standard deviation is

$$\sigma_P = \sqrt{(0.36)(0.0049)+(0.16)(0.0064)+2(0.60)(0.40)(0.07)(0.08)(0.50)}$$

$$= \text{about } 0.0643 \text{ or about } 6.43\%$$

We assume joint normality, that is to say the combined return of the currencies is normally distributed. The maximum one-month loss of the currency portfolio is determined by the lower boundary (the left tail) of the probability distribution, which is about 1.65 standard deviations away from the expected percentage change in the currency portfolio. Assuming an expected percentage change of 0% for each currency during the next month (and therefore an expected change of zero for the portfolio), the maximum one-month loss is:

Maximum one-month loss of currency portfolio $\quad= E(e_t) - (1.65 \times \sigma_p)$
$\qquad\qquad\qquad\qquad\qquad\qquad\qquad\qquad\quad= 0\% - (1.65 \times 6.43\%)$
$\qquad\qquad\qquad\qquad\qquad\qquad\qquad\qquad\quad= -0.1061, \text{ or } -10.61\%$

Compare this maximum one-month loss to that of the rupiah or the baht:

Maximum one month loss of rupiah $\qquad= 0\% - (1.65 \times 7\%)$
$\qquad\qquad\qquad\qquad\qquad\qquad\qquad\quad= -0.1155 \text{ or } -11.55\%$

Maximum one month loss of baht $\qquad= 0\% - (1.65 \times 8\%)$
$\qquad\qquad\qquad\qquad\qquad\qquad\qquad\quad= -0.132 \text{ or } -13.2\%$

Notice that the maximum one-month loss for the portfolio is less than the maximum loss for either individual currency, which is attributed to the diversification effects. Even if one currency experiences its maximum loss in a given month, the other currency is not likely to experience its maximum loss in that same month. The lower the correlation between the movements in the two currencies, the greater are the diversification benefits.

Given the maximum losses calculated here, Benny AB may decide to hedge its rupiah position, its baht position, neither position, or both positions. The decision of whether to hedge is discussed in the next chapter.

ECONOMIC EXPOSURE

The degree to which a firm's present value of future cash flows can be influenced by exchange rate fluctuations is referred to as **economic exposure** to exchange rates. All types of anticipated future transactions that cause transaction exposure also cause economic exposure because these transactions represent cash flows that can be influenced by exchange rate fluctuations. Thus economic exposure is the general term for the financial effects of exchange rates, it includes transaction exposure and indirect effects on revenues and costs.

EXAMPLE

Intel invoices about 65% of its chip exports in US dollars. Although Intel is not subject to transaction exposure for its dollar-denominated exports, it is subject to economic exposure. If the euro weakens against the dollar, the European importers of those chips from Intel will need more euros to pay for them. These importers are subject to transaction exposure and economic exposure. As their costs of importing the chips increase in response to the weak euro, they may decide to purchase chips from European manufacturers instead. Consequently, Intel's cash flows from its exports will be reduced, even though these exports are invoiced in dollars.

Some of the more common international business transactions that typically subject an MNC's cash flows to economic exposure are listed in the first column of Exhibit 10.9. Transactions listed in the exhibit that require conversion of currencies, and thus reflect transaction exposure, include exports denominated in foreign currency, interest received from foreign investments, imports denominated in foreign currency, and interest owed on foreign loans. The other transactions, which do not require conversion of currencies and therefore do not reflect transaction exposure, are also a form of economic exposure

Exhibit 10.9 Economic exposure to exchange rate fluctuations

Transactions that influence a firm's cash inflows in its home currency	Impact of home currency appreciation on transactions	Impact of home currency depreciation on transactions
Home sales (relative to foreign competition in home markets)	Decrease	Increase
Firm's exports denominated in home currency	Decrease	Increase
Firm's exports denominated in foreign currency	Decrease	Increase
Interest received from foreign investments	Decrease	Increase
Transactions that influence a firms' cash outflows in its home currency		
Firm's imported supplies denominated in home currency	No change	No change
Firm's imported supplies denominated in foreign currency	Decrease	Increase
Interest owed on foreign funds borrowed	Decrease	Increase

because the cash flows resulting from these transactions can be influenced by exchange rate movements. Indirect effects of exchange rates can be greater than the direct effects.

The second and third columns of Exhibit 10.9 indicate how each transaction can be affected by the appreciation and depreciation, respectively, of the firm's home (local) currency. The next sections discuss these effects in turn.

Economic exposure to home currency appreciation

The following discussion is related to the second column of Exhibit 10.9. With regard to the firm's cash inflows, its home sales are expected to decrease if the home currency appreciates because the firm will face increased foreign competition. Home customers will be able to obtain foreign substitute products cheaply with their strengthened currency. The extent of the decline in home sales will depend on the degree of foreign competition in the domestic market.

Cash inflows from exports denominated in the local currency are also likely to be reduced as a result of appreciation in that currency. The reason is that foreign importers will need more of their own currency to pay for these products.

EXAMPLE

Molone plc an Irish firm, arranged to sell software to UK customers. Its sales are invoiced in euros. Recently, the pound depreciated against the euro increasing the price of the software to British customers. Consequently, some British customers shifted their purchases to British software producers, and Molone's sales to Britian declined.

Exports and investment income denominated in the foreign currency are also likely to result in reduced cash inflows, but for a different reason. Inflows received in a currency that has depreciated, will convert to a reduced amount of local currency. Similarly, any interest or dividends received from foreign investments will also convert to a reduced amount if the local currency has strengthened.

With regard to the firm's cash outflows, the cost of imported supplies denominated in the *home* currency (e.g. a UK firm paying pounds for its imports) will not be directly affected by changes in exchange rates. If the home currency appreciates, however, the cost of imported supplies denominated in the *foreign* currency against which the pound is increasing in value, will be reduced. The reduction in cost will apply to all payments in such foreign currencies, including interest payments on borrowings.

Thus, appreciation in the firm's own home currency causes a reduction in both cash inflows and outflows. The impact on a firm's net cash flows will depend on whether the inflow transactions are affected more or less than the outflow transactions. If, for example, the firm is in the exporting business but obtains its supplies and borrows funds

MANAGING FOR VALUE
Philips Electronics exposure to exchange rate risk

Philips Electonics incurs much of its expenses in euros but earns substantial amounts in dollars and dollar-related currencies. When the dollar strengthens, Philips is at an advantage with respect to its US competitors as its euro costs reduce in comparison. When the dollar is relatively weak, the company can potentially lose. To manage this risk the company hedges the dollar value. A decline in the value of the dollar increases the value of its derivatives and therefore offsets the potential exchange rate losses. When the value of the dollar rises, the value of the derivatives falls and hence some of the gain is lost. In this way Philips is able to reduce the impact of its exposure to the dollar.

locally, its inflow transactions will be reduced by a greater degree than its outflow trans-actions. In this case, net cash flows will be reduced. Conversely, cash inflows of a firm concentrating its sales locally with little foreign competition will not be severely reduced by appreciation of the home currency. If such a firm obtains supplies and borrows funds overseas, its outflows will be reduced. Overall, this firm's net cash flows will be enhanced by the appreciation of its home currency.

Economic exposure to home currency depreciation

If the firm's home currency depreciates (see the third column of Exhibit 10.9), its trans-actions will be affected in a manner opposite to the way they are influenced by apprecia-tion. Home sales should increase due to reduced foreign competition, because prices denominated in strong foreign currencies will seem high to the home customers. The firm's exports denominated in the home currency will appear cheap to importers, thereby increasing foreign demand for those products. Even exports denominated in the foreign currency can increase cash flows because a given amount in foreign currency inflows to the firm will convert to a larger amount of the home currency. In addition, interest or dividends from foreign investments will now convert to more of the home currency.

With regard to cash outflows, imported supplies denominated in the home currency will not be directly affected by any change in exchange rates. The cost of imported sup-plies denominated in the foreign currency will rise, however, because more of the weak-ened home currency will be required to obtain the foreign currency needed. Any interest payments paid on financing in foreign currencies will increase.

In general, depreciation of the firm's home currency causes an increase in both cash inflows and outflows. A firm that concentrates on exporting and obtains supplies and borrows funds locally is likely to benefit from a depreciated home currency. This is the case for Philips Electronics and Renault both of whom earn substantial foreign income. Conversely, a firm that concentrates on home sales, has very little foreign competition, and obtains foreign supplies (denominated in foreign currencies), will likely be hurt by a depreciated home currency.

Economic exposure of domestic firms

Although our focus is on the financial management of MNCs, even purely domestic firms are affected by economic exposure.

EXAMPLE   Bridlington ltd is a UK manufacturer of steel that purchases all of its supplies locally and sells all of its steel locally. Because its transactions are solely in the home currency, Bridlington is not subject to transaction exposure. It is subject to economic exposure, however, because it faces foreign competition in its home markets. If the exchange rate of the foreign competitor's invoice currency depreciates against the pound, customers interested in steel products will shift their purchases toward the foreign steel producer. Consequently, demand for Bridlington's steel is likely to decrease, and so will its net cash inflows. Thus, Bridlington is subject to economic exposure even though it is not subject to transaction exposure.

Measuring economic exposure

Since MNCs are affected by economic exposure, they should assess the potential degree of exposure that exists and then determine whether to insulate themselves against it.

Sensitivity of earnings to exchange rates. One method of measuring an MNC's economic exposure is to forecast a range of exchange rates and for each rate develop a subjective prediction of the costs and revenues that make up the income statement for the firm. By reviewing how the earnings forecast in the income statement changes in response to alternative exchange rate scenarios, the firm can assess the influence of currency movements on its earnings and cash flows.

Unlike transaction exposure, the problem of economic exposure is that the original foreign currency amounts are uncertain due to the economic effects of a change in the exchange rate. A common cause of such uncertainty is a change in the volumes of sales and consequent change in the variable costs of production that both occur directly as a result of a change in the exchange rate. Although very evident in practice, it should be remembered that foreign costs are likely to vary with all sales including sales in the home market. Production for an MNC can be anywhere for any market.

Economic exposure therefore has a volume as well as a currency or price effect. A simple set of rules that ensures that both effects are included, is for each scenario to:

1. Calculate the volume changes *in the currency where they occur* – such change is typically as a result of a change in the level of sales. You may need to convert from pounds back to the original currency before applying the volume adjustment.
2. Convert to the reporting (home) currency at the exchange rate for the chosen scenario.

The following example illustrates the problem in context.

EXAMPLE

Mannerton plc is a UK-based MNC that conducts a portion of its business in Europe. Its UK sales are denominated in British pounds, while its European sales are denominated in euros. Its pro forma income statement for next year is shown in Exhibit 10.10 (a). The income statement items are segmented into those for the UK and for Europe. Note that Mannerton undertakes much of the manufacturing of UK goods in Europe. Assume that Mannerton plc desires to assess how its income statement items would be affected by three possible exchange rate scenarios for the euro over the period of concern: (1) £0.60, (2) £0.70, and (3) £0.80. The estimated impact is outlined in Exhibit 10.10 (b) and the implications for the profit and loss account are analyzed in the second, third, and fourth columns of Exhibit 10.10 (c).

Mannerton's sales in the UK are higher when the euro is stronger (Exhibit 10.10 (b)), because European competitors are priced out of the UK market.

The impact of an exchange rate on home sales for any firm will depend on the foreign competition. Historical data can be used to assess how home sales were affected by exchange rates in the past. It may be possible to construct a probability distribution from historic data or historic data may be used to inform an essentially subjective estimate of the effect of exchange rates.

We assume in Exhibit 10.10 (c) that the cost of sales and variable costs vary with volume and that the manufacturing in Europe is for UK as well as European goods. Given this information, Mannerton, plc, can determine how its pro forma statement would be affected by each exchange rate scenario, as shown in Exhibit 10.10 (c). The

EXAMPLE

Exhibit 10.10(a) Revenue and cost estimates based on an exchange rate of £0.60:1 euro: Mannerton plc

	UK Business £ million	European Business Millions of euros
Sales	300.00	40
less Cost of goods sold	50.00	200
Gross profit	250.00	−160
less Operating expenses:		
Fixed	30.00	—
Variable	30.72	—
Total	60.72	—
Earnings before interest and taxes (EBIT)	189.28	−160
less Interest expense	3.00	10
Earnings before taxes (EBT)	186.28	−170

Note:

■ European goods are translated from pounds to euros at a rate of approximately £0.60:1 euro so European sales represents 40m euros × £0.60 = £24 million or about 24/(300+24) = 7.4% of total sales.

Exhibit 10.10(b) Exchange rate scenarios with sales and volume changes

Possible values of the euro	Forecasted UK sales (in millions)	Volume increase over £0.75 rate assume no price changes
£0.60	£300	–
£0.70	304	$1^1/_3$ % (304/300 − 1)
£0.80	307	$2^1/_3$ % (307/300 − 1)

Note:
We assume that Mannerton's sales in Europe are not affected as a result of a more expensive euro.

assumed impact of exchange rates on UK sales is shown in line 1. Line 2 shows the amount in pounds to be received as a result of European sales (after converting the forecasted 40 million euros of European sales into pounds). Line 3 shows the estimated pounds to be received from total sales, which is determined by combining lines 1 and 2. Line 4 shows the cost of goods sold in the United Kingdom which is subject to the volume changes. Line 5 converts the estimated 200 million euro cost of goods sold into pounds after adjusting for volume changes. Line 6 measures the estimated pounds needed to cover the total cost of goods sold, which is determined by combining lines 4 and 5. Line 7 estimates the gross profit in pounds, determined by subtracting line 6 from line 3. Lines 8 through to 10 shows estimated operating expenses, and line 11 subtracts total operating expenses from gross profit to determine earnings before interest and taxes (EBIT). Line 12 estimates the interest expenses paid in the United Kingdom, while line 13 estimates the pounds needed to make interest payments in Europe. Line 14 combines lines 12 and 13 to estimate total pounds needed to make all interest payments. Line 15 shows earnings before taxes (EBT), estimated by subtracting line 14 from line 11.

The effect of exchange rates on Mannerton's revenues and costs can now be reviewed. Exhibit 10.10 (c) illustrates how both UK sales and the pound value of European sales would increase as a result of a stronger euro. Because Mannerton's European cost of

Exhibit 10.10(c) Impact of possible exchange rate movements in earnings of Mannerton plc – see "Mannerton ch10.xls" in support software for a spreadsheet version

Exchange Rate Scenarios			
		£ million	
	Scenario 1	**Scenario 2**	**Scenario 3**
Value of euro	£0.60	£0.70	£0.80
(1) UK sales	300.00	304.00	307.00
(2) European Sales (40 million euros in each scenario)	24.00	28.00	32.00
(3) Total	324.00	332.00	339.00
less Cost of goods sold:			
(4) UK costs	50.00	50.62	51.08
(5) European costs	120.00	141.73	163.46
(6) Total	170.00	192.35	214.54
(7) Gross profit	**154.00**	**139.65**	**124.46**
less Operating expenses:			
(8) UK: Fixed	30.00	30.00	30.00
less (9) UK: Variable costs (by volume of output)	30.72	31.10	31.38
(10) Total	60.72	61.10	61.38
(11) EBIT (earnings before interest and tax)	**93.28**	**78.56**	**63.08**
less Interest expense:			
(12) UK	3.00	3.00	3.00
(13) European 10 million euros	6.00	7.00	8.00
(14) Total	9.00	10.00	11.00
(15) EBT (earnings before tax)	**84.28**	**68.56**	**52.08**

Notes:
Total volume changes compared to Scenario 1: European sales are 0.074 or 7.4 % of total sales in Scenario 1 (see Exhibit 10.10 (a)) and do not change. So using the volume changes from Exhibit 10.10 (b) and taking a weighted average, the volume changes are: Scenario 2: $0.074 \times 0\% + (1-0.074) \times 1^1/3 \% = \mathbf{1.235\%}$; Scenario 3: $0.074 \times 0\% + (1-0.074) \times 2^1/3 \% = \mathbf{2.16\%}$ (0% represents no change to the European sales)

Line 4: UK cost of goods sold is variable and presumed to relate to all sales. Applying the volume changes (above) for Scenarios 2 and 3, $50 + 1.235 \% \times 50 = 50.62$ and $50 + 2.16\% \times 50 = 51.08$

Line 5: European costs are incurred in the production of both UK and European goods. So for scenarios 2 and 3 applying the volume changes above:
Scenario 2: $200 + 200 \times 1.235\% = 202.47$ euros
Scenario 3: $200 + 200 \times 2.16 \% = 204.32$ euros
And the £ valuations are Scenario 1: $200 \times 0.6 = 120$; Scenario 2: $202.47 \times 0.70 = 141.73$; Scenario 3: $204.32 \times 0.80 = 163.46$

Line 9: UK variable costs are subject to the volume changes above, 30.72 as given for Scenario 1, for Scenario 2 it is $30.72 + 1.235\% \times 30.72 = 31.10$ and $30.72 + 2.16\% \times 30.72 = 31.38$ for Scenarios 2 and 3.

goods sold exposure (200 million euro) is much greater than its European sales exposure (40 million euro), a strong euro has a negative overall impact on gross profit. The total amount in pounds needed to make interest payments is also higher when the euro is stronger. In general therefore, Mannerton, plc, would be adversely affected by a stronger euro. By the same argument, the company would be favourably affected by a weaker euro because the reduced value of total revenue would be more than offset by the reduced cost of goods sold and interest expenses.

A general conclusion from this example is that firms with more (less) in foreign costs than in foreign revenue will be unfavourably (favourably) affected by a stronger foreign currency. The precise anticipated impact, however, can be determined only by utilizing the procedure described here or some alternative procedure. The example is based on a one-period time horizon. If firms have developed forecasts of sales, expenses, and exchange rates for several periods ahead, they can assess their economic exposure over time. Their economic exposure will be affected by any change in operating characteristics over time.

Sensitivity of cash flows to exchange rates. A firm's economic exposure to currency movements can also be assessed by applying regression analysis to historical cash flow and exchange rate data as follows:

$$PCF_t = a_0 + a_1 e_t + \mu_t$$

where

PCF_t	=	percentage change in inflation-adjusted cash flows measured in the firm's home currency over period t
e_t	=	percentage change in the exchange rate of the currency over period t
μ_t	=	random error term
a_0	=	intercept
a_1	=	slope coefficient

The regression coefficient a_1, estimated by regression analysis, indicates the sensitivity of PCF_t to e_t. If the firm anticipates no major adjustments in its operating structure, it will expect the sensitivity detected from regression analysis to be somewhat similar in the future.

This regression model can be revised to handle more complex situations. For example, if additional currencies are to be assessed, they can be included in the model as additional independent variables. Each currency's impact is measured by estimating its respective regression coefficient. If an MNC is influenced by numerous currencies, it can measure the sensitivity of PCF_t to an index (or composite) of currencies.

The analysis just described for a single currency can also be extended over separate sub-periods, as the sensitivity of a firm's cash flows to a currency's movements may change over time. This would be indicated by a shift in the regression coefficient, which may occur if the firm's exposure to exchange rate movements changes.

Some MNCs may prefer to use their share price as a proxy for the firm's value and then assess how their share price changes in response to currency movements. Regression analysis could also be applied to this situation by replacing PCF_t with the percentage change in share price in the model specified here.

Some researchers, including Adler and Dumas,[1] suggest the use of regression analysis for this purpose. By assigning share returns as the dependent variable, regression analysis can indicate how the firm's value is sensitive to exchange rate fluctuations.

Some companies may assess the impact of exchange rates on particular corporate characteristics, such as earnings, exports, or sales.

---

1. Michael Adler and Bernard Dumas (1984) "Exposure to Currency Risk: Definition and Measurement", *Financial Management*, 13 (2) (Summer), 41–50.

EXAMPLE

Volkswagen AG engages in what it calls "natural hedging". By producing in Mexico and Brazil, they lower their exchange rate risk. Because the currency of these cash outflows matches better with the currency of Volkswagen's inflows from abroad, they reduce their exposure to exchange rate risk. If revenues fall due to the value of the currency of foreign sales falling against the euro, costs will also fall due to the fact that they are in similarly behaving currencies such as the Brazilian real and the Mexican peso.

TRANSLATION EXPOSURE

An MNC creates its financial statements by consolidating all of its individual subsidiaries' financial statements. A subsidiary's financial statement is normally measured in its local currency. To be consolidated, each subsidiary's financial statement must be translated into the currency of the MNC's parent. Since exchange rates change over time, the translation of the subsidiary's financial statement into a different currency is affected by exchange rate movements. The exposure of the MNC's consolidated financial statements to exchange rate fluctuations is known as **translation exposure**. In particular, subsidiary earnings translated into the reporting currency on the consolidated income statement are subject to changing exchange rates.

The process of consolidating financial statements is governed by accounting standards. In the UK the standard is Financial Reporting Standard 23, in the US the standard is set by the Financial Accounting Standards Board (FASB) in FASB 52. The International Accounting Standard is IAS 21 will represent the common accounting standard to be used by all major reporting countries. To obtain a quote on a stock exchange, companies must produce reports in conformity with the standard of that country. Standards also exist for translating currency derivative contracts, in the UK FRS 39.

Does translation exposure matter?

The relevance of translation exposure can be argued based on a cash flow perspective or a stock price perspective.

Cash flow perspective. Translation of financial statements for consolidated reporting purposes does not by itself affect an MNC's cash flows. The subsidiary earnings do not actually have to be converted into the parent's currency only reported in that currency. If a subsidiary's local currency is currently weak, the earnings could be retained rather than converted and sent to the parent. The earnings could be reinvested in the subsidiary's country if feasible opportunities exist.

An MNC's parent, however, may rely on funding from periodic remittances of earnings by the subsidiary. Even if the subsidiary does not need to remit any earnings today, it will remit earnings at some point in the future. To the extent that today's spot rate serves as a forecast of the spot rate that will exist when earnings are remitted, a weak foreign currency today results in a forecast of a weak exchange rate at the time that the earnings are remitted. In this case, the expected future cash flows are affected by the prevailing weakness of the foreign currency.

Stock price perspective. Many investors tend to use earnings when valuing firms, either by deriving estimates of expected cash flows from previous earnings or by applying a price-earnings (P/E) ratio to expected annual earnings to derive a value per share of stock. Since an MNC's translation exposure affects its consolidated earnings, it can affect the MNC's valuation. If the market is efficient, investors will realize that negative exchange rate adjustments to earnings are not necessarily actual cash flow losses. As long as the information is fully revealed to the market, investors will be able to make an unbiased valuation of the firm. The very open and detailed reports on risk (including currency risk) in the accounts of MNCs, are in recognition of this efficiency argument.

Determinants of translation exposure

Some MNCs are subject to a greater degree of translation exposure than others. An MNC's degree of translation exposure is dependent on the following:

- The proportion of its business conducted by foreign subsidiaries.
- The locations of its foreign subsidiaries, in particular, the volatility of the currency in relation to the home currency.
- The accounting methods that it uses.

Proportion of its business conducted by foreign subsidiaries. The greater the percentage of an MNC's business conducted by its foreign subsidiaries, the larger the percentage of a given financial statement item that is susceptible to translation exposure.

EXAMPLE

Locus ltd and Zeuss ltd each generate about 30% of their sales from foreign countries. However, Locus ltd generates all of its international business by exporting, whereas Zeuss ltd has a large subsidiary in India that generates all of its international business. Locus ltd is not subject to translation exposure (although it is subject to economic exposure), while Zeuss has substantial translation exposure.

Locations of foreign subsidiaries. The locations of the subsidiaries can also influence the degree of translation exposure because the financial statement items of each subsidiary are typically measured by the home currency of the subsidiary's country.

EXAMPLE

Zum ltd (UK) and Canton SA (France) each have one large foreign subsidiary that generates about 30% of their respective sales. However, Zum ltd is subject to a much higher degree of translation exposure because its subsidiary is based in India, and the rupee's value is volatile. In contrast, Canton's subsidiary is based in Switzerland, and the Swiss franc is very stable against the euro.

Accounting methods. An MNC's degree of translation exposure can be greatly affected by the accounting procedures it uses to translate when consolidating financial statement data. The guidelines for UK statement FRS 23 incorporates International Accounting Standard 21. The main points of IAS 21 are:

1. The functional currency of an entity is the currency of the economic environment in which the entity operates. This is normally the local currency where the subsidiary operates. But if the subsidiary is in India but sells and buys in France, the euro would be the functional currency. SAB (Miller) has a main quote on the London Stock Exchange but has the dollar as its functional (reporting) currency.
2. The current exchange rate as of the reporting date is used to translate monetary assets and liabilities of a foreign entity from its functional currency into the reporting or presentation currency. Non-monetary assets and liabilities are translated at the rate current when the transaction was recorded, or when there was a revaluation.
3. The weighted average exchange rate over the relevant period is used to translate revenue, expenses, and gains and losses of a foreign entity from its functional currency

into the reporting currency. The weights reflect the level of sales and expense activity. In some cases, such as depreciation, a simple average may be used.

4. Translated income gains or losses arise mainly due to the different rate applied to when the transaction took place and when the resultant assets and liabilities are reported. Thus, sales recorded at an average rate result in an increase in monetary assets (cash and debtors) recorded at the reporting date – hence the difference. These differences are due to presentation only and are not taken into the current period income or expense.

5. *Realized* income gains or losses due to foreign currency transactions are recorded in current net income, although there are some exceptions.

Under IAS 21, consolidated earnings are sensitive to the functional currency's weighted average exchange rate.

EXAMPLE

A US subsidiary of Provenance plc (a UK company) earned $10,000,000 in Year 1 and $10,000,000 in Year 2. When these earnings are consolidated along with other subsidiary earnings, they are translated into pounds at the weighted average exchange rate in that year. Assume the weighted average exchange rate of the dollar is £0.60 in Year 1 and £0.55 in Year 2. The translated earnings for each reporting period in British pounds are determined as follows:

Reporting period	Local earnings of US subsidiary	Weighted average exchange rate of the dollar over the period	Translated UK pound earnings of the US subsidiary
Year 1	$10,000,000	£0.60	£6,000,000
Year 2	$10,000,000	£0.55	£5,500,000

Notice that even though the subsidiary's earnings in dollars were the same each year, the translated consolidated pound earnings were reduced by £½ million in Year 2. The discrepancy here is due to the change in the weighted average of the British pound exchange rate. The drop in earnings is not the fault of the subsidiary, but rather of the weakened British pound that makes its Year 2 earnings look small (when measured in pounds).

Examples of translation exposure

Consolidated earnings of Black & Decker, Philips, Renault, The Coca-Cola Company, and other MNCs are very sensitive to exchange rates because more than a third of their assets and sales are overseas. Their earnings in foreign countries are reduced when foreign currencies depreciate against the dollar.

In the 2000–01 period, the weakness of the euro caused several US-based MNCs to report lower earnings than they had expected. In September 2000, when DuPont announced that its consolidated earnings would be affected by its translation exposure to the euro, investors responded quickly by dumping DuPont's shares. The stock price of DuPont declined 10% on that day. Other MNCs including Colgate-Palmolive, Gillette, Goodyear, and McDonald's followed with similar announcements.

In 2002 and 2003, however, the euro strengthened, and the consolidated income statements of US-based MNCs improved as a result. IBM stated that in the first quarter of 2003, more than half of its 11% increase in revenue was attributed to favourable translation effects. In that same quarter, translation effects accounted for more than two-thirds of Colgate-Palmolive's 20% increase in revenue.

Conversely, the strong euro and pound affected MNCs in Europe. In 2004 when the pound reached $1.88 and the euro was worth $1.31 difficulties were created for European MNCs, Volkswagen saw its US sales fall by 14%, whereas BMW were less affected as they had a production plant in South Carolina that supplied the US market. Adidas-Salomon were also protected in that the source of the majority of their products was from Asia and they were billed in dollars.

SUMMARY

- MNCs with less risk can obtain funds at lower financing costs. Since they may experience more volatile cash flows because of exchange rate movements, exchange rate risk can affect their financing costs. Thus, MNCs may benefit from hedging exchange rate risk.

- Transaction exposure is the exposure of an MNC's future cash transactions to exchange rate movements. MNCs can measure their transaction exposure by determining their future payables and receivables positions in various currencies, along with the variability levels and correlations of these currencies. From this information, they can assess how their revenue and costs may change in response to various exchange rate scenarios.

- Economic exposure is any exposure of an MNC's cash flows (direct or indirect) to exchange rate movements. MNCs can attempt to measure their economic exposure by determining the extent to which their cash flows will be affected by their exposure to each foreign currency.

- Translation exposure is the exposure of an MNC's consolidated financial statements to exchange rate movements. To measure translation exposure, MNCs can forecast their earnings in each foreign currency and then determine the potential exchange rate movements of each currency relative to their home currency.

CRITICAL DEBATE

Should investors care about an MNC's translation exposure?

Proposition. No. The present value of an MNC's cash flows is based on the cash flows that the parent receives. Any impact of the exchange rates on the financial statements is not important unless cash flows are affected. MNCs should focus their energy on assessing the exposure of their cash flows to exchange rate movements and should not be concerned with the exposure of their financial statements to exchange rate movements. Value is about cash flows, and investors focus on value.

Opposing view. Investors do not have sufficient financial data to derive cash flows. They commonly use earnings as a base, and if earnings are distorted, so will

be their estimates of cash flows. If they underestimate cash flows because of how exchange rates affected the reported earnings, they may underestimate the value of the MNC. Even if the value is corrected in the future once the market realizes how the earnings were distorted, some investors may have sold their stock by the time the correction occurs. Investors should be concerned about an MNC's translation exposure. They should recognize that the earnings of MNCs with large translation exposure may be more distorted than the earnings of MNCs with low translation exposure.

With whom do you agree? As well as looking at translation exposure, you might like to review the concept of market efficiency.

SELF TEST

Answers are provided in Appendix A at the back of the text.

1. Given that shareholders can diversify away an individual firm's exchange rate risk by investing in a variety of firms, why are firms concerned about exchange rate risk?

2. Brume SA (France) considers importing its supplies from either Switzerland (denominated in Swiss francs) or South Africa (denominated in rand) on a monthly basis. The quality is the same for both sources. Once the firm completes the agreement with a supplier, it will be obliged to continue using that supplier for at least three years. Based on existing exchange rates, the euro amount to be paid (including transportation costs) will be the same. The firm has no other exposure to exchange rate movements. Given that the firm prefers to have less exchange rate risk, which alternative is preferable? Explain.

3. Assume your firm Paris SA (France) currently exports to the US on a monthly basis. The goods are priced in dollars. Once material is received from a source, it is quickly used to produce the product in France, and then the product is exported. Currently, you have no other exposure to exchange rate risk. You have a choice of purchasing the material from Canada (denominated in C$), from the US (denominated in dollars), or from within Europe (denominated in euros). The quality and your expected cost are similar across the three sources. Which source is preferable, given that you prefer minimal exchange rate risk?

4. Using the information in the previous question, consider a proposal to price the exports to the US in euros and to use the French source for material. Would this proposal eliminate the exchange rate risk?

5. Assume that the euro is expected to strengthen against the dollar over the next several years. Explain how this will affect the consolidated earnings of Europe-based MNCs with subsidiaries in the US.

QUESTIONS AND APPLICATIONS

1. **Transaction versus economic exposure.** Compare and contrast transaction exposure and economic exposure. Why would an MNC consider examining only its "net" cash flows in each currency when assessing its transaction exposure?

2. **Assessing transaction exposure.** Your employer, a large MNC, has asked you to assess its transaction exposure. Its projected cash flows are as follows for the next year:

Currency	Total inflow	Total outflow	Value of currency
C$ (Canadian dollar)	C$ 3.2m	C$ 2.56m	£0.43
$ (US dollar)	$2m	$1m	£0.60

Provide your assessment as to your firm's degree of transaction exposure (as to whether the exposure is high or low). Explain your answer.

3. **Factors that affect a firm's transaction exposure.** What factors affect a firm's degree of transaction exposure in a particular currency? For each factor, explain the desirable characteristics that would reduce transaction exposure.

4. **Currency correlations.** Kopetsky SA (Poland) has net receivables in several currencies that are highly correlated with each other. What does this imply about the firm's overall degree of transaction exposure? Are currency correlations perfectly stable over time? What does your answer imply about Kopetsky or any other firm using past data on correlations as an indicator for the future?

5. **Currency effects on cash flows.** How should appreciation of a firm's home currency generally affect its cash inflows? How should depreciation of a firm's home currency generally affect its cash outflows?

6. **Transaction exposure.** Fischer ltd exports products from Europe to the US. It obtains supplies and borrows funds locally. How would the appreciation of the dollar be likely to affect its net cash flows? Why?

7. **Exposure of domestic firms.** Why are the cash flows of a purely domestic firm exposed to exchange rate fluctuations?

8. **Measuring economic exposure.** Boston ltd (UK) hires you as a consultant to assess its degree of economic exposure to exchange rate fluctuations. How would you handle this task? Be specific.

9. **Factors that affect a firm's translation exposure.** What factors affect a firm's degree of translation exposure? Explain how each factor influences translation exposure.

10. **Translation exposure.** Consider a period in which the US dollar weakens against the euro. How will this affect the reported earnings of a European-based MNC with US subsidiaries? Consider a period in which the US dollar strengthens against most foreign currencies. How will this affect the reported earnings of a European-based MNC with subsidiaries all over the world?

11. **Transaction exposure.** Aggie plc (UK) produces chemicals. It is a major exporter to the United States, where its main competition is from other European exporters. All of these companies invoice the products in US dollars. Is Aggie's transaction exposure likely to be significantly affected if the euro strengthens or weakens? Explain. If the euro weakens for several years, can you think of any change that might occur in the global chemicals market?

12. **Economic exposure.** Holbein BV (Netherlands) produces hospital equipment. Most of its revenues are in the United States. About half of its expenses are in Philippine pesos (to pay for Philippine materials). Most of Holbein's competition is from US firms that have no international business at all. How will Holbein be affected if the peso strengthens?

13. **Economic exposure.** Enid ltd (UK) produces furniture and has no international business. Its major competitors import most of their furniture from Brazil and then sell it out of retail stores in the United Kingdom. How will Enid be affected if Brazil's currency (the real) strengthens over time?

14. **Economic exposure.** Laurette SA is a French wholesale company that imports expensive high-quality luggage and sells it to retail stores around Europe. Its main competitors also import high-quality luggage and sell it to retail stores. None of these competitors hedge their exposure to exchange rate movements. The treasurer of Laurette told the board of directors that the firm's performance would be more volatile over time if it hedged its exchange rate exposure. How could a firm's cash flows be more stable as a result of such high exposure to exchange rate fluctuations?

15. **PPP and economic exposure.** Boulder plc exports chairs to the US (invoiced in euros) and competes against local US companies. If purchasing power parity exists, why would Boulder not benefit from a stronger dollar?

16. **Measuring changes in economic exposure.** Renault SA measures the sensitivity of its profits to the pound and dollar exchange rate (relative to the euro). Explain how regression analysis could be used for such a task. Identify the expected sign of the regression coefficient if Renault primarily exports to the United States. If Renault established new plants in the United States, how might the regression coefficient on the exchange rate variable change?

17. **Impact of exchange rates on earnings.** Cieplak NV is a Dutch-based MNC that has expanded into Asia. Its Dutch parent exports to some Asian countries, with its exports denominated in the Asian currencies. It also has a large subsidiary in Malaysia that serves that market. Offer at least two reasons related to exposure to exchange rates why Cieplak's earnings were reduced during the Asian crisis.

ADVANCED QUESTIONS

18. **Speculating based on exposure.** During the Asian crisis in 1998, there were rumours that China would weaken its currency (the yuan) against the US dollar and many European currencies. This caused investors to sell stocks in Asian countries such as Japan, Taiwan, and

Singapore. Offer an intuitive explanation for such an effect. What types of Asian firms would have been affected the most?

19. **Dual currency.** In the early 1990s the UK government suggested that what is now called the euro could be used alongside local currencies. How would such a currency arrangement affect MNCs?

20. **Using regression analysis to measure exposure.**
   a. How can a UK company use regression analysis to assess its economic exposure to fluctuations in the euro?
   b. In using regression analysis to assess the sensitivity of cash flows to exchange rate movements, what is the purpose of breaking the database into sub-periods?
   c. Assume the regression coefficient based on assessing economic exposure was much higher in the second sub-period than in the first sub-period. What does this tell you about the firm's degree of economic exposure over time? Why might such results occur?

21. **Transaction exposure.** Crediton plc is a UK firm that exports most of its products to Europe. It historically invoiced its products in euros to accommodate the importers. However, it was adversely affected when the euro weakened against the British pound. Since Crediton did not hedge, its euro receivables were converted into a relatively small amount of pounds. After a few more years of continual concern about possible exchange rate movements, Crediton called its customers and requested that they pay for future orders with pounds instead of euros. At this time, the European pound was valued at £0.81. The customers decided to oblige, since the number of euros to be converted into pounds when importing the goods from Crediton was still slightly smaller than the number of euros that would be needed to buy the product from a European manufacturer. Based on this situation, has transaction exposure changed for Crediton plc? Has economic exposure changed? Explain.

22. **Measuring economic exposure.** Using the following cost and revenue information shown for DeKalb plc (UK) determine how the costs, revenue, and earnings items would be affected by three possible exchange rate scenarios for the New Zealand dollar (NZ$): (1) NZ$ = £0.40, (2) NZ$ = £0.44, and (3) NZ$ = £0.48. (Assume UK sales will be unaffected by the exchange rate.) Assume that NZ$ earnings will be remitted to the UK parent at the end of the period.

Revenue and cost estimates for DeKalb plc		
	UK business £m	New Zealand business NZ$m
Sales	800	800
Cost of goods sold	500	100
Gross profit	300	700
Operating expenses	300	0
Earnings before and taxes interest	0	700
Interest expense	100	0
Earnings before taxes	−100	700

23. **Changes in economic exposure.** Walt Disney World built an amusement park in France that opened in 1992. How do you think this project has affected Disney's economic exposure to exchange rate movements? Think carefully before you give your final answer. There is more than one way in which Disney's cash flows may be affected. Explain.

24. **Lagged effects of exchange rate movements.** Uton plc is an exporter of products to Singapore. It wants to know how its share price is affected by changes in the Singapore dollar's exchange rate. It believes that the impact may occur with a lag of one to three quarters. How could regression analysis be used to assess the impact?

25. **Potential effects if the United Kingdom adopted the euro.** The British pound's interest rate has historically been higher than the euro's interest rate. The United Kingdom has considered adopting the euro as its currency. There have been many arguments about whether it should do so.
   Discuss the likely effects on the UK economy if the United Kingdom were to adopt the euro. For each of the ten statements below, insert either *increase* or *decrease* in the first blank and complete the statement by adding a clear, short explanation (perhaps one to three sentences) as to why

the United Kingdom's adoption of the euro would have that effect.

To help you narrow your focus, follow these guidelines. Do not base your answer on whether the pound would have been stronger than the euro in the future. Also, do not base your answer on an unusual change in economic growth in the United Kingdom or in the euro zone if the euro is adopted.

a. The economic exposure of British firms that are heavy exporters to the euro zone would _____ because …

b. The translation exposure of firms based in the euro zone that have British subsidiaries would _____ because …

c. The economic exposure of US firms that conduct substantial business in the United Kingdom and have no other international business would _____ because…

d. The translation exposure of US firms with British subsidiaries would _____ because …

e. The economic exposure of US firms that export to the United Kingdom and whose only other international business is importing from firms based in the euro zone would _____ because …

f. The discount on the forward rate paid by US firms that periodically use the forward market to hedge payables of British imports would _____ because …

g. The earnings of a foreign exchange department of a British bank that executes foreign exchange transactions desired by its European clients would _____ because …

h. Assume that the Swiss franc is more highly correlated with the British pound than with the euro (the opposite is in fact the case). A US firm has substantial monthly exports to the United Kingdom denominated in the British currency and also has substantial monthly imports of Swiss supplies (denominated in Swiss francs). The economic exposure of this firm would _____ because …

i. Assume that the Swiss franc is more highly correlated with the British pound than with the euro. A US firm has substantial monthly exports to the United Kingdom denominated in the British currency and also has

substantial monthly exports to Switzerland (denominated in Swiss francs). The economic exposure of this firm would _____ because …

j. The British government's reliance on monetary policy (as opposed to fiscal policy) as a means of fine-tuning the economy would _____ because …

26. **Invoicing policy to reduce exposure.** Blackstone is a UK firm that exports its products to Canada. It faces competition from many firms in Canada. Its price to customers in Canada has generally been lower than those of the competitors, primarily because the British pound has been strong. It prices its exports in Canadian dollars, and then converts the Canadian dollar receivables into pounds. All of its expenses are in the the UK and are paid for with pounds. It is concerned about its economic exposure. It considers a change in its pricing policy, in which it will price its products in pounds instead of Canadian dollars. Offer your opinion on why this will or will not significantly reduce its economic exposure.

27. **Exposure of an MNC's subsidiary.** Le Rozier SA is a French firm with a Chinese subsidiary that produces cell phones in China and sells them in Japan. This subsidiary pays its wages and its rent in Chinese yuan, which is presently tied to a basket of major currencies. The cell phones sold to Japan are denominated in Japanese yen. Assume that Le Rozier SA expects that the Chinese yuan will continue to stay fixed against the dollar. The subsidiary's main goal is to generate profits for itself and it reinvests the profits. It does not plan to remit any funds to the French parent.

a. Assume that the Japanese yen strengthens against the euro over time. How would this be expected to affect the profits earned by the Chinese subsidiary?

b. If Le Rozier SA had established its subsidiary in Tokyo, Japan instead of China, would its subsidiary's profits be more exposed or less exposed to exchange rate risk?

c. Why do you think that Le Rozier SA established the subsidiary in China instead of Japan? Assume no major country risk barriers.

d. If the Chinese subsidiary needs to borrow money to finance its expansion and wants to reduce its exchange rate risk, should it borrow euros, Chinese yuan, or Japanese yen?

28. **Daily exchange rates and annual reports.** The following website provides daily exchange rate data for several currencies over the last few months: http://www.oanda.com.
    a. Use this website to assess the volatility of recent daily exchange rates of the euro and US dollar over the last two months. Which currency appears to be more volatile? What are the implications for UK firms with cash flows denominated in US dollars and euros?
    b. The following website contains lists of the worlds top 2000 companies http://www.forbes.com. Select *lists* and then *Forbes 2000*, then select "Sort list by" *country*. Select a Continental European country (Germany, France, Netherlands etc.). By clicking on the

firm's name you will be able to access the homepage of the company and by following the financial links *investor relations* or *annual accounts* find the latest annual report stored as a pdf file (choose another firm if your first selection does not work, the more well-known firms are usually more informative). By searching on the word "risk" review the company's policy on transaction exposure, economic exposure, and translation exposure. Summarize the MNC's exposure based on the comments in the annual report.

DISCUSSION IN THE BOARDROOM

This exercise can be found on the companion website at www.cengage.co.uk/madura_fox.

RUNNING YOUR OWN MNC

This exercise can be found on the companion website at www.cengage.co.uk/madura_fox.

Essays/discussion and articles can be found at the end of Part 3

BLADES PLC CASE STUDY
Assessment of exchange rate exposure

Blades plc is currently exporting roller blades to Thailand and importing certain components needed to manufacture roller blades from that country. Under a fixed contractual agreement, Blades' primary customer in Thailand has committed itself to purchase 180,000 pairs of roller blades annually at a fixed price of 4,594 Thai baht (THB) per pair. Blades is importing rubber and plastic components from various suppliers in Thailand at a cost of approximately THB2,871 per pair, although the exact price (in baht) depends on current market prices. Blades imports materials sufficient to manufacture 72,000 pairs of roller blades from Thailand each year. The decision to import materials from Thailand was reached because rubber and plastic components needed to manufacture Blades' products are inexpensive, yet high quality, in Thailand. Blades has also conducted business with a

Japanese supplier in the past. Although Blades' analysis indicates that the Japanese components are of a lower quality than the Thai components, Blades has occasionally imported components from Japan when the prices were low enough. Currently, Ben Holt, Blades' finance director, is considering importing components from Japan more frequently. Specifically, he would like to reduce Blades' baht exposure by taking advantage of the recently high correlation between the baht and the yen. Since Blades has net inflows denominated in baht and would have outflows denominated in yen, its net transaction exposure would be reduced if these two currencies were highly correlated. If Blades decides to import components from Japan, it would probably import materials sufficient to manufacture 1,700 pairs of roller blades annually at a price of ¥7,440 per pair.

Holt is also contemplating further expansion into foreign countries. Although he would eventually like to establish a subsidiary or acquire an existing business overseas, his immediate focus is on increasing Blades' foreign sales. Holt's primary reason for this plan is that the profit margin from Blades' imports and exports exceeds 25%, while the profit margin from Blades' domestic production is below 15%. Consequently, he believes that further foreign expansion will be beneficial to the company's future.

Though Blades' current exporting and importing practices have been profitable, Ben Holt is contemplating extending Blades' trade relationships to countries in different regions of the world. One reason for this decision is that various Thai roller blade manufacturers have recently established subsidiaries in the United Kingdom. Furthermore, various Thai roller blade manufacturers have recently targeted the UK market by advertising their products over the Internet. As a result of this increased competition from Thailand, Blades is uncertain whether its primary customer in Thailand will renew the current commitment to purchase a fixed number of roller blades annually. The current agreement will terminate in two years. Another reason for engaging in transactions with other, non-Asian, countries is that the Thai baht has depreciated substantially recently, which has somewhat reduced Blades' profit margins. The sale of roller blades to other countries with more stable currencies may increase Blades' profit margins.

While Blades will continue exporting to Thailand under the current agreement for the next two years, it may also export roller blades to Jogs Inc a US retailer. Preliminary negotiations indicate that Jogs would be willing to commit itself to purchase 200,000 pairs of "Speedos", Blades' primary product, for a fixed price of $80 per pair.

Holt is aware that further expansion would increase Blades' exposure to exchange rate fluctuations, but he believes that Blades can supplement its profit margins by expanding. He is vaguely familiar with the different types of exchange rate exposure but has asked you, a financial analyst at Blades plc to help him assess how the contemplated changes would affect Blades' financial position. Among other concerns, Holt is aware that recent economic problems in Thailand have had an effect on Thailand and other Asian countries. Whereas the correlation between Asian currencies such as the Japanese yen and the Thai baht is generally not very high and very unstable, these recent problems have increased the correlation among most Asian currencies. Conversely, the correlation between the British pound and the Asian currencies is quite low. To aid you in your analysis, Holt has provided you with the following data:

Currency	Expected exchange rate	Range of possible exchange rates
US dollar	£0.67	£0.68 to £0.65
Japanese yen	£0.0055	£0.0053 to £0.0058
Thai baht	£0.016	£0.013 to £0.019

Holt has asked you to answer the following questions:

1. What type(s) of exposure (i.e., transaction, economic, or translation exposure) is Blades subject to? Why?
2. Using a spreadsheet, conduct a consolidated net cash flow assessment of Blades plc and estimate the range of net inflows and outflows for Blades for the coming year. Assume that Blades enters into the agreement with Jogs Inc.
3. If Blades does not enter into the agreement with the US firm and continues to export to Thailand and import from Thailand and Japan, do you think the increased correlations between the Japanese yen and the Thai baht will increase or reduce Blades' transaction exposure?
4. Do you think Blades should import components from Japan to reduce its net transaction exposure in the long run? Why or why not?
5. Assuming Blades enters into the agreement with Jogs Inc, how will its overall transaction exposure be affected?
6. Given that Thai roller blade manufacturers located in Thailand have begun targeting the UK roller blade market, how do you think Blades' UK sales were affected by the depreciation of the Thai baht? How do you think its exports to Thailand and its imports from Thailand and Japan were affected by the depreciation?

SMALL BUSINESS DILEMMA
Assessment of exchange rate exposure by the Sports Exports Company

At the current time, the Sports Exports Company (Ireland) is willing to receive payments in British pounds for the monthly exports it sends to the United Kingdom. While all of its receivables are denominated in pounds, it has no payables in pounds or in any other foreign currency. Jim Logan, owner of the Sports Exports Company, wants to assess his firm's exposure to exchange rate risk.

1. Would you describe the exposure of the Sports Exports Company to exchange rate risk as transaction exposure? Economic exposure? Translation exposure?
2. Jim Logan is considering a change in the pricing policy in which the foreign importer must pay in euros, so that Jim will not have to worry about converting pounds to euros every month. If implemented, would this policy eliminate the transaction exposure of the Sports Exports Company? Would it eliminate Sports Exports' economic exposure? Explain.
3. If Jim decides to implement the policy described in the previous question, how would the Sports Exports Company be affected (if at all) by appreciation of the pound? By depreciation of the pound? Would these effects on Sports Exports differ if Jim retained his original policy of pricing the exports in British pounds?

CHAPTER 11

MANAGING TRANSACTION EXPOSURE

RECALL FROM THE PREVIOUS chapter that a multinational corporation (MNC) is exposed to exchange rate fluctuations in three ways: (1) transaction exposure, (2) economic exposure, and (3) translation exposure. This chapter focuses on the management of transaction exposure, while the following chapter focuses on the management of economic and translation exposure. By managing transaction exposure, financial managers may be able to increase cash flows and enhance the value of their MNCs.

THE SPECIFIC OBJECTIVES OF THIS CHAPTER ARE TO:

■ identify the commonly used techniques for hedging transaction exposure,

■ explain how each technique can be used to hedge future payables and receivables,

■ compare the advantages and disadvantages of the different hedging techniques, and

■ suggest other methods of reducing exchange rate risk when hedging techniques are not available.

Transaction exposure

Transaction exposure exists when the anticipated future cash transactions of a firm are affected by exchange rate fluctuations. A UK-based MNC that *purchases* French goods may need euros to buy the goods. Though it may know exactly how many euros it will need, it doesn't know how many British pounds will be needed to be exchanged for those euros. This uncertainty occurs because the exchange rate between euros and the pound fluctuates over time. A UK-based MNC that will be receiving a foreign currency is exposed because it does not know how many pounds it will obtain when it exchanges the foreign currency for pounds, though here again it may know the foreign currency units it expects to receive.

If transaction exposure exists, the firm faces three major tasks. First, it must identify its degree of transaction exposure. Second, it must decide whether to hedge this exposure. Finally, if it decides to hedge part or all of the exposure, it must choose among the various hedging techniques available. Each of these tasks is discussed in turn.

Identifying net transaction exposure

Before an MNC makes any decisions related to hedging, it should identify the individual net transaction exposure on a currency-by-currency basis. The term net here refers to the consolidation of all expected inflows and outflows for a particular time and currency. The management of each subsidiary plays a vital role in reporting its expected inflows and outflows. Then a centralized group consolidates the subsidiary reports to identify, for the MNC as a whole, the expected net positions in each foreign currency during several upcoming periods.

The MNC can identify its exposure by reviewing this consolidation of subsidiary positions. For example, one European subsidiary may have net receivables in dollars three months from now, while a different subsidiary has net payables in dollars. If the dollar appreciates, this will be favourable to the first subsidiary and unfavourable to the second subsidiary. For the MNC as a whole, however, the impact is at least partially offset. Each subsidiary may desire to hedge its net currency position in order to avoid the possible adverse impacts on its performance due to fluctuation in the currency's value. The overall performance of the MNC, however, may already be insulated by the offsetting positions between subsidiaries. Therefore, hedging the position of each individual subsidiary may not be necessary.

Adjusting the invoice policy to manage exposure

In some circumstances, the UK firm may be able to modify its pricing policy to hedge against transaction exposure. That is, the firm may be able to invoice (price) its exports in the same currency that will be needed to pay for imports.

EXAMPLE

Clarkson plc (UK) has continual payables in euros because a German exporter sends goods to Clarkson invoiced in euros. Clarkson also exports products (invoiced in UK pounds) to other corporations in Germany. If Clarkson changes its invoicing policy from pounds to euros, it can use the euro receivables from its exports to pay off its future payables in euros. It is unlikely, however, that Clarkson would be able to: (1) invoice the precise amount of euro receivables to match the euro payables, and (2) perfectly time the inflows and outflows to match each other.

MANAGING FOR VALUE
Centralized management of exposure

Fiat, the Italian auto manufacturer, implemented a centralized system to monitor 421 subsidiaries dispersed among 55 countries. It uses a comprehensive reporting system that keeps track of its aggregate cash flows in each currency. The net inflow or outflow position for each currency can then be assessed to determine whether and how the position should be balanced out.

Cadbury Schweppes plc (UK) seeks to relate its borrowings to the trading cash flows, matching receipts as far as possible with interest payments in that currency.

Renault SA (France) are monitored through Renault's Central Cash Management and Financing Department. The transactions are executed by its specialist subsidiary Renault Financing. Where cash surpluses are reported in weak currencies deposits are made in strong currencies where possible.

DuPont Co uses a centralized approach to determine its net inflow or outflow in each currency. Using this approach, it recently anticipated a net inflow position of more than 1 billion British pounds. It used hedging techniques to hedge almost all of its net exposure in pounds. The hedge generated substantial savings for DuPont because the pound's value had declined by the time the pounds were received.

The important point here is that a hedging decision cannot be made until the firm has determined its exposure to all currencies. The centralized approach enables the MNC to determine its net transaction exposure in each currency so that it can decide whether to hedge these individual positions having considered the complete picture.

Because the matching of inflows and outflows in foreign currencies does have its limitations, an MNC will normally be exposed to some degree of exchange rate risk and, therefore, should consider the various hedging techniques identified next.

TECHNIQUES TO ELIMINATE TRANSACTION EXPOSURE

If an MNC decides to hedge part or all of its transaction exposure, it may select from the following hedging techniques:

- Futures hedge
- Forward hedge
- Money market hedge
- Currency option hedge

Before selecting a hedging technique, MNCs normally compare the cash flows that would be expected from each technique along with the reduced risk associated with the hedging. Hedging techniques can vary over time, as the relative advantages of the various techniques may change over time. Each technique is discussed in turn, with examples provided. After all techniques have been discussed, a comprehensive example illustrates how all the techniques can be compared to determine the appropriate technique to hedge a particular position.

Futures hedge

Currency futures can be used by firms that desire to hedge transaction exposure.

Purchasing currency futures. A firm that buys a currency futures contract is entitled to receive a specified amount in a specified currency for a stated price on a specified date. To hedge a payment on future payables in a foreign currency, the firm may purchase a currency futures contract for the currency it will need in the near future. By holding this contract, it locks in the amount of its home currency needed to make the payment. There is therefore no risk associated with this method of hedging.

Selling currency futures. A firm that sells a currency futures contract is entitled to sell a specified amount in a specified currency for a stated price on a specified date. To hedge the home currency value of future receivables in a foreign currency, the firm may sell a currency futures contract for the currency it will be receiving. Therefore, the firm knows how much of its home currency it will receive after converting the foreign currency receivables into its home currency. By locking in the exchange rate at which it will be able to exchange the foreign currency for its home currency, the firm insulates the value of its future receivables from the fluctuations in the foreign currency's spot rate over time.

Forward hedge

Like futures contracts, forward contracts can be used to lock in the future exchange rate at which an MNC can buy or sell a currency. A forward contract hedge is very similar to a futures contract hedge, except that forward contracts are commonly used for large transactions, whereas futures contracts tend to be used for smaller amounts. Also, MNCs can request forward contracts that specify the exact number of units that they desire, whereas futures contracts represent a standardized number of units for each currency.

Forward contracts are commonly used by large companies that desire to hedge. For example, DuPont Co often has the equivalent of $300 million to $500 million in forward contracts at any one time to cover open currency positions. To recognize the uses of forward contracts, consider the following quotations from the annual reports of MNCs:

> *To manage their foreign exchange risk arising from future commercial transactions and recognised assets and liabilities, companies in the Group use forward contracts … The Group also enters into forward exchange contracts to hedge the foreign exchange exposure in respect of intra-Group loans to and from its overseas subsidiaries…The Group has investments in foreign operations whose net assets are exposed to foreign currency translation risk. The Group finances certain overseas investments in the euro and US dollar through the use of foreign currency borrowings and forward exchange contracts to hedge the net foreign currency investment… The Group does not hedge the foreign exchange risk in respect of the translation of the results of overseas operations into sterling.*
>
> (Gallaher Group plc, Annual Report, 2005, 76)

> *The Group has transactional currency exposures arising from sales or purchases by operating subsidiaries in currencies other than the subsidiaries' functional currency. Under the Group's foreign exchange policy, such transactional exposures are hedged once they are known.*
>
> (GKN plc, Annual Report, 2004, 29)

> *Our most significant foreign currency exposures relate to Japan, Korea, Taiwan and western European countries. We selectively enter into foreign exchange forward and option contracts with durations generally 15 months or less to hedge our exposure to exchange rate risk on foreign source income and purchases. The hedges are scheduled to mature coincident with the timing of the underlying foreign currency commitments and transactions. The objective of these contracts is to neutralize the impact of exchange rate movements on our operating results. We also enter into foreign exchange forward contracts when situations arise where our foreign subsidiaries or Corning enter into lending situations, generally on an intercompany basis, denominated in currencies other than their local currency.*
>
> (Owens Corning Co., Annual Report, 2004, 98)

Forward contracts. Recall that forward contracts are negotiated between the firm and a commercial bank and specify the currency, the exchange rate, and the date of the forward transaction. MNCs that need a foreign currency in the future can negotiate a forward contract to purchase the currency forward, thereby locking in the exchange rate at which they will obtain the currency on a future date. MNCs wishing to sell a foreign currency in the future can negotiate a forward contract to sell the currency forward, thereby locking in the exchange rate at which they sell the currency on a future date.

Forward hedge versus no hedge on payables. Although forward contracts are easy to use for hedging, that does not mean that every exposure to exchange rate movements should be hedged. In some cases, an MNC may prefer not to hedge its exposure to exchange rate movements. It may decide that the gains and losses will even themselves out or it may have offsetting transactions such that its net exposure is low.

Forward rates for hedging Forward rates are available for the euro, US dollar, and Japanese yen for 1-month, 3-month, and 12-month maturities at http://www.marketprices.ft.com/markets/currencies/ab. These forward rates indicate the exchange rates at which positions in these currencies can be hedged for specific time periods.

The decision as to whether to hedge a position with a forward contract or to keep it unhedged can be made by comparing the known result of hedging to the possible results of remaining unhedged.

EXAMPLE

Durham plc (UK) will need $100,000 in 90 days to pay for US imports. Today's 90-day forward rate of the US dollar is £0.55 to the dollar. To assess the future value of the US dollar, Durham may develop a probability distribution, as shown in Exhibit 11.1. This is graphically illustrated in Exhibit 11.2, which breaks down the probability distribution. Both exhibits can be used to determine the probability that a forward hedge will be more costly than no hedge. This is achieved by estimating the expected cost of hedging payables (ECH_p). The expected cost of hedging measures the overall expected additional expenses beyond those incurred without hedging. The expected cost of payables when hedged is measured as:

$$ECH_p = \sum[(CH_p - CNH_p) \times P_i]$$

Where

ECH_p	=	expected cost of hedged payables (see total of column 6)
CH_p	=	cost of payables when hedged for a given possible exchange rate (column 2, Exhibit 11.1)
CNH_p	=	cost of payables *without* hedging for a given possible exchange rate (column 3, Exhibit 11.1)
P_i	=	probability of given exchange rate (column 5, Exhibit 11.1)
$\sum[.]$	=	overall average being the total of the expression in the squared brackets for all possible exchange rates (see total of column 6, Exhibit 11.1)

When the expected cost of hedging payables is negative, this implies that hedging is more favourable than not hedging. The cost of hedging for each exchange rate scenario ($CH_p - CNH_p$) is estimated for each exchange rate scenario (column 4, Exhibit 11.1). While CH_p is certain, CNH_p is uncertain, causing ECH_p to be uncertain.

Exhibit 11.1 Feasibility analysis for hedging

1	2	3	4	5	6
Possible spot rate of dollar in 90 days (pounds to the dollar)	Cost of *hedging* $100,000 using the forward rate of £0.55:$1. (*CH*)	Amount in £s needed to buy *$100,000* if firm remains *unhedged* (column 1 × $100,000 – CNH)	Cost of hedging for each possible spot (column 2 – column 3)	Probability (%) of spot in column 1 occurring (*P$_i$*)	Expected value calculation (column 4 × column 5)
£0.45:$1	£55,000	£45,000	£10,000	5%	£500
0.47	55,000	47,000	8,000	10	800
0.49	55,000	49,000	6,000	15	900
0.51	55,000	51,000	4,000	20	800
0.53	55,000	53,000	2,000	20	400
0.55	55,000	55,000	0	15	0
0.57	55,000	57,000	−2,000	10	-200
0.59	55,000	59,000	−5,000	5	-250
				100%	
		Overall expected cost of hedged payables (*ECH$_p$*)			£2,950

Though Durham plc doesn't know the actual cost of hedging in advance, it can at least use the information in Exhibits 11.1 and 11.2 to decide whether a hedge is feasible. The spread of possible returns is as important as the expected return. An informal review of the range of possible outcomes shows that there is a 15% chance that the cost of hedging will be cheaper than the unhedged position (the last two entries in column 4). But the unhedged position is anticipated to cost less or as much for 85% of the time. So Durham is faced with losing out by an expected £2,950 through hedging with only a 15% chance of the actual cost of hedging being cheaper. Providing that the potential cost of buying the $100,000 at £57,000 and £59,000 is bearable (has no special consequences), Durham would do better not to hedge.

The hedge-versus-no-hedge decision is based on the firm's degree of risk aversion. Firms with a greater desire to avoid risk (in the case of Durham, the possibility of paying £57,000 or £59,000) will hedge their open positions in foreign currencies more often than firms that are less concerned about risk.

If the forward rate is an accurate predictor of the future spot rate, the expected cost of hedging will be zero. This means that although in practice the forward rate will sometimes underestimate or overestimate the future spot rate for any particular period, on average, the actual cost of hedging will be zero over time. On that basis hedging would seem worthwhile because on average it will not be costly and in any one particular period it will avoid possible adverse outcomes. For instance, if the actual rate turned out to be £0.59 to the US dollar in the Durham example, the company will be pleased to have hedged and purchased at the forward price of only £0.55 to the dollar. Even if on average the hedged position proves to be more expensive, the firm might still choose to hedge. If there are potentially very adverse outcomes that could happen in a period, for example a 40% depreciation in the value of foreign currency earnings, then avoiding such outcomes by hedging might be seen as worthwhile. Companies are accountable to shareholders on an annual basis and might well feel uncomfortable with arguing that their losses in one year will be recouped in future years.

Forward hedge versus no hedge on receivables. For firms with exposure in receivables, the expected cost of hedging receivables (ECH_r) can be estimated as with payables namely:

$$ECH_r = \sum [(CNH_r - CH_r) \times P_i]$$

Where

ECH_r = expected cost of hedging receivables
CH_r = receivables when hedged for a given possible exchange rate
CNH_r = receivables when *not* hedged for a given possible exchange rate
P_i = probability of a given exchange rate
$\sum[.]$ = overall average being the total of the expression in the squared brackets for all possible exchange rates

The terms in the "( )" above are reversed so that a positive value means that hedging is more costly than not hedging as with the previous cost equation.

As with payable positions, firms can determine whether to hedge receivable positions by first developing a probability distribution for the future spot rate and then using it to develop a probability distribution of possible outcomes as in Exhibit 11.2. Again the consideration is of the expected value and the range of possible outcomes. An MNC might consider as with payables that a year on year net cost of hedging as opposed to not hedging might be worthwhile if the immediate consequences of exceptionally adverse exchange rate movements can be avoided.

Exhibit 11.2 Comparison of costs of hedging versus no hedge

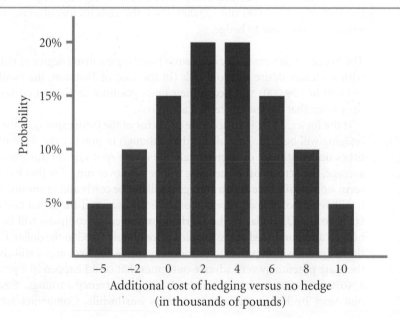

Note that a hedge that avoids an exceptionally adverse exchange rate movement can only do so for a limited period, and that the MNC will eventually have to face the new rate. The value of the hedge is that it will have avoided the immediate effect, but also for the longer term, it will have "bought time" for the MNC to restructure its affairs to lessen the impact of the currency change.

Measuring the cost of hedging with forward contracts. The cost of hedging has been defined here in terms of the currency of the MNC's home country. It can also be expressed as a percentage of the hedged amount. This may be a useful measurement when comparing the cost of hedging for various currencies. A percentage expected cost of hedging applies to all currencies as an easily applicable measure.

The cost of hedging has two uncertainties, first, the exchange rate, and second, the actual amount involved. Generally, firms are reluctant to hedge for estimated amounts and prefer to hedge known payments or receipts. The benefits of hedging for any currency has been positive in some periods and negative in others. In the 2000–01 period, many currencies such as the euro and the pound weakened against the strengthening dollar. As this weakness was not reflected in the forward rate as interest rates were not significantly higher (see covered interest rate arbitrage Chapter 7), the cost to a UK firm of hedging *receivables* in dollars was positive in this period, i.e. it would not have been worthwhile. Whereas the cost of hedging *payables* in dollars was negative and was worthwhile – hedging would have protected against the strengthening dollar required for purchasing. In the 2002–03 period, however, these currencies strengthened against a weakening dollar. The positions were reversed. Hedging receivables in dollars became beneficial and hedging payables not worthwhile.

Money market hedge

A **money market hedge** involves taking a money market position to cover a future payables or receivables position (see Exhibit 11.3). Money market hedges on payables and receivables will be discussed separately.

Money market hedge on payables. If a firm has a payment required in a foreign currency in six months time, it can buy the required amount of foreign currency now and deposit it in a bank account denominated in that currency. In six months time the money can be used to make the payment. In this way, uncertainty due to exchange rate fluctuation can be avoided. Furthermore, the firm will not have to convert the full amount of the payment. Only the discounted value will need to be converted. When the payment is due, the converted sum plus interest will amount to the payment.

EXAMPLE

Ashland plc needs NZ$1,000,000 (New Zealand dollars) in 30 days, and it can earn 6% annualized (0.5% for 30 days) on a New Zealand security over this period. In this case, the amount needed to purchase a New Zealand one-month security is:

$$\text{Deposit amount to hedge NZ\$ payables} = \frac{\text{NZ\$1,000,000}}{(1+0.005)} = \text{NZ\$995,025}$$

Assuming that the New Zealand dollar's spot rate is £0.40, then £398,010 is needed to purchase the New Zealand security (computed as NZ$995,025 × £0.40). In 30 days, the security will mature and provide NZ$1,000,000 to Ashland plc which can then use this money to cover its payables. Regardless of how the New Zealand dollar exchange rate changes over this period, Ashland's investment in the New Zealand security will be able to cover its payables position.

In many cases, MNCs prefer to hedge payables without using their own cash balances. A money market hedge can still be used in this situation, but it requires two money market positions: (1) borrowed funds in the home currency, and (2) a short-term investment in the foreign currency.

EXAMPLE

Reconsider the previous example, in which Ashland plc needs NZ$1,000,000 in 30 days. Recall that £398,010 is needed to obtain the investment of NZ$995,025, which in turn will accumulate to the NZ$1,000,000 needed in 30 days. If Ashland has no excess cash, it can borrow £398,010 from a UK bank and exchange those pounds for New Zealand dollars in order to purchase the New Zealand security.

Because the New Zealand investment will cover Ashland's future payables position, the firm needs to be concerned only about the pounds owed on the loan in 30 days. The firm's money market hedge used to hedge payables can be summarized as follows:

Step 1. Borrow £398,010 from a UK bank; assume a 0.7% interest rate over the 30-day loan period.

Step 2. Convert the £398,010 to NZ$995,025, given the exchange rate of £0.40 per New Zealand dollar.

Step 3. Use the New Zealand dollars to purchase a New Zealand security that offers 0.5% over one month.

Step 4. Pay the NZ$1million with the maturing security.

Step 5. Repay the UK loan in 30 days, plus interest; the amount owed is £400,796 (computed as £398,010 × 1.007).

Note that the cost of the exercise is the interest paid to the UK bank at 0.7% less the effective discount for early payment of 0.5% – a net cost of 0.2% (0.002) or more accurately: 400,000 – 398,010 = £1,990 saved through early payment at a cost of 398,010 × 0.007 = £2,786 a net cost of £796 (1,990 – 2,786). The approximate version is £400,000 × 0.002 = £800.

Money market hedge on receivables. If, in six months" time, a firm expects receivables in a foreign currency, it can hedge this position by borrowing the present value of the receivables now in that foreign currency and converting the amount into the home currency. The foreign receivable can then be left to repay the foreign borrowing and will therefore not be converted.

EXAMPLE

Bakerstown ltd is a UK firm that transports goods to Singapore and expects to receive 400,000 Singapore dollars (S$) in 90 days. To avoid exchange rate uncertainty, Bakerstown can today borrow Singapore dollars and convert the amount into British pounds. The Singapore dollar receipt can then be "left" to repay the Singapore dollar loan in 90 days. Assuming an annualized interest rate of 8%, or 2% over the 90-day period, the amount of Singapore dollars to be borrowed to hedge the future receivables is:

$$\text{Borrowed amount to hedge the S\$ receivables} = \frac{\text{S\$400,000}}{1+0.02}$$

$$= \text{S\$392,157}$$

Exhibit 11.3 Money market hedges

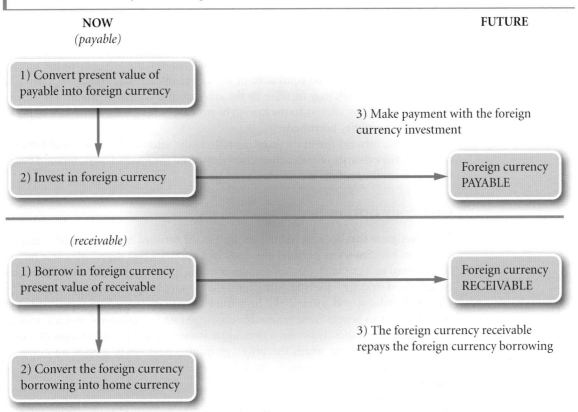

NOW	FUTURE
(payable)	

1) Convert present value of payable into foreign currency

2) Invest in foreign currency

3) Make payment with the foreign currency investment

Foreign currency PAYABLE

(receivable)

1) Borrow in foreign currency present value of receivable

Foreign currency RECEIVABLE

3) The foreign currency receivable repays the foreign currency borrowing

2) Convert the foreign currency borrowing into home currency

If Bakerstown borrows S$392,157 now and converts those Singapore dollars to British pounds, then it can use the receivables of S$400,000 to pay off the Singapore dollar loan in 90 days. Meanwhile, the converted value of the S$392,157 can now be used by Bakerstown. The company will not be affected by any change in the S$ value as it will not be converting the receivables in 90 days. The cost is the interest rate on borrowing in Singapore dollars less the benefit of receiving the converted money early (not shown here).

Hedging with a money market hedge versus a forward hedge. Should an MNC implement a forward contract hedge or a money market hedge? The forward hedge and the money market hedge are directly comparable. Both eliminate currency risk. The forward rate guarantees a rate now for the future point in time; whereas the money market hedge converts the present value of the receivable or payable at the current spot rate. As the effect is the same for the MNC, the cost cannot differ greatly. However, the money market hedge is a drain on the working capital of the MNC. Box 1 in Exhibit 11.3 for receivables and payables both represent an increase in the MNC's short-term liabilities (overdraft) either through borrowing now (the receivable) or paying early (the payable). For this reason the money market hedge is less attractive when considering the strategies in isolation. If the MNC was borrowing anyway, then hedging the receivable by switching borrowing to the currency of the receivable would be an attractive money market hedge. If the MNC had surplus cash, hedging the payable by depositing the present value of the payable in the foreign currency might also be an attractive prospect.

Implications of IRP for the money market hedge. If interest rate parity (IRP) exists, and transaction costs do not exist, the money market hedge will yield the same results as the forward hedge. This is so because, as establised in Chapter 5, the forward premium on the forward rate reflects the interest rate differential between the two currencies. The money market hedge also reflects the interest rate differential. The position for payables and receivables is illustrated in Exhibit 11.3. For payables, the MNC earns the foreign interest rate but "pays" the equivalent of the home interest rate by paying early (for example, the overdraft may increase by the amount of the early payment). For receivables, the MNC pays interest on the foreign borrowing but earns the equivalent of home interest on the money borrowed.

Even if the forward premium generally reflects the interest rate differential between countries, the existence of transaction costs may cause the results from a forward hedge to differ from those of the money market hedge.

Currency option hedge

Firms recognize that hedging techniques such as the forward hedge and money market hedge can backfire when payables are made in a currency that depreciates or a receivables earned in a currency that appreciates over the hedged period. In these situations, an unhedged strategy is likely to outperform the forward hedge or money market hedge. The ideal hedge would insulate the firm from adverse exchange rate movements but allow the firm to benefit from favourable exchange rate movements. Currency options exhibit these attributes. However, a firm must assess whether the advantages of a currency option hedge are worth the price (premium) paid for it. Details on currency options are provided in Chapter 5. The following discussion illustrates how they can be used in hedging.

Hedging payables with currency call options. A currency call option provides the right to buy a specified amount of a particular currency at a specified price (the exercise price) within a given period of time. Yet, unlike a futures or forward contract, the currency call option *does not oblige* its owner to buy the currency at that price. If the spot rate of the currency remains lower than the exercise price throughout the life of the option, the firm can let the option expire and simply purchase the currency at the existing spot rate. On the other hand, if the spot rate of the currency appreciates over time, the call option allows the firm to purchase the currency at the exercise price. That is, the firm owning a call option has locked in a maximum price (the exercise price) to pay for the currency. Yet, it also has the flexibility to let the option expire and obtain the currency at the existing spot rate when the currency is to be sent for payment.

EXAMPLE

Clement ltd (UK) has payables of $100,000 to be made 90 days from now. Assume there is a call option available with an exercise price of £0.62 for one dollar. Assume also that the option premium is £0.03 per unit. For options that cover the 100,000 units, the total premium is £3,000 (100,000 × £0.03). If the cost of a dollar at the time of maturity is below the option strike price of £0.62 per dollar, Clement will not have to exercise the option.

Clement expects the spot rate of the dollar to be either £0.58, £0.63, or £0.66 when the payables are due. The effect of each of these scenarios on Clement's cost of payables is shown in Exhibit 11.4. Columns 1 and 2 simply identify the scenario to be analyzed. Column 3 applies the rule for exercising: where spot is greater than the exercise price it is cheaper to buy using the option, therefore the option is exercised; if the spot is less

Exhibit 11.4 Use of currency call options for hedging the US dollar payables for a UK company (exercise price = £0.62; Premium £0.03)

(1)	(2)	(3)	(4)	(5)	(6) = (5) + (4)	(7) = (6) × $100,000
Scenario	Spot rate when payables are due	Exercise price £0.62 per $ Exercise?	Premium per unit paid on call options	Amount paid per unit when owning call options	Total amount paid per unit (including the premium) when owning call options	£ amount paid for $100,000 when owning a call option on dollars
1	£0.58	NO	£0.03	£0.58	£0.61	£61,000
2	0.63	YES	0.03	0.62	0.65	65,000
3	0.66	YES	0.03	0.62	0.65	65,000

than the exercise price then it is cheaper to buy on the spot market and not exercise the option. Column 4 shows the premium per unit paid on the option, which is the same regardless of the spot rate that occurs when payables are due – note that this is a fixed or sunk cost and should not play a part in our decision whether or not to exercise. Column 5 shows the amount that Clement would pay per dollar for the payables under each scenario, the amount varies depending on whether or not the option is exercised. If Scenario 1 occurs, Clement will let the options expire and purchase dollars on the spot market for £0.58 each. If Scenario 2 occurs Clement will exercise the option because the option price is £0.62 which is less than the spot of £0.63. Similarly for Scenario 3, the spot cost of the dollar is greater than the option cost and therefore it is cheaper to buy dollars using the spot rate. Column 6, which is the sum of Columns 4 and 5, shows the amount paid per unit when the premium paid on the call option is included. Note that the Scenario 2 total cost of £0.65 is higher than the spot rate of £0.63. It is a common error to argue that the option should therefore not have been exercised. The premium, however, is a sunk cost. If the option had not been exercised in Scenario 2, the premium would still have to be paid and therefore the total cost would have been £0.66 (i.e. £0.63 + £0.03), more than if the option had been exercised. Column 7 converts Column 6 into a total dollar cost, based on the $100,000 hedged.

Hedging receivables with currency put options. Like currency call options, currency put options can be a valuable hedging device. A currency put option provides the right to sell a specified amount in a particular currency at a specified price (the exercise price) within a given period of time. Firms can use a currency put option to hedge future receivables in foreign currencies, since it guarantees a certain price (the exercise price) at which the future receivables can be sold. The currency put option *does not oblige* its owner to sell the currency at a specified price. If the existing spot rate of the foreign currency is above the exercise price when the firm receives the foreign currency, the firm can sell the currency received at the spot rate and let the put option expire.

EXAMPLE

Lebenstadt GmbH (Germany), transports goods to Brazil (the real, R$) and expects to receive R$600,000 in about 90 days. Because Lebenstadt is concerned that the Brazilian real may depreciate against the euro, the company is considering purchasing put options to cover its receivables. The Brazilian real put options considered here have an exercise price of 0.32 euros and a premium of 0.02 euros per unit. Lebenstadt anticipates that the spot rate of the real in 90 days will be either 0.30 euros, 0.32 euros or 0.35 euros. The amount to be received as a result of owning currency put options is shown in Exhibit

11.5. Columns 2 through to 6 are on a per-unit basis. Column 7 is determined by multi-plying the per-unit amount received in Column 5 by 600,000 units.

Exhibit 11.5 Use of currency put options to hedge a Brazilian real receivable to be converted to euros (exercise price 0.32 euros for R$1; premium 0.02 euros)

(1)	(2)	(3)	(4)	(5)	(6) = (5) − (4)	(7) = (6) × R$600,000
Scenario	Spot rate when receivables are received	Exercise price 0.32 euros for R$1 Exercise?	Premium per unit paid on Put Options	Amount received per unit when owning Put Options	Net amount received per unit (after paying the premium) when owning Put Options.	Euro amount received for R$600,000 when owning Put options
1	0.30 euros	YES	0.02euros	0.32 euros	0.30 euros	R$180,000
2	0.33	NO	0.02	0.33	0.31	186,000
3	0.35	NO	0.02	0.35	0.33	198,000

Hedging contingent exposure. Currency call options are also useful for hedging contingent exposure, in which an MNC's exposure is contingent on a specific event happening.

James plc (UK) is negotiating to acquire an Australian company in three months, but the deal is contingent on approval by the Australian government. The British pound price that will be paid for the company is dependent on the value of the Australian dollar in three months. James wants to lock in the rate at which it will exchange pounds for Australian dollars because it is worried that the Australian dollar may appreciate. Yet, it does not want to be obliged to obtain Australian dollars unless the acquisition is approved. It can purchase call options on Australian dollars to hedge its contingent exposure.

Comparison of hedging techniques

Each of the hedging techniques is briefly summarized in Exhibit 11.6. When using a futures hedge, forward hedge, or money market hedge, the firm can estimate the funds (denominated in its home currency) that it will need for future payables, or the funds that it will receive after converting foreign currency receivables. Thus, it can compare the costs or revenue and determine which of these hedging techniques is appropriate. In contrast, the cash flow associated with the currency option hedge cannot be determined with certainty because the costs of purchasing payables and the revenue generated from receivables are not known ahead of time. Therefore, firms need to forecast cash flows from the option hedge based on possible exchange rate outcomes.

Comparison of techniques to hedge payables. A comparison of hedging techniques should focus on obtaining a foreign currency at the lowest possible cost. To reinforce an understanding of the hedging techniques, a comprehensive example is provided here.

Exhibit 11.6 Review of techniques for hedging transaction exposure

Hedging Technique	To Hedge Payables	To Hedge Receivables
1. Futures hedge	Purchase a currency futures contract (or contracts) representing the currency and amount related to the payables.	Sell a currency futures contract (or contracts) representing the currency and amount related to the receivables.
2. Forward hedge	Negotiate a forward contract to purchase the amount of foreign currency needed to cover the payables.	Negotiate a forward contract to sell the amount of foreign currency that will be received as a result of the receivables.
3. Money market hedge	Borrow local currency and convert to currency denominating payables. Invest these funds until they are needed to cover the payables.	Borrow the currency denominating the receivables, convert it to the local currency, and invest it. Then pay off the loan with cash inflows from the receivables.
4. Currency option hedge	Purchase a currency call option (or options) representing the currency and amount related to the payables.	Purchase a currency put option (or options) representing the currency and amount related to the receivables.

E X A M P L E

Assume that Bracken ltd (UK) will need $200,000 in 180 days. It considers using: (1) a forward hedge, (2) a money market hedge, (3) an option hedge, or (4) no hedge. Its analysts develop the following information, which can be used to assess the alternative solutions:

- Spot rate of the dollar as of today = £0.60 for $1
- 180-day forward rate of pound as of today = £0.61 for $1

Interest rates are as follows:

	UK	US
180-day deposit rate	4.5%	4%
180-day borrowing rate	5.5%	5%

- A call option on pounds that expires in 180 days has an exercise price of £0.61 and a premium of $0.021.
- A put option on pounds that expires in 180 days has an exercise price of £0.59 and a premium of £0.004.

Bracken forecasts the future spot rate in 180 days as follows:

Possible outcomes	Probability
0.75	1%
0.70	9
0.66	22
0.63	33
0.59	23
0.56	10
0.53	2
	100%

Bracken then assesses the alternative solutions, as shown in Exhibit 11.7. Each alternative is analyzed to estimate the cost of paying in pounds for the payables denominated in dollars.

The cost is known with certainty for the forward rate hedge and money market hedge. When using the call option or leaving the payment unhedged, the cost is dependent on the spot rate 180 days from now. The costs of the four alternatives are illustrated using probability distributions as shown in Exhibit 11.8. A review of this exhibit shows that the money market hedge is superior to the forward hedge by £269 (£122,000 − £121,731) This is a very small amount and the order could be easily reversed by differing tax treatments or further administration cost differences.

Whereas the forward and the money market hedges are offering a single known exchange rate, both the option and the no hedge positions have uncertain outcomes. There is in Exhibit 11.8, an estimated 35% chance that the call option will be cheaper than a money market or forward hedge. A cheaper outcome could be £110,200 (2%) or 116,200 (10%) or 120,200 (23%), the total percentage probability of these outcomes is 35%. There is also a 65% chance that it will cost about 3½% more than the forward hedge at £126,200 (i.e. (126,200 − 122,000) / 122,000 = 0.034 or about 3½%) and similarly so for the money market hedge. For the no hedge position the outcomes and probabilities are: £150,000 (1%), 140,000 (9%), 132,000 (22%), 126,000 (33%), 118,000 (23%), 112,000 (10%), 106,000 (2%). Here again, there is a 35% chance that the cost of the $200,000 payable could be cheaper than either the forward or money market hedges.

There is no clear decision as to which is the best form of hedge. A company may well be prepared to take a 65% chance of paying about 3½% more in order to potentially benefit from the 35% chance of paying less than the cost of a fixed hedge.

Often there are too many transactions in a company to take the decision on a transaction by transaction basis. Company policy will offer overall guidance. As an example, for transactions up to a certain size, the company may as a matter of policy use options; but above a certain size, decide on a transaction by transaction basis whether or not to use forward rates. As well as looking at transactions, a company may well look at its overall exposure across all transactions for selected currencies. Where a certain overall exposure level for each currency is reached, the company may well decide to take out protection against variation in the currency by means of a futures or forward contract.

Comparison of techniques to hedge receivables. If a firm desires to hedge receivables, it will conduct a similar analysis of transaction exposure. From an MNC's perspective, the comparison should focus on selecting a technique that will maximize the dollars to be received as a result of hedging.

E X A M P L E

Haytor plc will receive $300,000 in 180 days. The same information on the spot, forward, and options prices as in the previous example is used to compare hedging techniques and an unhedged strategy. The dollar amounts to be received from each of the four alternatives are compared in Exhibits 11.9 and 11.10.

Haytor can firstly compare the two certain hedges. These are offering exactly the same form of protection, a guaranteed rate but for slightly differing prices. Unless there are tax or transaction costs that account for the difference between the money market hedge and the forward hedge, in this example, the forward hedge appears preferable in that it is offering £3,858 more (i.e. £183,000 − 179,142).

The decision between the forward hedge and the option or no hedge positions is more difficult. In making the decision, as for the payable, the company has to trade off risk for

Exhibit 11.7 Comparison of hedging alternatives for Bracken ltd wishing to purchase $200,000 in 180 days' time (point of comparison is in 180 days' time)

Forward Hedge

To purchase dollars 180 days forward

British pounds needed in 180 days = forward rate of dollar × payables in dollars

$$= £0.61 × \$200,000$$
$$= £122,000$$

Money Market Hedge

Borrow in pounds the present value of the payable, convert to dollars and invest, then allow the investment to pay the payable when due.

$$\text{Amount in dollars that has to be invested} = \frac{\$200,000}{(1 + 0.04)}$$
$$= \$192,308$$

Amount in £s needed to convert into $s for investment = $192,308 × £0.60 = £115,385

Interest and principal owed on £ loan after 180 days = £115,385 × (1 + 0.055) = **£121,731**

Call Option

Exercise price £0.61, premium = £0.021

Possible spot rate in 180 days	Premium per unit paid for option	Exercise option at £0.61 per dollar	Total price (including option premium) paid per unit	Total Price paid for $200,000	Probability
£0.75	£0.021	YES	£0.631	£126,200	1%
0.70	0.021	YES	0.631	126,200	9
0.66	0.021	YES	0.631	126,200	22
0.63	0.021	YES	0.631	126,200	33
0.58	0.021	NO	0.601	120,200	23
0.56	0.021	NO	0.581	116,200	10
0.53	0.021	NO	0.551	110,200	2
			Expected value	123,500	

Remain Unhedged

Possible Spot Rate in 180 days	British pounds needed to pay for $200,000	Probability
£0.75	£150,000	1%
0.70	140,000	9
0.66	132,000	22
0.63	126,000	33
0.58	116,000	23
0.56	112,000	10
0.53	106,000	2
Expected value	124,720	

Exhibit 11.8 British pound cost of dollar denominated payables

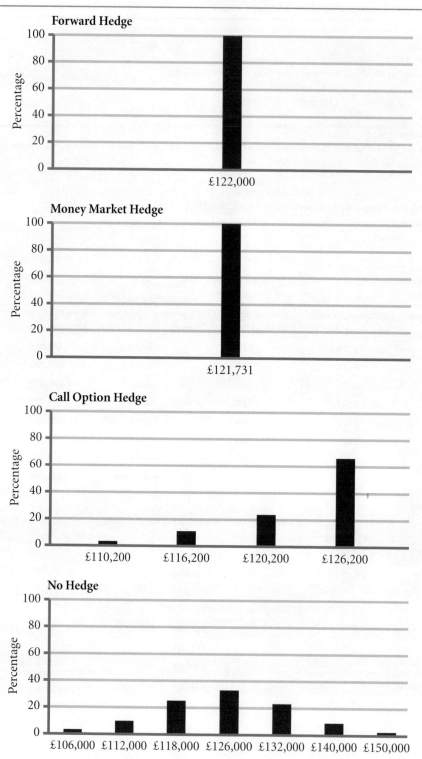

Exhibit 11.9 Comparison of hedging alternatives for Haytor plc wishing to sell $300,000 in 180 days' time

Forward hedge

To sell dollars 180 days forward

British pounds value of dollars in 180 days = forward rate of dollar × receivables in dollars

$$= £0.61 × \$300,000$$

$$= £183,000$$

Money market hedge

Borrow in dollars the present value of the receivable, convert to pounds then allow the dollar receivable to repay the borrowing when due.

Amount in dollars borrowed $= \dfrac{\$300,000}{(1 + 0.05)}$

$$= \$285,714$$

£s received from converting $s = \$285,714 × £0.60 = £171,428

Interest and principal on £s invested 180 days = £171,428 × (1 + 0.045) = **£179,142**

(this is done to compare with other hedges all valued in 180 days' time)

Put option

Exercise price £0.59, premium = £0.004

Possible spot rate in 180 days	Premium per unit paid for option	Exercise option at £0.61 per dollar	Total price (net of option premium) received per unit	Total price received for $300,000	Probability
£0.75	£0.004	NO	£0.746	£223,800	1%
0.70	0.004	NO	0.696	208,800	9
0.66	0.004	NO	0.656	196,800	22
0.63	0.004	NO	0.626	187,800	33
0.58	0.004	YES	0.586	175,800	23
0.56	0.004	YES	0.586	175,800	10
0.53	0.004	YES	0.586	175,800	2
			Expected value	187,830	

Remain Unhedged

Possible spot rate in 180 days	British pounds received from converting $300,000	Probability
£0.75	£225,000	1%
0.70	210,000	9
0.66	198,000	22
0.63	189,000	33
0.58	174,000	23
0.56	168,000	10
0.53	159,000	2
Expected value	187,080	

Exhibit 11.10 British pound value of dollar denominated receivables for Haytor plc wishing to sell $300,000 in 180 days' time

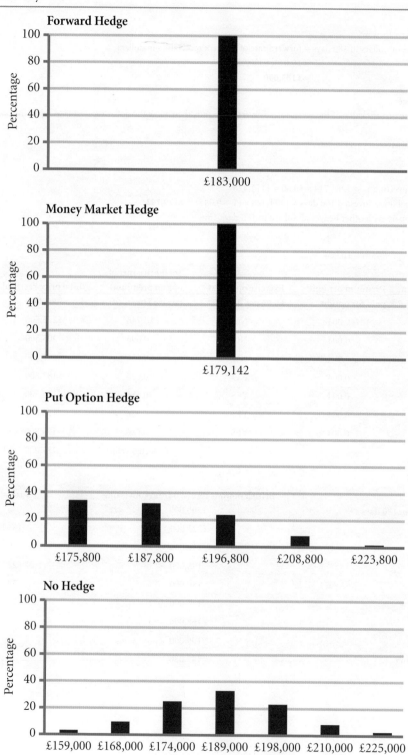

expected return. The expected value of the option is £187,830 (i.e. 223,800 × 1% + 208,800 × 9% + 196,800 × 22% + 187,800 × 33% + 175,800 × 35%). As this is higher than the forward hedge, is it preferable? The expected value is the risk neutral position and one suspects that for a large company the risk neutral position would be preferred as these gains and losses would be relatively small. But, in looking at the possible outcomes of the option, note that there is a 35% chance of the receipts being only £175,800 or some £7,200 less than the forward hedge. A more risk averse company may well rationally choose to avoid this possibility by preferring the forward hedge even though such a choice would mean foregoing a 65% possibility of earning *at least* £4,800 more (£187,800 − 183,000 = £4,800).

The no hedge position has an expected value of £187,080 (i.e. £225,000 × 0.01 + 210,000 × 0.09 + 198,000 × 0.22 + 189,000 × 0.33 + 174,000 × 0.23 + 168,000 × 0.10 + 159,000 × 0.02). Not only is this £750 less than the option, there is a possibility of receiving only £159,000 from the $300,000 receivable. This is some £16,800 less than the lowest option value of £175,800 (i.e. 175,800 − 159,000 = 16,800); at other rates the gain is only £1,200 more than the option position (the difference is due to the cost of the option being $300,000 × £0.004 = £1,200). The option contract looks better than the unhedged position for all but the risk loving company – normally companies are risk averse.

To sum up, the choice is between the option contract and the forward contract. The more risk averse companies will choose the forward contract; the less risk averse the option contract. As with the payable, it should be apparent that making a separate decision for each transaction is not practical. Firms will usually devise a policy guideline to ensure that the decision can be made more simply and consistently across all net cash flows in a currency (receivables less payables). An example of a policy would be to use options for all such cash flows except for very large amounts when a forward contract may be preferable.

Comparing alternative currency option contracts. Although the preceding example assessed only one particular currency option, several alternative currency options are normally available with different exercise prices. When hedging payables, a firm can reduce the premium paid by choosing a call option with a higher exercise price. Of course, the tradeoff is that the maximum amount to be paid for the payables will be higher. Similarly, a firm hedging receivables can reduce the premium paid by choosing a put option with a lower exercise price. In this case, the tradeoff is that the minimum amount to be received for the receivables will be lower. Firms generally compare the available options first to determine which is most appropriate. Then, this particular option is compared to the other hedging techniques to determine which technique (if any) should be used.

When MNCs purchase call options to hedge payables, they can finance their purchase by selling put options. This was outlined in Appendix B Chapter 5.

EXAMPLE

Haytor in the previous example was considering a put option at £0.59 to the dollar exercise price, the spot being £0.60 to the dollar. Although the premium was only £0.004 per dollar, the total cost was $300,000 × 0.004 = £1,200. One way of "paying" for the option is to offer (probably to the seller of the option) a call contract for that same amount ($300,000) at a similar premium. Using the Black Scholes formula (not shown here) such a strike price would be at about £0.67. In other words, to pay for the put, Haytor can sell a call at a strike price of 0.67 for a premium of £0.004 per dollar. The company is now is a position of having to pay £0.004 for the put and receive £0.004 for selling or writing the call. Therefore no net payment need be made. If the counterparty is a bank, then

Exhibit 11.11 Comparison of returns between no hedge (■) and a purchase put and written call position (▨)

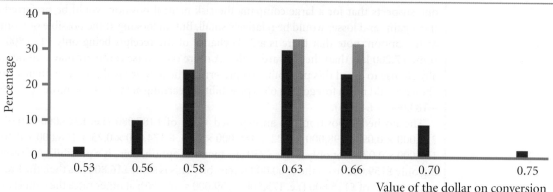

Haytor would be fully compensated by the bank if the value of the dollar falls below £0.59 to the dollar. To pay for this service, if the value of the dollar rises above £0.67, Haytor will in effect have paid the bank the difference out of its converted $300,000 revenue at a higher rate. So Haytor will at most convert the receivables at £0.67 (anything above that amount is paid to the bank). In return Haytor will not receive anything less than £0.59 for each dollar of revenue. Anything less is compensated by the bank. The spread of possible returns for Haytor is shown in Exhibit 11.11.

Note that if the amount were to be a payment, then Haytor could purchase a call and finance the purchase by writing a put option. The graph in Exhibit 11.11 would be similar.

Hedging policies of MNCs

In general, hedging policies vary with the MNC management's degree of risk aversion. An MNC may choose to hedge most of its exposure, to hedge none of its exposure, or to selectively hedge.

Hedging most of the exposure. Some MNCs hedge most of their exposure so that their value is not highly influenced by exchange rates. MNCs that hedge most of their exposure do not necessarily expect that hedging will always be beneficial. In fact, such MNCs may even use some hedges that are likely to result in slightly worse outcomes than no hedges at all, just to avoid the possibility of a major adverse movement in exchange rates. They prefer to know what their future cash inflows or outflows in terms of their home currency will be in each period because this improves corporate planning. A hedge allows the firm to know the future cash flows (in terms of the home currency) that will result from any foreign transactions that have already been negotiated.

Hedging none of the exposure. MNCs that are well diversified across many countries may consider not hedging their exposure. This strategy may be driven by the view that a diversified set of exposures will limit the actual impact that exchange rates will have on the MNC during any period.

LIMITATIONS OF HEDGING

Although hedging transaction exposure is effective and widely practised by multinationals, the protection it offers is limited in a number of ways.

MANAGING FOR VALUE
BP hedging strategy

BP, Philips Electrical and Cadbury Schweppes and a number of other European multinationals have considerable sales in dollars. In the case of BP its major source of revenue, oil, is priced in dollars. Some of the costs as in its Alaskan oil fields will be in dollars as well; so a fall in the price of dollars will not only mean a fall in the value of revenues but also in the case of the Alaskan oil, a fall in the cost of drilling. Exposure will only be for the net earnings in dollars. In other oil fields such as the North Sea and the Middle East revenues will still be in dollars but costs will be in other currencies and a fall in the value of the dollar will directly affect profits. The company is able to protect itself from some of the differences through lags in market adjustment to exchange rate differences. In other words, a contract at an agreed exchange rate will provide protection from short-term changes. The company can also switch to other sup-pliers in reaction to exchange rate changes. Nevertheless there remains a significant exposure to the dollar in particular. To manage its hedging strategy the group has a central coordinating body that takes the net of inflows and outflows of each currency from whatever source throughout the company. BP then uses a range of derivatives such as futures and options as well as swaps, over the counter options and forward contracts to manage the residual exposure. As it is predominantly hedging revenues, it will take out futures contracts to sell dollars and buy put options. Finally, in order to increase the level of dollar payments to set off against the revenues, BP borrows mostly in dollars or will hedge any movement in the borrowed currency against the dollar so that it will be as if the borrowing were in dollars. Interest rates are also mainly swapped into dollars.

Limitation of hedging an uncertain amount

Some international transactions involve an uncertain amount of goods ordered and therefore involve an uncertain transaction amount in a foreign currency. Consequently, an MNC may create a hedge for a larger number of units than it will actually need and hedging can then easily turn into speculating.

EXAMPLE

Recall the previous example on hedging receivables, which assumed that Haytor plc will receive $300,000 in 180 days. Now assume that the receivables amount could actually be much lower. If Haytor sells the $300,000 forward and the receivables amount to only $200,000, it will in effect be speculating on the $100,000 balance. If the future spot value of the dollar is above the forward rate, the company will lose out; if below, it will gain by the difference over $300,000, more than the revenue it was trying to hedge.

This example shows how **over-hedging** (hedging a larger amount in a currency than the actual transaction amount) can adversely affect a firm. A solution to avoid over-hedging is to hedge only known amounts. As a result an MNC will tend to be under-hedged and more exposed to currency fluctuations. In our example, if the future receivables were as low as $200,000, Haytor could hedge this amount. Under these conditions, however, the firm may not have completely hedged its position. If the actual transaction amount turns out to be $300,000 as expected, Haytor will be only partially hedged and will need to sell the extra $100,000 in the spot market.

Firms commonly face this type of dilemma because the precise amount to be received in a foreign currency at the end of a period can be uncertain, especially for firms heavily involved in exporting. Based on this example, it should be clear that most MNCs cannot completely hedge all of their transactions. Nevertheless, by hedging a portion of those transactions that affect them, they can reduce the sensitivity of their cash flows to exchange rate movements.

Limitation of repeated short-term hedging

The continual hedging of repeated transactions that are expected to occur in the near future has limited effectiveness over the long run. A hedge gives the MNC time to rearrange its affairs. If the company still has to purchase goods in an appreciating currency, the higher rate will have to be paid after the period of protection afforded by the hedge. Similarly for a depreciating currency, revenues in a depreciating currency can be protected for the period of the hedge, but beyond that period the revenues will translate at the lower value.

E X A M P L E   Renghini SpA (Italy) is an importer that specializes in importing particular CD players in one large shipment per year and then selling them to retail stores throughout the year. Assume that today's exchange rate of the Japanese yen is worth 0.005 euro and that the CD players are worth ¥60,000, or 300 euro. The forward rate of the yen generally exhibits a small premium over the currency spot. But such a premium may be absorbed by a strengthening yen. Exhibit 11.12 shows the euro value of the yen to be paid by the importer over time. As the spot rate changes, the forward rate will change by a similar amount given that the interest rate differential will not change greatly. Thus, if the spot rate increases by 10% over the year, the forward rate will increase by about the same amount and the importer will pay 10% more for next year's shipment (assuming no change in the yen price quoted by the Japanese exporter).

The use of a one-year forward contract during a strong-yen cycle is preferable to no hedge in this case but will still result in subsequent increases in prices paid by the importer each year under existing conditions. The hedge does however give the importer time to rearrange finances to account for the change in the value of the currency. Renghini may seek to negotiate lower prices. The company may look elsewhere for supplies. Or the company may try to earn revenues in yen. All these actions would help to reduce the financial cost of an appreciating currency.

Exhibit 11.12 The spot and forward rate when a currency is appreciating (a simulation)

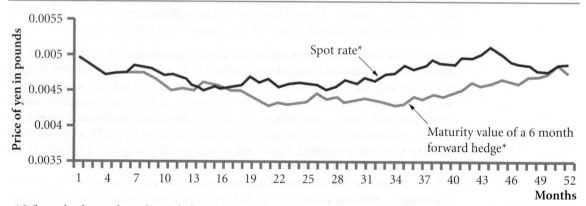

* Where the forward rate line is below the spot line, the forward contract will have been worthwhile for purchasing yen. Otherwise the spot rate will have been cheaper.

If the hedging techniques can be applied to longer-term periods, they can more effectively insulate the firm from exchange rate risk over the long run. That is, Renghini could, as of Time 0, create a hedge for shipments to arrive at the end of each of the next several years. During a strong-yen cycle, such a strategy would save a substantial amount of money but there could be large losses if the yen were to weaken. It should be remembered that hedging is a person to person contract and that any gains by Renghini will be paid for by the losses of the counterparty. In an efficient market, those gains and losses should even out. With this in mind, Renghini should find that the longer-term forward contracts will offer increasingly less attractive rates for purchasing the yen compared to converting at spot. No strategy offers the prospect of certain gains in the financial markets.

HEDGING LONG-TERM TRANSACTION EXPOSURE

Some MNCs are almost certain of having cash flows of a certain amount denominated in foreign currencies for several years and attempt to use long-term hedging. For example, Walt Disney Co hedged its Japanese yen cash flows that will be remitted to the United States (from its Japanese theme park) 20 years ahead.

Firms that can accurately estimate foreign currency payables or receivables that will occur several years from now commonly use three techniques to hedge such long-term transaction exposure:

- Long-term forward contract
- Currency swap
- Parallel loan
- Borrowing policy

Each technique is discussed in turn.

Long-term forward contract

Until recently, **long-term forward contracts**, or long forwards, were seldom used. Today, the long forward is quite popular. Most large international banks routinely quote forward rates for terms of up to five years for British pounds, Canadian dollars, Japanese yen, and Swiss francs. Long forwards are especially attractive to firms that have set up fixed-price exporting or importing contracts over a long period of time and want to protect their cash flow from exchange rate fluctuations.

Like a short-term forward contract, the long forward can be tailored to accommodate the specific needs of the firm. Maturities of up to ten years or more can sometimes be set up for the major currencies. Because a bank trusts that the firm will fulfil its long-term obligation specified in the forward contract, it will consider only very creditworthy customers.

Currency swap

A **currency swap** is a second technique for hedging long-term transaction exposure to exchange rate fluctuations. It can take many forms. One type of currency swap accommodates two firms that have different long-term needs.

E X A M P L E   Bellevue ltd, a UK firm, is hired to build an oil pipeline in Alaska. It expects to receive payment in US dollars in five years when the job is completed. At the same time, a US firm is hired by a UK bank for a long-term consulting project. Assume that this US firm will be paid in British pounds and that much of the payment will occur in five years.

Thus, Bellevue ltd will be receiving US dollars in five years, and the US firm will be receiving pounds in five years. These two firms could arrange a currency swap that allows for an exchange of pounds for dollars in five years at some negotiated exchange rate. In this way, Bellevue can lock in the number of pounds the US dollar earnings will convert to in five years. Likewise, the US firm can lock in the number of US dollars its earnings will convert to in five years. This is an example of disintermediation in the forward market. Instead of going to the forward market and taking out long forwards, the same protection is gained by cutting out the market and having a person to person swap deal.

In practice the other party to swap may well be a bank and is likely to be a member of the International Swaps and Derivatives Association (http://www.isda.org/). Large banks and investment firms employ brokers who act as intermediaries for swaps. Corporations that want to eliminate transaction exposure to specific currencies at certain future dates contact a broker. The role of the broker is to find one firm that needs a currency and another firm that wants to sell the same currency and then match them up. The broker receives a fee for the service. A swap may be non-deliverable, as in the case where one of the currencies is restricted. In such cases payments are made between the two parties to reflect the net effect of an actual swap.

In the above example the swap was of a single amount. Often a firm will be engaged in earning regular amounts in a foreign currency and want some form of protection against exchange rate fluctuations over time. In such cases interest payments on loans can be exchanged. Suppose that in the above example Bellevue, as is normal for businesses, had a number of loans in British pounds requiring regular interest payments in pounds. The company may want to swap the interest payments it makes on its borrowings for dollar interest payments. The dollar payments would not be of the exact amount of dollar earnings nor would they be at the same time. But if the value of the dollar were to decrease, the less expensive interest payments would help offset the decline in value of the dollar earnings. Such a swap arrangement is likely to be cheaper for the company than an equivalent series of long forwards.

Over time, the currency swap obligation may become undesirable to one of the parties involved. The parties can mutually agree to end the arrangement. Or a contract with opposite offsetting terms can be drawn up either with the original counterparty (as a mirror swap) or with another party. As with closing out of futures contracts, if one is due to receive £x and pay £x at the same time, the net liability is zero. Finally, an arrangement similar to daily settlement may require periodic payments from one party to the other to account for exchange rate movements. Such an arrangement will reduce the possibility that one party will not fulfil its obligation by the time the exchange of currencies is supposed to occur.

Parallel loan

A **parallel loan** (or "back-to-back loan") involves an exchange of loans in different currencies between two parties, they then agree to pay the interest on each other's loan and repay the amount borrowed on maturity. A parallel loan is interpreted by accountants as a loan and is therefore recorded on financial statements. At first this behaviour may seem rather odd. The critical aspect of the arrangement is that companies will find themselves paying interest in the currency of their choice which due to circumstances may not be the currency of the original loan (similar to the swap arrangement discussed above). If an MNC finds that it has significant yen revenues and wants to protect itself from changes in the value of the yen, it can do so by arranging more of its payments in yen.

Borrowing policy

For many MNCs the exposure of their profits to exchange rate changes will be predictable as the pattern of trade will not change greatly. For such companies such knowledge will over time guide their choice of currency in which to borrow.

> *The currency disposition of the borrowings is used as a partial, long-term hedge of the cash flows arising from investments overseas and as a hedge against any future business disposal proceeds. Consequently, a large part of the Group's borrowings (after taking account of swaps and forward contracts) are denominated in US Dollars.*
>
> (ICI Annual Report 2005, 22)

ALTERNATIVE HEDGING TECHNIQUES

A firm may engage in a number of less direct hedging activities which reduce exposure to exchange rate fluctuation. Such methods include the following:

- Leading and lagging
- Cross-hedging
- Currency diversification

Each method is discussed in turn.

Leading and lagging

Leading and lagging strategies involve adjusting the timing of a payment request or disbursement to reflect expectations about future currency movements.

EXAMPLE

Zlatica AG is based in Austria and has subsidiaries dispersed around the world. The focus here will be on a subsidiary in the United States that has built up a considerable cash surplus. If Zlatica AG expects that the dollar will soon depreciate against the euro, it may attempt to make the payment before the dollar depreciates. This strategy is referred to as **leading**.

As a second scenario, assume that the US subsidiary expects the dollar to appreciate against the euro soon. In this case, the US subsidiary may attempt to stall its payment until after the dollar appreciates. This strategy is referred to as **lagging**.

MNCs commonly use leading and lagging strategies in countries that allow them. In some countries, the government limits the length of time involved in leading and lagging strategies so that the flow of funds into or out of the country is not disrupted. However, the form of payment is varied and not easy to control. It may include tightening or extending credit, early or late settlement of inter-subsidiary accounts, reinvesting funds or repatriating them, adjusting transfer prices and dividend payments. There are, in short, many ways in which an MNC can minimize the time it has funds denominated in weakening currencies and maximize the length of time funds are held in strengthening currencies.

Cross-hedging

Cross-hedging is a common method of reducing transaction exposure when the currency cannot be hedged.

EXAMPLE

Greeley plc, a UK firm, has payables in zloty (Poland's currency) 90 days from now. Because it is worried that the zloty may appreciate against the British pound, it may desire to hedge this position. If forward contracts and other hedging techniques are not possible for the zloty, Greeley may consider cross-hedging. In this case, it needs to first identify a currency that can be hedged and is highly correlated with the zloty. Greeley notices that the euro has recently been moving in tandem with the zloty and decides to set up a 90-day forward contract on the euro. If the movements in the zloty and euro continue to be highly correlated relative to the British pound (that is, they move in a similar direction and degree against the British pound), then the exchange rate between these two currencies should be somewhat stable over time. By buying euros using a 90-days forward contract, Greeley plc will gain if the euro unexpectedly gains in value, because the euro is highly correlated with the zloty, that gain will help offset the more expensive zloty.

How much protection in euros should Greeley take out? The amount will depend on the relative standard deviations of the euro and zloty and the correlation between the two. If there is perfect correlation and the standard deviations are the same then the same amount in euros as the revenue in zloty should be covered in euro forwards. If the standard deviation of the euro is less than the zloty then more euros will need to be sold forward. The more highly correlated the currencies, the more effective the strategy (see Appendix 11A).

Currency diversification

A third method for reducing transaction exposure is **currency diversification**, which can limit the potential effect of any single currency's movements on the value of an MNC. Some MNCs claim that their exposure to exchange rate movements is significantly reduced because they diversify their business among numerous countries.

The dollar value of future inflows in foreign currencies will be more stable if the foreign currencies received are *not* highly positively correlated. The reason is that lower positive correlations or negative correlations can reduce the variability of the dollar value of all foreign currency inflows. If the foreign currencies were highly correlated with each other, diversifying among them would not be a very effective way to reduce risk. If one of the currencies substantially depreciated, the others would do so as well, given that all these currencies move in tandem.

SUMMARY

■ MNCs use the following techniques to hedge transaction exposure: (1) futures hedge, (2) forward hedge, (3) money market hedge, and (4) currency options hedge.

■ To hedge payables, a futures or forward contract on the foreign currency can be purchased. Alternatively, a money market hedge strategy can be used; in this case, the MNC borrows its home currency and converts the proceeds into the foreign currency that will be needed in the future. Finally, call options on the foreign currency can be purchased.

■ To hedge receivables, a futures or forward contract on the foreign currency can be sold. Alternatively, a money market hedge strategy can be used. In this case, the MNC borrows the foreign currency to be received and converts the funds into its home currency; the loan is to be repaid by the receivables.

Finally, put options on the foreign currency can be purchased.

■ Futures contracts and forward contracts normally yield similar results. Forward contracts are more flexible because they are not standardized. The money market hedge yields results similar to those of the forward hedge if interest rate parity exists. The currency options hedge has an advantage over the other hedging techniques in that the options do not have to be exercised if the MNC would be better off unhedged. A premium must be paid to purchase the currency options, however, so there is a cost for the flexibility they provide.

■ When hedging techniques are not available, there are still some methods of reducing transaction exposure, such as leading and lagging, cross-hedging, and currency diversification.

CRITICAL DEBATE

Should MNCs hedge?

Proposition. No. when investors buy shares in an MNC they are in part wanting to benefit from the currency risk that they believe that the MNC is exposed to when trading. If the dollar is unexpectedly strong, UK investors may choose a company that has strong sales in the US. If the MNC hedges all its dollar revenues the hedging losses caused by a strong dollar will offset any benefits. The shareholder will be deceived. The only benefit of hedging is to protect the jobs and bonuses of current management. The accounts state clearly the effect of exchange rates on profits and the shareholders can use this information to isolate their effect when judging the management. The better quality company reports also tell you the effect on profits of a 1% change in their major trading currencies. Shareholders who want protection from currency changes can invest in bonds or in other shares less sensitive but the market should not be denied this important source of risk.

Opposing view. MNCs should hedge. Foreign exchange variation is not really part of a business. Predicting its value is not in the expertise of companies whose goals are to make profits through providing goods or services or both. It is also the duty of management to maintain steady profits so that shareholders who have to sell their shares because they are faced with unexpected bills, do not have to do so when the companies' price is low due to adverse currency conditions. Dividend payments should also be kept as regular as possible for investors who want steady income. Large exchange rate losses could jeopardize such payments. Shareholders wanting to benefit from a strong dollar could take out futures contracts instead.

With whom do you agree? Examine the arguments on both sides. How well do the points made support the case? Whom do you support and why?

SELF TEST

Answers are provided in Appendix A at the back of the text.

1. Montclair plc, a UK firm, plans to use a money market hedge to hedge its payment of 3,000,000 Australian dollars for Australian goods in one year. The UK interest rate is 7%, while the Australian interest rate is 12%. The spot rate of the Australian dollar is £0.45, while the one-year forward rate is £0.44. Determine the amount of British pounds needed in one year if a money market hedge is used.

2. Using the information in the previous question, would Montclair be better off hedging the payables with a money market hedge or with a forward hedge?

3. Using the information about Montclair from the first question, explain the possible advantage of a currency option hedge over a money market hedge for Montclair. What is a possible disadvantage of the currency option hedge?

4. Sanibel ltd purchases US goods (and pays in dollars) every month. It negotiates a one-month forward contract at the beginning of every month to hedge its payables. Assume the US dollar appreciates consistently over the next five years. Will Sanibel be affected? Explain.

5. Using the information from question 4, suggest how Sanibel ltd could more effectively insulate itself from the possible long-term appreciation of the US dollar.

6. Hopkins ltd transported goods to Switzerland and will receive 2,000,000 Swiss francs in three months. It believes the three-month forward rate will be an accurate forecast of the future spot rate. The three-month forward rate of the Swiss franc is £0.35. A put option is available with an exercise price of £0.36 and a premium of £0.02. Would Hopkins prefer a put option hedge to no hedge? Explain.

QUESTIONS AND APPLICATIONS

1. **Consolidated exposure.** Quincy Corp. estimates the following cash flows in 90 days at its subsidiaries as follows:

Net position in each currency measured in the parent's currency (in 100s of units)			
Subsidiary	Currency 1	Currency 2	Currency 3
A	+200	−300	−100
B	+100	−40	−10
C	−180	+200	−40

Determine the consolidated net exposure of the MNC to each currency.

2. **Money market hedge on receivables.** Assume that Hartland Point ltd (UK) has net receivables of 100,000 Singapore dollars in 90 days. The spot rate of the S$ is £0.32, and the Singapore interest rate is 2% over 90 days. Suggest how the UK firm could implement a money market hedge. Be precise.

3. **Money market hedge on payables.** Assume that Belmont plc has net payables of 200,000 Mexican pesos in 180 days. The Mexican interest rate is 7% over 180 days, and the spot rate of the Mexican peso is £0.05. Suggest how the UK firm could implement a money market hedge. Be precise.

4. **Invoicing strategy.** Assume that Citadel plc purchases some goods in Chile that are denominated in Chilean pesos. It also sells goods denominated in British pounds to some firms in Chile. At the end of each month, it has a large net payables position in Chilean pesos. How can it use an invoicing strategy to reduce this transaction exposure? List any limitations on the effectiveness of this strategy.

5. **Hedging with futures.** Explain how a UK company could hedge net receivables in US dollars with futures contracts. Explain how a UK company could hedge net payables in Japanese yen with futures contracts.

6. **Hedging with forward contracts.** Explain how a UK company could hedge net receivables in Malaysian ringgit with a forward contract.

Explain how a UK company could hedge payables in euros with a forward contract.

7. **The cost of hedging payables.** Assume that Loras (UK) ltd imported goods from New Zealand and needs 100,000 New Zealand dollars 180 days from now. It is trying to determine whether to hedge this position. Loras has developed the following probability distribution for the New Zealand dollar:

Possible value of the New Zealand dollar in 180 days	Probability
£0.40	5%
0.45	10
0.48	30
0.50	30
0.53	20
0.55	5
	100%

The 180-day forward rate of the New Zealand dollar is £0.52. The spot rate of the New Zealand dollar is £0.49. Develop a table showing a feasibility analysis for hedging. That is, determine the possible differences between the costs of hedging versus no hedging. What is the probability that hedging will be more costly to the firm than not hedging? Determine the expected value of the additional cost of hedging.

8. **Benefits of hedging.** If hedging is expected to be more costly than not hedging, why would a firm even consider hedging?

9. **Cost of hedging payables.** Assume that Suffolk plc negotiated a forward contract to purchase $200,000 in 90 days. The 90-day forward rate was £0.70 to the US dollar. The dollars to be purchased were to be used to purchase US supplies. On the day the dollars were delivered in accordance with the forward contract, the spot rate of the British pound was £0.69. What was the cost of hedging the payables for this UK firm compared with not hedging?

10. **Cost of hedging receivables.** Assume that Bentley ltd negotiated a forward contract to sell 100,000 Canadian dollars in one year. The one-year forward rate on the Canadian dollar was £0.55. This strategy was designed to hedge receivables in Canadian dollars. On the day the Canadian

dollars were to be sold in accordance with the forward contract, the spot rate of the Canadian dollar was £0.53. What was the cost of hedging receivables for this UK firm compared with not hedging?

Repeat the question, except assume that the spot rate of the Canadian dollar was £0.60 on the day the Canadian dollars were to be sold in accordance with the forward contract. What was the cost of hedging receivables in this example compared with not hedging?

11. **Forward versus money market hedge on payables.** Assume the following information:

90-day UK interest rate	4%
90-day Malaysian interest rate	3%
90-day forward rate of Malaysian ringgit	£0.25
Spot rate of Malaysian ringgit	£0.2525

Assume that Saint Barnabus plc in the UK will need 300,000 ringgit in 90 days. It wishes to hedge this payables position. Would it be better off using a forward hedge or a money market hedge? Substantiate your answer with estimated costs for each type of hedge.

12. **Forward versus money market hedge on receivables.** Assume the following information:

90-day UK interest rate	8%
90-day US interest rate	9%
90-day forward rate of US dollar	£0.65
Spot rate of US dollar	£0.64

Assume that Riverside ltd (UK) will receive $400,000 in 180 days. Would it be better off using a forward hedge or a money market hedge? Substantiate your answer with estimated revenue for each type of hedge.

13. **Currency options.** Relate the use of currency options to hedging net payables and receivables. That is, when should currency puts be purchased, and when should currency calls be purchased?

Why would Bristol ltd consider hedging net payables or net receivables with currency options rather than forward contracts? What are the disadvantages of hedging with currency options as opposed to forward contracts?

14. **Currency options.** Can Birstall plc determine whether currency options will be more or less

expensive than a forward hedge when considering both hedging techniques to cover net payables in euros? Why or why not?

15. **Long-term hedging.** How can a firm hedge long-term currency positions? Elaborate on each method.

16. **Leading and lagging.** Under what conditions would Zoot ltd's subsidiary consider using a "leading" strategy to reduce transaction exposure? Under what conditions would Zoot's subsidiary consider using a "lagging" strategy to reduce transaction exposure?

17. **Cross-hedging.** Explain how a firm can use cross-hedging to reduce transaction exposure.

18. **Currency diversification.** Explain how a firm can use currency diversification to reduce transaction exposure.

19. **Hedging with put options.** As treasurer of Tupperman (a UK exporter to New Zealand), you must decide how to hedge (if at all) future receivables of 250,000 New Zealand dollars 90 days from now. Put options are available for a premium of £0.02 per unit and an exercise price of £0.24 per New Zealand dollar. The forecasted spot rate of the NZ$ in 90 days follows:

Future spot rate	Probability
£0.25	30%
0.24	50
0.22	20

Given that you hedge your position with options, create a probability distribution for British pounds to be received in 90 days.

20. **Forward hedge.** Would Devon ltd's cost of hedging Australian dollar payables every 90 days have been positive, negative, or about zero on average over a period in which the British pound weakened unexpectedly? What does this imply about the forward rate as an unbiased predictor of the future spot rate? Explain.

21. **Implications of IRP for hedging.** If interest rate parity exists, would a forward hedge be more favourable, equally favourable, or less favourable than a money market hedge on euro payables? Explain.

22. **The cost of hedging.** Would Monkton ltd's cost of hedging Japanese yen receivables have been positive, negative, or about zero on average over a period in which the British pound unexpectedly weakened? Explain.

23. **Forward versus options hedge on payables.** If you are a US importer of Mexican goods and you believe that today's forward rate of the peso is a very accurate estimate of the future spot rate, do you think Mexican peso call options would be a more appropriate hedge than the forward hedge? Explain.

24. **Forward versus options hedge on receivables.** You are an exporter of goods to the United States and you believe that today's forward rate of the US dollar substantially underestimates the future spot rate. Company policy requires you to hedge your dollar receivables in some way. Would a forward hedge or a put option hedge be more appropriate? Explain.

25. **Forward hedging.** Explain how a Malaysian firm can use the forward market to hedge periodic purchases of UK goods denominated in British pounds. Explain how a French firm can use forward contracts to hedge periodic sales of goods sold to the United States that are invoiced in dollars. Explain how a British firm can use the forward market to hedge periodic purchases of Japanese goods denominated in yen.

26. **Continuous hedging.** Cornwall ltd (UK) purchases computer chips denominated in euros on a monthly basis from a Dutch supplier. To hedge its exchange rate risk, this UK firm negotiates a three-month forward contract three months before the next order will arrive. In other words, Cornwall is always covered for the next three monthly shipments. Because Cornwall consistently hedges in this manner, it is not concerned with exchange rate movements. Is Cornwall insulated from exchange rate movements? Explain.

27. **Hedging payables with currency options.** Malibu, inc, is a US company that imports British goods. It plans to use call options to hedge payables of £100,000 in 90 days. Three call options are available that have an expiration date 90 days from now. Fill in the number of dollars needed to pay for the payables (including the option

premium paid) for each option available under each possible scenario.

Scenario	Spot rate of pound 90 days from now	Exercise price = $1.74; premium = $.06	Exercise price = $1.76; premium = $.05	Exercise price = $1.79; premium = $.03
1	$1.65			
2	1.70			
3	1.75			
4	1.80			
5	1.85			

If each of the five scenarios had an equal probability of occurrence, which option would you choose? Explain.

28. **Forward hedging.** Wedco Technology (UK) exports plastics products to the United States. Wedco decided to price its exports in British pounds. Telematics International plc (of Scotland) exports computer network systems to the United States (denominated in US dollars) and other countries. Telematics decided to use hedging techniques such as forward contracts to hedge its exposure.
   a. Does Wedco's strategy of pricing its materials for European customers in dollars avoid economic exposure? Explain.
   b. Explain why the earnings of Telematics International plc were affected by changes in the value of the pound. Why might Telematics leave its exposure unhedged sometimes?

29. **The long-term hedge dilemma.** St Weonards ltd which relies on exporting, denominates its exports in euros and receives euros every month. It expects the euro to weaken over time. St Weonards recognizes the limitation of monthly hedging. It also recognizes that it could remove its transaction exposure by denominating its exports in British pounds but it would still be subject to economic exposure. The long-term hedging techniques are limited, and the firm does not know how many euros it will receive in the future, so it would have difficulty even if a long-term hedging method was available. How can this business realistically reduce its exposure over the long term?

30. **Long-term hedging.** Since Llancloudy ltd conducts much business in Japan, it is likely to have cash flows in yen that will periodically be remitted by its Japanese subsidiary to the UK parent. What are the limitations of hedging these remittances one year in advance over each of the next 20 years? What are the limitations of creating a hedge today that will hedge these remittances over each of the next 20 years?

31. **Hedging during the Asian crisis.** Describe how the Asian crisis could have reduced the cash flows of a UK firm that exported products (denominated in British pounds) to Asian countries. How could a UK firm that exported products (denominated in British pounds) to Asia, and anticipated the Asian crisis before it began, have insulated itself from any currency effects while continuing to export to Asia?

ADVANCED QUESTIONS

32. **Comparison of techniques for hedging receivables.**
   a. Assume that Carbondale ltd expects to receive S$500,000 in one year. The existing spot rate of the Singapore dollar is £0.40. The one-year forward rate of the Singapore dollar is £0.41. Carbondale created a probability distribution for the future spot rate in one year as follows:

Future Spot Rate	Probability
£0.41	20%
0.43	50
0.47	30

Assume that one-year put options on Singapore dollars are available, with an exercise price of £0.40 and a premium of £0.025 per unit. One-year call options on Singapore dollars are available with an exercise price of £0.39 and a premium of £0.02 per unit. Assume the following money market rates:

	UK	Singapore
Deposit rate	8%	5%
Borrowing rate	9	6

Given this information, determine whether a forward hedge, a money market hedge, or a currency options hedge would be most appropriate. Then compare the most appropriate hedge to an unhedged strategy, and decide whether Carbondale should hedge its receivables position.

b. Assume that Black Rod plc expects to need S$1 million in one year. Using any relevant information in part (a) of this question, determine whether a forward hedge, a money market hedge, or a currency options hedge would be most appropriate. Then, compare the most appropriate hedge to an unhedged strategy, and decide whether Black Rod should hedge its payables position.

33. **Comparison of techniques for hedging payables.** SMU ltd has future receivables of 4,000,000 New Zealand dollars (NZ$) in one year. It must decide whether to use options or a money market hedge to hedge this position. Use any of the following information to make the decision. Verify your answer by determining the estimate (or probability distribution) of dollar revenue to be received in one year for each type of hedge.

Spot rate of NZ$	£0.36	
One-year call option	Exercise price = £0.33; premium = £0.046	
One-year put option	Exercise price = £0.35; premium = £0.02	
	UK	New Zealand
One-year deposit rate	9%	6%
One-year borrowing rate	11	8
	Rate	Probability
Forecasted spot rate of NZ$	£0.33	20%
	0.34	50
	0.35	30

34. **Devon ltd** manufactures plastic moulding machines. Annual company sales are £3 million in the UK and £12 million in the rest of Europe (invoiced in euros, average exchange rate £0.60:1 euro). The cost of goods sold are £11 million, half of which is incurred in the euro area again at £0.60:1 euro (about half the product is actually made in Europe and half in the UK). Devon estimates that for every 1% increase in the value of the euro its UK sales increase by 0.2% and its euro sales decrease by 0.5%. Profits are generally translated into British pounds at the end of the year.

a. Calculate the percentage change in the gross profit based on a 10% increase in the value of the euro. Explain your result.

b. Suggest how gross profits might be made less sensitive to the value of the euro.

35. **Hedging with a bull spread.** (See the chapter appendix.) Evar Imports ltd buys chocolate from Switzerland and resells it in the United Kingdom. It just purchased chocolate invoiced at SFr62,500. Payment for the invoice is due in 30 days. Assume that the current exchange rate of the Swiss franc is £0.49. Also assume that three call options for the franc are available. The first option has a strike price of £0.49 and a premium of £0.02; the second option has a strike price of £0.51 and a premium of £0.005; the third option has a strike price of £0.53 and a premium of £0.004. Evar Imports is concerned about a modest appreciation in the Swiss franc.

a. Describe how Evar Imports could construct a bull spread using the first two options. What is the cost of this hedge? When is this hedge most effective? When is it least effective?

b. Describe how Evar Imports could construct a bull spread using the first option and the third option. What is the cost of this hedge? When is this hedge most effective? When is it least effective?

c. Given your answers to parts (a) and (b), what is the tradeoff involved in constructing a bull spread using call options with a higher exercise price?

36. **Hedging with a bear spread.** (See the chapter appendix.) Marsden ltd has customers in Canada and frequently receives payments denominated in Canadian dollars (C$). The current spot rate for the Canadian dollar is £0.50. Two call options on Canadian dollars are available. The first option has an exercise price of £0.47 and a premium of £0.02. The second option has an exercise price of £0.49 and a premium of £0.01. Marsden ltd would like to use a bear spread to hedge a receivable

position of C$50,000, which is due in one month. Marsden is concerned that the Canadian dollar may depreciate to £0.48 in one month.

a. Describe how Marsden ltd could use a bear spread to hedge its position.

b. Assume the spot rate of the Canadian dollar in one month is £0.48. Was the hedge effective?

37. **Hedging with forward versus option contracts.** As treasurer of Temple plc you are confronted with the following problem. Assume the one-year forward rate of the US dollar is £0.62. You plan to receive 1 million pounds in one year. A one-year put option is available. It has an exercise price of £0.63. The spot rate as of today is £0.63 and the option premium is £0.03 per unit. Your forecast of the percentage change in the spot rate was determined from the following regression model:

$$e_t = a_0 + a_1 DINF_{t-1} + a_1 DINT_t + \varepsilon$$

where:

e_t = percentage change in British pound value over period t

$DINF_{t-1}$ = differential in inflation between the United States and the United Kingdom in period $t - 1$

$DINT_t$ = average differential between US interest rate and British interest rate over period t

a_0, a_1, and a_2 = regression coefficients

ε = error term

The regression model was applied to historical annual data, and the regression coefficients were estimated as follows:

$a_0 = 0.0$

$a_1 = 1.1$

$a_2 = 0.6$

Assume last year's inflation rates were 3% for the United States and 8% for the United Kingdom. Also assume that the interest rate differential ($DINT_t$) is forecasted as follows for this year:

Forecast of $DINT_t$	Probability
1%	40%
2	50
3	10

Using any of the available information, should the treasurer choose the forward hedge or the put option hedge? Show your work.

38. **Hedging with straddles.** (See the chapter appendix.) Bach GmbH (a German company) imports wood from Morocco. The Moroccan exporter invoices in Moroccan dirham. The current exchange rate of the dirham is 0.10 euro. Bach has just purchased wood for 2 million dirham and should pay for the wood in three months. It is also possible that Bach will receive 4 million dirham in three months from the sale of refinished wood in Morocco. Bach is currently in negotiations with a Moroccan importer about the refinished wood. If the negotiations are successful, Bach will receive the 4 million dirham in three months, for a net cash inflow of 2 million dirham. The following option information is available:

- Call option premium on Moroccan dirham = 0.003 euro.

- Put option premium on Moroccan dirham = 0.002 euro.

- Call and put option strike price = 0.098 euro.

- One option contract represents 500,000 dirham.

a. Describe how Bach could use a straddle to hedge its possible positions in dirham.

b. Consider three scenarios. In the first scenario, the dirham's spot rate at option expiration is equal to the exercise price of 0.98 euro. In the second scenario, the dirham depreciates to 0.08 euro. In the third scenario, the dirham appreciates to 0.11 euro. For each scenario, consider both the case when the negotiations are successful and the case when the negotiations are not successful. Assess the effectiveness of the long straddle in each of these situations by comparing it to a strategy of using long call options to hedge.

39. **Hedging with straddles versus strangles.** (See the chapter appendix.) Refer to the previous problem. Assume that Bach believes the cost of a long straddle is too high. However, call options with an exercise price of 0.105 euro and a premium of 0.002 euro and put options with an exercise price of 0.09 euro and a premium of 0.001 euro are also available on Moroccan dirham. Describe how Bach could use a long strangle to hedge its possible dirham positions. What is the tradeoff involved in using a long strangle versus a long straddle to hedge the positions?

40. **Hedging decision.** You believe that IRP presently exists. The nominal annual interest rate in Mexico is 14%. The nominal annual interest rate in the United Kingdom is 6%. You expect that annual inflation will be about 4% in Mexico and 5% in the United Kingdom. The spot rate of the Mexican peso is £0.65. Put options on pesos are available with a one-year expiration date, an exercise price of £0.70, and a premium of £0.07 per unit. You will receive 1 million pesos in one year.
    a. Determine the expected amount of British pounds that you will receive if you use a forward hedge.
    b. Determine the expected amount of pounds that you will receive if you do not hedge and believe in purchasing power parity.
    c. Determine the amount of pounds that you will expect to receive if you use a currency put option hedge. Account for the premium you would pay on the put option.

41. **Evaluating exchange rate movement** Find the homepage of a large multinational by referring to the lists on the site http://www.forbes.com and find the latest annual report – including all the accounting policies.
    a. Review the annual report of your choice. Look for any comments in the report that describe the MNC's hedging of transaction exposure. Summarize the MNC's hedging of transaction exposure based on the comments in the annual report (an easy way to find the right section is to use the search function using the word "risk").
    b. The following website provides exchange rates: http://www.oanda.com, select the FXhistory option. Based on the exposure of the MNC you assessed in part (a), determine whether the exchange rate movements of whatever currency (or currencies) the MNC is exposed to moved in a favourable or unfavourable direction over the last few months.

DISCUSSION IN THE BOARDROOM

This exercise can be found on the companion website at www.cengage.co.uk/madura_fox.

RUNNING YOUR OWN MNC

This exercise can be found on the companion website at www.cengage.co.uk/madura_fox.

Essays/discussion and articles can be found at the end of Part 3

BLADES PLC CASE STUDY
Management of transaction exposure

Blades plc has recently decided to expand its international trade relationship by exporting to the United States. Jogs Inc a US retailer, has committed itself to the annual purchase of 200,000 pairs of "Speedos", Blades' primary product, for a price of $80 per pair. The agreement is to last for two years, at which time it may be renewed by Blades and Jogs.

In addition to this new international trade relationship, Blades continues to export to Thailand. Its primary customer there, a retailer called Entertainment Products, is committed to the purchase of 180,000 pairs of Speedos annually for another two years at a fixed price of 4,594 Thai baht per pair. When the agreement terminates, it may be renewed by Blades and Entertainment Products.

Blades also incurs costs of goods sold denominated in Thai baht. It imports materials sufficient to manufacture 72,000 pairs of Speedos annually from Thailand. These imports are denominated in baht, and the price depends on current market prices for the rubber and plastic components imported.

Under the two export arrangements, Blades sells quarterly amounts of 50,000 and 45,000 pairs of Speedos to Jogs and Entertainment Products, respectively. Payment for these sales is made on the first of January, April, July, and October. The annual amounts are spread over quarters in order to avoid excessive inventories for the British and Thai retailers. Similarly, in order to avoid excessive inventories, Blades usually imports materials sufficient to manufacture 18,000 pairs of Speedos quarterly from Thailand. Although payment terms call for payment within 60 days of delivery, Blades generally pays for its Thai imports upon delivery on the first day of each quarter in order to maintain its trade relationships with the Thai suppliers. Blades feels that early payment is beneficial, as other customers of the Thai supplier pay for their purchases only when it is required.

Since Blades is relatively new to international trade, Ben Holt, Blades' chief financial officer (CFO), is concerned with the potential impact of exchange rate fluctuations on Blades' financial performance. Holt is vaguely familiar with various techniques available to hedge transaction exposure, but he is not certain whether one technique is superior to the others. Holt would like to know more about the forward, money market, and option hedges and has asked you, a financial analyst at Blades, to help him identify the hedging technique most appropriate for Blades. Unfortunately, no options are available for Thailand, but dollar call and put options are available for $50,000 per option.

Ben Holt has gathered and provided you with the following information for Thailand and the United States:

	Thailand (baht)	United States (dollar)
Current spot rate	£0.0153	£0.66
90-day forward rate	£0.0143	£0.67
Put option premium	Not available	£0.013 per unit
Put option exercise price	Not available	£0.68
Call option premium	Not available	£0.010 per unit
Call option exercise price	Not available	£0.68
90-day borrowing rate (non-annualized)	4%	2%
90-day lending rate (non-annualized)	3.5%	1.8%

In addition to this information, Ben Holt has informed you that the 90-day borrowing and lending rates in the United States are 2.3% and 2.1%, respectively, on a non-annualized basis. He has also identified the following probability distributions for the exchange rates of the British pound and the Thai baht in 90 days:

Probability	Spot Rate for the dollar in 90 Days	Spot Rate for the Thai baht in 90 Days
5%	£0.690	£0.0133
20	0.680	0.0142
30	0.675	0.0145
25	0.671	0.0147
15	0.666	0.0153
5	0.658	0.0157

Blades' next sales to and purchases from Thailand will occur one quarter from now. If Blades decides to hedge, Holt will want to hedge the entire amount subject to exchange rate fluctuations, even if it requires overhedging (i.e., hedging more than the needed amount). Currently, Holt expects the imported components from Thailand to cost approximately 3,000 baht per pair of Speedos. Holt has asked you to answer the following questions for him:

1. Using a spreadsheet, compare the hedging alternatives for the Thai baht with a scenario under which Blades remains unhedged. Do you think Blades should hedge or remain unhedged? If Blades should hedge, which hedge is most appropriate?
2. Using a spreadsheet, compare the hedging alternatives for the dollar receivables with a scenario under which Blades remains unhedged. Do you think Blades should hedge or remain unhedged? Which hedge is the most appropriate for Blades?
3. In general, do you think it is easier for Blades to hedge its inflows or its outflows denominated in foreign currencies? Why?

4. Would any of the hedges you compared in question 2 for the dollars to be received in 90 days require Blades to overhedge? Given Blades' exporting arrangements, do you think it is subject to overhedging with a money market hedge?
5. Could Blades modify the timing of the Thai imports in order to reduce its transaction exposure? What is the tradeoff of such a modification?
6. Could Blades modify its payment practices for the Thai imports in order to reduce its transaction exposure? What is the tradeoff of such a modification?
7. Given Blades' exporting agreements, are there any long-term hedging techniques Blades could benefit from? For this question only, assume that Blades incurs all of its costs in the United Kingdom.

SMALL BUSINESS DILEMMA
Hedging decisions by the Sports Exports Company

Jim Logan, owner of the Sports Exports Company (Ireland), will be receiving about £10,000 about one month from now as payment for exports produced and sent by his firm. Jim is concerned about his exposure because he believes that there are two possible scenarios: (1) the pound will depreciate by 3% over the next month, or (2) the pound will appreciate by 2% over the next month. There is a 70% chance that Scenario 1 will occur. There is a 30% chance that Scenario 2 will occur.

Jim notices that the prevailing spot rate of the pound is 1.45 euros, and the one-month forward rate is about 1.445 euros. Jim can purchase a put option over the counter from a securities firm that has an exercise (strike) price of 1.445 euros, a premium of 0.020 euros, and an expiration date of one month from now.

1. Determine the amount of euros received by the Sports Exports Company if the receivables to be received in one month are not hedged under each of the two exchange rate scenarios.
2. Determine the amount of euros received by the Sports Exports Company if a put option is used to hedge receivables in one month under each of the two exchange rate scenarios.
3. Determine the amount of euros received by the Sports Exports Company if a forward hedge is used to hedge receivables in one month under each of the two exchange rate scenarios.
4. Summarize the results of euros received based on an unhedged strategy, a put option strategy, and a forward hedge strategy. Select the strategy that you prefer based on the information provided.

APPENDIX 11A

CALCULATING THE OPTIMAL SIZE OF A CROSS CURRENCY HEDGE

Suppose I expect to receive Polish zloty to the value of £10,000 with a standard deviation of £1,000 at current spot rates in 90 days. If there is no market for a forward or futures rate with the zloty (giving a guaranteed exchange rate in 90 days), a cross hedge can be arranged with a closely correlated currency – the euro for example. Instead of taking out a forward contract to sell zloty for a fixed rate, a forward contract is taken out to sell euro at a fixed rate. The idea is that if the value of the zloty unexpectedly falls, the euro value will also fall as the two currencies are well correlated. A forward euro contract in such circumstances will have gained (buy the now unexpectedly cheaper euros and sell at the higher fixed forward rate); but this gain will depend on the correlation between the euro and the zloty. If the correlation between euros and zloty were perfect positive and the standard deviation were the same, then one would take out a contract for £10,000 worth of euros. The gain in the euro forward contract would exactly offset the loss due to the fall in value of the zloty. But where the standard deviations are different and the correlation not perfect, one wants to know the ratio of euro to zloty in taking out a forward contract that would afford the best protection (e.g. the ratio could be euros to the value of 1.2 times the £10,000 or 0.8 times the £10,000 and so on). The formula for the optimum ratio and hence the amount to invest in euros is:

$(\sigma_{zloty}/\sigma_{euro}) \times$ correlation (zloty, euro).

If the correlation coefficient between euros and zloty is 0.75 and the standard deviation of £10,000 worth of euros is £666.66 (and £1,000 for zloty), maximum protection (i.e. minimum overall variance of cash flows) is gained through taking out a forward sell on euros. The ratio is: $1000/666.66 \times 0.75 = 1.125$, therefore the size of the cross hedge is: £10,000 × 1.125 = £11,250. Any less, and one could lower prospective variation by increasing the euros being sold forward, any more and euro variation would actually increase the overall variation in the total returns.

The expected variation of the combined return from the forward contract and the zloty can be calculated by using a variance/covariance matrix with weights of 1 for the zloty receipt and –1 for the euro forward contract. The expected return on the euro would be 0 as it is a forward contract and the standard deviation would be £666.66 × £11,250/£10,000 = £750. The zloty return and standard deviations are £10,000 and £1,000 respectively. Place these values in the portfolio cash flow model spreadsheet (see support material) as follows:

	Weights	SD	Returns
zloty	1	£1,000	£10,000
euro	−1	£750	£0
Correlation (zloty/euro) = 0.75			

The variance covariance matrix is:

	zloty	euro
zloty	1,000,000	−562,500
euro	−562,500	562,500

where $1,000 \times 750 \times 1 \times -1 \times 0.75 = 562,500$, see notes on the variance covariance matrix. The total of the matrix is the variance $1,000,000 - 562,500 = £437,500$. The standard deviation of the returns to the zloty and euro combination is the square root i.e. $£437,500^{1/2} = £661.44$. Thus the variation in zloty is countered by the euro forward variation having an opposite effect.

More generally the formula is:

$$R = (\sigma_{hedged} / \sigma_{hedging}) \times \rho_{(hedged, hedging)}$$

Where:

R = Ratio of hedging amount to hedged currency

σ_{hedged} and $\sigma_{hedging}$ = expected standard deviation of the hedged and hedging currency respectively.

$\rho_{(hedged, hedging)}$ = correlation of hedged and hedging currency

NON-TRADITIONAL HEDGING TECHNIQUES

While traditional hedging techniques were covered in the chapter, many other techniques may be appropriate for an MNC's particular situation. Some of these non-traditional techniques are described in this appendix.

HEDGING WITH CURRENCY STRADDLES

In reality, some MNCs do not know whether they will have net cash inflows or outflows as a result of their transactions in a specific currency over a particular period of time. A long straddle (purchase of a call option and put option with the same exercise price) is an effective tool to hedge under these conditions.

EXAMPLE

Hunter ltd conducts business in Switzerland and expects to need SFr 4,000,000 to cover specific expenses. If it is unable to renew a business deal with the Swiss government (its biggest customer), it will receive a total of SFr 3,000,000 in revenue in one month, which will result in net cash flows of −SFr 1,000,000. Conversely, if it is able to renew the business deal with the government, it will receive a total of SFr5,000,000, which will result in net cash flows of +SFr1,000,000. The prevailing spot rate of the Swiss franc is £0.45. If Hunter has excess Swiss francs in one month, it will convert them to British pounds. Conversely, if Hunter does not have enough Swiss francs in one month, it will use pounds to obtain the amount that it needs. Hunter would like to hedge its exchange rate risk, regardless of which scenario occurs.

Currently, call options for Swiss francs with settlement dates in one month are available with an exercise price of £0.45 (the same as the spot rate) and a premium of £0.004 per franc. Put options for Swiss francs with the same exercise price and settlement date of one month are available for a premium of £0.005 per franc. Options for Swiss francs are denominated in 250,000 francs per option contract.

Hunter could hedge its possible position of having positive net cash flows of SFr1,000,000 by purchasing put options on Swiss francs. It would pay a premium of £5,000 (1,000,000 units × £0.005). It could hedge its possible position of needing SFr1,000,000 by purchasing call options. It would pay a premium of £4,000 (1,000,000 units × £0.004). Assume that Hunter constructs a straddle to hedge both possible outcomes and pays £9,000 for the call options and put options on francs. Assume that Hunter exercises the options in one month, if at all.

Consider the following scenarios that could occur one month from now:

1. If Hunter has net cash flows of +SFr1,000,000 and the franc's value is £0.51, it would let its put options expire and would convert its francs to pounds in the spot market, receiving £510,000 (1,000,000 units × £0.51) from this transaction. It would also exercise its call option by purchasing 1,000,000 francs at £0.45 and selling them in the spot market for £0.51. This transaction would generate a gain of (0.51 − 0.45) × 1,000,000 = £60,000. Overall, Hunter would receive £510,000 + £60,000 = £570,000, minus the £9,000 in premiums paid for the options.

2. If Hunter has net cash flows of +SFr1,000,000 and the franc depreciates to £0.44, it would exercise its put options and let the call options expire. Overall, Hunter would

Exhibit 11B.1(a) Possible scenarios for Hunter Co. when hedging with a straddle

Panel A: Hunter has net cash flows of +SFr 1,000,000 in one month

SFr value > £0.45 in one month	▪ Hunter converts excess Swiss francs to pounds in the spot market. ▪ It lets the put options expire. ▪ It exercises its call options and sells the francs obtained from this transaction in the spot market; the proceeds recapture part of the premiums that were paid for the options.
SFr value < £0.45 in one month	▪ Hunter converts excess francs to pounds at £0.45, by exercising its put options. ▪ It lets the call options expire.
SFr value = £0.45 in one month	▪ Hunter converts excess francs to pounds in the spot market. ▪ It lets its call options and put options expire.

Panel B: Hunter has net cash flows of −SFR1,000,000 in one month

SFr value > £0.45 in one month	▪ Hunter converts pounds to francs by exercising its call options. ▪ It lets the put options expire.
SFr value < £0.45 in one month	▪ It lets the call options expire. ▪ It buys francs in the spot market and sells the francs obtained by exercising the put options; the proceeds recapture part of the premiums that were paid for the options.
SFr = £0.45 in one month	▪ Hunter converts pounds to francs in the spot market. ▪ It lets its call and put options expire.

Exhibit 11B.1(b) Contengency diagram for hedging with a straddle (Hunter ltd)

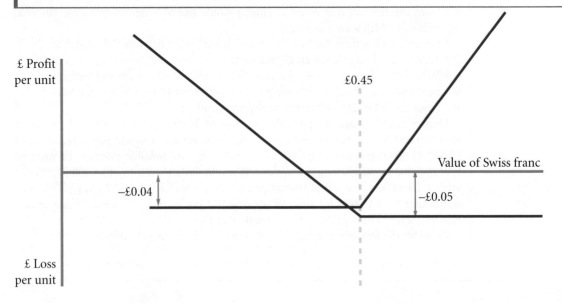

receive £450,000 (1,000,000 units × £0.45) from exercising the options, minus the £9,000 in premiums paid for the options.

3. If Hunter has net cash flows of +SFr1,000,000 and the franc is £0.45, it would let its call and put options expire. It would receive £450,000 (1,000,000 × £0.45) from selling francs in the spot market, minus the £9,000 in premiums paid for the options.

4. If Hunter has net cash flows of −SFr1,000,000, and the franc's value is £0.51, it would exercise its call options and let its put options expire. Overall, Hunter would pay a total of £459,000, which consists of the £450,000 (1,000,000 × £0.45) from exercising the call option and the £9,000 in premiums paid for the options.

5. If Hunter has net cash flows of −SFr1,000,000 and the franc's value is £0.44, it would let its call options expire and buy francs in the spot market. It would also buy 1,000,000 francs and then sell them by exercising its put options. This transaction would generate a gain of (0.45 − 0.44) × 1,000,000 = £10,000. Overall, Hunter would pay a total of £439,000, which consists of the £440,000 paid to obtain the francs it needs, plus the £9,000 in premiums paid for the options, minus the £10,000 gain generated from its put options.

6. If Hunter has net cash flows of −SFR1,000,000 and the franc's value is £0.45, it would let its call and put options expire. It would pay a total of £459,000, which consists of the £450,000 paid to obtain francs and the £9,000 in premiums paid for the options. Many other scenarios could also occur, but a summary of the possible scenarios and the actions taken by Hunter appears in Exhibit 11B.1 (a) and (b).

HEDGING WITH CURRENCY STRANGLES

In the hedging example just provided for Hunter ltd, consider that the expected value of the amount that Hunter would pay or receive based on today's spot rate is £450,000 (SFr1,000,000 × £0.45). The option premiums paid for the options (£9,000) represent 2% of that expected value. Thus, the straddle is a relatively expensive means of hedging. The exercise price at which Hunter hedged was equal to the spot rate ("at the money"). If Hunter is willing to accept exposure to small exchange rate movements in the Swiss franc, it could reduce the premiums paid for the options. Specifically, it would use a *long strangle* by purchasing a call option and a put option that have different exercise prices. By purchasing a call option that has an exercise price higher than £0.45, and a put option that has an exercise price lower than £0.45, Hunter can reduce the premiums it will pay on the options (see Exhibit 11B.2).

Reconsider the example in which Hunter ltd expects that it will have net cash flows of either +SFr1,000,000 or −SFr1,000,000 in one month. To reduce the premiums it pays for hedging with options, it can purchase options that are out of the money. Assume that it can obtain call options for Swiss francs with an expiration date of one month, an exercise price of £0.455, and a premium of £0.002 per Swiss franc. It can also obtain put options for Swiss francs with an expiration date of one month, an exercise price of £0.445, and a premium of £0.003 per Swiss franc.

Hunter ltd could hedge its possible position of needing SFr1,000,000 by purchasing call options. It would pay a premium of £2,000 (1,000,000 units × £0.002) – note that the term units is used instead of the particular currency involved, in this case Swiss francs. It could also hedge its possible position of having positive net cash flows of SFr1,000,000 by purchasing put options. It would pay a premium of £3,000 (1,000,000 units × £0.003). Overall, Hunter would pay £5,000 for the call options and put options on francs, which is substantially less than the £9,000 it would pay for the straddle in the previous example. However, the options do not offer protection until the spot rate deviates by more than

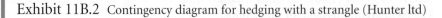

Exhibit 11B.2 Contingency diagram for hedging with a strangle (Hunter ltd)

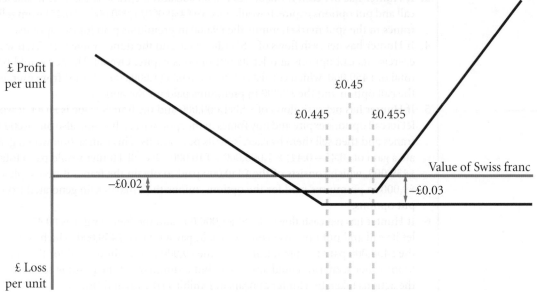

Note:
■ Notice the smaller costs compared with the straddle (Exhibit 11B.1) and the reduced protection.

£0.005 from its existing level. If the spot rate remains within the range of the two exercise prices (from £0.445 to £0.455), Hunter will not exercise either option.

This example of hedging with a strangle is a compromise between hedging with the straddle in the previous example and no hedge. For the range of possible spot rates between £0.445 and £0.455, there is no hedge. For scenarios in which the spot rate moves outside the range, Hunter is hedged. It will have to pay no more than £0.455 if it needs to obtain francs and will be able to sell francs for at least £0.445 if it has francs to sell.

HEDGING WITH CURRENCY BULL SPREADS

In certain situations, MNCs can use currency bull spreads to hedge their cash outflows denominated in a foreign currency, as the following example illustrates.

E X A M P L E

Peak ltd needs to order US raw materials to use in its production process. The US exporter typically invoices Peak in US dollars. Assume that the current exchange rate for the US dollar ($) is £0.55 and that Peak needs $100,000 in three months. Two call options for US dollars with expiration dates in three months and the following additional information are available:

■ Call Option 1 premium on US dollars = £0.015.
■ Call Option 2 premium on US dollars = £0.008.
■ Call Option 1 strike price = £0.55.
■ Call Option 2 strike price = £0.60.
■ One option contract represents $50,000.

To lock into a future price for the $100,000, Peak could buy two Option 1 contracts, paying 2 × 50,000 × £0.015 = £1,500. This would effectively lock in a maximum price of

£0.55 that Peak would pay in three months, for a total maximum outflow of £56,500 (100,000 × £0.55 + £1,500). If the spot price for US dollars at option settlement is below £0.55, Peak has the right to let the options expire and buy the $100,000 in the open market for the lower price. Naturally, Peak would still have paid the £1,500 total premium in this case.

If Peak believes that the US dollar will appreciate in the next three months but is very unlikely to be above £0.60, it should consider constructing a bull spread to hedge its US dollar payables. To do so, Peak would purchase two Option 1 contracts. To help finance this cost Peak should *write* (or sell) two Option 2 contracts (see Exhibit 11B.3). The total cash outflow necessary to construct this bull spread is 2 × $50,000 × (£0.015 − £0.008) = £700, since Peak would receive the premiums from writing the two Option 2 contracts. Constructing the bull spread has reduced the cost of hedging by £800 (£1,500 − £700).

Exhibit 11B.3 Contingency diagram for hedging with a bull spread (Peak ltd) per unit (dollars) and total cost (not drawn to scale)

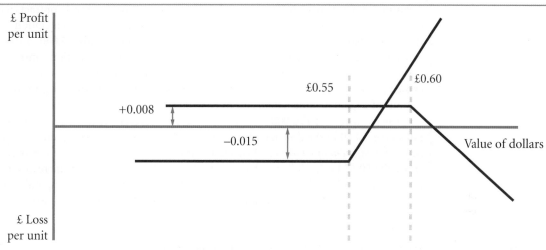

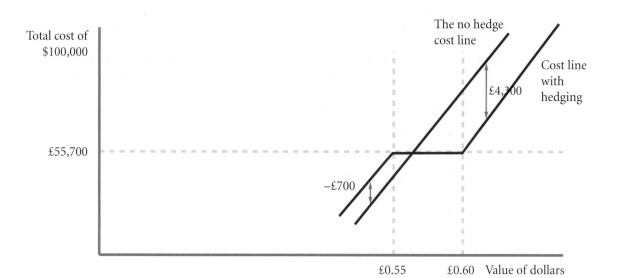

If the spot price of the US dollar at option expiration is below the £0.60 strike price, the bull spread will have provided an effective hedge. For example, if the spot price at option expiration is £0.58, Peak will exercise the two Option 1 contracts it purchased, for a total maximum outflow of £55,700 ($100,000 × £0.55 + $700). If Peak had not hedged then the cost would have been £58,000 ($100,000 × £0.58), so there has been a saving of £2,300 (£58,000 − £55,700). The buyer of the two Option 2 contracts Peak wrote would let those options expire. If the US dollar depreciates below the lower strike price of £0.55, both options will expire worthless. Peak would purchase the US dollars at the prevailing spot rate, having paid the difference in option premiums and therefore be worse off by £700 compared to the no hedge position.

Now consider what will happen if the US dollar appreciates above the higher exercise price of £0.60 prior to option settlement. In this case, the bull spread will still reduce the total cash outflow and therefore provide a partial hedge. However, the hedge will not protect against differences above £0.60 as any gain on the purchased calls is lost on the written calls. The maximum benefit will be (£0.60 − £0.55) × $100,000 − £700 = £4,300.

To illustrate, assume the US dollar appreciates to a spot price of £0.70 in three months. Peak will still exercise the two Option 1 contracts it purchased. However, the two Option 2 contracts it wrote will also be exercised. The gain on the two Option 1 contracts will be (£0.70 − £0.55) × 100,000 = £15,000. But Peak will lose on the two written Option 2 contracts by (£0.60 − £0.70) × 100,000 = £10,000, a net gain of only £5,000 (£15,000 − £10,000). The gain of £5,000 has been at the cost of purchasing the option contracts at a cost of £700 (see above) so the net gain is £4,300. The total cost to Peak will be the purchase at spot of the $100,000, so $100,000 × £0.70 = £70,000 less the net gain from the options of £4,300 making a total cost of £65,700 (£70,000 − £4,300), still better than the no protection cost of £70,000. To repeat, for every £0.01 or penny increase in the spot rate above £0.60 to the dollar, Option 1 *pays to Peak £0.01* per $1 covered but Option 2 *requires a payment of £0.01* per $1 covered. The two contracts cancel out for movements above the £0.60 to the dollar exchange rate. So Peak is not covered for increases in spot rates above £0.60 to the dollar. Consequently, MNCs should hedge using bull spreads only for relatively stable currencies that are not expected to appreciate drastically prior to option settlement.

HEDGING WITH CURRENCY BEAR SPREADS

In certain situations, MNCs can use currency bear spreads to hedge their receivables denominated in a foreign currency.

EXAMPLE

Weber ltd has some Canadian customers, Weber typically bills these customers in Canadian dollars. Assume that the current exchange rate for the Canadian dollar (C$) is £0.48 and that Weber expects to receive C$50,000 in three months. The following options for Canadian dollars are available.

- Call Option 1 premium on Canadian dollars = £0.015.
- Call Option 2 premium on Canadian dollars = £0.008.
- Call Option 1 strike price = £0.48.
- Call Option 2 strike price = £0.50.
- One option contract represents C$50,000.

If Weber believes the Canadian dollar will not appreciate above £0.48, it can construct a bear spread to hedge the receivable. Weber will buy Call Option 2 and write Call Option

1 to establish this bear spread. The total cash *inflow* resulting from this bear spread is C$50,000 × ($0.015 − $0.008) = £350 with no further receipts or payments *if* both contracts are out of the money. Constructing a bear spread will always result in a net cash inflow, since the spreader writes the call option with the lower exercise price and, therefore, the higher premium (see Exhibit 11B.4).

What will happen if the Canadian dollar appreciates to £0.487? At this rate Weber will have to pay £0.007 (£0.487 − £0.48) on Option 1 and will receive nothing on Option 2. The benefit per Canadian dollar of £0.007 (£0.015 − £0.008) will therefore have been paid out on Option 1. Now assume that the spot rate for the Canadian dollar is £0.53 at option settlement. In this case, the written contract 1 would require a payout of (£0.53 − £0.48) = £0.05 per Canadian dollar but the contract 2 option to purchase at £0.50 would help offset this loss as it would pay Weber £0.53 − £0.50 = £0.03 per Canadian dollar

Exhibit 11B.4 Contingency diagram for hedging with a bull spread (Weber ltd) per unit (Canadian dollars) and total cost (not drawn to scale)

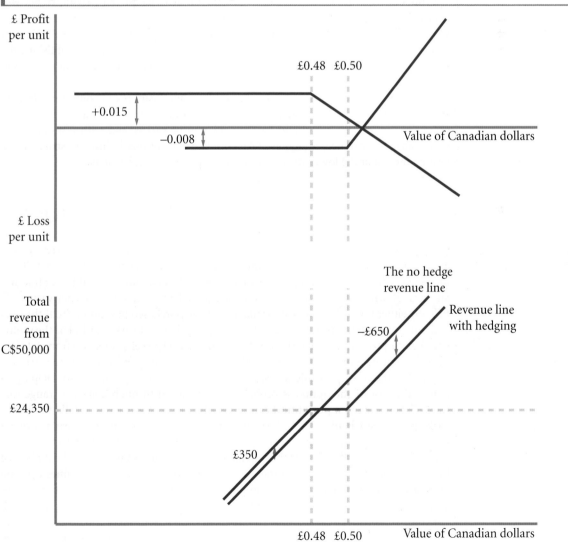

covered. For increases above £0.50 for the Canadian dollar, the loss on contract 1 is offset by the gain on contract 2. The loss *at* £0.50 to the Canadian dollar is £0.02 (£0.48 – £0.50) or £0.02 × C$50,000 = £1,000. As movements above the £0.50 rate are covered, this represents the maximum loss at settlement – the net loss would be £1,000 – £350 = £650. The maximum gain will be £350 when the price at settlement is at or below £0.48 – both contracts will be out of the money and hence Weber will collect the difference in premiums.

The bear spread also provides an effective hedge if the spot price of the Canadian dollar at option expiration is above the lower strike price of £0.48 but below the break even price of £0.487. In this case, however, the benefit is reduced. For instance, if the spot price at option expiration is £0.485, Weber will let Option 2 expire. The buyer of Option 1 will exercise it, and Weber will sell the receivables at the exercise price of £0.48 to fulfil its obligation. This will result in a total cash inflow of £24,350 (C$50,000 × £0.48 + £350) after including the net premium received from establishing the spread. If Weber had not hedged, the revenue would have been C$50,000 × £0.485 = £24,250, there is therefore an opportunity loss of £100 (£24,250 – £24,350) = –£100.

If the Canadian dollar depreciates below the lower strike price of £0.48, Weber will realize the maximum gain from the bear spread, but will have to sell the receivables at the low prevailing spot rate. For example, if the spot rate at option expiration is £0.45, both options will expire worthless, but Weber would have received £350 from establishing the spread. If Weber sells the receivables at the spot rate, the net cash inflow will be £22,850 (i.e. C$50,000 × £0.45 + £350).

In summary, MNCs should hedge receivables using bear spreads only for relatively stable currencies that are expected to depreciate modestly, but not drastically, prior to option expiration. Both bull and bear spreads can be carried out with put options as well. Weber, for instance, could have taken out two put options at different strike prices, writing the put at the lower strike to finance the put at the higher strike.

EVALUATION OF NON-TRADITIONAL HEDGING TECHNIQUES

Options used in combination offer a very flexible form of protection from currency variation. Many such combinations are popular with speculators who want to benefit from imagined patterns in currency prices or who want to take out unusual bets. Straddles and strangles, for example, are bets on the standard deviation, if the currency varies sufficiently either up or down a profit is made with the purchased puts and calls. If the puts and calls are written, a profit is made if the currency does not vary greatly. For the multinational the protection is likely to be rather simpler. MNCs seek protection from extreme rates. Such protection avoids unexpected losses and gives the company time to rearrange affairs. For the most part this would involve buying a put or a call option. Helping to reduce the cost of the option is probably best achieved through collars or range forwards. Thus, buying a put option can in part be financed by selling a call at a higher strike price (see Chapter 5). A cheap put at a low strike price protects from revenue values being translated at an unexpectedly low price. If the price is unexpectedly high, some of the "joy" will be lost as the purchaser of the call option will claim the difference between the high call strike and the even higher spot. How an MNC defines extreme rates and high and low will depend on the financial circumstances. Where margins are small, transactions infrequent and significant, a high level of protection may be desired. For companies with larger margins and frequent transactions there will be greater tolerance of currency changes. For such companies, protection may only be desired for large adverse changes. In any event, the rationale for non-traditional options must be carefully worked out as it is very easy to accidentally start to speculate on currencies when the original intention was simply to protect against adverse movements. See Appendix 5B and the companion website for a spreadsheet that models two option combinations.

CHAPTER 12

MANAGING ECONOMIC EXPOSURE AND TRANSLATION EXPOSURE

WHEN THE BRITISH POUND value of the Argentine peso changes, the cost in pounds of all goods and services denominated in pesos will change. Any transaction by an MNC that involves converting pounds to pesos or pesos to pounds will be directly affected (transaction exposure). There will also be indirect effects caused by changes in the pattern of demand for goods and services as a result of the new exchange rate. Together these risks are termed economic exposure.

Even if an MNC is protected from all economic exposure, the reported profits of an MNC may still be affected by exchange rate changes. This is because reported profits are in the home currency and therefore a conversion of foreign sales etc. has to be made even if no such conversion has taken place. Accounting conventions help to clarify and minimize the effect of converting currencies for reporting purposes, but there remains a concern that a loss that is solely as a result of reporting practices may yet reflect badly on MNCs. This form of risk is termed translation exposure.

In this chapter we examine how an MNC may organize its affairs and use the financial markets to protect itself from both forms of exposure.

THE SPECIFIC OBJECTIVES OF THIS CHAPTER ARE TO:

- explain how an MNC's economic exposure can be hedged, and
- explain how an MNC's translation exposure can be hedged.

ECONOMIC EXPOSURE

From a multinational's perspective, transaction exposure represents only the exchange rate risk when *converting* net foreign cash inflows to its home currency or when making payments in foreign currency. Economic exposure includes this concept but also represents *any* impact of exchange rate fluctuations on a firm's future cash flows. A firm whose production and sales are in the home market with no sales or purchases from abroad can be affected by foreign currency movements *if* competitors are affected. Therefore, firms cannot focus just on hedging their foreign currency payables or receivables but must also attempt to determine how all their cash flows will be affected by possible exchange rate movements.

EXAMPLE

Adidas's economic exposure comes in various forms. First, it is subject to transaction exposure because of its numerous purchase and sale transactions in foreign currencies, particularly dollars. This transaction exposure is a subset of economic exposure. Second, any remitted earnings from foreign subsidiaries to the German parent also reflect transaction exposure. Third, a change in exchange rates that affects the demand for shoes at other athletic shoe companies (such as Nike) can indirectly affect the demand for Adidas' athletic shoes. All these effects when taken together amount to economic exposure. Adidas gives special mention to options as a means of protecting against an appreciation of the dollar and at the same time allowing the firm to benefit from a depreciation. Adidas also purchase forward contracts and engage in currency swaps as well as trying to increase purchases in the currency of their sales. The company attempts to hedge some of its transaction exposure typically up to 18 months in advance, but it cannot eliminate transaction exposure because it cannot predict all future transactions ahead of time. Moreover, even if it could eliminate its transaction exposure, it cannot perfectly hedge its remaining economic exposure; it is difficult to determine exactly how a specific exchange rate movement will affect the demand for a competitor's athletic shoes and, therefore, how it will indirectly affect the demand for Adidas' shoes.

The following comments by PepsiCo summarize the dilemma faced by many MNCs that assess economic exposure.

> *Operating in international markets involves exposure to movements in currency exchange rates. Currency exchange rate movements typically affect economic growth, inflation, interest rates, governmental actions and other factors. These changes, if material, can cause us to adjust our financing and operating strategies. The discussion of changes in currency below does not incorporate these other important economic factors. The sensitivity analysis presented below does not take into account the possibility that rates can move in opposite directions and that gains from one category may or may not be offset by losses from another category.*
>
> (PepsiCo Annual Report, 1998)

Use of the income statement to assess economic exposure

An MNC must determine its economic exposure before it can manage its exposure. It can determine its exposure to each currency in terms of its cash inflows and cash outflows. The income statements for each subsidiary can be used to derive estimates.

http://

See **http://www. renault.com** as an example of an MNC's website and a wealth of good quality financial information in the annual report. The websites of various MNCs make available financial statements such as annual reports that describe the use of financial derivatives to hedge interest rate risk and exchange rate risk.

EXAMPLE

Recall from Chapter 10 that Mannerton plc is subject to economic exposure. Mannerton can assess its economic exposure to exchange rate movements by determining the sensitivity of its expenses and revenue to various possible exchange rate scenarios.

Exhibit 12.1 reproduces Mannerton's revenue and expense information from Exhibit 10.10 (c) of Chapter 10. The UK revenues are assumed to be sensitive to different exchange rate scenarios because of the foreign competition. Regardless of the exchange rate scenario, European sales are expected to be 40 million euros, but the British pound amount received from these sales will depend on the scenario. The cost of goods sold attributable to UK orders is assumed to be £50 million for Scenario 1; Scenarios 2 and 3 are sensitive to the volume effects on UK sales of exchange rate. The cost of goods sold attributable to European and UK orders is 200 million euros for Scenario 1. The British pound amount of this cost varies with the exchange rate scenario *and* the volume changes in UK sales as a result of the differing exchange rates. The gross profit shown in Exhibit 12.1 is determined by subtracting the total pound value of cost of goods sold from the total pound value of sales.

Operating expenses are separated into fixed and variable categories. The fixed expenses are £30 million per year, while the projected variable expenses are dictated by projected sales volumes. The earnings before interest and taxes are determined by the total British pound amount of gross profit minus the total British pound amount of operating expenses. The interest owed to UK banks is insensitive to the exchange rate scenario, but the projected amount of pounds needed to pay interest on existing European loans varies with the exchange rate scenario. Earnings before taxes are estimated by subtracting total interest expense from earnings before interest and taxes.

Exhibit 12.1 enables Mannerton to assess how its income statement items will be affected by different exchange rate movements. A stronger euro increases Mannerton's UK sales and the pound value of the revenue earned from European sales. On the negative side, there is also a large increase in Mannerton's cost of materials purchased from Europe and the pound amount needed to pay interest on loans from European banks.

The higher expenses more than offset the higher revenue in this scenario. Hence, the amount of Mannerton's earnings before taxes is inversely related to the strength of the euro. A 17% rise in the value of the euro (£0.70 / £0.60 − 1 = 0.17) results in an estimated fall in profits of 19% (£68.56m / £84.28m − 1 = 0.19). Equivalent figures for Scenario 3 are a 33% rise in the value of the euro compared to Scenario 1 resulting in a 38% fall in profits. To convey some idea of this risk, Mannerton could report in the annual accounts that a 1% rise in the value of the euro will result in an estimated £0.9m fall in profits ((84.28 − 68.56) / 17 ≈ 0.9). Renault SA report their exposure as follows: "*Based on the structure of its results and its operating cash flows in 2004, the Group estimates that a 1% appreciation of the euro against all other currencies would have a negative impact of 41m euro on operating margins*" (about 1.7% of operating profit) (Renault SA).

If the euro strengthens consistently over the long run, Mannerton's cost of goods sold and interest expense will rise at a higher rate than its UK revenues. Consequently, it may wish to institute some policies to ensure that movements of the euro will have a more balanced impact on its revenue and expenses. At the current time, Mannerton's high exposure to exchange rate movements occurs because its expenses are more susceptible than its revenue to the changing value of the euro.

Now that Mannerton has assessed its exposure, it recognizes that it can reduce this exposure by either increasing European sales or reducing orders of European materials. These actions would allow some offsetting of cash flows and therefore reduce its economic exposure.

Exhibit 12.1 Original impact of exchange rate movements on earnings: Mannerton plc

		Exchange Rate Scenarios		
Item		**Scenario 1**	**Scenario 2**	**Scenario 3**
	value of euro	£0.60	£0.70	£0.80
		£ million		
	(1) UK sales	300.00	304.00	307.00
(2) European Sales (40 million euros in each scenario)		24.00	28.00	32.00
(3) Total		324.00	332.00	339.00
less Cost of goods sold:				
(4) UK costs		50.00	50.62	51.08
	(5) European costs	120.00	141.73	163.46
	(6) Total	170.00	192.35	214.54
	(7) Gross profit	**154.00**	**139.65**	**124.46**
less Operating expenses:				
	(8) UK: Fixed	30.00	30.00	30.00
less (9) UK: Variable costs (by volume of output)		30.72	31.10	31.38
(10) Total		60.72	61.10	61.38
(11) EBIT (earnings before interest and tax)		**93.28**	**78.56**	**63.08**
less Interest expense:				
(12) UK		3.00	3.00	3.00
(13) European 10 million euros		6.00	7.00	8.00
(14) Total		9.00	10.00	11.00
(15) EBT		**84.28**	**68.56**	**52.08**

Notes:

Total volume changes compared to Scenario 1: European sales are 0.074 or 7.4% of total sales in Scenario 1 (see Exhibit 10.10 (a)) and do not change. So using the volume changes from Exhibit 10.10 (b) and taking a weighted average, the volume changes are: Scenario 2: $0.074 \times 0\% + (1-0.074) \times 1^1/_3\%$ = **1.235%**; Scenario 3: $0.074 \times 0\% + (1-0.074) \times 2^1/_3\%$ = **2.16%**.

Line 4: cost of goods sold is variable and presumed to relate to all sales. Applying the volume changes (above) for Scenarios 2 and 3, $50 + 1.235\% \times 50 = 50.62$ and $50 + 2.16\% \times 50 = 51.08$

Line 5: European costs are incurred in the production of both UK and European goods. So for Scenarios 2 and 3 applying the volume changes above:

Scenario 2: $200 + 200 \times 1.235\% = 202.47$ euros

Scenario 3: $200 + 200 \times 2.16\% = 204.32$ euros

And the £ valuations are Scenario 1: $200 \times 0.6 = 120$; Scenario 2: $202.47 \times 0.70 = 141.73$; Scenario 3: $204.32 \times 0.80 = 163.46$

Line 9: UK variable costs are subject to the volume changes above, 30.72 as given for Scenario 1, for Scenario 2 it is $30.72 + 1.235\% \times 30.72 = 31.10$ and $30.72 + 2.16\% \times 30.72 = 31.38$ for Scenarios 2 and 3.

How restructuring can reduce economic exposure

MNCs may restructure their operations to reduce their economic exposure. The restructuring involves shifting the sources of costs or revenue to other locations in order to match cash inflows and outflows in foreign currencies.

EXAMPLE

Reconsider the previous example of Mannerton plc which has more cash outflows than cash inflows in euros as it produces mainly in Europe. Mannerton could create more balance by increasing European sales. It believes that it can achieve European sales of 60 million euro if it spends £2 million more on advertising (which is part of its fixed operating expenses). The increased sales will also require an additional expenditure of £10 million on materials from UK suppliers and a £1m increase in variable operating expenses. In addition, it plans to reduce its reliance on European suppliers and increase its reliance on UK suppliers. Mannerton anticipates that this strategy will reduce the cost of goods sold attributable to European suppliers by 100 million euros and increase the cost of goods sold attributable to UK suppliers by £70 million (not including the £10 million increase resulting from increased sales to the European market). Furthermore, it plans to borrow additional funds in the United Kingdom and retire some existing loans from European banks. The result will be an additional interest expense of £3.5 million to UK banks and a reduction of 5 million euros owed to European banks. Exhibit 12.2 shows the anticipated impact of these strategies on Mannerton's income statement. For each of the three exchange rate scenarios, the initial projections are in the left column, and the revised projections (as a result of the proposed strategy) are in the right column.

Note first that there is an increase in projected total sales in response to Mannerton's plan to penetrate the European market. Second, the UK cost of goods sold is now £130 million higher as a result of the £10 million materials increase to accommodate increased European sales and the £70 million increase due to the shift from European suppliers to UK suppliers. The European cost of goods sold decreases from 200 million euros to 100 million euros as a result of this shift to the UK. The revised fixed operating expenses of $32 million include the increase in advertising expenses necessary to penetrate the European market. The variable operating expenses are revised by £1m because of revised estimates for total sales. The interest expenses are revised because of the increased loans from the UK banks and reduced loans from European banks.

If Mannerton increases its euro inflows and reduces its euro outflows as proposed, its revenue and expenses will be affected by movements of the euro. Exhibit 12.3 illustrates the sensitivity of Mannerton's earnings before taxes to the three exchange rate scenarios (derived from Exhibit 12.2). The reduced sensitivity of Mannerton's proposed restructured operations to exchange rate movements is clear. There is nevertheless a cost to be considered. Taking Scenario 1 to be the most likely, Mannerton is in effect having to consider reducing its earnings in the most likely scenario in order to improve earnings in the less favourable but less likely scenarios.

The way a firm restructures its operations to reduce economic exposure to exchange rate risk depends on the form of exposure. For Mannerton plc future expenses are more sensitive than future revenue to the possible values of a foreign currency. Therefore, it can reduce its economic exposure by increasing the sensitivity of revenue and reducing the sensitivity of expenses to exchange rate movements. Firms that have a greater level of exchange rate-sensitive revenue than expenses, however, would reduce their economic exposure by decreasing the level of exchange rate-sensitive revenue or by increasing the level of exchange rate-sensitive expenses. The net effect is to match as far as possible revenues and costs in each currency.

Exhibit 12.2 Impact of possible exchange rate movements on earnings under two alternative operational structures (in millions)

£ million	Scenario 1 £0.60:1euro		Scenario 2 £0.70:1euro		Scenario 3 £0.80:1euro	
	original	proposed	original	proposed	original	proposed
(1) UK sales	300.00	300.00	304.00	304.00	307.00	307.00
(2) European Sales						
(40 million euros and 60 million – proposed)	24.00	36.00	28.00	42.00	32.00	48.00
(3) Total	324.00	336.00	306.80	346.00	339.00	355.00
Cost of goods sold:						
(4) UK	50.00	130.00	50.62	131.55	51.08	132.71
(5) European costs	120.00	60.00	141.73	70.83	163.46	81.67
(6) Total	170.00	190.00	192.53	202.38	214.54	214.38
(7) Gross profit	**154.00**	**146.00**	**139.65**	**143.62**	**124.46**	**140.63**
Operating expenses:						
(8) UK: Fixed	30.00	32.00	30.00	32.00	30.00	32.00
(9) UK: Variable (by volume of output)	30.72	31.72	31.10	32.10	31.38	32.38
(10) Total	60.72	63.72	61.10	64.10	61.38	64.38
(11) EBIT	**93.28**	**82.28**	**78.55**	**79.52**	**63.08**	**76.24**
Interest expense:						
(12) UK	3.00	6.50	3.00	6.50	3.00	6.50
(13) European 10 million euros	6.00	3.00	7.00	3.50	8.00	4.00
(14) Total	9.00	9.50	10.00	10.00	11.00	10.50
(15) EBT	**84.28**	**72.78**	**68.55**	**69.52**	**52.08**	**65.74**

Summary of strategy

European sales increase of 20 million euro from spending £2 million more on advertising (which is part of its fixed operating expenses) £10 million on materials from UK suppliers and £1m on operating expenses.

Reduce the European cost of goods sold by 100 million euros and increase the UK cost of goods sold by £50 million (not including the £10 million increase resulting from increased sales to the European market).

Increase UK borrowing by £3.5 million to UK banks and reduce borrowing from European banks by 5 million euros.

For Scenarios 2 and 3 the volume effects are applied as outlined in Chapter 10.

Line 2: European sales increased to 60m euros so Scenario 1: 60 × 0.60 = 36.00 etc.

Line 4: £10m for European sales plus £50m switch from European costs, Scenario 1 £50m + £10m + £70m = £110m.

Line 5: Decrease in costs of 100m euros so Scenario 1: £120m − 100m euros × 0.6 = £60m etc.

Line 8: plus the £2m on advertising.

Line 9: plus the £1m on operating expenses for European sales.

See Exhibit 10.10(c) for the orginal plan.

Some revenue or expenses may be more sensitive to exchange rates than others. An increase in the value of the euro in the previous example could mean a very large increase in domestic demand as big customers switch to Mannerton's products. The volume effects of economic exposure mean that the simple matching of costs and revenues may not be sufficient. The firm can best evaluate a proposed restructuring of operations by forecasting various income statement items for various possible exchange rate scenarios (as shown in Exhibit 12.2) and then assessing the sensitivity of earnings to these different scenarios as in Exhibit 12.3.

Exhibit 12.3   Economic exposure – earnings in different scenarios

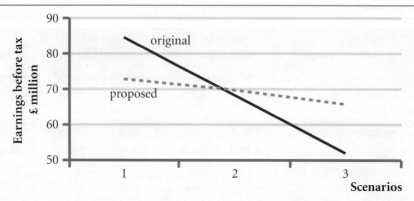

Note:

These are earnings in different scenarios: the steeper the slope the greater the risk. Note that the proposed changes lessen the risk faced by the company but offers a lower overall spread of returns – see "mannerton ch.12.xls" in the support software at www.cengage.co.uk/madura_fox.

Using computer spreadsheets.   Determining the sensitivity of earnings before taxes to alternative exchange rate scenarios can be helped by using a computer to create a spreadsheet similar to Exhibit 12.2. The analyst then inputs forecasts for items such as sales, cost of goods sold, and fixed operating expenses. A formula is used to define the remaining items so that the computer can provide estimates after the forecasts are input. For example, the exchange rate forecast influences projections of: (1) pounds received from European sales, (2) cost of goods sold attributable to purchases of European materials, and (3) amount in dollars needed to cover the European interest payments. By revising the input to reflect various possible restructurings, the analyst can determine how each operational structure would affect the firm's economic exposure.

Recall that Mannerton plc assessed one alternative operational structure in which it increased European sales by 20 million euros, reduced its purchases of European materials by 100 million euros, and reduced its interest owed to European banks by 5 million euros. By using a computerized spreadsheet, Mannerton can easily assess the impact of alternative strategies, such as increasing European sales by other amounts and/or reducing the European expenses by other amounts. This provides Mannerton with more information about its economic exposure under various operational structures and enables it to devise the operational structure that will reduce its economic exposure to the degree desired.

http://

A spreadsheet of the Mannerton example is available from the textbook website at **www·cengage.co. uk/madura_fox** (see Mannerton.xls)

Issues involved in the restructuring decision

Restructuring operations to reduce economic exposure is a more complex task than hedging any single foreign currency transaction. By managing economic exposure, however, the firm is developing a long-term solution because once the restructuring is complete, it should reduce economic exposure over the long run. In contrast, the hedging of transaction exposure deals with each foreign currency transaction separately. Note, however, that it can be very costly to reverse or eliminate restructuring that was undertaken to reduce economic exposure. Therefore, MNCs must be very confident about the potential benefits before they decide to restructure their operations.

When deciding how to restructure operations to reduce economic exposure, one must address the following questions:

Exhibit 12.4   How to restructure operations to balance the impact of currency changes

Type of operation	Recommended action when a company has net cash inflows in the foreign currency	Recommended action when a company has net cash outflows in the foreign currency
Sales in foreign currency units	Reduce foreign currency sales	Increase foreign currency sales
Reliance on foreign supplies	Increase foreign supply orders (costs)	Reduce foreign supply orders (costs)
Proportion of debt structure representing foreign debt	Restructure debt to increase debt payments in foreign currency	Restructure debt to reduce debt payments in foreign currency

- Should the firm attempt to increase or reduce sales in new or existing foreign markets?

- Should the firm increase or reduce its dependency on foreign suppliers?

- Should the firm establish or eliminate production facilities in foreign markets?

- Should the firm increase or reduce its level of debt denominated in foreign currencies?

Each of these questions reflects a different part of the firm's income statement. The first relates to foreign cash inflows and the remaining ones to foreign cash outflows. Some of the more common solutions to balancing a foreign currency's inflows and outflows are summarized in Exhibit 12.4. Any restructuring of operations that can reduce the periodic difference between a foreign currency's inflows and outflows can reduce the firm's economic exposure to that currency's movements.

MNCs that have production and marketing facilities in various countries may be able to reduce any adverse impact of economic exposure by shifting the allocation of their operations.

E X A M P L E

Hartland plc produces products in the United Kingdom, Japan, and France and sells these products to several countries. The products are denominated in the currency where they are produced – so Japanese production is sold in yen even when exported. If the Japanese yen strengthens against many currencies, Hartland may boost production in France, expecting a decline in demand for the Japanese subsidiary's exported products. Hartland may even transfer some machinery from Japan to France and allocate more marketing funds to the French subsidiary at the expense of the Japanese subsidiary. By following this strategy, however, Hartland may have to forgo economies of scale that could be achieved if it concentrated production at one subsidiary while other subsidiaries focused on warehousing and distribution.

A CASE STUDY IN HEDGING ECONOMIC EXPOSURE

The complexity of MNC operations presents further difficulties. First, an MNC's economic exposure may not be so obvious. An analysis of the income statement for an entire MNC may not necessarily detect its economic exposure. The MNC may be composed of various business units, each of which attempts to achieve high performance for its shareholders. Each business unit may have a unique cost and revenue structure. One unit of an MNC may focus on computer consulting services in the United Kingdom and have no exposure to exchange rates. Another unit may also focus on sales of personal computers in the United Kingdom, but this unit may be adversely affected by weak foreign currencies because its UK customers may buy computers from foreign firms.

MANAGING FOR VALUE
How auto manufacturers restructure to reduce exposure

To illustrate how the shifting of production can reduce economic exposure, consider the actual case of Honda, the Japanese automobile producer. By developing plants in the United States to produce automobiles for sale there, Honda not only circumvents possible trade restrictions but also reduces its economic exposure to exchange rate risk. When Honda exported automobiles to the United States, the US demand for Hondas would decline if the yen appreciated because the dollar cost of the autos would increase. Thus, Honda's cash flows were adversely affected when a strong yen reduced demand for its exports. By producing automobiles in the United States and invoicing them in dollars, Honda has reduced the sensitivity of US demand for its automobiles to the value of the Japanese yen. Nevertheless, Honda is not completely insulated from exchange rate risk for two reasons. First, the Honda plants in the United States purchase various components from Japan (invoiced in yen), so the dollar costs of these components rises when the yen appreciates. Second, earnings remitted from Honda's plants in the United States to its parent in Japan convert to a smaller number of yen when the yen appreciates. Nevertheless, by transferring production to the location where the product is sold, Honda has reduced its economic exposure.

Honda's British subsidiary has also restructured to reduce the adverse effects of its economic exposure. When the euro declined against the British pound, consumers throughout Europe reduced their demand for vehicles produced at Honda's subsidiary in the United Kingdom and denominated in pounds. Consequently, Honda shifted some of its supply sources from the United Kingdom to European countries that have adopted the euro. This strategy is intended to reduce the impact of the euro on the performance of Honda's British subsidiary. When the euro declines, the decline in revenue (because of a reduced demand for Hondas produced in the United Kingdom) is partially offset by a decline in the costs of obtaining supplies denominated in euros. When the euro's value increases, Honda's cost of euro-denominated supplies rises, but the demand for its pound-denominated vehicles (and therefore its revenue) also increases (see Exhibit 12.5). By shifting its operations, Honda has reduced its exposure to exchange rate risk, thereby increasing its value.

As a result of Honda's decision to use suppliers in the euro-zone countries to hedge its exposure, it is buying less from suppliers in the United Kingdom. Thus, the UK auto suppliers have lost local business because of Honda's desire to offset its exposure. Ironically, these auto suppliers are subject to increased economic exposure as a result of Honda's decision to reduce its exposure.

Exhibit 12.5 Honda's decision to obtain supplies outside the United Kingdom

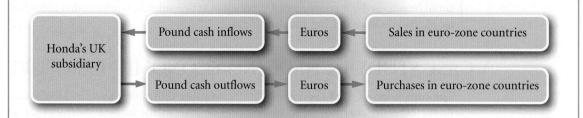

- ■ Weak euro: weak European demand for Honda's pound denominated vehicles offset by reduced cost of euro denominated supplies.
- ■ Strong euro: strong European demand for Honda's pound denominated vehicles offsets high cost of euro denominated supplies.

A multinational can more effectively hedge its economic exposure if it can pinpoint the underlying source of the exposure. Yet, even if the MNC can pinpoint the underlying source of the exposure, there may not be a perfect hedge. No textbook formula can provide the perfect solution, but a combination of actions may reduce the economic exposure to a tolerable level, as illustrated in the following example.

Silverton ltd's dilemma

Silverton ltd (a UK firm), is primarily concerned with its exposure to the euro. It wants to pinpoint the source of its exposure so that it can determine a hedging strategy. Silverton has three units that conduct some of their business in Europe. Because each unit has established a wide variety of business arrangements, it is not obvious whether all three units have a similar exposure. Each unit tends to be independent of the others, and the managers of each unit are compensated according to that unit's performance. Silverton may want to hedge its economic exposure, but it must first determine whether it is exposed and the source of the exposure.

Assessment of economic exposure

Because the exact nature of its economic exposure to the euro is not obvious, Silverton attempts to assess the relationship between the euro's movements and each unit's cash flows over the last nine quarters. A firm may want to use more data, but nine quarters are sufficient to illustrate the point. The cash flows and movements in the euro are shown in Exhibit 12.6. First, Silverton applies regression analysis (as discussed in the previous chapter) to determine whether the percentage change in its total cash flow (*PCF*, shown in Column 5) is related to the percentage change in the euro (%Δeuro, shown in Column 6) over time:

$$PCF_t = a_0 + a_1 (\%\Delta euro)_t + \mu$$

Regression analysis derives the values of the constant, a_0, and the slope coefficient, a_1. The slope coefficient represents the sensitivity of PCF_t to movements in the euro. Based

Exhibit 12.6 Assessment of Silverton's cash flows and the euro's movements

(1) Quarter	(2) % change in unit A's cash flows	(3) % change in unit B's cash flows	(4) % change in unit C's cash flows	(5) % change in total cash flows	(6) % change in unit the value of the euro
1	−3	2	1	0	2
2	0	1	3	4	5
3	6	−6	−1	−1	−3
4	−1	1	−1	−1	0
5	−4	0	−1	−5	−2
6	−1	−2	−2	−5	−5
7	1	−3	3	1	4
8	−3	2	1	0	2
9	4	−1	0	3	−4

on this analysis, the slope coefficient is positive and statistically significant, which implies that the cash flows are positively related to the percentage changes in the euro. That is, a negative change in the euro adversely affects Silverton's total cash flows. The r-squared statistic is 0.31, which suggests that 31% of the variation in Silverton's cash flows can be explained by movements in the euro. The evidence presented so far strongly suggests that Silverton is exposed to exchange rate movements of the euro, but does not pinpoint the source of the exposure.

Assessment of each unit's exposure

To determine the source of the exposure, Silverton applies the regression model separately to each individual unit's cash flows. The results are shown here (apply the regression analysis yourself as an exercise):

Unit	Slope coefficient
A	Not significant
B	Not significant
C	Coefficient = 0.45, which is statistically significant (r-squared = 0.80)

The results suggest that the cash flows of Units A and B are not subject to economic exposure. However, Unit C is subject to economic exposure. Approximately 80% of Unit C's cash flows can be explained by movements in the value of the euro over time. The regression coefficient suggests that for a 1% decrease in the value of the euro, the unit's cash flows will decline by about 0.45%. Exhibit 12.6, which shows the euro's exchange rate movements and the cash flows for Silverton's individual units, confirms the strong relationship between the euro's movements and Unit C's cash flows.

Identifying the source of the unit's exposure

Now that Silverton has determined that one unit is the cause of the exposure, it can pinpoint the characteristics of that unit that cause the exposure. Silverton believes that the key components that affect Unit C's cash flows are income statement items such as its UK revenue, its cost of goods sold, and its operating expenses. This unit conducts all of its production in the United Kingdom.

Silverton first determines the value of each income statement item that affected the unit's cash flows in each of the last nine quarters. It then applies regression analysis to determine the relationship between the percentage change in the euro and each income statement item over those quarters. Assume that it finds:

- A significant positive relationship between Unit C's sales and the euro's value.
- No relationship between the unit's cost of goods sold and the euro's value.
- No relationship between the unit's operating expenses and the euro's value.

These results suggest that when the euro weakens, the unit's revenue from UK customers declines substantially. Its UK customers shift their demand to foreign competitors when the euro weakens and they can obtain imports at a low price. Thus, Silverton's economic exposure could be due to foreign competition. A firm's economic exposure is not always obvious, however, and regression analysis may detect exposure that was not suspected by the firm or its individual units. Furthermore, regression analysis can be used to provide a more precise estimate of the degree of economic exposure, which can be useful when deciding how to manage the exposure.

It is important to stress, however, that findings from regression analysis should be supported by other evidence. In this case, customers may not be sensitive to a weakening euro. It could be that the regression happened to be measured during a period of weakening euro when customers were moving away from Silverton's products for entirely different reasons. A correlation, no matter how strong, must be supported by other evidence before being acted upon.

Possible strategies to hedge economic exposure

Now that Silverton has identified the source of its economic exposure, it can develop a strategy to reduce that exposure.

Pricing policy. Silverton recognizes that there will be periods in the future when the euro will depreciate against the pound. Under these conditions, Unit C may attempt to be more competitive by reducing its prices. If the euro's value declines by 10% and this reduces the prices that UK customers pay for the foreign products by 10%, then Unit C can attempt to remain competitive by discounting its prices by 10%. Although this strategy can retain market share, the lower prices will result in less revenue and therefore less cash flows. Therefore, this strategy does not completely eliminate Silverton's economic exposure. Nevertheless, this strategy may still be feasible, especially if the unit can charge relatively high prices in periods when the euro is strong and UK customers have to pay higher prices for European products. In essence, the strategy might allow the unit to generate abnormally high cash flows in a strong-euro period to offset the abnormally low cash flows in a weak-euro period. The adverse effect during a weak-euro period will still occur, however. Given the limitations of this strategy, other strategies should be considered.

Hedging with forward contracts. Silverton's Unit C could sell euros forward for the period in which it wants to hedge against the adverse effects of the weak euro. Assume the spot and three-month forward rates on the euro are £0.80. If the euro weakens, the cash flows from normal operations will still be adversely affected. However, the unit would generate a gain on the forward contract because it will be able to purchase euros at the spot rate at the end of the period at a lower exchange rate than the rate at which it will have to sell those euros to fulfil the forward contract. The weaker the euro, the more pronounced will be the adverse effects on the unit's cash flows from normal operations, but the gains from the forward contract will also be more pronounced.

Using a forward contract has definite limitations, however. Since the economic exposure is likely to continue indefinitely, the use of a forward contract in the manner described here hedges only for the period of the contract. It does not serve as a continuous long-term hedge against economic exposure.

Purchasing foreign supplies. Another possibility is for the unit to purchase its materials in Europe, a strategy that would reduce its costs (and enhance its cash flows) during a weak-euro period to offset the adverse effects of the weak euro. However, the cost of buying European materials may be higher than the cost of buying local materials, especially when transportation expenses are considered.

Financing with foreign funds. The unit could also reduce its economic exposure by financing a portion of its business with loans in euros. It could convert the loan proceeds to pounds and use the pounds to support its business. It will need to make periodic loan repayments in euros. If the euro weakens, the unit will need fewer pounds to cover the loan repayments. This favourable effect can partially offset the adverse effect of a weak euro on the unit's revenue. If the euro strengthens, the unit will need more pounds to cover the loan repayments, but this adverse effect will be offset by the favourable effect of the strong euro on the unit's revenue. This type of hedge is more effective than the pricing hedge because it can offset the adverse effects of a weak euro in the same period (whereas the pricing policy attempts to make up for lost cash flows once the euro strengthens).

This strategy also has some limitations. First, the strategy only makes sense if Silverton needs some debt financing. It should not borrow funds just for the sake of hedging its economic exposure. Second, Silverton might not desire this strategy when the euro has a very high interest rate. Though borrowing in euros can reduce its economic exposure, it may not be willing to enact the hedge at a cost of higher interest expenses than it would pay in the United Kingdom.

Third, this strategy is unlikely to create a perfect hedge against Silverton's economic exposure. Even if the company needs debt financing and the interest rate charged on the foreign loan is low, Silverton must attempt to determine the amount of debt financing that will hedge its economic exposure. The amount of foreign debt financing necessary to fully hedge the exposure may exceed the amount of funding that Silverton needs.

Revising operations of other units. Given the limitations of hedging Unit C's economic exposure by adjusting the unit's operations, Silverton may consider modifying the operations of another unit in a manner that will offset the exposure of Unit C. However, this strategy may require changes in another unit that will not necessarily benefit that unit. For example, assume that Unit C could partially hedge its economic exposure by borrowing euros (as explained above) but that it does not need to borrow as much as would be necessary to fully offset its economic exposure. Silverton's top management may suggest that Units A and B also obtain their financing in euros, so that the MNC's overall economic exposure is hedged. Thus, a weak euro would still adversely affect Unit C because the adverse effect on its revenue would not be fully offset by the favourable effect on its financing (debt repayments). Yet, if the other units have borrowed euros as well, the combined favourable effects on financing for Silverton overall could offset the adverse effects on Unit C.

However, Units A and B will not necessarily desire to finance their operations in euros. Recall that these units are not subject to economic exposure. Also recall that the managers of each unit are compensated according to the performance of that unit. By agreeing to finance in euros, Units A and B could become exposed to movements in the euro. If the euro strengthens, their cost of financing increases. So, by helping to offset the exposure of Unit C, Units A and B could experience weaker performance, and their managers would receive less compensation.

A solution is still possible if Silverton's top managers who are not affiliated with any unit can remove the hedging activity from the compensation formula for the units' managers. That is, top management could instruct Units A and B to borrow funds in euros, but could reward the managers of those units based on an assessment of the units' performance that excludes the effect of the euro on financing costs. In this way, the managers will be more willing to engage in a strategy that increases their economic exposure while reducing Silverton's.

Silverton's hedging solution

In summary, Silverton's initial analysis of its units determined that only Unit C was highly subject to economic exposure. Unit C could attempt to use a pricing policy that would maintain market share when the euro weakens, but this strategy would not eliminate the economic exposure because its cash flows would still be adversely affected. Borrowing euros can be an effective strategy to hedge Unit C's exposure, but it does not need to borrow the amount of funds necessary to offset its exposure. The optimal solution for Silverton is to instruct its other units to do their financing in euros as well. This strategy effectively increases their exposure, but in the opposite manner of Unit C's exposure, so that the MNC's economic exposure overall is reduced. The units' managers should be willing to cooperate if their compensation is not reduced as a result of increasing the exposure of their individual units.

Limitations of Silverton's optimal hedging strategy

Even if Silverton is able to achieve the hedge described above, the hedge will still not be perfect. The impact of the euro's movements on Silverton's cash outflows needed to repay the loans is known with certainty. But the impact of the euro's movements on Silverton's cash inflows (revenue) is uncertain and can change over time. If the amount of foreign competition increases, the sensitivity of Unit C's cash flows to exchange rates would increase. To hedge this increased exposure, it would need to borrow a larger amount of euros. An MNC's economic exposure can change over time in response to shifts in foreign competition or other global conditions, so it must continually assess and manage its economic exposure.

HEDGING EXPOSURE TO FIXED ASSETS

Up to this point, the focus has been on how economic exposure can affect periodic cash flows. The effects may extend beyond periodic cash flows, however. When an MNC has fixed assets (such as buildings or machinery) in a foreign country, the cash flows to be received from the ultimate sale of these assets is subject to exchange rate risk.

EXAMPLE

Wagner ltd a UK firm, pursued a six-year project in Russia. It purchased a manufacturing plant from the Russian government in April 1998 for 500 million roubles. Since the rouble was worth £0.10 at the time of the investment, Wagner needed £50 million to purchase the plant. The Russian government guaranteed that it would repurchase the plant for 500 million roubles in July 2005 when the project was completed. In July 2005, however, the rouble was worth only £0.02, so Wagner received only £10 million (computed as 500 million × £0.02) from selling the plant. Even though the price of the plant in roubles at the time of the sale was the same as the price at the time of the purchase, the sales price of the plant in pounds at the time of the sale was 80% less than the purchase price.

Some MNCs may not worry about the exchange rate effect on fixed assets because they normally expect to retain the assets for several years. Given the frequent restructuring of global operations, however, MNCs should consider hedging against the possible sale of these assets in the distant future. A sale of fixed assets can be hedged by creating a liability that matches the expected value of the assets at the point in the future when they may be sold. In essence, the sale of the fixed assets generates a foreign currency cash inflow that can be used to pay off the liability that is denominated in the same currency.

EXAMPLE

In the previous example, Wagner could have financed part of its investment in the Russian manufacturing plant by borrowing roubles from a local bank, with the loan structured to have zero interest payments and a lump-sum repayment value equal to the expected sales price set for the date when Wagner expected to sell the plant. Thus, the loan could have been structured to have a lump-sum repayment value of 500 million roubles in July 2005. Any loss in expected revenue would therefore be matched by the reduced cost of repaying the loan.

The limitations of hedging a sale of fixed assets are that an MNC does not necessarily know the date when it will sell the assets or the price in local currency at which it will sell them. Consequently, it is unable to create a liability that perfectly matches the date and amount of the sale of the fixed assets. Nevertheless, any hedging strategy that reduces the time the exposure is unhedged is valuable – any residual unhedged periods will be much shorter and therefore present far less risk to the firm.

EXAMPLE

Even if the Russian government would not guarantee a purchase price of the plant, Wagner could create a liability that reflects the earliest possible sale date and the lowest expected sale price. If the sale date turns out to be later than the earliest possible sale date, Wagner might be able to extend its loan period to match the sale date. By structuring the lump-sum loan repayment to match the minimum sale price, Wagner will not be perfectly hedged if the fixed assets turn out to be worth more than the minimum expected amount. Nevertheless, Wagner would at least have reduced its exposure by offsetting a portion of the fixed assets with a liability in the same currency.

Long-term forward contracts may also be a possible way to hedge the distant sale of fixed assets in foreign countries, but they may not be available for many emerging market currencies.

MANAGING TRANSLATION EXPOSURE

Translation exposure occurs when an MNC translates each subsidiary's financial data to its home currency for consolidated financial statements. Even if translation exposure does not affect cash flows, it is a concern of many MNCs because it can reduce an MNC's consolidated earnings and risks causing a decline in its share price. Thus, some MNCs may consider hedging their translation exposure. Annual reports of multinationals for the most part make statements along the lines of: "*While the Group uses short term hedging for trading activities, the Company does not believe that it is appropriate or practicable to hedge long term translation exposure*" (Cadbury Schweppes).

A statement that does not preclude the following: "*In addition the Group hedges balance sheet risk selectively*" (Adidas).

Occasionally more committed statements are made: "*The company does not hedge the exposure arising from translation exposure of net income in foreign entities. Translation exposure of equity invested in consolidated foreign entities financed by equity is partially hedged*" (Philips).

The phrase "the Company does not believe that it is appropriate" in the first quote is interesting. Changes in profits due solely to reporting practices are not relevant to the future prosperity of the firm because they do not represent actual transactions. Hedging a translation exposure should not further the wealth of the shareholders and therefore is not appropriate as expenditure. But this argument critically relies on the semi-strong form of efficient market, namely, that all public information is interpreted in a timely and unbiased manner (i.e. without consistent errors). The company has every chance in the annual report to distinguish translation exposure from other types of exposure. If the market interprets the information correctly and sees that shareholder wealth is not affected, there should indeed be no need to hedge such exposure. Nevertheless, multinationals are perfectly entitled to hedge translation risk. Some companies are very exposed to such risk and may well argue that a failure to protect against such risk may be interpreted as a signal of weakness on the part of management. The consequent fall in share price would affect the wealth of shareholders and therefore justify hedging.

Use of forward contracts to hedge translation exposure

MNCs can use forward contracts or futures contracts to hedge translation exposure. Specifically, they can sell the currency forward that their foreign subsidiaries receive as earnings. In this way, they create a cash outflow in the currency to offset the earnings received in that currency.

EXAMPLE

Callia SA, is a Greek-based MNC with just one subsidiary. As of the beginning of its fiscal year, the subsidiary, which is located in the United Kingdom, forecasts that its annual earnings will be £20 million. The subsidiary plans to reinvest the entire amount of earnings within the United Kingdom and does not plan to remit any earnings back to the parent in Greece. While there is no foreseeable transaction exposure in the near future from the future earnings (since the pounds will remain in the United Kingdom), Callia is exposed to translation exposure.

In the consolidated profit and loss account, the British earnings will be translated at the weighted average value of the pound over the course of the year. If the British pound is currently worth 1.30 euros and its value remains constant during the year, the forecasted translation of British earnings into euros would be 26 million euros (computed as £20 million × 1.30 euros per pound).

Callia SA, may be concerned that the translated value of the British earnings will be reduced if the pound's value declines during the year. To hedge this translation exposure, Callia can implement a forward hedge using futures contracts on the expected earnings by selling £20 million one year forward. Assume the futures rate at that time is 1.30 euros, the same as the spot rate. At the end of the year, if the spot rate has fallen to, say, 1.2 euros to the pound, Callia *will have received* the difference of 0.1 euros × £20m or £200,000 through daily settlement. This amount matches the arbitrage profit on maturity that the Greek company could have made by buying £20m at the spot rate of 1.2 euros and selling at the higher futures rate of 1.3 euros. If the pound appreciates during the fiscal year, then Callia will be have to pay the difference between 1.3 euros and the higher rate. This payment or loss reflects the operation of buying £20m at the above 1.3 euro rate and fulfilling the contract by selling at the lower 1.2 euro rate. In such a case Callia will have incurred a real loss in a failed attempt to save a potential paper loss.

The precise level of income generated by the forward contract will depend on the spot rate of the pound at the end of the fiscal year. Under conditions in which the pound depreciates, the translation loss will be somewhat offset by the gain generated from the forward contract position.

Limitations of hedging translation exposure

There are five limitations in hedging translation exposure.

Inaccurate earnings forecasts. A subsidiary's forecasted earnings for the end of the year are not guaranteed. In the previous example involving Callia SA, British earnings were projected to be £20 million. If the actual earnings turned out to be much higher, and if the pound weakens during the year, the translation loss would likely exceed the gain generated from the forward contract strategy.

Inadequate forward contracts for some currencies. A second limitation is that forward contracts are not available for all currencies. Thus, an MNC with subsidiaries in some smaller countries may not be able to obtain forward contracts for the currencies of concern.

Accounting distortions. A third limitation is that the forward rate gain or loss reflects the difference between the forward rate and the future spot rate, whereas the translation gain or loss reflects the difference between the average exchange rate over the period of concern and the future spot rate. In addition, the translation losses are not tax deductible, whereas gains on forward contracts used to hedge translation exposure are taxed.

Increased transaction exposure. The fourth and most critical limitation with a hedging strategy (forward or money market hedge) on translation exposure is that the MNC may be increasing its transaction exposure. For example, consider a situation in which the subsidiary's currency appreciates during the fiscal year, resulting in a translation gain. If the MNC enacts a hedge strategy that results in losses if the foreign currency appreciates, this strategy will generate a transaction (real) loss that will partly offset the translation gain.

A translation loss is not a real loss. It has already been noted that reporting a loss that is due purely to accounting conventions rather than actual losses should not affect the value of a multinational in an efficient stock market. A translation gain is simply a paper gain arising out of the need to report in one currency. In the Callia example, none of the British pound earnings were translated into the home currency of euros; but an appreciation of the pound would have increased the accounting profits of Callia overall. The appreciation of the pound does affect expectations of future profits, but whether or not one reporting convention is used as opposed to another should not affect the valuation of the company. As actual cash flows are not affected, the value of the company should not be affected in an efficient stock market. Conversely, the loss resulting from a hedge strategy is a *real* loss; that is, the net cash flow to the parent will be reduced due to this loss. Incurring a real loss to avoid a paper loss is not a policy that is actively pursued by multinationals as the extract from accounts given above illustrate.

SUMMARY

- Economic exposure can be managed by balancing the sensitivity of revenue and expenses to exchange rate fluctuations. To accomplish this, however, the firm must first recognize how its revenue and expenses are affected by exchange rate fluctuations. For some firms, revenue is more susceptible. These firms are most concerned that their home currency will appreciate against foreign currencies, since the unfavourable effects on revenue will more than offset the favourable effects on expenses. Conversely, firms whose expenses are more sensitive to exchange rates than their revenue are most concerned that their home currency will depreciate against foreign currencies. When firms reduce their economic exposure, they reduce not only these unfavourable effects but also the favourable effects if the home currency value moves in the opposite direction.

■ Translation exposure can be reduced by selling forward the foreign currency used to measure a subsidiary's income. If the foreign currency depreciates against the home currency, the adverse impact on the consolidated income statement can be offset by the gain on the forward sale in that currency. If the foreign currency appreciates over the time period of concern, there will be a loss on the forward sale that is offset by a favourable effect on the reported consolidated earnings. However, many MNCs would not be satisfied with a "paper gain" that offsets a "cash loss".

CRITICAL DEBATE

Should an MNC reduce expected profits by hedging as in the Mannerton example in order to limit losses in less likely scenarios?

Proposition. Yes. Extreme losses will disrupt the running of the company and put future earnings in jeopardy. By protecting against such losses the company is protecting shareholders' long-term interests.

Opposing view. No. Investors know the risk. Part of the reason for investing in a multinational is to benefit from the exchange rate risk. If a company hedges against such risk, they are only protecting themselves at the expense of the shareholders.

With whom do you agree? Which argument do you support? Offer your own opinion on this issue.

SELF TEST

Answers are provided in Appendix A at the back of the text.

1. Salem Exporting ltd (UK) purchases chemicals from UK sources and uses them to make pharmaceutical products that are exported to US hospitals. Salem prices its products in dollars and is concerned about the possibility of the long-term depreciation of the dollar against the pound. It periodically hedges its exposure with short-term forward contracts, but this does not insulate against the possible trend of continuing dollar depreciation. How could Salem offset some of its exposure resulting from its export business?

2. Using the information in question 1, give a possible disadvantage of offsetting exchange rate exposure from the export business.

3. Neve NV is a Dutch firm with a subsidiary in the United States. It expects that the dollar will depreciate this year. Explain Neve's translation exposure. How could Neve hedge its translation exposure?

4. Cheriton plc has substantial translation exposure in US subsidiaries. The treasurer of Cheriton plc suggests that the translation effects are not relevant because the earnings generated by the US subsidiaries are not being remitted to the UK parent, but are simply being reinvested in the US. Nevertheless, the director of finance of Cheriton plc is concerned about translation exposure because the stock price is highly dependent on the consolidated earnings, which are dependent on the exchange rates at which the earnings are translated. Who is correct?

5. Lincolnshire ltd manufactures wholly in the UK and exports 80% of its total production of goods to Latin American countries. Kalafa ltd sells all the goods it produces to Latin America, but it has a subsidiary in Spain that usually generates about 20% of its total earnings. Compare the translation exposure of these two UK firms.

QUESTIONS AND APPLICATIONS

1. **Reducing economic exposure.** Banter plc is an Irish based MNC that obtains 10% of its supplies from US manufacturers. Of its revenues, 60% are due to exports to the US, where its product is invoiced in dollars. Explain how Banter can attempt to reduce its economic exposure to exchange rate fluctuations in the dollar.

2. **Reducing economic exposure.** UVA ltd is a UK-based MNC that obtains 40% of its foreign supplies from Thailand. It also borrows Thailand's currency (the baht) from Thai banks and converts the baht to pounds to support UK operations. It currently receives about 10% of its revenue from Thai customers. Its sales to Thai customers are denominated in baht. Explain how UVA ltd can reduce its economic exposure to exchange rate fluctuations.

3. **Reducing economic exposure.** Alright ltd is a UK-based MNC that has a large government contract with Australia. The contract will continue for several years and generate more than half of Albany's total sales volume. The Australian government pays Albany in Australian dollars. About 10% of Albany's operating expenses are in Australian dollars; all other expenses are in pounds. Explain how Alright can reduce its economic exposure to exchange rate fluctuations.

4. **Tradeoffs when reducing economic exposure.** When an MNC restructures its operations to reduce its economic exposure, it may sometimes forgo economies of scale. Explain.

5. **Exchange rate effects on earnings.** Explain how an MNC's consolidated earnings are affected when foreign currencies depreciate.

6. **Hedging translation exposure.** Explain how a firm can hedge its translation exposure.

7. **Limitations of hedging translation exposure.** Bartunek Co is a US-based MNC that has European subsidiaries and wants to hedge its translation exposure to fluctuations in the euro's value. Explain some limitations when it hedges translation exposure.

8. **Effective hedging of translation exposure.** Would a more established MNC or a less established MNC be better able to effectively hedge its given level of translation exposure? Why?

9. **Comparing degrees of economic exposure.** Carlton ltd and Palmer ltd are UK-based MNCs with subsidiaries in Brazil that distribute medical supplies (produced in the United Kingdom) to customers throughout Latin America. Both subsidiaries purchase the products at cost and sell the products at 90% markup. The other operating costs of the subsidiaries are very low.

   Carlton has a research and development centre in the United Kingdom that focuses on improving its medical technology. Palmer has a similar centre based in Brazil. The parent of each firm subsidizes its respective research and development centre on an annual basis. Which firm is subject to a higher degree of economic exposure? Explain.

10. **Comparing degrees of translation exposure.** Nelson ltd is a UK firm with annual export sales to Singapore of about £20 million. Its main competitor is Hamilton ltd also based in the United Kingdom, with a subsidiary in Singapore that also generates about £20 million in annual sales. Any earnings generated by the subsidiary are reinvested to support its operations.

    Based on the information provided, which firm is subject to a higher degree of translation exposure? Explain.

ADVANCED QUESTIONS

11. **Managing economic exposure.** St Paul ltd (a UK company) does business in the United Kingdom and New Zealand. In attempting to assess its economic exposure, it compiled the following information.
    a. St Paul's UK sales are somewhat affected by the value of the New Zealand dollar (NZ$), because it faces competition from New Zealand exporters. It forecasts the UK sales based on the following three exchange rate scenarios:

Exchange rate of NZ$	Revenue from UK business (in millions)
NZ$ = £0.32	£100
NZ$ = 0.33	105
NZ$ = 0.36	110

b. Its New Zealand dollar revenues on sales to New Zealand invoiced in New Zealand dollars are expected to be NZ$600 million.

c. Its anticipated cost of goods sold is estimated at £200 million from the purchase of UK materials and NZ$100 million from the purchase of New Zealand materials.

d. Fixed operating expenses are estimated at £30 million.

e. Variable operating expenses are approximated as 20% of total sales (after including New Zealand sales, translated to a pound amount).

f. Interest expense is estimated at £20 million on existing UK loans, and the company has no existing New Zealand loans.

Create a forecasted income statement for St Paul under each of the three exchange rate scenarios. Explain how St Paul's projected earnings before taxes are affected by possible exchange rate movements. Explain how it can restructure its operations to reduce the sensitivity of its earnings to exchange rate movements without reducing its volume of business in New Zealand.

12. **Assessing economic exposure.** Alhambra plc plans to create and finance a subsidiary in Argentina that produces computer components at a low cost and exports them to other countries. It has no other international business. The subsidiary will produce computers and export them to Africa and will invoice the products in pounds. The values of the currencies in Africa are expected to remain very stable against the pound. The subsidiary will pay wages, rent, and other operating costs in Argentine pesos. The subsidiary will remit earnings monthly to the parent.

a. Would Alhambra's cash flows be favourably or unfavourably affected if the Argentine peso depreciates over time?

b. Assume that Alhambra considers partial financing of this subsidiary with peso loans from Argentine banks instead of providing all the financing with its own funds. Would this alternative form of financing increase, decrease, or have no effect on the degree to which Alhambra is exposed to exchange rate movements of the peso?

13. **Hedging continual exposure.** Consider this common real-world dilemma faced by many firms that rely on exporting. Clearlake ltd produces its products in its factory in the UK and exports most of the products to Europe each month. The exports are denominated in euros. Clearlake recognizes that hedging on a monthly basis does not really protect against long-term movements in exchange rates. It also recognizes that it could eliminate its transaction exposure by denominating the exports in British pounds, but that it still would have economic exposure because European consumers would reduce demand if the euro weakened. Clearlake does not know how many euros it will receive in the future, so it would have difficulty even if a long-term hedging method were available. How can Clearlake realistically deal with this dilemma and reduce its exposure over the long term? (There is no perfect solution, but in the real world, there rarely are perfect solutions.)

PROJECT WORKSHOP

14. **Researching MNCs and exposure.** The following website provides annual reports of numerous MNCs: http://reportgallery.com. You may also access annual reports via the FT website at http://www.ft.com and international reports via http://www.forbes.com choosing lists.

a. Review an annual report of an MNC of your choice. Look for any comments that relate to the MNC's economic or translation exposure. Does it appear that the MNC hedges its economic exposure or translation exposure? If so, what methods does it use to hedge its exposure?

b. The following website provides exchange rate movements between currencies over time: http://www.oanda.com.

Based on the translation exposure of the MNC you assessed in exercise (a), determine whether the exchange rate movements of whatever currency (or currencies) it is exposed to moved in a favourable or unfavourable direction over the reporting period.

Further notes: search the annual reports using the keyword "risk". You will find the MNC's policy on currency risk. Fuller details are given by the major multinationals. These can include: estimates of the sensitivity of profits to a 1% currency change; derivative returns from currency change; the main types of hedging used and principal type of exposure. Do not just report their calculations; make your own estimates from the data provided.

DISCUSSION IN THE BOARDROOM

This exercise can be found on the companion website at www.cengage.co.uk/madura_fox.

RUNNING YOUR OWN MNC

This exercise can be found on the companion website at www.cengage.co.uk/madura_fox.

Essays/discussion and articles can be found at the end of Part 3

BLADES PLC CASE STUDY
Assessment of economic exposure

Blades plc has been exporting to Thailand since its decision to supplement its declining UK sales by exporting there. Furthermore, Blades has recently begun exporting to a retailer in the United States. The suppliers of the components needed by Blades for roller blade production (such as rubber and plastic) are located in the United Kingdom and Thailand. Blades decided to use Thai suppliers for rubber and plastic components needed to manufacture roller blades because of cost and quality considerations. All of Blades' exports and imports are denominated in the respective foreign currency; for example, Blades pays for the Thai imports in baht.

The decision to export to Thailand was supported by the fact that Thailand had been one of the world's fastest growing economies in recent years. Furthermore, Blades found an importer in Thailand that was willing to commit itself to the annual purchase of 180,000 pairs of Blades' "Speedos", which are among the highest quality roller blades in the world. The commitment began last year and will last another two years, at which time it may be renewed by the two parties. Due to this commitment, Blades is selling its roller blades for 4,594 baht per pair (approximately £60 at current exchange rates) instead of the usual £72 per pair. Although this price represents a substantial

discount from the regular price for a pair of Speedo blades, it still constitutes a considerable markup above cost. Because importers in other Asian countries were not willing to make this type of commitment, this was a decisive factor in the choice of Thailand for exporting purposes. Although Ben Holt, Blades' financial director, believes the sports product market in Asia has very high future growth potential, Blades has recently begun exporting to Jogs ltd, a US retailer. Jogs has committed itself to purchase 200,000 pair of Speedos annually for a fixed price of $80 per pair.

For the coming year, Blades expects to import rubber and plastic components from Thailand sufficient to manufacture 80,000 pairs of Speedos, at a cost of approximately 3,000 baht per pair of Speedos.

You, as Blades' financial analyst, have pointed out to Ben Holt that events in Asia have fundamentally affected the economic condition of Asian countries, including Thailand. For example, you have pointed out that the high level of consumer spending on leisure products such as roller blades has declined considerably. Thus, the Thai retailer may not renew its commitment with Blades in two years. Furthermore, you are worried that the current economic conditions in Thailand may lead to a substantial depreciation of the Thai baht, which would affect Blades negatively.

Despite recent developments, however, Ben Holt remains optimistic; he is convinced that South East Asia will exhibit high potential for growth when the impact of recent events in Asia subsides. Consequently, Holt has no doubt that the Thai customer will renew its commitment for another three years when the current agreement terminates. In your opinion, Holt is not considering all of the factors that might directly or indirectly affect Blades. Moreover, you are worried that he is ignoring Blades' future in Thailand even if the Thai importer renews its commitment for another three years. In fact, you believe that a renewal of the existing agreement with the Thai customer may affect Blades negatively due to the high level of inflation in Thailand.

Since Holt is interested in your opinion and wants to assess Blades' economic exposure in Thailand, he has asked you to conduct an analysis of the impact of the value of the baht on next year's earnings to assess Blades' economic exposure. You have gathered the following information:

- Blades has forecasted sales in the United Kingdom of 520,000 pairs of Speedos at regular prices; exports to Thailand of 180,000 pairs of Speedos for 4,594 baht a pair; and exports to the United States of 200,000 pairs of Speedos for $80 per pair.

- Cost of goods sold for 80,000 pairs of Speedos are incurred in Thailand; the remainder is incurred in the United States, where the cost of goods sold per pair of Speedos runs to approximately £70.

- Fixed costs are £2 million, and variable operating expenses other than costs of goods sold represent approximately 11% of UK sales. All fixed and variable operating expenses other than cost of goods sold are incurred in the United States.

- Events in Asia have increased the uncertainty regarding certain Asian currencies considerably, making it extremely difficult to forecast the value of the baht at which the Thai revenues will be converted. The current spot rate of the baht is £0.0147, and the current spot rate of the dollar is £0.67. You have created three scenarios and derived an expected value on average for the upcoming year based on each scenario:

Scenario	Effect on the average value of the baht	Average value of the baht	Average value of the dollar
1	No change	£0.015	£0.654
2	Depreciate by 5%	£0.01425	0.6213
3	Depreciate by 10%	£0.0135	£0.5886

- Blades currently has no debt in its capital structure. However, it may borrow funds in Thailand if it establishes a subsidiary in the country.

Ben Holt has asked you to answer the following questions:

1. How will Blades be negatively affected by the high level of inflation in Thailand if the Thai customer renews its commitment for another three years?

2. Holt believes that the Thai importer will renew its commitment in two years. Do you think his assessment is correct? Why or why not? Also, assume that the Thai economy returns to the high growth level that existed prior to the recent unfavourable economic events. Under this assumption, how likely is it that the Thai importer will renew its commitment in two years?

3. For each of the three possible values of the Thai baht and the dollar, use a spreadsheet to construct a pro forma income statement for the next year. Briefly comment on the level of Blades' economic exposure.

4. Now repeat your analysis in question 3 but assume that the British pound and the Thai baht are perfectly correlated. For example, if the baht depreciates by 5%, the pound will also depreciate by 5%. Under this assumption, is Blades subject to a greater degree of economic exposure? Why or why not?

5. Based on your answers to the previous three questions, what actions could Blades take to reduce its level of economic exposure to Thailand?

SMALL BUSINESS DILEMMA

Hedging the Sports Exports Company's economic exposure to exchange rate risk

Jim Logan, owner of the Sports Exports Company (Ireland), remains concerned about his exposure to exchange rate risk. Even if Jim hedges his transactions from one month to another, he recognizes that a long-term trend of depreciation in the British pound could have a severe impact on his firm. He believes that he must continue to focus on the British market for selling his basketballs. However, he plans to consider various ways in which he can reduce his economic exposure. At the current time, he obtains material from a local manufacturer and uses a machine to produce the basketballs, which are then exported. He still uses his garage as a place of production and would like to continue using his garage to maintain low operating expenses.

1. How could Jim adjust his operations to reduce his economic exposure? What is a possible disadvantage of such an adjustment?

2. Offer another solution to hedging the economic exposure in the long run as Jim's business grows. What are the disadvantages of this solution?

EXCHANGE RATE RISK MANAGEMENT

Vogel ltd is a UK firm conducting a financial plan for the next year. It has no foreign subsidiaries, but more than half of its sales are from exports. Its foreign cash inflows to be received from exporting and cash outflows to be paid for imported supplies over the next year are shown in the following table:

Currency	Total Inflow	Total Outflow
Canadian dollar (C$)	C$32,000,000	C$2,000,000
New Zealand dollar (NZ$)	NZ$5,000,000	NZ$1,000,000
Mexican peso (MXP)	MXP11,000,000	MXP10,000,000
Singapore dollar (S$)	S$4,000,000	S$8,000,000

The spot rates and one-year forward rates as of today are shown below:

Currency	Spot Rate	One-Year Forward Rate
C$	£0.60	£0.63
NZ$	0.40	0.39
MXP	0.14	0.12
S$	0.42	0.41

Questions

1. Based on the information provided, determine Vogel's net exposure to each foreign currency in dollars.
2. Assume that today's spot rate is used as a forecast of the future spot rate one year from now. The New Zealand dollar, Mexican peso, and Singapore dollar are expected to move in tandem against the British pound over the next year. The Canadian dollar's movements are expected to be unrelated to movements of the other currencies. Since exchange rates are difficult to predict, the forecasted net pound cash flows per currency may be inaccurate. Do you anticipate any offsetting exchange rate effects from whatever exchange movements do occur? Explain.
3. Given the forecast of the Canadian dollar along with the forward rate of the Canadian dollar, what is the expected increase or decrease in dollar cash flows that would result from hedging the net cash flows in Canadian dollars? Would you hedge the Canadian dollar position?
4. Assume that the Canadian dollar net inflows may range from C$20,000,000 to C$40,000,000 over the next year. Explain the risk of hedging C$30,000,000 in net inflows. How can Vogel ltd avoid such a risk? Is there any tradeoff resulting from your strategy to avoid that risk?
5. Vogel recognizes that its year-to-year hedging strategy hedges the risk only over a given year and does not insulate it from long-term trends in the Canadian dollar's value. It has considered establishing a subsidiary in Canada. The goods would be sent from the United Kingdom to the Canadian subsidiary and distributed by the subsidiary. The proceeds received would be reinvested by the Canadian subsidiary in Canada. In this way, Vogel would not have to convert Canadian dollars to pounds each year. Has Vogel eliminated its exposure to exchange rate risk by using this strategy? Explain.

1. Bodnar, G.M. (1999) "Derivative Usage in Risk Management by US and German Non Financial Firms", *Journal of International Financial Management and Accounting*, 10, (3), 153–87.

   Q *Describe the usage of derivatives by US and German firms. Discuss possible trends in Europe, will usage inevitably become more like the US model?*

2. Dominguez, K.M.E. and L.L. Tesar (2006) "Exchange Rate Exposure", *Journal of International Economics*, 68, 188–218. Some relatively simple regression analysis looking at MNC valuation and exchange rates.

   Q *What can be learned from the Dominguez and Tesar article that can be of practical use to a Finance Director of an MNC? Discuss.*

3. Dhanani, A. (2003) "Foreign Exchange Risk Management: A Case in the Mining Industry", *British Accounting Review*, 35, 35–63. An excellent review and case study.

   Q *Evaluate the way in which the exchange rate risk management of ABC plc in the mining industry (as described by Dhanani) differs from the exchange rate risk management of other multinationals. More generally, how important are the activities of multinationals in determining exchange rate risk policy?*

4. Solomon, J.F. (1999) "Do Institutional Investors in the UK Adopt a Dual Strategy for Managing Foreign Exchange Risk", *British Accounting Review*, 31, 205–24. This is, in fact, an excellent survey of the factors influencing foreign investment.

   Q *Combine the survey results in Solomon's article to produce an overall description of the factors influencing portfolio investment. Assess the extent to which practice differs from theory.*

5. Dhanani, A. and R. Groves (2001) "The Management of Strategic Exchange Risk: Evidence from Corporate Practices", *Accounting and Business Research*, 31 (4), 275–90.

   Q *From a reading of the Dhanani and Groves article, discuss the organizational issues involved in managing exchange rate risk.*

6. Makar, S.D. J. deBruin and S.P. Huffman (1999) 2The Management of Foreign Currency Risk: Derivatives Use and the Natural Hedge of Geographic Diversification", *Accounting & Business Research*, 29 (3), 229–37.

   Q *Explain the hypothesis advanced by Makar et al. concerning the use of derivatives. Assess the strength of their findings.*

LONG-TERM ASSET AND LIABILITY MANAGEMENT

PART 4 (CHAPTERS 13 THROUGH 18) focuses on how multinational corporations (MNCs) manage long-term assets and liabilities. Chapter 13 explains how MNCs can benefit from international business. Chapter 14 describes the information MNCs must have when considering multinational projects and demonstrates how the capital budgeting analysis is conducted. Chapter 15 identifies the common forms of multinational restructuring and illustrates

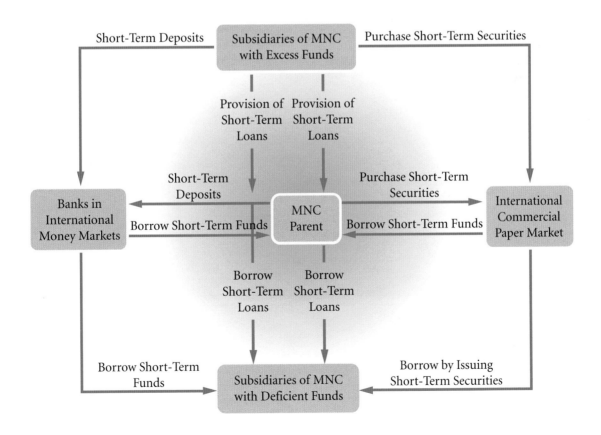

how to assess the feasibility of proposed forms of restructuring. Chapter 16 explains how MNCs assess country risk associated with their prevailing projects as well as with their proposed projects. Chapter 17 explains the capital structure decision for MNCs, which affects the cost of financing new projects. Chapter 18 describes the MNC's long-term financing decision.

CHAPTER 13

FOREIGN DIRECT INVESTMENT

MNCs COMMONLY CAPITALIZE ON foreign business opportunities by engaging in foreign direct investment (FDI), which is investment in real assets (such as land, buildings, or even existing plants) in foreign countries. They engage in joint ventures with foreign firms, acquire foreign firms, and form new foreign subsidiaries. Any of these types of FDI (involving ownership interest in a legally recognized foreign entity) can generate high returns when managed properly. However, FDI requires a substantial investment and can therefore put much capital at risk. Moreover, if the investment does not perform as well as expected, the MNC may have difficulty selling the foreign project it created. Given these return and risk characteristics of FDI, MNCs tend to carefully analyze the potential benefits and costs before implementing any type of FDI. Financial managers must understand the potential return and risk associated with FDI so that they can make investment decisions that maximize the MNC's value.

THE SPECIFIC OBJECTIVES OF THIS CHAPTER ARE TO:

- describe common motives for initiating foreign direct investment and
- illustrate the benefits of international diversification.

MOTIVES FOR FOREIGN DIRECT INVESTMENT

MNCs commonly consider foreign direct investment because it can improve their profitability and enhance shareholder wealth. In most cases, MNCs engage in FDI because they are interested in boosting revenues, reducing costs, or both.

Revenue-related motives

The following are typical motives of MNCs that are attempting to boost revenues:

■ *Attract new sources of demand.* A corporation often reaches a stage when growth is limited in its home country, possibly because of intense competition. Even if it faces little competition, its market share in its home country may already be near its potential peak. Thus, the firm may consider foreign markets where there is potential demand. Many developing countries, such as Argentina, Chile, Mexico, Hungary, and China, have been perceived as attractive sources of new demand. Many MNCs have penetrated these countries since barriers have been removed. Because the consumers in some countries have historically been restricted from purchasing goods produced by firms outside their countries, the markets for some goods are not well established and offer much potential for penetration by MNCs.

EXAMPLE

Blockbuster Entertainment Corp. (a US company) has recently established video stores in Australia, Chile, Japan, and several European countries where the video-rental concept is relatively new. With over 2,000 stores in the United States, Blockbuster's growth potential in the United States was limited.

China has also attracted MNCs. Motorola recently invested more than $1 billion in joint ventures in China. The Coca-Cola Co. has invested about $500 million in bottling facilities in China, and Scottish and Newcastle have purchased a 20% stake in one of the top five breweries. Siemens' (electrical goods and electrical engineering) sales were 2.9 billion euros in 2004 in China.

■ *Enter profitable markets.* If other corporations in the industry have proved that superior earnings can be realized in other markets, an MNC may also decide to sell in those markets. It may plan to undercut the prevailing, excessively high prices. A common problem with this strategy is that previously established sellers in a new market may prevent a new competitor from taking away their business by lowering their prices just when the new competitor attempts to break into this market.

■ *Exploit monopolistic advantages.* Firms may become internationalized if they possess resources or skills not available to competing firms. If a firm possesses advanced technology and has exploited this advantage successfully in local markets, the firm may attempt to exploit it internationally as well. In fact, the firm may have a more distinct advantage in markets that have less advanced technology.

■ *React to trade restrictions.* In some cases, MNCs use FDI as a defensive rather than an aggressive strategy. Specifically, MNCs may pursue FDI to circumvent trade barriers.

EXAMPLE

Japanese automobile manufacturers (notably Toyota and Honda) established plants in the United Kingdom in anticipation that their exports to the European Union would be subject to more stringent trade restrictions. Japanese companies recognized that trade barriers could be established that would limit or prohibit their exports. By producing automobiles in the United Kingdom, Japanese manufacturers could avoid such trade barriers.

- *Diversify internationally.* Since the economies of countries do not move perfectly in tandem over time, net cash flow from sales of products across countries should be more stable than comparable sales of the products in a single country. By diversifying sales (and possibly even production) internationally, a firm can make its net cash flows less volatile. Thus, the possibility of a liquidity deficiency is less likely. In addition, the firm may enjoy a lower cost of capital as shareholders and creditors perceive the MNC's risk to be lower as a result of more stable cash flows. Potential benefits to MNCs that diversify internationally are examined more thoroughly later in the chapter.

Cost-related motives

MNCs also engage in FDI in an effort to reduce costs. The following are typical motives of MNCs that are trying to cut costs:

- *Fully benefit from economies of scale.* A corporation that attempts to sell its primary product in new markets may increase its earnings and shareholder wealth due to **economies of scale** (lower average cost per unit resulting from increased production). Firms that utilize much machinery are most likely to benefit from economies of scale.

EXAMPLE

The removal of trade barriers within the European Union by the Single European Act allowed MNCs to achieve greater economies of scale. Some US-based MNCs consolidated their European plants because the removal of tariffs between countries in the European Union (EU) enabled firms to achieve economies of scale at a single European plant without incurring excessive exporting costs. The act also enhanced economies of scale by making regulations on television ads, automobile standards, and other products and services uniform across the EU. As a result, Colgate-Palmolive Co. and other MNCs are manufacturing more homogeneous products that can be sold in all EU countries. The adoption of the euro also encouraged consolidation by eliminating exchange rate risk within these countries.

- *Use foreign factors of production.* Labour and land costs can vary dramatically among countries. MNCs often attempt to set up production in locations where land and labour are cheap. Due to market imperfections (as discussed in Chapter 1) such as imperfect information, relocation transaction costs, and barriers to industry entry, specific labour costs do not necessarily become equal among markets. Thus, it is worthwhile for MNCs to survey markets to determine whether they can benefit from cheaper costs by producing in those markets.

EXAMPLE

Many MNCs have established subsidiaries in Mexico to achieve lower labour costs.

Mexico has attracted almost $5 billion in FDI from firms in the automobile industry, primarily because of the low-cost labour. Mexican workers at General Motors' subsidiaries who manufacture estates and trucks earn daily wages that are less than the average hourly rate for similar workers in the United Kingdom. Ford is also producing trucks at subsidiaries based in Mexico.

Volkswagen produces its Beetle in Mexico. DaimlerChrysler manufactures its 12-wheeler trucks in Mexico, and Nissan Motor Co. of Japan produces some of its wagons in Mexico.

Other Japanese companies are also increasingly using Mexico and other low-wage countries for production. For example, Sony Corp. recently established a plant in Tijuana. Matsushita Electrical Industrial Co. has a large plant in Tijuana.

- *Use foreign raw materials.* Due to transportation costs, a corporation may attempt to avoid importing raw materials from a given country, especially when it plans to sell the finished product back to consumers in that country. Under such circumstances, a more feasible solution may be to develop the product in the country where the raw materials are located.

- *Use foreign technology.* Corporations are increasingly establishing overseas plants or acquiring existing overseas plants to learn the technology of foreign countries. This technology is then used to improve their own production processes and increase production efficiency at all subsidiary plants around the world.

- *React to exchange rate movements.* When a firm perceives that a foreign currency is undervalued, the firm may consider FDI in that country, as the initial outlay should be relatively low.

   A related reason for such FDI is to offset the changing demand for a company's exports due to exchange rate fluctuations. For example, when Japanese automobile manufacturers build plants in the United States, they can reduce exposure to exchange rate fluctuations by incurring dollar costs for their production that offset dollar revenues. Although MNCs do not engage in large projects simply as an indirect means of speculating on currencies, the feasibility of proposed projects may be dependent on existing and expected exchange rate movements.

Cost-related motives in the expanded European Union. Several countries that became part of the European Union in 2004 were targeted for new FDI by MNCs that wanted to reduce manufacturing costs.

EXAMPLE

General Motors (Vauxhall and Opel) expanded its production in Poland, Peugeot increased its production in the Czech Republic, Toyota expanded its production in Slovakia, Audi expanded in Hungary, and Renault expanded in Romania. Volkswagen recently expanded its capacity in Slovenia, and cut jobs in Spain. While it originally established operations in Spain because the wages were about half of those in Germany, wages in Slovenia are less than half of those in Spain. Peugeot has recently also moved production from the UK to Eastern Europe. The expansion of the EU allows new member countries to transport products throughout Europe at reduced tariffs.

The shifts to low-wage countries will make manufacturers more efficient and competitive, but the tradeoff is thousands of jobs lost in Western Europe. However, it may be argued that the high unionized wages encouraged the firms to seek growth in productivity elsewhere. European labour unions tend to fight layoffs, but recognize that manufacturers might move completely out of the Western European countries where unions have more leverage, and move into the low-wage countries in Eastern Europe.

Comparing benefits of FDI among countries

The optimal way for a firm to penetrate a foreign market is partially dependent on the characteristics of the market. For example, foreign direct investment by US firms is common in Europe but not so common in Asia, where the people are accustomed to

http://

Also, visit **http://www.imf.org** and click on "country info" **http://www.worldbank.org** and click on "countries".

purchasing products from Asians. Thus, licensing arrangements or joint ventures may be more appropriate when firms are expanding into Asia.

Exhibit 13.1 summarizes the possible benefits of FDI and explains how MNCs can use FDI to achieve those benefits. Most MNCs pursue FDI based on their expectations of capitalizing on one or more of the potential benefits summarized in Exhibit 13.1. Although most attempts to increase international business are motivated by one or more of the benefits listed here, some disadvantages are also associated with FDI.

USING THE WEB

FDI indicators Visit Morgan Stanley's Global Economic Forum at http://www.morganstanley.com/GEFdata/digests/latest-digest.html for analyses, discussions, statistics, and forecasts related to non-US economies.

EXAMPLE

Plymouth ltd, a large clothing manufacturer, is thinking of producing clothes in the Philippines. The company determines that the direct costs of production would be lower in the Philippines. However, there are some other indirect costs of FDI that should also be considered. Plymouth ltd determines that economic conditions in the Philippines are uncertain, that government restrictions might be imposed on a subsidiary there, and that inflation and exchange rate movements might be unfavourable. Most importantly, the safety of employees who would be sent there to manage the subsidiary might be threatened by terrorist groups. After considering all the costs, Plymouth ltd decides not to pursue FDI in the Philippines.

Exhibit 13.1 Summary of motives for foreign direct investment

Revenue-related Motives	Means of Using FDI to Achieve This Benefit
1. Attract new sources of demand.	Establish a subsidiary or acquire a competitor in a new market.
2. Enter markets where superior profits are possible.	Acquire a competitor that has controlled its local market.
3. Exploit monopolistic advantages.	Establish a subsidiary in a market where competitors are unable to produce the identical product; sell products in that country.
4. React to trade restrictions.	Establish a subsidiary in a market where tougher trade restrictions will adversely affect the firm's export volume.
5. Diversify internationally.	Establish subsidiaries in markets whose business cycles differ from those where existing subsidiaries are based.
Cost-related Motives	
6. Fully benefit from economies of scale.	Establish a subsidiary in a new market that can sell products produced elsewhere; this allows for increased production and possibly greater production efficiency.
7. Use foreign factors of production.	Establish a subsidiary in a market that has relatively low costs of labour or land; sell the finished product to countries where the cost of production is higher.
8. Use foreign raw materials.	Establish a subsidiary in a market where raw materials are cheap and accessible; sell the finished product to countries where the raw materials are more expensive.
9. Use foreign technology.	Participate in a joint venture in order to learn about a production process or other operations.
10. React to exchange rate movements.	Establish a subsidiary in a new market where the local currency is weak but is expected to strengthen over time.

| USING THE WEB | **Foreign direct investment** Valuable updated country data that can be considered when making FDI decisions is provided at http://www.worldbank.org. |

Comparing benefits of FDI over time

As conditions change over time, so do possible benefits from pursuing foreign direct investment in various countries. Thus, some countries may become more attractive targets while other countries become less attractive. The choice of target countries for FDI has changed over time. Canada now receives a smaller proportion of total FDI than it received in the past, while Europe, Latin America, and Asia receive a larger proportion than in the past. More than one-half of all FDI by US firms is in European countries. The opening of the Eastern European countries and the expansion of the EU account for some of the increased FDI in Europe, especially Eastern Europe. The increased focus on Latin America is partially attributed to its high economic growth, which has encouraged MNCs to capitalize on new sources of demand for their products. In addition, MNCs have targeted Latin America and Asia to use factors of production that are less expensive in foreign countries than in the United States.

| EXAMPLE | Rodez SA (a French firm) is contemplating FDI in Thailand where it would produce and sell mobile phones. It had decided that costs were too high. Now it is reconsidering because costs in Thailand have declined. Rodez could rent office space at a low cost. It could also purchase a manufacturing plant at a lower cost because factories that recently failed are standing empty. In addition, the Thai baht has depreciated substantially against the euro, so Rodez could invest in Thailand at a time when the British pounds can be exchanged at a favourable exchange rate. |

MANAGING FOR VALUE
Yahoo!'s decision to expand internationally

Laminar Medica, a UK-based manufacturer of transport systems for healthcare facilities, has so far invested 1.7m euro in constructing a plant in the Czech Republic. The 204 square metre operation is located at Vodnany, south of Prague, in Bohemia. "We started the search for a suitable site in eastern Europe two years ago", said Stuart Allcock, managing director of Laminar. "We were looking for ways to enhance our service to an expanding customer base on the eastern side of Western Europe. We considered other options – namely Poland and, to a lesser extent, Hungary and Austria."

A key player in the establishment of the Vodnany operation was CzechInvest, the inward investment organization. "It saved us a lot of leg work", Mr Allcock said. "The agency gave us phenomenal help with our research, and also set up meetings with local officials and helped us pinpoint suitable sites." Identifying local staff presented no problems. With about 9% unemployment in the area, there were a lot of enthusiastic potential employees to choose from, said Mr Allcock. The Vodnany plant is expected to become as large as Laminar's UK operation within five years.

Crucial in the early stages of production is the initial qualifying process, which is undertaken directly with customers, according to regulations set down by the regulatory bodies. This can take months, but it is vital that products made at the plant are of a consistent quality to those produced at the company's Tring HQ in the UK.

Mr Allcock conceded that lower costs in the Czech Republic would help to take cost out of the delivered products. "Costs are significantly lower than they are in the UK. I'd be naïve to say that wasn't of interest, but the main reason for setting up in Vodnany was strategic. It will be a huge benefit for our customers on the eastern side of Europe to have greater access to our service to enhance their cold chain", he said.

Laminar Medica was established in 1975 and, with the backing of the CliniMed Group since 1996, is now the leading manufacturer and supplier of insulated shipping systems in Europe.

(Financial Times (FDI, Internet magazine, 1 August 2005))

Rodez also discovers, however, that while the cost-related characteristics have improved, the revenue-related characteristics are now less desirable. A new subsidiary in Thailand might not attract new sources of demand due to the country's weak economy. In addition, Rodez might be unable to earn excessive profits there because the weak economy might force existing firms to keep their prices very low in order to survive. Rodez must compare the favourable aspects of FDI in Thailand with the unfavourable aspects by using multinational capital budgeting, which is explained in the following chapter.

BENEFITS OF INTERNATIONAL DIVERSIFICATION

An international project can reduce a firm's overall risk as a result of international diversification benefits. The key to international diversification is selecting foreign projects whose performance levels are not highly correlated over time. In this way, the various international projects should not experience poor performance simultaneously.

EXAMPLE

Merriweather ltd (a UK firm) plans to invest in a new project in either the UK or the US. Once the project is completed, it will constitute 30% of the firm's total funds invested. The remaining 70% of its investment is exclusively in the United Kingdom. Characteristics of the proposed project are forecasted for a five-year period for both a US and a British location, as shown in Exhibit 13.2.

Merriweather ltd plans to assess the feasibility of each proposed project based on expected risk and return, using a five-year time horizon. Its expected annual after-tax return on investment on its prevailing business is 20%, and its variability of returns (as measured by the standard deviation) is expected to be 0.10. The firm can assess its expected overall performance based on developing the project in the United States and in the United Kingdom. In doing so, it is essentially comparing two portfolios. In the first portfolio, 70% of its total funds are invested in its prevailing UK business, with the remaining 30% invested in a new project located in the United Kingdom. In the second portfolio, again 70% of the firm's total funds are invested in its prevailing business, but the remaining 30% are invested in a new project located in the United States. Therefore, 70% of the portfolios' investments are identical. The difference is in the remaining 30% of funds invested.

If the new project is located in the United Kingdom, the firm's overall expected after-tax return (r_p) is:

$r_p =$	(70%	×	20%)	+	(30%	×	25%)	= 21.5%
	% of funds invested in prevailing business		Expected return on prevailing business		% of funds invested in new UK project		Expected return on new UK project	Firm's overall expected return

This computation is based on weighting the returns according to the percentage of total funds invested in each investment.

If the firm calculates its overall expected return with the new project located in the United States instead of the United Kingdom, the results are unchanged. This is because the new project's expected return happens in this case to be the same regardless of the country of location. Therefore, in terms of return, neither new project has an advantage.

With regard to risk, the new project is expected to exhibit slightly less variability in returns during the five-year period if it is located in the United Kingdom (see Exhibit 13.2). Since firms typically prefer more stable returns on their investments, this is an

Exhibit 13.2 Evaluation of proposed projects in alternative locations

	Characteristics of Proposed Project	
	If Located in the United Kingdom	If Located in the United States
Mean expected annual return on investment (after taxes)	25% (0.25)	25% (0.25)
Standard deviation of expected annual after-tax returns on investment	0.09	0.11
Correlation of expected annual after-tax returns on investment with after-tax returns of prevailing UK business	0.80	0.02

advantage. However, estimating the risk of the individual project without considering the overall firm would be a mistake. The expected correlation of the new project's returns with those of the prevailing business must also be considered. Recall that portfolio variance is determined by the individual variability of each component as well as their pairwise correlations. The variance of a portfolio (Var (P)) composed of only two investments (A and B) is computed as:

$$Var\ (P) = w^2_A\ var\ (A) + w^2_B\ var(B) + 2\ w_A\ w_B\ stdev\ (A)\ stdev\ (B)\ corr\ (A,B)$$

where w_A and w_B represent the percentage of total funds allocated to Investments A and B, respectively; $stdev\ (A)\ stdev\ (B)$ are the standard deviations of returns on Investments A and B, respectively, and $corr\ (A,B)$ is the correlation coefficient of returns between Investments A and B. This equation for portfolio variance can be applied to the problem at hand. The portfolio reflects the overall firm. First, compute the overall firm's variance in returns assuming it locates the new project in the United Kingdom (based on the information provided in Exhibit 13.2). This variance (Var (P)) is:

$$
\begin{aligned}
Var\ (P_{UK}) \ &= \ (0.70)^2\ (0.10)^2 + (0.30)^2\ (0.09)^2 + 2\ (0.70)\ (0.30)\ (0.10)\ (0.09)\ (0.80) \\
&= \ (0.49)\ (0.01) + (0.09)(0.0081) + 0.003024 \\
&= \ 0.0049 + 0.000729 + 0.003024 \\
&= \ 0.008653
\end{aligned}
$$

If Merriweather ltd decides to locate the new project in the United States instead of the United Kingdom, its overall variability in returns will be different, because that project differs from the new UK project in terms of individual variability in returns and correlation with the prevailing business. The overall variability of the firm's returns based on locating the new project in the United States is estimated by variance in the portfolio returns (Var(P)):

$$
\begin{aligned}
Var\ (P_{US}) \ &= \ (0.70)^2\ (0.10)^2 + (0.30)^2\ (0.11)^2 + 2\ (0.70)\ (0.30)\ (0.10)\ (0.11)\ (0.02) \\
&= \ (0.49)\ (0.01) + (0.09)(0.0121) + 0.0000924 \\
&= \ 0.0049 + 0.001089 + 0.0000924 \\
&= \ 0.0060814
\end{aligned}
$$

Thus, Merriweather will generate more stable returns if the new project is located in the United States. The firm's overall variability in returns is almost 29.7% less if the new project is located in the United States rather than in the United Kingdom.

The variability is reduced when locating in the foreign country because of the correlation of the new project's expected returns with the expected returns of the prevailing business. If the new project is located in Merriweather's home country (the United Kingdom), its returns are expected to be more highly correlated with those of the prevailing business than they would be if the project was located in the United States. When economic conditions of two countries (such as the United Kingdom and the United States) are not highly correlated, then a firm may reduce its risk by diversifying its business in both countries instead of concentrating in just one.

Diversification analysis of international projects

Like any investor, an MNC with projects positioned around the world is concerned with the risk and return characteristics of the projects. The portfolio of all projects reflects the MNC in aggregate.

EXAMPLE

Virginia plc considers a global strategy of developing projects as shown in Exhibit 13.3. Each point on the graph reflects a specific project that either has been implemented or is being considered. The return axis may be measured by potential return on assets or return on equity. The risk may be measured by potential fluctuation in the returns generated by each project.

Exhibit 13.3 shows that Project A has the highest expected return of all the projects. While Virginia could devote most of its resources toward this project to attempt to achieve such a high return, its risk is possibly too high by itself. In addition, such a project may not be able to absorb all available capital anyway if its potential market for customers is limited. Other projects in Exhibit 13.3 offer lower risk at the cost of a lower return. It should be stressed at this point that risk refers to the spread of *expected* returns. A high-risk project could be, for instance, a failed dot.com venture. In other words the *actual* returns on a high-risk venture may be negative – as with a bet on a horse with high odds. On the other hand a high-risk venture might be successful and earn high returns, the success of Google being an instance of success in the dot.com market. Lower risk brings with it the increasing likelihood of a positive return. In choosing a portfolio, Virginia has to decide how much extra return is needed to compensate for extra risk – or how much expected return the company is willing to sacrifice in order to lower risk.

If Virginia combines projects, its project portfolio may be able to achieve a risk-return tradeoff exhibited by any of the points on the curve in Exhibit 13.3. This curve represents a frontier of efficient project portfolios that exhibit desirable risk-return characteristics, in that no single project could outperform any of these portfolios for a given risk level. The term *efficient* refers to a maximum return for a given level of risk. Project portfolios outperform the individual projects considered by Virginia plc because of the diversification attributes discussed earlier. The lower the correlation in project returns over time, the lower will be the project portfolio risk. As new projects are proposed, the frontier of efficient project portfolios available to Virginia plc may shift.

Comparing portfolios along the frontier. Along the frontier of efficient project portfolios, no portfolio can be singled out as "optimal" for all MNCs. This is because MNCs vary in their willingness to accept risk. If the MNC is very conservative and has the choice of any portfolios represented by the frontier in Exhibit 13.3, it will probably prefer one that exhibits low risk (near the bottom of the frontier). Conversely, a more aggressive strategy would be to implement a portfolio of projects that exhibits risk-return characteristics such as those near the top of the frontier.

Exhibit 13.3 Risk-return analysis of international projects

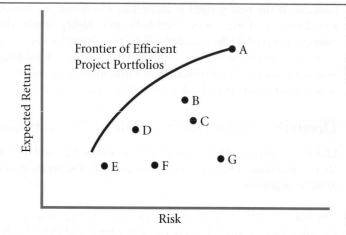

Comparing frontiers among MNCs. The actual location of the frontier of efficient project portfolios depends on the business in which the firm is involved. Some MNCs have frontiers of possible project portfolios that are more desirable than the frontiers of other MNCs.

EXAMPLE

Eurosteel plc sells steel solely to European nations and is considering other related projects. Its frontier of efficient project portfolios exhibits considerable risk (because it sells just one product to countries whose economies move in tandem). In contrast, Global Products plc sells a wide range of products to countries all over the world and due to its diversified range has a lower degree of project portfolio risk. This comparison is illustrated in Exhibit 13.4. Of course, this comparison assumes that Global Products plc is knowledgeable about all of its products and the markets where it sells.

Exhibit 13.4 Risk-return advantage of a diversified MNC

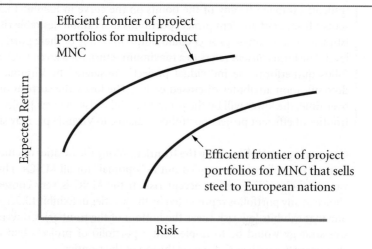

Our discussion suggests that MNCs can achieve more desirable risk-return characteristics from their project portfolios if they sufficiently diversify among products and geographic markets. This also relates to the advantage an MNC has over a purely domestic firm with only a local market. The MNC may be able to develop a more efficient portfolio of projects than its domestic counterpart.

Diversification among countries

Exhibit 13.5 shows the growth in the inflation-adjusted gross domestic product (GDP) for six major countries. Notice that the growth rates vary among countries, which suggests that MNCs may be able to reduce their exposure to economic conditions by spreading their business among various economies. This strategy reduces the proportion of their business that may be subject to a weak economy at any point in time. In some periods, however, countries may simultaneously experience a recession, so even MNCs that are diversified across countries will be highly exposed to weak economic conditions.

Exhibit 13.5 Comparison of economic growth (annualized) among countries

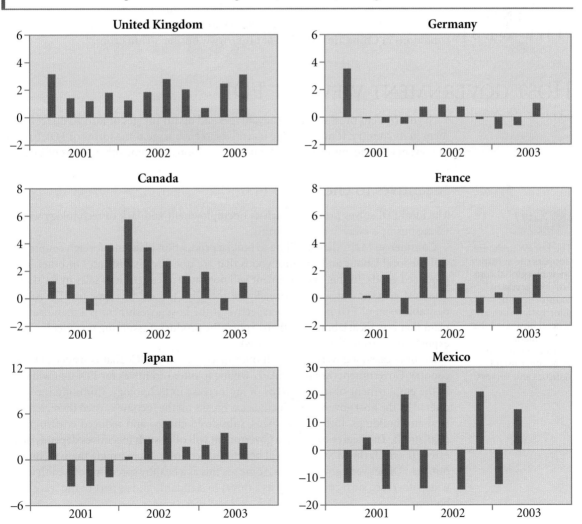

Exhibit 13.5 shows that in the 2001–02 period, most countries experienced relatively weak economic growth.

DECISIONS SUBSEQUENT TO FDI

Once foreign direct investment takes place, periodic decisions are necessary to determine whether further expansion should take place in a given location. In addition, as the project generates earnings, the MNC must decide whether to have the funds remitted to the parent or used by the subsidiary. If the subsidiary has a use for the funds that would be of more value than the parent's use, the subsidiary should retain the funds. Of course, a certain percentage of the funds will be needed to maintain operations, but the remaining funds can be sent to the parent, sent to another subsidiary, or reinvested for expansion purposes.

Facts relevant to the decision of whether the subsidiary should reinvest the earnings should be analyzed on a case-by-case basis. The appropriate decision depends on the economic conditions in the subsidiary's country and the parent's country, as well as restrictions imposed by the host country government.

USING THE WEB

FDI information for a particular country Foreign direct investment in specific countries can be assessed by reviewing websites focused on those countries. For example, conditions in China are described at http://www.business-china.com.

HOST GOVERNMENT VIEWS OF FDI

Each government must weigh the advantages and disadvantages of foreign direct investment in its country. It may provide incentives to encourage some forms of FDI, barriers to prevent other forms of FDI, and impose conditions on some other forms of FDI.

Incentives to encourage FDI

http://

The PriceWaterhouse Coopers site at **http://www.pwcglobal.com** provides access to country-specific information such as general business rules and regulations, tax environments, and some other useful statistics and surveys.

The ideal FDI solves problems such as unemployment and lack of technology without taking business away from local firms.

Consider an MNC that is willing to build a production plant in a foreign country that will use local labour and produce goods that are not direct substitutes of other locally produced goods. In this case, the plant will not cause a reduction in sales by local firms. The host government would normally be receptive toward this type of FDI. Another desirable form of FDI from the perspective of the host government is a manufacturing plant that uses local labour and then exports the products (assuming no other local firm exports such products to the same areas).

In some cases, a government will offer incentives to MNCs that consider FDI in its country. Governments are particularly willing to offer incentives for FDI that will result in the employment of local citizens or an increase in technology. Common incentives offered by the host government include tax breaks on the income earned there, rent-free land and buildings, low-interest loans, subsidized energy, and reduced environmental regulations. The degree to which a government will offer such incentives depends on the extent to which the MNC's FDI will benefit that country. Increasingly there is competition for FDI between governments. Some see this as a healthy spreading of wealth worldwide; others see such competition as a threat to standards and as part of the "race to the bottom".

The decision by Allied Research Associates, Inc. (a US-based MNC), to build a production facility and office in Belgium was highly motivated by Belgian government subsidies. The Belgian government subsidized a large portion of the expenses incurred by Allied Research Associates and offered tax concessions and favourable interest rates on loans to Allied.

While many governments encourage FDI, they use different types of incentives. France has periodically sold government land at a discount, while Finland and Ireland attracted MNCs in the late 1990s by imposing a very low corporate tax rate on specific businesses.

Barriers to FDI

Barriers that protect local firms or consumers. When MNCs consider engaging in FDI by acquiring a foreign company, they may face various barriers imposed by host government agencies. All countries have one or more government agencies that monitor mergers and acquisitions. The acquisition activity in any given country is influenced by the regulations enforced by these agencies.

In France, the Treasury can reject any deal if the acquirer is based outside the European Union. The French government may also reject a deal if the target is in some closely monitored industry, such as defence or health care. The Monopolies Commission of France also reviews acquisitions to prevent any combined firms from controlling more than 25% of an industry or from severely reducing competition.

The European Union Commission assesses mergers that may affect competition in Europe. The EU Commission rejected the merger between General Electric and Honeywell because it believed that the merger would have resulted in a monopoly.

Acquisitions in Japan are reviewed by the Fair Trade Commission. Japan has historically imposed barriers to discourage international acquisitions. Recently, however, these barriers have been reduced (as long as the Japanese target is agreeable), enabling US-based MNCs such as Corning Glass Works, Data General, Eastman Kodak, and Motorola to acquire Japanese firms.

Acquisitions in the United States are also reviewed by several agencies, including the Securities and Exchange Commission, which regulates the conduct of acquisitions, and the Justice Department and Federal Trade Commission, which analyze the potential impact on competition.

Barriers that restrict ownership. Some governments restrict foreign ownership of local firms. Such restrictions may limit or prevent international acquisitions.

Many governments in Asia and Latin America have traditionally restricted foreign majority ownership. In recent years, however, these restrictions have been reduced. Governments of Asian countries removed restrictions on international acquisitions during the Asian crisis to encourage MNCs to develop new business there. Mexico also recently announced that it would allow foreign companies to own 100% of their subsidiaries established in Mexico.

"Red tape" barriers. An implicit barrier to FDI in some countries is the "red tape" involved, such as procedural and documentation requirements. An MNC pursuing FDI is subject to a different set of requirements in each country. Therefore, it is difficult for an MNC to become proficient at the process unless it concentrates on FDI within a single foreign country. The current efforts to make regulations uniform across Europe have simplified the paperwork required to acquire European firms.

Industry barriers. The local firms of some industries in particular countries have substantial influence on the government and will likely use their influence to prevent competition from MNCs that attempt FDI. MNCs that consider FDI need to recognize the influence that these local firms have on the local government.

Political instability. The governments of some countries may prevent FDI. If a country is susceptible to abrupt changes in government and political conflicts, the feasibility of FDI may be dependent on the outcome of those conflicts. MNCs want to avoid a situation in which they pursue FDI under a government that is likely to be removed after the FDI occurs.

Government-imposed conditions to engage in FDI

Some governments allow international acquisitions but impose special requirements on MNCs that desire to acquire a local firm. For example, the MNC may be required to ensure pollution control for its manufacturing or to structure the business to export the products it produces so that it does not threaten the market share of other local firms. The MNC may even be required to retain all the employees of the target firm so that unemployment and general economic conditions in the country are not adversely affected.

EXAMPLE

Mexico requires that a specified minimum proportion of parts used to produce automobiles there are made in Mexico. The proportion is lower for automobiles that are to be exported.

Spain's government allowed Ford Motor Co to set up production facilities in Spain only if it would abide by certain provisions. These included limiting Ford's local sales volume to 10% of the previous year's local automobile sales. In addition, two-thirds of the total volume of automobiles produced by Ford in Spain must be exported. The idea behind these provisions was to create jobs for workers in Spain without seriously affecting local competitors. Allowing a subsidiary that primarily exports its product achieved this objective.

SUMMARY

- MNCs may be motivated to initiate foreign direct investment in order to attract new sources of demand or to enter markets where superior profits are possible. These two motives are normally based on opportunities to generate more revenue in foreign markets. Other motives for using FDI are typically related to cost efficiency, such as using foreign factors of production, raw materials, or technology. In addition MNCs may engage in FDI to protect their foreign market share, to react to exchange rate movements, or to avoid trade restrictions.

- International diversification is a common motive for foreign direct investment. It allows an MNC to reduce its exposure to domestic economic conditions. In this way, the MNC may be able to stabilize its cash flows and reduce its risk. Such a goal is desirable because it may reduce the firm's cost of financing. International projects may allow MNCs to achieve lower risk than is possible from only domestic projects without reducing their expected returns. International diversification tends to be better able to reduce risk when the FDI is targeted to countries whose economies are somewhat unrelated to an MNC's home country economy.

CRITICAL DEBATE

Should MNCs avoid FDI in countries with liberal child labour laws?

Proposition. Yes. An MNC should maintain its hiring standards, regardless of what country it is in. Even if a foreign country allows children to work, an MNC should not lower its standards. Although the MNC forgoes the use of low-cost labour, it maintains its global credibility.

Opposing view. No. An MNC will not only benefit its shareholders, but will create employment for some children who need support. The MNC can provide reasonable working conditions and perhaps may even offer educational programmes for its employees.

With whom do you agree? Review sites such as http://www.corporatewatch.org and contrast http://www.cleanclothes.org/companies/adidas00-05-05.htm with http://www.adidas-group.com/en/overview/corporate_governance/sea/default.asp.

Also see http://cbae.nmsu.edu/~dboje/AA/academics _reebok.html, for a more sympathetic view of MNCs see http://www.fdimagazine.com/ (keywords being "Corporatewatch", "Adidas", "Cleanclothes", "Standards of Engagement", "academics studying" and "FDI"). But remember that these sites and others are not impartial and often present a distorted picture. *You must take care to think of both sides of the argument.*

SELF TEST

Answers are provided in Appendix A at the back of the text.

1. Offer some reasons why UK firms might prefer to direct their foreign direct investment (FDI) to Europe rather than Latin America.

2. Offer some reasons why UK firms might prefer to direct their FDI to Latin America rather than Europe.

3. One UK executive said that Europe was not considered as a location for FDI because of the euro's value. Interpret this statement.

4. Why do you think UK firms commonly use joint ventures as a strategy to enter China?

5. Why would the United Kingdom offer a foreign automobile manufacturer large incentives for establishing a production subsidiary in the United Kingdom? Isn't this strategy indirectly subsidizing the foreign competitors of UK firms?

QUESTIONS AND APPLICATIONS

1. **Motives for FDI.** Describe some potential benefits to an MNC as a result of foreign direct investment (FDI). Elaborate on each type of benefit. Which motives for FDI do you think encouraged Nike (a US company) to expand its footwear production in Latin America?

2. **Impact of a weak currency on feasibility of FDI.** Tilda AB, a Swedish producer of computer disks, plans to establish a subsidiary in the Ukraine in order to penetrate the Middle Eastern market. Tilda's executives believe that the Ukrainian hryvnia's value is relatively strong and will weaken against the Swedish Krone over time. If their

expectations about the hryvnia's value are correct, how will this affect the feasibility of the project? Explain.

3. **FDI to achieve economies of scale.** Max AG and Marie AG are German automobile manufacturers that desire to benefit from economies of scale. Max has decided to establish distributorship subsidiaries in various countries, while Marie has decided to establish manufacturing subsidiaries in various countries. Which firm is more likely to benefit from economies of scale?

4. **FDI to reduce cash flow volatility.** Rideau Chemical SA and Robert Sarl (both French

companies) have similar intentions to reduce the volatility of their cash flows. Rideau implemented a long-range plan to establish 40% of its business in Canada. Robert implemented a long-range plan to establish 30% of its business in Europe and Asia, scattered among 12 different countries. Which company will more effectively reduce cash flow volatility once the plans are achieved?

5. **Impact of import restrictions.** If the United Kingdom imposed long-term restrictions on imports, would the amount of FDI by non-UK MNCs in the United Kingdom increase, decrease, or be unchanged? Explain.

6. **Capitalizing on low-cost labour.** Some MNCs establish a manufacturing facility where there is a relatively low cost of labour. Yet, they sometimes close the facility later because the cost advantage dissipates. Why do you think the relative cost advantage of these countries is reduced over time? (Ignore possible exchange rate effects.)

7. **Opportunities in less developed countries.** Offer your opinion on why economies of some less developed countries with strict restrictions on international trade and FDI are somewhat independent from economies of other countries. Why would MNCs desire to enter such countries? If these countries relaxed their restrictions, would their economies continue to be independent of other economies? Explain.

8. Consider the effects on FDI of a major **political incident** involving the host country of the MNC making the investment.

9. **FDI strategy.** Luigi SpA (an Italian company) has decided to establish a subsidiary in Taiwan that will produce stereos and sell them there. It expects that the cost of producing these stereos will be one-third the cost of producing them in Italy. Assuming that its production cost estimates are accurate, is Luigi's strategy sensible? Explain.

10. **Risk resulting from international business.** This chapter concentrates on possible benefits to a firm that increases its international business.
    a. What are some risks of international business that may not exist for local business?
    b. What does this chapter reveal about the relationship between an MNC's degree of international business and its risk?

11. **Motives for FDI.** Starter ltd (UK) produces sportswear that is licensed by professional sports teams. It recently decided to expand in Europe. What are the potential benefits for this firm from using FDI?

12. **Disney's FDI motives.** What potential benefits do you think were most important in the decision of the Walt Disney Co. to build a theme park in France?

13. **FDI strategy.** Once an MNC establishes a subsidiary, FDI remains an ongoing decision. What does this statement mean?

14. **Host government incentives for FDI.** Why would foreign governments provide MNCs with incentives to undertake FDI there?

ADVANCED QUESTIONS

15. **FDI strategy.** J.C. Penney (a real US company) has recognized numerous opportunities to expand in foreign countries and has assessed many foreign markets, including Brazil, Greece, Mexico, Portugal, Singapore, and Thailand. It has opened new stores in Europe, Asia, and Latin America. In each case, the firm was aware that it did not have sufficient understanding of the culture of each country that it had targeted. Consequently, it engaged in joint ventures with local partners who knew the preferences of the local customers.
    a. What comparative advantage does J.C. Penney have when establishing a store in a foreign country, relative to an independent variety store?
    b. Why might the overall risk of J.C. Penney decrease or increase as a result of its recent global expansion?
    c. J.C. Penney has been more cautious about entering China. Explain the potential obstacles associated with entering China.

16. **FDI location decision.** Pimlico ltd is a UK firm with a Chinese subsidiary that produces mobile phones in China and sells them in Japan. This subsidiary pays its wages and its rent in Chinese yuan, which is presently tied to the dollar. The mobile phones sold to Japan are denominated in Japanese yen. Assume that Pimlico ltd expects

that the Chinese yuan will continue to stay fixed against the dollar. The subsidiary's main goal is to generate profits for itself and reinvest the profits. It does not plan to remit any funds to the UK parent.

a. Assume that the Japanese yen strengthens against the US dollar over time. How would this be expected to affect the profits earned by the Chinese subsidiary?

b. If Pimlico ltd had established its subsidiary in Tokyo, Japan instead of China, would its subsidiary's profits be more exposed or less exposed to exchange rate risk?

c. Why do you think that Pimlico ltd established the subsidiary in China instead of Japan? Assume no major country risk barriers.

d. If the Chinese subsidiary needs to borrow money to finance its expansion and wants to reduce its exchange rate risk, should it borrow US dollars, Chinese yuan, or Japanese yen?

PROJECT WORKSHOP

17. Select three articles from the online *FDI* magazine (registration for the search function is free) at http://www.fdimagazine.com/. For search-words choose well-known MNCs or countries. For each article assess what good and what bad aspects of FDI are supported by the article.

DISCUSSION IN THE BOARDROOM

This exercise can be found on the companion website at www.cengage.co.uk/madura_fox.

RUNNING YOUR OWN MNC

This exercise can be found on the companion website at www.cengage.co.uk/madura_fox.

Essays/discussion and articles can be found at the end of Part 4

BLADES PLC CASE STUDY
Consideration of foreign direct investment

For the last year, Blades plc has been exporting to Thailand in order to supplement its declining UK sales. Under the existing arrangement, Blades sells 180,000 pairs of roller blades annually to Entertainment Products, a Thai retailer, for a fixed price denominated in Thai baht. The agreement will last for another two years. Furthermore, to diversify internationally and to take advantage of an attractive offer by Jogs Inc a US retailer, Blades has recently begun exporting to the United States. Under the resulting agreement, Jogs will purchase 200,000 pairs of "Speedos", Blades' primary product, annually at a fixed price of $80 per pair.

Blades' suppliers of the needed components for its roller blade production are located primarily in the United Kingdom, where Blades incurs the majority of its cost of goods sold. Although prices for inputs

needed to manufacture roller blades vary, recent costs have run approximately £70 per pair. Blades also imports components from Thailand because of the relatively low price of rubber and plastic components and because of their high quality. These imports are denominated in Thai baht, and the exact price (in baht) depends on prevailing market prices for these components in Thailand. Currently, inputs sufficient to manufacture a pair of roller blades cost approximately 3,000 Thai baht per pair of roller blades.

Although Thailand had been among the world's fastest growing economies, recent events in Thailand have increased the level of economic uncertainty. Specifically, the Thai baht, which had been pegged to the dollar, is now a freely floating currency and has depreciated substantially in recent months. Furthermore, recent levels of inflation in Thailand have been very high. Hence, future economic conditions in Thailand are highly uncertain.

Ben Holt, Blades' financial director, is seriously considering FDI in Thailand. He believes that this is a perfect time to either establish a subsidiary or acquire an existing business in Thailand because the uncertain economic conditions and the depreciation of the baht have substantially lowered the initial costs required for FDI. Holt believes the growth potential in Asia will be extremely high once the Thai economy stabilizes.

Although Holt has also considered FDI in the United States, he would prefer that Blades invest in Thailand as opposed to the United States. Forecasts indicate that the demand for roller blades in the United States is similar to that in the United Kingdom; since Blades' UK sales have recently declined because of the high prices it charges, Holt expects that FDI in the United States will yield similar results. Furthermore, both domestic and foreign roller blade manufacturers are relatively well established in the United States, so the growth potential there is limited. Holt believes the Thai roller blade market offers more growth potential.

Blades can sell its products at a lower price but generate higher profit margins in Thailand than it can in the United Kingdom. This is because the Thai customer has committed itself to purchase a fixed number of Blades' products annually only if it can purchase Speedos at a substantial discount from the UK price. Nevertheless, since the cost of goods sold incurred in Thailand is substantially below that incurred in the United States, Blades has managed to generate higher profit margins from its Thai exports and imports than in the United Kingdom.

As a financial analyst for Blades plc you generally agree with Ben Holt's assessment of the situation. However, you are concerned that Thai consumers have not been affected yet by the unfavourable economic conditions. You believe that they may reduce their spending on leisure products within the next year. Therefore, you think it would be beneficial to wait until next year, when the unfavourable economic conditions in Thailand may subside, to make a decision regarding FDI in Thailand. However, if economic conditions in Thailand improve over the next year, FDI may become more expensive both because target firms will be more expensive and because the baht may appreciate. You are also aware that several of Blades' UK competitors are considering expanding into Thailand in the next year.

If Blades acquires an existing business in Thailand or establishes a subsidiary there by the end of next year, it would fulfil its agreement with Entertainment Products for the subsequent year. The Thai retailer has expressed an interest in renewing the contractual agreement with Blades at that time if Blades establishes operations in Thailand. However, Holt believes that Blades could charge a higher price for its products if it establishes its own distribution channels.

Holt has asked you to answer the following questions:

1. Identify and discuss some of the benefits that Blades plc could obtain from FDI.
2. Do you think Blades should wait until next year to undertake FDI in Thailand? What is the tradeoff if Blades undertakes the FDI now?
3. Do you think Blades should renew its agreement with the Thai retailer for another three years? What is the tradeoff if Blades renews the agreement?
4. Assume a high level of unemployment in Thailand and a unique production process employed by Blades inc. How do you think the Thai government would view the establishment of a subsidiary in Thailand by firms such as Blades? Do you think the Thai government would be more or less supportive if firms such as Blades acquired existing businesses in Thailand? Why?

SMALL BUSINESS DILEMMA
Foreign direct investment decision by the Sports Exports Company

Jim Logan's business, the Sports Exports Company (Ireland), continues to grow. His primary product is the basketballs he produces and exports to a distributor in the United Kingdom. However, his recent joint venture with a British firm has also been successful. Under this arrangement, a British firm produces other sporting goods for Jim's firm; these goods are then delivered to that distributor. Jim intentionally started his international business by exporting because it was easier and cheaper to export than to establish a place of business in the United Kingdom. However, he is considering establishing a firm in the United Kingdom to produce the basketballs there instead of in Ireland. This firm would also produce the other sporting goods that he now sells, so he would no longer have to rely on another British firm (through the joint venture) to produce those goods.

1. Given the information provided here, what are the advantages to Jim of establishing the firm in the United Kingdom?
2. Given the information provided here, what are the disadvantages to Jim of establishing the firm in the United Kingdom?

CHAPTER 14

MULTINATIONAL CAPITAL BUDGETING

MULTINATIONAL CORPORATIONS (MNCs) EVALUATE international projects by using multinational capital budgeting, which compares the benefits and costs of these projects. Given that many MNCs spend more than £100 million per year on international projects, multinational capital budgeting is a critical function. Many international projects are irreversible and cannot be easily sold to other corporations at a reasonable price. Proper use of multinational capital budgeting can identify the international projects worthy of implementation.

The most popular method of capital budgeting involves determining the project's net present value by estimating the present value of the project's future cash flows and subtracting the initial outlay required for the project. Multinational capital budgeting typically uses a similar process. However, special circumstances of international projects that affect the future cash flows or the discount rate used to discount cash flows make multinational capital budgeting more complex. Financial managers must understand how to apply capital budgeting to international projects, so that they can maximize the value of the MNC.

THE SPECIFIC OBJECTIVES OF THIS CHAPTER ARE TO:

- compare the capital budgeting analysis of an MNC's subsidiary versus its parent,

- demonstrate how multinational capital budgeting can be applied to determine whether an international project should be implemented, and

- explain how the risk of international projects can be assessed.

SUBSIDIARY VERSUS PARENT PERSPECTIVE

Should capital budgeting for a multinational project be conducted from the viewpoint of the subsidiary that will administer the project or the parent that will most likely finance much of the project? Some would say the subsidiary's perspective should be used because it will be responsible for administering the project and there will be shareholders with interests only in the subsidiary. However, if the parent is financing the project, then it should be evaluating the results from its point of view. The feasibility of the capital budgeting analysis can vary with the perspective because the net after-tax cash inflows to the subsidiary can differ substantially from those to the parent. Such differences can be due to several factors, some of which are discussed here.

Tax differentials

If the earnings due to the project will someday be remitted to the parent, the MNC needs to consider how the parent's government taxes these earnings. If the parent's government imposes a high tax rate on the remitted funds, the project may be feasible from the subsidiary's point of view, but not from the parent's point of view. Under such a scenario, the parent should not consider implementing the project, even though it appears feasible from the subsidiary's perspective.

Restricted remittances

Consider a potential project to be implemented in a country where government restrictions require that a percentage of the subsidiary earnings remain in the country. Since the parent may never have access to these funds, the project is not attractive to the parent, although it may be attractive to the subsidiary. One possible solution is to let the subsidiary obtain partial financing for the project within the host country. In this case, the portion of funds not allowed to be sent to the parent can be used to cover the financing costs over time.

Excessive remittances

Consider a parent that charges its subsidiary very high administrative fees because management is centralized at the headquarters. To the subsidiary, the fees represent an expense. To the parent, the fees represent revenue that may substantially exceed the actual cost of managing the subsidiary. In this case, the project's earnings may appear low from the subsidiary's perspective and high from the parent's perspective. The feasibility of the project again depends on perspective. In most cases, neglecting the parent's perspective will distort the true value of a foreign project.

Exchange rate movements

When earnings are remitted to the parent, they are normally converted from the subsidiary's local currency to the parent's currency. The amount received by the parent is therefore influenced by the existing exchange rate. If the subsidiary project is assessed from the subsidiary's perspective, the cash flows forecasted for the subsidiary do not have to be converted to the parent's currency.

Summary of factors

Exhibit 14.1 illustrates the process from the time earnings are generated by the subsidiary until the parent receives the remitted funds. The exhibit shows that the earnings are reduced initially by corporate taxes paid to the host government. Then, some of the earnings are retained by the subsidiary (either by the subsidiary's choice or according to the host government's rules), with the residual targeted as funds to be remitted. Those funds that are remitted may be subject to a withholding tax by the host government. The remaining funds are converted to the parent's currency (at the prevailing exchange rate) and remitted to the parent.

Given the various factors shown here that can drain subsidiary earnings, the cash flows actually remitted by the subsidiary may represent only a small portion of the earn-

Exhibit 14.1 Process of remitting subsidiary earnings to the parent

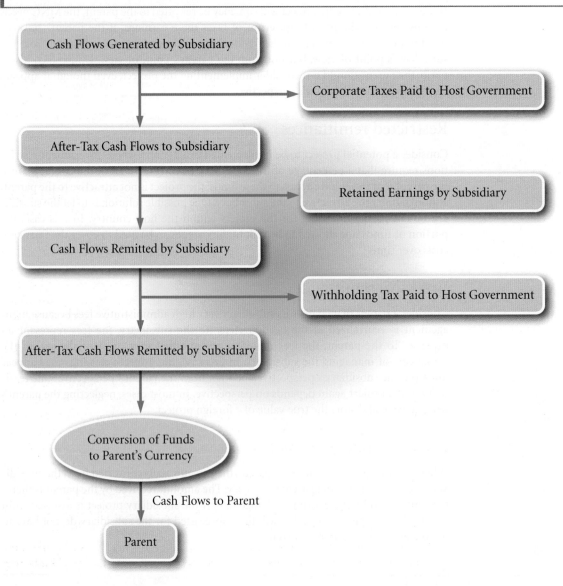

ings it generates. The feasibility of the project from the parent's perspective is dependent not on the subsidiary's cash flows but on the cash flows that the parent ultimately receives.

The parent's perspective is appropriate in attempting to determine whether a project will enhance the firm's value. Given that the parent's shareholders are its owners, it should make decisions that satisfy its shareholders. Each project, whether foreign or domestic, should ultimately generate sufficient cash flows to the parent to enhance shareholder wealth. Any changes in the parent's expenses should also be included in the analysis. The parent may incur additional expenses for monitoring the new foreign subsidiary's management or consolidating the subsidiary's financial statements. Any project that can create a positive net present value for the parent should enhance shareholder wealth.

One exception to the rule of using a parent's perspective occurs when the foreign subsidiary is not wholly owned by the parent and the foreign project is partially financed with retained earnings of the parent and of the subsidiary. In this case, the foreign subsidiary has a group of shareholders that it must satisfy. Any arrangement made between the parent and the subsidiary should be acceptable to the two entities only if the arrangement enhances the values of both. The goal is to make decisions in the interests of both groups of shareholders and not to transfer wealth from one entity to another.

Although this exception occasionally occurs, most foreign subsidiaries of MNCs are wholly owned by the parents. Examples in this text implicitly assume that the subsidiary is wholly owned by the parent (unless noted otherwise) and therefore focus on the parent's perspective.

INPUT FOR MULTINATIONAL CAPITAL BUDGETING

http://

The website **http://quote.yahoo.com/m2?u** provides information on the recent performance of country stock indexes (the location of this page may move within the Yahoo site). This is sometimes used as a general indication of economic conditions in various countries and may be considered by MNCs that assess the feasibility of foreign projects.

Regardless of the long-term project to be considered, an MNC will normally require forecasts of the economic and financial characteristics related to the project. Each of these characteristics is briefly described here:

- *Initial investment.* The parent's initial investment in a project may constitute the major source of funds to support a particular project. Funds initially invested in a project may include not only whatever is necessary to start the project but also additional funds, such as working capital, to support the project over time. Such funds are needed to finance inventory, wages, and other expenses until the project begins to generate revenue. Because cash inflows will not always be sufficient to cover upcoming cash outflows, working capital is needed throughout a project's lifetime.

- *Consumer demand.* When projecting a cash flow schedule, an accurate forecast of consumer demand for a product is very valuable, but future demand is often difficult to forecast. For example, if the project is a plant in Germany that produces automobiles, the MNC must forecast what percentage of the auto market in Germany it can pull from prevailing auto producers. Once a market share percentage is forecasted, projected demand can be computed. Demand forecasts can sometimes be aided by historical data on the market share other MNCs in the industry pulled when they entered this market, but historical data are not always an accurate indicator of the future. In addition, many projects reflect a first attempt, so there are no predecessors to review as an indicator of the future.

- *Price.* The price at which the product could be sold can be forecasted using competitive products in the markets as a comparison. A long-term capital budgeting analysis requires projections for not only the upcoming period but the expected lifetime of the project as well. The future prices will most likely be responsive to the future inflation rate in the host country (where the project is to take place), but the future inflation rate is not known. Thus, future inflation rates must be forecasted in order to develop projections of the product price over time.

- *Variable cost.* Like the price estimate, variable-cost forecasts can be developed from assessing prevailing comparative costs of the components (such as hourly labour costs and the cost of materials). Such costs should normally move in tandem with the future inflation rate of the host country. Even if the variable cost per unit can be accurately predicted, the projected total variable cost (variable cost per unit times quantity produced) may be wrong if the demand is inaccurately forecasted.

- *Fixed cost.* On a periodic basis, the fixed cost may be easier to predict than the variable cost since it normally is not sensitive to changes in demand. It is, however, sensitive to any change in the host country's inflation rate from the time the forecast is made until the time the fixed costs are incurred.

- *Project lifetime.* Some projects have indefinite lifetimes that can be difficult to assess, while other projects have designated specific lifetimes, at the end of which they will be liquidated. This makes the capital budgeting analysis easier to apply. It should be recognized that the MNC does not always have complete control over the lifetime decision. In some cases, political events may force the firm to liquidate the project earlier than planned. The probability that such events will occur varies among countries.

- *Salvage (liquidation) value.* The after-tax salvage value of most projects is difficult to forecast. It will depend on several factors, including the success of the project and the attitude of the host government toward the project. As an extreme possibility, the host government could take over the project without adequately compensating the MNC.

- *Restrictions on fund transfers.* In some cases, a host government will prevent a subsidiary from sending its earnings to the parent. This restriction may reflect an attempt to encourage additional local spending or to avoid excessive sales of the local currency in exchange for some other currency. Since the restrictions on fund transfers prevent cash from coming back to the parent, projected net cash flows from the parent's perspective will be affected. If the parent is aware of these restrictions, it can incorporate them when projecting net cash flows. Sometimes, however, the host government adjusts its restrictions over time; in that case, the MNC can only forecast the future restrictions and incorporate these forecasts into the analysis.

- *Tax laws.* The tax laws on earnings generated by a foreign subsidiary or remitted to the MNC's parent vary among countries. Under some circumstances, the MNC receives tax deductions or credits for tax payments by a subsidiary to the host country (see the chapter appendix for more details). Because after-tax cash flows are necessary for an adequate capital budgeting analysis, international tax effects must be determined on any proposed foreign projects.

- *Exchange rates.* Any international project will be affected by exchange rate fluctuations during the life of the project, but these movements are often very difficult to forecast. There are methods of hedging against them, though most hedging techniques are used to cover short-term positions. While it is possible to hedge over longer periods (with long-term forward contracts or currency swap arrangements), the MNC has no way of knowing the amount of funds that it should hedge. This is because it is only guessing at its future costs and revenue due to the project. Thus, the MNC may decide not to hedge the projected foreign currency net cash flows.

■ *Required rate of return.* Once the relevant cash flows of a proposed project are estimated, they can be discounted at the project's required rate of return, which may differ from the MNC's cost of capital because of that particular project's risk. Additional considerations will be discussed after a simplified multinational capital budgeting example is provided. In the real world, magic numbers aren't provided to MNCs for insertion into their computers. The challenge revolves around accurately forecasting the variables relevant to the project evaluation. If garbage (inaccurate forecasts) is input into the computer, the analysis output by the computer will also be garbage. Consequently, an MNC may take on a project by mistake. Since such a mistake may be worth millions of pounds, MNCs need to assess the degree of uncertainty for any input that is used in the project evaluation. This is discussed more thoroughly later in this chapter.

MULTINATIONAL CAPITAL BUDGETING EXAMPLE

Capital budgeting for the MNC is a necessary stage of planning for all projects. Projects may range from a small scale expenditure that can be accommodated in a single budget, to large-scale strategic decisions that will be significant over the medium to long term. This section presents a medium-term example involving the possible development of a new subsidiary. It begins with assumptions that simplify the capital budgeting analysis. Then, additional considerations are introduced to emphasize the potential complexity of such an analysis.

This example illustrates only one approach to budget planning; one that is founded on current views of best practice. Keep in mind that a real-world problem may be approached differently and may have aspects related to the problem not represented here.

Background

Spartan ltd is considering the development of a subsidiary in Singapore that would manufacture and sell tennis rackets locally. Spartan's management has asked various departments to supply relevant information for a capital budgeting analysis. In addition, some Spartan executives have met with government officials in Singapore to discuss the proposed subsidiary. All relevant information follows.

1. *Initial investment.* An estimated 20 million Singapore dollars (S$), which includes funds to support working capital, would be needed for the project. Given the existing spot rate of £0.33 per Singapore dollar, the value of the parent's initial investment is £7 million.
2. *Project life.* The project is expected to end in four years. The host government of Singapore has promised to purchase the plant from the parent after four years.
3. *Price and demand.* The estimated price and demand schedules during each of the next four years are shown here:

Year	Price per Racket	Demand in Singapore
1	S$350	60,000 units
2	S$350	60,000 units
3	S$360	100,000 units
4	S$380	100,000 units

4. *Costs.* The variable costs (for materials, labour, etc.) per unit have been estimated and consolidated as shown here:

Year	Variable Costs per Racket
1	S$200
2	S$200
3	S$250
4	S$260

The expense of leasing extra office space is S$1 million per year. Other annual overhead expenses are expected to be S$1 million per year.

5. *Exchange rates.* The spot exchange rate of the Singapore dollar is £0.33. Spartan uses the spot rate as its best forecast of the exchange rate that will exist in future periods. Thus, the forecasted exchange rate for all future periods is £0.33.

6. *Host country taxes on income earned by subsidiary.* The Singapore government will allow Spartan ltd to establish the subsidiary and will impose a 20% tax rate on income. In addition, it will impose a 10% withholding tax (see appendix to this chapter) on any funds remitted by the subsidiary to the parent.

7. *UK government taxes on income earned by Spartan subsidiary.* The UK government will allow a tax credit on taxes paid in Singapore; therefore, earnings remitted to the UK parent will not be taxed by the UK government.

8. *Cash flows from Spartan subsidiary to parent.* The Spartan subsidiary plans to send all net cash flows received back to the parent firm at the end of each year. The Singapore government promises no restrictions on the cash flows to be sent back to the parent firm but does impose a 10% withholding tax on any funds sent to the parent, as mentioned earlier.

9. *Depreciation.* The Singapore government will allow Spartan's subsidiary to depreciate the cost of the plant and equipment at a maximum rate of S$2 million per year, which is the rate the subsidiary will use.

10. *Salvage value.* The Singapore government will pay the parent S$12 million to assume ownership of the subsidiary at the end of four years. Assume that there is no capital gains tax on the sale of the subsidiary.

11. *Required rate of return.* Spartan ltd requires a 15% return on this project.

Analysis

The capital budgeting analysis will be conducted from the parent's perspective, based on the assumption that the subsidiary is intended to generate cash flows that will ultimately be passed on to the parent. Thus, the net present value (*NPV*) from the parent's perspective is based on a comparison of the present value of the cash flows received by the parent to the initial outlay by the parent. As explained earlier in this chapter, an international project's *NPV* is dependent on whether a parent or subsidiary perspective is used. Since the UK parent's perspective is used, the cash flows of concern are the pounds ultimately received by the parent as a result of the project.

The initial outlay of concern is the investment by the parent. The required rate of return is based on the cost of capital used by the parent to make its investment, with an adjustment for the risk of the project. For the establishment of the subsidiary to benefit Spartan's parent, the present value of future cash flows (including the salvage value) ultimately received by the parent should exceed the parent's initial outlay.

The capital budgeting analysis to determine whether Spartan ltd should establish the subsidiary is provided in Exhibit 14.2 (review this exhibit as you read on). The first step is to incorporate demand and price estimates in order to forecast total revenue (see lines 1 through 3). Then, the expenses are summed up to forecast total expenses (see lines 4 through 9). Next, before-tax earnings are computed (in line 10) by subtracting total expenses from total revenues. Host government taxes (line 11) are then deducted from before-tax earnings to determine after-tax earnings for the subsidiary (line 12).

Exhibit 14.2 Capital budgeting analysis: Spartan ltd

	Year 0	Year 1	Year 2	Year 3	Year 4
1. Demand		60,000	60,000	100,000	100,000
2. Price per unit		S$350	S$350	S$360	S$380
3. Total revenue = (1) × (2)		S$21,000,000	S$21,000,000	S$36,000,000	S$38,000,000
4. Variable cost per unit		S$200	S$200	S$250	S$260
5. Total variable cost = (1) × (4)		S$12,000,000	S$12,000,000	S$25,000,000	S$26,000,000
6. Annual lease expense		S$1,000,000	S$1,000,000	S$1,000,000	S$1,000,000
7. Other fixed annual expenses		S$1,000,000	S$1,000,000	S$1,000,000	S$1,000,000
8. Non-cash expense (depreciation)		S$2,000,000	S$2,000,000	S$2,000,000	S$2,000,000
9. Total expenses = (5) + (6) + (7) + (8)		S$16,000,000	S$16,000,000	S$29,000,000	S$30,000,000
10. Before-tax earnings of subsidiary = (3) − (9)		S$5,000,000	S$5,000,000	S$7,000,000	S$8,000,000
11. Host government tax (20%)		S$1,000,000	S$1,000,000	S$1,400,000	S$1,600,000
12. After-tax earnings of subsidiary		S$4,000,000	S$4,000,000	S$5,600,000	S$6,400,000
13. Net cash flow to subsidiary = (12) + (8)		S$6,000,000	S$6,000,000	S$7,600,000	S$8,400,000
14. S$ remitted by subsidiary (100% of net cash flow)		S$6,000,000	S$6,000,000	S$7,600,000	S$8,400,000
15. Withholding tax on remitted funds (10%)		S$600,000	S$600,000	S$760,000	S$840,000
16. S$ remitted after withholding taxes		S$5,400,000	S$5,400,000	S$6,840,000	S$7,560,000
17. Salvage value					S$12,000,000
18. Exchange rate of S$		£0.33	£0.33	£0.33	£0.33
19. Cash flows to parent		£1,782,000	£1,782,000	£2,257,200	£6,454,800
20. *PV* of parent cash flows (15% discount rate)		£1,549,565	£1,347,448	£1,484,146	£3,690,553
21. Initial investment by parent	£6,500,000				
22. CUMULATIVE *NPV*		−£4,950,435	−£3,602,987	−£2,118,841	£1,571,712

The depreciation expense is added to the after-tax subsidiary earnings to compute the net cash flow to the subsidiary (line 13). All of these funds are to be remitted by the subsidiary, so line 14 is the same as line 13. The subsidiary can afford to send all net cash flow to the parent since the initial investment provided by the parent includes working capital. The funds remitted to the parent are subject to a 10% withholding tax (line 15), so the actual amount of funds to be sent after these taxes is shown in line 16. The salvage value of the project is shown in line 17. The funds to be remitted must first be converted into pounds at the exchange rate (line 18) existing at that time. The parent's cash flow from the subsidiary is shown in line 19. The periodic funds received from the subsidiary are not subject to UK corporate taxes since it was assumed that the parent would receive credit for the taxes paid in Singapore that would offset taxes owed to the UK government.

Although several capital budgeting techniques are available, a commonly used technique is to estimate the cash flows and salvage value to be received by the parent and compute the *NPV* of the project, as shown here:

$$NPV = -IO + \left(\sum_{t=1}^{n} \frac{CF_t}{(1+k)^t} \right) + \frac{SV_n}{(1+k)^n}$$

where:

IO = initial outlay (investment)
CF_t = cash flow in period t
SV_n = salvage value
k = required rate of return on the project
n = lifetime of the project (number of periods)

The *present value (PV)* of each period's net cash flow is computed using a 15% discount rate (line 20). The discount rate should reflect the parent's cost of capital with an adjustment for the project's risk. Finally, the cumulative *NPV* (line 22) is determined by consolidating the discounted cash flows for each period and subtracting the initial outlay (in line 21). For example, as of the end of Year 2, the cumulative *NPV* was £–3,602,987. This was determined by consolidating the £1,549,565 in Year 1, the £1,347,448 in Year 2, and subtracting the initial investment of £6,500,000. The cumulative *NPV* in each period measures how much of the initial outlay has been recovered up to that point by the receipt of discounted cash flows. Thus, it can be used to estimate how many periods it will take to recover the initial outlay. For some projects, the cumulative *NPV* remains negative in all periods, which suggests that the discounted cash flows never exceed the initial outlay. That is, the initial outlay is never fully recovered. The critical value in line 22 is the one for the last period because it reflects the *NPV* of the project.

In our example, the cumulative *NPV* as of the end of the last period is $2,229,867. Because the *NPV* is positive, Spartan ltd may accept this project assuming that the discount rate of 15% has fully accounted for the project's market risk. However, the currency risk statements of MNCs in their annual accounts almost always state that individual transactions are hedged. Clearly, MNCs also consider the risk of individual transactions and hence individual projects. The following section looks at how such risk might also be considered.

FACTORS TO CONSIDER IN MULTINATIONAL CAPITAL BUDGETING

The example of Spartan ltd ignored a variety of factors that may affect the capital budgeting analysis, such as:

- Exchange rate fluctuations
- Inflation
- Financing arrangement
- Blocked funds
- Uncertain salvage value
- Impact of project on prevailing cash flows
- Host government incentives
- Real options

Each of these factors is discussed in turn.

Exchange rate fluctuations

Recall that Spartan ltd uses the Singapore dollar's current spot rate (£0.33) as a forecast for all future periods of concern. The company realizes that the exchange rate will typically change over time, but it does not know whether the Singapore dollar will strengthen or weaken in the future. Though the difficulty in accurately forecasting the exchange rate itself is well known, it is nevertheless possible to forecast the standard deviation of the exchange rate. This is useful information because it enables Spartan to look at possible scenarios and have some idea as to their probability.

From the parent's point of view an appreciation of the Singapore dollar would be favourable since the Singapore dollar inflows would someday be converted to more British pounds. Conversely, depreciation would be unfavourable since the weakened Singapore dollars would convert to fewer British pounds over time.

Exhibit 14.3 examines the cash flows under a strong Singapore dollar regime and under a weak regime. The question arises as to how strong and how weak should the estimates be? Intuitively, if the currency value varies greatly over time we would want to look at scenarios that account for quite a wide variation. Alternatively, if the exchange rate with the pound has been stable over many years the strong and weak scenarios would realistically be not greatly different from the existing picture, i.e. not very strong and not very weak. Using past variation seems a sensible idea to predict future variation. There is however another effect. The further ahead we look the less certain we can be about the possible spread of returns. So as well as looking at the past, we need help to broaden our prediction the further ahead we look. Fortunately, statistics can help in both processes.

Using the past to predict the future requires that we look at past values of the exchange rate. Rather than take the actual rate, we detrend the data by taking the changes in the rates. Taking the past year as typical of future behaviour, it is a simple matter to work out the standard deviation of daily changes in the exchange rate. If the past year was not typical then a representative period has to be found. For the year 2005 the standard deviation of daily changes in the exchange of the Singapore dollar with the British pound was 0.0037 or 0.37%. To convert a daily standard deviation to an estimate of the standard deviation of the future year, two years, three and four years, we can use the formula explained in Chapter 10.

$$\sigma_t = \sigma_m \times \sqrt{(t/m)}$$

where:

t = the longer time period
m = shorter time period, both expressed in common time units
σ = standard deviation of the foreign currency

So to calculate the annual standard deviation of the percentage change the value is:

$$\sigma_t = \sigma_m \times \sqrt{(t/m)}$$

$$0.07 = 0.0037 \times \sqrt{(360 \times 1)} \text{ or } 7\% \text{ so } 0.07 \times £0.33 = £0.0231$$

and for 2, 3 and 4 years it is:

$$0.10 = 0.0037 \times \sqrt{(360 \times 2)} \text{ or } 10\% \text{ so } 0.10 \times £0.33 = £0.0330$$

$$0.12 = 0.0037 \times \sqrt{(360 \times 3)} \text{ or } 12\% \text{ so } 0.12 \times £0.33 = £0.0396$$

$$0.14 = 0.0037 \times \sqrt{(360 \times 4)} \text{ or } 14\% \text{ so } 0.14 \times £0.33 = £0.0462$$

remembering that by convention 360 is taken as the number of days in the year. So the standard deviation of changes in the exchange rate for 1 to 4 years ahead is 7%, 10%, 12% and 14%. A strong and weak currency is part of the traditional set of three, i.e. strong, medium and weak. Assuming a normal distribution, three outcomes have the probabilities 25%, 50% and 25% for strong, medium and weak respectively (i.e. this is the closest approximation, see Appendix B). The mid point of the 25% top and bottom bands will have half the 25%, i.e. 12½% above and below. From the normal distribution tables that is 1.15 standard deviations above and below the mean (see Exhibit 14.3).

The strong and weak exchange rates can now be defined more clearly as in Exhibit 14.4.

Exhibit 14.3 Distribution properties of high, medium and low outcomes for a normal distribution

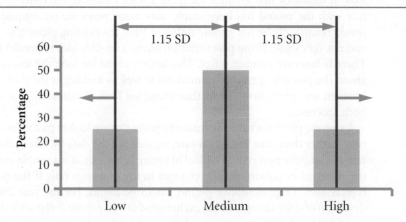

Exhibit 14.4 High, medium and low estimates of the exchange rate with the Singapore dollar

	Estimates of the value of the Singapore dollar		
Year	low	medium	high
1	£0.30	£0.33	£0.36
2	0.29	0.33	0.37
3	0.28	0.33	0.38
4	0.28	0.33	0.38

Notes:

■ Low, medium and high have probabilities of 25%, 50% and 25% respectively.

■ The annual standard deviation of the percentage changes in the Singapore dollar for 1 to 4 years ahead are as calculated in the text above. So, for example, year 4 "high" is 0.33 + 1.15 × 0.0462 = 0.38 (rounded); "low" is 0.33 − 1.15 × 0.0462 = 0.28 (rounded).

http://

You may vary the assumptions in calculating high, medium and low by using the spreadsheet "Spartan ltd" which can be found on the companion website.

Variations on the definition of high and low are, of course, possible. For example, Spartan might want an exchange rate with only a 5% chance of being lower. A more extreme calculation such as this would be appropriate if considering hedging. From normal distribution tables, a 5% chance of being lower would be 1.65 standard deviations below the mean. The year 4 low rate would be £0.254 (i.e. £0.33 − 1.65 × 0.0462) to the Singapore dollar in such a case.

All the above calculations are intended only to assist the manager.

Ultimately the definition of high and low is a management decision. All the above calculations assume that the distribution of exchange rates is normal and that their movement follows a random walk over time. This is not always the case; currencies can be subject to "jumps". Subjective estimates of high, medium and low are therefore a perfectly valid approach to estimating. The above calculations serve as a starting point for such a process.

Exhibit 14.5 Analysis using different exchange rate scenarios: Spartan ltd

	Year 0	Year 1	Year 2	Year 3	Year 4
S$ remitted to parent – line 16 &17 Exhibit 14.2		S$5,400,000	S$5,400,000	S$6,840,000	S$19,560,000
Strong-S$ Scenario					
Exchange rate of S$		£0.36	£0.37	£0.38	£0.38
Cash flows to parent		£1,944,000	£1,998,000	£2,599,200	£7,432,800
PV of cash flows (15% discount rate)		£1,690,435	£1,510,775	£1,709,016	£4,249,728
Initial investment by parent	£6.5m				
Cumulative *NPV*		−4,809,565	−3,298,790	−1,589,774	2,659,954
Weak-S$ Scenario					
Exchange rate of S$		£0.30	£0.29	£0.28	£0.28
Cash flows to parent		£1,620,000	£1,566,000	£1,915,200	£5,476,800
PV of cash flows (15% discount rate)		£1,408,696	£1,184,121	£1,259,275	£3,131,378
Initial investment by parent	£6.5m				
Cumulative *NPV*		−£5,091,304	-£3,907,183	−£2,647,908	£483,470

Exhibit 14.5 illustrates both a strong Singapore dollar (top half) scenario and a weak Singapore dollar (bottom half) scenario. At the top of the table, the anticipated after-tax Singapore dollar cash flows (including salvage value) are shown for the subsidiary from lines 16 and 17 in Exhibit 14.2. The amount in British pounds that these Singapore dollars convert to depends on the exchange rates existing in the various periods when they are converted. The number of Singapore dollars multiplied by the forecasted exchange rate will determine the estimated number of pounds received by the parent.

Notice from Exhibit 14.6 how the cash flows received by the parent differ depending on the scenario. A strong Singapore dollar is clearly beneficial, as indicated by the increased pound value of the cash flows received. The large differences in cash flow received by the parent in the different scenarios illustrate the impact of exchange rate expectations on the feasibility of an international project.

The *NPV* forecasts based on projections for exchange rates are illustrated in Exhibit 14.6. The estimated *NPV* is highest if the Singapore dollar is expected to strengthen and lowest if it is expected to weaken. The acceptability of the project will depend on the risk aversion of Spartan. It may be that the Directors of Spartan judge that the negative figures for the second and third years for the low outcome are simply too negative and that the eventual positive outcome is too close to being negative. If this is the case, the Directors may well abandon this project in favour of one that offers better returns year on year.

Some projects are in countries where the local currency is tied to the dollar or some other currency. Typically, such ties are periodically broken causing a large and sometimes catastrophic change in the exchange rate. The value of the Argentine peso between the years 2000 to 2004 serves as a warning (see Exhibit 14.7).

There is a danger in such circumstances that the risk will be underestimated because the sample of past exchange rates did not include a readjustment. Therefore, the MNC may re-estimate the project's *NPV* based on a particular devaluation scenario that it believes could possibly occur. If the project is still feasible under this scenario, the MNC may be more comfortable pursuing the project.

Exhibit 14.6 Sensitivity of the project's *NPV* to different exchange rate scenarios: Spartan ltd

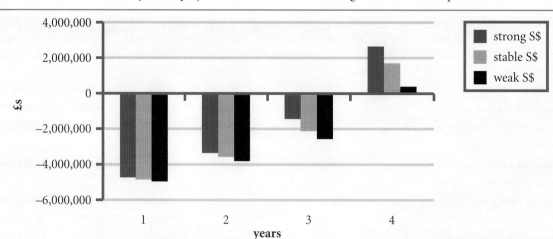

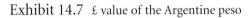

Exhibit 14.7 £ value of the Argentine peso

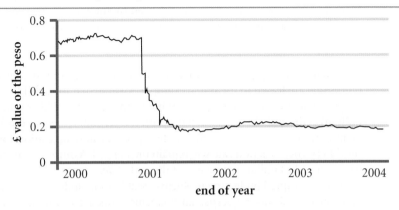

Inflation

Capital budgeting analysis may either *include* or *exclude* inflation in the calculations. When inflation is significant, calculations can appear confusing as the numbers are unrecognizably high. So it can be helpful to work with inflation adjusted estimates instead.

If inflation is to be *included* in the figures, revenues and costs must be estimates of the actual costs and revenues that the firm expects to pay and receive *at the time*. The discount rate must be the nominal rate or rate as one would see in the newspapers plus market risk for the project, and the exchange rate estimates should be based on the actual exchange rates. The inflation rate included in the discount rate should be that of the currency of the calculation. So for Spartan ltd, the rate should be for the pound. The difference between the pound inflation and inflation in Singapore is, according to PPP, adjusted for in the exchange rate. In the case of Spartan, the future estimate was based on the current spot rate. By implication there was therefore an assumption that the difference in inflation between the two countries was not going to be significant.

The joint impact of inflation in the foreign currency and devaluation of the exchange rate will therefore produce an offsetting effect from the viewpoint of the parent. Thus, even if subsidiary earnings are inflated, they will be deflated when converted into the parent's home currency (if the subsidiary's currency has weakened). Such an offsetting effect is not exact or consistent, though. Because inflation is only one of many factors that influence exchange rates, there is no guarantee that a currency will depreciate when the local inflation rate is relatively high. Therefore, one cannot ignore the impact of inflation and exchange rates on net cash flows.

If inflation is to be *excluded*, then the revenues and costs are in today's values and will be more familiar to managers. The current exchange rate should be used and predictions should not include a trend element caused by inflation differences between the two countries. It may be tempting to predict a fall in currency value particularly as the use of current values is more likely to occur for currencies where there is high inflation. Over the year 1999, for example, the Turkish lira devalued by 40%. Calculations at the end of that year using current values should however have resisted the temptation to predict a further 40% fall, because that fall offset a rampant inflation in Turkey and project figures that have excluded inflation should not therefore include a devaluing currency.

Financing arrangement

Many foreign projects are partially financed by foreign subsidiaries. To illustrate how this foreign financing can influence the feasibility of the project, consider the following revisions in the example of Spartan ltd.

Subsidiary financing. Assume that the subsidiary borrows S$10 million to purchase the offices that are leased in the initial example. Assume that the subsidiary will make interest payments on this loan (of S$1 million) annually and will pay the principal (S$10 million) at the end of Year 4, when the project is terminated. Since the Singapore government permits a maximum of S$2 million per year in depreciation for this project, the subsidiary's depreciation rate will remain unchanged. Assume the offices are expected to be sold for S$10 million after taxes at the end of Year 4.

Domestic capital budgeting problems would not include debt payments in the measurement of cash flows because all financing costs are captured by the discount rate. Foreign projects are more complicated, however, especially when the foreign subsidiary partially finances the investment in the foreign project. Although consolidating the initial investments made by the parent and the subsidiary simplifies the capital budgeting process, it can cause significant estimation errors. The estimated foreign cash flows that are ultimately remitted to the parent and are subject to exchange rate risk will be overstated if the foreign interest expenses are not explicitly considered as cash outflows for the foreign subsidiary. Thus, a more accurate approach is to separate the investment made by the subsidiary from the investment made by the parent. The capital budgeting analysis can focus on the parent's perspective by comparing the present value of the cash flows received by the parent to the initial investment by the parent.

Given the revised assumptions, the following revisions must be made to the capital budgeting analysis:

1. Since the subsidiary is borrowing funds to purchase the offices, the lease payments of S$1 million per year will not be necessary. However, the subsidiary will pay interest of S$1 million per year as a result of the loan. Thus, the annual cash outflows for the subsidiary are still the same.
2. The subsidiary must pay the S$10 million in loan principal at the end of four years. However, since the subsidiary expects to receive S$10 million (in four years) from the sale of the offices it purchases with the funds provided by the loan, it can use the proceeds of the sale to pay the loan principal.

Since the subsidiary has already taken the maximum depreciation expense allowed by the Singapore government before the offices were considered, it cannot increase its annual depreciation expenses. In this example, the cash flows ultimately received by the parent when the subsidiary obtains financing to purchase offices are similar to the cash flows determined in the original example (when the offices are to be leased). If the numbers were not offsetting, the capital budgeting analysis would be repeated to determine whether the *NPV* from the parent's perspective is higher than in the initial example.

Parent financing. Consider one more alternative arrangement, in which, instead of the subsidiary leasing the offices or purchasing them with borrowed funds, the parent uses its own funds to purchase the offices. Thus, its initial investment is £9.8 million, composed of the original £6.5 million investment as explained earlier, plus an additional £3.3 million to obtain an extra S$10 million to purchase the offices. This example illustrates how the capital budgeting analysis changes when the parent takes a bigger stake in the investment. If the parent rather than the subsidiary purchases the offices, the following revisions must be made to the capital budgeting analysis:

1. The subsidiary will not have any loan payments (since it will not need to borrow funds) because the parent will purchase the offices. Since the offices are to be purchased, there will be no lease payments either.
2. The parent's initial investment is £9.8 million instead of £6.5 million.
3. The salvage value to be received by the parent is S$22 million instead of S$12 million because the offices are assumed to be sold for S$10 million after taxes at the end of Year 4. The S$10 million to be received from selling the offices can be added to the S$12 million to be received from selling the rest of the subsidiary.

The capital budgeting analysis for Spartan ltd under this revised financing strategy in which the parent finances the entire £9.8 million investment is shown in Exhibit 14.8. This analysis uses our original exchange rate projections of £0.33 per Singapore dollar for each period. The numbers that are directly affected by the revised financing arrangement are bracketed. Other numbers are also affected indirectly as a result. For example, the subsidiary's after-tax earnings increase as a result of avoiding interest or lease payments on its offices. The *NPV* of the project under this alternative financing arrangement is positive but less than in the original arrangement. Given the higher initial outlay of the parent and the lower *NPV*, this arrangement is not as feasible as the arrangement in which the subsidiary either leases the offices or purchases them with borrowed funds.

Comparison of parent versus subsidiary financing. One reason that the subsidiary financing is more feasible than complete parent financing is that the financing rate on the loan is lower than the parent's required rate of return on funds provided to the subsidiary. If local loans had a relatively high interest rate, however, the use of local financing would likely not be as attractive.

In general, this revised example shows that the increased investment by the parent increases the parent's exchange rate exposure for the following reasons. First, since the parent provides the entire investment, no foreign financing is required. Consequently, the subsidiary makes no interest payments and therefore remits larger cash flows to the parent. Second, the salvage value to be remitted to the parent is larger. Given the larger payments to the parent, the cash flows ultimately received by the parent are more susceptible to exchange rate movements.

The parent's exposure is not as large when the subsidiary purchases the offices because the subsidiary incurs some of the financing expenses. The subsidiary financing essentially shifts some of the expenses to the same currency that the subsidiary will receive and therefore reduces the amount that will ultimately be converted into dollars for remittance to the parent.

Financing with other subsidiaries' retained earnings. Some foreign projects are completely financed with retained earnings of existing foreign subsidiaries. These projects are difficult to assess from the parent's perspective because their direct effects are normally felt by the subsidiaries. One approach is to view a subsidiary's investment in a project as an opportunity cost, since the funds could be remitted to the parent rather than invested in the foreign project. Thus, the initial outlay from the parent's perspective is the amount of funds it would have received from the subsidiary if the funds had been remitted rather than invested in this project. The cash flows from the parent's perspective

Exhibit 14.8 Analysis with an alternative financing arrangement: Spartan ltd

	Year 0	Year 1	Year 2	Year 3	Year 4
1. Demand		60,000	60,000	100,000	100,000
2. Price per unit		S$350	S$350	S$360	S$380
3. Total revenue = (1) × (2)		S$21,000,000	S$21,000,000	S$36,000,000	S$38,000,000
4. Variable cost per unit		S$200	S$200	S$250	S$260
5. Total variable cost = (1) × (4)		S$12,000,000	S$12,000,000	S$25,000,000	S$26,000,000
6. Annual lease expense		S$0	S$0	S$0	S$0
7. Other fixed annual expenses		S$1,000,000	S$1,000,000	S$1,000,000	S$1,000,000
8. Non-cash expense (depreciation)		S$2,000,000	S$2,000,000	S$2,000,000	S$2,000,000
9. Total expenses = (5) + (6) + (7) + (8)		S$15,000,000	S$15,000,000	S$28,000,000	S$29,000,000
10. Before-tax earnings of subsidiary = (3) − (9)		S$6,000,000	S$6,000,000	S$8,000,000	S$9,000,000
11. Host government tax (20%)		S$1,200,000	S$1,200,000	S$1,600,000	S$1,800,000
12. After-tax earnings of subsidiary		S$4,800,000	S$4,800,000	S$6,400,000	S$7,200,000
13. Net cash flow to subsidiary = (12) + (8)		S$6,800,000	S$6,800,000	S$8,400,000	S$9,200,000
14. S$ remitted by subsidiary (100% of net cash flow)		S$6,800,000	S$6,800,000	S$8,400,000	S$9,200,000
15. Withholding tax on remitted funds (10%)		S$680,000	S$680,000	S$840,000	S$920,000
16. S$ remitted after withholding taxes		S$6,120,000	S$6,120,000	S$7,560,000	S$8,280,000
17. Salvage value					S$22,000,000
18. Exchange rate of S$		£0.33	£0.33	£0.33	£0.33
19. Cash flows to parent		£2,019,600	£2,019,600	£2,494,800	£9,992,400
20. *PV* of parent cash flows (15% discount rate)		£1,756,174	£1,527,108	£1,640,371	£5,713,187
21. Initial investment by parent	−£9,800,000				
22. CUMULATIVE *NPV*		−£8,043,826	−£6,516,718	−£4,876,347	£836,840

reflect those cash flows ultimately received by the parent as a result of the foreign project.

Even if the project generates earnings for the subsidiary that are reinvested by the subsidiary, the key cash flows from the parent's perspective are those that it ultimately receives from the project. In this way, any international factors that will affect the cash flows (such as withholding taxes and exchange rate movements) are incorporated into the capital budgeting process.

Blocked funds

In some cases, the host country may block funds that the subsidiary attempts to send to the parent. Some countries require that earnings generated by the subsidiary be reinvested locally for at least three years before they can be remitted. Such restrictions can affect the accept/reject decision on a project.

Reconsider the example of Spartan ltd assuming that all funds are blocked until the subsidiary is sold. Thus, the subsidiary must reinvest those funds until that time. Blocked funds penalize a project if the return on the reinvested funds is less than the required rate of return on the project.

Exhibit 14.9 Capital budgeting with blocked funds: Spartan ltd

	Year 0	Year 1	Year 2	Year 3	Year 4
S$ to be remitted by subsidiary		S$6,000,000	S$6,000,000	S$7,600,000	S$8,400,000
					S$7,980,000
S$ accumulated by reinvesting funds to be remitted					S$6,615,000
					S$6,945,750
					S$29,940,750
Withholding tax (10%)					S$2,994,075
S$ cash flow after withholding tax					S$26,946,675
Salvage value					S$12,000,000
Total S$ remitted					S$38,946,675
Exchange rate					£0.33
Cash flows to parent					£12,852,240
PV of parent cash flows (15% discount rate)					£7,348,310
Initial investment by parent	–£6.5m				
Cumulative NPV		–£6,500,000	–£6,500,000	–£6,500,000	**£848,310**

Assume that the subsidiary uses the funds to purchase marketable securities that are expected to yield 5% annually after taxes. A re-evaluation of Spartan's cash flows (from Exhibit 14.2) to incorporate the blocked-funds restriction is shown in Exhibit 14.9. The withholding tax is not applied until the funds are remitted to the parent, which is in Year 4. The original exchange rate projections are used here. All parent cash flows depend on the exchange rate four years from now. The NPV of the project with blocked funds is still positive, but it is substantially less than the NPV in the original example.

If the foreign subsidiary has a loan outstanding, it may be able to better utilize the blocked funds by repaying the local loan. For example, the S$6 million at the end of Year 1 could be used to reduce the outstanding loan balance instead of being invested in marketable securities, assuming that the lending bank allows early repayment.

Uncertain salvage value

The salvage value of an MNC's project typically has a significant impact on the project's NPV. When the salvage value is uncertain, the MNC may incorporate various possible outcomes for the salvage value and re-estimate the NPV based on each possible outcome. It may even estimate the break-even salvage value (also called break-even terminal value), which is the salvage value necessary to achieve a zero NPV for the project. If the actual salvage value is expected to equal or exceed the break-even salvage value, the project is feasible. The break-even salvage value (called SV_n) can be determined by setting NPV equal to zero and rearranging the capital budgeting equation, as follows:

$$NPV = -IO + \sum_{t=1}^{n} \frac{CF_t}{(1+k)^t} + \frac{SV_n}{(1+k)^n}$$

$$0 = -IO + \sum_{t=1}^{n} \frac{CF_t}{(1+k)^t} + \frac{SV_n}{(1+k)^n}$$

the only unknown is now SV_n, which can be solved as follows:

$$SV_n = \left(IO - \sum_{t=1}^{n} \frac{CF_t}{(1+k)^t} \right)(1+k)^n$$

Reconsider the Spartan ltd example and assume that Spartan is not guaranteed a price for the project. The break-even salvage value for the project can be determined by: (1) calculating the present value of all cash flows *except* the salvage value (the value in the brackets above); and (2) calculating the salvage value required to make the project just acceptable (as in the above formula). Using the original cash flow information from Exhibit 14.2, the present value of cash flows can be determined:

$$\text{PV of cash flows to parent} = \frac{£1,782,000}{(1.15)^1} + \frac{£1,782,000}{(1.15)^2} + \frac{£2,257,200}{(1.15)^3} + \frac{(S\$7,560,000 \times £0.33)}{(1.15)^4}$$

$$= £1,549,565 + £1,347,448 + £1,484,146 + £1,426,410$$

$$= £5,807,569$$

The year 4 value excludes the salvage value and therefore has to be recalculated as above. Given the present value of cash flows and the estimated initial outlay, the break-even salvage value is determined as:

$$SV_n = \left(IO - \sum_{t=1}^{n} \frac{CF_t}{(1+k)^t} \right)(1+k)^n$$

$$= (£6,500,000 - £5,807,569) \quad (1.15)^4$$

$$= £1,211,066$$

Given the original information in Exhibit 14.2, Spartan ltd will accept the project only if the salvage value is estimated to be at least £1,211,066 (assuming that the project's required rate of return is 15%).

Assuming the forecasted exchange rate of £0.33 per Singapore dollar, the project must sell for more than S\$3,669,897 (computed as £1,211,066 divided by £0.33) to exhibit a positive *NPV* (assuming no taxes are paid on this amount). If Spartan did not have a guarantee from the Singapore government, it could assess the probability that the subsidiary would sell for more than the break-even salvage value and then incorporate this assessment into its decision to accept or reject the project.

Impact of project on prevailing cash flows

Thus far, in our example, we have assumed that the new project has no impact on prevailing cash flows. In reality, however, there may often be an impact.

Reconsider the Spartan ltd example, assuming this time that: (1) Spartan currently exports tennis rackets from its UK plant to Singapore; (2) Spartan ltd still considers establishing a subsidiary in Singapore because it expects production costs to be lower in Singapore than in the United States; and (3) without a subsidiary, Spartan's export business to Singapore is expected to generate net cash flows of £600,000 over the next four

Exhibit 14.10 Capital budgeting when prevailing cash flows are affected: Spartan ltd

	Year 0	Year 1	Year 2	Year 3	Year 4
Cash flows to parent, ignoring impact on existing home cash flows (line 19 Exhibit 14.2)		£1,782,000	£1,782,000	£2,257,200	£6,454,800
Impact of project on existing home cash flows		£600,000	£600,000	£600,000	£600,000
Cash flows to parent, incorporating impact on existing home cash flows		£1,182,000	£1,182,000	£1,657,200	£5,854,800
PV of cash flows to parent (15% discount rate)		£1,027,826	£893,762	£1,089,636	£3,347,501
Initial investment (line 21 Exhibit 14.2)	−£6,500,000				
Cumulative NPV		−£5,472,174	−£4,578,412	−£3,488,776	−£141,275

years. With a subsidiary, these cash flows would be forgone. The effects of these assumptions are shown in Exhibit 14.10. The previously estimated cash flows to the parent from the subsidiary (drawn from line 19 Exhibit 14.2) are restated in Exhibit 14.10. These estimates do not account for forgone cash flows since the possible export business was not considered. If the export business is established, however, the forgone cash flows attributable to this business must be considered, as shown in Exhibit 14.10. The adjusted cash flows to the parent account for the project's impact on prevailing cash flows.

The present value of adjusted cash flows and cumulative NPV are also shown in Exhibit 14.10. The project's NPV is now negative as a result of the adverse effect on prevailing cash flows. Thus, the project will not be feasible if the exporting business to Singapore is eliminated.

Some foreign projects may have a favourable impact on prevailing cash flows.

EXAMPLE

Colgate established a joint venture with the Chinese company Sanxiao in 2000 to manufacture toothbrushes. The company has a large share of the Chinese market. As it also had a 30% cost advantage over Colgate's existing production, the company now produces for the international market producing cost savings on Colgate's existing production.

Host government incentives

Foreign projects proposed by MNCs may have a favourable impact on economic conditions in the host country and are therefore encouraged by the host government. Any incentives offered by the host government must be incorporated into the capital budgeting analysis. For example, a low-rate host government loan or a reduced tax rate offered to the subsidiary will enhance periodic cash flows. If the government subsidizes the initial establishment of the subsidiary, the MNC's initial investment will be reduced.

EXAMPLE

Hyundai/Kia, the South Korean car manufacturer has set up car production in Slovakia. The plant is expected to employ some 3,000 workers by 2009. As part of the incentive package, the Slovakian government is providing subsidies expected to amount to 15% of the initial investment and will also improve road and rail links and will build extra school facilities. Tax breaks of up to 50% can be granted for ten years for small manufacturing enterprises in the automotive industry.

Real options

Some capital budgeting projects contain real options, in that they may allow for additional business opportunities. Since these opportunities can generate cash flows, they can enhance the value of a project.

EXAMPLE

Topeka ltd considers undertaking a project requested by the government of Ukraine. This specific project would require a significant outlay for materials. Topeka determines that this project has a slight negative *NPV*. However, the project would allow Topeka to establish a relationship with the Ukrainian government, so that it would be well positioned to expand its business in Ukraine if the country's economy becomes more market oriented over time. Without a business relationship with the government, Topeka will not be positioned to expand in Ukraine. Thus, the government contract contains an implicit call option (to expand its business in Ukraine) that Topeka could exercise someday if Ukraine's economy becomes more market oriented. When the value of this real option is considered, the *NPV* of the government project becomes positive. Therefore, Topeka decides to undertake the project.

The value of a real option within a project is primarily influenced by two factors: (1) the probability that the real option will be exercised, and (2) the *NPV* that will result from exercising the real option. In the previous example, Topeka's real option is influenced by: (1) the probability that Ukraine's economy will become market oriented, and (2) the *NPV* of opportunities that would be pursued under this condition. The danger of the real options argument is that it becomes an excuse for unprofitable projects. The option must be for a different activity. For example, a business that is involved in unprofitable brewing interests in China, may view the current lack of profits as a payment of sorts for greater profits in the future. This is not an option but merely a project with a long period of losses in the early years. For the project to have an option element in this case, the brewing investment should in some sense qualify the company to engage in other activities in China that it would not otherwise have been able to undertake.

ADJUSTING PROJECT ASSESSMENT FOR RISK

Finance theory recommends that projects are discounted at the rate demanded by the stock market as derived from the Capital Asset Pricing Model (CAPM). The discount rate required by the model depends on the beta for the project – as defined by the model. The beta of a company engaged in similar projects can be used to calculate the appropriate discount rate (usually, this will be the beta of the company undertaking the project itself). The calculation of the return itself is simply the risk free rate of interest plus a proportion of the market risk premium (the market return less the risk free rate) – beta determines for each project the amount of market risk premium to include. So if the risk free rate is 4% and the market risk premium is, say, 10%, then a firm or project with a beta of 1 would have a required market return of 4% + (1 × 10%) = 14%. This rate is the same as the market rate because, by definition, the market rate is the risk free rate plus the risk premium. Therefore betas of greater than 1 require an above market return and below 1, a below market return. Whereas the mechanics seem simple enough, the problems are in measurement.

The market return is the return on the market index, or in the case of the UK, the percentage change in the FTSE index. But is any one index appropriate for multinational companies who have investors worldwide? Volkswagen AG, for example, use the DAX index to calculate their cost of capital, but their shares are quoted on exchanges world-wide; for many investors, the DAX index of European companies will be of little interest, and basing a discount rate on that particular index would not be relevant. Measuring the risk free rate also poses problems. Which country's risk free rate should be used? There are no simple answers.

In outline, the rationale is that investors can diversify their risk from all effects except that of the overall market return. The risk that they want their investments to account for is therefore the market-related element in their investment portfolio. The problem for MNCs is that the market-related element will be very different amongst such a diverse shareholder community. One approach to the problem is to test to see to which markets in particular the MNC shares are sensitive. It turns out that the market-related element for MNCs is that of their home county's market index. Simple correlations between the movement of share price of the MNC and the market indices show that there is little relationship with market indices of other countries. Thus, a UK multinational such as GlaxoSmithKlein although it has over half its sales outside Europe let alone the UK, will nevertheless have a share price that varies principally with the London Stock Exchange even though it is also quoted on the US Stock Exchange. So it is a poor diversification for investors in the London Stock Exchange but good for diversification for investors in shares whose home countries are abroad.

> *The calculation of the return requirement is based on the weighted average cost of capital (WACC) according to the capital asset pricing model (CAPM). This capital cost is restated as a return requirement per country with consideration of local tax rates and interest levels. The discount factor before tax for Eniro units varied between 8.5 and 9.0%*

> (Eniro AB (Swedish) Annual Accounts, 2004).

In addition to the concerns over the international interpretation of finance theory, there are also questions as to the importance of CAPM type analysis for MNCs. Although annual accounts occasionally make statements as in the example of the Eniro example, the safe conclusion is that the influence is small. Questionnaire surveys give scant reference to betas and the now extensive statements on risk in the annual reports are almost wholly concerned with the risk of the company itself rather than market risk. Until there is greater clarity in this field and greater evidence of the theory's practical importance, it is sensible to view projects and their risk from an MNC rather than market perspective. This is the approach taken here.

In adjusting for risk therefore, three methods are commonly used:

- Risk-adjusted discount rate
- Sensitivity analysis
- Simulation

Each method is described in turn.

Risk-adjusted discount rate

The greater the uncertainty about a project's forecasted cash flows, the larger should be the discount rate applied to cash flows, other things being equal. This risk-adjusted discount rate is intended to reduce the worth of a project by a degree that reflects the risk the project exhibits. Often this will be a constant rate such as 10% per period. The compound process will mean that the risk discount for future periods will increase significantly. In the case of a 10% risk discount the reduction in cash flows in year 3 will be some 35% (calculated as $(1-1.15^{-3})$. If the projected cash flows over periods have different degrees of uncertainty that do not match the constant rate approach, separate adjustments can be made. For instance, a firm might not want to look more than five years ahead and effectively have an infinite discount rate after five years. The probability of blocked funds, expropriation, a destabilized political situation and other adverse events would more than justify such an approach (finance theory ignores all such threats).

Despite its subjectivity, the risk-adjusted discount rate is a commonly used technique, perhaps because of the ease with which it can be applied. In addition, there is no alternative technique that will perfectly adjust for risk, although in certain cases some others (discussed next) may better reflect a project's risk.

Sensitivity analysis

Once the MNC has estimated the *NPV* of a proposed project, it may want to consider alternative estimates for its input variables. Recall that the demand for the Spartan subsidiary's tennis rackets (in our earlier example) was estimated to be 60,000 in the first two years and 100,000 in the next two years. If demand turns out to be 60,000 in all four years, how will the *NPV* results change? Alternatively, what if demand is 100,000 in all four years? Use of such *what-if* scenarios is referred to as sensitivity analysis. A simple spreadsheet is ideal for sensitivity analysis. The objective is to determine how sensitive the *NPV* is to alternative values of the input variables. The estimates of any input variables can be revised to create new estimates for *NPV*. If the *NPV* is consistently positive during these revisions, then the MNC should feel more comfortable about the project. If it is negative in many cases, the accept/reject decision for the project becomes more difficult.

The two exchange rate scenarios developed earlier represent a form of sensitivity analysis. Sensitivity analysis can be more useful than simple point estimates because it reassesses the project based on various circumstances that may occur. It is a particularly useful technique when considering events that lie outside normal business risk, examples would include blocked funds, a devaluation of a fixed currency or expropriation.

MANAGING FOR VALUE
Senior plc's decision to set up in Cape Town

Senior plc manufacture parts for the automotive industry and produce products at a range of locations. In the late 1990s it chose Cape Town as the location to set up a plant manufacturing catalytic converters and connectors for exhausts and seals. On the plus side of the investment was low labour costs, a good supply of raw materials (steel in particular), excellent air and sea transport to supply the world's vehicle manufacturers, cheap land and electricity and a well-educated workforce for what was a capital intensive process. On the negative side was a reputation for a lack of security, though Senior found that the security was very good in their case. Regulations for foreign workers were restrictive and personal tax rates were high. In 2005, the company moved to a much larger factory producing a wider product range. More recently demand has increased due to a weak local currency and customers changing from UK and US suppliers to the South African provider. Currency risks are managed by a centralized treasury department. The group has a policy of hedging its net investment in overseas operations by borrowing in the same currency and also by taking out forward contracts. Such contracts are taken out on a 12 month rolling basis and therefore provide time to avoid the worst effects of the most adverse of currency movements.

Simulation

Simulation can be used for a variety of tasks, including the generation of a probability distribution for *NPV* based on a range of possible values for one or more input variables. Simulation is typically performed with the aid of a computer package.

Reconsider Spartan ltd, and assume that it expects the exchange rate to depreciate by 3 to 7% per year (with an equal probability of all values in this range occurring). Unlike a single point estimate, simulation can consider the range of possibilities for the Singapore dollar's exchange rate at the end of each year. It considers all point estimates for the other variables and randomly picks one of the possible values of the Singapore dollar's depreciation level for each of the four years. Based on this random selection process, the *NPV* is determined.

The procedure just described represents one iteration. Then the process is repeated: the Singapore dollar's depreciation for each year is again randomly selected (within the range of possibilities assumed earlier), and the *NPV* of the project is computed. The simulation program may be run for, say, 100 iterations. This means that 100 different possible scenarios are created for the possible exchange rates of the Singapore dollar during the four-year project period. Each iteration reflects a different scenario. The *NPV* of the project based on each scenario is then computed. Thus, simulation generates a distribution of *NPVs* for the project. The major advantage of simulation is that the MNC can examine the range of possible *NPVs* that may occur. From the information, it can determine the probability that the *NPV* will be positive or greater than a particular level. The greater the uncertainty of the exchange rate, the greater will be the uncertainty of the *NPV*. The risk of a project will be greater if it involves transactions in more volatile currencies, other things being equal.

In reality, many or all of the input variables necessary for multinational capital budgeting may be uncertain in the future. Probability distributions can be developed for all variables with uncertain future values. The final result is a distribution of possible *NPVs* that might occur for the project. The simulation technique does not put all of its emphasis on any one particular *NPV* forecast but instead provides a distribution of the possible outcomes that may occur.

The project's cost of capital can be used as a discount rate when simulation is performed. The probability that the project will be successful can be estimated by measuring the area within the probability distribution in which the *NPV* > 0. This area represents the probability that the present value of future cash flows will exceed the initial outlay. An MNC can also use the probability distribution to estimate the probability that the project will backfire by measuring the area in which *NPV* < 0.

Simulation is difficult to do manually because of the iterations necessary to develop a distribution of *NPVs*. Computer programs can run 100 iterations and generate results within a matter of seconds. The user of a simulation program must provide the probability distributions for the input variables that will affect the project's *NPV*. As with any model, the accuracy of results generated by simulation will be determined by the accuracy of the input.

SUMMARY

- Capital budgeting may generate different results and a different conclusion depending on whether it is conducted from the perspective of an MNC's subsidiary or from the perspective of the MNC's parent. The subsidiary's perspective does not consider possible exchange rate and tax effects on cash flows transferred by the subsidiary to the parent. When a parent is deciding whether to implement an international project, it should determine whether the project is feasible from its own perspective.

- Multinational capital budgeting requires any input that will help estimate the initial outlay, periodic cash flows, salvage value, and required rate of return on the project. Once these factors are estimated, the international project's net present value can be estimated, just as if it were a domestic project. However, it is normally more difficult to estimate these factors for an international project.

Exchange rates create an additional source of uncertainty because they affect the cash flows ultimately received by the parent as a result of the project. Other international conditions that can influence the cash flows ultimately received by the parent include the financing arrangement (parent versus subsidiary financing of the project), blocked funds by the host government, and host government incentives.

- The risk of international projects can be accounted for by adjusting the discount rate used to estimate the project's net present value. However, the adjustment to the discount rate is subjective. An alternative method is to estimate the net present value based on various possible scenarios for exchange rates or any other uncertain factors. This method is facilitated by the use of sensitivity analysis or simulation.

CRITICAL DEBATE

Should MNCs use net present value techniques to value foreign projects?

Proposition. Yes. Net present value is the most widely accepted technique for valuing investments. It provides a measure of return in terms of cash flows and the required return in the form of the discount rate. The rate includes risk however defined. All projects with a positive *NPV* should be accepted – a clear criterion.

Opposing view. No. An MNC should use its own valuation techniques including payback, decision tree analysis and sensitivity analysis. NPV calculations are too limited a consideration of a complex problem.

With whom do you agree? Which argument do you support? Offer your own opinion on this issue.

SELF TEST

Answers are provided in Appendix A at the back of the text.

1. Two managers of Marshall ltd assessed a proposed project in Jamaica. Each manager used exactly the same estimates of the earnings to be generated by the project, as these estimates were provided by other employees. The managers agree on the proportion of funds to be remitted each year, the life of the project, and the discount rate to be applied. Both managers also assessed the project from the

UK parent's perspective. Nevertheless, one manager determined that this project had a large net present value, while the other manager determined that the project had a negative net present value. Explain the possible reasons for such a difference.

2. Pinpoint the parts of a multinational capital budgeting analysis for a proposed sales distribution centre in Ireland that are sensitive when the forecast of a stable economy in Ireland is revised to predict a recession.

3. Hampshire ltd produces small computer components, which are then sold to India. It plans to expand by establishing a plant in India that will produce the components and sell them locally. This plant will reduce the amount of goods that are transported from the UK. The firm has determined that the cash flows to be earned in India would yield a positive net present value after accounting for tax and exchange rate effects, converting cash flows to pounds, and discounting them at the proper discount rate. What other major factor must be considered to estimate the project's *NPV*?

4. Explain how the present value of the salvage value of an Indonesian subsidiary will be affected (from the UK parent's perspective) by: (a) an increase in the risk of the foreign subsidiary, and (b) an expectation that Indonesia's currency (rupiah) will depreciate against the pound over time.

5. William ltd and Niles ltd (both from the UK) are assessing the acquisition of the same firm in Thailand and have obtained the future cash flow estimates (in Thailand's currency, baht) from the firm. William would use its retained earnings from UK operations to acquire the subsidiary. Niles would finance the acquisition mostly with a term loan (in baht) from Thai banks. Neither firm has any other business in Thailand. Which firm's pound cash flows would be affected more by future changes in the value of the baht (assuming that the Thai firm is acquired)?

6. Review the capital budgeting example of Spartan ltd discussed in this chapter. Identify the specific variables assessed in the process of estimating a foreign project's net present value (from a UK perspective) that would cause the most uncertainty about the *NPV*.

QUESTIONS AND APPLICATIONS

1. **MNC parent's perspective.** Why should capital budgeting for subsidiary projects be assessed from the parent's perspective? What additional factors that normally are not relevant for a purely domestic project deserve consideration in multinational capital budgeting?

2. **Accounting for risk.** What is the limitation of using point estimates of exchange rates in the capital budgeting analysis? List the various techniques for adjusting risk in multinational capital budgeting. Describe any advantages or disadvantages of each technique. Explain how simulation can be used in multinational capital budgeting. What can it do that other risk adjustment techniques cannot?

3. **Uncertainty of cash flows.** Using the capital budgeting framework discussed in this chapter, explain the sources of uncertainty surrounding a proposed project in Hungary by a UK firm. In what ways is the estimated net present value of this project more uncertain than that of a similar project in a more developed European country?

4. **Accounting for risk.** Your employees have estimated the net present value of project X to be £1.2 million. Their report says that they have not accounted for risk, but that with such a large

NPV, the project should be accepted since even a risk-adjusted *NPV* would likely be positive. You have the final decision as to whether to accept or reject the project. What is your decision?

5. **Impact of exchange rates on *NPV*.**
   a. Describe in general terms how future appreciation of the euro will likely affect the value (from the parent's perspective) of a project established in Germany today by a UK-based MNC. Will the sensitivity of the project value be affected by the percentage of earnings remitted to the parent each year?
   b. Repeat this question, but assume the future depreciation of the euro.

6. **Impact of financing on *NPV*.** Explain how the financing decision can influence the sensitivity of the net present value to exchange rate forecasts.

7. **Impact of events.** An MNC in the euro area is thinking of investing outside the area. For each continent, think of events outside the project that might adversely affect cash flows.

8. **Assessing a foreign project.** Huskie SA, a French-based MNC, considers purchasing a small manufacturing company in the US that sells products only within the States. Huskie has no other

existing business in the US and no cash flows in dollars. Would the proposed acquisition likely be more feasible if the dollar is expected to appreciate or depreciate over the long run? Explain.

9. **Relevant cash flows in Disney's French theme park.** When Walt Disney World considered establishing a theme park in France, were the forecasted revenues and costs associated with the French park sufficient to assess the feasibility of this project? Were there any other "relevant cash flows" that deserved to be considered?

10. **Capital budgeting logic.** Athens GmbH (Germany) established a subsidiary in the United Kingdom that was independent of its operations in Germany. The subsidiary's performance was well above what was expected. Consequently, when a British firm approached Athens about the possibility of acquiring the subsidiary, Athens' chief financial officer implied that the subsidiary was performing so well that it was not for sale. Comment on this strategy.

11. **Capital budgeting logic.** Lehigh SA (France) established a subsidiary in Switzerland that was performing below the cash flow projections developed before the subsidiary was established. Lehigh anticipated that future cash flows would also be lower than the original cash flow projections. Consequently, Lehigh decided to inform several potential acquiring firms of its plan to sell the subsidiary. Lehigh then received a few bids. Even the highest bid was very low, but Lehigh accepted the offer. It justified its decision by stating that any existing project whose cash flows are not sufficient to recover the initial investment should be divested. Comment on this statement.

12. **Impact of reinvested foreign earnings on *NPV*.** Greet BV is a Dutch-based firm with a subsidiary in Mexico. It plans to reinvest its earnings in Mexican government securities for the next ten years since the interest rate earned on these securities is so high. Then, after ten years, it will remit all accumulated earnings to the Netherlands. What is a drawback of using this approach? (Assume the securities have no default or interest rate risk.)

13. **Capital budgeting example.** Cleto Srl (Spain) has just constructed a manufacturing plant in Ghana. The construction cost 9 billion Ghanian

cedi. Cleto intends to leave the plant open for three years. During the three years of operation, cedi cash flows are expected to be 3 billion cedi, 3 billion cedi, and 2 billion cedi, respectively. Operating cash flows will begin one year from today and are remitted back to the parent at the end of each year. At the end of the third year, Cleto expects to sell the plant for 5 billion cedi. Cleto has a required rate of return of 17%. It currently takes 8,700 cedi to buy one euro, and the cedi is expected to depreciate by 5% per year.

a. Determine the *NPV* for this project. Should Cleto build the plant?

b. How would your answer change if the value of the cedi was expected to remain unchanged from its current value of 8,700 cedi per euro over the course of the three years? Should Cleto construct the plant then?

14. **Impact of financing on NPV.** Ventura plc a UK-based MNC, plans to establish a subsidiary in Japan. It is very confident that the Japanese yen will appreciate against the pound over time. The subsidiary will retain only enough revenue to cover expenses and will remit the rest to the parent each year. Will Ventura benefit more from exchange rate effects if its parent provides equity financing for the subsidiary or if the subsidiary is financed by local banks in Japan? Explain.

15. **Accounting for changes in risk.** Santa Monica SA (Portugal) was considering establishing a consumer products division in Germany, which would be financed by German banks. Santa Monica completed its capital budgeting analysis in August. Then, in November, the government leadership stabilized and political conditions improved in Germany. In response, Santa Monica increased its expected cash flows by 20% but did not adjust the discount rate applied to the project. Should the discount rate be affected by the change in political conditions?

16. **Estimating the *NPV*.** Assume that a less developed country called LDC encourages foreign direct investment (FDI) in order to reduce its unemployment rate, currently at 15%. Also assume that several MNCs are likely to consider FDI in this country. The inflation rate in recent years has averaged 4%. The hourly wage in LDC for manufacturing work is the equivalent of about $5 per hour. When Piedmont SpA (Italy)

develops cash flow forecasts to perform a capital budgeting analysis for a project in LDC, it assumes a wage rate of 5 euros in Year 1 and applies a 4% increase for each of the next ten years. The components produced are to be exported to Piedmont's headquarters in Italy, where they will be used in the production of computers. Do you think Piedmont will overestimate or underestimate the net present value of this project? Why? (Assume that LDC's currency is tied to the euro and will remain that way.)

17. **PepsiCo's project in Brazil.** PepsiCo recently decided to invest more than $300 million for expansion in Brazil. Brazil offers considerable potential because it has 150 million people and their demand for soft drinks is increasing. However, the soft drink consumption is still only about one-fifth of the soft drink consumption in the United States. PepsiCo's initial outlay was used to purchase three production plants and a distribution network of almost 1,000 trucks to distribute its products to retail stores in Brazil. The expansion in Brazil was expected to make PepsiCo's products more accessible to Brazilian consumers.

   a. Given that PepsiCo's investment in Brazil was entirely in dollars, describe its exposure to exchange rate risk resulting from the project. Explain how the size of the parent's initial investment and the exchange rate risk would have been affected if PepsiCo had financed much of the investment with loans from banks in Brazil.

   b. Describe the factors that PepsiCo likely considered when estimating the future cash flows of the project in Brazil.

   c. What factors did PepsiCo likely consider in deriving its required rate of return on the project in Brazil?

   d. Describe the uncertainty that surrounds the estimate of future cash flows from the perspective of the US parent.

   e. PepsiCo's parent was responsible for assessing the expansion in Brazil. Yet, PepsiCo already had some existing operations in Brazil. When capital budgeting analysis was used to determine the feasibility of this project, should the project have been assessed from a Brazilian perspective or a US perspective? Explain.

18. **Impact of Asian crisis.** Assume that Fordham plc was evaluating a project in Thailand (to be financed with British pounds). All cash flows generated from the project were to be reinvested in Thailand for several years. Explain how the Asian crisis would have affected the expected cash flows of this project and the required rate of return on this project. If the cash flows were to be remitted to the UK parent, explain how the Asian crisis would have affected the expected cash flows of this project.

19. **Tax effects on NPV.** When considering the implementation of a project in one of various possible countries, what types of tax characteristics should be assessed among the countries? (See the chapter appendix.)

20. **Capital budgeting analysis.** A project in South Korea requires an initial investment of 2 billion South Korean won. The project is expected to generate net cash flows to the subsidiary of 3 billion and 4 billion won in the two years of operation, respectively. The project has no salvage value. The current value of the won is 1,800 won per pound, and the value of the won is expected to remain constant over the next two years.

   a. What is the NPV of this project if the required rate of return is 13%?

   b. Repeat the question, except assume that the value of the won is expected to be 2,000 won per pound after two years. Further assume that the funds are blocked and that the parent company will only be able to remit them back to the United Kingdom in two years. How does this affect the NPV of the project?

21. **Accounting for exchange rate risk.** Carson ltd is considering a ten-year project in Hong Kong, where the Hong Kong dollar is tied to the US dollar. Carson ltd uses sensitivity analysis that allows for alternative exchange rate scenarios. Why would Carson use this approach rather than using the pegged exchange rate as its exchange rate forecast in every year?

22. **Decisions based on capital budgeting.** Marathon plc considers a one-year project with the Belgian government. Its euro revenue would be guaranteed. Its consultant states that the percentage change in the euro is represented by a normal distribution based on a 95% confidence interval, the

percentage change in the euro is expected to be between 0% and 6%. Marathon uses this information to create three scenarios: 0%, 3% and 6% for the euro. It derives an estimated *NPV* based on each scenario and then determines the mean *NPV*. The *NPV* was positive for the 3% and 6% scenarios, but was slightly negative for the 0% scenario. This led Marathon to reject the project. Its manager stated that it did not want to pursue a project that had a one-in-three chance of having a negative *NPV*. Do you agree with the manager's interpretation of the analysis? Explain.

23. **Estimating cash flows of a foreign project.** Assume that Nike decides to build a shoe factory in Brazil; half the initial outlay will be funded by the parent's equity and half by borrowing funds in Brazil. Assume that Nike wants to assess the project from its own perspective to determine whether the project's future cash flows will provide a sufficient return to the parent to warrant the initial investment. Why will the estimated cash flows be different from the estimated cash flows of Nike's shoe factory in New Hampshire? Why will the initial outlay be different? Explain how Nike can conduct multinational capital budgeting in a manner that will achieve its objective.

ADVANCED QUESTIONS

24. **Break-even salvage value.** A project in Malaysia costs £4,000,000. Over the next three years, the project will generate total operating cash flows of £3,500,000, measured in today's pounds using a required rate of return of 14%. What is the break-even salvage value of this project?

25. **Capital budgeting analysis.** Zistine plc considers a one-year project in New Zealand so that it can capitalize on its technology. It is risk-averse, but is attracted to the project because of a government guarantee. The project will generate a guaranteed NZ$8 million in revenue, paid by the New Zealand government at the end of the year. The payment by the New Zealand government is also guaranteed by a credible UK bank. The cash flows earned on the project will be converted to British pounds and remitted to the parent in one year. The prevailing nominal one-year interest rate in

New Zealand is 8% while the nominal one-year interest rate in the United Kingdom is 2%. Zistine's chief executive officer believes that the movement in the New Zealand dollar is highly uncertain over the next year, but his best guess is that the change in its value will be in accordance with the international Fisher effect (IFE). He also believes that interest rate parity holds. He provides this information to three recent finance graduates that he just hired as managers and asks them for their input.

a. The first manager states that due to the parity conditions, the feasibility of the project will be the same whether the cash flows are hedged with a forward contract or are not hedged. Is this manager correct? Explain.

b. The second manager states that the project should not be hedged. Based on the interest rates, the IFE suggests that Zistine will benefit from the future exchange rate movements, so the project will generate a higher *NPV* if Zistine does not hedge. Is this manager correct? Explain.

c. The third manager states that the project should be hedged because the forward rate contains a premium and, therefore, the forward rate will generate more US dollar cash flows than the expected amount of dollar cash flows if the firm remains unhedged. Is this manager correct? Explain.

26. **Accounting for uncertain cash flows.** Blustream ltd considers a project in which it will sell the use of its technology to firms in South Africa. It already has received orders from South African firms that will generate R2,000,000 in revenue at the end of the next year. However, it might also receive a contract to provide this technology to the South African government. In this case, it will generate a total of R5,000,000 at the end of the next year. It will not know whether it will receive the government order until the end of the year.

Today's spot rate of the rand is £0.11. The one-year forward rate is £0.09. Blustream expects that the spot rate of the rand will be £0.10 one year from now. The only initial outlay will be £200,000 to cover development expenses (regardless of whether the South African government purchases the technology). Blustream will pursue the project only if it can satisfy its required rate of return of 18%. Ignore possible tax effects. It decides to hedge the maximum amount of revenue that it will receive from the project.

a. Determine the *NPV* if Blustream receives the government contract.

b. If Blustream does not receive the contract, it will have hedged more than it needed to and will offset the excess forward sales by purchasing rand in the spot market at the time the forward sale is executed. Determine the *NPV* of the project assuming that Blustream does not receive the government contract.

c. Now consider an alternative strategy in which Blustream only hedges the minimum rand revenue that it will receive. In this case, any revenue due to the government contract would not be hedged. Determine the *NPV* based on this alternative strategy and assume that Blustream receives the government contract.

d. If Blustream uses the alternative strategy of only hedging the minimum rand revenue that it will receive, determine the *NPV* assuming that it does not receive the government contract.

e. If there is a 50% chance that Blustream will receive the government contract, would you advise Blustream to hedge the maximum amount or the minimum amount of revenue that it may receive? Explain.

f. Blustream recognizes that it is exposed to exchange rate risk whether it hedges the minimum amount or the maximum amount of revenue it will receive. It considers a new strategy of hedging the minimum amount it will receive with a forward contract and hedging the additional revenue it might receive with a put option on South African rand. The one-year put option has an exercise price of £0.11 and a premium of £0.01. Determine the *NPV* if Blustream uses this strategy and receives the government contract. Also, determine the *NPV* if Blustream uses this strategy and does not receive the government contract. Given that there is a 50% probability that Blustream will receive the government contract, would you use this new strategy or the strategy that you selected in question (e)?

27. Capital budgeting analysis. Wolverine GmbH (Germany) currently has no existing business in New Zealand but is considering establishing a subsidiary there. The following information has been gathered to assess this project:

■ The initial investment required is 50 million euros in New Zealand dollars (NZ$). Given the existing spot rate of 0.50 euros per New Zealand dollar, the initial investment is 25 million euros. In addition to the NZ$50 million initial investment for plant and equipment, NZ$20 million is needed for working capital and will be borrowed by the subsidiary from a New Zealand bank. The New Zealand subsidiary will pay interest only on the loan each year, at an interest rate of 14%. The loan principal is to be paid in ten years.

■ The project will be terminated at the end of Year 3, when the subsidiary will be sold.

■ The price, demand, and variable cost of the product in New Zealand are as follows:

Year	Price	Demand	Variable Cost
1	NZ$500	40,000 units	NZ$30
2	NZ$511	50,000 units	NZ$35
3	NZ$530	60,000 units	NZ$40

■ The fixed costs, such as overhead expenses, are estimated to be NZ$6 million per year.

■ The exchange rate of the New Zealand dollar is expected to be 0.52 euros at the end of Year 1, 0.54 euros at the end of Year 2, and 0.56 euros at the end of Year 3.

■ The New Zealand government will impose an income tax of 30% on income. In addition, it will impose a withholding tax of 10% on earnings remitted by the subsidiary. The US government will allow a tax credit on the remitted earnings and will not impose any additional taxes.

■ All cash flows received by the subsidiary are to be sent to the parent at the end of each year. The subsidiary will use its working capital to support ongoing operations.

■ The plant and equipment are depreciated over ten years using the straight-line depreciation method. Since the plant and equipment are initially valued at NZ$50 million, the annual depreciation expense is NZ$5 million.

- In three years, the subsidiary is to be sold. Wolverine plans to let the acquiring firm assume the existing New Zealand loan. The working capital will not be liquidated but will be used by the acquiring firm that buys the subsidiary. Wolverine expects to receive NZ$52 million after subtracting capital gains taxes. Assume that this amount is not subject to a withholding tax.

- Wolverine requires a 20% rate of return on this project.

a. Determine the net present value of this project. Should Wolverine accept this project?

b. Assume that Wolverine is also considering an alternative financing arrangement, in which the parent would invest an additional 10 million euros to cover the working capital requirements so that the subsidiary would avoid the New Zealand loan. If this arrangement is used, the selling price of the subsidiary (after subtracting any capital gains taxes) is expected to be NZ$18 million higher. Is this alternative financing arrangement more feasible for the parent than the original proposal? Explain.

c. From the parent's perspective, would the *NPV* of this project be more sensitive to exchange rate movements if the subsidiary uses New Zealand financing to cover the working capital or if the parent invests more of its own funds to cover the working capital? Explain.

d. Assume Wolverine used the original financing proposal and that funds are blocked until the subsidiary is sold. The funds to be remitted are reinvested at a rate of 6% (after taxes) until the end of Year 3. How is the project's *NPV* affected?

e. What is the break-even salvage value of this project if Wolverine uses the original financing proposal and funds are not blocked?

f. Assume that Wolverine decides to implement the project, using the original financing proposal. Also assume that after one year, a New Zealand firm offers Wolverine a price of 27 million euros after taxes for the subsidiary and that Wolverine's original forecasts for Years 2 and 3 have not changed. Compare the present value of the expected cash flows if Wolverine keeps the subsidiary to the selling price. Should Wolverine divest the subsidiary? Explain.

28. **Capital budgeting with hedging.** Baxter Co. (US) considers a project with Thailand's government. If it accepts the project, it will definitely receive one lump sum cash flow of 10 million Thai baht in five years. The spot rate of the Thai baht is presently $0.03. The annualized interest rate for a five-year period is 4% in the United States and 17% in Thailand. Interest rate parity exists. Baxter plans to hedge its cash flows with a forward contract. What is the dollar amount of cash flows that Baxter will receive in five years if it accepts this project?

29. **Capital budgeting and financing.** Cantoon plc is considering the acquisition of a unit from the French government. Its initial outlay would be £2.6 million. It will reinvest all the earnings in the unit. It expects that at the end of eight years, it will sell the unit for 12 million euros after capital gains taxes are paid. The spot rate of the euro is £0.8 and is used as the forecast of the euro in the future years. Cantoon has no plans to hedge its exposure to exchange rate risk. The annualized UK risk-free interest rate is 5% regardless of the maturity of the debt, and the annualized risk-free interest rate on euros is 7%, regardless of the maturity of debt. Assume that interest rate parity exists. Cantoon's cost of capital is 20%. It plans to use cash to make the acquisition.

a. Determine the *NPV* under these conditions.

b. Rather than use all cash, Cantoon could partially finance the acquisition. It could obtain a loan of 3 million euros today that would be used to cover a portion of the acquisition. In this case, it would have to pay a lump sum total of 7 million euros at the end of eight years to repay the loan. There are no interest payments on this debt. The way in which this financing deal is structured, none of the payment is tax-deductible. Determine the *NPV* if Cantoon uses the forward rate instead of the spot rate to forecast the future spot rate of the euro, and elects to partially finance the acquisition. You need to derive the eight-year forward rate for this specific question.

30. **MNC investment prospects.** Consult the online section for the Foreign Investment Magazine at http://www.fdimagazine.com/ and register to use the search option. Selecting articles from this site, compare the investment conditions for foreign companies wishing to invest in the European Union with the conditions for Brazil. Use the search words: "Brazil investment regulations" to make the first search and "European investment regulations" for a second search.

This exercise can be found on the companion website at www.cengage.co.uk/madura_fox.

This exercise can be found on the companion website at www.cengage.co.uk/madura_fox.

Essays/discussion and articles can be found at the end of Part 4

BLADES PLC CASE STUDY
Decision by Blades to invest in Thailand

Since Ben Holt, Blades' financial director, believes the growth potential for the roller blade market in Thailand is very high, he, together with Blades' board of directors, has decided to invest in Thailand. The investment would involve establishing a subsidiary in Bangkok consisting of a manufacturing plant to produce "Speedos", Blades' high-quality roller blades. Holt believes that economic conditions in Thailand will be relatively strong in ten years, when he expects to sell the subsidiary.

Blades will continue exporting to the United States under an existing agreement with Jogs co. a US retailer. Furthermore, it will continue its sales in the United Kingdom. Under an existing agreement with Entertainment Products, Inc., a Thai retailer, Blades is committed to selling 180,000 pairs of Speedos to the retailer at a fixed price of 4,594 Thai baht per pair. Once operations in Thailand commence, the agreement will last another year, at which time it may be renewed. Thus, during its first year of operations in Thailand, Blades will sell 180,000 pairs of roller blades to Entertainment Products under the existing agreement whether it has operations in the country or not. If it establishes the plant in Thailand, Blades will produce 108,000 of the 180,000 Entertainment Products Speedos at the plant during the last year of the agreement. Therefore, the new subsidiary would

need to import 72,000 pairs of speedos from the United Kingdom so that it can accommodate its agreement with Entertainment Products. It will save the equivalent of 300 baht per pair in variable costs on the 108,000 pairs not previously manufactured in Thailand.

Entertainment Products has already declared its willingness to renew the agreement for another three years under identical terms. Because of recent delivery delays, however, it is willing to renew the agreement only if Blades has operations in Thailand. Moreover, if Blades has a subsidiary in Thailand, Entertainment Products will keep renewing the existing agreement as long as Blades operates in Thailand. If the agreement is renewed, Blades expects to sell a total of 300,000 pairs of Speedos annually during its first two years of operation in Thailand to various retailers, including 180,000 pairs to Entertainment Products. After this time, it expects to sell 400,000 pairs annually (including 180,000 to Entertainment Products). If the agreement is not renewed, Blades will be able to sell only 5,000 pairs to Entertainment Products annually, but not at a fixed price. Thus, if the agreement is not renewed, Blades expects to sell a total of 125,000 pairs of Speedos annually during its first two years of operation in Thailand and 225,000 pairs annually thereafter. Pairs not sold under the contractual agreement with Entertainment Products will be sold for 5,000 Thai baht per pair, since Entertainment Products had required a lower price to compensate it for the risk of being unable to sell the pairs it purchased from Blades.

Ben Holt wishes to analyze the financial feasibility of establishing a subsidiary in Thailand. As a Blades' financial analyst, you have been given the task of analyzing the proposed project. Since future economic conditions in Thailand are highly uncertain, Holt has also asked you to conduct some sensitivity analyses. Fortunately, he has provided most of the information you need to conduct a capital budgeting analysis. This information is detailed here:

■ The building and equipment needed will cost 550 million Thai baht. This amount includes additional funds to support working capital.

■ The plant and equipment, valued at 300 million baht, will be depreciated using straight-line depreciation. Thus, 30 million baht will be depreciated annually for ten years.

■ The variable costs needed to manufacture Speedos are estimated to be 3,500 baht per pair next year.

■ Blades' fixed operating expenses, such as administrative salaries, will be 25 million baht next year.

■ The current spot exchange rate of the Thai baht is £0.0153. Blades expects the baht to depreciate by an average of 2% per year for the next ten years.

■ The Thai government will impose a 25% tax rate on income and a 10% withholding tax on any funds remitted by the subsidiary to Blades. Any earnings remitted to the United Kingdom will not be taxed again.

■ After ten years, Blades expects to sell its Thai subsidiary. It expects to sell the subsidiary for about 650 million baht, after considering any capital gains taxes.

■ The average annual inflation in Thailand is expected to be 12%. Unless prices are contractually fixed, revenue, variable costs, and fixed costs are subject to inflation and are expected to change by the same annual rate as the inflation rate. Blades could continue its current operations of exporting to and importing from Thailand, which have generated a return of about 20%. Blades requires a return of 25% on this project in order to justify its investment in Thailand. All excess funds generated by the Thai subsidiary will be remitted to Blades and will be used to support UK operations.

Ben Holt has asked you to answer the following questions:

1. Should the sales and the associated costs of 180,000 pairs of roller blades to be sold in Thailand under the existing agreement be included in the capital budgeting analysis to decide whether Blades should establish a subsidiary in Thailand? Should the sales resulting from a renewed agreement be included? Why or why not?
2. Using a spreadsheet, conduct a capital budgeting analysis for the proposed project, assuming that Blades renews the agreement with Entertainment Products. Should Blades establish a subsidiary in Thailand under these conditions?
3. Using a spreadsheet, conduct a capital budgeting analysis for the proposed project assuming that Blades does not renew the agreement with Entertainment Products. Should Blades establish a subsidiary in Thailand under these conditions? Should Blades renew the agreement with Entertainment Products?
4. Since future economic conditions in Thailand are uncertain, Ben Holt would like to know how critical the salvage value is in the alternative you think is most feasible.
5. The future value of the baht is highly uncertain. Under a worst case scenario, the baht may depreciate by as much as 5% annually. Revise your spreadsheet to illustrate how this would affect Blades' decision to establish a subsidiary in Thailand. (Use the capital budgeting analysis you have identified as the most favourable from questions 2 and 3 to answer this question.)

SMALL BUSINESS DILEMMA
Multinational capital budgeting by the Sports Exports Company

Jim Logan, owner of the Sports Exports Company (Ireland), has been pleased with his success in the United Kingdom. He began his business by producing basketballs and exporting them to the United Kingdom. While American-style basketball is still not nearly as popular in the United Kingdom as it is in the United States, his firm controls the market in the United Kingdom. Jim is considering an application of the same business in the US. He would produce the basketballs in Ireland and export them to a distributor of sporting goods in the US, who would sell the basketballs to retail stores. The distributor would likely want to pay for the product each month in dollars. Jim would need to hire one full-time employee in Ireland to produce the basketballs. He would also need to lease one more warehouse.

1. Describe the capital budgeting steps that would be necessary to determine whether this proposed project is feasible, as related to this specific situation.
2. Explain why there is uncertainty surrounding the cash flows of this project.

APPENDIX 14

INCORPORATING INTERNATIONAL TAX LAWS IN MULTINATIONAL CAPITAL BUDGETING

Tax laws can vary among countries in many ways, but any type of tax causes an MNC's after-tax cash flows to differ from its before-tax cash flows. To estimate the future cash flows that are to be generated by a proposed foreign project (such as the establishment of a new subsidiary or the acquisition of a foreign firm), MNCs must first estimate the taxes that they will incur due to the foreign project. This appendix provides a general background on some of the more important international tax characteristics that an MNC must consider when assessing foreign projects. Financial managers do not necessarily have to be international tax experts because they may be able to rely on the MNC's international tax department or on independent tax consultants for guidance. Nevertheless, they should at least be aware of international tax characteristics that can affect the cash flows of a foreign project and recognize how those characteristics can vary among the countries where foreign projects are considered.

VARIATION IN TAX LAWS AMONG COUNTRIES

Each country generates tax revenue in different ways. The United Kingdom relies on corporate and individual income taxes for federal revenue. Other countries may depend more on a *value-added tax (VAT)* or excise taxes. Since each country has its own philosophy on whom to tax and how much, it is not surprising that the tax treatment of corporations differs among countries. Because each country has a unique tax system and tax rates, MNCs need to recognize the various tax provisions of each country where they consider investing in a foreign project. The more important tax characteristics of a country to be considered in an MNC's international tax assessment are: (1) corporate income taxes, (2) withholding taxes, (3) personal and excise tax rates, (4) provision for carrybacks and carryforwards, (5) tax treaties, (6) tax credits, and (7) taxes on income from intercompany transactions. A discussion of each characteristic follows.

Corporate income taxes

In general, countries impose taxes on corporate income generated within their borders, even if the parents of those corporations are based in other countries. Each country has its unique corporate income tax laws. The United States, for example, taxes the world-wide income of US *persons*, a term that includes corporations. As a general rule, however, foreign income of a foreign subsidiary of a US company is not taxed until it is transferred to the US parent by payment of dividends or a liquidation distribution. This is the concept of deferral.

An MNC planning direct foreign investment in foreign countries must determine how the anticipated earnings from a foreign project will be affected. Tax rates imposed on income earned by businesses (including foreign subsidiaries of MNCs) or income remitted to a parent are shown in Exhibit 14A.1 for several countries. The tax rates may be lower than what is shown for corporations that have relatively low levels of earnings. This exhibit shows the extent to which corporate income tax rates can vary among host countries and illustrates why MNCs closely assess the tax guidelines in any foreign country where they consider conducting direct foreign investment. Given differences in tax deductions, depreciation, business subsidies, and other factors, corporate tax differentials cannot be measured simply by comparing quoted tax rates across countries.

Corporate tax rates can also differ within a country, depending on whether the entity is a domestic corporation. Also, if an unregistered foreign corporation is considered to have a permanent establishment in a country, it may be subject to that country's tax laws on income earned within its borders. Generally, a permanent establishment includes an office or fixed place of business or a specified kind of agency (*independent* agents are

http://

The PriceWaterhouse Coopers site at http://www.pwcglobal.com provides access to country-specific information such as general business rules and regulations and tax environments.

Exhibit 14A.1 Comparison of tax characteristics among countries

Country	Corporate Income Tax	Country	Corporate Income Tax
Argentina	35%	Israel	36
Australia	30	Italy	37
Austria	34	Japan	42
Belgium	34	Korea	30
Brazil	34	Malaysia	28
Canada	36	Mexico	33
Chile	17	Netherlands	35
China	33	New Zealand	33
Czech Republic	28	Singapore	22
France	34	Spain	35
Germany	38	Switzerland	24
Hong Kong	17	Taiwan	25
Hungary	16	United Kingdom	30
India	36	United States	35
Indonesia	30	Venezuela	34
Ireland	13		

Source: Worldwide Corporate Tax Guide, Ernst & Young. The numbers provided are for illustrative purposes only, as the actual tax rate may depend on specific characteristics of the MNC.

normally excluded) through which active and continuous business is conducted. In some cases, the tax depends on the industry or on the form of business used (e.g., corporation, branch, partnership).

Withholding taxes

The following types of payments by an MNC's subsidiary are commonly subject to a withholding tax by the host government: (1) a subsidiary may remit a portion of its earnings, referred to as *dividends*, to its parent since the parent is the shareholder of the subsidiary; (2) the subsidiary may pay interest to the parent or to other non-resident debtholders from which it received loans; (3) the subsidiary may make payments to the parent or to other non-resident firms in return for the use of patents (such as technology) or other rights. The payment of dividends reduces the amount of reinvestment by the subsidiary in the host country. The payments by the subsidiary to non-resident firms to cover interest or patents reflect expenses by the subsidiary, which will normally reduce its taxable income and therefore will reduce the corporate income taxes paid to the host government. Thus, withholding taxes may be a way for host governments to tax MNCs that make interest or patent payments to non-resident firms.

Since withholding taxes imposed on the subsidiary can reduce the funds remitted by the subsidiary to the parent, the withholding taxes must be accounted for in a capital budgeting analysis conducted by the parent. As with corporate tax rates, the withholding tax rate can vary substantially among countries.

Reducing exposure to withholding taxes. Withholding taxes can be reduced by income tax treaties (discussed shortly). Because of tax treaties between some countries, the withholding taxes may be lower when the MNC's parent is based in a county participating in the treaties.

If the host country government of a particular subsidiary imposes a high withholding tax on subsidiary earnings remitted to the parent, the parent of the MNC may instruct the subsidiary to temporarily refrain from remitting earnings and to reinvest them in the host country instead. As an alternative approach, the MNC may instruct the subsidiary to set up a research and development division that will enhance subsidiaries elsewhere. The main purpose behind this strategy is to efficiently use the funds abroad when the funds cannot be sent to the parent without excessive taxation. Since international tax laws can influence the timing of the transfer of funds to the parent, they affect the timing of cash flows on proposed foreign projects. Therefore, the international tax implications must be understood before the cash flows of a foreign project can be estimated.

Personal and excise tax rates

An MNC is more likely to be concerned with corporate tax rates and withholding tax rates than individual tax rates because its cash flows are directly affected by the taxes incurred. However, a country's individual tax rates can indirectly affect an MNC's cash flows because the MNC may have to pay higher wages to employees in countries (such as in Europe) where personal income is taxed at a relatively high rate. In addition, a country's value-added tax or excise tax may affect cash flows to be generated from a foreign project because it may make the products less competitive on a global basis (reducing the expected quantity of products to be sold).

Provision for carrybacks and carryforwards

Negative earnings from operations can often be carried back or forward to offset earnings in other years. The laws pertaining to these so-called **net operating loss carrybacks** and **carryforwards** can vary among countries. An MNC generally does not plan to generate negative earnings in foreign countries. If negative earnings do occur, however, it is desirable to be able to use them to offset other years of positive earnings. Most foreign countries do not allow negative earnings to be carried back but allow some flexibility in carrying losses forward. Since many foreign projects are expected to result in negative earnings in the early years, the tax laws for the country of concern will affect the future tax deductions resulting from these losses and will therefore affect the future cash flows of the foreign project.

Tax treaties

Countries often establish income tax treaties, whereby one partner will reduce its taxes by granting a credit for taxes imposed on corporations operating within the other treaty partner's tax jurisdiction. Income tax treaties help corporations avoid exposure to double taxation. Some treaties apply to taxes paid on income earned by MNCs in foreign countries. Other treaties apply to withholding taxes imposed by the host country on foreign earnings that are remitted to the parent.

Without such treaties, subsidiary earnings could be taxed by the host country and then again by the parent's country when received by the parent. To the extent that the parent uses some of these earnings to provide cash dividends for shareholders, triple taxation could result (since the dividend income is also taxed at the shareholder level). Because income tax treaties reduce taxes on earnings generated by MNCs, they help stimulate direct foreign investment. Many foreign projects that are perceived as feasible would not be feasible without income tax treaties because the expected cash flows would be reduced by excessive taxation.

Tax credits

Even without income tax treaties, an MNC may be allowed a credit for income and withholding taxes paid in one country against taxes owed by the parent if it meets certain requirements. Like income tax treaties, tax credits help to avoid double taxation and stimulate direct foreign investment.

Tax credit policies vary somewhat among countries, but they generally work like this. Consider a UK-based MNC subject to a UK tax rate of 30%. Assume that a foreign subsidiary of this corporation has generated earnings taxed at less than 30% by the host country's government. The earnings remitted to the parent from the subsidiary will be subject to an additional amount of UK tax to bring the total tax up to 30%. From the parent's point of view, the tax on its subsidiary's remitted earnings are 30% overall, so it does not matter whether the host country of the subsidiary or the United Kingdom receives most of the taxes. From the perspective of the governments of these two countries, however, the allocation of taxes is very important. If subsidiaries of UK corporations are established in foreign countries, and if these countries tax income at a rate close to 30%, they can generate large tax revenues from income earned by the subsidiaries. The host countries receive the tax revenues at the expense of the parent's country (the United Kingdom, in this case). The UK has double taxation agreements with over 100 countries.

If the corporate income tax rate in a foreign country is greater than 30%, the United Kingdom generally does not impose any additional taxes on earnings remitted to a UK parent by foreign subsidiaries in that country. In fact, some countries allow the excess foreign tax to be credited against other taxes owed by the parent, due on the same type of income generated by subsidiaries in other lower-tax countries. In a sense, this suggests that some host countries could charge abnormally high corporate income tax rates to foreign subsidiaries and still attract direct foreign investment. If the MNC in our example has subsidiaries located in some countries with low corporate income taxes, the UK tax on earnings remitted to the UK parent will normally bring the total tax up to 30%. Yet, credits against excessive income taxes by high-tax countries on foreign subsidiaries could offset these taxes that would otherwise be paid to the UK government. Due to tax credits, therefore, an MNC might be more willing to invest in a project in a country with excessive tax rates.

Basic information on a country's current taxes may not be sufficient for determining the tax effects of a particular foreign project because tax incentives may be offered in particular circumstances, and tax rates can change over time. Consider an MNC that plans to establish a manufacturing plant in Country Y rather than Country X. Assume that while many economic characteristics favour Country X, the current tax rates in Country Y are lower. However, whereas tax rates in Country X have been historically stable and are expected to continue that way, they have been changing every few years in Country Y. In this case, the MNC must assess the future uncertainty of the tax rates. It cannot treat the current tax rate of Country Y as a constant when conducting a capital budgeting analysis. Instead, it must consider possible changes in the tax rates over time and, based on these possibilities, determine whether Country Y's projected tax advantages *over time* sufficiently outweigh the advantages of Country X. One approach to account for possible changes in the tax rates is to use sensitivity analysis, which measures the sensitivity of the net present value (*NPV*) of after-tax cash flows to various possible tax changes over time. For each tax scenario, a different *NPV* is projected. By accounting for each possible tax scenario, the MNC can develop a distribution of possible *NPVs* that may occur and can then compare these for each country.

Two critical, broadly defined functions are necessary to determine how international tax laws affect the cash flows of a foreign project. The first is to be aware of all the current (and possible future) tax laws that exist for each country where the MNC does (or plans to do) business. The second is to take the information generated from the first function and apply it to forecasted earnings and remittances to determine the taxes, so that the proposed project's cash flows can be estimated.

Taxes on income from intercompany transactions

Many of an MNC's proposed foreign projects will involve intercompany transactions. For example, a US-based MNC may consider acquiring a foreign firm that will produce and deliver supplies to its UK subsidiaries. Under these conditions, the MNC must use transfer pricing, which involves pricing the transactions between two entities (such as subsidiaries) of the same corporation. When MNCs consider new foreign projects, they must incorporate their transfer pricing to properly estimate cash flows that will be generated from these projects. Therefore, before the feasibility of a foreign project can be determined, transfer pricing decisions must be made on any anticipated intercompany transactions that would result from the new project. MNCs are subject to some guidelines on transfer pricing, but they usually have some flexibility and tend to use a transfer pricing policy that will minimize taxes while satisfying the guidelines.

EXAMPLE

Oakland ltd has established two subsidiaries to capitalize on low production costs. One of these subsidiaries (called Hitax Sub) is located in a country whose government imposes a 50% tax rate on before-tax earnings. Hitax Sub produces partially finished products and sends them to the other subsidiary (called Lotax Sub) where the final assembly takes place. The host government of Lotax Sub imposes a 20% tax on before-tax earnings. To simplify the example, assume that no dividends are to be remitted to the parent in the near future. Given this information, pro forma income statements would be as shown in the top part of Exhibit 14A.2 for Hitax Sub (second column), Lotax Sub (third column), and the combined subsidiaries (last column). The income statement items are reported in UK pounds to illustrate how a revised transfer pricing policy can affect earnings and cash flows.

The sales level shown for Hitax Sub matches the cost of goods sold for Lotax Sub, indicating that all Hitax Sub sales are to Lotax Sub. The additional expenses incurred by Lotax Sub to complete the product are classified as operating expenses.

Notice from Exhibit 14A.2 that both subsidiaries have the same earnings before taxes. Yet, because of the different tax rates, Hitax Sub's after-tax income is £7.5 million less

Exhibit 14A.2 Impact of transfer pricing adjustment on pro forma earnings and taxes: Oakland ltd (in thousands)

	Original Estimates		
	Hitax Sub	Lotax Sub	Combined
Sales	£100,000	£150,000	£150,000
Less: Cost of goods sold	50,000	100,000	50,000
Gross profit	50,000	50,000	100,000
Less: Operating expenses	20,000	20,000	40,000
Earnings before interest and taxes	30,000	30,000	60,000
Interest expense	5,000	5,000	10,000
Earnings before taxes	25,000	25,000	50,000
Taxes (50% for Hitax and 20% for Lotax)	12,500	5,000	17,500
Earnings after taxes	£12,500	£20,000	£32,500
	Revised Estimates Based on Adjusting Transfer Pricing Policy		
	Hitax Sub	Lotax Sub	Combined[1]
Sales	£80,000	£150,000	£150,000
Less: Cost of goods sold	50,000	80,000	50,000
Gross profit	30,000	70,000	100,000
Less: Operating expenses	20,000	20,000	40,000
Earnings before interest and taxes	10,000	50,000	60,000
Interest expense	5,000	5,000	10,000
Earnings before taxes	5,000	45,000	50,000
Taxes (50% for Hitax and 20% for Lotax)	2,500	9,000	11,500
Earnings after taxes	£2,500	£36,000	£38,500

Note: The combined numbers are shown here for illustrative purposes only and do not reflect the firm's official consolidated financial statements. When consolidating sales and cost of goods sold, intercompany transactions have been eliminated. This example is intended simply to illustrate how total taxes paid by subsidiaries are lower when transfer pricing is structured to shift some gross profit from a high-tax subsidiary to a low-tax subsidiary.

than Lotax Sub's. If Oakland ltd can revise its transfer pricing, its combined earnings after taxes will be increased. To illustrate, suppose that the price of products sent from Hitax Sub to Lotax Sub is reduced, causing Hitax Sub's sales to decline from £100 million to £80 million. This also reduces Lotax Sub's cost of goods sold by £20 million. The revised pro forma income statement resulting from the change in the transfer pricing policy is shown in the bottom part of Exhibit 14A.2. The two subsidiaries' forecasted earnings before taxes now differ by £40 million, although the combined amount has not changed. Because earnings have been shifted from Hitax Sub to Lotax Sub, the total tax payments are reduced to £11.5 million from the original estimate of £17.5 million. Thus, the corporate taxes imposed on earnings are now forecasted to be £6 million lower than originally expected.

It should be mentioned that possible adjustments in the transfer pricing policies may be limited because host governments may restrict such practices when the intent is to avoid taxes. Transactions between subsidiaries of a firm are supposed to be priced using the principle of "arm's-length" transactions. That is, the price should be set as if the buyer is unrelated to the seller and should not be adjusted simply to shift tax burdens.

Nevertheless, there is some flexibility on transfer pricing policies, enabling MNCs from all countries to attempt to establish policies that are within legal limits, but also reduce tax burdens. Even if the transfer price reflects the "fair" price that would normally be charged in the market, one subsidiary can still charge another for technology transfers, research and development expenses, or other forms of overhead expenses incurred.

The actual mechanics of international transfer pricing go far beyond the example provided here. The UK laws in this area are particularly strict. Nevertheless, there are various ways that MNCs can justify increasing prices at one subsidiary and reducing them at another.

There is substantial evidence that MNCs based in numerous countries use transfer pricing strategies to reduce their taxes. Moreover, transfer pricing restrictions can be circumvented in several ways. Various fees can be implemented for services, research and development, royalties, and administrative duties. Although the fees may be imposed to shift earnings and minimize taxes, they have the effect of distorting the actual performance of each subsidiary. To correct for any distortion, the MNC can use a centralized approach to account for the transfer pricing strategy when assessing the performance of each subsidiary.

USING THE WEB

Country corporate tax rates An MNC must determine a country's corporate tax rates before it can properly estimate its cash flows from establishing direct foreign investment there. Information about taxes imposed by each country is provided at http://www.pwcglobal.com/uk/eng/main/home/ enter "tax" into the search section and review information about corporate income taxes, dividend withholding tax, interest withholding tax, and royalties and fees withholding tax.

CHAPTER 15

MULTINATIONAL RESTRUCTURING

MULTINATIONAL CORPORATIONS (MNCs) COMMONLY engage in restructuring their assets and liabilities. **Multinational restructuring** decisions involve restructuring the composition and location of multinational assets or liabilities. The differing economies and currencies makes borrowing and investing a more complex process than the purely domestic equivalent. Thus, multinational restructuring decisions not only determine the types of assets, but also the countries where those assets are located and the currencies used to finance those assets. Financial managers must understand how to assess restructuring alternatives so that they can make restructuring decisions that maximize the value of the MNC.

THE SPECIFIC OBJECTIVES OF THIS CHAPTER ARE TO:

■ provide a background on how MNCs use international acquisitions as a form of multinational restructuring,

■ explain how MNCs conduct valuations of foreign target firms,

■ explain why valuations of a target firm vary among MNCs that plan to restructure by acquiring a target, and

■ identify other types of multinational restructuring besides international acquisitions

BACKGROUND ON MULTINATIONAL RESTRUCTURING

Decisions by an MNC to build a new subsidiary in the Netherlands, to acquire a company in Italy, to sell its Singapore subsidiary, to downsize its operations in New Zealand, or to shift some production from its US subsidiary to its Mexican subsidiary all represent forms of multinational restructuring. Even the most successful MNCs continuously assess possible forms of multinational restructuring so that they can capitalize on changing economic, political, or industry conditions across countries.

MNCs re-evaluate their existing businesses and other proposed projects when determining the ideal composition of assets to employ and the locations where the assets are employed. Even if an existing business adds value to the MNC, it may be worth while to assess whether the business would generate more value to the MNC if it was restructured.

Trends in international acquisitions

The volume of foreign acquisitions tends to vary greatly over the years for the UK. The number of foreign acquisitions increased in 2004 from 243 to 305 according to the Office for National Statistics; but in 1999 the number was nearly double. The UK is also a target for foreign investors and is listed as the third most popular destination after the US and Norway for foreign investment according UN figures. The size of foreign investments is reflected in the fact that one third of global trade is intra firm, that is trade between parts of the same multinational company. The type of trade is also shifting to the service sector, rising from about 25% in the 1970s to about 60% today. For the UK the bond with the US remains strong. US firms acquire more targets in the United Kingdom than in any other country. British and Canadian firms are the most common non-US acquirers of US targets.

Model for valuing a foreign target

An MNC's decision to invest in a foreign company is similar to the decision to invest in other projects, in that it is based on a comparison of benefits and costs as measured by net present value. From an MNC's parent's perspective, the foreign target's value can be

---

MANAGING FOR VALUE
International acquisitions

In 2002 the Chinese company Fook Tin ("rich field") purchased the French bathroom and kitchen scales manufacturer Terraillon adding to its existing purchase in 2000 of Scaime (France) a global leader in magnitude sensors. The Hong Kong-based company now manufactures scales in Shenzen province (China) where it is seeking to expand. Thus French design, Chinese manufacturing and Hong Kong entrepreneurial spirit is combined. Andre Terraillon founded the company that bore his name in 1947 in France at a location near Switzerland (Haute Savoie near Geneva). Making watches and scales are similar activities, in this sense it could be regarded as part of an investment cluster. After initial success, the company experienced difficulties in the 1980s, affected by competition and rising costs. It was taken over in 1981 by Bernard Tapie, a well-known French entrepreneur, who was unable to revive the company's fortunes. Eventually an Irish venture capital fund purchased the company from the Credit Lyonnais bank and improved the company's fortunes. It was then bought out by an American electronics company MSI who met with stock market disapproval and sold it on to Fook Tin. Terraillon represents a fairly typical example of the history of an MNC – a tale of sale and acquisition.

estimated as the present value of cash flows that it would receive from the target, as the target would become a foreign subsidiary owned by the parent.

The MNC's parent would consider investing in the target only if the estimated present value of the cash flows it would ultimately receive from the target over time exceeds the initial outlay necessary to purchase the target. Thus, capital budgeting analysis can be used to determine whether a firm should be acquired. The net present value of a company from the acquiring firm's perspective (NPV_a) is

$$NPV_a = -IO_a + \left(\sum_{t=1}^{n} \frac{CF_{a,t}}{(1+k)^t} \right) + \frac{SV_a}{(1+k)^n}$$

where:

IO_a = initial outlay needed by the acquiring firm to acquire the target
$CF_{a,t}$ = cash flow to be generated by the target for the acquiring firm
k = required rate of return on the acquisition of the target
SV_a = salvage value of the target (expected selling price of the target at a point in the future)
n = time when the target will be sold by the acquiring firm

The capital budgeting analysis of a foreign target must account for the exchange rate of concern. For example, consider a UK-based MNC that assesses the acquisition of a foreign company. The initial outlay (IO_{UK}) needed by the UK firm is determined by the acquisition price in foreign currency units (IO_f) and the spot rate of the foreign currency (S):

$$IO_{UK} = IO_f(S)$$

The pound denominated cash flows to the UK firm is determined by the foreign currency cash flows ($CF_{f,t}$) per period remitted to the United Kingdom and the spot rate at that time (S_t):

$$CF_{a,t} = CF_{f,t}(S)$$

This ignores any withholding taxes or blocked-funds restrictions imposed by the host government and any income taxes imposed by the UK government. The pound salvage value to the UK firm is determined by the salvage value in foreign currency units (SV_f) and the spot rate at the time (period n) when it is converted to pounds (S_n):

$$SV_a = (SV_f)S_n$$

The net present value of a foreign target can be derived by substituting the equalities just described in the capital budgeting equation:

$$NPV_a = -IO_a + \left(\sum_{t=1}^{n} \frac{CF_{a,t}}{(1+k)^t} \right) + \frac{SV_a}{(1+k)^n}$$

$$NPVa = -(IO^f)S + \left(\sum_{t=1}^{n} \frac{(CF_{f,t})S_t}{(1+k)^t} \right) + \frac{(SV_f)S_n}{(1+k)^n}$$

Assessing potential acquisitions after the Asian crisis

Although the Asian crisis had devastating effects, it created an opportunity for some MNCs to pursue new business in Asia. The initial outlay for acquiring a firm in Asia was lower as a result of the crisis. First, property values in Asia had declined. Second, the parent's currency (for parents in the United States or Europe) had more purchasing power due to the weakening of the Asian currencies. Third, many firms in Asia were near bankruptcy and were unable to obtain necessary funding. Fourth, the governments in these countries were more willing to allow foreign acquisitions of local firms (especially those that were failing) as a means of resolving the crisis. Consequently, some US and European firms pursued direct foreign investment in Asia during the Asian crisis.

In the first six months of 1998, US firms invested more than $8 billion in Asia – more than double the amount they had invested there in all of 1997. Procter & Gamble agreed to acquire Sanyong Paper (a large conglomerate in South Korea) during the crisis. Citicorp obtained a large stake of First City Bank in Thailand.

Firms that made aquistions had to consider the obvious adverse effects of the crisis in their capital budgeting analysis. The lower economic growth meant that most Asian projects would generate lower cash flows, and the weak currencies reduced the amount of cash flows (in the parent's currency) that would ultimately be received as a return on the parent's investment.

To the extent that the firms believed that the Asian currency values had hit bottom and would rebound, they could assume that any new acquisitions of Asian firms would benefit from future exchange rate movements. Firms could initiate their investment in Asia by investing their home currency in exchange for the weak Asian currency. Then, if the Asian currency appreciated over time, the earnings generated there would be worth more (in terms of the parent's currency) when remitted to the parent.

Assessing potential acquisitions in Europe

Before the adoption of the euro, MNCs had to separately consider the exchange rate effects from acquiring firms in different European countries. For example, Italy's currency (the lira) was considered more likely to weaken against the dollar than some of the other European currencies, and this could affect the decision of whether to acquire an Italian firm versus a firm in Germany or France. The adoption of the euro as the local currency by several European countries has simplified the analysis for an MNC that is comparing possible target firms in those countries. The MNC can still be affected by future movements in the euro's value against the dollar, but those effects will occur regardless of whether the MNC purchases a firm in Italy or in any other euro-zone country. Thus, the MNC can make its decision on which firm to acquire within these countries without being concerned about differential exchange rate effects. If the MNC is also considering firms in European countries that have not adopted the euro as their currency, however, it will still have to compare the potential exchange rate effects that could result from the acquisition.

FACTORS THAT AFFECT THE EXPECTED CASH FLOWS OF THE FOREIGN TARGET

When an MNC estimates the future cash flows that it will ultimately receive after acquiring a foreign target, it considers several factors that reflect either conditions in the country of concern or conditions of the target itself.

Target-specific factors

The following characteristics of the foreign target are typically considered when estimating the cash flows that the target will provide to the parent.

Target's previous cash flows. Since the foreign target has been conducting business, it has a history of cash flows that it has generated. The recent cash flows per period may serve as an initial base from which future cash flows per period can be estimated after accounting for other factors.

A company's previous cash flows are not necessarily an accurate indicator of future cash flows, however, especially when the target's future cash flows would have to be converted into the acquirer's home currency as they are remitted to the parent. Therefore, the MNC needs to carefully consider all the factors that could influence the cash flows that will be generated from a foreign target.

Managerial talent of the target. An acquiring firm must assess the target's existing management so that it can determine how the target firm will be managed after the acquisition. The way the acquirer plans to deal with the managerial talent will affect the estimated cash flows to be generated by the target.

If the MNC acquires the target, it may allow the target firm to be managed as it was before the acquisition. Under these conditions, however, the acquiring firm may have less potential for enhancing the target's cash flows.

A second alternative for the MNC is to downsize the target firm after acquiring it. For example, if the acquiring firm introduces new technology that reduces the need for some of the target's employees, it can attempt to downsize the target. Downsizing reduces expenses but may also reduce productivity and revenue, so the effect on cash flows can vary with the situation. In addition, an MNC may encounter significant barriers to increasing efficiency by downsizing in several countries. Governments of some countries are likely to intervene and prevent the acquisition if downsizing is anticipated.

A third alternative for the MNC is to maintain the existing employees of the target but restructure the operations so that labour is used more efficiently. For example, the MNC may infuse its own technology into the target firm and then restructure operations so that many of the employees receive new job assignments. This strategy may cause the acquirer to incur some additional expenses, but there is potential for improved cash flows over time.

Country-specific factors

An MNC typically considers the following country-specific factors when estimating the cash flows that will be provided by the foreign target to the parent.

Target's local economic conditions. Potential targets in countries where economic conditions are strong are more likely to experience strong demand for their products in the future and may generate higher cash flows. However, some firms are more sensitive to economic conditions than others. Also, some acquisitions of firms are intended to focus on exporting from the target's home country, so the economic conditions in the target's country may not be as important. Economic conditions are difficult to predict over a long-term period, especially for emerging countries.

Target's local political conditions. Potential targets in countries where political conditions are favourable are less likely to experience adverse shocks to their cash flows. The sensitivity of cash flows to political conditions is dependent on the firm's type of business. Political conditions are also difficult to predict over a long-term period, especially for emerging countries.

Target's industry conditions. Industry conditions within a country can cause some targets to be more desirable than others. Some industries in a particular country may be extremely competitive while others are not. In addition, some industries exhibit strong potential for growth in a particular country, while others exhibit very little potential. When an MNC assesses targets among countries, it would prefer a country where the growth potential for its industry is high and the competition within the industry is not excessive.

Target's currency conditions. If a UK-based MNC plans to acquire a foreign target, it must consider how future exchange rate movements may affect the target's local currency cash flows. It must also consider how exchange rates will affect the conversion of the target's remitted earnings to the UK parent. In the typical case, ideally the foreign currency would be weak at the time of the acquisition (so that the MNC's initial outlay is low) but strengthen over time as funds are periodically remitted to the UK parent. There can be exceptions to this general statement, but the point is that the MNC forecasts future exchange rates and then applies those forecasts to determine the impact on cash flows.

Target's local stock market conditions. Potential target firms that are publicly held are continuously valued in the market, so their stock prices can change rapidly. As the target firm's stock price changes, the acceptable bid price necessary to buy that firm will likely change as well. Thus, there can be substantial swings in the purchase price that would be acceptable to a target. This is especially true for publicly traded firms in emerging markets in Asia, Eastern Europe, and Latin America where stock prices commonly change by 5% or more in a week. Therefore, an MNC that plans to acquire a target would prefer to make its bid at a time when the local stock market prices are generally low.

Taxes applicable to the target. When an MNC assesses a foreign target, it must estimate the expected after-tax cash flows that it will ultimately receive in the form of funds remitted to the parent. Thus, the tax laws applicable to the foreign target are used to derive the after-tax cash flows. First, the applicable corporate tax rates are applied to the estimated future earnings of the target to determine the after-tax earnings. Second, the after-tax proceeds are determined by applying any withholding tax rates to the funds that are expected to be remitted to the parent in each period. Third, if the acquiring firm's government imposes an additional tax on remitted earnings or allows a tax credit, that tax or credit must be applied.

EXAMPLE OF THE VALUATION PROCESS

Lincoln ltd desires to expand in Latin America or Canada. The methods Lincoln uses to initially screen targets in various countries and then to estimate a target's value are discussed next.

International screening process

Lincoln considers the factors just described when it conducts an initial screening of prospective targets. It has identified prospective targets in Mexico, Brazil, Colombia, and Canada, as shown in Exhibit 15.1. The target in Mexico has no plans to sell its business and is unwilling to even consider an offer from Lincoln. Therefore, this firm is no longer considered. Lincoln anticipates potential political problems that could create barriers to an acquisition in Colombia, even though the Colombian target is willing to be acquired. Stock market conditions are not favourable in Brazil, as the stock prices of most Brazilian companies have recently risen substantially. Lincoln does not want to pay as much as the Brazilian target is now worth based on its prevailing market value.

Based on this screening process, the only foreign target that deserves a closer assessment is the target in Canada. According to Lincoln's assessment, Canadian currency conditions are slightly unfavourable, but this is not a reason to eliminate the target from further consideration. Thus, the next step would be for Lincoln to obtain as much information as possible about the target and conditions in Canada. Then Lincoln can use this information to derive the target's expected cash flows and to determine whether the target's value exceeds the initial outlay that would be required to purchase it, as explained next.

Estimating the target's value

Once Lincoln has completed its initial screening of targets, it conducts a valuation of all targets that passed the screening process. Lincoln can estimate the present value of future cash flows that would result from acquiring the target. This estimation is then used to determine whether the target should be acquired.

Continuing with our simplified example, Lincoln's screening process resulted in only one eligible target, a Canadian firm. Assume the Canadian firm has conducted all of its business locally. Assume also that Lincoln expects that it can obtain materials at a lower cost than the target can because of its relationships with some Canadian suppliers and

Exhibit 15.1 Example of process used to screen foreign targets

Target based in	Is the target receptive to an acquisition	Local economic and industry conditions	Local political conditions	Local currency conditions	Prevailing stock market prices	Tax laws
Mexico	No	Favourable	OK	OK	OK	May change
Brazil	Maybe	OK	OK	OK	Too high	May change
Colombia	Yes	Favourable	Volatile	Favourable	OK	Reasonable
Canada	Yes	OK	Favourable	Slightly unfavourable	OK	Reasonable

that it also expects to implement a more efficient production process. Lincoln also plans to use its existing managerial talent to manage the target and thereby reduce the administrative and marketing expenses incurred by the target. It also expects that the target's revenue will increase when its products are sold under Lincoln's name. Lincoln expects to maintain prices of the products.

The target's expected cash flows can be measured by first determining the revenue and expense levels in recent years and then adjusting those levels to reflect the changes that would occur after the acquisition.

Revenue. The target's annual revenue has ranged between C$80 million and C$90 million in Canadian dollars (C$) over the last four years. Lincoln expects that it can improve sales, and forecasts revenue to be C$100 million next year, C$93.3 million in the following year, and C$121 million in the year after. The cost of goods sold has been about 50% of the revenue in the past, but Lincoln expects it will fall to 40% of revenue because of improvements in efficiency. The estimates are shown in Exhibit 15.2.

Expenses. Selling and administrative expenses have been about C$20 million annually, but Lincoln believes that through restructuring it can reduce these expenses to C$15 million in each of the next three years. Depreciation expenses have been about C$10 million in the past and are expected to remain at that level for the next three years. The Canadian tax rate on the target's earnings is expected to be 30%.

Earnings and cash flows. Given the information assumed here, the after-tax earnings that the target would generate under Lincoln's ownership are estimated in Exhibit 15.2. The cash flows generated by the target are determined by adding the depreciation

Exhibit 15.2 Valuation of Canadian target based on the assumptions provided (in millions of Canadian dollars)

	Last Year	Year 1	Year 2	Year 3
Revenue	C$90	C$100	C$93.3	C$121
Cost of goods sold	45	40	37.3	48.4
Gross profit	45	60	56	72.6
Selling & administrative expenses	20	15	15	15
Depreciation	10	10	10	10
Earnings before taxes	15	35	31	47.6
Tax (30%)	4.5	10.5	9.3	14.28
Earnings after taxes	10.5	24.5	21.7	33.32
+Depreciation		10	10	10
−Funds to reinvest		5	5	5
Sale of firm				230
Cash flows in C$		29.5	26.7	268.32
Exchange rate of C$		£0.50	£0.50	£0.50
Cash flows in £		£14.75	£13.35	£134.16
PV (20% discount rate)		£12.29	£9.27	£77.64
Cumulative PV		£12.29	£21.56	£99.20

expenses back to the after-tax earnings. Assume that the target will need C$5 million in cash each year to support existing operations (including the repair of existing machinery) and that the remaining cash flow can be remitted to the UK parent. Assume that the target firm is financially supported only by its equity. It currently has 10 million shares of stock outstanding that are priced at C$17 per share.

Cash flows to parent. Since Lincoln's parent wishes to assess the target from its own perspective, it focuses on the cash flows that it expects to receive. Assuming no additional taxes, the expected cash flows generated in Canada that are to be remitted to Lincoln's parent are converted into pounds at the expected exchange rate at the end of each year. Lincoln uses the prevailing exchange rate of the Canadian dollar (which is £0.50) as the expected exchange rate for the Canadian dollar in future years.

Estimating the target's future sales price. If Lincoln purchases the target, it will sell the target in three years, after improving the target's performance. Lincoln expects to receive C$230 million (after capital gains taxes) from the sale. The price at which the target can actually be sold will depend on its expected future cash flows from that point forward, but those expected cash flows are partially dependent on its performance prior to that time. Thus, Lincoln can enhance the sales price by improving the target's performance over the three years it plans to own the target.

Valuing the target based on estimated cash flows. The expected pound cash flows to Lincoln over the next three years are shown in Exhibit 15.2. The high cash flow in Year 3 is due to Lincoln's plans to sell the target at that time. Assuming that Lincoln has a required rate of return of 20% on this project, the cash flows are discounted at that rate to derive the present value of target cash flows. From Lincoln's perspective, the present value of the target is about £99.20 million.

Given that the target's shares are currently valued at C$17 per share, the 10 million shares are worth C$170 million. At the prevailing exchange rate of £0.50 per pound, the target is currently valued at £85 million by the market (computed as C$170 million × £0.50). Lincoln's valuation of the target of about £99.2 million is about 17% above the market valuation. However, Lincoln will have to pay a premium on the shares to persuade the target's board of directors to approve the acquisition. Premiums commonly range from 10% to 40% of the market price. If Lincoln allows for a premium of 10% above the prevailing stock price of C$17 per share, it would pay C$18.7 per share for the target. At this price per share, the price paid for the Canadian firm would be C$187 million, or £93.5 million at the existing exchange rate. This price is less than the perceived net present value of the target, so Lincoln may be willing to pay this amount.

Lincoln recognizes that the target may reject its offer of a 10% premium and ask for a higher premium, but it will not pay more than its estimate of the target's net present value. Since Lincoln values the target at about £99.2 million, it will not pay more than about C$198 million at the prevailing exchange rate (computed as £99.2 million divided by £0.50 per Canadian dollar), or a share price of C$19.80 (computed as C$198 million divided by 10 million shares).

Sources of uncertainty. This example shows how the acquisition of a publicly traded foreign firm differs from the creation of a new foreign subsidiary. Although the valuation of a publicly traded foreign firm can utilize information about an existing business, the cash flows resulting from the acquisition are still subject to uncertainty for several reasons, which can be identified by reviewing the assumptions made in the valuation process. First, the growth rate of revenue is subject to uncertainty. If this rate is overestimated (perhaps because Canadian economic growth is overestimated), the earnings generated in Canada will be lower, and cash flows remitted to the UK parent will be lower as well.

Second, the cost of goods sold could exceed the assumed level of 40% of revenue, which would reduce cash flows remitted to the parent. Third, the selling and administrative expenses could exceed the assumed amount of C$15 million, especially when considering that the annual expenses were C$20 million prior to the acquisition. Fourth, Canada's corporate tax rate could increase, which would reduce the cash flows remitted to the parent. Fifth, the exchange rate of the Canadian dollar may be weaker than assumed, which would reduce the cash flows received by the parent. Sixth, the estimated selling price of the target three years from now could be incorrect for any of the previous five reasons, and this estimate is very influential on the valuation of the target today.

Since one or more of these conditions could occur, the estimated net present value of the target could be overestimated. Consequently, it is possible for Lincoln to acquire the target at a purchase price exceeding its actual value. In particular, the future cash flows are very sensitive to exchange rate movements. This can be illustrated by using sensitivity analysis and re-estimating the value of the target based on different scenarios for the exchange rate over time.

Changes in valuation over time

If Lincoln ltd decides not to bid for the target at this time, it will need to redo its analysis if it later reconsiders acquiring the target. As the factors that affect the expected cash flows or the required rate of return from investing in the target change, so will the value of the target.

Impact of stock market conditions. A change in stock market conditions affects the price per share of each stock in that market. Thus, the value of publicly traded firms in that market will change. Remember that an acquirer needs to pay a premium above the market valuation to acquire a foreign firm.

Continuing with our example involving Lincoln's pursuit of a Canadian target, assume that the target firm has a market price of C$17 per share, representing a valuation of C$170 million, but that before Lincoln makes its decision to acquire the target, the Canadian stock market level rises by 20%. If the target's stock price rises by this same percentage, the firm is now valued at

$$\text{New stock price} = \text{C\$170} \times 1.2$$
$$= \text{C\$204 million}$$

Using the 10% premium assumed in the earlier example, Lincoln must now pay C$224.4 million (computed as C$204 million × 1.1) if it wants to acquire the target. This example illustrates how the price paid for the target can change abruptly simply because of a change in the general level of the stock market.

Impact of stock market conditions on the value of private firms. Even if a target is privately held, general stock market conditions will affect the amount that an acquirer has to pay for the target because a privately held company's value is influenced by the market price multiples of related firms in the same country. A simple method of valuing a private company is to apply the price-earnings (P/E) ratios of publicly traded firms in the same industry to the private company's annual earnings.

For example, if the annual earnings of a private Canadian company are C$8 million and the average P/E ratio of publicly traded Canadian firms in the same industry is 15, the company's market valuation can be estimated as

$$
\begin{aligned}
\text{Market valuation} \quad &= \text{earnings} \times \text{average P/E ratio} \\
&= \text{C\$8 million} \times 15 \\
&= \text{C\$120 million}
\end{aligned}
$$

If the stock market level rises by 20%, the average P/E ratio of the firms in the same industry is likely to rise by about 20%, which represents an increase in the P/E ratio from 15 to 18. The new market valuation of the Canadian firm will be C$144 (i.e. C$8 × 18).

As this example illustrates, private companies also become more expensive targets when local stock market conditions improve.

Impact of exchange rates. Whether a foreign target is publicly traded or private, a UK acquirer must convert pounds to the local currency to purchase the target. If the foreign currency appreciates by the time the acquirer makes payment, the acquisition will be more costly. The cost of the acquisition changes in the same proportion as the change in the exchange rate.

Combined stock market and exchange rate effects. In reality, stock market levels and exchange rates change simultaneously. The effects on the cost of acquiring a foreign target are especially pronounced in emerging markets where stock and currency values are volatile.

EXAMPLE

For example, assume that Mizner plc, a UK firm, wants to acquire a firm in the Czech Republic so that it can expand its business in Eastern Europe. Also assume that the Czech target's valuation moves in tandem with general Czech stock market conditions. Exhibit 15.3, which is based on actual data from a recent period, shows how the cost to Mizner of acquiring the Czech target could change over time, even though the performance of the firm itself does not change. During the period shown, the cost of acquisition could have increased by 20% in a single month (December of Year 1) as a result of a very strong stock market in that month and also appreciation of the Czech currency (koruna). At the other extreme, the cost of the acquisition declined by 20% in a single month (March of Year 2) as a result of a weakening stock market and koruna over that month. This exhibit illustrates how sensitive the cost of an acquisition of a foreign target is to foreign market conditions.

Impact of market anticipation regarding the target. The stock price of the target may increase if investors anticipate that the target will be acquired, since they are aware that stock prices of targets rise abruptly after a bid by the acquiring firm. Thus, it is important that Lincoln keep its intentions about acquiring the target confidential.

WHY VALUATIONS OF A TARGET MAY VARY AMONG MNCS

Most MNCs that consider acquiring a specific target will use a somewhat similar process for valuing the target. Nevertheless, their valuations will differ because of differences in the way the MNC's estimate the key determinants of a given target's valuation: (1) cash

Exhibit 15.3 Influence of Czech stock market and currency conditions on the cost of acquiring a Czech target

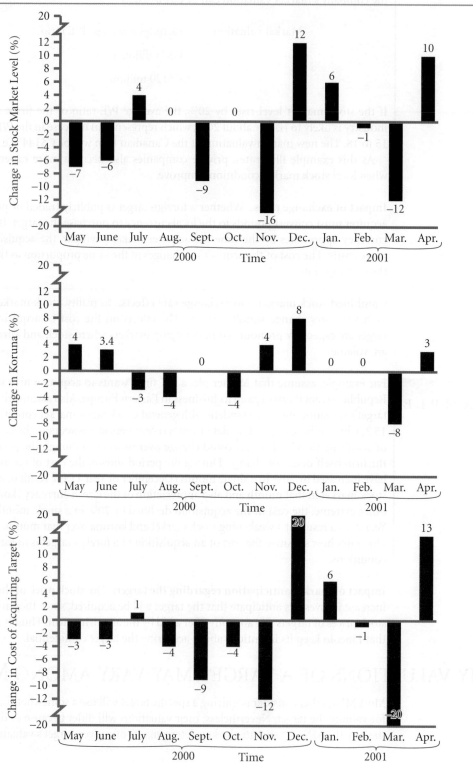

flows to be generated by the target, (2) exchange rate effects on funds remitted to the MNC's parent, and (3) the required rate of return when investing in the target.

Estimated cash flows of the foreign target

The target's expected future cash flows will vary among MNCs because the cash flows will be dependent on the MNC's management or oversight of the target's operations. If an MNC can improve the production efficiency of the target without reducing the target's production volume, it can improve the target's cash flows.

Each MNC may have a different plan as to how the target will fit within its structure and how the target will conduct future operations. The target's expected cash flows will be influenced by the way it is utilized. An MNC with production plants in Asia that purchases another Asian production plant may simply be attempting to increase its market share and production capacity. This MNC's cash flows change because of a higher production and sales level. Conversely, an MNC with all of its production plants in the United Kingdom may purchase an Asian production plant to shift its production where costs are lower. This MNC's cash flows change because of lower expenses.

Tax laws can create competitive advantages for acquirers based in some countries. Acquirers based in low-tax countries may be able to generate higher cash flows from acquiring a foreign target than acquirers in high-tax countries simply because they are subject to lower taxes on the future earnings remitted by the target (after it is acquired).

Exchange rate effects on the funds remitted

The valuation of a target can vary among MNCs simply because of differences in the exchange rate effects on funds remitted by the foreign target to the MNC's parent. If the target remits funds frequently in the near future, its value will be partially dependent on the expected exchange rate of the target's local currency in the near future. If the target does not remit funds in the near future, its value is more dependent on its local growth strategy and on exchange rates in the distant future.

Required return of acquirer

The valuation of the target could also vary among MNCs because of differences in their required rate of return from investing funds to acquire the target. If an MNC targets a successful foreign company with plans to continue the target's local business in a more efficient manner, the risk of the business will be relatively low, and therefore the MNC's required return from acquiring the target will be relatively low. Conversely, if an MNC targets the company because it plans to turn the company into a major exporter, the risk is much higher. The target has not established itself in foreign markets, so the cash flows that would result from the exporting business are very uncertain. Thus, the required return to acquire the target company will be relatively high as well.

If potential acquirers are based in different countries, their required rates of return from a specific target will vary even if they plan to use the target in similar ways. Recall that an MNC's required rate of return on any project is dependent on the local risk-free interest rate (since that influences the cost of funds for that MNC). Therefore, the required rate of return for MNCs based in countries with relatively high interest rates such as Brazil and Venezuela may differ from MNCs based in low-interest-rate countries such as the United States or Japan. The higher required rate of return for MNCs based in Latin American countries will not necessarily lead to a lower valuation. The target's currency might be expected to appreciate substantially against Latin American currencies (since some Latin American currencies have consistently weakened over time), which would enhance the amount of cash flows received as a result of remitted funds and could possibly offset the effects of the higher required rate of return.

OTHER TYPES OF MULTINATIONAL RESTRUCTURING

Besides acquiring foreign firms, MNCs can engage in multinational restructuring through international partial acquisitions, acquisitions of privatized businesses, international alliances, and international divestitures. Each type is described in turn.

International partial acquisitions

In many cases, an MNC may consider a partial international acquisition of a firm, in which it purchases part of the existing stock of a foreign firm. A partial international acquisition requires less funds because only a portion of the foreign target's shares are purchased. With this type of investment, the foreign target normally continues operating and may not experience the employee turnover that commonly occurs after a target's ownership changes. Nevertheless, by acquiring a substantial fraction of the shares, the MNC may have some influence on the target's management and be in a position to complete the acquisition in the future. Some MNCs buy substantial stakes in foreign companies to have some control over their operations. For example, Coca-Cola has purchased stakes in many foreign bottling companies that bottle its syrup. In this way, it can ensure that the bottling operations meet its standards.

Valuation of a foreign firm that may be partially acquired. When an MNC considers a partial acquisition in which it will purchase sufficient shares so that it can control the firm, the MNC can conduct its valuation of the target in much the same way as when it purchases the entire firm. If the MNC buys only a small proportion of the firm's shares, however, the MNC cannot restructure the firm's operations to make it more efficient. Therefore, its estimates of the firm's cash flows must be made from the perspective of a passive investor rather than as a decision maker for the firm.

International acquisitions of privatized businesses

In recent years, government-owned businesses of many developing countries in Eastern Europe and South America have been sold to individuals or corporations. Many MNCs have capitalized on this wave of so-called privatization by acquiring businesses being sold by governments. These businesses may be attractive because of the potential for MNCs to increase their efficiency.

Valuation of a privatized business. An MNC can conduct a valuation of a foreign business that was owned by the government in a developing country by using capital budgeting analysis, as illustrated earlier. However, the valuation of such businesses is difficult for the following reasons:

- The future cash flows are very uncertain because the businesses were previously operating in environments of little or no competition. Thus, previous sales volume figures may not be useful indicators of future sales.
- Data concerning what businesses are worth are very limited in some countries because there are not many publicly traded firms in their markets, and there is

limited disclosure of prices paid for targets in other acquisitions. Consequently, there may not be any benchmarks to use when valuing a business.

- Economic conditions in these countries are very uncertain during the transition to a market-oriented economy.

- Political conditions tend to be volatile during the transition, as government policies for businesses are sometimes unclear or subject to abrupt changes.

- If the government retains a portion of the firm's equity, it may attempt to exert some control over the firm. Its objectives may be very different from those of the acquirer, a situation that could lead to conflict.

Hungary serves as a model country for privatizations. More than 25,000 MNCs have a foreign stake in Hungary's businesses. Hungary's government has been quick and efficient at selling off its assets to MNCs.

International alliances

MNCs commonly engage in international alliances such as joint ventures and licensing agreements with foreign firms. International alliances are quite different from international acquisitions. The initial outlay is typically smaller because the MNC is not acquiring a foreign firm, and the cash flows to be received are typically smaller as well.

EXAMPLE

Lasceaux Sarl (French) plans to provide a Brazilian firm with technology. In return, the Brazilian firm will pay royalties amounting to 10% of its future sales of products resulting from use of this technology over the next five years. Lasceaux's initial outlay for this international alliance is the initial expense incurred as a result of providing the technology. Lasceaux can estimate the cash flows to be received from the Brazilian firm by first forecasting the Brazilian firm's annual sales (in Brazilian real) of products based on the technology. Lasceaux will receive 10% of this amount. Then, it must forecast the value of the real over each of the next five years so that it can determine the euro cash flows resulting from these royalties. It must also consider any tax effects.

International divestitures

http://

Visit the World Bank's website at **http://www.worldbank.org** for data on socioeconomic development and performance indicators as well as links to statistical and project-oriented publications and analyses.

An MNC should periodically reassess its direct foreign investments to determine whether they should be retained or sold (divested). Some foreign projects may no longer be feasible as a result of the MNC's increased cost of capital, increased host government taxes, increased political risk in the host country, or revised projections of exchange rates. Many divestitures occur as a result of a revised assessment of industry or economic conditions. For example, Warner-Lambert Co, Johnson & Johnson, and several other US-based MNCs recently divested some of their Latin American subsidiaries when economic conditions deteriorated there.

Assessing whether to divest existing operations in Asia. During the Asian crisis in the 1997–98 period, some MNCs with direct foreign investment in Asia reassessed the feasibility of their existing operations. The expected cash flows that these operations would generate for the parent had declined in many cases for two obvious reasons. First, the rate of economic growth in Asia declined, which led to a decline in expected local sales by the foreign subsidiaries and therefore a decline in the expected level of foreign currency cash flow. Second, the weak currencies of Asian countries led to a decline in the expected amount of the parent's currency to be received when foreign subsidiaries in

Asian countries remitted funds. At the same time, however, market valuations had declined so much that any operations could be divested only if the parent was willing to sell them at a low price. The low prices deterred some divestitures.

Valuation of an international project that may be divested. The valuation of a proposed international divestiture can be determined by comparing the present value of the cash flows if the project is continued to the proceeds that would be received (after taxes) if the project is divested.

EXAMPLE

Reconsider the example from the previous chapter in which Spartan ltd considered establishing a Singapore subsidiary. Assume that the Singapore subsidiary was created and, after two years, the spot rate of the Singapore dollar (S\$) is £0.33. In addition, forecasts have been revised for the remaining two years of the project, indicating that the Singapore dollar should be worth £0.29 in Year 3 and £0.27 in the project's final year. Because these forecasted exchange rates have an adverse effect on the project, Spartan, Inc, considers divesting the subsidiary. For simplicity, assume that the original forecasts of the other variables remain unchanged and that a potential acquirer has offered S\$13 million (after adjusting for any capital gains taxes) for the subsidiary if the acquirer can retain the existing working capital.

Spartan can conduct a divestiture analysis by comparing the after-tax proceeds from the possible sale of the project (in pounds) to the present value of the expected pound inflows that the project will generate if it is not sold. This comparison will determine the net present value of the divestiture (NPV_d), as illustrated in Exhibit 15.4. Since the present value of the subsidiary's cash flows from Spartan's perspective exceeds the price at which it can sell the subsidiary, the divestiture is not feasible. Thus, Spartan should not divest the subsidiary at the price offered. Spartan may still search for another firm that is willing to acquire the subsidiary for a price that exceeds its present value.

RESTRUCTURING DECISIONS AS REAL OPTIONS

Some restructuring issues faced by MNCs involve **real options**, or implicit options on real assets (such as buildings, machinery, and other assets used by MNCs to facilitate

Exhibit 15.4 Divestiture analysis Spartan ltd (from Exhibit 14.2)

	End of year 2 (today)	End of year 3 (one year from today)	End of year 4 (two years from today)
16. S\$ remitted after withholding taxes		S\$6,840,000	S\$7,560,000
17. Salvage value			S\$12,000,000
Selling price	S\$13,000,000		
18. Exchange rate of S\$	£0.33	£0.29	£0.27
19a. Cash flows to parent (if divested)	£4,290,000		
19b. Cash flows to parent (if not divested)		£1,983,600	£5,281,200
20a. *PV* of parent cash flows (if divested)	£4,290,000		
20b. *PV* of parent cash flows if not divested (15% discount rate)		(£1,724,870 + £4,401,663) =6.126.533	
Divest – retain	£4,290,000 – 6,126,533 = –£1,836,533		

their production). A real option can be classified as a call option on real assets or a put option on real assets, as explained next.

Call option on real assets

A **call option on real assets** represents a proposed project that contains an option of pursuing an additional venture that may or may not be undertaken. The additional venture has in some sense to rely on the original project being undertaken. Some possible forms of restructuring by MNCs contain a call option on real assets. Multinational capital budgeting can be conducted in a manner to account for the option.

Coral plc, a clothing firm in the United Kingdom, is considering the acquisition of a clothing manufacturer in Morocco. Coral estimates and discounts the expected pound cash flows that would result from acquiring this business and compares them to the initial outlay. At this time, the present value of the future cash flows that are directly attributable to the Moroccan business is slightly lower than the initial outlay that would be required to purchase that business, so the business appears to be an unprofitable investment.

A Brazilian clothing firm is also likely to come up for sale in the following year for a given value, but its owners will only sell the business to a firm that they know and trust, and Coral plc has no relationship with this business. A possible advantage of the Moroccan firm that is not measured by the traditional multinational capital budgeting analysis is that it frequently does business with the Brazilian firm and could use its relationship to help Coral acquire the Brazilian firm. If Coral purchases the Moroccan business, it estimates that in about one year's time it will in effect have an option to also acquire the clothing firm in Brazil. In essence, Coral will have a call option on real assets (of the Brazilian firm), because it will have the option (not the obligation) to purchase the Brazilian firm.

The extra or premium that Coral would be willing to pay for the right to bid for the Brazilian firm is an extra benefit for the Moroccan investment – it is a hidden benefit that should be included in the original calculations.

The difficulty is in valuing this option. If the clothing market prospers, Coral should value the Brazilian cash flows with a low risk discount and almost certainly take up the option. If the clothing market is subsequently poor it should apply a higher risk discount and possibly not take up the option. In the terminology of options (see earlier chapters) the expected purchase price of the Brazilian firm serves as the exercise or strike price in the call option on real assets. Coral's valuation serves as the spot price on maturity of the option and the premium is the benefit that Coral has acquired in having this option when taking over the Moroccan firm.

In theory the Black Scholes option pricing model can be used to estimate the value of the option. The problem with using the model is that whereas in a financial market context many of the input variables can be estimated from data, in a real investment context, input variables are subject to as much uncertainty as the object of estimation (i.e. the premium). Thus, in this case, the value of the Brazilian firm has to be estimated as does the volatility of the market, however defined. There are also further complications if the exercise price is not wholly independent of Coral's valuation (the spot); this seems likely in that if the market is good, the price for the Brazilian firm is likely to be higher.

The true value of the option approach is to highlight possible avenues that would otherwise not be available and to alert investors to the value of having the option to take up these opportunities. The Black Scholes approach to valuing such options is in many ways problematic and MNCs would do well to evaluate possible scenarios and use probability to approximate the expected benefits.

Put option on real assets

A **put option on real assets** represents a proposed project that contains an option of divesting part or all of the project. As with a call option on real assets, a put option on real assets can be accounted for by multinational capital budgeting.

EXAMPLE

Jade ltd a UK office supply firm, is considering the acquisition of a similar business in Italy. Jade believes that if future economic conditions in Italy are favourable, the net present value of this project is positive. However, given that weak economic conditions in Italy are more likely, the proposed project appears to be unprofitable.

Assume now that Jade knows that it has the option to sell the Italian firm at a specified price to another firm over the next four years. In this case, Jade has an implied put option attached to the project.

Jade can treat the option to sell as a put option where the selling price is the strike or exercise price, the actual value of the firm is the spot price and the premium is the value of this option. Jade should add the value of the option (i.e. the premium) to the net present value of the project before coming to a decision. Analysis as to the direct application of option theory to value the option is the same as for the above call option example. To have a guaranteed price over the next four years irrespective of actual market conditions is indeed a valuable offer that would for most investors affect the valuation of the Italian business. The valuation process can be entirely subjective, use the Black Scholes model with subjective input or employ the scenario approach – all with approximate results. The benefit of analysis is that it will have structured the decision and indicated approximate value.

MANAGING FOR VALUE
Mazda's decision to restructure

Mazda's main production facilities are based in Japan, but it relies heavily on exports to the United States and Europe. In 1996, Ford Motor Co purchased about one-third of Mazda's shares. In the late 1990s, Mazda's performance was weak despite Ford's efforts to improve its operations. It had an excessive amount of debt. It was also highly susceptible to the weakness of the euro in the 1999–2000 period. When the euro weakened against the yen, the European demand for exports made in Japan (and priced in Japanese yen) was reduced. Mazda's costs of producing its vehicles in Japan were not reduced, however, because those costs were denominated in yen. In the first six months of 2000, Mazda experienced losses of more than $9 billion yen (about $90 million), and much of the loss was attributed to the euro's weakness.

In November 2000, Mazda decided to engage in major multinational restructuring to resolve its financial problems. It shifted some of its production from Japan to Europe so that its expenses and revenue from its sales in Europe would be denominated in the same currency. This strategy reduced Mazda's exposure to exchange rate risk because it could sell the cars in Europe at a markup above the cost (in euros) necessary to produce them. The euro's movements against other currencies would not have a direct effect on the European demand for Mazdas. This multinational restructuring was politically tense because it required the closing of some facilities in Japan, which resulted in layoffs. Since the restructuring, however, the value of the firm has increased; thus, the shareholders have benefited from Mazda's decision.

SUMMARY

- International acquisitions are one of the most common types of multinational restructuring. MNCs can use capital budgeting to determine whether a foreign target is worth acquiring. The expected cash flows of a foreign target are affected by target-specific factors (such as the target's previous cash flows and its managerial talent) and country-specific factors (such as economic conditions, political conditions, currency conditions, and stock market conditions).

- In the typical valuation process, an MNC initially screens prospective targets based on willingness to be acquired and country barriers. Then, each prospective target is valued by estimating its cash flows, based on target-specific characteristics and the target's country characteristics, and by discounting the expected cash flows. Then the perceived value is compared to the target's market value to determine whether the target can be pur-

chased at a price that is below the perceived value from the MNC's perspective.

- Valuations of a foreign target may vary among potential acquirers because of differences in estimates of the target's cash flows or exchange rate movements or differences in the required rate of return among acquirers. These differences may be especially pronounced when the acquirers are from different countries.

- Besides international acquisitions of firms, the more common types of multinational restructuring include international partial acquisitions, international acquisitions of privatized businesses, international alliances (such as international licensing or joint ventures), and international divestitures. Each of these types of multinational restructuring can be assessed by applying multinational capital budgeting.

CRITICAL DEBATE

Can a foreign target be assessed like any other asset?

Proposition. Yes. The value of a foreign target to an MNC is the present value of the future cash flows to the MNC. The process of estimating a foreign target's value is the same as the process of estimating a machine's value. A target has expected cash flows, which can be derived from information about previous cash flows.

Opposing view. No. A target's behaviour will change after it is acquired by an MNC. Its efficiency may improve depending on the ability of the MNC to integrate the target with its own operations. The MNC's performance may also change. It is not enough to just have one valuation figure. A range of possible scenarios must be considered.

With whom do you agree? Which argument do you support? Offer your own opinion on this issue.

SELF TEST

Answers are provided in Appendix A at the back of the text.

1. Explain why more acquisitions have taken place in Europe in recent years.

2. What are some of the barriers to international acquisitions?

3. Why might MNCs prefer to establish a foreign subsidiary rather than acquire an existing firm in a foreign country?

4. Provoke ltd (based in the UK), has been considering the divestiture of a Swedish subsidiary that produces ski equipment and sells it locally. A Swedish firm has already offered to acquire this Swedish subsidiary. Assume that the UK parent has just revised its projections of the Swedish krona's value downward. Will the proposed divestiture now seem more or less feasible than it did before? Explain.

QUESTIONS AND APPLICATIONS

1. **Motives for restructuring.** Why do you think MNCs continuously assess possible forms of multinational restructuring, such as foreign acquisitions or downsizing of a foreign subsidiary?

2. **Exposure to country regulations.** Maude ltd a UK-based MNC, has recently acquired a firm in Singapore. To eliminate inefficiencies, Maude downsized the target substantially, eliminating two-thirds of the workforce. Why might this action affect the regulations imposed on the subsidiary's business by the Singapore government?

3. **Global expansion strategy.** Toki ltd a UK-based MNC, is considering expanding into Thailand because of decreasing profit margins in the UK. The demand for Toki's product in Thailand is very strong. However, forecasts indicate that the baht is expected to depreciate substantially over the next three years. Should Toki expand into Thailand? What factors may affect its decision?

4. **Alternatives to international acquisitions.** Rastelle SA a French-based MNC, is considering the acquisition of a Russian target to produce personal computers (PCs) and market them throughout Russia, where demand for PCs has increased substantially in recent years. Assume that the stock market conditions are not favourable in Russia, as the stock prices of most Russian companies rose substantially just prior to Rastelle's assessment of the target. What are some alternatives available to Rastelle?

5. **Comparing international projects.** Savannah SA (Spain), a manufacturer of clothing, wants to increase its market share by acquiring a target producing a popular clothing line in the US. This clothing line is well established. Forecasts indicate a relatively stable euro over the life of the project. Marquette SA wants to increase its market share in the personal computer market by acquiring a target in Thailand that currently produces radios and converting the operations to produce PCs. Forecasts indicate a depreciation of the baht over the life of the project. Funds resulting from both projects will be remitted to the respective Spanish parents on a regular basis. Which target do you think will result in a higher net present value? Why?

6. **Privatized business valuations.** Why are valuations of privatized businesses previously owned by the governments of developing countries more difficult than valuations of existing firms in developed countries?

7. **Valuing a foreign target.** Blore plc a UK-based MNC, has screened several targets. Based on economic and political considerations, only one eligible target remains in Malaysia. Blore would like you to value this target and has provided you with the following information:

   ■ Blore expects to keep the target for three years, at which time it expects to sell the firm for 300 million Malaysian ringgit (MYR) after any taxes.

   ■ Blore expects a strong Malaysian economy. The estimates for revenue for the next year are MYR200 million. Revenues are expected to increase by 8% in each of the following two years.

   ■ Cost of goods sold is expected to be 50% of revenue.

   ■ Selling and administrative expenses are expected to be MYR30 million in each of the next three years.

   ■ The Malaysian tax rate on the target's earnings is expected to be 35%.

   ■ Depreciation expenses are expected to be MYR20 million per year for each of the next three years.

   ■ The target will need MYR7 million in cash each year to support existing operations.

   ■ The target's stock price is currently MYR30 per share. The target has 9 million shares outstanding.

   ■ Any remaining cash flows will be remitted by the target to Blore plc. Blore uses the prevailing exchange rate of the Malaysian ringgit as the expected exchange rate for the next three years. This exchange rate is currently £0.25.

   ■ Blore's required rate of return on similar projects is 20%.

a. Prepare a worksheet to estimate the value of the Malaysian target based on the information provided.

b. Will Blore plc be able to acquire the Malaysian target for a price lower than its valuation of the target?

8. **Uncertainty surrounding a foreign target.** Refer to question 7. What are some of the key sources of uncertainty in Blore's valuation of the target? Identify two reasons why the expected cash flows from an Asian subsidiary of a UK-based MNC would have been lower as a result of the Asian crisis.

9. **Divestiture strategy.** The reduction in expected cash flows of Asian subsidiaries as a result of the Asian crisis likely resulted in a reduced valuation of these subsidiaries from the parent's perspective. Explain why a European-based MNC might not have sold its Asian subsidiaries.

10. **Why a foreign acquisition may backfire.** Provide two reasons why an MNC's strategy of acquiring a foreign target will backfire. That is, explain why the acquisition might result in a negative *NPV*.

ADVANCED QUESTIONS

11. **Pricing a foreign target.** Alaska ltd would like to acquire Estoya EIRL which is located in Peru. In initial negotiations, Estoya has asked for a purchase price of 1 billion Peruvian new sol. If Alaska completes the purchase, it would keep Estoya's operations for two years and then sell the company. In the recent past, Estoya has generated annual cash flows of 500 million new sol per year, but Alaska believes that it can increase these cash flows by 5% each year by improving the operations of the plant. Given these improvements, Alaska believes it will be able to resell Estoya in two years for 1.2 billion new sol. The current exchange rate of the new sol is £0.19, and exchange rate forecasts for the next two years indicate values of £0.19 and £0.18, respectively. Given these facts, should Alaska ltd pay 1 billion new sol for Estoya Corp. if the required rate of return is 18%? What is the maximum price Alaska should be willing to pay?

12. **Global strategy.** Senser GmbH (Germany) established a subsidiary in Russia two years ago. Under its original plans, Senser intended to operate the subsidiary for a total of four years. However, it would like to reassess the situation, since exchange rate forecasts for the Russian rouble indicate that it may depreciate from its current level of 0.033 euros to 0.028 euros next year and to 0.025 euros in the following year. Senser could sell the subsidiary today for 5 million roubles to a potential acquirer. If Senser continues to operate the subsidiary, it will generate cash flows of 3 million roubles next year and 4 million rubles in the following year. These cash flows would be remitted back to the parent in Germany. The required rate of return of the project is 16%. Should Senser continue operating the Russian subsidiary?

13. **Divestiture decision.** Collumpton Springs ltd plans to divest either its Singapore or its Canadian subsidiary. Assume that if exchange rates remain constant, the pound cash flows each of these subsidiaries would provide to the parent over time would be somewhat similar. However, the firm expects the Singapore dollar to depreciate against the British pound, and the Canadian dollar to appreciate against the pound. The firm can sell either subsidiary for about the same price today. Which one should it sell?

14. **Divestiture decision.** San Gabriel SA (Spain) recently considered divesting its Italian subsidiary and determined that the divestiture was not feasible. The required rate of return on this subsidiary was 17%. In the last week, San Gabriel's required return on that subsidiary increased to 21%. If the sales price of the subsidiary has not changed, explain why the divestiture may now be feasible.

15. **Divestiture decision.** Ethridge plc has a subsidiary in India that produces products and sells them throughout Asia. In response to a recent downturn in domestic sales Ethridge decided to conduct a capital budgeting analysis to determine whether it should divest the subsidiary. Why might this decision be different if Ethridge were doing well? Describe the general method for determining whether the divestiture is financially feasible.

16. **Feasibility of a divestiture.** Flowerdew ltd has a subsidiary in Bulgaria that it fully finances with its own equity. Last week, a firm offered to buy

the subsidiary from Flowerdew for £60 million in cash, and the offer is still available this week as well. The annualized long-term risk-free rate in the United Kingdom increased from 7% to 8% this week. The expected monthly cash flows to be generated by the subsidiary have not changed since last week. The risk premium that Flowerdew applies to its projects in Bulgaria was reduced from 11.3% to 10.9% this week. The annualized long-term risk-free rate in Bulgaria declined from 23% to 21% this week. Would the *NPV* to Flowerdew from divesting this unit be more or less than the *NPV* determined last week? Why? (No analysis is necessary, but make sure that your explanation is very clear.)

17. **Accounting for government restrictions.** Sunveldt NV (Dutch) plans to purchase a firm in Indonesia. It believes that it can install its operating procedure in this firm, which would significantly reduce the firm's operating expenses. However, the Indonesian government may approve the acquisition only if Sunveldt does not lay off any workers. How can Sunveldt possibly increase efficiency without laying off workers? How can Sunveldt account for the Indonesian government's position as it assesses the *NPV* of this possible acquisition?

Project workshop

18. **Current events affecting MNCs.** Use an online news source to review international events in the last week. Select three economic events that could affect economic or political conditions in foreign countries and explain how an MNC might restructure its business in response to these events. Would the MNC increase or reduce its business in that country due to that event?

19. Go to the web page of the United Nations Conference on Trade and Development http://www.unctad.org and enter on the search box: 'OFDI' and the name of the country, e.g. Argentina or Russia. Look for a pdf report on outward foreign investment from that country. From the report summarize the motives for FDI and the examples given. Consider the motives and rank them in order of importance giving your reasons.

Discussion in the boardroom

This exercise can be found on the companion website at www.cengage.co.uk/madura_fox.

Running your own MNC

This exercise can be found on the companion website at www.cengage.co.uk/madura_fox.

Essays/discussion and articles can be found at the end of Part 4

BLADES PLC CASE STUDY
Assessment of an acquisition in Thailand

Recall that Ben Holt, Blades' financial director, has suggested to the board of directors that Blades proceed with the establishment of a subsidiary in Thailand. Due to the high growth potential of the roller blade market in Thailand, his analysis suggests that the venture will be profitable. Specifically, his view is that Blades should establish a subsidiary in Thailand to manufacture roller blades, whether an existing agreement with Entertainment Products (a Thai retailer) is renewed or not. Under this agreement, Entertainment Products is committed to the purchase of 180,000 pairs of "Speedos", Blades' primary product, annually. The agreement was initially for three years and will expire two years from now. At this time, the agreement may be renewed. Due to delivery delays, Entertainment Products has indicated that it will renew the agreement only if Blades establishes a subsidiary in Thailand. In this case, the price per pair of roller blades would be fixed at 4,594 Thai baht per pair. If Blades decides not to renew the agreement, Entertainment Products has indicated that it would purchase only 5,000 pairs of Speedos annually at prevailing market prices.

According to Ben Holt's analysis, renewing the agreement with Entertainment Products and establishing a subsidiary in Thailand will result in a net present value (NPV) of some £1,760,000. Conversely, if the agreement is not renewed and a subsidiary is established, the resulting NPV is about £5,830,000. Consequently, Holt has suggested to the board of directors that Blades establish a subsidiary without renewing the existing agreement with Entertainment Products.

Recently, a Thai roller blade manufacturer called Skates'n'Stuff contacted Holt regarding the potential sale of the company to Blades. Skates'n'Stuff entered the Thai roller blade market a decade ago and has generated a profit in every year of operation. Furthermore, Skates'n'Stuff has established distribution channels in Thailand. Consequently, if Blades acquires the company, it could begin sales immediately and would not require an additional year to build the plant in Thailand. Initial forecasts indicate that Blades would be able to sell 280,000 pairs of roller blades annually. These sales are incremental to the acquisition of

Skates'n'Stuff. Furthermore, all sales resulting from the acquisition would be made to retailers in Thailand. Blades' fixed expenses would be 20 million baht annually. Although Holt has not previously considered the acquisition of an existing business, he is now wondering whether aquiring Skates'n'Stuff may be a better course of action than building a subsidiary in Thailand.

Holt is also aware of some disadvantages associated with such an acquisition. Skates'n'Stuff's CFO has indicated that he would be willing to accept a price of 1 billion baht (one thousand million) in payment for the company, which is clearly more expensive than the 550 million baht outlay that would be required to establish a subsidiary in Thailand. However, Skates'n'Stuff's CFO has indicated that it is willing to negotiate. Furthermore, Blades' employs a high-quality production process, which enables it to charge relatively high prices for roller blades produced in its plants. If Blades acquires Skates'n'Stuff, which uses an inferior production process (resulting in lower quality roller blades), it would have to charge a lower price for the roller blades it produces there. Initial forecasts indicate that Blades will be able to charge a price of 4,500 Thai baht per pair of roller blades without affecting demand. However, because Skates'n'Stuff uses a production process that results in lower-quality roller blades than Blades' Speedos, operating costs incurred would be similar to the amount incurred if Blades establishes a subsidiary in Thailand. Thus, Blades estimates that it would incur operating costs of about 3,500 baht per pair of roller blades.

Ben Holt has asked you, a financial analyst for Blades, Inc, to determine whether the acquisition of Skates'n'Stuff is a better course of action for Blades than the establishment of a subsidiary in Thailand. Acquiring Skates'n'Stuff will be more favourable than establishing a subsidiary if the present value of the cash flows generated by the company exceeds the purchase price by more than £5,830,000, the NPV of establishing a new subsidiary. Thus, Holt has asked you to construct a spreadsheet that determines the NPV of the acquisition.

To aid you in your analysis, Holt has provided the following additional information, which he gathered from various sources, including unaudited financial statements of Skates'n'Stuff for the last three years:

- Blades, requires a return on the Thai acquisition of 25%, the same rate of return it would require if it established a subsidiary in Thailand.

- If Skates'n'Stuff is acquired, Blades, Inc., will operate the company for ten years, at which time Skates'n'Stuff will be sold for an estimated 1.1 million baht.

- Of the 1 billion baht purchase price, 600 million baht constitutes the cost of the plant and equipment. These items are depreciated using straight-line depreciation. Thus, 60 million baht will be depreciated annually for ten years.

- Sales of 280,000 pairs of roller blades annually will begin immediately at a price of 4,500 baht per pair.

- Variable costs per pair of roller blades will be 3,500 per pair.

- Fixed operating costs, including salaries and administrative expenses, will be 20 million baht annually.

- The current spot rate of the Thai baht is $0.023. Blades expects the baht to depreciate by an average of 2% per year for the next ten years.

- The Thai government will impose a 25% tax on income and a 10% withholding tax on any funds remitted by Skates'n'Stuff to Blades, plc. Any earnings remitted to the United Kingdom will not be taxed again in the United Kingdom. All earnings generated by Skates'n'Stuff will be remitted to Blades plc.

- The average inflation rate in Thailand is expected to be 12% annually. Revenues, variable costs, and fixed costs are subject to inflation and are expected to change by the same annual rate as the inflation rate.

In addition to the information outlined above, Ben Holt has informed you that Blades, will need to manufacture all of the 180,000 pairs to be delivered to Entertainment Products this year and next year in Thailand. Since Blades previously only used components from Thailand (which are of a lower quality but cheaper than UK components) sufficient to manufacture 72,000 pairs annually, it will incur cost savings of 32.4 million baht this year and next year. However, since Blades will sell 180,000 pairs of Speedos annually to Entertainment Products this year and next year whether it acquires Skates'n'Stuff or not, Holt has urged you not to include these sales in your analysis. The agreement with Entertainment Product will not be renewed at the end of next year.

Ben Holt would like you to answer the following questions:

1. Using a spreadsheet, determine the *NPV* of the acquisition of Skates'n'Stuff. Based on your numerical analysis, should Blades establish a subsidiary in Thailand or acquire Skates'n'Stuff?

2. If Blades negotiates with Skates'n'Stuff, what is the maximum amount (in Thai baht) Blades should be willing to pay?

3. Are there any other factors Blades should consider in making its decision? In your answer, you should consider the price Skates'n'Stuff is asking relative to your analysis in question 1, other potential businesses for sale in Thailand, the source of the information your analysis is based on, the production process that will be employed by the target in the future, and the future management of Skates'n'Stuff.

SMALL BUSINESS DILEMMA

Multinational restructuring by the Sports Exports Company

The Sports Exports Company (Ireland) has been successful in producing basketballs in Ireland and exporting them to the United Kingdom. Recently, Jim Logan (owner of the Sports Exports Company) has considered restructuring his company by expanding throughout Europe. He plans to export basketballs and other sporting goods that were not already popular in Europe to one large sporting goods distributor in Germany; the goods will then be distributed to any retail sporting goods stores throughout Europe that are willing to purchase these goods. This distributor will make payments in euros to the Sports Exports Company.

1. Are there any reasons why the business that has been so successful in the United Kingdom will not necessarily be successful in other European countries?

2. If the business is diversified throughout Europe, will this substantially reduce the exposure of the Sports Exports Company to exchange rate risk?

3. Now that several countries in Europe participate in a single currency system, will this affect the performance of new expansion throughout Europe?

CHAPTER 16

COUNTRY RISK ANALYSIS

AN MNC CONDUCTS COUNTRY risk analysis when assessing whether to continue conducting business in a particular country. The analysis can also be used when determining whether to implement new projects in foreign countries. Country risk can be partitioned into the country's political risk and its financial risk. Financial managers must understand how to measure country risk so that they can make investment decisions that maximize their MNC's value.

THE SPECIFIC OBJECTIVES OF THIS CHAPTER ARE TO:

- identify the common factors used by MNCs to measure a country's political risk,
- identify the common factors used by MNCs to measure a country's financial risk,
- explain the techniques used to measure country risk, and
- explain how MNCs use the assessment of country risk when making financial decisions.

WHY COUNTRY RISK ANALYSIS IS IMPORTANT

Country risk is the potentially adverse impact of a country's environment on an MNC's cash flows. Investments with all the normal business guarantees attached against non-payment, including government guarantees, can become worthless overnight. Loan repayments can be delayed or reduced without warning. Such financial crises are a regular phenomenon in international finance. If the credit risk level of a particular country begins to increase, the MNC may consider divesting its subsidiaries located there. MNCs can also use country risk analysis as a screening device to avoid conducting business in countries with excessive risk. Events that heighten country risk tend to discourage direct foreign investment in that particular country.

Country risk analysis is not restricted to predicting major crises. An MNC may also use this analysis to revise its investment or financing decisions in light of recent events. In any given week, the following unrelated international events might occur around the world:

- A terrorist attack.
- A major labour strike in an industry.
- A political crisis due to a scandal within a country.
- Concern about a country's banking system that may cause a major outflow of funds.
- The imposition of trade restrictions on imports.
- A declaration of non-payment of debts by a government.

Any of these events could affect the potential cash flows to be generated by an MNC or the cost of financing projects and therefore affect the value of the MNC.

Even if an MNC reduces its exposure to all such events in a given week, a new set of events will occur in the following week. For each of these events, an MNC must consider whether its cash flows will be affected and whether there has been a change in policy to which it should respond. Country risk analysis is an ongoing process. Most MNCs will not be affected by every event, but they will pay close attention to any events that may have an impact on the industries or countries in which they do business. They also recognize that they cannot eliminate their exposure to all events but may at least attempt to limit their exposure to any single country-specific event.

POLITICAL RISK FACTORS

An MNC must assess country risk not only in countries where it currently does business but also in those where it expects to export or establish subsidiaries. Several risk characteristics of a country may significantly affect performance, and the MNC should be concerned about the likely degree of impact for each.

As one might expect, many country characteristics related to the political environment can influence an MNC. An extreme form of political risk is the possibility that the host country will take over a subsidiary. In some cases of expropriation, some compensation (the amount decided by the host country government) is awarded. In other cases, the assets are confiscated and no compensation is provided. Expropriation can take place peacefully or by force. The following are some of the more common forms of country-related risk:

- Attitude of consumers in the host country.
- Actions of host government.
- Blockage of fund transfers.
- Currency inconvertibility.
- War.
- Bureaucracy.
- Corruption.

Each of these characteristics will be examined.

Attitude of consumers in the host country

A mild form of political risk (to an exporter) is a tendency of residents to purchase only locally produced goods. Even if the exporter decides to set up a subsidiary in the foreign country, this philosophy could prevent its success. All countries tend to exert some pressure on consumers to purchase from locally owned manufacturers. (In the United Kingdom, consumers have in the past been encouraged to purchase locally made goods under the "buy British" slogan.) MNCs that consider entering a foreign market (or have already entered that market) must monitor the general loyalty of consumers toward locally produced products. If consumers are very loyal to local products, a joint venture with a local company may be more feasible than an exporting strategy.

Actions of host government

Various actions of a host government can affect the cash flow of an MNC. For example, a host government might impose pollution control standards (which affect costs) and additional corporate taxes (which affect after-tax earnings) as well as withholding taxes and fund transfer restrictions (which affect after-tax cash flows sent to the parent).

EXAMPLE

In 2004, the Chinese government enacted a law requiring computer chips to include security technology that is licensed by Chinese firms. In addition, China imposes a 17% tax on computer chips sold there, but provides a rebate of up to 14% for chips produced locally. This may discourage chip manufacturers such as Intel and Broadcom from selling chips in China.

Some MNCs use turnover in government members or political beliefs as a proxy for a country's political risk. While this can significantly influence the MNC's future cash flows, it alone does not serve as a suitable representation of political risk. A subsidiary will not necessarily be affected by changing governments. Furthermore, a subsidiary can be affected by new policies of the host government or by a changed attitude toward the subsidiary's home country (and therefore the subsidiary), even when the host government has no risk of being overthrown.

A host government can use various means to make an MNC's operations coincide with its own goals. It may, for example, require the use of local employees for managerial positions at a subsidiary. In addition, it may require social facilities (such as an exercise room or non-smoking areas) or special environmental controls (such as air pollution controls). Furthermore, it is not uncommon for a host government to require special permits, impose extra taxes, or subsidize competitors. All of these actions represent political risk, in that they reflect a country's political characteristics and could influence an MNC's cash flows.

EXAMPLE

In March 2004, antitrust regulators representing the European Union countries decided to fine Microsoft about 500 million euros (equivalent to about $610 million at the time) for abusing its monopolistic position in computer software. They also imposed restrictions on how Microsoft can bundle its Windows MediaPlayer (needed to access music or videos) in its portable computer sold in Europe. Microsoft argued that the fine was unfair because it was not subject to such restrictions in its home country, the United States. Some critics argue, however, that the European regulators are not being too strict, but rather that the US regulators are being too lenient.

Lack of restrictions. In some cases, MNCs are adversely affected by a lack of restrictions in a host country, which allows illegitimate business behaviour to take market share. One of the most troubling issues for MNCs is the failure by host governments to enforce copyright laws against local firms that illegally copy the MNC's product. For example, local firms in Asia commonly copy software produced by MNCs and sell it to customers at lower prices. Software producers lose an estimated £2 billion in sales annually in Asia for this reason. Furthermore, the legal systems in some countries do not adequately protect a firm against copyright violations or other illegal means of obtaining market share.

Blockage of fund transfers

Subsidiaries of MNCs often send funds back to the headquarters for loan repayments, purchases of supplies, administrative fees, remitted earnings, or other purposes. In some cases, a host government may block fund transfers, which could force subsidiaries to undertake projects that are not optimal (just to make use of the funds). Alternatively, the MNC may invest the funds in local securities that provide some return while the funds are blocked. But this return may be inferior to what could have been earned on funds remitted to the parent.

Currency inconvertibility

Some governments do not allow the home currency to be exchanged into other currencies. Thus, the earnings generated by a subsidiary in these countries cannot be remitted to the parent through currency conversion. When the currency is inconvertible, an MNC's parent may need to exchange it for goods to extract benefits from projects in that country.

War

Some countries tend to engage in constant conflicts with neighbouring countries or experience internal turmoil. This can affect the safety of employees hired by an MNC's subsidiary or by salespeople who attempt to establish export markets for the MNC. In addition, countries plagued by the threat of war typically have volatile business cycles, which make the MNC's cash flows generated from such countries more uncertain. The terrorist attack on the United States on September 11, 2001, aroused the expectation that the United States would be involved in a war. MNCs were adversely affected by their potential exposure to terrorist attacks, especially if their subsidiaries were located in countries where there might be anti-US sentiment. Even if an MNC is not directly damaged due to a war, it may incur costs from ensuring the safety of its employees.

The 2003 war in Iraq. As a result of the 2003 war in Iraq, MNCs' cash flows were affected in various ways. The war caused friction between the United States and some countries in the Middle East. Consequently, MNCs faced the possibility that their buildings or offices overseas might be destroyed and that their employees might be attacked. Furthermore, demand for US products and services by consumers in the Middle East declined. In addition, because of friction between the United States and France over how the situation in Iraq should be handled, French demand for some products produced by US-based MNCs also declined. To a lesser extent, there were protests by citizens in other countries, which could have reduced the demand for products produced by US firms. This form of country risk is not limited to US-based MNCs. Friction periodically arises between many countries. Just as French consumers reduced their demand for US products during the war, US consumers reduced their demand for French wine and reduced their travel to France. The French Government Tourist Office estimated that revenue received in France due to US tourism in 2003 was about $500 million less than in the previous year.

Even if MNCs were not directly affected by the various protests, there was substantial uncertainty about how the war might adversely affect MNCs by weakening economic conditions. There was concern that oil prices would rise because of the possible destruction of oil wells, and higher oil prices have a direct impact on transportation and energy costs. Higher interest rates were feared because of the substantial funding needed to finance the military spending. Some of the more pessimistic predictions suggested there would be a major world recession combined with high inflation. Thus, MNCs were concerned about the potential higher costs of supplies and the potential impact of high US inflation or interest rates on exchange rates. Given all this uncertainty, MNCs restricted their expansion until the impact of the war on oil prices, the US budget deficit, and the political relationships between the United States and other countries was clear.

Bureaucracy

http://

For information and surveys on political and country risk visit the portal site: http://www.countryrisk.com/.

Another country risk factor is government bureaucracy, which can complicate an MNC's business. Although this factor may seem irrelevant, it was a major deterrent for MNCs that considered projects in Eastern Europe in the early 1990s. Many of the Eastern European governments were not experienced at facilitating the entrance of MNCs into their markets.

Corruption

http://

A corruption index is derived for major countries by Transparency International (see http://www.transparency.org). The index for selected countries is shown in Exhibit 16.1.

Corruption can adversely affect an MNC's international business because it can increase the cost of conducting business or it can reduce revenue. Various forms of corruption can occur between firms or between a firm and the government. For example, an MNC may lose revenue because a government contract is awarded to a local firm that paid off a government official. Laws and their enforcement vary among countries, however. For example, in the United States, it is illegal to make a payment to a high-ranking government official in return for political favours, but it is legal in most countries for companies to make contributions to political parties.

Exhibit 16.1 Corruption index ratings for selected countries (Maximum rating = 10. High ratings indicate low corruption.)

Country rank	Country	TI 2005 Corruption Perceptions Index		
		2005 CPI score*	Confidence range**	Surveys used***
1	Iceland	9.7	9.5–9.7	8
2	Finland	9.6	9.5–9.7	9
	New Zealand	9.6	9.5–9.7	9
4	Denmark	9.5	9.3–9.6	10
5	Singapore	9.4	9.3–9.5	12
6	Sweden	9.2	9.0–9.3	10
7	Switzerland	9.1	8.9–9.2	9
8	Norway	8.9	8.5–9.1	9
9	Australia	8.8	8.4–9.1	13
10	Austria	8.7	8.4–9.0	9
11	Netherlands	8.6	8.3–8.9	9
	United Kingdom	8.6	8.3–8.8	11
13	Luxembourg	8.5	8.1–8.9	8
14	Canada	8.4	7.9–8.8	11
15	Hong Kong	8.3	7.7–8.7	12
16	Germany	8.2	7.9–8.5	10
17	USA	7.6	7.0–8.0	12
18	France	7.5	7.0–7.8	11
19	Belgium	7.4	6.9–7.9	9
	Ireland	7.4	6.9–7.9	10
21	Chile	7.3	6.8–7.7	10
	Japan	7.3	6.7–7.8	14
23	Spain	7.0	6.6–7.4	10
24	Barbados	6.9	5.7–7.3	3
25	Malta	6.6	5.4–7.7	5
26	Portugal	6.5	5.9–7.1	9
27	Estonia	6.4	6.0–7.0	11
28	Israel	6.3	5.7–6.9	10
	Oman	6.3	5.2–7.3	5
30	United Arab Emirates	6.2	5.3–7.1	6
31	Slovenia	6.1	5.7–6.8	11
32	Botswana	5.9	5.1–6.7	8
	Qatar	5.9	5.6–6.4	5
	Taiwan	5.9	5.4–6.3	14
	Uruguay	5.9	5.6–6.4	6
36	Bahrain	5.8	5.3–6.3	6
37	Cyprus	5.7	5.3–6.0	5
	Jordan	5.7	5.1–6.1	10

TI 2005 Corruption Perceptions Index				
Country rank	Country	2005 CPI score*	Confidence range**	Surveys used***
39	Malaysia	5.1	4.6–5.6	14
40	Hungary	5.0	4.7–5.2	11
	Italy	5.0	4.6–5.4	9
	South Korea	5.0	4.6–5.3	12
43	Tunisia	4.9	4.4–5.6	7
44	Lithuania	4.8	4.5–5.1	8
45	Kuwait	4.7	4.0–5.2	6
46	South Africa	4.5	4.2–4.8	11
47	Czech Republic	4.3	3.7–5.1	10
	Greece	4.3	3.9–4.7	9
	Namibia	4.3	3.8–4.9	8
	Slovakia	4.3	3.8–4.8	10
51	Costa Rica	4.2	3.7–4.7	7
	El Salvador	4.2	3.5–4.8	6
	Latvia	4.2	3.8–4.6	7
	Mauritius	4.2	3.4–5.0	6
55	Bulgaria	4.0	3.4–4.6	8
	Colombia	4.0	3.6–4.4	9
	Fiji	4.0	3.4–4.6	3
	Seychelles	4.0	3.5–4.2	3
59	Cuba	3.8	2.3–4.7	4
	Thailand	3.8	3.5–4.1	13
	Trinidad and Tobago	3.8	3.3–4.5	6
62	Belize	3.7	3.4–4.1	3
	Brazil	3.7	3.5–3.9	10
64	Jamaica	3.6	3.4–3.8	6
65	Ghana	3.5	3.2–4.0	8
	Mexico	3.5	3.3–3.7	10
	Panama	3.5	3.1–4.1	7
	Peru	3.5	3.1–3.8	7
	Turkey	3.5	3.1–4.0	11
70	Burkina Faso	3.4	2.7–3.9	3
	Croatia	3.4	3.2–3.7	7
	Egypt	3.4	3.0–3.9	9
	Lesotho	3.4	2.6–3.9	3
	Poland	3.4	3.0–3.9	11
	Saudi Arabia	3.4	2.7–4.1	5
	Syria	3.4	2.8–4.2	5
77	Laos	3.3	2.1–4.4	3
78	China	3.2	2.9–3.5	14
	Morocco	3.2	2.8–3.6	8

	TI 2005 Corruption Perceptions Index		
Country rank	**Country**	**2005 CPI score***	**Confidence range****	**Surveys used*****
	Senegal	3.2	2.8–3.6	6
	Sri Lanka	3.2	2.7–3.6	7
	Suriname	3.2	2.2–3.6	3
83	Lebanon	3.1	2.7–3.3	4
	Rwanda	3.1	2.1–4.1	3
85	Dominican Republic	3.0	2.5–3.6	6
	Mongolia	3.0	2.4–3.6	4
	Romania	3.0	2.6–3.5	11
88	Armenia	2.9	2.5–3.2	4
	Benin	2.9	2.1–4.0	5
	Bosnia and Herzegovina	2.9	2.7–3.1	6
	Gabon	2.9	2.1–3.6	4
	India	2.9	2.7–3.1	14
	Iran	2.9	2.3–3.3	5
	Mali	2.9	2.3–3.6	8
	Moldova	2.9	2.3–3.7	5
	Tanzania	2.9	2.6–3.1	8
97	Algeria	2.8	2.5–3.3	7
	Argentina	2.8	2.5–3.1	10
	Madagascar	2.8	1.9–3.7	5
	Malawi	2.8	2.3–3.4	7
	Mozambique	2.8	2.4–3.1	8
	Serbia and Montenegro	2.8	2.5–3.3	7
103	Gambia	2.7	2.3–3.1	7
	Macedonia	2.7	2.4–3.2	7
	Swaziland	2.7	2.0–3.1	3
	Yemen	2.7	2.4–3.2	5
107	Belarus	2.6	1.9–3.8	5
	Eritrea	2.6	1.7–3.5	3
	Honduras	2.6	2.2–3.0	7
	Kazakhstan	2.6	2.2–3.2	6
	Nicaragua	2.6	2.4–2.8	7
	Palestine	2.6	2.1–2.8	3
	Ukraine	2.6	2.4–2.8	8
	Vietnam	2.6	2.3–2.9	10
	Zambia	2.6	2.3–2.9	7
	Zimbabwe	2.6	2.1–3.0	7
117	Afghanistan	2.5	1.6–3.2	3
	Bolivia	2.5	2.3–2.9	6
	Ecuador	2.5	2.2–2.9	6
	Guatemala	2.5	2.1–2.8	7

TI 2005 Corruption Perceptions Index				
Country rank	Country	2005 CPI score*	Confidence range**	Surveys used***
	Guyana	2.5	2.0–2.7	3
	Libya	2.5	2.0–3.0	4
	Nepal	2.5	1.9–3.0	4
	Philippines	2.5	2.3–2.8	13
	Uganda	2.5	2.2–2.8	8
126	Albania	2.4	2.1–2.7	3
	Niger	2.4	2.2–2.6	4
	Russia	2.4	2.3–2.6	12
	Sierra Leone	2.4	2.1–2.7	3
130	Burundi	2.3	2.1–2.5	3
	Cambodia	2.3	1.9–2.5	4
	Congo, Republic of	2.3	2.1–2.6	4
	Georgia	2.3	2.0–2.6	6
	Kyrgyzstan	2.3	2.1–2.5	5
	Papua New Guinea	2.3	1.9–2.6	4
	Venezuela	2.3	2.2–2.4	10
137	Azerbaijan	2.2	1.9–2.5	6
	Cameroon	2.2	2.0–2.5	6
	Ethiopia	2.2	2.0–2.5	8
	Indonesia	2.2	2.1–2.5	13
	Iraq	2.2	1.5–2.9	4
	Liberia	2.2	2.1–2.3	3
	Uzbekistan	2.2	2.1–2.4	5
144	Congo, Democratic Republic	2.1	1.8–2.3	4
	Kenya	2.1	1.8–2.4	8
	Pakistan	2.1	1.7–2.6	7
	Paraguay	2.1	1.9–2.3	7
	Somalia	2.1	1.6–2.2	3
	Sudan	2.1	1.9–2.2	5
	Tajikistan	2.1	1.9–2.4	5
151	Angola	2.0	1.8–2.1	5
152	Cote d'Ivoire	1.9	1.7–2.1	4
	Equatorial Guinea	1.9	1.6–2.1	3
	Nigeria	1.9	1.7–2.0	9
155	Haiti	1.8	1.5–2.1	4
	Myanmar	1.8	1.7–2.0	4
	Turkmenistan	1.8	1.7–2.0	4
158	Bangladesh	1.7	1.4–2.0	7
	Chad	1.7	1.3–2.1	6

Explanatory notes

* **CPI score** relates to perceptions of the degree of corruption as seen by business people and country analysts and ranges between 10 (highly clean) and 0 (highly corrupt).

****Confidence range** provides a range of possible values of the CPI score. This reflects how a country's score may vary, depending on measurement precision. Nominally, with 5% probability the score is above this range and with another 5% it is below. However, particularly when only few sources (n) are available an unbiased estimate of the mean coverage probability is lower than the nominal value of 90%.

*****Surveys used** refers to the number of surveys that assessed a country's performance. 16 surveys and expert assessments were used and at least three were required for a country to be included in the CPI.

Source: Transparency International 2005

FINANCIAL RISK FACTORS

Along with political factors, financial factors should be considered when assessing country risk. One of the most obvious financial factors is the current and potential state of the country's economy. An MNC that exports to a country or develops a subsidiary in a country is highly concerned about that country's demand for its products. This demand is, of course, strongly influenced by the country's economy. A recession in the country could severely reduce demand for the MNC's exports or products sold by the MNC's local subsidiary. In the early 1990s and again in the 2000–02 period, the European business performance of Ford Motor Co, Nike, Walt Disney Co, and many other US-based MNCs was adversely affected by a weak European economy.

Indicators of economic growth

A country's economic growth is dependent on several financial factors:

- *Interest rates.* Higher interest rates tend to slow the growth of an economy and reduce demand for the MNC's products. Lower interest rates often stimulate the economy and increase demand for the MNC's products.

- *Exchange rates.* Exchange rates can influence the demand for the country's exports, which in turn affects the country's production and income level. A strong currency may reduce demand for the country's exports, increase the volume of products imported by the country, and therefore reduce the country's production and national income. A very weak currency can cause speculative outflows and reduce the amount of funds available to finance growth by businesses.

- *Inflation.* Inflation can affect consumers' purchasing power and therefore their demand for an MNC's goods. It also indirectly affects a country's financial condition by influencing the country's interest rates and currency value. A high level of inflation may also lead to a decline in economic growth.

Most financial factors that affect a country's economic conditions are difficult to forecast. Thus, even if an MNC considers them in its country risk assessment, it may still make poor decisions because of an improper forecast of the country's financial factors.

Some financial conditions may be caused by political risk. For example, the September 11, 2001 terrorist attack on the United States affected US-based MNCs because of political risk and financial risk. Political uncertainty caused uncertainty about economic conditions, which resulted in a reduction in spending by consumers and, therefore, a reduction in cash flows of MNCs.

Types of country risk assessment

Although there is no consensus as to how country risk can best be assessed, some guidelines have been developed. The first step is to recognize the difference between: (1) an overall risk assessment of a country without consideration of the MNC's business, and (2) the risk assessment of a country as it relates to the MNC's type of business. The first type can be referred to as **macroassessment** of country risk and the latter type as a **microassessment**. Each type is discussed in turn.

Macroassessment of country risk

A macroassessment involves consideration of all variables that affect country risk except those unique to a particular firm or industry. This type of risk is convenient in that it remains the same for a given country, regardless of the firm or industry of concern; however, it excludes relevant information that could improve the accuracy of the assessment. Although a macroassessment of country risk is not ideal for any individual MNC, it serves as a foundation that can then be modified to reflect the particular business of the MNC.

Any macroassessment model should consider both political and financial characteristics of the country being assessed:

- *Political factors.* Political factors include the relationship of the host government with the MNC's home country government, the attitude of people in the host country toward the MNC's government, the historical stability of the host government, the vulnerability of the host government to political takeovers, and the probability of war between the host country and neighbouring countries. Consideration of such political factors will indicate the probability of political events that may affect an MNC and the magnitude of the impact.

- *Financial factors.* The financial factors of a macroassessment model should include GDP growth, inflation trends, government budget levels (and the government deficit), interest rates, unemployment, the country's reliance on export income, the balance of trade, and foreign exchange controls. The list of financial factors could easily be extended several pages. The factors listed here represent just a subset of the financial factors considered when evaluating the financial strength of a country.

Uncertainty surrounding a macroassessment. There is clearly a degree of subjectivity in identifying the relevant political and financial factors for a macroassessment of country risk. There is also some subjectivity in determining the importance of each factor for the overall macroassessment for a particular country. For instance, one assessor may assign a much higher weight (degree of importance) to real GDP growth than another assessor. Finally, there is some subjectivity in predicting these financial factors. Because of these various types of subjectivity, it is not surprising that risk assessors often arrive at different opinions after completing a macroassessment of country risk.

Microassessment of country risk

While a macroassessment of country risk provides an indication of the country's overall status, it does not assess country risk from the perspective of the particular business of concern. A microassessment of country risk is needed to determine how the country risk relates to the specific MNC.

Since Adidas conducts a large amount of international business, it must monitor country risk in many countries. Adidas could be affected by country risk in several ways. First, a conflict between Europe and a specific foreign country could cause either the foreign country's government or its people to vent their anger against an Adidas subsidiary in that country. Thus, Adidas could be a target simply because it is viewed as a European company, even if all the employees at that subsidiary are locals. Second, a change in a foreign government could result in new tax laws and other restrictions imposed on subsidiaries of European firms or firms from any other country that are based there. Third, other local shoe manufacturers could possibly use government ties to impose more restrictions against Adidas so that they could have a competitive advantage in the country of concern. Fourth, Adidas' subsidiary could be adversely affected by other political problems that cause a deterioration in economic conditions in that country. Any of these events could cause an increase in the subsidiary's expenses or a decline in its revenue.

The specific impact of a particular form of country risk can affect MNCs in different ways.

Country Z has been assigned a relatively low macroassessment by most experts due to its poor financial condition. Two MNCs are deciding whether to set up subsidiaries in Country Z. Carco ltd is considering developing a subsidiary that would produce automobiles and sell them locally, while Milco ltd plans to build a subsidiary that would produce military supplies. Carco's plan to build an automobile subsidiary does not appear to be feasible, unless there is a shortage of automobile producers in Country Z.

Country Z's government may be committed to purchasing a given amount of military supplies, regardless of how weak the economy is. Thus, Milco's plan to build a military supply subsidiary may still be feasible, even though Country Z's financial condition is poor.

It is possible, however, that Country Z's government will order its military supplies from a locally owned firm because it wants its supply needs to remain confidential. This possibility is an element of country risk because it is a country characteristic (or attitude) that can affect the feasibility of a project. Yet, this specific characteristic is relevant only to Milco ltd and not to Carco.

This example illustrates how an appropriate country risk assessment varies with the firm, industry, and project of concern and therefore why a macroassessment of country risk has its limitations. A microassessment is also necessary when evaluating the country risk related to a particular project proposed by a particular firm.

In addition to political variables, financial variables must also be included in a microassessment of country risk. Microfactors include the sensitivity of the firm's business to real GDP growth, inflation trends, interest rates, and other factors. Due to differences in business characteristics, some firms are more susceptible to the host country's economy than others. Exhibit 16.2 reports a survey of risk factors as perceived by large MNCs.

In summary, the overall assessment of country risk consists of four parts:

1. Macropolitical risk
2. Macrofinancial risk
3. Micropolitical risk
4. Microfinancial risk

Exhibit 16.2 Survey of top 1,000 multinationals (2004) – percentage of total respondents listing item as a critical risk

Most critical risk to firm operations	%
Govt Regulations/legal decisions	64
Country financial risk	60
Currency interest rate volatility	51
Political and social disturbances	46
Corporate governance	30
Absence of rule of law	29
Theft of intellectual property	28
Terrorist attack	26
Security threats to employees and assets	26
Disruption of key supplier/customer/partner	23
Product quality and safety problems	20
IT disruption	19
Employee fraud or sabotage	10
Natural disasters	6
Activist attacks on global or corporate brands	5

Source: FDI Confidence Index, Copyright A.T. Kearney, 2004. All rights reserved. Reprinted with permission

Although these parts can be consolidated to generate a single country risk rating, it may be useful to keep them separate so that an MNC can identify the various ways its direct foreign investment or exporting operations are exposed to country risk.

TECHNIQUES TO ASSESS COUNTRY RISK

Once a firm identifies all the macro- and microfactors that deserve consideration in the country risk assessment, it may wish to implement a system for evaluating these factors and determining a country risk rating. Various techniques are available to achieve this objective. The following are some of the more popular techniques:

■ Checklist approach
■ Delphi technique
■ Quantitative analysis
■ Inspection visits
■ Combination of techniques

Each technique is briefly discussed in turn.

Checklist approach

A checklist approach involves making a judgement on all the political and financial factors (both macro and micro) that contribute to a firm's assessment of country risk. Ratings are assigned to a list of various financial and political factors, and these ratings are then consolidated to derive an overall assessment of country risk. Some factors (such as real GDP growth) can be measured from available data, while others (such as probability of entering a war) must be subjectively measured.

A substantial amount of information about countries is available on the Internet. This information can be used to develop ratings of various factors used to assess country risk. The factors are then converted to some numerical rating in order to assess a particular country. Those factors thought to have a greater influence on country risk should be assigned greater weights. Both the measurement of some factors and the weighting scheme implemented are subjective.

Delphi technique

The **Delphi technique** involves the collection of independent opinions on country risk without group discussion by the assessors (such as employees or outside consultants) who provide these opinions. Though the Delphi technique can be useful, it is based on subjective opinions, which may vary among assessors. The MNC can average these opinions in some manner and even assess the degree of disagreement by measuring the dispersion of opinions.

Quantitative analysis

Once the financial and political variables have been measured for a period of time, models for quantitative analysis can attempt to identify the characteristics that influence the level of country risk. For example, regression analysis may be used to assess risk, since it can measure the sensitivity of one variable to other variables. A firm could regress a measure of its business activity (such as its percentage increase in sales) against country characteristics (such as real growth in GDP) over a series of previous months or quarters. Results from such an analysis will indicate the susceptibility of a particular business to a country's economy. This is valuable information to incorporate into the overall evaluation of country risk.

Although quantitative models can quantify the impact of variables on each other, they do not necessarily indicate a country's problems before they actually occur (preferably before the firm's decision to pursue a project in that country). Nor can they evaluate subjective data that cannot be quantified. In addition, historical trends of various country characteristics are not always useful for anticipating an upcoming crisis.

Inspection visits

Inspection visits involve travelling to a country and meeting with government officials, business executives, and/or consumers. Such meetings can help clarify any uncertain opinions the firm has about a country. Indeed, some variables, such as intercountry relationships, may be difficult to assess without a trip to the host country.

Combination of techniques

A survey of 193 corporations heavily involved in foreign business found that about half of them have no formal method of assessing country risk. This does not mean that they neglect to assess country risk, but rather that there is no proven method to use. Consequently, many MNCs use a variety of techniques, possibly using a checklist approach to develop an overall country risk rating and then using the Delphi technique, quantitative analysis, and inspection visits to assign ratings to the various factors.

EXAMPLE

Mission ltd recognizes that it must consider several financial and political factors in its country risk analysis of the Ukraine, where it plans to establish a subsidiary. Mission creates a checklist of several factors and assigns a rating to each factor. It uses the Delphi technique to rate various political factors. It uses quantitative analysis to predict future economic conditions in the Ukraine so that it can rate various financial factors. It conducts an inspection visit to complement its assessment of the financial and political factors.

MEASURING COUNTRY RISK

Deriving an overall country risk rating using a checklist approach requires separate ratings for political and financial risk. First, the political factors are assigned values within some arbitrarily chosen range (such as values from 1 to 5, where 5 is the best value/lowest risk). Next, these political factors are assigned weights (representing degree of importance), which should add up to 100%. The assigned values of the factors times their respective weights can then be summed to derive a political risk rating.

The process is then repeated to derive the financial risk rating. All financial factors are assigned values (from 1 to 5, where 5 is the best value/lowest risk). Then the assigned values of the factors times their respective weights can be summed to derive a financial risk rating.

Once the political and financial ratings have been derived, a country's overall country risk rating as it relates to a specific project can be determined by assigning weights to the political and financial ratings according to their perceived importance. The importance of political risk versus financial risk varies with the intent of the MNC. An MNC considering direct foreign investment to attract demand in that country must be highly concerned about financial risk. An MNC establishing a foreign manufacturing plant and planning to export the goods from there should be more concerned with political risk.

If the political risk is thought to be much more influential on a particular project than the financial risk, it will receive a higher weight than the financial risk rating (together both weights must total 100%). The political and financial ratings multiplied by their respective weights will determine the overall country risk rating for a country as it relates to a particular project.

EXAMPLE

Assume that Cougar plc plans to build a steel plant in the Country X. It has used the Delphi technique and quantitative analysis to derive ratings for various political and financial factors. The discussion here focuses on how to consolidate the ratings to derive an overall country risk rating.

Exhibit 16.3 illustrates Cougar's country risk assessment of Country X. Notice in Exhibit 16.3 that two political factors and five financial factors contribute to the overall country risk rating in this example. Cougar plc will consider projects only in countries that have a country risk rating of 3.5 or higher, based on its country risk rating.

EXAMPLE

Cougar plc has assigned the values and weights to the factors as shown in Exhibit 16.4. In this example, the company generally assigns the financial factors higher ratings than the political factors. The financial condition of Country X has therefore been assessed more favourably than the political condition. Industry growth is the most important financial factor in Country X, based on its 40% weighting. The bureaucracy is thought to be the most important political factor, based on a weighting of 70%; regulation of international fund transfers receives the remaining 30% weighting. The political risk

Exhibit 16.3 Determining the overall country risk rating

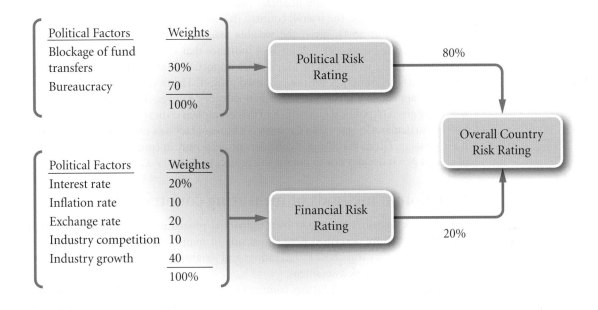

Exhibit 16.4 Derivation of the overall country risk rating for country based on assumed information

(1)	(2) Rating Assigned by company to factor within a range of 1–5	(3) Weight Assigned by company to factor according to importance	(4) = (2) × (3) Weighted value of factor
Blockage of fund transfers	4	30%	1.2
Bureaucracy	3	70	2.1
Financial Risk Factors		100%	3.3 = **Political risk rating**
Interest rate	5	20%	1.0
Inflation rate	4	10	0.4
Exchange rate	4	20	0.8
Industry competition	5	10	0.5
Industry growth	3	40	1.2
		100%	3.9 = **Financial risk rating**
(1)	(2)	(3)	(4) = (2) × (3)
Weight Assigned	Rating as determined above	Weight assigned by company to each risk factor	Weighted Rating
Political risk	3.3	80%	2.64
Financial risk	3.9	20	0.78
		100%	3.42 = **Overall country risk rating**

rating is estimated at 3.3 by adding the products of the assigned ratings (Column 2) and weights (Column 3) of the political risk factors.

The financial risk is computed to be 3.9, based on adding the products of the assigned ratings and the weights of the financial risk factors. Once the political and financial ratings are determined, the overall country risk rating can be derived (as shown at the bottom of Exhibit 16.4), given the weights assigned to political and financial risk. Column 3 at the bottom of Exhibit 16.4 indicates that Cougar perceives political risk (receiving an 80% weight) to be much more important than financial risk (receiving a 20% weight) in Country X for the proposed project. The overall country risk rating of 3.42 may appear low given the individual category ratings. This is due to the heavy weighting given to political risk, which in this example is critical from the firm's perspective. In particular, Cougar views Country X's bureaucracy as a critical factor and assigns it a low rating. Given that Cougar considers projects only in countries that have a rating of at least 3.5; it decides not to pursue the project in Country X.

Variation in methods of measuring country risk

Country risk assessors have their own individual procedures for quantifying country risk. The procedure described here is just one of many. Most procedures are similar, though, in that they somehow assign ratings and weights to all individual characteristics relevant to country risk assessment.

The number of relevant factors comprising both the political risk and the financial risk categories will vary with the country being assessed and the type of corporate operations planned for that country. The assignment of values to the factors, along with the degree of importance (weights) assigned to the factors, will also vary with the country being assessed and the type of corporate operations planned for that country.

Using the country risk rating for decision making

If the country risk is too high, then the firm does not need to analyze the feasibility of the proposed project any further. Some firms may contend that no risk is too high when considering a project. Their reasoning is that if the potential return is high enough, the project is worth undertaking. When employee safety is a concern, however, the project may be rejected regardless of its potential return.

Even after a project is accepted and implemented, the MNC must continue to monitor country risk. With a labour-intensive MNC, the host country may feel it is benefiting from a subsidiary's existence (due to the subsidiary's employment of local people), and the chance of expropriation may be low. Nevertheless, several other forms of country risk could suddenly make the MNC consider divesting the project. Furthermore, decisions regarding subsidiary expansion, fund transfers to the parent, and sources of financing can all be affected by any changes in country risk. Since country risk can change dramatically over time, periodic reassessment is required, especially for less stable countries.

Regardless of how country risk analysis is conducted, MNCs are often unable to predict crises in various countries. MNCs should recognize their limitations when assessing country risk and consider ways they might limit their exposure to a possible increase in that risk.

COMPARING RISK RATINGS AMONG COUNTRIES

An MNC may evaluate country risk for several countries, perhaps to determine where to establish a subsidiary. One approach to comparing political and financial ratings among countries, advocated by some foreign risk managers, is a **foreign investment risk matrix (FIRM)**, which displays the financial (or economic) and political risk by intervals ranging across the matrix from "poor" to "good". Each country can be positioned in its appropriate location on the matrix based on its political rating and financial rating.

USING THE WEB

Country risk ratings If an MNC wants to consider a country risk assessment by outside evaluators, it can obtain a country risk rating for any country at http://www.oecd.org and search for "Country Risk Classification" within the site.

ACTUAL COUNTRY RISK RATINGS ACROSS COUNTRIES

http://

Visit **http://www.duke.edu/~charvey** for the results of Campbell R. Harvey's political, economic, and financial country risk analysis.

Country risk ratings are shown in Exhibit 16.5. This exhibit is not necessarily applicable to a particular MNC that wants to pursue international business because the risk assessment here may not focus on the factors that are relevant to that MNC. Nevertheless, the exhibit illustrates how the risk rating can vary substantially among countries. Many industrialized countries have high ratings, indicating low risk. Emerging countries tend to have lower ratings. Country risk ratings change over time in response to the factors that influence a country's rating.

INCORPORATING COUNTRY RISK IN CAPITAL BUDGETING

If the risk rating of a country is in the tolerable range, any project related to that country deserves further consideration. Country risk can be incorporated in the capital budgeting analysis of a proposed project by adjusting the discount rate or by adjusting the estimated cash flows. Each method is discussed here.

Adjustment of the discount rate

The discount rate of a proposed project is supposed to reflect the required rate of return on that project. Thus, the discount rate can be adjusted to account for the country risk. The lower the country risk rating, the higher the perceived risk and the higher the discount rate applied to the project's cash flows. This approach is convenient in that one adjustment to the capital budgeting analysis can capture country risk. However, there is no precise formula for adjusting the discount rate to incorporate country risk. The adjustment is somewhat arbitrary and may therefore cause feasible projects to be rejected or infeasible projects to be accepted.

Adjustment of the estimated cash flows

Perhaps the most appropriate method for incorporating forms of country risk in a capital budgeting analysis is to estimate how the cash flows would be affected by each form of risk. For example, if there is a 20% probability that the host government will temporarily block funds from the subsidiary to the parent, the MNC should estimate the project's net present value (NPV) under these circumstances, realizing that there is a 20% chance that this NPV will occur.

Exhibit 16.5 Country risk ratings among countries (maximum rating is 100)

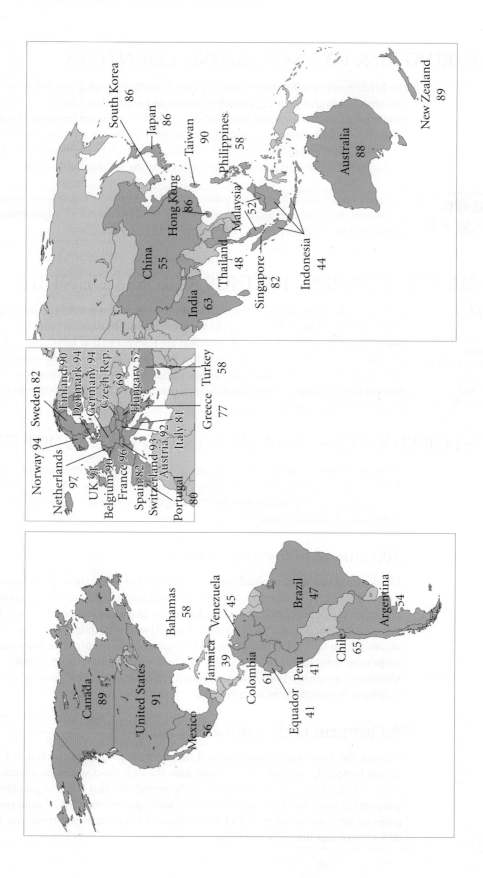

In 1995 Ireland's Electricity Supply Board (ESB) a government owned firm started looking to build electricity power plants abroad and supply electricity abroad. The legal framework for such development was not in place in either Germany or France. They eventually chose Spain as offering a suitable legal framework. The area they chose was the Basque Country because of its good infrastructure, education and local supply of natural gas needed to produce the electricity. They set up a wholly owned subsidiary called Bizkaia Energia and waited for reports by the central government and the Basque parliament concerning the environmental impact of their plans. They also have to take into account the possibility of terrorist group ETA demanding Basque independence. ESB estimated that ETA would not be a threat. Reasons were not given, indeed MNCs rarely report their precise country risk calculations as such

judgements are obviously politically sensitive. In this case, one would have good reason to believe that ETA would not see an Irish company as hostile or as a symbol of suppression. Ireland historically had been part of the British Empire and had to fight for its freedom, a path that ETA aspired to. It is also a part of the Celtic fringe of Europe along with Brittany, Wales and Scotland with whom the Basque maintained cultural links. In fact over the subsequent nine years there were no incidents with employees. In 2005, the company sold 50% of its electricity producing plant to a Japanese multinational Osaka Gas. Shell will sell gas to and buy electricity from the ESB plant in Spain. By judging the political risk correctly at a national and local level and by having certain cultural advantages, ESB was able to develop electricity supply before other major MNCs.

If there is a chance that a host government takeover will occur, the foreign project's *NPV* under these conditions should be estimated. Each possible form of risk has an estimated impact on the foreign project's cash flows and therefore on the project's *NPV*. By analyzing each possible impact, the MNC can determine the probability distribution of *NPV*s for the project. Its accept/reject decision on the project will be based on its assessment of the probability that the project will generate a positive *NPV*, as well as the size of possible *NPV* outcomes. Though this procedure may seem somewhat tedious, it directly incorporates forms of country risk into the cash flow estimates and explicitly illustrates the possible results from implementing the project. The more convenient method of adjusting the discount rate in accordance with the country risk rating does not indicate the probability distribution of possible outcomes.

EXAMPLE

Reconsider the example of Spartan ltd that was discussed in Chapter 14. Assume for the moment that all the initial assumptions regarding Spartan's initial investment, project life, pricing policy, exchange rate projections, and so on still apply. Now, however, we will incorporate two country risk characteristics that were not included in the initial analysis. First, assume that there is a 30% chance that the withholding tax imposed by the Singapore government will be at a 20% rate rather than a 10% rate. Second, assume that there is a 40% chance that the Singapore government will provide Spartan a payment (salvage value) of S$7 million rather than S$12 million. These two possibilities represent a form of country risk.

Assume that these two possible situations are unrelated. To determine how the *NPV* is affected by each of these scenarios, a capital budgeting analysis similar to that shown in Exhibit 14.2 in Chapter 14 can be used. If this analysis is already on a spreadsheet, the *NPV* can easily be estimated by adjusting line items no. 15 (withholding tax on remitted funds) and no. 17 (salvage value). The capital budgeting analysis measures the effect of a 20% withholding tax rate in Exhibit 16.6. Since items before line no. 14 are not affected, these items are not shown here. If the 20% withholding tax rate is imposed, the *NPV* of the four-year project is £926,427.

Now consider the possibility of the lower salvage value, while using the initial assumption of a 10% withholding tax rate. The capital budgeting analysis accounts for the lower salvage value in Exhibit 16.7. The estimated *NPV* is £628,319, based on this scenario.

Finally, consider the possibility that both the higher withholding tax and the lower salvage value occur. The capital budgeting analysis in Exhibit 16.8 accounts for both of these situations. The *NPV* is estimated to be –£16,966.

Once estimates for the *NPV* are derived for each scenario, Spartan ltd can attempt to determine whether the project is feasible. There are two country risk variables that are uncertain, and there are four possible *NPV* outcomes, as illustrated in Exhibit 16.9. Given the probability of each possible situation and the assumption that the withholding tax outcome is independent from the salvage value outcome, joint probabilities can be determined for each pair of outcomes by multiplying the probabilities of the two outcomes of concern. Since the probability of a 20% withholding tax is 30%, the probability of a 10% withholding tax is 70%. Given that the probability of a lower salvage value is 40%, the probability of the initial estimate for the salvage value is 60%. Thus, scenario

Exhibit 16.6   Analysis of the original project (Exhibit 14.2) with a 20% withholding tax: Spartan ltd

14. S$ remitted by subsidiary (100% of net cash flow)	S$6,000,000	S$6,000,000	S$7,600,000	S$8,400,000
15. Withholding tax on remitted funds (**20%**)	S$1,200,000	S$1,200,000	S$1,520,000	S$1,680,000
16. S$ remitted after withholding taxes	S$4,800,000	S$4,800,000	S$6,080,000	S$6,720,000
17. Salvage value				S$12,000,000
18. Exchange rate of S$	£0.33	£0.33	£0.33	£0.33
19. Cash flows to parent	£1,584,000	£1,584,000	£2,006,400	£6,177,600
20. *PV* of parent cash flows (15% discount rate)	£1,377,391	£1,197,732	£1,319,241	£3,532,063
21. Initial investment by parent	–£6,500,000			
22. CUMULATIVE *NPV*		–£5,122,609	–£3,924,877	–£2,605,636	£926,427

Exhibit 16.7   Analysis of the original project (Exhibit 14.2) with a reduced salvage value: Spartan ltd

14. S$ remitted by subsidiary (100% of net cash flow)	S$6,000,000	S$6,000,000	S$7,600,000	S$8,400,000
15. Withholding tax on remitted funds (10%)	S$600,000	S$600,000	S$760,000	S$840,000
16. S$ remitted after withholding taxes	S$5,400,000	S$5,400,000	S$6,840,000	S$7,560,000
17. Salvage value				S$7,000,000
18. Exchange rate of S$	£0.33	£0.33	£0.33	£0.33
19. Cash flows to parent	£1,782,000	£1,782,000	£2,257,200	£4,804,800
20. *PV* of parent cash flows (15% discount rate)	£1,549,565	£1,347,448	£1,484,146	£2,747,160
21. Initial investment by parent	£6,500,000			
22. CUMULATIVE *NPV*		–£4,950,435	–£3,602,987	–£2,118,841	£628,319

Exhibit 16.8 Analysis of project based on a 20% withholding tax *and* a reduced salvage value: Spartan ltd

14. S$ remitted by subsidiary (100% of net cash flow)		6,000,000	6,000,000	7,600,000	8,400,000
15. Withholding tax on remitted funds (20%)		1,200,000	1,200,000	1,520,000	1,680,000
16. S$ remitted after withholding taxes		4,800,000	4,800,000	6,080,000	6,720,000
17. Salvage value					7,000,000
18. Exchange rate of S$		£0.33	£0.33	£0.33	£0.33
19. Cash flows to parent		£1,584,000	£1,584,000	£2,006,400	£4,527,600
20. *PV* of parent cash flows (15% discount rate)		£1,377,391	£1,197,732	£1,319,241	£2,588,670
21. Initial investment by parent	£6,500,000				
22. CUMULATIVE *NPV*		−£5,122,609	−£3,924,877	−£2,605,636	−£16,966

Exhibit 16.9 Summary of estimated *NPV*s across the possible scenarios: Spartan ltd

Scenario	Withholding Tax Imposed by Singapore Government	Salvage Value of Project	NPV	Probability
1 (Exhibit 14.2)	10%	S$12,000,000	£1,571,712	(70%)(60%) = **42%**
2 (Exhibit 16.5)	20%	S$12,000,000	£926,427	(30%)(60%) = **18%**
3 (Exhibit 16.6)	10%	S$7,000,000	£628,319	(70%)(40%) = **28%**
4 (Exhibit 16.7)	20%	S$7,000,000	−£16,966	(30%)(40%) = **12%**
	E(NPV)	= £1,571,712 (42%)		
		+ £926,427 (18%)		
		+ £628,319 (28%)		
		−£16,966 (12%)		
		= £1,000,769		

no. 1 (10% withholding tax and S$12 million salvage value) created in Chapter 14 has a joint probability (probability that both outcomes will occur) of 70% × 60% = 42%.

In Exhibit 16.9, scenario no. 4 is the only scenario in which there is a negative *NPV*. Since this scenario has a 12% chance of occurring, there is a 12% chance that the project will adversely affect the value of the firm. Put another way, there is an 88% chance that the project will enhance the firm's value. The expected value of the project's *NPV* can be measured as the sum of each scenario's estimated *NPV* multiplied by its respective probability across all four scenarios, as shown at the bottom of Exhibit 16.8. Most MNCs would accept the proposed project, given the likelihood that the project will have a positive *NPV* and the limited loss that would occur under even the worst case scenario.

Using an electronic spreadsheet to account for uncertainty. In the previous example, the initial assumptions for most input variables were used as if they were known with certainty. However, Spartan ltd could account for the uncertainty of country risk characteristics (as in our current example) while also allowing for uncertainty in the other variables as well. This process can be facilitated if the analysis is on a computer spreadsheet (a spreadsheet for Spartan ltd is included in the support material).

EXAMPLE

If Spartan ltd wishes to allow for three possible exchange rate trends, it can adjust the exchange rate projections for each of the four scenarios assessed in the current example. Each scenario will reflect a specific withholding tax outcome, a specific salvage value outcome, and a specific exchange rate trend. There will be a total of 12 scenarios, with each scenario having an estimated *NPV* and a probability of occurrence. Based on the estimated *NPV* and the probability of each scenario, Spartan ltd can then measure the expected value of the *NPV* and the probability that the *NPV* will be positive, which leads to a decision regarding whether the project is feasible.

How country risk affects financial decisions

Country risk analysis is a separate source of risk particular to international investment. Unlike other sources of risk, country risk tends to be concerned with the possibility of sudden big events described as crises. This can be in the form of a sudden collapse in the value of the currency, such as the Russian rouble (see below). Or it can be in the form of a sudden collapse in the economy, or both. In contrast, other sources of risk in international investment, such as business risk and currency risk, lead to outcomes that can be represented by the normal probability curve. They offer a range of outcomes from being a little better or worse than expected to being much better or worse than expected. The normal probability curve captures the greater likelihood of smaller deviations from expectations compared to larger deviations. But where a crisis is anything more than a very remote possibility, combining such a one off risk with currency and business risk becomes difficult. Scenario analysis can be useful, particularly worst case scenarios. As a result, two investments offering the same return may be chosen on the basis of their ability to cope with crises rather than the normal measure of risk, i.e. the standard deviation of returns. The history of international finance (see Chapter 6), is littered with such crises as the following further examples illustrate.

Gulf War. As a result of the crisis that culminated in the Gulf War in 1991, many MNCs attempted to reassess country risk. Terrorism became a major concern. MNCs used various methods to protect against terrorism. Cross-country travel by executives was reduced, as MNCs used teleconference calls instead. Some MNCs with subsidiaries in Saudi Arabia temporarily closed some of their operations, allowing employees from other countries to return home. Some projects that were being considered for countries that could be subject to terrorist attacks were postponed. Even projects that appeared to be feasible from a financial perspective were postponed because of the potential danger to employees.

In addition to the threat of terrorism, the crisis influenced cash flows of MNCs in many other ways. The effects varied with the characteristics of each MNC. The more obvious effects of the crisis were reduced travel and higher oil prices. The reduction in travel adversely affected airlines, hotels, restaurants, luggage manufacturers, tourist attractions, rental car agencies, and cruise lines.

Asian crisis. As a result of the 1997–98 Asian crisis, MNCs realized that they had underestimated the potential financial problems that could occur in the high-growth Asian countries. Country risk analysts had concentrated on the high degree of economic growth, even though the Asian countries had high debt levels and their commercial banks had massive loan problems. The loan problems were not obvious because commercial banks were typically not required to disclose much information about their loans. Some MNCs recognized the potential problems in Asia, though, and discontinued their exports to those Asian businesses that were not willing to pay in advance.

Russian crisis. Large government budget deficits in 1996 and 1997 led to a build up of government debts. To reduce the debt the government introduced austerity packages which resulted in political unrest and discontent with the Prime Minister. In July of 1998 the IMF made a loan to the Russian government of $15bn which was accompanied by $22.6bn from international lenders. In addition the Asian crisis led to withdrawal by investors in emerging markets, such as Russia, causing adverse balances on the financial (capital) account. On 17 August 1998 the government set a partial moratorium (nonpayment) on foreign debt, the currency fell by 10%. The following day the parliament called for the President Boris Yeltsin to resign. On the 23rd the President sacked the Prime Minister. The Russian stock market fell. On the 25th, the government announced rouble debt restructuring that foreign investors say amounts to default. On 26 August rouble–dollar trading was suspended by the central bank and there was a run on Russian banks (customers withdrew their deposits in cash). Many banks were unable to meet their commitments. September 4, inflation was reported as having jumped to 15% per month; the value of the rouble had fallen by 64% compared to 25 August. September 11, the government failed to pay $685 million in interest payments. October 21, the State backed railway company defaulted on its bond payments. The gross domestic product (value of all output) was reported as having fallen by 10% year on year. Inflation was over 50% higher than the previous year and shares hit all time lows. The following year Putin became Prime Minister and subsequently President. The effect of these events on the value of the rouble is illustrated in Exhibit 16.10.

The Russian crisis combined with the earlier Asian crisis is also thought to have prompted the Brazilian crisis in January 1999 when the Brazilian real abandoned its

Exhibit 16.10 Russian currency crisis

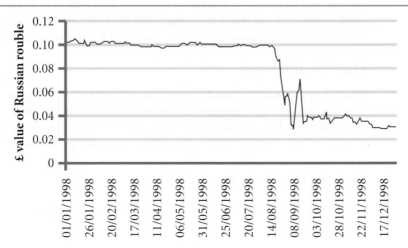

crawling peg arrangement and became freely floating. During that month the real declined by 40% against the British pound.

REDUCING EXPOSURE TO HOST GOVERNMENT TAKEOVERS

Although direct foreign investment offers several possible benefits, country risk can offset such benefits. The most severe country risk is a host government takeover. This type of takeover may result in major losses, especially when the MNC does not have any power to negotiate with the host government.

The following are the most common strategies used to reduce exposure to a host government takeover:

- Use a short-term horizon.
- Rely on unique supplies or technology.
- Hire local labour.
- Borrow local funds.
- Purchase insurance.
- Use project finance.

Use a short-term horizon

An MNC may concentrate on recovering cash flow quickly so that in the event of expropriation, losses are minimized. An MNC would also exert only a minimum effort to replace worn-out equipment and machinery at the subsidiary. It may even phase out its overseas investment by selling off its assets to local investors or the government in stages over time.

Rely on unique supplies or technology

If the subsidiary can bring in supplies from its headquarters (or a sister subsidiary) that cannot be duplicated locally, the host government will not be able to take over and operate the subsidiary without those supplies. Also the MNC can cut off the supplies if the subsidiary is treated unfairly.

If the subsidiary can hide the technology in its production process, a government takeover will be less likely. A takeover would be successful in this case only if the MNC would provide the necessary technology, and the MNC would do so only under conditions of a friendly takeover that would ensure that it received adequate compensation.

Hire local labour

If local employees of the subsidiary would be affected by the host government's takeover, they can pressure their government to avoid such action. However, the government could still keep those employees after taking over the subsidiary. Thus, this strategy has only limited effectiveness in avoiding or limiting a government takeover.

Borrow local funds

If the subsidiary borrows funds locally, local banks will be concerned about its future performance. If for any reason a government takeover would reduce the probability that the banks would receive their loan repayments promptly, they might attempt to prevent a takeover by the host government. However, the host government may guarantee repayment to the banks, so this strategy has only limited effectiveness. Nevertheless, it could still be preferable to a situation in which the MNC not only loses the subsidiary but also still owes home country creditors.

Purchase insurance

Insurance can be purchased to cover the risk of expropriation. For example, the UK government provides insurance through the Export Credit Guarantee Department (ECGD). The insurance premiums paid by a firm depend on the degree of insurance coverage and the risk associated with the firm. Typically, however, any insurance policy will cover only a portion of the company's total exposure to country risk.

Many home countries of MNCs have investment guarantee programmes that insure to some extent the risks of expropriation, wars, or currency blockage. Some guarantee programmes have a one-year waiting period or longer before compensation is paid on losses due to expropriation. Also, some insurance policies do not cover all forms of expropriation. Furthermore, to be eligible for such insurance, the subsidiary might be required by the country to concentrate on exporting rather than on local sales. Even if a subsidiary qualifies for insurance, there is a cost. Any insurance will typically cover only a portion of the assets and may specify a maximum duration of coverage, such as 15 or 20 years. A subsidiary must weigh the benefits of this insurance against the cost of the policy's premiums and potential losses in excess of coverage. The insurance can be helpful, but it does not by itself prevent losses due to expropriation.

In 1993, Russia established an insurance fund to protect MNCs against various forms of country risk. The Russian government took this action to encourage more direct foreign investment in Russia.

The World Bank has established an affiliate called the Multilateral Investment Guarantee Agency (MIGA) to provide political insurance for MNCs with direct foreign investment in less developed countries. MIGA offers insurance against expropriation, breach of contract, currency inconvertibility, war, and civil disturbances.

Use project finance

Many of the world's largest infrastructure projects are structured as "project finance" deals, which limit the exposure of the MNCs. First, project finance deals are heavily financed with credit. Thus, the MNC's exposure is limited because it invests only a limited amount of equity in the project. Second, a bank may guarantee the payments to the MNC. Third, project finance deals are unique in that they are secured by the project's future revenues from production. That is, the project is separate from the MNC that manages the project. The loans are "non-recourse" in that the creditor cannot pursue the MNC for payment but only the assets and cash flows of the project itself. Thus, the cash flows of the project are relevant, and not the credit risk of the borrower. Because of the transparency of the process arising from the single purpose and finite plan for termination, project finance allows projects to be financed that otherwise would likely not obtain financing under conventional terms. A host government is unlikely to take over this type of project because it would have to assume the existing liabilities due to the credit arrangement.

EXAMPLE   The largest project financed by the International Financial Corp. (IFC) is the $1.34 billion Mozal aluminium smelter in Mozambique. The IFC's investment in the smelter involves the extension of $133 million of credit, which is more than Mozambique's annual GDP. The credit risk of the government of Mozambique is very high, as is the political risk inherent in the project, especially since the country has experienced 20 years of civil war. The project is managed by Mitsubishi, BHB Billiton, and the Industrial Development Corp. of South Africa. The plant and the aluminium output serve as collateral for the loan. The project has had a major impact on the economy of Mozambique.

SUMMARY

- The factors used by MNCs to measure a country's political risk include the attitude of consumers toward purchasing locally produced goods, the host government's actions toward the MNC, the blockage of fund transfers, currency inconvertibility, war, bureaucracy, and corruption. These factors can increase the costs of international business.

- The factors used by MNCs to measure a country's financial risk are the country's interest rates, exchange rates, and inflation rates.

- The techniques typically used by MNCs to measure the country risk are the checklist approach, the Delphi technique, quantitative analysis, and inspection visits. Since no one technique covers all aspects of country risk, a combination of these techniques is commonly used. The measurement of country risk is essentially a weighted average of the political

or financial factors that are perceived to comprise country risk. Each MNC has its own view as to the weights that should be assigned to each factor. Thus, the overall rating for a country may vary among MNCs.

- Once country risk is measured, it can be incorporated into a capital budgeting analysis by adjustment of the discount rate. The adjustment is somewhat arbitrary, however, and may lead to improper decision making. An alternative method of incorporating country risk analysis into capital budgeting is to explicitly account for each factor that affects country risk. For each possible form of risk, the MNC can recalculate the foreign project's net present value under the condition that the event (such as blocked funds, increased taxes, etc.) occurs.

CRITICAL DEBATE

Does country risk analysis make other forms of risk meaningless?

Proposition. Where there is a risk of a 40% fall or more in the value of a currency, worrying about a 3% standard deviation makes no sense. Firms should analyze their ability to cope with such disaster scenarios and use this analysis to decide whether the expected returns are worthwhile.

Opposing view. No. These kinds of risks can affect all firms and in a sense is an unavoidable risk of international finance. The lessons of diversification and currency protection from looking at lower levels of risk are all the more relevant given country risk.

With whom do you agree? Which argument do you support? Offer your own opinion on this issue.

Self test

Answers are provided in Appendix A at the back of the text.

1. Key West Co. (a US company) exports highly advanced phone system components to its subsidiary shops on islands in the Caribbean. The components are purchased by consumers to improve their phone systems. These components are not produced in other countries. Explain how political risk factors could adversely affect the profitability of Key West Co.

2. Using the information in question 1, explain how financial risk factors could adversely affect the profitability of Key West Co.

3. Given the information in question 1, do you expect that Key West Co is more concerned about the adverse effects of political risk or of financial risk?

4. Explain how a terrorist attack might affect an MNC.

5. Rockford ltd plans to expand its successful business by establishing a subsidiary in France. However, it is concerned that after two years the French government will either impose a special tax on any income sent back to the US parent or order the subsidiary to be sold at that time. The executives have estimated that either of these scenarios has a 15% chance of occurring. They have decided to add four percentage points to the project's required rate of return to incorporate the country risk that they are concerned about in the capital budgeting analysis. Is there a better way to more precisely incorporate the country risk of concern here?

Questions and applications

1. **Forms of country risk.** List some forms of country risk other than a takeover of a subsidiary by the host government, and briefly elaborate on how each factor can affect the risk to the MNC. Identify common financial factors for an MNC to consider when assessing country risk. Briefly elaborate on how each factor can affect the risk to the MNC.

2. **Country risk assessment.** Describe the steps involved in assessing country risk once all relevant information has been gathered.

3. **Uncertainty surrounding the country risk assessment.** Describe the possible errors involved in assessing country risk. In other words, explain why country risk analysis is not always accurate.

4. **Diversifying away country risk.** Why do you think that an MNC's strategy of diversifying projects internationally could achieve low exposure to country risk?

5. **Monitoring country risk.** Once a project is accepted, country risk analysis for the foreign country involved is no longer necessary, assuming that no other proposed projects are being evaluated for that country. Do you agree with this statement? Why or why not?

6. **Country risk analysis.** If the potential return is high enough, any degree of country risk can be tolerated. Do you agree with this statement? Why or why not? Do you think that a proper country risk analysis can replace a capital budgeting analysis of a project considered for a foreign country? Explain.

7. **Country risk analysis.** Niagra ltd has decided to call a well-known country risk consultant to conduct a country risk analysis in a small country where it plans to develop a large subsidiary. Niagra prefers to hire the consultant since it plans to use its employees for other important corporate functions. The consultant uses a computer program that has assigned weights of importance linked to the various factors. The consultant will evaluate the factors for this small country and insert a rating for each factor into the computer. The weights assigned to the factors are not adjusted by the computer, but the factor ratings are adjusted for each country that the consultant assesses. Do you think Niagra ltd should use this consultant? Why or why not?

8. **Microassessment.** Explain the microassessment of country risk.

9. **Incorporating country risk in capital budgeting.** How could a country risk assessment be used to adjust a project's required rate of return? How could such an assessment be used instead to adjust a project's estimated cash flows?

10. **Reducing country risk.** Explain some methods of reducing exposure to existing country risk, while maintaining the same amount of business within a particular country.

11. **Managing country risk.** Why do some subsidiaries maintain a low profile as to where their parents are located?

12. **Country risk analysis.** When Jerrik ApS (Danish) considered establishing a subsidiary in Zenland, it performed a country risk analysis to help make the decision. It first retrieved a country risk analysis performed about one year earlier, when it had planned to begin a major exporting business to Zenland firms. Then it updated the analysis by incorporating all current information on the key variables that were used in that analysis, such as Zenland's willingness to accept exports, its existing quotas, and existing tariff laws. Is this country risk analysis adequate? Explain.

13. **Reducing country risk.** MNCs such as Alcoa, DuPont, Heinz, and IBM donated products and technology to foreign countries where they had subsidiaries. How could these actions have reduced some forms of country risk?

14. **Country risk ratings.** Assauer ltd would like to assess the country risk of Glovanskia. Assauer has identified various political and financial risk factors, as shown below.

Political Risk Factor	Assigned Rating	Assigned Weight
Blockage of fund transfers	5	40%
Bureaucracy	3	60%

Financial Risk Factor	Assigned Rating	Assigned Weight
Interest rate	1	10%
Inflation	4	20%
Exchange rate	5	30%
Competition	4	20%
̇h	5	20%

Assauer has assigned an overall rating of 80% to political risk factors and of 20% to financial risk factors. Assauer is not willing to consider Glovanskia for investment if the country risk rating is below 4.0. Should Assauer consider Glovanskia for investment?

15. Buxton plc is thinking of investing in Country Y. The expected return is 20% with a standard deviation due to currency movements of 5%. However, ten years ago Country Y's currency fell by 40%. How should Buxton assess this risk?

ADVANCED QUESTIONS

16. **How country risk affects NPV.** Hoosier ltd is planning a project in the United States. It would lease space for one year in a shopping mall to sell expensive clothes manufactured in the United Kingdom. The project would end in one year, when all earnings would be remitted to Hoosier ltd. Assume that no additional corporate taxes are incurred beyond those imposed by the UK government. Since Hoosier ltd would rent space, it would not have any long-term assets in the United States and expects the salvage (terminal) value of the project to be about zero.

Assume that the project's required rate of return is 18%. Also assume that the initial outlay required by the parent to fill the store with clothes is £200,000. The pretax foreign earnings are expected to be $300,000 at the end of one year. The British pound is expected to be worth $1.60 at the end of one year, when the after-tax earnings are converted to pounds and remitted to the United Kingdom. The following forms of country risk must be considered:

- The US economy may weaken (probability = 30%), which would cause the expected pretax earnings to be $200,000.

- The US corporate tax rate on income earned by British firms may increase by 25% (probability = 20%).

These two forms of country risk are independent.

Calculate the expected value of the project's net present value (*NPV*) and determine the probability that the project will have a negative *NPV*.

17. **How country risk affects *NPV*.** Explain how the capital budgeting analysis in the previous question would need to be adjusted if there were three possible outcomes for the British pound along with the possible outcomes for the British economy and corporate tax rate.

18. **J.C. Penney's country risk analysis.** Recently, J.C. Penney (an actual US company) decided to consider expanding into various foreign countries; it applied a comprehensive country risk analysis before making its expansion decisions. Initial screenings of 30 foreign countries were based on political and economic factors that contribute to country risk. For the remaining 20 countries where country risk was considered to be tolerable, specific country risk characteristics of each country were considered. One of J.C. Penney's biggest targets is Mexico, where it planned to build and operate seven large stores.

    a. Identify the political factors that you think may possibly affect the performance of the J.C. Penney stores in Mexico.

    b. Explain why the J.C. Penney stores in Mexico and in other foreign markets are subject to financial risk (a subset of country risk).

    c. Assume that J.C. Penney anticipated that there was a 10% chance that the Mexican government would temporarily prevent conversion of peso profits into dollars because of political conditions. This event would prevent J.C. Penney from remitting earnings generated in Mexico and could adversely affect the performance of these stores (from the US perspective). Offer a way in which this type of political risk could be explicitly incorporated into a capital budgeting analysis when assessing the feasibility of these projects.

    d. Assume that J.C. Penney decides to use dollars to finance the expansion of stores in Mexico. Second, assume that J.C. Penney decides to use one set of dollar cash flow estimates for any project that it assesses. Third, assume that the stores in Mexico are not subject to political risk. Do you think that the required rate of return on these projects would differ from the required rate of return on stores built in the United States at that same time? Explain.

    e. Based on your answer to the previous question, does this mean that proposals for any new stores in the United States have a higher probability of being accepted than proposals for any new stores in Mexico?

19. **How country risk affects *NPV*.** Monk ltd is considering a capital budgeting project in Tunisia. The project requires an initial outlay of 1 million Tunisian dinar; the dinar is currently valued at £0.48. In the first and second years of operation, the project will generate 700,000 dinar in each year. After two years, Monk will terminate the project, and the expected salvage value is 300,000 dinar. Monk has assigned a discount rate of 12% to this project. The following additional information is available:

    ■ There is currently no withholding tax on remittances to the United Kingdom, but there is a 20% chance that the Tunisian government will impose a withholding tax of 10% beginning next year.

    ■ There is a 50% chance that the Tunisian government will pay Monk 100,000 dinar after two years instead of the 300,000 dinar it expects.

    ■ The value of the dinar is expected to remain unchanged over the next two years.

    a. Determine the net present value (*NPV*) of the project in each of the four possible scenarios.

    b. Determine the joint probability of each scenario.

    c. Compute the expected *NPV* of the project and make a recommendation to Monk regarding its feasibility.

20. **How country risk affects *NPV*.** In the previous question, assume that instead of adjusting the estimated cash flows of the project, Monk had decided to adjust the discount rate from 12% to 17%. Re-evaluate the *NPV* of the project's expected scenario using this adjusted discount rate.

21. **The risk and cost of potential kidnapping.** In 2004 following the war in Iraq, some MNCs capitalized on opportunities to rebuild Iraq. However, in April 2004, some employees were kidnapped by local militant groups. How should an MNC

account for this potential risk when it considers foreign direct investment (FDI) in any particular country? Should it avoid FDI in any country in which such an event could occur? If so, how would it screen the countries to determine which are acceptable? For whatever countries that it is willing to consider, should it adjust its feasibility analysis to account for the possibility of kidnapping? Should it attach a cost to reflect this possibility or increase the discount rate when estimating the net present value? Explain.

22. **Integrating country risk and capital budgeting.** Tovar Cie is a French firm that has been asked to provide consulting services to help Gredia Company (in Country Y) improve its performance. Tovar would need to spend 300,000 euros today on expenses related to this project. In one year, Tovar will receive payment from Gredia, which will be tied to Gredia's performance during the year. There is uncertainty about Gredia's performance and about Gredia's tendency for corruption.

Tovar expects that it will receive 400,000 euros if Gredia achieves strong performance following the consulting job. However, there are two forms of country risk that are a concern to Tovar. There is an 80% chance that Gredia will achieve strong performance. There is a 20% chance that Gredia will perform poorly, and in this case, Tovar will receive a payment of only 200,000 euros.

While there is a 90% chance that Gredia will make its payment to Tovar, there is a 10% chance that Gredia will become corrupt, and in this case, Gredia will not submit any payment to Tovar.

Assume that the outcome of Gredia's performance is independent of whether Gredia becomes corrupt. The prevailing spot rate of country Y's currency is 0.6 euros to the Y, but Tovar expects that currency Y will depreciate by 10% in one year, regardless of Gredia's performance or whether it is corrupt.

Tovar's cost of capital is 26%. Determine the expected value of the project's net present value. Determine the probability that the project's *NPV* will be negative.

23. **Political considerations** Enter the terms: "Financial crisis", "chronology", "date" and "country". Select a reasonably long article in a search engine of newspaper articles. Your institution should have access to such resources.
    a. Select events from the financial crisis that would be of concern to a multinational operating in the country.
    b. From each of the events of the financial crisis, consider how an MNC with investments in that country would be affected and how the MNC might best react.

This exercise can be found on the companion website at www.cengage.co.uk/madura_fox.

This exercise can be found on the companion website at www.cengage.co.uk/madura_fox.

Essays/discussion and articles can be found at the end of Part 4

BLADES PLC CASE STUDY
Country risk assessment

Recently, Ben Holt, Blades' chief financial officer (CFO), has assessed whether it would be more beneficial for Blades to establish a subsidiary in Thailand to manufacture roller blades or to acquire an existing manufacturer, Skates'n'Stuff, which has offered to sell the business to Blades for 1 billion Thai baht. In Holt's view, establishing a subsidiary in Thailand yields a higher net present value (NPV) than acquiring the existing business. Furthermore, the Thai manufacturer has rejected an offer by Blades plc for 900 million baht. A purchase price of 900 million baht for Skates'n'Stuff would make the acquisition as attractive as the establishment of a subsidiary in Thailand in terms of NPV. Skates'n'Stuff has indicated that it is not willing to accept less than 950 million baht.

Although Holt is confident that the NPV analysis was conducted correctly, he is troubled by the fact that the same discount rate, 25%, was used in each analysis. In his view, establishing a subsidiary in Thailand may be associated with a higher level of country risk than acquiring Skates'n'Stuff. Although either approach would result in approximately the same level of financial risk, the political risk associated with establishing a subsidiary in Thailand may be higher then the political risk of operating Skates'n'Stuff. If the establishment of a subsidiary in Thailand is associated with a higher level of country risk overall, then a higher discount rate should have been used in the analysis. Based on these considerations, Holt wants to measure the country risk associated with Thailand on both a macro and a micro level and then to re-examine the feasibility of both approaches.

First, Holt has gathered some more detailed political information for Thailand. For example, he believes that consumers in Asian countries prefer to purchase goods produced by Asians, which might prevent a subsidiary in Thailand from being successful. This cultural characteristic might not prevent an acquisition of Skates'n'Stuff from succeeding, however, especially if Blades retains the company's management and employees. Furthermore, the subsidiary would have to apply for various licences and permits to be allowed to operate in Thailand, while Skates'n'Stuff obtained these licences and permits long ago. However, the number of licences required for Blades' industry is

relatively low compared to other industries. Moreover, there is a high possibility that the Thai government will implement capital controls in the near future, which would prevent funds from leaving Thailand. Since Blades ltd has planned to remit all earnings generated by its subsidiary or by Skates'n'Stuff back to the United Kingdom, regardless of which approach to direct foreign investment it takes, capital controls may force Blades to reinvest funds in Thailand.

Ben Holt has also gathered some information regarding the financial risk of operating in Thailand. Thailand's economy has been weak lately, and recent forecasts indicate that a recovery may be slow. A weak economy may affect the demand for Blades' products, roller blades. The state of the economy is of particular concern to Blades since it produces a leisure product. In the case of an economic turndown, consumers will first eliminate these types of purchases. Holt is also worried about the high interest rates in Thailand, which may further slow economic growth if Thai citizens begin saving more. Furthermore, Holt is also aware that inflation levels in Thailand are expected to remain high. These high inflation levels can affect the purchasing power of Thai consumers, who may adjust their spending habits to purchase more essential products than roller blades. However, high levels of inflation also indicate that consumers in Thailand are still spending a relatively high proportion of their earnings.

Another financial factor that may affect Blades' operations in Thailand is the baht–pound exchange rate. Current forecasts indicate that the Thai baht may depreciate in the future. However, recall that Blades will sell all roller blades produced in Thailand to Thai consumers. Therefore, Blades is not subject to a lower level of UK demand resulting from a weak baht. Blades will remit the earnings generated in Thailand back to the United Kingdom, however, and a weak baht would reduce the pound amount of these translated earnings.

Based on these initial considerations, Holt feels that the level of political risk of operating may be higher if Blades decides to establish a subsidiary to manufacture roller blades (as opposed to acquiring Skates'n'Stuff). Conversely, the financial risk of operating in Thailand will be roughly the same whether

Blades establishes a subsidiary or acquires Skates'n'Stuff. Holt is not satisfied with this initial assessment, however, and would like to have numbers at hand when he meets with the board of directors next week. Thus, he would like to conduct a quantitative analysis of the country risk associated with operating in Thailand. He has asked you, a financial analyst at Blades, to develop a country risk analysis for Thailand and to adjust the discount rate for the riskier venture (i.e., establishing a subsidiary or acquiring Skates'n'Stuff). Holt has provided the following information for your analysis:

- Since Blades produces leisure products, it is more susceptible to financial risk factors than political risk factors. You should use weights of 60% for financial risk factors and 40% for political risk factors in your analysis.

- You should use the attitude of Thai consumers, capital controls, and bureaucracy as political risk factors in your analysis. Holt perceives capital controls as the most important political risk factor. In his view, the consumer attitude and bureaucracy factors are of equal importance.

- You should use interest rates, inflation levels, and exchange rates as the financial risk factors in your analysis. In Holt's view, exchange rates and interest rates in Thailand are of equal importance, while inflation levels are slightly less important.

- Each factor used in your analysis should be assigned a rating in a range of 1 to 5, where 5 indicates the most unfavourable rating.

Ben Holt has asked you to provide answers to the following questions for him, which he will use in his meeting with the board of directors:

1. Based on the information provided in the case, do you think the political risk associated with Thailand is higher or lower for a manufacturer of leisure products such as Blades as opposed to, say, a food producer? That is, conduct a microassessment of political risk for Blades, Inc.

2. Do you think the financial risk associated with Thailand is higher or lower for a manufacturer of leisure products such as Blades as opposed to, say, a food producer? That is, conduct a microassessment of financial risk for Blades plc. Do you think a leisure product manufacturer such as Blades will be more affected by political or financial risk factors?

3. Without using a numerical analysis, do you think establishing a subsidiary in Thailand or acquiring Skates'n'Stuff will result in a higher assessment of political risk? Of financial risk? Substantiate your answer.

4. Using a spreadsheet, conduct a quantitative country risk analysis for Blades plc using the information Ben Holt has provided for you. Use your judgement to assign weights and ratings to each political and financial risk factor and determine an overall country risk rating for Thailand. Conduct two separate analyses for: (a) the establishment of a subsidiary in Thailand, and (b) the acquisition of Skates'n'Stuff.

5. Which method of direct foreign investment should utilize a higher discount rate in the capital budgeting analysis? Would this strengthen or weaken the tentative decision of establishing a subsidiary in Thailand?

SMALL BUSINESS DILEMMA
Country risk analysis at the Sports Exports Company

The Sports Exports Company (Ireland) produces basketballs and exports them to the United Kingdom. It also has an ongoing joint venture with a British firm that produces some sporting goods for a fee. The Sports Exports Company is considering the establishment of a small subsidiary in the United Kingdom.

1. Under the current conditions, is the Sports Exports Company subject to country risk?

2. If the firm does decide to develop a small subsidiary in the United Kingdom, will its exposure to country risk change? If so, how?

CHAPTER 17

MULTINATIONAL COST OF CAPITAL AND CAPITAL STRUCTURE

An MNC FINANCES ITS operations by using a mixture of fixed interest borrowing and equity financing that can minimize the overall cost of capital (the weighted average of its interest rate and dividend payments). By minimizing the cost of capital used to finance a given size and risk of operations, financial managers can maximize the value of the company and therefore maximize shareholder wealth.

THE SPECIFIC OBJECTIVES OF THIS CHAPTER ARE TO:

- explain how corporate and country characteristics influence an MNC's cost of capital,

- explain why there are differences in the costs of capital among countries, and

- explain how corporate and country characteristics are considered by an MNC when it establishes its capital structure.

BACKGROUND ON COST OF CAPITAL

Apart from working capital, a firm's capital consists of equity (retained earnings and funds obtained by issuing shares) and debt (borrowed funds). With these funds a firm invests in a portfolio of projects, each project potentially offering different risks and different returns. The interest rate that the firm applies or charges to these projects (the cost of using the firm's capital) will therefore vary according to the project's particular risk. Profitable investment in this context is where the firm invests in projects that achieve returns greater than that required by their risk. A project that achieves a 20% return from investing in car parks (safe) is arguably a better performer than a project achieving a 25% return from financing a musical show (risky) – for convenience, rather than use *NPV* terminology we use the closely related IRR (internal rate of return) concept of return. Remember that *NPV* calculations are based on the cash flows that the firm *hopes* to achieve in the future, it is ex ante or before the event and is calculated as follows:

$$NPV = -I_0 + \frac{E(CF_1)}{(1+r)^1} + \frac{E(CF_2)}{(1+r)^2} + \frac{E(CF_3)}{(1+r)^3} + \frac{E(CF_4)}{(1+r)^4} + \frac{E(CF_5)}{(1+r)^5} \cdots + \frac{E(CF_n)}{(1+r)^n}$$

where:

r	=	required return for the project
$E(CF_1)$	=	expected cash flow in period 1
n	=	last period of the project
NPV	=	net present value
$-I_0$	=	initial investment

Actual outcome is just one of the possible anticipated range of outcomes. The next musical show may do much better or much worse; the next car park may do a little better or a little worse if it is less risky.

A project is simply a defined set of activities evaluated in finance by their cash flows. The firm itself can, of course, be viewed as a project. In some cases, e.g. car manufacturers or food retailers, the activities (or sub-projects) of the company are in similar markets and will be charged similar interest rates. In the case of a conglomerate such as Invensys plc the widely varying projects, from rail signalling systems to a control system in a Venezuelan chemical plant, will be charged differing rates according to the differing risks of the projects. For an MNC it is likely that the firm will be engaging in projects of widely varying risks. Even if it is the same physical activity, for example Michelin and tyre manufacturing, the differing international markets will present a range of risks.

The firm can be valued as one would value any project. The combined cash flows from each activity or sub-project should be discounted with an interest rate that includes a premium for the risks of each sub-project. The overall discount rate to be applied would be the firm's weighted average cost of capital. The problem for an investor is that firms do not disclose sufficient details about their individual projects to make this approach possible.

The traditional and more accessible way of valuing the firm is to measure return as dividends and share price growth and to calculate the weighted average cost of capital (the effective discount rate to be applied to the returns) by taking a weighted average of the returns demanded by shareholders and debt holders, i.e. all the lenders to the firm. Like any individual project, value is maximized by achieving a cash flow higher than required by the cost of capital.

Calculating the cost of capital in a single market

An MNC as with other firms, is financed through two principal sources of finance. Equity or shares and fixed interest debt often in the form of debentures or bonds. The main financial difference between the two types of lending is risk. A share represents part ownership of the company, shareholders appoint the managing director and through this influence have the most important voice in running the company. A share is rewarded through the payment of dividends. Dividends are not fixed and may not be paid at all. The value of the share entirely depends on the profitability of the company from which the dividends are paid. If the company fails, the shareholder will be last in line to receive anything from selling off the assets. Holding shares is risky; whereas holding debentures is less risky. Debentures are rewarded through the payment of interest, that is, a guaranteed amount irrespective of the performance of the company. The terms of the debenture will normally include a lien or "hold" on assets. If interest payments are not made, a meeting of creditors can be held and the company declared bankrupt. In such a case the debenture holders will have a right to sell off the assets held under a lien in order to repay interest and the value of their investment. As the debenture has more assurances as to returns than shares, the cost for the company of financing with debentures is less. As in all efficient markets, a less risky investment requires less return.

A firm's weighted average cost of capital (referred to as k_c) can be measured as

$$k_c = \left(\frac{D}{D+E}\right)k_d(1-t) + \left(\frac{E}{D+E}\right)k_e$$

Where:

D	=	market value of firm's debt
k_d	=	the before-tax cost of its debt
t	=	the corporate tax rate
E	=	the firm's equity at market value, and
k_e	=	the cost of financing with equity.

The ratios reflect the percentage of capital represented by debt and equity, respectively. In total the cost of capital, k_c is the average cost of all providers of finance to the firm.

Initially, using cheaper fixed interest debt (D) to finance company projects may seem attractive. The drawback is that the greater the percentage of overall finance in the form of fixed interest debt, the more variable (risky) the prospective returns to shareholders. To see this, think of a firm with very high debt and therefore very high fixed interest payments (a highly geared firm). These payments have to be made in good times and bad times. Imagine if such a firm is doing badly and is able to just cover its interest payments, there will be nothing left for the shareholder. At very high levels of borrowing, profits may not be sufficient to pay interest charges and the firm could be declared bankrupt, so there is the additional risk of bankruptcy. But if the same company is financed mainly by shares (a low geared firm) there would have been much more for the shareholder. In bad times the low geared equivalent company will be able to pay out more because its interest rate bill will be lower. Calculation will also show that in good times the low geared equivalent company will pay out less than its high geared counterpart. This is because when the company is making profits, shareholders gain from high levels of borrowing at relatively low interest rates. The variation in returns to a low geared firm will therefore be less (more money available to pay as dividends in bad times and less in good times) and the company will therefore be seen as less risky.

Fundamental to the idea of the cost of capital are the propositions by Modigilani and Miller.[1] They demonstrate that, given a free market, the cost of capital should be constant at all proportions of debt that the company may wish to adopt. So, low geared companies being financed by only 10% fixed interest debt and 90% equity, ranging to a high geared companies being financed by, say, 80% debt and only 20% of its finances being provided by shareholders, would all have the same *overall* cost of capital (k_c as above). They showed that a shareholder in a low geared firm could, without selling the shares, obtain the same return as if holding shares in a company with identical earnings but with high gearing. This can be done by *personal* gearing, borrowing and investing money in the same low geared firm. If gearing can be changed by shareholders independently of the company, then gearing cannot play a part in the valuation of the company – it is not relevant. The cost of capital is central to valuing the company, it is the rate at which future cash flows are discounted (see Chapter 1). Therefore, if changing debt levels does not affect the discount rate nor (with some assumptions) the cash flows, the value of the company is unchanged.

Looking at the cost of capital formula it is a simple matter of arithmetic to show that if k_c is to remain constant at higher levels of D, then the cost of equity capital (k_e) must increase to compensate, as the cost of debt k_d is less than the cost of equity and is fixed.

There are two general exceptions. The first is that at a very high level of debt, for example if 90% of a firm's finance were from fixed interest borrowings, there would be a risk of bankruptcy due to non-payment of the interest charges. So one would therefore expect to see an increase in the cost of capital at high levels of debt. The second exception is tax. Debt is tax deductible for companies but not for individuals. Moderate levels of debt enable the company to obtain savings otherwise not accessible to shareholders as individuals. Where the shareholder is an investment company or insurance company, this will not be the case.

The tradeoff between debt's advantage (tax deductibility of interest) and its disadvantage (increased risk of bankruptcy is illustrated in Exhibit 17.1). As the exhibit shows, the firm's cost of capital initially decreases as the ratio of debt to total capital increases. However, after some point (labelled X in Exhibit 17.1), the cost of capital rises as the ratio of debt to total capital increases. This suggests that the firm should increase its use of debt financing until the point at which the bankruptcy probability becomes large enough to offset the tax advantage of using debt. To go beyond that point would increase the firm's overall cost of capital.

Exhibit 17.1 Determining the appropriate capital structure

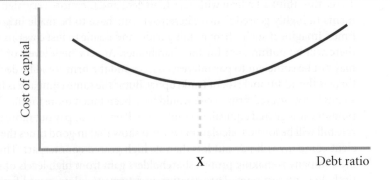

1   For example see P. Vernimmen (2005) *Corporate Finance: Theory and Practice*, New York: Wiley, pp.660 *et seq*

COST OF CAPITAL FOR MNCS

The cost of capital for MNCs may differ from that for domestic firms because of the following characteristics that differentiate MNCs from domestic firms:

- *Size of firm.* An MNC that often borrows substantial amounts may receive preferential treatment from creditors, thereby reducing its cost of capital. Furthermore, its relatively large issues of stocks or bonds allow for reduced flotation costs (as a percentage of the amount of financing). Note, however, that these advantages are due to the MNC's size and not to its internationalized business. A domestic corporation may receive the same treatment if it is large enough. Nevertheless, a firm's growth is more restricted if it is not willing to operate internationally. Because MNCs may more easily achieve growth, they may be more able than purely domestic firms to reach the necessary size to receive preferential treatment from creditors.

- *International diversification.* An MNC has a greater opportunity to exploit profitable investment. As markets are not highly correlated, these opportunities can help offset poor performance in the home market. So, to the extent that individual economies are independent of each other, net cash flows from a portfolio of subsidiaries should exhibit less variability, which may reduce the probability of bankruptcy and therefore reduce the cost of capital.

- *Exposure to exchange rate change.* All investments denominated in a foreign currency are unavoidably exposed to changes in the value of that currency. PPP suggests that exchange rate change will offset higher or lower inflation in that currency. So the translated value of the foreign currency will have the same inflation as the home currency (compare year 1 with year 0 in Exhibit 17.2). The exposure to exchange rate risk is therefore to changes in the real value of the currency, that is to say, those changes that are not explained by inflation differences, assuming PPP (compare year 2 with year 1 in Exhibit 17.2).

E X A M P L E

Bude plc (UK) is investing in Country N (currency the N). Last year's returns were N1 million at an exchange rate of N4 to the British pound or £0.25 for 1 N. The translated value was therefore N1m × 0.25 = £250,000. For the coming year, inflation in N is expected to be 20% compared to 2% in the UK. Bude's foreign earnings are expected to be in line with inflation, so expected earnings are N 1,200,000 (1 million × (1 + 0.20)).

If the exchange rate behaves according to PPP, the value of the N will change to £0.25 × 1.02 / 1.20 = £0.2125. The translated value for the coming year is expected to be N1,200,000 × 0.2125 = £255,000. This is the same value as if the British pound value of the earnings (£250,000) had been earned in the UK where it would have experienced UK inflation of 2%, because £250,000 × 1.02 = £255,000. Thus the exchange rate change has simply protected Bude's investors from the effects of foreign inflation.

For the *following* year inflation is again expected to be 20% in N and 2% in the UK and earnings are again expected to be in line with inflation. In terms of Ns, the earnings are expected to be N1,200,000 × (1 + 0.20) = N1,440,000.

Only this time because of concerns about the economic effects of inflation there is expected to be a 5% fall in the real value of the N. The total change in the value of the N relative to the British pound will therefore be: 1.02 / (1.20 × 1.05) − 1 = −0.190476 or 19.0476%. The new expected exchange rate will be £0.2125 × (1 − 0.190476) = 0.17202385. So earnings converted to British pounds will be N1,440,000 × 0.17202385 = £247,714. If it were not for the fall in the real value of the N, earnings would have been 5% higher at

$247,714 \times (1 + 0.05) = £260,100$. As a check, UK inflation will have been 2%, so if the earnings had performed as well, only in the UK, UK earnings will be expected to be $£255,000 \times (1 + 0.02) = £260,100$. It is therefore only real changes in the value of foreign currency that affects the value of translated earnings if IFE prevails.

Expected change in the real value of the currency is the effect of the currency risk premium. It is that change in the value of a foreign currency that is not compensated by a difference in inflation. In the above example (Exhibit 17.2) the expected fall in the real value of N by 5% reflects a concern about the state of the economy. This concern includes the possibility that the expected revenues from Bude will not be as high as expected. The exchange rate therefore not only accounts for a difference in the expected inflation rates but also a difference in the expected overall risk between the two countries (the risk differential would not exist if the UK economy were thought to be equally precarious).

For MNCs therefore, exposure is to changes in the real value of the foreign currency. That does not imply that PPP has to hold, merely that some of the changes in the exchange rate will do no more than account for the inflation differences between the two countries, any further anticipated change will affect the translated value of the currency.

- *Access to international capital markets.* MNCs are normally able to obtain funds through the international capital markets. Since the cost of funds can vary among markets, the MNC's access to the international capital markets may allow it to obtain funds at a lower cost than that paid by domestic firms. In addition, subsidiaries may be able to obtain funds locally at a lower cost than that available to the parent if the prevailing interest rates in the host country are relatively low.

Exhibit 17.2 The effect of exchange rates on translated foreign earnings

| | Translated £ value of MNC earnings in Country N (N 1 million per year in year 0 values) | | | | | | |
| | Country N | | | | | UK | |
	Country N inflation	Change in real value of N	Foreign Earnings N1m per year in year 0 terms	Exchange rate £s per N assuming PPP	Translated £ value	UK inflation	Current Value of £250,000 in year 0
Previous year (0)	0%	0%	N1 million	£0.25	£250,000	0%	£250,000
The coming year (1)	20%	0%	N1,200,000	£0.2125	£255,000	2%	£255,000
The following year (2)	20%	–5%	N1440,000	£0.17202385	£247,714	2%	£260,100

Notes:

Year 0: The MNC earns N1m which is translated into £s, N1m × 0.25 = £250,000.

Year 1: Country N earnings have kept pace with Country N inflation. PPP assumes that the exchange rate has adjusted for the inflation differential £0.25 × 1.02 / 1.20 = £0.2125 for 1N. Hence the 0% change in real value. The translated earnings (N1,200,000 × 0.2125 = £255,000) are therefore in line with UK inflation as in this case the change in the value of N is exactly in line with PPP.

Year 2: Country N earnings have kept pace with Country N inflation. PPP type changes are still assumed to apply except that there has also been a 5% fall in the real value of the N. The new exchange rate will now change by 1.02 / (1.20 × 1.05) − 1 = −0.190476 or 19.0476%. So the new rate will now be: be 0.2125 × (1− 0.190476) = 0.17202385. As a result, translated foreign earnings of N1,440,000 × 0.17202385 = £247,714 are 5% lower than the domestic equivalent: 247,714 × (1 + 0.05) = £260,100.

The use of foreign funds can reduce the MNC's exposure to exchange rate risk. Firms can borrow in the currency in which they earn (sometimes referred to in reports as "natural hedging"). A British MNC earning in dollars will suffer if it translates its earnings into pounds when the dollar is weak. To offset this loss, if it *borrows* in dollars then the reduced revenue value from the weak dollar will be partially compensated by the reduced cost of the interest payments that are made in dollars. The disadvantage of this approach is that when the dollar is strong, some of the benefit will be lost because interest payments will be higher. The exposure to the effects of *variability* of the foreign currency is nevertheless reduced.

- *Exposure to country risk.* An MNC that establishes foreign subsidiaries is subject to the possibility that a host country government may seize a subsidiary's assets. The probability of such an occurrence is influenced by many factors, including the attitude of the host country government and the industry of concern.

  Other forms of country risk, such as changes in a host government's tax laws, could also affect an MNC's subsidiary's cash flows.

  An MNC must decide whether or not the country risks being contemplated are a part of normal business risk or whether they should be considered separately. These issues were considered in the previous chapter.

EXAMPLE ExxonMobil has much experience in assessing the feasibility of potential projects in foreign countries. If it detects a radical change in government or tax policy, it adds a premium to the required return of related projects. Country risk is therefore treated as part of its normal business risk.

THE INTERNATIONAL CAPITAL ASSET PRICING MODEL (ICAPM)

The International Capital Asset Pricing Model (ICAPM) can be regarded as more formal treatment of the cost of capital elements in the previous section. The model is an international extension of the Capital Asset Pricing Model (CAPM). The CAPM addresses a single currency area and single financial market where there are no restrictions on financial transactions. The ICAPM extends this analysis to multiple currency areas and multiple financial markets. Both models seek to answer the question: "What discount rate should be applied to the future cash flows of a particular project?" The 'project' may be a venture managed from the Head Office, or it may be being run by a wholly owned subsidiary, or it may be applied to the MNC as a whole by a potential or existing investor. But in essence it is an outlay followed by a series of expected positive cash flows that need to be discounted by an interest rate that is appropriate to the required return of the cash flows.

The following outline looks first at the CAPM, addressing a single currency area; then the following section extends the analysis to the ICAPM.

The CAPM

The answer to the question: "What discount rate should be applied to the future cash flows of a particular project?" is simple in outline. The discount (interest) rate that should be applied must reflect all required returns that cannot be diversified away by holding a portfolio of projects. In a single market non-diversifiable elements will include time preference, inflation and that element of project risk that is related to the risk of the market as a whole. These elements of the discount rate for the CAPM are examined in turn.

Time preference. If you are seeking to save £100 and the bank offered you a return in one year's time to the value of £100 today (i.e. the same purchasing power), you would probably be dissatisfied. Most savers would want a guaranteed return value that is more than just the value of the original saving. More is required because saving means not consuming now and is an inconvenience for which investors will want a reward. The same is true for MNCs. On behalf of their shareholders, they need to earn a return in terms of today's money to reward investors even if the project is perfectly safe. One may wonder if such returns differ on average between countries. The answer is yes, for reasons that are not clear. Some economies are less prone to saving than others, for example, two thirds of credit card debt in Europe is incurred by UK citizens suggesting a greater impatience and higher time preference in the UK. In Germany, on the other hand, people are compulsive savers. But in general, reward for saving is required by all investors hence it is a part of all interest rates.

Inflation. The decision not to consume (spend) earnings now but delay by saving the money would be most unattractive if the investor could not buy at least the same goods as could be purchased now. Investors want savings to keep pace at least with inflation. Otherwise, the investor may well find that he or she will not be able to buy as much after having saved than before. So a reward for inflation in the currency of calculation is required by investors as inflation cannot be avoided.

Risk. The element of risk that cannot be diversified away for the CAPM is market risk. How market risk is defined in the CAPM is a considerable practical problem. As CAPM deals with a single economy, the market risk is the return from investing in a weighted average of investments in that economy. In many cases this is approximated in the UK as the return on the Financial Times Stock Exchange (FTSE) index. In practice, an individual or firm may invest in assets outside the Stock Exchange, such as land and private businesses. The assumption is that the returns from changes in land prices and businesses outside the exchange somehow are reflected in the returns of at least some of the businesses that are quoted. The investments of an MNC, it is argued, can through diversification avoid all risk except that element of risk that is common to all investments in the economy. Hence the extent to which the returns of a particular project move in line with the market is important in assessing its unavoidable or systematic risk. All other sources of risk, termed individual risk, can be diversified away by having a range of investments.

To assess required rates of return for purely domestic projects, the capital asset pricing model (CAPM) can be applied. It defines the required return (k_j) on a project or a share (j) as:

$$k_j = R_f + \beta_j (R_m - R_f)$$

where:

R_f = risk free rate of return (time preference and inflation)
R_m = market return (return on the FTSE index)
β = beta of a particular share or a project

The CAPM suggests that the required return on a firm's stock is a positive function of: (1) the risk-free rate of interest, (2) the market rate of return, and (3) the stock's beta.

The beta represents the sensitivity of the stock's returns to market returns (a stock market index). If the beta is one, the returns on the investment are perfectly correlated with the market returns. The model will charge the whole of the market risk premium ($R_m - R_f$) to the investment. As the model adds back the risk free element R_f, the cost of capital where beta is 1.0 is R_m, the market return. Some simple examples will confirm that if beta is less than 1.0 the required return will be less than the market return; if beta is greater than 1.0, the required return will be greater than the market return. Thus the CAPM defines the required return in relation to the overall market return known as the systematic risk. The overall risk of a project, defined as the variance of returns can therefore be broken down into two elements: (1) unsystematic variability in cash flows unique to the firm, and (2) systematic risk. Capital asset pricing theory suggests that the unsystematic risk of projects can be ignored because it will be diversified away.

However, systematic risk (measured by the beta of an investment) is not diversified away because all projects are similarly affected. The lower a project's beta, the lower is the project's systematic risk and the lower its required rate of return. Note that in theory at least, as individual risk can be ignored, it would be possible in the CAPM world to have a project with a higher total risk (variance of returns) but with a lower k_e due to a lower systematic risk.

The ICAPM

The ICAPM extends the analysis of the CAPM to a multimarket, multicurrency scenario. Essentially the ICAPM is the relevant model for MNCs as they are able to invest in a range of stock markets and have investments in a range of currencies. The ability of an MNC to diversify is therefore much greater. As with the CAPM the required return is the non-diversifiable risk.

The risk free element in the ICAPM is the risk free rate in the currency in which the overall returns are being measured. Thus if the MNC is measuring its returns in British pounds the rate will be the pound risk free rate; if measured in euros, the rate will be the risk free rate for the euro.

The market return and the sensitivity of the investments to markets returns will remain as an element in the ICAPM. Thus projects will still have betas. The change is in the measure of the market. Instead of the FTSE index, the measure is of a world index. MNCs can invest in differing markets worldwide and can therefore avoid all risk through diversification except world risk. The beta for a particular project will therefore be with a world risk premium or $\beta_j (R_w - R_f)$ where R_f is the risk free rate in the valuation currency and R_w is the return on a world index.

Additionally, projects will have exposure to non-diversifiable currency risks. A business will need to know how the returns translated into the home currency are likely to be affected by changes in the value of the foreign currency. This exposure will vary from project to project and will depend on the hedging policy adopted by the MNC. If all revenues are in the foreign currency and costs in the domestic currency with no futures, forwards or options taken out, the currency exposure risk will be much greater than if some of the costs are in the foreign currency and the company has hedged its returns. Additionally, some currencies have greater real exchange rate risk than others (as a reminder, real exchange rate risk is the movement in the value of a foreign currency that is not compensated by the higher or lower inflation in that country (see Exhibit 17.2). The sensitivity of a project to currency variation is sometimes referred to as the currency beta.

CAPM and ICAPM application issues

The application of the CAPM model and the ICAPM model presents considerable practical problems for an MNC. The company first has to find a like project of a similar risk class to identify an appropriate beta. If the project is like all the other projects being undertaken by the firm, then the company's cost of capital will serve the task. But if there is a sufficient difference between projects because maybe the project is in a very different economy or is a different activity not normally carried out by the company, then the beta of another company that undertakes similar projects would be more appropriate. The choice of such companies is not an exact science. The measurement of market return is also problematic. To what extent does the market return represent the return on all potential investments in society? Highly correlated measures of return can nevertheless produce very different betas.

There is also a problem of meaning. Why a beta is particularly high or low or why it changes is not easy to explain. Selecting the appropriate beta may well not be easy. Beyond beta being some measure of correlation with the market return, the actual beta score can easily appear as a *deus ex machina* (Greek for 'a god from a machine'). The prospect for an MNC is that a project is rejected due to a measure over which there is much approximation and little understanding. The more user friendly subjective probability estimation appears attractive in comparison. Even why the return on the Stock Market has been so high over the years is also not well understood (this is known as the equity premium puzzle). Briefly, investment can be seen as deferred or delayed consumption. So another way of approximating risk for the investment market as a whole is to look at the variation in the growth rate of consumption. It turns out that historically this variance has been far too low to justify the fact that in real terms (i.e. excluding inflation) the US stock market has been 7.8 percentage points (i.e. 8.4% − 0.6%) above the riskless return in the post-war period and in the UK the stock market has been 4.6 percentage points above the market over a similar period (Mehra 2003).[2]

A final critique is that the model is not complete. The application of the ICAPM or any discount cash flow model does not account for the role of real options in investments. For the MNC, the option to abandon is a very important safeguard in estimating country risk – this is effectively an American style put option on an investment. Also, many would dispute that the market is the only non-diversifiable risk source, exposure to interest rate changes and changes in the price of oil are also not easily diversified away.

EXAMPLE

Blat plc is considering building a factory in country X or country Y. Both factories will serve the European market. In country X the costs are much lower than in Y and the net present value of the project is much higher. But in country Y the government has given a guarantee that Blat can sell the factory back to them at the purchase price and that all labour liabilities will be taken over by the government. This option can be exercised at any time. Blat decides that country Y is the better prospect even though the net present value of the project is lower.

Implications of the ICAPM and CAPM for an MNC's risk

In view of the issues raised in the previous section it is natural to think that there may indeed be few implications for the CAPM and ICAPM in estimating risk for an MNC. This would be wrong. These models clearly have measurement problems and it would be wrong to see them as formulas that can be applied as a simple numerical calculation.

2. R. Mehra (2003) "The Equity Premium: Why Is It A Puzzle?", *Financial Analysts Journal*, 54–69.

Their value is that they provide a logical construct around which an MNC can formulate its thinking.

Capital asset pricing theory suggests that the cost of capital should be generally lower for MNCs than for domestic firms. MNCs have a greater opportunity to diversify across different financial markets. The systematic or non-diversifiable element of their investments should be lower. However, investing abroad is risky, more risky than domestic investment. The non-systematic part of risk may therefore reasonably be expected to be greater. For particular MNCs diversification opportunities may be limited. Michelin make tyres, GlaxoSmithKlein formulate medicines and SABMiller brew beer. Different markets are possible, but the product and demand for the product is fairly narrow. The extensive use of derivatives by MNCs is an attempt to lower such risk.

At present it is still the case that MNC shares react predominantly to their home stock market index. Those indexes are over time increasingly becoming international as companies are quoted in more than one market. In the case of SABMiller (South African Breweries) the share is quoted on the London Stock Exchange, its functional (i.e. reporting) currency is the US dollar. It calculates its weighted average cost of capital as being a lowly 8.75%. Its attitude to risk is summarized in the Managing for Value section below.

We cannot say with certainty whether an MNC will have a lower cost of capital than a purely domestic firm in the same industry. However, we can use this discussion to understand how an MNC may attempt to take full advantage of the favourable aspects that reduce its cost of capital, while minimizing exposure to the unfavourable aspects that increase its cost of capital.

Costs of capital across countries

An understanding as to why the cost of capital can vary among countries is relevant for three reasons. First, it can explain why MNCs based in some countries may have a competitive advantage over others. Just as technology and resources differ across countries, so does the cost of capital. MNCs based in some countries will have a larger set of feasible (positive net present value) projects because their cost of capital is lower; thus, these MNCs can more easily increase their world market share. MNCs operating in countries

Managing for value
SABMiller

SABMiller is quoted on the London Stock exchange and is in the FTSE100 index. The group's weighted average cost of capital in the 2005 accounts is stated as 8.75% after taking into account "relevant individual country profiles and the group's overall debt profile". To reduce currency risk, the group borrows in euro, Polish zloty, Czech krone and US dollars. That is the fixed and variable interest rate costs of this borrowing is set off against earnings in those currencies. Its reporting currency is the dollar. Its policy is to hedge against currency movements such that a 10% change in the value of the currency, for example the Polish zloty, will not affect overall profits (which are reported in dollars) by more than 1%. Any transaction over $60m is therefore hedged. In fact it reports that its exposure to foreign currency movment, described as a simultaneous change of 10% in all the foreign (non-US) currencies would affect profits by about half that amount. Interest rate risk and occasional commodity risk (aluminium) is also hedged. Thus in working out its cost of capital, SABMiller recognize currency risk, the weighted average cost of capital and country risk. No detailed calculations are provided but at least the ICAPM model has pointed to the principal factors. Note that risk is defined by the company in relation to its functional currency the dollar despite the fact that it is quoted on the London Stock Exchange.

with a high cost of capital will be forced to decline projects that might be feasible for MNCs operating in countries with a low cost of capital.

Second, MNCs may be able to adjust their international operations and sources of funds to capitalize on differences in the cost of capital among countries. Third, differences in the costs of each capital component (debt and equity) can help explain why MNCs based in some countries tend to use a more debt-intensive capital structure than MNCs based elsewhere. Country differences in the cost of debt are discussed next, followed by country differences in the cost of equity.

Country differences in the cost of debt

The cost of debt to a firm is primarily determined by the prevailing risk-free interest rate in the currency borrowed and the risk premium required by creditors. The cost of debt for firms is higher in some countries than in others because the corresponding risk-free rate is higher at a specific point in time or because the risk premium is higher (see Exhibit 17.3). Explanations for country differences in the risk-free rate and in the risk premium follow.

Differences in the risk-free rate. The risk-free rate is determined by the interaction of the supply of and demand for funds. Any factors that influence the supply and/or demand will affect the risk-free rate. These factors include tax laws, demographics, monetary policies, and economic conditions, all of which differ among countries.

Tax laws in some countries offer more incentives to save than those in others, which can influence the supply of savings and, therefore, interest rates. A country's corporate tax laws related to depreciation and investment tax credits can also affect interest rates through their influence on the corporate demand for funds.

A country's demographics influence the supply of savings available and the amount of loanable funds demanded. Since demographics differ among countries, so will supply and demand conditions and, therefore, nominal interest rates. Countries with younger populations are likely to experience higher interest rates because younger households tend to save less and borrow more.

The monetary policy implemented by a country's central bank influences the supply of loanable funds and therefore influences interest rates. Each central bank implements its own monetary policy, and this can cause interest rates to differ among countries. One exception is the set of European countries that rely on the European Central Bank to control the supply of euros. All of these countries now have the same risk-free rate because they use the same currency.

Since economic conditions influence interest rates, they can cause interest rates to vary across countries. The cost of debt is much higher in many less developed countries than in industrialized countries, primarily because of economic conditions. Countries such as Brazil and Russia commonly have a high risk-free interest rate, which is partially attributed to high inflation. Investors in these countries will invest in a firm's debt securities only if they are compensated beyond the degree to which prices of products are expected to increase.

If interest parity were to hold, higher foreign risk free interest rates would be offset by a depreciating currency; lower foreign interest rates would be compensated for by an appreciating currency. Looking at historic data, interest parity does not appear to hold well.

Differences in the risk premium. The risk premium on debt must be large enough to compensate creditors for the risk that the borrower may be unable to meet its payment obligations. This risk can vary among countries because of differences in economic conditions, relationships between corporations and creditors, government intervention, and degree of financial leverage.

When a country's economic conditions tend to be stable, the risk of a recession in that country is relatively low. Thus, the probability that a firm might not meet its obligations is lower, allowing for a lower risk premium.

Corporations and creditors have closer relationships in some countries than in others. In Japan, creditors stand ready to extend credit in the event of a corporation's financial distress, which reduces the risk of illiquidity. The cost of a Japanese firm's financial problems may be shared in various ways by the firm's management, business customers, and consumers. Since the financial problems are not borne entirely by creditors, all parties involved have more incentive to see that the problems are resolved. Thus, there is less likelihood (for a given level of debt) that Japanese firms will go bankrupt, allowing for a lower risk premium on the debt of Japanese firms.

Exhibit 17.3 Costs of risk free debts across countries

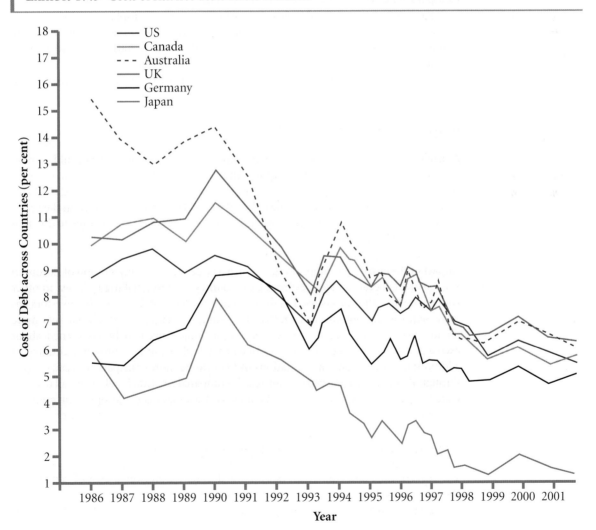

Governments in some countries are more willing to intervene and rescue failing firms. In China and Russia large energy companies tend to be partly state owned. It may be in the government's best interest to rescue firms that it partially owns. Even if the government is not a partial owner, it may provide direct subsidies or extend loans to failing firms. Increasingly, government rescues are less likely because taxpayers prefer not to bear the cost of corporate mismanagement. In Europe government subsidies are likely to break EU competition policy. Where the probability that a failing firm will be rescued by the government is lower the risk premium on a given level of debt may be higher than for firms of other countries.

Firms in some countries have greater borrowing capacity because their creditors are willing to tolerate a higher degree of financial leverage. For example, firms in Japan and Germany have a higher degree of financial leverage than firms in the United States. If all other factors were equal, these high-leverage firms would have to pay a higher risk premium to their shareholders. However, all other factors are not equal. In fact, these firms are allowed to use a higher degree of financial leverage because of their unique relationships with the creditors and governments.

Comparative costs of debt across countries. The before-tax cost of debt (as measured by high-rated corporate bond yields) for various countries is displayed in Exhibit 17.3. There is some positive correlation between country cost-of-debt levels over time. The nominal cost of debt for firms in many countries declined in 2001–02 due to a global recession. However, some rates declined more than others. The disparity in the cost of debt among the countries is due primarily to the disparity in their risk-free interest rates.

Country differences in the cost of equity

A firm's cost of equity represents an opportunity cost: what shareholders could earn on investments with similar risk if the equity funds were distributed to them. This return on equity can be measured as a risk-free interest rate that could have been earned by shareholders, plus a premium to reflect the risk of the firm. For reasons explained in the previous section, the risk premium and hence the cost of equity will vary according to different economic environments.

Impact of the euro. The adoption of the euro has facilitated the integration of European stock markets because investors from each country are more willing to invest in other countries where the euro is used as the currency. As demand for shares by investors has increased, trading volume has increased, making the European stock markets more liquid. Investors in one euro-zone country no longer need to be concerned about exchange rate risk when they buy stock of a firm based in another euro-zone country. In addition, the euro allows the valuations of firms to be more transparent because firms throughout the euro-zone can be more easily compared since their values are all denominated in the same currency. Given the increased willingness of European investors to invest in stocks, MNCs based in Europe may obtain equity financing at a lower cost.

Combining the costs of debt and equity

The costs of debt and equity can be combined to derive an overall cost of capital (see above). The relative proportions of debt and equity used by firms in each country must be applied as weights to reasonably estimate this cost of capital. Given the differences in the costs of debt and equity across countries, it is understandable that the cost of capital may be lower for firms based in specific countries. Japan, for example, commonly has a relatively low cost of capital. It usually has a relatively low risk-free interest rate, which not only affects the cost of debt but also indirectly affects the cost of equity. In addition, the price-earnings multiples of Japanese firms are usually high, allowing these firms to obtain equity funding at a relatively low cost. MNCs can attempt to access capital from countries where capital costs are low, but when the capital is used to support operations in other countries, the cost of using that capital is exposed to exchange rate risk. Thus, the cost of capital may ultimately turn out to be higher than expected. As stated above, the international Fisher effect predicts that the exchange rate should offset any differences, thus the value of the yen should increase relative to other currencies to offer a similar return.

Estimating the cost of debt and equity

When financing new projects, MNCs estimate their cost of debt and equity from various sources. They consider these estimates when they decide on the capital structure to use for financing the projects.

The after-tax cost of debt can be estimated with reasonable accuracy using public information on the present costs of debt (bond yields) incurred by other firms whose risk level is similar to that of the project. The cost of equity is an opportunity cost: what investors could earn on alternative equity investments with similar risk. The MNC can attempt to measure the expected return on a set of stocks that exhibit the same risk as its project. This expected return can serve as the cost of equity. The required rate of return on the project will be the project's weighted cost of capital, based on the estimates as explained here.

EXAMPLE

Lexon plc, a successful UK-based MNC, is considering how to obtain funding for a project in Argentina during the next year. It considers the following information:

- UK risk-free rate = 6%.
- Argentine risk-free rate = 10%.
- Risk premium on pound-denominated debt provided by UK creditors = 3%.
- Risk premium on Argentine peso-denominated debt provided by Argentine creditors = 5%.
- Beta of project (expected sensitivity of project returns to UK investors in response to the UK market) = 1.5.
- Expected UK market return = 14%.
- UK corporate tax rate = 30%.
- Argentine corporate tax rate = 30%.
- Creditors are likely to allow no more than 50% of the financing to be in the form of debt, which implies that equity must provide at least half of the financing.

Lexon's Cost of Each Component of Capital	
Cost of pound-denominated debt	$= (6\% + 3\%) \times (1 - 0.3) = 6.3\%$
Cost of Argentine peso-denominated debt	$= (10\% + 5\%) \times (1 - 0.3) = 10.5\%$
Cost of pound-denominated equity	$= 6\% + 1.5 (14\% - 6\%) = 18\%$

Exhibit 17.4 Lexon's estimated weighted average cost of capital (WACC) for financing a project

Possible Capital Structure	UK Debt (Cost = 6.3%)	Argentine Debt (Cost = 10.5%)	Equity (Estimated Cost)	Estimated WACC
30% UK debt, 70% equity	30% × 6.3% = 1.89%		70% × 18% = 12.6%	14.49%
50% UK debt, 50% UK equity	50% × 6.3% = 3.15%		50% × 20% = 10%	13.15%
20% UK debt, 30% Argentine debt, 50% UK equity	20% × 6.3% = 1.26%	30% × 10.5% = 3.15%	50% × 20% = 10%	14.41%
50% Argentine debt, 50% UK equity		50% × 10.5% = 5.25%	50% × 20% = 10%	15.25%

Note:

The cost of equity will vary according to the level of borrowing (leverage). We assume a constant exchange rate.

Notice that Lexon's cheapest source of funds is pound-denominated debt. However, creditors have imposed restrictions on the total amount of debt funding that Lexon can obtain.

Lexon considers four different capital structures for this new project, as shown in Exhibit 17.4. Its weighted average cost of capital (WACC) for this project can be derived by summing the products of the weight times the cost for each component of capital. The weight assigned to each component is the proportion of total funds obtained from that component.

The exhibit shows that lowest estimate of the WACC results from a capital structure of 50% UK debt and 50% equity. Although it is useful to estimate the costs of possible capital structures as shown here, the estimated WACC does not account for the exposure to exchange rate risk. Thus, Lexon will not necessarily choose the capital structure with the lowest estimated WACC. Lexon can attempt to incorporate the exchange rate effects in various ways, as explained in the following section.

USING THE COST OF CAPITAL FOR ASSESSING FOREIGN PROJECTS

When an MNC's parent proposes an investment in a foreign project that has the same risk as the MNC itself, it can use its weighted average cost of capital as the required rate of return for the project. However, many foreign projects exhibit different risk levels than the risk of the MNC. There are various ways for an MNC to account for the risk differential in its capital budgeting process.

Derive net present values based on the weighted average cost of capital

EXAMPLE

Recall that Lexon estimated that its WACC will be 13.15% if it uses 50% pound-denominated debt and 50% equity. It considers assessing the project in Argentina based on a required rate of return of 13.15%. Yet, by financing the Argentine project completely with pounds, Lexon will likely be highly exposed to exchange rate movements. It can attempt to account for the way in which expected exchange rate movements will affect its cash flows when it conducts its capital budgeting analysis.

Furthermore, Lexon could account for the risk within its cash flow estimates. Many possible values for each input variable (such as exchange rate, demand, price, labour cost, etc.) can be incorporated into the estimated future cash flows. Risk may then be assessed independently by looking at the returns and their probability and standard deviation of those returns. The standard deviation as a measure of risk can then be translated into a discount rate and *NPV* processes applied. Alternatively, Lexon may wish to look at worst case scenarios and value options available. Computer software programs that perform sensitivity analysis and simulation can be used to facilitate the process.

Adjust the weighted average cost of capital for the risk differential

An alternative method of accounting for a foreign project's risk is to adjust the firm's weighted average cost of capital for the risk differential. For example, if the foreign project is thought to exhibit more risk than the MNC exhibits, a premium can be added to the WACC to derive the required rate of return on the project. Then, the capital budgeting process will incorporate this required rate of return as the discount rate. If the foreign project exhibits lower risk, the MNC will use a required rate of return on the project that is less than its WACC.

EXAMPLE   Lexon estimated that its WACC will be 13.15% if it uses the capital structure of 50% pound-denominated debt and 50% equity. But it recognizes that its Argentine project will be exposed to exchange rate risk and that this project is exposed to more risk than its normal operations. Lexon considers adding a risk premium of 6 percentage points to the estimated WACC to derive the required rate of return. In this case, the required rate of return would be 13.15% + 6% = 19.15%.

The usefulness of this method is limited because the risk premium is arbitrarily determined and is subject to error. The risk premium is dependent on the manager who conducts the analysis. Thus, the decision to accept or reject the foreign project, which is based on the estimated *NPV* of the project, could be dependent on the manager's decision about the risk premium to use within the required rate of return. Such judgements are inevitable given that the Argentine peso exhibited great stability and then in 2001/02 devalued suddenly by 40%. Statistics cannot easily cope with such jumps.

Derive the net present value of the equity investment

The two methods described up to this point discount cash flows based on the total cost of the project's capital. That is, they compare the *NPV* of the project's cash flows to the initial capital outlay. They ignore debt payments because the cost of debt is captured within the required rate of return on the capital to be invested in the project. When an MNC is considering financing a portion of the foreign project within that country, these methods are less effective because they do not measure how the debt payments could affect pound cash flows. Some of the MNC's debt payments in the foreign country may reduce its exposure to exchange rate risk, which affects the cash flows that will ultimately be received by the parent.

To explicitly account for the exchange rate effects, an MNC can assess the project by measuring the *NPV* of the equity investment in the project. All debt payments are explicitly accounted for when using this method, so the analysis fully accounts for the effects of expected exchange rate movements. Then, the present value of all cash flows received by the parent can be compared to the parent's initial equity investment in the project. The MNC can conduct this same analysis for various financing alternatives to determine the one that yields the most favourable *NPV* for the project.

EXAMPLE

To illustrate, reconsider Lexon plc, which might finance the Argentine project with partial financing from Argentina. More details are needed to illustrate this point. Assume that Lexon would need to invest 80 million Argentine pesos (AP) in the project. Since the peso is currently worth £0.30, Lexon needs the equivalent of £26 million. It will use equity for 50% of the funds needed, or £13 million. It will use debt to obtain the remaining capital. For its debt financing, Lexon decides that it will either borrow pounds and convert the funds into pesos or borrow pesos. The project will be terminated in one year; at that time, the debt will be repaid, and any earnings generated by the project will be remitted to Lexon's parent in the United Kingdom. The project is expected to result in revenue of AP200 million, and operating expenses in Argentina will be AP10 million. Lexon expects that the Argentine peso will be valued at £0.24 in one year.

This project will not generate any revenue in the United Kingdom, but Lexon does expect to incur operating expenses of £6 million in the United Kingdom. It will also incur pound-denominated interest expenses if it finances the project with pound-denominated debt. Any pound-denominated expenses provide tax benefits, as the expenses will reduce UK taxable income from other operations. The amount of debt used in each country affects the interest payments incurred and the taxes paid in that country.

The previous two methods are not effective for analyzing this type of financing decision. To compare the two financing alternatives, the analysis needs to incorporate the debt payments directly into the cash flow estimates. Consequently, the focus is on comparing the present value of pound cash flows earned on the equity investment to the initial equity outlay. If neither alternative has a positive *NPV*, the proposed project will not be undertaken. If both alternatives have positive *NPVs*, the project will be financed with the capital structure that is expected to generate a higher *NPV*.

As with the capital budgeting analysis in Chapter 14, it is necessary to assess the project from the perspective of the parent's local equity holders. A project should be considered only if it is beneficial to the parent's shareholders. The payments from Lexon to any creditors in the United Kingdom or in a foreign country should be explicitly accounted for in order to measure the cash flows that flow back to the parent's shareholders after payments have been made to creditors. This allows for a more accurate measure of the remitted cash flows that are exposed to exchange rate movements. Cash flows to the parent are discounted at the parent's cost of equity, which represents the required rate of return on the project by the parent's shareholders. Since the debt payments are explicitly accounted for, the analysis compares the present value of the project's cash flows to the initial equity investment that would be invested in the project.

The analysis of the two financing alternatives is provided in Exhibit 17.5. If Lexon uses pound-denominated debt, a larger amount of funds will be remitted and thus will be subject to the exchange rate effect. Conversely, if Lexon uses peso-denominated debt, the amount of remitted funds is smaller. The analysis shows that the project generates an *NPV* of –£1.42 million if the project is partially financed with pound-denominated debt versus an *NPV* of £1.26 million if it is partially financed with peso-denominated debt.

Since the peso is expected to depreciate significantly over the year, Lexon will be better off using the more expensive peso-denominated debt than the pound-denominated debt. That is, the higher cost of the debt is more than offset by the reduced exposure to adverse exchange rate effects. Consequently, Lexon should finance this project with a capital structure that includes the peso-denominated debt, even though the interest rate on this debt is high.

Relationship between project's net present value and capital structure. The *NPV* of the foreign project is dependent on the project's capital structure for two reasons. First, the capital structure can affect the cost of capital. Second, the capital structure influences the amount of cash flows that are distributed to creditors in the local country before taxes are imposed and funds are remitted to the parent. Since the capital structure influences the tax and exchange rate effects, it affects the cash flows that are ultimately received by the parent.

Tradeoff when financing in developing countries. The results here do not imply that foreign debt should always be used to finance a foreign project. The advantage of using foreign debt to offset foreign revenue (reduce exchange rate risk) must be weighed against the cost of that debt. Many developing countries commonly have high interest rates on debt, but their local currencies tend to weaken against the dollar. Thus, US-based MNCs must either tolerate a high cost of local debt financing or borrow in dollars but be exposed to significant exchange rate risk. The tradeoff can best be assessed by estimating the *NPV* of the MNC's equity investment under each financing alternative, as illustrated in the previous example.

Accounting for multiple periods. The preceding example focused on just one period to illustrate how the analysis is conducted. The analysis can easily be adapted to assess multiple periods, however. The same analysis shown for a single year in Exhibit 17.5 could be applied to multiple years. For each year, the revenue and expenses would be recorded, with the debt payments explicitly accounted for. The tax and exchange rate effects would be measured to derive the amount of cash flows received in each year. A discount rate that reflects the required rate of return on equity would be applied to measure the present value of the cash flows to be received by the parent. The discount rate would reflect the risk applicable to the estimates.

Comparing alternative debt compositions. In the Lexon example, the focus was on whether the debt should be in pesos or in pounds. Other debt compositions could also have been considered, such as the following:

- 75% of the debt denominated in Argentine pesos, and the remaining debt denominated in pounds.
- 50% of the debt denominated in Argentine pesos, and the remaining debt denominated in pounds.
- 25% of the debt denominated in Argentine pesos, and the remaining debt denominated in pounds.

The analysis can also account for different debt maturity structures. For example, if an MNC is considering a short-term Argentine loan that would be paid off in one year, it can estimate the cash outflow payments associated with the debt repayment. If it is considering a medium-term or long-term loan denominated in pesos, the payments will be spread out more and incorporated within the cash outflows over time. The analysis can

Exhibit 17.5 Analysis of Lexon's project based on two financing alternatives (numbers are in millions)

(Currency in millions)	Rely on UK Debt (£13 million Borrowed) and Equity of £13 million	Rely on Argentine Debt (40 million pesos Borrowed) and Equity of £13 million
Argentine revenue	AP200	AP200
− Argentine operating expenses	−AP10	−AP10
− Argentine interest expenses (15% rate)	−AP0	−AP6
= Argentine earnings before taxes	= AP190	= AP184
− Taxes (30% tax rate)	−AP57	−AP55.2
= Argentine earnings after taxes	= AP133	= AP128.8
− Principal payments on Argentine debt	−AP0	−AP40
= Amount of pesos to be remitted =	AP133	= AP88.8
× Expected exchange rate of AP	×£0.24	×£0.24
= Amount of pounds received from converting pesos	= £31.92	= £21.31
− UK operating expenses	−£6	−£6
− UK interest expenses (9% rate)	−£1.17	−$0
+ UK tax benefits on UK expenses (based on 30% tax rate)	+£2.15	+£1.8
− Principal payments on UK debt	−£13	−£0
= Pound cash flows	= £13.90	= £17.11
Present value of pound cash flows, discounted at the cost of equity (assumed to be 20%)	£11.58	£14.26
− Initial equity outlay	£13	£13
= NPV	= − £1.42	= £1.26

easily account for a combination of short-term loans in Argentina and long-term loans in the UK or vice versa. It can account for floating-rate loans that adjust to market interest rates by developing one or more scenarios for how market interest rates will change in the future. The key is that all interest and principal payments on the debt are accounted for, along with any other cash flows. Then the present value of the cash flows can be compared to the initial outlay to determine whether the equity investment is feasible.

Comparing alternative capital structures. In the example of Lexon plc the proportion of debt versus equity was held constant for both alternatives that were analyzed. In reality, the capital structure decision will consider not only the composition of the debt, but also the proportion of equity versus debt that should be obtained. The same type of analysis could have been used to compare different capital structures, such as the following:

- 50% equity and 50% debt.
- 60% equity and 40% debt.
- 70% equity and 30% debt.

If Lexon in the previous example used more UK equity, there would be three obvious effects:

1. A higher initial equity investment would be needed.
2. The higher the level of debt the greater the gearing and hence the risk to equity. The cost of equity capital will therefore increase. Modigliani and Miller argue that the increase in the required return to equity capital is such that the overall cost of capital will remain constant.
3. With the lower debt level, the cash outflows needed to make debt payments would be reduced, so the present value of cash flows would increase but the required return on equity would increase to compensate.

The first effect would reduce the *NPV* of the equity investment in the project, whereas the second effect would increase it. As in the previous example, an analysis would have to be conducted to determine whether using more equity would result in a higher *NPV* generated by the equity investment.

Assessing alternative exchange rate scenarios. The example used only one exchange rate scenario, which may not be realistic. A spreadsheet can easily compare the *NPV*s of the two alternatives based on other exchange rate projections. This type of analysis would show that because of the greater exposure, the *NPV* of the project will be more sensitive to exchange rate scenarios if the project is financed with pound-denominated debt than if it is financed with peso-denominated debt. The reason is simply that setting costs in a currency (interest payments) against revenues in that currency reduces the exposure to exchange rate changes as it is only the net amount that will affect the wealth of the MNC.

Considering foreign stock ownership. Some capital structure decisions also include foreign shareholders, but the analysis can still be conducted in the same manner. The analysis becomes complicated only if the foreign ownership changes the corporate governance in some way that affects the firm's cash flows. Many MNCs have issued stock in foreign countries where they do business. They will consider issuing stock only in countries where there is a sufficient demand for it. When there is not sufficient foreign demand, an MNC can more easily place its stock in its home market.

Normally, an MNC will focus its stock offerings in a few countries where it does most of its business. The stock will be listed on the local stock exchange in the countries where the shares are issued and will be denominated in the local currency. The listing is necessary to create a secondary market for the stock in the foreign country. Many investors will consider purchasing a stock only if there is a local secondary market where they can easily sell their shares.

THE MNC'S CAPITAL STRUCTURE DECISION

An MNC's capital structure decision involves the choice of debt versus equity financing within all of its subsidiaries. Thus, its overall capital structure is essentially a combination of all of its subsidiaries' capital structures. MNCs recognize the tradeoff between using debt and using equity for financing their operations. The advantages of using debt as opposed to equity vary with corporate characteristics specific to each MNC and specific to the countries where the MNC has established subsidiaries. Some of the more relevant corporate characteristics specific to an MNC that can affect its capital structure are identified first, followed by country characteristics.

Influence of corporate characteristics

Characteristics unique to each MNC can influence its capital structure. Some of the more common firm-specific characteristics that affect the MNC's capital structure are identified here.

Stability of MNC's cash flows. MNCs with more stable cash flows can handle more debt because there is a constant stream of cash inflows to cover periodic interest payments. Conversely, MNCs with erratic cash flows may prefer less debt because they are not assured of generating enough cash in each period to make larger interest payments on debt. MNCs that are diversified across several countries may have more stable cash flows since the conditions in any single country should not have a major impact on their cash flows. Consequently, these MNCs may be able to handle a more debt-intensive capital structure.

MNC's credit risk. MNCs that have lower credit risk (risk of default on loans provided by creditors) have more access to credit. Any factors that influence credit risk can affect an MNC's choice of using debt versus equity. For example, if an MNC's management is thought to be strong and competent, the MNC's credit risk may be low, allowing for easier access to debt. MNCs with assets that serve as acceptable collateral (such as buildings, trucks, and adaptable machinery) are more able to obtain loans and may prefer to emphasize debt financing. Conversely, MNCs with assets that are not marketable have less acceptable collateral and may need to use a higher proportion of equity financing.

MNC's access to retained earnings. Highly profitable MNCs may be able to finance most of their investment with retained earnings and therefore use an equity-intensive capital structure. Conversely, MNCs that have small levels of retained earnings may rely on debt financing. Growth-oriented MNCs are less able to finance their expansion with retained earnings and tend to rely on debt financing. MNCs with less growth need less new financing and may rely on retained earnings (equity) rather than debt.

MNC's guarantees on debt. If the parent backs the debt of its subsidiary, the subsidiary's borrowing capacity might be increased. Therefore, the subsidiary might need less equity financing. At the same time, however, the parent's borrowing capacity might be reduced, as creditors will be less willing to provide funds to the parent if those funds might be needed to rescue the subsidiary.

MNC's agency problems. If a subsidiary in a foreign country cannot easily be monitored by investors from the parent's country, agency costs are higher. To maximize the firm's stock price, the parent may ask the subsidiary to issue stock rather than debt in the local market so that its managers there will be monitored. In this case, the foreign subsidiary is referred to as "partially owned" rather than "wholly owned" by the MNC's parent. This strategy can affect the MNC's capital structure. It may be feasible when the MNC's parent can enhance the subsidiary's image and presence in the host country or can motivate the subsidiary's managers by allowing them partial ownership.

   One concern about a partially owned foreign subsidiary is a potential conflict of interest, especially when its managers are minority shareholders. These managers may make decisions that can benefit the subsidiary at the expense of the MNC overall. For example, they may use funds for projects that are feasible from their perspective but not from the parent's perspective.

Influence of country characteristics

In addition to characteristics unique to each MNC, the characteristics unique to each host country can influence the MNC's choice of debt versus equity financing and therefore influence the MNC's capital structure. Specific country characteristics that can influence an MNC's choice of equity versus debt financing are described here.

Visit **http://www.worldbank.org** for country profiles, analyses, and sectoral surveys.

Stock restrictions in host countries. In some countries, governments allow investors to invest only in local stocks. Even when investors are allowed to invest in other countries, they may not have complete information about stocks of companies outside their home countries. This represents an implicit barrier to cross-border investing. Furthermore, potential adverse exchange rate effects and tax effects can discourage investors from investing outside their home countries. Such impediments to worldwide investing can cause some investors to have fewer stock investment opportunities than others. Consequently, an MNC operating in countries where investors have fewer investment opportunities may be able to raise equity in those countries at a relatively low cost. This could entice the MNC to use more equity by issuing stock in these countries to finance its operations.

Interest rates in host countries. Because of government-imposed barriers on capital flows along with potential adverse exchange rate, tax, and country risk effects, loanable funds do not always flow to where they are needed most. Thus, the price of loanable funds (the interest rate) can vary across countries. MNCs may be able to obtain loanable funds (debt) at a relatively low cost in specific countries, while the cost of debt in other countries may be very high. Consequently, an MNC's preference for debt may depend on the costs of debt in the countries where it operates. If markets are somewhat segmented and the cost of funds in the subsidiary's country appears excessive, the parent may use its own equity to support projects implemented by the subsidiary.

Strength of host country currencies. If an MNC is concerned about the potential weakness of the currencies in its subsidiaries' host countries, it may attempt to finance a large proportion of its foreign operations by borrowing those currencies instead of relying on parent funds. In this way, the subsidiaries will remit a smaller amount in earnings because they will be making interest payments on local debt. This strategy reduces the MNC's exposure to exchange rate risk.

If the parent believes that a subsidiary's local currency will appreciate against the parent's currency, it may have the subsidiary retain and reinvest more of its earnings. The parent may also provide an immediate cash infusion to finance growth in the subsidiary. As a result, there will be a transfer of internal funds from the parent to the subsidiary, possibly resulting in more external financing by the parent and less debt financing by the subsidiary.

Country risk in host countries. A relatively mild form of country risk is the possibility that the host government will temporarily block funds to be remitted by the subsidiary to the parent. Subsidiaries that are prevented from remitting earnings over a period may prefer to use local debt financing. This strategy reduces the amount of funds that are blocked because the subsidiary can use some of the funds to pay interest on local debt.

If an MNC's subsidiary is exposed to risk that a host government might confiscate its assets, the subsidiary may use much debt financing in that host country. Then local creditors that have lent funds will have a genuine interest in ensuring that the subsidiary is treated fairly by the host government. In addition, if the MNC's operations in a foreign country are terminated by the host government, it will not lose as much if its operations are financed by local creditors. Under these circumstances, the local creditors will have to negotiate with the host government to obtain all or part of the funds they have lent after the host government liquidates the assets it confiscates from the MNC.

A less likely way to reduce exposure to a high degree of country risk is for the subsidiary to issue stock in the host country. Minority shareholders benefit directly from a profitable subsidiary. Therefore, they could pressure their government to refrain from imposing excessive taxes, environmental constraints, or any other provisions that would reduce the profits of the subsidiary. Having local investors own a minority interest in a subsidiary may also offer some protection against threats of adverse actions by the host government. Another advantage of a partially owned subsidiary is that it may open up additional opportunities in the host country. The subsidiary's name will become better known when its shares are acquired by minority shareholders in that country.

Tax laws in host countries. Foreign subsidiaries of an MNC may be subject to a withholding tax when they remit earnings. By using local debt financing instead of relying on parent financing, they will have to make interest payments on the local debt and thus may be able to reduce the amount to be remitted periodically. Thus, they may reduce the withholding taxes by using more local debt financing. Foreign subsidiaries may also consider using local debt if the host governments impose high corporate tax rates on foreign earnings; in this way, the subsidiaries can benefit from the tax advantage of using debt where taxes are high (unless the higher taxes paid would be fully offset by tax credits received by the parent).

Revising the capital structure in response to changing conditions

As economic and political conditions in a country change or an MNC's business changes, the costs or benefits of each component cost of capital can change as well. An MNC may revise its capital structure in response to the changing conditions.

1. A firm discontinues its business in Argentina and decides to reduce its Argentine debt. It no longer has Argentine peso revenue that it used to offset to reduce exchange rate risk.
2. The UK government reduces taxes on dividends, which makes stocks more attractive to investors than investing in debt securities. Thus, the cost of equity has decreased, causing some MNCs to shift their capital structure.
3. Interest rates in Europe increase, causing some UK-based MNCs to support their European operations with pound-denominated debt.
4. Interest rates in Singapore decrease, causing some UK-based MNCs with operations in Singapore to increase their use of debt denominated in Singapore dollars.
5. Political risk in Peru increases, causing some UK-based MNCs to finance more of their business there with local debt so that they have some support from local institutions with political connections.

In recent years, MNCs have revised their capital structures to reduce their withholding taxes on remitted earnings by subsidiaries.

EXAMPLE

Clayton plc is a UK-based MNC whose parent plans to raise £50 million of capital in the United Kingdom by issuing stock in the United Kingdom. The parent plans to convert the £50 million into 100 million Australian dollars (A$) and use the funds to build a subsidiary in Australia. Since the parent may need some return on this capital to pay its shareholders' dividends, it will require that its Australian subsidiary remit A$4 million per year. Assume that the Australian government will impose a withholding tax of 10% on the remitted earnings, which will amount to A$400,000 per year. Clayton plc can revise its capital structure in several different ways to reduce or avoid this tax. Most solutions involve reducing the reliance of the subsidiary on the parent's capital.

First, Clayton's Australian subsidiary could borrow funds in Australia as its main source of capital instead of relying on the UK parent. Thus, it would use some of its earnings to pay its local creditors interest instead of remitting a large amount of earnings to the UK parent. This financing strategy minimizes the amount of funds that would be

Exhibit 17.6 Adjusting the multinational capital structure to reduce withholding taxes

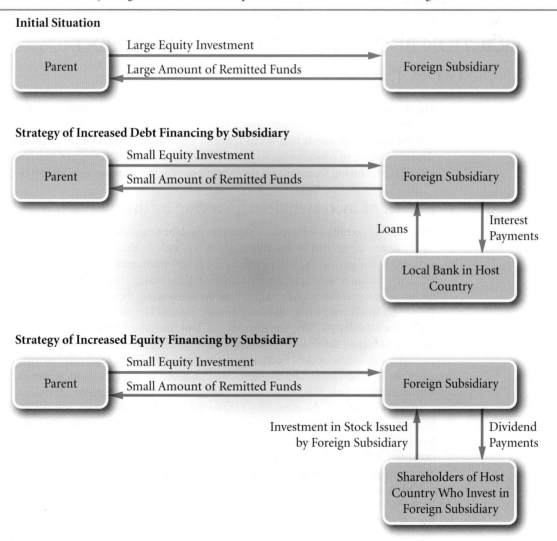

remitted and can therefore minimize the withholding taxes that would be paid to the Australian government. In addition, the subsidiary would not need as much equity investment from the parent. One limitation of this strategy is that the subsidiary may increase its debt to an excessive level.

If Clayton prefers not to increase the subsidiary's debt, the subsidiary could raise funds by issuing stock in the host country. In this case, the subsidiary would use a portion of its funds to pay dividends to local shareholders rather than remit those funds to the parent. Once again, withholding taxes are minimized because the subsidiary would not remit much money to the parent. The issuance of stock would create a minority owner-ship in Australia, which reduces the parent's control over the subsidiary. The parent could retain control, however, by instructing the subsidiary to issue non-voting stock.

Both strategies minimize Clayton's withholding tax, but the first strategy reflects a more debt-intensive capital structure while the second strategy reflects a more equity-intensive capital structure. The two strategies are illustrated in Exhibit 17.6. These strate-gies could also have been used to reduce Clayton's exposure to exchange rate risk because they minimize the amount of Australian dollars that will be converted into British pounds.

INTERACTION BETWEEN SUBSIDIARY AND PARENT FINANCING DECISIONS

The decision by a subsidiary to use internal equity financing (retaining and reinvesting its earnings) or obtain debt financing can affect its degree of reliance on parent financing and the amount of funds that it can remit to the parent. Thus, its financing decisions should be made in consultation with the parent. The potential impact of two common subsidiary financing situations on the parent's capital structure are explained next.

Impact of increased debt financing by the subsidiary

When global conditions increase a subsidiary's debt financing, the amount of internal equity financing needed by the subsidiary is reduced. As these extra internal funds are remitted to the parent, the parent will have a larger amount of internal funds to use for financing before resorting to external financing. Assuming that the parent's operations absorb all internal funds and require some debt financing, there are offsetting effects on the capital structures of the subsidiary and the parent. The increased use of debt financ-ing by the subsidiary is offset by the reduced debt financing of the parent. Nevertheless, the cost of capital for the MNC overall could have changed for two reasons. First, the revised composition of debt financing (more by the subsidiary, less by the parent) could affect the interest charged on the debt. Second, it could affect the MNC's overall expo-sure to exchange rate risk and therefore influence the risk premium on capital.

In some situations, the subsidiary's increased use of debt financing will not be offset by the parent's reduced debt financing. For example, if there are any restrictions or exces-sive taxes on remitted funds, the parent may not be able to rely on the subsidiary and may need some debt financing as well. In this case, international conditions that encour-age increased use of debt financing by the subsidiary will result in a more debt-intensive capital structure for the MNC. Again, for reasons already mentioned, the cost of capital to the MNC could be affected by the subsidiary's increased debt financing. In addition, the use of a higher proportion of debt financing for the MNC overall would also affect the cost of capital.

Exhibit 17.7   Effect of global conditions on financing

	Amount of Local Debt Financing by Subsidiary	Amount of Internal Funds Available to Parent	Amount of Debt Financing Provided by Parent
Higher country risk	Higher	Higher	Lower
Higher interest rates	Lower	Lower	Higher
Lower interest rates	Higher	Higher	Lower
Expected weakness of local currency	Higher	Higher	Lower
Expected strength of local currency	Lower	Lower	Higher
Blocked funds	Higher	Higher	Lower
High withholding taxes	Higher	Higher	Lower
Higher corporate taxes	Higher	Higher	Lower

Impact of reduced debt financing by the subsidiary

When global conditions encourage the subsidiary to use less debt financing, the subsidiary will need to use more internal financing. Consequently, it will remit fewer funds to the parent, reducing the amount of internal funds available to the parent. If the parent's operations absorb all internal funds and require some debt financing, there are offsetting effects on the capital structures of the subsidiary and parent. The subsidiary's reduced use of debt financing is offset by the parent's increased use. For reasons expressed earlier, the cost of capital may change even if the MNC's overall capital structure does not.

If the parent's operations can be fully financed with internal funds, the parent will probably not use debt financing. Thus, the subsidiary's reduced debt financing is not offset by the parent's increased debt financing, and the MNC's overall capital structure becomes more equity-intensive. MNC's will have an overall target for the level of debt financing. Changing currency exposure, the maturity of old debts and new finance requirements will mean a constant review of borrowing policy.

Summary of interaction between subsidiary and parent financing decisions

Exhibit 17.7 provides a summary of some of the more relevant characteristics of the host country that can affect a subsidiary's preference for debt or equity financing. The decision by a subsidiary to finance with local debt affects the amount of funds remitted to the parent and therefore affects the amount of internal financing available to the parent. Since the subsidiary's local debt financing decisions are influenced by country-specific characteristics like those shown in Exhibit 17.7, the MNC's overall capital structure is partially influenced by the locations of the foreign subsidiaries.

LOCAL VERSUS GLOBAL TARGET CAPITAL STRUCTURE

An MNC may deviate from its "local" target capital structure in each country where financing is obtained, yet still achieve its "global" target capital structure (based on consolidating the capital structures of all its subsidiaries). The following examples of particular foreign country conditions illustrate the motive behind deviating from a local target capital structure while still satisfying a global target capital structure.

Offsetting a subsidiary's high degree of financial leverage

First, consider that Country A does not allow MNCs with headquarters elsewhere to list their stocks on its local stock exchange. Under these conditions, an MNC's subsidiary that desires to expand its operations is likely to borrow funds by issuing bonds or obtaining bank loans rather than by issuing stock in this country. By being forced to use debt financing here, the MNC may deviate from its target capital structure, which could raise its overall cost of capital. The parent might offset this concentration in debt by using more equity financing for its own operations.

Alternatively, consider an MNC that desires financing in Country B, which is experiencing political turmoil. The use of local bank loans would be most appropriate since local banks may be able to prevent the subsidiary's operations from being affected by political conditions in that country. If the local banks serve as creditors to the MNC's subsidiary, it is in their interest to ensure that the subsidiary's operations are sufficiently profitable to repay its loans. Since the subsidiary may have more financial leverage than is desired for the MNC overall, the parent may use less financial leverage to finance its own operations in order to achieve its overall ('global') target capital structure.

Offsetting a subsidiary's low degree of financial leverage

Suppose that Country C allows the MNC's subsidiary to issue stock there and list its stock on its local exchange. Also assume that the project to be implemented in that country will not generate net cash flows for five years, thereby limiting the subsidiary's ability to generate internal financing. In this case, equity financing by the subsidiary may be more appropriate. The subsidiary could issue stock, and, by paying low or zero dividends, it could avoid any major cash outflows for the next five years. The parent might offset the subsidiary's concentration in equity by instructing one of its other foreign subsidiaries in some other host country to use mostly debt financing. Alternatively, the parent could use more debt financing to support its own operations.

Limitations in offsetting a subsidiary's abnormal degree of financial leverage

The examples provided up to this point suggest that the parent can offset the imbalance created by a foreign subsidiary by adjusting the way it finances its own operations. However, the revision of the parent's capital structure may result in a higher cost of capital for the parent. Given that the subsidiary's financing decision could affect the parent's capital structure and therefore affect the parent's cost of capital, the subsidiary must consider the impact of its decision on the parent. The subsidiary's decision to use an unusually high or low degree of financial leverage should be made only if the benefits outweigh any costs for the MNC overall.

The strategy of ignoring a "local" target capital structure in favour of a "global" target capital structure is rational as long as it is acceptable to foreign creditors and investors. However, if foreign creditors and investors monitor each subsidiary's local capital structure, they may require a higher rate of return on funds provided to the MNC. For example, the "local" target capital structures for the subsidiaries based in Country A (from the earlier example) and in Country B are debt-intensive. Creditors in these two countries may penalize the subsidiary for its highly leveraged local capital structure, even though the MNC's global capital structure is more balanced, because they believe that the subsidiary may be unable to meet its high debt repayments. If the parent plans to back the subsidiaries, however, it could guarantee debt repayment to the creditors in the foreign countries, which might reduce their risk perception and lower the cost of the debt. Many MNC parents stand ready to financially back their subsidiaries because, if they did not, their subsidiaries would be unable to obtain adequate financing.

SUMMARY

- The cost of capital may be lower for an MNC than for a domestic firm because of characteristics peculiar to the MNC, including its size, its access to international capital markets, and its degree of international diversification. Yet, some characteristics peculiar to an MNC can increase the MNC's cost of capital, such as exposure to exchange rate risk and to country risk.

- Costs of capital vary across countries because of country differences in the components that comprise the cost of capital. Specifically, there are differences in the risk-free rate, the risk premium on debt, and the cost of equity among countries. Countries with a higher risk-free rate tend to exhibit a higher cost of capital.

- An MNC's capital structure decision is influenced by corporate characteristics such as the stability of the MNC's cash flows, its credit risk, and its access to earnings. The capital structure is also influenced by characteristics of the countries where the MNC conducts business, such as stock restrictions, interest rates, strength of local currencies, country risk, and tax laws. Some characteristics favour an equity-intensive capital structure because they discourage the use of debt. Other characteristics favour a debt-intensive structure because of the desire to protect against risks by creating foreign debt. Given that the relative costs of capital components vary among countries, the MNC's capital structure may be dependent on the specific mix of countries in which it conducts operations.

CRITICAL DEBATE

Is the cost of capital really relevant for valuing projects?

Proposition. No. The cost of capital is a discount rate that is applied when using the *NPV* approach to valuing projects similar to the average risk project of the company. An MNC looking at a project in another country will find that the individual risks are very high and outweigh any idea of an average. Valuing the option to abandon, the risk of bankruptcy, the risk of a collapse in the currency are more important than worrying about whether or not the discount rate should be 12% or 10%. In any case looking ahead a number of years is impossible when the individual risk of a project is high.

Opposing view. Although the risks of failure are there, they are not as great as imagined. Otherwise there

would not be the great increase in MNC activity that we see today. Levels of borrowing and the market risk of a project do matter. If the WACC does not provide the right risk measure, the ICAPM will provide a measure in effect using the cost of capital of a more appropriate firm. When a firm accepts a project or carries on with an existing project, by implication, it accepts that it is better off as a result. Measuring how much better off by using the CAPM makes good sense.

With whom do you agree? Provide a reasoned argument as to why you agree or disagree with one of the above views.

SELF TEST

Answers are provided in Appendix A at the back of the text.

1. When Goshen ltd (UK) focused only on domestic business in the United Kingdom, it had a low debt level. As it expanded into other countries, it increased its degree of financial leverage (on a consolidated basis). What factors would have caused Goshen to increase its financial leverage (assuming that country risk was not a concern)?

2. Lynde ltd is a UK-based MNC with a large subsidiary in the Philippines financed with equity from the parent. In response to news about a possible change in the Philippine government, the subsidiary revised its capital structure by borrowing from local banks and transferring the equity investment back to the UK parent. Explain the likely motive behind these actions.

3. Duever ltd (a UK firm) noticed that its financial leverage was substantially lower than that of most successful firms in Germany and Japan in the same industry. Is Duever's capital structure less than optimal?

4. Atlanta plc has a large subsidiary in Venezuela, where interest rates are very high and the currency is expected to weaken. Assume that Atlanta perceives the country risk to be high. Explain the tradeoff involved in financing the subsidiary with local debt versus an equity investment from the parent.

5. Reno SA (France) is considering a project to establish a plant for producing and selling consumer goods in an undeveloped country. Assume that the host country's economy is very dependent on oil prices, the local currency of the country is very volatile, and the country risk is very high. Also assume that the country's economic conditions are unrelated to European conditions. Should the required rate of return (and therefore the risk premium) on the project be higher or lower than that of other alternative projects in Europe?

QUESTIONS AND APPLICATIONS

1. **Capital structure of MNCs.** Present an argument in support of an MNC's favouring a debt-intensive capital structure. Present an argument in support of an MNC's favouring an equity-intensive capital structure.

2. **Optimal financing.** Wizard plc has a subsidiary in a country where the government allows only a small amount of earnings to be remitted to the United Kingdom each year. Should Wizard finance the subsidiary with debt financing by the parent, equity financing by the parent, or financing by local banks in the foreign country?

3. **Country differences.** Describe general differences between the capital structures of firms based in the United Kingdom and those of firms based in Japan. Offer an explanation for these differences.

4. **Local versus global capital structure.** Why might a firm use a "local" capital structure at a particular subsidiary that differs substantially from its "global" capital structure?

5. **Cost of capital.** Explain how characteristics of MNCs can affect the cost of capital.

6. **Capital structure and agency issues.** Explain why managers of a wholly owned subsidiary may be more likely to satisfy the shareholders of the MNC.

7. **Target capital structure.** LaSalle SA is a French-based MNC with subsidiaries in various less developed countries where stock markets are not well established. How can LaSalle still achieve its "global" target capital structure of 50% debt and 50% equity, if it plans to use only debt financing for the subsidiaries in these countries?

8. **Financing decision.** Drexel ltd is a UK-based company that is establishing a project in a politically unstable country. It is considering two possible sources of financing. Either the parent could

provide most of the financing, or the subsidiary could be supported by local loans from banks in that country. Which financing alternative is more appropriate to protect the subsidiary?

9. **Financing decision.** Veer NV is a Netherlands-based MNC that has most of its operations in Japan. Since the Japanese companies with which it competes use more financial leverage, it has decided to adjust its financial leverage to be in line with theirs. With this heavy emphasis on debt, Veer should reap more tax advantages. It believes that the market's perception of its risk will remain unchanged, since its financial leverage will still be no higher than that of its Japanese competitors. Comment on this strategy.

10. **Financing tradeoffs.** Pullman ltd, a UK firm, has been highly profitable, but prefers not to pay out higher dividends because its shareholders want the funds to be reinvested. It plans for large growth in several less developed countries. Pullman would like to finance the growth with local debt in the host countries of concern to reduce its exposure to country risk. Explain the dilemma faced by Pullman, and offer possible solutions.

11. **Costs of capital across countries.** Explain why the cost of capital for a UK-based MNC with a large subsidiary in Brazil is higher than for a UK-based MNC in the same industry with a large subsidiary in Japan. Assume that the subsidiary operations for each MNC are financed with local debt in the host country.

12. **WACC.** An MNC has total assets of £100 million and debt of £20 million. The firm's before-tax cost of debt is 12%, and its cost of financing with equity is 15%. The MNC has a corporate tax rate of 40%. What is this firm's weighted average cost of capital?

13. **Cost of equity.** Wiley plc, an MNC, has a beta of 1.3. The UK stock market is expected to generate an annual return of 11%. Currently, Treasury bills yield 2%. Based on this information, what is Wiley's estimated cost of equity?

14. **WACC.** Blues plc is an MNC located in the United Kingdom. Blues would like to estimate its weighted average cost of capital. On average, bonds issued by Blues yield 9%. Currently, T-bill rates are 3%. Furthermore, Blues' shares have a beta of 1.5, and the return on the FTSE stock index is expected to be 10%. Blues' target capital structure is 30% debt and 70% equity. If Blues is in the 35% tax bracket, what is its weighted average cost of capital?

15. **Political unrest.** Rose plc of Tralee (Ireland) needed to infuse capital into its foreign subsidiaries to support their expansion. It planned to issue stock in the United Kingdom. Recent political unrest in the subsidiary countries has made Rose change its plans to issuing long-term debt. Explain how political unrest could have altered the two forms of capital.

16. **Adidas' cost of capital.** If Adidas decides to expand further in South America, why might its capital structure be affected? Why will its overall cost of capital be affected?

ADVANCED QUESTIONS

17. **Interaction between financing and investment.** Charleston Corp is considering establishing a subsidiary in either Germany or the United Kingdom. The subsidiary will be mostly financed with loans from the local banks in the host country chosen. Charleston has determined that the revenue generated from the British subsidiary will be slightly more favourable than the revenue generated by the German subsidiary, even after considering tax and exchange rate effects. The initial outlay will be the same, and both countries appear to be politically stable. Charleston decides to establish the subsidiary in the United Kingdom because of the revenue advantage. Do you agree with its decision? Explain.

18. **Financing decision.** In recent years, several European firms have penetrated Mexico's market. One of the biggest challenges is the cost of capital to finance businesses in Mexico. Mexican interest rates tend to be much higher than European interest rates. In some periods, the Mexican government does not attempt to lower the interest rates because higher rates may attract foreign investment in Mexican securities.

  a. How might European-based MNCs expand in Mexico without incurring the high Mexican interest expenses when financing the expansion? Are any disadvantages associated with this strategy?

b. Are there any additional alternatives for the Mexican subsidiary to finance its business itself after it has been well established? How might this strategy affect the subsidiary's capital structure?

19. **Financing decision.** Forest Co produces goods in the United States, Germany, and Australia and sells the goods in the areas where they are produced. Foreign earnings are periodically remitted to the US parent. As the euro's interest rates have declined to a very low level, Forest has decided to finance its German operations with borrowed funds in place of the parent's equity investment. Forest will transfer the US parent's equity investment in the German subsidiary over to its Australian subsidiary. These funds will be used to pay off a floating-rate loan, as Australian interest rates have been high and are rising. Explain the expected effects of these actions on the consolidated capital structure and cost of capital of Forest Co.

    Given the strategy to be used by Forest, explain how its exposure to exchange rate risk may have changed.

20. **Financing in a high-interest-rate country.** Fairfield plc a UK firm, recently established a subsidiary in a less developed country that consistently experiences an annual inflation rate of 80% or more. The country does not have an established stock market, but loans by local banks are available with a 90% interest rate. Fairfield has decided to use a strategy in which the subsidiary is financed entirely with funds from the parent. It believes that in this way it can avoid the excessive interest rate in the host country. What is a key disadvantage of using this strategy that may cause Fairfield to be no better off than if it paid the 90% interest rate?

21. **Cost of foreign debt versus equity.** Carazona SA is a Spanish firm that has a large subsidiary in Indonesia. It wants to finance the subsidiary's operations in Indonesia. However, the cost of debt is currently about 30% there for firms like Carazona or government agencies that have a very strong credit rating. A consultant suggests to Carazona that it should use equity financing there to avoid the high interest expense. He suggests that since Carazona's cost of equity in Europe is about 14%, the Indonesian investors should be satisfied with a return of about 14% as well. Clearly explain why the consultant's advice is not logical. That is, explain why Carazona's cost of equity in Indonesia would not be less than Carazona's cost of debt in Indonesia.

22. **Integrating cost of capital and capitial budgeting.** Zylon plc is a UK firm that provides technology software for the government of Singapore. It will be paid S$7,000,000 at the end of each of the next five years. The entire amount of the payment represents earnings since Zylon created the technology software years ago. Zylon is subject to a 30% corporate income tax rate in the United Kingdom. Its other cash inflows (such as revenue) are expected to be offset by its other cash outflows (due to operating expenses) each year, so its profits on the Singapore contract represent its expected annual net cash flows. Its financing costs are not considered within its estimate of cash flows. The Singapore dollar (S$) is presently worth £0.40, and Zylon uses that spot exchange rate as a forecast of future exchange rates.

    The risk-free interest rate in the United Kingdom is 6% while the risk-free interest rate in Singapore is 14%. Zylon's capital structure is 60% debt and 40% equity. Zylon is charged an interest rate of 12% on its debt. Zylon's cost of equity is based on the CAPM. It expects that the UK annual market return will be 12% per year. Its beta is 1.5.

    Quiso SA a French firm, wants to acquire Zylon and offers Zylon a price of 8,000,000 euros.

    Zylon's owner must decide whether to sell the business at this price and hires you to make a recommendation. Estimate the *NPV* to Zylon as a result of selling the business, and make a recommendation about whether Zylon's owner should sell the business at the price offered.

PROJECT WORKSHOP

23. **The cost of debt.** The Bloomberg website provides interest rate data for many countries and various maturities. Its address is http://www.bloomberg.com.

    Go to the "Market data2 section and then to "Rates and Bonds". Assume that an MNC would pay 1% more on borrowed funds than the risk-free (government) rates shown at the Bloomberg website. Determine the cost of debt (use a ten-year maturity) for an MNC that borrows dollars. Then determine the cost of funds for a foreign subsidiary in Japan that borrows funds locally. Then determine the cost of debt for a subsidiary in Germany that borrows funds locally. Offer some explanations as to why the cost of debt may vary among the three countries.

DISCUSSION IN THE BOARDROOM

This exercise can be found on the companion website at www.cengage.co.uk/madura_fox.

RUNNING YOUR OWN MNC

This exercise can be found on the companion website at www.cengage.co.uk/madura_fox.

Essays/discussion and articles can be found at the end of Part 4

BLADES PLC CASE STUDY
Assessment of cost of capital

Recall that Blades has tentatively decided to establish a subsidiary in Thailand to manufacture roller blades. The new plant will be utilized to produce "Speedos", Blades' primary product. Once the subsidiary has been established in Thailand, it will be operated for ten years, at which time it is expected to be sold. Ben Holt, Blades' financial director, believes the growth potential in Thailand will be extremely high over the next few years. However, his optimism is not shared by most economic forecasters, who predict a slow recovery of the Thai economy, which has been very negatively affected by recent events in that country. Furthermore, forecasts for the future value of the baht indicate that the currency may continue to depreciate over the next few years.

Despite the pessimistic forecasts, Ben Holt believes Thailand is a good international target for Blades' products because of the high growth potential and lack of competitors in Thailand. At a recent meeting of the board of directors, Holt presented his capital budgeting analysis and pointed out that the establishment of a subsidiary in Thailand had a net present value (*NPV*) of over £5 million even when a 25% required rate of return is used to discount the cash flows resulting from the project. Blades' board of directors, while favourable to the idea of international expansion, remained sceptical. Specifically, the directors wondered where Holt obtained the 25% discount rate to conduct his capital budgeting analysis and

whether this discount rate was high enough. Consequently, the decision to establish a subsidiary in Thailand has been delayed until the directors' meeting next month.

The directors also asked Holt to determine how operating a subsidiary in Thailand would affect Blades' required rate of return and its cost of capital. The directors would like to know how Blades' characteristics would affect its cost of capital relative to roller blade manufacturers operating solely in the United Kingdom. Furthermore, the capital asset pricing model (CAPM) was mentioned by two directors, who would like to know how Blades' systematic risk would be affected by expanding into Thailand. Another issue that was raised is how the cost of debt and equity in Thailand differ from the corresponding costs in the United Kingdom, and whether these differences would affect Blades' cost of capital. The last issue that was raised during the meeting was whether Blades' capital structure would be affected by expanding into Thailand. The directors have asked Holt to conduct a thorough analysis of these issues and report back to them at their next meeting.

Ben Holt's knowledge of cost of capital and capital structure decisions is somewhat limited, and he requires your help. You are a financial analyst for Blades plc. Holt has gathered some information regarding Blades' characteristics that distinguish it from roller blade manufacturers operating solely in the United Kingdom, its systematic risk, and the costs of debt and equity in Thailand, and he wants to know whether and how this information will affect Blades' cost of capital and its capital structure decision.

Regarding Blades' characteristics, Holt has gathered information regarding Blades' size, its access to the Thai capital markets, its diversification benefits from a Thai expansion, its exposure to exchange rate risk, and its exposure to country risk. Although Blades' expansion into Thailand classifies the company as an MNC, Blades is still relatively small compared to UK roller blade manufacturers. Also, Blades' expansion into Thailand will give it access to the capital and money markets there. However, negotiations with various commercial banks in Thailand indicate that Blades will be able to borrow at interest rates of approximately 15%, versus 8% in the United Kingdom.

Expanding into Thailand will diversify Blades' operations. As a result of this expansion, Blades would be subject to economic conditions in Thailand as well as the United Kingdom. Ben Holt sees this as a major advantage since Blades' cash flows would no longer be solely dependent on the UK economy. Consequently, he believes that Blades' probability of bankruptcy would be reduced. Nevertheless, if Blades establishes a subsidiary in Thailand, all of the subsidiary's earnings will be remitted back to the UK parent, which would create a high level of exchange rate risk. This is of particular concern because current economic forecasts for Thailand indicate that the baht will depreciate further over the next few years. Furthermore, Holt has already conducted a country risk analysis for Thailand, which resulted in an unfavourable country risk rating.

Regarding Blades' level of systematic risk, Holt has determined how Blades' beta, which measures systematic risk, would be affected by the establishment of a subsidiary in Thailand. Holt believes that Blades' beta would drop from its current level of 2.0 to 1.8 because the firm's exposure to UK market conditions would be reduced by the expansion into Thailand. Moreover, Holt estimates that the risk-free interest rate is 5% and the required return on the market is 12%.

Holt has also determined that the costs of both debt and equity are higher in Thailand than in the United Kingdom. Lenders such as commercial banks in Thailand require interest rates higher than UK rates. This is partially attributed to a higher risk premium, which reflects the larger degree of economic uncertainty in Thailand. The cost of equity is also higher in Thailand than in the United Kingdom. Thailand is not as developed as the United Kingdom in many ways, and various investment opportunities are available to Thai investors, which increases the opportunity cost. However, Holt is not sure that this higher cost of equity in Thailand would affect Blades, as all of Blades' shareholders are located in the United Kingdom.

Ben Holt has asked you to analyze this information and to determine how it may affect Blades' cost of capital and its capital structure. To help you in your analysis, Holt would like you to provide answers to the following questions:

1. If Blades expands into Thailand, do you think its cost of capital will be higher or lower than the cost of capital of roller blade manufacturers operating solely in the United Kingdom? Substantiate your answer by outlining how Blades' characteristics distinguish it from domestic roller blade manufacturers.

2. According to the CAPM, how would Blades' required rate of return be affected by an expansion into Thailand? How do you reconcile this result with your answer to question 1? Do you think Blades should use the required rate of return resulting from the CAPM to discount the cash flows of the Thai subsidiary to determine its *NPV*?

3. If Blades borrows funds in Thailand to support its Thai subsidiary, how would this affect its cost of capital? Why?

4. Given the high level of interest rates in Thailand, the high level of exchange rate risk, and the high (perceived) level of country risk, do you think Blades will be more or less likely to use debt in its capital structure as a result of its expansion into Thailand? Why?

SMALL BUSINESS DILEMMA
Multinational capital structure decision at the Sports Exports Company

The Sports Exports Company (Ireland) has considered a variety of projects, but all of its business is still in the United Kingdom. Since most of its business comes from exporting basketballs (denominated in pounds), it remains exposed to exchange rate risk. On the favourable side, the British demand for its basketballs has risen consistently every month. Jim Logan, the owner of the Sports Exports Company, has retained more than 100,000 euros (after the pounds were converted into euros) in earnings since he began his business. At this point in time, his capital structure is mostly his own equity, with very little debt. Jim has periodically considered establishing a very small subsidiary in the United Kingdom to produce the basketballs there (so that he would not have to export them from Ireland). If he does establish this subsidiary, he has several options for the capital structure that would be used to support it: (1) use all of his equity to invest in the firm, (2) use pound-denominated long-term debt, or (3) use euro-denominated long-term debt. The interest rate on British long-term debt is slightly higher than the interest rate on euro long-term debt.

1. What is an advantage of using equity to support the subsidiary? What is a disadvantage?
2. If Jim decides to use long-term debt as the primary form of capital to support this subsidiary, should he use dollar-denominated debt or pound-denominated debt?
3. How can the equity proportion of this firm's capital structure increase over time after it is established?

CHAPTER 18

LONG-TERM FINANCING

MULTINATIONAL CORPORATIONS (MNCs) typically use long-term sources of funds to finance long-term projects. They have access to both domestic and foreign sources of funds. It is worthwhile for MNCs to consider all possible forms of financing before making their final decisions. Financial managers must be aware of their sources of long-term funds so that they can finance international projects in a manner that maximizes the wealth of the MNC.

THE SPECIFIC OBJECTIVES OF THIS CHAPTER ARE TO:

- explain why MNCs consider long-term financing in foreign currencies,

- explain how to assess the feasibility of long-term financing in foreign currencies, and

- explain how the assessment of long-term financing in foreign currencies is adjusted for bonds with floating interest rates.

LONG-TERM FINANCING DECISION

Since MNCs commonly invest in long-term projects, they rely heavily on long-term financing. Generally, long-term projects take longer to generate funds and are more appropriately financed by investors who are prepared to deposit their funds for the longer term. Shorter-term funding would mean constant need for refinancing that is to say repaying one short-term fund by taking out another. The risk is that further funds might not be forthcoming, particularly if the project is at a difficult stage of its development. Those seeking short-term security might be worried that on maturity of their short-term loans the funds might not be available. Equity is one of the major sources of long-term funding able to raise large sums of money. Long-term debt, in the form of debentures is the other major source. The decision to use equity funding versus debt funding was covered in the previous chapter. Once that decision is made, the MNC must consider the possible sources of equity or debt and the cost and risk associated with each source.

Sources of equity

MNCs may consider a domestic equity offering in their home country, in which the funds are denominated in their local currency. Second, they may consider a global equity offering, in which they issue stock in their home country and in one or more foreign countries. They may consider this approach to obtain partial funding in a currency that they need to finance a foreign subsidiary's operations. In addition, the global offering may provide them with some name recognition. Investors in a foreign country will be more interested in a global offering if the MNC places a sufficient number of shares in that country to provide liquidity. The stock will be listed on an exchange in the foreign country so that investors there can sell their holdings of the stock.

Third, MNCs may offer a private placement of equity to financial institutions in their home country. Fourth, they may offer a private placement of equity to financial institutions in the foreign country where they are expanding. Private placements are beneficial because they may reduce transaction costs. However, MNCs may not be able to obtain all the funds that they need with a private placement. The funding must come from a limited number of large investors who are willing to maintain the investment for a long period of time, because the equity has very limited liquidity.

Sources of debt

When MNCs consider debt financing, they have a similar set of options. They can engage in a public placement of debt in their own country or a global debt offering. In addition, they can engage in a private placement of debt in their own country or in the foreign country where they are expanding.

Most MNCs obtain equity funding in their home country. In contrast, debt financing is frequently done in foreign countries. Thus, the focus of this chapter is on how debt financing decisions can affect the MNC's cost of capital and risk.

COST OF DEBT FINANCING

An MNC's long-term financing decision is commonly influenced by the different interest rates that exist among currencies. The actual cost of long-term financing is based on both the quoted interest rate and the percentage change in the exchange rate of the

Exhibit 18.1   London Stock Exchange new and further issues by method 2005

2005	Total	
	No. of co's / issues	Money raised (£m)
Equities		
New companies		
Public offer	54	6,804.68
Placing	22	3,132.87
Placing and public offer	9	611.50
Totals	**103**	**10,549.05**
Further issues		
Public offer	309	818.93
Placing	104	4,175.79
Placing and public offer	27	789.57
Rights issues	19	2,886.90
Employee shares/options	366	0.00
Totals	**825**	**8,671.19**
Grand totals	**928**	**19,220.24**
Fixed interest		
New and further issues		
Debentures and loans	2	40.00
Preference	12	971.05
Total company	**14**	**1,011.05**
Eurobonds	2,550	269,386.34
other	2	314.41
Grand totals	**3,243**	**270,711.80**

Notes:

■ The total money raised is the equivalent of about 20% of UK Gross Domestic Product.

■ Fixed interest includes refinancing unlike the equity issues.

■ Eurobonds are bonds denominated in currencies other than British pounds.

■ The data includes MNCs with their main listing in London and MNCs with their main listing elsewhere. About 30% of the equity and 45% of the debt is raised by non-domestic MNCs.

■ Further details are available at Main Market Factsheet http://www.londonstockexchange.com.

Source: London Stock Exchange by kind permission.

currency borrowed over the loan life. Just as interest rates on short-term bank loans vary among currencies, so do bond yields. Exhibit 18.2 illustrates the long-term bond yields for several different countries. The wide differentials in bond yields among countries reflect a different cost of debt financing for firms in different countries.

Because bonds denominated in foreign currencies sometimes have lower yields, MNCs often consider issuing bonds denominated in those currencies (see Exhibit 18.1). Since the total financing cost to an MNC issuing a foreign currency-denominated bond is affected by that currency's value relative to the MNC's main (functional) currency there is no guarantee that the bond will be less costly than a home currency-denominated bond. The borrowing firm must make coupon payments in the currency denominating the bond. If this currency appreciates against the firm's home currency, more funds will be needed to make the coupon payments. For this reason, a firm will not always denominate debt in a currency that exhibits a low interest rate.

To make the long-term financing decision, the MNC must: (1) determine the amount of funds needed, (2) forecast the price at which it can issue the bond, and (3) forecast periodic exchange rate values for the currency denominating the bond. This information can be used to determine the bond's financing costs, which can be compared with the financing costs the firm would incur using its home currency. The uncertainty of the actual financing costs to be incurred from foreign financing must be accounted for as well.

Measuring the cost of financing

The cost of financing in a foreign currency is influenced by the value of that currency when the MNC makes coupon payments to its bondholders and when it pays off the principal at the time the bond reaches maturity.

EXAMPLE

Piedmont plc needs to borrow £1 million over a three-year period. This reflects a relatively small amount of funds and a short time period for bond financing but will allow for a more simplified example. Piedmont believes it can sell pound-denominated bonds at par value if it provides a coupon rate of 14%. It also has the alternative of denominating the bonds in Singapore dollars (S$), in which case it would convert its borrowed Singapore dollars to pounds to use as needed. Then, it would need to obtain Singapore dollars annually to make the coupon payments. Assume that the current exchange rate of the Singapore dollar is £0.3333.

Piedmont needs S$3 million in loans (computed as £1 million / £0.3333 per Singapore dollar) to obtain the £1 million it initially needs. It believes it can sell the Singapore dollar-denominated bonds at par value if it provides a coupon rate of 10%.

The costs of both financing alternatives are illustrated in Exhibit 18.2, which provides the outflow payment schedule of each financing method. The outflow payments if Piedmont finances with UK pound denominated debt fixed interest capital are known. In addition, if Piedmont finances with Singapore dollar-denominated bonds, the number of Singapore dollars needed at the end of each period is known. Yet, because the future exchange rate of the Singapore dollar is uncertain, the number of pounds needed to obtain the Singapore dollars each year is uncertain. If exchange rates do not change, the annual cost of financing with Singapore dollars is 10%, which is less than the 14% annual cost of financing with pounds.

A comparison between the costs of financing with the two different currencies can be conducted by determining the annual cost of financing with each bond, from Piedmont's perspective. The comparison is shown in the last column of Exhibit 18.2. The annual cost of financing represents the discount rate at which the future outflow payments must be discounted so that their present value equals the amount borrowed. This is similar to the so-called yield to maturity but is assessed here from the borrower's perspective rather than from the investor's perspective. When the price at which the bonds are initially issued equals the par value and there is no exchange rate adjustment, the annual cost of financing is simply equal to the coupon rate. Thus, the annual cost of financing for the British pound-denominated bonds would be 14%.

Exhibit 18.2 Financing with bonds denominated in British pounds versus Singapore dollars

Financing Alternative	End of Year: 1	End of Year: 2	End of Year: 3	Annual Cost of Financing
(1) British pound-denominated debt (coupon rate = 14%) borrow £1 million	£140,000	£140,000	£1,140,000	14%
or				
(2) Singapore dollar-denominated bonds (coupon rate = 10%) borrow S$3,000,000	S$300,000	S$300,000	S$3,300,000	—
(2) Forecasted exchange rate of S$	£0.3333	£0.3333	£0.3333	—
(2) Payments in pounds	£100,000	£100,000	£1,100,000	10%

Notes:
- At an exchange rate of £0.33 financing with Singapore dollars (2) is cheaper.
- The exchange rate would have to increase to 14% / 10% × £0.3333 = £0.46662 for the Singapore loan to be as expensive, this is unlikely unless inflation is higher by about 4% in the UK.

For Piedmont, the Singapore dollar-denominated debt appears to be less costly. However, it is unrealistic to assume that the Singapore dollar will remain stable over time. Consequently, some MNCs may choose to issue UK pound-denominated debt, even though it appears more costly. The potential savings from issuing bonds denominated in a foreign currency must be weighed against the potential risk of such a method. In this example, risk reflects the possibility that the Singapore dollar will appreciate to a degree that causes Singapore dollar-denominated bonds to be more costly than UK fixed interest debt. There would in fact have to be a considerable change in the exchange rate (40%) for the Singapore loan to be more expensive, as explained in the notes to Exhibit 18.2.

Normally, exchange rates are more difficult to predict over longer time horizons. Thus, the time when the principal is to be repaid may be so far away that it is virtually impossible to have a reliable estimate of the exchange rate at that time. For this reason, some firms may be uncomfortable issuing bonds denominated in foreign currencies.

Impact of a strong currency on financing costs. If the currency that was borrowed appreciates over time, an MNC will need more funds to cover the coupon or principal payments. This type of exchange rate movement increases the MNC's financing costs.

EXAMPLE

After Piedmont decides to issue Singapore dollar-denominated bonds, assume that the Singapore dollar appreciates from £0.3333 to £0.40 at the end of Year 1, to £0.45 at the end of Year 2, and to £0.50 by the end of Year 3. In this case, the payments made by Piedmont are displayed in Exhibit 18.3. By comparing the pound outflows in this scenario with the outflows that would have occurred from a British pound-denominated bond, the risk to a firm from denominating a bond in a foreign currency is evident. The period of the last payment is particularly crucial for bond financing in foreign currencies because it includes not only the final coupon payment but the principal as well. Based on the exchange rate movements assumed here, financing with Singapore dollars was more expensive than financing with pounds would have been.

Exhibit 18.3 Financing with Singapore dollars during a strong S$ period

	End of year:			
	1	2	3	Annual Cost of Financing
Payments in Singapore dollars	S$300,000	S$300,000	S$3,300,000	—
Forecasted exchange rate of Singapore dollar	£0.40	£0.45	£0.50	—
Payments in pounds	£120,000	£135,000	£1,650,000	26.20%

Notes:
The annual cost (discount rate) is calculated by trial and error on a spreadsheet such that:

$$£1,000,000 = \frac{120,000}{(1+0.262)} + \frac{135,000}{(1+0.262)^2} + \frac{1,650,000}{(1+0.262)^3}$$

an appreciating foreign currency increases the cost of borrowing in that currency.

Exhibit 18.4 Financing with Singapore dollars during a weak –S$ period

	End of year:			
	1	2	3	Annual Cost of Financing
Payments in Singapore dollars	S$300,000	S$300,000	S$3,300,000	—
Forecasted exchange rate of Singapore dollar	£0.32	£0.30	£0.28	—
Payments in pounds	£96,000	£90,000	£924,000	3.90%

Note:
The annual cost (discount rate) is calculated by trial and error on a spreadsheet such that:

$$£1,000,000 = \frac{96,000}{(1+0.039)} + \frac{96,000}{(1+0.039)^2} + \frac{924,000}{(1+0.039)^3}$$

a depreciating foreign currency lowers the cost of borrowing in that currency.

Impact of a weak currency on financing costs. Whereas an appreciating currency increases the periodic outflow payments of the bond issuer, a depreciating currency will reduce the issuer's outflow payments and therefore reduce its financing costs.

EXAMPLE

Reconsider the case of Piedmont plc, except assume that the Singapore dollar depreciates from £0.3333 to £0.32 at the end of Year 1, to £0.30 at the end of Year 2, and to £0.28 by the end of Year 3. In this case, the payments made by Piedmont are shown in Exhibit 18.4. When one compares the pound outflows in this scenario with the outflows that would have occurred from a UK fixed interest debt, the potential savings from foreign financing are evident.

Exhibit 18.5 compares the effects of a weak currency on financing costs to the effects of a stable or a strong currency. An MNC that denominates bonds in a foreign currency may achieve a major reduction in costs, but could incur high costs if the currency denominating the bonds appreciates over time.

Exhibit 18.5   Exchange rate effects on outflow payments for Singapore dollar-denominated bonds

| | Payment in UK pounds at End of Year: | | | |
| | End of year: | | | |
Exchange Rate Scenario	1	2	3	Annual Cost of Financing
Scenario 1: No change in S$ value	£100,000	£100,000	£1,100,000	10.00%
Scenario 2: Strong	£120,000	£135,000	£1,650,000	26.20%
Scenario 3: Weak	£96,000	£90,000	£924,000	3.90%

Actual effects of exchange rate movements on financing costs

To recognize how exchange rate movements have affected the cost of bonds denominated in a foreign currency, consider the following example, which uses actual exchange rate data for the British pound from 1980 to 2004.

EXAMPLE

In January 1980, Parkside, Inc, sold bonds denominated in British pounds with a par value of £10 million and a 10% coupon rate, thereby requiring coupon payments of £1 million at the end of each year. Assume that this US firm had no existing business in the United Kingdom and therefore needed to exchange dollars for pounds to make the coupon payments each year. Exhibit 18.6 shows how the dollar payments would fluctuate each year according to the actual exchange rate at that time.

In 1980, when the pound was worth $2.3950, the coupon payment was $2,395,000. Just four years later, the pound was worth $1.1592, causing the coupon payment to be $1,159,200. Thus, the firm's dollar coupon payment in 1984 was less than half of that paid in 1980, even though the same number of pounds was needed (£1 million) each year.

In general, the dollar coupon payments increased during the late 1980s (as the pound appreciated) and then declined during the early 1990s (as the pound depreciated). The pound was less volatile in the middle and late 1990s, so its effect on the coupon payment was not so pronounced. As the pound appreciated in 2002 and 2003, the dollar coupon payments increased again. The influence of exchange rate movements on the cost of financing with bonds denominated in a foreign currency is very obvious in this exhibit. The actual effects would vary with the currency of denomination, since exchange rates do not move in perfect tandem against the dollar.

ASSESSING THE EXCHANGE RATE RISK OF DEBT FINANCING

Given the importance of the exchange rate when issuing bonds in a foreign currency, an MNC needs a reliable method to account for the potential impact of exchange rate fluctuations. It can use a point estimate exchange rate forecast of the currency used to denominate its bonds for each period in which an outflow payment will be provided to bondholders. However, a point estimate forecast does not account for uncertainty surrounding the forecast, which varies depending on the volatility of the currency. From a US borrower's perspective, for example, a bond denominated in Canadian dollars is

Exhibit 18.6 Actual costs of annual financing with pound-denominated bonds from a US perspective

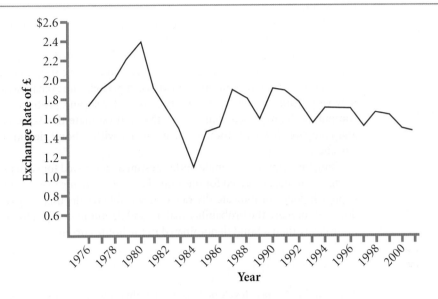

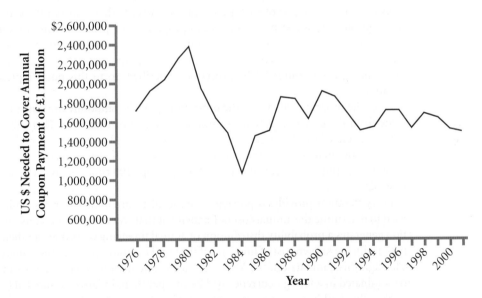

subject to less exchange rate risk than a bond denominated in most other foreign currencies (assuming the borrower has no offsetting position in these currencies). The Canadian dollar exhibits less variability against the US dollar over time and therefore is less likely to deviate far from its projected future exchange rate. A similar argument can be made for companies in the euro-zone and the Swiss franc. The variability of the euro with the Swiss franc is less than with other currencies. The uncertainty surrounding a point estimate forecast can be accounted for by using probabilities or simulation, as described next.

Use of exchange rate probabilities

One approach to using point estimates of future exchange rates is to develop a probability distribution for an exchange rate for each period in which payments will be made to bondholders. The *expected value* of the exchange rate can be computed for each period by multiplying each possible exchange rate by its associated probability and totalling the products. Then, the exchange rate's expected value can be used to forecast the cash outflows necessary to pay bondholders over each period. The exchange rate's expected value may vary from one period to another. After developing probability distributions and computing the expected values, the MNC can estimate the expected cost of financing and compare that with the cost of financing with a bond denominated in the home currency.

Using this approach, a single outflow estimate is derived for each payment period, and a single estimate is derived for the annual cost of financing over the life of the bond. This approach does not indicate the range of possible results that may occur, however, so it does not measure the probability that a bond denominated in a foreign currency will be more costly than a bond denominated in the home currency.

Use of simulation

After an MNC has developed its probability distributions of the foreign currency's exchange rate at the end of each period, as just described, it can feed those probability distributions into a computer simulation program. The program will randomly draw one possible value from the exchange rate distribution for the end of each year and determine the outflow payments based on those exchange rates. Consequently, the cost of financing is determined. The procedure described up to this point represents one iteration.

Next, the program will repeat the procedure by again randomly drawing one possible value from the exchange rate distribution at the end of each year. This will provide a new schedule of outflow payments reflecting those randomly selected exchange rates. The cost of financing for this second iteration is also determined. The simulation program continually repeats this procedure, perhaps 100 times or so (as many times as desired).

Every iteration provides a possible scenario of future exchange rates, which is then used to determine the annual cost of financing if that scenario occurs. Thus, the simulation generates a probability distribution of annual financing costs that can then be compared with the known cost of financing if the bond is denominated in the home currency. Through this comparison, the MNC can determine the probability that issuing bonds denominated in a foreign currency will be cheaper than dollar-denominated bonds.

Note that in this context we are using actual exchange rates whereas in earlier chapters we have used exchange rate movements. What is the difference? The point has been made earlier but is worth repeating. Exchange rate movements are used when looking at actual past data. Therefore if the probability distributions were drawn up by looking at actual data, only the movements of the exchange rate should be used. This is because actual data contains trends (is non-stationary) or is liable to do so. These trends are only clear after the event, so they cannot be used for profit. The actual rate a few years ago may be out of date, but the tendency to change will be relevant to today. To get back to actual rates, the percentage changes can be applied to some future expected value. So, if one expects that the value of the dollar one year hence will be £0.60 and historical analysis suggests that there is a 25% chance of a 5% increase in value, then there is a 25%

chance that the future value of the dollar will be £0.60 × 1.05 = £0.63. The other approach is to make direct subjective estimates of the future rates and their probabilities. In such cases the actual rate can be used without reference to percentage changes, or indeed, past data.

REDUCING EXCHANGE RATE RISK

The exchange rate risk from financing with bonds in foreign currencies can be reduced by using one of the alternative strategies described next.

Offsetting cash inflows

Some firms may have inflow payments in particular currencies, which could offset their outflow payments related to bond financing. Thus, a firm may be able to finance with bonds denominated in a foreign currency that exhibits a lower coupon rate without becoming exposed to exchange rate risk. Nevertheless, it is unlikely that the firm would be able to perfectly match the timing and amount of the outflows in the foreign currency denominating the bond to the inflows in that currency. Therefore, some exposure to exchange rate fluctuations will exist. The exposure can be substantially reduced, though, if the firm receives inflows in the particular currency denominating the bond. This can help to stabilize the firm's cash flow.

EXAMPLE

GlaxoSmithKlein policy is to minimize the exposure of overseas operating subsidiaries to transaction risk by matching local currency income with local currency costs… A significant proportion of Group borrowing including the commercial paper programme, is in US dollars, to benefit from the liquidity of US denominated capital markets. Certain of these and other borrowings are swapped into other currencies as required for group purposes. The Group seeks to denominate borrowings in the currencies of its principal assets.

(GSK Annual Report, 2004)

Offsetting cash flows. MNCs may be able to offset their exposure to exchange rate risk by issuing bonds denominated in the local currency. Issuing debt denominated in the currencies of some developing countries such as Brazil, Indonesia, Malaysia, and Thailand is an example. If an MNC issues bonds denominated in the local currency in one of those countries, there may be a natural offsetting effect that will reduce the MNC's exposure to exchange rate risk because it can use its cash inflows in that currency to repay the debt.

Alternatively, the MNC might obtain debt financing in its home currency at a lower interest rate, but it will not be able to offset its earnings in the foreign currency. Recall that countries where bond yields are high tend to have a high risk-free interest rate and that a high risk-free interest rate usually occurs where inflation is high (the Fisher effect). Also consider that the currencies of countries with relatively high inflation tend to weaken over time (as suggested by purchasing power parity). Thus, a UK-based MNC could be highly exposed to exchange rate risk when using pound-denominated debt to finance business in a country with high costs of local debt because it would have to convert cash inflows generated in a potentially depreciated currency to cover the debt repayments. Thus, MNCs face a dilemma when they consider obtaining long-term financing: issue debt in the local currency and reduce exposure to exchange rate risk, or issue debt denominated in its home currency at a lower interest rate but with considerable exposure to exchange rate risk. Neither solution is without problems.

General Electric is a well-diversified MNC that produces lighting products, automation devices, electrical equipment, and many other products. It has subsidiaries scattered throughout the world, which produce products that are sold locally. General Electric obtains funds from many different markets to finance a portion of its investment in foreign countries. It has issued bonds denominated in Australian dollars, British pounds, Japanese yen, New Zealand dollars, and Polish zloty to finance its foreign operations. Its subsidiaries in Australia use Australian dollar inflows to pay off their Australian debt. Its subsidiaries in Japan use Japanese yen inflows to pay off their yen-denominated debt. By using various debt markets, General Electric can match its cash inflows and outflows in a particular currency. The decision to obtain debt in currencies where it receives cash inflows reduces the company's exposure to exchange rate risk. If it used dollars to finance all of its foreign investment, the subsidiaries would have to convert much of the local currency they receive to dollars to repay their debt. During periods when the foreign currencies depreciate against the dollar, General Electric would need more foreign currency to pay off the dollar-denominated debt. Thus, by considering its source of cash inflows, General Electric is able to make financing decisions that reduce its exposure to exchange rate risk and maximize its value.

Implications of the euro for financing to offset cash inflows. Since the adoption of the euro by Austria, Belgium, Finland, France, Germany, Greece, Ireland, Italy, Luxembourg, Netherlands, Portugal, Spain (but not Sweden, Denmark or the United Kingdom) MNCs from member countries have not had to worry about exchange risk for trade within their area. Exchange rate risk is also lower for MNCs from outside the area as they no longer are exposed to exchange rate risk of sometimes quite small economies. Nevertheless, there is a lessening of the possibilities for diversification. The management of the euro is still a relatively new process that has not had the test of a major financial crisis. There are therefore still considerable currency risks to be hedged.

FORWARD CONTRACTS

When a bond denominated in a foreign currency has a lower coupon rate than the firm's home currency, the firm may consider issuing bonds denominated in that currency and simultaneously hedging its exchange rate risk through the forward market. Because the forward market can sometimes accommodate requests of five years or longer, such an approach may be possible. The firm could arrange to purchase the foreign currency forward for each time at which payments are required. However, the forward rate for each horizon will most likely be above the spot rate. Consequently, hedging these future outflow payments may not be less costly than the outflow payments needed if a dollar-denominated bond were issued. The relationship implied here reflects the concept of interest rate parity, which was discussed in earlier chapters, except that the point of view in this chapter is long term rather than short term.

CURRENCY SWAPS

A currency swap enables firms to exchange currencies at periodic intervals. The motive for such swaps is to make payments in a currency where revenues are being earned and thereby reduce exposure to exchange rate movements.

EXAMPLE

Milltop plc a UK firm, desires to issue a bond denominated in euros because it could make payments with euro revenues to be generated from existing operations. However, Milltop is not well known to investors who would consider purchasing euro-denominated bonds. Meanwhile Beck GmbH of Germany desires to issue pound-denominated bonds because it has large revenues in pounds. However, it is not well known to the investors who would purchase these bonds.

If Milltop is known in the pound-denominated market while Beck is known in the euro-denominated market, the following transactions are appropriate. Milltop issues pound-denominated bonds, while Beck issues euro-denominated bonds. Milltop will provide euro payments to Beck in exchange for pound payments from Beck. The two companies will in effect swap their interest rate bills. They will also typically swap the principal. This swap of currencies allows the companies to lower their exchange rate exposure by making interest payments in a revenue earning currency.

This type of currency swap is illustrated in Exhibit 18.7.

The swap just described was successful in reducing exchange rate risk for both Milltop and Beck. Milltop essentially passes the euros it receives from ongoing operations through to Beck and passes the pounds it receives from Beck through to the investors in the pound-denominated bonds. Thus, even though Milltop receives euros from its ongoing foreign operations, the effect of a change in value of the euro is reduced in that it now makes offsetting interest payments in euros. The same logic applies to Beck GmbH on the other side of the transaction.

Many MNCs simultaneously swap interest payments and currencies at agreed rates. Rates can also be fixed with forwards and futures. The Gillette Co engaged in swap agreements that converted $500 million in fixed rate dollar-denominated debt into multiple currency variable rate debt. PepsiCo enters into interest rate swaps and currency swaps to reduce borrowing costs.

The differing conditions for each of the loans mean that a mutually agreed arrangement can be difficult. The large commercial banks that serve as financial intermediaries

Exhibit 18.7 Illustration of an interest rate swap

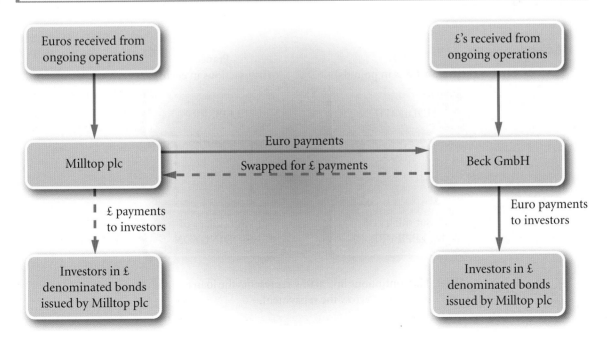

for currency swaps sometimes take positions. That is, they may agree to swap currencies with firms, rather than simply search for suitable swap candidates.

Parallel loans

Firms can also obtain financing in a foreign currency through a parallel (or back-to-back) loan, which occurs when two parties provide simultaneous loans with an agreement to repay at a specified point in the future.

EXAMPLE

A UK company, Siddington ltd operates a subsidiary in France and a French company LePierre SA operates a subsidiary in the UK. Both wish to invest in their respective subsidiaries but wish to avoid exchange rate risks. LePierre therefore lends euros to the French subsidiary of Siddington and in return Siddington lends to the UK subsidiary of LePierre. The loans are repaid in the same currencies as shown in Exhibit 18.8.

Using parallel loans to hedge exchange rate risk for foreign projects. The ability to reduce or eliminate exchange rate risk can also affect the attractiveness of projects in foreign countries. Sometimes, parallel loans can function as a useful alternative to forward or futures contracts as a way to finance foreign projects. The use of parallel loans is particularly attractive if the MNC is conducting a project in a foreign country, will receive the cash flows in the foreign currency, and is worried that the foreign currency will depreciate substantially. If the foreign currency is not heavily traded, other hedging alternatives, such as forward or futures contracts, may not be available, and the project may have a negative net present value (*NPV*) if the cash flows remain unhedged.

Exhibit 18.8 Illustration of a parallel loan

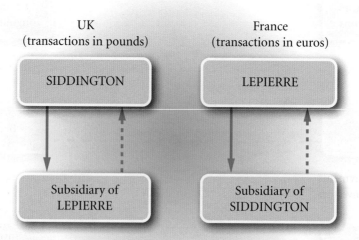

Note: The continuous line arrow represents the loan and the
dashed line arrow the repayment.

EXAMPLE

Spell ltd has been approached by the government of Malaysia to engage in a project there over the next year. The investment in the project totals 1 million Malaysian ringgit (MYR), and the project is expected to generate cash flows of MYR1.4 million next year. The project will terminate at that time.

The current value of the ringgit is £0.15, but Spell believes that the ringgit will depreciate substantially over the next year. Specifically, it believes the ringgit will have a value of either £0.12 or £0.10 next year. Furthermore, Spell will have to borrow the funds necessary to undertake the project and will incur financing costs of 13%.

If Spell undertakes the project, it will incur a net outflow now of MYR1,000,000 × £0.15 = £150,000. Next year, it will also have to pay the financing costs of £150,000 × 13% = £22,500. If the ringgit depreciates to £0.12, then Spell will receive MYR1,400,000 × £0.12 = £168,000 next year. If the ringgit depreciates to £0.10, it will receive MYR1,400,000 × £0.10 = £140,000 next year. For each year, the cash flows are summarized below.

Scenario 1: ringgit depreciates to £0.12

	Year 0 (i.e. start of Year 1)	Year 1
Investment	−£150,000	
Interest payment (financing cost: £150,000 × 13%)		−£19,500
Project cash flow (MYR1,400,000 × £0.12)	0	£168,000
Net	−£150,000	£148,500

Ignoring the time value of money, the combined cash flows are:

$$£148,000–£150,000 = –£1,500.$$

Scenario 2: ringgit depreciates to £0.10

	Year 0 (i.e. start of Year 1)	Year 1
Investment	−£150,000	
Interest payment (financing cost: £150,000 × 13%)		−£19,500
Project cash flow (MYR1,400,000 × £0.10)	0	£140,000
Net	−£150,000	£120,500

Ignoring the time value of money, the combined cash flows are £120,500 − £150,000 = −£29,500. Although this example includes the interest payment in the cash flows and ignores discounting for illustrative purposes, it is obvious that the project is not attractive for Spell. Furthermore, no forward or futures contracts are available for ringgit, so Spell cannot hedge its cash flows from exchange rate risk.

Now assume that the Malaysian government offers a parallel loan to Spell. According to the loan, the Malaysian government will give Spell MYR1,000,000 in exchange for a loan by Spell of £250,000 to the Malaysian government at the current exchange rate. The two amounts will be returned by both parties at the end of the project. Initially, this arrangement sounds rather odd. It is perhaps best seen as a loan by the Malaysian government to Spell and Spell's loan as a security deposit with the government. As all the rates are fixed at the beginning of the loans, exchange rate risk is eliminated. The Malaysian government could set the interest rate such that there is no difference in interest rates received and paid and they are netted off. In this example there is a small difference resulting in a net payment by Spell to the government.

Next year, Spell will pay the Malaysian government 15% interest on the MYR1,000,000, and the Malaysian government will pay Spell 7% interest on the pound loan. The parallel loan would be as follows:

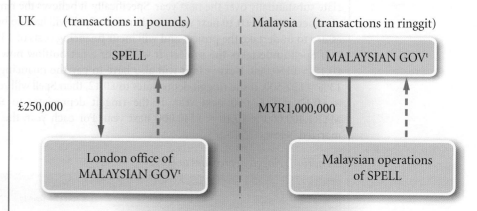

Notes: The continuous line arrow represents the loans at the beginning of year 1 i.e. year 0 and the dashed line arrow the repayment at the end of year 1. The repayment would include interest.

By using the parallel loan, Spell is able to reduce the net cash flows denominated in Malaysian ringgit it will receive in one year. Consider both the ringgit and pound cash flows:

Spell's Cash Flows

	Ringgit cash flows	
	Year 0 (i.e. start of Year 1)	Year 1
Loan from Malaysian Government	MYR1,000,000	
Investment in project	−MYR1,000,000	
Interest paid to Malaysian Govt (MYR1,000,000 × 15%)		−MYR150,000
Return of loan to Malaysian Govt		−MYR1,000,000
Project cash flow		MYR1,400,000
Net cash flow to be converted into British pounds	MYR0	MYR250,000

	British pound cash flows	
	Year 0 (i.e. start of Year 1)	Year 1
Loan to Malaysian Government	−£150,000	
Interest payment by Spell (financing cost: £150,000 × 13%)		−£19,500
Interest received from Malaysian Govt (£150,000 × 7%)		£10,500
Return of loan to Spell	0	£150,000
Net	−£150,000	£141,000

We therefore have a position of having incurred a net cost of £141,000 − £150,000 = −£9,000 in lending to the Malaysian government. This cost has been incurred because the loan to the government was at the low rate of 7% whereas Spell had to pay 13% to obtain the finance in the first place 150,000 × (7% − 13%) = −£9,000. In return, Spell has earned MYR250,000. This sum has to be converted back to pounds. Two scenarios are being considered:

Scenario 1: Ringgit depreciates to £0.12

The net cash flow in Year 1 of MYR250,000 is converted to pounds at the £0.12 spot rate to generate MYR250,000 × £0.12 = £30,000. Thus, the total pound cash flows using the parallel loan are as follows:

Malaysian earnings converted to pounds at £0.12	£30,000
less	
Cost of lending to the Malaysian Government	£9,000
Net cash flow from the investment	£21,000

Scenario 2: Ringgit depreciates to £0.10

The net cash flow in Year 1 of MYR 250,000 is converted to pounds at the £0.10 spot rate to generate MYR250,000 × £0.10 = £25,000. Thus, the total pound cash flows using the parallel loan are as follows:

Malaysian earnings converted to pounds at £0.10	£25,000
less	
Cost of lending to the Malaysian Government	£9,000
Net cash flow from the investment	£16,000

Notice that the cash flows have improved dramatically by using the parallel loan, as the following table illustrates:

	Scenario 1	Scenario 2
Net cash flow without parallel loan	−£1,500	−£29,500
Net cash flow with parallel loan	£21,000	£16,000

Not only was Spell able to reduce its exchange rate risk by financing the project through the loan, but it was also able to generate positive total cash flows. The reason for this is that the very large expected percentage depreciation in the ringgit (20% or 40%) exceeds the incremental cost of financing (15% − 7% = 8%). By using the parallel loan, Spell has reduced the ringgit amount it must convert to pounds at project termination from MYR1.4 million to MYR250,000. It was therefore able to reduce the amount of its cash flows that would be subject to the expected depreciation of the ringgit.

The Malaysian government also benefits from the loan because it receives incremental interest payments of 8% from the arrangements. Of course, the Malaysian government also incurs the implicit cost of the depreciating ringgit since it must re-exchange ringgit for pounds after one year. Nevertheless, it may offer such a loan if its expectations for the ringgit's value differ from those of Spell. That is, the government may expect the ringgit to appreciate or to depreciate by less than Spell expects. In addition, the government may not have many other options for completing the project if local companies do not have the expertise to perform the work.

Diversifying among currencies

A UK firm may denominate bonds in several foreign currencies, rather than a single foreign currency, so that substantial appreciation of any one currency will not drastically increase the number of pounds needed to cover the financing payments.

EXAMPLE

Never plc, a UK-based MNC, is considering four alternatives for issuing bonds to support its US operations:

1. Issue bonds denominated in British pounds (14%).
2. Issue bonds denominated in Japanese yen (8%).
3. Issue bonds denominated in US dollars (8%).
4. Issue some bonds denominated in Japanese yen and some bonds denominated in US dollars.

Never plc has no net exposure in either Japanese yen or US dollars. The coupon rate for a UK pound-denominated bond is 14%, while the coupon rate is 8% for a yen- or US dollar-denominated bond. It is expected that any of these bonds could be sold at par value. The foreign currency would then be converted to British pounds for use and then at the end of the term of the bond Never will have to purchase the foreign currency to repay the loan. The exchange rate movement over the life of the loan will affect the cost of the loan.

If the US dollar appreciates against the British pound by more than 14% − 8% = 6%, Never's actual financing cost from issuing US dollar-denominated bonds may be higher than that of the British pound-denominated bonds. If the Japanese yen appreciates substantially against the British pound, Never's actual financing cost from issuing yen-denominated bonds may be higher than that of the British pound-denominated bonds. If the exchange rates of the US dollar and Japanese yen move in opposite directions against the British pound, then both types of bonds could not simultaneously be more costly than British pound-denominated bonds, so financing with both types of bonds would almost ensure that the Never's overall financing cost would be less than the cost from issuing British pound-denominated bonds.

There is no guarantee that the exchange rates of the US dollar and Japanese yen will move in opposite directions. The movements of these two currencies are not highly correlated, however, so it is unlikely that both currencies will simultaneously appreciate to an extent that will offset their lower coupon rate advantages. Therefore, financing in bonds denominated in more than one foreign currency can increase the probability that the overall cost of foreign financing will be less than that of financing with the dollars. Never decides to issue bonds denominated in US dollars and in yen.

The preceding example involved only two foreign currencies. In reality, a firm may consider several currencies that they feel are going to cost less after taking into account the interest rate of the bond and the expected exchange rate movement and issue a portion of its bonds in each of these currencies. Such a strategy can increase the other costs (advertising, printing, etc.) of issuing bonds, but those costs may be offset by a reduction in cash outflows to bondholders.

Currency cocktail bonds. A firm can finance in several currencies without issuing various types of bonds (thus avoiding higher transaction costs) by developing a **currency cocktail bond**, denominated in not one, but a mixture (or "cocktail" or "basket") of currencies. A currency cocktail simply reflects a multicurrency unit of account. Several currency cocktails have been developed to denominate international bonds, and some have already been used in this manner. One of the more popular currency cocktails is the special drawing right (SDR), which was originally devised as a unit of account for the IMF and is made up of a cocktail of currencies but is now also used to denominate bonds and bank deposits and to price various services. With the creation of the euro, the use of currency cocktail bonds in Europe is limited because numerous European countries now use a single currency.

INTEREST RATE RISK FROM DEBT FINANCING

Regardless of the currency that an MNC uses to finance its international operations, it must also decide on the maturity that it should use for its debt. Its goal is to use a maturity that will minimize the total payments on the debt needed for each business unit. Normally, an MNC will not use a maturity that exceeds the expected life of the business in that country.

When it uses a relatively short maturity, the MNC is exposed to interest rate risk, or the risk that interest rates will rise, forcing it to refinance at a higher interest rate. It can avoid this exposure by issuing a long-term bond (with a fixed interest rate) that matches the expected life of the operations in the foreign country. The disadvantage of this strategy is that long-term interest rates may decline in the near future, but the MNC will be obliged to continue making its debt payments at the higher rate. There is no perfect solution, but the MNC should consider the expected life of the business and the yield curve of the country in question when weighing the tradeoff. The yield curve is the difference in the per annum rate for bonds of differing maturities (e.g. a ten year bond may charge 7% per annum but a three year bond may charge 5% per annum). The difference is shaped by the demand for and supply of funds at various maturity levels in a country's debt market.

The debt maturity decision

Before making the debt maturity decision, MNCs assess the yield curves of the countries in which they need funds. Examples of yield curves as of February 2004 for six different countries are shown in Exhibit 18.9. First, notice that at any given debt maturity, the interest rate varies among countries. Second, notice that the shape of the yield curve can vary among countries. For example, the United States typically has an upward-sloping yield curve, which means that the per annum interest rates are lower for short-term debt than for long-term debt. One argument for the upward slope is that investors may require a higher rate of return on long-term debt as compensation for lower liquidity. The market value of long-term debt is more sensitive to market interest rate movements, so investors face a greater risk of a loss if they need to sell the debt before its maturity. Even in the United States, the yield curve is not always upward sloping because other forces such as interest rate expectations may affect the demand and supply conditions for debt at various maturity levels. In some countries, the yield curve is commonly flat or downward sloping for longer maturities.

Some MNCs may use a country's yield curve to compare annualized rates among debt maturities, so that they can choose a maturity that has a relatively low rate. Other MNCs use a yield curve to assess the prevailing market demand for and supply of funds for particular debt maturities, which may indicate the future movement in interest rates. This type of information may help an MNC decide whether to lock in a long-term rate or borrow for a short-term period and re-finance in the near future.

Exhibit 18.9   Yield curves among foreign countries (as of 6 February 2001)

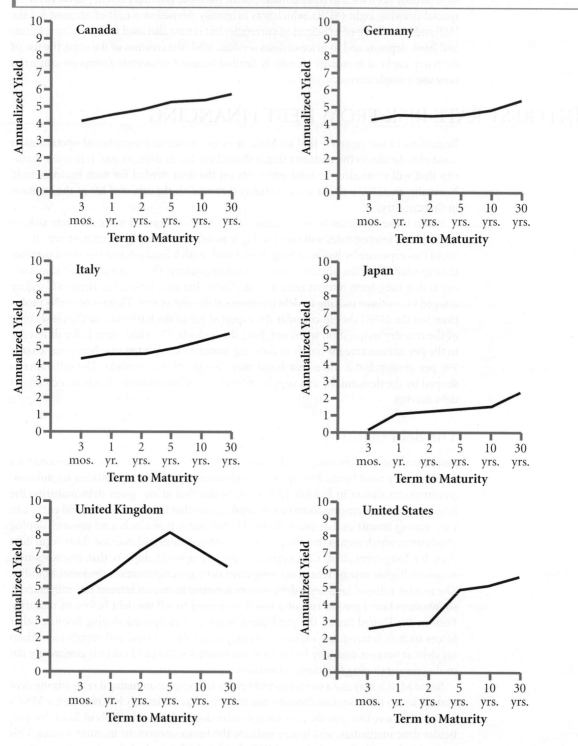

Withington ltd expects to generate earnings in Indonesia, Malaysia, and Thailand for the next ten years. It expects that the Indonesian rupiah and Malaysian ringgit will weaken substantially against the pound over that period, and therefore plans to finance the respective operations with local debt from those countries. Its earnings from Thailand may be discontinued in five years when a contract with the Thai government expires.

Withington's best guess is that the Thai baht's future value will be similar to today's spot rate, but it is concerned about the exchange rate risk of its baht-denominated revenue. The ten-year bond yield is about 12% for each country, but the yield curve is upward sloping (implying lower annualized yields for shorter debt maturities) in Malaysia and Thailand and downward sloping (higher annualized yields for shorter debt maturities) in Indonesia. It expects that future interest rates in these countries should be somewhat stable over time.

Withington ltd decides to issue Thai notes with a maturity of five years to finance the Thai operations because it does not want to have debt in the business beyond the period when its operations may be discontinued. In addition, the upward-sloping yield curve allows it to issue five-year notes at a lower annualized yield than a ten-year bond in Thai baht. Withington decides to issue ten-year bonds to finance its operations in Indonesia; because the yield curve is downward sloping, if it issued shorter-term debt, it would have to pay a higher annualized yield and would then be exposed to the possibility of higher interest rates when it re-finances the debt. Finally, it decides to issue short-term debt to finance its operations in Malaysia because it will pay a lower annualized yield on short-term debt. In this case, Withington will be exposed to the possibility that interest rates will increase by the time it refinances the debt.

The fixed versus floating rate decision

MNCs that wish to use a long-term maturity but wish to avoid the prevailing fixed rate on long-term bonds may consider floating rate bonds. In this case, the coupon rate will fluctuate over time in accordance with interest rates. For example, the coupon rate is frequently tied to the London Interbank Offer Rate (LIBOR), which is a rate at which banks lend funds to each other. As LIBOR increases, so does the coupon rate of a floating rate bond. A floating coupon rate can be an advantage to the bond issuer during periods of decreasing interest rates, when otherwise the firm would be locked in at a higher coupon rate over the life of the bond. It can be a disadvantage during periods of rising interest rates. In some countries, such as those in South America, most long-term debt has a floating interest rate.

If the coupon rate is floating, then forecasts are required for interest rates as well as for exchange rates. Simulation can be used to incorporate possible outcomes for the exchange rate and for the coupon rate over the life of the loan and can develop a probability distribution of annual costs of financing.

Hedging with interest rate swaps

When MNCs issue bonds that expose them to interest rate risk, they may use interest rate *swaps* to hedge the risk. Interest rate swaps enable a firm to exchange fixed rate payments for variable rate payments. Bonds issuers use interest rate swaps because they may reconfigure the future cash flows in a manner that offsets their outflow payments to bondholders. In this way, MNCs can reduce their exposure to interest rate movements.

Financial institutions such as commercial and investment banks and insurance companies often act as dealers in interest rate swaps. Financial institutions can also act as brokers in the interest rate swap market. As a broker, the financial institution simply arranges an interest rate swap between two parties, charging a fee for the service, but does not actually take a position in the swap. MNCs frequently engage in interest rate swaps to hedge or to reduce financing costs.

Note that as with much in finance there are alternative ways of achieving the same result. In this case, a firm may take out a futures contract on bonds. A bond price varies inversely with any change in the interest rate. If interest rates go up, bond prices fall to offer a similarly attractive return and vice versa. Selling bonds on the futures market will mean that an MNC will receive money (through daily settlement) when interest rates go up and consequently bond prices fall and the MNC will pay out when interest rates fall and bond prices go up. Closing out will ensure that no bonds are actually sold on the forward market. So the price of a swap must not be greater than this alternative approach.

Plain vanilla swap

A plain vanilla swap is a standard contract without any unusual contract additions. In a plain vanilla swap, the floating rate payer is typically highly sensitive to interest rate changes and seeks to reduce interest rate risk. A firm with a large amount of highly interest rate-sensitive assets may seek to exchange floating rate payments for fixed rate payments. In general, the floating rate payer, at the time of arranging the loan, believes interest rates are going to decline. The fixed rate payer in a plain vanilla interest rate swap, on the other hand, expected that interest rates were going to rise and hence chose to make fixed rate payments. Fixed rate payers may include firms with a large amount of highly interest rate-sensitive liabilities or a relatively large proportion of fixed rate assets.

EXAMPLE

Two firms plan to issue bonds:

■ Quality plc is a highly rated firm that prefers to borrow at a variable interest rate.

■ Risky plc is a low-rated firm that prefers to borrow at a fixed interest rate.

Assume that the rates these companies would pay for issuing either floating (variable) rate or fixed rate bonds are as follows:

	Fixed Rate Bond	Variable Rate Bond
Quality plc (prefers variable)	9%	LIBOR + ½%
Risky plc (prefers fixed)	10½%	LIBOR + 1%

LIBOR changes over time. Based on the information given, Quality plc has an advantage when issuing either fixed rate or variable rate bonds, but more of an advantage with fixed rate bonds. Quality plc could issue fixed rate bonds while Risky plc issues variable rate bonds; then, Quality could provide variable rate payments to Risky in exchange for fixed rate payments.

Assume that Quality plc negotiates with Risky plc to provide variable rate payments at LIBOR + ½% in exchange for fixed rate payments of 9½%. The interest rate swap arrangement is shown in Exhibit 18.10. Quality plc benefits because the fixed rate payments it receives on the swap exceed the payments it owes to bondholders by ½%. Its variable rate payments to Risky plc are the same as what it would have paid if it had issued variable rate bonds. Risky plc is receiving LIBOR + ½% on the swap, which is ½%

Exhibit 18.10 Illustration of an interest rate swap

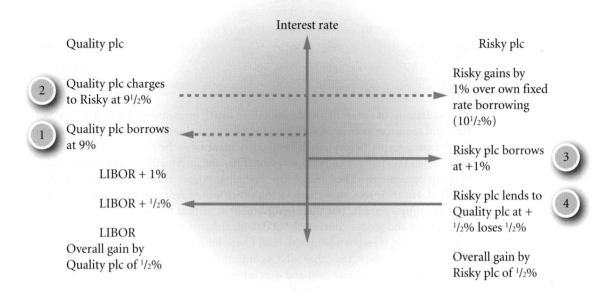

Notes:

- Risky wants a fixed rate loan; Quality a variable rate loan.

- Risky's position: Paying a fixed rate at $9^1/2\%$ is 1% cheaper than issuing at $10^1/2\%$ at a cost of losing $1/2\%$ on the variable (LIBOR) rate deal. Net gain $1/2\%$.

- Quality's position: Variable loan is the same as if it had issued directly. But by issuing at fixed rate instead and charging $9^1/2\%$ to Risky, it gains $1/2\%$.

less than what it must pay on its variable rate bonds. Yet, it is making fixed rate payments of 9½%, which is 1% less than what it would have paid if it had issued fixed rate bonds. Overall, Risky plc saves ½% per year of financing costs.

Determining swap payments. The payments in an interest rate swap are typically determined using some **notional value** agreed upon by the parties to the swap and established contractually. Importantly, the notional amount itself is never exchanged between the parties, but is used only to determine the swap payments. Once the swap payments have been determined using the notional amount, the parties periodically exchange only the net amount owed instead of all payments. Payments are typically exchanged either annually or semi-annually.

EXAMPLE

Continuing with the previous example involving Quality plc and Risky plc, assume that the notional value agreed upon by the parties is £50 million and that the two firms exchange net payments annually.

From Quality plc's viewpoint, the complete swap arrangement now involves payment of LIBOR +½% annually, based on a notional value of £50 m. From Risky plc's viewpoint, the swap arrangement involves a fixed payment of 9½% annually based on a notional value of £50 m. The following table below illustrates the payments based on LIBOR over time.

Year	LIBOR	Quality plc Payment	Risky plc Payment	Net Payment
1	8.0%	8.5% × £50 m = £4.25 m	9.5% × £50 m = £4.75 m	Risky pays Quality £0.5 m
2	7.0%	7.5% × £50 m = £3.75 m	9.5% × £50 m = £4.75 m	Risky pays Quality £1 m
3	5.5%	6.0% × £50 m = £3 m	9.5% × £50 m = £4.75 m	Risky pays Quality £1.75 m
4	9.0%	9.5% × £50 m = £4.75 m	9.5% × £50 m = £4.75 m	No payment is made
5	10.0%	10.5% × £50 m = £5.25 m	9.5% × £50 m = £4.75 m	Risky pays Quality £0.5 m

Two limitations of the swap just described are worth mentioning. First, there is a cost of time and resources associated with searching for a suitable swap candidate and negotiating the swap terms. Second, each swap participant faces the risk that the counterparty could default on payments. For this reason, financial intermediaries are usually involved in swap agreements. They match up participants and also assume the default risk involved. For their role, they charge a fee, which would reduce the estimated benefits in the preceding example, but their involvement is critical to effectively match up swap participants and reduce concern about default risk.

Ashland, Inc, Campbell Soup Co, Intel Corp, Johnson Controls, Union Carbide, and Adidas Salomon and many other MNCs commonly use interest rate swaps. Ashland, Inc, commonly issues fixed rate debt and uses interest rate swaps to achieve lower borrowing costs on variable rate debt. Campbell Soup Co uses interest rate swaps to minimize its worldwide financing costs and to achieve a targeted proportion of fixed rate versus variable rate debt. Adidas use interest rate swaps and cross currency interest rate swaps, thereby reducing foreign currency exposure as well.

Other types of interest rate swaps. Continuing financial innovation has resulted in various additional types of interest rate swaps in recent years. Listed below are some examples:

- *Accretion swap.* An accretion swap is a swap in which the notional value is increased over time.
- *Amortizing swap.* An amortizing swap is essentially the opposite of an accretion swap. In an amortizing swap, the notional value is reduced over time.
- *Basis (floating-for-floating) swap.* A basis swap involves the exchange of two floating rate payments. For example, a swap between one-year LIBOR and six-month LIBOR is a basis swap.
- *Callable swap.* As the name suggests, a callable swap gives the fixed rate payer the right to terminate the swap. The fixed rate payer would exercise this right if interest rates fall substantially.
- *Forward swap.* A forward swap is an interest rate swap that is entered into today. However, the swap payments start at a specific future point in time.
- *Putable swap.* A putable swap gives the floating rate payer the right to terminate the swap. The floating rate payer would exercise this right if interest rates rise substantially.
- *Zero-coupon swap.* In a zero-coupon swap, all fixed interest payments are postponed until maturity and are paid in one lump sum when the swap matures. However, the floating rate payments are due periodically.

- *Swaption.* A swaption gives its owner the right to enter into a swap. The exercise price of a swaption is a specified fixed interest rate at which the swaption owner can enter the swap at a specified future date. A payer swaption gives its owner the right to switch from paying floating to paying fixed interest rates at the exercise price. A receiver swaption gives its owner the right to switch from receiving floating rate to receiving fixed rate payments at the exercise price.

Standardization of the swap market. As the swap market has grown in recent years, one association in particular is frequently credited with its standardization. The International Swaps and Derivatives Association (ISDA) is a global trade association representing leading participants in the privately negotiated derivatives industry. This encompasses interest rate, currency, commodity, credit, and equity swaps, as well as related products such as caps, collars, floors, and swaptions. The ISDA was chartered in 1985, after a group of 18 swap dealers began work in 1984 to develop standard terms for interest rate swaps. Today, the ISDA has over 600 member institutions from 46 countries. These members include most of the world's major institutions that deal in derivative instruments, as well as leading end-users of privately negotiated derivatives and associated service providers and consultants.

Since its inception, the ISDA has pioneered efforts to identify and reduce the sources of risk in the derivatives and risk management business. The ISDA's two primary objectives are: (1) the development and maintenance of derivatives documentation to promote efficient business conduct practices, and (2) the promotion of the development of sound risk management practices.

One of the ISDA's most notable accomplishments is the development of the ISDA Master Agreement. This agreement provides participants in the private derivatives markets with the opportunity to establish the legal and credit terms between them for an ongoing business relationship. The key advantage of such an agreement is that the general legal and credit terms do not have to be renegotiated each time the parties enter into a transaction. Consequently, the ISDA Master Agreement has contributed greatly to the standardization of the derivatives market (see http://www.isda.org).

USING THE WEB

Long-term foreign interest rates Long-term interest rates for major currencies such as the Canadian dollar, Japanese yen, and British pound for various maturities are provided at http://www.bloomberg.com. You can develop a yield curve from this information.

SUMMARY

- Some MNCs may consider long-term financing in foreign currencies to offset future cash inflows in those currencies and therefore reduce exposure to exchange rate risk. Other MNCs may consider long-term financing in foreign currencies to reduce financing costs. If a foreign interest rate is relatively low or the foreign currency borrowed depreciates over the financing period, long-term financing in that currency can result in low financing costs.

- An MNC can assess the feasibility of financing in foreign currencies by applying exchange rate forecasts to the periodic coupon payments and the principal payment. In this way, it determines the amount of its home currency that is necessary per period to cover the payments. The annual cost of financing can be estimated by determining the discount rate that equates the periodic payments on the foreign financing to the initial amount borrowed (as measured in the domestic currency). The discount rate derived from this exercise represents the annual cost of financing in the foreign currency, which can be compared to the cost of

domestic financing. The cost of long-term financing in a foreign currency is dependent on the currency's exchange rate over the financing period and therefore is uncertain. Thus, the MNC will not automatically finance with a foreign currency that has a lower interest rate, since its exchange rate forecasts are subject to error. For this reason, the MNC may estimate the costs of foreign financing under various exchange rate scenarios over time.

- For bonds that have floating interest rates, the coupon payment to be paid to investors is uncertain. This creates another uncertain variable (along with exchange rates) in estimating the amount in the firm's domestic currency that is required per period to make the payments. This uncertainty can be accounted for by estimating the coupon payment amount necessary under various interest rate scenarios over time. Then, with the use of these estimates, the amount of the firm's domestic currency required to make the payments can be estimated, based on various exchange rate scenarios over time.

CRITICAL DEBATE

Are swaps deceiving the market?

Proposition. Yes. Interest rates are charged to firms because the market estimates that the risk is appropriate for the borrower. For MNCs to then swap the loans is to ignore this judgement and puts lenders at risk and hence the interests of the shareholders.

Opposing view. No. The difference in rates is often small and hardly related to non-payment. There are

other reasons for swaps to do with currencies and changing the nature of the loan, so there is no second guessing the market.

With whom do you agree? Provide a reasoned argument as to why you agree or disagree with one of the above views.

SELF TEST

Answers are provided in Appendix A at the back of the text.

1. Explain why a firm may issue a bond denominated in a currency different from its home currency to finance local operations. Explain the risk involved.

2. Trulane plc is considering issuing a 20-year Swiss franc-denominated bond. The proceeds are to be converted to pounds to support the firm's UK

operations. Trulane has no Swiss operations but prefers to issue the bond in francs rather than pounds because the coupon rate is 2 percentage points lower. Explain the risk involved in this strategy. Do you think the risk here is greater or less than it would be if the bond proceeds were used to finance Swiss operations? Why?

3. Some large companies based in Latin American countries could borrow funds (through issuing

bonds or borrowing from UK banks) at an interest rate that would be substantially less than the interest rates in their own countries. Assuming that they are perceived to be creditworthy in the United Kingdom, why might they still prefer to borrow in their local countries when financing local projects (even if they incur interest rates of 80% or more)?

4. A respected economist recently predicted that even though Japanese inflation would not rise, Japanese interest rates would rise consistently over the next five years. Abend GmbH a German firm with no foreign operations, has recently issued a Japanese yen-denominated bond to finance German opera-

tions. It chose the yen denomination because the coupon rate was low. Its vice president stated, "I'm not concerned about the prediction because we issued fixed rate bonds and are therefore insulated from risk." Do you agree? Explain.

5. Long-term interest rates in some Latin American countries commonly exceed 100% annually. Offer your opinion as to why these interest rates are so much higher than those of industrialized countries and why some projects in these countries are feasible for local firms, even though the cost of funding the projects is so high.

QUESTIONS AND APPLICATIONS

1. **Floating rate bonds**
   a. What factors should be considered by a UK firm that plans to issue a floating rate bond denominated in a foreign currency?
   b. Is the risk of issuing a floating rate bond higher or lower than the risk of issuing a fixed rate bond? Explain.
   c. How would an investing firm differ from a borrowing firm in the features (i.e., interest rate and currency's future exchange rates) it would prefer a floating rate foreign currency-denominated bond to exhibit?

2. **Risk from issuing foreign currency-denominated bonds.** What is the advantage of using simulation to assess the bond financing position?

3. **Exchange rate effects**
   a. Explain the difference in the cost of financing with foreign currencies during a strong-pound period versus a weak-pound period for a UK firm.
   b. Explain how a UK-based MNC issuing bonds denominated in euros may be able to offset a portion of its exchange rate risk.

4. **Bond offering decision.** Columbia plc is a UK company with no foreign currency cash flows. It plans to issue either a bond denominated in euros with a fixed interest rate or a bond denominated in UK pounds with a floating interest rate. It estimates its periodic pound cash flows for each bond. Which bond do you think would have

greater uncertainty surrounding these future pound cash flows? Explain.

5. **Currency diversification.** Why would a UK firm consider issuing bonds denominated in multiple currencies?

6. **Financing that reduces exchange rate risk.** Kerr plc a major UK exporter of products to Japan, denominates its exports in pounds and has no other international business. It can borrow pounds at 9% to finance its operations or borrow yen at 3%. If it borrows yen, it will be exposed to exchange rate risk. How can Kerr borrow yen and possibly reduce its economic exposure to exchange rate risk?

7. **Exchange rate effects.** Katina plc is a UK firm that plans to finance with bonds denominated in euros to obtain a lower interest rate than is available on pound-denominated bonds. What is the most critical point in time when the exchange rate will have the greatest impact?

8. **Financing decision.** Ivax plc (based in Germany) is a drug company that has attempted to capitalize on new opportunities to expand in Eastern Europe. The production costs in most Eastern European countries are very low, often less than one-fourth of the cost in Germany or Switzerland. Furthermore, there is a strong demand for drugs in Eastern Europe. Ivax penetrated Eastern Europe by purchasing a 60% stake in Galena AS, a Czech firm that produces drugs.

a. Should Ivax finance its investment in the Czech firm by borrowing euros that would then be converted into koruna (the Czech currency) or by borrowing koruna from a local Czech bank? What information do you need to know to answer this question?

b. How can borrowing koruna locally from a Czech bank reduce the exposure of Ivax to exchange rate risk?

c. How can borrowing koruna locally from a Czech bank reduce the exposure of Ivax to political risk caused by government regulations?

ADVANCED QUESTIONS

9. **Bond financing analysis.** Sambuka plc can issue bonds in either UK pounds or in Swiss francs. Pound-denominated bonds would have a coupon rate of 15%; Swiss franc-denominated bonds would have a coupon rate of 12%. Assuming that Sambuka can issue bonds worth £10,000,000 in either currency, that the current exchange rate of the Swiss franc is £0.47, and that the forecasted exchange rate of the franc in each of the next three years is £0.50, what is the annual cost of financing for the franc-denominated bonds? Which type of bond should Sambuka issue?

10. **Bond financing analysis.** Hatton ltd just agreed to a long-term deal in which it will export products to Japan. It needs funds to finance the production of the products that it will export. The products will be denominated in pounds. The prevailing UK long-term interest rate is 9% versus 3% in Japan. Assume that interest rate parity exists, and that Hatton believes that the international Fisher effect holds.

a. Should Hatton finance its production with yen and leave itself open to exchange rate risk? Explain.

b. Should Hatton finance its production with yen and simultaneously engage in forward contracts to hedge its exposure to exchange rate risk?

c. How could Hatton plc achieve low-cost financing while eliminating its exposure to exchange rate risk?

11. **Cost of financing.** Assume that Seminole plc considers issuing a Singapore dollar-denominated bond at its present coupon rate of 7%, even though it has no incoming cash flows to cover the bond payments. It is attracted to the low financing rate, since UK pound-denominated bonds issued in the United Kingdom would have a coupon rate of 12%. Assume that either type of bond would have a four-year maturity and could be issued at par value. Seminole needs to borrow £10 million. Therefore, it will issue either UK pound-denominated bonds with a par value of £10 million or bonds denominated in Singapore dollars with a par value of S$20 million. The spot rate of the Singapore dollar is £0.33. Seminole has forecasted the Singapore dollar's value at the end of each of the next four years, when coupon payments are to be paid:

End of Year	Pound Exchange Rate of Singapore
1	£0.34
2	0.35
3	0.38
4	0.33

Determine the expected annual cost of financing with Singapore dollars. Should Seminole plc issue bonds denominated in UK pounds or Singapore dollars? Explain.

12. **Interaction between financing and invoicing policies.** Assume that Hurricane plc is a UK company that exports products to the United States, invoiced in pounds. It also exports products to Denmark, invoiced in pounds. It currently has no cash outflows in foreign currencies, and it plans to issue bonds in the near future. Hurricane could issue bonds at par value in: (1) pounds with a coupon rate of 12%, (2) Danish kroner with a coupon rate of 9%, or (3) dollars with a coupon rate of 15%. It expects the kroner and dollar to strengthen over time. How could Hurricane revise its invoicing policy and make its bond denomination decision to achieve low financing costs without excessive exposure to exchange rate fluctuations?

13. **Swap agreement.** Grant plc is a well-known UK firm that needs to borrow 10 million dollars to support a new business in the United States. However, it cannot obtain financing from US banks because it is not yet established within the United States. It decides to issue pound-

denominated debt (at par value) in the United Kingdom, for which it will pay an annual coupon rate of 10%. It then will convert the pound proceeds from the debt issue into dollars at the prevailing spot rate (the prevailing spot rate is one pound = $1.70). Over each of the next three years, it plans to use the revenue in dollars from the new business in the United States to make its annual debt payment. Grant plc engages in a currency swap in which it will convert dollars to pounds at an exchange rate of $1.70 per pound at the end of each of the next three years. How many pounds must be borrowed initially to support the new business in the United States? How many dollars should Grant plc specify in the swap agreement that it will swap over each of the next three years in exchange for pounds so that it can make its annual coupon payments to the UK creditors?

14. **Interest rate swap.** Janutis plc has just issued fixed rate debt at 10%. Yet, it prefers to convert its financing to incur a floating rate on its debt. It engages in an interest rate swap in which it swaps variable rate payments of LIBOR plus 1% in exchange for payments of 10%. The interest rates are applied to an amount that represents the principal from its recent debt issue in order to determine the interest payments due at the end of each year for the next three years. Janutis plc expects that the LIBOR will be 9% at the end of the first year, 8.5% at the end of the second year, and 7% at the end of the third year. Determine the financing rate that Janutis plc expects to pay

on its debt after considering the effect of the interest rate swap.

PROJECT WORKSHOP

15. **Long-term cost of debt.** The Bloomberg website provides interest rate data for many countries and various maturities. Its address is http://www.bloomberg.com.

Go to the "Market Data" section of the website and then to "Rates and Bonds". Consider a subsidiary of a US-based MNC that is located in Australia. Assume that when it borrows in Australian dollars, it would pay 1% more than the risk-free (government) rates shown on the website. What rate would the subsidiary pay for one-year debt? For five-year debt? For ten-year debt? Assuming that it needs funds for ten years, do you think it should use one-year debt, five-year debt, or ten-year debt? Explain your answer.

DISCUSSION IN THE BOARDROOM

This exercise can be found on the companion website at www.cengage.co.uk/madura_fox.

RUNNING YOUR OWN COMPANY

This exercise can be found on the companion website at www.cengage.co.uk/madura_fox.

Essays/discussion and articles can be found at the end of Part 4

BLADES PLC CASE STUDY
Use of long-term foreign financing

Recall that Blades plc is considering the establishment of a subsidiary in Thailand to manufacture "Speedos", Blades' primary roller blade product. Alternatively, Blades could acquire an existing manufacturer of roller blades in Thailand, Skates'n'Stuff. At the most recent meeting of the board of directors of Blades plc, the directors voted to establish a subsidiary in Thailand

because of the relatively high level of control it would afford Blades.

The Thai subsidiary is expected to begin production by early next year, and the construction of the plant in Thailand and the purchase of necessary equipment to manufacture Speedos are to commence immediately. Initial estimates of the plant and equipment required to establish the subsidiary in Bangkok indicate costs of approximately 550 million Thai baht. Since the current exchange rate of the baht is £0.0153, this translates to a pound cost of £8.43 million. Blades currently has £1.76 million available in cash to cover a portion of the costs. The remaining £6.67 million (436 million baht), however, will have to be obtained from other sources.

The board of directors has asked Ben Holt, Blades' financial director, to line up the necessary financing to cover the remaining construction costs and purchase of equipment. Holt realizes that Blades is a relatively small company whose stock is not widely held. Furthermore, he believes that Blades' stock is currently undervalued because the company's expansion into Thailand has not been widely publicized at this point. Because of these considerations, Holt would prefer debt to equity financing to raise the funds necessary to complete construction of the Thai plant.

Ben Holt has identified two alternatives for debt financing: issue the equivalent of £8.43 million yen-denominated notes or issue the equivalent of approximately £8.43 million baht-denominated notes. Both types of notes would have a maturity of five years. In the fifth year, the face value of the notes will be repaid together with the last annual interest payment.

Due to recent unfavourable economic events in Thailand, expansion into Thailand is viewed as relatively risky; Holt's research indicates that Blades would have to offer a coupon rate of approximately 10% on the yen-denominated notes to induce investors to purchase these notes. Conversely, Blades could issue baht-denominated notes at a coupon rate of 15%. Whether Blades decides to issue baht- or yen-denominated notes, it would use the cash flows generated by the Thai subsidiary to pay the interest on the notes and to repay the principal in five years. For example, if Blades decides to issue yen-denominated notes, it would convert baht into yen to pay the interest on these notes and to repay the principal in five years.

Although Blades can finance with a lower coupon rate by issuing yen-denominated notes, Ben Holt suspects that the effective financing rate for the yen-denominated notes may actually be higher than for

the baht-denominated notes. This is because forecasts for the future value of the yen indicate an appreciation of the yen (versus the baht) in the future. Although the precise future value of the yen is uncertain, Holt has compiled the following probability distribution for the annual percentage change of the yen versus the baht:

Annual % Change in Yen (versus the baht)	Probability
0%	20%
2	50
3	30

Holt suspects that the effective financing cost of the yen-denominated notes may actually be higher than for the baht-denominated notes once the expected appreciation of the yen (versus the baht) is taken into consideration.

Holt has asked you, a financial analyst at Blades plc to answer the following questions for him:

1. Given that Blades expects to use the cash flows generated by the Thai subsidiary to pay the interest and principal of the notes, would the effective financing cost of the baht-denominated notes be affected by exchange rate movements? Would the effective financing cost of the yen-denominated notes be affected by exchange rate movements? How?

2. Construct a spreadsheet to determine the annual effective financing percentage cost of the yen-denominated notes issued in each of the three scenarios for the future value of the yen. What is the probability that the financing cost of issuing yen-denominated notes is higher than the cost of issuing baht-denominated notes?

3. Using a spreadsheet, determine the expected annual effective financing percentage cost of issuing yen-denominated notes. How does this expected financing cost compare with the expected financing cost of the baht-denominated notes?

4. Based on your answers to the previous questions, do you think Blades should issue yen- or baht-denominated notes?

5. What is the tradeoff involved?

SMALL BUSINESS DILEMMA
Long-term financing decision by the Sports Exports Company

The Sports Exports Company continues to focus on producing basketballs in Ireland and exporting them to the United Kingdom. The exports are denominated in pounds, which has continually exposed the firm to exchange rate risk. It is now considering a new form of expansion where it would sell specialty sporting goods in the United States. If it pursues this US project, it will need to borrow long-term funds. The dollar-denominated debt has an interest rate that is slightly lower than the pound-denominated debt.

1. Jim Logan, owner of the Sports Exports Company, needs to determine whether dollar-denominated debt or pound-denominated debt would be most appropriate for financing this expansion, if he does expand. He is leaning toward financing the US project with dollar-denominated debt, since his goal is to avoid exchange rate risk. Is there any reason why he should consider using pound-denominated debt to reduce exchange rate risk?

2. Assume that Jim decides to finance his proposed US business with dollar-denominated debt, if he does implement the US business idea. How could he use a currency swap along with the debt to reduce the firm's exposure to exchange rate risk?

LONG-TERM ASSET AND LIABILITY MANAGEMENT

Gandor plc is a UK firm that is considering a joint venture with a Chinese firm to produce and sell videocassettes. Gandor will invest £12 million in this project, which will help to finance the Chinese firm's production. For each of the first three years, 50% of the total profits will be distributed to the Chinese firm, while the remaining 50% will be converted to dollars to be sent to the United Kingdom. The Chinese government intends to impose a 20% income tax on the profits distributed to Gandor. The Chinese government has guaranteed that the after-tax profits (denominated in yuan, the Chinese currency) can be converted to British pounds at an exchange rate of £0.13 per yuan and sent to Gandor plc each year. At the current time, no withholding tax is imposed on profits sent to the United Kingdom as a result of joint ventures in China. Assume that after considering the taxes paid in China, an additional 10% tax is imposed by the UK government on profits received by Gandor plc. After the first three years, all profits earned are allocated to the Chinese firm.

The expected total profits resulting from the joint venture per year are as follows:

Year	Total Profits From Joint Venture (in yuan)
1	60 million
2	80 million
3	100 million

Gandor's average cost of debt is 13.8% before taxes. Its average cost of equity is 18%. Assume that the corporate income tax rate imposed on Gandor is normally 30%. Gandor uses a capital structure composed of 60% debt and 40% equity. Gandor automatically adds 4 percentage points to its cost of capital when deriving its required rate of return on international joint ventures. Though this project has particular forms of country risk that are unique, Gandor plans to account for these forms of risk within its estimation of cash flows.

Gandor is concerned about two forms of country risk. First, there is the risk that the Chinese government will increase the corporate income tax rate from 20% to 40% (20% probability). If this occurs, additional tax credits will be allowed, resulting in no UK taxes on the profits from this joint venture. Second, there is the risk that the Chinese government will impose a withholding tax of 10% on the profits that are sent to the United Kingdom (20% probability). In this case, additional tax credits will not be allowed, and Gandor will still be subject to a 10% UK tax on profits received from China. Assume that the two types of country risk are mutually exclusive. That is, the Chinese government will adjust only one of its taxes (the income tax or the withholding tax), if any.

Questions

1. Determine Gandor's cost of capital. Also, determine Gandor's required rate of return for the joint venture in China.
2. Determine the probability distribution of Gandor's net present values for the joint venture. Capital budgeting analyses should be conducted for these three scenarios:

- *Scenario 1.* Based on original assumptions.
- *Scenario 2.* Based on an increase in the corporate income tax by the Chinese government.
- *Scenario 3.* Based on the imposition of a withholding tax by the Chinese government.

3. Would you recommend that Gandor participate in the joint venture? Explain.
4. What do you think would be the key underlying factor that would have the most influence on the profits earned in China as a result of the joint venture?
5. Is there any reason for Gandor to revise the composition of its capital (debt and equity) obtained from the United Kingdom when financing joint ventures like this?
6. When Gandor was assessing this proposed joint venture, some of its managers recommended that Gandor borrow the Chinese currency rather than dollars to obtain some of the necessary capital for its initial investment. They suggested that such a strategy could reduce Gandor's exchange rate risk. Do you agree? Explain

1. Buch, C.M., J. Kleinert, A. Lipponer and F. Toubal (2005) "Determinants and Effects of Foreign Direct Investment: Evidence from German firms level data", *Economic Policy*, Jan., 51–110.

   Q *Evaluate the principal determinants of FDI as reported by Buch et al. in their survey of German firms. Is there any clear lesson for the future?*

2. Doukas, John A. and L.H.P. Lang (2003) "Foreign Direct Investment, Diversification and Firm Performance", *Journal of International Business Studies*, 34 (2), 153–72.

   Q *A study of differing types of international investment – some technical content. Writing as a Finance Director, prepare a report outlining the main findings in this paper and assessing their significance for a non-diversified multinational. Take care to assess the size as well as significance of any relationships.*

3. Blonigen, B.A. (2005) "A Review of the Empirical Literature on FDI Determinants", *Atlantic Economic Journal*, 3, 383–403. A review of the issues, a bit heavy going especially as the studies are not particularly conclusive. Nevertheless it does give a good idea of the issues and problems.

   Q *From a reading of Blonigen's review, select the three most convincing (partial) models of FDI. Evaluate these models and explain why you think these models have the potantial for greater development.*

4. Brink, N. and W. Viviers (2003) "Obstacles on Attracting Increased Portfolio Investment into Southern Africa'" *Development Southern* Africa, 20 (2), 213–36. This is an excellent study of portfolio investment in the widely differing economies of Southern Africa.

   Q *With reference to the Brink and Viviers article, is there a mismatch? Discuss (you are being asked to discuss the ways in which the economies of southern Africa fail to meet the needs of foreign investors and evaluate the extent to which foreign investment fails to meet the development needs of southern Africa).*

5. Xing, Y. and G. Wan (2006) "Exchange Rates and Competition for FDI in Asia", *The World Economy*, 29 (4), 419–34.

   Q *How important are exchange rates in determining the significance of FDI? Discuss.*

6. Demirag, I.S. (1986) "The Treatment of Exchange Rates in Internal Performance Evaluation", *Accounting & Business Research*, 16 (2), 157–64.

   Q *Describe the differing methods of treating exchange rates in the budget process. Discuss how a survey today might differ from Demirag's findings.*

PART 5

SHORT-TERM ASSET AND LIABILITY MANAGEMENT

. . . .

PART 5 (CHAPTERS 19 TO 21) focuses on the MNC's management of short-term assets and liabilities. Chapter 19 describes methods by which MNCs can finance their international trade. Chapter 20 identifies sources of short-term funds and explains the criteria used by MNCs to make their short-term financing decisions. Chapter 21 describes how MNCs optimize their cash flows and explains the criteria used to make their short-term investment decisions.

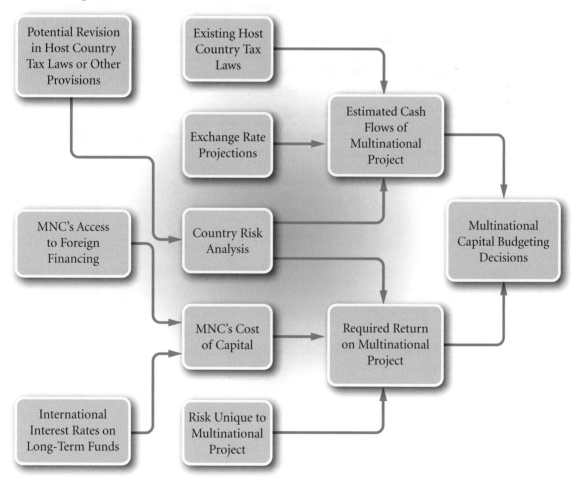

CHAPTER 19

FINANCING INTERNATIONAL TRADE

THE INTERNATIONAL TRADE ACTIVITIES of MNCs have grown in importance over time. This trend is attributable to the increased globalization of the world economies and the availability of trade finance from the international banking community. Although banks also finance domestic trade, their role in financing international trade is more critical due to the additional complications involved. First, the exporter might question the importer's ability to make payment. Second, even if the importer is creditworthy, the government might impose exchange controls that prevent payment to the exporter. Third, the importer might not trust the exporter to ship the goods ordered. Fourth, even if the exporter does ship the goods, trade barriers or time lags in international transportation might delay arrival time. Financial managers must recognize methods that they can use to finance international trade so that they can conduct exporting or importing in a manner that maximizes the value of an MNC.

THE SPECIFIC OBJECTIVES OF THIS CHAPTER ARE TO:

- describe methods of payment for international trade,
- explain common trade finance methods, and
- describe the major agencies that facilitate international trade with export insurance and/or loan programmes.

Payment methods for international trade

In any international trade transaction, credit is provided by the supplier (exporter), the buyer (importer), one or more financial institutions, or any combination of these. The supplier may have sufficient cash flow to finance the entire trade cycle, beginning with the production of the product by the exporter until payment is eventually made by the importer. This form of credit is known as **supplier credit**. In some cases, the exporter may require bank financing to augment its cash flow. On the other hand, the exporter may not desire to provide financing, in which case the buyer will have to finance the transaction itself, either internally or externally, through its bank. Banks on both sides of the transaction can thus play an integral role in trade financing.

In general, five basic methods of payment are used to settle international transactions, each with a different degree of risk to the exporter and importer (Exhibit 19.1):

- Prepayment
- Letters of credit
- Drafts (sight/time)
- Consignment
- Open account

Prepayment

Under the **prepayment** method, the exporter will not ship the goods until the buyer has remitted payment to the exporter. Payment is usually made in the form of an international wire (electronic) transfer to the exporter's bank account or foreign bank draft (an order by the importer's bank to a bank local to the exporter to pay the exporter in its own currency). As technology progresses, electronic commerce will allow firms engaged in international trade to make electronic credits and debits through an intermediary bank. This method affords the supplier the greatest degree of protection, and it is normally requested of first-time buyers whose creditworthiness is unknown or whose countries are in financial difficulty. Most buyers, however, are not willing to bear all the risk by prepaying an order.

Letters of credit (L/C)

A **letter of credit (L/C)** is an instrument issued by a bank on behalf of the importer (buyer) promising to pay the exporter (beneficiary) upon presentation of shipping documents in compliance with the terms stipulated therein. In effect, the bank is substituting its credit for that of the buyer. This method is a compromise between seller and buyer because it affords certain advantages to both parties. The exporter is assured of receiving payment from the issuing bank as long as it presents documents in accordance with the L/C. An important feature of an L/C is that the issuing bank is obliged to honour drawings under the L/C regardless of the buyer's ability or willingness to pay. On the other hand, the importer does not have to pay for the goods until shipment has been made and the documents are presented in good order. However, the importer must still rely upon the exporter to ship the goods as described in the documents, since the L/C does not guarantee that the goods purchased will be those invoiced and shipped. Letters of credit will be described in greater detail later in this chapter.

Drafts

A **draft** (or **bill of exchange**) is an unconditional promise drawn by one party, usually the exporter, instructing the buyer to pay the face amount of the draft upon presentation. The draft represents the exporter's formal demand for payment from the buyer. By signing or accepting a draft the importer has a legal liability to pay. A draft affords the exporter less protection than an L/C, because the banks are not obliged to honour payments on the buyer's behalf.

Most trade transactions handled on a draft basis are processed through banking channels. In banking terminology, these transactions are known as **documentary collections**. In a documentary collection transaction, banks on both ends act as intermediaries in the processing of shipping documents and the collection of payment. If shipment is made under a sight draft, the exporter is paid once shipment has been made and the draft is presented to the buyer for payment. The buyer's bank will not release the shipping documents to the buyer until the buyer has paid the draft. This is known as **documents against payment**. It provides the exporter with some protection, since the banks will release the shipping documents only according to the exporter's instructions. The buyer needs the shipping documents to pick up the merchandise. The buyer does not have to pay for the merchandise until the draft has been presented.

If a shipment is made under a time draft, the exporter instructs the buyer's bank to release the shipping documents against acceptance (signing) of the draft. This method of payment is sometimes referred to as **documents against acceptance**. By accepting the draft, the buyer is promising to pay the exporter at the specified future date. This accepted draft is also known as a **trade acceptance**, which is different from a banker's acceptance (discussed later in the chapter). In this type of transaction, the buyer is able to obtain the merchandise prior to paying for it.

The exporter is providing the financing and is dependent upon the buyer's financial integrity to pay the draft at maturity. Shipping on a time draft basis provides some added comfort in that banks at both ends are used as collection agents. In addition, a draft serves as a binding financial obligation in case the exporter wishes to pursue litigation on uncollected receivables. The added risk is that if the buyer fails to pay the draft at maturity, the bank is not obliged to honour payment. The exporter is assuming all the risk.

Consignment

Under a **consignment** arrangement, the exporter ships the goods to the importer while still retaining actual title to the merchandise. The importer has access to the items but does not have to pay for the goods until they have been sold to a third party. The exporter is trusting the importer to remit payment for the goods sold at that time. If the importer fails to pay, the exporter has limited recourse because no draft is involved and the goods have already been sold. As a result of the high risk, consignments are seldom used except by affiliated and subsidiary companies trading with the parent company. Some equipment suppliers allow importers to hold some equipment on the sales floor as demonstrator models. Once the models are sold or after a specified period, payment is sent to the supplier.

Open account

The opposite of prepayment is the **open account transaction** in which the exporter ships the merchandise and expects the buyer to remit payment according to the agreed-

Exhibit 19.1 Comparison of payment methods

Method	Usual Time of Payment	Goods Available to Buyers	Risk to Exporter	Risk to Importer
Prepayment	Before shipment	After payment	None	Relies completely on exporter to ship goods as ordered
Letter of credit	When shipment is made	After payment	Very little or none, depending on credit terms	Assured shipment made, but relies on exporter to ship goods described in documents
Sight draft; documents against payments	On presentation of draft to buyer	After payment	If draft unpaid must dispose of goods	Same as above unless importer can inspect goods before payment
Time draft; documents against acceptance	On maturity of drafts	Before payment	Relies on buyer to pay drafts	Same as above
Consignment	At time of sale by buyer	Before payment	Allows importer to sell inventory before paying exporter	None; improves cash flow of buyer
Open account	As agreed	Before payment	Relies completely on buyer to pay account as agreed	None

upon terms. The exporter is relying fully upon the financial creditworthiness, integrity, and reputation of the buyer. As might be expected, this method is used when the seller and buyer have mutual trust and a great deal of experience with each other. Where there is a trading relationship there are repeated exports. There is therefore a natural incentive for payment in the sense that the importer will want to continue to receive the goods. Despite the risks, open account transactions are widely utilized, particularly among the industrialized countries in North America and Europe.

TRADE FINANCE METHODS

As mentioned in the previous section, banks on both sides of the transaction play a critical role in financing international trade. The following are some of the more popular methods of financing international trade:

- Accounts receivable financing
- Factoring
- Letters of credit (L/Cs)
- Banker's acceptances
- Working capital financing
- Medium-term capital goods financing (forfaiting)
- Countertrade

Each of these methods is described in turn.

Accounts receivable financing

In some cases, the exporter of goods may be willing to ship goods to the importer without an assurance of payment from a bank. This could take the form of an open account shipment or a time draft. Prior to shipment, the exporter should have conducted its own credit check on the importer to determine creditworthiness. If the exporter is willing to wait for payment, it will extend credit to the buyer.

If the exporter needs funds immediately, it may require financing from a bank. In what is referred to as **accounts receivable financing**, the bank will provide a loan to the exporter secured by an assignment of the account receivable as security. The bank's loan is made to the exporter based on the creditworthiness of the account. In the event the buyer fails to pay the exporter for whatever reason, the exporter is still responsible for repaying the bank.

Accounts receivable financing involves additional risks, such as government restrictions and exchange controls that may prevent the buyer from paying the exporter. As a result, the loan rate is often higher than domestic accounts receivable financing. The length of a financing term is usually one to six months. To mitigate the additional risk of a foreign receivable, exporters and banks often require export credit insurance before financing foreign receivables.

Factoring

When an exporter ships goods before receiving payment, the accounts receivable (or debtors) balance increases. Unless the exporter has received a loan from a bank, it is initially financing the transaction and must monitor the collections of receivables. Since there is a danger that the buyer will never pay at all, the exporting firm may consider selling the accounts receivable to a third party, known as a **factor**. In this type of financing, the exporter sells the accounts receivable without recourse (i.e. any further responsibilites). The factor then assumes all administrative responsibilities involved in collecting from the buyer and the associated credit exposure. The factor performs its own credit approval process on the foreign buyer before purchasing the receivable. For providing this service, the factor usually purchases the receivable at a discount and also receives a flat processing fee.

Factoring provides several benefits to the exporter. First, by selling the accounts receivable, the exporter does not have to worry about the administrative duties involved in maintaining and monitoring an accounts receivable accounting ledger. Second, the factor assumes the credit exposure to the buyer, so the exporter does not have to maintain personnel to assess the creditworthiness of foreign buyers. Finally, by selling the receivable to the factor, the exporter receives immediate payment and improves its cash flow. A disadvantage is that customer relations may be adversely affected by the debt collection policies of the factor. Also, marketing strategies will not be able to extend to the payment process.

Since it is the importer who must be creditworthy from a factor's point of view, **cross-border factoring** is often used. This involves a network of factors in various countries who assess credit risk. The exporter's factor contacts a correspondent factor in the buyer's country to assess the importer's creditworthiness and handle the collection of the receivable. Factoring services are usually provided by the factoring subsidiaries of commercial banks, commercial finance companies, and other specialized finance houses. Factors often utilize export credit insurance to mitigate the additional risk of a foreign receivable.

Letters of credit (L/C)

Introduced earlier, the letter of credit (L/C) is one of the oldest forms of trade finance still in existence. Because of the protection and benefits it accords to both exporter and importer, it is a critical component of many international trade transactions. The L/C is an undertaking by a bank to make payments on behalf of a specified party to a beneficiary under specified conditions. The beneficiary (exporter) is paid upon presentation of the required documents in compliance with the terms of the L/C. The L/C process normally involves two banks, the exporter's bank and the importer's bank. The issuing bank is substituting its credit for that of the importer. It has essentially guaranteed payment to the exporter, provided the exporter complies with the terms and conditions of the L/C.

Sometimes the exporter is uncomfortable with the issuing bank's promise to pay because the bank is located in a foreign country. Even if the issuing bank is well known worldwide, the exporter may be concerned that the foreign government will impose exchange controls or other restrictions that would prevent payment by the issuing bank. For this reason, the exporter may request that a local bank confirm the L/C and thus assure that all the responsibilities of the issuing bank will be met. The confirming bank is obliged to honour drawings made by the beneficiary in compliance with the L/C regardless of the issuing bank's ability to make that payment. Consequently, the confirming bank is trusting that the foreign bank issuing the L/C is sound. The exporter, however, need worry only about the credibility of the confirming bank.

EXAMPLE

Nike can attribute part of its international business growth in the 1970s to the use of L/Cs. In 1971, Nike (which was then called BSR) was not well known to businesses in Japan or anywhere else. Nevertheless, by using L/Cs, it was still able to subcontract the production of athletic shoes in Japan. The L/Cs assured the Japanese shoe producer that it would receive payment for the shoes it would send to the United States and thus facilitated the flow of trade without concern about credit risk. Banks served as the guarantors in the event that the Japanese shoe company was not paid in full after transporting shoes to the United States. Thus, because of the backing of the banks, the L/Cs allowed the Japanese shoe company to do international business without having to worry that the counterparty in its agreement would not fulfil its obligation. Without such agreements, Nike (and many other firms) would not be able to order shipments of goods.

Types of letters of credit. Trade-related letters of credit are known as **commercial letters of credit** or **import/export letters of credit**. There are basically two types: revocable and irrevocable. A **revocable letter of credit** can be cancelled or revoked at any time without prior notification to the beneficiary, and it is seldom used. An **irrevocable letter of credit** (see Exhibit 19.2) cannot be cancelled or amended without the beneficiary's consent. The bank issuing the L/C is known as the **"issuing" bank**. The correspondent bank in the beneficiary's country to which the issuing bank sends the L/C is commonly referred to as the **"advising" bank**. An irrevocable L/C obliges the issuing bank to honour all drawings presented in conformity with the terms of the L/C. Letters of credit are normally issued in accordance with the provisions contained in "Uniform Customs and Practice for Documentary Credits", published by the International Chamber of Commerce.

The bank issuing the L/C makes payment once the required documentation has been presented in accordance with the payment terms. The importer must pay the issuing bank the amount of the L/C plus accrued fees associated with obtaining the L/C. The importer usually has established an account at the issuing bank to be drawn upon for

Exhibit 19.2   Example of an irrevocable letter of credit

Name of issuing bank
Address of issuing bank
Name of exporter
Address of exporter

We establish our irrevocable letter of credit: for the account of (*importer name*), in the amount of (*value of exports*), expiring (*date*), available by your draft at (*time period*) days sight and accompanied by: (any invoices, packing lists, bills of lading, etc., that need to be presented with the letter of credit) Insurance provided by (*exporter or importer*) covering shipment of (*merchandise description*)

From: (*port of shipment*)

To: (*port of arrival*)

(Authorized Signature)

_____

payment, so that the issuing bank does not tie up its own funds. However, if the importer does not have sufficient funds in its account, the issuing bank is still obliged to honour all valid drawings against the L/C. This is why the bank's decision to issue an L/C on behalf of an importer involves an analysis of the importer's creditworthiness and is analogous to the decision to make a loan. The documentary credit procedure is depicted in the flowchart in Exhibit 19.3. In what is commonly referred to as a *re-financing of a sight L/C*, the bank arranges to fund a loan to pay out the L/C instead of charging the importer's account immediately. The importer is responsible for repaying the bank both the principal and interest at maturity. This is just another method of providing extended payment terms to a buyer when the exporter insists upon payment at sight.

The bank issuing the L/C makes payment to the beneficiary (exporter) upon presentation of documents that meet the conditions stipulated in the L/C. Letters of credit are payable either at sight (upon presentation of documents) or at a specified future date. The typical documentation required under an L/C includes a draft (sight or time), a commercial invoice, and a bill of lading. Depending upon the agreement, product, or country, other documents (such as a certificate of origin, inspection certificate, packing list, or insurance certificate) might be required. The three most common documents to accompany L/Cs are drafts, bills of lading and commercial invoices.

Draft. Also known as a bill of exchange, a draft (introduced earlier) is an unconditional promise drawn by one party, usually the exporter, requesting the importer to pay the face amount of the draft at sight or at a specified future date. If the draft is drawn at sight, it is payable upon presentation of documents. If it is payable at a specified future date (a time draft) and is accepted by the importer, it is known as a trade acceptance. A **banker's acceptance** is a time draft drawn on and accepted by a bank. When presented under an L/C, the draft represents the exporter's formal demand for payment. The time period, or **tenor**, of most time drafts is usually anywhere from 30 to 180 days.

Exhibit 19.3 Documentary credit procedure

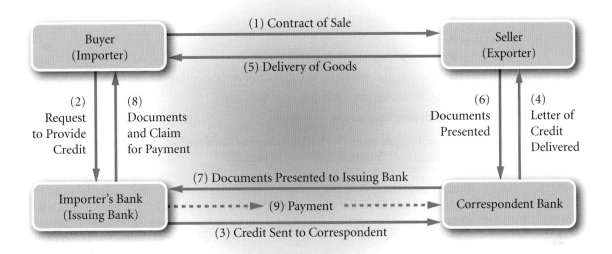

Bill of lading. The key document in an international shipment under an L/C is the **bill of lading (B/L)**. It serves as a receipt for shipment and a summary of freight charges; most importantly, it conveys title to the merchandise. If the merchandise is to be shipped by boat, the carrier will issue what is known as an **ocean bill of lading**. When the merchandise is shipped by air, the carrier will issue an **airway bill**. The carrier presents the bill to the exporter (shipper), who in turn presents it to the bank along with the other required documents.

A significant feature of a B/L is its negotiability. When a B/L is made out to order, it is said to be in negotiable form. The exporter normally endorses the B/L to the bank once payment is received from the bank.

The bank will not endorse the B/L over to the importer until payment has been made. The importer needs the original B/L to pick up the merchandise. With a **negotiable B/L**, title passes to the holder of the endorsed B/L. Because a negotiable B/L grants title to the holder, banks can take the merchandise as collateral. A B/L usually includes the following provisions:

- A description of the merchandise
- Identification marks on the merchandise
- Evidence of loading (receiving) ports
- Name of the exporter (shipper)
- Name of the importer
- Status of freight charges (prepaid or collect)
- Date of shipment

Commercial invoice. The exporter's (seller's) description of the merchandise being sold to the buyer is the **commercial invoice**, which normally contains the following information:

- Name and address of seller
- Name and address of buyer
- Date
- Terms of payment
- Price, including freight, handling, and insurance if applicable
- Quantity, weight, packaging, etc.
- Shipping information

Under an L/C shipment, the description of the merchandise outlined in the invoice must correspond exactly to that contained in the L/C.

Variations of the L/C. There are several variations of the L/C that are useful in financing trade. A **standby letter of credit** can be used to guarantee invoice payments to a supplier. It promises to pay the beneficiary if the buyer fails to pay as agreed. Internationally, standby L/Cs often are used with government-related contracts and serve as bid bonds, performance bonds, or advance payment guarantees. In an international or domestic trade transaction, the seller will agree to ship to the buyer on standard open account terms as long as the buyer provides a standby L/C for a specified amount and term. As long as the buyer pays the seller as agreed, the standby L/C is never funded. However, if the buyer fails to pay, the exporter may present documents under the L/C and request payment from the bank. The buyer's bank is essentially guaranteeing that the buyer will make payment to the seller.

A **transferable letter of credit** is a variation of the standard commercial L/C that allows the first beneficiary to transfer all or a part of the original L/C to a third party. The new beneficiary has the same rights and protection as the original beneficiary. This type of L/C is used extensively by brokers, who are not the actual suppliers.

E X A M P L E

A broker asks a foreign buyer to issue an L/C for £100,000 in his favour. The L/C must contain a clause stating that the L/C is transferable. The broker has located a supplier who will provide the product for £80,000, but requests payment in advance from the broker. With a transferable L/C, the broker can transfer £80,000 of the original L/C to the supplier under the same terms and conditions, except for the amount, the latest shipment date, the invoice, and the period of validity. When the supplier ships the product, it presents its documents to the bank. When the bank pays the L/C, £80,000 is paid to the supplier and £20,000 goes to the broker. In effect, the broker has utilized the credit of the buyer to finance the entire transaction.

http://

Many banks have a website that explains the variety of trade financing that they can provide for firms. Try, for example, "nat west bank letter of credit" in Google.

Another type of L/C is the **assignment of proceeds**. In this case, the original beneficiary of the L/C pledges (or assigns) the proceeds under an L/C to the supplier. The supplier has assurance from the bank that if and when documents are presented in compliance with the terms of the L/C, the bank will pay the supplier according to the assignment instructions. This assignment is valid only if the beneficiary presents documents that comply with the L/C. The supplier must recognize that the issuing bank is under no obligation to pay the supplier if the original beneficiary never ships the goods or fails to comply with the terms of the L/C.

Exhibit 19.4 Banker's acceptance

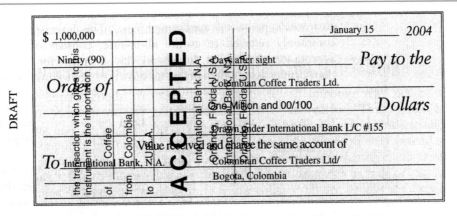

Banker's acceptance

Introduced earlier, a banker's acceptance (shown in Exhibit 19.4) is a bill of exchange, or time draft, drawn on and accepted by a bank. It is the accepting bank's obligation to pay the holder of the draft at maturity.

For the first step in creating a banker's acceptance, the importer orders goods from the exporter. The importer then requests its local bank to issue an L/C on its behalf. The L/C will allow the exporter to draw a time draft on the bank in payment for the exported goods. The exporter presents the time draft along with shipping documents to its local bank, and the exporter's bank sends the time draft along with shipping documents to the importer's bank. The importer's bank accepts the draft, thereby creating the banker's acceptance. If the exporter does not want to wait until the specified date to receive payment, it can request that the banker's acceptance be sold in the money market. By doing so, the exporter will receive less funds from the sale of the banker's acceptance than if it had waited to receive payment. This discount reflects the time value of money.

A money market investor may be willing to buy the banker's acceptance at a discount and hold it until payment is due. This investor will then receive full payment because the banker's acceptance represents a future claim on funds of the bank represented by the acceptance. The bank will make full payment at the date specified because it expects to receive this amount plus an additional fee from the importer.

If the exporter holds the acceptance until maturity, it provides the financing for the importer as it does with accounts receivable financing. In this case, the key difference between a banker's acceptance and accounts receivable financing is that a banker's acceptance guarantees payment to the exporter by a bank. If the exporter sells the banker's acceptance in the secondary market, however, it is no longer providing the financing for the importer. The holder of the banker's acceptance is financing instead.

A banker's acceptance can be beneficial to the exporter, importer, and issuing bank. The exporter does not need to worry about the credit risk of the importer and can therefore penetrate new foreign markets without concern about the credit risk of potential customers. In addition, the exporter faces little exposure to political risk or to exchange controls imposed by a government because banks normally are allowed to meet their payment commitments even if controls are imposed. In contrast, controls could prevent an importer from paying, so without a banker's acceptance, an exporter might not receive payment even though the importer is willing to pay. Finally, the exporter can sell the banker's acceptance at a discount before payment is due and thus obtain funds up front from the issuing bank.

The importer benefits from a banker's acceptance by obtaining greater access to foreign markets when purchasing supplies and other products. Without banker's acceptances, exporters may be unwilling to accept the credit risk of importers. In addition, due to the documents presented along with the acceptance, the importer is assured that goods have been shipped. Even though the importer has not paid in advance, this assurance is valuable because it lets the importer know if and when supplies and other products will arrive. Finally, because the banker's acceptance allows the importer to pay at a later date, the importer's payment is financed until the maturity date of the banker's acceptance. Without an acceptance, the importer is likely to be forced to pay in advance, thereby tying up funds.

The bank accepting the drafts benefits in that it earns a commission for creating an acceptance. The commission that the bank charges the customer reflects the customer's perceived creditworthiness. The interest rate charged to the customer, commonly referred to as the **all-in-rate,** consists of the discount rate plus the acceptance commission. In general, the all-in-rate for acceptance financing is lower than prime-based borrowings, as shown in the following comparison:

	Loan	Acceptance
Amount:	£1,000,000	£1,000,000
Term:	180 days	180 days
Rate:	Prime + 1.5%	Banker's Acceptance rate + 1.5%
	10.0% + 1.5% = 11.5%	7.60% + 1.5% = 9.10%
Interest cost:	£57,500	£45,500

In this case, the savings in interest for a six-month period is £12,000 (i.e. £57,500 − £45,500). Since the banker's acceptance is a marketable instrument with an active secondary market, the rates on acceptances usually fall between the rates on short-term Treasury bills and the rates on commercial paper. Investors are usually willing to purchase acceptances as an investment because of their yield, safety, and liquidity. When a bank creates, accepts, and sells the acceptance, it is actually using the investor's money to finance the bank's customer. As a result, the bank has created an asset at one price, sold it at another, and retained a commission (spread) as its fee.

EXAMPLE

Slow Bank has accepted a time draft from WellKnown plc for £1,500,000 to be paid to WellKnown in six months' time. WellKnown wants the money now and has asked its own bank, MyBank, to sell the bill. MyBank charges a 10% discount to WellKnown. So WellKnown receives £1,500,000 × (1 − 10%) = £1,350,000. MyBank then sells the bill to BigInsurance plc for £1,400,000. In effect, MyBank has operated as a go-between and has created an asset, the bill to be paid by Slow Bank, for a cost of £1,350,000 (buying it from WellKnown) and sold it for £1,400,000. BigInsurance plc has purchased this asset and in effect has used its spare cash ultimately to help provide finance to WellKnown. Big Insurance will collect £1,500,000 from Slow bank in six months' time a return of (£1,500,000 − £1,400,000) / £1,500,000 = 0.0666 or 6.66%. This is a return of $1.066^2 - 1$ = 0.136 or 13.6% per year and presumably it is a good return given the low risk of non-payment by Slow Bank.

Banker's acceptance financing can also be arranged through the refinancing of a sight letter of credit. In this case, the beneficiary of the L/C (the exporter) may insist on

Exhibit 19.5 Life cycle of a typical banker's acceptance (B/A)

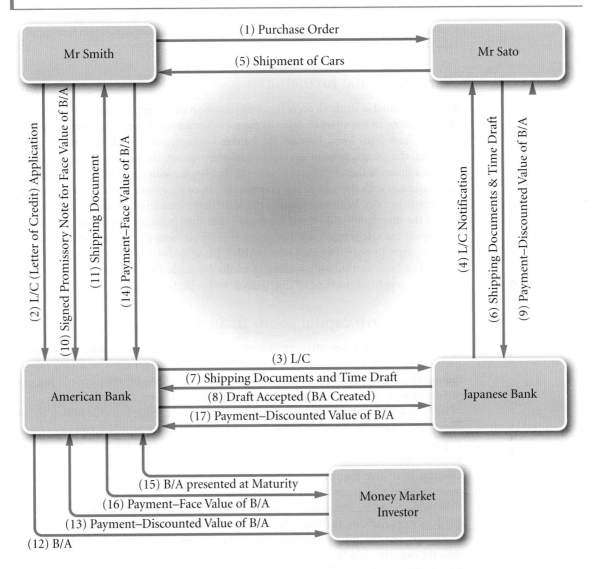

payment at sight. The bank arranges to finance the payment of the sight L/C under a separate acceptance-financing agreement. The importer (borrower) simply draws drafts upon the bank (a "you, the bank, owe me" note), the bank in turn accepts and discounts the drafts (i.e. sells the bills on the money markets) on condition that the importer will pay with say a promissory note. The proceeds are used to pay the exporter. At maturity of the discounted acceptance, the money market investor presents the bill to the bank, who pay, and the importer then pays the money to the bank honouring the promissory note. Why is it done in this way? Well, it is important that to the money markets the bank is the debtor – the discount will be less. So the bank creates this debt to the importer with the backing that the importer will pay.

Acceptance financing can also be arranged without the use of an L/C under a separate acceptance agreement. Similar to a regular loan agreement, it stipulates the terms and conditions under which the bank is prepared to finance the borrower using acceptances instead of promissory notes. As long as the acceptances meet one of the underlying transaction requirements, the bank and borrower can utilize banker's acceptances as an alternative financing mechanism. The life cycle of a banker's acceptance is illustrated in Exhibit 19.5.

Working capital financing

As just explained, a banker's acceptance can allow an exporter to receive funds immediately, yet allow an importer to delay its payment until a future date. The bank may even provide short-term loans beyond the banker's acceptance period. In the case of an importer, the purchase from overseas usually represents the acquisition of inventory. The loan finances the working capital cycle that begins with the purchase of inventory and continues with the sale of the goods, creation of an account receivable, and finally conversion to cash. With an exporter, the short-term loan might finance the manufacture of the merchandise destined for export (pre-export financing) or the time period from when the sale is made until payment is received from the buyer. For example, the firm may have imported foreign beer, which it plans to distribute to grocery and liquor stores. The bank can provide a letter of credit for trade finance, and also finance the importer's cost from the time of distribution and collection of payment.

Medium-term capital goods financing (forfaiting)

Because capital goods are often quite expensive, an importer may not be able to make payment on the goods within a short time period. Thus, longer-term financing may be required here. The exporter might be able to provide financing for the importer but may not desire to do so, since the financing may extend over several years. In this case, a type of trade finance known as **forfaiting** could be used. The forfaiter buys the bills or promissory notes from the exporter. These financial obligations are usually guaranteed by the importer (payer's) bank. The importer thus finds that payment has to be made to a financial institution rather than the exporter. Thus, for a fee, the forfaiter enables the exporter to receive the money immediately and the importer at the same time has a period of credit before payment has to be made.

In some respects, forfaiting is similar to factoring, in that the forfaiter (or factor) assumes responsibility for the collection of payment from the buyer, the underlying credit risk, and the risk pertaining to the countries involved. Since the forfaiter rather than the exporter now bears the risk of non-payment, it should assess the creditworthiness of the importer as if it were extending a medium-term loan. Forfait transactions normally are supported (collateralized) by a bank guarantee or letter of credit issued by the importer's bank for the term of the transaction. Since obtaining financial information about the importer is usually difficult, the forfaiter (a bank or financial institution) places a great deal of reliance on the bank guarantee as the collateral in the event the buyer fails to pay as agreed. It is this guarantee backing the transaction that has fostered the growth of the forfait market, particularly in Europe, as a practical means of trade finance.

Forfaiting transactions are usually in excess of £250,000 and can be denominated in most currencies. For some larger transactions, more than one bank may be involved as the forfaiter. In this case, a syndicate is formed wherein each participant assumes a proportionate share of the underlying risk and profit. A forfaiting firm may decide to sell the promissory notes of the importer to other financial institutions willing to purchase them. However, the forfaiting firm is still responsible for payment on the notes in the event the importer is unable to pay.

Countertrade

The term **countertrade** denotes all types of foreign trade transactions in which the sale of goods to one country is linked to the purchase or exchange of goods from that same country. Some types of countertrade, such as barter, have been in existence for thousands of years. Only recently, however, has countertrade gained popularity and importance. The growth in various types of countertrade has been fuelled by large balance-of-payment disequilibriums, foreign currency shortages, the debt problems of less developed countries and stagnant worldwide demand. As a result, many MNCs have encountered countertrade opportunities, particularly in Asia, Latin America, and Eastern Europe. The most common types of countertrade include barter, compensation, and counterpurchase.

Barter is the exchange of goods between two parties without the use of any currency as a medium of exchange. Most barter arrangements are one-time transactions governed by one contract. An example would be the exchange of 100 tons of wheat from Canada for 20 tons of shrimp from Ecuador.

In a **compensation** or clearing-account arrangement, the delivery of goods to one party is compensated for by the seller's buying back a certain amount of the product from that same party. The transaction is governed by one contract, and the value of the goods is expressed in monetary terms. The buy-back arrangement could be for a fraction of the original sale (**partial compensation**) or more than 100% of the original sale (**full compensation**). An example of compensation would be the sale of phosphate from Morocco to France in exchange for purchasing a certain percentage of fertilizer. In some countries, this is also referred to as an industrial cooperation arrangement. Such arrangements often involve the construction of large projects, such as power plants, in exchange for the purchase of the project's output over an extended period of time. For example, Brazil sold a hydroelectric plant to Argentina and in exchange purchased a percentage of the plant's output under a long-term contract.

The term **counterpurchase** denotes the exchange of goods between two parties under two distinct contracts expressed in monetary terms. Delivery and payment of both goods are technically separate transactions.

Despite the economic inefficiencies of countertrade, it has become much more important in recent years. The primary participants are governments and MNCs, with assistance provided by specialists in the field, such as attorneys, financial institutions, and trading companies. The transactions are usually large and very complex. Many variations of countertrade exist, and the terminology used by the various market participants is still forming as the countertrade market continues to develop.

GOVERNMENT AGENCIES FOR INTERNATIONAL TRADE

Due to the inherent risks of international trade, government institutions and the private sector offer various forms of export credit, export finance, and guarantee programmes to reduce risk and stimulate foreign trade. The private sector is generally reluctant to provide financial support for investments with high risk. Usually such investments are in countries with poorly developed or unreliable financial systems. To provide cover for such transactions most developed countries have a government backed agency whose principal goal is to provide credit and finance for exports.

In the UK export services are provided by the Export Credit Guarantee Department (ECGD). For a fee, it provides a guarantee of payment to UK exporters on transactions ranging from £25,000 to over £100 million. As with a forfaiter, it will also offer loans to importers thus enabling exporters to receive payment immediately and at the same time give time for foreign importers to pay in accordance with the conditions of the loan. Government backing of the ECGD and like organizations elsewhere ensures that the guarantees are well respected in the marketplace and may of themselves be sufficient for a company to then get private finance to support an export transaction. The ECGD also offers insurance against political risk for UK investors of up to 15 years.

As with all government agencies a moral as well as a practical rationale is required to justify their role. On the virtuous side, Third World countries termed Heavily Indebted Poor Countries (HIPC – this is an official IMF term) often have poor credit records. Credit guarantees and loans to importers in those countries encourage trade with HIPCs helping their economies to grow. Thus the ECGD, by offering generous credit terms to HIPCs is providing a form of foreign aid. It is arguable that such help is much better than straight gift-based aid in that trade is encouraged, and trade is generally seen as the principal means of becoming a developed economy.

Some trade is, of course, with governments. The ECGD holds most of the sovereign (government) debt owed to the UK. The agency therefore has a crucial role in any debt relief programme. HIPCs are supported by IMF and World Bank programmes. Satisfactory compliance is measured as achieving a "completion point" that triggers a debt relief programme. Developed countries in the form of the Paris Club will reduce payments to a sustainable level for countries that achieve their completion point, and in the case of the UK, will write off old debts completely. Thus the ECGD is heavily involved in aid packages.

There is also, surprisingly, a less virtuous argument. First, IMF debt relief programmes are seen by some as intrusive, unaccountable and ineffective (visit the IMF website – http://www.imf.org – and search under the term "ineffective" for example see: http://www.imf.org/external/pubs/ft/scr/2005/cr05433.pdf). The progress towards developed nation status is generally recognized as having been slow to non-existent for most HIPCs over the last 50 years. This leads to the second counter argument that the true purpose of the ECGD is to finance and thereby subsidize domestic industry with little real concern for the recipient country. The aid given to Third World countries to purchase exports from developed countries is in fact a way of helping MNCs sell goods to customers of doubtful credit. Although such aid purports to be to help the customer, the suspicion is that the real purpose is to help the MNC. Arms sales, in particular, are difficult to justify as necessary for a developing country. In tacit acknowledgement of this critique the ECGD sets out a broad mission statement that includes a commitment that: "ECGD will when considering support look not only at the payment risks but also at the underlying quality of the project including its environmental, social and human rights impact" (Statement of ECGD Business Principles, 2000). There is also a special procedure over financial help for arms exports (some 24% of ECGD business). In addition to the special licences, for less developed countries it also applies a "productive expenditure test". The relevant form asks:

Please explain how it (the project) will contribute to economic and social development:
  You may care to give details of how the project will:

■ *Meet priority human development needs;*

■ *Promote the inclusion of the poor in economic activity;*

- *Build or rehabilitate essential infrastructure;*
- *Promote economic growth; or*
- *Promote development of the indigenous private sector.*

For some, these stated intentions are not borne out by practice and there is a campaign for European Credit Agencies (ECAs) to improve their practices (see http://www.fern.org/pages/eca/eucamp.html). Undoubtedly, financing international trade has a political dimension. Similar issues can be found in examining "soft loans" policies, for more information see http://www.bankwatch.org and search for 'EIB'. MNCs need to be aware that requesting government help requires an ethical as well as a financial justification.

Summary

- The common methods of payment for international trade are: (1) prepayment (before goods are sent), (2) letters of credit, (3) drafts, (4) consignment, and (5) open account.

- The most popular methods of financing international trade are: (1) accounts receivable financing, (2) factoring, (3) letters of credit, (4) banker's acceptances, (5) working capital financing, (6) medium-term capital goods financing (forfaiting), and (7) countertrade.

- The major agencies that facilitate international trade with export insurance and/or loan programmes are: (1) Export-Import Bank, (2) Private Export Funding Corporation, and (3) Overseas Private Investment Corporation.

Critical debate

Do government agencies promoting exports benefit the recipient country?

Proposition. Yes. They enable countries to import vital supplies needed to develop their economies. The commercial world would not necessarily export to these countries because of the risks that they face. They are in a catch 22 position, they cannot get credit unless they are developed and they cannot develop unless they have credit to purchase goods. Government agencies are the ideal bodies to break this vicious circle. In addition, the agencies can and do promote a social and economic agenda working with the World Bank and the IMF.

Opposing view. No. The commercial world will lend to these countries and has done so to a greater extent in colonial days before World War I. Developing countries must realize that a stable currency and a stable economy is a top priority and that instability is more than just a technical problem. Corruption, over ambitious economic policies and social unrest caused by oppression all result in unstable economies. Giving credit and guarantees to these countries has unfortunately served to support poor government practice rather than cure it. Developed countries are concerned with helping their own firms in competition with other developed countries and any desire to promote standards is lost in the need to protect home industry against competition.

With whom do you agree? Reread the section on the ECGD and follow the website links.

SELF TEST

Answers are provided in Appendix A at the back of the text.

1. Explain why so many international transactions require international trade credit facilitated by commercial banks.

2. Explain the difference in the risk to the exporter between accounts receivable financing and factoring.

3. Explain how the Export-Import Bank can encourage UK firms to export to less developed countries where there is political risk.

QUESTIONS AND APPLICATIONS

1. **Banker's acceptances.**
   a. Describe how foreign trade would be affected if banks did not provide trade-related services.
   b. How can a banker's acceptance be beneficial to an exporter, an importer, and a bank?

2. **Export financing.**
   a. Why would an exporter provide financing for an importer?
   b. Is there much risk in this activity? Explain.

3. **Role of factors.** What is the role of a factor in international trade transactions?

4. **ECGD**
   a. What is the role today of the ECGD?
   b. Describe the basis of the political opposition to the ECGD.

5. **Bills of lading.** What are bills of lading, and how do they facilitate international trade transactions?

6. **Forfaiting.** What is forfaiting? Specify the type of traded goods for which forfaiting is applied.

7. Should the **World Bank** be in charge of providing finance for exports?

8. **Government programmes.** What motivates a government to establish/intervene in the credit markets?

9. **Countertrade.** What is countertrade?

10. **Impact of a financial crisis.** What steps should Brunch take if a crisis occurs in country X which is a major exporting destination for Brunch ltd?

ADVANCED QUESTIONS

11. **Letters of credit.** Channel Traders (UK) is a firm based in Grimsby, that specializes in seafood exports and commonly uses letters of credit (L/Cs) to ensure payment. It recently experienced a problem, however. Channel Traders had an irrevocable L/C issued by a Russian bank to ensure that it would receive payment upon shipment of 16,000 tons of fish to a Russian firm. This bank backed out of its obligation, however, stating that it was not authorized to guarantee commercial transactions.
   a. Explain how an irrevocable L/C would normally facilitate the business transaction between the Russian importer and Channel Traders (the UK exporter).
   b. Explain how the cancellation of the L/C could create a trade crisis between the UK and Russian firms.
   c. Why do you think situations like this (the cancellation of the L/C) are rare in industrialized countries?
   d. Can you think of any alternative strategy that the UK exporter could have used to protect itself better when dealing with a Russian importer?

PROJECT WORKSHOP

12. Compare and contrast the web provision for exporters from the UK and the US. For the US provision visit http://www.exim.gov and for the UK provision visit http://www.ecgd.gov.

DISCUSSION IN THE BOARDROOM

This exercise can be found on the companion website at www.cengage.co.uk/madura_fox.

RUNNING YOUR OWN MNC

This exercise can be found on the companion website at www.cengage.co.uk/madura_fox.

Essays/discussion and articles can be found at the end of Part 5

BLADES PLC CASE STUDY
Assessment of international trade financing in Thailand

Blades plc has recently decided to establish a subsidiary in Thailand to produce "Speedos", Blades' primary roller blade product. In establishing the subsidiary in Thailand, Blades was motivated by the high growth potential of the Thai roller blade market. Furthermore, Blades has decided to establish a subsidiary, as opposed to acquiring an existing Thai roller blade manufacturer for sale, in order to maintain its flexibility and control over the operations in Thailand. Moreover, Blades has decided to issue yen-denominated notes to partially finance the cost of establishing the subsidiary. Blades has decided to issue notes denominated in yen instead of baht to avoid the high effective interest rates associated with the baht-denominated notes.

Currently, Blades plans to sell all roller blades manufactured in Thailand to retailers in Thailand. Furthermore, Blades plans to purchase all components for roller blades manufactured in Thailand from Thai suppliers. Similarly, all of Blades' roller blades manufactured in the United Kingdom will be sold to retailers in the United Kingdom and all components needed for Blades' UK production will be purchased from suppliers in the UK. Consequently, Blades will have no exports and imports once the plant in Thailand is operational, which is expected to occur early next year.

Construction of the plant in Thailand has already begun, and Blades is currently in the process of purchasing the machinery necessary to produce Speedos. Besides these activities, Ben Holt, Blades' financial director, has been actively lining up suppliers of the needed rubber and plastic components in Thailand and identifying Thai customers, which will consist of various sports product retailers in Thailand.

Although Holt has been successful in locating both interested suppliers and interested customers, he is discovering that he has neglected certain precautions for operating a subsidiary in Thailand. First, although Blades is relatively well known in the United States, it is not recognized internationally. Consequently, the suppliers Blades would like to use in Thailand are not

familiar with the firm and have no information about its reputation. Moreover, Blades' previous activities in Thailand were restricted to the export of a fixed number of Speedos annually to one customer, a Thai retailer called Entertainment Products. Holt has little information about the potential Thai customers that would buy the roller blades produced by the new plant. He is aware, however, that although letters of credit (L/Cs) and drafts are usually employed for exporting purposes, these instruments are also used for trade within a country between relatively unknown parties.

Of the various potential customers Blades has identified in Thailand, four retailers of sports products appear particularly interested. Because Blades is not familiar with these firms and their reputations, it would like to receive payment from them as soon as possible. Ideally, Blades would like its customers to prepay for their purchases, as this would involve the least risk for Blades. Unfortunately, none of the four potential customers have agreed to a prepayment arrangement. In fact, one potential customer, Cool Runnings inc, insists on an open account transaction. Payment terms in Thailand for purchases of this type are typically "net 60", indicating that payment for the roller blades would be due approximately two months after a purchase was made. Two of the remaining three retailers, Sports Equipment inc, and Major Leagues inc, have indicated that they would also prefer an open account transaction; however, both of these retailers have indicated that their banks would act as intermediaries for a time draft. The fourth retailer, Sports Gear, Inc., is indifferent as to the specific payment method but has indicated to Blades that it finds a prepayment arrangement unacceptable.

Blades also needs a suitable arrangement with its various potential suppliers of rubber and plastic components in Thailand. Because Blades' financing of the Thai subsidiary involved a UK bank, it has virtually no contacts in the Thai banking system. Because Blades is relatively unknown in Thailand, Thai suppliers have indicated that they would prefer pre-payment or at least a guarantee from a Thai bank that Blades will be able to make payment within 30 days of purchase. Blades does not currently have accounts receivable in Thailand. It does, however, have accounts receivable in the United Kingdom resulting from its UK sales.

Ben Holt would like to please Blades' Thai customers and suppliers in order to establish strong business relationships in Thailand. However, he is worried that Blades may be at a disadvantage if it accepts all of the Thai firms' demands. Consequently, he has asked you, a financial analyst for Blades plc to provide him with some guidance regarding international trade financing. Specifically, Holt has asked you to answer the following questions for him:

1. Assuming that banks in Thailand issue a time draft on behalf of Sports Equipment inc, and Major Leagues inc, would Blades receive payment for its roller blades before it delivers them? Do the banks issuing the time drafts guarantee payment on behalf of the Thai retailers if they default on the payment?

2. What payment method should Blades suggest to Sports Gear inc? Substantiate your answer.
3. What organization could Blades contact in order to insure its sales to the Thai retailers? What type of insurance does this organization provide?
4. How could Blades use accounts receivable financing or factoring, considering that it does not currently have accounts receivable in Thailand? If Blades uses a Thai bank to obtain this financing, how do you think the fact that Blades does not have receivables in Thailand would affect the terms of the financing?
5. Assuming that Blades is unable to locate a Thai bank that is willing to issue an L/C on Blades' behalf, can you think of a way Blades could utilize its bank in the United Kingdom to effectively obtain an L/C from a Thai bank?
6. What organizations could Blades contact to obtain working capital financing? If Blades is unable to obtain working capital financing from these organizations, what are its other options to finance its working capital needs in Thailand?

SMALL BUSINESS DILEMMA
Ensuring payment for products exported by the Sports Exports Company

The Sports Exports Company (Ireland) produces basketballs and exports them to a distributor in the United Kingdom. It typically sends basketballs in bulk and then receives payment after the distributor receives the shipment. The business relationship with the distributor is based on trust. Although the relationship has worked thus far, Jim Logan (owner of the Sports Exports Company) is concerned about the possibility that the distributor will not make its payment.

1. How could Jim use a letter of credit to ensure that he will be paid for the products he exports?

2. Jim has discussed the possibility of expanding his export business through a second sporting goods distributor in the United States; this second distributor would cover a different territory than the first distributor. The second distributor is only willing to engage in a consignment arrangement when selling basketballs to retail stores. Explain the risk to Jim beyond the typical types of risk he incurs when dealing with the first distributor. Should Jim pursue this type of business?

CHAPTER 20

SHORT-TERM FINANCING

ALL FIRMS MAKE SHORT-TERM financing decisions periodically. Beyond the trade financing discussed in the previous chapter, MNCs obtain short-term financing to support other operations as well. Because MNCs have access to additional sources of funds, their short-term financing decisions are more complex than those of other companies. Financial managers must understand the possible advantages and disadvantages of short-term financing with foreign currencies so that they can make short-term financing decisions that maximize the value of the MNC.

THE SPECIFIC OBJECTIVES OF THIS CHAPTER ARE TO:

- explain why MNCs consider foreign financing,
- explain how MNCs determine whether to use foreign financing, and
- illustrate the possible benefits of financing with a portfolio of currencies.

SOURCES OF SHORT-TERM FINANCING

MNC parents and their subsidiaries typically use various methods of obtaining short-term funds to satisfy their liquidity needs. When financing in a foreign currency, it is increasingly the case that the bank or financial market providing the finance will not be in the country of the currency. When this is the case the term "euro" is used. Thus a eurodollar bank account is an account that will probably be situated in London and will be denominated in dollars. A eurobank is a bank that makes loans and accepts deposits in foreign currencies.

Euronotes

One method increasingly used in recent years is the issuing of **euronotes**, or unsecured debt securities. These are bonds issued by MNCs with an interest payment and a fixed term after which the MNC will repay the nominal (agreed) amount. The interest rates on these notes are based on LIBOR (the interest rate eurobanks charge on interbank loans). Euronotes typically have maturities of one, three, or six months. Some MNCs continually roll them over as a form of intermediate-term financing. That is to say, they issue new euronotes to repay ones that are maturing need to be repaid by the MNC. The MNCs in this way extend the term of the loan to themselves. Commercial banks underwrite the notes for MNCs, and some commercial banks purchase them for their own investment portfolios.

Euro-commercial paper

In addition to euronotes, MNCs also issue **euro-commercial paper** to obtain short-term financing. Dealers issue this paper for MNCs without the backing of an underwriting syndicate, so a selling price is not guaranteed to the issuers. Maturities can be tailored to the issuer's preferences. Dealers make a secondary market by offering to repurchase euro-commercial paper before maturity.

Eurobank loans

Direct loans from eurobanks, which are typically utilized to maintain a relationship with eurobanks, are another popular source of short-term funds for MNCs. If other sources of short-term funds become unavailable, MNCs rely more heavily on direct loans from eurobanks. Most MNCs maintain credit arrangements with various banks around the world. Some MNCs have credit arrangements with more than 100 foreign and domestic banks.

INTERNAL FINANCING BY MNCs

Before an MNC's parent or subsidiary in need of funds searches for outside funding, it should check other subsidiaries' cash flow positions to determine whether any internal funds are available.

EXAMPLE

The French subsidiary of Shrimport ltd (UK) has experienced strong earnings and invested a portion of the earnings locally in money market securities. Meanwhile, Shrimport's Mexican subsidiary has generated lower earnings recently but needs funding to support expansion. Shrimport can instruct the French subsidiary to loan some of its excess funds to the Mexican subsidiary.

This process is especially useful during periods when the cost of obtaining funds in the parent's home country is relatively high.

Parents of MNCs can also attempt to obtain financing from their subsidiaries by increasing the markups on supplies they send to the subsidiaries. In this case, the funds the subsidiary gives to the parent will never be returned. This method of supporting the parent can sometimes be more feasible than obtaining loans from the subsidiary because it may circumvent restrictions or taxes imposed by national governments. In some cases, though, this method itself may be restricted or limited by host governments where subsidiaries are located. The practice may also transgress double taxation agreements where intra (within) company trade should be conducted "at arms length", i.e. as if they were independent companies.

Why MNCs consider foreign financing

Regardless of whether an MNC parent or subsidiary decides to obtain financing from subsidiaries or from some other source, it must also decide which currency to borrow. Even if it needs its home currency, it may prefer to borrow a foreign currency. Reasons for this preference follow.

Foreign financing to offset foreign currency inflows

A large firm may finance in a foreign currency to offset a net receivables position in that foreign currency.

EXAMPLE

Plenty ltd (UK) has net receivables denominated in dollars and needs pounds now for liquidity purposes. It can borrow dollars and convert them to British pounds to obtain the needed funds. Then, the net receivables in dollars will be used to pay off the loan. In this example, financing in a foreign currency reduces the firm's exposure to fluctuating exchange rates. This strategy is especially appealing if the interest rate of the foreign currency is low and the currency is not appreciating.

How Avon used foreign financing during the Asian crisis. During the Asian crisis in 1997 and 1998, many MNCs with Asian subsidiaries were adversely affected by the weakening of Asian currencies against the dollar. Avon Products inc used various methods to reduce its economic exposure to the weak Asian currencies. Given that Avon had more cash inflows than cash outflows in Asian currencies, it used strategies that reduced the excess of cash inflows denominated in those currencies. First, it purchased more materials locally. Second, it borrowed funds locally to finance its operations so that it could use some of its cash inflows in Asian currencies to repay the debt. Third, it hired more local salespeople (rather than relying on marketing from the United States) to help sell its products locally. Fourth, it began to remit its earnings more frequently so that excess cash flows denominated in Asian currencies would not accumulate.

Foreign financing to reduce costs

Even when an MNC parent or subsidiary is not attempting to cover foreign net receivables, it may still consider borrowing foreign currencies if the interest rates on those currencies are relatively low and the currency stable. Since interest rates vary among currencies, the cost of borrowing can vary substantially among countries. MNCs that conduct business in countries with high interest rates and a currency that is not depreciating to compensate,

Exhibit 20.1   Short-term interest rates for various countries

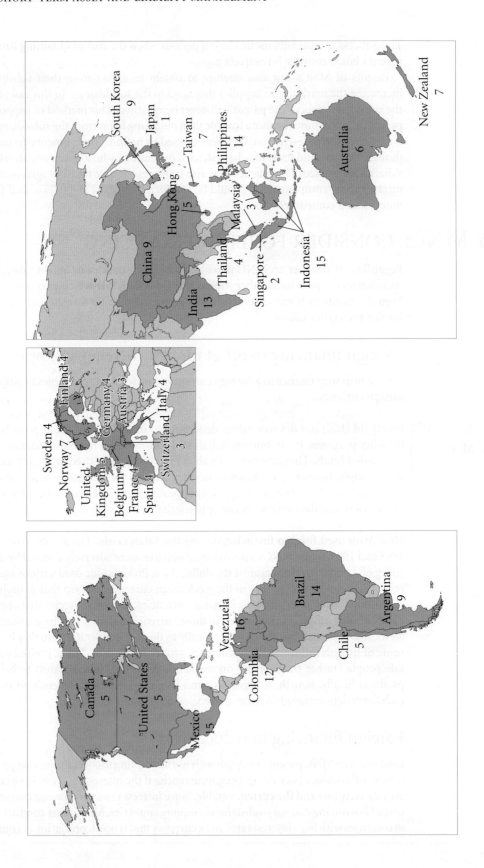

incur a high cost of short-term financing if they finance in the local currency. Thus, they may consider financing with another currency that has a lower interest rate. By shaving 1 percentage point off its financing rate, an MNC can save £1 million annually on debt of £100 million. Thus, MNCs are motivated to consider in detail various currencies when financing their operations.

Exhibit 20.1 compares short-term interest rates among countries for a given point in time. In most periods, the interest rate in Japan is relatively low, while the interest rates in many developing countries are relatively high. Countries with a high rate of inflation tend to have high interest rates.

EXAMPLE

Salon SA is a French firm that needs euros to expand its EU operations. Assume the euro financing rate is 9%, while the Japanese yen financing rate is 4%. Salon can borrow Japanese yen and immediately convert those yen to euros for use. When the loan repayment is due, Salon will need to obtain Japanese yen to pay off the loan. If the value of the Japanese yen in terms of euros has not changed since the time Salon obtained the loan, it will pay 4% on that loan. If, however, the Japanese yen has increased in value by 2% over the period then the total cost of the loan will be the 4% plus the extra 2% of the cost of buying the yen to repay the loan (using the approximate method). The total cost will therefore be 4% + 2% = 6%, still much cheaper than the 9% cost of borrowing in euros. So when choosing a currency for the loan, Salon has to decide whether the lower interest rate in a foreign currency is going to be taken up by the increasing value of that currency. The international Fisher effect (IFE) suggests that the currency will increase in value such that any saving in interest rates will be taken up entirely by the increase in value of the currency and hence the cost of repayment. Salon is hoping that the IFE will not hold if it decides to borrow in yen.

USING THE WEB

Forecasts of interest rates When an MNC borrows funds in a specific currency, its choice of a maturity is partially based on expectations of future interest rates in that country. Forecasts of interest rates in the near future for each country are provided by a number of websites that can be accessed by search engines, try: http://www.investica.co.uk/rateforecasts.htm.

DETERMINING THE EFFECTIVE FINANCING RATE

As has been pointed out, the actual cost of financing by the debtor firm will depend on: (1) the interest rate charged by the bank that provided the loan, and (2) the movement in the borrowed currency's value over the life of the loan. Thus, the actual or "effective" financing rate may differ from the quoted interest rate. This point is further illustrated in the following example.

EXAMPLE

Deckborn ltd (UK) obtains a two-year loan in New Zealand dollars (NZ$) worth £1,000,000 at the quoted interest rate of 8% – a full 2% less than an equivalent loan offered to Deckborn in the UK. When Deckborn receives the New Zealand loan, it converts the New Zealand dollars to British pounds to pay a supplier for materials. The exchange rate at that time is £0.40 per New Zealand dollar, so the NZ$2,500,000 is converted to £1,000,000 (computed as NZ$2,500,000 × £0.40 per NZ$ = £1,000,000). One year later, Deckborn pays interest of NZ$200,000 (computed as 8% × NZ$2,500,000). Two years later, Deckborn pays back the loan of NZ$2,500,000 plus a second interest payment instalment of NZ$200,000 a total of NZ$2,700,000. Assume that the New Zealand dollar unexpectedly appreciates from £0.40 to £0.50 shortly after receiving the loan and before any repayments are made. The interest payment at the end of the first year will therefore cost Deckborn NZ$200,000 × 0.50 or £100,000. At the end of the second year Deckborn will have a bill for NZ$2,700,000, this will cost £1,350,000 (computed as NZ$2,700,000 × £0.50 per NZ$). The cash flows are as follows:

	Start of period 1 or t_0	End of period 1 or t_1	End of period 2 or t_2
Cash flows in NZ$s	NZ$2,500,000	NZ$200,000	NZ$2,700,000
Exchange rate £s per NZ$	£0.40	£0.40	£0.40
Cash flows in £s	+£1,000,000	−£80,000	−£1,080,000

	Start of period 1 or t_0	End of period 1 or t_1	End of period 2 or t_2
Cash flows in NZ$s	NZ$2,500,000	NZ$200,000	NZ$2,700,000
Exchange rate £s per NZ$	£0.40	£0.50	£0.50
Cash flows in £s	+£1,000,000	−£100,000	−£1,350,000

The effective cost is the interest rate that "equates" the repayments with the initial loan. The interest rate is a cost so the basic formula is repayment less cost equals the original loan. The formula is:

$$\text{Initial loan} +£1,000,000 = \frac{-£100,000 + \text{repayment}}{(1+r)^1} + \frac{-£1,350,000 \text{ repayment}}{(1+r)^2}$$

Cost of borrowing

A two period model can be solved by formula but the simplest approach is to solve such problems by trial and error using a spreadsheet (where the cost of borrowing is placed in cell C9 (10% = 0.10 etc.) the formula for the present value in another cell is =1,000,000−100,000/(1+C9) − 1,350,000/(1+C9)²). A sufficiently close result is achieved with an interest rate of 21.3% thus:

$$+£1,000,000 = \frac{-£100,000}{(1+0.213)^1} + \frac{-1,350,000}{(1+0.213)^2}$$

Originally, Deckborn was seeking to obtain a loan for 8% some 2% cheaper than the UK equivalent. But because of the increase in the value of the NZ dollar, Deckborn is now having to pay 21.3%.

MANAGING FOR VALUE
Outsourcing short-term asset and liability management

SkyePharma is a UK-based drug delivery company, focused on the development of prescription pharmaceuticals utilizing proprietary controlled release technologies. In May 1996 the company listed on the main board of the London Stock Exchange and in 1998 achieved a US NASDAQ listing.

In June 2000, SkyePharma issued a five year 6% convertible bond raising £60 million to fund key research and development projects. The company's strategy is to earn a greater share of product revenues and profits through: 1) providing customers with a wider range of services, and 2) taking selected key products to later stages in the development process independently.

Given this background, SkyePharma's finance function was focused on value added support activities such as strategic risk management rather than day-to-day operational treasury activities.

SkyePharma has specific requirements with regard to the management of the convertible bond proceeds:

- Credit risk has to be diversified across a number of institutions to a minimum credit rating of A+.
- Cash has to be managed in line with stated cash burn obtaining a consistently competitive rate of return.

In addition it was recognized that, to help support the stated business strategy, SkyePharma would require access to an active foreign exchange and interest rate deal execution and hedging resource going forward.

Driven by the costs and management time involved in providing these services in house, a strategic decision was taken to outsource this function. The Royal Bank of Scotland's Agency Treasury Services team was chosen as the preferred outsourcing supplier. The bank was mandated to act as SkyePharma's agent and deal with all aspects of treasury risk.

The services provided fall into three categories:

- Liquidity management.
- Foreign exchange and interest rate risk management.
- Treasury administration and support.

Liquidity management

As a first step, an investment model was created for management of the convertible bond proceeds, which reflected SkyePharma's cash flow requirements and risk/reward parameters. This model covered:

- Credit limits – maximum maturity to be authorized.
- Counterparty list – list of authorized banks/financial institutions and credit ratings.
- Instruments permitted – range of authorized financial instruments and approved amount per instrument.
- Time limits – tenor per counterparty and financial instrument.
- Authorized signatories – list of designated personnel who could approve changes to the agreed investment policy.

This model provides the basis for SkyePharma's investment portfolio. Liquidity is managed out to a pre-agreed panel of counterparties using a competitive tender approach. Working to an ongoing cashflow forecast, cash is repatriated in line with requirements and the portfolio is constantly updated to reflect both ongoing investment needs and alterations in the shape of the sterling yield curve.

Foreign exchange and interest rate risk management

With overseas operations in Europe and the United States, SkyePharma has forex exposures in the Swiss franc, euro and US dollar. To ensure effective control over management of foreign exchange risk, a hedging policy has been pre-agreed. Similar in nature to the liquidity management policy, it covers products, tenors, credit limits and authorized signatories.

In practice, as soon as a foreign exchange exposure has been identified, it is notified to the bank. Under the terms of the outsourcing mandate, it is analyzed and a range of solutions to hedge the risk arising are created for approval. SkyePharma select the solution most appropriate to business needs, and this is then executed on the company's behalf in the marketplace.

In terms of interest rate risk management, early on an opportunity was identified to lower the servicing costs on the convertible bond through interest rate risk management. The structuring, execution and settlement aspects of this issue were also outsourced.

Treasury administration and support

To reduce costs within the finance function, SkyePharma has outsourced all confirmations, settlements, payments and transfers activity. A performance benchmarking service forms part of the outsourcing mandate, with performance reported on a monthly basis against a pre-agreed benchmark. This benchmark is appropriate to the service being utilized, i.e. a LIBID-related benchmark for liquidity management and appropriate foreign exchange budget rates (LIBID is the London Interbank bid rate, the rate banks offer to buy eurocurrency deposits hence determining the interest rate).

Conclusion

Outsourcing is a growing trend in finance, following proven successes in IT, HR and other operational areas. In today's uncertain economic climate, corporations are looking for innovative ways to generate further efficiencies and protect competitive positions. For SkyePharma, outsourcing this part of our business has allowed us to concentrate on strategies for growing the company and has helped us to optimize the value our treasury exposures represent.

Source: gtnews.com and SkyePharma plc by kind permission

Interest rates can be broken down into differing elements. The relationship is multiplicative. Thus if the overall rate is called the effective financing rate (denoted as r_{eff}) then breaking the rate down into two elements can be represented as:

$$r_{eff} = (1+r_1)(1+r_2) - 1$$

or three elements as:

$$r_{eff} = (1+r_1)(1+r_2)(1+r_3) - 1$$

When managing international loans a natural division to examine is how much of the effective interest rate is due to foreign interest rates (i_f) and how much due to the percentage change in the exchange rate (e_f). Thus

$$r_{eff} = (1+i_f)(1+e_f)$$

Taking the case of Deckborn, $i_f = 0.08$ or 8% and the effective rate is 21.3%. So the portion of the effective rate due to changes in the exchange rate (e_f) is:

$$0.213 = (1+0.08)(1+e_f) - 1$$

thus

$$e_f = 1.213 / 1.08 - 1$$
$$= 0.123 \text{ or } 12.3\%$$

Deckborn was charged 8% interest but incurred a further 12.3% due to the fact that the value of the NZ$ went up from £0.40 to £0.50. As a result interest payments in NZ$s were more expensive and the loan was also more expensive to repay. But the value of the NZ$ could have fallen in which case the loan could have been even cheaper.

Assume the same details as in the previous example, only the value of the NZ$ fell from £0.40 per NZ$ to £0.35 per NZ$.

	Start of period 1 or t_0	End of period 1 or t_1	End of period 2 or t_2
Cash flows in NZ$s	NZ$2,500,000	NZ$200,000	NZ$2,700,000
Exchange rate £s per NZ$	£0.40	£0.35	£0.35
Cash flows in £s	+£1,000,000	−£70,000	−£945,000

We are now seeking a rate of return that will solve the following equation:

$$+£1,000,000 = \frac{-£70,000}{(1+r)^1} + \frac{-945,000}{(1+r)^2}$$

Again using trial and error and a spreadsheet the solution is 0.77% so:

$$+£1,000,000 = \frac{-£70,000}{(1+0.0077)^1} + \frac{-945,000}{(1+0.0077)^2}$$

If the NZ dollar were to fall in value in this way, the loan would virtually be free. Thus Deckborn is taking a risk by borrowing in a foreign currency, the cost could be much cheaper than a domestic loan, on the other hand, if the value of the foreign currency increases the cost of the loan could be greater. An MNC should therefore consider the expected rate of appreciation or depreciation as well as the quoted interest rates of foreign currencies.

USING
THE WEB

Short-term foreign interest rates Short-term interest rates for major currencies such as the Canadian dollar, Japanese yen, and British pound for various maturities are provided at http://www.bloomberg.com. The short-term interest rates provided at this site reflect the government cost of borrowing; an MNC would have to pay a slightly higher interest rate than the rate shown. A review of the data illustrates how short-term interest rates can vary among currencies at a given point in time.

CRITERIA CONSIDERED FOR FOREIGN FINANCING

A more formal consideration of the factors relevant to short-term financing should include:

- Interest rate parity
- Exchange rate forecasts

These criteria can influence the MNC's decision regarding which currency or currencies to borrow. Each is discussed in turn.

Interest rate parity

Recall that covered interest arbitrage was described as a short-term foreign investment with a simultaneous forward sale of the foreign currency denominating the foreign investment. From a financing perspective, covered interest arbitrage can be conducted as follows. First, borrow a foreign currency and convert that currency to the home currency for use. Also, simultaneously purchase the foreign currency forward to lock in the exchange rate of the currency needed to pay off the loan. If the foreign currency's interest rate is low, this may appear to be a feasible strategy. However, such a currency will, in an efficient market, exhibit a forward premium that offsets the differential between its interest rate and the home interest rate. Therefore borrowing in the foreign currency will incur the same cost as borrowing domestically. So if a foreign interest rate is 2% cheaper, the currency on the forward market will exhibit a 2% premium (i.e. be more expensive by 2%) and this premium will offset the lower interest rate. Thus there is no benefit through borrowing from abroad.

More formally interest rate parity can be expressed as:

$$r_{eff} = (1 + i_f)(1 + p) - 1$$

where:

r_{eff} = the overall cost of financing in a foreign currency
i_f = foreign currency interest rate
p = the forward rate premium – currency more expensive (or discount – currency cheaper)

If interest rate parity exists then

$$r_{eff} = i_h$$

where:

i_h = home interest rate

and therefore

$$i_h = (1 + i_f)(1 + p) - 1$$

and

$$p = \frac{(1 + i_h)}{(1 + i_f)} - 1 \text{ and approximately for small differences } p = i_h - i_f$$

which is a more formal way of saying that the premium will reflect the difference in interest rates.

Covered interest rate arbitrage is one of the relationships that hold well in the marketplace. If there are differences with domestic returns than administration costs or restrictions will ensure that no riskless (arbitrage) profit can be made.

An MNC has a choice when borrowing internationally, in can cover its position by taking out a forward or futures contract thus ensuring a return similar to domestic returns. Alternatively it can leave its position uncovered. In such a case:

$$r_{eff} = (1 + i_f)(1 + e_f) - 1$$

where;

e_f = the change in value of the foreign currency.

The forward rate premium (p) had to reflect the difference in interest rates to avoid arbitrage profits; but in this case interest rate parity may or may not exist as there is no implied forward or futures contract in e_f. So a firm may have experiences as in the Deckborn example.

Finally, an MNC may choose to half cover its position by taking out a derivative such as a forward or futures or option contract that protects against some of the risk. In the case of forwards and futures, taking out contracts that do not fully cover the position would mean that some risk remains. In the Deckborn example the New Zealand loan was 2% cheaper therefore the forward rate for the first year can be expected to be 2% more expensive to offset the difference. The current spot was £0.40 per NZ$ so the forward rate should be £0.408 per NZ$ for the first year (i.e. (0.408 – 0.40) / 0.40 = 0.02 or 2%). If Deckborn only covers (by taking out a forward or futures contract) for NZ$100,000 of the NZ$200,000 due after the first year, then there is no cover for the cost of repaying the remaining NZ$100,000, there may be gains or losses compared to domestic lending. Alternatively, an option may be taken out. In this case, Deckborn may take out a call option to buy NZ$200,000 at £0.42. So that if the NZ$ increased by more than 5% (i.e. (0.42 – 0.40) / 0.40 = 0.05 or 5%) Deckborn could exercise the option and lock in a maximum effective interest rate of 3% more than the domestic (UK) equivalent (5% extra at the £0.42 rate less the 2% lower NZ charge compared to the domestic charge). Similar calculations can be made for the year 2 payments.

Exhibit 20.2 summarizes the implications of a variety of scenarios relating to interest rate parity.

Finally, an issue dealt with in Chapter 18 and earlier, is the effect of the borrowing on the overall exchange rate exposure of the MNC. Short-term financing in a foreign cur-

Exhibit 20.2 Financing alternatives and immediate implications

Scenario	Implications
1. All repayments fully covered by forward or futures contracts.	The effective interest rate will be about the same as the domestic rate (there may be differences due to transaction costs and market imperfections).
2. All repayments made at the prevailing exchange rate.	If interest parity holds, the effective rate will be similar to the domestic rate. If interest rate parity does not hold, the effective cost could be higher or lower than the domestic rate depending on the change in value of the foreign currency.
3. Some repayments covered by a futures or forwards contract.	As in scenario 1 for the elements covered by the contract and as in scenario 2 for the uncovered element.
4. Repayments covered by options.	Assuming that the option is out of the money (the exercise price is above the currency spot), if the value of the foreign currency goes above the level determined by the strike or exercise price, the option will be exercised and the increased cost of payment restricted to that of the exercise price.

rency implies cash outflows in that currency. Where there are earnings in that currency as well, the borrowing will give a degree of protection from exchange rate exposure. So, if the value of the currency falls, the adverse effect on translation of earnings into the home currency will be offset partially (or even fully) by the saving made by the cheaper cost home currency of payments of interest and capital in the foreign currency. The matching is not an exact science but setting any cash outflow in a currency against an inflow will help protect against the effects of changes in the value of that currency.

Exchange rate forecasts

While the forecasting capabilities of firms are somewhat limited, some firms may make decisions based on their estimation of the future value of the currency. The estimate may be based on market forecasts through a stockbroker subscription service or the quoted futures rate may be taken as a prediction of the future rate (effectively assuming that interest rate parity holds. Or a firm may use its own in-house economists to make an estimate. Methods of prediction used by staff may range from sophisticated econometric techniques to purely subjective judgements.

A point estimate or prediction of a single rate is rarely sufficient. Most MNCs will want to have an idea of the potential variation in the rate that could occur in the future. Only by knowing these possibilities can some impression of risk be gained. In looking at future possibilities two approaches are common. The first is to develop a probability distribution, looking at the varying rates and their probabilities. This is the dominant approach in financial theory leading to measures of spread such as the standard deviation and also to measures of association as in covariance or correlation. A second approach is to assess scenarios. Probabilities may or may not be used, for instance, if a firm wants to adopt a policy of protecting against the three worst scenarios, no probability calculations would be required. Scenarios are not confined to predicting the value of the exchange rate. There may, for instance, be a series of scenarios whereby the value of the foreign currency falls by 5%, but the differences in the scenarios is what is happening to other exchange rates or to international regulations or government policies. So this approach is more than merely approximating a distribution of exchange rates.

Starting with a prediction of a single future rate, once the firm develops a forecast or series of forecasts for the exchange rate's percentage change over the financing period (e_f), it can use this forecast along with the foreign interest rate to forecast the effective financing rate of a foreign currency. The forecasted rate can then be compared to the domestic financing rate.

EXAMPLE

Danya ltd (Ireland) needs funds for one year and is aware that the one-year interest rate in euros is 12% while the interest rate from borrowing Swiss francs is 8%. Danya forecasts that the Swiss franc will appreciate from its current rate of 0.64 euros to 0.6528 euros or by 2% over the next year. The expected value for e_f [written as $E(e_f)$] will therefore be 2%. Thus, the expected effective financing rate $[E(r_f)]$ will be:

$$E(r_{eff}) = (1 + i_f)(1 + E(e_f)) - 1$$
$$= (1 + 0.08)(1 + 0.02) - 1$$
$$= 0.1016 \text{ or } 10.16\%$$

In this example, financing in Swiss francs is expected to be less expensive than financing in euros. However, the value for e_f is forecasted and therefore is not known with certainty. Thus, there is no guarantee that foreign financing will truly be less costly.

Deriving a value for e_f that equates domestic and foreign rates. Continuing from the previous example, Danya ltd may attempt at least to determine what value of e_f would make the effective rate from foreign financing the same as domestic financing. To determine this value, note that e_f plays the same role as "p" above so:

$$e_f = \frac{(1 + i_h)}{(1 + i_f)} - 1 \text{ and approximately for small differences } e_f = i_h - i_f$$

i_h = 12% and i_f = 8% so the change in value of foreign currency (e_f) that equates domestic and foreign rates is 12% − 8% = 4%. The more accurate calculation is:

$$ef = \frac{(1 + 0.12)}{(1 + 0.08)} = 0.037037 \text{ or } 3.704\%$$

This suggests that the Swiss franc would have to appreciate by about 3.7% over the loan period to make the Swiss franc loan as costly as a loan in euros. Any smaller degree of appreciation would make the Swiss franc loan less costly. Danya can use this information when determining whether to borrow euros or Swiss francs. If it expects the Swiss franc to appreciate by more than 3.7% over the loan life, it should prefer borrowing in euros. If it expects the Swiss franc to appreciate by less than 3.7% or to depreciate, its decision is more complex. If the potential savings from financing with the foreign currency outweigh the risk involved, then the firm should choose that route. The final decision here will be influenced by Danya's degree of risk aversion.

Use of probability distributions. To gain more insight about the financing decision, a firm may wish to develop a probability distribution for the percentage change in value for a particular foreign currency over the financing horizon. Since forecasts are not always accurate, it is sometimes useful to develop a probability distribution instead of relying on a single point estimate. Using the probability distribution of possible percentage changes in the currency's value, along with the currency's interest rate, the firm can determine the probability distribution of the possible effective financing rates for the currency. Then, it can compare this distribution to the known financing rate of the home currency in order to make its financing decision.

Caroline ltd (UK) is deciding whether to borrow Swiss francs for one year. It finds that the bank quote for Caroline to borrow in Swiss francs is 8% and the quoted rate for the pound is 15%. It then develops a probability distribution for the Swiss franc's possible percentage change in value over the life of the loan.

The probability distribution is displayed in Exhibit 20.3. The first row in Exhibit 20.3 shows that there is a 5% probability of a 6% depreciation in the Swiss franc over the loan life. If the Swiss franc does depreciate by 6%, the effective financing rate would be 1.52%. Thus, there is a 5% probability that Caroline will incur a 1.52% effective financing rate on its loan. The second row shows that there is a 10% probability of a 4% depreciation in the Swiss franc over the loan life. If the Swiss franc does depreciate by 4%, the effective financing rate would be 3.68%. Thus, there is a 10% probability that Caroline will incur a 3.68% effective financing rate on its loan.

For each possible percentage change in the Swiss franc's value, there is a corresponding effective financing rate. We can associate each possible effective financing rate (third column) with its probability of occurring (second column). By multiplying each possible effective financing rate by its associated probability, we can compute an expected value for the effective financing rate of the Swiss franc. Based on the information in Exhibit 20.3, the expected value of the effective financing rate, referred to as $E(r_f)$, is computed as:

$$E(r_f) = 5\%(1.52\%) + 10\%(3.68\%) + 15\%(6.92\%) + 20\%(9.08\%) +$$
$$20\%(12.32\%) + 15\%(14.48\%) + 10\%(16.64\%) + 5\%(18.80\%)$$

$$= 0.076\% + 0.368\% + 1.038\% + 1.816\% + 2.464\% + 2.172\% + 1.664\% + 0.94\%$$

$$= 10.538\%$$

Thus, the decision for Caroline is whether to borrow pounds (at 15% interest) or Swiss francs (with an expected value of 10.538% for the effective financing rate). Using Exhibit 20.3, the risk reflects the 5% chance (probability) that the effective financing rate on Swiss francs will be 18.8% and the 10% chance that the effective financing rate on Swiss francs will be 16.64%. Either of these possibilities represents a greater expense to Caroline than it would incur if it borrowed British pounds.

To further assess the decision regarding which currency to borrow, the information in the second and third columns of Exhibit 20.3 is used to develop the probability distribution in Exhibit 20.4. This exhibit illustrates the probability of each possible effective financing rate that may occur if Caroline borrows Swiss francs. Notice that the UK interest rate (15%) is included in Exhibit 20.4 for comparison purposes. There is no distribution of possible outcomes for the UK rate since the rate of 15% is known with certainty (no exchange rate risk exists). There is a 15% probability that the UK rate will be lower than the effective rate on Swiss francs and an 85% chance that the UK rate will be higher than the effective rate on Swiss francs. This information can assist the firm in its financing decision. Given the potential savings relative to the small degree of risk, Caroline decides to borrow Swiss francs.

Exhibit 20.3 Analysis of financing with a foreign currency

Possible Rate of Change in the Swiss Franc over the Life of the Loan	Probability of Occurrence	Effective Financing Rate if this Rate of Change in the (e_f) Swiss Franc Does Occur (r_{eff})
−6%	5%	$(1.08)[1 + (−6\%)] − 1 = 1.52\%$
−4	10	$(1.08)[1 + (−4\%)] − 1 = 3.68$
−1	15	$(1.08)[1 + (−1\%)] − 1 = 6.92$
+1	20	$(1.08)[1 + (1\%)] − 1 = 9.08$
+4	20	$(1.08)[1 + (4\%)] − 1 = 12.32$
+6	15	$(1.08)[1 + (6\%)] − 1 = 14.48$
+8	10	$(1.08)[1 + (8\%)] − 1 = 16.64$
+10	5	$(1.08)[1 + (10\%)] − 1 = 18.80$
	100%	

Exhibit 20.4 Probability distribution of effective financing rates

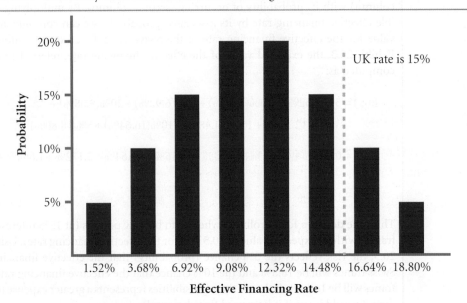

ACTUAL RESULTS FROM FOREIGN FINANCING

The fact that some firms utilize foreign financing suggests that they believe reduced financing costs can be achieved. To assess this issue, the effective financing rates of the Swiss franc and the US dollar are compared in Exhibit 20.5 from the perspective of a US firm. The data are segmented into annual periods.

In the 1999–2000 period, the Swiss franc weakened against the dollar, and a US firm that borrowed Swiss francs would have incurred a negative effective financing rate. In the 2002–03 period, however, the Swiss franc appreciated against the dollar. The effective financing rate of Swiss francs from a US perspective was 22% in 2002 and 11% in 2003. These rates were much higher than the US interest rate and illustrate the risk to an MNC that finances operations with a foreign currency.

Exhibit 20.5 Comparison of financing with Swiss francs versus dollars

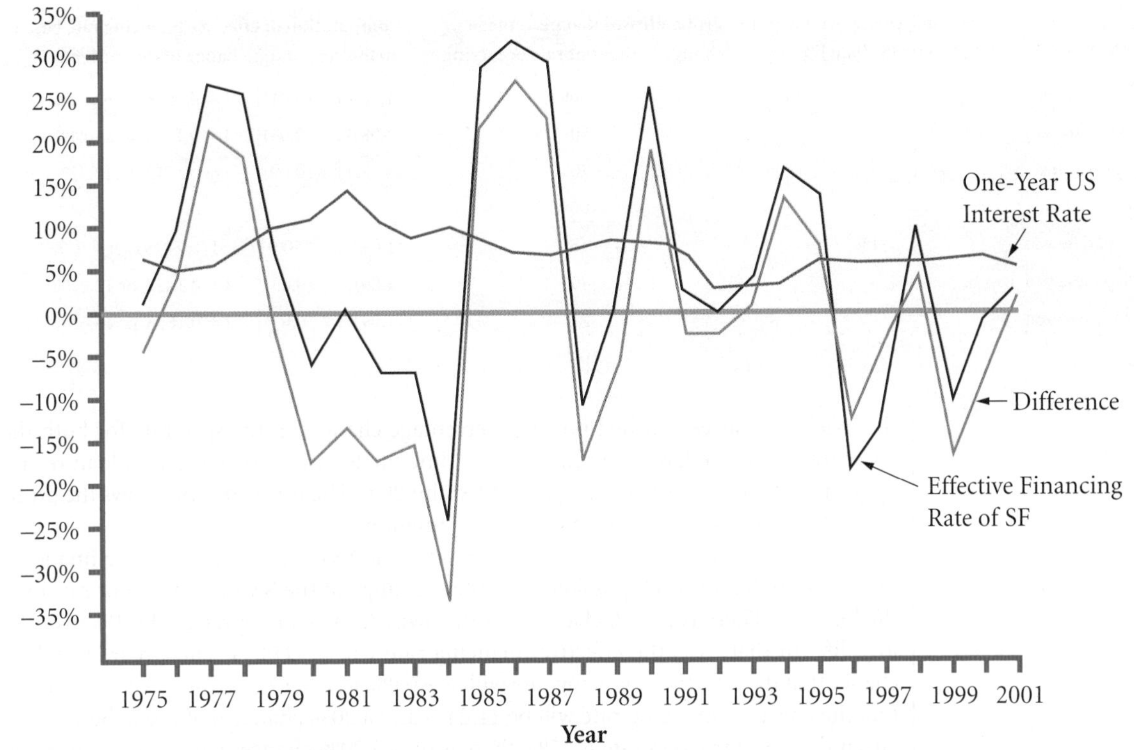

Exhibit 20.5 demonstrates the potential savings in financing costs that can be achieved if the foreign currency depreciates against the firm's home currency. It also demonstrates how foreign financing can backfire if the firm's expectations are incorrect and the foreign currency appreciates over the financing period.

FINANCING WITH A PORTFOLIO OF CURRENCIES

Although foreign financing can result in significantly lower financing costs, the variance in foreign financing costs over time is higher. MNCs may be able to achieve lower financing costs without excessive risk by financing with a portfolio of foreign currencies, as demonstrated here.

EXAMPLE Niels BV (Netherlands) needs to borrow 100,000 euros for one year and obtains the following interest rate quotes:

- Interest rate for a one-year loan in euros = 15%
- Interest rate for a one-year loan in Swiss francs = 8%
- Interest rate for a one-year loan in Japanese yen = 9%

Since the quotes for a loan in Swiss francs or Japanese yen are relatively low, Niels may desire to borrow in a foreign currency. If Niels decides to use foreign financing, it has three choices based on the information given: (1) borrow only Swiss francs, (2) borrow only Japanese yen, or (3) borrow a portfolio of Swiss francs and Japanese yen. Assume

Exhibit 20.6 Derivation of possible effective financing rates

Currency	Possible change in the spot rate over the loan life	Probability of that percentage change in the spot rate occurring	Computation of effective financing rate based on the percentage change in the spot rate
Swiss franc	1%	30%	$(1.08)[1 + (0.01)] - 1 = 0.0908$, or 9.08%
Swiss franc	3	50	$(1.08)[1 + (0.03)] - 1 = 0.1124$, or 11.24%
Swiss franc	9	20	$(1.08)[1 + (0.09)] - 1 = 0.1772$, or 17.72%
		100%	
Japanese yen	−1%	35%	$(1.09)[1 + (-0.01)] - 1 = 0.0791$, or 7.91%
Japanese yen	3	40	$(1.09)[1 + (0.03)] - 1 = 0.1227$, or 12.27%
Japanese yen	7	25	$(1.09)[1 + (0.07)] - 1 = 0.1663$, or 16.63%
		100%	

that Niels BV has established possible percentage changes in the spot rate for both the Swiss franc and the Japanese yen from the time the loan would begin until loan repayment, as shown in the second column of Exhibit 20.6. The third column shows the probability that each possible percentage change might occur.

Based on the assumed interest rate of 8% for the Swiss franc, the effective financing rate is computed for each possible percentage change in the Swiss franc's spot rate over the loan life. There is a 30% chance that the Swiss franc will appreciate by 1% over the loan life. In that case, the effective financing rate will be 9.08%. Thus, there is a 30% chance that the effective financing rate will be 9.08%. Furthermore, there is a 50% chance that the effective financing rate will be 11.24% and a 20% chance that it will be 17.72%. Given that the euro loan rate is 15%, there is only a 20% chance that financing in Swiss francs will be more expensive than domestic financing.

The lower section of Exhibit 20.6 provides information on the Japanese yen. For example, the yen has a 35% chance of depreciating by 1% over the loan life, and so on. Based on the assumed 9% interest rate and the exchange rate fluctuation forecasts, there is a 35% chance that the effective financing rate will be 7.91%, a 40% chance that it will be 12.27%, and a 25% chance that it will be 16.63%. Given the 15% rate on euro financing, there is a 25% chance that financing in Japanese yen will be more costly than domestic financing. Before examining the third possible foreign financing strategy (the portfolio approach), determine the expected value of the effective financing rate for each foreign currency by itself. This is accomplished by totalling the products of each possible effective financing rate and its associated probability as follows:

Currency	Computation of Expected Value of Effective Financing Rate
Swiss francs	30% (9.08%) + 50% (11.24%) + 20% (17.72%) = 11.888%
Japanese yen	35% (7.91%) + 40% (12.27%) + 25% (16.63%) = 11.834%

The expected financing costs of the two currencies are almost the same. The individual degree of risk (that the costs of financing will turn out to be higher than domestic financing) is about the same for each currency. If Niels chooses to finance with only one of these foreign currencies, it is difficult to pinpoint (based on our analysis) which currency is more appropriate. Now, consider the third and final foreign financing strategy: the portfolio approach.

Based on the information in Exhibit 20.6, there are three possibilities for the Swiss franc's effective financing rate. The same holds true for the Japanese yen. If Niels BV borrows half of its needed funds in each of the foreign currencies, then there will be nine possibilities for this portfolio's effective financing rate, as shown in Exhibit 20.7. Columns 1 and 2 list all possible joint effective financing rates. Column 3 computes the joint probability of that occurrence assuming that exchange rate movements of the Swiss franc and Japanese yen are independent. Column 4 shows the computation of the portfolio's effective financing rate based on the possible rates shown for the individual currencies.

An examination of the top row will help to clarify the table. This row indicates that one possible outcome of borrowing both Swiss francs and Japanese yen is that they will exhibit effective financing rates of 9.08% and 7.91%, respectively. The probability of the Swiss franc's effective financing rate occurring is 30%, while the probability of the Japanese yen rate occurring is 35%. Recall that these percentages were given in Exhibit 20.6. The joint probability that both of these rates will occur simultaneously is (30%) (35%) = 10.5% (given that there is no correlation between the two rates). Assuming that half (50%) of the funds needed are to be borrowed from each currency, the portfolio's effective financing rate will be 0.5 (9.08%) + 0.5 (7.91%) = 8.495% (if those individual effective financing rates occur for each currency).

A similar procedure was used to develop the remaining eight rows in Exhibit 20.7. From this table, there is a 10.5% chance that the portfolio's effective financing rate will be 8.495%, a 12% chance that it will be 10.675%, and so on.

Exhibit 20.8 displays the probability distribution for the portfolio's effective financing rate that was derived in Exhibit 20.7. This exhibit shows that financing with a portfolio (50% financed in Swiss francs with the remaining 50% financed in Japanese yen) has only a 5% chance of being more costly than domestic financing. These results are more favourable than those of either individual foreign currency. Therefore, Niels decides to borrow the portfolio of currencies.

Exhibit 20.7 Analysis of financing with two foreign currencies based on no correlation between yen and Swiss franc changes in value

(1) Swiss franc	(2) Japanese yen	(3) Computation of joint probability assuming no correlation between yen and Swiss franc changes in value	(4) Computation of effective financing rate of portfolio (50% of total funds borrowed in each currency
9.08%	7.91%	(30%)(35%) = 10.5%	0.5(9.08%) + 0.5(7.91%) = 8.495%
9.08	12.27	(30%)(40%) = 12.0	0.5(9.08%) + 0.5(12.27%) = 10.675
9.08	16.63	(30%)(25%) = 7.5	0.5(9.08%) + 0.5(16.63%) = 12.855
11.24	7.91	(50%)(35%) = 17.5	0.5(11.24%) + 0.5(7.91%) = 9.575
11.24	12.27	(50%)(40%) = 20.0	0.5(11.24%) + 0.5(12.27%) = 11.755
11.24	16.63	(50%)(25%) = 12.5	0.5(11.24%) + 0.5(16.63%) = 13.935
17.72	7.91	(20%)(35%) = 7.0	0.5(17.72%) + 0.5(7.91%) = 12.815
17.72	12.27	(20%)(40%) = 8.0	0.5(17.72%) + 0.5(12.27%) = 14.995
17.72	16.63	(20%)(25%) = 5.0	0.5(17.72%) + 0.5(16.63%) = 17.175
		100.0%	

Exhibit 20.8 Probability distribution of the portfolio's effective financing rate

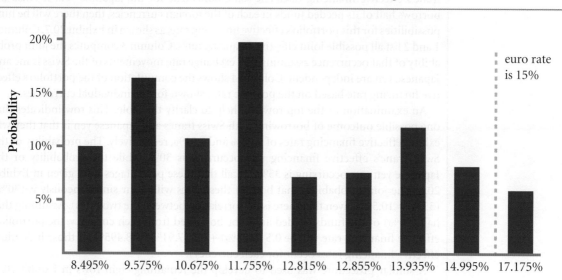

Portfolio diversification effects

When both foreign currencies are borrowed, the only way the portfolio will exhibit a higher effective financing rate than the domestic rate is if *both* currencies experience their maximum possible level of appreciation (which is 9% for the Swiss franc and 7% for the Japanese yen). If only one does, the severity of its appreciation will be somewhat offset by the other currency's not appreciating to such a large extent. The probability of maximum appreciation is 20% for the Swiss franc and 25% for the Japanese yen. The joint probability of both of these events occurring simultaneously is (20%) (25%) = 5%. This is an advantage of financing in a portfolio of foreign currencies. Niels has a 95% chance of attaining lower costs with the foreign portfolio than with domestic financing.

The expected value of the effective financing rate for the portfolio can be determined by multiplying the percentage financed in each currency by the expected value of that currency's individual effective financing rate. Recall that the expected value was 11.888% for the Swiss franc and 11.834% for the Japanese yen. Thus, for a portfolio representing 50% of funds borrowed in each currency, the expected value of the effective financing rate is 0.5 (11.888%) + 0.5 (11.834%) = 11.861%. Based on an overall comparison, the expected value of the portfolio's effective financing rate is very similar to that from financing solely in either foreign currency. However, the risk (of incurring a higher effective financing rate than the domestic rate) is substantially less when financing with the portfolio.

In the example, the computation of joint probabilities requires the assumption that the two currencies move independently. If movements of the two currencies are actually highly positively correlated, then financing with a portfolio of currencies will not be as beneficial as demonstrated because there is a strong likelihood of both currencies experiencing a high level of appreciation simultaneously. If the two currencies are not highly correlated, they are less likely to simultaneously appreciate to such a degree. Thus, the chances that the portfolio's effective financing rate will exceed the UK rate are reduced when the currencies included in the portfolio are not highly positively correlated.

The example included only two currencies in the portfolio. Financing with a more diversified portfolio of additional currencies that exhibit low interest rates might increase the probability that foreign financing will be less costly than domestic financing; several currencies are unlikely to move in tandem and therefore unlikely to simultaneously appreciate enough to offset the advantage of their low interest rates. Again, the degree to which these currencies are correlated with each other is important. If all currencies are highly positively correlated with each other, financing with such a portfolio would not be very different from financing with a single foreign currency.

Repeated financing with a currency portfolio

A firm that repeatedly finances with a currency portfolio would normally prefer to compose a financing package that exhibits a somewhat predictable effective financing rate on a periodic basis. The more volatile a portfolio's effective financing rate over time, the more uncertainty (risk) there is about the effective financing rate that will exist in any period. The degree of volatility depends on the standard deviations and paired correlations of effective financing rates of the individual currencies within the portfolio.

We can use the portfolio variance as a measure of the degree of volatility. The variance of a two-currency portfolio's effective financing rate $[VAR(r_p)]$ over time is computed as

$$VAR\,(r_p) = I^2{}_A\sigma^2{}_A + w^2{}_B\sigma^2{}_B + 2w_Aw_B\sigma_A\sigma_B CORR_{AB}$$

where $w^2{}_A$ and $w^2{}_B$ represent the percentage of total funds financed from Currencies A and B, respectively; $\sigma^2{}_A$ and $\sigma^2{}_B$ represent the individual variances of each currency's effective financing rate over time, and $CORR_{AB}$ reflects the correlation coefficient of the two currencies' effective financing rates. Since the percentage change in the exchange rate plays an important role in influencing the effective financing rate, it should not be surprising that $CORR_{AB}$ is strongly affected by the correlation between the exchange rate fluctuations of the two currencies. A low correlation between movements of the two currencies may force $CORR_{AB}$ to be low.

EXAMPLE

Valparaiso SA (Spain) considers borrowing a portfolio of Japanese yen and Swiss francs to finance its euro operations. Half of the needed funding would come from each currency. To determine how the variance in this portfolio's effective financing rate is related to characteristics of the component currencies, assume the following information based on historical information for several three-month periods:

- Mean effective financing rate of Swiss franc for three months = 3% or 0.03
- Mean effective financing rate of Japanese yen for three months = 2% or 0.02
- Standard deviation of Swiss franc's effective financing rate = 0.04
- Standard deviation of Japanese yen's effective financing rate = 0.09
- Correlation coefficient of effective financing rates of these two currencies = 0.10

Given this information, the mean effective rate on a portfolio (r_p) of funds financed 50% by Swiss francs and 50% by Japanese yen is determined by totalling the weighted individual effective financing rates:

$$r_p = w_{SFr}r_{SFr} + w_{Yen}r_{Yen}$$
$$= 0.50\,(0.03) + 0.50\,(0.02)$$
$$= 0.015 + 0.01$$
$$= 0.025 \text{ or } 2.5\%$$

The variance of this portfolio's effective financing rate over time is:

$$VAR\ (r_p) = 0.5^2\ (0.04)^2 + 0.5^2\ (0.09)^2 + 2\ (0.5)\ (0.5)\ (0.04)\ (0.09)\ (0.10)$$

$$= 0.25\ (0.0016) + 0.25\ (0.0081) + 0.00018$$

$$= 0.002605$$

The standard deviation of the portfolio is:

$$\sqrt{0.002605} = 0.051 \text{ or } 5.1\%$$

Valparaiso can use this same process to compare various financing packages to see which package would be most appropriate. It may be more interested in estimating the mean return and variability for repeated financing in a particular portfolio in the future. There is no guarantee that past data will be indicative of the future. Yet, if the individual variability and paired correlations are somewhat stable over time, the historical variability of the portfolio's effective financing rate should provide a reasonable forecast.

To recognize the benefits from financing with two currencies that are not highly correlated, reconsider how the variance of the portfolio's effective financing rate would have been affected if the correlation between the two currencies was 0.90 (very high correlation) instead of 0.10. The variance would be 0.004045, which is more than 50% higher than the variance when the correlation was assumed to be 0.10.

The assessment of a currency portfolio's effective financing rate and variance is not restricted to just two currencies. The mean effective financing rate for a currency portfolio of any size will be determined by totalling the respective individual effective financing rates weighted by the percentage of funds financed with each currency. Solving the variance of a portfolio's effective financing rate becomes more complex as more currencies are added to the portfolio; the underlying model, however, is the variance/covariance matrix first encountered in Chapter 3.

SUMMARY

- MNCs may use foreign financing to offset anticipated cash inflows in foreign currencies so that exposure to exchange rate risk will be minimized. Alternatively, some MNCs may use foreign financing in an attempt to reduce their financing costs. Foreign financing costs may be lower if the foreign interest rate is relatively low or if the foreign currency borrowed depreciates over the financing period.

- MNCs can determine whether to use foreign financing by estimating the effective financing rate for any foreign currency over the period in which financing will be needed. The expected effective financing rate is dependent on the quoted interest rate of the foreign currency and the forecasted percentage change in the currency's value over the financing period.

- When MNCs borrow a portfolio of currencies that have low interest rates, they can increase the probability of achieving relatively low financing costs if the currencies' values are not highly correlated.

CRITICAL DEBATE

Do MNCs increase their risk when borrowing foreign currencies?

Proposition. Yes. MNCs should borrow the currency that matches their cash inflows. If they borrow a foreign currency to finance business in a different currency, they are essentially speculating on the future exchange rate movements. The results of the strategy are uncertain, which represents risk to the MNC and its shareholders.

Opposing view. No. If MNCs expect that they can reduce the effective financing rate by borrowing a foreign currency, they should consider borrowing that currency. This enables them to achieve lower costs and improves their ability to compete. If they take the most conservative approach by borrowing whatever currency matches their inflows, they may incur higher costs and have a greater chance of failure.

With whom do you agree? Which argument do you support? Offer your own opinion on this issue.

SELF TEST

Answers are provided in Appendix A at the back of the text.

1. Assume that the interest rate in New Zealand is 9%. A UK firm plans to borrow New Zealand dollars, convert them to UK pounds, and repay the loan in one year. What will be the effective financing rate if the New Zealand dollar depreciates by 6%? If the New Zealand dollar appreciates by 3%?

2. Using the information in question 1 and assuming a 50% chance of either scenario occurring, determine the expected value of the effective financing rate.

3. Assume that the Japanese one-year interest rate is 5%, while the UK one-year interest rate is 8%. What percentage change in the Japanese yen would cause a UK firm borrowing yen to incur the same effective financing rate as it would if it borrowed pounds?

4. The spot rate of the Australian dollar is £0.40. The one-year forward rate of the Australian dollar is £0.38. The Australian one-year interest rate is 9%. Assume that the forward rate is used to forecast the future spot rate. Determine the expected effective financing rate for a UK firm that borrows Australian dollars to finance its UK business.

5. Omaha SA (France) plans to finance its UK operations by repeatedly borrowing two currencies with low interest rates whose exchange rate movements are highly correlated. Will the variance of the two-currency portfolio's effective financing rate be much lower than the variance of either individual currency's effective financing rate? Explain.

QUESTIONS AND APPLICATIONS

1. **Financing from subsidiaries.** Explain why an MNC parent would consider financing from its subsidiaries.

2. **Foreign financing.**
   a. Explain how a firm's degree of risk aversion enters into its decision of whether to finance in a foreign currency or a local currency.
   b. Discuss the use of specifying a break-even point when financing in a foreign currency.

3. **Probability distribution.**
   a. Discuss the development of a probability distribution of effective financing rates when financing in a foreign currency. How is this distribution developed?
   b. Once the probability distribution of effective financing rates from financing in a foreign currency is developed, how can this distribution be used in deciding whether to finance in the foreign currency or the home currency?

4. **Financing and exchange rate risk.** How can a UK firm finance in euros and not necessarily be exposed to exchange rate risk?

5. **Short-term financing analysis.** Assume that Tilly ltd needs £3 million for a one-year period. Within one year, it will generate enough British pounds to pay off the loan. It is considering three options: (1) borrowing pounds at an interest rate of 6%, (2) borrowing Japanese yen at an interest rate of 3%, or (3) borrowing Canadian dollars at an interest rate of 4%. Tilly expects that the Japanese yen will appreciate by 1% over the next year and that the Canadian dollar will appreciate by 3%. What is the expected "effective" financing rate for each of the three options? Which option appears to be most feasible? Why might Tilly not necessarily choose the option reflecting the lowest effective financing rate?

6. **Effective financing rate.** How is it possible for a firm to incur a negative effective financing rate?

7. **IRP application to short-term financing.**
   a. If interest rate parity does not hold, what strategy should Connect ltd consider when it needs short-term financing?
   b. Assume that Connect ltd needs pounds. It borrows euros at a lower interest rate than that for pounds. If interest rate parity exists and if the forward rate of the euro is a reliable predictor of the future spot rate, what does this suggest about the feasibility of such a strategy?
   c. If Connect ltd expects the current spot rate to be a more reliable predictor of the future spot rate, what does this suggest about the feasibility of such a strategy?

8. **Break-even financing.** Akron ltd needs dollars. Assume that the local one-year loan rate is 15%, while a one-year loan rate on euros is 7%. By how much must the euro appreciate to cause the loan in euros to be more costly than a UK loan?

9. **IRP application to short-term financing.** Assume that interest rate parity exists. If a firm believes that the forward rate is an unbiased predictor of the future spot rate, will it expect to achieve lower financing costs by consistently borrowing a foreign currency with a low interest rate?

10. **Effective financing rate.** Boca, SA (Spain) needs 4 million euros for one year. It currently has no business in Japan but plans to borrow Japanese yen from a Japanese bank because the Japanese interest rate is 3 percentage points lower than the euro rate. Assume that interest rate parity exists; also assume that Boca believes that the one-year forward rate of the Japanese yen will exceed the future spot rate one year from now. Will the expected effective financing rate be higher, lower, or the same as financing with euros? Explain.

11. **IRP application to short-term financing.** Assume that the UK interest rate is 7% and the euro's interest rate is 4%. Assume that the euro's forward rate has a premium of 4% (is 4% more expensive in terms of £s?). Determine whether the following statement is true: "Interest rate parity does not hold; therefore, UK firms could lock in a lower financing cost by borrowing euros and purchasing euros forward for one year". Explain your answer.

12. **Break-even financing.** Orlando plc is a UK-based MNC with a subsidiary in Mexico. Its Mexican subsidiary needs a one-year loan of 10 million pesos for operating expenses. Since the Mexican interest rate is 70%, Orlando is considering borrowing pounds, which it would convert to pesos to cover the operating expenses. By how much would the pound have to appreciate against the peso to cause such a strategy to backfire? (The one-year UK interest rate is 9%.)

13. **Financing in a crisis.** What actions can a firm take with regard to its short-term financing when there are concerns that there might be a currency crisis in the country of one of its subsidiaries.

14. **Effects of currency change.** Homewood ltd commonly finances some of its expansion in Europe by borrowing in euros. The interest rate for the euro then increases with no prospect of a fall in value of the euro against the pound. Should Homewood re-finance in pounds? Explain.

ADVANCED QUESTIONS

15. **Probability distribution of financing costs.** Missoula ltd decides to borrow Japanese yen for one year. The interest rate on the borrowed yen is 8%. Missoula has developed the following probability distribution for the yen's degree of fluctuation against the pound:

Possible degree of fluctuation of yen against the pound	Percentage probability
−4%	20%
−1	30
0	10
3	40

Given this information, what is the expected value of the effective financing rate of the Japanese yen from Missoula's perspective?

16. **Analysis of short-term financing.** Jackson ltd is a UK-based firm that needs £600,000. It has no business in Japan but is considering one-year financing with Japanese yen because the annual interest rate would be 5% versus 9% in the United Kingdom. Assume that interest rate parity exists.
    a. Can Jackson benefit from borrowing Japanese yen and simultaneously purchasing yen one year forward to avoid exchange rate risk? Explain.
    b. Assume that Jackson does not cover its exposure and uses the forward rate to forecast the future spot rate. Determine the expected effective financing rate. Should Jackson finance with Japanese yen? Explain.
    c. Assume that Jackson does not cover its exposure and expects that the Japanese yen will appreciate by either 5%, 3%, or 2%, and with equal probability of each occurrence. Use this information to determine the probability distribution of the effective financing rate. Should Jackson finance with Japanese yen? Explain.

17. **Financing with a portfolio.** Pfeffer GmbH (Germany) considers obtaining 40% of its one-year financing in Canadian dollars and 60% in Japanese yen. The forecasts of appreciation in the Canadian dollar and Japanese yen for the next year are as follows:

Currency	Possible percentage change in the spot rate over the loan life	Probability of that percentage change in the spot rate occurring
Canadian dollar	4%	70%
Canadian dollar	7	30
Japanese yen	6	50
Japanese yen	9	50

The interest rate on the Canadian dollar is 9%, and the interest rate on the Japanese yen is 7%. Develop the possible effective financing rates of the overall portfolio and the probability of each possibility based on the use of joint probabilities (assume independence).

18. **Financing with a portfolio.**
    a. Does borrowing a portfolio of currencies offer any possible advantages over the borrowing of a single foreign currency?
    b. If a firm borrows a portfolio of currencies, what characteristics of the currencies will affect the potential variability of the portfolio's effective financing rate? What characteristics would be desirable from a borrowing firm's perspective?

19. **Financing with a portfolio.** Raleigh ltd needs to borrow funds for one year to finance an expenditure in the United States. The following interest rates are available:

	Borrowing Rate
US	10%
Canada	6
Japan	5

The percentage changes in the spot rates of the Canadian dollar and Japanese yen over the next year are as follows:

Canadian dollar		Japanese yen	
Probability	Percentage change in spot rate	Probability	Percentage change in spot rate
10%	5%	20%	6%
90	2	80	1

If Raleigh ltd borrows a portfolio, 50% of funds from Canadian dollars and 50% of funds from yen, determine the probability distribution of the effective financing rate of the portfolio. What is the probability that Raleigh will incur a higher effective financing rate from borrowing this portfolio than from borrowing US dollars?

PROJECT WORKSHOP

20. **Yields for foreign currencies.** The Bloomberg website provides interest rate data for many

different foreign currencies over various maturities. Its address is: http://www.bloomberg.com.

a. Go to the section that shows yields for different foreign currencies. Review the three-month yields of currencies. Assume that you could borrow at a rate 1 percentage point above the quoted yield for each currency. Which currency would offer you the lowest quoted yield?

b. As a cash manager of a UK-based MNC that needs dollars to support UK operations, where would you borrow funds for the next three months? Explain.

DISCUSSION IN THE BOARDROOM

This exercise can be found on the companion website at www.cengage.co.uk/madura_fox.

RUNNING YOUR OWN MNC

This exercise can be found on the companion website at www.cengage.co.uk/madura_fox.

Essays/discussion and articles can be found at the end of Part 5

BLADES PLC CASE STUDY
Use of foreign short-term financing

Blades plc just received a special order for 120,000 pairs of "Speedos", its primary roller blade product. Ben Holt, Blades' financial director, needs short-term financing to finance this large order from the time Blades orders its supplies until the time it will receive payment. Blades will charge a price of 5,000 baht per pair of Speedos. The materials needed to manufacture these 120,000 pairs will be purchased from Thai suppliers. Blades expects the cost of the components for one pair of Speedos to be approximately 3,500 baht in its first year of operating the Thai subsidiary.

Because Blades is relatively unknown in Thailand, its suppliers have indicated that they would like to receive payment as early as possible. The customer that placed this order insists on open account transactions, which means that Blades will receive payment for the roller blades approximately three months subsequent to the sale. Furthermore, the production cycle necessary to produce Speedos, from purchase of the materials to the eventual sale of the product, is approximately three months. Because of these considerations, Blades expects to collect its revenues approximately six months after it has paid for the materials, such as rubber and plastic components, needed to manufacture Speedos.

Ben Holt has identified at least two alternatives for satisfying Blades' financing needs. First, Blades could borrow Japanese yen for six months, convert the yen to Thai baht, and use the baht to pay the Thai suppliers. When the accounts receivable in Thailand are collected, Blades would convert the baht received to yen and repay the Japanese yen loan. Second, Blades could borrow Thai baht for six months in order to pay its Thai suppliers. When Blades collects its accounts receivable, it would use these receipts to repay the baht loan. Thus, Blades will use revenue generated in Thailand to repay the loan, whether it borrows the money in yen or in baht.

Holt's initial research indicates that the 180-day interest rates available to Blades in Japan and in Thailand are 4% and 6%, respectively. Consequently, Holt favours borrowing the Japanese yen, as he believes this loan will be cheaper than the baht-denominated loan. He is aware that he should somehow incorporate the future movements of the yen–baht exchange rate in his analysis, but he is unsure how to accomplish this. However, he has identified the following probability distribution of the change in the value of the Japanese yen with respect to the Thai baht and of the change in the value of the Thai baht with respect to the dollar over the six-month period of the loan:

Possible rate of change in the Japanese yen relative to the Thai baht over the life of the loan	Possible rate of change in the Thai baht relative to the pound over the life of the loan	Probability of occurrence
2%	−3%	30%
1	−2	30
0	−1	20
1	0	15
2	1	5

Holt has also informed you that the current spot rate of the yen (in baht) is THB0.347826, while the current spot rate of the baht (in pounds) is £0.0015.

As a financial analyst for Blades, you have been asked to answer the following questions for Ben Holt:

1. What is the amount, in baht, that Blades needs to borrow to cover the payments due to the Thai suppliers? What is the amount, in yen, that Blades needs to borrow to cover the payments due to the Thai suppliers?

2. Given that Blades will use the receipts from the receivables in Thailand to repay the loan and that Blades plans to remit all baht-denominated cash flows to the UK parent whether it borrows in baht or yen, does the future value of the yen with respect to the baht affect the cost of the loan if Blades borrows in yen?

3. Using a spreadsheet, compute the expected amount (in pounds) that will be remitted to the United Kingdom in six months if Blades finances its working capital requirements by borrowing baht versus borrowing yen. Based on your analysis, should Blades obtain a yen- or baht-denominated loan?

SMALL BUSINESS DILEMMA
Short-term financing by the Sports Exports Company

At the current time, the Sports Exports Company (Ireland) focuses on producing basketballs and exporting them to a distributor in the United Kingdom. The exports are denominated in British pounds. Jim Logan, the owner, plans to develop other sporting goods products besides the basketballs that he produces. His entire expansion will be focused on the United Kingdom, where he is trying to make a name for his firm. He remains concerned about his firm's exposure to exchange rate risk but does not plan to let that get in the way of his expansion plans because he believes that his firm can continue to penetrate the British sporting goods market. He has just negotiated a joint venture with a British firm that will produce other sporting goods products that are popular in the United States but will be sold in the United Kingdom. Jim will pay the British manufacturer in British pounds. These products will be delivered directly to the British distributor rather than to Jim, and the distributor will pay Jim with British pounds.

Jim's expansion plans will result in the need for additional funding. Jim would prefer to borrow on a short-term basis now. Jim has an excellent credit rating and collateral and therefore should be able to obtain short-term financing. The British interest rate is one-fourth of a percentage point above the US interest rate.

1. Should Jim borrow dollars or pounds to finance his joint venture business? Why?

2. Jim could also borrow euros at an interest rate that is lower than the US or British rate. The values of the euro and pound tend to move in the same direction against the dollar but not always by the same degree. Would borrowing euros to support the British joint venture result in more exposure to exchange rate risk than borrowing pounds? Would it result in more exposure to exchange rate risk than borrowing dollars?

CHAPTER 21

INTERNATIONAL CASH MANAGEMENT

THE TERM CASH MANAGEMENT can be broadly defined to mean optimization of cash flows and investment of excess cash. From an international perspective, cash management is very complex because laws pertaining to cross-border cash transfers differ among countries. In addition, exchange rate fluctuations can affect the value of cross-border cash transfers. Financial managers need to understand the advantages and disadvantages of investing cash in foreign markets so that they can make international cash management decisions that maximize the value of the MNC.

THE SPECIFIC OBJECTIVES OF THIS CHAPTER ARE TO:

- explain the difference in analyzing cash flows from a subsidiary perspective and from a parent perspective,

- explain the various techniques used to optimize cash flows,

- explain common complications in optimizing cash flows, and

- explain the potential benefits and risks from foreign investing.

CASH FLOW ANALYSIS: SUBSIDIARY PERSPECTIVE

The management of working capital (such as inventory, accounts receivable and payable – debtors and creditors – and cash) has a direct influence on the amount and timing of cash flows. Working capital management and the management of cash flow are integrated. First, we discuss these elements before focusing on cash management.

Subsidiary expenses

Begin with outflow payments by the subsidiary to purchase raw materials or supplies. The subsidiary will normally have a more difficult time forecasting future outflow payments if its purchases are international rather than domestic because of exchange rate fluctuations. In addition, there is a possibility that payments will be substantially higher due to appreciation of the invoice currency. Consequently, the firm may wish to maintain a large inventory of supplies and raw materials so that it can draw from its inventory and cut down on purchases if the invoice currency appreciates. Still another possibility is that imported goods from another country could be restricted by the host government (through quotas, etc.). In this event, a larger inventory would give a firm more time to search for alternative sources of supplies or raw materials. A subsidiary with domestic supply sources would not experience such a problem and therefore would not need such a large inventory.

Outflow payments for supplies will be influenced by future sales. If the sales volume is substantially influenced by exchange rate fluctuations, its future level becomes more uncertain, which makes its need for supplies more uncertain. Such uncertainty may force the subsidiary to maintain larger cash balances to cover any unexpected increase in supply requirements.

Subsidiary revenue

If subsidiaries export their products, their sales volume may be more volatile than if the goods were only sold domestically. This volatility could be due to the fluctuating exchange rate of the invoice currency. Importers' demand for these finished goods will most likely decrease if the invoice currency appreciates. The sales volume of exports is also susceptible to business cycles of the importing countries. If the goods were sold domestically, the exchange rate fluctuations would not have a direct impact on sales, although they would still have an indirect impact since the fluctuations would influence prices paid by local customers for imports from foreign competitors.

Sales can often be increased when credit standards are relaxed. However, it is important to focus on cash inflows due to sales rather than on sales themselves. Looser credit standards may cause a slowdown in cash inflows from sales, which could offset the benefits of increased sales. Accounts receivable management is an important part of the subsidiary's working capital management because of its potential impact on cash inflows.

Subsidiary dividend payments

The subsidiary may be expected to periodically send dividend payments and other fees to the parent. These fees could represent royalties or charges for overhead costs incurred by the parent that benefit the subsidiary. An example is research and development costs incurred by the parent, which improve the quality of goods produced by the subsidiary. Whatever the reason, payments by the subsidiary to the parent are often necessary. When dividend payments and fees are known in advance and denominated in the subsidiary's currency, forecasting cash flows is easier for the subsidiary. The level of dividends paid by subsidiaries to the parent is dependent on the liquidity needs of each subsidiary, potential uses of funds at various subsidiary locations, expected movements in the currencies of the subsidiaries, and regulations of the host country government.

Subsidiary liquidity management

After accounting for all outflow and inflow payments, the subsidiary will find itself with either excess or deficient cash. It uses liquidity management to either invest its excess cash or borrow to cover its cash deficiencies. If it anticipates a cash deficiency, short-term financing is necessary, as described in the previous chapter. If it anticipates excess cash, it must determine how the excess cash should be used. Investing in foreign currencies can sometimes be attractive, but exchange rate risk makes the effective yield uncertain. This issue is discussed later in this chapter.

Liquidity management is a crucial component of a subsidiary's working capital management. Subsidiaries commonly have access to numerous lines of credit and overdraft facilities in various currencies. Therefore, they may maintain adequate liquidity without substantial cash balances. While liquidity is important for the overall MNC, it cannot be properly measured by liquidity ratios. Potential access to funds is more relevant than cash on hand.

CENTRALIZED CASH MANAGEMENT

Each subsidiary should manage its working capital by simultaneously considering all of the points discussed thus far. Often, though, each subsidiary is more concerned with its own operations than with the overall operations of the MNC. Thus, a **centralized cash management** group may need to monitor, and possibly manage, the parent–subsidiary and intersubsidiary cash flows. This role is critical since it can often benefit individual subsidiaries in need of funds or overly exposed to exchange rate risk.

EXAMPLE

The treasury department of Kraft Foods is centralized to manage liquidity, funding, and foreign exchange requirements of its global operations. And Monsanto has a centralized system for pooling different currency balances from various subsidiaries in Asia that saves hundreds of thousands of dollars per year.

Exhibit 21.1 is a complement to the following discussion of cash flow management. It is a simplified cash flow diagram for an MNC with two subsidiaries in different countries. Although each MNC may handle its payments in a different manner, Exhibit 21.1 is based on simplified assumptions that will help illustrate some key concepts of international cash management. The exhibit reflects the assumption that the two subsidiaries periodically send loan repayments and dividends to the parent or send excess cash to the parent (where the centralized cash management process is assumed to take place). These cash flows represent the incoming cash to the parent from the subsidiaries. The parent's cash outflows to the subsidiaries can include loans and the return of cash previously invested by the subsidiaries. The subsidiaries also have cash flows between themselves because they purchase supplies from each other.

While each subsidiary is managing its working capital, there is a need to monitor and manage the cash flows between the parent and the subsidiaries, as well as between the individual subsidiaries. This task of international cash management should be delegated

Exhibit 21.1 Cash flow of the overall MNC

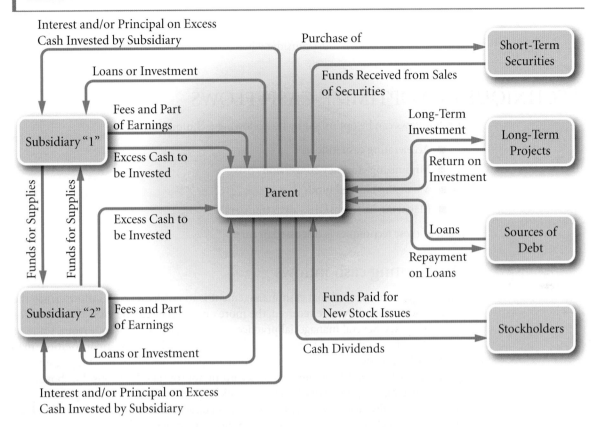

to a centralized cash management group. International cash management can be segmented into two functions: (1) optimizing cash flow movements, and (2) investing excess cash. These two functions are discussed in turn.

The centralized cash management division of an MNC cannot always accurately forecast events that affect parent–subsidiary or intersubsidiary cash flows. It should, however,

<hr>

MANAGING FOR VALUE
Flexsys's decision to use a multibank payments system

Flexsys is a large chemical company with more than 20 subsidiaries in Europe, the United States, and Asia. To improve its liquidity, it wanted to create a system that would enable its treasury department to continuously monitor all payments at each subsidiary. Since the inception of the euro, Flexsys has had euro balances at several subsidiaries and consolidates these balances so that it can maximize the interest earned on the balances. It uses technology that allows all payments due to be recorded and transmitted to the treasury department. The treasury nets all payments due between subsidiaries so that only net payments need to be made to cover the payments due

between subsidiaries. Flexsys' system is especially effective because it is "transparent", meaning that the payments due at each subsidiary can be easily monitored by the subsidiaries.

Flexsys uses multiple banks rather than branches of a single bank so that each subsidiary can use the bank it prefers. Having a multibank system complicates the reporting of payments, but allows each subsidiary to choose the bank that provides it with the best service. Thus, Flexsys' decision to use a multibank system can ensure optimal service at its subsidiaries. At the same time, however, its centralized payments network ensures that cash is utilized properly so that it can maximize its value.

be ready to react to any event by considering: (1) any potential adverse impact on cash flows, and (2) how to avoid such an adverse impact. If the cash flow situation between the parent and subsidiaries results in a cash squeeze on the parent, it should have sources of funds (credit lines) available. On the other hand, if it has excess cash after considering all outflow payments, it must consider where to invest funds. This decision is thoroughly examined shortly.

TECHNIQUES TO OPTIMIZE CASH FLOWS

Cash inflows can be optimized by the following techniques:

- Accelerating cash inflows
- Minimizing currency conversion costs
- Managing blocked funds
- Managing intersubsidiary cash transfers

Each of these techniques is discussed in turn.

Accelerating cash inflows

The first goal in international cash management is to accelerate cash inflows, since the more quickly the inflows are received, the more quickly they can be invested or used for other purposes. Several managerial practices are advocated for this endeavour, some of which may be implemented by the individual subsidiaries. First, a corporation may establish **lockboxes** around the world, which are post office boxes to which customers are instructed to send payment. When set up in appropriate locations, lockboxes can help reduce mailing time (**mail float**). A bank usually processes incoming checks at a lockbox on a daily basis. Second, cash inflows can be accelerated by using **preauthorized payments**, which allow a corporation to charge a customer's bank account up to some limit. Both preauthorized payments and lockboxes are also used in a domestic setting. Because international transactions may have a relatively long mailing time, these methods of accelerating cash inflows can be quite valuable for an MNC.

Minimizing currency conversion costs

Another technique for optimizing cash flow movements, **netting**, can be implemented with the joint effort of subsidiaries or by the centralized cash management group. This technique optimizes cash flows by reducing the administrative and transaction costs that result from currency conversion.

EXAMPLE

Mount plc has subsidiaries located in France and in Hungary. Whenever the French subsidiary needs to purchase supplies from the Hungarian subsidiary, it needs to convert euros into Hungary's currency (the forint) to make payment. Hungary's subsidiary must convert its forint into euros when purchasing supplies from the French subsidiary. Mount plc has instructed both subsidiaries to net their transactions on a monthly basis so that only one net payment is made at the end of each month. By using this approach, both subsidiaries avoid (or at least reduce) the transaction costs of currency conversion.

Over time, netting has become increasingly popular because it offers several key benefits. First, it reduces the number of cross-border transactions between subsidiaries, thereby reducing the overall administrative cost of such cash transfers. Second, it reduces the need for foreign exchange conversion since transactions occur less frequently, thereby reducing the transaction costs associated with foreign exchange conversion. Third, the netting process imposes tight control over information on transactions between subsidiaries. Thus, all subsidiaries engage in a more coordinated effort to accurately report and settle their various accounts. Finally, cash flow forecasting is easier since only net cash transfers are made at the end of each period, rather than individual cash transfers throughout the period. Improved cash flow forecasting can enhance financing and investment decisions.

A **bilateral netting system** involves transactions between two units: between the parent and a subsidiary, or between two subsidiaries. A **multilateral netting system** usually involves a more complex interchange among the parent and several subsidiaries. For most large MNCs, a multilateral netting system would be necessary to effectively reduce administrative and currency conversion costs. Such a system is normally centralized so that all necessary information is consolidated. From the consolidated cash flow information, net cash flow positions for each pair of units (subsidiaries, or whatever) are determined, and the actual reconciliation at the end of each period can be dictated. The centralized group may even maintain inventories of various currencies so that currency conversions for the end-of-period net payments can be completed without significant transaction costs.

MNCs commonly monitor the cash flows between their subsidiaries with the use of an intersubsidiary payments matrix.

EXAMPLE

Exhibit 21.2 (a) is an example of an intersubsidiary payments matrix that totals each subsidiary's individual payments to each of the other subsidiaries. The first row indicates that the Canadian subsidiary owes the equivalent of £40,000 to the French subsidiary, the equivalent of £90,000 to the Japanese subsidiary, and so on. During this same period, these subsidiaries have also received goods from the Canadian subsidiary, for which payment is due. The second column (under Canada) shows that the Canadian subsidiary is owed the equivalent of £60,000 by the French subsidiary, the equivalent of £100,000 by the Japanese subsidiary, and so on.

Since subsidiaries owe each other, the first step is to charge only the net amounts between each other as illustrated in 21.2 (b) and (c). Since the Canadian subsidiary owes the French subsidiary the equivalent of £40,000 but is owed the equivalent of £60,000 by the French subsidiary, the net payment required is the equivalent of £20,000 from the French subsidiary to the Canadian subsidiary. This is known as bilateral netting.

Exhibit 21.2 (a) Intersubsidiary payments matrix

Payments OWED BY Subsidiary Located in:	British pound Value (in Thousands) OWED TO Subsidiary Located in:				
	Canada	*France*	*Japan*	*Switzerland*	*UK*
Canada	—	40	90	20	40
France	60	—	30	60	50
Japan	100	30	—	20	30
Switzerland	10	50	10	—	50
UK	10	60	20	20	—

Exhibit 21.2 (b)   Bilateral netting (arrows show the example of Canada)

Payments OWED BY Subsidiary Located in:	British pound Value (in Thousands) OWED TO Subsidiary Located in:				
	Canada	France	Japan	Switzerland	UK
Canada	—	40	90	20	40
France	60	—	30	60	50
Japan	100	30	—	20	30
Switzerland	10	50	10	—	50
UK	10	60	20	20	—

Exhibit 21.2 (c)   Bilateral netting – the net position (arrows show the example of Canada)

Payments OWED BY Subsidiary Located in:	British pound Value (in Thousands) OWED TO Subsidiary Located in:				
	Canada	France	Japan	Switzerland	UK
Canada	—	0	0	10	30
France	20	—	0	10	0
Japan	10	0	—	10	10
Switzerland	0	0	0	—	30
UK	0	10	0	0	—

Exhibit 21.3   Multilateral netting schedule

Payments OWED BY Subsidiary Located in:	British pound Value (in Thousands) OWED TO Subsidiary Located in:					Total owed by:	Net payments by:
	Canada	France	Japan	Switzerland	UK		
Canada	—	0	0	10	30	40	10
France	20	—	0	10	0	30	20
Japan	10	0	—	10	10	30	30
Switzerland	0	0	0	—	30	30	0
UK	0	10	0	0	—	10	0
Total owed to:	30	10	0	30	70		
Net owed to:	0	0	0	0	60		60

Further economies can be made through multilateral netting (Exhibit 21.3). Canada owes £40,000 in total and is owed £30,000 in total and therefore can clear net indebtedness by paying £10,000. The Canadian subsidiary would not be especially concerned as to which other subsidiary it paid the net indebtedness. Similarly, France owes a net amount of £20,000.

The only country owed money is the UK, so if Canada pays £10,000, France £20,000 and Switzerland £30,000 all to the UK, all debts will have been paid. Thus three payments will have accounted for a payments schedule that at the outset amounted to 20 payments! Note that the bilateral stage could be skipped by simply totalling the columns and rows in the original matrix and making the net payers pay the net receivers.

Managing blocked funds

Cash flows can also be affected by a host government's blockage of funds, which might occur if the government requires all funds to remain within the country in order to create jobs and reduce unemployment. To deal with funds blockage, the MNC may implement the same strategies used when a host country government imposes high taxes. To make efficient use of these funds, the MNC may instruct the subsidiary to set up a research and development division, which incurs costs and possibly generates revenues for other subsidiaries.

Another strategy is to use transfer pricing in a manner that will increase the expenses incurred by the subsidiary. A host country government is likely to be more lenient on funds sent to cover expenses than on earnings remitted to the parent. Most tax treaties require that transfer pricing be conducted at market rates. Therefore a policy of artificially inflated transfer prices resulting in subsidiaries in developing countries paying very high prices for "services" or "goods" from Head Office is of dubious legality and ethics.

When subsidiaries are restricted from transferring funds to the parent, the parent may instruct the subsidiary to obtain financing from a local bank rather than from the parent. By borrowing through a local intermediary, the subsidiary is assured that its earnings can be distributed to pay off previous financing. Overall, most methods of managing blocked funds are intended to make efficient use of the funds by using them to cover expenses that are transferred to that country.

EXAMPLE

Wittenberg GmbH a German-based MNC, has a subsidiary in the Philippines. During a turbulent period, the subsidiary was prevented from exchanging its Philippine pesos into euros to be sent home. Wittenberg held its corporate meeting in Manila so that it could use the pesos to pay the expenses of the meeting (hotel, food, etc.) in pesos. In this way, it was able to use local funds to cover an expense that it would have incurred anyway. Ordinarily, the corporate meeting would have been held in the parent's country, and the parent would have paid the expenses.

Managing intersubsidiary cash transfers

Proper management of cash flows can also be beneficial to a subsidiary in need of funds.

EXAMPLE

Essex ltd has two foreign subsidiaries called Short Sub and Long Sub. Short Sub needs funds, while Long Sub has excess funds. If Long Sub purchases supplies from Short Sub, it can provide financing by paying for its supplies earlier than necessary. This technique is often called leading. Alternatively, if Long Sub sells supplies to Short Sub, it can provide financing by allowing Short Sub to lag its payments. This technique is called lagging.

The leading or lagging strategy can make efficient use of cash and thereby reduce debt. Some host governments prohibit the practice by requiring that a payment between subsidiaries occur at the time the goods are transferred. Thus, an MNC needs to be aware of any laws that restrict the use of this strategy.

COMPLICATIONS IN OPTIMIZING CASH FLOW

Most complications encountered in optimizing cash flow can be classified into three categories:

- Company-related characteristics
- Government restrictions
- Characteristics of banking systems

Each complication is discussed in turn.

Company-related characteristics

In some cases, optimizing cash flow can become complicated due to characteristics of the MNC. If one of the subsidiaries delays payments to other subsidiaries for supplies received, the other subsidiaries may be forced to borrow until the payments arrive. A centralized approach that monitors all intersubsidiary payments should be able to minimize such problems.

Government restrictions

The existence of government restrictions can disrupt a cash flow optimization policy. Some governments prohibit the use of a netting system, as noted earlier. In addition, some countries periodically prevent cash from leaving the country, thereby preventing net payments from being made. These problems can arise even for MNCs that do not experience any company-related problems. Countries in Latin America commonly impose restrictions that affect an MNC's cash flows.

Characteristics of banking systems

The abilities of banks to facilitate cash transfers for MNCs vary among countries. Banks in the developed world are advanced in this field, but banks in some other countries do not offer services. MNCs prefer some form of zero-balance account, where excess funds can be used to make payments but earn interest until they are used. In addition, some MNCs benefit from the use of lockboxes. Such services are not available in some countries.

In addition, a bank may not update the MNC's bank account information sufficiently or provide a detailed breakdown of fees for banking services. Without full use of banking resources and information, the effectiveness of international cash management is limited. In addition, an MNC with subsidiaries in, say, eight different countries will typically be dealing with eight different banking systems. Much progress has been made in foreign banking systems in recent years. As time passes and a more uniform global banking system emerges, such problems may be alleviated.

INVESTING EXCESS CASH

Many MNCs have at least £100 million in cash balances across banks in various countries. If they can find a way to earn an extra 1% on those funds, they will generate an extra £1 million each year on cash balances of £100 million. Thus, their short-term investment decision affects the amount of their cash inflows. Their excess funds can be

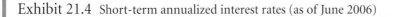

Exhibit 21.4 Short-term annualized interest rates (as of June 2006)

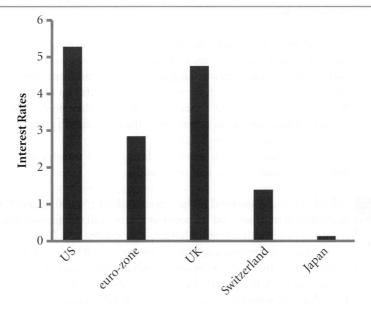

invested in domestic or foreign short-term securities. In some periods, foreign short-term securities will have higher interest rates than domestic interest rates. The differential can be substantial, as illustrated in Exhibit 21.4. However, firms must account for the possible exchange rate movements when assessing the potential yield on foreign investments.

How to invest excess cash

International money markets have grown to accommodate corporate investments of excess cash. MNCs may use international money markets in an attempt to earn higher returns than they can achieve domestically.

Eurocurrency deposits are one of the most commonly used international money market instruments. Many MNCs establish large deposits in various currencies in the eurocurrency market, with eurodollar deposits being the most popular. The dollar volume of eurodollar deposits has more than doubled since 1980. eurodollar deposits commonly offer MNCs a slightly higher yield than bank deposits in the United States. Though eurodollar deposits still dominate the market, the relative importance of non-dollar currencies has increased over time.

In addition to using the eurocurrency market, MNCs can also purchase foreign Treasury bills and commercial paper. Improved telecommunications systems have increased access to these securities in foreign markets and allow for a greater degree of integration among money markets in various countries.

Centralized cash management

An MNC's short-term investing policy can either maintain separate investments for all subsidiaries or employ a centralized approach. Recall that the function of optimizing cash flows can be improved by a centralized approach, since all subsidiary cash positions can be monitored simultaneously. With regard to the investing function, centralization allows for more efficient usage of funds and possibly higher returns. Here the term *centralized* means that excess cash from each subsidiary is pooled until it is needed by a particular subsidiary.

Centralization when subsidiaries use the same currency. To understand the advantages of a centralized system, consider that the rates paid on short-term investments such as bank deposits are often higher for larger amounts. Thus, if two subsidiaries have excess cash of £50,000 each for one month, the rates on their individual bank deposits may be lower than the rate they could obtain if they pooled their funds into a single £100,000 bank deposit. In this manner, the centralized (pooling) approach generates a higher rate of return on excess cash.

The centralized approach can also facilitate the transfer of funds from subsidiaries with excess funds to those that need funds.

EXAMPLE

Subsidiary A of Moorhead ltd has excess cash of £50,000 during the next month, while Subsidiary B of Moorhead ltd needs to borrow £50,000 for one month. If cash management is not centralized, Subsidiary A may use the £50,000 to purchase a one-month bank certificate earning, say, 10% (on an annualized basis). At the same time, Subsidiary B may borrow from a bank for one month at a rate of, say, 12%. The bank must charge a higher rate on loans than it offers on deposits. With a centralized approach, Subsidiary B can borrow Subsidiary A's excess funds, thereby reducing its financing costs.

Centralized cash management of multiple currencies. Centralized cash management is more complicated when the MNC uses multiple currencies. All excess funds could be pooled and converted to a single currency for investment purposes. However, the advantage of pooling may be offset by the transaction costs incurred when converting to a single currency.

Centralized cash management can still be valuable, though. The short-term cash available among subsidiaries can be pooled together so that there is a separate pool for each currency. Then excess cash in a particular currency can still be used to satisfy other subsidiary deficiencies in that currency. In this way, funds can be transferred from one subsidiary to another without incurring transaction costs that banks charge for exchanging currencies. This strategy is especially feasible when all subsidiary funds are deposited in branches of a single bank so that the funds can easily be transferred among subsidiaries.

Another possible function of centralized cash management is to invest funds in securities denominated in the foreign currencies that will be needed by the subsidiaries in the future. MNCs can use excess cash to invest cash in international money market instruments so that they can cover any payables positions in specific foreign currencies. If they have payables in foreign currencies that are expected to appreciate, they can cover such positions by creating short-term deposits in those currencies. The maturity of a deposit would ideally coincide with the date at which the funds are needed.

Impact of technology on centralized cash management. International cash management requires timely information across subsidiaries regarding each subsidiary's cash positions in each currency, along with interest rate information about each currency. A centralized cash management system needs a continual flow of information about currency positions so that it can determine whether one subsidiary's shortage of cash can be covered by another subsidiary's excess cash in that currency. Given the major improvements in online technology in recent years, all MNCs can easily and efficiently create a multinational communications network among their subsidiaries to ensure that information about cash positions is continually updated.

EXAMPLE

To understand how such a communications network works, consider Jax plc which creates a cash balances website that specifies the cash balance of every currency for each subsidiary. Near the end of each day, each subsidiary revises the website to provide the latest update of its cash balance for each currency. Each subsidiary also specifies the period of time in which the excess or deficiency will persist. The parent's treasury department monitors the updated data and determines whether any cash needs identified by a subsidiary in a particular currency can be accommodated by another subsidiary that has excess cash in that same currency. The treasury department then e-mails instructions to the subsidiaries about fund transfers. If it notices that the Canadian subsidiary has an excess of Canadian dollars for the next 26 days, and the Belgian subsidiary needs Canadian dollars tomorrow (but will have inflows of Canadian dollars in 17 days), it provides the following instructions: "The Canadian subsidiary should transfer C$60,000 to the Belgian subsidiary and will be repaid by the Belgian subsidiary in 17 days". The fund transfers are essentially short-term loans, so a subsidiary that borrows funds will repay them with interest. The interest charged on a loan creates an incentive for subsidiaries to make their excess cash available and an incentive for subsidiaries with cash deficiencies to return the funds as soon as possible.

The electronic communications network may be more sophisticated than the one described here, but this description illustrates how easy it is for an MNC's parent to continuously monitor the cash balances of each subsidiary and communicate instructions among subsidiaries. The process of transferring funds among subsidiaries may be especially easy when all the MNC's subsidiaries use branches of the same bank. A communications network allows the MNC to make the best use of each subsidiary's cash, which can reduce the amount of external financing needed and reduce the MNC's exchange rate risk.

Determining the effective yield

Firms commonly consider investing in a deposit denominated in a currency with a high interest rate and then converting the funds back to dollars when the deposit matures. This strategy will not necessarily be feasible, since the currency denominating the deposit may depreciate over the life of the deposit. If it does, the advantage of a higher interest rate may be more than offset by the depreciation in the currency representing the deposit.

Consequently, it is the deposit's **effective yield**, not its interest rate, that is most important to the cash manager. The effective yield of a bank deposit considers both the interest rate and the rate of appreciation (or depreciation) of the currency denominating the deposit and can therefore be very different from the quoted interest rate on a deposit denominated in a foreign currency. An example follows to illustrate this point.

EXAMPLE

Quant plc a large UK corporation with £1,000,000 in excess cash, could invest in a one-year deposit at 6% but is attracted to higher interest rates in Australia. It creates a one-year deposit denominated in Australian dollars (A$) at 9%. The exchange rate of the Australian dollar at the time of the deposit is £0.45. The British pounds are first converted to A$2,222,222 (since £1,000,000/£0.45 = $2,222,222) and then deposited in a bank.

One year later, Quant receives A\$2,422,222, which is equal to the initial deposit plus 9% interest on the deposit. At this time, Quant plc has no use for Australian dollars and converts them into pounds. Assume that the exchange rate at this time is £0.48. The funds will convert to £1,162,667 (computed as A\$2,422,222 × £0.48 per A\$). Thus, the yield on this investment is:

$$\frac{£1,162,667 - £1,000,000}{£1,000,000} = 0.1627 \text{ or } 16.27\%$$

The high yield is attributed to the relatively high interest rate earned on the deposit, plus the appreciation in the currency denominating the deposit over the investment period.

If the currency had depreciated over the investment period, however, the effective yield to Quant plc would have been less than the interest rate on the deposit and could even have been lower than the interest rate available on UK investments. For example, if the Australian dollar had *depreciated* from £0.45 at the beginning of the investment period to £0.43 by the end of the investment period, Quant plc would have received £1,041,555 (computed as A\$2,422,222 × £0.43 per A\$). In this case, the yield on the investment to the UK company would have been:

$$\frac{£1,041,555 - £1,000,000}{£1,000,000} = 0.0416 \text{ or } 4.16\%$$

The preceeding example illustrates how appreciation of the currency denominating a foreign deposit over the deposit period will force the effective yield to be above the quoted interest rate. Conversely, depreciation will create the opposite effect.

The previous computation of the effective yield on foreign deposits was conducted in a real world setting. A quicker method is shown here:

$$r = (1 + i_f)(1 + e_f) - 1$$

The effective yield on the foreign deposit is represented by r (for simpler notation the r_{eff} from the previous chapter has been dropped here), i_f is the quoted interest rate, and e_f is the percentage change (from the day of deposit to the day of withdrawal) in the value of the currency representing the foreign deposit. The term i_f was used in Chapter 20 to represent the interest rate when borrowing a foreign currency. In this chapter, the interest rate of concern is the deposit rate on the foreign currency.

EXAMPLE

Given the information for Quant plc, the effective yield on the Australian deposit can be estimated. The term e_f represents the percentage change in the Australian dollar (against the pound) from the date Australian dollars are purchased (and deposited) until the day they are withdrawn (and converted back to pounds). The Australian dollar appreciated from £0.45 to £0.48, or by 6.66% over the life of the deposit. Using this information as well as the quoted deposit rate of 9%, the effective yield to the UK firm on this deposit denominated in Australian dollars is:

$$
\begin{aligned}
r &= (1 + i_f)(1 + e_f) - 1 \\
&= (1 + 0.09)(1 + 0.0666) \\
&= 0.1627 \text{ or } 16.27\%
\end{aligned}
$$

This estimate of the effective yield corresponds with the return on investment determined earlier for Quant plc.

If the currency had depreciated, Quant plc would have earned an effective yield that was less than the interest rate.

In the revised example for Quant plc the Australian dollar depreciated from £0.45 to £0.43, or by 4.44%. Based on the quoted interest rate of 9% and the depreciation of 4.44%, the effective yield is:

$$r = (1+i_f)(1+e_f)-1$$
$$= (1+0.09)(1+-0.0444)$$
$$= 0.0416 \text{ or } 4.16\%$$

which is the same rate computed earlier for this revised example.

The effective yield can be negative if the currency denominating the deposit depreciates to an extent that more than offsets the interest accrued from the deposit.

Northampton ltd invests in a bank deposit denominated in euros that provides a yield of 9%. The euro depreciates against the dollar by 12% over the one-year period. The effective yield is:

$$r = (1+i_f)(1+e_f)-1$$
$$= (1+0.09)(1+-0.12)$$
$$= 0.0408 \text{ or } -4.08\%$$

This result indicates that Northamption will end up with 4.08% less in funds than it initially deposited.

As with bank deposits, the effective yield on all other securities denominated in a foreign currency is influenced by the fluctuation of that currency's exchange rate. Our discussion will continue to focus on bank deposits for short-term foreign investment, but the implications of the discussion can be applied to other short-term securities as well.

Implications of interest rate parity

Recall that covered interest arbitrage is described as a short-term foreign investment with a simultaneous forward sale of the foreign currency denominating the foreign investment. One might think that a foreign currency with a high interest rate would be an ideal candidate for covered interest arbitrage. However, such a currency will normally exhibit a forward discount that reflects the differential between its interest rate and the investor's home interest rate. This relationship is based on the theory of interest rate parity. Investors cannot lock in a higher return when attempting covered interest arbitrage if interest rate parity exists.

Even if interest rate parity does exist, short-term foreign investing may still be feasible but would have to be conducted on an uncovered basis (without use of the forward market). That is, short-term foreign investing may result in a higher effective yield than domestic investing, but it cannot be guaranteed.

Use of the forward rate as a forecast

If interest rate parity exists, the forward rate serves as a break-even point to assess the short-term investment decision. When investing in the foreign currency (and not covering the foreign currency position), the effective yield will be more than the domestic yield if the spot rate of the foreign currency after one year is more than the forward rate at the time the investment is undertaken. Conversely, the yield of a foreign investment will be lower than the domestic yield if the spot rate of the foreign currency after one year turns out to be less than the forward rate at the time the investment is undertaken.

Relationship with the international Fisher effect. When interest rate parity exists, MNCs in the UK that use the forward rate as a predictor of the future spot rate expect the yield on foreign deposits to equal that on UK deposits. Though the forward rate is not necessarily an accurate predictor, it may provide unbiased forecasts of the future spot rate. If the forward rate is unbiased, it does not consistently underestimate or overestimate the future spot rate with equal frequency. Thus, the effective yield on foreign deposits is equal to the domestic yield, on average. MNCs that consistently invest in foreign short-term securities would earn a yield similar on average to what they could earn on domestic securities.

Our discussion here is closely related to the international Fisher effect (IFE). Recall that the IFE suggests that the exchange rate of a foreign currency is expected to change by an amount reflecting the differential between its interest rate and the UK interest rate. The rationale behind this theory is that a high nominal interest rate reflects an expectation of high inflation, which could weaken the currency (according to purchasing power parity).

If interest rate parity exists, the forward premium or discount reflects that interest rate differential and represents the expected percentage change in the currency's value when the forward rate is used as a predictor of the future spot rate. The IFE suggests that firms cannot consistently earn short-term yields on foreign securities that are higher than those on domestic securities because the exchange rate is expected to adjust to the interest rate differential on average. If interest rate parity holds and the forward rate is an unbiased predictor of the future spot rate, we can expect the IFE to hold.

A look back in time reveals that the IFE is supported for some currencies in some periods. Moreover, it may be difficult for an MNC to anticipate when the IFE will hold and when it will not. For virtually any currency, it is possible to identify previous periods when the forward rate substantially underestimated the future spot rate, and an MNC

Exhibit 21.5 Considerations when investing excess cash	
Scenario	**Implications for Investing in Foreign Money Markets**
1. Interest rate parity exists.	Covered interest arbitrage is not worthwhile.
2. Interest rate parity exists, and the forward rate is an accurate forecast of the future spot rate.	An uncovered investment in a foreign security is not worthwhile.
3. Interest rate parity exists, and the forward rate is an unbiased forecast of the future spot rate.	An uncovered investment in a foreign security will on average earn an effective yield similar to an investment in a domestic security.
4. Interest rate parity exists, and the forward rate is expected to overestimate the future spot rate.	An uncovered investment in a foreign security is expected to earn a lower effective yield than an investment in a domestic security.
5. Interest rate parity exists, and the forward rate is expected to underestimate the future spot rate.	An uncovered investment in a foreign security is expected to earn a higher effective yield than an investment in a domestic security.
6. Interest rate parity does not exist; the forward premium (discount) exceeds (is less than) the interest rate differential.	Covered interest arbitrage is feasible for investors residing in the home country.
7. Interest rate parity does not exist; the forward premium (discount) is less than (exceeds) the interest rate differential.	Covered interest arbitrage is feasible for foreign investors but not for investors residing in the home country.

would have earned very high returns from investing short-term funds in a foreign money market security. However, it is also possible to identify other periods when the forward rate substantially overestimated the future spot rate, and the MNC would have earned low or even negative returns from investing in that same foreign money market security.

Conclusions about the forward rate. The key implications of interest rate parity and the forward rate as a predictor of future spot rates for foreign investing are summarized in Exhibit 21.5. This exhibit explains the conditions in which investment in foreign short-term securities is feasible.

Use of exchange rate forecasts

Although MNCs do not know how a currency's value will change over the investment horizon, they can use the formula for the effective yield provided earlier in this chapter and plug in their forecast for the percentage change in the foreign currency's exchange rate (e_f). Since the interest rate of the foreign currency deposit (i_f) is known, the effective yield can be forecasted given a forecast of e_f. This projected effective yield on a foreign deposit can then be compared with the yield when investing in the firm's local currency.

EXAMPLE

Latrobe SA is a French firm with funds available to invest for one year. It is aware that the one-year interest rate on a euro deposit is 11% and the interest rate on an Australian deposit is 14%. Assume that the French firm forecasts that the Australian deposit will depreciate from its current rate of 0.60 euros to 0.594 euros, or a 1% decrease. The expected value for e_f [$E(e_f)$] will therefore be −1%. Thus, the expected effective yield [$E(r)$] on an Australian dollar-denominated deposit is:

$$E(r) = (1+i_f)(1+E(e_f))-1$$
$$= (1+0.14)(1+-0.01)$$
$$= 0.1286 \text{ or } 12.86\%$$

Thus, this example, investing in an Australian dollar deposit is expected to be more rewarding than investing in a euro denominated deposit.

Keep in mind that the value for e_f is forecasted and therefore is not known with certainty. Thus, there is no guarantee that foreign investing will truly be more lucrative.

Deriving the value of e_f that equates foreign and domestic yields. From the preceding example, Latrobe may attempt to at least determine what value of e_f would make the effective yield from foreign investing the same as that from investing in a euro deposit. To determine this value, begin with the effective yield formula and solve for e_f as follows:

$$r = (1+i_f)(1+e_f)-1$$

$$(1+r) = (1+i_f)(1+e_f)$$

$$(1+e_f) = \frac{(1\_r)}{(1+i_f)}$$

$$e_f = \frac{(1+r)}{(1+i_f)} - 1$$

Since the euro deposit rate was 11% in our previous example, that is the rate to be plugged in for r. We can also plug in 14% for i_f, so the break-even value of e_f would be:

$$e_f = \frac{(1+r)}{(1+i_f)} - 1$$

$$= \frac{(1+0.11)}{(1+0.14)} - 1$$

$$= -2.63\%$$

This suggests that the Australian dollar must depreciate by about 2.63% to make the Australian dollar deposit generate the same effective yield as a deposit in euros. With any smaller degree of depreciation, the Australian dollar deposit would be more rewarding. Latrobe SA can use this information when determining whether to invest in a euro or Australian dollar deposit. If it expects the Australian dollar to depreciate by more than 2.63% over the deposit period, it will prefer investing in euros. If it expects the Australian dollar to depreciate by less than 2.63%, or to appreciate, its decision is more complex. If the potential reward from investing in the foreign currency outweighs the risk involved, then the firm should choose that route. The final decision here will be influenced by the firm's degree of risk aversion.

Use of probability distributions. Since even expert forecasts are not always accurate, it is sometimes useful to develop a probability distribution instead of relying on a single prediction. An example of how a probability distribution is applied follows.

EXAMPLE

Opera ltd (UK) is deciding whether to invest in Australian dollars for one year. It finds that the quoted interest rate for the Australian dollar is 14%, and the quoted interest rate for a pound deposit is 11%. It then develops a probability distribution for the Australian dollar's possible percentage change in value over the life of the deposit.

The probability distribution is displayed in Exhibit 21.6. From the first row in the exhibit, we see that there is a 5% probability of a 10% depreciation in the Australian dollar over the deposit's life. If the Australian dollar does depreciate by 10%, the effective yield will be 2.60%. This indicates that there is a 5% probability that Opera ltd will earn

Exhibit 21.6   Analysis of investing in a foreign currency

Possible rate of change in the Australian dollar over the life of the investment (e_f)	Probability of occurrence	Effective yield if this rate of change in the Australian dollar does occur (combining the 14% interest rate with the change in the value of the currency)
−10%	5%	(1.14) [1 + (−0.10)] − 1 = 0.0260, or 2.60%
−8	10	(1.14) [1 + (−0.08)] − 1 = 0.0488, or 4.88%
−4	15	(1.14) [1 + (−0.04)] − 1 = 0.0944, or 9.44%
−2	20	(1.14) [1 + (−0.02)] − 1 = 0.1172, or 11.72%
+1	20	(1.14) [1 + (0.01)] − 1 = 0.1514, or 15.14%
+2	15	(1.14) [1 + (0.02)] − 1 = 0.1628, or 16.28%
+3	10	(1.14) [1 + (0.03)] − 1 = 0.1742, or 17.42%
+4	5	(1.14) [1 + (0.04)] − 1 = 0.1856, or 18.56%
	100%	

a 2.60% effective yield on its funds. From the second row in the exhibit, there is a 10% probability of an 8% depreciation in the Australian dollar over the deposit period. If the Australian dollar does depreciate by 8%, the effective yield will be 4.88%, which means there is a 10% probability that Opera will generate a 4.88% effective yield on this deposit.

For each possible percentage change in the Australian dollar's value, there is a corresponding effective yield. Each possible effective yield (third column) is associated with a probability of that yield occurring (second column). An *expected value* of the effective yield of the Australian dollar is derived by multiplying each possible effective yield by its corresponding probability. Based on the information in Exhibit 21.6, the expected value of the effective yield, referred to as $E(r)$, is computed this way:

$$
\begin{aligned}
E(r) &= 5\%\,(2.60\%) + 10\%\,(4.88\%) + 15\%\,(9.44\%) + 20\%\,(11.72\%) + 20\% \\
&\quad (15.14\%) + 15\%\,(16.28\%) + 10\%\,(17.42\%) + 5\%\,(18.56\%) \\
&= 0.13\% + 0.488\% + 1.416\% + 2.344\% + 3.028\% + 2.422\% + 1.742\% + \\
&\quad 0.928\% \\
&= 12.518\%
\end{aligned}
$$

Thus, the expected value of the effective yield when investing in Australian dollars is approximately 12.5%.

To further assess the question of which currency to invest in, the information in the second and third columns from Exhibit 21.6 is used to develop a probability distribution in Exhibit 21.7, which illustrates the probability of each possible effective yield that may occur if Opera ltd invests in Australian dollars. Notice that the UK interest rate (11%) is known with certainty and is included in Exhibit 21.7 for comparison purposes. A comparison of the Australian dollar's probability distribution against the UK interest rate suggests that there is a 30% probability that the UK rate will be more than the effective yield from investing in Australian dollars and a 70% chance that it will be less.

If Opera ltd invests in a British pound deposit, it knows with certainty the yield it will earn from its investment. If it invests in Australian dollars, its risk is the 5% chance

Exhibit 21.7 Probability distribution of effective yields

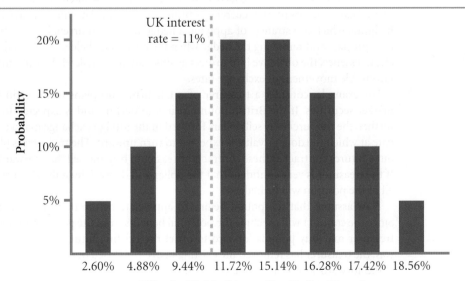

(probability) that the effective yield on the Australian dollar deposit will be 2.60%, or the 10% chance that the effective yield on the Australian dollar deposit will be 4.88%, or the 15% chance that the effective yield on Australian dollars will be 9.44%. Each of these possibilities represents a lower return to Opera ltd than what it would have earned had it invested in a UK deposit. Opera ltd concludes that the potential return on the Australian deposit is not high enough to compensate for the risk and decides to invest in the UK deposit.

Diversifying cash across currencies

Because an MNC is not sure how exchange rates will change over time, it may prefer to diversify cash among securities denominated in different currencies. Limiting the percentage of excess cash invested in each currency will reduce the MNC's exposure to exchange rate risk.

The degree to which a portfolio of investments denominated in various currencies will reduce risk depends on the currency correlations. Ideally, the currencies represented within the portfolio will exhibit low or negative correlations with each other. When currencies are likely to be affected by the same underlying event, their movements tend to be more highly correlated, and diversification among these types of currencies does not substantially reduce exposure to exchange rate risk.

EXAMPLE

In 1997, the interest rates in most Asian countries were higher than the interest rate in the United Kingdom. However, Asian currencies, such as the Indonesian rupiah, the Malaysian ringgit, the South Korean won, and the Thailand baht, depreciated by more than 50% against the pound in less than one year. Consequently, subsidiaries based outside Asia that attempted to benefit from the high Asian interest rates earned negative effective yields on their investments, so they received less than what they initially invested. Diversification of cash among these currencies was not beneficial in this case because all of the currencies weakened in response to the Asian crisis.

Dynamic hedging

Some MNCs continually adjust their short-term positions in currencies in response to revised expectations of each currency's future movement. They may engage in **dynamic hedging**, which is a strategy of applying a hedge when the currencies held are expected to depreciate and removing the hedge when the currencies held are expected to appreciate. In essence, the objective is to protect against downside risk while benefiting from the favourable movement of exchange rates.

For example, consider a treasurer of a UK firm who plans to invest in US money market securities. If the British pound begins to decline and is expected to depreciate further, the treasurer may sell dollars forward in the foreign exchange market for a future date at which the dollar's value is expected to turn upward. The treasurer is likely to take out a futures contract as these contracts are easier to buy and sell than forward contracts. If the treasurer is very confident that the dollar will depreciate in the short run, most or all of the position will be hedged.

Now assume that the pound begins to appreciate before the futures contract date. Since the contract will preclude the potential benefits from the pound's appreciation, the treasurer may buy pounds forward to offset the existing futures sale contracts. In this way, the treasurer has removed the existing hedge (or closed out the position). Of course, if the forward rate at the time of the futures purchase exceeds the forward rate that existed at the time of the futures sale, a cost is incurred to offset the hedge.

The treasurer may decide to remove only part of the hedge, offsetting only some of the existing futures sales with futures purchases. With this approach, the position is still partially protected if the pound depreciates further. Overall, the performance from using dynamic hedging is dependent on the treasurer's ability to forecast the direction of exchange rate movements.

SUMMARY

■ Each subsidiary of an MNC can assess its cash flows by estimating expected cash inflows and outflows to forecast its balance in each currency. This will indicate whether it will have excess cash to invest or a cash deficiency. The MNC's parent may prefer to use a centralized perspective, which consolidates the cash flow positions of all subsidiaries. In this way, funds can be transferred among subsidiaries to accommodate cash deficiencies at particular subsidiaries.

■ The common techniques to optimize cash flows are: (1) accelerating cash inflows, (2) minimizing currency conversion costs, (3) managing blocked funds, and (4) implementing intersubsidiary cash transfers.

■ The efforts by MNCs to optimize cash flows are complicated by: (1) company-related characteristics, (2) government restrictions, and (3) characteristics of banking systems.

■ MNCs can possibly achieve higher returns when investing excess cash in foreign currencies that either have relatively high interest rates or may appreciate over the investment period. If the foreign currency depreciates over the investment period, however, this may offset any interest rate advantage of that currency.

CRITICAL DEBATE

Should an MNC's subsidiaries operate their own cash management policies?

Proposition. Yes. Ultimately cash management means that everything is controlled from the centre. Different countries and indeed different products have very different working capital requirements. Centralization could easily lead to poor working capital management and cash flow difficulties.

Opposing view. No. Trade between subsidiaries accounts for about a large percentage of world exports,

there has to be coordination between subsidiaries, also customers can be MNC's so coordination is also required in debt collection. Also, there are considerable exchange rate savings to be made.

With whom do you agree? Think carefully about the arguments for and against allowing subsidiaries to manage their own cash. What are the problems with each of the arguments? Is there a solution that avoids the main drawbacks?

SELF TEST

Answers are provided in Appendix A at the back of the text.

1. Country X typically has a high interest rate, and its currency is expected to strengthen against the pound over time. Country Y typically has a low interest rate, and its currency is expected to weaken against the pound over time. Both countries have imposed a "blocked funds" restriction over the

next four years on the two subsidiaries owned by a UK firm. Which subsidiary will be more adversely affected by the blocked funds, assuming that there are limited opportunities for corporate expansion in both countries?

2. Assume that the Australian one-year interest rate is 14%. Also assume that the Australian dollar is expected to appreciate by 8% over the next year

against the British pound. What is the expected effective yield on a one-year deposit in Australia by a UK firm?

3. Assume that the one-year forward rate is used as the forecast of the future spot rate. The Malaysian ringgit's spot rate is £0.12, while its one-year forward rate is £0.11. The Malaysian one-year interest rate is 11%. What is the expected effective yield on a one-year deposit in Malaysia by a UK firm?

4. Assume that the Venezuelan one-year interest rate is 90%, while the UK one-year interest rate is 6%. Determine the break-even value for the percentage change in Venezuela's currency (the bolivar) that would cause the effective yield to be the same for a one-year deposit in Venezuela as for a one-year deposit in the United Kingdom.

5. Assume interest rate parity exists. Would European firms possibly consider placing deposits in countries with high interest rates? Explain.

QUESTIONS AND APPLICATIONS

1. **International cash management.** Discuss the general functions involved in international cash management. Explain how the MNC's optimization of cash flow can distort the profits of each subsidiary.

2. **Netting.** Explain the benefits of netting. How can a centralized cash management system be beneficial to the MNC?

3. **Leading and lagging.** How can an MNC implement leading and lagging techniques to help subsidiaries in need of funds?

4. **International Fisher effect.** If a US firm believes that the international Fisher effect holds, what are the implications regarding a strategy of continually attempting to generate high returns from investing in currencies with high interest rates?

5. **Investing strategy.** Trumpington ltd has £2 million in excess cash that it has invested in Mexico at an annual interest rate of 60%. The UK interest rate is 9%. By how much would the Mexican peso have to depreciate to cause such a strategy to backfire?

6. **Investing strategy.** Why would a UK firm consider investing short-term funds in euros even when it does not have any future cash outflows in euros?

7. **Covered interest arbitrage.** Granville SA has 2 million euro in cash available for 90 days. It is considering the use of covered interest arbitrage, since the euro's 90-day interest rate is higher than the euro interest rate. What will determine whether this strategy is feasible?

8. **Effective yield.** Corlins plc has £1 million in cash available for 30 days. It can earn 1% on a 30-day investment in the United Kingdom. Alternatively, if it converts the pounds to South African rand, it can earn 1½% on a rand deposit. The spot rate of the rand is £0.09. The spot rate 30 days from now is expected to be £0.08. Should Corlins invest its cash in the United Kingdom or in South Africa? Explain your answer.

9. **Effective yield.** Rollins plc has £3 million in cash available for 180 days. It can earn 7% on a UK Treasury bill or 9% on a US Treasury bill. The US investment does require conversion of pounds to dollars. Assume that interest rate parity holds and that Rollins believes the 180-day forward rate is a reliable predictor of the spot rate to be realized 180 days from now. Would the British investment provide an effective yield that is below, above, or equal to the yield on the US investment? Explain your answer.

10. **Effective yield.** Repeat question 9, but this time assume that Rollins plc expects the 180-day forward rate of the dollar to substantially overestimate the spot rate to be realized in 180 days.

11. **Effective yield.** Repeat question 9, but this time assume that the Rollins plc expects the 180-day forward rate of the dollar to substantially underestimate the spot rate to be realized in 180 days.

12. **Effective yield.** Assume that the one-year UK interest rate is 10% and the one-year US interest rate is 13%. If a UK firm invests its funds in the US, by what percentage will the dollar have to depreciate to make its effective yield the same as

the UK interest rate from the UK firm's perspective?

13. **Investing in a currency portfolio.** Why would a firm consider investing in a portfolio of foreign currencies instead of just a single foreign currency?

14. **Interest rate parity.** Trellis ltd has determined that the interest rate on euros is 16% while the UK interest rate is 11% for one-year Treasury bills. The one-year forward rate of the euro has a discount of 7%. Does interest rate parity exist? Can Trellis achieve a higher effective yield by using covered interest arbitrage than by investing in UK Treasury bills? Explain.

15. **Diversified investments.** Hofstra ltd has no business outside the UK but has cash invested in six European countries, each of which uses the euro as its local currency. Are Hofstra's short-term investments well diversified and subject to a low degree of exchange rate risk? Explain.

16. **Investing strategy.** Should McNeese ltd consider investing funds in Latin American countries where it may expand facilities? The interest rates are high, and the proceeds from the investments could be used to help support the expansion. When would this strategy backfire?

17. **Impact of a crisis.** Palos SA (Spain) commonly invests some of its excess euros in foreign government short-term securities in order to earn a higher short-term interest rate on its cash. Describe how the potential return and risk of this strategy may be affected by financial crisis.

ADVANCED QUESTIONS

18. **Investing in a portfolio.** Poppleton ltd plans to invest its excess cash in South African rand for one year. The one-year South African interest rate is 19%. The probability of the rand's percentage change in value during the next year is shown below:

Possible rate of change in the South African rand over the life of the investment	Probability of occurrence
−15%	20%
−4	50%
0	30%

What is the expected value of the effective yield based on this information? Given that the UK interest rate for one year is 7%, what is the probability that a one-year investment in pesos will generate a lower effective yield than could be generated if Poppleton ltd simply invested domestically?

19. **Effective yield of portfolio.** Ithaca (Greece) considers placing 30% of its excess funds in a one-year Singapore dollar deposit and the remaining 70% of its funds in a one-year US dollar deposit. The Singapore one-year interest rate is 15%, while the US one-year interest rate is 10%. The possible percentage changes in the two currencies for the next year are forecasted as follows:

Currency	Possible percentage change in the spot rate over the investment horizon	Probability of that change in the spot rate occurring
Singapore dollar	−2%	20%
Singapore dollar	1	60
Singapore dollar	3	20
US dollar	1	50
US dollar	4	40
US dollar	6	10

Given this information, determine the possible effective yields of the portfolio and the probability associated with each possible portfolio yield. Given a one-year euro interest rate of 8%, what is the probability that the portfolio's effective yield will be lower than the yield achieved from investing in the United States? (Assume that the movements on the two currencies are not correlated.)

PROJECT WORKSHOP

20. **Foreign currency yields.** The Bloomberg website provides interest rate data for many different foreign currencies over various maturities. Its address is http://www.bloomberg.com.
    a. Go to the section that shows yields for different foreign currencies. Review the one-year yields of currencies. Assume that you could borrow at a rate 1 percentage point above the quoted yield for each currency. Which

currency would offer you the highest quoted yield?

b.   As a cash manager of an MNC based in the United Kingdom that has extra pounds that can be invested for one year, where would you invest funds for the next year? Explain.

c.   If you were working for a foreign subsidiary based in Japan and could invest Japanese yen for one year until the yen are needed to support local operations, where would you invest the yen? Explain.

DISCUSSION IN THE BOARDROOM

This exercise can be found on the companion website at www.cengage.co.uk/madura_fox.

RUNNING YOUR OWN MNC

This exercise can be found on the companion website at www.cengage.co.uk/madura_fox.

> **Essays/discussion and articles can be found at the end of Part 5**

BLADES PLC CASE STUDY
International cash management

Recall from Chapter 20 that the new Thailand subsidiary of Blades plc received a one-time order from a customer for 120,000 pairs of "Speedos", Blades' primary product. There is a six-month lag between the time when Blades needs funds to purchase material for the production of the Speedos and the time when it will be paid by the customer. Ben Holt, Blades' chief financial officer (CFO), has decided to finance the cost by borrowing Thai baht at an interest rate of 6% over a six-month period. Since the average cost per pair of Speedos is approximately 3,500 baht, Blades will borrow 420 million baht. The payment for the order will be used to repay the loan's principal and interest.

Ben Holt is currently planning to instruct the Thai subsidiary to remit any remaining baht-denominated cash flows back to the United Kingdom. Just before Blades receives payment for the large order, however, Holt notices that interest rates in Thailand have increased substantially. Blades would be able to invest funds in Thailand at a relatively high interest rate compared to the UK rate. Specifically, Blades could invest the remaining baht-denominated funds for one year in Thailand at an interest rate of 15%.

If the funds are remitted back to the UK parent, the excess pound volume resulting from the conversion of baht will either be used to support the UK production of Speedos, if needed, or be invested in the United Kingdom. Specifically, the funds will be used to cover cost of goods sold in the UK manufacturing plant. Since Blades used a significant amount of cash to finance the initial investment to build the plant in Thailand and purchase the necessary equipment, its UK operations are strapped for cash. Consequently, if the subsidiary's earnings are not remitted back to the United Kingdom, Blades will have to borrow funds at an interest rate of 10% to support its UK operations. Any funds remitted by the subsidiary that are not used to support UK operations will be invested in the United States at an interest rate of 8%. Holt estimates that approximately 60% of the remitted funds will be needed to support UK operations and that the remaining 40% will be invested in the United Kingdom. Consequently, Holt must choose between two alternative plans. First, he could instruct the Thai subsidiary to repay the baht loan (with interest) and invest any remaining funds in Thailand at an interest rate of 15%. Second, he could instruct the Thai subsidiary to repay the baht loan and remit any remaining funds back to the United Kingdom, where 60% of the funds would be used to support UK operations and 40% would be invested at an interest rate of 8%. Assume no income or withholding taxes on the earnings generated in Thailand.

Ben Holt has contacted you, a financial analyst at Blades plc to help him analyze these two options. Holt has informed you that the current spot rate of the Thai baht is £0.015 and that the baht is expected to depreciate by 5% over the coming year. He has provided you with the following list of questions he would like you to answer.

1. There is a tradeoff between the higher interest rates in Thailand and the delayed conversion of baht into pounds. Explain what this means.
2. If the net baht received from the Thailand subsidiary are invested in Thailand, how will UK operations be affected?
3. Construct a spreadsheet that compares the cash flows resulting from the two plans. Under the first plan, net baht-denominated cash flows (received today) will be invested in Thailand at 15% for a one-year period, after which the baht will be converted to pounds. Under the second plan, net baht-denominated cash flows are converted to pounds immediately and 60% of the funds will be used to support UK operations, while 40% are invested in the United Kingdom for one year at 8%. Which plan is superior given the expectation of the baht's value in one year?

SMALL BUSINESS DILEMMA
Cash management at the Sports Exports Company

Ever since Jim Logan began his Sports Exports Company (Ireland), he has been concerned about his exposure to exchange rate risk. The firm produces basketballs and exports them to a distributor in the United Kingdom, with the exports being denominated in British pounds. Jim has just entered into a joint venture in the United Kingdom in which a British firm produces sporting goods for Jim's firm and sells the goods to the British distributor. The distributor pays pounds to Jim's firm for these products. Jim recently borrowed pounds to finance this venture, which created some cash outflows (interest payments) that partially offset his cash inflows in pounds. The interest paid on this loan is equal to the British Treasury bill rate plus 3 percentage points. His original business of exporting has been very successful recently, which has caused him to have revenue (in pounds) that will be retained as excess cash. Jim must decide whether to pay off part of the existing British loan, invest the cash in the euro denominated Treasury bills, or invest the cash in British Treasury bills.

1. If Jim invests the excess cash in UK Treasury bills, would this reduce the firm's exposure to exchange rate risk?
2. Jim decided to use the excess cash to pay off the British loan. However, a friend advised him to invest the cash in British Treasury bills, stating that "the loan provides an offset to the pound receivables, so you would be better off investing in British Treasury bills than paying off the loan". Is Jim's friend correct? What should Jim do?

SHORT-TERM ASSET AND LIABILITY MANAGEMENT

Kent plc is a large UK firm with no international business. It has two branches within the UK, a southern branch and a northern branch. Each branch currently makes investing or financing decisions independently, as if it were a separate entity. The northern branch has excess cash of £15 million to invest for the next year. It can invest its funds in Treasury bills denominated in pounds or in any of four foreign currencies. The only restriction enforced by the parent is that a maximum of £5 million can be invested or financed in any foreign currency.

The southern branch needs to borrow £15 million over one year to support its UK operations. It can borrow funds in any of these same currencies (although any foreign funds borrowed would need to be converted to pounds to finance the UK operations). The only restriction enforced by the parent is that a maximum equivalent of £5 million can be borrowed in any single currency. A large bank serving the international money market has offered Kent plc the following terms:

Currency	Annual interest rate on deposits	Annual interest rate charged on loans
British pound	6%	9%
Australian dollar	11	14
Canadian dollar	7	10
New Zealand dollar	9	12
Japanese yen	8	11

The parent of Kent plc has created one-year forecasts of each currency for the branches to use in making their investing or financing decisions:

Currency	Today's spot exchange rate	Forecasted annual percentage change in exchange rate
Australian dollar	11	14
Canadian dollar	7	10
New Zealand dollar	9	12
Japanese yen	8	11

Questions

1. Determine the investment portfolio composition for Kent's northern branch that would maximize the expected effective yield while satisfying the restriction imposed by the parent.
2. What is the expected effective yield of the investment portfolio?
3. Based on the expected effective yield for the portfolio and the initial investment amount of £15 million, determine the annual interest to be earned on the portfolio.
4. Determine the financing portfolio composition for Kent's southern branch that would minimize the expected effective financing rate while satisfying the restriction imposed by the parent.
5. What is the expected effective financing rate of the total amount borrowed?

6. Based on the expected effective financing rate for the portfolio and the total amount of £15 million borrowed, determine the expected loan repayment amount beyond the principal borrowed.

7. When the expected interest received by the northern branch and paid by the southern branch of Kent plc are consolidated, what is the net amount of interest received?

8. If the northern branch and the southern branch worked together, the northern branch could loan its £15 million to the southern branch. Nevertheless, one could argue that the branches could not take advantage of interest rate differentials or expected exchange rate effects among currencies. Given the data provided in this example, would you recommend that the two branches make their short-term investment or financing decisions independently, or should the northern branch lend its excess cash to the southern branch? Explain.

1. Shenk, C.R. (1997) "The Origins of the Eurodollar Market in London 1955–1963", *Explorations in Economic History*, 35, 221–38. A readable account of financial innovation being a mixture of market competition, margins and governments.
   Q *To what extent is the control of national financial economics out of the hands of any one government? Discuss in relation to international financial arrangements (the eurodollar market being one such example).*

2. Easterly, W. (2002) "How Did Heavily Indebted Poor Countries Become Heavily Indebted? Reviewing two decades of debt relief", *World Development*, 30 (10), 1677–96. Required reading for any discussion of debt relief.
   Q *Is it sensible for governments of rich countries to offer better trade terms for poorer countries? Discuss.*

3. Menzler-Hokkanen, I. (1989) "Countertrade Arrangements in International Trade: A Tool for Creating Competitive Advantage", *Scandinavian Journal of Management*, 5 (2), 105–22. Never mind the date; this paper looks at the relationship between business and finance – a subject that deserves more attention.
   Q *Use Menzler-Hokkanen's article to assess the advantages and disadvantages of using financial schemes to promote trade. In particular, what factors need to be considered?*

4. Durbin, E. and D. Ng (2005) "The Sovereign Ceiling and Emerging Market Corporate Bond Spreads", *Journal of International Money and Finance*, 24, 631–49. A look at bond spreads.
   Q *Based on the study by Durbin and Ng, assess the extent to which companies' credit is limited by their home countries' credit worthiness?*

5. De Boyrie, M.E., S.J. Pak and J.S. Zdaniwicz (2005) "Estimating the Magnitude of Capital Flight Due to Abnormal Pricing in International Trade, the Russia–USA Case", *Accounting Forum*, 29, 249–70. Over and under invoicing.
   Q *Describe how the authors establish mispricing of exports and imports. Discuss the effects of such mispricing – is it all bad?*

CHAPTER 22

CONCLUDING COMMENTS

Textbooks can easily appear to be manuals explaining how things work. This is not their intended role. A textbook is no more than an explanation of the current state of knowledge. As a reminder of this function, it is a valuable exercise to outline the areas where there have been gains and also where further development is required.

THE SIGNIFICANCE OF INTERNATIONAL FINANCIAL MANAGEMENT

One of the most significant facts in the world of finance is to be found in the rather dryly named "Triennial Central Bank Survey of Foreign Exchange and Derivatives Market Activity in April 2004" published by the Monetary and Economic Department of the Bank for International Settlements (http://www.bis.org/publ/rpfx04.pdf). Daily turnover of foreign exchange (spot, swaps and forward transactions) total $1.9 trillion (12 zeros). This is more than the gross national product of the UK. The sheer size of the international markets means that governments cannot pursue their own economic policies without the market's tacit approval. Currency crises that can follow a loss of confidence by the international markets as in Argentina, Asia, Russia, Mexico and elsewhere show how the countries can be brought to the point of social and economic chaos. Perhaps the loss of sovereignty by being a member of the euro-zone is not so great. In addition, the World Trade Organization pursues a policy of freer trade, reducing a government's ability to protect and subsidize its own industries. Multinational companies close factories in one country and open elsewhere with fewer restrictions than ever before. MNCs can borrow in any currency and increasingly invest freely. In sum, MNCs and international financial markets are experiencing greater influence and the nation state less influence over our economic lives.

Understanding the motives for international investment, the reasons for exchange rate changes and the problems of international financial management is becoming a study of the new "engine" of economic wealth. International financial management is, rather surprisingly, a topic of increasing importance beyond finance.

SUMMARY OF THE BOOK

This book has taken as its reference point, in what is a very broadly defined area, the MNC. The first two parts of the book examined the general international environment and financial environment with particular reference to the exchange rate. It is hoped that the reader now appreciates that the exchange rate is in many ways the "melting pot" where differences in economic policy, economic development, investment behaviour, trade and monetary operations are resolved. Certainly, it is much more than a mere technical problem. How the European Union will resolve these differences between member countries without the exchange rate as an adjustment factor will be one of the interesting developments in the next few years. But as the text illustrates, currency unions and fixed exchange rates have been made and unmade in the past – it is not a process that is ending. Understanding the driving forces of the exchange rate is important to MNC management. Dramatic devaluations as in Argentina and Russia directly affect profits; even movements between major currencies can be significant. The international financial markets allow MNCs to manage these risks to much finer levels of detail than in the past. Part 3 of the book explained the many market and non-market methods that MNCs can now use. Evidence of the increasing management of such risks is to be found in the expanding risk management sections of the Annual Reports of MNCs. MNCs even publish estimated sensitivities of their profits to exchange rate changes.

The final two parts of the book explored the financial management of long-term and short-term assets and liabilities in the international environment. The management and valuation of long-term projects and shorter-term cash flows need to account for international risks. Many of the issues represent an extension of single economy analysis focusing, in particular, on the currency risk analysis that is a feature of most international transactions.

ADVANCES

The biggest advance over the last 50 years from the perspective of the MNC has undoubtedly been the management of risk. Derivatives markets enable MNCs to choose what risk they want to take and how much of that risk to expose the company to. Some risk has to be taken, otherwise there will be no return, at least not in an efficient market. Financial markets themselves are now better understood. The risk return trade off, the concept of market efficiency and the significance of random walks all help MNCs to understand and manage their investments. Markets are now more open and more heavily scrutinized than ever before. The result is arguably greater stability in the marketplace and an improved ability to avoid panics and to adjust to change. Crashes still occur as does hyperinflation, but without the devastating consequences of the earlier part of the twentieth century.

REMAINING ISSUES

The early years of certainty over investment analysis have given way to increasing doubt. The Capital Asset Pricing Model in the international environment gives rise to difficult questions. How is the risk of investing in developing countries to be measured? It does not seem right to just apply systematic risk; such investments might even appear safer under such approaches. In a world where portfolios are imperfectly diversified, exactly what index to use and other relevant non-diversifiable risks are not clear. The size of the discount rate to apply is also problematic. The equity premium puzzle highlights the size of the market premium – it appears too large given the historic risk of such investment compared to safer fixed interest instruments. There is also the PPP puzzle. Why do exchange rates change so often when the underlying causes appear relatively static? Perhaps the information process itself or the opinion forming process should be included, or indeed, can they be included? Are there aspects of the process that are inherently not measurable?

There are more applied issues as well. IMF recovery packages (conditionality) are challenged by many as ineffective. The almost permanent status of many countries as less developed countries is depressing. Are free market policies, advocated by the IMF and others, the answer? Or should there be greater management and responsibility? Then there are trade issues. The persistence of price differential between countries is not well understood. The adjustment to the tremendous price differentials between Europe and developing countries such as China and India raises issues about the progress of globalization. To what extent should resources such as labour be transferable?

Most of these issues have been addressed or referenced in the main text. It should be said, of course, that with all the above questions, something is known of the answer, it is simply that the answers are evidently incomplete. In general, the improvement in managing the effect of international risks needs now to be matched by a better understanding of the causes. The need for more development merely supports and explains why international financial management remains a well-rewarded profession.

APPENDIX A Answers to self-test questions

ANSWERS TO SELF-TEST QUESTIONS FOR CHAPTER 1

1. MNCs can capitalize on comparative advantages. *Firm specific advantages*: i) proprietary technology – licensing; ii) managerial/marketing skills – franchising; iii) trademarks; iv) economies of scale; v) large capital requirements. *Internalization advantages*: i) high enforcement costs (e.g. weak legal systems mean that an MNC is better doing it itself rather than contracting with local companies); ii) buyer uncertainty over value; iii) need to control production; iv) tax. *Country specific advantages*: i) natural resources; ii) labour force (cheap); iii) trade barriers (e.g. a US multinational may seek to avoid barriers by producing in the EU). Many MNCs initially penetrate markets by exporting but ultimately establish a subsidiary in foreign markets and attempt to differentiate their products as other firms enter those markets (product cycle theory).

2. The European Union seeks to create a unified market across all member states. Common rules and regulations particularly on takeovers will make expansion for MNCs easier, though this area as the text explains remains restrictive. The euro as a common currency across most of the EU except for UK, Denmark and Sweden reduces exchange rates risk for MNCs. The large increase in portfolio investment by MNCs will be helped by this reduction in uncertainty. Eastern European countries also offer opportunities for MNCs to use relatively cheaper resources in countries such as the Czech Republic.

3. First, there is the risk of poor economic conditions in the foreign country. High inflation, a slump in demand, high interest rates, labour and material shortages can all severely affect MNC performance. Second, there is country risk, which reflects the risk of changing government or public attitudes towards the MNC. Funds can be blocked, taxes increased and regulations made more restrictive. Third, there is exchange rate risk, which can affect the financial performance of the MNC in the foreign country.

ANSWERS TO SELF-TEST QUESTIONS FOR CHAPTER 2

1. Each of the economic factors is described, holding other factors constant.
   a. *Inflation.* A relatively high UK inflation rate relative to other countries can make UK goods less attractive to UK and non-UK consumers, which results in fewer UK exports, more UK imports, and a lower (or more negative) current account balance. A relatively low UK inflation rate would have the opposite effect.
   b. *National income.* A relatively high increase in the UK national income (compared to other countries) tends to cause a large increase in demand for imports and can cause a lower (or more negative) current account balance. A relatively low increase in the UK national income would have the opposite effect.
   c. *Exchange rates.* A weaker pound tends to make UK products cheaper to non-UK firms and makes non-UK products expensive to UK firms. Thus, UK exports are expected to increase, while UK imports are expected to decrease. However, some conditions can prevent these effects from occurring, as explained in the chapter. Normally, a stronger pound causes UK exports to decrease and UK imports to

increase because it makes UK goods more expensive to non-UK firms and makes non-UK goods less expensive to UK firms.

    d. *Government restrictions.* When the UK government imposes new barriers on imports, UK imports decline, causing the UK balance of trade to increase (or be less negative). When non-UK governments impose new barriers on imports from the United Kingdom, the UK balance of trade may decrease (or be more negative). When governments remove trade barriers, the opposite effects are expected.

2. When the United Kingdom imposes tariffs on imported goods, foreign countries may retaliate by imposing tariffs on goods exported by the United Kingdom. Thus, there is a decline in UK exports that may offset any decline in UK imports.

3. The Asian crisis caused a decline in Asian income levels and therefore resulted in a reduced demand for UK exports. In addition, Asian exporters experienced problems, and some UK importers discontinued their relationships with the Asian exporters. The large devaluations in Asian currencies also attracted speculators looking for investments that appeared to be undervalued.

ANSWERS TO SELF-TEST QUESTIONS FOR CHAPTER 3

1. Sunny Bank is buying US dollars at £0.58 and selling dollars at £0.60. The spread is:

$$\text{Bid/Ask spread} = \frac{\text{Ask rate} - \text{Bid rate}}{\text{Ask rate}}$$

$$\text{Bid/Ask spread} = \frac{£0.60 - £0.58}{£0.60}$$

$$= 0.0333$$

$$= 3\tfrac{1}{3}\%$$

2. Cloudy Bank is buying the new sol at £0.09 and selling the new sol at £0.12. The spread is:

$$\text{Bid/Ask spread} = \frac{\text{Ask rate} - \text{Bid rate}}{\text{Ask rate}}$$

$$\text{Bid/Ask spread} = \frac{£0.12 - £0.09}{£0.12}$$

$$= 0.25$$

$$= 25\%$$

Greater currency variability, order costs, inventory costs and competition costs account for the difference in spreads (see chapter).

3. MNCs use the spot foreign exchange market to exchange currencies for immediate delivery. They use the forward foreign exchange market and the currency futures market to lock in the exchange rate at which currencies will be exchanged at a future point in time. They use the currency options market when they wish to lock in the maximum (minimum) amount to be paid (received) in a future currency transaction but maintain flexibility in the event of favourable exchange rate movements.

    MNCs use the eurocurrency market to engage in short-term investing or financing or the eurocredit market to engage in medium-term financing. They can obtain long-term financing by issuing bonds in the eurobond market or by issuing stock in the international markets.

ANSWERS TO SELF-TEST QUESTIONS FOR CHAPTER 4

1. Economic factors affect the yen's value as follows:
   a. If UK inflation is higher than Japanese inflation, the UK demand for Japanese goods may increase (to avoid the higher UK prices), and the Japanese demand for UK goods may decrease (to avoid the higher UK prices). Consequently, there is upward pressure on the value of the yen.
   b. If UK interest rates increase and exceed Japanese interest rates, the UK demand for Japanese interest-bearing securities may decline (since UK interest-bearing securities are more attractive), while the Japanese demand for UK interest-bearing securities may rise. Both forces place downward pressure on the yen's value in terms of British pounds.
   c. If UK national income increases more than Japanese national income, the UK demand for Japanese goods may increase more than the Japanese demand for UK goods. Assuming that the change in national income levels does not affect exchange rates indirectly through effects on relative interest rates, the forces should place upward pressure on the yen's value.
   d. If government controls reduce the UK demand for Japanese goods, they place downward pressure on the yen's value. If the controls reduce the Japanese demand for UK goods, they place upward pressure on the yen's value.

   The opposite scenarios of those described here would cause the expected pressure to be in the opposite direction.

2. UK capital flows with Country A may be larger than UK capital flows with Country B. Therefore, the change in the interest rate differential has a larger effect on the capital flows with Country A, causing the exchange rate to change. If the capital flows with Country B are non-existent, interest rate changes do not change the capital flows and therefore do not change the demand and supply conditions in the foreign exchange market.

3. Smart Banking plc should not pursue the strategy because a loss would result, as shown here.
   a. Borrow £5 million.
   b. Convert £5 million to $8,333,333 (based on the spot exchange rate of £0.60 per $).
   c. Invest the dollars at 9% annualized, which represents a return of 0.15% over six days, so the dollars received after six days = $8,345,833 (computed as $8,333,333 × [1 + 0.0015]).
   d. Convert the dollars received back to UK pounds after six days: $8,345,833 = £4,924,041 (based on anticipated exchange rate of £0.59 per dollar after six days).
   e. The interest rate owed on the UK pound loan is 0.10% over the six-day period. Thus, the amount owed as a result of the loan is £5,005,000 (computed as $5,000,000 × [1 + 0.001]).
   f. The strategy is expected to cause a loss of ($4,924,041 − $5,005,000) = −£80,959.

   In approximate terms the value of the dollar is expected to decline *in six days* from £0.60 to £0.59 or 1.66%. The difference in the lending and borrowing rate produces a small surplus of 3% (i.e. 9% − 6%) *over one year* – this is a six-day gain of approximately

3% / (360/6) = 0.0005 or 0.05% as in the calculations above. The benefit through borrowing at a low rate and investing at a higher rate is therefore considerably outweighed by expected decline in the value of the dollar.

ANSWERS TO SELF-TEST QUESTIONS FOR CHAPTER 5

1. The net profit to the speculator is £0.65 – £0.60 – £0.06 = –£0.01 per unit.

   The net profit to the speculator for one contract is –£500 (computed as –£.01 × 50,000 units).

   The spot rate would need to be £0.66 for the speculator to break even.

   The net profit to the seller of the call option is +£0.01 per unit calculated as £0.60 – 0.65 + 0.06 = +£0.1

2. The speculator should exercise the option.

   The net profit to the speculator is (£0.53 – £0.50) – £0.02 = £0.01 per unit.

   The net profit to the seller or writer of the put option is equal and opposite to –£0.01.

3. The premium paid is higher for options with longer expiration dates (other things being equal). Firms may prefer not to pay such high premiums.

ANSWERS TO SELF-TEST QUESTIONS FOR CHAPTER 6

1. Market forces cause the demand and supply of dollars and euros in the foreign exchange market to change, which causes a change in the equilibrium exchange rate. The central banks could intervene to affect the demand or supply conditions in the foreign exchange market, but they would not always be able to offset the changing market forces. For example, if there were a large increase in the US demand for euros and no increase in the supply of euros for sale, the central banks would have to increase the supply of euros in the foreign exchange market to offset the increased demand.

2. The ECB could use direct intervention by selling some of its euro reserves in exchange for dollars in the foreign exchange market. It could also use indirect intervention by attempting to reduce euro interest rates through monetary policy. Specifically, it could increase the euro money supply, which places downward pressure on euros interest rates (assuming that inflationary expectations do not change). The lower euro interest rates should discourage foreign investment in the euros area and encourage increased investment by euros investors in foreign securities. Both forces tend to weaken the euro's value.

3. A weaker home currency tends to increase the demand for home goods because the price paid for a specified amount in home currency by foreign firms is reduced. In addition, the home demand for foreign goods is reduced because it takes more home currency to obtain a specified amount in foreign currency once the home currency weakens. Both forces tend to stimulate the home economy and therefore improve productivity and reduce unemployment in the home country.

ANSWERS TO SELF-TEST QUESTIONS FOR CHAPTER 7

1. No. The pound buys $1.50 or C$2.00, the indirect or implied rate is $1.50 = C$2.00 as they are both worth £1. Taking $1.50 = C$2.00 and dividing both sides by 2.00 we

have C$1 = $0.75 which is the direct rate, so there is no gain to be made through triangular arbitrage.

2. Covered interest arbitrage involves the exchange of pounds for dollars. Assuming that the investors begin with £1 million (the starting amount will not affect the final conclusion), the pounds would be converted to dollars as shown here:

$$£1 \text{ million} \times \$1.50 = \$1,500,000$$

The US investment would accumulate interest over the 180-day period, resulting in

$$\$1,500,000 \times 1.03 = \$1,545,000$$

After 180 days, the dollars would be converted to pounds:

$$\$1,545,000 \times £0.673 \text{ per dollar} = \$1,039,785$$

This amount reflects a return of 3.9875% a small amount below the domestic return from investment of 4%. Thus, UK investors would earn less using the covered interest arbitrage strategy than investing in the United Kingdom.

3. No strong reaction. The forward rate premium on the dollar almost matches the interest rate difference between the two countries. It is likely that the margin required by banks, their bid and ask spreads and other transaction costs, would make any attempt to capitalize on those differences unprofitable.

4. If there is a discrepancy in the pricing of a currency, one may capitalize on it by using the various forms of arbitrage described in the chapter. As arbitrage occurs, the exchange rates will be pushed toward their appropriate levels because arbitrageurs will buy an underpriced currency in the foreign exchange market (increase in demand for currency places upward pressure on its value) and will sell an overpriced currency in the foreign exchange market (increase in the supply of currency for sale places downward pressure on its value).

5. The one-year forward premium on dollars in terms of £s would increase as a UK investor would lose a further 1% relative to UK investment by investing in the US. So what the UK investor loses in terms of interest rates must be made up for in terms of change in the value of the currency for interest rate parity to hold – the value of the dollar would therefore have to increase by 1% to offset the difference. Arbitrage would, in any case, ensure that the premium would rise.

ANSWERS TO SELF-TEST QUESTIONS FOR CHAPTER 8

1. If the Japanese prices rise because of Japanese inflation, the value of the yen should decline. Thus, even though the importer might need to pay more yen, it would benefit from a weaker yen value (it would pay fewer pounds for a given amount in yen). Thus, there could be an offsetting effect if PPP holds. The real value of the yen would therefore possibly remain the same, the higher inflation on its own increases the real value (purchasing power) of the yen and this is offset by the fall in the value of the yen on the exchange markets. If there were an exact offset there would be no change in the purchasing power of the yen (its real value) and hence no change in the cost of Japanese goods.

2. Purchasing power parity does not necessarily hold. In our example, Japanese inflation could rise (causing the importer to pay more yen), and yet the Japanese yen would not necessarily depreciate by an offsetting amount, or at all. Therefore, the pound amount to be paid for Japanese supplies could increase over time.

3. High inflation is likely to result in a decline in the value of the Eastern European currencies relative to the euro and the British pound. The higher prices in Eastern Europe will result in a decline in demand for their goods and an increase in demand by resident people and companies in Eastern Europe for euros and UK goods. On the foreign exchange there will be a decline in demand for Eastern European currency and an increase in the supply of Eastern European currency for euros and pounds. Both forces will result in a decline in the value of the Eastern European currencies. These forces will only cease when the decline in the value of Eastern European currencies offsets the change in relative inflation rates. So, using the approximate approach, if inflation in an Eastern European currency had increased by 5% more than in the UK, it is only after a 5% fall in the value of the Eastern European currency that the old levels of demand and supply will be restored. Demand for Eastern European goods will then pick up as they will now cost the same relative to UK and euro goods as before and Eastern European demand for UK and euro goods from Eastern Europe will decline as they become more expensive due to the fall in value of Eastern European currencies and the implied increase in value of the euro and the pound for holders of Eastern European currency.

4. The approximate formula is:
$$e_f = I_h - I_f$$
Taking the UK as the home currency
$$= 3\% - 4\%$$
$$= 0.01 \text{ or } -1\%$$
$$S_{t+1} = S_t(1+e_f)$$
$$= £0.57\ (1+(-0.01))$$
$$= £0.5643$$

5.
$$e_f = (1+i_h)\ /\ (1+i_f) - 1$$
$$= 1.06\ /\ 1.11 - 1$$
$$= -0.045 \text{ or } -4.5\% \text{ approximately}$$
$$S_{t+1} = S_t(1+e_f)$$
$$= £0.30\ (1+(-0.045))$$
$$= £0.2865$$

6. According to the IFE, the increase in interest rates by 5 percentage points reflects an increase in expected inflation by 5 percentage points.

   If the inflation adjustment occurs, the balance of trade should be affected, as Australian demand for UK goods rises while the UK demand for Australian goods declines. Thus, the Australian dollar should weaken.

   If UK investors believed in the IFE, they would not attempt to capitalize on higher Australian interest rates because they would expect the Australian dollar to depreciate over time.

ANSWERS TO SELF-TEST QUESTIONS FOR CHAPTER 9

1. UK four-year interest rate $= (1 + 0.07)^4 - 1 = 0.3108$ or 31.08%. Indian four-year interest rate $= (1 + 0.20)^4 - 1 = 1.0736$ or 107.36%.

   percentage change $= (1 + i_h)\ /\ (1 + i_f) - 1 = 1.3108\ /\ 2.0736 - 1 = -0.3679$ or -36.79% decline in the value of the Indian rupee offsetting any gain through higher interest rates.

2. Canadian dollar absolute of $[(0.80 - 0.82) / 0.82] = 2.44\%$

Japanese yen absolute of $[(0.012 - 0.011) / 0.011] = 9.09\%$

The forecast error was larger for the Japanese yen, remember that error is measured as a percentage so the yen error is greater even though the actual number is smaller.

3. Semistrong-form efficiency would be refuted since the currency values do not adjust immediately to useful public information.

4. The rouble should decline in value relative to the pound, the higher interest rates should compensate for higher inflation and PPP suggests that the rouble should decline in value to maintain the same real value or purchasing power.

5. As the chapter suggests, forecasts of currencies are subject to a high degree of error. Thus, if a project's success is very sensitive to the future value of the bolivar, there is much uncertainty. This project could easily result in losses because the future value of the bolivar is very uncertain.

ANSWERS TO SELF-TEST QUESTIONS FOR CHAPTER 10

1. Managers have more information about the firm's exposure to exchange rate risk than do shareholders and may be able to hedge it more easily than shareholders could. Shareholders may prefer that the managers hedge for them. Also, cash flows may be stabilized as a result of hedging, which can reduce the firm's cost of financing.

2. The Swiss supplies would have less exposure to exchange rate risk because historically the Swiss franc is less volatile with respect to the euro than the South African rand.

3. The US source would be preferable because the firm could use dollar inflows to make payments for material that is imported thus reducing your exposure to changes in the value of the dollar.

4. No. If exports are priced in euros, the euro cash flows received from exporting will depend on US demand, which will be influenced by the dollar's value. If the dollar depreciates, US demand for the French exports is likely to decrease. Exposure would be economic rather than translation exposure as there would now be no need to convert dollars to euros.

5. The earnings generated by the European subsidiaries will be translated to a smaller amount in euro earnings if the euro strengthens. Thus, the consolidated earnings of the Europe-based MNCs will be reduced.

ANSWERS TO SELF-TEST QUESTIONS FOR CHAPTER 11

1. Invest the present value of the payment in A$s by using borrowed money in £s and converting at the current spot rate (thus avoiding exchange rate risk).

The A$s to be invested today is A$3,000,000 / (1+ 0.12) = A$2,678,571

£s needed to be borrowed in order to buy these A$s: A$2,678,571 × £0.45 = £1,205,357. At a cost of 7%, the amount owing after one year will be 1,205,357 × 1.07 = £1,289,732.

2. The money market hedge would be more appropriate. Given a forward rate of £0.44, Montclair would need £1,320,000 in one year (computed as A$3,000,000 × £0.44) when using a forward hedge. Thus more is needed in one year's time using the forward hedge than the money market hedge where the amount needed is only £1,289,732.

3. Montclair could purchase currency call options in Australian dollars. The option could hedge against the possible appreciation of the Australian dollar. Yet, if the Australian dollar depreciates, Montclair could let the option expire and purchase the Australian dollars at the spot rate at the time it needs to send payment. A disadvantage of the currency call option is that a premium must be paid for it. Thus, if Montclair expects the Australian dollar to appreciate over the year, the money market hedge would probably be a better choice, since the flexibility provided by the option would not be useful in this case.

4. Even though Sanibel ltd is insulated from the beginning of a month to the end of the month, the forward rate will become higher each month because the forward rate moves with the spot rate. Thus, the firm will pay more dollars each month, even though it is hedged during the month. Sanibel will therefore be adversely affected by the consistent appreciation of the dollar. The effect will be lagged (delayed) by one month. If the appreciation is very high, it may use the delay gained from hedging to find an alternative supplier.

5. Sanibel ltd could engage in a series of forward contracts today to cover the payments in each successive month. In this way, it locks in the future payments today and does not have to agree to the higher forward rates that may exist in future months.

6. A put option allows Hopkins ltd to sell SFs at £0.36, higher than the expected future spot of £0.35. Unfortunately to sell at the rate of £0.36 will cost £0.02 per SF, so the net revenue will be £0.36 – £0.02 = £0.34 less than the expected future spot of £0.35. Hopkins has a difficult choice. Based on expected values, no hedge would be preferable. Such a decision would make sense if Hopkins were risk neutral and would be willing to risk a loss (i.e. below £0.35) for the possible gain (i.e. above £0.35). If Hopkins is satisfied with the forward rate of £0.35 but is worried that it might be less, then a forward contract at the £0.35 rate would be best. If Hopkins is willing to risk the possibility of getting only £0.34 but wants to take the chance that it might rise to above £0.35 then the option would be preferable. The amount of revenue involved (about £700,000) will affect Hopkins' attitude to risk. If this is a small amount for Hopkins, it is more likely that the company will be risk neutral.

ANSWERS TO SELF-TEST QUESTIONS FOR CHAPTER 12

1. Salem could attempt to purchase its chemicals from US sources. Then, if the $ depreciates, the reduction in dollar inflows resulting from its exports to the US will be partially offset by a reduction in dollar outflows needed to pay for the imports.

   An alternative possibility for Salem is to finance its business with US dollars, but this would probably be a less efficient solution.

2. A possible disadvantage is that Salem would forgo some of the benefits if the $ appreciated over time.

3. We do not know if the subsidiary is a net cost (say a production unit) or a net earner for Neve. If there are net earnings, the consolidated earnings of Neve will be adversely affected if the dollar depreciates because the dollar earnings will be translated into

euros for the consolidated income statement at a lower exchange rate. Neve could attempt to hedge its translation exposure by selling dollars forward. If the dollar depreciates, it will benefit from its forward position, which could help offset the translation effect. If the subsidiary is a net cost then the prospect of a depreciating dollar will be attractive as the translated cost will be lower.

4. This argument has no perfect solution. It appears that shareholders penalize the firm for poor earnings even when the reason for poor earnings is a weak euro that has adverse translation effects. It is possible that translation effects could be hedged to stabilize earnings, but Cheriton may consider informing the shareholders that the major earnings changes have been due to translation effects and not to changes in consumer demand or other factors. Perhaps shareholders would not respond so strongly to earnings changes if they were well aware that the changes were primarily caused by translation effects. In an efficient market, one would expect that the investors would appreciate that translation effects do not have direct wealth implications. It is up to Cheriton to point this out to their shareholders in the annual and interim reports.

5. Lincolnshire has no translation exposure since it has no foreign subsidiaries. Kalafa has translation exposure resulting from its subsidiary in Spain.

ANSWERS TO SELF-TEST QUESTIONS FOR CHAPTER 13

1. Possible reasons may include:
   - More demand for the product (depending on the product)
   - Better technology in Europe
   - Fewer restrictions (less political interference)
   - No exchange rate risk
   - Low political risk

2. Possible reasons may include:
   - More demand for the product (depending on the product)
   - Greater probability of earning superior profits (since many goods have not been marketed in Latin America in the past)
   - Cheaper factors of production (such as land and labour)
   - Possible exploitation of monopolistic advantages

3. UK firms normally would prefer that the foreign currency appreciate after they invest their pounds to develop the subsidiary. The executive's comment suggests that the euro is too strong and is likely to depreciate in the future, so any UK investment of pounds into Europe will lose value in the future.

4. It may be easier to engage in a joint venture with a Chinese firm, which is already well established in China, to circumvent barriers.

5. The government may attempt to stimulate the economy in this way.

ANSWERS TO SELF-TEST QUESTIONS FOR CHAPTER 14

1. In addition to earnings generated in Jamaica, the *NPV* is based on some factors not controlled by the firm, such as the expected host government tax on profits, the with-

holding tax imposed by the host government, and the salvage value to be received when the project is terminated. Furthermore, the exchange rate projections will affect the estimates of dollar cash flows received by the parent as earnings are remitted. All these are subjective estimates that will differ between different managers.

2. The most obvious effect is on the cash flows that will be generated by the sales distribution centre in Ireland. These cash flow estimates are likely to be revised downward (due to lower sales estimates). It is also possible that the estimated salvage value could be reduced. Exchange rate estimates could be revised as a result of revised economic conditions. Estimated tax rates imposed on the centre by the Irish government could also be affected by the revised economic conditions.

3. Hampshire must account for the cash flows that will be forgone as a result of the plant, because some of the cash flows that used to be received by the parent through its exporting operation will be eliminated. The *NPV* estimate will be reduced after this factor is accounted for.

4. a. An increase in the risk will cause an increase in the required rate of return on the subsidiary, which results in a lower discounted value of the subsidiary's salvage value.
   b. If the rupiah depreciates over time, the subsidiary's salvage value will be reduced because the proceeds will convert to fewer dollars.

5. The cash flows of William would be affected more because the periodic remitted earnings from Thailand to be converted to pounds would be larger. The pound cash flows of Niles would not be affected so much because interest payments would be made on the Thai loans before earnings could be remitted to the United Kingdom. Thus, a smaller amount in earnings would be remitted.

6. The demand for the product in the foreign country may be very uncertain, causing the total revenue to be uncertain. The exchange rates can be very uncertain, creating uncertainty about the cash flows received by the UK parent. The salvage value may be very uncertain; this will have a larger effect if the lifetime of the project is short (for projects with a very long life, the discounted value of the salvage value is small anyway).

ANSWERS TO SELF-TEST QUESTIONS FOR CHAPTER 15

1. Acquisitions have increased in Europe to capitalize on the inception of the euro, which created a single European currency for many European countries. This has not only eliminated the exchange rate risk on transactions between the participating European countries, but it has also made it easier to compare valuations among European countries to determine where targets are undervalued. The increasingly common regulation structure also reduces political risk.

2. Common restrictions include government regulations, such as antitrust restrictions, environmental restrictions, and red tape.

3. The establishment of a new subsidiary allows an MNC to create the subsidiary it desires without assuming existing facilities or employees. However, the process of building a new subsidiary and hiring employees will normally take longer than the process of acquiring an existing foreign firm.

4. The divestiture is now more feasible because the pound cash flows to be received by the UK parent are reduced as a result of the revised projections of the krona's value.

ANSWERS TO SELF-TEST QUESTIONS FOR CHAPTER 16

1. First, consumers on the islands could develop a philosophy of purchasing homemade goods. Second, they could discontinue their purchases of exports by Key West Co as a form of protest against specific US government actions. Third, the host governments could impose severe restrictions on the subsidiary shops owned by Key West Co (including the blockage of funds to be remitted to the US parent).

2. First, the islands could experience poor economic conditions, which would cause lower income for some residents. Second, residents could be subject to inflation that is greater than the increase in their salaries or higher interest rates, which would reduce the income that they could allocate toward exports. Depreciation of the local currencies could also raise the local prices to be paid for goods imported from the United States. All factors described here could reduce the demand for goods exported by Key West Co.

3. Financial risk is probably a bigger concern. The political risk factors are unlikely, based on the product produced by Key West Co and the absence of substitute products available in other countries. The financial risk factors deserve serious consideration.

4. A terrorist attack usually heightens concern about the particular target (office, underground, a checkpoint). Firms can seek to insure employees or seek safer ways of communicating. There may be cultural elements, some people will be more affected by such events than others. Projects may be delayed or redesigned or abandoned as a result of revised risk assessments.

5. Rockford ltd could estimate the net present value (*NPV*) of the project under three scenarios: (1) include a special tax when estimating cash flows back to the parent (probability of scenario = 15%), (2) assume the project ends in two years and include a salvage value when estimating the *NPV* (probability of scenario = 15%), and (3) assume no French government intervention (probability = 70%). This results in three estimates of *NPV*, one for each scenario. This method is less arbitrary than the one considered by Rockford's executives.

ANSWERS TO SELF-TEST QUESTIONS FOR CHAPTER 17

1. Growth may have caused Goshen to require a large amount for financing that could not be completely provided by retained earnings. In addition, the interest rates may have been low in these foreign countries to make debt financing an attractive alternative. Finally, the use of foreign debt can reduce the exchange rate risk since the amount in periodic remitted earnings is reduced when interest payments are required on foreign debt.

2. If country risk has increased, Lynde can attempt to reduce its exposure to that risk by removing its equity investment from the subsidiary. When the subsidiary is financed with local funds, the local creditors have more to lose than the parent if the host government imposes any severe restrictions on the subsidiary.

3. Not necessarily. German and Japanese firms tend to have more support from other firms or from the government if they experience cash flow problems and can therefore afford to use a higher degree of financial leverage than firms from the same industry in the United Kingdom.

4. Local debt financing is favourable because it can reduce the MNC's exposure to country risk and exchange rate risk. However, the high interest rates will make the local debt very expensive. If the parent makes an equity investment in the subsidiary to avoid the high cost of local debt, it will be more exposed to country risk and exchange rate risk.

5. The answer to this question is dependent on whether you believe unsystematic risk is relevant. If the CAPM is used as a framework for measuring the risk of a project, the risk of the foreign project is determined to be low, because the systematic risk is low. That is, the risk is specific to the host country and is not related to euro market conditions. However, if the project's unsystematic risk is relevant, the project is considered to have a high degree of risk. The project's cash flows are very uncertain, even though the systematic risk is low. The MNC may reasonably seek to protect against unsystematic risk if it believes that the shareholders will not be able to easily diversify in reaction to this investment. Lack of knowledge, time and effort are all reasons as to why the shareholders of Reno may prefer that the MNC protects against the unsystematic risk of this investment.

ANSWERS TO SELF-TEST QUESTIONS FOR CHAPTER 18

1. A firm may be able to obtain a lower coupon rate by issuing bonds denominated in a different currency. The firm converts the proceeds from issuing the bond to its local currency to finance local operations. Yet, there is exchange rate risk because the firm will need to make coupon payments and the principal payment in the currency denominating the bond. If that currency appreciates against the firm's local currency, the financing costs could become larger than expected. If there are revenues earned in that country then the bond payments will serve to reduce the company's net exposure to the currency and thereby reduce risk.

2. The risk is that the Swiss franc would appreciate against the pound over time since the European subsidiary will periodically convert some of its pound cash flows to francs to make the coupon payments.

   The risk here is less than it would be if the proceeds were used to finance UK operations. The Swiss franc's movement against the pound is much more volatile than the Swiss franc's movement against the euro. The Swiss franc and the euro have historically moved in tandem to some degree against the pound, which means that there is a somewhat stable exchange rate between the two currencies.

3. If these firms borrow pounds and convert them to finance local projects, they will need to use their own currencies to obtain pounds and make coupon payments. These firms would be highly exposed to exchange rate risk.

4. Abend GmbH is exposed to exchange rate risk. If the yen appreciates, the number of euros needed for conversion into yen will increase. To the extent that the yen strengthens, Abend's cost of financing when financing with yen could be higher than when financing with euros.

5. The nominal interest rate incorporates expected inflation (according to the Fisher effect). Therefore, the high interest rates reflect high expected inflation. Cash flows can be enhanced by inflation because a given profit margin converts into larger profits as a result of inflation, even if costs increase at the same rate as revenues.

ANSWERS TO SELF-TEST QUESTIONS FOR CHAPTER 19

1. The exporter may not trust the importer or may be concerned that the government will impose exchange controls that prevent payment to the exporter. Meanwhile, the importer may not trust that the exporter will ship the goods ordered and therefore may not pay until the goods are received. Commercial banks can help by providing guarantees to the exporter in case the importer does not pay.

2. In accounts receivable financing, the bank provides a loan to the exporter secured by the accounts receivable. If the importer fails to pay the exporter, the exporter is still responsible to repay the bank. Factoring involves the sales of accounts receivable by the exporter to a so-called factor, so that the exporter is no longer responsible for the importer's payment.

3. The Export Credit Guarantee Department provides medium-term protection against the risk of non-payment by the foreign buyer due to political risk.

ANSWERS TO SELF-TEST QUESTIONS FOR CHAPTER 20

1. If the New Zealand dollar depreciates by 6%, in approximate terms the return will be:

cost of borrowing in NZ$s	9%
less gain from reduction in value of the NZ$:	6%
net cost of borrowing	3%

Using the exact approach: $(1 + 9\%)(1 + -6\%) - 1 = 1.09 \times 0.94 - 1 = 0.0246$ or 2.46%.

If the New Zealand dollar appreciates by 3%, in approximate terms the return will be:

cost of borrowing in NZ$s	9%
plus loss due to increase in value of the NZ$:	3%
net cost of borrowing	12%

Using the exact approach: $(1 + 9\%)(1 + 3\%) - 1 = 1.09 \times 1.03 - 1 = 0.01227$ or 12.27%.

2. Using the exact measures $50\% \times 2.46\% + 50\% \times 12.27\% = 0.5 \times 2.46 + 0.5 \times 12.27 = 7.365\%$.

3. IFE is based on the notion that the cost of borrowing should be the same at home as abroad (there should be one price). Using the approximate method the IFE formula is $e_f = i_h - i_f$ or $i_h = i_f + e_f$. Plugging in the variables from the question we have 8% = 5% + e_f. By inspection we can see that e_f should take the value 3% for the same effective borrowing rate in the UK as in Japan. Using the exact approach IFE states that:

$$e_f = \frac{(1+i_h)}{(1+i_f)} = \frac{1.08}{1.05} = 1 = 0.286 \text{ or } 2.86\% \text{ or about } 3\%$$

4. The expected gain or loss from conversion will be due to the expected difference in the exchange rates

$$E(e_f) = (\text{Forward rate} - \text{sport rate})/\text{spot rate}$$
$$= (\pounds 0.38 - \pounds 0.40)/\pounds 0.40 = -0.05 \text{ or} -5\%$$

The expected effective financing rate $E(r_{eff}) = I(I) + I = -5\% + 9\%$ or 4% the exact rate would be $(1 + -5\%)(1 + 9\%) - 1 = 0.0355 = 3.55\%$.

5. The two-currency portfolio will not exhibit much lower variance than either individual currency because the currencies tend to move together. Thus, the diversification effect is limited.

ANSWERS TO SELF-TEST QUESTIONS FOR CHAPTER 21

1. The subsidiary in Country Y should be more adversely affected because the blocked funds will not earn as much interest over time. In addition, the funds will likely be converted to pounds at an unfavourable exchange rate because the currency is expected to weaken over time.

2. Well, when a firm invests abroad the returns are affected by the profitability of the operation in the country and changes in the exchange rate. Using the approximate method returns from investment in Australia is:

return on Australian investment in A\$s	= 14%
change in the value of the A\$	= 8%
total return	= 22%

Using the exact method the return is $(1 + 14\%)(1 + 8\%) - 1 = 0.2312$ or 23.12%.

3. The percentage change in the value of the ringgit is $(\pounds 0.11 - \pounds 0.12)/\pounds 0.12 = -0.0833$ or −8.33%. A one year investment earns 11%. Using the approximate method returns from investment in Malaysian is:

return on Malaysian investment in ringgit	= 11.00%
change in the value of the ringgit	= −8.33%
total return	= 2.67%

Using the exact method the return is $(1 + 11\%)(1 - 8.33\%) - 1 = 0.017537$ or 1.75%.

4. If the cost of borrowing should be the same at home as abroad according to the IFE (there should be one price). Using the approximate method the IFE formula is $e_f = i_h - i_f$ or $i_h = i_f + e_f$. Plugging in the variables from the question we have 6% = 90% + e_f, implying that $e_f = -84\%$. But caution should be advised because the approximate method is only suitable for relatively small interest rates. The exact method produces a very different rate:

$$e_f = \frac{(1+i_h)}{(1+i_f)} = \frac{1.06}{1.90} - 1 = -0.4421 \text{ or} -44.21\%$$

As a a a check, $1.90 \times (1 - 0.4421) -1 = 0.06001$, a small rounding error of 0.00001. Therefore, the point at which the returns would be the same is if the bolivar depreciates by less than 44.21% against the pound over the one-year period, a one-year deposit in Venezuela will generate a higher effective yield than a one-year UK deposit.

5. Well, only on the basis that interest rate parity will not actually hold. As long as the firms believe that the currency will not depreciate to offset the interest rate advantage, they may consider investing in countries with high interest rates.

This section is aimed specifically at students who are experiencing difficulties with the more numerate aspects of the text. It therefore offers a more descriptive version of measures used in the text as opposed to the mathematical definitions that are widely available. It may also serve as a quick reminder of basic issues to those who are experiencing less difficulty. Some attention is also paid to linguistic issues which is occasionally a problem where English is a second language. The subjects addressed are:

- Return
- Siegel's paradox
- Rounding
- Indexes
- Variance and standard deviation
- Covariance and correlation
- Regression analysis

RETURN

A return is the most fundamental measure in finance; it is therefore worth spending a little time considering its various forms. A return is a measure of an increase or decrease over an initial investment. If I invest £100 today and receive £110 tomorrow, I have made a return of £10 in absolute terms. Often the return is expressed as a percentage, this is a price paid by the borrower and received by the investor per £1 invested. So the return on the £100 above is:

$$\text{Return} = \frac{\text{End value} - \text{start value}}{\text{Start value}}$$

$$\frac{£110 - £100}{£100} = 0.10 \text{ or } 10\%$$

an alternative formulation that is arithmetically the same is:

$$\text{Return} = \frac{\text{End value}}{\text{Start value}} - 1$$

$$\frac{£110}{£100} - 1 = 0.10 \text{ or } 10\%$$

The end value can be defined as the value at the end of the period of any amount invested (the principal) plus any payments received or paid such as interest rates, dividends and so on. The start period is the start of that particular month if the period is defined as months. So monthly returns for a particular year would start with 1 January to 31 January, followed by 1 February to 28 February, then 1 March to 31 March and so on.

The problem with expressing the return as a percentage is that the investor (or the borrower) does not know how much will be received (or paid). This may sound trivial; surely the investor knows how much he or she is investing? To be told that the investment offers a return of 10% only requires a small calculation to work out that £100 invested will yield a return of £10. But in the text, we deal with investment in several different sources and look at the combined effect. To be told that the £100 will be invested in a combination of one venture that will yield a return of 10% and another that will yield a return of 5%, does not allow calculation of the overall return because we do not know how much is invested in each source. To measure that we need to know the weights, these are the proportions of the total investment in each source. So for two investments A and B the symbols w_A and w_B are used and they should add up to 1.00 so that the whole of the investment is explained. If A yields 10% and B yields 5% and 60% is invested in A implying that 40% is invested in B ($w_A = 0.60$ and $w_B = 0.40$) then the overall return is $0.60 \times 0.10 + 0.40 \times 0.05 = 0.08$ or 8%. For this reason, when looking at portfolio returns and standard deviation when a percentage is being used (e.g. the standard deviation is 3%), we need a weight (w_A etc.) to tell us how much of our total investment will be affected in this way. Note that this is not a problem if returns are expressed in absolute terms, thus one would be told that investment A has a return of £6 and investment B a return of £2 so it is immediately apparent that the overall return is £8 and as a percentage 8%. The problem with absolute returns is that they are unwieldy and difficult to generalize; percentage returns are much more 'portable' between problems.

When measuring return over time, there are three types of measure: simple, compound and continuous. In this text we use the most popular type namely compound. In words this means that interest is earned on interest and is credited per period. So investment of £100 for one year at 10% results in a return of £110 (£100 × 1.1); for two years it is this amount multiplied by 1.1 or (£100 × 1.1) × 1.1 = £100 × 1.1² = £121. Interest rates are expressed as being per year unless otherwise stated. In databases, all interest rates are expressed on an annual basis. So a 30-day rate is not the rate over 30 days but the 30-day rate over one year. So, without explanation, converting a 30-day rate quoted as an *annualized* rate to the rate for 30 days is calculated as follows:

30-day rate as quoted in the database: 8% implies a rate over 30 days of:

$(1 + 8\%)^{30/360} - 1 = (1.08)^{0.8333} - 1 = 0.006434$ or 0.6434%.

Note that 360 days rather than 365 days are used in finance, simply because it is easier to halve, quarter etc. It also results in a slightly higher charge by the lender (the bank) and is a hidden source of profit.

Sometimes a simple approach is used to approximate the amount, thus in the above example, the rate would be given as 8% × (30/360) = 0.6667% which is about the same as 0.6434%. Often in financial contracts, such as mortgages, the simple method is used to calculate payments. The reason for its use is because, as you can see from this example, the approximate or simple approach errs on the side of charging a higher amount – once again!

Generally, databases give very short-term, short-term, medium- and long-term rates. When comparing interest rates of different countries, it may not be possible to get an exact match of rates. Instead an approximate time match should be used. So, short-term rates should not be mixed with long-term rates, the risk profile is not comparable. As a rule, very short-term rate (often described as overnight rates) should be avoided altogether – its annualized rate is often very high.

There is frequent reference in the text to using the approximate method when combining returns. Thus, investment abroad results in a return from movement of the currency and a return from investing in the foreign share, bond or whatever. Suppose that these are 3% and 2% respectively. The combined return is $(1.03) \times (1.02) - 1 = 0.0506$ or 5.06% for the exact approach. This is approximately the same as 3% + 2% = 5% a method referred to as the approximate approach. This is always true for low rates. But if the rates were 30% and 20% then the exact approach gives $(1.30) \times (1.20) - 1 = 0.56$ or 56% whereas the approximate approach yields 30% + 20% = 50%, so 12% in error, whereas the earlier calculation was (5.06 – 5) / 5 = 1.2% in error. Whether or not these differences matter depends on the context of the question (see rounding below). The benefit of using the approximate method is that the analysis of return is much clearer – it is therefore almost always used in this text.

The language used for return differs according to the context. Where it is an investment in a bank or other financial institution it is an interest rate or borrowing rate. Where the return is from a change in the value of a currency the term premium (a positive return) or discount (a negative return) tends to be used. For convenience, often the term premium is used even where the return is negative, so one can have a negative premium. But the term "positive discount'" is never used! In investment analysis the terms "discount rate" or "internal rate of return" are used to describe the interest rate in net present value calculations. Finally, where the investment is in shares, return might be expressed as being a dividend.

SIEGEL'S PARADOX

In all examples the home country has been carefully specified. The reason for this is that in many problems, different answers are obtained depending on which country is designated as being the home country. Also, in triangular arbitrage going around the "triangle" in one direction does not yield an equal and opposite return from going around in the other direction. The effect is known as Siegel's paradox and is included here as a warning to the student who notices this phenomenon – do not spend hours checking your calculations! Occasionally the paradox is mentioned in the research literature but it is not currently thought to have any consequences. As a practical guide, one has to be aware that taking a different perspective may yield slightly differing results. The example in Exhibit B1 illustrates the effect.

| Exhibit B1 | Siegel's paradox |

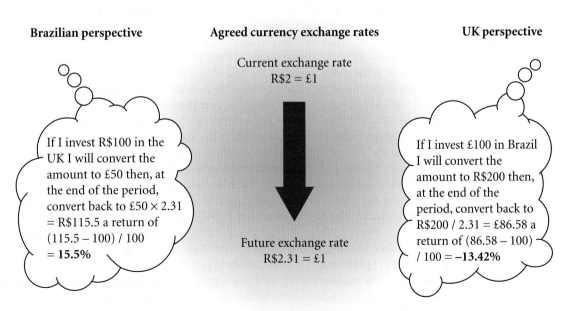

Notes:
- The paradox is that the returns are not equal and opposite: 15.5% × –1.0 is not equal to –13.42%.
- Note that the percentage change in the exchange rate is the e_f of the equations in the text, therefore the Brazilian perspective will be expecting different inflation and interest rate differences compared to the UK perspective.

ROUNDING

The most common issue raised by students is the problem of rounding. How accurate does one need to be? A practical response is to ask the lecturer. Some lecturers prefer to issue an overall guideline for the course such as all currencies are to be rounded to four decimal places; others prefer to leave the decision to the student.

Rounding is a problem in practice as well as in study. If you are translating $100 into British pounds in three months time and the bureau de change rounds the figure from the actual quote of $1.7277 to the pound to $1.73 saying that "it is our practice to round the rates for convenience", this will mean that you will receive $100 / 1.73 = £57.80 instead of £57.88 – not a great difference. However, if the amount is $1 million, then the translated amount should be £578,804 and you receive £578,035 a difference of £769. Why should their convenience cost you nearly £800? You will note that in illustrating this case, the figures themselves have been rounded, the translated amounts are to the nearest pound! So what is the basis for rounding? The simple answer is that it depends on the context. If rounding does not make much of a difference to the answer, then round. If there is a big difference, then do not round or at least round to a level that will only make a small difference to the answer. If the answer is simply a rate such as the exchange rate, then you again need to look at the context. If the problem concerns exchange rates that vary between, say, 1.7277 and 1.7315 then clearly the answer should be to four decimal places or even five places. If the problem is looking at exchange rates that vary between 1.7 and 1.9 then one decimal place possibly or two just to be safe! Managing the rounding problem forces one to look at the context of the problem and not just see it as a game of numbers – so it is useful to have to consider the issue.

INDEXES

In international finance indexes are almost always concerned with prices and exchange rates. Databases contain numerous consumer price indexes and manufacturing price indexes and so on. Price indexes can be thought of as "average prices"; a change in the index is a measure of the change in the average price and hence a measure of the rate of inflation. So if the index is 3245 at the end of month 1 and 3251 at the end of month 2 and 3576 at the end of month 3, the inflation over the second month is (3251 – 3245) / 3245 = 0.001849 (rounded) or 0.1849% and over the third month is (3576 – 3251) / 3251 = 0.10 or 10%. The type of index to use depends on the problem. If one is dealing with exports then an index of exported goods prices would seem appropriate. Note that in making up the average, the prices are weighted by the importance of the goods. So the price of high revenue earning exports would receive a higher weighting than low revenue items. Finally, there is sometimes a break in an index. Usually this occurs when the index number gets too high and unwieldy. Thus one might have a run of numbers such as: 8329, 9995, 12, 13. The first inflation rate is (9995 – 8329) / 8329 = 20% but the second is NOT (12 – 9995) / 9995 = –100%! The numbers have clearly been divided by 1000, no other number would give a sensible answer. Thus the second inflation rate is (12 – [9995/1000]) / [9995/1000] = 20%. The third rate is (13 – 12) / 12 = 8.33%. You should always check the numbers being used in a regression or correlation to ensure that there are no odd values such as –100%. Most regression packages will give outliers and these should be checked for just such errors.

VARIANCE AND STANDARD DEVIATION

In words, a variance is the average "squared distance from the mean". Where the input data is a history of actual exchange rates changes converted to a column of percentage changes from the past, you take the distance from the mean of each member of the sample, square that distance, and then find the average of these squared difference figures (dividing the total by the number in the sample less 1). Exhibit B2 illustrates this method. Where there is no relevant history and the estimates are of possible future rates accompanied by their probability, the squared differences are multiplied by their probabilities and totalled to get the variance – consult a statistics textbook for further details.

The variance figure often looks rather odd. To make it more intuitive, the standard deviation or the square root of the figure is often reported. As both measures order the level of spread in the same way (a larger variance implies a larger standard deviation), the term variance is often used in analysis even where the actual figure might be the standard deviation.

There are two types of variance in international finance, the variance in the prediction of an actual exchange rate and the variance in the prediction of *changes* in the exchange rate. Scenario analysis, as used extensively in this text, uses predictions of actual rates and their probability estimated subjectively (i.e. gut feeling). When looking at databases, the better approach is to estimate *changes* in the exchange rate and look at the average change and measure standard deviation of the changes in the exchange rate – this is illustrated in Exhibit B2. Why are changes in the rate a more interesting measure than

Exhibit B2 Prediction of a change in the exchange rate

1 year	2 exchange rate: $s to the £1	2a year on year change, e.g. $(1.1 - 1.3)/1.3 =$ −0.1538 or −15.38%	3 The difference from the mean: column 2a less 0.119	4 The square of the difference from the mean: square of column 3
1	1.3			
2	1.1	−0.1538	−0.2728	0.0744
3	1.8	0.6364	0.5174	0.2677
4	1.5	−0.1667	−0.2857	0.0816
5	1.6	0.0667	−0.0523	0.0027
6	1.94	0.2125	0.0935	0.0087
total			0.00000	0.4352
Average or mean change (e_f) =		0.1190 or 11.9%	Variance =	0.1088
			standard deviation =	0.3298 i.e. 32.98%

Notes:
- The variance is the total of column 4 divided by the number of observations less 1 i.e. 5 − 1 = 4. The 1 is concerned with degrees of freedom. So, variance = 0.4352 / (5 − 1) = 0.1088; standard deviation = $\sqrt{0.1088}$ = 0.3298.
- Note that this is the expected *change in the exchange rate* (11.9%) and the standard deviation of the *change* (32.98%). So, for example, 1 standard deviation above the change would be 11.9% + 32.98% = 44.88%.
- The expected change is the same as e_f in the text, it is therefore the object of prediction for IFE and PPP theories.

the actual rate? The answer is that, as in the Exhibit, the exchange rate from five years ago may not now be relevant because of trends and general changes in the economic environment. One does not expect the rate today to suddenly change to the rate five years ago! But we can expect the history of *change* to continue. Thus if the exchange rate habitually in the past changed 5% to 10% a year up or down, i.e. was extremely volatile, one can expect such behaviour to continue. So how the figures *changed* five years ago is relevant but not the actual figures. Variance of course does itself change over time and statistical methods do attempt to predict such change (the ARCH and GARCH models); but in using just the variance of past changes in exchange rate as a prediction of the future variance we assume no change. The statistical models do no more than try to identify patterns in past variances in the exchange rate, they do not provide explanatory variables such as interest rates etc. to attempt to explain why variance changes – the actual reasons for changes in variance is not well understood. With regard to predicting the actual rate, using the current rate is better than using past actual rates because market efficiency states that the current rate includes all information about the future value discounted into the current price. So the rate five years ago is definitely inferior. Also, although we cannot predict the actual future rate any better than the present price, the variance remains predictable. Unfortunately, one cannot make a profit from such knowledge because we do not know the direction of the change! Note also that IFE and PPP talk about the change in the value of a currency, not the actual rate. Again they take the current rate and current information as the starting point as advocated by market efficiency.

There are many other measures of spread. One could take the absolute distance from the mean, that is, simply treat the negatives as positive and take the average absolute distance from the mean. Alternatively, one could take just the downside variance, that is, the variance that is unattractive. With regard to a cost, unattractive variance would be the variation above the mean; with revenue, the variation below the mean would be unattractive. In practice, such measures do not produce radically different conclusions about the spread of a distribution. The advantage of the variance over the other methods is that the variance is more tractable – easier to manipulate in measurement generally – hence variance has remained the most popular measure of spread.

Exhibit B3 Intuitive measures of covariance

High covariance / correlation	Change in exchange rate 2 is *above* the average change	Change in exchange rate 2 is *below* the average change
When change in exchange rate 1 is *above* the average change	often	rarely
When change in exchange rate 1 is *below* the average change	rarely	often
Low covariance / correlation	Change in exchange rate 2 is *above* the average change	Change in exchange rate 2 is *below* the average change
When change in exchange rate 1 is *above* the average change	sometimes	occasionally
When change in exchange rate 1 is *below* the average change	occasionally	sometimes

COVARIANCE AND CORRELATION

A covariance is, as the name suggests, a measure as to what extent two variables co-vary or move together. Exhibit B3 illustrates the relation between the measure and one's intuitive idea of varying together. Notice that the measure is taken in relation to the mean, i.e. being above or below the mean. The calculation of the measure of covariance is in practice much like the measure of variance and is illustrated in Exhibit B4. The correlation, also illustrated in Exhibit B4, is based on the same differences from the mean of the dollar and the euro (columns 3 and 5). The effect of dividing the total differences (column 6) by the standard deviations of the two exchange rates is to map the covariance on to a scale of –1 for perfect negative correlation, to 0 for absolutely no correlation and

Exhibit B4 Correlation and covariance

1 year	2 exchange rate: $s to the £1 (dollar)	2a year on year % change (dollar)	3 column 2a less average (0.119) (dollar)	4 exchange rate: euros to the £1 (euro)	4a year on year % change (euro)	5 column 2a less –0.0302 (euro)	6 squared differences columns 3 × 5 (both)
1	1.3			1.4			
2	1.1	–0.1538	–0.2728	1.1	–0.2143	–0.1841	0.0502
3	1.8	0.6364	0.5174	1.2	0.0909	0.1211	0.0627
4	1.5	–0.1667	–0.2857	1.2	0.0000	0.0302	–0.0086
5	1.6	0.0667	–0.0523	0.9	–0.2500	–0.2198	0.0115
6	1.94	0.2125	0.0935	1.1	0.2222	0.2525	0.0236
total			0.00000			0.00000	0.1394
average		0.119			–0.0302		
standard deviation		0.3298			0.2009		

number of observations = 5

covariance = 0.1394 / 5 = 0.02788

correlation = 0.0279 / (0.3298 * 0.2009) × 4/5 = 0.526

Notes:

■ The ratio 4/5 reverses the degrees of freedom in the standard deviation. This adjustment becomes less important the larger the sample (normally the sample would be much larger in project work, 30 at least). For, say, 50 observations the adjustment would be 49/50. Note that the degree of freedom is only an issue for actual observations. If the variables are estimated using probabilities, the degree of freedom is not relevant.

■ To understand covariance, examine columns 3 and 5. For the dollar exchange rate (column 3) (–0.1538 – 0.119) = –0.2728, is quite a bit below the mean, whereas for the euro the same calculation is (–0.2143 – –0.0302) = –0.1841 again below the mean by the second highest amount. So the two currencies moved in similar directions in year 2. In year 3 they were both above their means, the dollar rate at 0.5174 and the euro at 0.1211, so the pound rose in value that year against both currencies. In year 4, however, there was a sharp fall in the dollars to the pound, the change was –0.2857 below the mean. Whereas for the euro there was no change, the no change was 0.0302 above the average negative change of that amount. So with respect to the mean the two currencies moved in opposite directions against the pound – note the resultant negative value in column 6 with the effect of lowering the covariance and correlation. In year 5 the change in the currencies are both less than the average change but the euro is more negative and in year 6 the changes are both more than the average changes and the euro is again moving rather more in that it is more positive than the dollar. It may be rather surprising that the changes in the euro value against the pound are on average less than the dollar (the standard deviation is less). The cause is the early years where the dollar is changing rather more, in particular the year 3 change is very large for the dollar. If the covariance is being used to apply to future changes then there may be concerns that the change in year 3 is exceptional and not relevant to predicting the future. The point here is that these exchange rate movements are more than mere numbers but rather are the result of economic events.

no relationship, to the highest value of 1 representing perfect positive correlation. A correlation is therefore a covariance mapped on to a –1 to 1 scale. Thus one may talk about a correlation when in fact the measure used is a covariance. As with standard deviations and variances the terms relate to the same phenomenon measures in a slightly different way. The spreadsheet for Exhibit B4 is available in the support material website.

REGRESSION ANALYSIS

Businesses often use **regression analysis** to measure relationships between variables when establishing policies. For example, a firm may measure the historical relationship between its sales and its accounts receivable. Using the relationship detected, it can then forecast the future level of accounts receivable based on a forecast of sales. Alternatively, it may measure the sensitivity of its sales to economic growth and interest rates so that it can assess how susceptible its sales are to future changes in these economic variables. In international financial management, regression analysis can be used to measure the sensitivity of a firm's performance (using sales or earnings or stock price as a proxy) to currency movements or economic growth of various countries.

Regression analysis can be applied to measure the sensitivity of exports to various economic variables. This example will be used to explain the fundamentals of regression analysis. The main steps involved in regression analysis are:

1. Specifying the regression model
2. Compiling the data
3. Estimating the regression coefficients
4. Interpreting the regression results

Specifying the regression model

Assume that your main goal is to determine the relationship between percentage changes in UK exports to Australia (called *CEXP*) and percentage changes in the value of the Australian dollar (called *CAUS*). The percentage change in the exports to Australia is the **dependent variable** since it is hypothesized to be influenced by another variable. Although you are most concerned with how *CAUS* affects *CEXP*, the regression model should include any other factors (or so-called **independent variables**) that could also affect *CEXP*. Assume that the percentage change in the Australian GDP (called *CGDP*) is also hypothesized to influence *CEXP*. This factor should also be included in the regression model. To simplify the example, assume that *CAUS* and *CGDP* are the only factors expected to influence *CEXP*. Also assume that there is a lagged impact of one quarter. In this case, the regression model can be specified as

$$CEXP_t = b_0 + b_1 (CAUS_{t-1}) + b_2(CGDP_{t-1}) + \mu_t$$

Where

b_0	=	a constant
b_1	=	regression coefficient that measures the sensitivity of $CEXP_t$ to $CAUS_{t-1}$
b_2	=	regression coefficient that measures the sensitivity of $CEXP_t$ to $CGDP_{t-1}$
μ_t	=	an error term

The *t* subscript represents the time period. Some models, such as this one, specify a *lagged impact* of an independent variable on the dependent variable and therefore use a *t*–1 subscript. In this case we assume that the lag is one year, the size of the lag is usually an educated guess. The lag could be two or even three years. Often researchers simply try differing lag patterns to see which is best by including independent variables with lags of one, two and three years in the same equation, in this case $CAUS_{t-1}$ $CAUS_{t-1}$ and $CAUS_{t-1}$ and $CGDP_{t-1}$ $CGDP_{t-1}$ and $CGDP_{t-1}$.

Compiling the data

Now that the model has been specified, data on the variables must be compiled. The data are normally input on to a spreadsheet or into a statistics package such as MINITAB or SPSS as follows:

Period (t)	CEXP	CAUS	CGDP
1	0.03	−0.01	0.04
2	−0.01	0.02	−0.01
3	−0.04	0.03	−0.02
4	0.00	0.02	−0.01
5	0.01	−0.02	0.02
.	...	...	...
.	...	...	...
.	...	...	...

The column specifying the period is not necessary to run the regression model but is normally included in the data set for convenience.

The difference between the number of observations (periods) and the regression coefficients (including the constant) represents the degrees of freedom. For our example, assume that the data covered 40 quarterly periods. The degrees of freedom for this example are $40 - 3 = 37$. As a general rule, analysts usually try to have at least 30 degrees of freedom when using regression analysis.

Some regression models involve only a single period. For example, if you desired to determine whether there was a relationship between a firm's degree of international sales (as a percentage of total sales) and earnings per share of MNCs, last year's data on these two variables could be gathered for many MNCs, and regression analysis could be applied. This example is referred to as **cross-sectional analysis**, whereas our original example is referred to as a **time-series analysis**.

Estimating the regression coefficients

Once the data have been input into a data file, a regression program can be applied to the data to estimate the **regression coefficients**. There are various packages such as Excel and Lotus, MINITAB and SPSS that contain a regression analysis application.

The actual steps conducted to estimate regression coefficients are somewhat complex. For more details on how regression coefficients are estimated, see any econometrics textbook.

Interpreting the regression results

Most regression programs provide estimates of the regression coefficients along with additional statistics. For our example, assume that the following information was provided by the regression programme:

	Estimated regression coefficient	Standard error of regression coefficient	t-statistic
Constant	0.002		
$CAUS_t-1$	80	0.32	2.50
$CGDP_t-1$	0.36	0.50	0.72
Coefficient of determination (R^2)	= 0.33		

The independent variable $CAUS_t-1$ has an estimated regression coefficient of 0.80, which suggests that a 1% increase in CAUS is associated with an 0.8% increase in the dependent variable CEXP in the following period. This implies a positive relationship between $CAUS_t-1$ and $CEXP_t$. The independent variable $CGDP_t-1$ has an estimated coefficient of 0.36, which suggests that a 1% increase in the Australian GDP is associated with a 0.36% increase in CEXP one period later.

Many analysts attempt to determine whether a coefficient is statistically different from zero. Regression coefficients may be different from zero simply because of a coincidental relationship between the independent variable of concern and the dependent variable. One can have more confidence that a negative or positive relationship exists by testing the coefficient for significance. A t-test is commonly used for this purpose, as follows:

Test to determine whether $CAUS_t-1$ affects $CEXP_t$

$$\text{Calculated } t - \text{statistic} = \frac{\text{Estimated regression coefficient for } CAUS_{t-1}}{\text{Standard error of the regression coefficient}} = \frac{0.80}{0.42} = 2.50$$

Test to determine whether $CGDP_t-1$ affects $CEXP_t$

$$\text{Calculated } t - \text{statistic} = \frac{\text{Estimated regression coefficient for } CGDP_{t-1}}{\text{Standard error of the regression coefficient}} = \frac{0.80}{0.42} = 2.50$$

The calculated t-statistic is sometimes provided within the regression results. It can be compared to the critical t-statistic to determine whether the coefficient is significant. The critical t-statistic is dependent on the degrees of freedom and confidence level chosen. For our example, assume that there are 37 degrees of freedom and that a 95 confidence level is desired. The critical t-statistic would be 2.02, which can be verified by using a t-table from any statistics book. Based on the regression results, the coefficient of $CAUS_t-1$ is significantly different from zero, while $CGDP_t-1$ is not. This implies that one can be confident of a positive relationship between $CAUS_t-1$ and $CEXP_t$, but the positive relationship between $CGDP_t-1$ and $CEXP_t$ may have occurred simply by chance.

In some particular cases, one may be interested in determining whether the regression coefficient differs significantly from some value other than zero. In these cases, the t-statistic reported in the regression results would not be appropriate. See an econometrics text for more information on this subject.

The regression results indicate the **coefficient of determination** (called R^2) of a regression model, which measures the percentage of variation in the dependent variable that can be explained by the regression model. R^2 can range from 0 to 100%. It is unusual for regression models to generate an R^2 of close to 100%, since the movement in a given dependent variable is partially random and not associated with movements in independent variables. In our example, R^2 is 33%, suggesting that one-third of the variation in CEXP can be explained by movements in $CAUS_t-1$ and $CGDP_t-1$.

Some analysts use regression analysis to forecast. For our example, the regression results could be used along with data for CAUS and CGDP to forecast CEXP. Assume that CAUS was 5% in the most recent period, while CGDP was −1% in the most recent period. The forecast of CEXP in the following period is derived from inserting this information into the regression model as follows:

$$
\begin{aligned}
CEXP_t &= b_0 + b_1(CAUS_{t-1}) + b_2(CGDP_{t-1}) \\
&= 0.002 + (0.80)(0.05) + (0.36)(-0.01) \\
&= 0.002 + 0.0400 - 0.0036 \\
&= 0.0420 - 0.0036 \\
&= 0.0384
\end{aligned}
$$

Thus, the CEXP is forecasted to be 3.84% in the following period. Some analysts might eliminate $CGDP_t-1$ from the model because its regression coefficient was not significantly different from zero. This would alter the forecasted value of CEXP.

When there is not a lagged relationship between independent variables and the dependent variable, the independent variables must be forecasted in order to derive a forecast of the dependent variable. In this case, an analyst might derive a poor forecast of the dependent variable even when the regression model is properly specified, if the forecasts of the independent variables are inaccurate.

As with most statistical techniques, there are some limitations that should be recognized when using regression analysis. These limitations are described in most statistics and econometrics textbooks.

Using Excel to conduct regression analysis

Various software packages are available to run regression analysis. The following example is run on Excel to illustrate the ease with which regression analysis can be run. Assume that a firm wants to assess the influence of changes in the value of the Australian dollar on changes in its exports to Australia based on the following data:

Period	Value (in thousands of dollars) of exports to Australia	Average exchange rate of Australian dollar over that period
1	110	$0.50
2	125	0.54
3	130	0.57
4	142	0.60
5	129	0.55
6	113	0.49
7	108	0.46
8	103	0.42
9	109	0.43
10	118	0.48
11	125	0.49
12	130	0.50

Period	Value (in thousands of dollars) of exports to Australia	Average exchange rate of Australian dollar over that period
13	134	0.52
14	138	0.50
15	144	0.53
16	149	0.55
17	156	0.58
18	160	0.62
19	165	0.66
20	170	0.67
21	160	0.62
22	158	0.62
23	155	0.61
24	167	0.66

Assume that the firm applies the following regression model to the data:

$$CEXP = b_0 + b_1 \, CAUS + \mu$$

Where

$CEXP$ = percentage change in the firm's export value from one period to the next

$CAUS$ = percentage change in the average exchange rate from one period to the next

μ = error term

The first step is to input the data for the two variables in two columns on a file using Excel. Then, the data can be converted into percentage changes. This can be easily performed with a COMPUTE statement in the third column (Column C) to derive $CEXP$ and another COMPUTE statement in the fourth column (Column D) to derive $CAUS$. These two columns will have a blank first row, since the percentage change cannot be computed without the previous period's data. Many students already know how to use Excel to create a COMPUTE statement and to apply the COMPUTE statement to all of the data within a column. If you do not, ask a friend for a few minutes of help.

Once you have derived $CEXP$ and $CAUS$ from the raw data, you can perform regression analysis as follows. On the main menu, select "Tools". This leads to a new menu, in which you should click on "Data Analysis". Next to the "Input Y Range", identify the range C2 to C24 for the dependent variable as C2:C24. Next to the "Input X Range", identify the range D2 to D24 for the independent variable as D2:D24. The "Output Range" specifies the location on the screen where the output of the regression analysis should be displayed. In our example, F1 would be an appropriate location, representing the upper-left section of the output. Then, click on OK, and within a few seconds, the regression analysis will be complete. For our example, the output is listed below:

SUMMARY OUTPUT

Regression statistics	
Multiple R	0.8852
R Square	0.7836
Adjusted R Square	0.7733
Standard error	2.9115
Observations	23.0000

ANOVA

	df	SS	MS	F	Significance F
Regression	1.0000	644.6262	644.6262	76.0461	0.0000
Residual	21.0000	178.0125	8.4768		
Total	22.0000	822.6387			

	Coefficients	Standard Error	t-Stat	P-value
Intercept	0.7951	0.6229	1.2763	0.2158
X Variable 1	0.8678	0.0995	8.7204	0.0000

	Lower 95%	Upper 95%	Lower 95.0%	Upper 95.0%
Intercept	−0.5004	2.0905	−0.5004	2.0905
X Variable 1	0.6608	1.0747	0.6608	1.0747

The estimate of the so-called slope coefficient is about 0.8678, which suggests that every 1% change in the Australian dollar's exchange rate is associated with a 0.8678% change (in the same direction) in the firm's exports to Australia. The t-statistic is also estimated to determine whether the slope coefficient is significantly different than zero. Since the standard error of the slope coefficient is about 0.0995, the t-statistic is $(0.8678/0.0995) =$ 8.72. This would imply that there is a significant relationship between *CAUS* and *CEXP*. The R-Square statistic suggests that about 78% of the variation in *CEXP* is explained by *CAUS*. The correlation between *CEXP* and *CAUS* can also be measured by the correlation coefficient, which is the square root of the R-Square statistic.

If you have more than one independent variable (multiple regression), you should place the independent variables next to each other in the file. Then, for the X-RANGE, identify this block of data. The output for the regression model will display the coefficient, standard error, and t-statistic for each of the independent variables. For multiple regression, the R-Square statistic is interpreted as the percentage of variation in the dependent variable explained by the model as a whole.

Using the "COPY" command

If you need to repeat a particular type of computation for several different cells, you can use the COPY command. You must highlight the particular cells in which the computation is performed and instruct Excel (by clicking on "Edit") to copy that computation to whatever range of cells you desire.